T0189353

Lecture Notes in Computer Science   11401

Commenced Publication in 1973
Founding and Former Series Editors:
Gerhard Goos, Juris Hartmanis, and Jan van Leeuwen

More information about this series at http://www.springer.com/series/7412

Ruben Vera-Rodriguez
Julian Fierrez · Aythami Morales (Eds.)

Progress in Pattern Recognition, Image Analysis, Computer Vision, and Applications

23rd Iberoamerican Congress, CIARP 2018
Madrid, Spain, November 19–22, 2018
Proceedings

 Springer

Editors
Ruben Vera-Rodriguez
Biometrics and Data Pattern Analytics Lab
Universidad Autonoma de Madrid
Madrid, Spain

Aythami Morales
Biometrics and Data Pattern Analytics Lab
Universidad Autonoma de Madrid
Madrid, Spain

Julian Fierrez
Biometrics and Data Pattern Analytics Lab
Universidad Autonoma de Madrid
Madrid, Spain

ISSN 0302-9743   ISSN 1611-3349 (electronic)
Lecture Notes in Computer Science
ISBN 978-3-030-13468-6   ISBN 978-3-030-13469-3   (eBook)
https://doi.org/10.1007/978-3-030-13469-3

Library of Congress Control Number: 2019931950

LNCS Sublibrary: SL6 – Image Processing, Computer Vision, Pattern Recognition, and Graphics

This Springer imprint is published by the registered company Springer Nature Switzerland AG
The registered company address is: Gewerbestrasse 11, 6330 Cham, Switzerland

Preface

After 23 editions, the Iberoamerican Congress on Pattern Recognition (CIARP) has become a key research event, and the most important in pattern recognition for the Iberoamerican community.

CIARP has always been an open international event, and this year CIARP received submissions from more than 20 countries. In this edition, the biggest presence is from Brazil, Chile, Colombia, Cuba, Mexico, Portugal, and Spain. On the other hand, there is also good presence from Algeria, France, Germany, Italy, Tunisia, UK, and USA; and also from countries like Japan, Russia, South Africa, and South Korea.

CIARP 2018 received 187 submissions. The review process for CIARP 2018 was diligent and required careful consideration of more than 550 reviews from 117 reviewers who spent significant time and effort in reviewing the papers. In the end 112 papers were accepted, which is an acceptance rate of 59.9%. To form the final program, 34 papers were selected for oral presentations (18.2% of all submissions) and 78 as poster presentations. The program comprised six oral sessions on the following topics: machine learning, computer vision (two sessions), classification, biometrics and medical applications, and brain signals. Three additional poster sessions included papers on all previous topics, and also on text and character analysis, human interaction, and sentiment analysis.

The pattern recognition community is witnessing a *deep* transformation, now increasingly dominated by advances occurring in industry in machine learning, computer vision, and related fields around pattern recognition. CIARP also considered this industrial vortex by incorporating a number of researchers and practitioners from key companies like IBM, Google, MathWorks, Microsoft, Nuance, and Telefonica, into a number of panel discussions.

The CIARP 2018 program was finally enhanced by four keynotes by eminent speakers: Jiri Matas, Johan Suykens, Björn Schuller, and Francisco Herrera.

We hope that these proceedings will result in a fruitful reference for the pattern recognition research community. Finally, we would like to thank all who made this possible, especially the authors, the reviewers, and the CIARP community at large.

January 2019

Julian Fierrez
Ruben Vera-Rodriguez
Aythami Morales

Organization

Organizing Committee

General Chair

Julian Fierrez   Universidad Autonoma de Madrid, Spain

Honorary Chairs

Anil K. Jain	Michigan State University, USA
Josef Kittler	University of Surrey, UK

CIARP Steering Committee

Bernardete Ribeiro	APRP, Portugal
Eduardo Bayro-Corrochano	MACVNR, Mexico
César Beltrán-Castañón	APeRP, Peru
Julian Fierrez	AERFAI, Spain
Andrés Gago Alonso	ACRP, Cuba
Marta Mejail	SARP, Argentina
Marcelo Mendoza	AChiRP, Chile
Joao Paulo Papa	SIGPR-BR, Brazil
Álvaro Pardo	APRU, Uruguay
María Trujillo	UniVa, Colombia
(Invited Member)	

Program Chairs

Ruben Vera-Rodriguez	Universidad Autonoma de Madrid, Spain
Sergio Velastin	Carlos III University of Madrid, Spain; Queen Mary University, London, UK
Manuel Montes-y-Gomez	INAOE, Mexico

Publication and Awards Chair

Aythami Morales   Universidad Autonoma de Madrid, Spain

Local Organization Chairs

Ruben Tolosana	Universidad Autonoma de Madrid, Spain
Alejandro Acien	Universidad Autonoma de Madrid, Spain

Local Arrangements

Ivan Bartolome	Universidad Autonoma de Madrid, Spain
Marta Blazquez	Universidad Autonoma de Madrid, Spain

Miguel Caruana	Universidad Autonoma de Madrid, Spain
David Diaz	Universidad Autonoma de Madrid, Spain
Berta Fernandez	Universidad Autonoma de Madrid, Spain
Marta Fernandez	Universidad Autonoma de Madrid, Spain
Carlos Gonzalez	Universidad Autonoma de Madrid, Spain
Mustafa Kocakulak	Universidad Autonoma de Madrid, Spain
Gustavo Manzano	Universidad Autonoma de Madrid, Spain
Victor Martinez	Universidad Autonoma de Madrid, Spain

Program Committee

Daniel Acevedo	Universidad de Buenos Aires, Argentina
Niusvel Acosta-Mendoza	Advanced Technologies Application Center (CENATAV), Cuba
Enrique Alegre	University of Leon, Spain
Luís A. Alexandre	UBI and Instituto de Telecomunicações, Portugal
Fernando Alonso-Fernandez	Halmstad University, Sweden
Leopoldo Altamirano	INAOE, Mexico
Arnaldo Araujo	Universidade Federal de Minas Gerais, Brazil
Mauricio Araya-López	Universidad Técnica Federico Santa Maria, Chile
Xiang Bai	Huazhong University of Science and Technology, China
Antonio Bandera	University of Malaga, Spain
Jose Miguel Benedi	Universitat Politécnica de València, Spain
Gunilla Borgefors	Centre for Image Analysis, Uppsala University, Sweden
Ramon F. Brena	Tecnologico de Monterrey, Mexico
María Elena Buemi	Universidad de Buenos Aires, Argentina
Leticia Cagnina	Universidad Nacional de San Luis, Argentina
Luis Vicente Calderita Estévez	University of Extremadura, Spain
Hiram Calvo	National Polytechnic Institute, Mexico
Jorge Camargo	National University of Colombia, Colombia
Cristina Carmona-Duarte	Universidad de Las Palmas de Gran Canaria, Spain
Jesus Ariel Carrasco-Ochoa	Instituto Nacional de Astrofísica, Óptica y Electrónica, Mexico
German Castellanos	Universidad Nacional de Colombia, Colombia
Rama Chellappa	University of Maryland, USA
Diego Sebastián Comas	Universidad Nacional del Mar del Plata, Argentina
Paulo Correia	Instituto de Telecomunicacoes – Instituto Superior Tecnico, Portugal
Raúl Cruz-Barbosa	Universidad Tecnológica de la Mixteca, Mexico
Abhijit Das	Inria, France
Jorge De La Calleja	Universidad Politécnica de Puebla, Mexico
Mauricio Delbracio	Universidad de La República, Uruguay
Cheng Deng	Xidian University, China
Moises Diaz	Universidad del Atlantico Medio, Spain

Esau Villatoro-Tello	Universidad Autónoma Metropolitana, Mexico
Arnold Wiliem	The University of Queensland, Australia
Gui-Song Xia	Wuhan University, China
Pablo Zegers	Universidad de los Andes, Chile

Contents

Computer Vision

Biometrics

Medical Applications and Brain Signals

Text and Characters Analysis

Human Interaction

Machine Learning

Large Scale Learning Techniques for Least Squares Support Vector Machines

Santiago Toledo-Cortés[✉], Ivan Y. Castellanos-Martinez[✉], and Fabio A. Gonzalez[✉]

MindLab Research Group, Universidad Nacional de Colombia, Bogotá, Colombia
{stoledoc,iycastellanosm,fagonzalezo}@unal.edu.co

Abstract. Although kernel machines allow a non-linear analysis through the transformation of their input data, their computational complexity makes them inefficient in terms of time and memory for the analysis of very large databases. Several attempts have been made to improve kernel methods performance, many of which are focused on approximate the kernel matrix or the feature mapping associated to it. Current trends in machine learning demands the capacity of dealing with large data sets while exploiting the capabilities of massively parallel architectures based on GPUs. This has been mainly accomplished by a combination of gradient descent optimization and online learning. This paper presents an online kernel-based model based on the dual formulation of Least Squared Support Vector Machine method, using the Learning on a Budget strategy to lighten the computational cost. This extends the algorithm capability to analyze very large or high-dimensional data without requiring high memory resources. The method was evaluated against other kernel approximation techniques: Nyström approximation and Random Fourier Features. Experiments made with different datasets show the effectiveness of the Learning on a Budget strategy compared with the other approximation techniques.

Keywords: Kernel Methods · Least Squared · Support Vector Machine · Nyström · Budget · Random Fourier Features

1 Introduction

The importance of kernel methods such as Support Vector Machines (SVM) lies in the fact that they can approximate very complex non-linear decision functions thanks to the kernel trick [5]. Using kernels as a similarity measure allows the user to involve domain knowledge that helps to shape the geometry of the data representation space. The use of the Reproducing Kernel Hilbert Space offers many advantages in machine learning, such as the possibility to define powerful and flexible models, and the possibility to generalize many results and algorithms for linear models in Euclidean spaces [5]. However, traditional kernel methods suffer many problems, especially with memory and time computational

© Springer Nature Switzerland AG 2019
R. Vera-Rodriguez et al. (Eds.): CIARP 2018, LNCS 11401, pp. 3–11, 2019.
https://doi.org/10.1007/978-3-030-13469-3_1

complexity, which grows at least quadratically in relation to the number of samples in the training dataset [2]. Thus, kernel methods are very successful with small datasets but do not scale well on their own to large datasets.

Given the fact that the size of the data has been growing exponentially, machine learning methods mostly point to more efficient optimizations strategies. In this sense, Stochastic Gradient Descent (SGD) rises as an effective procedure for large scale learning [3]. The classic formulation for the optimization problem in kernel-based methods does not permit an explicit implementation of SGD. However, it turned out to be possible in Least Squares Support Vector Machine (LS-SVM) [11]. Besides the SGD implementation, different approximation techniques can be used to relieve the computational cost of the Gram matrix. In this paper we use the Learning on a Budget strategy, which consists in taking only a reduced number of representative instances to compute the kernel matrix: the machine is trained with a budget kernel matrix. This strategy has already been applied in the automatic multi-label annotation problem [8], showing a significantly reduction of the computational complexity, with no losing of accuracy.

In the present work we evaluated and compared the performance of LS-SVM using Learning on a Budget with LS-SVM and using the Nyström approximation [4] instead of the budget. Also, an Online Random Fourier Features LS-SVM was proposed and implemented to compare the results with an state-of-the-art method. The Random Fourier Features (RFF) [9] gives an explicit feature mapping to a low dimensional feature space $\hat{\mathcal{F}}$. This permits to solve the LS-SVM primal optimization problem directly on $\hat{\mathcal{F}}$. As the primal problem also has an explicit summation over the error of each prediction, an SGD implementation is feasible. The rest of the paper is organized as follows. Section 2 contains theoretical background about the methods. Section 3 describes the proposed method. Results and discussions over experimental work is presented in Sect. 4. Finally, Sect. 5 has some concluding remarks.

2   Related Work

Approximated kernel methods have been widely studied due to their computational benefits [13]. One of the most used is the Nyström Method [4,10], which finds a low rank approximation of the kernel matrix from a matrix decomposition. It takes $\beta \ll n$ instances and construct the sub-matrix of X corresponding to those instances: B; this matrix is called the budget. Then it defines $C = k(X, B)$ and $W = k(B, B)$, and approximate Ω by $\tilde{\Omega} = CW^{-1}C^T$. This approximation saves memory of storage of the kernel matrix and time from calculating the overall loss in a training step. Nyström method can be extended to find a k-rank approximation of Ω. To make this, the best low k-rank approximation of W is used instead of the original W. As it uses an approximation of the full kernel matrix, this strategy shall not be used with an online implementation.

Another approximated kernel method broadly used is the RFF method [9,13], which states a relation between a shift invariant kernel k and a probability distribution p using the Bochner's theorem. This allows to approximate the feature map ϕ with linear projections on D random features and, gives a low dimensional representation $\hat{\mathcal{F}}$ of the feature space $\mathcal{F}$ induced by the kernel. Having an explicit representation of the approximated feature map $\hat{\phi}$ allows us to use the set of images of the training data as input in a simple linear learning algorithm, which does not require too much memory capabilities or does not have high computational complexity.

Recently, several works have used a different approach, using what is called Learning on a Budget [8,12]. In this method, the loss function in the SVM does not use the full kernel matrix, but only a small portion of it. The formulation of the SVM using Learning on a Budget enables to use SGD and thus online learning. Different versions of the Learning on a Budget strategy have been studied in recent years as in [6], in which the overall formulation of a LS-SVM was adapted to use a budget, therefore improving memory usage and time complexity. However, all the previous methods using the LS-SVM keep working with matricial systems which requires successive replacements of the entries of the matrix in case of an online implementation.

3   Method

The classic LS-SVM solves the optimization problem by means of a system of linear equations. Here we will describe an alternative to solve the convex dual problem by means of SGD, using just a portion of the training data.

3.1   Least Square Support Vector Machine

LS-SVM is a least squared version of the SVM for classification or regression problem. The problem considers equality constraints instead of inequalities as in classic SVM, this allows the solution to be reached by solving a system of linear equations. Given a set of training data $\{x_1, \ldots, x_n\} \subset X$ and the labels $\{y_i\}_{i=1}^n$, and given a nonlinear feature mapping $\phi : X \to \mathcal{F}$, associated to the kernel function k, the LS-SVM classifier defines the classification problem as [11]

$$\min_{w,b,e} J(w,b,e) = \frac{1}{2}w^T w + \gamma \frac{1}{2}\sum_{k=1}^{n} e_k^2, \tag{1}$$

subject to

$$y_k \left[w^T \phi(x_k) + b \right] = 1 - e_k, \quad k = 1, \ldots, N.$$

Once the Lagrangian is defined subject to Kuhn-Tucker conditions, the dual problem arises as a system of equations

$$\begin{bmatrix} \Omega + I_n/\gamma & 1_n \\ 1_n^T & 0 \end{bmatrix} \begin{bmatrix} \alpha \\ b \end{bmatrix} = \begin{bmatrix} y \\ 0 \end{bmatrix}, \tag{2}$$

where $\Omega_{ij} = k(x_i, x_j) = \langle \phi(x_i), \phi(x_j) \rangle$ is the kernel matrix, $1_n = [1, \ldots, 1]^T \in \mathbb{R}^n$, $\alpha = [\alpha_1, \ldots, \alpha_n]^T$ is the vector of Lagrange multipliers, $y = [y_1, \ldots, y_n]^T$, and I_n is the $n \times n$ identity matrix. Once the system is solved for α and b, the model is given by:

$$y(x) = w^T \phi(x) + b, \qquad (3)$$

where $w = \sum_{i=1}^n \alpha_i y_i \phi(x_i)$. The first attempts to apply LS-SVM to large datasets, required solving the linear system by means of an iterative method like Conjugate Gradient or Successive Over-Relaxation [11].

For the dual version, we take the Lagrangian of the original LS-SVM problem (1)

$$\mathcal{L}(w, b, e, \alpha) = J(w, b, e) - \sum_{k=1}^n \alpha_k \left(y_k \left[w^T \varphi(x_k) + b \right] - 1 + e_k \right), \qquad (4)$$

subject to $w = \sum_{k=1}^n \alpha_k y_k \varphi(x_i)$, $\sum_{k=1}^n \alpha_k y_k = 0$, and $\alpha_k = \gamma e_k$, $y_k \left[w^T \varphi(x_k) + b \right] - 1 + e_k = 0$ for $k = 1, \ldots n$. Plugging this into Eq. (4), we get the dual problem

$$\mathcal{L}(w, b, e, \alpha) = -\frac{1}{2}(\alpha y)^T k(X, X)(\alpha y) + \sum_{k=1}^n \alpha_k - \frac{\gamma}{2} \sum_{k=1}^n \left(1 - y_k \left[(\alpha y)^T k(X, x_k) + b \right] \right)^2, \quad (5)$$

where (αy) represents a pairwise product of α and y, and must be maximized for $\alpha_k, k = 1, \ldots, n$, and b.

3.2   Large Scale LS-SVM

Solving a system of linear equations is a way complicated procedure if an online implementation is required. Solving a quadratic optimization problem by means of SGD is a widely used strategy, for example in the training of deep network architectures [3].

Budget LS-SVM. The Learning on a Budget strategy can be implemented in LS-SVM as follows: instead of computing the entire kernel matrix, a random selection of $\beta \ll n$ instances will be made, selecting a sub-matrix B from the input data matrix X to train the machine. The loss function will be

$$\min_{\alpha, b} \mathcal{L}' = \frac{1}{2}(\alpha y)^T k(B, B)(\alpha y) - \sum_{k=1}^{\beta} \alpha_k + \frac{\gamma}{2} \sum_{k=1}^n \left(1 - y_k \left[(\alpha y)^T k(B, x_k) + b \right] \right)^2, \qquad (6)$$

Online Budget LS-SVM. SGD permits an online implementation as it updates the solution using a single training sample at time, which alleviates even more the memory requirements. Following this, given the derivatives

$$\frac{\partial \mathcal{L}'}{\partial \alpha_i} = \sum_{k=1}^{\beta} \alpha_k y_k y_i k(x_i, x_k) - 1 - \gamma \sum_{k=1}^n \left(1 - y_k \left[(\alpha y)^T k(B, x_k) + b \right] \right) y_k y_i k(x_i, x_k), \qquad (7)$$

the update rule is given by

$$\alpha_m = \alpha_m - \eta y_m (\alpha y)^T k(B, x_m) + \eta$$
$$+ \eta \gamma n \left(1 - y_j \left[(\alpha y)^T k(B, x_j) + b\right]\right) y_j y_m k(x_j, x_m), \tag{8}$$

where (x_j, y_j) is a randomly chosen instance of X. The entire procedure of the Online Budget LS-SVM is described in Algorithm 1.

Algorithm 1. Online Budget LS-SVM:

1. **Input:**
   - Training set X and labels y. $n = |X|$.
   - Budget size: β.
   - Initial values for α and b.
   - Step size: η.
2. Randomly choose β instances in X to build the budget matrix B.
3. Compute kernel matrix $k(B, B)$.
4. **Repeat** (until an approximate minimum is obtained):
   Randomly shuffle X.
   for $j \in \{1 \ldots n\}$:
      for $m = 1$ to β:

$$\alpha_m = \alpha_m - \eta y_m (\alpha y)^T k(B, x_m) + \eta$$
$$+ \eta \gamma n \left(1 - y_j \left[(\alpha y)^T k(B, x_j) + b\right]\right) y_j y_m k(x_j, x_m),$$
$$b = b - \eta \gamma n \left(1 - y_j \left[(\alpha y)^T k(B, x_j) + b\right] (-y_j)\right)$$

Nyström LS-SVM. As for the budget strategy, the Nyström method can be used in (5) to approximate the kernel matrix. The loss function will be

$$\min_{\alpha, b} \mathcal{L}' = \frac{1}{2} (\alpha y)^T \hat{k}(X, X)(\alpha y) - \sum_{k=1}^{\beta} \alpha_k + \frac{\gamma}{2} \sum_{k=1}^{n} \left(1 - y_k \left[(\alpha y)^T \hat{k}(X, x_k) + b\right]\right)^2, \tag{9}$$

where $\hat{k}$ is the dot function after the Nyström approximation of original k.

4   Experimental Evaluation

4.1   Experimental Setup

The proposed methods were implemented in the dataflow GPU TensorFlow framework [1], one of the most used interfaces to express and develop research over machine learning algorithms. All the datasets were partitioned 80% for training and 20% for test. The optimization process is performed by SGD

with the Adam optimizer [7], running until 1000 epochs. Four binary classification problems were chosen to test the proposed models using a RBF kernel.
The datasets are described in Table 1. The Online Budget LS-SVM was trained
with different budget proportions: 0.2, 0.4, 0.6, 0.8, 1.0 of the original data size.
The same proportions were taken to make the Nyström low rank matrix and
train the Nyström LS-SVM. In order to compare results with an state-of-the-art
method, an Online RFF LS-SVM (which solves (1) in the primal by means of
an approximation of the feature mapping ϕ and a linear learning algorithm) was
tested for five different features sizes: the same as budget sizes in each dataset.
After a parameter exploration for γ, we decided to fix $\gamma = 1.0$.

Table 1. Datasets details. In the case of Wine and Mnist only two classes where taken.

Dataset	Instances	Features	Positive samples	Negative samples
Wine	130	13	65	65
Spambase	4601	57	1813	2788
Mnist	12136	784	5834	6302
Bank	41118	16	4640	36548

4.2   Results

Each configuration was executed several times and the mean and standard deviation of the results are presented in Fig. 1. On Wine and on Spambase, the
Online Budget LS-SVM outperformed the Nyström LS-SVM, specially for the
bigger proportions of the budget. In Mnist and Bank, although Nyström reached
higher accuracy levels, the difference with the budget version is not quite high.
The RFF approach showed the worst performance in all the datasets, specially
in Mnist, where the accuracy level was almost constant equal to 0.5, indicating a null capacity of learning. As expected, in all the datasets the standard
deviation goes down as the dataset grows in size, and there is more stability in
the Nyström procedure as it recreates the entire kernel matrix. Regarding the

Table 2. Mean training times for each dataset. Times reported for Online Budget
LS-SVM correspond to the experiments trained with 20% of the data. For Nyström
LS-SVM, they correspond to the experiments with an approximated kernel matrix
made from 20% of the data, and for RFF LS-SVM, the number of selected features
equals the 20% of training set size.

Method	Wine	Spambase	Mnist	Bank
Online Budget LS-SVM	3.0243s	21.928s	176.35s	1132.15s
Nyström LS-SVM	1.9257s	34.386s	241.29s	2220.49s
RFF LS-SVM	3.2200s	6.0859s	17.856s	45.1223s

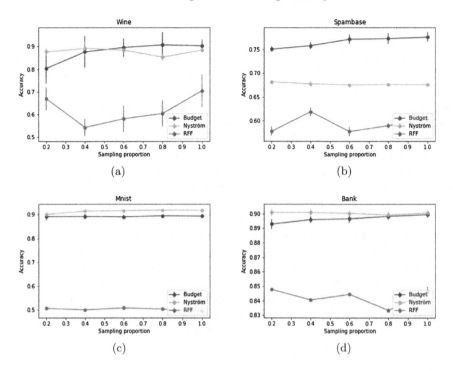

Fig. 1. Mean and standard deviation of the results reached by Online Budget LS-SVM, with the Nyström LS-SVM and with the Online RFF LS-SVM.

training times (Table 2), it is quite notable that in Wine the Nyström LS-SVM is faster than the Online Budget LS-SVM. However, as the size of the dataset gets bigger, Nyström LS-SVM became slower that the budget (as in Bank).

4.3   Discussion

Results show a similar performance between Online Budget LS-SVM and Nyström LS-SVM. There is not a significant dominance of one method over the other one. However, to solve the LS-SVM problem in the primal using the RFF approach has not shown any good performance independently of the number of features selected. The standard deviation reported using the budget strategy is higher than the reported with the Nyström approximation, which indicates more stability in the approximation of the kernel matrix. The running times show that the budget method works best for larger sets compared to the Nyström method. This is where the computational complexity of the Nyström approximation is evidenced.

5   Conclusions

In this work we presented the Online Budget LS-SVM, a large scale learning method based on the LS-SVM algorithm. It uses the Learning on a Budget technique to avoid the entire computation of the kernel matrix. In order to compare the performance with other state-of-the-art approximation methods, a Nyström approximation (Nyström LS-SVM) and a RFF approach are also implemented. Experimental results show that there is not a significant loss of accuracy when a random budget is selected to train the machine. Comparing the results of Online Budget LS-SVM with the LS-SVM Nyström, and with the Online RFF LS-SVM, the Online Budget LS-SVM is on par with the Nyström version of the method, sometimes even outperforming it. The execution times showed that, in large datasets, the computation required to obtain the Nyström low rank matrix approximation does not compensate any improvement in the performance of the method, as it is shown in the running times for the Bank datasets. Regarding the Online RFF LS-SVM, the results have shown a bad performance compared to the other methods, independently of the number of features. To conclude, the Learning on a Budget technique alleviates the computation of the kernel matrix, without significant loss of accuracy, speeding up the training process, and making kernel-based methods more scalable.

References

1. Abadi, M., et al.: TensorFlow: a system for large-scale machine learning. CoRR (2016)
2. Barreto, A.M.S., Precup, D., Pineau, J.: Practical kernel-based reinforcement learning. arXiv preprint arXiv:1407.5358, **17**, 1–70 (2014). http://arxiv.org/abs/1407.5358%5Cnpapers://6d7e3f19-aa00-4bdb-8e1b-85d8ff06c154/Paper/p9035
3. Bottou, L.: Large-scale machine learning with stochastic gradient descent. In: Lechevallier, Y., Saporta, G. (eds.) Proceedings of COMPSTAT 2010, pp. 177–186. Springer, Heidelberg (2010). https://doi.org/10.1007/978-3-7908-2604-3_16
4. Drineas, P., Mahoney, M.W.: On the Nyström method for approximating a gram matrix for improved kernel-based learning. J. Mach. Learn. R. **6**, 2153–2175 (2005)
5. Hofmann, T., Schölkopf, B., Smola, A.J.: Kernel methods in machine learning. Ann. Stat. **36**, 1171–1220 (2008)
6. Jian, L., Shen, S., Li, J., Liang, X., Li, L.: Budget online learning algorithm for least squares SVM. IEEE Trans. Neural Netw. Learn. Syst. **28**, 2076–2087 (2017)
7. Kingma, D.P., Ba, J.: Adam: a method for stochastic optimization. CoRR (2014)
8. Páez-Torres, A.E., González, F.A.: Online kernel matrix factorization. Progress in Pattern Recognition, Image Analysis, Computer Vision, and Applications. LNCS, vol. 9423, pp. 651–658. Springer, Cham (2015). https://doi.org/10.1007/978-3-319-25751-8_78
9. Rahimi, A., Recht, B.: Random features for large-scale kernel machines. In: Proceedings of the 20th International Conference on Neural Information Processing Systems, NIPS 2007, pp. 1177–1184. Curran Associates Inc. (2007)
10. Si, S., Hsieh, C.J., Dhillon, I.S.: Memory efficient kernel approximation. J. Mach. Learn. Res. **18**(1), 682–713 (2017)

11. Suykens, J., Vandewalle, J.: Least squares support vector machine classifiers. Neural Process. Lett. **9**(3), 293–300 (1999)
12. Wang, Z., Crammer, K., Vucetic, S.: Breaking the curse of kernelization: budgeted stochastic gradient descent for large-scale SVM training. J. Mach. Learn. Res. **13**(1), 3103–3131 (2012)
13. Yang, T., Li, Y.F., Mahdavi, M., Jin, R., Zhou, Z.H.: Nyström method vs random fourier features: a theoretical and empirical comparison. In: Pereira, F., Burges, C.J.C., Bottou, L., Weinberger, K.Q. (eds.) Advances in Neural Information Processing Systems, vol. 25, pp. 476–484. Curran Associates, Inc. (2012)

An Automatic Approximate Bayesian Computation Approach Using Metric Learning

W. González-Vanegas$^{(\boxtimes)}$, A. Álvarez-Meza, and A. Orozco-Gutiérrez

Faculty of Engineerings, Automatic Research Group,
Universidad Tecnológica de Pereira, Pereira, Colombia
wilgonzalez@utp.edu.co

Abstract. Recent progress in Bayesian inference has allowed for accurate posterior estimations in complex situations with no idea about a likelihood function. Currently, Approximate Bayesian Computation (ABC) techniques have emerged as a widely used set of free-likelihood methods. Although there is a large number of different ABC-based approaches across the literature, all they have in common a hard dependence on free parameters selection, demanding for expensive tuning procedures such as grid search or cross-validation. Here, we introduce an Automatic Metric Learning-based ABC approach, termed AML-ABC. Namely, AML-ABC matches the simulation and observation spaces within an ABC-based framework. Attained results on a synthetic dataset and a real-world ecological system show that our approach is a competitive method compared to other non-automatic state-of-the-art ABC techniques.

Keywords: Approximate Bayesian Computation · Kernel methods ·
Metric learning · Non-linear dynamic system · Statistical inference

1 Introduction

Bayesian-based statistical inference tasks require the calculation of the likelihood function, which performs an important role as long as it states the probability of the observed data under a particular model. Therefore, the Bayes' theorem leverages the inclusion of a priori knowledge about the studied phenomenon into the posterior distribution. Indeed, straightforward models gather an analytic expression for the likelihood function facilitating the evidence assessment; then, the posterior can be precisely computed. Notwithstanding, for complex models, to find an exact formula for the likelihood function is often intractable [13].

To deal with this intractability, free-likelihood techniques like Approximate Bayesian Computation (ABC) have emerged. ABC-based methods assess an auxiliary model with different parameter values drawn from a prior distribution to compute simulations that are compared to the observed data [13]. In particular, this comparison can be performed using statistics that summarize and characterize the information over large features and observations [5,10]. However, the

© Springer Nature Switzerland AG 2019
R. Vera-Rodriguez et al. (Eds.): CIARP 2018, LNCS 11401, pp. 12–19, 2019.
https://doi.org/10.1007/978-3-030-13469-3_2

selection of proper and sufficient summary statistic could be difficult for complex models, demanding for alternative approaches that rely on kernel functions to embed and compare distributions into a Reproducing Kernel Hilbert Space (RKHS) [4,9]. Recent advances in ABC-based inference have introduced kernel methods to accomplish more accurate posterior estimations. Authors in [6] developed a surrogate model as synthetic likelihood to define an adequate number of simulations within the ABC procedure via a Gaussian process-based framework. Mitrovic et al. [7] modeled the functional relationship between simulations and the optimal choice of summary statistics to encode the structure of a generative model using a kernel ridge regression for conditional distributions. Nonetheless, the techniques mentioned above require the estimation of different parameters related to the similarity computation among simulations to approximate the posterior. Then, expensive tuning procedures as grid search and cross-validation are carried out. Moreover, the user requires a vast knowledge concerning the ABC algorithm and the studied data to properly tune the free parameters, yielding to a high influence in the quality of the posterior approximation.

Here, we introduce an automatic version of an ABC algorithm to support Bayesian inference. Our approach, named AML-ABC, comprises a metric learning stage based on a Centered Kernel Alignment (CKA) to assess the matching between similarities defined over parameters and simulations [3]. Besides, a Mahalanobis distance is computed through CKA, and a graph representation is utilized to highlight local dependencies from both parameter and simulation spaces in ABC. Achieved results on synthetic and real-world inference problems demonstrate that our automatic extension of ABC infers competitive posteriors without requiring any manually fixing of free parameters.

The remainder of this paper is organized as follows: Sect. 2 describes the mathematical background. Section 3 describes the experimental set-up and the obtained result. Finally, the conclusions are outlined in Sect. 4.

2   Materials and Methods

ABC Fundamentals. In any Bayesian inference task, the central aim concerns the computation of a posterior $p(\theta|y)$, using a prior distribution $\zeta(\theta)$ and a likelihood function $p(y|\theta)$, where $y \in \mathcal{Y}$ stands for the observed data and $\theta \in \Theta$ holds the model parameters. Nonetheless, when the likelihood is intractable, neither exact nor sampled posterior $p(\theta|y) \propto p(y|\theta)\zeta(\theta)$ can be calculated. ABC approaches aim to facilitate such an inference via simulation of the likelihood through a generative model represented by a conditional probability $p(x|\theta)$, where $x \in \mathcal{Y}$ is a random variable standing for the simulated data [13]. Fundamentally, an ABC-based framework relies on the acceptance and rejection of simulated samples x using a distance function $d_{\mathcal{Y}} : \mathcal{Y} \times \mathcal{Y} \to \mathbb{R}^+$. In turn, an approximate posterior can be estimated such that: $\hat{p}(\theta|y;\epsilon) \propto \hat{p}(y|\theta;\epsilon)\zeta(\theta)$, where $\hat{p}(y|\theta;\epsilon) = \int_{\mathcal{B}(y;\epsilon)} p(x|\theta)dx$, $\mathcal{B}(y;\epsilon) = \{x : d_{\mathcal{Y}}(x,y) < \epsilon\}$, and $\epsilon \in \mathbb{R}^+$. Note that setting the value of ϵ is a crucial stage for obtaining an accurate posterior.

On the other hand, most of the times it is difficult to apply a distance directly on $\mathcal{Y}$ due to a large number of samples and features in real data. In such a case, some strategies use a mapping $s = \vartheta(x)$ before calculating the distance, where $s \in \mathcal{S}$ is a feature space and $\vartheta : \mathcal{Y} \to \mathcal{S}$ [5]. However, using $\vartheta(x)$ often leaks information for complex models. Then, some ABC-based approaches approximate $\hat{p}(y|\theta; \epsilon)$ as the convolution of the true likelihood $p(y|\theta)$ and a kernel function $\kappa : \mathcal{Y} \times \mathcal{Y} \to \mathbb{R}$, which imposes a constraint to the rejection of samples as the inner product $\kappa(x, y) = \langle \phi(x), \phi(y) \rangle_{\mathcal{H}}$ in a Reproducing Kernel Hilbert Space (RKHS), $\mathcal{H}$, where $\phi : \mathcal{Y} \to \mathcal{H}$ [9]. In practice, given N samples $\{x_n \backsim P_{X_n}\}_{n=1}^N$ drawn from $p(x|\theta_n)$, with $\theta_n \backsim \zeta(\theta)$, and the observation $y \backsim P_Y$, a weighted sample set $\Psi = \{(\theta_n, w_n)\}_{n=1}^N$ is calculated by fixing:

$$w_n = \kappa_G\left(d_{\mathcal{H}}(P_{X_n}, P_Y); \epsilon\right) \Big/ \sum\nolimits_{n=1}^N \kappa_G\left(d_{\mathcal{H}}(P_{X_n}, P_Y); \epsilon\right), \tag{1}$$

where κ_G is a Gaussian kernel with bandwidth ϵ. Eq. (1) is used to approximate $p(\theta|y)$ via posterior expectation as: $\hat{p}(\theta|y) = \sum_{n=1}^N w_n \kappa_G(d_e(\theta, \theta_n); \sigma_\theta)$, where d_e stands for the Euclidean distance and $\sigma_\theta \in \mathbb{R}^+$. Moreover, $d_{\mathcal{H}}(P_{X_n}, P_Y)$ represents a distance over distributions.

Automatic ABC Using Metric Learning. To avoid the influence of the ϵ value and the kernel parameters while computing the ABC-based posterior as in Eq. (1), we introduce an Automatic Metric Learning (AML) approach in the context of ABC, termed AML-ABC, for enhancing and automating the inference task. The idea behind AML-ABC is to include the information contained in the candidates $\{\theta_n\}_{n=1}^N$ to improve the comparison stage carried out over simulations and observations. Let $\Psi = \{\theta_n, x_n\}_{n=1}^N$ be the set of N candidates $\theta_n \in \mathbb{R}^P \backsim \zeta(\theta)$ and their corresponding simulations $x_n \in \mathbb{R}^Q \backsim p(x|\theta)$. Further, let the kernel function $\kappa_\theta : \Theta \times \Theta \to \mathbb{R}^+$ be a similarity measure between candidates in Θ, that define the kernel matrix $\mathbf{K}_\theta \in \mathbb{R}^{N \times N}$ holding elements:

$$\kappa_\theta(\theta_n, \theta_{n'}) = \begin{cases} \exp(-d_\Theta^2(\theta_n, \theta_{n'})), & \theta_n \in \Omega_{n'} \\ 0, & \text{otherwise,} \end{cases} \tag{2}$$

where $\Omega_{n'}$ is a set holding the M-nearest neighbors of $\theta_{n'}$ in the sense of the distance $d_\Theta : \Theta \times \Theta \to \mathbb{R}^+$. In this paper, to avoid large variations among components of θ_n we rely on the Mahalanobis distance $d_\Theta^2(\theta_n, \theta_{n'}) = (\theta_n - \theta_{n'})^T \Sigma_\Theta^{-1}(\theta_n - \theta_{n'})$, where $\Sigma_\Theta \in \mathbb{R}^{P \times P}$ is the sample covariance matrix of $\{\theta_n\}_{n=1}^N$. Concerning the feature space $\mathcal{S}$, we assess the similarity via the kernel $\kappa_s : \mathcal{S} \times \mathcal{S} \to \mathbb{R}^+$, $\kappa_s(\vartheta(x_n), \vartheta(x_{n'})) = \exp(-d_{\mathcal{S}}^2(\vartheta(x_n), \vartheta(x_{n'})))$, to build the matrix $\mathbf{K}_s \in \mathbb{R}^{N \times N}$, where $d_{\mathcal{S}}^2 : \mathcal{S} \times \mathcal{S} \to \mathbb{R}^+$ and $\vartheta : \mathcal{Y} \to \mathcal{S}$ is a feature mapping. To perform the pairwise comparison between simulations in $\mathcal{S}$ we use the Mahalanobis distance of the form [2]:

$$d_{\mathcal{S}}^2(\vartheta(x_n), \vartheta(x_{n'})) = (\vartheta(x_n) - \vartheta(x_{n'}))^T \mathbf{A}\mathbf{A}^T(\vartheta(x_n) - \vartheta(x_{n'})), \tag{3}$$

where $\Sigma_{\mathcal{S}}^{-1} = \mathbf{A}\mathbf{A}^T$ stands for the inverse covariance matrix of $\vartheta(x_n) \in \mathbb{R}^D$ and $\mathbf{A} \in \mathbb{R}^{D \times d}$. In this sense, we use the information concerning the similarity over candidates in Θ, represented via $\mathbf{K}_\theta$, to state the notion of similarity over simulations and observation in $\mathcal{S}$, represented via $\mathbf{K}_s$. In particular, we use a CKA-based measure between the above kernel matrices as [3]:

$$\hat{\rho}(\mathbf{K}_\theta, \mathbf{K}_s) = \frac{\langle \bar{\mathbf{K}}_\theta, \bar{\mathbf{K}}_s \rangle_{\mathrm{F}}}{\sqrt{\langle \bar{\mathbf{K}}_\theta \bar{\mathbf{K}}_\theta \rangle_{\mathrm{F}} \langle \bar{\mathbf{K}}_s \bar{\mathbf{K}}_s \rangle_{\mathrm{F}}}}, \tag{4}$$

where $\bar{\mathbf{K}}$ stands for the centered kernel as $\bar{\mathbf{K}} = \tilde{\mathbf{I}} \mathbf{K} \tilde{\mathbf{I}}$, being $\tilde{\mathbf{I}} = \mathbf{I} - \mathbf{1}^\top \mathbf{1}/N$ the empirical centering matrix, $\mathbf{I} \in \mathbb{R}^{N \times N}$ is the identity matrix, and $\mathbf{1} \in \mathbb{R}^N$ is the all-ones vector. Moreover, The notation $\langle \cdot, \cdot \rangle_{\mathrm{F}}$ represents the matrix-based Frobenius norm. In Eq. (4), $\hat{\rho}(\cdot, \cdot)$ is a data driven estimator that aims to quantify the similarity between the parameter space and the feature space. To find the projection matrix $\mathbf{A}$, we consider the following optimization problem:

$$\hat{\mathbf{A}} = \arg \max_{A} \log \left(\hat{\rho}(\mathbf{K}_s(\mathbf{A}), \mathbf{K}_\theta) \right), \tag{5}$$

where the logarithm function is used for mathematical convenience. The optimization problem in Eq. (5) can be solved using a gradient descent-based approach [2]. Moreover, we form the weighted sample set $\Psi = \{(\theta_n, w_n)\}_{n=1}^N$ by fixing $w_n = \kappa_E(z, z_n)/\sum_{n=1}^N \kappa_E(z, z_n)$, where $\kappa_E : \mathbb{R}^d \times \mathbb{R}^d \to \mathbb{R}$ is a similarity kernel defined as:

$$\kappa_E(z, z_n) = \begin{cases} \exp(-\|z - z_n\|_2^2), & z_n \in \Upsilon \\ 0, & \text{otherwise,} \end{cases} \tag{6}$$

where Υ is a set holding the M-nearest neighbors of $z = \vartheta(y)^\top \hat{\mathbf{A}}$ in the sense of the Euclidean distance. Algorithm 1 summarizes the AML-ABC approach.

Algorithm 1. AML-ABC algorithm

Input: Observed data: y, prior: $\zeta(\theta)$, mapping: ϑ, M-nearest neighbors, width: σ_θ.
Output: Posterior estimation: $\hat{p}(\theta|y)$.
Metric learning stage:
1: $\Psi' = \left\{ (\theta_n', x_n') \right\}_{n=1}^N$; $\theta_n' \frown \zeta(\theta),\, x_n' \frown p(x|\theta_n')$ ▷ Draw training data.
2: $\hat{\mathbf{A}} = \arg \max_A \log \left(\hat{\rho}(\mathbf{K}_s(\mathbf{A}), \mathbf{K}_\theta) \right)$ ▷ Compute CKA based on ϑ, M, θ_n', and x_n'.
Inference stage:
3: $\Psi = \{(\theta_n, x_n)\}_{n=1}^N$; $\theta_n \frown \zeta(\theta),\, x_n \frown p(x|\theta_n)$ ▷ Draw simulated data.
4: $z = \vartheta(y)^\top \hat{\mathbf{A}}$ ▷ Project features of observed data
5: **for** $n = 1, \cdots, N$ **do**
6:      $z_n = \vartheta(x_n)^\top \hat{\mathbf{A}}$ ▷ Project features of simulated data
7:      $\tilde{w}_n = \kappa_E(z, z_n)$ ▷ Compute the n-th weight value.
8: **end for**
9: $w_n = \tilde{w}_n / \sum_{n=1}^N \tilde{w}_n$ ▷ Normalize the weights
10: $\hat{p}(\theta|y) = \sum_{n=1}^N w_n \kappa_G(\mathrm{d}_e(\theta, \theta_n; \sigma_\theta))$ ▷ Compute the posterior.

---

3   Experiments and Results

To test the AML-ABC performance, we consider two experiments following [9]: a toy problem concerning synthetic data from a mixture model and a Bayesian inference problem for a real ecological dynamic system. To accomplish an automatic inference, we find the number of M-nearest neighbors as the median of the optimal number of neighbours per point according to the Local Neighborhood Selection (LNS) algorithm introduced in [1]. Moreover, the K2-ABC method is selected as benchmark due to its nice performance over other methods [9].

For the toy problem, we analyze a mixture of uniform distributions of the form: $p(x|\boldsymbol{\pi}) = \sum_{c=1}^{C} \pi_c \mathscr{U}(c-1, c)$, where $\boldsymbol{\pi} = \{\pi_c\}_{c=1}^{C}$ are the mixing coefficients holding $\sum_{c=1}^{C} \pi_c = 1$, and C is the number of components. Here, the aim is to estimate the posterior $p(\boldsymbol{\pi}|y)$ for $C=5$, given synthetic observations y drawn from the mixture with true parameters (target): $\boldsymbol{\pi}^* = \{0.25, 0.04, 0.33, 0.04, 0.34\}$. For concrete testing, we draw $N = 1000$ samples from a symmetric Dirichlet prior, $\boldsymbol{\pi} \sim \text{Dirichlet}(\mathbf{1})$, and then used the mixture model to form the simulated data by drawing 400 observations for each prior candidate. Moreover, we employ a histogram with 10 bins as feature mapping in AML-ABC, and kernel widths $\gamma = 0.1$, $\epsilon = 0.001$ in K2-ABC [9]. As quantitative assessment, we use the Euclidean distance $\mathcal{E} = ||\boldsymbol{\pi}^* - \hat{\boldsymbol{\pi}}||_2$, where $\hat{\boldsymbol{\pi}}$ is the expected value of the posterior using the weights $\{w_n\}_{n=1}^{N}$ obtained by each method.

For the real dataset experiment, we considere the problem of inferring the dynamics of an adult blowfly population as introduced in [14]. In particular, the population dynamics are modelled by a discretised differential equation of the form: $N_{t+1} = PN_{t-\tau} \exp(-N_{t-\tau}/N_0)e_t + N_t \exp(-\delta\epsilon_t)$, with N_{t+1} denoting the observation time at $t+1$ which is determined by the time-lagged observations N_t and $N_{t-\tau}$, where e_t and ϵ_t stand for Gamma distributed noise $e_t \sim \mathcal{G}(1/\sigma_p^2, \sigma_p^2)$ and $\epsilon_t \sim \mathcal{G}(1/\sigma_d^2, \sigma_d^2)$. Here, the aim is to estimate the posterior of the parameters $\boldsymbol{\theta} = \{P, N_0, \sigma_d, \sigma_p, \tau, \delta\}$ given observed data concerning a time series of 180 observations[1]. We adopt Log-normal distributions for setting priors over $\boldsymbol{\theta}$ [6]: $\log P \sim \mathcal{N}(2, 2^2)$, $\log N_0 \sim \mathcal{N}(6, 1)$, $\log \sigma_d \sim \mathcal{N}(-0.5, 1)$, $\log \sigma_p \sim \mathcal{N}(-0.5, 1)$, $\log \tau \sim \mathcal{N}(2.7, 1)$, $\log \delta \sim \mathcal{N}(-1, 0.4^2)$. For AML-ABC we draw $N = 5000$ samples from the prior and then assess the model to form the simulated data by drawing 180 observations for each prior candidate. Besides, as feature mapping, we selected the 10 statistics used in [9]. Moreover, we use the Euclidean distance $\mathcal{E} = ||\vartheta(y) - \vartheta(x_n|\hat{\boldsymbol{\theta}})||_2$ as quantitative assessment, where $x_n|\hat{\boldsymbol{\theta}}$ is a simulation from the model given the expected value of the posterior using each method. In particular, due to fluctuations produced by ϵ_t and e_t, we draw 100 simulation for each method and compute the median and standard deviation for $\mathcal{E}$ [9].

Toy Problem Results. Since this is a controlled experiment with known parameters $\boldsymbol{\pi}^*$, we can find the best possible performance of our AML-ABC by running the inference stage in Algorithm 1 with $\tilde{w}_n = \kappa_E(\boldsymbol{\pi}^*, \boldsymbol{\pi}_n)$. We refer to this approach as *Best*. The previous setting is equivalent to think that the CKA between

---

[1] Available on the supplementary materials of [14].

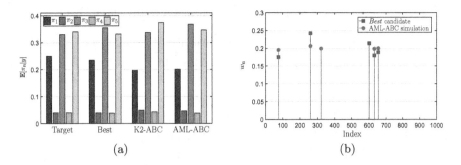

Fig. 1. Uniform mixture model results. (a) Estimated mean posterior of mixing coefficients using various methods (b) Weights of the 5 nearest neighbors in AML-ABC.

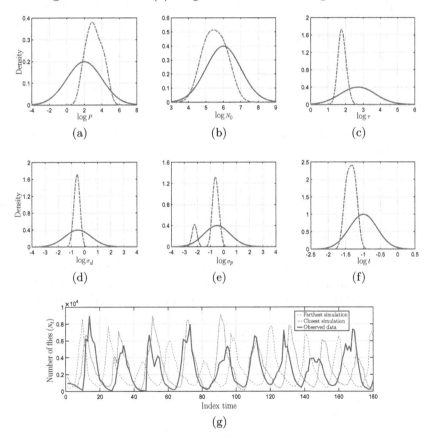

Fig. 2. Non-linear ecological dynamic system results. (a)–(f) Prior distribution (solid line) and AML-ABC-based posterior estimation (dashed line) of model parameters in the log-space. (g) Some realizations from the model using the expected value of the parameters found via AML-ABC.

Table 1. Performance of different ABC schemes over the blowfly dataset.

Method	Median $(\mathscr{E}) \pm$ std $(\mathscr{E})$
Kernel ABC [8]	5.2 ± 3.0
Indirect score ABC [11]	2.1 ± 1.8
Semi-Automatic ABC [10]	1.9 ± 1.2
Synthetic Likelihood ABC [14]	1.7 ± 1.3
K2-ABC [9]	$\mathbf{1.0 \pm 0.8}$
AML-ABC	$\mathbf{1.2 \pm 0.4}$

$\mathbf{K}_\theta$ and $\mathbf{K}_s$ is perfect ($\mathbf{K}_\theta = \mathbf{K}_s$). Figure 1 shows the *Best* performance along with K2-ABC and AML-ABC results over the uniform mixture problem. In Fig. 1(a), the expected value of the posterior computed for all methods is close to the target. In particular, we obtained $\mathscr{E}_{Best} = 0.030$, $\mathscr{E}_{\text{K2-ABC}} = 0.063$, and $\mathscr{E}_{\text{AML-ABC}} = 0.064$. These results show that our AML-ABC is a competitive estimator to K2-ABC with a significant advantage concerning the automatic selection of free parameters. In addition, to provide a better understanding of the AML-ABC effectiveness, in Fig. 1(b) we provide the weights for the 5 nearest neighbors (according to the LNS algorithm) used to compute the posteriors. As noted, the majority of the chosen simulations for AML-ABC match the selected candidates using the *Best*, although our approach never observes the target.

Real Dataset Results. Inferring the model parameters in this blowfly dataset is a very challenging task since the system dynamics can easily move from stable to chaotic regimes [6,14]. This states an interesting scenario to test the performance and robustness of the AML-ABC. In Figs. 2(a) to (f), we provide the prior and the posterior approximation for each parameter fixing σ_θ according to [12]. Notice how our proposal updates the beliefs about the model parameters leading to more concentrated posteriors. In the case of $\log \sigma_p$, two modes reflect different intervals with probable values for driving the noise realization associated with egg production in the blowfly population. However, there is a predominant mode that states higher probabilities for this parameter. Moreover, Fig. 2(g) shows the closest and farthest simulation to the observed data from 100 realization used to compute $\mathscr{E}$, showing a posterior in stable regime. Finally, Table 1 shows the performance of AML-ABC compared to different ABC-based methods tested on the blowfly dataset by authors in [9], where clearly the proposed method is a quite competitive approach to K2-ABC.

4   Conclusions

We propose an automatic enhancement of the well-known ABC algorithm devoted to Bayesian inference called AML-ABC. In particular, we include a Metric Learning approach based on a CKA methodology to quantify the matching between parameter and simulation spaces. Then, a Mahalanobis distance is learned through CKA and a graph representation is employed to reveal local relationships among parameter and simulation samples. Notably, our AML-ABC does not require the tuning of any free parameter. Besides, obtained results on a synthetic dataset and a real-world ecological system show the introduced AML-ABC is a competitive approach compared to other non-automatic state-of-the-art ABC methods. Future work includes the extension of AML-ABC for multi-dimensional problems and the inclusion of other dissimilarity measures, besides the Mahalanobis distance, to deal with complex and/or noisy data.

Acknowledgments. Research under grants provided by the project 1110-745-58696, funded by Colciencias, Colombia. Authors would like to thank the Master in Electrical Engineering program from Universidad Tecnológica de Pereira for partially funding this research. Moreover, author W. González-Vanegas was supported under the project E6-18-2, funded by Universidad Tecnológica de Pereira.

References

1. Álvarez-Meza, A., et al.: Global and local choice of the number of nearest neighbors in locally linear embedding. Pattern Recogn. Lett. **32**(16), 2171–2177 (2011)
2. Álvarez-Meza, A., et al.: Kernel-based relevance analysis with enhanced interpretability for detection of brain activity patterns. Frontiers Neurosci. **11**, 550 (2017)
3. Cortes, C., Mohri, M., Rostamizadeh, A.: Algorithms for learning kernels based on centered alignment. JMLR **13**, 795–828 (2012)
4. González-Vanegas, W., Alvarez-Meza, A., Orozco-Gutierrez, Á.: Sparse hilbert embedding-based statistical inference of stochastic ecological systems. In: Mendoza, M., Velastín, S. (eds.) CIARP 2017. LNCS, vol. 10657, pp. 255–262. Springer, Cham (2018). https://doi.org/10.1007/978-3-319-75193-1_31
5. Joyce, P., Marjoram, P., et al.: Approximately sufficient statistics and Bayesian computation. Stat. Appl. Genet. Molec. **7**(1), 26 (2008)
6. Meeds, E., Welling, M.: GPS-ABC: Gaussian process surrogate approximate Bayesian computation. arXiv preprint arXiv:1401.2838 (2014)
7. Mitrovic, J., Sejdinovic, D., Teh, Y.W.: DR-ABC: approximate Bayesian computation with kernel-based distribution regression. In: International Conference on Machine Learning, ICML 2016, vol. 48, pp. 1482–1491 (2016)
8. Nakagome, S., et al.: Kernel approximate Bayesian computation in population genetic inferences. Stat. Appl. Genet. Mol. Biol. **12**(6), 667–678 (2013)
9. Park, M., Jitkrittum, W., Sejdinovic, D.: K2-ABC: approximate Bayesian computation with kernel embeddings. arXiv preprint arXiv:1502.02558 (2015)
10. Paul, F., Dennis, P.: Constructing summary statistics for approximate Bayesian computation: semi-automatic approximate bayesian computation. J. Roy. Stat. Soc. Ser. B (Stat. Methodol.) **74**(3), 419–474 (2012)
11. Pigorsch, E.G.C.: Approximate Bayesian computation with indirect summary statistics. Technical report (2013)
12. Shimazaki, H., Shinomoto, S.: Kernel bandwidth optimization in spike rate estimation. J. Comput. Neurosci. **29**(1–2), 171–182 (2010)
13. Turner, B.M., Van Zandt, T.: A tutorial on approximate Bayesian computation. J. Math. Psychol. **56**(2), 69–85 (2012)
14. Wood, S.N.: Statistical inference for noisy nonlinear ecological dynamic systems. Nature **466**(7310), 1102–1104 (2010)

Generative Models for Deep Learning with Very Scarce Data

Juan Maroñas[1]([⊠]), Roberto Paredes[1], and Daniel Ramos[2]

[1] Pattern Recognition and Human Language Technology,
Universitat Politècnica de València, Valencia, Spain
rparedes@prhlt.upv.es, jmaronasm@gmail.com
[2] AUDIAS, Universidad Autónoma de Madrid, Madrid, Spain
daniel.ramos@uam.es

Abstract. The goal of this paper is to deal with a data scarcity scenario where deep learning techniques use to fail. We compare the use of two well established techniques, Restricted Boltzmann Machines and Variational Auto-encoders, as generative models in order to increase the training set in a classification framework. Essentially, we rely on Markov Chain Monte Carlo (MCMC) algorithms for generating new samples. We show that generalization can be improved comparing this methodology to other state-of-the-art techniques, e.g. semi-supervised learning with ladder networks. Furthermore, we show that RBM is better than VAE generating new samples for training a classifier with good generalization capabilities.

Keywords: Data scarcity · Generative models · Data augmentation · Markov Chain Monte Carlo algorithms

1 Introduction

In the last few years deep neural networks have achieved state-of-the-art performance in many task such as image recognition [18], object recognition [14], language modeling [10], machine translation [17] or speech recognition [7]. One of the key facts that increased this performance is the great amount of available data. This amount of data together with the high expressiveness of neural networks as functions approximators and appropriate hardware lead us to an unprecedented performance in challenging problems.

However, deep learning lacks of success in scenarios where the amount of labeled data is scarce. In this work we aim at providing a methodology in order to apply deep learning techniques to problems with *very* scarce available data. Some techniques are proposed to deal with such data size problem: semi supervised learning techniques such as the ladder network [13], Bayesian modeling [5] and data augmentation (DA) [19]. In particular, data augmentation uses to be referred to the techniques where the practitioners know the most common data variability, as in image recognition, and these variations can be applied to

© Springer Nature Switzerland AG 2019
R. Vera-Rodriguez et al. (Eds.): CIARP 2018, LNCS 11401, pp. 20–28, 2019.
https://doi.org/10.1007/978-3-030-13469-3_3

the available data in order to obtain new samples. On the other hand, there are other methods not assisted by practitioners to generate new samples: generative adversarial networks, GANs [6], variational models such as variational auto-encoder VAE [9,15] and autoregressive models [12].

In this work we study how we can apply deep learning techniques when the amount of data is very scarce. We simulate scenarios where not only the amount of labeled data is scarce, but all the available data. As mentioned before, some techniques can deal with such scenarios. Bayesian modeling incorporates the uncertainty in the model [3]. However Bayesian neural networks are a field under study and introduce several problems for which there is not a wide well established solution: Monte Carlo integration, variational approximations or sampling in high dimensional data spaces, among others.

On the other hand, semi supervised learning techniques need a great amount of unlabeled data to work well. For instance, the ladder network can achieve impressive results with only 100 labeled samples in the MNIST task but using 60000 unlabeled samples.

Finally, deep generative models (DGM) need great amounts of data to be able of generate good quality samples. Figure 1 shows a Variational Auto-encoder (VAE) trained with 100 and 60000 samples. We can see that although the reconstruction error is being minimized the VAE with few samples is unable to generate good samples.

To our knowledge, none of the above mentioned techniques (both semi supervised and DA with DGM) has been applied disruptively to train neural networks models in data scarce scenarios as the ones we propose. Moreover DA based on DGM has not achieved impressive results in neural networks training with lots of data. In this work we show that simple generative models as the Restricted Boltzmann Machines (RBM) [1] clearly outperforms the ladder network and DA based on a Deep Convolutional Variational Auto-encoder.

2 Methodology

In this work we simulate very scarce data scenarios. We train binary VAE and RBM using all the available samples. Details on these models can be found at [1,9,15]. Once these models are trained, we perform a sample generation following a MCMC procedure.

2.1 Sample Generation

For sample generation we rely on the theory of MCMC algorithms and define our transition operator as:

$$T(x'|x) = \int dh \, p(x'|h) \cdot p(h|x) \tag{1}$$

Where $p(x'|h)$ and $p(h|x)$ represents the likelihood distribution of an observed sample x given a latent variable h and, the posterior distribution over the latent

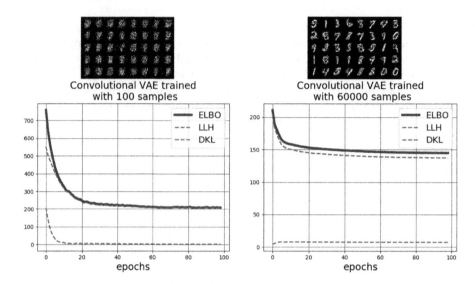

Fig. 1. Samples obtained by decoding a sample from the prior distribution with two VAEs trained on 100 (top left) and 60000 (top right) samples from the MNIST database. Below we plot the reconstruction error (red dashed line) showing that although we are minimizing it, we cannot generate good quality images. Acronyms: $ELBO$ evidence lower bound; D_{KL} Kullback-Lieber divergence and LLH log-likelihood. (Color figure online)

variable given an observed sample, respectively. We will assume that this transition operator generates an ergodic Markov Chain and thus as long as the number of generated samples goes to infinity we will be sampling from the model distribution $p(x)$ [2,3,11]. In case of VAEs, where the posterior distribution is approximated, see [15] appendix F for a proof of correctness.

In our models the likelihood distribution $p(x|h)$ is modeled with a Bernoulli distribution. The posterior distribution is modeled with a Bernoulli distribution for the RBM and with a factorized Gaussian distribution for the VAE. For generating a sample we follow the Contrastive Divergence [4] algorithm which

Input: x, N
Output: generated_chain
generated_chain=vector(N)
$x' = x$
for $i = 0$ *until* $N - 1$ **do**
    $h' \sim p(h|x')$
    $x' \sim p(x|h')$
    generated_chain[i]= x'
end

Algorithm 1. Running MCMC algorithm for data generation

  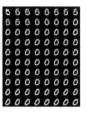

Fig. 2. This figure shows $\mathbb{E}_{x \sim p(x|h)}\{x\}$ of a Markov Chain run with a VAE trained on 60000 samples, starting from a test image (image on the top left corner). We can clearly see how the generated samples can change from class as we run the algorithm. Image in the middle starts from an 8, then, the two next generated samples are 9s to after generate 8s and finally generate 3s. Sample on the right starts from a 5, generate some 5 s and finally generate 0 s.

is based on Gibbs Sampling but starting from an observed sample. As example for generating 100 samples we follow Algorithm 1, where x is a sample from our dataset from which we will be generating new samples and N is the number of samples to generate.[1]

2.2   Labeling Process

We use the generated samples in two ways. As we stated, our approach is based on training a classifier on a set of labeled samples using additional generated samples from a VAE or a RBM. We associate the generated samples with the same label as the sample from the data distribution. In a first approach we use all the generated samples (and denote this approach in the experiments with letter n). In the second approach we classify the samples from the chain (using the same classifier we are training) and only the correctly classified samples are used for training (we denote this approach in the experiments with letter y). This has a great impact, as shown in the experiments, because long Markov Chains are likely to generate samples from other classes, as shown in Fig. 2.

Moreover, in case of the RBM we train two kind of models, named B-RBM ("bad RBM") and G-RBM ("good RBM"). The difference rely on the convergence of the model, i.e., how is the quality of the generated samples, see Fig. 3. We expect that with a B-RBM the injected noise is able to improve the generalization whereas the G-RBM is collapsing to a part of the model space where no generalization improvement will be obtained. Basically we do not let the model achieve the same minimum for the case of the B-RBM as we do with the G-RBM.

Finally, Fig. 4 shows images from the different trained models in this work. We can clearly see how the VAE is able to generate good quality samples only when more training samples are provided.

---

[1] In case of VAE $p(h|x)$ is replaced by $q(h|x)$ which is the Variational Distribution. Note that although a Gibbs sampler depends on all the previous generated dimensions of a sample, in this case we can sample all the feature dimensions in parallel and thus our method is highly efficient.

Fig. 3. Samples from a bad (left) and good (right) RBM. Figure shows a sample from a MCMC chain of 1 step starting from a test sample.

3   Experiments

For the experiments we use a binarized version from the MNIST database. This database has 60000 training samples and 10000 test samples. The pixels above 0.5 are saturated to value 1.0 and the rest are saturated to 0.0. In order to simulate a scarce data scenario, we randomly select a small set of samples, and assume that only a very small subset is labeled. We simulate three different scenarios with a total of 100, 1000 and 10000 samples where only 10, 100 and 1000 are labeled respectively. Note that for the first scenario we have only 1 labeled sample per class.

We use a binarized version of this database because, the expressions of the conditional distributions of the RBM models we use, are obtained assuming binary data distributions. Moreover, the VAE models for MNIST converge better when using Bernoulli decoders, ie binary cross entropy loss.

We trained 3 models, two fully connected (FC) and one convolutional (CNN). For fully connected we choose the following parameters, FC1: 784-1024-1024-10, FC2: 784-1000-500-250-250-250-10. For the convolutional counterpart we use, CONV1: 32@3x3-64@3x3-128@3x3-512-512-10. In all the topologies we inject Gaussian noise with $\sigma = 0.3$ in the input and we use batch norm (BN) [8] and dropout [16]).

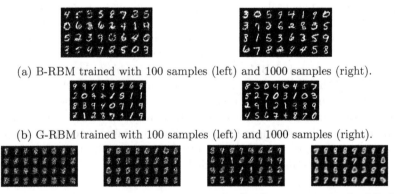

(a) B-RBM trained with 100 samples (left) and 1000 samples (right).

(b) G-RBM trained with 100 samples (left) and 1000 samples (right).

(c) Samples from a VAE trained with 100 samples (left), 1000 samples (middle left), 10000 samples (middle right) and $\mathbb{E}_{x \sim p(x|h)}\{x\}$ on 10000 samples (right)

Fig. 4. Samples from our proposed generative models

Table 1. Data augmentation for 10 labeled samples

	Baseline	B-RBM				G-RBM				VAE			
Chain length		500		1000		500		1000		500		1000	
Classify		y	n	y	n	y	n	y	n	y	n	y	n
FC1	53.71	44.71	47.87	**43.19**	47.56	53.49	52.55	53.91	52.5	80.25	51.49	84.48	50.56
FC2	58.88	**45.34**	47.18	46.4	46.26	54.74	55.27	57.43	57.96	78.14	56.91	78.79	56.66
CONV1	49.58	33.77	37.51	**32.26**	36.69	41.260	38.94	40.12	40.66	39.35	41.56	44.86	41.47

Table 2. Data augmentation for 100 labeled samples

	Baseline	B-RBM				G-RBM				VAE			
Chain length		500		1000		500		1000		500		1000	
Classify		y	n	y	n	y	n	y	n	y	n	y	n
FC1	26.56	**21.34**	21.61	21.41	22.43	26.83	26.51	28.41	26.86	52.01	37.00	-	-
FC2	28.39	19.72	21.31	**18.66**	22.31	26.95	26.98	25.96	26.54	64.82	43.99	-	-
CONV1	12.41	11.65	13.55	-	-	11.36	**11.25**	-	-	58.35	30.14	-	-

Table 3. Data augmentation for 1000 labeled samples

	Baseline	B-RBM				G-RBM				VAE			
Chain length		500		1000		500		1000		500		1000	
Classify		y	n	y	n	y	n	y	n	y	n	y	n
FC1	7.62	**5.55**	6.16	5.81	6.04	5.86	5.91	5.79	5.97	24.13	12.42	-	-
FC2	7.25	5.60	5.96	5.76	5.62	5.28	5.40	**4.70**	5.49	36.19	18.00	-	-
CONV1	3.11	3.26	3.89	-	-	**3.09**	3.54	-	-	10.19	4.85	-	-

Tables 1, 2 and 3 show the error percentage with the here proposed data augmentation showing that the B-RBM clearly outperforms other approaches. We generate Markov chains of 500 and 1000 samples to increase the data set and train the classifier[2]. It is interesting to see that although the deep FC (FC2) has worse performance than FC1 with 10 and 100 samples without DA, we can achieve better results in case of 100 samples with FC2 when using our proposed method.

We also see that a significant improvement is obtained with the most scarce scenario (see Table 1), where we are able to reduce 17% error on CONV1 (check B-RBM option y 1000 samples) and more than 10% in FC models (check B-RBM option y), which is the main objective of this work.

---

[2] Convolutional models on 10 labeled samples are trained with 850 instead of 1000 samples. Convolutional models for 100 and 1000 samples use chains of 100 samples. VAE model on 100 and 1000 samples for all the schemes generates 100 samples. We found a GPU-memory bottleneck because we performed a parameter update per batch with all its generated samples.

Table 4. A comparison with the ladder network. We represent error percentage.

Labeled samples	10	100	1000
Baseline	58.88	28.39	7.25
Ladder network	48.85	24.74	6.96
RBM DA	**45.34**	**18.66**	**5.60**

Finally, Table 4 shows a comparison with the ladder network. Ladder network can be considered the state-of-the art on semi-supervised learning on this dataset[3]. As can be seen we obtain better results on the three scenarios.

4   Conclusions

We can draw several conclusions from this work. We first show that in data scarcity scenarios simple generative models outperform deep generative models (like VAEs). We also see that a B-RBM is incorporating noise that is improving generalization. We can check that G-RBM and VAE works better when we do not classify the generated sample and this is in fact another way to incorporate noise into the classifier. However B-RBM is the best of the three. This also means that a generative model trained in this way (where latent variables capture high detail) is unable to generate samples that improve generalization. The G-RBM generates better quality images but is unable to improve classification accuracy as the B-RBM does.

This can also be noted when we add more training samples, where the difference between the baseline and the here proposed DA is lower, as with CNN. This is because the samples generated do not incorporate additional information to the model and are either quite similar between them or quite similar to the labeled samples. A possible hypothesis is that the generative model is collapsing to a part of the data feature space.

VAEs results were unexpected because despite the poor quality images generated it can improve performance over the baseline. We got this improvement always without classifying images, model n, and only in the case where few label samples are used. It is clear that the VAE is not a good model for these scenarios.

Finally, we also show that the here proposed approach outperforms and is clearly an alternative to semi supervised learning in data scarcity scenarios as shown in Table 4. Another important advantage is that RBM is robust and has a stable learning whether the ladder network and GAN frameworks have several training challenges. The ladder network has many hyper-parameters and its performance is really sensible to little changes on them and the GANs are quite sensible to hyper-parameters as well.

---

[3] Recently other proposed methods have achieved better results, but they are based on GANs and we showed here that DGM are not suitable for these scenarios. For that reason we compare with ladder network.

Acknowledgment. We gratefully acknowledge the support of NVIDIA Corporation with the donation of two Titan Xp GPU used for this research. The work of Daniel Ramos has been supported by the Spanish Ministry of Education by project TEC2015-68172-C2-1-P. Juan Maroñas is supported by grant FPI-UPV.

References

1. Bengio, Y.: Learning deep architectures for AI. Found. Trends Mach. Learn. **2**(1), 1–127 (2009)
2. Bengio, Y., et al.: Generalized denoising auto-encoders as generative models. In: Advances in Neural Information Processing Systems, vol. 26, pp. 899–907. Curran Associates, Inc. (2013)
3. Bishop, C.M.: Pattern Recognition and Machine Learning. Springer, New York (2006)
4. Carreira-Perpinan, M.A., et al.: On contrastive divergence learning. In: AISTATS, vol. 10, pp. 33–40. Citeseer (2005)
5. Gal, Y., Ghahramani, Z.: Bayesian convolutional neural networks with Bernoulli approximate variational inference. In: 4th International Conference on Learning Representations (ICLR) Workshop Track (2016)
6. Goodfellow, I., et al.: Generative adversarial nets. In: Advances in Neural Information Processing Systems, vol. 27, pp. 2672–2680. Curran Associates, Inc. (2014)
7. Hinton, G., et al.: Deep neural networks for acoustic modeling in speech recognition. IEEE Signal Process. Mag. **29**, 82–97 (2012)
8. Ioffe, S., et al.: Batch normalization: accelerating deep network training by reducing internal covariate shift. In: Proceedings of the 32nd International Conference on International Conference on Machine Learning, ICML 2015, vol. 37, pp. 448–456. JMLR.org (2015)
9. Kingma, D.P., et al.: Auto-encoding variational bayes (2013)
10. Mikolov, T., et al.: Efficient estimation of word representations in vector space (2013)
11. Neal, R.M.: Probabilistic inference using Markov Chain Monte Carlo methods (1993)
12. van den Oord, A., et al.: Conditional image generation with PixeLCNN decoders. In: Advances in Neural Information Processing Systems, vol. 29, pp. 4790–4798. Curran Associates, Inc. (2016)
13. Rasmus, A., et al.: Semi-supervised learning with ladder networks. In: Advances in Neural Information Processing Systems, vol. 28, pp. 3546–3554. Curran Associates, Inc. (2015)
14. Redmon, J., et al.: You only look once: unified, real-time object detection. In: 2016 IEEE Conference on Computer Vision and Pattern Recognition, CVPR 2016, Las Vegas, NV, USA, 27–30 June 2016, pp. 779–788 (2016)
15. Rezende, D.J., et al.: Stochastic backpropagation and approximate inference in deep generative models. In: Proceedings of the 31st International Conference on International Conference on Machine Learning, ICML 2014, vol. 32, pp. II-1278–II-1286. JMLR.org (2014)
16. Srivastava, N., et al.: Dropout: a simple way to prevent neural networks from overfitting. J. Mach. Learn. Res. **15**, 1929–1958 (2014)
17. Sutskever, I., et al.: Sequence to sequence learning with neural networks. In: Advances in Neural Information Processing Systems, vol. 27, pp. 3104–3112. Curran Associates, Inc. (2014)

18. Szegedy, C., et al.: Inception-v4, inception-ResNet and the impact of residual connections on learning (2016)
19. Tran, et al.: A Bayesian data augmentation approach for learning deep models. In: Guyon, I., et al. (eds.) Advances in Neural Information Processing Systems, vol. 30, pp. 2797–2806. Curran Associates, Inc. (2017)

Data Augmentation via Variational Auto-Encoders

Unai Garay-Maestre[1], Antonio-Javier Gallego[1(✉)], and Jorge Calvo-Zaragoza[2]

[1] Department of Software and Computing Systems,
University of Alicante, Alicante, Spain
`ugm2@alu.ua.es`, `jgallego@dlsi.ua.es`
[2] PRHLT Research Centre, Universitat Politècnica de València, Valencia, Spain
`jcalvo@prhlt.upv.es`

Abstract. Data augmentation is a widely considered technique to improve the performance of Convolutional Neural Networks during training. This step consists in synthetically generate new labeled data by perturbing the samples of the training set, which is expected to provide more robustness to the learning process. The problem is that the augmentation procedure has to be adjusted manually because the perturbations considered must make sense for the task at issue. In this paper we propose the use of Variational Auto-Encoders (VAEs) to generate new synthetic samples, instead of resorting to heuristic strategies. VAEs are powerful generative models that learn a parametric latent space of the input domain from which new samples can be generated. In our experiments over the well-known MNIST dataset, the data augmentation by VAEs improves the base results, yet to a lesser extent of that obtained by a well-adjusted conventional data augmentation. However, the combination of both conventional and VAE-guided data augmentations outperforms all the results, thereby demonstrating the goodness of our proposal.

Keywords: Data augmentation · Variational auto-encoders ·
Convolutional Neural Networks · MNIST dataset

1 Introduction

Supervised learning is the most considered approach for addressing automatic classification tasks. It is based on learning from a series of correct input-output pairs, from which a model is built with the aim of generalizing to correctly classify unseen inputs.

Convolutional Neural Networks (CNNs) have been one of the biggest breakthroughs of supervised classification [5], especially in the fields of computer vision and image processing. These networks allow learning a hierarchy of features suitable for the recognition task by means of a series of stacked convolutional layers. Although these networks were initially proposed decades ago, several factors have contributed to their eventual success [1].

© Springer Nature Switzerland AG 2019
R. Vera-Rodriguez et al. (Eds.): CIARP 2018, LNCS 11401, pp. 29–37, 2019.
https://doi.org/10.1007/978-3-030-13469-3_4

Within these factors, data augmentation has become a *de facto* standard to improve the learning process [4,6]. It is a step focused on generating a set of synthetic samples out of those in the training set. The intention of this process is twofold: (i) since these neural networks need to be trained on a large set of data, data augmentation might boost the performance by increasing the size of the original training set, (ii) if the augmentation procedure creates examples that mimic expected distortions, the CNN might be more robust to variations at test stage. There are several ways to do data augmentation, especially for images (rotation, color variation, random occlusions, etc.), although the goodness of each one is strongly dependent on the task at issue. Many augmentations can be combined to produce a higher number of new images.

Instead of resorting to hand-crafted procedures, this work proposes a learning-driven approach for the data augmentation stage by means of Variational Auto-Encoders (VAE) [3]. VAEs are powerful generative models that estimate a parametric distribution of the input domain from data. This allows us to generate synthetic samples that fit such distribution. Data augmentation needs to be adjusted manually to select a set of specific augmentations that are suitable to predict variations at the test stage. Nevertheless, a VAE is expected to learn these variations among input samples by itself, thereby offering a greater generalization to any type of classification task. Our experiments demonstrate the goodness of this approach on the MNIST dataset, improving the results obtained with the original training set and demonstrating its complementarity with conventional data augmentation techniques.

The rest of the paper is organized as follows: the proposed approach is elaborated in Sect. 2, our experimental results are presented in Sect. 3, and the main conclusions of our work are summarized in Sect. 4.

2   Method

2.1   Variational Auto-Encoders

Auto-Encoders (AE) are neural networks with an encoder-decoder structure [2,8]. Traditionally, the encoder takes the input and converts it into a smaller, dense representation, from which the decoder converts the input back. Depending on the size of the intermediate representation, the encoder has to learn to preserve as much of the relevant information as possible in the limited space, and intelligently discard irrelevant parts. The space in which the encoding projects the input is usually called *latent space*. Typically, the latent space of a conventional AE does not follow any constraint, and therefore it is difficult to interpret.

Variational Auto-Encoders (VAEs) follow the same topology of that of an AE, but the latent space they consider is forced to fit a parametric distribution [7], allowing easy random sampling and interpolation. Typically, this is achieved by forcing the latent space to behave as a normal distribution. Therefore, the encoder must yield two representations, instead of one: a vector of means, μ, and another vector of standard deviations, σ.

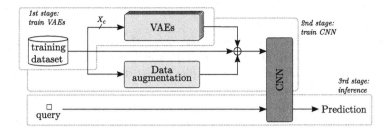

Fig. 1. General outline of the proposed methodology.

Two additional considerations are necessary for training a VAE. On the one hand, the loss function includes the minimization of a divergence between the distribution defined by μ and σ and the chosen distribution for the latent space. On the other hand, the decoder does not operate over the latent space itself, but its parameters are used to generate a random vector that follows the defined distribution. Therefore, the decoder must learn to reconstruct the inputs from sampled values of the distribution estimated by the encoder. This is known as the "re-parameterization trick".

As the latent space samples are somehow generated from the distribution defined by μ and σ, the decoder learns to not just decode single, specific points of the latent space, but the distribution itself. Once trained, decoding sampled vectors from the learned distribution should generate new images that fit within the distribution of the input domain, thus behaving as a generator of samples.

In this work we will train a different VAE per class, and so ensuring that each VAE generates samples that belong to the class that it has been provided during its training. Therefore, the generated samples can be reliably labeled for the classification task.

2.2 Methodology

Figure 1 shows an outline of the methodology proposed in this work. The process consists of three stages: first, different VAEs are trained for every class on the dataset in order to independently model the variations of each class. Once trained, new samples of each class can be created by sampling the latent space distribution. In the second stage, a CNN is trained with the samples generated by the VAEs and/or conventional data augmentation. In the last stage, the trained CNN is able to make predictions about the test samples.

3   Experiments

This section describes the experiments carried out to measure the goodness of the proposed approach.[1]

---

[1] For the sake of reproducible research, the code of the experiments is available at http://github.com/ugm2/DataAugmentation_VAE.

3.1   MNIST Dataset

The experimentation has been carried out using the MNIST dataset of hand-written digits (10 classes). Originally, this dataset is split into two parts: 60,000 samples of training data and 10,000 samples of test data. The training partition is used both to train the VAEs and the CNN. In order to measure the impact of our proposal, we consider reduced training sets. In particular, we consider training set of sizes 50, 100, 250, 500, and 1,000. Each of these sizes represent the total images, i.e. for the size of 50 only 5 samples per digit will be used. For the case of the VAEs, as there is one for every class of the dataset, a tenth of the amounts are used to train every class-wise VAE. From the training partition, 85% is used to train the VAEs, while the remaining 15% is used as validation to know when to stop. The evaluation part is performed with 700 images of each class (7,000 in total).

3.2   Architectures

Table 1 shows the architecture used for the VAEs and the CNN. The hidden layer of the VAE (marked with (*)) refers to two separated fully connected layers of the size of the latent space: one representing the mean vector (μ) and the other the standard deviation vector (σ). The lambda (λ) layer of the VAE (marked with (**)) is used to sample a vector with the dimensionality of the latent space, following the actual values of μ and σ. The dimensionality of the latent space will be studied empirically.

Table 1. VAE and CNN architectures. Notation: Conv(f, $w \times h$) stands for a layer with f convolutional operators of size $w \times h$; ConvT(f, $w \times h$) stands for a layer with f transposed convolutional operators of size $w \times h$; MaxPool($w \times h$) stands for the Max-Pooling operator with a $w \times h$ kernel; Drop(d) refers to Dropout with ratio d; FC(n) is a Fully-Connected layer with n neurons; LS denotes the dimensionality of the latent space.

Network	Part	Configuration			
VAE	Encoder	Conv(1, 2 × 2)	Conv(64, 2 × 2)	Conv(64, 3 × 3)	Conv(64, 3 × 3)
	Hidden	Flatten()	FC(128)	FC(LS[μ, σ])*	λ(sampling([μ, σ])**
	Decoder	FC(128)	ConvT(64, 3 × 3)	Conv(1, 2 × 2)	
		FC(12544)	ConvT(64, 3 × 3)		
		Reshape(14 × 14 × 64)	ConvT(64, 3 × 3)		
CNN	–	Conv(64, 3 × 3)	Conv(128, 3 × 3)	Flatten()	
		Conv(128, 3 × 3)	Conv(128, 3 × 3)	FC(128)	
		Ma × Poo(2 × 2)	Ma × Pool(2 × 2)	Drop(0.5)	
		Drop(0.5)	Drop(0.5)	FC(10)	

3.3   Training

3.3.1   VAE

For the training of the VAEs it has been employed the RMSprop optimizer, which uses the magnitude of recent gradients to normalize the gradients. The loss function consists of two terms: the binary cross-entropy and the Kullback-Leibler (KL) divergence. The first one evaluates "how wrong" the output of the decoder (y) matches the input of the encoder $(\hat{y})$. It is calculated as:

$$-\frac{1}{N}\sum_{i=1}^{n} y_i \cdot \log(\hat{y_i}) + (1 - y_i) \cdot \log(1 - \hat{y_i}) \tag{1}$$

The KL divergence measures the difference between $\mathcal{N}(0,1)$ and $\mathcal{N}(\mu,\sigma)$. It is computed as:

$$\sum_{i=1}^{n} \sigma_i^2 + \mu_i^2 - \log(\sigma_i) - 1 \tag{2}$$

The number of epochs used for training the VAEs has been adjusted manually according to the size of the initial training set.

3.3.2   CNN

For the training of the CNN, the Adam gradient descent optimization algorithm has been employed with a categorical cross entropy loss function. The training process was monitored using early stopping, which stops the training process if the validation loss of the training does not decrease after 10 epochs. Once the training process is stopped, the model of the epoch with the best validation loss is chosen.

For the use of conventional data augmentation during the training of the CNN, the following transformations of the data were applied: rotation range of $20°$, width shift range of 20%, and height shift range of 20%.

3.4   Results

In this section, we both analyze the generative power of the VAEs and the results of the proposed methodology. The classification performance metric considered in this work is the F_1 score. This metric is defined as the harmonic mean of the precision and the recall, and it properly summarizes the classification performance.

First, we show in Fig. 2 some examples of the digits that have been generated by the VAEs trained with 50 images each, and with varying sizes of the latent space. It seems that the digits generated when considering a latent space of 3 dimensions are the most realistic ones.

Figure 3 shows the effect of applying different types of transformations during the data augmentation process. The types of transformations applied go gradually from a possible lack of expert supervision (applying all the transformations possible) to suitable changes for the MNIST dataset. It has been used different

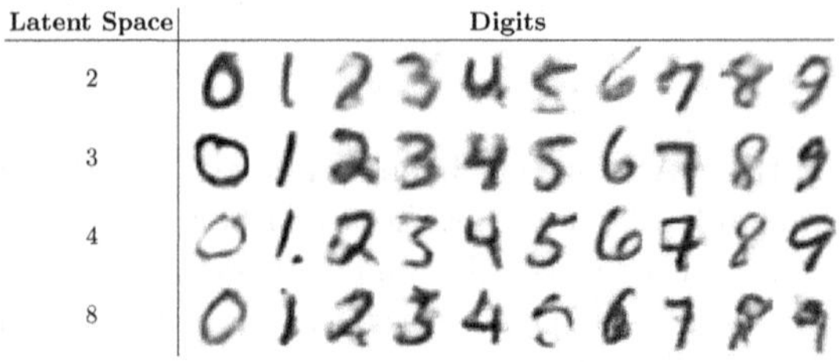

Latent Space	Digits
2	
3	
4	
8	

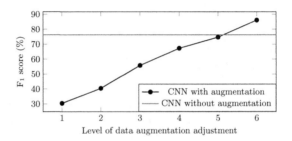

Fig. 2. Generated digits using VAEs with different latent space sizes.

levels of data augmentation adjustment to observe that in order to improve over the CNN without data augmentation (red line), it needs expert knowledge about which perturbations to do on the dataset at issue, as it could worsen the results otherwise.

Fig. 3. Comparison of the improvement obtained by gradually adjusting the transformations applied in the data augmentation process from inexpert hands to suitable changes for the corresponding dataset.

The final classification experiments are shown in Table 2, including the CNN without any augmentation method (CNN), using standard data augmentation (AUG), using the generated digits from VAEs (VAE), and using both standard data augmentation along with the digits of the VAEs (AUG + VAE).

At first sight, it turns out that the results with the VAE-generated data remarkably improves the training with the original data; however, the data augmentation process boosts the performance even more, as it has been manually adjusted to the MNIST dataset. Furthermore, considering both data augmentation and the generated samples from the VAEs, as well as the original dataset, the best figures are generally attained, improving the results of just considering data augmentation in most of the cases.

It is important to emphasize that our approach does work with limited training data. For instance, starting from 50 images as initial training set, the result of data augmentation combined with VAE-generated data from a latent space of 3 dimensions, achieves the outstanding result of almost 91% of F_1 score, which

Table 2. Results of the experiments performed: no augmentation method (CNN), standard data augmentation (AUG), digits generated from VAEs (VAE), and using both standard data augmentation and digits generated from VAEs (AUG+VAE)

Latent Space	Training Size	CNN	VAE	AUG	AUG+VAE
2	50	76.30	84.89	86.10	**89.05**
	100	84.38	90.90	**94.85**	94.50
	250	93.03	94.84	97.12	**98.00**
	500	94.28	95.65	98.11	**98.22**
	1000	96.54	97.24	98.36	**98.87**
3	50	76.30	85.40	86.10	**90.86**
	100	84.38	91.98	94.85	**95.15**
	250	93.03	95.93	97.12	**97.97**
	500	94.28	96.38	98.11	**98.26**
	1000	96.54	97.74	98.36	**98.87**
4	50	76.30	83.77	86.10	**89.67**
	100	84.38	91.75	94.85	**94.73**
	250	93.03	95.16	97.12	**97.86**
	500	94.28	96.28	98.11	**98.30**
	1000	96.54	97.38	98.36	**98.90**
8	50	76.30	84.46	86.10	**89.32**
	100	84.38	91.28	**94.85**	94.56
	250	93.03	95.24	97.12	**97.86**
	500	94.28	95.95	98.11	**98.41**
	1000	96.54	97.50	98.36	**98.79**

Table 3. Results obtained for the statistical significance tests comparing our approach with the other methods evaluated. Symbols ✓ and ✗ state that results achieved by elements in the rows significantly improve or decrease, respectively, to the results by the elements in the columns. Significance has been set to $p < 0.01$.

	CNN	VAE	AUG
VAE	✓	–	✗
AUG	✓	✓	–
AUG + VAE	✓	✓	✓

increases the result of the original dataset by 14.56% and the result of the conventional data augmentation by 4.76%.

The dimensionality of the latent space set to 3 seems to give the best results overall, being settled down as the sweet spot for this dataset in concrete. This confirms what was already observed, visually, in Table 2.

In order to draw more robust conclusions from the results obtained, statistical significance tests are performed between the different configurations, taking into account the results for the different sizes of the training set. Specifically, Wilcoxon signed-rank tests are considered, which compare the different approaches by pairs. Table 3 reports the outcomes of these tests. It can be observed that the statistical significance is directly related to the average results obtained, and therefore the conclusions drawn from Table 2 have a proper statistical significance.

4   Conclusions

A learning-driven approach for data augmentation has been proposed. It considers Variational Auto-Encoders (VAEs), which can be used to generate new samples after being trained to model the input domain of a specific class of the classification task.

Our experiments with the MNIST dataset has reported very promising results. It has been shown that including the samples generated by the VAEs in the training set leads to a better performance compared to that of just using the initial training set. Although using conventional data augmentation improves the actual accuracy even more, it should be noted that our approach does not need to be manually adjusted. In addition, the combination of traditional data augmentation with the samples generated by the VAEs provides the best overall results.

This work has been restricted to the MNIST dataset, and so the first avenue to explore is to study this approach in other, more challenging tasks. We are especially interested in checking the performance of our approach in those datasets for which traditional data augmentation is not advisable.

Acknowledgements. This work was supported by the Spanish Ministerio de Ciencia, Innovación y Universidades through HISPAMUS project (Ref. TIN2017-86576-R, partially funded by UE FEDER funds).

References

1. Goodfellow, I., Bengio, Y., Courville, A.: Deep Learning. MIT Press, Cambridge (2016)
2. Hinton, G.E., Salakhutdinov, R.R.: Reducing the dimensionality of data with neural networks. Science **313**(5786), 504–507 (2006)
3. Kingma, D.P., Welling, M.: Auto-encoding variational bayes. Computing Research Repository abs/1312.6114 (2013)
4. Krizhevsky, A., Sutskever, I., Hinton, G.E.: ImageNet classification with deep convolutional neural networks. In: 26th Annual Conference on Neural Information Processing Systems, pp. 1106–1114 (2012)
5. LeCun, Y., Bengio, Y., Hinton, G.: Deep learning. Nature **521**(7553), 436–444 (2015)
6. Lv, J.J., Cheng, C., Tian, G.D., Zhou, X.D., Zhou, X.: Landmark perturbation-based data augmentation for unconstrained face recognition. Signal Process. Image Commun. **47**, 465–475 (2016)

7. Rezende, D.J., Mohamed, S., Wierstra, D.: Stochastic backpropagation and approximate inference in deep generative models. In: 31th International Conference on Machine Learning, ICML 2014, Beijing, China, 21–26 June 2014, pp. 1278–1286 (2014)
8. Rumelhart, D.E., Hinton, G.E., Williams, R.J.: Learning internal representations by error propagation. In: Parallel Distributed Processing: Explorations in the Microstructure of Cognition, pp. 318–362. MIT Press, Cambridge (1986)

LSTM-Based Multi-scale Model for Wind Speed Forecasting

Ignacio A. Araya[1(✉)], Carlos Valle[2], and Héctor Allende[1]

[1] Departamento de Informática, Universidad Técnica Federico Santa María,
Valparaíso, Chile
{ignacio.araya.11,hector.allende}@usm.cl
[2] Departamento de Computación e Informática, Universidad de Playa Ancha,
Valparaíso, Chile
carlos.valle@upla.cl

Abstract. Wind speed forecasting is crucial for the penetration of wind energy sources in electrical systems, since accurate wind speed forecasts directly translates into accurate wind power predictions. A framework called Multi-scale RNNs specifically addresses the issue of learning long term dependencies in RNNs. Following that approach, we devised a LSTM-based Multi-scale model that learns to build different temporal scales from the original wind speed series that are then used as input for multiple LSTMs, whose final internal states are used to forecast wind speed future values. Results from two real wind speed datasets from northern Chile show that this approach outperforms the standard LSTM and its capable of working with very long input series without overfitting, while being computationally efficient regarding training times.

Keywords: Wind speed forecasting · Long Short-Term Memory ·
Multi-scale recurrent networks

1 Introduction

Wind energy is a renewable energy source that holds strong appeal given its low environmental impact, high availability and low costs. Since an electrical system must be able to estimate future power output coming from each energy source, penetration of this kind of energy in electrical systems is difficult due to wind speed's natural high variability and randomness. It is crucial then to have accurate wind speed forecasts, since wind power can be estimated from it using turbines power curves.

Among the many techniques in the literature used for forecasting, Recurrent Neural Networks (RNNs) are a widely used approach due to their natural capabilities of modeling complex temporal dynamics [1] which are often found in naturally occurring processes such as wind speed [2]. Specifically, in the wind speed forecasting task, it has been shown that these networks outperform ARIMA models [3] and have been successfully applied in hybrid approaches in which the

© Springer Nature Switzerland AG 2019
R. Vera-Rodriguez et al. (Eds.): CIARP 2018, LNCS 11401, pp. 38–45, 2019.
https://doi.org/10.1007/978-3-030-13469-3_5

original series are decomposed into multiple sub-series that are used to train RNNs, improving their generalization capabilities [4,5]. Although widely used in series forecasting tasks, these networks have a major problem by cause of their architecture; learning long-term temporal relations in the data using back-propagation is difficult due to the Vanishing Gradient problem [8]. In practice, this means that these networks do not benefit from being trained with long input series; instead they tend to overfit and underperform. An extensively used RNN that addresses this issue is the Long Short-Term Memory (LSTM) [7], whose internal nodes are memory blocks that can prevent the gradient from vanishing through its Constant Error Carrousel. In reality, however, very long term dependencies are still impossible to learn using only this approach. In the wind speed forecasting community, besides using the LSTM network as the Recurrent Network of choice [6], this problem has not been directly addressed.

A class of RNNs called Multi-scale RNNs [9] have been developed to mitigate this problem. Networks from this class have nodes that update their states with different frequencies and that are organized in a hierarchical manner, creating different pathways for the gradient to propagate. Specifically, low frequency nodes create short pathways between input and output values, thus excessive matrix multiplications and applications of squashing functions are avoided when computing gradients for these models. Their downside is that their training might be slow depending on how the nodes interact with one another. Networks belonging to this class have been devised and applied successfully in several sequential tasks, such as search query generation and words translation [10].

Resembling the aforementioned approach, in this work we devise a LSTM-based Multi-scale model for the wind speed forecasting task that uses Feed-forward neural networks to build coarser time-scale series than the original one, and then processes these series using LSTMs. This allows our model to work with very long input series and to integrate information from multiple series at once to make the forecasts, while still being computationally efficient in terms of training time.

The rest of the paper is organized as follows. In Sect. 2 we discuss the theoretical framework, outlining RNNs, the LSTM and Multi-scale RNNs. Next, in Sect. 3 our proposal is described. Section 4 is devoted to our experimental setting and results, and Sect. 5 to conclusions and future work.

2   Theoretical Framework

2.1   Recurrent Neural Networks

Recurrent Neural Networks (RNNs) are a class of artificial neural network with recurrent connections in its nodes that have been specially designed to work with sequences and time series. At each time-step, these networks update their nodes internal states using a vector from the series and their previous internal states. Mathematically, given a series $\{\mathbf{x}_t\}_{t=1}^N$ where $\mathbf{x}_t \in \mathbb{R}^l$ and considering a single layer network, let $\mathbf{s}_t$ be the states of its nodes at time t, $\mathbf{W}_i \in \mathbb{R}^{k \times l}$ the input weights of the network, $\mathbf{W}_r \in \mathbb{R}^{k \times k}$ its recurrent weights, $\mathbf{b} \in \mathbb{R}^k$ a vector bias and $f : \mathbb{R}^k \mapsto \mathbb{R}^k$ a non-linearity, then the model updates its states using the rule $s_{t+1} = f(\mathbf{W_i}\, x_t + \mathbf{W_r}\, s_t + \mathbf{b})$.

After processing a series, the final internal states can be used to compute the output of the network, which in the forecasting task could be the 1-step ahead forecasted value. When long input sequences are given to a RNN the Vanishing Gradient problem is exacerbated, since more updates imply more matrix multiplications and applications of squashing functions to the gradient.

The Long Short-Term Memory is a type of recurrent network that uses memory blocks as internal nodes. These memory blocks have internal gates with sigmoid activation functions in the range [0, 1] that control the internal flow of the network; the input gate and forget gate control how much information from the input value and from the previous internal states are considered when updating the internal states of the networks. If the forget gate value of a memory block is close to 1 in a certain time-step, then the entire previous internal state is used to compute the new one, and thus the gradient, at that time-step, has a free pathway where it avoids being diminished.

2.2   Multi-scale Recurrent Networks

A Recurrent Network is considered Multi-scale if it has recurrent nodes that update their internal state at different frequencies. As an example, if a Recurrent Network has two nodes and the first one updates its state every time an input from the sequence is given to the network (frequency 1), while the second one updates its states only once every two inputs are given (frequency 0.5), it is considered a Multi-scale network. The underlying idea behind this kind of structure is to help the model learn long term dependencies more easily; low frequency nodes are less prone to completely forget information from the past when new information arrives at the network. Another way to see it is in terms of backpropagation and the vanishing gradient problem: since there are fewer updates to the internal state of the node, the gradient is multiplied fewer times by values less than one, thus lessening its vanishing. Nodes in these networks are grouped in hierarchies, making these networks capable of learning complex long-term relationships and hierarchical temporal structures in the data. Yet, when having low frequency nodes receive information from those of higher frequency, computational times tend to increase substantially, since for low frequency nodes to be updated the higher frequency ones have to be updated multiple times before.

Another common feature of the networks already devised is that they make predictions based on the last layer in the hierarchy, which presumably contains all the necessary information to address the task at hand. Individual layers though might contain relevant information from its scale that would be hard to recover if only the last layer is taken into account when computing the forecast.

3   Proposal

In this section, we develop a LSTM-based Multi-scale model (LSTM-Ms) for the wind speed forecasting task. Our proposed network uses Feed-forward layers that learn to extract features from the original series to create sub-series at different temporal scales, built in a hierarchical manner, whose values are used as input for different LSTMs. LSTMs that process coarse scales are of low frequency, ensuring short pathways between inputs and outputs that lessen the vanishing gradient problem. The final internal states of these LSTMs are then used to make one step ahead wind speed forecasts with information from multiple scales. Since we are decoupling the scale construction mechanism from the recurrent processing of them, we can control how many inputs each LSTM receives and thus avoid excessive increases in computational costs when adding more scales to the model.

To construct sub-series with coarser temporal scales than the original one, a feature extractor defined by a one layer Feed-forward Network is moved along the series of input values, without overlapping segments, producing feature vectors (analogous to a convolutional filter). From these feature vectors, which are now regarded as a new sequence in time, new features are extracted by applying another Feed-forward Network, and so on. If the model builds M sub-series in this manner, we say it has M + 1 scales (taking into account the original one) and refer to the sub-series as scales. Since each sub-series is constructed from multiple values of the previous one, its length gets smaller. Each scale then has specific features that might be useful in order to forecast future values, thus, they are given as input to LSTMs to produce the network output value. To do this, the final internal states of all the LSTMs are concatenated to produce a

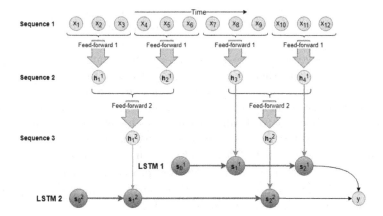

Fig. 1. An example of a LSTM-Ms with two scales built in a hierarchical manner, $\mathbf{h}^1$ and $\mathbf{h}^2$, plus the original one x. In this particular case, these two scales are given as inputs to LSTMs, while the original one is ignored. The LSTM networks are shown unfolded in the figure; $\mathbf{s}^1$ and $\mathbf{s}^2$ are the states of the LSTMs, red arrows represent recurrent connections and yellow ones input connections. LSTM 1 has a higher frequency than LSTM 2, since it updates its states once every 3 values from the original series are given to the network, while the second one does it every 6. Also, in this example, LSTM 1 processes only the last 2 values of its scale while LSTM 2 processes it completely, so $z_1 = z_2 = 2$ (Color figure online)

final vector, from which the output of the network is computed by means of a simple linear combination of its values.

Formally, let $\{x_{t+i}\}_{i=0}^{n}$ be a time series used to forecast x_{t+n+1}. Also, let $f_1 : \mathbb{R}^k \mapsto \mathbb{R}^{l_1}$ be a function representing a one layer Feed-forward network with l_1 hidden nodes. This function is applied to the vector $[x_t \oplus x_{t+1} \oplus ... \oplus x_{t+k}]^T$, where $\oplus$ is the concatenation operator, and produces an output vector $\mathbf{h}_1^1 \in \mathbb{R}_1^l$. Then its applied to $[x_{t+k+1} \oplus x_{t+k+2} \oplus ... \oplus x_{t+2k}]^T$, and so on, until reaching the end of the series. What we get after this process is a new series $\mathbf{h}^1 = \{\mathbf{h_n^1}\}_{n=1}^{n_1}$ from which a third series can be generated using a second Feed-forward operation.

After creating M scales, we use $M + 1$ LSTMs to process them sequentially: let $r_m : \mathbb{R}^{l_m + c_m} \mapsto \mathbb{R}^{c_m}$ be the update operation of the m-th LSTM with c_m memory blocks. Starting with an initial state $s_0^m \in \mathbb{R}^{c_m}$ then, this function is applied sequentially to the last z_m vectors from the m-th sequence $\mathbf{h}^m$, until reaching the end of the sequence and producing the final state $\mathbf{s}_{z_m}^m$. A final vector $\mathbf{s} = [\mathbf{s}_{z_0}^0 \oplus \mathbf{s}_{z_1}^1 \oplus ... \oplus \mathbf{s}_{z_m}^m]^T$ is used to compute the network output as $y = \mathbf{w}^T \mathbf{s}$.

Figure 1 illustrates this process. The entire mechanism of our model can be seen as the forward pass of one network whose parameters are the weights of the Feed-forward networks, the weights of each LSTM and the vector $\mathbf{w}$. Thus, given a proper loss function, the parameters can be learnt using back-propagation.

4   Experiments and Results

Our goal is to forecast wind speed from 1 to 24 h after the last observed measurement. To asses our proposal, we have used data from the Ministry of Energy, Chile, corresponding to average wind speed measurements, measured by wind prospecting towers 20 m high. Measurements coming from 2 towers placed in the Antofagasta Region (Northern Chile) but more than 200 kms apart have been used, and can be found online[1] under the names *e01* and *b08*. This series have 25719 and 19536 measurements respectively, but to asses performance, both of them have been divided into 10 smaller sub-series by applying a sliding window that creates a 30% difference between consecutive sub-series. If w is the length of the sliding window and it slides s values each time, then, the k sub-series corresponds to the set $\{x_i\}_{i=(k-1)s}^{(k-1)s+w}$. By this procedure, each sub-series from *e01* and *b08* gets 6950 and 5279 consecutive hourly measurements respectively. Each sub-series was normalized to the range $[0, 1]$.

Since our models learn from input series of N hourly measurements and forecasts the measurement that immediately follows that sequence, input series of length N were extracted for training from each sub-series, together with their corresponding output measurement values. The last 24 measurements from each sub-series were kept for testing and were not used at all when building the training input series/output measurement pairs.

---

[1] http://walker.dgf.uchile.cl/Mediciones/.

Performance on each dataset is measured using Mean Absolute Error (MAE) and Mean Squared Error (MSE) over the 24 forecasts and then averaging over the 10 sub-series:

$$\text{MAE} = \frac{1}{10}\sum_{j=1}^{10}\frac{1}{24}\sum_{i=1}^{24}|x^j_{h_j+i} - \hat{x}^j_{h_j+i}|, \quad \text{MSE} = \frac{1}{10}\sum_{j=1}^{10}\frac{1}{24}\sum_{i=1}^{24}(x^j_{h_j+i} - \hat{x}^j_{h_j+i})^2$$

Here, h_j refers to the index of the last value present in the j-th training sub-series, so $x^j_{h_j+i}$ is the ith of the last 24 values of the jth sub-series, while $\hat{x}^j_{h_j+i}$ is its unnormalized forecasted value. The 24 forecasts for each sub-series are calculated recursively by forecasting one value each time and using that value to create a new input series to be given to the model.

As baseline for our comparisons, a naive persistent model that just makes forecasts by repeating the previous 24 values was employed. Our LSTM-Ms models were built with up to 3 scales: the hourly scale; which is the original data series, a daily scale; built using every 24 values from the hourly scale, and a two days scale; built using every 2 values from the daily scale. In order to see if processing multiple scales is useful in terms of performance, we tried models with LSTMs only in the last scale, only in the last 2 scales, and in all 3 of them. We tried 5, 10, 15, 20 nodes and memory blocks, each Feed-Forward network and LSTM respectively; 1, 5, 10, 15, 20 values that were processed by each LSTM from each sub-series (z_m), and 5, 10, 15, 20 epochs to train the models.

Our models were compared against the standard LSTM with multiple stacked layers, since our models make use of multiple layers to extract relevant features as well. For these models, we tried 1, 2, 3, 4 stacked layers, 10, 20, ..., 50 memory blocks for each layer, input series for the model of length 12, 24, 36, ..., 96, and 5, 10, 15, 20 epochs.

Using a validation set we found best results were attained if we trained the models using batches of size 1. The optimization method known as Adadelta was also found to work well for all the models.

Experiments were repeated 5 times for each model for each possible configuration of parameters. Average MAE and MSE for the best parameter configuration of each model, for both datasets, are shown in Table 1. The sub-indexes in our proposal denote which scales were processed by LSTMs, being 1 the hourly scale, 24 the daily scale and 48 the two days one. As results show, the best models from our proposal outperform both the standard LSTM and the persistent model. In the dataset *b08*, both the best MAE and MSE were achieved by our LSTM-Ms$_{24,48}$. Whenever the hourly scale series was processed performance would get worse, which suggests that the daily scale and two days scale extracted all the necessary features from it. On the other hand, in *e01*, the best model was our LSTM-Ms$_{24}$. It seems that, in this case, the daily scale got all the meaningful features and adding more scales to it led to overfitting. In both cases, the feature extractors with 5 nodes only gave best results. It is important to point out that the best standard LSTM models for both datasets used a single layer and their best input series length values were 36 and 24 for the *b08* and *e01* sets

Table 1. MAE and MSE for the best configurations of every model are shown for each dataset. Best results across models are shown in bold.

Data	b08		e01	
Model	**MAE**	**MSE**	**MAE**	**MSE**
Persistent	1.266	2.659	2.271	9.286
LSTM	1.161 (0.032)	2.257 (0.265)	2.134 (0.072)	7.835 (0.482)
LSTM-Ms$_{1,24}$	1.117 (0.022)	2.143 (0.166)	1.993 (0.043)	6.934 (0.292)
LSTM-Ms$_{24}$	1.105 (0.012)	1.974 (0.123)	**1.954 (0.069)**	**6.920 (0.457)**
LSTM-Ms$_{1,24,48}$	1.097 (0.026)	2.004 (0.192)	1.990 (0.098)	6.993 (0.581)
LSTM-Ms$_{24,48}$	**1.081 (0.035)**	**1.895 (0.235)**	1.994 (0.050)	7.026 (0.290)
LSTM-Ms$_{48}$	1.092 (0.028)	1.941 (0.138)	2.077 (0.068)	7.396 (0.381)

respectively; adding depth to those models and considering more than 36 and 24 hourly values always decreased performance, besides making training very slow. In contrast, the best models from our proposal were able to use far longer input series without overfitting; in *e01*, the best configuration used 5 values from the daily scale, which amounts to using input series of length 120, while in *b08*, 10 values from the two-days scale were used, meaning input series of length 480 were processed. As it can bee seen, our models made effective use of far longer input series than the standard LSTM, which suggests that our models were able to learn long term dependencies the standard LSTM could not.

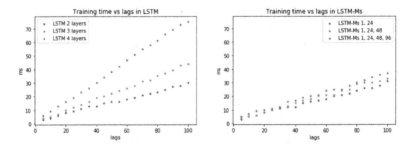

Fig. 2. Average time to compute gradients in stacked LSTMs and LSTM-Ms for a batch of one input series. All LSTMs had 5 memory blocks and all Feed-forward networks 5 nodes. Lags refers to the length of the input series that is given to the standard LSTM, and to how many values are given to each LSTM from its scale in the LSTM-Ms case (z_m parameter)

Finally, we compared how adding scales to our proposal and having LSTMs process them compares to stacking multiple layers in standard LSTMs in terms of computational time. Figure 2 shows the average time it takes to compute gradients in stacked LSTMs and LSTM-Ms, for a batch of just one input series. It can be seen that stacking layers of LSTMs greatly increases computational times, while in our proposal, adding more scales does not increase times significantly, showing the efficiency of our approach.

5   Conclusions and Future Work

In this paper, we proposed a LSTM-based Multi-scale model that uses Feed-forward networks to hierarchically construct multiple series of different temporal scales and LSTMs that process them to forecast hourly wind speed values one step-ahead. Experiments showed that the proposal outperformed both the persistence model and the standard LSTM. The experiments also confirmed that the proposal is capable of working with very long input series without overfitting and that there are benefits to integrating information from multiple scales in the forecast. Furthermore, adding scales to our model did not increase computational times significantly, making it also a very efficient approach. In future work we would like to explore working with convolutional filters and pooling layers for the construction of the series, since it might help the model locate very specific patterns within the series and make those features available for forecasting.

Acknowledgments. This work was supported in part by Fondecyt Grant 1170123, Basal Project FB0821 and the PIIC Research Project, DGIIP-UTFSM (Chile).

References

1. Hallas, M., Dorffner, G.: A comparative study on feedforward and recurrent neural networks in time series prediction using gradient descent learning (1998)
2. Barbounis, T.G., Theocharis, J.B., Alexiadis, M.C., Dokopoulos, P.S.: Long-term wind speed and power forecasting using local recurrent neural network models. IEEE Trans. Energy Convers. **21**(1), 273–284 (2006)
3. Cao, Q., Ewing, B.T., Thompson, M.A.: Forecasting wind speed with recurrent neural networks. Eur. J. Oper. Res. **221**(1), 148–154 (2012)
4. Wang, J., Zhang, W., Li, Y., Wang, J., Dang, Z.: Forecasting wind speed using empirical mode decomposition and Elman neural network. Appl. Soft Comput. **23**, 452–459 (2014)
5. Liu, H., Tian, H.Q., Liang, X.F., Li, Y.F.: Wind speed forecasting approach using secondary decomposition algorithm and Elman neural networks. Appl. Energy **157**, 183–194 (2015)
6. Liu, H., Mi, X.W., Li, Y.F.: Wind speed forecasting method based on deep learning strategy using empirical wavelet transform, long short term memory neural network and Elman neural network. Energy Convers. Manag. **156**, 498–514 (2018)
7. Hochreiter, S., Schmidhuber, J.: Long short-term memory. Neural Comput. **9**(8), 1735–1780 (1997)
8. Pascanu, R., Mikolov, T., Bengio, Y.: On the difficulty of training recurrent neural networks. In International Conference on Machine Learning, pp. 1310–1318, February 2013
9. Chung, J., Ahn, S., Bengio, Y.: Hierarchical multiscale recurrent neural networks. arXiv preprint arXiv:1609.01704 (2016)
10. Koutnik, J., Greff, K., Gomez, F., Schmidhuber, J.: A clockwork RNN. In: International Conference on Machine Learning, pp. 1863–1871, January 2014

Using Deep Learning to Classify Class Imbalanced Gene-Expression Microarrays Datasets

A. Reyes-Nava[1(✉)], H. Cruz-Reyes[2], R. Alejo[2], E. Rendón-Lara[2],
A. A. Flores-Fuentes[1], and E. E. Granda-Gutiérrez[1]

[1] UAEM University Center at Atlacomulco,
Universidad Autónoma del Estado de México,
Carretera Toluca-Atlacomulco km. 60, 50450 Atlacomulco, Mexico
`adriananava0@gmail.com`

[2] Division of Postgraduate Studies and Research, National Institute of Technology
of Mexico (TecNM), Campus Toluca, Av. Tecnológico s./n., 52149 Metepec, Mexico

Abstract. Performance of deep learning neural networks to classify class imbalanced gene-expression microarrays datasets is studied in this work. The low number of samples and high dimensionality of this type of datasets represent a challenging situation. Three sampling methods which have shown favorable results to deal with the class imbalance problem were used, namely: Random Over-Sampling (ROS), Random Under-Sampling (RUS) and Synthetic Minority Oversampling Technique (SMOTE). Moreover, artificial noise and greater class imbalance were included in the datasets in order to analyze these situations in the context of classification of gene-expression microarrays datasets. Results show that the noise or separability of the dataset is more determinant than its dimensionality in the classifier performance.

Keywords: Gene-expression microarrays · Deep neural networks · Class-imbalance

1 Introduction

Recently, the use of deep learning to solve a variety of real-life problems has attracted the interest of many researchers because these algorithms usually allow to obtain better results than traditional machine learning methods [14,21]. Multi-Layer Perceptron (MLP), the most common neural network, has been also translated to deep learning context [18]: Deep Learning MLP (DL-MLP) incorporates two or more hidden layers [13], thus increasing the computational cost of processing large size and high dimension datasets [12]. Nevertheless, when efficient frameworks are available, such as Apache-Spark [24] or Tensor-Flow, the advantage of the high performance, robustness to overfitting, and high processing capability of this deep neural networks could be taken.

© Springer Nature Switzerland AG 2019
R. Vera-Rodriguez et al. (Eds.): CIARP 2018, LNCS 11401, pp. 46–54, 2019.
https://doi.org/10.1007/978-3-030-13469-3_6

In the field of biomedical databases classification, the use of deep learning is gaining attention [18]; for instance, in the classification of gene-expression microarrays [6,12,17]. Typical applications with deep neural networks refer to problems in which both: dimensionality and number of samples are high [5,20]. However, in gene-expression microarrays databases, the number of samples is low, and the dimensionality is high, which represent a challenging situation. In some cases, the classes are imbalanced, where one class is highly underrepresented compared to the other class [3].

Class imbalance problem has been a hot topic in machine learning and datamining and more recently, in deep learning [9]. Usual techniques employed to handle the class imbalance problem have been the random sampling methods (under-sampling - RUS or over-sampling - ROS), mainly due to the independence of the underlying classifier [19]. ROS randomly replicates samples in the minority-class, while RUS randomly eliminates samples from the majority-class, biasing the discrimination process to compensate the imbalance of classes. Synthetic Minority Oversampling Technique (SMOTE) is also a helpful sampling technique which generates artificial samples from the minority class by interpolating existing instances that lie close together [11]; it has motivated the development of other over-samplings methods [16,19]. RUS is one of the most successful under-sampling methods, however, this method loses effectiveness when removes significant samples [19]. Other important under-sampling methods include a heuristic mechanism [16].

Usually in the state-of-the-art, machine learning methods have been used to classify gene-expression microarrays databases [6,10,17], but recent works have been focused in the application of deep learning [1,5,7,15,20,23]. In this scenario, common methods used to face the class imbalance have been ROS, RUS and SMOTE; however, results are not conclusive in different works. For example, in [4] SMOTE is better than others methods, while in [8] RUS presents better results. In this paper, performance of DL-MLP in the classification of gene-expression microarrays databases in presence of class imbalance problem is evaluated. In order to focus this study in the situation of class imbalance and noisy data, artificial scenarios were also included.

2   Deep Learning MLP

MLP is the most conventional neural network architecture, which is commonly based on three layers: input, output, and one hidden layer [18]. MLP can be translated into deep neural networks by incorporating more than two hidden layers, becoming a Deep Learning-MLP (DL-MLP); this allows to reduce the number of nodes per layer and uses fewer parameters, but in return this leads to a more complex optimization problem [12,13]. If an efficient framework, such as Apache-Spark [24] or Tensor-Flow, the advantage of high performance, robustness to overfitting, and high processing capability of DL-MLP could be taken.

Traditionally, a MLP has been trained with the back-propagation algorithm (based in the stochastic gradient descent) and its weights are randomly initialized. However, in the last versions of the DL-MLP, hidden layers are pre-trained by an unsupervised algorithm and weights are optimized by the back-propagation algorithm [18]. Alternatively, MLP uses sigmoid activation functions, such as the hyperbolic tangent or logistic function, but DL-MLP includes (commonly) the rectified linear unit (ReLU) $f(z) = \max(0, z)$, because typically it learns much faster in networks with many layers, allowing training a DL-MLP without supervised pre-training.

There are three variants of the descending gradient that differ in how many data are used to process the gradient of the objective function: (a) Batch Gradient Descendent, calculates the gradient of the cost function to the parameters for the entire training data set, (b) Stochastic Gradient Descendent, performs an update of parameters for each training example and (c) Mini-batch Gradient Descendent, takes the best of the two previous types and performs an update for each mini-batch of n training examples [22].

The most common algorithms of descending gradient optimization are: (a) Adagrad, it adapts the learning reason for the parameters, making bigger updates for less frequent parameters and smaller for the most frequent, (b) Adadelta, is an extension of Adagrad that seeks to reduce aggressiveness, monotonously decreasing the learning rate, instead of accumulating all the previous descending gradients, restricting accumulation to a fixed size and (c) Adam, calculates adaptations of the learning rate for each parameter and stores an exponentially decreasing average of past gradients. Other relevant algorithms are AdaMax, Nadam and RMSprop [22].

3   Related Works

Nowadays, the treatment of bioinformatic databases is increasingly common, including tasks for disease prediction, treatments and sick classification. Most efforts have focused on feature selection: for example, [6] presents a technique to classify microarrays of genetic expression by selection of characteristics, comparing 7 classifiers with 4 databases, obtaining the best results with HAM (proposed method) and Support Vector Machines (SVM). A similar case is presented by [10], where a cancer database is evaluated by using 6 classifiers, of which the MLP shows the best results with 98% accuracy. Likewise, in [17], several methods of selection and extraction of characteristics are presented to reduce the dimensionality of the microarray databases; this selection is made through filters, wrappers, and integrated techniques.

In literature, machine learning methods have been applied to treat biomedical information; however, the presented databases have high dimensionality. For example, in [20], a series of images of breast cancer is classified into 3 different groups; the method uses Restricted Boltzmann Machines (RBM) in a Deep Neural Network (DNN) that allows classifying faster and more accurately. In [5], multiple Recurrent Neural Networks (RNN) are used to make the classification of people with benign and malignant breast cancer; the proposed model consists of four RNN to extract the characteristics and one RNN to make the final classification. Reference [1] presented an automatic diagnosis system to detect breast cancer based on a deep belief network for the training phase followed by a back-propagation neuronal network. Reference [15] implemented deep bidirectional recurrent neuronal networks of short-term memory for the reduction of intrinsic protein disorder.

In works such as [7,23], a comparison is made to classify and identify relevant genes and perform cancer detection; the data used are the most important characteristics extracted through different methods, including the use of autoencoders. When the results of both works are analyzed, better classification results are obtained when deep learning methods are used.

Currently, there are several works dealing with the problem of imbalance of classes in bioinformatic databases, which contain biological information such as nucleotide sequence data, protein structures, genomes, genetic expression, metabolism and other similar data. Re-sampling techniques are applied to balance the classes in the set of samples; for example, in the work presented by [4], SMOTE is used to deal with the imbalance of databases of high dimensionality, presented in three databases with real and simulated data, where it is shown that in the case of the low dimensionality database, the accuracy of the classifier increases when applying SMOTE, however, in cases of high dimensionality, it is not advisable.

In problems of imbalance of classes in databases of gene expression microarrays, studies have been carried out by applying under and over sampling techniques. In [8], RUS, ROS and SMOTE were applied to treat the imbalance in bioinformatic databases through classifiers 5-NN and SVM; results show that RUS obtains the best results, in comparison with the work of [4] where they mention that SMOTE is significantly better to RUS when the k-NN classifier is applied.

4   Experimental Set-Up

In order to study the class imbalance problem on the classification of gene-expression microarrays datasets using deep neural networks, four microarray cancer data sets were used (see Table 1). Datasets were obtained from the Kent Ridge Biomedical DataSet Repository (http://datam.i2r.a-star.edu.sg/datasets/krbd). Original datasets were also modified to highlight the class imbalance (+HI) and to include artificial noise (+Noise). The modification consisted in random elimination (+HI) or change the label (+Noise) at ten samples from the minorities classes. Table 1 presents the main features of the new produced benchmarking datasets. For the experimental design, the hold out method was adopted (10 times), with 60% of the samples for training and 40% for testing.

In this work it is used a DL-MLP with two hidden layer, sigmoid (logistic) function in their nodes, and softmax function on the output layer nodes. The framework Apache-Spark [24] was used. The configuration of each hidden layer was 10 and 20 nodes respectively. Back-propagation was used for learning the model, and the logistic loss function for optimization. Then, Limited-memory Broyden-Fletcher-Goldfarb-Shanno algorithm (L-BFGS) was employed as an optimization routine.

Table 1. Description of the benchmarking datasets. The imbalance ratio (IR), which corresponds to the ratio of the majority class size to the minority class size is reported in the last column

Database	Features	Samples	Class 1	Class 2	IR
Ovarian	15154	253	162 Cancer	Normal 91	1.78
Ovarian+HI+Noise	15154	253	172 Cancer	Normal 81	2.12
Ovarian+HI	15154	243	162 Cancer	Normal 81	2
Colon	2000	62	22 Positive	Negative 40	1.82
Colon+HI+Noise	2000	62	12 Positive	Negative 50	4.16
Colon+HI	2000	52	12 Positive	Negative 40	3.33
Prostate	12600	136	77 Tumor	Normal 59	1.31
Prostate+HI+Noise	12600	136	87 Tumor	Normal 49	1.78
Prostate+HI	12600	126	77 Tumor	Normal 49	1.57
CNS	7129	60	21 Class1	Class0 39	1.86
CNS+HI+Noise	7129	60	11 Class1	Class0 49	4.45
CNS+HI	7129	50	11 Class1	Class0 39	3.54

In order to deal with the class imbalance problem, ROS, RUS and SMOTE were used to sample the training dataset to reach a relative class distribution balance on class imbalanced gene-expression microarrays datasets.

Area Under the Receiver Operating Characteristic Curve (AUROC) was used as measure criteria for the classifiers performance; it is one of most widely-used and accepted technique for the evaluation of binary classifiers in imbalanced domain [3].

Finally, a non-parametric statistical tests [19] of Friedman and Iman–Davenport was applied in order to detect whether differences in the results exist. If the null-hypothesis was rejected, the Holm-Shaffer post-hoc test was used to find the particular pairwise comparisons that produce statistical significant differences. These test were applied with a level of confidence $\gamma = 0.05$, by using the KEEL software [19].

5   Results and Discussion

In this section, main experimental results of this research are presented. Table 2 exhibits, in term of AUROC and rank values, the experimental results obtained to classify class imbalanced gene-expression microarrays datasets with DL-MLP. It is noted that when the class imbalance is increased and noise is included in the dataset (HI+Noise), the classification performance is harmed; however, increasing the class imbalance does not necessarily affect the performance of DL-MLP (see Prostate and Ovarian datasets). The worst performance of DL-MLP was obtained for original CNS and Colon datasets, in accordance to AUROC values (0.539 and 0.721 respectively), and the performance of the classifier is reduced when it includes noise (HI+Noise) or more imbalance (HI). It is assumed that these dataset are less separable than Prostate and Ovarian; thus, noise and imbalance do affect the classifier performance. These results agree with the reported in others works [2,3], which show that the class imbalance becomes a problem when the dataset is overlapped or less separable. Also, when SMOTE is applied to CNS, the performance of DL-MLP trained with this dataset exhibits the worst performance compared to the other methods; it occurs because SMOTE generates artificial samples, which could increase the overlapping or noise in the dataset. Table 2 also shows that Ovarian datasets produces good results for all methods: even RUS does not harm the performance of the classifier (remember RUS deletes about 50% of the size dataset), possibly because it is a highly separable dataset.

Table 2 does not show a direct relationship between the dimensionality dataset and its percentage of success. For example, Ovarian is the dataset with highest dimensionality (compared with other datasets used in this work) and the classification performance of the DL-MLP was close to 1. Thus, AUROC values obtained for CNS (which has about 50% less features than Ovarian) are close to 0.5, i.e., the prediction is not much better than just flipping a coin.

In general terms, it is noticed in Table 2 that RUS is not a good option to deal with the class imbalance problem: although it does not considerably deteriorate the classification performance, the tendency is that RUS presents results worse than other methods, even by using the original dataset. In contrast, it is noticeable than ROS and SMOTE improve the DL-MLP performance when class imbalanced gene-expression microarrays datasets are used.

Table 2. Classification performance of the DL-MLP on class imbalanced gene-expression microarrays datasets using the AUROC and average ranks (AR).

	ROS	SMOTE	ORIGINAL	RUS
Colon	0.865(1)	0.814(2)	0.721(3)	0.694(4)
Colon+HI+Noise	0.873(1)	0.866(2)	0.547(4)	0.563(3)
Colon+HI	0.883(2)	0.898(1)	0.667(3)	0.657(4)
CNS	0.642(2)	0.684(1)	0.539(3)	0.506(4)
CNS+HI+Noise	0.870(1)	0.754(2)	0.512(3)	0.462(4)
CNS+HI	0.781(1)	0.751(2)	0.510(4)	0.548(3)
Prostate	0.861(2)	0.896(1)	0.835(4)	0.839(3)
Prostate+HI+Noise	0.823(2)	0.826(1)	0.712(4)	0.774(3)
Prostate+HI	0.897(1)	0.878(2)	0.853(3)	0.798(4)
Ovarian	0.979(1)	0.978(2)	0.963(3)	0.962(4)
Ovarian+HI+Noise	0.942(1)	0.936(2)	0.886(4)	0.893(3)
Ovarian+HI	0.990(1.5)	0.990(1.5)	0.982(4)	0.949(3)
Average rank	1.375	1.625	3.416	3.583

Nevertheless, according to the results shown in this section, it is highly recommended to make a statistical analysis (see Sect. 4). Friedman and Iman−Davenport non-parametrical statistical tests report that considering a performance reduction distributed according to chi-square with 3 degrees of freedom, the Friedman statistic is set to 29.125, and p value computed by Friedman test is 2.108×10^{-6}. Considering a performance reduction distributed according to F-distribution with 3 and 33 degrees of freedom, Iman−Davenport statistic is 46.6, and p value computed by this test is 5.804×10^{-6}. Thus, the null hypothesis is rejected because both: Friedman's and Iman-Davenport's tests, indicate that significant differences exist. Upon these results, it is concluded that a post-hoc statistical analysis is required. Holm and Shaffer statistics values were obtained, as well as p-values (Table 3). Holm and Shaffer procedures rejects those hypotheses with an unadjusted p-value $\leq \{Holm$ and $Shaffer\}$ values, respectively.

In the Table 3, the Holm-Shaffer test demonstrates non-significant statistical differences between ROS and SMOTE; however, there is statistical differences between both methods and Original (i.e., the dataset without any preprocessing) and RUS. In addition, it shows that does not exist significant statistical differences between RUS and Original. These results confirm that the worst method to deal with the class imbalance problem is RUS, while ROS is very competitive with SMOTE; in other words, does not exist evidence of the predominance of any of these two methods.

Table 3. The accepted null hypothesis are typed in bold (p-values for $\alpha = 0.05$).

i	Algorithms	$z = (R_0 - R_i)/SE$	p	Holm	Shaffer
6	ROS vs. RUS	4.190018	0.000028	0.008333	0.008333
5	Original vs. ROS	3.873790	0.000107	0.010000	0.016667
4	RUS vs. SMOTE	3.715676	0.000203	0.012500	0.016667
3	Original vs. SMOTE	3.399448	0.000675	0.016667	0.016667
2	**ROS vs. SMOTE**	**0.474342**	**0.635256**	**0.025000**	**0.025000**
1	**Original vs. RUS**	**0.316228**	**0.75183**	**0.050000**	**0.050000**

6   Conclusion

The classification performance of the deep learning MLP to classify class imbalanced gene-expression microarrays datasets was analyzed. In accordance to the results, does not exist evidence of the predominance of ROS over SMOTE or viseversa, but the tendency is that RUS presents worse results than other methods, even when the original dataset is used. On the other hand, does not exists evidence (based on the datasets used in this work), of the relationship between its dimensionality and the classifier effectiveness on class imbalance scenarios. However, results show that the noise or separability of the dataset is more determinant than its dimensionality in the classifier performance.

References

1. Abdel-Zaher, A.M., Eldeib, A.M.: Breast cancer classification using deep belief networks. Expert Syst. Appl. **46**, 139–144 (2016)
2. Alejo, R., Monroy-de Jesús, J., Ambriz-Polo, J.C., Pacheco-Sánchez, J.H.: An improved dynamic sampling back-propagation algorithm based on mean square error to face the multi-class imbalance problem. Neural Comput. Appl. **28**(10), 2843–2857 (2017). https://doi.org/10.1007/s00521-017-2938-3
3. Alejo, R., Monroy-de Jesús, J., Pacheco-Sánchez, J., López-González, E., Antonio-Velázquez, J.: A selective dynamic sampling back-propagation approach for handling the two-class imbalance problem. Appl. Sci. **6**(7), 200 (2016). https://doi.org/10.3390/app6070200
4. Blagus, R., Lusa, L.: Smote for high-dimensional class-imbalanced data. BMC Bioinform. **14**(1), 106 (2013). https://doi.org/10.1186/1471-2105-14-106
5. Chen, D., Qian, G., Shi, C., Pan, Q.: Breast cancer malignancy prediction using incremental combination of multiple recurrent neural network. In: Liu, D., Xie, S., Li, Y., Zhao, D., El-Alfy, E.S. (eds.) ICONIP 2017. LNCS, vol. 10635, pp. 43–52. Springer, Cham (2017). https://doi.org/10.1007/978-3-319-70096-0_5
6. Cleofas-Sánchez, L., Sánchez, J.S., García, V.: Gene selection and disease prediction from gene expression data using a two-stage hetero-associative memory. Progress Artif. Intell. (2018). https://doi.org/10.1007/s13748-018-0148-6
7. Danaee, P., Reza, G., Hendrix, D.A.: A deep learning approach for cancer detection and relevant gene identification. In: Pacific Symposium on Biocomputing, Honolulu, pp. 219–229 (2016)
8. Dittman, D., Khoshgoftaar, T., Wald, R., Napolitano, A.: Comparison of data sampling approaches for imbalanced bioinformatics data. In: Proceedings of the 27th International Florida Artificial Intelligence Research Society Conference, FLAIRS 2014, pp. 268–271 (2014)
9. Dong, Q., Gong, S., Zhu, X.: Imbalanced deep learning by minority class incremental rectification. CoRR abs/1804.10851 (2018)
10. Dwivedi, A.K.: Artificial neural network model for effective cancer classification using microarray gene expression data. Neural Comput. Appl. **29**(12), 1545–1554 (2018). https://doi.org/10.1007/s00521-016-2701-1
11. Fernandez, A., Garcia, S., Herrera, F., Chawla, N.V.: SMOTE for learning from imbalanced data: progress and challenges, marking the 15-year anniversary. J. Artif. Intell. Res. **61**, 863–905 (2018)
12. Geman, O., Chiuchisan, I., Covasa, M., Doloc, C., Milici, M.-R., Milici, L.-D.: Deep learning tools for human microbiome Big Data. In: Balas, V.E., Jain, L.C., Balas, M.M. (eds.) SOFA 2016. AISC, vol. 633, pp. 265–275. Springer, Cham (2018). https://doi.org/10.1007/978-3-319-62521-8_21
13. Goodfellow, I., Bengio, Y., Courville, A.: Deep Learning. MIT Press, Cambridge (2016)
14. Guo, Y., Liu, Y., Oerlemans, A., Lao, S., Wu, S., Lew, M.S.: Deep learning for visual understanding: a review. Neurocomputing **187**, 27–48 (2016)
15. Hanson, J., Yang, Y., Paliwal, K., Zhou, Y.: Improving protein disorder prediction by deep bidirectional long short-term memory recurrent neural networks. Bioinformatics **33**, 685–692 (2016)
16. He, H., Garcia, E.: Learning from imbalanced data. IEEE Trans. Knowl. Data Eng. **21**(9), 1263–1284 (2009). https://doi.org/10.1109/TKDE.2008.239

17. Hira, Z., Gillies, D.F.: A review of feature selection and feature extraction methods applied on microarray data. Adv. Bioinform. **2015**, 1–13 (2015)
18. LeCun, Y., Bengio, Y., Hinton, G.: Deep learning. Nature **521**, 436–444 (2015)
19. López, V., Fernández, A., García, S., Palade, V., Herrera, F.: An insight into classification with imbalanced data: empirical results and current trends on using data intrinsic characteristics. Inf. Sci. **250**, 113–141 (2013). https://doi.org/10.1016/j.ins.2013.07.007
20. Maqlin, P., Thamburaj, R., Mammen, J.J., Manipadam, M.T.: Automated nuclear pleomorphism scoring in breast cancer histopathology images using deep neural networks. In: Prasath, R., Vuppala, A.K., Kathirvalavakumar, T. (eds.) MIKE 2015. LNCS (LNAI), vol. 9468, pp. 269–276. Springer, Cham (2015). https://doi.org/10.1007/978-3-319-26832-3_26
21. Reyes-Nava, A., Sánchez, J.S., Alejo, R., Flores-Fuentes, A.A., Rendón-Lara, E.: Performance analysis of deep neural networks for classification of gene-expression microarrays. In: Martínez-Trinidad, J.F., Carrasco-Ochoa, J.A., Olvera-López, J.A., Sarkar, S. (eds.) MCPR 2018. LNCS, vol. 10880, pp. 105–115. Springer, Cham (2018). https://doi.org/10.1007/978-3-319-92198-3_11
22. Ruder, S.: An overview of gradient descent optimization algorithms. CoRR abs/1609.04747 (2016)
23. Salaken, S.M., Khosravi, A., Khatami, A., Nahavandi, S., Hosen, M.A.: Lung cancer classification using deep learned features on low population dataset. In: IEEE 30th Canadian Conference on Electrical and Computer Engineering, Windsor, pp. 1–5 (2017)
24. Zaharia, M., et al.: Apache spark: a unified engine for Big Data processing. Commun. ACM **59**(11), 56–65 (2016). https://doi.org/10.1145/2934664

A Data Representation Approach to Support Imbalanced Data Classification Based on TWSVM

C. Jimenez$^{(\boxtimes)}$, A. M. Alvarez, and A. Orozco

Automatics Research Group, Universidad Tecnologica de Pereira, Pereira, Colombia
`craljimenez@utp.edu.co`

Abstract. Imbalance classification requires to represent the input data adequately to avoid biased results towards the class with the greater samples number. Here, we introduce an enhanced version of the famous twin support vector machine (TWSVM) classifier by incorporating an extended dual formulation of its quadratic programming optimization. Besides a centered kernel alignment (CKA)-based representation is used to avoid data overlapping. In particular, our approach, termed enhanced TWSVM (ETWSVM), allows representing the input samples in a high dimensional space (possibly infinite) after reformulation of the TWSVM dual form. Obtained results for binary classification demonstrate that our ETWSVM can reveal relevant data structures diminishing overlapping and biased classification results under imbalance scenarios. Moreover, ETWSVM notably adopts the lowest computational cost for training in comparison to state-of-the-art methods.

Keywords: TWSVM · Imabalanced data · Kernel enhacenment

1 Introduction

Imbalanced data refer to datasets in which one of the classes have a higher number of samples than the others. The class with the highest number of samples is called the majority class, while the class with the lowest number of samples is known as the minority class. Traditional classification models tend to deal with the minority class as noise, that is, the minority class inputs are deemed as rare patterns. Besides, in several applications, i.e., natural disaster prediction, cancer gene expression discrimination, fraudulent credit card transactions, the non-identification of minority class samples yields to a massive cost [1].

Some machine learning approaches have been developed in the past decade to deal with imbalanced data, most of which have been based on sampling techniques, ensemble methods, and cost-sensitive learning [2]. The sampling techniques are applied over data to balance the number of samples between classes; this is done by eliminating samples from the majority class (under-sampling) and/or creating synthetic samples of the minority one (over-sampling). However, these techniques can generate a loss of information by eliminating majority

© Springer Nature Switzerland AG 2019
R. Vera-Rodriguez et al. (Eds.): CIARP 2018, LNCS 11401, pp. 55–63, 2019.
https://doi.org/10.1007/978-3-030-13469-3_7

class samples, or overfitting due to the redundant information through generating synthetic minority class inputs [3]. Secondly, ensemble methods split the set of the majority class in several subsets with a size equal to the minority set. Then, this train as many classifiers as the number of majority class subsets. These approaches usually archive competitive performance; but, the computational cost is enormous since the number of classifiers to train [4]. In turn, cost-sensitive approaches modify the learning algorithm or the cost function by penalizing the misclassification of the minority class samples. Nevertheless, these techniques lead to overfitting, since it tends to bias the minority class [5]. In recent years, a twin support vector machines (TWSVM)-based algorithms take advantage of their generalization capacity and their low computational cost by constructing two non-parallel hyperplanes instead of only one hyperplane as the traditional support vector machine (SVM) [6]. Some TWSVM's extensions include a structural data representation a favor the generalization capacity of the classifier [7]. Additionally, TWSVM-based approaches have been proposed to counter the imbalanced data effect combining resampling techniques, coupling a between-class discriminant algorithm, and weighting the primal problem to prevent the overtraining [8,9]. Nonetheless, most of the TWSVM-based approaches do not include a suitable reproducing kernel Hilbert space (RKHS)-based representation, being difficult to incorporate an incorporate kernel approach within the optimization. Thus, they neglect the intrinsic formulation and virtues of a dual problem regarding kernel methods.

In this work, we propose a TWSVM-based cost-sensitive method that make a kernel-based enhancement of the TWSVM for imbalance data classification (ETWSVM), which allows representing the input samples in a high dimensional space. Also, we use a centered kernel alignment (CKA) method [10] with the objective of learning a kernel mapping to counteract inherent imbalanced issues, reduce the computational time and enhance the data representation. As benchmarks, we test the standard SVM classifier [11], a support vector machine with slack variables regulated [5], a SMOTE with SVM [12], and a weighted Lagrangian twin support vector machine (WLTSVM) [13] for binary classification. Results obtained from benchmarks databases of the state-of-the-art show that our approach outperforms the baseline methods concerning both the accuracy and the geometric mean-based classification assessment.

The remainder of this paper is organized as follows: Sect. 2 describes the material and methods of the approach proposed for classification. Sections 3 and 4 describe the experimental set-up and the results obtained, respectively. Finally, the concluding remarks are outlined in Sect. 5.

2   Enhanced TWSVM

Nonlinear Extension of the TWSVM Classifier. Let $\{x_n \in \mathbb{R}^P, y_n \in \{+1, -1\}\}_{n=1}^N$ be an input training set, where each sample x_n can belong to the minority class matrix $X^+ \in \mathbb{R}^{P \times N^+}$ ($y_n = +1$), or to the majority class matrix $X^- \in \mathbb{R}^{P \times N^-}$ ($y_n = -1$), being P the number of features and $N = N^+ + N^-$

the number of samples. The well-know extension of the SVM classifier, termed twin support vector machine (TWSVM), relaxes the SVM's quadratic programming optimization (QPP) by employing two non-parallel hyperplanes, as follows: $f^\ell(\boldsymbol{x}) = \boldsymbol{x}^\top \boldsymbol{w}^\ell + b^\ell = 0$, where $\ell \in \{+,-\}$, $\boldsymbol{w}^\ell \in \mathbb{R}^P$ is a normal vector concerning $f^\ell(\boldsymbol{x})$, and $b^\ell \in \mathbb{R}$ is a bias term. Traditionally, the non-linear extension of the TWSVM includes a kernel within the discrimination function as $f^\ell(\boldsymbol{x}) = \sum_{n=1}^N \kappa(\boldsymbol{x}, \boldsymbol{x}_n)\tilde{w}_n^\ell + b^\ell$, where $\tilde{w}_n^\ell \in \mathbb{R}$ is the n-th element of the vector $\tilde{\boldsymbol{w}}^\ell \in \mathbb{R}^N$, and $\kappa : \mathbb{R}^P \times \mathbb{R}^P \to \mathbb{R}$ is a kernel function. Nonetheless, such a non-linear extension does not consider directly a reproductive kernel Hilbert space (RKHS) within the empirical risk minimization-based cost function of the TWSVM, that is to say, it does not consider a mapping to a high dimensional (possible infinite) feature space.

So, we introduce a non-linear extension of the TWSVM, termed NTWSVM, optimization functional towards the mapping $\varphi : \mathbb{R}^P \to \mathbb{R}^D$, where $D \to \infty$. Thereby, the hyperplanes can be rewritten as: $f^\ell(\boldsymbol{x}) = \varphi(\boldsymbol{x})^\top \boldsymbol{w}^\ell + b^\ell = 0$. In particular, each hyperplane plays the role of a one-class classifier, aiming to enclose its corresponding class. Next, the NTWSVM's primal form yields:

$$\hat{\boldsymbol{w}}^\ell, \hat{b}^\ell, \hat{\boldsymbol{\xi}}^{\ell'} = \arg\min_{\boldsymbol{w},b,\boldsymbol{\xi}} \frac{c_1}{2}\left(\|\boldsymbol{w}\|_2^2 + b^2\right) + \frac{1}{2}\left\|\boldsymbol{w}^\top \boldsymbol{\Phi}^\ell + \boldsymbol{1}^\ell b\right\|_2^2 + c_2 \boldsymbol{1}^{\ell'}\boldsymbol{\xi} \tag{1}$$
$$\text{s.t.} \left(\boldsymbol{w}^\top \boldsymbol{\Phi}^{\ell'} + b\boldsymbol{1}^{\ell'}\right)\boldsymbol{\Delta}^{\ell'} + \boldsymbol{\xi}^\top \geq \boldsymbol{1}^{\ell'}, \boldsymbol{\xi} \geq \boldsymbol{0}; \quad \forall_{\ell,\ell' \in \{+,-\}},$$

where $\boldsymbol{\Phi}^\ell = [\varphi(\boldsymbol{x}_n)]_{n=1}^{N^\ell} \forall \{\boldsymbol{x}_n \mid y_n = \ell\}$, $\hat{\boldsymbol{\xi}}^{\ell'} \in \mathbb{R}^{N^{\ell'}}$ is a slack variable vector for the l-th class; $c_1, c_2 \in \mathbb{R}^+$ are regularization parameters, the first one regularizes the slack variables and the second one the model parameters $\hat{\boldsymbol{w}}^\ell$ and $\hat{b}^\ell$ (rules the margin maximization). Besides, $\boldsymbol{1}^\ell \in \mathbb{R}^{N^\ell}$ is an all ones row vector, $\boldsymbol{\Delta}^{\ell'} = \ell' \boldsymbol{I}_{N^{\ell'}}$ being $\boldsymbol{I}_{N^{\ell'}} \in \{0,1\}^{N^{\ell'} \times N^{\ell'}}$ an identity matrix, $\ell' = -\ell$, and $\|\cdot\|_2$ stands for the 2-norm. Later, the Wolfe dual form of Eq. (1) can be written as follows:

$$\hat{\boldsymbol{\alpha}}^{\ell'} = \arg\max_{\boldsymbol{\alpha}} -\frac{1}{2}\boldsymbol{\alpha}^\top \boldsymbol{M}\boldsymbol{B}\boldsymbol{\alpha} + \boldsymbol{1}^{\ell'}\boldsymbol{\alpha} \quad \text{s.t.} \quad \boldsymbol{0}^\top \leq \boldsymbol{\alpha}^\top \leq c_2 \boldsymbol{1}^{\ell'}, \tag{2}$$

where $\hat{\boldsymbol{\alpha}}^{\ell'} \in \mathbb{R}^{N^{\ell'}}$ is a Lagrangian multiplier, $\boldsymbol{M} \in \mathbb{R}^{N^{\ell'} \times N^{\ell'}}$ holds elements $M_{nn'} = \kappa\left(\boldsymbol{s}_n, \boldsymbol{s}_{n'} \mid \sigma^2 \boldsymbol{I}_{P+1}\right)$, $\kappa(\cdot,\cdot)$ is a multivariate Gaussian kernel, $\boldsymbol{s}_n = [\boldsymbol{x}_n; 1]$ is an extended column vector of the matrix $\boldsymbol{S}^{\ell'} \in \mathbb{R}^{(P+1) \times N^{\ell'}}$, $\boldsymbol{B} \in \mathbb{R}^{N^{\ell'} \times N^{\ell'}}$ holds elements $B_{nn'} = \kappa\left(\boldsymbol{s}_n, \boldsymbol{s}_m \mid \boldsymbol{\Sigma}\right)$, $\boldsymbol{\Sigma} = \left(c_1 \boldsymbol{I}_{D^\ell + 1} + \boldsymbol{S}^\ell (\boldsymbol{S}^\ell)^\top \boldsymbol{S}^\ell (\boldsymbol{S}^\ell)^\top\right)$, and $\boldsymbol{I}_{P+1}, \boldsymbol{I}_{D^\ell + 1}$ are identity matrix of proper size. Hence, the NTWSVM hyperplanes yields: $f^\ell(\boldsymbol{x}) = \boldsymbol{d}^\top \boldsymbol{B}\boldsymbol{\Delta}^{\ell'} \hat{\boldsymbol{\alpha}}^{\ell'}$, where $\boldsymbol{d} \in \mathbb{R}^{N^{\ell'}}$ holds elements $d_n = \kappa\left(\boldsymbol{s}, \boldsymbol{s}_n \mid \sigma^2 \boldsymbol{I}_{P+1}\right)$ and $\boldsymbol{s}_n \in \boldsymbol{S}^{\ell'}$. Finally, the label of the new input is computed as the distance to the closest hyperplane as $y^* = \arg\min_{\ell \in \{+,-\}} |f^\ell(\boldsymbol{x})|$, where $|\cdot|$ stands for the absolute value. It worth noting that due to the one-class foundation of the NTWSVM approach, the distance to the hyperplanes are proportional to the score magnitude.

CKA-Based Enhancement of the NTWSVM. To avoid instability issues concerning the inverse of the matrix $\boldsymbol{\Sigma}$ and to reveal relevant data structures for imbalance classification tasks, we use a centered kernel alignment (CKA)-based approach to infer $\boldsymbol{\Sigma}^{-1} = \boldsymbol{E}\boldsymbol{E}^{\top}$, where $\boldsymbol{E} \in \mathbb{R}^{(P+1)\times P'}$ ($P' \leq P+1$). In fact, we learn $\boldsymbol{E}$ as a linear projection to match the kernels $\boldsymbol{K}^x \in \mathbb{R}^{N \times N}$ and $\boldsymbol{K}^y \in \mathbb{R}^{N \times N}$, holding elements $\boldsymbol{K}^x_{nn'} = \kappa\left(\boldsymbol{x}_n, \boldsymbol{x}'_n \mid (\boldsymbol{E}\boldsymbol{E}^{\top})^{-1}\right)$, $\boldsymbol{K}^y_{ij} = \delta\left(y_i, y_j\right)$, being $\delta\left(\cdot\right)$ the delta function. Besides, the empirical estimate of the CKA alignment between $\boldsymbol{K}^x$ and $\boldsymbol{K}^y$ is defined as [10]:

$$\hat{\rho}\left(\tilde{\boldsymbol{K}}^x, \tilde{\boldsymbol{K}}^y\right) = \frac{\langle\tilde{\boldsymbol{K}}^x, \tilde{\boldsymbol{K}}^y\rangle_{\mathrm{F}}}{\sqrt{\langle\tilde{\boldsymbol{K}}^x, \tilde{\boldsymbol{K}}^x\rangle_{\mathrm{F}}\langle\tilde{\boldsymbol{K}}^y, \tilde{\boldsymbol{K}}^y\rangle_{\mathrm{F}}}}, \tag{3}$$

where $\tilde{\boldsymbol{K}}$ stands for the centered kernel matrix calculated as $\tilde{\boldsymbol{K}} = \tilde{\boldsymbol{I}}\boldsymbol{K}\tilde{\boldsymbol{I}}$, where $\tilde{\boldsymbol{I}} = \boldsymbol{I} - \boldsymbol{1}\boldsymbol{1}^{\top}/N$, $\boldsymbol{I} \in \mathbb{R}^{N \times N}$ is an identity matrix, and $\langle\cdot, \cdot\rangle_{\mathrm{F}}$ denotes the matrix-based Frobenius inner product. Later, to compute the projection matrix $\boldsymbol{E}$, the following learning algorithm is employed:

$$\hat{\boldsymbol{E}} = \arg\max_{\boldsymbol{E}} \log\left(\hat{\rho}\left(\tilde{\boldsymbol{K}}^x, \tilde{\boldsymbol{K}}^y; \boldsymbol{E}\right)\right). \tag{4}$$

Lastly, given $\boldsymbol{\Sigma}^{-1} = \hat{\boldsymbol{E}}\hat{\boldsymbol{E}}^{\top}$, the NTSVM is trained as above explained. For the sake of simplicity, we called our proposal as ETWSVM. A MatLab code of ETWSVM is publicly available[1]

3   Experimental Set-Up

Datasets and ETWSVM Training. A toy dataset comprising two classes belonging to Gaussian distribution with a mean vector of $\boldsymbol{0} \in \mathbb{R}^2$ and a variance matrix of $0.3\boldsymbol{I}_2$, the minority samples are the samples with a probability greater than 0.7 and rest as majority one; and twelve benchmark datasets originating from the well-known UCI machine learning repository are used to test the ETWSVM proposed[2]. Table 1 displays the main properties of the studied UCI repository datasets; the minority class is marked and rest as the majority one. As quality assessment, we employ the classification performance regarding the accuracy (ACC) and the geometric mean (GM) measures. The ACC is computed as $ACC = (TP + TN)/(TP + TN + FP + FN)$, where TP is the number of samples belonging to class $+1$ and classified as $+1$, FN codes the number of samples belonging to class $+1$ and classified as -1, TF is the number of samples belonging to class -1 and classified as -1, and FP is the number of samples belonging to class -1 and classified $+1$. Traditionally, The ACC measure is used for classification, but it can be biased for imbalanced datasets. Therefore, the GM is utilized to test imbalance classification as follows: $GM = \sqrt{\nu \times \zeta}$,

---

[1] https://github.com/cralji/ETWSVM.git.
[2] https://archive.ics.uci.edu/ml/index.php.

where $\nu = TP/(TP + FN)$ and $\zeta = TF/(TN + FP)$. Besides, a nested 10-fold cross-validation scheme is carried out for ETWSVM training. Regarding the free parameter tuning, the regularization value c_2 is fixed as $c_2 = N^-/N^+$, and the bandwidth is searched from the set $\sigma \in \{0.1\sigma_0, 0.2\sigma_0, \ldots, \sigma_0\}$, where σ_0 is the median of the input data Euclidean distances. Note that our CKA-based enhancement avoids the estimation of the c_1 value in Eq. (1).

Method Comparison. As baseline, four classification approaches are tested: SVM [11], SVM with regularized slack variables (SVM reg-slack) [5], SVM with synthetic minority oversampling technique (SMOTE) [12], and a weighted Lagrangian twin support vector machine (WLTSVM) [13]. All provided methods include a Gaussian kernel. So, we infer the kernel bandwidth as in the ETWSVM training. Also, the regularization parameter value is computed from the set $\{0.1, 1, 10, 100, 1000\}$ (for the WLTSVM technique we assume equal regularization parameter values). On the other hand, the k value for the SMOTE algorithm is fixed from the set $\{3, 5, 9, 10, 15\}$ and the relationship between minority and majority samples is set to 1:1. All the classifiers are implemented in MATLAB R2016b environment on a PC with Intel i5 processor (2.7 GHz) with 6 GB RAM.

Table 1. Benchmark datasets from the UCI machine learning repository.

Datasets	Imbalance ratio	Features	Data size	Minority class
Haberman	0.3600	4	306	2
Housing	0.0743	13	506	1 (CHAS)
Vehicle	0.3076	18	846	Van
Transfusion	0.3123	4	748	1
Ionosphere	0.5600	34	351	b
Balance	0.0851	4	625	Balanced
Biodeg	0.5093	41	1055	RB
cmc	0.2921	9	1473	2:Long-term
Pima-Indians	0.5360	8	768	1
BankNote	0.8005	4	1372	1
Iris	0.5000	4	150	Iris Virginica
Wisconsin	0.5938	30	569	Malignant

4   Results and Discussion

Figure 1 presents the ETWSVM results on the toy dataset. As seen in Figs. 1(a) and (b), which show the generated score by the minority and majority hyperplanes, respectively; the majority hyperplane generates a higher score for the samples associated with the minority class. Such behavior occurs reciprocally between the minority hyperplane and the examples of the majority class. Indeed, each hyperplane function is fixed depending on the slack variables of its counterpart. Therefore, the minority class's support vectors are selected from the

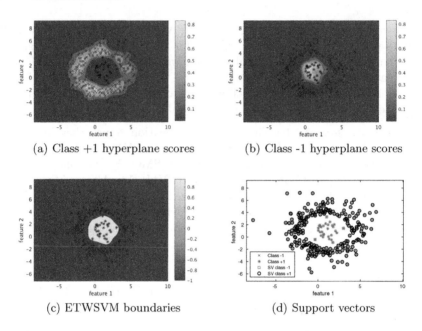

(a) Class +1 hyperplane scores

(b) Class -1 hyperplane scores

(c) ETWSVM boundaries

(d) Support vectors

Fig. 1. An illustrative example of the ETWSVM classifier. (a) and (b) show the scores hyperplane. (c) shows the decision boundary, where the yellow zone is classified as +1 and the blue as −1. (d) support vectors. (Color figure online)

majority hyperplane meanwhile the majority class's support vectors from the minority one. Also, the Fig. 1(d) exposes the support vectors obtained, where the majority hyperplane only requires three support vectors, but the minority hyperplane chooses all the majority samples as support vectors to reveal the central data structure. As expected, our ETWTSVM highlights the minority class data structure holding a higher number of support vectors than in the majority one. In turn, by combining the ETWSVM hyperplanes, Fig. 1(c) displays the classifier's boundaries that encodes the class patterns correctly.

Next, the attained classification results on the real-world datasets are summarized in Table 2 concerning the ACC and the GM assessments. As seen, the average ACC performances for the SVM reg-slack, the SVM, the SMOTE-SVM, and our ETWSVM are closely similar. Nonetheless, the SMOTE-SVM and our proposal achieve more reliable results regarding the standard deviation values. Further, for the GM, which is preferred for evaluating imbalance data classification, demonstrates that the SMOTE-SVM and the introduced ETWSVM allow revealing discriminative patterns to avoid biased results. Again, the low standard deviation values of such approaches probe their dominance to cope with imbalance problems. Notably, the CKA-based kernel learning in Eq. (4),

Table 2. Classification results on the UCI repository datasets. ACC: accuracy, GM: geometric mean. Testing scheme: nested 10-fold cross-validation.

Datasets	SVM reg-slack [11] ACC ± std (%) GM ± std (%)	SVM [4] ACC ± std (%) GM ± std (%)	SMOTE-SVM [12] ACC ± std (%) GM ± std (%)	WLTSVM [13] ACC ± std (%) GM ± std (%)	ETWSVM ACC ± std (%) GM ± std (%)
Haberman	62.82 ± 08.52	71.53 ± 05.03	61.76 ± 05.20	59.49 ± 16.26	**71.90 ± 08.88**
	53.42 ± 12.12	54.54 ± 09.53	56.24 ± 12.53	38.26 ± 22.86	**57.70 ± 14.93**
Housing	**91.91 ± 02.68**	88.55 ± 05.29	90.32 ± 03.65	44.86 ± 06.61	81.02 ± 07.61
	63.36 ± 16.72	67.73 ± 27.57	66.31 ± 25.13	46.18 ± 18.18	**72.11 ± 15.95**
Vehicle	97.52 ± 01.42	**97.88 ± 01.34**	97.63 ± 01.48	82.39 ± 04.62	92.19 ± 01.79
	97.66 ± 02.02	**97.71 ± 01.79**	96.85 ± 02.39	82.20 ± 03.96	93.33 ± 02.34
Transfusion	**69.12 ± 04.05**	68.04 ± 04.96	62.56 ± 10.27	35.95 ± 31.21	68.46 ± 06.65
	64.78 ± 05.91	59.73 ± 22.00	51.91 ± 28.18	39.18 ± 33.89	63.92 ± 07.48
Ionosphere	**94.59 ± 02.47**	94.01 ± 02.51	93.72 ± 04.96	82.40 ± 06.80	89.76 ± 06.29
	93.56 ± 03.11	93.12 ± 03.29	92.23 ± 06.71	82.49 ± 07.61	85.64 ± 09.83
Balance	90.70 ± 03.34	**90.70 ± 03.15**	83.83 ± 05.98	49.54 ± 20.70	59.71 ± 06.83
	81.10 ± 18.90	57.32 ± 11.22	69.31 ± 13.40	52.49 ± 16.49	65.58 ± 12.86
Biodeg	87.02 ± 02.86	87.30 ± 02.98	**87.77 ± 02.21**	77.82 ± 02.21	59.00 ± 40.78
	86.58 ± 02.78	86.49 ± 02.97	**86.84 ± 02.71**	75.23 ± 02.23	59.83 ± 41.33
cmc	26.75 ± 04.74	33.20 ± 03.16	**67.82 ± 06.23**	31.94 ± 22.44	61.71 ± 03.58
	19.88 ± 17.54	31.69 ± 04.05	58.76 ± 21.07	31.71 ± 22.56	**64.48 ± 04.08**
Prima-Indians	25.26 ± 04.66	24.99 ± 04.30	72.78 ± 04.95	65.36 ± 06.95	**73.29 ± 05.84**
	24.53 ± 05.56	24.47 ± 05.04	**72.71 ± 04.60**	68.27 ± 07.09	71.87 ± 06.23
Banknote	88.26 ± 03.66	92.34 ± 12.99	**97.45 ± 01.89**	91.84 ± 01.36	96.58 ± 01.65
	88.65 ± 03.62	86.64 ± 30.46	**97.42 ± 02.11**	92.18 ± 01.28	96.72 ± 01.64
Iris	86.00 ± 09.14	99.33 ± 02.11	99.33 ± 02.11	99.33 ± 02.11	**100.00 ± 00.00**
	73.92 ± 19.32	98.94 ± 03.34	98.94 ± 03.34	98.94 ± 03.34	**100.00 ± 00.00**
Wisconsin	51.34 ± 05.77	**97.19 ± 01.49**	97.18 ± 02.06	80.82 ± 05.55	97.01 ± 02.03
	46.55 ± 09.22	**96.96 ± 01.72**	96.84 ± 02.30	81.54 ± 05.50	96.42 ± 02.31
Average	72.61 ± 25.83	78.76 ± 25.21	**84.35 ± 14.35**	66.81 ± 22.34	79.22 ± 15.47
	66.17 ± 25.90	71.28 ± 26.02	**78.70 ± 18.00**	65.72 ± 23.11	77.30 ± 15.99

favors the ETWSVM hyperplane representation through a non-linear matching between the input data dependencies and the output labels. Moreover, despite that SMOTE-SVM reports the best GM performance in average, it requires the higher computational time to train the classification system (see Table 3). On the other hand, the GM results for the ETWSVM are competitive but requires the lowest computational cost for training. The later can be explained because our ETWSVM optimization takes advantage of the one-class foundation of the straightforward TWSVM, while decreasing the class overlapping based on the CKA matching. Finally, it is worth noting to mention that the ETWSVM requires to fix few free parameters and solves two smaller sized QPP in comparison to the state-of-the-art algorithms.

Table 3. Classification results on the UCI repository datasets. Required time in seconds for one fold training.

Datasets	SVM reg-slack [11]	SVM [4]	SMOTE-SVM [12]	WLTSVM [13]	ETWSVM
HaberMan	06.50 ± 04.26	34.07 ± 32.22	114.73 ± 34.05	17.21 ± 00.42	**03.59 ± 00.76**
Balance	15.67 ± 02.91	**01.58 ± 00.06**	358.45 ± 190.86	42.53 ± 01.41	10.88 ± 01.62
Housing	111.11 ± 67.86	**03.17 ± 00.28**	1064.70 ± 126.78	21.78 ± 00.26	07.14 ± 01.44
Iris	00.29 ± 00.03	**00.22 ± 00.03**	01.36 ± 00.04	03.78 ± 00.07	01.72 ± 00.39
Vehicle	31.20 ± 16.03	21.83 ± 09.59	300.71 ± 49.30	75.96 ± 04.24	**22.45 ± 05.84**
Ionosphere	88.18 ± 78.22	102.79 ± 104.61	777.84 ± 161.20	12.60 ± 00.33	**04.19 ± 00.15**
Prima-Indians	162.53 ± 75.23	157.81 ± 50.10	1175.29 ± 141.30	60.93 ± 02.95	**13.97 ± 00.70**
Banknote	**01.18 ± 00.96**	01.96 ± 02.19	07.51 ± 01.98	278.07 ± 14.83	57.72 ± 09.77
Wisconsin	11.52 ± 07.18	12.16 ± 06.24	73.96 ± 27.75	31.97 ± 00.99	**08.60 ± 01.54**
biodeg	466.33 ± 126.19	581.15 ± 430.96	3688.18 ± 658.75	126.74 ± 09.69	**39.80 ± 09.08**
Transfusion	**00.67 ± 00.40**	03.95 ± 10.26	04.92 ± 01.11	50.68 ± 01.65	13.34 ± 03.63
cmc	02.34 ± 01.59	**01.60 ± 01.06**	15.20 ± 07.91	233.00 ± 09.44	67.65 ± 08.69
Average	74.79 ± 134.26	76.86 ± 166.28	631.90 ± 1051.79	79.60 ± 89.17	**20.92 ± 22.14**

5 Conclusions

In this study, we propose an enhanced version of the well-known twin support vector machine classifier. In fact, our approach, called ETWSVM, includes a direct non-linear mapping within the quadratic programming optimization of the standard TWSVM, which allows representing the input samples in a high dimensional space (possibly infinite) after reformulation of the TWSVM dual form. Besides, a centered kernel alignment-based approach is proposed to learn the ETWSVM kernel mapping to counteract inherent imbalanced issues. Attained results on both synthetic and real-world datasets probe the virtues of our approach regarding classification and computational cost assessments. In particular, the real-world results related to some UCI repository datasets, show that the ETWSVM-based discrimination outperforms most of the standard SVM-based methods for imbalance classification and obtains competitive results in comparison to the SMOTE-SVM. However, ETWSVM notably adopts the lowest computational cost for training. As future work, authors plan to couple the ETWSVM approach with resampling methods to improve the classification performance. Moreover, a scalable multi-class extension could be an exciting research line. Finally, a couple the ETWSVM approach with a stochastic gradient descent for large scale problems.

Acknowledgments. Under grants support by the project: "Desarrollo de un sistema de posorte clínico basado en el procesamiento estócastico para mejorar la resolusión espacial de la resonancia magnética estructural y de difusión con aplicación al procedimiento de la ablación de tumores", code: 111074455860, funded by COLCIENCIAS. Moreover, C. Jimenez is partially financed by the project E6-18-09: "Clasificador de máquinas de vectores de soporte para problemas desbalanceados con selección automática de parámetros", funded by Vicerrectoria de Investigación, innovación y extension and by Maestría en Ingeniería Eléctrica, both from Universidad Tecnológica de Pereira.

References

1. Haixiang, G., et al.: Learning from class-imbalanced data: review of methods and applications. Expert Syst. Appl. **73**, 220–239 (2017)
2. Loyola-González, O., et al.: Study of the impact of resampling methods for contrast pattern based classifiers in imbalanced databases. Neurocomputing **175**, 935–947 (2016)
3. Branco, P., Torgo, L., Ribeiro, R.P.: A survey of predictive modeling on imbalanced domains. ACM Comput. Surv. **49**(2), 31 (2016)
4. García, S., et al.: Dynamic ensemble selection for multi-class imbalanced datasets. Inf. Sci. **445**, 22–37 (2018)
5. Xanthopoulos, P., Razzaghi, T.: A weighted support vector machine method for control chart pattern recognition. Comput. Ind. Eng. **70**, 134–149 (2014)
6. Tang, L., Tian, Y., Yang, C.: Nonparallel support vector regression model and its SMO-type solver. Neural Netw. (2018)
7. Qi, Z., Tian, Y., Shi, Y.: Structural twin support vector machine for classification. Knowl. Based Syst. **43**, 74–81 (2013)
8. Liu, L., et al.: Between-class discriminant twin support vector machine for imbalanced data classification. In: CAC 2017, pp. 7117–7122. IEEE (2017)
9. Xu, Y.: Maximum margin of twin spheres support vector machine for imbalanced data classification. IEEE Trans. Cybern. **47**(6), 1540–1550 (2017)
10. Alvarez-Meza, A., Orozco-Gutierrez, A., Castellanos-Dominguez, G.: Kernel-based relevance analysis with enhanced interpretability for detection of brain activity patterns. Front. Neurosci. **11**, 550 (2017)
11. Anandarup, R., et al.: A study on combining dynamic selection and data preprocessing for imbalance learning. Neurocomputing **286**, 179–192 (2018)
12. Piri, S., Delen, D., Liu, T.: A synthetic informative minority over-sampling (SIMO) algorithm leveraging support vector machine to enhance learning from imbalanced datasets. Decis. Support Syst. **106**, 15–29 (2018)
13. Shao, Y.H., et al.: An efficient weighted lagrangian twin support vector machine for imbalanced data classification. Pattern Recogn. **47**(9), 3158–3167 (2014)

Improving Regression Models by Dissimilarity Representation of Bio-chemical Data

Francisco Jose Silva-Mata, Catherine Jiménez, Gabriela Barcas,
David Estevez-Bresó, Niusvel Acosta-Mendoza[✉], Andres Gago-Alonso,
and Isneri Talavera-Bustamante

Advanced Technologies Application Center, 7th A Avenue # 21406 % 214 and 216,
Siboney, Playa, P.C. 12200, Havana, Cuba
{fjsilva,nacosta}@cenatav.co.cu

Abstract. The determination of characteristics by regression models using bio-chemical data from analytical techniques such as Near Infrared Spectrometry and Nuclear Magnetic Resonance is a common activity within the recognition of substances and their chemical-physical properties. The data obtained from the mentioned techniques are commonly represented as vectors, which ignore the continuous nature of data and the correlation between variables. This fact affects the regression modeling and calibration processes. For solving these problems, alternative representations of data have been previously used with good results, such as those ones based on functions and the others based on dissimilarity representation. By using the alternative based on dissimilarities, the obtained results improve the efficiency of the classification processes, but the experience in regression with this representation is scarce. For this reason, in this paper, in order to improve the quality of the regression models, we combine the dissimilarity representation with some adequate data pre-processing, in our case, we use the classical Partial Least Square regression as the modeling method. The evaluation of the results was carried out by using the coefficient of determination R^2 for each case and a statistical analysis of them is performed.

Keywords: Dissimilarity representation · Regression ·
Bio-chemical data

1 Introduction

Chemometrics, according to Massart [6], "is the chemical discipline that uses mathematical and statistical, and other methods that employ formal logic to design or select procedures and experiments for optimal measurement and to provide the relevant chemical information from the analysis of the chemical data". In this field, the development of classification methods, regression methods and analysis of substances from spectroscopic and chromatographic signals is one of

© Springer Nature Switzerland AG 2019
R. Vera-Rodriguez et al. (Eds.): CIARP 2018, LNCS 11401, pp. 64–71, 2019.
https://doi.org/10.1007/978-3-030-13469-3_8

the fundamental activities. The prediction of the concentration of a compound in a mixture spectrum or the properties of a material from its known structural parameters is a common task in chemistry [1].

Nowadays, instrumental techniques allow the analysis of pertinent data for different substances, such as: drugs, fuels, inks, medicines, etc. These data are usually represented as a sequence of independent values where each one can be: a measurement or observation made in time, response values for different wavelengths, etc. Usually, spectra are considered as vectors whose values correspond to the samples of the curve at a set of points, therefore, it ignores the continuous nature of data, the correlation between variables and, in many cases, it contains noisy and redundant information. In addition, the high dimension of data contrasts with the small number of samples that are usually counted in the laboratories. Each kind of spectroscopy and chromatography has its own characteristics, then the methods developed for a specific technique may not be applicable to the other ones. It is almost impossible to infer how a model will behave by simply making a reduction in the size of its variables. In order to lead with the mentioned problems, some alternative representations have reported, such as the known Dissimilarity Representation (DR) [7].

The DR allows that certain additional knowledge regarding data can be included making use of a measure of dissimilarity, which, in many cases, reduces the original dimension of data [13]. However, due to the physic-chemical nature of the measurement and the characteristics of each compound, not all dissimilarity measures achieve good results. The dissimilarity based approach has been used for the chemical substances classification, obtaining good results [8]; however, to the best of our knowledge, it has been purely applied in regression tasks [5,12]. Besides, it is not usually known which are the most appropriate dissimilarity measures for certain analytical techniques and what is their effect on the regression modeling.

Although the representation of data is a very important factor for the improvement of the regression model, it is not the only fact to take into account. The whole process to obtain a regression model is rather achieved through the combined use of an adequate pre-processing method and the selection of the most appropriated representation for each analytical technique. In case of using a representation based on dissimilarities, it is crucial the selection of the most appropriated dissimilarity measure.

The goal of this paper is to determine if regression models can be improved by using dissimilarities and which measures are more appropriated for each technique. We use the Partial Least Squares (PLS) as regression method, and Multiplicative Scatter Correction (MSC) and Standard Normal Variate (SNV) as pre-processing methods. For comparatively evaluating the quality of the regression models, the Coefficient of Determination (R^2) is used. It indicates the proportionate amount of variation in the response variable Y explained by the independent variables X in the linear regression model. The larger the R^2 is, the more variability is explained by the linear regression model.

This paper is organized in the following sections. In Sect. 2, we present a brief background. We detailed our proposal in Sect. 3. Section 4 is dedicated to the experiments description and the result analysis. In Sect. 5, the final conclusions of the work are presented.

2   Background

2.1   Pre-processing Methods

Data obtained from instrumental techniques often require that the differences in level and scale be eliminated, but must be known if is needed to pre-process the data and which is the adequate method to be used. MSC and SNV are probably the most widely used of pre-processing techniques for the Near Infrared technique (NIR) [9]. Imperfections, such as the effect of dispersions, are removed from the data matrix before modeling. MSC comprises two steps: (1) the estimation of the regression coefficients (additive and multiplicative contributions), and (2) the spectrum correction. The SNV concept is very similar to MSC except that the reference signal is not needed and each observation is processed separately.

2.2   Partial Least Squares

Partial Least-Squares Regression (PLS) is a widely used method in Chemometry for multivariate calibration. This method uses the information of the latent variables space (i.e. a combination of several variables to form a new one with a certain property). In PLS, the decomposition is carried out in such a way that the scores have the maximum covariance with the dependent variables. The covariance combines the large variances of the independent variables X and the high correlation with the response variable Y [3]. PLS is a linear model where the final latent variables predict the property and it is linear combinations of the original variables, supporting the collinearity between the variables. For modeling a single Y, the algorithm is known as PLS1 and for multivariate regression it is called PLS2.

2.3   Dissimilarity Representation

The Dissimilarity Representation (DR) is based on the role played by the proximity concept in classification problems, so the authors proposed to work in the space defined by the dissimilarity between objects [7]. When the objects to be classified are spectra or signals, the geometry and structure of them are used as discriminative characteristics between the different classes, depending on the used dissimilarity measure. Dissimilarity measures allow calculating and quantifying the differences between the samples; therefore, the selection of the appropriate measure for a given problem is a challenge and it depend on the characteristics of each particular problem. The use of the representation of data based on dissimilarities can be especially advantageous when the number of objects is very small or when the data are represented in high-dimensional spaces [8]. In DR, instead of having an $m \times n$ matrix where m represents the number of objects and n the measured variables, the data will be represented by an $m \times k$ matrix where k is the number of representative objects.

The commonly used dissimilarity measures are Chi-Square with a tolerance parameter epsilon of 0.1, Euclidean Distance (E), Kolmogorov-Smirnov Distance (KS), Cosine Distance (C), Shape Distance (Sh) with smoothing parameter $s = 2$, Spectral Angle Mapping (SAM), Pearson Correlation Coefficient (PCC), Bray-Curtis (BC), Correlation (Corr), Minkowski Distance (M) with $p = 5$ parameters, and Spearman Correlation (S).

3   Our Proposal

Our regression models can be explained by using the steps shown in Fig. 1. In general, we can obtain four possible regression model alternatives. The first one starts representing the original data by a vectorial representation which is modeled by using PLS and evaluated by using R^2 (see the sequence 1-4-5 of Fig. 1). The second alternative is similar to the first one but starting with a pre-processing step over the original data. The third alternative consists in representing the data in the dissimilarity space by using a selected measure over the vectorial representation of the original data (see the sequence 1-2-3-4-5 of Fig. 1). Finally, the fourth alternative is similar to the third one but starting with a pre-processing step over the original data. In this way, our four regression model are built, allowing us a comparison between the results of the regression model based on the space of the dissimilarities for different measures of similarity.

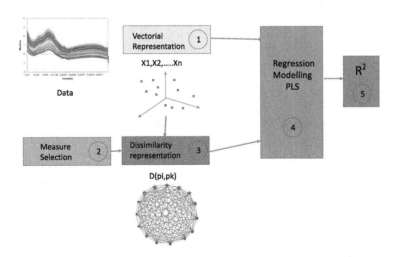

Fig. 1. Sequence steps to obtain the regression modelling.

4   Experiments

Following our four alternatives proposed in Sect. 3, we can evaluate the possible regression models. In our experiments, the PLS method was used with 10 components on each test. For comparing the regression models, the value of R^2 was calculated by each experiment. ANOVA is used to compare the experimental results because a higher value of R^2 does not guarantee a better model, for this fact, we want to verify that the difference between the values is not significant.

4.1   Used Datasets

The chosen dataset used in our experiments are Soil [10], Tecator [11], Cancer [2] (Metabolomic Cancer Diagnosis) and Wine [4] (see Fig. 2), where Soil and Tecator were obtained from the Near Infrared technique (NIR), while Cancer and Wine were obtained from the Nuclear Magnetic Resonance Technique (NMR). The Soil dataset is composed by soil samples originated in a field experiment in Abisko Sweden, where the samples comes from 36 parcels, with three subsamples of each parcel (in two different horizons, one of the inferior and two of the superior), giving a total of 108 samples, and the predicted values measured correspond to the ergosterol concentration. The Tecator dataset comes from the food industry and contains NIR spectra of meat samples, measured in a Tecator Infratec Food and Feed Analyzer. It has 215 samples consisting of 100 Absorbance values in the wavelength range 850 to 1050 nm and is associated with a description of the meat samples, obtained by a chemical that contains the percentage of fat, water and protein of each sample. The calibration problem addressed with this dataset consists in predicting the percentage of fat in the sample of meat from its NIR spectrum.

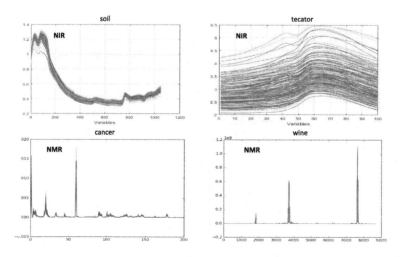

Fig. 2. NIR: Soil and Tecator (top) and NMR: Cancer and Wine (bottom) datasets.

The Cancer dataset was obtained by 1H-NMR spectroscopy (CPMG and NOESY-Presat) of human plasma samples (sodium citrate anticoagulant) and biomarker measurements (TIMP-1 and CEA). This study included patients undergoing to endoscopy of the large intestine due to symptoms that could be associated with ColoRectal Cancer (CRC), also known as bowel cancer and colon cancer. This dataset contains samples of control cases with one case of verified colorectal cancer and three controls for each case. The control group in this dataset correspond to subjects in which benign colorectal adenomas were found. The controls correspond to the age, sex and location of the tumors. The data of NMR are represented as PCA scores (first component) of the integrated peaks. Biomarker data is transformed into a record (base 2). It is known that TIMP-1 and CEA biomarkers change with the age and the genre. This has been corrected in the concentrations of biomarkers subtracting the concentration of a matched sample from another group of control (without findings). On the other hand, the Wine dataset is originated from the analysis by 1H-NMR of 40 table wines of different origin and color, where the value to predict is the pH of mentioned samples.

4.2 Experimental Results

The R^2 average results over each aforementioned dataset are shown in Fig. 3, which covers the four variant results. For each measure the results correspond to the use of the pre-processing step or not. From left to right (up to down) the first value is obtained without pre-processing, the second one is obtained by applying SNV and the third one is achieved by using MSC.

As it can be seen in the figures of Soil, the measures that had improvements with respect to the R^2 value using the vector representation without preprocessing were BC, E, SAM and Sh, measures that in turn have lower variance. Therefore, we can say that the model is more consistent when these measures are applied.

In the case of Tecator, except for the SAM, BC, E and M measures, the other seven measures reported improvements in the results of the dissimilarity, which is verified with the statistical analysis that having little variance in the results of R^2, the values obtained do not depend on the selected set.

For the Cancer dataset, R^2 values for BC, E, M, SAM and Sh measures increase by more than 30% and have the lowest variance values; while for the Wine dataset, the BC, E, M, SAM, Sh, S and X^2 measures present a high value of R^2, approximately 0.99 compared to 0.96 of the original data.

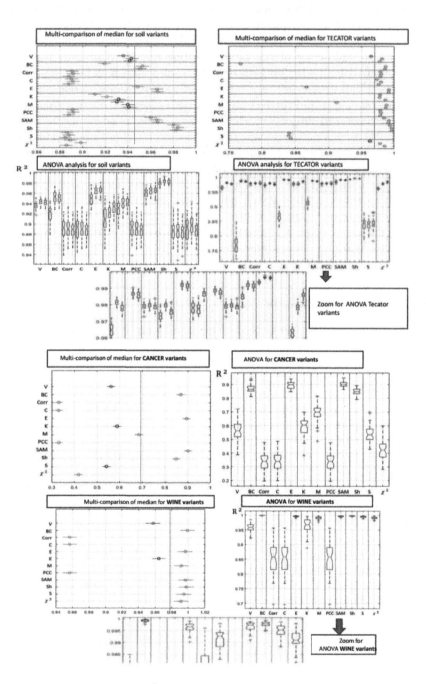

Fig. 3. Values of R^2, multicomparison and ANOVA analysis.

5 Conclusions and Future Work

The results indicate that the use of The Dissimilarity Representation with certain measures, in combination with a pre-processing (in cases where it is required), considerably improves the regression model in comparison with the model for the original feature based representation of data. The measures of dissimilarity that improved to a greater extent the models were: Euclidean, Shape and SAM, and those with the worst results were Kolmogorov-Smirnov and Cosine. The Dissimilarity Representation showed to be good alternative on obtaining the regression models in the selected chemical data for the analytical techniques NIR and NMR.

References

1. Brereton, R.G.: Chemometrics: Data Analysis for the Laboratory and Chemical Plant. Wiley, Chichester (2003)
2. Bro, R., et al.: Data fusion in metabolomic cancer diagnostics. Metabolomics **9**(1), 3–8 (2013)
3. Esbensen, K.H., Guyot, D., Westad, F., Houmoller, L.P.: Multivariate data analysis: in practice: an introduction to multivariate data analysis and experimental design. In: Multivariate Data Analysis (2002)
4. Larsen, F.H., van den Berg, F., Engelsen, S.B.: An exploratory chemometric study of 1H NMR spectra of table wines. J. Chemometr. J. Chemometr. Soc. **20**(5), 198–208 (2006)
5. Martin, Y.C., Lin, C.T., Hetti, C., DeLazzer, J.: PLS analysis of distance matrixes to detect nonlinear relationships between biological potency and molecular properties. J. Med. Chem. **38**(16), 3009–3015 (1995)
6. Massart, D.L.: Handbook of Chemometrics and Qualimetrics. Elsevier Science, Amsterdam (1997)
7. Pekalska, E., Duin, R.P.: Dissimilarity representations allow for building good classifiers. Pattern Recogn. Lett. **23**(8), 943–956 (2002)
8. Porro Munoz, D.: Classification of continuous multi-way data via dissimilarity representation (2013)
9. Rinnan, Å., van den Berg, F., Engelsen, S.B.: Review of the most common pre-processing techniques for near-infrared spectra. TrAC Trends Anal. Chem. **28**(10), 1201–1222 (2009)
10. Rinnan, R., Rinnan, Å.: Application of near infrared reflectance (NIR) and fluorescence spectroscopy to analysis of microbiological and chemical properties of arctic soil. Soil Biol. Biochem. **39**(7), 1664–1673 (2007)
11. Thodberg, H.: Statlib-datasets archive website (2018). http://lib.stat.cmu.edu/datasets/tecator
12. Zerzucha, P., Daszykowski, M., Walczak, B.: Dissimilarity partial least squares applied to non-linear modeling problems. Chemometr. Intell. Lab. Syst. **110**(1), 156–162 (2012)
13. Zerzucha, P., Walczak, B.: Concept of (dis)similarity in data analysis. TrAC Trends Anal. Chem. **38**, 116–128 (2012)

A Comparative Study on Unsupervised Domain Adaptation for Coffee Crop Mapping

Edemir Ferreira[✉], Hugo Oliveira[✉], Mário Sérgio Alvim[✉],
and Jefersson Alex dos Santos[✉]

Universidade Federal de Minas Gerais, Belo Horizonte, Brazil
{edemirm,oliveirahugo,msalvim,jefersson}@dcc.ufmg.br

Abstract. In this work, we investigate the application of existing unsupervised domain adaptation (UDA) approaches to the task of transferring knowledge between crop regions having different coffee patterns. Given a geographical region with fully mapped coffee plantations, we observe that this knowledge can be used to train a classifier and to map a new county with no need of samples indicated in the target region. Experimental results show that transferring knowledge via UDA strategies performs better than just applying a classifier trained in a region to predict coffee crops in a new one. However, UDA methods may lead to negative transfer, which may indicate that domains are excessively dissimilar, rendering transfer strategies ineffective. We observe a meaningful complementary contribution between coffee crop data; and a visual behavior suggests the existence of clusters of samples that are more likely to be drawn from a specific data.

Keywords: Unsupervised domain adaptation · Remote sensing · Transfer knowledge · Coffee crops

1 Introduction

Accessibility to large sets of Remote Sensing Images (RSIs) has increased over the years, and RSIs are currently a common source of information in many agribusiness applications. Identifying crops is essential for knowing and monitoring land use, defining new land expansion strategies, and estimating viable production value. In this work, we focus on the use of RSIs for a crucial agro-economic activity in the Brazilian state of Minas Gerais: the coffee crop mapping.

Automatic recognition of coffee plantations using RSIs is typically modeled as a supervised classification problem. However, this task is rather challenging, mainly because the relief and age of the crop may hinder the recognition process. Indeed, different spectral responses and texture patterns can be observed for different regions.

The authors would like to thank FAPEMIG (APQ-00449-17), CAPES and CNPq for their financial support to this research project.

© Springer Nature Switzerland AG 2019
R. Vera-Rodriguez et al. (Eds.): CIARP 2018, LNCS 11401, pp. 72–80, 2019.
https://doi.org/10.1007/978-3-030-13469-3_9

Because of this, spectral information may be significantly reduced or even totally lost. Moreover, since the growing of coffee is not a seasonal activity, there may be coffee plantations of different ages in different regions, which also affects the observed spectral patterns.

Although several approaches have advanced the state of the art in mapping coffee in recent years [5,6,8], one problem still remains: how to automatically obtain representative samples for classification of new geographic areas?

A strategy to obtain extra data for training models is to transfer knowledge from previously mapped regions. However, as Nogueira et al. [6] has shown, due to the aforementioned differences that may exist in the coffee patterns, the direct transfer does not yield satisfactory results.

In this work, we investigate the application of existing unsupervised domain adaptation (UDA) approaches to the task of transferring knowledge between crop regions with different coffee patterns. Our intent is to evaluate the effectiveness of UDA approaches to map new coffee crop areas. UDA methods allow labeled data to be employed from one or more prior datasets with the aim of creating a learning model for unseen or unlabeled data. As assumption of UDA, the source (prior labeled datasets) and target (new unlabeled data) domains have related but different probability distributions and the divergence between such distributions is called *domain shift*.

Since supervised learning methods typically expect both source and target data to follow the same distribution, the presence of domain shift can degrade the accuracy on target data if the training occurs directly in a source domain without domain adaptation. Ideally, we would like to learn a proper domain adaptation in an unsupervised manner. This task, however, is rather challenging, and its relation with realistic applications has been gathering attention in the last years [12].

Encouraged by these challenges, in this paper we perform a comparative experimental study of various methods for UDA in RSIs. We use the dataset composed of four remote sensing images of coffee crop agriculture in scenarios with different plant and terrain conditions.

Following sections of this paper are organized as follows: Sect. 2 presents an overview of UDA techniques. Sections 3 and 4 present, respectively, the evaluation protocol and experimental results of our analysis. We conclude this work in Sect. 5 with some remarks and the future directions in the research.

2   Unsupervised Domain Adaptation Approaches

Our experimental evaluation is focused on feature-based UDA methods [12]. Seven approaches were selected from the literature and are summarized in Table 1 according to their main properties. Note that they are grouped into three branches: Data-centric, Subspace centric, and Hybrid methods. We briefly introduce each UDA method according to their branch in the next subsections.

Table 1. Summary of Unsupervised Domain Adaptation Methods

	Approaches	Preserve variance	Marginal distribution	Conditional distribution	Reweight instances	Geometric structure
Data Centric	TCA [7]	✓	✓			
	JDA [3]	✓	✓	✓		
	TJM [4]	✓	✓		✓	
Subspace Centric	SA [1]	✓				
	GFK [2]	✓				✓
Hybrid	CORAL [10]	✓				✓
	JGSA [11]	✓	✓		✓	✓

2.1 Data Centric Approaches

To align source and target data, data-centric methods attempt to find a specific transformation that can project both domains into a domain-invariant space. The Divergence between domains is reduced, while preserving the data properties from the original spaces [3, 4, 7].

Transfer Component Analysis (TCA) [7]: its goal is to learn a set of transfer components in a Reproducing Kernel Hilbert Space. When projecting domain data onto the latent space spanned by the transfer components, the distance between different distributions across domains is reduced and variance is preserved.

Joint Distribution Adaptation (JDA) [3]: these approaches extend the Maximum Mean Discrepancy (MMD) to measure the difference in both marginal and conditional distributions. Despite minimizing the marginal distribution between the source and target data, TCA does not guarantee that conditional distributions are reduced in this formulation, which may lead to a poor adaptation. JDA improves TCA, and integrates MMD with Principal Component Analysis (PCA) to create a feature representation that is effective and robust for large domain shifts.

Transfer Joint Matching (TJM) [4]: aims at minimizing the distribution distance between domains while trying to properly reweigh the most discriminative instances in the final adaptation. Some instances from source data may have more relevance for classification task than others due to the differences in the data. TCA, JDA, and TJM rely on the assumption that there always exists a transformation function which can project the source and target data into a common subspace which, at the same time, reduce distribution difference and preserves most original information. This assumption, however, is not realistic: known problems arising from strong domain shifts suggest that there may not always exist such a space.

2.2 Subspace Centric Approaches

In contrast to data-centric methods, subspace-centric methods do not assume the existence of an unified transformation. They rely on a subspace manipulation of the source and target domains [1] or between them [2], upholding that separate subspaces have very optional particular features to be exploited.

Subspace Alignment (SA) [1]: this approach projects source and target data onto different subspaces using PCA. The method then learns a linear transformation matrix M that aligns the source subspace to the target one while minimizing the Frobenius norm of their difference.

Geodesic Flow Kernel (GFK) [2]: is an approach that integrates an infinite number of subspaces that lie on the geodesic flow from the source subspace to the target one using the kernel trick.

The main drawback of subspace-centric methods is that, while focused on reducing the geometrical shift between subspaces, the distribution shift between projected data of domains is not explicitly treated as in data-centric methods.

2.3 Hybrid Approaches

CORAL [10]: addresses the drawbacks of data and subspace-centric methods. Domain shift is minimized by aligning the covariance of the source and target distributions in the original data. In contrast to subspace-centric methods, CORAL suggests an alignment without the need of subspace projection, which would require intense compuatation and complex hyper-parameter tuning.

In addition, CORAL do not assume a unified transformation like data-centric methods; it uses, instead, an asymmetric transformation only on source data.

Joint Geometric Subspace Alignment (JGSA) [11]: aims to reduce the statistical and geometrical divergence between domains using common and specific properties of the source and target data. An overall objective function is created by taking into account five terms: target variance, the variance between/within classes, distribution shift, and subspace shift.

3 Methodology

We performed an extensive set of experiments on Brazilian Coffee Crops dataset in order to evaluate the robustness of UDA methods in a remote-sensing agriculture scenario. The experiments were designed to answer the following research questions:

1. Can knowledge transfer between coffee plantations datasets from different geographic regions yield complementary results?
2. Is it possible to infer a spatial relationship between coffee samples correctly predicted from learning models trained in different data sources?

To answer the question (1), we used Venn diagrams of predictions to analyze the complementarity among different coffee datasets.

Concerning question (2), we perform a visual analysis of samples which are correctly predicted by specific models, using two different methods to project the original representation of data in 2D-space: Principal Component Analysis and t-Distributed Stochastic Neighbor Embedding (TSNE).

3.1 Data

The Brazilian Coffee Scenes[1] dataset consists of four remote sensing images composed of multi-spectral scenes taken by the SPOT sensor in 2005, covering regions of coffee cultivation over four counties in the state of Minas Gerais, Brazil: Arceburgo (AR), Guaxupé (GX), Guaranésia (GA) and Monte Santo (MS). Each county is partitioned into multiple tiles of 64 × 64 pixels, which are divided into 2 classes (coffee and non-coffee). To mitigate the problem of imbalanced datasets, we applied a random under-sampling technique, balancing the data by randomly selecting a subset of data for the targeted classes. In our analysis, we considered each county as a different domain, thus we have four domains (AR, GX, GA, and MS) leading to 12 possible domain adaptation combinations. We used the low-level Border/Interior Pixel Classification (BIC) [9] for feature extraction. BIC is a very effective descriptor for coffee crops as shown in [5,8].

3.2 Setup and Implementation Details

We made a comparison between seven state-of-the-art methods: Transfer Component Analysis (TCA) [7], Geodesic Flow Kernel (GFK) [2], Subspace Alignment (SA) [1], Joint Distribution Analysis (JDA) [3], Transfer Joint Matching (TJM) [4], CORAL [10], Joint Geometrical and Statistical Alignment (JGSA) [11] and transfer with no adaptation (NA). A brief description of methods is shown in Sect. 2 (for more details we recommend the original papers). We follow a full training evaluation protocol, where a Support Vector Machine (SVM) is trained on the labeled source data, and tested on the unlabeled target data. In our experimental setup, tuning of parameters is always made in the source data, since it is impossible to use a cross-validation without labeled samples from the target domain. We evaluate all methods by empirically searching the parameter space for optimal parameter settings that yield the highest average kappa on all datasets, and we report the best accuracy results of each method.

4 Experimental Results and Discussion

In this section we compare different strategies of transferring knowledge between geographic domains in order to map coffee crops. SVM classifiers were trained with no adaptation (NA) and using the seven selected UDA approaches.

Table 2 presents cases of positive and negative transfer for the datasets using L2 Norm-Z-score normalization.

4.1 Complementarity of Cross-Domain Predictions

In this subsection, we select the pair (l2-Norm-Z-score/TCA) to analyze the complementarity of predictions between the source and target data. Given a target

---

[1] http://www.patreo.dcc.ufmg.br/2017/11/12/brazilian-coffee-scenes-dataset/.

data, each group from the diagram represents a source data wherein the pair (l2-Norm-Z-score/TCA) was trained. Intersections between sets show samples that were predicted correctly by both sets. The results were represented in Venn diagrams, as shown in Fig. 1.

Table 2. Positive (blue) and Negative (red) Transfer using L2 Norm - Z-score

Source	AR			GX			GA			MS			
Method / Target	GX	GA	MS	AR	GA	MS	AR	GX	MS	AR	GX	GA	Mean
NA	66.16	79.17	63.82	67.03	66.85	81.31	69.78	61.60	65.16	69.78	85.64	78.44	68.41
TCA	69.75	75.36	69.18	68.13	75.00	82.09	76.92	66.30	68.62	73.63	85.08	77.72	74.31
GFK	62.85	74.28	58.46	66.48	73.91	83.50	78.02	65.47	64.95	72.53	85.08	77.54	73.22
SA	61.46	73.91	56.98	64.84	71.74	83.64	76.37	67.54	65.66	72.53	84.53	76.81	72.13
JDA	61.33	71.56	62.83	66.48	77.54	79.27	77.47	66.30	68.55	70.33	84.94	75.18	70.94
TJM	61.88	73.91	64.74	64.84	77.90	80.25	74.73	63.67	70.03	69.23	84.81	77.54	71.97
CORAL	63.40	72.10	61.07	64.29	72.46	82.37	73.63	64.23	63.82	69.78	85.08	76.81	70.94
JGSA	54.01	65.76	71.37	64.84	81.52	72.92	51.10	67.13	71.93	68.68	72.24	72.46	70.02

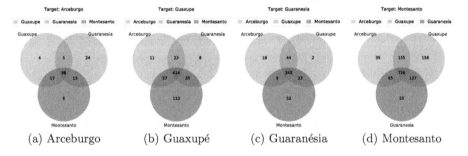

(a) Arceburgo   (b) Guaxupé   (c) Guaranésia   (d) Montesanto

Fig. 1. Venn diagram for samples correctly predicted in different target data. Target data: **(a)** Arceburgo. **(b)** Guaxupé. **(c)** Guaranesia. **(d)** Monte Santo.

As expected, most of the samples in all diagrams are at the intersection of three sets, i.e., the easiest samples are correctly predicted if trained in any of the available source datasets. However, it is possible to notice a considerable number of samples that were correctly predicted only from a single source.

This suggests the existence of complementary information that can be exploited to build a more reliable learning model. One can also notice a relationship of "similarity" between domains. That is, some pair of domains perform better than others. For instance, GX and MS in Fig. 1b.

However, this relationship is not always bidirectional, as exemplified by AR and GA in Fig. 1a. GA yields good results as a source domain, predicting correctly 76.92% of samples, but in Fig. 1c MS is more useful than AR, correctly classifying 77.71% of samples, compared with 75.36% from AR.

4.2   Visual Analysis

In this section we investigate the spatial relationship between the samples. Given a fix adaptation approach, we are focusing on samples that were correctly predicted exclusively for that source data in specific. For this purpose, we propose a visual analysis of these samples using two different methods to project the original representation of data in 2D-space: Principal Component Analysis and t-Distributed Stochastic Neighbor Embedding (TSNE). The projections from PCA and TSNE data are showed in Figs. 2 and 3 respectively.

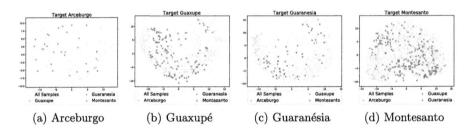

(a) Arceburgo   (b) Guaxupé   (c) Guaranésia   (d) Montesanto

Fig. 2. 2D-space projections using PCA

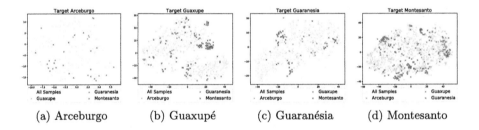

(a) Arceburgo   (b) Guaxupé   (c) Guaranésia   (d) Montesanto

Fig. 3. 2D-space projections using TSNE

With a visual analysis of the projections, it is possible to notice important aspects of data and the complementarity between source data. First, PCA projections show little insight into the spatial relationship of correctly predicted samples; instead, it shows sparsity over the features space. The PCA projection is a powerful dimensional reduction technique since it projects the original high-dimensional data in a low-dimensional space preserving the maximum variance as possible. However, PCA not preserve the local structure of original data, i.e., points that are close, regarding some metric, in original high-dimensional space do not remain close in the new low-dimensional space. Second, in contrast with PCA, TSNE using a non-linear manifold approach can successfully create a low-dimensional representations preserving local structures, as shown in Fig. 3. In addition, we can notice a leaning of a complementarity between learning models, since the samples corrected predict from different sources are tending to create clusters. This behavior in projections can be a suggestive interpretation of shared properties between the source and target data where the clusters show samples whose are more likely to be drawn from a specific source data. Another way of seeing the previous interpretation is taking in consideration the fact of remote sensing images can present a high intra-class variance due to the huge spatial extension explored. An entire image can be seen as a composition of several probabilities distributions which some of them are better explained from different sources of data.

5   Conclusion

This paper describes a comparative experimental analysis of seven UDA approaches to perform automatic coffee crop mapping. We conducted two sets of experiments with the intent of verifying whether existing approaches to unsupervised domain adaptation can assist in the transfer of knowledge between datasets of different geographic domains. The main conclusion is that employing a UDA strategy is more effective than performing transfer knowledge without any adaptation.

In terms of mean accuracy, TCA [7] presents the most suitable results. The negative transfer phenomenon is noticed in several experiments, supporting the importance of an effective adaptation. Analyzing the complementarity of predictions, we observed the existence of additional information that could be exploited from multiple source data to build a more reliable learning model. At last, a visual analysis was conducted to identify clusters between samples correctly predicted using different source data. This observation shows that some samples from target data are likely to be drawn from a specific source. This inspection indicates that a robust UDA approach needs to recognize the importance of multiples sources, considering that each source data has a different contribution for distinct samples from the target.

As future work, we intend to investigate ways for avoiding the negative transfer and employ UDA strategies in other vegetation mapping applications.

References

1. Fernando, B., Habrard, A., Sebban, M., Tuytelaars, T.: Unsupervised visual domain adaptation using subspace alignment. In: ICCV, pp. 2960–2967 (2013)
2. Gong, B., Shi, Y., Sha, F., Grauman, K.: Geodesic flow kernel for unsupervised domain adaptation. In: CVPR, pp. 2066–2073. IEEE (2012)
3. Long, M., Wang, J., Ding, G., Sun, J., Yu, P.S.: Transfer feature learning with joint distribution adaptation. In: ICCV, pp. 2200–2207 (2013)
4. Long, M., Wang, J., Ding, G., Sun, J., Yu, P.S.: Transfer joint matching for unsupervised domain adaptation. In: CVPR, pp. 1410–1417 (2014)
5. Nogueira, K., Penatti, O.A., dos Santos, J.A.: Towards better exploiting convolutional neural networks for remote sensing scene classification. Pattern Recognit. **61**, 539–556 (2017)

6. Nogueira, K., Schwartz, W.R., dos Santos, J.A.: Coffee crop recognition using multi-scale convolutional neural networks. In: Pardo, A., Kittler, J. (eds.) Progress in Pattern Recognition, Image Analysis, Computer Vision, and Applications. LNCS, vol. 9423, pp. 67–74. Springer, Cham (2015). https://doi.org/10.1007/978-3-319-25751-8_9

7. Pan, S.J., Tsang, I.W., Kwok, J.T., Yang, Q.: Domain adaptation via transfer component analysis. IEEE Trans. Neural Netw. **22**(2), 199–210 (2011)

8. dos Santos, J.A., Penatti, O.A.B., da Silva Torres, R.: Evaluating the potential of texture and color descriptors for remote sensing image retrieval and classification. In: VISAPP, Angers, France, May 2010

9. Stehling, R.O., Nascimento, M.A., Falcão, A.X.: A compact and efficient image retrieval approach based on border/interior pixel classification. In: CIKM, pp. 102–109. ACM (2002)

10. Sun, B., Feng, J., Saenko, K.: Return of frustratingly easy domain adaptation. In: AAAI, vol. 6, p. 8 (2016)

11. Zhang, J., Li, W., Ogunbona, P.: Joint geometrical and statistical alignment for visual domain adaptation. In: CVPR, pp. 1859–1867 (2017)

12. Zhang, J., Li, W., Ogunbona, P.: Transfer learning for cross-dataset recognition: a survey. arXiv preprint arXiv:1705.04396 (2017)

Analytical Comparison of Histogram Distance Measures

Manuel G. Forero$^{(\boxtimes)}$ ⓘ, Carlos Arias-Rubio,
and Brigete Tatiana González

Facultad de Ingeniería, Universidad de Ibagué, Ibagué, Colombia
manuel.forero@unibague.edu.co, caar93@hotmail.com,
tatigoq@hotmail.com

Abstract. This paper presents a comparative study of different distance measures used to compare histograms in applications such as pattern recognition, feature selection, image sorting, grouping, identification, indexing, and retrieval. The focus of the study is on how distance measures are affected by variations across images. Different distances between histograms were investigated and tested to compare their performance in retrieving gray scale and color images. A wide range of review papers on calculating distances between histograms was examined. One comparative study was found where histogram bins having zero value were discarded in the calculus of certain distances. We show that this is an inappropriate approach; our tests revealed that zero-value bins should be included to avoid erroneous calculations and achieve a performance advantage over other distance measures.

Keywords: Histogram distances · Bhattacharyya distance · Color distance

1 Introduction

In image analysis, a histogram is a graphical representation of the pixel distribution that describes the amount or frequency of different image intensity values.

When object classification is performed using histograms, the underlying model takes into account only the color of the object and ignores its shape and texture. It is also important to mention that a histogram does not contain spatial information about its corresponding image, i.e., the image cannot be recovered from the histogram and two different images can have the same histograms. Therefore, histograms can be latently identical in two different images, containing different objects but sharing color information. In other words, if there is no spatial or shape information, related objects of different colors may be identified as identical when comparing only the color histograms. Despite the difficulties, solutions like color histogram intersections, indexing constant color, cumulative color histograms, and color distances are used to compare images. While there are drawbacks of using histograms for image indexing and classification, employing real-time color in these tasks has several advantages. One of the advantages is that information is faster to compute compared to other approaches, and it has been shown that color-based methods can be effective in identifying objects of known location and appearance.

© Springer Nature Switzerland AG 2019
R. Vera-Rodriguez et al. (Eds.): CIARP 2018, LNCS 11401, pp. 81–90, 2019.
https://doi.org/10.1007/978-3-030-13469-3_10

There are studies that relate color histogram data with physical properties of objects in an image [1]. These studies have shown that physical properties may represent not only luminescence and color of an object but also image geometry and roughness, all together provide a better estimate of object luminescence and color. Different solutions to the issues associated with comparing color histograms are proposed in the literature, for example, Distance Measure. Among the most utilized measures of distance to calculate the degree of similarity between images are: Euclidean distance, histogram intersection, and quadratic distance. In addition, calculating correlation coefficients is applied. There are many papers discussing distance measures, we found, specifically, two studies in the context of histogram comparison for image analysis tasks. The first paper is a comparative study of histogram distances for object identification by Marín [2], whereas the second paper is itself entitled "On measuring the distance between histograms" by Cha et al. [3]. These two papers served as a basis for our study in which the aim is to compare distance measures for calculating the similarity between histograms for image analysis tasks. We also improve the accuracy of some distance measures when indeterminations were found.

In summary, this paper presents a comparative analysis of some of the most popular techniques for measuring distances between histograms. Modifications to the distances with indeterminations are also proposed. These modified algorithms can be employed in tasks such as pattern recognition, feature selection, image classification, grouping, identification, indexing, and retrieval.

2   Distances

2.1   Distances Between Histograms

Generally, a distance can be defined as a numerical metric that defines the shortest line between two points. The distance between two histograms A and B can be defined as a mathematical function that meets the following conditions:

(a) Non-negativity: $d(A, B) \geq 0$, where $d(A, B) = 0 \leftrightarrow A = B$;
(b) Symmetry: $d(A, B) = d(B, A)$;
(c) Triangular inequality: $d(A, C) \leq d(A, B) + d(B, C)$.

Two types of measures are used to calculate distances between histograms. One is called bin to bin; it compares corresponding bins in each of the two histograms one by one (i.e., the first bin of one histogram with the first bin of another one, and so on). The second type of distance measure is called cross-bin; it focuses on the bins adjacent to the one considered. We used the bin to bin measure, where each histogram bin is treated in an independent way, and distances can be calculated from additions and averages.

The definitions of the six different distance measures employed in this study are introduced below.

Bhattacharyya. Bhattacharyya distance is used to assess equality between two distributions; the response represents the nearest distance between them. The equation for the distance is given by [4] as follows:

$$d(H_1, H_2) = -\ln(BC(H_1, H_2)) \tag{1}$$

$$BC(H_1, H_2) = \sum_{I=0}^{N-1} \sqrt{H_1(I) * H_2(I)} \tag{2}$$

where $BC(H1, H2)$ is the Bhattacharyya coefficient for discrete probability distributions and N is the number of bins, usually 256, H_1 and H_2 are the first and the second histograms respectively, and $\overline{H_1}$, and $\overline{H_2}$ represent their means calculated as

$$\overline{H_K} = \frac{1}{N} \sum_{J=0}^{N-1} H_k(J) \tag{3}$$

Chi-square. Chi-square distance is a statistical measure that compares observed and expected values for a data set. It is defined by the following expression [5]:

$$d(H_1, H_2) = \sum_{I=0}^{N-1} \frac{(H_1(I) - H_2(I))^2}{H_1(I)} \tag{4}$$

Correlation. Correlation is a measure of describing the degree of linear dependence between two histograms. Its value varies between −1 and +1. If the result is zero, it means that there is no linear association between the two histograms being compared. It is calculated as follows [5]:

$$d(H_1, H_2) = \frac{\sum_{I=0}^{N-1} \left(H_1(I) - \overline{H_1}\right)\left(H_2(I) - \overline{H_2}\right)}{\sqrt{\sum_{I=0}^{N-1} \left(H_1(I) - \overline{H_1}\right)^2 * \sum_{I=0}^{N-1} \left(H_2(I) - \overline{H_2}\right)^2}} \tag{5}$$

Intersection. Intersection metric is a measure that considers the intersection of two histograms and tells how many gray levels from the first histogram are present in the second one. The equation is provided below [5]:

$$d(H_1, H_2) = \sum_{I=0}^{N-1} \min(H_1(I), H_2(I)) \tag{6}$$

Kullback-Leibler (KL). Kullback-Leibler pseudo-distance is an asymmetrical measure that does not meet the condition (b) of the distance definition introduced earlier. This measure originated from the information theory for handling relative entropy. It is used to measure the average bit number required to identify an event from a set of possibilities, and numerically indicates how two histograms resemble each other. It is defined by the following equation [6]:

$$d(H_1, H_2) = \sum_{I=0}^{N-1} H_1(I) \log \frac{H_1(I)}{H_2(I)} \tag{7}$$

Euclidian. Euclidean distance is frequently used for evaluating distances in numerical spaces. It is used to determine the bin to bin distance between two histograms and is calculated according to the following equation [3]:

$$d(H_1, H_2) = \sqrt{\sum_{I=0}^{N-1} (H_1(I) - H_2(I))^2} \tag{8}$$

2.2   Indetermination

As it can be seen from Eqs. (4) and (7), the chi-square and KL distances can be undefined. In his work, Marín [2] simply discard the bins that are zero to avoid this indetermination. However, this solution is inappropriate. For example, according to Marín the two histograms shown in Fig. 1(a) and (b) would be defined as equal [2]. Given that zero bins are discarded making $D_{\text{chi-square}}$ (A, B) and D_{KL} (A, B) to be zero. However, according to the distance definition, distance between two histograms A and B is zero only when A = B. Therefore, in order to solve the indetermination, we considered the following solutions:

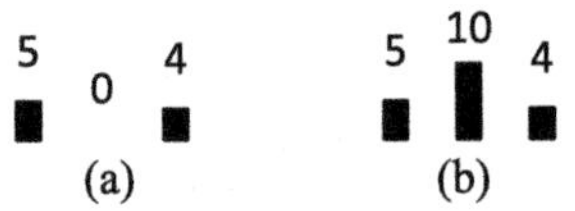

Fig. 1. Example of a critical case when measuring distance between two histograms (a) and (b).

Chi-square. Indetermination can be solved by using Eq. (9) instead of Eq. (4):

$$\sum_{I=0}^{N-1} \frac{[H_1(I) - H_2(I)]^2}{H_1(I) + 1} \tag{9}$$

This solution is equal to adding one count to both histograms given that

$$\sum_{I=0}^{N-1} \frac{[(H_1(I) + 1 - (H_2(I) + 1)]^2}{H_1(I) + 1} = \sum_{I=0}^{N-1} \frac{[(H_1(I) - H_2(I)]^2}{H_1(I) + 1} \tag{10}$$

This solution simply produces a reduction in each one of the addends. Note that a very small value ε must not be added because it would produce a very big addend introducing an error in distance computation. Figures 2(a, b) provide a graphical representation of both the original and the proposed formulas showing how close they are.

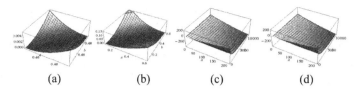

(a)   (b)   (c)   (d)

Fig. 2. Graphical representation of chi-square and KL functions: (a, c) original equations, (b, d) modified equations.

KL. Contrary to chi-square, the indetermination in KL distances can be avoided by using the following expression:

$$\sum_{I=0}^{N-1} H_1(I) * Log\left(\frac{H_1(I) + \varepsilon}{H_2(I) + \varepsilon}\right) \tag{11}$$

where ε is a small quantity (epsilon). We took $\varepsilon = 0.0001$ for our calculation. We do not take $\varepsilon = 1$ because when $H_1(I)$ and $H_2(I)$ are considerably small, $Log\left(\frac{H_1}{H_2}\right)$ is very different to that of $Log\left(\frac{H_1+1}{H_2+1}\right)$. However, as seen in Figs. 2(c, d), $Log\left(\frac{H_1}{H_2}\right) \cong Log\left(\frac{H_1+\varepsilon}{H_2+\varepsilon}\right)$, when ε is considerably small.

3 Proposal

To test the introduced distances, we considered five synthetic images designed by one of the team members of our University (see Fig. 3), four synthetic histograms were implemented (see Fig. 4), two microscopy images having a background taken with different illumination conditions (see Fig. 5), four microscopy images of a rat brain (acquired from the Instituto de Neurociencias de Castilla y León, Salamanca, Spain, see Fig. 6), and two images of the same objects but with different magnification (see Fig. 7). Distances were calculated for the following cases: between the image in Fig. 3 (a) and each one of its modified variations presented in Figs. 3(b–e); between histograms a, b, c, and d in Fig. 4; and between the images in Figs. 5, 6, and 7. Distances were implemented as plugins for the open source program ImageJ [8].

4 Results

Results are shown in Tables 1, 2, 3, 4 and 5. In column 1 are of the distance between a histogram and itself. It can be seen that, every distance is zero except that for the correlation and intersection. This is because these two measures are not true distances according to the distance definition provided in Sect. 2.1. The correlation distance can even have negative values. Also, the intersection can have a zero value if there are not common bins between two histograms, but it is maximal when they are equal.

In Tables 1, 2, 3, 4 and 5, beside each distance name are indicators in quotes, which correspond to the best equality approximation between histograms, for instance, the best result for Intersection is the largest value, the Correlation distance equals to one, the Chi-square, Bhattacharyya, KL, and Euclidian are all equal to zero. Chi-square distances are very similar between the original and the inverted images than between the original and the high gloss images, which are quite different, since the synthetic image has very few gray levels.

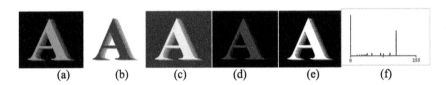

(a)   (b)   (c)   (d)   (e)   (f)

Fig. 3. Synthetic images: (a) original, (b) inverted, (c) high gloss, (d) low gloss, (e) high contrast, (f) histogram of (a).

Table 1. Distances between images in Fig. 3.

Distances	1. Original – Original	2. Original – Inverted	3. Original – High gloss	4. Original – Low gloss	5. Original – Contrast
Chi-square '0'	0.0	9.6771E8	9.676E8	2.834E7	3.4928E7
Intersection '≫'	39831.0	0.0	341.0	30797.0	30702.07
Correlation '1'	1.0	−0.006445	−0.006281	0.9721	0.9669
Bhattacharyya '0'	0.0	1.0	0.9929	0.4386	0.4735
KL '0'	0.0	326107.83	320314.15	64025.39	64340.34
Euclidian '0'	0.0	43992.50	43988.91	7983.16	8013.51

Table 1 shows the distances between synthetic images with a low quantity of gray levels. It can be seen from Table 1 that distances for the original and inverted images are quite dissimilar and there is no correlation between them. Results are appropriate only for the original vs. low gloss and original vs. contrast measures.

The results obtained for synthetic histograms Fig. 4 are shown in Table 2.

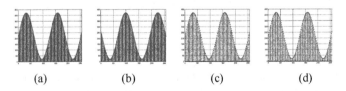

(a)   (b)   (c)   (d)

Fig. 4. Synthetic histograms: (a) original (b) inverted, (c) only odd values – "odd hist", (d) only even values – "even hist".

Table 2. Distances between synthetic histograms in Fig. 4.

Distances	1. Original – Original	2. Original – Inverted	3. Original – Odd hist	4. Odd hist – Even hist
Chi-square '0'	0.0	296673.98	28084.34	8761770.34
Intersection '≫'	56401.0	24474.0	28190.0	0.0
Correlation '1'	1.0	−0.9824	0.4725	−0.5525
Bhattacharyya '0'	0.0	0.5037	0.5394	1.0
KL '0'	0.0	27809.51	181815.72	181671.72
Euclidian '0'	0.0	4466.46	2945.744	4164.706

As seen in Table 2, correlation gives a good indication that the histogram in Fig. 4 (b) is the inverted histogram in Fig. 4(a). When comparing "odd hist" with "even hist", it can be noticed that they are very similar, whereas, the intersection is 0, given that there is no intersection between them. The correlation also does not indicate that these are similar histograms.

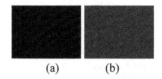

(a)   (b)

Fig. 5. Microscopy images: (a) intensity 1, (b) intensity 2.

Table 3. Distances between images in Fig. 5.

Distances	1. Intensity 1 – Intensity 1	2. Intensity 1 – Intensity 2
Chi-square '0'	0.0	3. 9795E11
Intersection '≫'	1428988.0	0.0
Correlation '1'	1.0	−0.01538
Bhattacharyya '0'	0.0	1.0
KL '0'	0.0	1.375019E7
Euclidian '0'	0.0	1046609.95

Column 2 in Table 3 shows that the images in Fig. 5 are quite different.

Color images in Fig. 6 were compared in the RGB color space by measuring the distance between each channel histogram and averaging the result as suggested by Prashant [7]. Distances calculated between the images in Fig. 6 are shown in Table 4. As seen in Table 4, the variation in the object intensity can make the distances to indicate that histograms are quite different. This suggests that image intensities must be similar to enable histogram comparison. At the same time, the Bhattacharyya distance is the most robust for intensity variations.

(a)   (b)   (c)   (d)

Fig. 6. Images of a rat brain: (a) normal intensity (CRnorm), (b) low light intensity (CRlow), (c) high light intensity (CRhigh), (d) contrast adjustment (CRcontr). (Color figure online)

Table 4. Results of distance measures between the respective images in Fig. 6.

Distances	1. CRnorm – Crnorm	2. CRnorm – CRlow	3. CRnorm – CRhigh	4. CRnorm – CRcontr
Chi-square '0'	0.0	1.6388E11	3.8845E13	8.19834E12
Intersection '≫'	1.253E7	457896.66	1421693.6	5003024.33
Correlation '1'	1.0	−0.2619	−0.0539	0.2354
Bhattacharyya '0'	0.0	0.6416	0.32919	0.0
KL '0'	0.0	1.115001E8	2.47538E7	8332926.72
Euclidian '0'	0.0	2442346.47	5865264.03	2537838.93

Columns 2 and 3 in Table 4 show that brightness variation increase distances. This occurs for all distances except the Bhattacharyya distance in columns 3 and 4, where the most similar values are obtained. To verify this observation, comparisons of RGB color photographs showing objects with similar light intensities at different distances were performed.

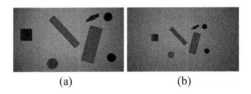

(a)   (b)

Fig. 7. Images of the same objects: (a) Dist1, (b) Dist2.

Table 5. Distances between images in Fig. 7.

Distances	1. Dist1 – Dist1	2. Dist1 – Dist2
Chi-square '0'	0.0	661342.262
Intersection '≫'	2073600.0	1603531.0
Correlation '1'	1.0	0.8253
Bhattacharyya '0'	0.0	0.2647
KL '0'	0.0	461700.1
Euclidian '0'	0.0	105320.75

The results in Table 5 show that histogram distances are not good indicators of how close two images are when their lightning is quite different. The Bhattacharyya distance shows the best performance even when intensities are dissimilar. When lightning is similar, the correlation and the Bhattacharyya distance show the best results.

The last experiment also shows that other problem in calculating distances occurs if histograms do not contain spatial information about the images and two different images may coincide in their histogram representations.

5   Conclusions

In this work, the performance of six distances measures the similarity between histograms in image analysis tasks was compared. Some of the considered distance measures are not true distances, namely KL distance and correlation.

The chi-square and KL distances were modified to avoid indeterminations when bins are equal to zero. We showed how the proposed solution is more effective compared to the one introduced originally; it prevents two different histograms to appear as equal when indetermination occurs.

It was found that the considered distance measures show bad results when histograms are not continuous, or images of the same objects have a high-intensity variation; only the Bhattacharyya distance showed that two images with the same objects were close when their intensity was very different. When lightning was similar, the Bhattacharyya distance and the correlation performed the best. It was also found that while the correlation is not a true distance, it can be useful for comparing histograms to show how two histograms are related.

In the future, we want to analyze a greater number of distance measures such as the EMD (Earth's moving distance) and test their performance in a higher number of images using histograms from more color spaces.

Acknowledgements. This work was supported by project # 17-461-INT Universidad de Ibagué. We thank Professor Dolores Lopez of the Instituto de Neurociencias de Castilla y León, Universidad de Salamanca for providing the microscopy images.

References

1. Novak, C., Shafer, S.: Method for estimating scene parameters from color histograms. J. Opt. Soc. Am. A **11**(11), 3020–3036 (1994)
2. Marín, P.: Estudio comparativo de medidas de distancia para histogramas en problemas de re-identificación (2015)
3. Cha, S.-H., Srihari, S.: On measuring the distance between histograms. Pattern Recogn. Soc. **35**, 1355–1370 (2002)
4. Bhattacharyya, A.: On a measure of divergence between two statistical populations defined by their probability distributions. Bull. Calcutta Math. Soc. **35**, 99–109 (1943). https://mathscinet.ams.org/mathscinet-getitem?mr=0010358
5. OpenCV Histogram Comparison. http://docs.opencv.org/2.4/doc/tutorials/imgproc/histograms/histogram_comparison/histogram_comparison.html. Accessed 30 June 2018

6. Kullback, S.: The Kullback-Leibler distance. Am. Stat. **41**(4), 340–341 (1987)
7. Prashant, I.: Histogram comparison (2013). https://es.scribd.com/doc/168216107/Histogram-Similarity. Accessed 20 May 2018
8. Rasband, W.S., ImageJ. U. S. National Institutes of Health, Bethesda, Maryland, USA (1997–2016). https://imagej.nih.gov/ij/. Accessed 01 Aug 2018

Gaussian Processes Regression with Multiple Annotators: When the Annotator Performance Is Not Homogeneous

Julián Gil González$^{(\boxtimes)}$, Andrés Marino Álvarez, and Álvaro Angel Orozco

Faculty of Engineering, Universidad Tecnológica de Pereira, 660003 Pereira, Colombia
{jugil,andres.alvarez1,aaog}@utp.edu.co

Abstract. In supervised learning problems, the right label (also known as the gold standard or the ground truth) is not available because the label acquisition can be expensive or infeasible. Instead of that gold standard, we have access to some annotations provided by multiple annotators with different levels of expertise. Hence, trivial methods such as majority voting (or average in regression problems) are not suitable since they assume homogeneity between the expertise of the labelers. In this work, we introduce a regression approach based on Gaussian processes, where we consider that the expertise of the labelers is non-homogeneous across the input space–(GPR-MANH). The idea is to assume that the input space can be represented by a defined number of regions where each annotator exhibit a particular level of expertise. Experimental results show that our methodology can estimate the performance of annotators even if the gold standard is not available, defeating state-of-the-art techniques.

1 Introduction

A typical supervised learning scenario comprises the computation of a function, which maps from inputs (samples) to outputs (labels), where it is assumed that exists an oracle who gives the correct label (also known as ground truth or gold standard) for each sample in the training set [1]. However, in many real-world applications, the gold standard is not available, because the process to acquire it is expensive, unfeasible, time-consuming or the label corresponds to a subjective assessment [2]. Instead of the ground truth, it is possible to access several labels provided by multiple annotators or sources. This information can be acquired using web sources, crowdsourcing platforms or the opinion of multiple experts. For instance, social networks (e.g., Twitter, Facebook) can be used to obtain information about a specific problem such as product rating or sentiment analysis [3]. Likewise, in problems where the gold standard is not available, we can use platforms like Amazon Mechanical Turk (AMT), LabelMe, Crowdflower.[1]

---

[1] www.mturk.com; labelme2.csail.mit.edu/; crowdflower.com.

© Springer Nature Switzerland AG 2019
R. Vera-Rodriguez et al. (Eds.): CIARP 2018, LNCS 11401, pp. 91–99, 2019.
https://doi.org/10.1007/978-3-030-13469-3_11

This kind of platforms offers a cost-effective, and efficient way to obtain labeled data [4]. On the other hand, in problems of computer-aided diagnosis, we can obtain subjective assessment provided by different experts [5,6]. Nevertheless, the information collected from these multiple sources could be subjective, noisy or even misleading [6]. Trivial solutions to deal with multiple labelers scenarios include *(i) to consider as the gold standard the output from one of the labelers,* and *(ii) to assume the majority voting (or the average in the case of regression) from the annotations as an estimation for the ground truth.* However, these approaches are not suitable due to they assume homogeneity between the performance of the annotators [2].

On the other hand, *Learning from crowds* is a particular area of supervised learning, which deals with different machine learning paradigms in the presence of multiple annotators, including classification, sequence labeling, and regression. Among the methodologies developed in the area of learning from crowds, we can identify two main groups. The first group named label aggregation are focused only on estimating the gold standard, which is then used to train a supervised learning scheme. On the other hand, the second group comprises the works that are focused on training supervised learning models directly from the labels of multiple sources. Regarding the classification paradigm, we recognize the approach proposed in [6], which comprises the estimation of the annotator expertise (in terms of sensitivity and specificity) through a maximum likelihood-based approach from repeated responses (labels). In this sense, this model estimate jointly the gold standard and the classifier parameters using a logistic regression-based framework. Similarly, the authors in [7] propose an extension of the work proposed in [6] aiming to introduce a Gaussian processes model as the classification scheme. On the other hand, with respect to real-valued label (i.e. Regression models), the authors in [1] propose a Gaussian processes model to deal with multiple annotators, where the performance of the labelers is coded by including a per-annotator variance in the likelihood function–(GPR-MAH). However, they assume that the labeler performance is homogeneous across the input space, which is a weak assumption as was demonstrated in [8]. The above assumption was relaxed by the work in [9]. This approach codes the performance using a Gaussian process model, which estimates the annotators expertise as a non-linear function of the gold standard and the input space.

In this work, we present a regression approach based on Gaussian processes, where the expertise of the labelers is non-homogeneous across the input space–(GPR-MANH). Our approach follows the idea of GPR-MAH, in the sense that we use a Gaussian processes method to model the regression function and assign a per-annotator variance to capture the performance of the labelers. However, unlike GPR-MAH, our methodology relaxes the assumption that the performance of each annotator is homogeneous across the input space by considering that the input space can be represented by a number specific of clusters, where each annotator exhibits different performances. We empirically show, using simulated annotators, that our methodology can be used to learn regression models using noisy data from multiple sources, outperforming state-of-the-art techniques. The remainder of this paper is organized as follows. Section 2 describes the background of our approach. Sections 3 and 4 present the experiments and discuss the results obtained. Finally, Sect. 5 outlines the conclusions and future work.

2   Probabilistic Formulation

A regression scenario has the primary goal to estimate a function $f : \mathcal{X} \to \mathcal{Z}$ using a training set $\{\mathbf{x}_n, z_n\}_{n=1}^N$, where $\mathbf{x}_n \in \mathcal{X} \subseteq \mathbb{R}^P$ is a $P-$dimensional input feature vector corresponding to the $n-$th instance with output $z_n \in \mathcal{Z} \subseteq \mathbb{R}$. In a typical regression configuration, each sample $\mathbf{x}_n$ is assigned to a single output z_n, i.e., the ground truth. However, in many real-world regression problems instead of the ground truth we have multiple labels provided by R sources with different levels of expertise [1]. Moreover, we assume that each annotator annotates $N_r \leq N$ observations. In this sense, it is possible to build a data set for the annotator $r \in \{1, 2, \dots, R\}$, $\mathscr{D}_r = \{\mathbf{X}_r, \mathbf{y}_r\}$, where $\mathbf{X}_r \in \mathbb{R}^{N_r \times P}$ and $\mathbf{y}_r \in \mathcal{Y}_r \subseteq \mathbb{R}$ are the input feature matrix and the labels given by the r-th annotator, respectively. Besides, $\mathbf{X}_r$ holds row vectors $\mathbf{x}_n^r$ and $\mathbf{y}_r$ is composed by elements y_n^r, where y_n^r is the m-th annotation of sample $\mathbf{x}_n^r$. Now given the data set from multiple annotators $\mathscr{D} = \{\mathbf{X} = \cup_{r=1}^R \mathbf{X}_r, \mathbf{Y} = \{\mathbf{y}_1, \dots, \mathbf{y}_R\}\}$, our goals are: First, to estimate the unknown gold standard for the instances in the training set $\mathbf{z} = [z_1, \dots, z_N]$. Second, to compute the performance of the labelers as a function of the ground truth and the input space. Finally, the third objective is to build a regression model based on Gaussian processes which generalizes well on unseen data.

Concerning this, we follow the model for the labels proposed in [1], $y_n^r = z_n + \mathcal{N}(0, \sigma_r^2)$, where they consider that the parameter σ_r^2 (related to the performance of the r-th annotator) is homogeneous across the input space. However, as we established previously, the principal aim of our work is to model the annotator expertise based on the assumption that it is no-homogeneous across the input space. For doing so, we assume that the input space $\mathcal{X}$ can be represented using K clusters based on the input space Euclidean distances, where each annotator exhibits a particular performance. Accordingly, the model proposed for the labels y_n^r follows $y_n^r = z_n + \mathcal{N}(0, (\sigma_k^r)^2)$, where $(\sigma_k^r)^2 \in \mathbb{R}^+$ is the variance for the r-th labeler in the cluster $k \in \{1, 2, \dots, K\}$. Assuming independence between annotators, and the fact that each annotator labels $\mathbf{x}_n$ independently, the likelihood is given as follows

$$p(\mathbf{Y}|\mathbf{z}) = \prod_k \prod_{n \sim k} \prod_{r \sim n} \mathcal{N}\left(y_n^r | z_n, (\sigma_k^r)^2\right) = c\mathcal{N}\left(\hat{\mathbf{y}}|\mathbf{z}, \hat{\boldsymbol{\Sigma}}\right), \tag{1}$$

where $c \in \mathbb{R}$ is independent of $\mathbf{z}$, the diagonal matrix $\hat{\boldsymbol{\Sigma}} \in \mathbb{R}^{N \times N}$ has elements $\hat{\sigma}_{nk}^2$, the vector $\hat{\mathbf{y}} \in \mathbb{R}^N$ has entries $\hat{y}_{nk}$. Also, $\hat{\sigma}_{nk}^{-2} = (\sum_{r \sim n} 1/(\sigma_k^r)^2)^{-1}$, $\hat{y}_{nk} = \hat{\sigma}_{nk}^2 \sum_{r \sim n} y_n^r/(\sigma_k^r)^2$. The notation $r \sim n$ refers to "take into account only the labelers who annotated the n-th observation" and $n \sim k$ indicates the sample n belonging to the k-th cluster. Assuming a Gaussian process prior for $\mathbf{z}$ given as $p(\mathbf{z}) = \mathcal{N}(\mathbf{z}|\mathbf{0}, \mathbf{K})$, with kernel matrix $\mathbf{K}$ computed using a particular kernel function $k : \mathbb{R}^P \times \mathbb{R}^P \rightarrow \mathbb{R}$, the posterior over the latent variable $\mathbf{z}$ is computed as follows $p(\mathbf{z}|\mathbf{Y}, \mathbf{X}) = \mathcal{N}(\mathbf{z}|\mathbf{m}, \mathbf{V})$, where $\mathbf{m} = (\mathbf{K}^{-1} + \hat{\boldsymbol{\Sigma}}^{-1})^{-1}\hat{\boldsymbol{\Sigma}}^{-1}\hat{\mathbf{y}}$, and $\mathbf{V} = (\mathbf{K}^{-1} + \hat{\boldsymbol{\Sigma}}^{-1})^{-1}$. In turn, it can be shown that the posterior over a new observation $f(\mathbf{x}_*)$ follows

$$p(f(\mathbf{x}_*)|\mathbf{Y}) = \mathcal{N}(f(\mathbf{x}_*)|\bar{f}(\mathbf{x}_*), k(\mathbf{x}_*, \mathbf{x}'_*)), \tag{2}$$

where $\bar{f}(\mathbf{x}_*) = k(\mathbf{x}_*, \mathbf{X})(\mathbf{K} + \hat{\boldsymbol{\Sigma}})^{-1}\hat{\mathbf{y}}$ and $k(\mathbf{x}_*, \mathbf{x}'_*) = k(\mathbf{x}_*, \mathbf{x}'_*) - k(\mathbf{x}_*, \mathbf{X})(\mathbf{K} + \hat{\boldsymbol{\Sigma}})^{-1}k(\mathbf{X}, \mathbf{x}'_*)$. The free parameters related to the model (the hyper-parameters of the kernel function, and the variances associated to the annotators in each region) are estimated by optimizing the negative log of the evidence, which is given as

$$-\log p(\mathbf{Y}) = \frac{1}{2}\log|\mathbf{K} + \hat{\boldsymbol{\Sigma}}| + \frac{1}{2}\hat{\mathbf{y}}^\top(\mathbf{K} + \hat{\boldsymbol{\Sigma}})^{-1}\hat{\mathbf{y}} - \frac{1}{2}\log|\hat{\boldsymbol{\Sigma}}|$$
$$+ \frac{1}{2}\sum_k \sum_{n \sim k} \sum_{r \sim n} \frac{(y_n^r)^2}{(\sigma_k^r)^2} - \frac{1}{2}\sum_k \sum_{n \sim k} \frac{\hat{y}_{nk}^2}{\hat{\sigma}_{nk}^2} - \sum_k \sum_{n \sim k} \sum_{r \sim n} \log\frac{1}{\sigma_k^r} + \frac{\zeta}{2}\log 2\pi,$$

where $\zeta = \sum_{r=1}^R N_r$. To summarize, we propose a regression scheme with multiple annotators based on Gaussian processes, where the performance of the annotators is coded by including a per-annotator variance in the likelihood function. Unlike GPR-MAH, we assume that the input space is represented by K regions, where the annotators exhibit a particular performance, which is represented by a variance $(\sigma_k^r)^2$.

3   Experimental Set-Up

Testing Datasets. To test our GPR-MANH, we use three datasets for regression of the well-known *UCI repository*[2]. The used datasets include: *Auto MPG*–(Auto), *Concrete Compressive Strength*–(Concrete), and *Boston Housing Data*–(Housing). The above datasets were chosen based on state-of-the-art works [1,9].

Simulated Annotations. The datasets from the UCI repository are mainly focused on supervised learning without multiple sources. Thus, we establish two methods for simulating multiple annotators: *(i)* Homogeneous Gaussian noise [1], that samples a random number $\varepsilon_n^r \in \mathbb{R}$ from a Gaussian distribution with zero mean and variance $\tau_r^2 \in \mathbb{R}^+$; then the annotations are simulated as, $y_n^r = z_n + \varepsilon_n^r$. Accordingly, τ_r^2 codes the performance of the annotators, the higher is its value, the lower the expertise level of the r-th labeler. *(ii)* Non-homogeneous Gaussian noise [8]. This simulation approach comprises the following steps: First, we split the data into L clusters using the k-means algorithm. Next, the annotations

---

[2] http://archive.ics.uci.edu/ml.

given by the r-th annotator for samples in the l-th cluster follows, $y_{nl}^r = z_n + \mathcal{N}\left(0, \lambda_{lr}^2\right)$, where $\lambda_{lr}^2 \in \mathbb{R}^+$ codes the labeler expertise in the region l. Hence, we simulate labelers where its expertise varies depending on the input space.

Validation Approaches and Learning Assessments. Aiming to validate the performance of our approach, we take into account the following state-of-the-art models. *(i) Gaussian Process-based regression with majority voting*–(GPR-Av), where a typical regression model is trained using as the gold standard the average from the annotations. The kernel hyperparameters related to this Gaussian processes are estimated by optimizing the marginal likelihood [11]. *(ii) Learning from Multiple Observers with Unknown Expertise*–(LMO), that uses a Gaussian process to code the expertise of the labelers as a function of the gold standard and the input samples. The parameter estimation is carried out using a Maximum a Posterior (MAP) approach [9]. *(iii) Learning from Multiple Annotators with Gaussian Processes*–(GPR-MA), where a per-annotator variance is included in the likelihood function to capture the information from multiple annotators. The hyperparameters related to the kernel function and the variances of each annotator are estimated by minimizing the minus log of the evidence.

Furthermore, the validation is carried out by estimating the regression performance in terms of the mean squared error (note that we have access to the gold standard). A cross-validation scheme is carried out with 30 repetitions (70% of the samples as training and 30% as testing).

4   Results and Discussions

First, we perform a controlled experiment aiming to verify the capability of our approach for dealing with regression setting in the context of multiple sources. For this first experiment, the training samples $\mathbf{X}$ are generated by randomly selecting 60 points in the interval $[0,1]$, and the ground truth is computed as $z_n = \sin(2\pi x_n)\sin(6\pi x_n)$. The instances for testing are formed with 600 equally spaced samples from the interval $[0,1]$. We simulate three labelers with different levels of expertise by using the simulation methods described in Sect. 3. For the "Homogeneous Gaussian noise" we use $\tau = (0.25,\ 0.5,\ 0.75)$. On the other hand, for the "Non-homogeneous Gaussian noise", we split the input space into three regions and use the following parameters:

$$\boldsymbol{\Lambda} = \begin{pmatrix} 0 & 0.65 & 1.0 \\ 0.25 & 0 & 0.75 \\ 0.1 & 0.75 & 0 \end{pmatrix}.$$

Here, the matrix $\boldsymbol{\Lambda}$ is formed by elements λ_{lr}^2, which indicates the variance for the r-th annotator in the cluster l. For testing our approach, we use a clustering algorithm based on *affinity propagation* [12] aiming to obtain a proper representation of the input space $\mathcal{X}$. Similarly, for the Gaussian processes model, the kernel is fixed as a squared exponential function [11]. Figure 1 shows a visual comparison among the performance of our GRP-MANH and the methods considered for validation (GPR-Av, LMO, GPR-MA), considering the case when the

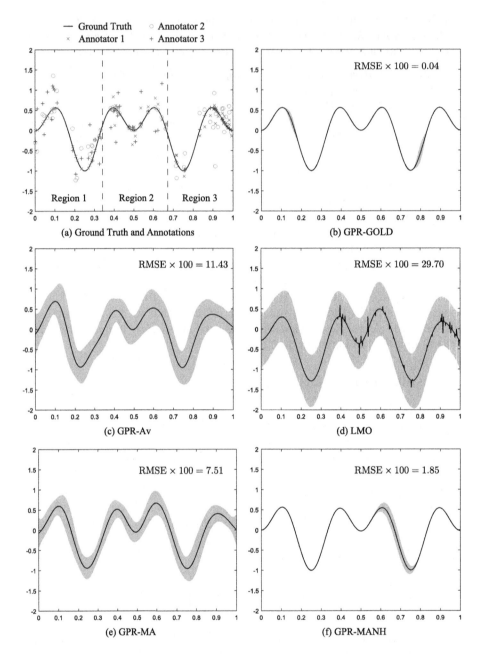

Fig. 1. Results for the first experiment. In (a) we expose the ground truth and the synthetic annotations, which are generated using the simulation method "Non-homogeneous Gaussian noise". In (b), (c), (d), (e), and (f) we respectively show the regression results for GPR-GOLD, GPR-Av, LMO, GPR-MA, and GPR-MANH. Shaded areas represent the variance for the predictions.

data from multiple annotators are generated using "Non-homogeneous Gaussian noise". Remarkably, we note that our approach can perform regression settings in scenarios where the gold standard is not available, and the expertise of the annotators is not homogeneous across the input space. In fact, it is possible to observe that the uncertainty of the predictions of our approach is remarkably lower when compared with the validation methodologies. The above can be explained in the sense that our GRP-MANH can perform a better codification of the annotator expertise.

Now, we carry out regression experiments using three datasets from the UCI repository, where we simulate three annotators with different levels of expertise using the simulation parameters described below. Table 1 reports the mean and the standard deviation for the root mean squared error–(RMSE) predicted. Besides, the method with the highest performance is highlighted in bold, excluding the upper bound (GPR-GOLD), which is a Gaussian Processes for regression trained with the true labels. As seen, most of the regression methods from multiple annotators considered in this work (GPR-MA, and GPR-MANH) outperform the average baseline (GPR-av) in most cases, which is not surprising, since this baseline does not consider differences between the expertise of the labelers. Furthermore, we empirically demonstrated that our approach is not affected where the performance of the annotators is not homogeneous across the input space. In fact, our GRP-MANH outperforms all the models considered in this work for validation under the two methods used for generating the synthetic annotations (homogeneous Gaussian noise and non-homogeneous Gaussian noise). The above can be explained in the sense that due to GPR-MANH is based on the assumption that

Table 1. UCI repository regression results. Bold: the method with the highest performance excluding the upper bound (target) classifier GPR-GOLD

(a) Homogeneous Gaussian noise					
Method	GPR-GOLD	GPR-Av	LMO	GPR-MA	GPR-MANH
	RMSE $\times$ 100				
Auto	35.40 ± 3.10	59.41 ± 7.03	70.30 ± 9.90	39.07 ± 9.41	$\mathbf{37.93 \pm 3.58}$
Concrete	40.05 ± 2.16	58.43 ± 1.95	71.89 ± 13.28	44.63 ± 2.39	$\mathbf{43.92 \pm 2.31}$
Housing	38.87 ± 5.90	56.85 ± 4.46	68.65 ± 11.48	38.96 ± 4.44	$\mathbf{38.92 \pm 4.50}$
Average	38.10	58.23	70.28	40.89	**40.26**
(b) Non-homogeneous Gaussian noise					
Method	GPR-GOLD	GPR-Av	LMO	GPR-MA	GPR-MANH
	RMSE $\times$ 100				
Auto	35.40 ± 3.10	54.49 ± 10.56	67.52 ± 10.91	36.82 ± 3.18	$\mathbf{36.42 \pm 3.14}$
Concrete	40.05 ± 2.16	54.46 ± 2.48	84.60 ± 8.67	43.96 ± 2.37	$\mathbf{42.28 \pm 2.13}$
Housing	38.87 ± 5.90	54.62 ± 3.86	74.72 ± 11.56	45.56 ± 5.81	$\mathbf{39.93 \pm 5.21}$
Average	38.10	54.52	75.61	42.11	**39.54**

the input space can be represented by a defined number of partitions, where each annotator exhibits a particular performance in each cluster. We highlight that the promising results of our approach are achieved based only on the responses from multiple annotators without considering any prior information.

5   Conclusion

In this paper, we presented a probabilistic framework based on Gaussian processes, termed GPR-MANH, to deal with regression problems in the presence of multiple annotators. Our approach relaxes the assumption that the performance of each annotator is homogeneous across the input space. GPR-MANH assume that the input space can be divided into K regions, where each annotator exhibit a particular level of expertise, which is coded by a variance $(\sigma_k^r)^2$. Then, the annotations are modeled as a version of the gold standard corrupted by additive and non-homogeneous Gaussian noise with zero mean and variance $(\sigma_k^r)^2$. Furthermore, we tested our approach using synthetic datasets from the UCI repository and simulate the annotations from multiple annotators following two different models (see Sect. 3). The results show that the proposed method can be used to perform regression problems in the context of multiple labelers with different levels of expertise. In fact, in most cases, our approach achieves better results when compared to different state-of-the-art techniques [1,9].

Finally, note that GPR-MANH loosens the assumption that the performance of the annotators only depends on the ground truth labels. As future work, this could be taken a step further by modeling the performance of the annotators as a function of the gold standard and the input samples through a Heteroscedastic Gaussian processes approach. Also, our method assumes independence between the opinions of the annotators; though it is suitable to consider that the labelers make their decisions independently, it is not true that these opinions are independent, due to there are possible correlations between the expert views. Accordingly, we expect to relax this assumption by using a probabilistic framework that allows to code the inter-annotator dependencies.

Acknowledgments. This work was funded by Colciencias under the project with code: 1110-744-55958. J. Gil González is funded by the program "Doctorados Nacionales - Convocatoria 785 de 2017". A. Orozco was partially funded by Maestría en ingeniería eléctrica from the Universidad Tecnológica de Pereira.

References

1. Groot, P., Birlutiu, A., Heskes, T.: Learning from multiple annotators with Gaussian processes. In: Honkela, T., Duch, W., Girolami, M., Kaski, S. (eds.) ICANN 2011. LNCS, vol. 6792, pp. 159–164. Springer, Heidelberg (2011). https://doi.org/10.1007/978-3-642-21738-8_21
2. Wolley, C., Quafafou, M.: Learning from multiple annotators: when data is hard and annotators are unreliable. In: 2012 IEEE 12th International Conference on Data Mining Workshops (ICDMW), pp. 514–521. IEEE (2012)

3. Mozetič, I., Grčar, M., Smailović, J.: Multilingual Twitter sentiment classification: the role of human annotators. PloS One **11**(5), e0155036 (2016)
4. Rodrigues, F., Lourenco, M., Ribeiro, B., Pereira, F.C.: Learning supervised topic models for classification and regression from crowds. IEEE Trans. Pattern Anal. Mach. Intell. **39**(12), 2409–2422 (2017)
5. González, J.G., Álvarez, M.A., Orozco, Á.A.: Automatic assessment of voice quality in the context of multiple annotations. In: 2015 37th Annual International Conference of the IEEE Engineering in Medicine and Biology Society (EMBC), pp. 6236–6239. IEEE (2015)
6. Raykar, V.C., et al.: Learning from crowds. J. Mach. Learn. Res. **11**, 1297–1322 (2010)
7. Rodrigues, F., Pereira, F.C., Ribeiro, B.: Gaussian process classification and active learning with multiple annotators. In: ICML, pp. 433–441 (2014)
8. Yan, Y., Rosales, R., Fung, G., Subramanian, R., Dy, J.: Learning from multiple annotators with varying expertise. Mach. Learn. **95**(3), 291–327 (2014)
9. Xiao, H., Xiao, H., Eckert, C.: Learning from multiple observers with unknown expertise. In: Pei, J., Tseng, V.S., Cao, L., Motoda, H., Xu, G. (eds.) PAKDD 2013. LNCS (LNAI), vol. 7818, pp. 595–606. Springer, Heidelberg (2013). https://doi.org/10.1007/978-3-642-37453-1_49
10. Bishop, C.M.: Pattern recognition. Mach. Learn. **128**, 1–58 (2006)
11. Rasmussen, C.E.: Gaussian Processes for Machine Learning. MIT Press, Cambridge (2006)
12. Frey, B.J., Dueck, D.: Clustering by passing messages between data points. Science **315**(5814), 972–976 (2007)

Linear Projection Learned from Hybrid CKA for Enhancing Distance-Based Classifiers

Diego Collazos-Huertas$^{(\boxtimes)}$, David Cárdenas-Peña,
and German Castellanos-Dominguez

Signal Processing and Recognition Group, Universidad Nacional de Colombia,
Km 7 via al Magdalena, Manizales, Colombia
{dfcollazosh,dcardenasp,cgcastellanosd}@unal.edu.co

Abstract. Most machine learning approaches are classified into either supervised or unsupervised. However, joining generative and discriminative functions in the learning process may beneficially influence each other. Using the centered kernel alignment similarity, this paper proposes a new hybrid cost function based on the linear combination of two computed terms: a discriminative component that accounts for the affinity between projected data and their labels, and a generative component that measures the similarity between the input and projected distributions. Further, the data projection is assumed as a linear model so that a matrix has to be learned by maximizing the proposed cost function. We compare our approach using a kNN classifier against the raw features and a multi-layer perceptron machine. Attained results on a handwritten digit recognition database show that there exists a trade-off value other than the trivial ones that provide the highest accuracy. Moreover, the proposed approach not only outperforms the baseline machines but also becomes more robust to several noise levels.

Keywords: Centered kernel aligment · Projection learning ·
Hybrid cost function

1 Introduction

In the last decade, machine learning algorithms have experienced a big boost due to improvements in both learning fields, unsupervised and supervised. Often, the task of selecting a relevant data representation that encodes the studied phenomenon becomes difficult due to the input matrix space is ill-posed, that is, a huge number of features and a limited number of vector samples. Hence, the reduction dimension approaches based on feature embedding appear as an important step in dealing with large dimensions. So, the optimized representation of the inputs allows visualizing the similarity between input vectors in both scenarios, unsupervised and supervised [4]. Generally, these approaches for selecting the suitable data representation comprises linear and nonlinear methodologies.

© Springer Nature Switzerland AG 2019
R. Vera-Rodriguez et al. (Eds.): CIARP 2018, LNCS 11401, pp. 100–108, 2019.
https://doi.org/10.1007/978-3-030-13469-3_12

Some linear strategies extract the relevant information from sample covariances, but regardless of including their unsupervised or supervised estimations, they lead to unsatisfactory results [8]. In [7], Centered Kernel Alignment (CKA) is proposed to learn a linear projection, encoding discriminative input features and benefiting from the nonlinear notion of similarity of kernel methods. The approach takes advantage of the joint information associating the available labels to the corresponding input samples, so achieving competitive results in object recognition [5] and computer-aided diagnosis [6] tasks. Nonetheless, encoding generative and discriminative information into a linear projection may influence favorable each other if they are combined during training, outperforming the conventional alignment [11].

Instead, the non-linear approaches aim to preserve the similarity structure using more elaborate methods of reduction dimension like kernel analysis [1] or manifold learning [9]. A particular case is the Artificial Neural Networks (ANN) that map the weighted inputs to the output of each neuron embedded in a nonlinear activation function. If there is a lack of a priori knowledge to model the architecture, ANN-based method splits the training into two separate models: unsupervised pre-training model and supervised fine-tuning model [10]. This strategy seems to be neither biologically plausible, nor optimal when it comes to optimization, as carefully designed stopping criteria have to be implemented to prevent over- or under-fitting [11]. Moreover, a direct interpretability from a nonlinear-based mapping is not always possible [2].

In this work, we introduce a linear projection learning procedure for data representation using kernel alignment approach. In particular, we define a hybrid CKA similarity by joining generative and discriminative functions, controlled by a trade-off parameter λ. It turns out that by annealing λ, when solving this unconstrained non-convex optimization problem, the model cope with the shortcomings described above. The present manuscript is organized as follows: Sect. 2.1 firstly describes the mathematical background of learning linear projections using CKA for classification. Section 3 introduces the developed experiments and achieved results. Then, performance results are discussed in Sect. 4. Finally, Sect. 5 presents the conclusions and future research directions.

2   Materials and Methods

2.1   Linear Projection Learning Through Hybrid Cost Function

Let $\boldsymbol{X} = \{\boldsymbol{x}_i \in \mathcal{X} : \forall i \in \{1, \ldots, N\}\}$ be an input data matrix of N P-sized vector samples drawn from the random process $\mathcal{X} \subset \mathbb{R}^P$ and $\boldsymbol{L} = \{l_i \in \mathcal{L} : \forall i \in \{1, \ldots, N\}\}$ that contains N output vectors $l_i \in \{1, \ldots, C\}$ representing C mutually exclusive classes. We define the classification problem in a similarity-based framework so that the model aims to maximize the distance between two samples if $l_i \neq l_i$ and minimize it if $l_i = l_i$. Given the dataset $\{\boldsymbol{X}, \boldsymbol{L}\}$, we consider the generalized inner product to measure the similarity between a couple of input vectors implemented through the kernel function $\kappa(\boldsymbol{x}_i, \boldsymbol{x}_j) = \langle \varphi(\boldsymbol{x}_i), \varphi(\boldsymbol{x}_j) \rangle : \forall i, j \in \{1, \ldots, N\}$, where notation $\langle \cdot, \cdot \rangle$ stands for the inner product and $\varphi(\cdot) : \mathbb{R}^P \to \mathcal{H}$ maps from the original domain, $\mathbb{R}^P$, into a Reproduced Kernel Hilbert Space (RKHS), $\mathcal{H}$, so that $|\mathcal{H}| \gg P$. The well-known *kernel trick* is employed for computing kernel function $\kappa(:)$ due to there is no need for computing $\varphi(\cdot)$ directly. Particularly, an introduced distance function parameterizes a positive definite and infinitely divisible kernel function as $k_{ij} = \kappa(\boldsymbol{x}_i, \boldsymbol{x}_j) = \kappa(\mathrm{d}_{\boldsymbol{W}}(\boldsymbol{x}_i, \boldsymbol{x}_j))$, being $\mathrm{d}_{\boldsymbol{W}}:\mathbb{R}^P \times \mathbb{R}^P \mapsto \mathbb{R}^+$ the Mahalanobis distance operator so that the pairwise comparison between input vectors $\boldsymbol{x}_i$ and $\boldsymbol{x}_j$ is carried out as follows, $\mathrm{d}_{\boldsymbol{W}}(\boldsymbol{x}_i, \boldsymbol{x}_j) = (\boldsymbol{x}_i - \boldsymbol{x}_j)\boldsymbol{W}\boldsymbol{W}^\top(\boldsymbol{x}_i - \boldsymbol{x}_j)^\top$, then the parameter matrix $\boldsymbol{W} \in \mathbb{R}^{P \times Q}$ linearly projects the samples $\boldsymbol{y}_i = \boldsymbol{x}_i\boldsymbol{W}$ ($\boldsymbol{y}_i \in \mathbb{R}^Q$ and $Q \leq P$), and $\boldsymbol{W}\boldsymbol{W}^\top$ implements the inverse covariance matrix of the Mahalanobis distance in the input feature space. Hence, a kernel matrix $\boldsymbol{K}_{\boldsymbol{W}} \in \mathbb{R}^{N \times N}$, resulting from the application of κ over each sample pair in $\boldsymbol{X}$, estimates the covariance of the random process $\mathcal{X}$ over $\mathcal{H}$.

To make our proposal suitable for a supervised learning task, we introduce the prior knowledge about the feasible sample membership in the computation of $\boldsymbol{W}$. To this end, we firstly enclose the target similarities in a matrix $\boldsymbol{K}_{\mathcal{L}} \in \mathbb{R}^{N \times N}$ with elements $k_{ij} = \kappa_l(l_i, l_j) = \delta(l_i - l_j)$. Thus, the matrix $\boldsymbol{W}$ can be learned by maximizing the similarity between $\{\boldsymbol{K}_{\boldsymbol{W}}, \boldsymbol{K}_{\mathcal{L}}\}$ through the following real-valued function, $\rho(\cdot, \cdot) \in [0, 1]$, that is termed as Centered Kernel Alignment (CKA) [3]:

$$\rho(\boldsymbol{K}_{\boldsymbol{W}}, \boldsymbol{K}_{\mathcal{L}}) = \frac{\langle \boldsymbol{H}\boldsymbol{K}_{\boldsymbol{W}}\boldsymbol{H}, \boldsymbol{H}\boldsymbol{K}_{\mathcal{L}}\boldsymbol{H}\rangle_F}{\|\boldsymbol{H}\boldsymbol{K}_{\boldsymbol{W}}\boldsymbol{H}\|_F \|\boldsymbol{H}\boldsymbol{K}_{\mathcal{L}}\boldsymbol{H}\|_F} \tag{1}$$

where $\boldsymbol{H} = \boldsymbol{I} - N^{-1}\boldsymbol{1}\boldsymbol{1}^\top$ is a centering matrix ($\boldsymbol{H} \in \mathbb{R}^{N \times N}$), $\boldsymbol{1} \in \mathbb{R}^N$ is an all-ones vector, and notations $\langle \cdot, \cdot \rangle_F$ and $\|\cdot, \cdot\|_F$ stand for the Frobenius inner product and norm, respectively.

Aiming to favor the system performance, we further encode discriminative and generative information during the tuning of $\boldsymbol{W}$ by proposing the hybrid cost function as follows:

$$J(\boldsymbol{W}|\lambda) = \lambda\rho(\boldsymbol{K}_{\boldsymbol{W}}, \boldsymbol{K}_{\boldsymbol{X}}) + (1 - \lambda)\rho(\boldsymbol{K}_{\boldsymbol{W}}, \boldsymbol{K}_{\mathcal{L}}) \tag{2}$$

where $\boldsymbol{K}_{\boldsymbol{X}} \in \mathbb{R}^{N \times N}$ encodes the all pair-wise similarities between input vectors into a kernel matrix with elements computed as $k_{ij} = \kappa(\mathrm{d}_{\boldsymbol{X}}(\boldsymbol{x}_i, \boldsymbol{x}_j))$, $\mathrm{d}_{\boldsymbol{X}}: \mathbb{R}^P \times \mathbb{R}^P \mapsto \mathbb{R}^+$ is the Euclidean distance operator, and the real-valued parameter $\lambda \in [0, 1]$ is a trade-off searching for a compromise between the generative (first term) and discriminative (second term) parts. As a result, the CKA hybrid cost function highlights relevant features by learning the matrix $\boldsymbol{W}$ that best match all relations between the projected vectors and the input samples, as well as the relations between the resulting feature vectors and provided target classes. Consequently, we state the following optimization problem to compute the projection matrix:

$$\boldsymbol{W}^\star = \arg\max_{\boldsymbol{W}} J(\boldsymbol{W}|\lambda), \tag{3}$$

where the obtained $\boldsymbol{W}^\star$ holds the linear projection $\boldsymbol{Y} = \boldsymbol{W}^\star\boldsymbol{X}$ that optimizes the similarity-based classification by assessing distances with $\mathrm{d}_{\boldsymbol{W}}(\cdot, \cdot)$. The optimization details for Eq. (3) are described as below.

2.2 Gradient Descent Optimization of Hybrid CKA

The proposed cost function stated in a conventional minimization problem by transforming each term in Eq. (2) into explicit minimization functions as [3]:

$$\hat{\rho}\left(\boldsymbol{K}_W, \boldsymbol{K}_{\mathcal{Z}}\right) = \log\left(\operatorname{tr}\left(\boldsymbol{K}_W\left(\boldsymbol{W}\right)\tilde{\boldsymbol{I}}\boldsymbol{K}_{\mathcal{Z}}\tilde{\boldsymbol{I}}\right)\right)$$
$$-\tfrac{1}{2}\log\left(\operatorname{tr}\left(\boldsymbol{K}_W\left(\boldsymbol{W}\right)\tilde{\boldsymbol{I}}\boldsymbol{K}_W\left(\boldsymbol{W}\right)\tilde{\boldsymbol{I}}\right)\right) + \rho_0, \quad (4)$$

being $\boldsymbol{K}_{\mathcal{Z}}$ either the target label $\left(\boldsymbol{K}_{\mathcal{L}}\right)$ or the input $\left(\boldsymbol{K}_X\right)$ kernel matrix, and $\rho_0 \in \mathbb{R}$ corresponds to a constant independent on $\boldsymbol{W}$. In this case, we consider the widely known Gaussian kernel for computing $\boldsymbol{K}_X$ and $\boldsymbol{K}_W$ defined as $\kappa\left(\mathrm{d}_W\left(\boldsymbol{x}_i, \boldsymbol{x}_j\right)\right) = \exp\left(-\mathrm{d}_W^2\left(\boldsymbol{x}_i, \boldsymbol{x}_j\right)/2\sigma^2\right)$, where the kernel bandwidth $\sigma \in \mathbb{R}^+$ is adjusted by maximizing the variance of the information forces among samples [2].

Here, we solve the optimization problem at hand using the iterative gradient descent algorithm and the derivative of each term in the hybrid cost function (Eq. (2)) with respect to the projection matrix $\boldsymbol{W}$ given by:

$$\nabla_W\left(J\left(\boldsymbol{W}|\lambda\right)\right) = \lambda\nabla_W\left(\hat{\rho}\left(\boldsymbol{K}_W, \boldsymbol{K}_X\right)\right)$$
$$+(1-\lambda)\nabla_W\left(\hat{\rho}\left(\boldsymbol{K}_W, \boldsymbol{K}_{\mathcal{L}}\right)\right), \quad (5)$$

$$\nabla_W\left(\hat{\rho}\left(\boldsymbol{K}_W, \boldsymbol{K}_X\right)\right) = -4(\boldsymbol{W})^\top\left((\boldsymbol{G}_X \circ \boldsymbol{K}_W\left(\boldsymbol{W}\right))\right.$$
$$\left.- \operatorname{diag}\left(\mathbf{1}^\top\left(\boldsymbol{G}_X \circ \boldsymbol{K}_W\left(\boldsymbol{W}\right)\right)\right)\right)\boldsymbol{W}, \quad (6)$$

$$\nabla_W\left(\hat{\rho}\left(\boldsymbol{K}_W, \boldsymbol{K}_{\mathcal{L}}\right)\right) = -4(\boldsymbol{W})^\top\left((\boldsymbol{G}_{\mathcal{L}} \circ \boldsymbol{K}_W\left(\boldsymbol{W}\right))\right.$$
$$\left.- \operatorname{diag}\left(\mathbf{1}^\top\left(\boldsymbol{G}_{\mathcal{L}} \circ \boldsymbol{K}_W\left(\boldsymbol{W}\right)\right)\right)\right)\boldsymbol{W}, \quad (7)$$

where notations $\operatorname{diag}(\cdot)$ and $\circ$ denote the diagonal operator and the Hadamard product, respectively. $\boldsymbol{G}_{\mathcal{Z}} \in \mathbb{R}^{N \times N}$ is the gradient of each term in the cost function with respect to $\boldsymbol{K}_W$, calculated as follows:

$$\boldsymbol{G}_{\mathcal{Z}} = \nabla_{K_W}\left(\hat{\rho}\left(\boldsymbol{K}_W, \boldsymbol{K}_{\mathcal{Z}}\right)\right) = \frac{\tilde{\boldsymbol{I}}\boldsymbol{K}_{\mathcal{Z}}\tilde{\boldsymbol{I}}}{\operatorname{tr}\left(\boldsymbol{K}_W\tilde{\boldsymbol{I}}\boldsymbol{K}_{\mathcal{Z}}\tilde{\boldsymbol{I}}\right)} - \frac{\tilde{\boldsymbol{I}}\boldsymbol{K}_W\tilde{\boldsymbol{I}}}{\operatorname{tr}\left(\boldsymbol{K}_W\tilde{\boldsymbol{I}}\boldsymbol{K}_W\tilde{\boldsymbol{I}}\right)}, \quad (8)$$

that yields the following updating rule for $\boldsymbol{W}$, provided an initial guess $\boldsymbol{W}_o$:

$$\boldsymbol{W}_{t+1} = \boldsymbol{W}_t - \mu_t\left(\lambda\nabla_{W_t}\left(\hat{\rho}\left(\boldsymbol{K}_W, \boldsymbol{K}_X\right)\right) + (1-\lambda)\nabla_{W_t}\left(\hat{\rho}\left(\boldsymbol{K}_W, \boldsymbol{K}_{\mathcal{L}}\right)\right)\right), \quad (9)$$

where $\mu_t \in \mathbb{R}^+$ is the step size of the learning rule at optimization epoch t.

3   Experimental Set-Up and Results

We validate the proposed data representation method based on learning the
linear projection through hybrid cost function within a classification framework.
The methodological development of this approach comprises the following stages:
(i) image preprocessing that includes noise injection procedure, *(ii)* linear projection learning that we carry out using the kernel alignment, and *(iii)* training
the classifier using resulting data projection. Later, we assess the trained model
performance by means of the classification accuracy in a cross-validation scheme.

3.1   Tested Database

We evaluate our proposed approach for classifying handwritten digits on the
well-known MNIST collection that holds 60.000 training images and 10.000 test
images sizing 28×28 pixels and 256 level gray-scale of digits between 0 and 9
(as shown in Fig. 1a). In order to evaluate the compromise between generative
and discriminative terms in Eq. (2), we corrupt each image using *salt-and-pepper*
noise with six density levels corresponding to the probability of occurrence of
noisy pixels $\eta \in \{2\%, 5\%, 8\%, 10\%, 15\%, 20\%\}$. Figure 1 illustrates one handwritten digit image affected by the noise levels.

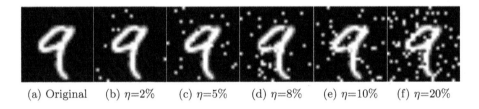

(a) Original   (b) η=2%   (c) η=5%   (d) η=8%   (e) η=10%   (f) η=20%

Fig. 1. Noise influence on the handwritten digit image within a range of α values.

3.2   Performance Assessment

The proposed linear projection learning based on CKA is performed per training
batch. Once the projection matrix W is estimated following Eq. (9), the linearly
projected data Y is computed and then used to tune the distance-based classifier.
Finally, the classification accuracy is computed as the average performance on
the test data batches. We carry out the experiments using the widely known
k-nearest neighbors (kNN) algorithm as the distance-based classifier.

For the sake of the model robustness, we compute the linear projection from
the corrupted data with different noise levels. Then, the average classification
performance is computed along a range of λ values using $k = 3$ neighbors. As seen
in Fig. 2, as the noise level increases the classification accuracy decreases, i.e.,
the problem becomes more complex. However, the results hold the compromise

between both terms of the cost function, yielding an optimal trade-off of $\lambda = 0.4$ for noise levels. As a result, the model demands a major contribution of the discriminative part without turning off the generative one.

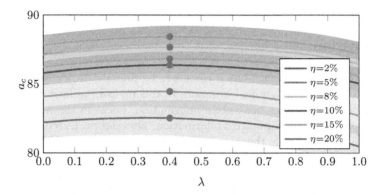

Fig. 2. Mean and standard deviation of the kNN accuracy performed within the tested data affected by the considered noise levels. The red dot marks the best-reached accuracy value. (Color figure online)

Lastly, we compare our proposal with the classification performance attained by the kNN classifier employing non-projected data. Additionally, we evaluate the performance of a conventional Multi-Layer Perceptron approach (MLP), as it implements linear projection estimations with the addition of saturating nonlinear activation functions. Table 1 displays the classification performance accomplished by each compared linear projection methodology under different noise conditions, where the best result is marked in boldface for each noise density level. In either scenario of comparison, all algorithms are evaluated in

Table 1. Classification performance on the testing group for the considered methodologies under evaluation criteria.

Noise density $\eta(\%)$	Accuracy a_c (%)		
	kNN (raw data)	MLP (raw data)	kNN (projected data)
0	87.1 ± 0.9	82.3 ± 3.9	$\mathbf{88.9 \pm 0.9}$
2	86.5 ± 0.9	80.8 ± 4.5	$\mathbf{88.4 \pm 0.8}$
5	85.4 ± 0.9	80.1 ± 3.1	$\mathbf{87.7 \pm 0.9}$
8	84.2 ± 1.0	76.9 ± 5.4	$\mathbf{86.8 \pm 1.0}$
10	83.2 ± 1.2	75.2 ± 8.9	$\mathbf{86.4 \pm 1.0}$
15	80.3 ± 1.0	71.9 ± 8.1	$\mathbf{84.5 \pm 1.2}$
20	76.9 ± 1.3	67.3 ± 8.4	$\mathbf{82.5 \pm 1.3}$
Average	83.4 ± 1.1	76.4 ± 6.1	$\mathbf{86.4 \pm 1.0}$

terms of their classification performance, accuracy (a_c) and standard deviation. Overall, the proposed approach outperforms the baselines techniques in terms of the studied performance measures. Hence, the estimated linear projection based on kernel alignment using hybrid cost function enhances the performance in similarity-based classification problems, facilitating the class discrimination.

4   Discussion

This paper enhances distance-based classifiers by linearly projecting data based on the centered kernel alignment function. In this regard, we introduce a hybrid cost function that encodes generative information, between the input and projected samples, and discriminative information, between projected data and the target label kernel. From the obtained results, upon the MNIST dataset for handwritten digit recognition, the following aspects are considered important:

As seen in Fig. 2, the resulting performance curves illustrate that despite the images being corrupted with a particular level of *salt and pepper* noise, there exists a trade-off between generative and discriminative terms of the objective cost function that attains the best classification accuracy. Therefore, the learned linear projection based on the hybrid CKA similarity function enhances the distance-based classification, achieving the highest accuracy with the additional benefit of robustness to the data representation.

Table 1 holds the average and standard deviation of performed accuracy for MNIST testing data. The MLP approach performs the worst (76.36 ± 6.06) which indicates that the learned non-linear projection randomly initialized limit the classification accuracy. Furthermore, the objective function of network training stage is purely discriminative and lacks information to model data inherent properties. Then, the kNN approach using raw data (83.36 ± 1.07) can only account for the original data distribution, so that noise corruption reduces its performance. Lastly, application of kNN on projected data, learned through the hybrid cost function, outperforms the baseline approaches (86.45 ± 1.02). As a result, estimating mapping matrices W based on a compromise between generative and discriminative terms allows capturing both the inherent input information while forcing the samples to be projected into a space with higher class separability.

5   Conclusion

This paper discusses the linear projection learning for data representation through hybrid cost function controlled by a trade-off parameter within a kNN-based classification framework. To this end, we make use of the centered kernel alignment criterion in order to encode generative and discriminative information available in the data into a projection matrix and enhance the class discrimination. We implement a similarity-based classification problem to evaluate the linear projection performance. For this purpose, we corrupt data with different noise levels in order to observe the behavior of classification accuracy in a range of trade-off values. In addition, we compare our proposal against a conventional MLP. Attained results for handwritten digit recognition show that our proposal improves other approaches in all of the considered performance measures, reduce data dimension, and add robustness to the data representation.

As a future research direction, we will evaluate our learning approach, exploring new classification and regression problems. We will also introduce constraints to the cost function, as linear independence, to account for other data properties, and explore other combination approaches, as the geometric average, for dealing with more complex relations among inherent distributions and labels.

Acknowledgment. This work was supported by Doctorados Nacionales 2017 - Conv 785 and the research project 111974454838, both funded by COLCIENCIAS.

References

1. Alvarez-Meza, A., Lee, J., Verleysen, M., Castellanos-Dominguez, G.: Kernel-based dimensionality reduction using renyi's α-entropy measures of similarity. Neurocomputing **222**, 36–46 (2017). https://doi.org/10.1016/j.neucom.2016.10.004
2. Álvarez-Meza, A.M., Cárdenas-Peña, D., Castellanos-Dominguez, G.: Unsupervised kernel function building using maximization of information potential variability. In: Bayro-Corrochano, E., Hancock, E. (eds.) CIARP 2014. LNCS, vol. 8827, pp. 335–342. Springer, Cham (2014). https://doi.org/10.1007/978-3-319-12568-8_41
3. Brockmeier, A.J., Choi, J.S., Kriminger, E.G., Francis, J.T., Principe, J.C.: Neural decoding with kernel-based metric learning. Neural Comput. **26**(6), 1080–1107 (2014). https://doi.org/10.1162/NECO_a_00591
4. Brockmeier, A.J., et al.: Information-theoretic metric learning: 2-D linear projections of neural data for visualization. In: 2013 35th Annual International Conference of the IEEE Engineering in Medicine and Biology Society (EMBC), pp. 5586–5589. IEEE (2013). https://doi.org/10.1109/EMBC.2013.6610816
5. Cárdenas-Peña, D., Collazos-Huertas, D., Álvarez-Meza, A., Castellanos-Dominguez, G.: Supervised kernel approach for automated learning using general stochastic networks. Eng. Appl. Artif. Intell. **68**, 10–17 (2018). https://doi.org/10.1016/j.engappai.2017.10.003
6. Cárdenas-Peña, D., Collazos-Huertas, D., Castellanos-Dominguez, G.: Centered kernel alignment enhancing neural network pretraining for mri-based dementia diagnosis. Comput. Math. Methods Med. **2016**, 1–10 (2016). https://doi.org/10.1155/2016/9523849
7. Cortes, C., Mohri, M., Rostamizadeh, A.: Algorithms for learning kernels based on centered alignment. J. Mach. Learn. Res. **13**, 795–828 (2012). http://dl.acm.org/citation.cfm?id=2503308.2188413
8. Cowley, B.R., et al.: DataHigh: graphical user interface for visualizing and interacting with high-dimensional neural activity. J. Neural Eng. **10**(6), 066012 (2013). https://doi.org/10.1088/1741-2560/10/6/066012

9. Harandi, M., Salzmann, M., Hartley, R.: Dimensionality reduction on spd manifolds: the emergence of geometry-aware methods. IEEE Trans. Pattern Anal. Mach. Intell. **40**(1), 48–62 (2018). https://doi.org/10.1109/TPAMI.2017.2655048

10. Hinton, G.E., Srivastava, N., Krizhevsky, A., Sutskever, I., Salakhutdinov, R.R.: Improving neural networks by preventing co-adaptation of feature detectors. arXiv preprint arXiv:1207.0580 (2012)

11. Zöhrer, M., Pernkopf, F.: General stochastic networks for classification. In: Ghahramani, Z., Welling, M., Cortes, C., Lawrence, N.D., Weinberger, K.Q. (eds.) Advances in Neural Information Processing Systems, vol. 27, pp. 2015–2023. Curran Associates, Inc. (2014). http://dl.acm.org/citation.cfm?id=2969033. 2969052

Evaluation of Bag-of-Word Performance for Time Series Classification Using Discriminative SIFT-Based Mid-Level Representations

Raquel Almeida[1], Hugo Herlanin[1], Zenilton Kleber G. do Patrocinio Jr.[1($\boxtimes$)], Simon Malinowski[2], and Silvio Jamil Ferzoli Guimarães[1]

[1] Computer Science Department, Pontifical Catholic University of Minas Gerais, Belo Horizonte, MG, Brazil
zenilton@pucminas.br
[2] Université de Rennes 1, IRISA, Rennes, France

Abstract. Time series classification has been widely explored over the last years. Amongst the best approaches for that task, many are based on the Bag-of-Words framework, in which time series are transformed into a histogram of word occurrences. These words represent quantized features that are extracted beforehand. In this paper, we aim to evaluate the use of accurate mid-level representations in order to enhance the Bag-of-Words representation. More precisely, this kind of representation enables to reduce the loss induced by feature quantization. Experiments show that these representations are likely to improve time series classification accuracy compared to Bag-of-Words and some of them are very competitive to the state-of-the-art.

Keywords: Time series · Mid-level representations · SIFT-based descriptors

1 Introduction

Time series can be seen as series of ordered measurements. They contain temporal information that needs to be taken into account when dealing with such data. Time series classification (TSC) could be defined as follows: given a collection of unlabeled time series, one should assign each time series to one of a predefined set of classes. TSC is a challenge that is receiving more and more attention recently due to its most diverse applications in real life problems involving, for example, data mining, statistics, machine learning and image processing.

An extensive comparison of TSC approaches is performed in [1]. Two particular methods stand out from other core classifiers for their accuracy:

This work received funding from CAPES (STIC-AmSUD TRANSFORM 88881. 143258/2017-01), FAPEMIG (PPM 00006-16), and CNPq (Universal 421521/2016-3 and PQ 307062/2016-3).

© Springer Nature Switzerland AG 2019
R. Vera-Rodriguez et al. (Eds.): CIARP 2018, LNCS 11401, pp. 109–116, 2019.
https://doi.org/10.1007/978-3-030-13469-3_13

COTE [2] and BOSS [12]. BOSS is a dictionary-based approach based on the extraction of Fourier coefficients from time series windows. Many other dictionary-based approaches have been proposed recently [3,4]. These methods share the same overall steps: (i) extraction of feature vectors from time series; (ii) creation of a codebook (composed of codewords) from extracted feature vectors; and (iii) representation of time series as a histogram of codeword appearances, called a Bag-of-Words (BoW).

Dictionary-based approaches are well adapted for TSC. Nevertheless, two drawbacks with such methods can be pointed out: (i) global temporal information is lost when representing a time series as a BoW; and (ii) extracted features are quantized using a dictionary inherently inducing a loss in the precision of time series representation. In this paper, we tackle this second issue. Particularly, we study the impact of mid-level representations (widely used for image and video analysis) on time series classification. We focus on mid-level features that aim at enhancing the BoW representation by more accurate description of the distribution of feature vectors related to an object. To the best of our knowledge, such representations have never been used for time series. Vector of Locally Aggregated Descriptors [8] and Locality-constrained Linear Coding [14] are examples of such mid-level representations.

This paper is organized as follows. Section 2 gives the related works about time series classification. Section 3 explains the background about SIFT-based descriptors extracted from time series. In Sect. 4, we present a methodology for time series classification by using powerful mid-level representations on SIFT-based descriptors. Section 5 details the experimental setup and results to validate the method, and finally, some conclusions are drawn in Sect. 6.

2   Related Work

In this section, we give an overview about the related work on TSC. One of the earliest methods for that task is the combination of 1-nearest-neighbor classifier and the Dynamic Time Warping. It has been a baseline for TSC for many years thanks to its good performance. Recently, more sophisticated approaches have been designed for TSC.

Shapelets, for instance, were introduced in [15]. They represent existing subsequences able to discriminate classes. Hills *et al.* proposed the shapelet transform [6], which consists in transforming a time series into a vector whose components represent the distance between the time series and different shapelets, extracted beforehand. Classifiers, such as SVM, can then be used with the vectorial representations of time series.

Numerous approaches have been designed based on the Bag-of-Word framework. This framework consists in extracting feature vectors from time series, creating a dictionary of words using these extracted features, and then representing each time series as a histogram of words occurrence. The different approaches proposed in the literature differ mainly on the kind of features that are extracted. Local features such as mean, variance and extrema are considered in [4] and Fourier coefficients in [12]. SAX coefficients are used in [9]. Recently, SIFT-based descriptors adapted to time series have been considered as feature vectors in [3].

All the methods based on the BoW framework create a dictionary of words by quantizing the set (or a subset) of extracted features. This quantization step induces a loss when representing time series as histogram of words occurrence. In this paper, we aim at improving the accuracy of time series representations such as BoW through the adoption of specially designed mid-level representations.

3   Background on SIFT-Based Feature Extraction

The work proposed in this paper aims at improving classical BoW representation for time series. More precisely, the idea is to build an accurate vectorial representation that models a set of feature vectors extracted from time series. The mid-level representations that we have used in this paper can be applied with any kind of feature vectors extracted from time series. We choose in this paper to use SIFT-based descriptors that were proposed in [3], illustrated in Fig. 1. We quickly explain in this section how such descriptors are computed.

First, key-points are extracted regularly every τ_{step} instants. Then, each key-point is described by different feature vectors representing its neighborhood at different scales. More precisely, let $L(\mathcal{S}, \sigma)$ be the convolution of a time series $\mathcal{S}$ with a Gaussian function $G(t, \sigma)$ of width σ computed by $L(\mathcal{S}, \sigma) = \mathcal{S} * G(t, \sigma)$ in which

$$G(t, \sigma) = \frac{1}{\sqrt{2\pi}\sigma} e^{-t^2/2\sigma^2} \tag{1}$$

For description, n_b blocks of size a are selected in $L(\mathcal{S}, \sigma)$ around each key-point. Each of these blocks is described by the gradient magnitudes of the points in the block. More precisely, the sum of positive gradients and the sum of negative gradients are computed in each block. Hence, the size of a key-point feature vector is $2 \times n_b$. The key-points are described at many different scales, thereby transforming a time series into a set of feature vectors. More details about SIFT-based descriptors can be found in [3].

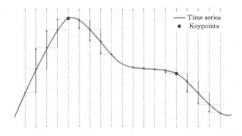

Fig. 1. SIFT-based descriptors for time series proposed in [3]: A time series and its extracted key-points. A keypoint is described by vectors representing the gradients in its neighborhood, at different scales.

4   Classification of Time Series by Using Their Mid-Level Representation

The methodology for classifying time series by using mid-level representation can be divided into four main steps: (i) dense extraction and description of key-points in time series; (ii) coding of the key-point descriptors, using clustering methods; (iii) feature encoding following by vector concatenation in order to create a final mid-level representation; and (iv) classification of time series by using their mid-level representation. Here, it is important to note that each time series is represented by only one mid-level description. In the following, we shortly discuss about some of the representations that were used here for describing a set of low features.

Let $\mathbb{X} = \left\{ \mathbf{x}_j \in \mathbb{R}^d \right\}_{j=1}^N$ be an unordered set of d-dimensional descriptors $\mathbf{x}_j$ extracted from the data. Let also $\mathbb{C} = \{ \mathbf{c}_m \in \mathbb{R}^d \}_{m=1}^M$ be the codebook learned by an unsupervised clustering algorithm, composed by a set of M code-words, also called prototypes or representatives. Consider $\mathbb{Z} \in \mathbb{R}^M$ as the final vector mid-level representation. As formalized in [5], the mapping from $\mathbb{X}$ to $\mathbb{Z}$ can be decomposed into three successive steps: (i) coding; (ii) pooling; and (iii) concatenation, as follows:

$$\alpha_j = f(\mathbf{x}_j), j \in [1, N] \qquad \text{(coding)} \qquad (2)$$

$$h_m = g(\alpha_m = \{\alpha_{m,j}\}_{j=1}^N), m \in [1, M] \qquad \text{(pooling)} \qquad (3)$$

$$z = [h_1^T, \ldots, h_M^T] \qquad \text{(concatenation)} \qquad (4)$$

In vector quantization (VQ) [13], the coding function f aims to minimize the distance to codewords and pooling function leverages these distances, as follows:

$$\alpha_{m,j} = 1 \text{ iff } j = \underset{1 \leq m \leq M}{\arg\min} \, D(\mathbf{c}_m, \mathbf{x}_j) \qquad (5)$$

$$h_m = \frac{1}{N} \sum_{j=1}^N \alpha_{m,j} \qquad (6)$$

in which $D(\mathbf{c}_m, \mathbf{x}_j)$ is the Euclidean distance between j-th descriptor and m-th codeword. A soft version of this approach, so-called soft-assignment (SA), attributes $\mathbf{x}_j$ to the n nearest codewords, and usually presents better results than the hard version. Fisher vector (FV), that is derived from Fisher kernel [7], is another mid-level representation which is a generic framework that combines the benefits of generative and discriminative approaches. FV was introduced for large-scale image categorization in [11] by using an improved Fisher vector.

Vector of Locally Aggregated Descriptors (VLAD) [8] can be viewed as a simplification of the Fisher kernel representation keeping the first-order statistics.

Fisher kernel combines the benefits of generative and discriminative approaches and it based on computation of two gradients as follows [11],

$$\mathcal{G}^{\mathbf{x}_j}_{\mu,k} = \frac{1}{\sqrt{\pi_k}}\gamma_k\left(\frac{\mathbf{x}_j - \mu_k}{\sigma_k}\right), \tag{7}$$

$$\mathcal{G}^{\mathbf{x}_j}_{\sigma,k} = \frac{1}{\sqrt{2\pi_k}}\gamma_k\left[\frac{(\mathbf{x}_j - \mu_k)^2}{\sigma_k^2} - 1\right], \tag{8}$$

where γ_k, μ_k and σ_k and are the weight of local descriptor, mean and standard deviation, respectively, related to the kth Gaussian Mixture. The final Fisher vector is the concatenation of these gradients for K models and is defined by

$$\text{FV}: \quad \mathcal{S} = [\mathcal{G}^{\mathbf{x}_j}_{\mu,1}, \mathcal{G}^{\mathbf{x}_j}_{\sigma,1}, \ldots, \mathcal{G}^{\mathbf{x}_j}_{\mu,K}, \mathcal{G}^{\mathbf{x}_j}_{\sigma,K}] \tag{9}$$

Furthermore, Vector of Locally Aggregated Descriptors (VLAD) can be defined as follows:

$$\text{VLAD}: \quad \mathcal{S} = [\mathbf{0}, \ldots, \mathbf{s}(i)(\mathbf{x}_j - \mathbf{d}_i), \ldots, \mathbf{0}] \tag{10}$$

in which $\mathbf{s}(i)$ is the ith element of VQ and is equal to 1; and $\mathbf{d}_i$ is the closest visual word to $\mathbf{x}_j$. Locality-constrained Linear Coding (LLC) [14] is a mid-level strategy which incorporates a linear reconstruction term during the coding step. It aims to iteratively optimize the produced code using the Coordinate Descent method. At each iteration, each descriptor is weighted and projected into the coordinate system using its locality constraint. At the end, the basis vectors which most minimizes the distance between the descriptor and the codebooks are selected and all other coefficients are set to zero.

5   Experimental Analysis

In this section, we describe our experiments in order to investigate the impact, in terms of classification performances, of more powerful encoding methods applied to dense extracted features to for TSC.

5.1   Experimental Setup

Experiments are conducted on the 84 currently available datasets from the UCR repository, the largest on-line database for time series classification. We ignored 2 datasets: (i) StarLightCurves, due the large amount of instances; and (ii) ItalyPowerDemand, due the small length of the series. All datasets are split into a training and a test set, whose size varies between less than 20 and more than 8,000 time series. For a given dataset, all time series have the same length, ranging from 24 to more than 2,500 points. For computing the mid-level representation, we have extracted SIFT-based descriptors proposed in [3] by using

Table 1. Comparison to the state-of-the-art in terms of classification rates and ranking.

Method	State-of-the-art				Mid-level representations using SIFT-based descriptors						
	D-BoTSW	BOSS	BoP	COTE	D-VQ	D-SA		D-LLC		D-VLAD	D-FV
						Max	Sum	Max	Sum		
Rate	0.819	**0.831**	0.742	**0.855**	0.814	0.780	0.806	0.797	0.821	**0.827**	0.806
Ranking	5.2	5.5	9.2	**3.6**	5.8	7.7	5.1	6.0	**4.5**	**4.3**	5.8

dense sampling. For computing the codebook and GMM, we have used the following number of clusters $\{16, 32, 64, 128, 256, 512, 1024\}$ considering a sampling of 30% of the descriptors. The representations are normalized by a L2-norm. The best sets of parameters are obtained by a 5-fold cross-validation to be used in a SVM with RBF kernel for the classification. In the following, we present specific details of the setup for these representations. It is important to note that we have adapted the framework proposed in [10] which was used for evaluating video action recognition.

Here, "D" means SIFT-based descriptor by using dense sampling as low level feature. For D-VQ, we followed VQ [16] and the final representation is obtained by *sum pooling*. For D-LLC, the final representation is obtained by *max* and *sum pooling*. For D-SA, we set the number of nearest codewords to 5, and we have used *max* and *sum pooling* for the final representation. For D-VLAD, we used $n = 5$ for the nearest codewords and *sum pooling*.

5.2   Comparison to the State-of-the-Art Methods

In order to study the impact of specially designed mid-level representations on TSC. We focus on two different analysis. In the first one, we compare the studied representations, namely D-VLAD and D-LLC, to D-VQ and D-BoTSW, which are our baselines. In the second one, we present a comparative analysis between the state-of-the-art, namely D-BoTSW [3], BoP [9], BOSS [12] and COTE [2], and the new proposed use of mid-level description. In both cases, we used the average accuracy rate and rank and summarized it in Table 1. As illustrated, D-VLAD obtained the best results among the studied mid-representation, and it is very competitive to the state-of-the-art, being better than D-BoTSW, BoP and BOSS. When compared to our baseline D-BoTSW, D-VLAD statistically outperformed D-BoTSW taking into account the paired t-test with 70% of confidence, and for rates of confidence greater than 70% in the paired t-test, our baseline D-BoTSW and D-VLAD are statistically equivalent. Concerning the comparison of D-LLC and D-VLAD to D-VQ, we have observed: (i) the studied specially designed mid-level representations presented better performances than D-VQ, which confirms the our initial assumptions; and (ii) D-VLAD presented the best results in terms of classification rates and average rank of a single mid-level representation. Moreover, as illustrated in Fig. 2, the pairwise comparisons involving several tested representation showed that D-VLAD outperformed all SIFT-based representations and BOSS. Furthermore, COTE statistically outperformed all tested representations.

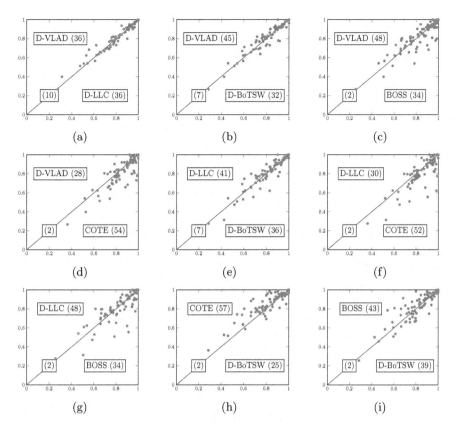

Fig. 2. Pairwise comparison of classification rates between SIFT-based mid-level representations and the state-of-the-art.

6   Conclusions

Time series classification is a challenge task due to its most diverse applications in real life. Among the several kind of approaches, dictionary-based ones have received much attention in the last years. In a general way, these ones are based on the extraction of feature vectors from time series, creation of codebook from the extracted feature vectors and finally representation of time series as traditional Bag-of-Words. In this work, we studied the impact of more discriminative and accurate mid-level representations for describing the time series taking into account SIFT-based descriptors [3].

According to our experiments, D-VLAD and D-LLC outperform the classical BoW representation, namely vector quantization (VQ). Moreover, we achieve competitive results when compared to the state-of-the-art methods, mainly with D-VLAD. By using, the average rank as a comparative criterion, D-VLAD is very competitive with COTE, which represents the state-of-the-art. However, despite the pairwise comparison (Fig. 2) involving both methods, COTE is slightly better than D-VLAD in terms of average rank. Thus, the use of more accurate mid-level representation in conjunction with SIFT-based descriptor seems to be a very interesting approach to cope with time series classification. From our results and observations, we believe that a future study of the normalization and distance functions could be interesting in order to understand their impact in our method, since according to [8] the reduction of frequent codeword influence could be profitable.

References

1. Bagnall, A., Lines, J., Bostrom, A., Large, J., Keogh, E.: The great time series classification bake off: a review and experimental evaluation of recent algorithmic advances. Data Min. Knowl. Discov. **31**(3), 606–660 (2017)
2. Bagnall, A., Lines, J., Hills, J., Bostrom, A.: Time-series classification with cote: the collective of transformation-based ensembles. IEEE Trans. Knowl. Data Eng. **27**(9), 2522–2535 (2015)
3. Bailly, A., Malinowski, S., Tavenard, R., Chapel, L., Guyet, T.: Dense bag-of-temporal-SIFT-words for time series classification. In: Douzal-Chouakria, A., Vilar, J.A., Marteau, P.-F. (eds.) AALTD 2015. LNCS (LNAI), vol. 9785, pp. 17–30. Springer, Cham (2016). https://doi.org/10.1007/978-3-319-44412-3_2
4. Baydogan, M.G., Runger, G., Tuv, E.: A bag-of-features framework to classify time series. IEEE PAMI **35**(11), 2796–2802 (2013)
5. Boureau, Y.L., Bach, F., LeCun, Y., Ponce, J.: Learning mid-level features for recognition. Proc. CVPR **2010**, 2559–2566 (2010)
6. Hills, J., Lines, J., Baranauskas, E., Mapp, J., Bagnall, A.: Classification of time series by shapelet transformation. Data Min. Knowl. Discov. **28**(4), 851–881 (2014)
7. Jaakkola, T., Haussler, D.: Exploiting generative models in discriminative classifiers. In: Advances in Neural Information Processing Systems, pp. 487–493 (1999)
8. Jegou, H., Perronnin, F., Douze, M., Sánchez, J., Perez, P., Schmid, C.: Aggregating local image descriptors into compact codes. IEEE PAMI **34**(9), 1704–1716 (2012)
9. Lin, J., Khade, R., Li, Y.: Rotation-invariant similarity in time series using bag-of-patterns representation. J. Intell. Inf. Syst. **39**(2), 287–315 (2012)
10. Peng, X., Wang, L., Wang, X., Qiao, Y.: Bag of visual words and fusion methods for action recognition: comprehensive study and good practice. Comput. Vis. Image Underst. **150**, 109–125 (2016)
11. Perronnin, F., Sánchez, J., Mensink, T.: Improving the fisher kernel for large-scale image classification. In: Daniilidis, K., Maragos, P., Paragios, N. (eds.) ECCV 2010. LNCS, vol. 6314, pp. 143–156. Springer, Heidelberg (2010). https://doi.org/10.1007/978-3-642-15561-1_11
12. Schäfer, P.: The BOSS is concerned with time series classification in the presence of noise. Data Min. Knowl. Discov. **29**(6), 1505–1530 (2014)
13. Sivic, J., Zisserman, A.: Video Google: a text retrieval approach to object matching in videos. In: Proceedings of the ICCV 2003, Nice, France, pp. 1470–1477 (2003)
14. Wang, J., Yang, J., Yu, K., Lv, F., Huang, T., Gong, Y.: Locality-constrained linear coding for image classification. Proc. CVPR **2010**, 3360–3367 (2010)
15. Ye, L., Keogh, E.: Time series shapelets: a new primitive for data mining. In: Proceedings of the 15th ACM SIGKDD International Conference on Knowledge Discovery and Data Mining, pp. 947–956. ACM (2009)
16. Zhang, J., Marszalek, M., Lazebnik, S., Schmid, C.: Local features and kernels for classification of texture and object categories: a comprehensive study. In: Proceedings of the CVPR 2006, p. 13. IEEE (2006)

Color Classification Methods for Perennial Weed Detection in Cereal Crops

Manuel G. Forero[1](✉) (iD), Sergio Herrera-Rivera[1],
Julián Ávila-Navarro[1], Camilo Andres Franco[2], Jesper Rasmussen[3],
and Jon Nielsen[3]

[1] Facultad de Ingeniería, Universidad de Ibagué, Ibagué, Colombia
{manuel.forero,sergio.herrera,
julian.avila}@unibague.edu.co
[2] Departamento de Ingeniería Industrial, Universidad de los Andes,
Bogotá, Colombia
[3] Department of Plant and Environmental Sciences, University of Copenhagen,
Copenhagen, Denmark

Abstract. *Cirsium arvense* is an invasive plant normally found in cold climates that affects cereal crops. Therefore, its detection is important to improve crop production. A previous study based on the analysis of aerial photographs focused on its detection using deep learning techniques and established methods based on image processing. This study introduces an image processing technique that generates even better results than those found with machine learning algorithms; this is reflected in aspects such as the accuracy and speed of the detection of the weeds in the cereal crops. The proposed method is based on the detection of the extreme green color characteristic of this plant with respect to the crops. To evaluate the technique, it was compared to six popular machine learning methods using images taken from two different heights: 10 and 50 m. The accuracy obtained with the machine learning techniques was 97.07% at best with execution times of more than 2 min with 200×200-pixel subimages, while the accuracy of the proposed image processing method was 98.23% and its execution time was less than 3 s.

Keywords: Automated weed classification · Machine learning ·
Deep learning · Image processing · Cereal crops

1 Introduction

The presence of *Cirsium arvense*, also known as Canadian thistle, and other types of weeds in organic cereal crops is a major concern in Nordic countries such as Norway and Denmark [2], primarily because they result in significant losses in crop efficiency, causing an average of 29.2% production losses worldwide if weed control is not applied [3]. Therefore, there is a need to identify areas with weeds so that farmers can take the appropriate actions. These weeds are usually controlled via the application of glyphosate before or after harvest [4], which can sometimes lead to the indiscriminate use of these chemicals, increasing production costs, soil depletion, and environmental contamination [5, 6].

© Springer Nature Switzerland AG 2019
R. Vera-Rodriguez et al. (Eds.): CIARP 2018, LNCS 11401, pp. 117–123, 2019.
https://doi.org/10.1007/978-3-030-13469-3_14

Site-specific weed management (SSWM) is a precision agriculture approach that refers to the variable application of weed control to minimize the use of herbicides [7]. Currently, different machine learning based methods are being implemented to detect specific areas of weed-growing cultures. For example, Gao et al. [8] implemented a method based on randomized forests and compared it to the K-nearest neighbors method to recognize weeds in corn crops using hyperspectral images and obtained accuracies higher than 93%. Image processing methods have also been used; Pérez et al. [9] detected broadleaf weeds by analyzing the colors and shapes to discriminate bottom vegetation and obtained better results than human experts. In a study focused on the detection of *Cirsium arvense* conducted by Sorensen [1], convolutional neural networks (CNNs) were implemented, obtaining accuracies higher than 97%, based on detecting the excess of green (ExG) characteristic of the weed.

In this study, we introduce a tool based on image processing that allows the easy and rapid detection of perennial weeds in cereal crops. To determine its efficiency, the results are compared to those produced by other popular techniques based on machine learning such as naive Bayes, descendant gradient, decision trees, nearest neighbors, neural networks, and support vector machine. Similarly, a comparative study was performed using previous results based on CNNs.

2   Materials

In this study, 26 photographs of cereal crops showing the presence of the *Cirsium arvense* (weed) plant, taken by a Canon PowerShot G15 camera with a size of 4000×3000 pixels, were used, among which 13 were taken at a height of 10 m and the rest were taken at a height of 50 m [1]. The images were cut from the original photographs to reduce the computational cost required by the process. A database of 800 samples of 5×5 pixels obtained from 20 of the images was constructed for use in the learning and adjustment of the machine learning based algorithms, as illustrated in Fig. 1. Half of the samples correspond to weeds (positive samples) and the rest to culture (negative samples). A total of 30 subimages of 200×200 pixels each (see Fig. 2) were obtained from the remaining six images and were used to validate and compare the methods.

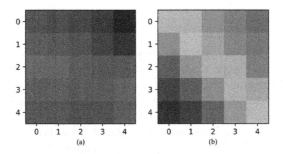

Fig. 1. Sample 5×5 pixel images used for the estimation and training of the machine learning algorithms: (a) weed and (b) crop images.

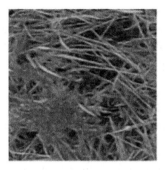

Fig. 2. Example of an image employed for the validation of the algorithms.

The study used an HP-2840 computer with 15.6 GB of memory, an Intel Xeon processor (R) CPU E5-2650v4 @ 2.20 GHz × 24, a NVIDIA Quadro P600 graphics card, and a Linux-Ubuntu operating system 16.04LTS. The machine learning algorithms were implemented in Python 2.7 using the OpenCV, Scikit-learn, NumPy, and Time releases. The image processing method was implemented using the free access software ImageJ.

3   Methods

A visual analysis of the photographs indicates that the RGB color space is not the most appropriate one for learning as it is difficult to recognize the areas where the weed is found, as shown in Fig. 3a. This observation was corroborated via a learning analysis with a reduced number of samples, where it was found that the accuracy was very low. Transforming the images into the Lab color space provides a better visual differentiation, particularly in channel a*, as shown in Fig. 3b.

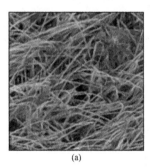
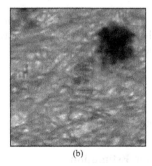

(a)   (b)

Fig. 3. Cereal crops: (a) original RGB image and (b) channel a* of the Lab color space.

To train the learning algorithms, 80% of the extracted data were used (600 samples of 5 × 5 pixels) for the estimation of the parameters. The remaining 20% of the extracted data were used to find the optimal values of each classifier according to the precision, as presented in Table 1. Finally, the classification was performed and the accuracies of the methods listed in Table 1 were evaluated using 30 validation images.

In Sorensen's original article [1], it is mentioned the areas where the weeds are found correspond to points where excess green is found, i.e., where the green intensity is very high; therefore, a processing technique was developed for images based on this idea. To find the areas where weeds are found, the green end areas are searched for in the photographs. To do this, a monochromatic image is obtained using the standard BT.601 given in Eq. 1 because it provides the image in gray based on the human vision model. Then, this image is subtracted from the green channel one. As shown in Fig. 4b, most of the image corresponding to the crop remains in the background and areas of extreme green are detected as objects of interest. Then, the next step is to binarize the image to isolate the pixels whose extreme green values are above a given value. It was empirically found that a value of 3 resulted in the best segmentation between the background and the object. As seen in Fig. 4c, some isolated pixels are also selected as part of the object; these pixels are produced by noise in the image. To eliminate them, morphological erosion is performed, so that the final image contains only the regions of interest. The resulting image is shown in Fig. 4d. The results obtained using this method were compared to those of the techniques listed in Table 1, and the precision provided by the algorithm was calculated, comparing the pixels of the images that were segmented manually and those that were chosen via the algorithms.

$$Y = 0.299R + 0.5876G + 0.114B \tag{1}$$

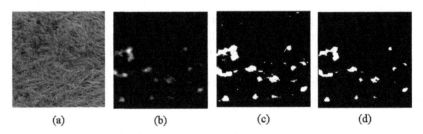

| (a) | (b) | (c) | (d) |

Fig. 4. Steps of the image processing method: (a) original RGB image, (b) result of the subtraction of the green channel from the grayscale image, (c) resulting binarized image, and (d) eroded image. (Color figure online)

4   Results

The results obtained for each of the analyzed algorithms are summarized below.

4.1   Parameter Estimation

Considering the selected parameters of interest and their qualitative or quantitative nature, the values shown in Table 1 were obtained, for which the analyzed learning techniques present better accuracies based on the estimation data.

Table 1. Parameters selected for the different machine learning algorithms.

Algorithm	Parameter	Value
Stochastic gradient descent	Loss function	Logarithmic
Decision trees	Number of samples per division	82
Nearest neighbors	Number of neighbors	11
Support vector machines	Kernel	Linear
Neural network	Number of neurons per layer	50

4.2   Classification

Once the parameters of interest for each of the analyzed algorithms were selected, we proceeded with the training and precision calculations. The times required to perform the training classification of the selected samples are shown in Table 2.

Table 2. Execution times and accuracy of the methods.

Times and accuracy required by the methods

Method	Import database and parameter estimation [s]	Training and classification [s]	Total [s]	General accuracy [%]
Image processing method	–	–	3	98.23
Naive Bayes Gaussian	3.571.061	0.923	3571.984	96.50
Stochastic gradient descent	3.571.061	0.826	3571.887	97.07
Decision trees	3.571.061	0.919	3571.980	96.09
K-nearest neighbors	3.571.061	9.875	3580.936	96.33
Support vector machines	3.571.061	78.966	3650.027	96.42
Neural network	3.571.061	14.950	3586.011	95.99

The accuracies generated by each of the studied algorithms are summarized in Table 2, along with Figs. 5 and 6, which show the operating characteristic curve of the receiver (ROC) for each of the analyzed methods and the white color demarcation of the areas in which the presence of weeds was detected in one of the images used for validation, respectively.

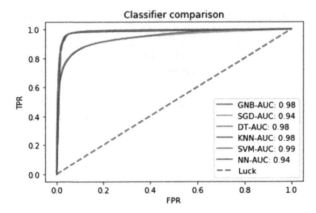

Fig. 5. Operating characteristic curve of the receiver (ROC) for the different classifiers.

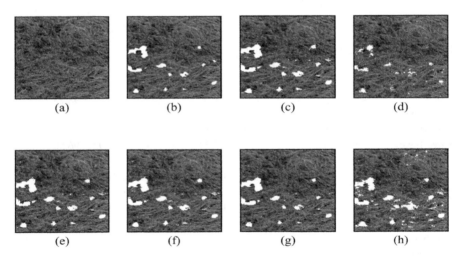

Fig. 6. Results obtained using the different methods: (a) original image, (b) image processing method, (c) Gaussian naive Bayes, (d) stochastic gradient descent, (e) decision trees, (f) nearest neighbors, (g) support vector machines, and (h) neural network.

5   Discussion

Table 2 show that the machine learning and image processing algorithms present similar results and comparable to the results obtained in [1], also can be observe that the execution times for algorithms Naive Bayes Gaussian, Stochastic Gradient Descent and Decision Trees are roughly equal. However, the method of image processing is computationally efficient because it does not require training and does not require a large amount of memory and computer resources. In addition, it presented the highest precision of the studied algorithms. Among the other methods, the SVM presented the highest precision, even though it requires a long analysis time. The Bayesian classifier, conversely, was the fastest algorithm and had a precision close to that of the SVM, making this case the best option for this type of method.

6 Conclusions

In this study, a new method was presented for the classification of *Cirsium arvense* based on image processing and was compared to other methods based on machine learning. Contrary to expectations, this new method is not only faster but also more accurate than the other methods because it does not require training and previous adjustments; therefore, a complete image can be directly processed and the classification can be performed with low execution times and computational cost. Similarly, it was confirmed that good image classification accuracy can be obtained using algorithms with a reduced level of complexity, such as the Stochastic Gradient Descent and Gaussian naive Bayes.

Therefore, the results show that, even though techniques based on machine learning are very powerful, methods based on image processing should not be forgotten and these methods can be combined with learning techniques to make the identification of patterns increasingly efficient when there are large amounts of information available and the basic principles of image theory can be used.

References

1. Sorensen, R.A., Rasmussen, J., Nielsen, J., Jorgensen, R.N.: Thistle detection using convolutional neural networks. In: EFITA 2017 Presentation, pp. 1–15 (2017)
2. Salonen, J., Hyvonen, T., Jalli, H.: Weeds in spring cereal fields in Finland - a third survey. Agric. Food Sci. Finland **10**(4), 347–364 (2001)
3. Dogan, M.N., Ünay, A., Boz, Ö., Albay, F.: Determination of optimum weed control timing in maize (Zea mays L.). Turk. J. Agric. Forest. **28**, 349–354 (2004)
4. Brandsæter, L.O., Mangerud, K., Helgheim, M., Berge, T.W.: Control of perennial weeds in spring cereals through stubble cultivation and mouldboard ploughing during autumn or spring. Crop Prot. **98**, 16–23 (2017)
5. Kataoka, T., Kaneko, T., Okamoto, H., Hata, S.: Crop growth estimation system using machine vision. In: Proceedings 2003 IEEE/ASME International Conference on Advanced Intelligent Mechatronics (AIM 2003), vol. 2, pp. b1079–b1083 (2003)
6. Åstrand, B., Baerveldt, A.J.: A vision based row-following system for agricultural field machinery. Mechatronics **15**(2), 251–269 (2005)
7. Shaw, D.R.: Remote sensing and site-specific weed management. Front. Ecol. Environ. **3**(10), 526–532 (2005)
8. Gao, J., Nuyttens, D., Lootens, P., He, Y., Pieters, J.G.: Recognising weeds in a maize crop using a random forest machine-learning algorithm and near-infrared snapshot mosaic hyperspectral imagery. Biosyst. Eng. **170**, 39–50 (2018)
9. Pérez, A.J., López, F., Benlloch, J.V., Christensen, S.: Colour and shape analysis techniques for weed detection in cereal fields. Comput. Electron. Agric. **25**(3), 197–212 (2000)

Hierarchical Graph-Based Segmentation in Detection of Object-Related Regions

Rafael Machado Ribeiro, Silvio Jamil Ferzoli Guimarães,
and Zenilton Kleber G. Patrocínio Jr.$^{(\boxtimes)}$

Computer Science Department, Pontifical Catholic University of Minas Gerais,
Belo Horizonte, MG, Brazil
rafaelmdribeiro@outlook.com, {sjamil,zenilton}@pucminas.br

Abstract. Object detection is an important task in computer vision. Recently, several unsupervised approaches have been proposed to cope with this problem in a category-independent manner. This work evaluates the adoption of a hierarchical graph-based segmentation along with an state-of-the-art method to detect object-related regions. A hierarchical segmentation approach produces a set of partitions at different detail levels, in a way that a coarser level can be obtained by a simple merge of finer ones. Experimental results show that our proposal obtains an increase of 11% in object detection rate.

Keywords: Object detection · Hierarchical image segmentation ·
Object segmentation · Object localization

1 Introduction

Recently, several models have been proposed to identify some categories of objects in images, such as face identification in digital cameras [13]. The difficulty of these approaches is that distinct models may be needed to identify different object classes. An idea to cope with this scenario is to create some strategy which is capable to identify image regions with a high probability of containing objects, *i.e.* object-related regions. According to [12], an approach to object detection should group pixels into uniform and homogeneous regions with respect to some characteristic(s) in a way that leads to the separation between the foreground objects and the background, making this task closely related to *figure-ground segmentation* and/or to *semantic image segmentation* [13].

Segmentation methods divide images into regions (or disjoint segments) that, in an ideal situation, are equivalent to (parts of) real objects portrayed by them. State-of-the-art methods to detect object-related regions generally depend on image segmentation [2,3,5]. In this work, we hypothesize that having an accurate segmentation method is essential for improving object detection rates. A hierarchical segmentation method generates multiple disjoint segments at different

This work received funding PUC Minas, CAPES (PVE 125000/2014-00), FAPEMIG (PPM 00006-16), and CNPq (Universal 421521/2016-3 and PQ 307062/2016-3).

R. Vera-Rodriguez et al. (Eds.): CIARP 2018, LNCS 11401, pp. 124–132, 2019.
https://doi.org/10.1007/978-3-030-13469-3_15

levels of detail (see Fig. 1 for an example). A coarse level of detail can be generated by simple merges of segments belonging to finer detail levels [9]. According to [8], a hierarchical method must respect two principles of multi-scale analysis: (i) causality principle, which states that a contour of a region on a given scale (or level of detail) k_1 must be present on any other scale $k_2 < k_1$; (ii) location principle, which says that contours of the regions should not change or deform when there is a change of scale. This work evaluates the adoption of the Hierarchical Graph-Based segmentation method (**hGB**) [9, 10] to compute ***Superpixel Straddling (SS) measure*** used in the state-of-the-art object detection approach proposed by [2]. We also evaluate the use of **SLIC** [1] (a state-of-the-art method to generate *superpixels*), since **SS measure** is intended to quantify the relationship between an object-related window and the *superpixels* intersected by it. The main contributions of this work are two-fold: (i) it shows that the use of hierarchical segmentation outperforms the non-hierarchical one; and (ii) it gives evidence that the use of a state-of-the-art method to generate *superpixels* does not seem to obtain the same improvement.

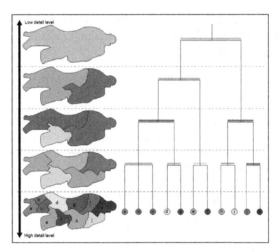

Fig. 1. Example of obtained result by a hierarchical image segmentation method.

The paper is organized as follows. Section 2 presents related works, while Sect. 3 describes *objectness measurement* in details. Section 4 presents concepts about hierarchical graph-based segmentation used in this work. Section 5 presents experimental results of our approach together with a comparative analysis. Finally, we draw some conclusions in Sect. 6.

2   Related Work

In [3], the authors use foreground and background seeds, which are group of pixels with a regular size. The input image is mapped onto a weighted graph. So, graph cuts are used with different parameters and seeds to obtain regions.

Each generated segment is ranked based a learned scoring function. Similarly, in [5], the method generates background and foreground segments which are then ranked. In [11], multiple segmentations are computed using the Graph-Based method (**GB**) [7] on different colour spaces. Afterwards, these segments are grouped and reported as object-related regions. Finally, in [2] the authors proposed a method which creates a random collection of windows over the image. Then, windows are scored and ranked based on a *objectness measurement*. Since this measurement is used in this work, it will be describe with more details in Sect. 3.

3   Objectness Measurement

In [2], the authors proposed a window score, named *objectness measurement*, which combines some measures in order to positively identify an object inside a given window. Several measures were investigated in [2], but the authors were able to demonstrate that the three most important are as follows.

Multiscale Saliency (MS): this is based on a saliency measure and analyzes the spectral residual of the FFT image. The saliency map I of image f is calculated (for each pixel p) using Eq. 1.

$$I(p) = g(p) * \mathcal{F}^{-1}[exp(\mathcal{R}(f) + \mathcal{P}(f))]^2 \tag{1}$$

in which $\mathcal{F}$ is the FFT, $\mathcal{R}(f)$ and $\mathcal{P}(f)$ are the spectral residual and the phase spectrum of image f, respectively; and g is a Gaussian filter. This calculation is done in different scales (see Fig. 2a) and for each color channel. For each scale s, Eq. 1 was used to calculate saliency $I_{MS}^s(p)$. Then, the saliency of a window w at scale s is calculated using Eq. 2.

$$MS(w, \theta_{MS}^s) = \sum_{\{p \in w \mid I_{MS}^s(S) \geq \theta_{MS}^s\}} \frac{I_{MS}^s(p) \times |\{p \in w \mid I_{MS}^s(p) \geq \theta_{MS}^s\}|}{|w|} \tag{2}$$

Color Contrast (CC): this measure calculates the dissimilarity between a window w and a surrounding window $Surr(w, \theta_{CC})$ which is bigger than w by a factor of θ_{CC} – see Eq. 3.

$$\frac{|Surr(w, \theta_{CC})|}{|w|} = \theta_{CC}^2 - 1 \tag{3}$$

The CC score is calculated by χ^2 distance between their LAB histograms h, as stated by Eq. 4.

$$CC(w, \theta_{CC}) = \chi^2(h(w), h(Surr(w, \theta_{CC}))) \tag{4}$$

Superpixel Straddling (SS): according to [2], a "bad" *superpixel* s_p (defined as a small region of uniform color or texture, that ideally preserves object boundaries) occurs when it straddles (surpasses) the borders of a window w. Thus, a window with fewer number of straddling *superpixels* should have a higher score. This score is calculated using Eq. 5.

$$SS(w, \theta_{SS}) = 1 - \sum_{s_p \in S(\theta_{SS})} \frac{min(|s_p \backslash w|, |s_p \cap w|)}{|w|} \tag{5}$$

in which $S(\theta_{SS})$ is the set of *superpixels* obtained using a segmentation method (the authors in [2] used **GB** method described in [7]) with a *"scale"* parameter θ_{SS}, $|s_p \backslash w|$ represents the area of s_p outside w, while $|s_p \cap w|$ stands for the area of s_p inside w.

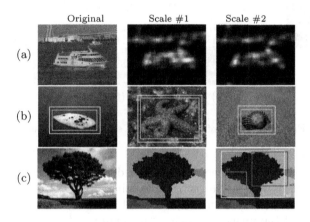

Fig. 2. Example of the three measures used: (a) **MS** (Multiscale Saliency); (b) **CC** (Color Contrast); and (c) **SS** (*Superpixel* Straddling). (Color figure online)

Learning the Parameters: in [2], using a supervised training, the best parameter values $\theta_{MS}^s, \theta_{CC}, \theta_{SS}$ related to each measure were calculated in order to maximize the object detection rate. Finally, several combinations of measures were tested, and the combination using all three measures described before (**MS+CC+SS**) has obtained the best object detection results.

4   Hierarchical Graph-Based Segmentation

According to [8], a hierarchical segmentation method must respect two principles of multi-scale analysis. Thus, hierarchical segmentation is able to maintain spatial and neighborhood information between segments, even when changing the scale [9]. Actually, in [9], the authors proposed a strategy for transforming a non-hierarchical method into a completely hierarchical one; and they have applied that approach to **GB** in order to obtained a new method called **hGB**, which is able to compute a hierarchy of partitions for all scales, as shown in Fig. 1. A comparison between **GB** and **hGB** segmentation results is shown in Fig. 3.

One can easily noticed that, for **GB** method [7], the number of regions does not decrease when scale parameter increases, neither contours of the regions are stable (see Fig. 3b–d). In contrast, **hGB** method [9,10] respects both causality and location principles (see Fig. 3e–g).

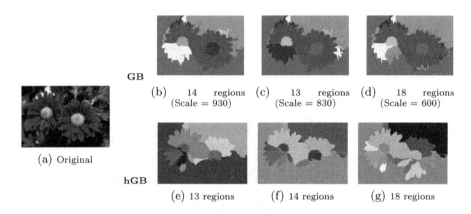

(a) Original

GB

(b)   14   regions
(Scale = 930)

(c)   13   regions
(Scale = 830)

(d)   18   regions
(Scale = 600)

hGB

(e) 13 regions

(f) 14 regions

(g) 18 regions

Fig. 3. Example of **GB** and **hGB** segmentation results.

In both methods, an image is transformed into an undirected graph $G = (V, E)$, in which V is a finite set (representing pixels) and E is a subset of $\{\{x, y\} \subseteq V \mid x \neq y\}$ (representing pixel neighborhood). To every tree T spanning the set V of the image pixels, to every map $w : E \mapsto \mathbb{N}$ that weights the edges of T and to every threshold $\lambda \in \mathbb{N}$, one may associate the partition $\mathcal{P}_\lambda^w$ of V induced by the connected components of the graph made from V and the edges with weight below λ. It is well known [4] that for any two values λ_1 and λ_2 such that $\lambda_1 \geq \lambda_2$, the partitions $\mathcal{P}_{\lambda_1}^w$ and $\mathcal{P}_{\lambda_2}^w$ are *nested* and $\mathcal{P}_{\lambda_1}^w$ is *coarser* than $\mathcal{P}_{\lambda_2}^w$. Hence, the set $\mathcal{H}^w = \{\mathcal{P}_\lambda^w \mid \lambda \in \mathbb{N}\}$ is a *hierarchy of partitions induced by the weight map* w.

The method **hGB** [9] does not explicitly produce a hierarchy of partitions, but instead produces a weight map L (scales of observations) from which the desired hierarchy $\mathcal{H}^L$ can be inferred on a given T. It starts from a minimum spanning tree T of the edge-weighted graph built from the image. In order to compute the scale $L(e)$ associated with each edge of T, **hGB** method iteratively considers the edges of T in a non-decreasing order of their original weights w. For every edge e, the new weight map $L(e)$ is initialized to ∞; then for each edge e linking two vertices x and y the following steps are performed:

(i) Find the region X of $\mathcal{P}_{w(e)}^w$ that contains x;
(ii) Find the region Y of $\mathcal{P}_{w(e)}^w$ that contains y;
(iii) Compute the hierarchical observation scale $L(e)$.

At step (iii), the *hierarchical scale* $S_Y(X)$ of X relative to Y is needed to obtain the value $L(e)$. Intuitively, $S_Y(X)$ is the lowest observation scale at which some sub-region of X, namely X^*, will be merged to Y. Then, the hierarchical scale $L(e)$ is simply set to:

$$L(e) = \max\{S_Y(X), S_X(Y)\}, \tag{6}$$

in which,

$$S_Y(X) = [Dif(X, Y) - Int(X)] \times |X| \tag{7}$$

with $Dif(X, Y)$ and $Int(X)$ defined (analogously to [7]). Thus, the *internal difference* $Int(X)$ of a region X is the highest edge weight among all the edges linking two vertices of X in MST; and the *difference* $Dif(X, Y)$ between two neighboring regions X and Y is the smallest edge weight among all the edges that link X to Y. Due to lack of space, additional details were omitted and the reader should refer to [9].

5   Experimental Results

In order to evaluate the adoption of **hGB** method [9] as a tool for solving object detection problem, we use the well-known PASCAL VOC 2007 dataset [6] with 20 object categories, which is also used in [2]. Similar to [2], during supervised training for obtaining parameter values, the *train+val* subsets were used and only images belonging to 06 categories (bird, car, cat, cow, dog, and sheep) were used, ignoring images marked as difficult. Therefore, 1,183 images from a total of 1,587 were selected for training. The **SS** measure was trained 03 times, *i.e.* one distinct training for each segmentation approach **GB**, **hGB** and **SLIC** in order to get the best θ_{SS} value for each one (for **GB** and **hGB**, θ_{SS} represents scale value used to obtain a partition; while, in **SLIC**, it is the number of *superpixels*).

During testing, the *test* subset of the dataset was used, selecting only images belonging to categories that were not used in training. According to [2], this is a way to show the effectiveness of the proposed approach. In addition, images marked as difficult have also been ignored during testing. Thus, 2,941 images from a total of 7,610 were selected. Since windows are chosen randomly for each new image, during tests, we use the same list of random windows to evaluate all combinations of measures for a given image.

Following the criterion adopted on PASCAL VOC 2007 challenge [6], if W and O represent the window area to be tested and the object area in the *ground-truth* image, respectively; an object appearing in the *ground-truth* image is considered covered if $|W \cap O|/|W \cup O|$ is greater than 0.5. To assess the results as in [2], we adopt the same test methodology. So, the evaluation was executed changing the number of random windows up to the limit of 1,000 windows; and the detection rate DR (*i.e.*, the percentage of objects covered by random windows) is calculated. The evaluation was executes 10 times; and average results are shown in Fig. 4, where the average DR values are presented for distinct combinations of measures as a function of the number of random windows (#WIN). The area under the curve (AUC) for each combination is also shown.

As one can see in the Fig. 4, the **hGB** method helps improving object detection rate when 100 or more windows are used. Despite of this, a big difference

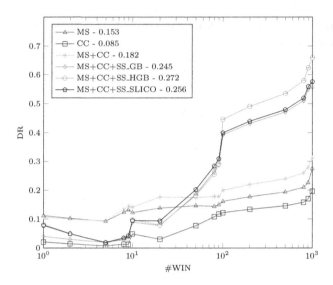

Fig. 4. Results – average DR × #WIN.

can be noticed when reaching 1000 windows, which could indicate that segments obtained by **hGB** (which respects causality and location principles) are more likely to have a positive impact on the result as the number of windows increases. In contrast, the use of **SLIC** method does not seem to have a significant impact on detection rate, when it is compared with **GB** for 100 or more windows.

As shown by AUC values, **hGB** outperforms both **GB** and **SLIC** by 11% and 6.25%, respectively. However, **hGB** (and also **SLIC**) presents a higher average execution time compared to **GB** – see Table 1.

Finally, a qualitative assessment indicates that **hGB** seems to be better for detecting more than one object in the same image. This can be seen in Fig. 5, where heatmaps are used to show the object probability distribution (warmer regions represent stronger evidence of object presence in the original image).

Table 1. Average execution time per image of each combination (in seconds).

Combination	Time (s)			
	#WIN = 1	#WIN = 10	#WIN = 100	#WIN = 1,000
MS	1.026	1.056	1.456	1.932
CC	0.970	1.151	1.443	1.777
MS+CC	1.697	1.935	2.203	2.966
MS+CC+SS_GB	2.163	2.251	3.360	4.132
MS+CC+SS_HGB	3.121	3.748	8.892	8.989
MS+CC+SS_SLIC	4.096	5.457	8.091	9.015

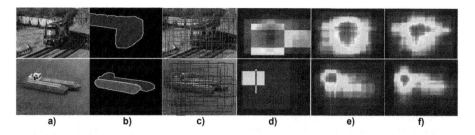

Fig. 5. Comparison between results: (a) original image; (b) ground-truth; (c) random windows over image; (d) heatmap for MS+CC+SS_GB; (e) heatmap for MS+CC+SS_SLIC; and (f) heatmap for MS+CC+SS_HGB.

6   Conclusion and Future Work

This paper proposed the use of a hierarchical graph-based segmentation to improve object detection. Experimental results have shown that the modified approach outperforms by 11% the previous state-of-the-art version, but with a high average execution time. When compared to a state-of-the-art method to generate *superpixels*, the modified approach consumes almost the same amount of time per image, still exhibiting an improvement of 6.25% in detection rate.

As future work, we plan to investigate the use of segments of different detail levels, to produce the best score for a current window. This could help dealing with partially occluded objects and with cluttered scenes.

References

1. Achanta, R., Shaji, A., Smith, K., Lucchi, A., Fua, P., Susstrunk, S.: SLIC superpixels compared to state-of-the-art superpixel methods. IEEE TPAMI **34**(11), 2274–2282 (2012)
2. Alexe, B., Deselaers, T., Ferrari, V.: Measuring the objectness of image windows. IEEE TPAMI **34**(11), 2189–2202 (2012)
3. Carreira, J., Sminchisescu, C.: CPMC: automatic object segmentation using constrained parametric min-cuts. IEEE TPAMI **34**(7), 1312–1328 (2012)
4. Cousty, J., Najman, L.: Incremental algorithm for hierarchical minimum spanning forests and saliency of watershed cuts. In: Soille, P., Pesaresi, M., Ouzounis, G.K. (eds.) ISMM 2011. LNCS, vol. 6671, pp. 272–283. Springer, Heidelberg (2011). https://doi.org/10.1007/978-3-642-21569-8_24
5. Endries, I., Hoiem, D.: Category-independent object proposals with diverse ranking. IEEE TPAMI **36**(2), 222–234 (2014)
6. Everingham, M., Van Gool, C., Williams, C., Winn, J., Zisserman, A.: The pascal visual object classes challenge (2007). http://host.robots.ox.ac.uk/pascal/VOC/voc2007/
7. Felzenszwalb, P.F., Huttenlocher, D.P.: Efficient graph-based image segmentation. IJCV **59**(2), 167–181 (2004)
8. Guiges, L., Cocquerez, J., Men, H.L.: Scale-sets image analysis. IJCV **68**(3), 289–317 (2006)

9. Guimarães, S.J.F., Kenmochi, Y., Cousty, J., Patrocínio Jr., Z.K.G., Najman, L.: Hierarchizing graph-based image segmentation algorithms relying on region dissimilarity: the case of the Felzenszwalb-Huttenlocher method. Math. Morphol. Theory Appl. **2**, 55–75 (2017)

10. Guimarães, S.J.F., Cousty, J., Kenmochi, Y., Najman, L.: A hierarchical image segmentation algorithm based on an observation scale. In: Gimel'farb, G., et al. (eds.) SSPR/SPR 2012. LNCS, vol. 7626. Springer, Heidelberg (2012). https://doi.org/10.1007/978-3-642-34166-3_13

11. van de Sande, K.E.A., Uijlings, J.R.R., Gevers, T., Smeulders, A.W.M.: Segmentation as selective search for object recognition. In: ICCV 2011, pp. 1879–1886 (2011)

12. Zhang, H., Fritts, J.E., Goldman, S.A.: Image segmentation evaluation: a survey of unsupervised methods. CVIU **110**(3), 260–280 (2008)

13. Zhang, X., Yang, Y.H., Han, Z., Wang, H., Gao, C.: Object class detection: a survey. ACM Comput. Surv. **46**(1), 10:1–10:53 (2013)

Dealing with Heterogeneous Google Earth Images on Building Area Detection Task

Cassio Almeida[1,2]([✉]), William Fernandes[1], Simone Barbosa[1], and Hélio Lopes[1]

[1] Departamento de Informática, PUC-Rio, Rio de Janeiro, Brazil
[2] ENCE-IBGE, Rio de Janeiro, Brazil
`cassio.almeida@ibge.gov.br`

Abstract. This paper proposes the use of a convolutional neural network in the building detection task, using as data source the high resolution heterogeneous Google Earth RGB images. This is a challenging task not only because it is necessary to build a training dataset, but also because the learning model has to respond well to the diversity of images taking into account a relatively small training dataset. We use images from Brazil that have a very diverse geography due to their continental dimension. In this case, Google Earth images are very heterogeneous and represent a great challenge. We use an adapted U-net and another convolutional neural network classification method recently proposed in the literature for solving this particular task. The use of U-net shows promising results.

Keywords: Convolution neural network · Image segmentation ·
Build detection

1 Introduction

The task of automatic object detection from satellite and aerial images is playing an increasingly important role in several remote sensing applications [4]. In particular, building detection [17] is considered a difficult task mainly because building areas and their surroundings have a high variability in color intensity values and complex attributes [7,11,13,15].

The methods proposed in the literature to solve the building detection task are mainly distinguished according to data source (LiDAR [3], aerial images [18], Google Earth images [22], etc) and classification method (active contours [15], textural features and Adaboost [2], convolutional neural networks [11,12], etc.).

This work aims to study the building detection task using RGB images. We use Google Earth (GE) images because they are freely and easily accessible. However, to deal with these images is very challenging since they show discrepancies, different brightness and shadows. Such characteristics occur mainly because they are acquired from different sources and with variation of the acquisition data, resolution and radiometric quality [9]. In particular, this work focus on GE images from Brazil. Considering the dimensions of this country, the GE

© Springer Nature Switzerland AG 2019
R. Vera-Rodriguez et al. (Eds.): CIARP 2018, LNCS 11401, pp. 133–140, 2019.
https://doi.org/10.1007/978-3-030-13469-3_16

images present a wide diversity of geographical aspects, besides the variation of image quality. These two facts make this particular building detection task much more difficult than with less diverse, higher quality images.

Several methods to detect buildings on GE images have been proposed recently [8,9,11,22]. In general, methods for solving the building detection task rely on segmentation and feature extraction [13,20]. Many solutions of these recent works evaluate a particular region on Earth [14]. Moreover, they still depend on handcrafted resources [4]. These facts limit applications in large scale, since it affects their generability to other domains. This paper focuses on methods that uses Deep Learning as a fundamental tool, which provides an alternative approach to automatically learn effective features from a training set. However, as Zhang et al. (2016) [21] and Karpatne et al. (2016) [13] note, there are still some interesting challenges to the use of Deep Learning to solve remote sensing tasks: (a) How to retain the representation learning performance on the Deep Learning methods with fewer adequate training samples and (b) How to cope with the complexity of remote sensing images, with large variance in both the backgrounds and the objects, which makes it difficult to learn robust and discriminative representations of scenes and objects with Deep Learning.

The U-net, proposed by Ronnenberger et al. [19] in 2015, was originally applied to the segmentation of biomedical images with excellent performance. We adapted the U-net to RGB images to be suitable for the building detection task, considering all the challenges cited above. We compare its results to the convolution neural network, the patch-based method proposed in [11].

The main contribution of this work is that we found a unique model with good performance for solving the building detection task in RGB images with large intra-class and background variation, and with a large variation in terms of image quality, while requiring only a small set of images for training. A secondary contribution is an annotated dataset composed of 126 annotated images from Brazil, which is publicly available at [1].

The remainder of this paper is organized as follows. Section 2 discusses relevant related work. Section 3 briefly introduces the two CNN architectures tested in this paper. Section 4 presents the dataset. Section 5 describes the test procedure and results. Finally, Sect. 6 concludes this paper by making some final remarks and suggesting future work.

2   Related Work

Since this study is dedicated to automatic building detection of Google Earth images using Deep Learning, we mainly focus on previous work related to building detection on Google Earth images, and on the use of Deep Learning in remote sensing tasks.

In recent years, Convolutional Neural Networks (CNNs) have been widely used to solve different remote sensing tasks. Zhang et al. [21] proposed a CNN that is composed of multiple feature-extraction stages, each one comprising a sequence of a convolutional layer. Related to the building detection task, we find a number of related works. Zhang et al. [22] proposed a deep CNN-based method to detect suburban buildings from GE images from the Yunnan province, China. Guo et al. [11] used supervised machine learning methods, including a CNN model, to identify village buildings using GE images from the Kaysone area, Laos. Also, Kampffmeyer et al. [12] used different deep learning approaches for land cover mapping in urban remote sensing, and tested them on a set of aerial images from Vaihingen, Germany.

According to Kampffmeyer et al. [12], there are two main approaches to segment images by the use of CNNs. The first one, called the *patch-based* approach, predicts every pixel in the image by looking at the small enclosing region (patch) of the pixel. The second one, called the *pixel-based* approach semantic segmentation using end-to-end learning [16], classifies each pixel in the image using a downscaling-upscaling approach. Guo et al.'s work [11] is an example of the patch-based approach, and Kampffmeyer et al.'s [12] is an example of the pixel-based approach.

The main classifiers that use CNNs are patch-based. Recent models, such as ALexNET, ZFNet, GoogleLeNet, VGGNet and RESNet, have been built to improve the performance on the ImageNet dataset, which is composed by millions of patches with 224×224 pixels associated to thousands of categories [10].

A survey on object detection in optical remote sensing images can be found in [4]. In particular, [17] proposed a survey for building detection. Finally, we recommend [21] for a survey on Deep Learning for remote sensing data.

3 CNN Architecture

This section describes the two CNN architectures that we tested in this work. The first one was proposed in [11], henceforth called the Patch-based Classification Model (PCM). The second one is the U-net proposed in [19].

The PCM is a simple network. It is composed by two convolutional layers, each one followed by a pooling layer with stride 2 for downsampling. Here we include a dense layer with one neuron at the end to perform the classification. The first convolutional layer contains six 5×5 filters and the second contains 12 4×4 filters. It considers as an input an RGB patch of size 18×18 pixels.

The U-net is only composed by CNN layers, with no dense layers at the end. It has two paths, a contracting path (left side) and an expansive path (right side). Each path has 4 steps of CNN. On the contracting side, each step consists of two sequential applications of: 3×3 convolutions filter, a rectified linear unit (ReLU) operation, and a 2×2 max-pooling operation for downsampling. On the other side of the U-net, each step of the expansive path is composed of an upsampling layer followed by a 2×2 convolution (blue box), a concatenation with the corresponding cropped feature map from the contracting path, and two 3×3 convolutions. Finally, a 1×1 convolution is used at the final layer to map each 64-component feature vector to the desired number of classes. For more details about the U-net see [19].

We selected the CNN model proposed by Guo et al. [11] to compare with the U-net because it is a recent work used to solve building detection on GE images, which is exactly our task.

(a)   (b)   (c)   (d)   (e)   (f)

Fig. 1. Some images from the dataset: diversity of the urbanist characteristics and image quality. (a) N.Mutum; (b) Trairí; (c) RJ-Botafogo;(d) RJ-B.Sucesso; (e) RJ-Tijuca; (f) Rio Bonito

4   Dataset

In this work we annotated 126 RGB images, each one with approximate 900 × 900 pixels. These images have been collected from GE by the use of the Google Maps API. We selected 12 location distributed in different regions of Brazil. They are distant in many hundred kilometers and they represent in a very concise and simplified way the diversity of image scenarios in this huge country. Figure 1 presents six examples of the collected images. They illustrate the diversity of the urbanist characteristics in the country and the variability of image quality. To each image in this dataset, we manually added a layer that indicates, in binary form, where there is a building or not. This annotated dataset is available in [1].

We divided the 126 annotated images in two subsets: one with 114 for training and validation and other with one images of each one of 12 selected areas in Brazil, for testing.

The PCM and the U-net models require input data in different formats. For PCM, we generated approximately 600,000 patches of 18×18 pixels from the 126 RGB images joined with the classification layer. To each patch a binary label was assigned indicating whether there is a building in that patch or not. For the U-net, we use a moving window strategy (with a stride of 150 pixels) to extract 772 images of size 572×572 pixels from the 126 RGB images and their corresponding classification layer.

5   Test Procedure and Results

We implemented the PCM and the U-net models in python with Keras [5]. We executed the training process of each model in an Intel i7 CPU with 64 GB of RAM and with an NVidia Titan X GPU. Each model were trained in numbers of epochs sufficient to have the best prediction performance without evidence of overfitting. This evaluation was performed comparing performance using F1 statistic, in the

Table 1. PCM and U-net model prediction statistics in the test dataset, using pixel by pixel evaluation, in the format *mean (standard deviation)*.

Model	Precision	Recall	F1-score
PCM - Patch	68.1% (15.1%)	87.6% (11.0%)	75.1% (11.7%)
PCM - Pixel	46.5% (15.1%)	80.3% (11.6%)	57.2% (14.5%)
U-net	80.5% (7.7%)	85.6% (9.1%)	82.6% (6.6%)

training and validation data set. For the PCM model training phase we executed 250 epochs in 2.7 h. For the U-net model training phase we executed 450 epochs in about 45 h. It is important to record here that we used the image generator functionality from Keras to augment our training examples. For each image in each epoch, we applied a random transformation not only to prevent overfitting, but also to improve the model performance [6]. More precisely, we applied vertical flips, horizontal flips, and scaling ranging from 0.9 to 1. In the results below, the prediction value in the PCM model refers to the 18×18 patch classification. The prediction result can be evaluated by comparing it with the truth classification layer either patch by patch or pixel by pixel, which results in different performance values. In the training and validation process, we use patch by patch comparison for the PCM model and pixel by pixel comparison for the U-net model. The measures for evaluation were Precision, Recall e F1-score.

A positive classification means value 1 ("has building") in the classification layer. Table 1 shows the results for the test dataset using patch by patch and pixel by pixel evaluation for the PCM, and pixel by pixel evaluation for the U-net. We selected 6 images from these locations to illustrate the results.

In the training and validation phases the U-net model produced better results, with F1-score = 93.9% in the validation against 86.6% for the PCM model. In the test phase (see Table 1), the results obtained by the PCM model using pixel by pixel evaluation are very similar to those reported by Guo et al. [11], which runs the model on a village in Laos: *Precision* = 41.9%; *Recall* = 94.0%; F1-score = 58.0%. However, the PCM model produced worse results than the U-net model. The mean precision with PCM was 68.1% using the patch by patch evaluation and 46.5% using the pixel by pixel evaluation, which means that the PCM made several false positive predictions. Figures 2c and a exemplify the PCM predictions with several false positive areas. On these two images the PCM model precision are 38.3% and 59.9% (patch by patch evaluation), respectively (as one can see in Table 2).

We notice that when the images have a low density of building areas, the performance of the PCM shows worse results when compared with the U-Net, since it generates several false positives (see Figs. 2a and c for the PCM and Figs. 2b and d for the U-net). The precision of the PCM model for the images in Figs. 2g and e are 71.3% and 57.0% respectively, using pixel by pixel evaluation. In these images that have high density building areas, one can observe that the PCM model predicted all streets as building areas. The relative high precision in

Table 2. Aggregated prediction statistics for 12 locations in the test dataset.

Image	Model	Precision	Recall	F1-score
N. Mutum - MT	PCM-Pixel	38.5	78.7	51.3
	U-net	83.8	66.8	74.2
RJ (Botafogo)	PCM-Pixel	57.0	90.5	69.7
	U-net	81.9	94.9	87.9
RJ (B.Sucesso)	PCM-Pixel	71.3	89.0	79.1
	U-net	93.7	93.0	93.3
RJ (Tijuca)	PCM-Pixel	58.2	90.0	70.7
	U-net	82.6	98.2	89.7
Rio Bonito - RJ	PCM-Pixel	50.1	71.9	58.8
	U-net	75.7	87.8	81.2
Trairí - CE	PCM-Pixel	17.9	77.0	28.9
	U-net	73.2	80.8	76.6

RJ-B.Sucesso-PCM is due to the high density of buildings in the image. In those test images, we could observe that the errors were probably due to the PCM model classifying a 18×18 patch. As a patch could partially include building areas, the PCM model would generate false positives, wrongly classifying streets and green areas as buildings. The image of RJ-Botafogo-U-net (Fig. 1c) shows a region with high buildings, parking areas, and shadows. These artifacts generated false positive areas in the result of both algorithms (see Figs. 2e and f). In images that have a medium level of building density, for example in residential area, the PCM model (see Figs. 2i and k) still present high incidence of false positives. However, the brightness contrast in these images also generates false positive and false negative areas. Both PCM and U-net generate more false negatives in images with high brightness.

We observe in Table 1 that U-net shows a good mean F1-score of 82.6%, with a low standard deviation of 6.6%, considering all images in the test dataset. Figures 2b and h illustrate the good precision of the U-net on these test images. However, we notice that the lowest U-net recall was 66.8% for the Nova Mutum area (Fig. 2b). This indicates a high occurrence of false negatives, which are mainly concentrated on the object boundaries. We can also observe that in the images in Fig. 2 the streets and green area are well identified. Incorrect classifications have usually occurred in areas with high concentration of buildings, Figs. 2e and f, due to higher occurrence of shadows in these cases. However, in the prediction by PCM, Fig. 2g and i, we verified a great incidence of false positives on the streets. Considering the high density of constructions, this difference is not evident in the statistics in Table 2. In these examples, the U-net F1-scores vary between 74.2% and 93.3% and PCM-Pixel F1-scores vary between 28.9% and 79.1%. This indicates that the U-net model shows to be quite robust, considering the high variability on the building characteristics, the different regions backgrounds, and the different levels of quality of the images.

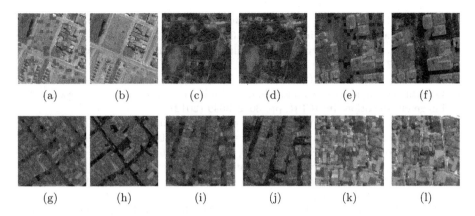

Fig. 2. Prediction output in different building density area. Green pixels represent True Positives, red pixels represent False Positives, and yellow pixels represent False Negatives. (a) N.Mutum-PCM; (b) N.Mutum-U-Net; (c) Trairí-PCM; (d) Trairí-U-Net; (e) RJ-Botafogo-PCM; (f) RJ-Botafogo-U-Net; (g) RJ-B. Sucesso-PCM; (h) RJ-B. Sucesso-U-Net; (i) RJ-Tijuca-PCM; (j) RJ-Tijuca-U-Net; (k) Rio Bonito-PCM; (l) Rio Bonito-U-Net (Color figure online)

6   Conclusions

In this work we found a unique model with good performance in solving the building detection task. It is relevant considering that we have used a single model to perform the task in a dataset with large intra-class and background variation, and also with a large variation in terms of image quality. Moreover, the results were obtained using a small set of training data. This annotated data is also a contribution of this work. Thus, we can conclude that U-net adapted to RGB images is a very promising net architecture to deal with the challenges of using Deep Learning to solve build detection tasks. In the future, we plan to increase the dataset to include more regions in order to achieve better generalization and precision.

Acknowledgements. We gratefully acknowledge the support of NVIDIA Corporation with the donation of the GPU used for this research. We would also like to thank Google Earth and their partners for the images utilized in this study. We also thanks CAPES and CNPq for their partial support.

References

1. Almeida, C.F.P., Fernandes, W.P.D., Barbosa, S.D.J., Lopes, H.: Using U-net to identify building areas on Google earth images from Brazil - annotated images (2017)
2. Cetin, M., Halici, U., Aytekin, Ö.: Building detection in satellite images by textural features and Adaboost. In: 2010 IAPR Workshop on PRRS, pp. 1–4. IEEE (2010)

3. Chen, L., Zhao, S., Han, W., Li, Y.: Building detection in an urban area using lidar data and quickbird imagery. IJRS **33**(16), 5135–5148 (2012)
4. Cheng, G., Han, J.: A survey on object detection in optical remote sensing images. ISPRS **117**, 11–28 (2016)
5. Chollet, F., et al.: Keras (2015). https://github.com/fchollet/keras
6. Cireşan, D., Meier, U., Schmidhuber, J.: Multi-column deep neural networks for image classification. In: ICPR, pp. 3642–3649 (2012)
7. Dornaika, F., Moujahid, A., El, Y., Ruichek, Y.: Building detection from orthophotos using a machine learning approach: an empirical study on image segmentation and descriptors. Expert Syst. Appl. **58**, 130–142 (2016)
8. Ghaffarian, S., Ghaffarian, S.: Automatic building detection based on Purposive FastICA (PFICA) algorithm using monocular high resolution Google Earth images. ISPRS **97**, 152–159 (2014)
9. Guo, J., Liang, L., Gong, P.: Removing shadows from google earth images. Int. J. Remote Sens. **31**(6), 1379–1389 (2010)
10. Guo, Y., Liu, Y., Oerlemans, A., Lao, S., Wu, S., Lew, M.S.: Deep learning for visual understanding: a review. Neurocomputing **187**, 27–48 (2016)
11. Guo, Z., Shao, X., Xu, Y., Miyazaki, H., Ohira, W., Shibasaki, R.: Identification of village building via google earth images and supervised machine learning methods. Remote Sens. **8**(4), 271 (2016)
12. Kampffmeyer, M., Salberg, A.B., Jenssen, R.: Semantic segmentation of small objects and modeling of uncertainty in urban remote sensing images using deep convolutional neural networks. In: CVPRW, pp. 1–9. IEEE (2016)
13. Karpatne, A., Jiang, Z., Vatsavai, R.R., Shekhar, S., Kumar, V.: Monitoring land-cover changes: a machine-learning perspective. IEEE GRSM **4**(2), 8–21 (2016)
14. Längkvist, M., Kiselev, A., Alirezaie, M., Loutfi, A.: Classification and segmentation of satellite orthoimagery using CNN. Remote Sens. **8**, 329 (2016)
15. Liasis, G., Stavrou, S.: Building extraction in satellite images using active contours and colour features. IJRS **37**(5), 1127–1153 (2016)
16. Long, J., Shelhamer, E., Darrell, T.: Fully convolutional networks for semantic segmentation. In: CVPR, 07–12 June 2015, pp. 3431–3440 (2015)
17. Mishra, A., Pandey, A., Baghel, A.S.: Building detection and extraction techniques: a review. In: Computing for Sustainable Global Development, pp. 3816–3821 (2016)
18. Quang, N.T., Thuy, N.T., Sang, D.V., Binh, H.T.T.: An efficient framework for pixel-wise building segmentation from aerial images. In: SoICT, pp. 282–287. ACM (2015)
19. Ronneberger, O., Fischer, P., Brox, T.: U-net: convolutional networks for biomedical image segmentation. In: Navab, N., Hornegger, J., Wells, W.M., Frangi, A.F. (eds.) MICCAI 2015. LNCS, vol. 9351, pp. 234–241. Springer, Cham (2015). https://doi.org/10.1007/978-3-319-24574-4_28
20. Yang, Y., Newsam, S.: Bag-of-visual-words and spatial extensions for land-use classification. In: Proceedings of the 18th SIGSPATIAL International Conference on Advances in Geographic Information Systems, pp. 270–279. ACM (2010)
21. Zhang, L., Zhang, L., Kumar, V.: Deep learning for remote sensing data. IEEE Geosci. Remote. Sens. Mag. **4**(2), 18 (2016)
22. Zhang, Q., Wang, Y., Liu, Q., Liu, X., Wang, W.: CNN based suburban building detection using monocular high resolution Google earth images. In: IGARSS, pp. 661–664. IEEE (2016)

Evaluation of Scale-Aware Realignments of Hierarchical Image Segmentation

Milena M. Adão, Silvio Jamil Ferzoli Guimarães,
and Zenilton K. G. Patrocínio Jr.[✉]

Computer Science Department, Pontifical Catholic University of Minas Gerais,
Belo Horizonte, MG, Brazil
milena.adao@gmail.com, {sjamil,zenilton}@pucminas.br

Abstract. A hierarchical image segmentation is a set of image segmentations at different detail levels. However, objects may appear at different scales due to their size or to their distance from the camera. One possible solution to cope with that is to realign the hierarchy such that every region containing an object is at the same level (or scale). In this work, we explore the use of regression to predict the best scale value for given region, which is then used to realign the entire hierarchy. Experimental results are presented for two different segmentation methods; along with an analysis of the adoption of different combination of mid-level features to describe regions.

Keywords: Hierarchical image segmentation ·
Alignment of hierarchy · Regression · Random forest · Neural network

1 Introduction

In the last two decades, a huge amount of multimedia data has been stored and made available through the Internet, which has attracted attention from research community to multimedia processing and analysis and, more specifically, to computer vision. Recent research results have pointed out that scale-awareness seems to be helpful in improving final results in many computer vision tasks [6, 11–13]. Even though Deep Convolutional Neural Networks (DCNNs) have improved the performance of computer vision systems, they still face some challenges including the existence of objects at multiple scales [5].

The adoption of a hierarchical approach which incorporates information from multiple scales is an alternative to deal with this issue. And, since segmentation is one of the first step involved in almost every computer vision task, the use of a hierarchical segmentation method has helped improving results for different tasks [3, 15, 16]. Specifically in image context, a hierarchical image segmentation

This work received funding from PUC Minas, CAPES (PVE 125000/2014-00), FAPE-MIG (PPM 00006-16), and CNPq (Universal 421521/2016-3 and PQ 307062/2016-3).

© Springer Nature Switzerland AG 2019
R. Vera-Rodriguez et al. (Eds.): CIARP 2018, LNCS 11401, pp. 141–149, 2019.
https://doi.org/10.1007/978-3-030-13469-3_17

is a set of image segmentations at different detail levels in which the segmentations at coarser detail levels can be produced from simple merges of regions from segmentations at finer detail levels [10].

Hierarchical segmentation methods [2,10] have been successfully used. These methods create a hierarchy of partitions that can be represented as a tree (Fig. 1). Moreover, the final results can be represented as an Ultrametric Contour Map (UCM) [1], which allows to obtain a particular segmentation (at a given observation scale) through a simple thresholding (Fig. 2). The hierarchies are typically computed by an unsupervised process that is susceptible to under-segmentation at coarse levels and over-segmentation at fine levels. Thus, objects (or even parts of the same object) may appear at different scales due to their size or to their distance from the camera. To cope with that one may explore the use of non-horizontal cuts [8,9]. Another possible solution is to flatten the hierarchy into a single non-trivial (or non-horizontal) segmentation, such as in [17].

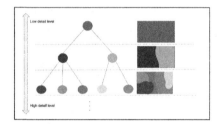

Fig. 1. Example of obtained result by a hierarchical image segmentation method.

In [7], the authors proposed to modify the final result of a hierarchical algorithm by improving its alignment, *i.e.*, by trying to modify the depth of the regions in the tree to better couple depth and scale and, therefore, putting (almost) all objects (and their parts) at the same level (or scale). To do that, they first train a regressor to predict the scale of regions using mid-level features. Then, they create a set of regions that better balance between over and under-segmentation, named *anchor slice*. Finally, the original hierarchy is realigned using the *anchor slice*, *i.e.*, adjusting the hierarchy such that every region in the *anchor slice* is at the same level (or scale) – see Fig. 3.

Fig. 2. Example of obtained result by a hierarchical image segmentation method: (left) original image; and (right) Ultrametric Contour Map (UCM).

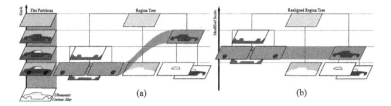

Fig. 3. Example from [7] showing the realignment of a hierarchical image segmentation: (a) original hierarchy; and (b) realigned hierarchy.

In this work, we explore the use of regression to predict the best scale value for given region, which is then used to realign the entire hierarchy. In our assessment, we used two different hierarchical image segmentation methods: **gPb-owt-ucm** [2] and **hGB** [10]. The main contributions of this work are: (i) impact analysis of a learning strategy on prediction of scale values for distinct hierarchical methods; and (ii) evaluation of the use of different combination of mid-level features to describe regions.

The paper is organized as follows. Section 2 describes the hierarchical segmentation methods used. In Sect. 3, we present the realignment approach for hierarchies. Section 4 presents experimental results. Finally, we draw some conclusions in Sect. 5.

2   Hierarchical Image Segmentation

There is a rich literature of hierarchical image segmentation. But here, in the following, we only describe the hierarchical methods used in this work: **gPb-owt-ucm** [2] and **hGB** [10].

Method gPb-owt-ucm. A widely-used state-of-the-art hierarchical segmentation method proposed in [2]. Discriminative features are learned for local boundary detection and spectral clustering is applied to it for boundary globalization. Afterwards, a hierarchical segmentation is built by exploring the information on the contour signal. The authors of [2] proposed a variant of the watershed transform, named Oriented Watershed Transform (OWT), for producing a set of initial regions from contour detection output. Then, an UCM is generated from the boundaries of these initial regions.

Method hGB. According to [10], a hierarchical segmentation should be able to maintain spatial and neighborhood information between segments, even when changing the scale. Thanks to that, one can compute the hierarchical observation scales for any graph, in which the adjacent graph regions are evaluated depending on the order of their merging in the fusion tree. The core of **hGB** [10] is the identification of the smallest scale value that can be used to merge the largest region to another one while guaranteeing that the internal differences of these merged regions are greater than the value calculated for smaller scales.

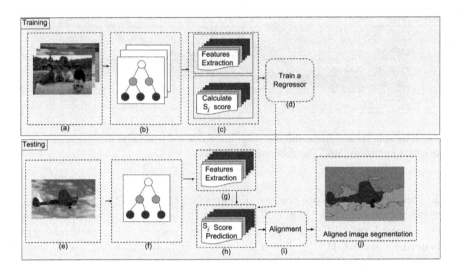

Fig. 4. Realign approach.

Starting with simple regions representing single image pixels, **hGB** is able to produce a hierarchy of partitions for the entire image. It has been successfully applied not only to image segmentation [10], but also to several other tasks, such as: video segmentation [16]; video summarization [3]; and video cosegmentation [15].

3   Realignment Approach

The realignment approach used in this work is illustrated in Fig. 4. First, a set of training images (Fig. 4a) is used to produce the corresponding set of hierarchies (Fig. 4b) using **gPb-owt-ucm** [2] or **hGB** [10]. Then, all regions belonging to training hierarchies are described with a set of features (see Sect. 3.1) and have their S_i scores (Eq. 1) calculated (Fig. 4c). These data is used to train a regression method (Fig. 4d). During testing, for each test image (Fig. 4e) the corresponding hierarchy is produced (Fig. 4f); and features are computed for every region (Fig. 4g). These features are used with the trained regressor to predict the best scale value (using S_i scores) for each region (Fig. 4h). Finally, the predicted scores/scales are used to realign (see Sect. 3.3) the original hierarchy (Fig. 4i), which is used to produce a final segmentation (Fig. 4j).

3.1   Features Extraction

The mid-level features were extracted from all regions of each hierarchy. Similar to [7], the chosen features were the following:

- **Graph partition properties:** cut, ratio cut, normalized cut, unbalanced normalized cut;

- **Region properties:** area, perimeter, bounding box size, major and minor axis lengths of the equivalent ellipse, eccentricity, orientation, convex area, Euler number;
- **Gestalt properties:** inter- and intra-region texton similarity, inter- and intra-region brightness similarity, inter- and intra-region contour energy, curvilinear continuity, convexity.

We have also explored features to encode **color properties**, such as color mean, and color histogram. Color-related features are calculated for each channel (in RGB color space) and histograms are generated with 04 bins per channel (in RGB color space). More details about these features could be found in [4].

3.2 Training and Predicting

A regression forest (with 100 trees) was trained using all regions R_i from each hierarchy. For each region R_i, its corresponding *ground-truth* region G_i is identified and used to calculate S_i score by Eq. 1.

$$S_i = \frac{|G_i| - |R_i|}{\max(|G_i|, |R_i|)} \tag{1}$$

in which $|R_i|$ and $|G_i|$ represent the size of region R_i and of its corresponding *ground-truth* region G_i, respectively. Similar to [7], the most-overlapping human-annotated segment is taken as the corresponding *ground-truth*. When S_i score is a negative value, it indicates that the region R_i is under-segmented, while a positive value stands for over-segmented (and, 0 for properly segmented). In order to describe the region properties, all features described before were extracted. In this step, regions whose area is less than 50 pixels were excluded.

After training the regression approach, they are used to make prediction. For that, the same set of features were extracted from all regions belonging to each hierarchy generated for the test subset and used to predict the best scale value.

3.3 Alignment of Hierarchical Image Segmentation

Following [7], each node belonging to a hierarchy should be labeled as: -1, 0, and $+1$ indicating under-, properly- and over-segmented, respectively. This could be done solving a problem that penalizes two cases: (i) segments in the group of under-segmented with positive scores; and (ii) segments in the group of over-segmented with negative scores. The resulting problem can be solved via dynamic programming. The *anchor slice* consists of regions labeled as 0.

After that, a local linear transform (the same used in [7]) is performed on the UCM corresponding to the hierarchy, and the *anchor slice* is aligned to scale value of 0.5 (for the convenience and later use).

Table 1. Average results for regression with random forest.

	SC ↑		PRI ↑		VI ↓		F_b ↑	
	ODS	OIS	ODS	OIS	ODS	OIS	ODS	OIS
gPb-owt-ucm w/no-alignment	0.59	0.65	0.83	0.86	1.69	1.48	0.73	0.76
gPb-owt-ucm w/alignment (c+gr+s)	0.58	0.64	0.82	0.85	1.75	1.49	0.69	0.76
gPb-owt-ucm w/alignment (c+s)	0.55	0.61	0.79	0.83	1.81	1.58	0.69	0.74
hGB w/no-alignment	0.43	0.62	0.74	0.80	2.34	1.88	0.49	0.50
hGB w/alignment (c+ge+gr+s)	0.38	0.53	0.75	0.81	2.45	1.89	0.50	0.50
hGB w/alignment (ge+gr+s)	0.39	0.53	0.74	0.81	2.45	1.89	0.50	0.50
hGB w/alignment (c+s)	0.43	0.62	0.74	0.80	2.34	1.88	0.49	0.50

4   Experimental Results

In order to evaluate the realignment of hierarchies generated by **gPb-owt-ucm** [2] and **hGB** [10], we use the BSDS500 dataset [2], which includes 500 images (200 for training, 100 for validation, and 200 for testing). As segmentation evaluation measures, we adopted: (i) Segmentation Covering (SC); (ii) Probabilistic Rand Index (PRI); (iii) Variation of Information (VI); and (iv) F-measure for boundary (F_b); all four computed at Optimal Dataset Scale (ODS) and Optimal Image Scale (OIS) – see [14] for a review of these measures and scales. Note that for all measures a large value is better, except for VI.

Average results obtained for regression made with random forest are shown in Table 1. In that table, 'c' stands form color based features (such as color mean and color histogram), 's' is used to represent region shape features (such as area, perimeters, etc.), 'gr' stands for graph features (such as cut, ratio cut, etc.), and 'ge' is used to represent gestalt features (such as texton similarities, brightness similarities, etc.). For **gPb-owt-ucm**, the realignment exhibits a improvement in average VI score when a set of color, graph and shape features is used, while for **hGB**, there is no difference in any metric (on average). But a closer look in some specific final results may help us understanding better those results.

In Figs. 5 and 6, we illustrate some examples in which the realignment of original hierarchies produces quite interesting results when the scale is set to 0.5 (which corresponds to the *anchor slice*). For **gPb-owt-ucm**, in Fig. 5(a) the results are showed without the realignment, while Fig. 5(b) illustrates the realigned results obtained. One can easily see the improvements related to SC, PRI, and VI measures. But this has some negative impact on F_b scores obtained by **gPb-owt-ucm**, specially for second example – see Fig. 5(b).

Similarly, for **hGB**, in Fig. 6(a) the results are showed without the realignment, while Fig. 6(b) illustrates the realigned results obtained. Again, it is easy to verify the improvements related to SC, PRI, and VI measures. But the main difference is that F_b scores obtained by **hGB** are not affected in this case. That could explain the decrease in average F_b scores in the realigned results for **gPb-owt-ucm** shown at Table 1.

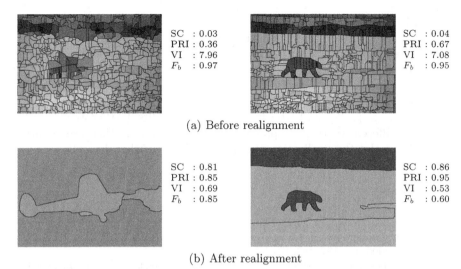

(a) Before realignment

(b) After realignment

Fig. 5. Examples of segmentations results before and after the realignments by using **gPb-owt-ucm** for computing the hierarchy.

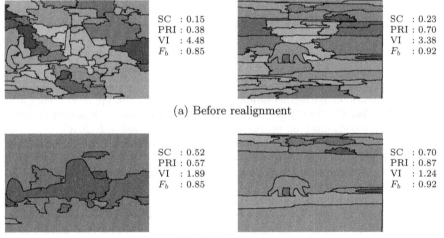

(a) Before realignment

(b) After realignment

Fig. 6. Examples of segmentations results before and after the realignments by using **hGB** for computing the hierarchy.

5   Conclusion

In this work, we explored the use of regression to predict the best scale value for given region, which is then used to realign the entire hierarchy.

Experimental results are presented for two different segmentation methods; along with an analysis of the adoption of different combination of mid-level features to describe regions.

For **gPb-owt-ucm**, the realignment exhibits a improvement in average VI score when a set of color, graph and shape features is used, while for **hGB**, there is no difference in any metric (on average). But a closer look in some specific final results seems to indicate that the realignment of hierarchies generated by **gPb-owt-ucm** has some negative impact on F_b scores, while this is not observed for hierarchies produced by **hGB**.

In order to improve and better understand our results, further works involve training of different regression approaches and adoption of other segmentation methods; and also the application of our proposal to another datasets.

References

1. Arbelaez, P.: Boundary extraction in natural images using ultrametric contour maps. In: Conference on Computer Vision and Pattern Recognition Workshop, CVPRW 2006, pp. 182–182. IEEE (2006)
2. Arbelaez, P., Maire, M., Fowlkes, C., Malik, J.: Contour detection and hierarchical image segmentation. IEEE TPAMI **33**(5), 898–916 (2011)
3. Belo, L.S., Caetano, C.A., Patrocínio Jr., Z.K.G., Guimaãres, S.J.F.: Summarizing video sequence using a graph-based hierarchical approach. Neurocomputing **173**, 1001–1016 (2016)
4. Carreira, J., Sminchisescu, C.: Constrained parametric min-cuts for automatic object segmentation. In: IEEE CVPR 2010, pp. 3241–3248. IEEE (2010)
5. Chen, L.C., Papandreou, G., Kokkinos, I., Murphy, K., Yuille, A.L.: Deeplab: semantic image segmentation with deep convolutional nets, atrous convolution, and fully connected CRFs. IEEE TPAMI **40**(4), 834–848 (2018)
6. Chen, L.C., Yang, Y., Wang, J., Xu, W., Yuille, A.L.: Attention to scale: scale-aware semantic image segmentation. In: IEEE CVPR 2016, pp. 3640–3649 (2016)
7. Chen, Y., Dai, D., Pont-Tuset, J., Van Gool, L.: Scale-aware alignment of hierarchical image segmentation. In: IEEE CVPR 2016, pp. 364–372 (2016)
8. Cousty, J., Najman, L.: Morphological floodings and optimal cuts in hierarchies. In: IEEE ICIP 2014, pp. 4462–4466 (2014)
9. Guiges, L., Cocquerez, J., Men, H.L.: Scale-sets image analysis. IJCV **68**(3), 289–317 (2006)
10. Guimarães, S.J.F., Kenmochi, Y., Cousty Jr., J., Z.K.G.P., Najman, L.: Hierarchizing graph-based image segmentation algorithms relying on region dissimilarity: the case of the Felzenszwalb-Huttenlocher method. Math. Morphol. Theory Appl. **2**, 55–75 (2017)
11. Hao, Z., Liu, Y., Qin, H., Yan, J., Li, X., Hu, X.: Scale-aware face detection. In: IEEE CVPR 2017, pp. 1913–1922 (2017)
12. Jie, Z., Liang, X., Feng, J., Lu, W.F., Tay, E.H.F., Yan, S.: Scale-aware pixelwise object proposal networks. IEEE TIP **25**(10), 4525–4539 (2016)
13. Li, J., Liang, X., Shen, S., Xu, T., Feng, J., Yan, S.: Scale-aware fast R-CNN for pedestrian detection. IEEE Trans. Multimed. **20**(4), 985–996 (2018)
14. Pont-Tuset, J., Marques, F.: Supervised evaluation of image segmentation and object proposal techniques. IEEE TPAMI **38**(7), 1465–1478 (2016)
15. Rodrigues, F., et al.: Graph-based hierarchical video cosegmentation. In: Battiato, S., Gallo, G., Schettini, R., Stanco, F. (eds.) ICIAP 2017. LNCS, vol. 10484, pp. 15–26. Springer, Cham (2017). https://doi.org/10.1007/978-3-319-68560-1_2

16. Souza, K.J.F., Araújo, A.A., Patrocínio Jr., Z.K.G., Guimarães, S.J.F.: Graph-based hierarchical video segmentation based on a simple dissimilarity measure. PRL **47**, 85–92 (2014)
17. Xu, C., Whitt, S., Corso, J.J.: Flattening supervoxel hierarchies by the uniform entropy slice. In: IEEE ICCV 2013, pp. 2240–2247 (2013)

3D SfM as a Measuring Technique for Human Body Transformation

Alessandro Marro$^{(\boxtimes)}$, Stefan Wiesen, Max Langbein, and Hans Hagen

TU Kaiserslautern, Kaiserslautern, Germany
marro@rhrk.uni-kl.de
https://hci.uni-kl.de/

Abstract. The tracking of fat loss as well as muscle gain has always been one of the most important steps during a person's fitness journey. It does not only motivate to continue practicing exercises, but also helps to develop specific workout plans to enhance particular body parts of athletes. Structure for Motion (SfM), unlike other reconstruction techniques, produces acceptable results from low-quality inputs. This makes the method applicable for ubiquitous equipment like a smartphone camera, while still being scalable to professional environments with proper equipment. In order to track overall body transformation, we propose a photogrammetry workflow employing SfM, reproducibly generating a model of the human body in different stages of a fitness plan. For visualization, we do a mesh alignment step followed by a comparison between the reconstructed body models of the subject, resulting in color-mapped meshes. Following this workflow the transformation of specific body regions can be analyzed in detail, only using consumer hardware.

Keywords: Body transformation · SfM · Photogrammetry

1 Introduction and Related Work

Simple indicators of health condition and fitness level are changes in human body shape. They motivate people physically and psychologically. Some of the methods tracking body transformations are targeted to internal changes, like fat loss and muscle gain [4]. Others measure body shape, including volumes and dimensions, to track external body transformations. *3D Body Scanners* (3D-BS) were used by the clothing market and *3D Photonic Scanners* (3D-PS) in medical clinics to take volumetric measurements of the human body [6,8,9]. They have shown high validity and reliability. However, most of this equipment is too expensive for general consumers, like personal trainers, nutritionists and coaches. Simpler measurements, such as skinfold thickness (SF) and body mass index (BMI) are also used, but their outcome is a crude index of the body shape and can not differentiate fat and lean mass. For further readings, Wells et al. [7] discuss about the different techniques for measuring body composition.

© Springer Nature Switzerland AG 2019
R. Vera-Rodriguez et al. (Eds.): CIARP 2018, LNCS 11401, pp. 150–158, 2019.
https://doi.org/10.1007/978-3-030-13469-3_18

Table 1. Comparison of different techniques from best (green) to worst (red)

	SF/BMI	3D-BS	3D-PS	Our Method
Cost				
Accessibility				
Accuracy				
Level of Detail				
Speed				

The Problems can be summarized in difficulties such as expense, access to hardware and portability, single variable to describe the body and lack of visual outcome to represent the changes to the body. *Our Proposed Solution* uses SfM employed in a photogrammetry pipeline to reconstruct, up to a scale factor, the subject's body as a 3D model, which is later on rescaled to real world scale and aligned to previous reconstructions. As a result, one can analyze the physical progress made at specific body parts. Figure 1 shows the outcome of the whole process as well as each performed stage. SfM has been used previously as main method of reconstruction by known research projects [2,3,5], and since then it has become widely used by commercial softwares. Due to the method's concept of taking several photos of a still scene in different time steps, static objects are reliably rebuilt. However, when applied to subjects that change their shape or move relatively to the scene, aberrations occur. One solution to that problem are layers of cameras which are synchronized to shoot at the same time, but this is expensive due to the number of cameras needed. Our solution is to help the

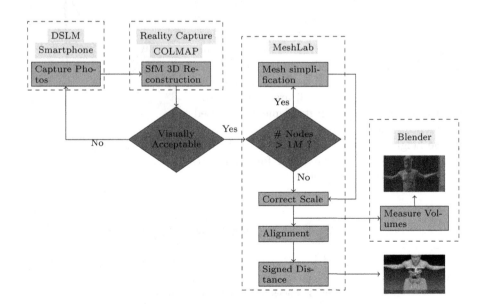

Fig. 1. Data processing pipeline

subject to keep a relaxed pose under the constraint of having all important body parts non-occluded, using two tripods as a handle. According to Wells [9] most of the unsuccessful scans made with 3D-PS were primarily due to body movement, or software inability to reconstruct the desired shape, which also applies to our method. Table 1 shows a basic comparison between the cited methods.

2   Method

2.1   Image Capturing

Location and Situation. Before we got to our final location we tested several areas with varying sizes, heights and light conditions. The best overall results were achieved in a subsection of the gym at TU Kaiserslautern with the dimensions $18 \times 27 \times 9$ m (LxWxH). The area is well illuminated by three tent-shaped skylights and light gray walls, floor (with colored stripes) and ceiling (Fig. 2).

Fig. 2. Dimensions and location

In general it should be considered to have a comparable uniformly lit environment, with enough space to walk around the person. Furthermore a closed, quiet area with no movement in the background and no other people in scene is important.

Base and Reference. The base (Fig. 3) consists of a flat PVC flooring sized 2×1.5 m, with fixed positions for tripods (used as handles) and cubes, size-corresponding footprints and markers composed of facing letters (A & T, U & W) surrounding the footprints. Two 3D-printed 10 cm wide cubes, color-coded and textured with shapes and letters, as shown in Fig. 4, are added as size reference. The base and all its elements are used as reference. The distances between every tripod leg, the height of the handles (1.40 m each) and the cubes are known values used for scaling to have a true-sized reconstruction.

Fig. 3. Base plane, cubes, markers and tripods

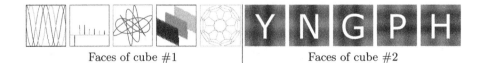

Faces of cube #1   Faces of cube #2

Fig. 4. Faces of the reference cubes

Test Person and Position. The test person stands upright on the fixed marked positions for their feet with stretched arms grabbing the handles (tripods). The tripods define the height (z-coordinate) and the local position (x- and y-coordinate) of the hands. In this position the hands and arms are accurately located in the same way for every capturing process. It is necessary to stretch the arms in a way like this to capture all parts of the upper body and the arms. The T-shaped stand provides a straight back and horizontal stretched arms. This position generates a little tension on the shoulder and arm muscles by rising up the arms and grasping the prepared handles. It is important that the test person is not moving during the capturing process, excluding subconscious body functions like breathing, blinking etc. This relative comfortable and mostly relaxed posture and the controlled environment are necessary.

Camera Position and Movement. The capturing process should be done as fast as possible to have a minimum of movement of the test person. To generalize it: the lower the capturing time and the lower the movement of the person, the higher the reconstruction quality.

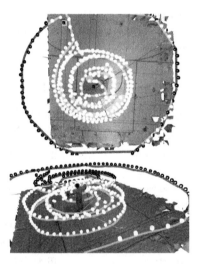

Considering this we developed a routine for the capturing process. All images are shot in portrait format. The following numbers are representative for the work with the DSLM camera from Table 2. The first set of images (around 50–60 pictures) need to be captured in a wide circle with a radius of ≈6 m around the test person with equal distances from the lower/upper end of the subject to the image border. The focus should be fixed at the center of the upper body. This set is needed to capture the whole setup and to match fur-

Fig. 5. Camera positions for capturing, top and side view

ther detail images to the body. The second set is needed to get more detailed images, starting with a turn in chest level with a ≈2–3 m distance around the person. After completing this turn the camera is risen in a overhead position (≈40–50 cm above) so that the test person and the base are visible. After every full turn around the subject the height decreases so that the camera positions are spherically arranged with the person in center. This second step should produce around 230 to 270 pictures. Now the base plane and the cubes with the lower body of the person are captured, so that the person can start relaxing the upper body. The focus is set to automatic continuous mode and the camera release is programmed to shoot every second to have an overlap of >60% and an angle of ≈15 between two consecutive images. In total it takes between 360 s and 440 s to take all pictures. The test person is not allowed to move 300 s to 380 s. The instructions defined are the ones that worked best in our condition, but they can vary depending on how much space is available. If the person keeps the T-shaped stand and all angles have being captured with sharp images, the reconstruction will be acceptable.

Doing the same process with a smartphone, the duration of the procedure and the amount of pictures taken will decrease, because of a wider angle of view of 78.3°. In total around 260 photos in about 370 s were produced. The test person needs to stand still for abound 300 s. The smartphone was released manually (Fig. 5).

Equipment. For the experiments we need besides the location, the base plane materials and tripods a smartphone and a camera for image capturing. The used devices are technically described in Table 2.

Table 2. Hardware specification smartphone and DSLM

Type	DSLM	Smartphone
Name	Fujifilm X-T1	Samsung Galaxy S7
Sensor size	23.6 mm × 15.6 mm (APS-C)	5.76 mm × 4.29 mm (IMX260 1/2.55″)
Sensor surface	368.16 mm^2	24.71 mm^2
Resolution	16.3 MP	12.2 MP
Pixel size	22.5865 μm^2	2.0255 μm^2
Lens (focal length)	27 mm f2.8	4.2 mm f1.7
Aperture	f6.4	f1.7 (fixed aperture)
ISO	3200	50-800 (auto ISO)
Full frame equivalent	41 mm f10	26.6 mm f10
Angle of view	55.7	78.3

2.2   3D Reconstruction Using SfM

SfM output quality depends on the quality of the images taken in the previous step. Images out of focus, with low resolution and/or high distortion, bad lighting conditions, among other factors will probably lead to low quality reconstructions, filled with strange artifacts, holes, deformations, i.e. unacceptable results. Even if a set of images with acceptable quality is used, other factors can lead to poor outputs, such as occluded body parts and lack of reference points. Therefore, the image capturing workflow explained previously need to be followed in order to achieve acceptable reconstructions. For this step, the paid software Reality Capture was used. For a reliable free alternative COLMAP could also be used. Since the proposal of this work is to present more accessible alternatives to expensive body measuring devices, Fig. 11 shows that it is possible to achieve acceptable results using COLMAP and a smartphone camera. Reality Capture performs the usual SfM pipeline. First, it starts by aligning images using detected features presented in each image and matched in between pairs. An initial model is then calculated as a sparse point cloud by triangulating matched feature points. After that, several optimizations

Fig. 6. Results: edge length cube: 99.92 mm - height of test person: 1806.5 mm

are done by calculating the error of reprojection of each triangulated point. At this moment, the positions of the cameras are recalculated based on the found error and the images are realigned. A dense point cloud can be estimated after the new optimized camera registration. The mesh is then extracted and textured (Fig. 6). To ensure precision, we measured the height of the person's model and the length of edges of the reference cube model in Meshlab [1], both resulting in 180.6 cm and 9.99 cm, respectively. In comparison to the real measurements of 180.4 cm and 10 cm, which were acquired using a measuring tape, the person's height was off by 0.2 cm and the cube's edge by 0.01 cm.

2.3   Mesh Alignment

A mesh alignment step is a mandatory process to prepare the models for comparison. The final result of the reconstruction step is a representative model of the subject on its local coordinate system. Therefore, each mesh is in its own orientation, position and scale. The alignment starts by rescaling the meshes to real world scale, that can be easily done due to our reference cubes. Having all meshes in the same scale, we perform a user-defined point alignment. It works by selecting a set of points in each of the models, which are used to estimate a transformation matrix containing translation and rotation information. The "moving mesh" is transformed to align the defined "fixed mesh". Figure 7 illustrates the whole procedure done in Meshlab. In our case, we defined the vertices of our reference cubes as the set of points, totalizing 16 points in each mesh. The alignment of the meshes is a hard task, especially when dealing with human or animal subjects, which are in constant movement. We tried to counteract this by posing the subject as relaxed as possible using the tripods, and always positioning his feet over the markers in every photo section. Otherwise, the alignment would not be practicable without independently modifying parts of the mesh, that would cause unacceptable changes in the body volumes and measurements.

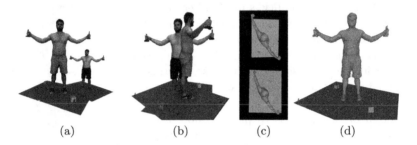

(a)   (b)   (c)   (d)

Fig. 7. Alignment process: (a) Before scale (b) After scale (c) Point-wise alignment (d) Aligned models

2.4   Comparison Between Models

In order to visualize in detail the body transformations, a per vertex computation of the signed distance between a mesh and a reference mesh is performed. The pair of vertices is defined by the closest distance. We also use Meshlab to perform this task (Fig. 8).

An *evaluation* of single reconstructions was performed by comparing the height and abdomen measurements of the subject's digital model to his real measurements, respectively (Figs. 6 and 10).

3   Results

On three different days, a mesh of the subject's body has been produced. The complete acquisition and processing of one model was done in around four hours. The resulting meshes are of good quality and the difference (shorts should not be considered) between two of those meshes is shown in Fig. 8. To demonstrate the results of the alignment and comparison procedure for larger body transformations, we modified two of the models using a

Fig. 8. Comparison

sculpting software. The second model (Fig. 9(b)) was mostly changed on the abdominal regions, adding more muscles and making the waist thinner. The third model (Fig. 9(c)) have even more developed muscles on the abdominal area, the trapezius muscle was enhanced near the neck and the biceps were also reworked. As visible in Figs. 9(d–f), these transformations are well represented in the visualizations.

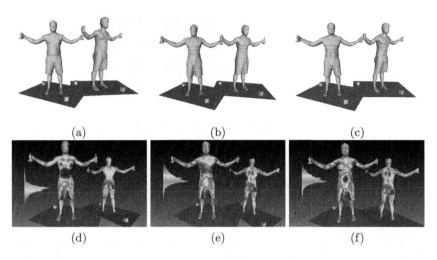

(a)   (b)   (c)

(d)   (e)   (f)

Fig. 9. Models and comparisons in millimeters (histogram). **(a)** Original model of day 1. **(b)** & **(c)** Modified models. Comparison **(d)** of (b) to (a), **(e)** of (c) to (b), **(f)** of (c) to (a)

4   Conclusion

We demonstrated that using SfM employed in a photogrammetry pipeline can be a tool to measure body transformations. As proposed, it is an easily accessible alternative to expensive commercial devices, yet scaling towards precision if using advanced equipment. For future works, we would like to test the concept with other subjects and build a framework to automatically handle all the performed operations. The *Contribution* of this work

Fig. 10. Blender measurements.

defines a workflow for measuring body transformation that works with accessible, ubiquitous equipment and free software, yet producing acceptable results (Fig. 11). It also scales in precision when using high-end devices and/or using commercial high-end softwares. The output of mutually aligned 3D meshes allows to employ all mesh-based analyses, including the measurement of volume and other dimensions (Fig. 10), but also more elaborated mesh comparison algorithms, and 3D visualizations. Finally, using these analyses and visualizations, a better understanding of the body transformation can be achieved.

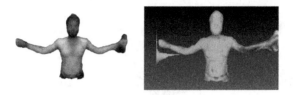

Fig. 11. Smartphone & COLMAP.

References

1. Cignoni, P., Callieri, M., Corsini, M., Dellepiane, M., Ganovelli, F., Ranzuglia, G.: MeshLab: an open-source mesh processing tool. In: Eurographics Italian Chapter Conference (2008)
2. Schaffalitzky, F., Zisserman, A.: Multi-view matching for unordered image sets, or "How Do I Organize My Holiday Snaps?". In: Heyden, A., Sparr, G., Nielsen, M., Johansen, P. (eds.) ECCV 2002. LNCS, vol. 2350, pp. 414–431. Springer, Heidelberg (2002). https://doi.org/10.1007/3-540-47969-4_28
3. Schonberger, J.L., Frahm, J.M.: Structure-from-motion revisited. In: Proceedings of the IEEE Conference on Computer Vision and Pattern Recognition, pp. 4104–4113 (2016)
4. Shaw, M.P., Robinson, J., Peart, D.J.: Comparison of a mobile application to estimate percentage body fat to other non-laboratory based measurements. Biomed. Hum. Kinet. **9**(1), 94–98 (2017)
5. Snavely, N., Seitz, S.M., Szeliski, R.: Photo tourism: exploring photo collections in 3D. ACM Trans. Graph. (TOG) **25**, 835–846 (2006)
6. Wang, J., Gallagher, D., Thornton, J.C., Yu, W., Horlick, M., Pi-Sunyer, F.X.: Validation of a 3-dimensional photonic scanner for the measurement of body volumes, dimensions, and percentage body fat–. Am. J. Clin. Nutr. **83**(4), 809–816 (2006)
7. Wells, J., Fewtrell, M.: Measuring body composition. Arch. Dis. Childhood **91**(7), 612–617 (2006)
8. Wells, J., Ruto, A., Treleaven, P.: Whole-body three-dimensional photonic scanning: a new technique for obesity research and clinical practice. Int. J. Obes. **32**(2), 232 (2008)
9. Wells, J.C., et al.: Acceptability, precision and accuracy of 3D photonic scanning for measurement of body shape in a multi-ethnic sample of children aged 5–11 years: the slic study. PLoS One **10**(4), e0124193 (2015)

Outlier Detection for Line Matching

Roi Santos$^{(\boxtimes)}$, Xose M. Pardo, and Xose R. Fdez-Vidal

Centro de Investigación en Tecnoloxías da Información (CiTIUS),
Universidade de Santiago de Compostela, Santiago de Compostela, Spain
{roi.santos,xose.pardo,xose.vidal}@usc.es

Abstract. Finding counterparts for straight lines over multiple images
is a fundamental task in image processing, and the base for 3D reconstruction methods using segments. This paper introduces novel insights
to improve the state-of-the-art unsupervised line matching over groups of
images, aimed to source geometrical relations for 3D reconstruction algorithms. Most of the line-based 3D reconstruction methods published are
ballasted as a consequence of sourcing the correspondences from matching methods that are not designed for this purpose. The repetitive line
patterns present in many man-made structure turns difficult to came up
with an outliers-free set of segment correspondences. The presented approach integrates an outliers detector based on 3D structure into a state
of the art line matching algorithm.

Keywords: 3D reconstruction · Line matching ·
Structure-From-Motion

1 Introduction

A line matching method comprises a set of algorithms which put in correspondence segments across different images showing common environment, elements,
or regions of interest. A 3D reconstruction, abstraction or spatial sketch based
on line correspondences is an estimation for the position of singular primitives
captured in several images, relative to the position of the camera that captured
them. The proposed approach is framed in the group of line matching methods
aimed for 3D reconstruction from pictures of objects built by humans, buildings,
urban structures, industrial elements or computer generated models.

The vast majority of the current approaches for feature matching are based
on 2D appearance. The point-based algorithms are the most common, including steerable filters [3], moment invariants [12], SIFT [9], and more recently
KAZE [1]. In order for these Structure-From-Motion (SfM) pipelines to generate
initial estimations for the location of points in 3D space, the feature points in
correspondence are triangulated [4].

Supported by Xunta de Galicia and European Union.

R. Vera-Rodriguez et al. (Eds.): CIARP 2018, LNCS 11401, pp. 159–167, 2019.
https://doi.org/10.1007/978-3-030-13469-3_19

The logical evolution of the environment abstraction from multiple views is to incorporate line segments. This addition for SfM provides geometrical information independently of described points. Beside, coplanar line primitives can be intersected to further reveal observed information.

Our proposed line matching algorithm is aimed for application altogether with 3D line based abstraction, and it takes advantage of a segment detection method using the Gaussian scale-space, an iterative voting algorithm running in groups of lines with the same structural distribution [10], and the robustness of an outliers rejection algorithm that uses 3D structures to discriminate potential outliers. The main hypothesis is that an outliers detection algorithm based on coplanar line intersections can improve the result of line matching algorithms. The inputs for the segment matching method are both the images and the intrinsic parameters of the camera, being the output the relation of matched lines among the images.

1.1 Related Work Based on Lines

A group of proposed solutions are exclusively based on the exploitation of 2D observations on the images. MLSD [15] encode a SIFT-like description of the different regions of a line into a description matrix. This method firstly avoids overlapped regions within the detections. In order to put each segment in correspondence in other images, the algorithm compares the mean and standard deviation of the gradient of the pixel values stored in the columns of the description matrix. LBD [17] improved MLSD by adding geometric constraints and an outliers topological filter. The method LJL [7] features another way to pick matching candidates, by finding detected line touching each other in one of their endpoints, and referred as junctions. Secondly, it compares intensity changes along the segments, the angle that the pair of segments is drawing, and the neighboring line junctions. Finally, sole lines that are observed close to a junction are grouped and become matching candidates to the segments detected close to the junction counterpart on other images. [16] uses appearance and structure for hypothesis generation, but adding feature point descriptor SIFT for outliers detection and removal. Another approach to match images pairwisely is by drawing convex hull around groups of close segments, and exploiting affine invariants in the hull [10]. The ratios of the areas of triangles drawn inside the hull are compared. This method has been improved for the proposed paper.

Another group of methods is employing homography constraints in order to obtain the relations. The method LJL [7] was evolved to VJ [8] by adding homography constraints from the intersections of the elongations of closely located pairs of line segments. The method LPI [2] shows how to team line detection with feature point detector and descriptor. It exploits the line-points affine invariants analogously to the methods of the first group, and takes advantage of the projective homography invariants by using four feature points beside the line. A recent evolution of this method is CLPI [5], that construct the line-points projective invariant on the intersections of coplanar lines. The drawback is that for both exploitations they had to suppose that all points and the line are coplanar, and often the lines resemble the limits of two planar surfaces.

The proposed outliers removal extension employs line based SfM to group lines according to their coplanarity. The method is described in Sect. 2. Section 3 exposes the quantitative comparison altogether with several other state of the art line matching methods. Section 4 goes through the conclusions.

2   Description of the Outlier Detection Method

The employed line matching algorithm is the same used in [10]. A matching outlier is a line whose counterpart in the other image does not correspond to the same human perceived segment. The purpose of the outlier detection algorithm

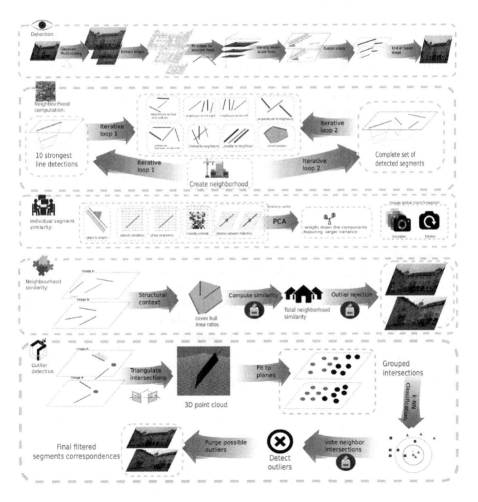

Fig. 1. Process of line matching

is to double-check the final set of line correspondences by performing geometric relations among their mutual intersections. A line crossing several intersections in different order than its counterpart is prone to be a matching outlier. The output of the algorithm is a set of line correspondences flagged as not trustworthy. The integration of the outlier detection in the line matching method is depicted in Fig. 1, and the outlier detection is shown in the lowest section of the figure.

Matched segments are extended to intersect neighbors within the image boundaries. This intersection and its counterpart in the other image are stored if they are apart from each segment a distance shorter than two times the length of the shortest originating segment, and the inner angle drawn by the intersecting lines is greater than $\pi/6$. These requirements are implemented because the location of intersections will carry the uncertainty just in the direction of both crossing lines.

The camera matrix $\boldsymbol{K}$ is provided in this problem, nevertheless the camera poses $\mathcal{P} = \{\boldsymbol{P}^i, \boldsymbol{P}^j\}$ are unknown. We have chosen to estimate them from a SfM pipeline based on KAZE [1] features, through the segments endpoints can be used for the same task. The Essential Matrix $\mathbf{E}$ is estimated by using the Five-Point Algorithm [13]. Having $\mathbf{E} = \boldsymbol{R}[\boldsymbol{t}]_\times$ and the set of 3D points $\mathcal{Y}$, the relative camera rotation and translation among the first pair of cameras $\boldsymbol{P}^j = \boldsymbol{K} \times [\boldsymbol{R}|\boldsymbol{t}]$ are estimated by using cheirality check [13] and discarding the triangulated points of $\mathcal{Y}$ that are not in front of the cameras.

The goal of the final stage is to divide the set of intersections and their counterparts on the other image $\mathcal{I} = \{\mathcal{I}^i, \mathcal{I}^j\}$ into groups according to their coplanarity: $\mathcal{I}^i = \{\mathcal{I}^i_1, \mathcal{I}^i_2, \cdots \mathcal{I}^i_V\}$ being V the total number of planes that were fitted taking 10 or more 3D estimations for the intersections. These new points obtained by intersecting lines are projected into space from the cameras, then the obtained 3D points are fit to planes. RANSAC is employed for the generation of hypothetical groups of these 3D points. A minimum threshold of 10 points is required to resemble a valid plane, and the 3D points that are not related to any plane after 100 iterations will be discarded for the rest of the algorithm. Therefore, each fitted plane gets related to a group of known corresponding intersections. Within each group, a search for neighboring coplanar intersections is performed by a k-Nearest-Neighbors (kNN) algorithm, as shown in the main loop of Algorithm 1. The relative 2D position of the intersections within these groups are checked and compared on both images. The output is a subset of $\mathcal{Y}$ comprised by the intersections that are most likely to be outliers. Any matched segment that originates four or more suspicious intersections is quarantined, as written in the last condition of the Algorithm 1.

Algorithm 1. Line matching outliers detection

Data: Set of matched lines $\{l_1^i, l_1^j\}, \{l_2^i, l_2^j\} \cdots \{l_L^i, l_L^j\}$ and their intersections on both
images $\{\mathcal{I}^i, \mathcal{I}^j\}$; K
Result: Most probable matching outliers $\mathcal{Z}$
initialization;
Selection criteria for intersections $\rightarrow \{\mathcal{I}^i, \mathcal{I}^j\}$ Linear Triangulation for $\{\mathcal{I}^i, \mathcal{I}^j\} \rightarrow$ 3D
points $\mathcal{Y}$, camera poses $\{P^i, P^j\}$
Fit $\mathcal{Y}$ to V different planes; $v \in V$
for $(\{c_{AB}^i, c_{AB}^j\}) \in \{\mathcal{I}_v^i, \mathcal{I}_v^j\}$ **do**
$\quad$ k-NN: Find 5 Nearest Neighbors of $\{c_{AB}^i, c_{AB}^j\} \rightarrow \{d^i, d^j\}$
$\quad d^i = \{d_1^i, d_2^i, d_3^i, d_4^i, d_5^i\} \in \mathcal{I}_v^i$
$\quad d^j = \{d_1^j, d_2^j, d_3^j, d_4^j, d_5^j\} \in \mathcal{I}_v^j$
$\quad$ **for** $u \in [1, 5]$ **do**
$\quad\quad$ **if** $Counterpart\ of\ d_u^i \in d^j$ **then**
$\quad\quad\quad$ $Score(\{c_{AB}^i, c_{AB}^j\}) = Score(\{c_{AB}^i, c_{AB}^j\}) + 1$
$\quad\quad$ **end**
$\quad$ **end**
$\quad$ **if** $Score(\{c_{AB}^i, c_{AB}^j\}) < 2$ **then**
$\quad\quad$ $\{l_A^i, l_A^j\}$ and $\{l_B^i, l_B^j\}$ are potential outliers and stored in $\mathcal{Z}$.
$\quad$ **end**
end

---

3 Experimental Results

The goal of this section is to quantitatively evaluate the proposed method with
the outliers rejection algorithm, against public datasets of pairs of images, altogether with other state-of-the-art line matching method. These public datasets
are selected looking for a fair compromise of scenes with and without texture,
transformations that include camera translation, moderate global rotations, and
changes in illumination conditions. The dataset "Castle" comprises the pictures
$\{0, 1\}$ of the dataset [11]. It features a viewpoint change with a camera rotation,
unveiling repetitive structures that can be tricky to identify. It was chosen in
order to evaluate the structural cohesion of the line neighborhoods. The rest of
datasets were obtained from [6]. The pairs "Low Texture" and "Textureless corri-
dor" portrait a complicated classical interior of a building, featuring few observed
long segments, and are selected to evaluate the resilience of the method to an
absence of texture information. "Outdoor light" and "Leuven" are included to
test changes of illumination in two different scenarios. Finally, "Drawer" combine a change of light exposition with a viewpoint change, and the scene feature
repetitive similar line patterns. The proposed method is quantitatively compared against the state-of-the-art methods addressed in the introduction of this
paper CLPI [5], LBD [17] and LJL [7]. The implementations for all the methods are provided by their respective corresponding authors, and its applicability
is restricted to pairs of views. These are executed by a notebook with Intel i7
3720QM Quad-Core and 16 GB DDR3. The average results are shown in Table 1.

The Ground Truth evaluation of the methods adopted an approach similar
to [14]: A line is marked as correct match if located 5 or less pixels apart from
the human-perceived line in the orthogonal direction, and if the difference in line
direction respect to the Ground Truth match of the counterpart is less than $5°$

of rotation. It has to be noted that for short atomic segments it is difficult to assess if the angle is correct compared to the Ground Truth. Despite the ratio of matching inliers compared to Ground Truth brings up meaningful information of the performance of each method, it is not possible to extract an unique global score to compare methods as a whole, as some can perform better in specific scenarios, and the characteristics of the extracted corresponding structures of lines will vary from one method to another.

The results show that the proposed method extracts line correspondences featuring longer, less fragmented lines that the competition. In addition these segments of are more similar in length to their respective counterparts compared with the results of other methods. Full length and non-fragmented matched lines profit when the method is applied to line-based 3D reconstruction from three or more images. Therefore, an average segment length has been extracted from all the results, and shown in Table 1. Besides this data, it is shown the total number of pixels covered by the matched segments on one image. Another measure that is crucial for the success of spacial reconstructions is the similarity between features in correspondence. This measure is valuable if the zoom global transformation is not featured in the image datasets, like in the ones included in this study. It is computed as the absolute value of the difference of lengths of the lines in correspondence, divided by the length of the longer segment. A better score is given to a result if both segments in correspondence are of similar length. This mark penalises correspondences of atomic short segments, as they return poor geometric information of the scene. The best average matched segment length is obtained by the proposed method, with an average of 105.1 pixels. It is distantly followed by the other methods, with resulting average lengths of less than two thirds the number of pixels covered by the segments put in correspondence by the presented method. This proposed method also returns the best average dissimilarity score of 0.14. This result shows a high advantage compared to the other methods in this mixed comparative, because the second on the line is CLPI [5] with an average dissimilarity score of 0.23. The last column in the Table 1 shows the processing times in seconds for each specific method on the evaluated dataset. The highest processing times were taken by LJL [7].

The main measure in the comparison is the number of correct correspondences. The overall score was computed as the ratio of inliers. The method CLPI [5] failed to return any correspondence from pairs of images featuring low texture and repetitive patterns. The method LJL [7] was the second on the line, just with downs in the images that present the segments more isolated. On the other hand, LBD [17] performed poorly in almost all the scenarios, showing a lackluster understanding of the structure cohesion. The goal of the proposed matching method is to obtain a result that serve as input for a 3D reconstruction pipeline based on straight lines. Therefore, it is critical that every human perceived line segment is represented by one sole complete entity. The most severe fragmentation was observed on the results of the methods LBD [17] and LJL [7].

The candidate outliers detection algorithm, based on coplanar line intersections, has been evaluated separately. Two examples of the matching outliers

Table 1. Quantitative comparison. Line matching accuracy and processing times.

Method	Inlier ratio	Avg. length	Avg. dissimilarity	Processing time (s)
CLPI	27.25%	67.3 pix.	0.23	39
LJL	85.91%	59.3 pix.	0.33	154
LBD	24.27%	66.6 pix.	0.40	2
Proposed	92.22%	105.1 pix.	0.14	39

detection are shown in Fig. 2. The first row of pictures is showing the matching results. The second row shows the suspicious line intersections. Lines crossing this point are flagged as possible outliers. These flagged segments are marked in the third row of pictures.

On the left hand side example, the outliers detection algorithm extracts the most noticeable segment correspondence outlier which is surrounded by lines visible on both images. There are other outliers on the figure, but the structural context is not enough the minimum number of neighbor intersections. On the right hand side of the figure it can be seen that from 13 suspicious line matches that are indicated, just 4 are actual correct matches, and 9 are real outliers.

The outliers detection algorithm is only applicable when there is a noticeable change of viewpoint among both images. Therefore results have been extracted for both datasets featuring perspective change. These results shown on Table 2 brings up to the validity of the proposed outliers detection method. The addition of the outliers detection improves the results on both datasets, without increasing the processing times.

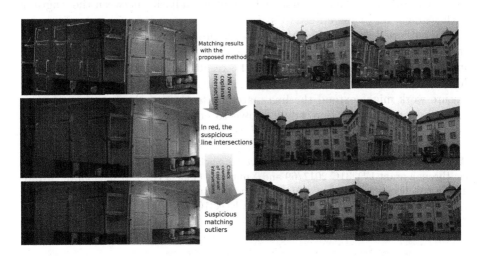

Fig. 2. Examples of the search for outliers using coplanar neighbor intersections.

Table 2. Average line matching accuracy and processing times from the results.

Dataset	Outliers detection	Correspondences	GT inliers	Inliers ratio	Processing time (s)
Castle	Without outliers detection	110	95	86%	46
	With outliers rejection	97	92	95%	46
Drawer	Without outliers detection	46	37	80%	20
	With outliers rejection	45	37	82%	20

4   Conclusions

The present paper proposes a method for multi-view matching of straight segments. The search for line counterparts starts by describing individual segments by the appearance properties and creating geometrical relations among groups of segments. The method has been quantitatively compared altogether with three different state-of-the-art methods, against public image datasets. The chosen images feature different man-made scenarios, including low texture, high texture with complex structures, changes of illumination, global rotations, camera viewpoint change, and a change of scale. The presented results show that the proposed method outperforms the competition against the segment matching inlier ratio, by returning longer and more structurally meaningful straight segment relations, and featuring noticeably higher similarity between the length of each segment and its counterpart's.

An outliers detection algorithm has been proposed to team with the method. It is rooted on the hypothesis that geometric relations between coplanar line intersections unveil inconsistencies in the resulting sets of correspondences. It has been proved advantageous by reducing the ratio of outliers in two datasets. Future work might extend the line matching to three and more views. In this case, the outliers detection would evolve to employ 3D planes obtained from advanced SfM based algorithms.

Acknowledgment. This work has received financial support from the Xunta de Galicia through grant ED431C 2017/69 and Xunta the Galicia (Centro singular de investigacin de Galicia accreditation 2016-2019) and the European Union (European Regional Development Fund - ERDF) through grant ED431G/08.

References

1. Alcantarilla, P.F., Bartoli, A., Davison, A.J.: KAZE features. In: Fitzgibbon, A., Lazebnik, S., Perona, P., Sato, Y., Schmid, C. (eds.) ECCV 2012. LNCS, vol. 7577, pp. 214–227. Springer, Heidelberg (2012). https://doi.org/10.1007/978-3-642-33783-3_16
2. Fan, B., Wu, F., Hu, Z.: Robust line matching through line-point invariants. Pattern Recognit. **45**(2), 794–805 (2012)
3. Freeman, W.T., et al.: The design and use of steerable filters. IEEE Trans. Pattern Anal. Mach. Intell. **13**(9), 891–906 (1991)
4. Hartley, R.I., Sturm, P.: Triangulation. Comput. Vis. Image Underst. **68**(2), 146–157 (1997)
5. Jia, Q., Gao, X., Fan, X., Luo, Z., Li, H., Chen, Z.: Novel coplanar line-points invariants for robust line matching across views. In: Leibe, B., Matas, J., Sebe, N., Welling, M. (eds.) ECCV 2016. LNCS, vol. 9912, pp. 599–611. Springer, Cham (2016). https://doi.org/10.1007/978-3-319-46484-8_36
6. Li, K., Yao, J., Lu, M., Heng, Y., Wu, T., Li, Y.: Line segment matching: a benchmark. In: 2016 IEEE Winter Conference on Applications of Computer Vision (WACV), pp. 1–9. IEEE (2016)
7. Li, K., Yao, J., Lu, X., Li, L., Zhang, Z.: Hierarchical line matching based on line-junction-line structure descriptor and local homography estimation. Neurocomputing **184**, 207–220 (2016)
8. Li, K., Yao, J., Xia, M., Li, L.: Joint point and line segment matching on wide-baseline stereo images. In: 2016 IEEE Winter Conference on Applications of Computer Vision (WACV), pp. 1–9. IEEE (2016)
9. Lowe, D.G.: Object recognition from local scale-invariant features. In: The Proceedings of the Seventh IEEE International Conference on Computer Vision, vol. 2, pp. 1150–1157. IEEE (1999)
10. Lpez, J., Santos, R., Fdez-Vidal, X.R., Pardo, X.M.: Two-view line matching algorithm based on context and appearance in low-textured images. J. Pattern Recognit. **48**(7), 2164 (2015)
11. Mikolajczyk, K., et al.: A comparison of affine region detectors. Int. J. Comput. Vis. **65**(1–2), 43–72 (2005)
12. Mindru, F., Tuytelaars, T., Van Gool, L., Moons, T.: Moment invariants for recognition under changing viewpoint and illumination. Comput. Vis. Image Underst. **94**(1), 3–27 (2004)
13. Nistér, D.: An efficient solution to the five-point relative pose problem. IEEE Trans. Pattern Anal. Mach. Intell. **26**(6), 756–770 (2004)
14. Verhagen, B., Timofte, R., Van Gool, L.: Scale-invariant line descriptors for wide baseline matching. In: 2014 IEEE Winter Conference on Applications of Computer Vision (WACV), pp. 493–500. IEEE (2014)
15. Wang, Z., Wu, F., Hu, Z.: MSLD: a robust descriptor for line matching. Pattern Recognit. **42**(5), 941–953 (2009)
16. Zeng, J., Zhan, L., Fu, X., Wang, B.: Straight line matching method based on line pairs and feature points. IET Comput. Vis. **10**(5), 459–468 (2016)
17. Zhang, L., Koch, R.: An efficient and robust line segment matching approach based on LBD descriptor and pairwise geometric consistency. J. Vis. Commun. Image Represent. **24**(7), 794–805 (2013)

Detection of Small Portions of Water in VIS-NIR Images Acquired by UAVs

Daniel Trevisan Bravo, Stanley Jefferson de Araujo Lima,
Sidnei Alves de Araujo[(✉)], and Wonder Alexandre Luz Alves

Informatics and Knowledge Management Graduate Program,
Universidade Nove de Julho (UNINOVE), São Paulo, SP, Brazil
{danieltbravo,saraujo,wonder}@uni9.pro.br,
stanleyjefferson@outlook.com

Abstract. Water bodies detection in aerial images is a problem widely known and explored in the literature. However, the detection of small portions of water in satellite images is not usual due to their low spatial resolution. With the increasing use of Unmanned Aerial Vehicle (UAVs), this task becomes feasible from the point of view of spatial resolution, but suffers from the problem of low spectral resolution of the acquired images. In this sense, we have new challenges in dealing with an old problem. In this work we proposed an approach that combines Visible (VIS) and Near Infrared (NIR) aerial images, commonly acquired by sensors used in UAVs, for providing an indicative index for detecting small portions of water. This approach also includes a scheme to reconstitute visible spectral bands contaminated by the use of a special lens, coupled to visible RGB camera, to provide NIR spectral band. Experimental results evidenced the good accuracy of proposed approach in mapping small portions of water such as pools and fountains in VIS-NIR images, even in the cases where there is only a thin layer of water.

Keywords: Aerial images · Small portions of water · UAVs ·
Spectral bands · Genetic Algorithm

1 Introduction

The recognition of water features from remote sensing images has been widely explored in the last decades. It is usually solved using specific spectral bands, captured by sensors carried on satellites, which facilitates the creation of spectral signatures to characterize the patterns assigned to water bodies well as other elements such as soil and vegetation. Thus, several indices have been developed for detecting different features such as NDVI (Normalized Difference Vegetation Index), NDWI (Normalized Difference Water Index) and WII (Water Indicator Index).

In the last decade, we can find several proposals addressing the detection of large water bodies, such as oceans, rivers and lakes. Among them, we can cite Portz et al. [10], Qiao et al. [11], Zhao et al. [12] and Colet et al. [4].

© Springer Nature Switzerland AG 2019
R. Vera-Rodriguez et al. (Eds.): CIARP 2018, LNCS 11401, pp. 168–176, 2019.
https://doi.org/10.1007/978-3-030-13469-3_20

The use of Unmanned Aerial Vehicle (UAVs), also known as drones, is an excellent alternative in remote sensing tasks, since they have the advantages of low cost, enabling flights closer to the ground and can produce high spatial resolution images. Thus, they have been widely used in recent years, especially in fields such as precision agriculture [2,6], geosciences [5,9] and health [1,3,7].

If on the one hand, the sensors carried by UAVs can acquire aerial images with high spatial resolution allowing the identification of small objects, on the other hand, they are very limited in terms of spectral resolution. Thus, new challenges have arisen such as the development of indices to characterize water, soil, vegetation and other elements, considering such limitations.

Murugan et al. [8] proposed an algorithm to select optimal subsets of spectral bands, aiming at the creation of indices indicative of water bodies and vegetation in satellite images. This algorithm makes an exhaustive search in 242 available spectral ranges, which may require a high computational cost. Nevertheless, the indices proposed for satellite-acquired images cannot be used in UAV-acquired images, since they have low spectral resolution and different ranges for the spectral bands.

Recently, Agarwal et al. [1] and Mehra et al. [7] addressed the identification of possible foci of the mosquito Aedes aegypti by means of image analysis, which were acquired by several types of devices, including UAVs' sensors. However, such works considers only the description of the scenes by means of a bag of features extracted from the images, without considering the detection of water features.

In fact, there are many approaches to detect large water bodies in satellite images. However, no work addressing the recognition of small portions of water in images acquired by UAVs was found in our literature review. One of the reasons may be the high cost of multispectral cameras with specific sensors, that can be used for detecting water. In this context, we explore in this paper how to detect small portions of water in aerial images acquired by a low-cost UAV equipped with a visible RGB camera adapted with a lens to capture the NIR spectral band. The procedures proposed in this work could, for example, make more robust the approach developed by Murugan et al. [8], which constitutes an important practical application for detecting foci of the mosquito Aedes aegypti.

2   Materials and Methods

For conducting the experiments, we acquired a dataset of 50 images from an area of the campus of São Paulo University – USP (central coordinate with latitude/longitude -23.5614311 and -46.7198984), located in the city of São Paulo/Brazil. We employed a DJI Phantom 3 professional UAV carrying on board a Sony EXMOR camera of 12.4 MP, capable of acquiring images of 4000×3000 pixels. Using a special lens (focal length 3.97 mm; aperture 2.8; 16 MP; 82°) this camera can provide the NIR spectral band. The flight was carried out 50 m above the ground, with a planned spatial resolution of 2.2 cm, on September 5, 2016 at 11:00 am, with a duration of approximately 20 min. We chose an area of the campus containing small portions of water discovered such as pools and fountains.

Each pixel of the acquired images is described as follows: $I\_NIR(x,y) = \{NIR(x,y), \tilde{G}(x,y), \tilde{R}(x,y)\}$, where NIR, $\tilde{G}$ and $\tilde{R}$ are the Near Infrared, green and red bands, respectively. It is important to highlight that the lens coupled in the RGB camera to obtain NIR has larger bandwidths and captures the data at different wavelengths causing nonlinear reflectance contamination in the bands G and R. Thus, we denote these contaminated bands as $\tilde{G}$ and $\tilde{R}$.

Since this contamination causes imprecision in the computation of indices indicative of water that depend on these bands, we proposed a procedure to reconstitute them using a Multilayer Perceptron Artificial Neural Network (MLP-ANN). In other words, we employed this procedure to generate an RGB image from I_NIR. To train the MLP-ANN, we also acquired 5 images from the same area of the USP using the RGB camera without the NIR lens, maintaining the same UAV flying parameters. An image of this second dataset is represented as: $I\_VIS(x,y) = \{R(x,y), G(x,y), B(x,y)\}$, where R, G and B are the visible bands red, green and blue. Such images were correlated with NIR images, using an image registration operation, to compose 5 pairs VIS-NIR from which we extracted the training set.

Finally, a Genetic Algorithm (GA) was designed to produce an optimized indicative index of water (OIIW), which is useful to filter pixels representing small portion of water in the images.

The experiments described in this work were performed using MATLAB R2015 running on an Intel i7 processor of 2.5 GHz speed and 8 GB RAM.

3   Proposed Approach

The proposed approach includes 3 parts: reconstitution of visible spectral bands, creation of the optimized indicative index of water (OIIW) and detection of small portions of water, which are described in Sects. 3.1 to 3.3.

3.1   Reconstitution of Visible Spectral Bands

Due to the contamination in the bands $\tilde{G}$ and $\tilde{R}$, already explained in the previous section, a MLP-ANN was employed to reconstitute I_VIS from I_NIR, as illustrated in Fig. 1.

To compose the dataset for training the MLP-ANN, we extracted manually 60 sub images with 50×50 pixels from the 5 pairs (used only for training) of correlated VIS-NIR images. In summary, for each pixel chosen in an RGB image, it was extracted a sub image from that image and from its correspondent NIR at the same position. Thus, each instance of training is described by the following 6 attributes: $NIR, \tilde{G}, \tilde{R}, R, G, B$, being the first three extracted from I_NIR (inputs) and the last three from I_VIS sub images (expected outputs).

Formally, the function of developed MLP-ANN is to map each set $\{NIR(x,y), \tilde{G}(x,y), \tilde{R}(x,y)\}$ into another set $\{R(x,y), G(x,y), B(x,y)\}$. Then, all mapped sets make up the pixels of the reconstituted RGB image. This procedure is important because it avoids the conduction of two complete missions to acquire the RGB and NIR images from the same area, impacting directly on the time spent in the image acquisition task as well as saving the battery of the UAV. In addition, the proposed OIIW depends on VIS and NIR spectral bands.

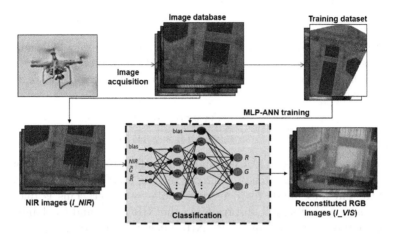

Fig. 1. Working of proposed approach for reconstitution of visible spectral bands.

3.2   Creation of the Optimized Indicative Index of Water (OIIW)

A Genetic Algorithm (GA) was designed to provide the OIIW, as illustrated in Fig. 2. Each chromosome of GA encodes a set of 4 values (c_1, b_1, c_2 and b_2) that compose the index, as follows: $OIIW = \frac{c_1 b_1 - c_2 b_2}{c_1 b_1 + c_2 b_2}$, where $b_i \in [1, 4]$ indicate the selected bands from the set NIR, R, G, B and $c_i \in [0.1, 10.0]$ are the weights applied to these bands. Obviously, b_i are integer values while c_i are real values.

The objective function (f) to evaluate the solutions of GA (Eq. 1) consists in minimizing the total similarity S between pairs of images (in our case, 3 pairs), each one consisting of an image provided by using of OIIW encoded in a GA solution (I_OIIW) and another binary image annotated manually to indicate the expected result (I_EXP). Examples of these images are shown in Fig. 3.

$$Minimize \quad f(c_1, b_1, c_2, b_2) = \sum_{j=1}^{3} S(I\_OIIW_j, I\_EXP_j) \tag{1}$$

In the experiments, we adopted the Mean Absolute Error (MAE), described in Eq. 2, to measure the similarity (S) between a pair of images:

$$S(I\_OIIW, I\_EXP) = \frac{1}{MN} \sum_{m=0}^{M-1} \sum_{n=0}^{N-1} |I\_OIIW_{m,n} - I\_EXP_{m,n}| \tag{2}$$

where M and N are the dimensions of the images being compared. It is important to emphasize that any other measure of similarity could be employed in Eq. 2.

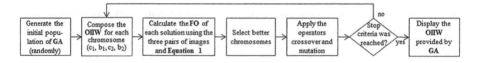

Fig. 2. Steps of designed GA to provide the OIIW.

Some GA configuration parameters were: population size $= 250$; number of generations $= 400$ (used as stop criteria); population rate of replacement $= 0.8$; crossover $= 0.85$; mutation rate $= 0.10$. After the convergence of GA, we obtained the OIIW given by Eq. 3.

$$OIIW = \frac{6.855NIR - 2.3475B}{6.855NIR + 2.3475B} \tag{3}$$

The bands suggested by GA to compose the OIIW are in consonance with the literature, since many researches in remote sensing area indicate a combination of the NIR and VIS bands for detecting bodies of water. This is due to the fact that water presents high absorption in the NIR range and the bands of the visible spectrum, when combined with NIR, allow to characterize water quality. Finally, the importance of determination the weights for each band, made by GA, must be highlighted. Such weights are responsible for the fine adjustment in the indices and, as may be observed in the literature, they are usually obtained empirically or exhaustively.

In Fig. 3 it can be observed that the images generated using proposed OIIW (column d) were very similar to the annotated images (column c), evidencing the good results obtained. In both columns, the regions of images containing water are indicated by gray levels near to black.

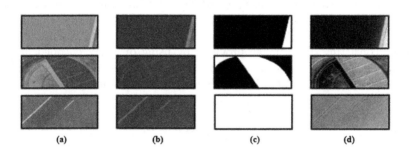

(a)   (b)   (c)   (d)

Fig. 3. Some results obtained with the created OIIW. (a) RGB images (I_VIS); (b) NIR images (I_NIR); (c) Images with the expected results (annotated images); (d) Images generated by OIIW considering the bands NIR and B extracted from images shown in columns a and b.

3.3   Detection of Small Portions of Water

The detection of small portions of water from a pair VIS-NIR images is performed by calculating the Eq. 3 (OIIW), which considers NIR and B spectral bands. This procedure generates a greyscale image I_GRAY in which the pixels are real values ranging from 0.0 to 1.0, being the portions of water represented by gray levels near to zero (black).

The final step consists in converting I_GRAY in a binary image I_BIN through a simple binarization algorithm using a threshold of 0.85 (obtained empirically). Thus, the pixels of I_BIN with value 0 indicate water.

4   Experimental Results

In this section, we present qualitative and quantitative results obtained in the experiments conducted. First, we apply the MLP-ANN in the 50 NIR images of the main dataset, to reconstitute their corresponding RGB versions aiming at the decontamination of spectral bands $\tilde{G}$ and $\tilde{R}$. Two reconstituted images are shown in the column c of Fig. 4. When comparing these images with the original RGB images, showed in the column b, it can be observed that the results are very satisfactory. Also based on a qualitative analysis, it is possible to observe from the images depicted in the columns d and e that the proposed approach for detection small portions of water presented good results.

Fig. 4. Results of detection of small portions of water. (a) NIR images (I_NIR); (b) Original RGB images (I_VIS); (c) Reconstituted RGB images; (d) Images resulting from the application of the OIIW (I_GRAY); (e) Binary images (I_BIN).

In the Table 1 we present some quantitative results obtained with the application of OIIW on a subset of 10 images (this subset includes all images containing bodies of water), for which we manually create the annotated versions with regions containing water highlighted in black. The quality of results is indicated by the measures Mean Absolute Error (MAE) and Structural Similarity Index ($SSIM$), which are widely used to express the similarity between images. It is possible to observe that the results were satisfactory, since the values obtained by MAE very close to 0. In addition, the average value of $SSIM$ (0.9768) also indicates that the resulting images are very similar to their annotated versions, considering that the maximum similarity between two images occurs when the value of $SSIM$ is equal to 1.

Finally, it is important to highlight that although the proposed procedure for providing OIIW considers only 4 spectral bands, it could be easily adapted for a larger number of bands adjusting the GA chromosome. In addition, our approach is much more efficient, in terms of computational cost, than that proposed by Murugan et al. [8].

Table 1. Quantitative results obtained from experiments considering annotated images (first and forth lines: annotated images; second and fifth lines: images generated by applying OIIW; third and sixth lines: MAE and SSIM values, respectively)

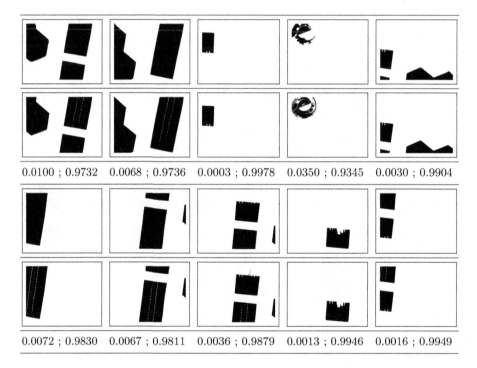

5 Conclusion

In this work, we proposed an approach to detect small portions of water in aerial images acquired by UAVs. It includes an optimized indicative index of water (OIIW) and a procedure do decontaminate visible spectral bands in images acquired by a RGB camera using a special lens to provide NIR band. Regarding the detection of water, the obtained results show that, in general, the proposed approach presents a good precision in detecting pools and fountains even in the cases where there is only a thin layer of water. Thus, this approach could be employed, for example, to map possible foci of Aedes aegypti mosquitoes. With respect to the experiments involving the reconstitution of visible spectral bands, it can be verified that the resulting images were well reconstituted, being very useful to compute OIIW. In future works we intend to carry out new experiments replacing the techniques of Neural Networks and Genetic Algorithms by a Deep Convolutional Neural Network.

Acknowledgements. The authors would like to thank UNINOVE by financial support and CNPq for the research scholarship granted to S. A. de Araújo (Proc. 311971/2015-6).

References

1. Agarwal, A., Chaudhuri, U., Chaudhuri, S., Seetharaman, G.: Detection of potential mosquito breeding sites based on community sourced geotagged images. In: SPIE 9089, Geospatial InfoFusion and Video Analytics IV and Motion Imagery for ISR and Situational Awareness II (2014). https://doi.org/10.1117/12.2058121
2. Candido, A.K.A.A., Silva, N.M., Filho, A.C.P.: High resolution images of unmanned aerial vehicles (UAV) in the planning of land use and occupation. Anuario do Instituto de Geociencias - UFRJ **38**, 147–156 (2015)
3. Capolupo, A., Pindozzi, S., Okello, C., Boccia, L.: Indirect field technology for detecting areas object of illegal spills harmful to human health: applications of drones, photogrammetry and hydrological models. Geospatial Health **8**(3), 699–707 (2014). https://doi.org/10.4081/gh.2014.298
4. Colet, M.E., Braun, A., Manssour, I.H.: A new approach to turbid water surface identification for autonomous navigation. In: 24th International Conference in Central Europe on Computer Graphics, Visualization and Computer Vision (WSCG 2016), pp. 317–326 (2016)
5. Gaitani, N., Burud, I., Thiis, T., Santamouris, M.: High-resolution spectral mapping of urban thermal properties with unmanned aerial vehicles. Build. Environ. **121**, 215–224 (2017)
6. Long, D., McCarthy, C.L., Jensen, T.: Row and water front detection from UAV thermal-infrared imagery for furrow irrigation monitoring. In: 2016 IEEE International Conference on Advanced Intelligent Mechatronics (AIM), pp. 300–305 (2016)
7. Mehra, M., Bagri, A., Jiang, X., Ortiz, J.: Image analysis for identifying mosquito breeding grounds. In: 2016 IEEE International Conference on Communication and Networking (SECON Workshops), pp. 1–6 (2016). https://doi.org/10.1109/SECONW.2016.7746808
8. Murugan, P., Sivakumar, R., Pandiyan, R., Annadurai, M.: Algorithm to select optimal spectral bands for hyperspectral index of feature extraction. Indian J. Sci. Technol. **9**(37), 1–13 (2016)
9. Oliveira, L.S.B., Bezerra, F.H.R.: Karstification fault identification in the potiguar using UAV/drone images. In: XVII Brazilian Symposium on Remote Sensing, pp. 6148–6152 (2015)
10. Portz, L., Guasselli, L.A., Correa, I.C.S.: Spatial and temporal variation of NDVI in lagoa do peixe. Revista Brasileira de Geografia Fisica **4**(5), 897–908 (2011)

11. Qiao, C., Luo, J., Sheng, Y., Shen, Z., Zhu, Z., Ming, D.: An adaptive water extraction method from remote sensing image based on NDWI. Indian Soc. Remote Sens. **40**(3), 421–433 (2012)
12. Zhao, Y., Deng, Y., Pan, C., Guo, L.: Research of water hazard detection based on color and texture features. Sens. Transducers **157**(10), 428–433 (2013)

Predicting City Safety Perception Based on Visual Image Content

Sergio F. Acosta and Jorge E. Camargo$^{(\boxtimes)}$

UnSecureLab Research Group,
Universidad Nacional de Colombia, Bogotá, Colombia
{sfacostale,jecamargom}@unal.edu.co

Abstract. Safety perception measurement has been a subject of interest in many cities of the world. This is due to its social relevance, and to its effect on some local economic activities. Even though people safety perception is a subjective topic, sometimes it is possible to find out common patterns given a restricted geographical and sociocultural context. This paper presents an approach that makes use of image processing and machine learning techniques to detect with high accuracy urban environment patterns that could affect citizen's safety perception.

1 Introduction

Cities are spatial structures of a significant size. In the case of Bogotá-Colombia, the city has an urban area of 307,36 km^2, and it is divided into 20 well defined zones that are named localities. This attribute makes it difficult to appreciate and experience them completely in just one round. This is the reason why the individual perception of a city is the result of a mixture of own experiences and experiences from others. Neighborhoods often differ in their demographics, such as income, and ethnicity of people that inhabits them, but also on how safe they are perceived [6]. Some of the recent works about automatic urban perception prediction have been based on Convolutional Neural Networks (CNN) [7], sets of between 100,000 and 1,000,000 images and with a wider territory scale approach. This work presents an approach based on a restricted geographical and sociocultural context, a modest image set, and on a technique called transfer learning. According to [3], perception of security can be defined as:

> Perception of security (PoS) refers to the subjective assessment of the risk and the magnitude of its consequences. The risk can be defined as the likelihood that an individual will experience the effect of danger, threats, or any adverse events.

Projects such as [2,8,9] and [10] have been focused on how to structure computational models that make it possible the automatic characterization of cities. These works have based their research on the visual appearance of city streets, and its association with the people perception. Misclassification is mainly caused by the huge variability in the set of images associated to the same group or tag.

© Springer Nature Switzerland AG 2019
R. Vera-Rodriguez et al. (Eds.): CIARP 2018, LNCS 11401, pp. 177–185, 2019.
https://doi.org/10.1007/978-3-030-13469-3_21

In [1] it is proposed that the activation output of inner layer of a CNN trained for some other classification task can be used as a visual feature of an image in a different classification task. Based on this idea, the first urban perception model based CNN was proposed in [10]. CNN approach is also implemented in [2], where a CNN architecture is implemented in order to build a worldwide urban perception model.

The methodology described in [11] involves an image score estimation using the fraction of times this is selected over another image, then this is corrected by the "win" and "loss" ratios of all images with which it was compared during a visual survey. In [8], people perception obtained through visual surveys is converted to a ranked score for each image using the Microsoft Trueskill algorithm [4]. In [2] and [10] it is proposed to predict pairwise comparisons by training a CNN model directly from image pairs and their crowd-sourced comparisons, which is used to generate "synthetic" comparisons by taking random image pairs as input.

Our paper presents an alternative approach in the construction of a computational model whose purpose is to predict how safe may be a given Bogotá city zone. This has been carried out in a restricted sociocultural and geographical context. In order to restrict sociocultural context, just people living in Bogotá was invited to take the visual survey. Safety perception like humor can depend on a particular sociocultural context. This is why sometimes a joke that is fun in the USA may not be fun in Germany. Geographical context restriction means that just local street images were used. One motivation for not using foreign street images is that many of the urban environment found in other countries, e.g. Washington or Germany, does not exist in Bogotá. It is expected that these restrictions reduce the variability of the underling distribution as well as the noisy of data. The presented approach makes use of a technique called transfer learning. This takes a piece of a model that has already been trained on a related task and reusing it in a new model. In particular VGG19 [12] model, loaded with weights trained on ImageNet, has been used for generic image feature extraction. A particular city zone of $40\,km^2$ was chosen for this work, and local people were asked to participate in the visual survey. Since Bogotá has an extremely heterogeneous urban environment, this restriction still guarantees a significant image variability. As a result, a model with an accuracy of 81% was obtained, and it was used to predict a safety perception score for two other neighboring localities. In order to detect different patterns, prediction on neighboring localities was performed using their particular image sets.

2   Materials and Methods

2.1   Dataset Construction

Street Image Crawler. A city street image crawler was built using the Google Street View API V3.0 along with a file that contained geographical limits of the target zones.

Image Filtering. Since some collected images have no a wide view of a street, but a close-up of a building facade, or a totally black image, it was required to remove these images from the collected set. This was done by extracting SIFT local descriptors from each image, and excluding images with a descriptor count less than 420.

Visual Survey. Visual surveys was carried out through a public web site. On this, users were shown two geotagged street city images, and asked to click on one in response to the questions "which place looks safer?". In this way a bit of citizenship perception is obtained. An image pair and its associated comparison are the unit of information that will be used during the training task. The visual survey tool is online in http://wmodi.com/. Figure 1 shows this site.

Fig. 1. Visual survey site

Image Serving Policies. Image pair serving policy and database housekeeping try to fulfill the following requirements.

- Each image should have the same vote share.
- Repeated image pair comparisons should be reduced to a single or no vote.
- Same image comparison is not allowed and should be removed.
- Comparisons of near images should be removed.

Vote Coding and Database Structures. In each visual survey session, two street images were presented to the user. The user was asked to click on one image or on the equal button in order to answer the question: Which place looks safer? Once the user click on an image or a button, the vote is coded as follows: If click on image 0 (left side image), vote is coded as 1; if click on button *equal* vote is coded as 0. Finally, if click on image 1 (right side image), vote is coded as 2. For each visual survey session, the resulting vote code along with the involved left and right image identifiers were stored. There is also a database structure associated to each published image. This holds the image identifier, a positive perception counter, a negative perception counter and a neutral perception counter. If user click on image 0 (left side image), this image positive perception counter is increased by 1 and image 1 (right side image) negative perception counter is increased by 1. Same logic applies if user click on image 1 (right side image). Finally, if user click on button *equal* both images neutral perception counter is increased by 1. This counters are used for each image basic perception percentage estimation.

Collected Data. 5,505 images of the target zone were published. In one year, 17,703 image pair votes were collected. Each image participated in 6 ± 1 image pair comparison session. The collected vote distribution based on its code is as follow: 5,657 code 0 votes, 5,946 code 1 votes, and 6,100 code 2 votes.

2.2   Image Feature Extraction

IN THE VGG19 Keras[1] model it was removed its fully-connected layer at the top of the network and loaded with the weights trained on ImageNet. Then, this model was used to obtain a row vector representation of each published image. This is a 512 values vector, i.e, the model is used like an image feature extractor and no training is required for this task. It is important to note that the goal of this research is to train a model that will be able to predict a visual survey vote based on a vector representation of a pair of city street images. That is, each training item is composed of two image feature vectors and their associated vote code.

2.3   Training Set Construction

The construction of the training set involved the transformation of the collected visual survey votes into number vectors and its associated label (vote code). This task starts with the elaboration of a list of all the votes found in the database. From this list, image identifiers are replaced by their associated vector descriptors. Finally, images descriptors associated to each single vote are concatenated and annotated with the respective $\{1, 2\}$. Ties (code 0 votes) were not used, but just charged votes were used. If an actual vote has been annotated with vote code 1, it means that left image was better perceived than the right image. This means also that if image positions are exchanged, the resulting vote should be annotated with vote code 2. This fact has been used to double the initial data set size. The resulting set of 24,092 ($5,946 * 2 + 6,100 * 2$) votes was split into training, validation and testing sets. A distribution of 65-7-28 was used. In this way 15,636 votes were used for training, 1,754 for validation and 6,702 votes for testing. Each descriptor vector corresponding to each image of the VGG19 was normalized applying the following expression,

$$f_{i,j} = (f_{i,j} - \mu_i)/\sigma_i,$$

---

[1] https://keras.io/.

where $f_{i,j}$ is the j-th component of the i-th vector, (μ) the mean, and (σ) the standard deviation. Each feature i of each row vector j is normalized by subtracting the associated mean and scaled by the associated standard deviation. Same normalization scheme was used on the image set of the neighboring localities, the model was used to predict on.

Training Phase. Training sessions were performed using the TensorFlow[2] machine learning framework. The implemented neural network configuration is shown in Fig. 2.

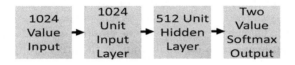

Fig. 2. Full connected neural network setup

The input data is the concatenation of image 0 and 1 VGG19 based on a 512 vector descriptor. This is a 1024 bin vector. A dropout technique was used as regularization method. Dropout rates of 0.5, 0.45 and 0.3 were applied to the input, hidden and output layers, respectively. The learning rate was set to 0.00001, and a mini-batch size was defined as 64. The AdamOptimizer [5] method was used along with Cross Entropy Loss. Figure 3 shows training session cost curves.

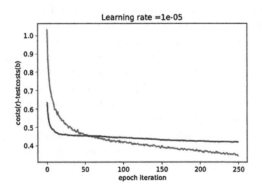

Fig. 3. Training session cost curves

Accuracy Report. Table 1 presents the confusion matrix for the testing set, for which an accuracy of 81.5% was achieved.

---

[2] https://www.tensorflow.org/.

Table 1. Testing confusion matrix

	Predicted Vote Code		Total
	1	2	
1	2,777	574	3,351
2	663	2,688	3,351
Total	3,440	3,262	6,702

Synthetic Vote Generation. Synthetic votes were generated dividing each locality collected image set into two same size groups. Each group holds images homogeneously distributed over the target locality area. Each group was divided into 10 subgroups. Then, each image from one group was paired with a randomly (uniform) selected image from each subgroup in the other group.

Synthetic Vote Prediction. In order to be able to make a map based on synthetic votes, the initial dummy vote label must be substituted by one based on the model prediction. The output of the softmax layer was used for this purpose. At first, the option with the higher probability was used to annotate the associated vote as 1 or 2. However, the absolute difference between the two probabilities must be higher than 0.25, otherwise the vote was annotated with the code 0. At the same time each image positive, negative and neutral perception counters were updated.

Image Score Based on Perception Counters. In section "Vote Coding and Database Structures" it was mentioned that published images had an structure associated to them and how its fields are updated during a visual survey session. This holds the image identifier, a positive perception counter, a negative perception counter and a neutral perception counter. Every image used in the synthetic vote prediction task has the same structure, and its perception counters are updated in the same way as during a visual survey session. If an image neutral perception counter is greater than 0, this value is redistributed between this image positive and negative counters. This redistribution is done by factors that are worked out form the perception counter summation of all images, which this image tied with. Finally, each image counter summation is normalized [0, 1] and each counter turned into positive, negative and neutral safety perception percentages.

3   Results

3.1   Actual and Synthetic Vote Maps of Same Zone

For the initial target zone training images were obtained, and a perception maps was built based on both, actual and synthetic votes. This was done in order to verify that colors patterns found in actual vote perception map are present in the synthetic vote perception map. For further exploration, actual[3] and synthetic[4] vote perception map are available in the project web site.

Figure 4 shows the color gradient used on the map set. Here left green end indicates a 100% percent of positive safety perception, and right red end 0%.

Fig. 4. Color gradient reference for image safety perception score (Color figure online)

3.2 Safety Perception Score Prediction for Other Localities

Model was used to generate synthetic votes on image pairs of different city zones. These image maps are available on line at left[5] and right[6] image map links (Fig. 5).

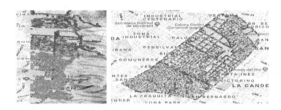

Fig. 5. Left: *Usaquen* zone 94,780 synthetic votes safety perception score map. Right: *Martires* zone 37,880 synthetic votes safety perception score map

3.3 Predicted Image Set

Figures 6 and 7 are samples of other zone images whose score has been predicted by the system based on synthetic votes. It is worth noting that the trained model predicts with high precision the perception of test images. For instance, the predicted vote of left image in Fig. 6 captures negative perception safety characteristics such as dirty houses, lonely streets, trash, etc., whilst the predicted vote of image in right image in Fig. 7 captures positive perception safety characteristics such illumination, green zones, clean streets, etc.

---

[3] http://wmodi.com/chapinero_17703actualvote_jun04_2018_imgscore.

[4] http://wmodi.com/chapinero_55040NNsyntheticvote_jun04_2018_imgscore.

[5] http://wmodi.com/usaquen_94780NNsyntheticvote_jun04_2018_imgscore.

[6] http://wmodi.com/martires_37880NNsyntheticvote_jun04_2018_imgscore.

Fig. 6. *Martires* zone: 0%, 49%, 86% positive safety perception images

Fig. 7. *Usaquen* zone: 6%, 41%, 87% positive safety perception images (Color figure online)

4   Conclusion and Future Work

This paper presented a model that allows to predict citizen's safety perception using visual information of street images. The obtained results show a prediction accuracy of 81%, which is higher than results obtained in recent state of the art methods. Up to our knowledge, this is the first time that this analysis is performed to Bogotá city. The presented method does not require a high computing capacity, that is, 1 model iterations per hour can be performed. This feature makes this approach appropriate for the development of an online tool. It is expected to carry out more exhaustive evaluations in order determine the robustness of the predictions as well as statistical stability. All these results and the results of an earlier model evaluated by us based on SVM with a smaller amount of votes are available at http://wmodi.com/.

References

1. Donahue, J., et al.: DeCAF: a deep convolutional activation feature for generic visual recognition (2013)
2. Dubey, A., Naik, N., Parikh, D., Raskar, R., Hidalgo, C.A.: Deep learning the city: quantifying urban perception at a global scale. In: Leibe, B., Matas, J., Sebe, N., Welling, M. (eds.) ECCV 2016. LNCS, vol. 9905, pp. 196–212. Springer, Cham (2016). https://doi.org/10.1007/978-3-319-46448-0_12
3. Gómez, F., Torres, A., Galvis, J., Camargo, J., Martínez, O.: Hotspot mapping for perception of security. In: IEEE 2nd International Smart Cities Conference: Improving the Citizens Quality of Life, ISC2 2016 - Proceedings, pp. 0–5 (2016)

4. Herbrich, R., Minka, T., Graepel, T.: TrueSkill: a Bayesian skill rating system. In: Advances in Neural Information Processing Systems, vol. 20, pp. 569–576 (2006)
5. Kingma, D.P., Ba, J.: Adam: a method for stochastic optimization. CoRR, abs/1412.6980 (2014)
6. Kominers, S.D., et al.: Do People Shape Cities, or Do Cities Shape People? The Co-evolution of Physical, Social, and Economic Change in Five Major U.S. Cities (2015)
7. Krizhevsky, A., Sutskever, I., Hinton, G.E.: ImageNet classification with deep convolutional neural networks. In: Advances in Neural Information Processing Systems, pp. 1–9 (2012)
8. Naik, N., Philipoom, J., Raskar, R.: Streetscore - Predicting the Perceived Safety of One Million Streetscapes (2014)
9. Ordonez, V., Berg, T.L.: Learning high-level judgments of urban perception. In: Fleet, D., Pajdla, T., Schiele, B., Tuytelaars, T. (eds.) ECCV 2014. LNCS, vol. 8694, pp. 494–510. Springer, Cham (2014). https://doi.org/10.1007/978-3-319-10599-4_32
10. Porzi, L., Buló, S.R., Lepri, B., Ricci, E.: Predicting and Understanding Urban Perception with Convolutional Neural Networks, pp. 139–148 (2015)
11. Salesses, P., Schechtner, K., Hidalgo, C.A.: The collaborative image of the city: mapping the inequality of urban perception. PLoS ONE **8**, e68400 (2013)
12. Simonyan, K., Zisserman, A.: Very deep convolutional networks for large-scale image recognition. CoRR, abs/1409.1556 (2014)

Analysis and Classification of MoCap Data by Hilbert Space Embedding-Based Distance and Multikernel Learning

Juan Diego Pulgarin-Giraldo[1,2(✉)], Andres Marino Alvarez-Meza[2],
Steven Van Vaerenbergh[3], Ignacio Santamaría[3],
and German Castellanos-Dominguez[2]

[1] G-BIO Research Group, Universidad Autónoma de Occidente, Cali, Colombia
[2] Signal Processing and Recognition Group, Universidad Nacional de Colombia,
Manizales, Colombia
jdpulgaring@unal.edu.co
[3] Department of Communications Engineering, University of Cantabria,
Santander, Spain

Abstract. A framework is presented to carry out prediction and classification of Motion Capture (MoCap) multichannel data, based on kernel adaptive filters and multi-kernel learning. To this end, a Kernel Adaptive Filter (KAF) algorithm extracts the dynamic of each channel, relying on the similarity between multiple realizations through the Maximum Mean Discrepancy (MMD) criterion. To assemble dynamics extracted from all MoCap data, center kernel alignment (CKA) is used to assess the contribution of each to the classification tasks (that is, its relevance). Validation is performed on a database of tennis players, performing a good classification accuracy of the considered stroke classes. Besides, we find that the relevance of each channel agrees with the findings reported in the biomechanical analysis. Therefore, the combination of KAF together with CKA allows building a proper representation for extracting relevant dynamics from multiple-channel MoCap data.

Keywords: Multichannel data · Kernel adaptive filters ·
Maximum Mean Discrepancy · Center kernel alignment

1 Introduction

In human action recognition using MoCap data, the primary efforts are directed at extracting adequately robust dynamics to model the movements accomplished under given actions [1]. In practice, the models are mostly oriented to classify accurately executed actions, accounting for the relevance of the extracted feature sets but voiding the contribution of the body segments and articulations

© Springer Nature Switzerland AG 2019
R. Vera-Rodriguez et al. (Eds.): CIARP 2018, LNCS 11401, pp. 186–193, 2019.
https://doi.org/10.1007/978-3-030-13469-3_22

(i.e., channel relevance). One of the restraints to assess the channel relevance is the need of developing spatial filtering methods that may provide an adequate interpretation of biomechanical generation.

To deal with this issue, compact, meaningful *dictionaries* or *codebooks*, that match physiological principles are built. To this end, Kernel Adaptive Filters (KAFs) are widely employed in time-series prediction task that enables encoding the salient elements of signals [2], avoiding the segmentation step within the feature extraction stage of human action recognition [3]. Furthermore, the combination of multiple dynamic models by kernels methods can be implemented through different feasible approaches like CKA proposed in [4].

Provided a set of output labels, the supervised CKA algorithm employs a distance that measures the dissimilarity/similarity between each basis kernel and the target kernel, yielding the combination weights that estimate the relevance of each input kernel. In channel relevance tasks of MoCap multichannel time series, however, construction of adequate basis kernel sets, which must be in independent from each other, is still a challenging issue.

Here, to reveal the contribution of channels involved in each action execution, a channel relevance methodology is presented to improve the performance of prediction and classification tasks using MoCap multichannel data. Initially, from input data, the Kernel Adaptive Filter build a *codebook* set as well a vector of predicted outputs, which are further mapped in a Reproducing Kernel Hilbert Space. Relying on the similarity between multiple realizations through the Maximum Mean Discrepancy criterion, we construct a basis kernel per channel. Then, CKA aligns the whole basis kernel set, using the label set. As a result, we find that the relevance of each channel agrees with the findings reported in the biomechanical analysis. Therefore, the combination of KAF together with CKA allows building a proper representation for extracting relevant dynamics from multiple-channel MoCap data.

2 Theoretical Framework

2.1 Dynamical Channel Model Encoded by Kernel Adaptive Filtering

We assume a scenario in which a set of J time series $\mathbf{x}_j[t]$ are obtained from sensor measurements, with $j = 1, \ldots, J$. For each time series, T time steps are available, i.e. $t = 1, \ldots, T$. We collect the entire set of measurements in the matrix $\boldsymbol{X} \in \mathbb{R}^{J \times T}$, which contains the J time series as its rows as follows:

$$\boldsymbol{X} = \begin{bmatrix} x_1[1] & x_1[2] & \ldots & x_1[T] \\ x_2[1] & x_2[2] & \ldots & x_2[T] \\ \vdots & \vdots & \ddots & \vdots \\ x_J[1] & x_J[2] & \ldots & x_J[T] \end{bmatrix} \tag{1}$$

Thorough this paper, we assume that multiple sets are available, where the n-th set is represented as $\boldsymbol{X}^n$, with $n = 1, \ldots, N$. Also, to indicate that a time series belongs to a particular set n, we use notation $\mathbf{x}_j^n[t]$.

With the aim of modeling properly each time series $\mathbf{x}_j$, its dynamic behavior is represented through Kernel Adaptive Filters (KAFs) so that the problem non-linearities can be represented as a kernel expansion in terms of the training data:

$$f(\mathbf{x}_j) = \sum_{r=1}^{R} \alpha_r \kappa(\mathbf{x}_j[r], \mathbf{x}_j), \tag{2}$$

where α_r is built using kernel least-mean-square algorithms (KLMS). Here, we employ KAFs that enable tracking of non-stationary data with nonlinear relationships. Among KAF algorithms, we are interested in those that construct a dictionary set or *codebook* composed of R elements, each one including the most representative data points learned from the quantization process.

2.2   Model Construction and Similarity Measure

The KRLS tracker introduced in [5], assumes a set of ordered input-output pairs $\{\mathbf{x}_j[t], y_j[t]\}$ in which the input data is taken as the time-embedded version of the series with L lags, $\mathbf{x}_j[t] = [x_j[t], x_j[t-1], \dots, x_j[t-L+1]]$, and the desired output is the next sample, $y_j[t] = x_j[t+1]$. In addition to the obtained channel predictor (see Eq. (2)), we get a codebook $\mathbf{c}_j[r]$ and their estimated latent function outputs or desired values $d[r]$, applying the KRLS tracker [5]. Consequently, we define a model associated to each time series as $\mathcal{M}_j = \{\mathbf{c}_j[r], d_j[r], \ r = 1, ..., R\}$.

Further, we perform the similarity measure between models. Namely, let us consider two different models $\mathbf{p}_r = (\mathbf{c}_p[r], d_p[r])$ and $\mathbf{q}_r = (\mathbf{c}_q[r], d_q[r])$. The elements of each model or model samples, as given by KRLST, are not ordered. Therefore, any permutation or reordering of the elements represents the same model. Bearing this in mind, we interpret each model as a cluster of points in the input space. We now define a mapping from the set of models $\mathcal{Z}$ to a RKHS as $\Phi : \mathcal{Z} \longrightarrow \mathcal{H}$, which maps $\{\mathbf{p}_r\}_{r=1}^{R} \longmapsto \{\Phi(\mathbf{p}_r)\}_{r=1}^{R}$. A model can be interpreted as a distribution function $\mathcal{P}$ from which R realizations are available. Then, to define a distance between models we resort to the Maximum Mean Discrepancy (MMD) defined by Gretton in [6]. Given two models $\mathcal{P}$ and $\mathcal{Q}$, the MMD criterion computes the distance between them as

$$\eth^2(\mathcal{P}, \mathcal{Q}) = \left\| \frac{1}{R} \sum_{r=1}^{R} \Phi(\mathbf{p}_r) - \frac{1}{R} \sum_{r=1}^{R} \Phi(\mathbf{q}_r) \right\|_2^2. \tag{3}$$

Assuming a separable model that decouples the influence of the input and the output [7], the distance between models in Eq. (3) can be rewritten in terms of kernel matrices as

$$\eth^2(\mathcal{P}, \mathcal{Q}) = \frac{1}{R^2} \left(\mathbf{d}_p^T \boldsymbol{K}_{pp} \mathbf{d}_p + \mathbf{d}_q^T \boldsymbol{K}_{qq} \mathbf{d}_q - 2\mathbf{d}_p^T \boldsymbol{K}_{pq} \mathbf{d}_q \right), \tag{4}$$

where $\boldsymbol{K}_{pq}(r, r') = \exp(-\|\mathbf{c}_p[r] - \mathbf{c}_q[r']\|^2 / 2\sigma_c^2)$, and $\mathbf{d}(r, r') = \mathbf{d}[r]\mathbf{d}[r']$ is a linear kernel for the output of each model.

2.3 Relevance Assessment by Multikernel Learning

Let $\boldsymbol{X}^n \in \mathbb{R}^{J \times T}$, $n = 1, \ldots, N$ be a labeled set of J-dimensional time series. For the n-th multichannel time series we have a collection of J models that we denote as $\{\mathcal{M}_j[n]\}_{j=1}^J$. Let us denote as $\boldsymbol{K}_j$ the $N \times N$ kernel matrix that measures the (di)similarities for the j-th channel between the N time series in the training data set. The element (n, m) of this kernel matrix is given by $\boldsymbol{K}_j(n, m) = \exp - \left(\frac{\eth^2(\mathcal{M}_j[n], \mathcal{M}_j[m])}{2\sigma_\eth^2} \right)$, where $\eth^2(\mathcal{M}_j[n], \mathcal{M}_j[m])$ is the pairwise distance between models described in Sect. 2.2 (Eq. (4)).

To combine the information from the J channels we propose to use a multikernel constructed as follows

$$\hat{\boldsymbol{K}} = \sum_{j=1}^J \alpha_j \boldsymbol{K}_j, \tag{5}$$

where the weights α_j $j = 1, \ldots, J$ are yet to be determined. To find informative weights that allow us to quantify the relevance of individual channels, we propose to use a centered kernel alignment procedure [4]. The basic idea is to find the optimal α_j^* maximizing the alignment between the multikernel matrix $\boldsymbol{K}$ and the target kernel matrix $\boldsymbol{K}_l = \boldsymbol{l}\boldsymbol{l}^T$, which is calculated from the known label classes $\boldsymbol{l} = \{l[i]\}_{i=1}^N$. For a given set of weights α_j, the centered correlation or alignment between matrix kernels $\boldsymbol{K}$ and $\boldsymbol{K}_l$ is given by

$$\rho(\boldsymbol{K}, \boldsymbol{K}_l; \alpha) = \frac{\langle \boldsymbol{HKH}, \boldsymbol{HK}_l\boldsymbol{H} \rangle}{\|\boldsymbol{HKH}\|_F \|\boldsymbol{HK}_l\boldsymbol{H}\|_F}, \qquad \rho \in [0, 1] \tag{6}$$

where $\boldsymbol{H} = \boldsymbol{I} - N^{-1}\boldsymbol{1}\boldsymbol{1}^\top$ is a centering matrix, $\boldsymbol{I} \in \mathbb{R}^{N \times N}$ is the identity matrix, $\boldsymbol{1} \in \mathbb{R}^N$ is an all-ones vector, and notations $\langle \cdot, \cdot \rangle$ and $\|\cdot, \cdot\|_F$ stand for the inner product and the Frobenius norm, respectively.

Then, the optimal relevance weights are $\alpha^* = \operatorname{argmax} \rho(\boldsymbol{K}, \boldsymbol{K}_l, \alpha)$ subject to the constraint $\|\alpha^*\| = 1$. This problem is solved by the Centered Kernel Alignment (CKA) algorithm [4].

3 Experimental Setup

3.1 Database Description

The data were collected from 17 high-performance tennis players of the Caldas-Colombia tennis league. Infrared videography with 23 optical markers was collected from six cameras to acquire sagittal, frontal, and lateral planes and skeleton and multichannel time series were estimated in Optitrack Arena®. All subjects were encouraged to hit the ball with the same velocity and action just as they would in a match. They were instructed to hit one series continuously by 30 s of each indicated stroke. The strokes indicated in each record were: serve, forehand, backhand, volley, backhand volley and smash.

3.2   MoCap Data Preprocessing

Let $U \in \mathbb{R}^{T \times (J \times D)}$ be a multi-channel input matrix that holds T frames and $J \times D$ channels, where J is the number of joints of the body model. Each $U_j = \{ \mathbf{u}_{ij} \in \mathbb{R}^D : i \in T \}$ assembles time behavior of D-dimensional body-joint j. Initially, all channels are centered respect to the limb center. Then, to describe the time behavior of the j-th body-joint from U_j, we perform a dimensional reduction stage from $\mathbb{R}^D \to \mathbb{R}$ to obtain a compact representation of its time behavior. In this case, from the covariance matrix $W \in \mathbb{R}^{D \times D}$ we consider only the first principal eigenvector $\mathbf{w}_1$, obtained from the first column of the covariance matrix. Then, we obtain the linear projection $\mathbf{x}_j = U_j \mathbf{w}_1$, where $\mathbf{w}_1 \in \mathbb{R}^{D \times 1}$.

3.3   Model Estimation and Similarity Measure

We compute each model $\mathcal{M}_j$ through a KRLST algorithm with parameters set as follows: forgetting factor 1, time embedding $L = 6$, codebook size $R = 50$, regularization parameter $\lambda = 10^{-6}$, a Gaussian kernel with σ calculated as the median value of channel $\mathbf{x}_j$ and the initial codebooks are built directly from the input time series $\mathbf{x}_j \in \mathbb{R}^{T \times 1}$. Each model is validated doing a simple task: predict $x(t + 1)$ from data available up to time t.

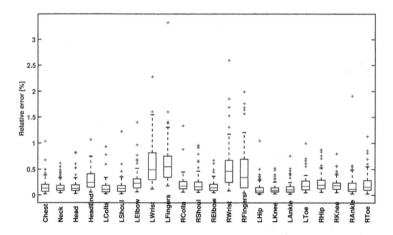

Fig. 1. Relative error results for each joint model $\mathcal{M}_j^n$ estimated over N records with six different classes

Figure 1 shows the mean prediction error in each channel j for all sets of multichannel data, in this case, N = 102. Although the number of outliers looks high, it shows a low and regular mean error, which is significant due to the high variability of both: inter-subject and inter-class variability. Besides, our approach works with the 30 s full-long one take videos where several and continuous actions were recorded. There are approximately 12 to 16 strokes in each individual record. It is worth saying that segmentation and selection of actions are not required in our modeling process.

Besides, our proposed functional $\mathfrak{d}^2$ allows us to construct a kernel similarity measure $\kappa(\mathcal{M}_j[n], \mathcal{M}_j[m])$ which highlights each group of actions without previous information about the classes. In Fig. 2(a) we can see the block diagonal structure of the Gram matrix K constructed over records of the right wrist joint. In fact, KPCA 2D-embedding in Fig. 2(b) shows the separability between groups of records that are colored according to its true label.

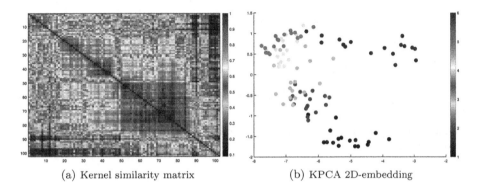

(a) Kernel similarity matrix   (b) KPCA 2D-embedding

Fig. 2. Model similarity comparison for right wrist body-joint over 102 records. In both plots, most classes of 17 strokes records are distinguishable.

4   Relevance and Classification Results

Once the multikernel $\hat{K}$ from Eq. (5) is constructed it allows us compare multi-channel data, so that we can apply any kernel-based classifier. In this work, we use a kernel nearest neighbor (KNN). The KNN classifier finds the k samples in the training dataset closest to test data (with maximum similarity) and carries out majority vote. Classification performance and relevance are computed using a cross-validation scheme.

Figure 3 shows the attained α values in a boxplot. Particularly, the body joints at the end of the limbs are the most relevant. These channels highlight the difference between the six classes of action executed. Nonetheless, the variability observed in the most relevant channels implies a strong dependency in the execution, namely, the angle of the racquet in the hit moment varies with the wrist and fingers channels relation.

Regarding to the classification results, as can be seen in Fig. 4(a), accuracies over 90% are attained for a number of nearest neighbors ranging from 1 to 9. In Fig. 4(b), the lowest results must be analyzed in confrontation with the action, where backhand presents low ball speeds after the impact and it were closer to speeds obtained in volley strokes executions. Nevertheless, each record classified contains 12 to 16 continuously stroke executions without segmentation, so the confused actions depend of execution's speed after 30 s.

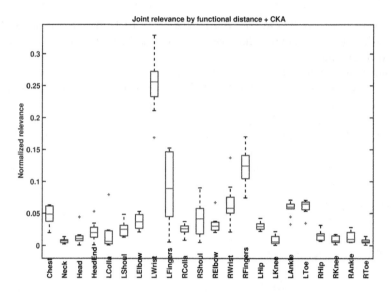

Fig. 3. Relevance body joint analysis in six activities. 10 folds in cross-validation were used over 102 records

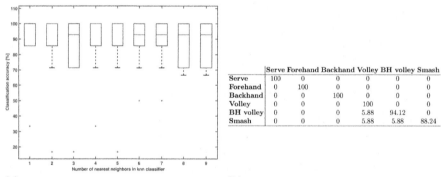

	Serve	Forehand	Backhand	Volley	BH volley	Smash
Serve	100	0	0	0	0	0
Forehand	0	100	0	0	0	0
Backhand	0	0	100	0	0	0
Volley	0	0	0	100	0	0
BH volley	0	0	0	5.88	94.12	0
Smash	0	0	0	5.88	5.88	88.24

(a) Classification performance versus number of nearest neighbors in KNN classifier classifier

(b) Confussion matrix with three nearest neighbors. Accuracy results in %

Fig. 4. Classification results in six activities. 10 folds in cross-validation were used over 102 records.

4.1 Discussion and Concluding Remarks

The proposed framework for MoCap multichannel analysis presents a methodology that first: obtains an appropriate and individual representation of the dynamic of each channel; and second: this channel representation based on KAFs allows us to combine similarity between several realizations. In fact, this framework easily matches with a multikernel algorithm as CKA, which merges multiple channels into just one kernel that can be used in classification tasks. It can be seen that CKA reveals the most significant channels in a set of actions, and these results are congruent with biomechanic theory in tennis actions execution [8].

This framework should be expanded to analyze optimal number and placement of sensors in human action recognition tasks, regardless of its source: optical markers, inertial sensors or depth cameras. Besides, human motion action involves an interaction between all body segments: every action has a biomechanical chain that produces it, so relevance of channels must give information about the most relevant body segments involved across the time. The results encourage us to develop an algorithm for biomechanical chain generation without kinetic information, just from skeleton representations of actions.

As future work, this framework must be validated in larger action datasets, as well as be evaluated in assessment motor disorders to check whether relevance shows alterations in specific body segments or articulations.

Acknowledgments. This work is supported by the project 36075 and mobility grant 8401 funded by Universidad Nacional de Colombia sede Manizales, by program "Doctorados Nacionales 2014" number 647 funded by COLCIENCIAS, as well as PhD financial support from Universidad Autónoma de Occidente.

References

1. Ofli, F., Chaudhry, R., Kurillo, G., Vidal, R., Bajcsy, R.: Sequence of the most informative joints (SMIJ): a new representation for human skeletal action recognition. J. Vis. Commun. Image Represent. **25**(1), 24–38 (2014)
2. Van Vaerenbergh, S., Santamaría, I.: A comparative study of kernel adaptive filtering algorithms. In: 2013 IEEE DSP/SPE Meeting, pp. 181–186, August 2013. Software available at https://github.com/steven2358/kafbox/
3. Pulgarin-Giraldo, J.D., Alvarez-Meza, A.M., Melo-Betancourt, L.G., Ramos-Bermudez, S., Castellanos-Dominguez, G.: A similarity indicator for differentiating kinematic performance between qualified tennis players. In: Beltrán-Castañón, C., Nyström, I., Famili, F. (eds.) CIARP 2016. LNCS, vol. 10125, pp. 309–317. Springer, Cham (2017). https://doi.org/10.1007/978-3-319-52277-7_38
4. Cortes, C., Mohri, M., Rostamizadeh, A.: Algorithms for learning kernels based on centered alignment. J. Mach. Learn. Res. **13**(1), 795–828 (2012)
5. Van Vaerenbergh, S., Lazaro-Gredilla, M., Santamaria, I.: Kernel recursive least-squares tracker for time-varying regression. IEEE Trans. Neural Netw. Learn. Syst. **23**(8), 1313–1326 (2012)
6. Gretton, A., Borgwardt, K.M., Rasch, M.J., Schölkopf, B., Smola, A.: A kernel two-sample test. J. Mach. Learn. Res. **13**, 723–773 (2012)
7. Álvarez, M.A., Rosasco, L., Lawrence, N.D.: Kernels for vector-valued functions: a review. Found. Trends Mach. Learn. **4**(3), 195–266 (2012)
8. Landlinger, J., Lindinger, S., Stoggl, T., Wagner, H., Muller, E.: Key factors and timing patterns in the tennis forehand of different skill levels. J. Sports Sci. Med. **9**, 643–651 (2010)

An Out of Sample Version of the EM Algorithm for Imputing Missing Values in Classification

Sergio Campos[1]([✉]), Alejandro Veloz[2], and Hector Allende[1]

[1] Departamento de Informática, Universidad Técnica Federico Santa María,
Valparaíso, Chile
sergio0.1@gmail.com
[2] Departamento de Ingeniería Biomédica, Universidad de Valparaíso,
Valparaíso, Chile

Abstract. Finding real-world applications whose records contain missing values is not uncommon. As many data analysis algorithms are not designed to work with missing data, a frequent approach is to remove all variables associated with such records from the analysis. A much better alternative is to employ data imputation techniques to estimate the missing values using statistical relationships among the variables.

The Expectation Maximization (EM) algorithm is a classic method to deal with missing data, but is not designed to work in typical Machine Learning settings that have training set and testing set.

In this work we present an extension of the EM algorithm that can deal with this problem. We test the algorithm with ADNI (Alzheimer's Disease Neuroimaging Initiative) data set, where about 80% of the sample has missing values.

Our extension of EM achieved higher accuracy and robustness in the classification performance. It was evaluated using three different classifiers and showed a significant improvement with regard to similar approaches proposed in the literature.

Keywords: Missing data · Imputation · Classification · ADNI · EM · Out of Sample

1 Introduction

Nowadays, data are generated from several distinct sources: sensor networks, opinion polls about political and socio-economical topic, medical diagnosis, social networks, recommendation systems, etc. Many of these real-world applications suffer from a common drawback, missing or unknown data (incomplete feature vector). This problem makes it very difficult to mine them using Machine Learning (ML) methods that can work only with complete data. The missing data

This work was supported by the Fondecyt Grant 1170123 and in part by Fondecyt Grant FB0821.

problem can be handled in two ways. Firstly, all samples having a missing record are removed before any analysis takes place. This is a reasonable approach when the percentage of removed samples is low so that a possible bias in the study can be discarded. Secondly, the missing values can be estimated from the incomplete measured data. This approach is known as *imputation* [6] and is recommended when the adopted data analysis techniques are not designed to work with missing entries as is the case of almost all ML techniques.

The Alzheimer's Disease Neuroimaging Initiative[1] (ADNI) is a well-known example of a missing data problem [5,11]. Most of the research related to the ADNI database is made with the purpose of contributing to the development of biomarkers for the early detection (diagnostic) and tracking (prognostic) of Alzheimer Disease (AD). The features belonging to this dataset are derived from longitudinal clinical, medical images (PET, MRI, fMRI), genetic, and biochemical data from patients with Alzheimer disease (AD), mild cognitive impairment (MCI), and healthy controls (HC).

Pattern analysis in ADNI is strongly hampered by missing data, i.e. patients with incomplete records, cases where the different data modalities are partially or fully absent due to several reasons: high measurement cost, equipment failure, unsatisfactory data quality, patients missing appointments or dropping out of the study, and unwillingness to undergo invasive procedures. About 80% of the ADNI patients have missing records. Thus, resorting to missing data imputation becomes mandatory in order to find useful patterns of clinical significance.

Among the most prominent approaches used for data imputation, it can be found the well-known and widely used Expectation-Maximization (EM) algorithm. On its classic form, the EM algorithm is an iterative and general method to estimate the parameters θ of a probability distribution by means of likelihood maximization. The method, proposed by Dempster [1], can be summarized in the E-Step and the M-Step. The E-Step computes a function for the expectation of the log-likelihood function using the current estimate of the parameters. Then, the M-Step computes the new values of the parameters maximizing the expected.

Many subsequent improvements based on the original EM algorithm idea can be found in the literature. Consider the work of Schneider [8] in which a new step of imputation is added based on a regression framework.

Existing approaches for imputation of missing data rely on the necessity of the whole incomplete data matrix and do not allow to evaluate new samples once the model is trained. This characteristic makes some existing methods for imputation, including Schneider method, not suitable for most Machine Learning algorithms. In this context, some authors [3,10] call to the methods can be evaluate new samples: Out-of-Sample version.

This work presents an out-of-sample extension for applying the EM algorithm in missing data problems. The idea behind the proposed method is to introduce a new version of the EM algorithm to impute missing data in ADNI and then using the imputed data to improve the classification of subjects.

---

[1] http://adni.loni.usc.edu/.

The Paper is Organized as Follow: In Sect. 2 we provide further background on the reguralized EM (regEM, Schneider proposal) and EM Out-of-Sample (regEM-oos) version (proposal of this work). Section 3 details the experimental settings on which we tested the different classification problems with regEM and regEM-oos, discussing our findings. Final remarks and future work are examined in Sect. 4.

2   Proposal

This section introduces the proposed approach for feature imputation. Let us begin by introducing the notation used through this work. A data matrix $X_{n \times d}$ can be represented by $\mathbf{X} = [\mathbf{x}_1, \mathbf{x}_2, \ldots, \mathbf{x}_j, \ldots, \mathbf{x}_d]$, where d is the total number of variables (or features) and n is the total number of examples (or subjects). When $\mathbf{X}$ has missing data, X is represented by concatenating two submatrices, i.e. $\mathbf{X} = [\mathbf{X}_o, \mathbf{X}_m]$, where $\mathbf{X}_o$ is the matrix of fully observed features and $\mathbf{X}_m$ is the matrix that encompasses features with missing values.

Our proposal leverages the *EM* algorithm and the approach proposed by Schneider [8] for missing data imputation. This method will be summarized as follows. The algorithm iterates between three steps, the E-Step, the M-step and the imputation step. In the E-step, the expected of the log-likelihood function is computed using the current estimate of the log-likelihood parameters. During the M-step, new estimates of the log-likelihood function parameters are obtained using the previous log-likelihood estimates obtained during the E-step. Formally, the E-Step and M-Step can be expressed as:

$$\text{E-Step} : Q(\theta_t) = E[l(\theta|\mathbf{X}_o, \mathbf{X}_m)]$$
$$\text{M-Step} : \theta_{t+1} = \arg\max_{\theta} Q(\theta_t)$$

where θ_t is the vector of parameters in the iteration t and $l(\cdot)$ is the log-likelihood function.

The imputation step is made by using a linear regression model that connects the variables with missing values and the variables without missing values:

$$x_m = \mu_m + (x_o - \mu_o)\beta + e \tag{1}$$

where $x_o \in \mathbb{R}^{1 \times p_o}$ is the sub-vector of p_o variables with observable data, $x_m \in \mathbb{R}^{1 \times p_m}$ is the sub-vector of p_m variables with missing values, $\mu_o \in \mathbb{R}^{1 \times p_o}$ is the sub-vector with the mean of the variables with observable data and $\mu_m \in \mathbb{R}^{1 \times p_m}$ is the sub-vector with the mean of the variables with missing values. $\beta \in \mathbb{R}^{p_o \times p_m}$ is the coefficients regression matrix and $e \in \mathbb{R}^{1 \times p_m}$ is a random vector with mean 0 (zero) and an unknown covariance matrix $C \in \mathbb{R}^{p_m \times p_m}$.

$\widehat{\beta} = \widehat{\Sigma}_{oo}^{-1} \widehat{\Sigma}_{om}$, where $\widehat{\Sigma}_{oo}$ is the covariance matrix estimated from variables with observable values and $\widehat{\Sigma}_{om}$ is the covariance matrix estimated from variables with missing and observable values.

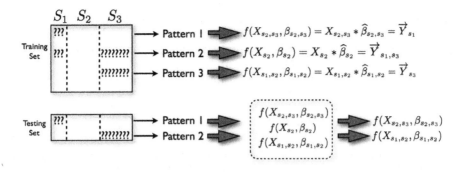

Fig. 1. Each missing values (MV) pattern in the training set has a regression model. Then, these regression models are used to impute the missing values in the testing set.

In the Schneider's approach [8], the inverse of the covariance matrix of the observed data, $\widehat{\Sigma}_{oo}^{-1}$, is iteratively estimated according to the expression:

$$\widehat{\Sigma}_{oo}^{-1} \longleftarrow (\widehat{\Sigma}_{oo} + h^2\widehat{D})^{-1} \tag{2}$$

where $\widehat{D} = Diag(\widehat{\Sigma}_{oo})$ is the diagonal matrix consisting of the diagonal elements of the covariance matrix $\widehat{\Sigma}_{oo}$ and h is a regularization parameter. That is, the ill-conditioned inverse $\widehat{\Sigma}_{oo}^{-1}$ is replaced with the inverse of the matrix that results from the covariance matrix $\widehat{\Sigma}_{oo}^{-1}$ when the diagonal elements are amplified.

This version of the EM algorithm (regEM) is used in several works [7,9], where the datasets have missing values and it is necessary to perform the classification task. In this context, the typical way to use this algorithm is to apply it to the training set and then, separately, to use it in the testing set. This way of using it, we consider that it is not correct, since every algorithm that works with a training set, must create a model, which will be later applied to the testing set. This methodology is always performed with the classification algorithms (ANN, SVM, etc.) and should also be applied with pre-processing algorithms, such as dimensionality reduction techniques, and missing values imputation algorithms.

In addition to the above mentioned remarks, our approach solves the problem that arises when the testing set arrives one data point at a time (very typical in real situations), since the original proposal can not construct the imputation model, since it is based on a regression model.

We will call this new version: regEM-Out of Sample (regEM-oos). regEM-oos can be applied in scenarios where both the training set and the testing set have missing values. Once used in the training set, the algorithm creates a general model that consists of as many regression models as missing patterns exist in the training set. These regression models are based on the Eq. 1, therefore in addition to using the matrix β, the vector of mean μ must be used. An example of this procedure, with three information sources S_i and three missing values patterns is shown in Fig. 1.

Although it is very rare, it may occur that a new MV pattern appears in the testing set. This means that this MV pattern does not have a regression model and therefore the imputation can not be made directly. To solve this, it is necessary to return to the training set and build a model for this new pattern. With the training set already imputed, we proceed to generate the new pattern found in the testing set, but in a synthetic way. With this, an imputation model of the new pattern found is obtained to make future imputations in the testing set.

3   Experimental Results

With the purpose of illustrating how well our approach performs, we consider three baseline ADNI modalities: cerebrospinal fluid (CSF), magnetic resonance imaging (MRI) and positron emission tomography (PET). The modalities were preprocessed according to [4], with 43 out of 819 subjects excluded for not passing the quality control. The CSF source contains three variables that measure the levels of some proteins and amino acids that are crucially involved in AD. The MRI source provides volumetric features of 83 brain anatomical regions. The PET source (with FDG radiotracer) provides the average brain function, in terms of the rate of cerebral glucose metabolism, within the 83 anatomical regions. Hence, each subject consists of 169 features. Table 1 shows details of the data distribution.

Table 1. Details of the data. First column shows the amount of examples for each class. The other columns show the amount of examples with MV per modalities. Individuals with MCI can be divided into two groups: those who remained in a stable condition (s-MCI) and those who later progressed to AD (p-MCI).

	ADNI	CSF	MRI	PET
AD	185	85	0	114
HC	210	107	0	141
pMCI	164	80	0	102
sMCI	217	114	0	132
Total	776	386	0	489

We consider three experiments: AD/HC with 395 subjects and MCI/HC with 591 subjects and pMCI/sMCI with 381 subjects. In each experiment we used 75% of the data to train three classifiers, a K-Nearest Neighbors (K-NN), a ν-Support Vector Machine (ν-SVM) and a Random Forest (RF) models, evaluated over 100 runs to avoid bias. The remaining 25% of the data was used for testing. We employed the implementations found in the scikit-learn library[2]. The number K and *metric_distance* for K-NN, ν and σ for ν-SVM and the number of trees and number of features for RF were determined using 5-fold CV.

---

[2] scikit-learn.org/stable.

We performed a normalization process before of the classification step following the Out-of-sample strategy. Considering we want the features had an interval $[0, 1]$, the testing set was normalized with:

$$X^{te}_{norm} = \frac{X^{te}_{raw} - X^{tr}_{min}}{X^{tr}_{max} - X^{tr}_{min}} \tag{3}$$

where X^{tr}_{min} and X^{tr}_{max} are the minimum and maximum from the training set respectively, and X^{te}_{raw} is the original values from the testing set.

For completeness, we include the results when the classifiers are trained solely with the reduced set of subjects having complete records and thus no imputation is needed. The number of subjects in this case is 72 for AD/HC, 110 for MCI/HC and 75 for pMCI/sMCI and is represented with *none* in the tables.

Tables 2, 3 and 4 show the classification results for the experiments based on ROC analysis [2].

Table 2. AD/HC multi-modality classification accuracy (acc.), area under the curve (AUC), sensitivity (sens.), specificity (spec.), and F-measure (F). Results are expressed as mean (standard deviation).

Classifier	Imputation	Acc. (%)	AUC (%)	Sens. (%)	Spec. (%)	F (%)
K-NN	*none*	82.2(8.9)	**93.1**(6.4)	90.4(10.9)	**76.5**(14.1)	82.6(9.3)
	regEM	82.9(4.4)	91.3(3.3)	94.3(3.7)	69.4(10.4)	85.6(3.5)
	regEM-oos	**84.6**(3.6)	91.8(2.8)	**94.3**(3.0)	73.4(7.1)	**86.8**(3.2)
SVM	*none*	84.7(8.9)	91.8(12.4)	83.4(16.0)	**86.7**(12.3)	83.1(11.1)
	regEM	87.7(3.4)	93.5(2.5)	90.8(5.1)	84.0(6.5)	88.7(3.5)
	regEM-oos	**88.3**(3.1)	**93.7**(2.5)	**91.6**(3.3)	84.6(5.4)	**89.4**(2.9)
RF	*none*	83.0(8.6)	92.0(6.8)	83.6(14.7)	83.7(11.6)	81.9(10.1)
	regEM	84.2(4.1)	92.4(2.5)	86.3(9.2)	81.5(9.2)	85.2(5.2)
	regEM-oos	**86.5**(3.6)	**93.0**(2.5)	**88.3**(4.6)	**84.5**(6.0)	**87.5**(3.3)

It can be noted that the classification improves when the full data set is used, imputing the missing values. This clearly provides more information to discriminate among the different diagnostic groups.

These experiments suggest that regEM-oos have the best performance in AD/HC, MCI/HC and pMCI/sMCI considering that when the difference is small, a lower standard deviation is preferred.

The classifiers present similar performances in each experiment, but a remarkable point is that their robustness (low variance) is increased in cases in which imputation is performed. Additionally, regEM-oos has the least variance in almost all experiments.

Regarding to execution time, an important feature of regEM-oos is that is faster than the regEM approach in about 27%. This is because regEM creates

Table 3. MCI/HC multi-modality classification accuracy (acc.), area under the curve (AUC), sensitivity (sens.), specificity (spec.), and F-measure (F). Results are expressed as mean (standard deviation).

Classifier	Imputation	Acc. (%)	AUC (%)	Sens. (%)	Spec. (%)	F (%)
K-NN	*none*	70.3(7.2)	72.5(10.4)	33.8(17.9)	**87.3**(8.8)	39.2(16.5)
	regEM	70.2(4.0)	76.2(4.2)	55.4(11.1)	78.9(6.3)	56.6(7.4)
	regEM-oos	**70.5**(3.9)	**76.3**(4.0)	**57.7**(9.0)	78.0(5.5)	**58.1**(6.1)
SVM	*none*	70.6(9.8)	70.7(17.1)	49.7(24.5)	**80.0**(17.9)	48.1(19.2)
	regEM	69.7(7.9)	**74.8**(13.0)	56.4(14.6)	77.1(15.0)	56.7(8.3)
	regEM-oos	**70.6**(8.1)	73.9(15.7)	**59.7**(12.7)	76.7(13.6)	**59.1**(7.7)
RF	*none*	**72.9**(7.2)	73.4(9.6)	42.6(18.2)	**87.1**(7.6)	47.6(16.8)
	regEM	71.8(3.9)	77.5(3.9)	45.2(13.1)	86.9(5.1)	52.4(10.8)
	regEM-oos	72.7(3.5)	**78.0**(3.5)	**53.6**(7.4)	83.7(4.1)	**58.3**(5.2)

Table 4. pMCI/sMCI multi-modality classification accuracy (acc.), area under the curve (AUC), sensitivity (sens.), specificity (spec.), and F-measure (F). Results are expressed as mean (standard deviation).

Classifier	Imputation	Acc. (%)	AUC (%)	Sens. (%)	Spec. (%)	F (%)
K-NN	*none*	53.7(10.1)	58.6(11.9)	**55.4**(17.5)	55.8(22.1)	**55.8**(11.4)
	regEM	**63.7**(4.7)	69.8(5.0)	46.1(11.9)	**77.2**(8.5)	51.4(8.5)
	regEM-oos	63.5(4.8)	**69.9**(4.9)	47.1(11.2)	76.3(8.6)	51.9(8.0)
SVM	*none*	52.6(11.5)	52.6(13.7)	**55.9**(22.0)	51.4(25.7)	**54.6**(14.6)
	regEM	63.2(4.3)	67.5(7.8)	51.3(13.8)	**72.4**(10.2)	53.4(9.1)
	regEM-oos	**63.3**(4.1)	**68.9**(4.7)	52.2(12.4)	72.0(9.4)	54.1(8.1)
RF	*none*	57.3(8.3)	60.9(10.9)	**64.9**(14.1)	50.2(17.1)	**62.3**(8.4)
	regEM	62.9(4.2)	68.7(5.0)	49.0(12.5)	**73.4**(9.5)	52.2(8.6)
	regEM-oos	**64.0**(4.5)	**70.3**(4.5)	53.9(7.8)	72.0(7.2)	56.0(5.5)

a new model for the testing set and regEM-oos use the model created from the training set. Obviously, while the testing set is larger, the time saving would become more significant.

4 Conclusions and Future Work

We have seen how imputation techniques allow using additional information, that in absence of accurate imputation methods would be discarded. In our experiments we have showed that using our imputation method we can achieve more accurate results in the task of determining the diagnostic groups to which ADNI's subjects belong.

Our results showed that training classifiers with imputed data is better than constructing a predictive model with a reduced number of subjects with complete records. This is supported in part by the fact that the imputation techniques increase both performance metrics and robustness of the classifiers.

It is necessary to use the Out-of-sample version of the algorithms when we are working in classification problems. Creating a model with the training set, and then using it in the testing set is one of the most relevant principles in Machine Learning. This issue is not typically taken into account within the imputation and dimensionality reduction literature.

In this work we presented a straightforward Out-of-sample version of regEM (regEM-oos) that improves the performance of the original algorithm, considering execution time and metrics based on ROC analysis.

Future work includes studying the performance of regEM-oos with other data sets and from the theoretical point of view. Furthermore, there is an interest in analyzing the relationship between the imputation and classification accuracies.

An interesting approach would be to consider the information of the labels from the training set to create a model for each class. With an ad-hoc model for each class we believe that the imputation and classification will be better, but the problem that must be addressed is how to decide which model should be used when new testing data becomes available.

References

1. Dempster, A.P., Laird, N.M., Rubin, D.B.: Maximum likelihood from incomplete data via the EM algorithm. J. Roy. Stat. Soc. B **39**(1), 1–38 (1977)
2. Fawcett, T.: An introduction to ROC analysis. Pattern Recogn. Lett. **27**(8), 861–874 (2006)
3. Gisbrecht, A., Lueks, W., Mokbel, B., Hammer, B.: Out-of-sample kernel extensions for nonparametric dimensionality reduction. In: ESANN 2012, pp. 531–536 (2012)
4. Gray, K., Aljabar, P., Heckemann, R.A., Hammers, A., Rueckert, D.: Random forest-based similarity measures for multi-modal classification of Alzheimer's disease. NeuroImage **65**, 167–175 (2013)
5. Jie, B., Zhang, D., Cheng, B., Shen, D.: Manifold regularized multitask feature learning for multimodality disease classification. Hum. Brain Mapp. **36**, 489–507 (2015)
6. Little, R.J.A., Rubin, D.B.: Statistical Analysis with Missing Data, 2nd edn. Wiley-Interscience, New York (2002)
7. Rahman, M.G., Islam, M.Z.: Missing value imputation using a fuzzy clustering-based EM approach. Knowl. Inf. Syst. **46**(2), 389–422 (2016)
8. Schneider, T.: Analysis of incomplete climate data: estimation of mean values and covariance matrices and imputation of missing values. J. Clim. **14**, 853–871 (2001)
9. Thung, K.H., Wee, C.Y., Yap, P.T., Shen, D.: Neurodegenerative disease diagnosis using incomplete multi-modality data via matrix shrinkage and completion. NeuroImage **91**, 386–400 (2014)

10. Van Der Maaten, L., Postma, E., Van den Herik, J.: Dimensionality reduction: a comparative review. J. Mach. Learn. Res. **10**, 66–71 (2009)
11. Yuan, L., Wang, Y., Thompson, P.M., Narayan, V.A., Ye, J.: Multi-source feature learning for joint analysis of incomplete multiple heterogeneous neuroimaging data. NeuroImage **61**(3), 622–632 (2012)

Multi-granulation Strategy via Feature Subset Extraction by Using a Genetic Algorithm and a Rough Sets-Based Measure of Dependence

Ariam Rivas[1]([✉]), Ricardo Navarro[2]([✉]), Chyon Hae Kim[2], and Rafael Bello[3]

[1] Universidad de Holguín, Holguín, Cuba
arivasm90@gmail.com
[2] Iwate University, Morioka, Japan
ricardonrcu@gmail.com, tenkai@iwate-u.ac.jp
[3] Universidad Central de Las Villas, Santa Clara, Cuba
rbellop@uclv.edu.cu

Abstract. Rough Set Theory (RST) is an effective technique for data analysis, which aims at approximate any concept (domain subset) by a pair of exact sets called the lower and upper approximations. In this research, we develop a machine learning method based on contexts (sets of attributes). It performs a multi-granulation based on a genetic algorithm in a way that it searches for the subsets of features having best values for the measure at hand (the degree of dependence from RST), but at the same time more distinct from each other. Then, an ensemble algorithm of the models obtained in each granule is applied. The proposed *Genetic Algorithm and Rough Sets-based Multi-Granulation* method exhibits satisfactory results compared to outstanding state-of-the-art algorithms.

Keywords: Rough sets · Multi-granulation · Genetic algorithm · Classification

1 Introduction

Granular computing (GC) [16] is a new paradigm in information processing. This term was coined to label a subset of Zadeh's granular mathematics [17]. Among several Artificial Intelligence (AI) strategies, GC is used for knowledge discovery. When using data instead of knowledge, it is hard to work with the least amount of information possible without losing the quality of the solution. A clear example appears in problem solving via rough sets. In this case, it is of interest to define the lowest possible equivalence relation, that is, the equivalence relation that includes the minimum amount of attributes keeping the same quality with the use of approximate sets.

Rough Set Theory (RST) has proven to be effective to develop machine learning techniques [9, 10]. RST approaches based on multi-granulation (MG) start from the existence of different granulations determined by the relationships $A_1, A_2, \ldots, A_m \subseteq A_T$; which allows to have different perspectives of the data, where A_T is the set of

© Springer Nature Switzerland AG 2019
R. Vera-Rodriguez et al. (Eds.): CIARP 2018, LNCS 11401, pp. 203–211, 2019.
https://doi.org/10.1007/978-3-030-13469-3_24

features, and the A_i are subsets of features called contexts. In reviewed papers [6, 9] on the combination of RST and MG (RST+MG), authors introduced those contexts A_i without any clear explanation about how they were determined. In the less common way to extract contexts, each A_i is clearly identified by experts in the application domain. In this research, we tackle this problem by building the contexts, which is indeed the most used option to solve this problem. Such variant is very appropriate, especially in domains with many predictive features, and in those where the contexts are not clear. This MG-based RST approach is similar to learning multi-views [15].

Unlike single-view learning, multi-views learning introduces a function to model a particular view and optimizes all functions at a time, exploiting redundant views over the input data. In such a configuration, each view may contain some knowledge that other views do not have. Multiple views can be used to describe data exhaustively and accurately [12]. In the review of the literature on learning from multi-views, this matter was found to be closely related to other topics of machine learning, such as active learning and ensemble learning. The idea of ensemble learning can be briefly depicted as the use of multiple learning models and combine their predictions [5, 12]. In addition, co-training is one of the oldest schemes for learning multi-views [12].

In this research, we propose a method to construct each A_i, which can be seen as multi-views. It uses a genetic algorithm (GA) and a measure of dependence between features; an ensemble algorithm similar to co-training is applied. However, our method differs from co-training in that it does not use any information provided by previous classifiers. In our ensemble algorithm, after separately obtaining the models of multiple views, an average probability vote is used to make the *classification*, which is the specific task of machine learning that we are dealing with. Classification is aim at inferring a function $F: P \rightarrow Y$ from a labeled training data $\{(P_1, Y_1),..., (P_m, Y_m)\}$ where P_i is a vector of values (the input) and Y_i is a class value (the output).

The remainder of this paper elaborates aspects on the computational methodology, in Sect. 2. Section 3 introduces our method *Genetic Algorithm and Rough Sets-based Multi-Granulation* (GA-RS-MG). Section 4 presents the experimental framework and results, while conclusions and future work remarks are given in Sect. 5.

2 Computational Methodology

To assess resulting contexts, we built an ensemble algorithm based on MLP classifier. It reveals the much the generation of contexts benefits machine learning methods.

2.1 Rough Set Theory

RST is an efficient tool for data mining, suitable for discovering dependencies between data, discovering patterns, estimating data significance, reducing data and so forth [2, 4, 13]. In particular, it has been remarkably applied to the field of medicine [9]. RST aims at approximate any concept $X \subseteq U$ (subset of the domain universe) by a pair of exact sets, the *lower and upper approximations*. The lower approximation $B_*(X)$ of a set X is defined as the collection of cases (objects of the universe U) whose equivalence classes [2, 13] are totally contained in X. The upper approximation $B^*(X)$ contains only those objects of U which belong to the equivalence classes that are at least partially contained in the set, i.e. generated by the inseparability relation containing at least one object x belonging to X. They are formally described as follows:

$$B_*(X) = \{x \in U \mid B(x) \subseteq X\} \tag{1}$$

$$B^*(X) = \{x \in U \mid B(x) \cap X \neq \phi\} \tag{2}$$

The classic RST works with discrete data to define the *separability* between objects based on the strict equality between values. When data have features of continuous domains, these are discretized in order to obtain the degree of dependence through equivalence relations; otherwise, it would be necessary to use similarity relations.

Dependence Between Contexts and Decision Features. Discovering dependencies between attributes is a key in data analysis [2]. Let B and D be subsets of set of attributes A in the information system (U, A). $B \Rightarrow \sigma D$ denotes that D depends on B in a degree of σ ($0 \leq \sigma \leq 1$). D depends partially on B in case $\sigma < 1$, whereas $B \Rightarrow D$ if the degree of dependence $\sigma = 1$, i.e. D depends totally on B, which happens when all values of the features in D are uniquely determined by the values of the features in B.

$$\sigma(B, D) = \frac{|POS_B(D)|}{|U|} \tag{3}$$

$$\text{where } POS_B(D) = \bigcup_{X \in U/D} B_*(X) \tag{4}$$

2.2 Random Forest and Multilayer Perceptron

Random Forest (RF) [3] is a general method to build a set of L tree-based classifiers. The data set of each classifier includes a subset of variables. The number of trees in the forest and the number of variables in the subset should be set a priori. The number of subsets of variables is calculated as $F = \log_2 M + 1$, where M is the number of attributes of the original data set. Each tree is built to its maximum depth and no pruning procedure is applied after that. The predicted class for any given example is determined by adding the predictions of the set of decision trees through a majority vote.

On the other hand, artificial neural networks (ANNs) are mathematical tools for modeling problems. They reveal functional relationships between the data in classification tasks, pattern recognition, regressions, etc. Applied ANN consists of Multilayer Perceptron (MLP) [11], ones of the most popular ANN models. As for training, MLP uses the backpropagation (BP) learning algorithm to adapt its computation function to the needs of each particular problem.

2.3   Problem Formulation

Usually, a decision system DS $= (U, A \cup \{d\})$ is seen as a single set, where A is the set of predictive features and d means the decision feature [1, 6, 8, 14]. However, in a DS it is possible to define different contexts (subsets of features $A_i \subset A$) that bear a certain relationship with d. Thus, such contexts reveal distinct viewpoints on the relationships between the predictive and decisive attributes. Several decision subsystems $DS_i = (U, A_i \cup \{d\})$ can be obtained by using different contexts A_i. Those contexts can emerge from any set of predictive feature in a natural way. Let us consider a DS with information of college students, where A includes few features on their social status, others about high school grades, others regarding entrance examination, and so forth. Each of those sets of features offers a unique outlook on the student.

In real-world scenarios, it is not easy to create proper contexts A_i from predictive features. Thus, it is needed to tackle the problem of creating suitable contexts to apply machine learning methods on them. That is indeed the problem that we approach in this paper by introducing a method to build contexts to be used in classification tasks.

3   Proposed Method

Genetic Algorithm and Rough Sets-based Multi-Granulation (GA-RS-MG) is the method that we propose to carry out a multi-granulation from the features viewpoint, in order to develop context-based machine learning methods. Our method bases on a GA to automatically determine the contexts of each DS. It uses a generational model with elitist replacement: the fittest individual of the previous population survives to current one. In this specific case, chromosomes (individuals) have as many genes as predictive features exist in the DS. Chromosomes have a binary representation, where value 1 indicates that the corresponding feature is selected, and it is set to 0 if not.

We used the measure of dependence described by Eq. (3) as fitness function, where each chromosome represents a context. For each decision class D_i, $B_*(D_i)$ is calculated by Eq. (1). The overall sum of the number of objects in each lower approximation is divided by the cardinality of the universe U, which in this case is the number of instances in the DS. In this way, we evaluate the degree of dependence of each chromosome with respect to the decision feature. In the last GA population, among the most mutually dependent individuals, the most different ones are selected.

Pseudocode in Table 1 describes the algorithmic basis of GA-RS-MG. **Line 1** initializes the population: every gene value is set to 1 or 0 with a probability of 0.5. Then, the fitness of each individual is evaluated. A maximum of 100 iterations is used as stop condition for the evolutionary loop (**line 2**), and the population size s = 44. We set pc = 0.7 as crossover probability and pm = 0.09 as mutation probability. The election of values for all the aforementioned parameters has an empirical nature.

In **line 16**, the best current individual replaces the worst descendant. We figure the number of contexts (**line 19**) according to a uniform distribution between a minimum level of 3 individuals and a maximum level of one third of the population size

Table 1. Genetic Algorithm and Rough Sets-based Multi-Granulation (GA-RS-MG).

Inputs:		
DS: decision system	pc: crossover probability	s: population size
m: number of iterations	pm: mutation probability	

Process:

1. initialize (population, DS)   // evaluate individuals with its 'degree of dependence'
2. **for** k = 1 **to** m **do**   // evolutionary loop of the genetic algorithm
3.   **for** i = 1 **to** s, i += 2, **do**
4.   parent1 = rouletteSelection (population)
5.   parent2 = rouletteSelection (population)
6.   **if** (random() <= pc)
7.   child1, child2 = crossoverOnePoint (parent1, parent2)
8.   **if** (random() <= pm) {
9.   mutateBinary (child1)
10.   mutateBinary (child2)
11.   }
12.   child1 = functionDependence (child1, DS)
13.   child2 = functionDependence (child2, DS)
14.   offspring.Add (child1, child2)
15.   **end for**
16.   replaceWorstChildren (offspring, population)   // by the fittest in 'population'
17.   replacement (offspring, population)   // offspring replace entire population
18. **end for**   // end of the evolutionary loop
19. nGranules = getGranulation (s)
20. selectBest (nGranules, population) {
21.   functionEvaluation (population) {
22.   calculate the global distance of each *i-th* individual: 'glDistance_i'
23.   evaluate each individual: (degreeOfDependence_i + glDistance_i) / 2
24.   }
25.   pop1 = select the granulation ('nGranules') that leads to fittest population
26.   **return** pop1
27. }

Output:
28.   data = convertToDataset (pop1, DS)

(s/3 individuals). We select the best individuals by the degree of dependence (**line 20**); we prefer those being more dependent but also more different from each other. Two given individuals (chromosomes) are distinct if they differ at any *i-th* position (gene). We try to obtain best contexts at once; we intend to assure that they are different regarding predictive features. Finally, selected best individuals become into output data set.

4 Results and Discussion

For experiment, we used data sets (see Table 2) from the University of California at Irvine (UCI) repository. The degree of dependence between contexts by GA-RS-MG and the decision feature satisfies the condition $\sigma(A_i, d) \geq 0.75$. Contexts found for each single DS do not have the same number of attributes. We assessed the suitability of such contexts by applying MLP to discover knowledge on them. For MLP and RF we used the default parametric setups given in WEKA data-mining tool, version 3.8.

Table 2. Benchmark decision systems: description and generated contexts.

DS	Attributes	Instances	Mixed data	Balanced	#Class values	#Contexts
Dermatology	34	366	No	No	6	11
Hepatitis	20	155	Yes	No	2	13
ADA	49	4147	Yes	No	2	6
Audiology	70	226	No	No	24	4
Autos	26	205	Yes	No	6	8
Flags	30	194	Yes	No	8	13
Segment	20	2310	No	Yes	7	10
Soybean	36	683	No	No	19	13
Waveform	41	5000	No	Yes	3	10
Primary-tumor	18	339	No	No	21	6
Lung-cancer	57	32	No	Yes	3	11
Heart-disease	14	303	Yes	No	2	11

To assure statistical robustness we made a 10-folds cross-validation with one run per DS. Besides, the built model of each original DS was added to a voting algorithm along with the remaining models of the corresponding contexts by GA-RS-MG. Such an ensemble algorithm has MLP as base classifier. Table 3 shows results (for *weighted precision* (WP) and *mean absolute error* (MAE) evaluation measures) achieved by the proposed ensemble method with MLP as base classifier (VoteMLP), as well as by MLP and RF. Highlighted (†) values are the overall best results for each DS. VoteMLP exhibits the one with the best results regarding WP.

Figure 1 depicts the mean and the standard deviation of the classification algorithms, concerning both WP and MAE. VoteMLP and MLP reached the best performance. To detect significant differences in the group of methods, we applied Friedman test on results for WP and MAE. Table 4 shows the average ranking of each method. The p-values computed by the Friedman test were 0.2636 and 4.1770E−05, for the case of WP and MAE respectively. According to that, there are significant differences among the three algorithms regarding the MAE, for a level of significance $\alpha = 0.05$. Consequently, in a post-hoc stage, we applied the Holm test in order to detect significant differences between all pairs of algorithms, as recommended in [7].

Table 3. Experimental results.

DS	MLP		VoteMLP		RF	
	WP	MAE	WP	MAE	WP	MAE
Dermatology	0.9702	0.0130	† 0.9757	0.0254	0.9729	0.0494
Hepatitis	0.8891	0.1251	† 0.8933	0.1406	0.8329	0.2068
ADA	0.8338	0.1735	† 0.8434	0.1837	0.8428	0.2020
Audiology	† 0.7908	0.0187	0.7618	0.0356	0.7548	0.0346
Autos	† 0.8869	0.0381	0.8847	0.0482	0.8813	0.0714
Flags	† 0.6237	0.0936	0.5529	0.1215	0.5891	0.1542
Segment	0.9710	0.0099	† 0.9745	0.0123	0.9719	0.0281
Soybean	0.9262	0.0098	0.9412	0.0120	† 0.9419	0.0242
Waveform	0.8310	0.1142	0.8437	0.1442	† 0.8508	0.2328
Primary-tumor	0.3996	0.0560	† 0.4174	0.0578	0.3697	0.0621
Lung-cancer	0.4202	0.3746	0.4261	0.3840	† 0.5135	0.4022
Heart-disease	0.8020	0.0822	0.8220	0.0827	† 0.8249	0.0957

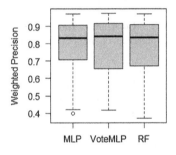
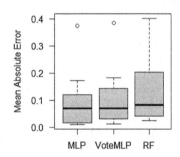

Fig. 1. Box plot of evaluation measures.

Table 4 shows the adjusted p-values by Holm test for each pair of methods in the comparison hypotheses. Results reveal significant differences between any pair of algorithms, for a level of significance $\alpha = 0.05$. Regarding weighted precision, MLP is outperformed by RF, which is in turn outperformed by VoteMLP. However, none of such superiorities is statistically significant. In contrast, while comparing them in terms of mean absolute error, MLP significantly outperforms both VoteMLP and RF, and the poorest results belong to RF, also significantly outperformed by VoteMLP. Considering all the aforementioned, MLP and VoteMLP exhibit the best performance.

Table 4. Friedman test and Holm test.

a) Friedman test: PW

Method	Rank
VoteMLP	1.6667
RF	2.0
MLP	2.3333

b) Friedman test: MAE

Method	Rank
MLP	1.0833
VoteMLP	2.0
RF	2.9167

c) Adjusted p-values by Holm test: MAE

Pair of methods	p-value	
MLP vs. RF	2.1293E-05	Hypotheses Rejected
MLP vs. VoteMLP	0.0495	
VoteMLP vs. RF	0.0495	

5 Conclusions

We propose *Genetic Algorithm and Rough Sets-based Multi-Granulation*, which creates granules (contexts) based on a GA. Each context must fulfill a certain degree of dependence with respect to the decision feature. Besides, obtained models are simpler and more precise as a whole. We consider models of contexts and the original DS for classification by an ensemble. The proposed method shows suitable results, statistically assessed by comparing the performance of MLP, VoteMLP and RF classifiers.

VoteMLP was superior to both MLP and RF in terms of weighted precision, while RF outperformed MLP, but in any case significantly. In addition, regarding the mean absolute error, VoteMLP significantly outperforms RF, and MLP outperforms them both. The results of the proposed approach are comparable with RF. Even in the case when RF performs better, our method has an extra advantage: RF uses 100 trees to find a solution but our method creates as many trees as built contexts (see Table 2). That is a good point to assess not only its effectiveness but also its efficiency.

References

1. Azuraliza, A.B., Zulaiha, A.O., Abdul, R.H., Rozianiwati, Y., Ruhaizan, I.: An agent based rough classifier for data mining. In: 8th International Conference on Intelligent Systems Design and Applications, pp. 145–151 (2008)
2. Bello, R., García, M., Pérez, J.N.: Teoría de los conjuntos aproximados. Conceptos y métodos computacionales (Rough set theory. Foundations and computational methods). Editorial UD, Colombia (2012)
3. Breiman, L.: Random forests. Mach. Learn. **45**(1), 5–32 (2001)
4. Chen, Y.-S., Cheng, C.-H.: A Delphi-based rough sets fusion model for extracting payment rules of vehicle license tax in the government sector. Expert Syst. Appl. **37**, 2161–2174 (2010)
5. Dietterichl, T.G.: Ensemble learning. In: Arbib, M.A. (ed.) The Handbook of Brain Theory and Neural Networks, pp. 405–408. MIT Press, Cambridge (2002)
6. Eissa, M.M., Elmogy, M., Hashem, M.: Rough-granular neural network model for making treatment decisions of hepatitis C. In: 9th International Conference on Informatics and Systems, Data Engineering and Knowledge Management Track, pp. 19–26 (2014)
7. García, S., Herrera, F.: An extension on "statistical comparisons of classifiers over multiple data sets" for all pairwise comparisons. J. Mach. Learn. Res. **9**, 2677–2694 (2008)
8. Qian, Y., Liang, X., Lin, G., Guo, Q., Liang, J.: Local multigranulation decision-theoretic rough sets. Int. J. Approximate Reasoning **82**, 119–137 (2017)
9. Kumar, S.S., Inbarani, H.H.: Optimistic multi-granulation rough set based classification for medical diagnosis. Procedia Comput. Sci. **47**, 374–382 (2015)
10. Li, J., Ren, Y., Mei, C., Qian, Y., Yang, X.: A comparative study of multigranulation rough sets and concept lattices via rule acquisition. Knowl. Based Syst. **91**, 152–164 (2016)
11. Haykin, S.: Neural Networks and Learning Machines, 3rd edn. Prentice Hall, Pearson Education, Inc., New Jersey (2009)
12. Nigam, K., Ghani, R.: Analyzing the effectiveness and applicability of co-training. In: 9th International Conference on Information and Knowledge Management, pp. 86–93 (2000)

13. Polkowski, L.: Rough Sets Mathematical Foundations. Physica-Verlag, Heidelberg (2003)
14. Sikder, I.U., Munakata, T.: Application of rough set and decision tree for characterization of premonitory factors of low seismic activity. Expert Syst. Appl. **36**, 102–110 (2009)
15. Xu, C., Tao, D., Xu, C.: A Survey on Multi-view Learning. Cornell University Library, arXiv:1304.5634 [cs.LG] (2013)
16. Yao, Y.Y.: Granular computing: basic issues and possible solutions. In: 5th Joint Conference on Information Sciences, pp. 186–189 (2000)
17. Zadeh, L.A.: Some reflections on soft computing, granular computing and their roles in the conception, design and utilization of information/intelligent systems. Soft. Comput. **2**, 23–25 (1998)

Boosting Collaborative Filters
for Drug-Target Interaction Prediction

Cristian Orellana M.[1](✉), Ricardo Ñanculef[1], and Carlos Valle[2]

[1] Department of Informatics,
Federico Santa María Technical University, Valparaíso, Chile
cristian.orellanam@alumnos.usm.cl, jnancu@inf.utfsm.cl
[2] Department of Computer Science and Informatics,
University of Playa Ancha, Valparaíso, Chile
carlos.valle@upla.cl

Abstract. In-silico prediction of interactions between drugs and proteins has become a crucial step in pharmaceutical sciences to reduce the time and cost required for drug discovery and repositioning. Even if the problem may be approached using standard recommendation algorithms, the accurate prediction of unknown drug-target interactions has shown to be very challenging due to the relatively small number of drugs with information of their target proteins and viceversa. This issue has been recently circumvent using regularization methods that actively exploit prior knowledge regarding drug similarities and target similarities. In this paper, we show that an additional improvement in terms of accuracy can be obtained using an ensemble approach which learns to combine multiple regularized filters for prediction. Our experiments on eight drug-protein interaction datasets show that most of the time this method outperforms a single predictor and other recommender systems based on multiple filters but not specialized to the drug-target interaction prediction task.

Keywords: Drug-target interaction prediction ·
Collaborative filtering · Ensemble methods

1 Introduction

Discovering novel drug-target interactions (DTI) is one of the fundamental tasks in pharmaceutical sciences [3]. As in-vivo experimental methods are extremely costly and time-consuming, computational approaches capable to select the most promising candidates for a further validation have become of great importance in the last years [3,9]. From a machine learning perspective, a DTI problem can be approached as a recommendation task, where for a given drug (or target) a ranking of "expected" target proteins (or drugs) interactions is generated.

Similar to implicit recommendation tasks, in DTI problems, only sparse information for interacting pairs is available. That means one cannot assume

© Springer Nature Switzerland AG 2019
R. Vera-Rodriguez et al. (Eds.): CIARP 2018, LNCS 11401, pp. 212–220, 2019.
https://doi.org/10.1007/978-3-030-13469-3_25

non-interacting pairs as truly negatives, because some of them correspond to interacting pairs not discovered yet. DTI prediction is also challenging because publicly available databases contain a extremely small amount of validated pairs [8]. Even if sparsity is also a challenging feature of other recommendation tasks, most settings assume a minimum of $s > 1$ annotations exist for each user and item. This context suggests that the use of knowledge beyond the known interactions may be of crucial importance to successfully address DTI problems.

Contribution. In this paper, we investigate the use of AdaBoost for DTI. Relying on a probabilistic formulation for DTI, it is possible to obtain a principled ensemble algorithm that learns to combine predictions to produce more accurate recommendations. This idea is in line with previous contributions in the collaborative filtering and DTI literature [12,13]. However, up to our knowledge, we are the first to study the use of Adaboost to build an ensemble of collaborative filters for DTI. Previous methods are based on other ensemble paradigms (e.g. stacking [15]) without collaborative filters or do not employ DTI methods as base learners (e.g. decision trees [10]). In a nutshell, our method consists in solving re-weighted versions on an objective function that has been successfully used by NRLMF, a state-of-the-art method for DTI. Our experiments on standard benchmarks show that, in general, the proposed method outperforms a single predictor and an ensemble method not specialized for DTI.

The rest of this article is organized as follows. In Sect. 2 we formalize the DTI problem and briefly discuss related work. In Sect. 3, we formulate our ensemble method. In Sect. 4 we present experimental results that demonstrate the performance of our algorithm on eight DTI datasets. Section 5 closes the article with the conclusions and final remarks.

2 Problem Statement and Related Work

Problem Definition. Given a set of drugs $D = \{d_i\}_{i=1}^{m} \subset \mathcal{D}$, a set of target proteins $T = \{t_j\}_{j=1}^{n} \subset \mathcal{T}$ and a binary matrix $R^* \in \mathbb{R}^{m \times n}$ where $R_{ij}^* = 1$ if and only if drug d_i interact with target t_j, a DTI problem consists in predicting R^* from a matrix $R \in \mathbb{R}^{m \times n}$ where some interactions has been removed, that is, $R_{ij} = 0$ but $R_{ij}^* = 1$. This definition implies that the negative examples in R are only implicit, in the sense that $R_{ij} = 0$ can represent either an interacting pair not yet discovered or a truly non-interacting pair. Besides the interaction matrix R, similarity information regarding drugs and targets can be available. This information is encoded into the form of similarity matrices $S^{(d)} \in \mathbb{R}^{m \times m}$ and $S^{(t)} \in \mathbb{R}^{n \times n}$ where a high value $S_{kl}^{(d)}$ (respectively $S_{kl}^{(t)}$) represents a high similarity between drugs d_k and d_l (respectively proteins t_k and t_l).

Related Work. Compared to more traditional recommendation tasks, DTI problems are challenging because publicly available databases contains a very small amount of validated pairs [8]. This context explains why many state of the art methods rely on knowledge beyond the partially observed matrix R. Indeed, many machine learning approaches integrating information on drug or target similarity have been investigated in the last years. In [5], Gönen proposed a Bayesian matrix factorization model which encodes chemical similarity between compounds and genomic similarity between proteins using kernels functions [11]. This allow to perform predictions for drugs/proteins without annotations (cold start). Zheng proposed in [16] a matrix factorization approach able to accept more than one similarity matrix over drugs, as well as over targets, and able to automatically learn weights over the multiple similarity matrices in order to fit the latent matrix factors. Cobanoglu et al. adapted in [2] a probabilistic matrix factorization to DTI, demonstrating that this technique allowed to identify functionally similar drugs even in the absence of 3D shape similarity. More recently, Liu et al. has extended in [9] logistic matrix factorization (LMF) [6] to more actively exploit drug/target similarities. Neighborhood-based regularizers are incorporated into the objective function in order to constraint the latent factors of similar drugs/targets to be similar. This method, referred to as NRLMF, is shown to outperform state-of-the-art methods, including [5] and [16].

Aside matrix factorization techniques, some ensemble methods have been used for DTI problems. One of them is DrugE-Rank [15], which trains multiple similarity-based methods and use each output as feature to train a ranking learner for DTI predictions (stacking ensemble). Another ensemble approach for DTI is formulated in [10], where a boosting framework is utilized to combine multiple features for drug-target pairs, using decision trees as base learners.

A Probabilistic Model for DTI. LMF and NRMLF rely on a probabilistic model for DTI. LMF decomposes the interaction matrix R as the product $R = UV^T$ of two latent matrices $U \in \mathbb{R}^{m \times r}$ and $V \in \mathbb{R}^{n \times r}$. Each row of U, u_i, encodes a latent representation for drug d_i, whereas each row of V, v_j encodes a latent representation for protein t_j. While standard matrix factorization methods models the interaction between a drug d_i and target t_j using a score $s_{ij} = u_i v_j^T$, LMF models the probability of interaction p_{ij} for a pair (d_i, t_j) using the model $p_{ij} = \sigma(s_{ij})$, where $\sigma(\xi) = \exp(\xi)/(1 + \exp(\xi))$ is the sigmoid function. The latent matrices U, V are learnt from data by maximizing the log-likelihood

$$\ell_0(U, V) = \sum_{i,j} c R_{ij} \log p_{ij} + (1 - R_{ij}) \log(1 - p_{ij}) - \frac{\lambda_d}{2} \|U\|_F^2 - \frac{\lambda_t}{2} \|V\|_F^2 , \quad (1)$$

where $c \in \mathbb{R}$ is a parameter controlling the relative importance of positive versus negative examples and $\lambda \in \mathbb{R}$ is a regularization parameter enforcing sparsity in the latent representations. Liu et al. [9] propose to regularize this objective function in such a way that similar proteins/drugs obtain similar latent representations. Let $N(d_i)$ be the set of k_1 nearest neighbours of drug d_i computed according to the similarity matrix $S^{(d)}$ and $N(t_j)$ be the set of k_2 nearest neighbours of protein t_j according to the similarity matrix $S^{(t)}$. The new objective takes the form

$$\ell_1(U, V) = \ell_0(U, V) - \alpha/2 \sum_{i,j} a_{ij} \|u_i - u_j\|_2^2 - \beta/2 \sum_{i,j} b_{ij} \|v_i - v_j\|_2^2 , \quad (2)$$

where $a_{ij} = s_{ij}^{(d)}$ if $d_j \in N(d_i)$, $a_{ij} = 0$ if $d_j \notin N(d_i)$, $b_{ij} = s_{ij}^{(t)}$ if $t_j \in N(t_i)$, $b_{ij} = 0$ if $t_j \notin N(t_i)$ and α, β are new regularization parameters. The obtained objective function is differentiable and can be optimized using gradient ascent.

3   Proposed Method

In this section we formulate an ensemble method specialized for DTI. Essentially, we demonstrate that a principled way to combine DTI filters consists in solving weighted versions of the objective function used by LMF or NRMLF.

Boosting Procedure. Let $P : \mathcal{D} \times \mathcal{T} \to [0, 1]$ be the probability distribution generating pairs (d, t) from $\mathcal{D} \times \mathcal{T}$ and $Y(d, t)$ a binary random variable such that $Y(d, t) = 1$ if (d, t) is an interacting pair and $Y(d, t) = -1$ otherwise. We cast the problem of learning an ensemble $F(d, t)$ of DTI filters as that of approximating the logit of the interaction probability, i.e.,

$$F(d, t) = \log \frac{P(Y = 1|d, t)}{1 - P(Y = 1|d, t)} = \log P(Y = 1|d, t) - \log P(Y = -1|d, t). \quad (3)$$

It is well known in machine learning that a way to obtain a hypothesis of the previous form consists in training a learner to minimize the following objective

$$J(F) = \mathbb{E}\left\{ Q(Y(d, t), F(d, t))|d, t \right\}, \quad (4)$$

where $Q(Y(d, t), F(d, t)) = \exp(-Y(d, t)F(d, t))$ is known as the exponential loss. To optimize (4) we can adopt the stage-wise approach characteristic of boosting algorithms, i.e. we can implement F using an additive model of the form $F^{(k)} = \sum_{\ell}^{k} f^{(\ell)}$, where each $f^{(\ell)} : \mathcal{D} \times \mathcal{T} \to [-1, 1]$ is a DTI filter, and train $f^{(1)}, f^{(2)}, \dots$ one after the other to improve the value of the objective function $J(F)$. It is not difficult to show indeed (see e.g. [4]) that taking a gradient descent step to expand $F^{(k)} = \sum_{\ell=1}^{k} f^{(\ell)}$ at a given iteration k correspond to choose

$$f_{*}^{(k+1)}(d, t) = \frac{1}{2} \log \frac{P^{(k)}(Y = 1|d, t)}{(1 - P^{(k)}(Y = 1|d, t))}, \quad (5)$$

where $P^{(k)}(Y = 1) = W^{(k)}(d, t)P(Y(d, t) = 1)$ and

$$W^{(k)}(d, t) \propto \exp(-Y(d, t)F^{(k)}(d, t)), \quad (6)$$

represents a weighting distribution enforcing the hypothesis $f^{(k+1)}$ built at step k of the boosting procedure to focus on drug-target pairs (d, t) that the ensemble $F^{(k)}$ has incorrectly identified or has identified with a small "margin" $\eta(d, t) = Y(d, t)F^{(k)}(d, t)$. In order to implement the hypothesis in (5), we can first train a probabilistic classifier $\hat{P}^{(k)}(d, t)$ to approximate $P^{(k)}(Y = 1|d, t)$ and then set the $k + 1$-th filter in the ensemble to be

$$f^{(k+1)}(d, t) = \frac{1}{2} \log \frac{\hat{P}^{(k)}(d, t)}{(1 - \hat{P}^{(k)}(d, t))}. \quad (7)$$

Now, a method commonly used in machine learning to approximate a distribution $q(\xi)$ from a model $\hat{q}(\xi)$ consists in minimizing the so-called cross-entropy loss $J(\hat{q}, q) = -q(\xi) \log \hat{q}(\xi) - (1 - q(\xi)) \log(1 - \hat{q}(\xi))$ on a set of training examples distributed according to $q(\xi)$. We can obtain examples distributed according to our target distribution $P^{(k)}(Y = 1 | d, t)$ from the interaction matrix R by defining $R_{ij}^{(k)} = W^{(k)}(d_i, t_j) R_{ij}$. The probabilistic model $\hat{P}^{(k)}(d, t)$ at iteration k can thus be trained to minimize

$$J^{(k)} = -\sum_{i,j} R_{ij}^{(k)} \log \hat{P}^{(k)}(d_i, t_j) + (1 - R_{ij}^{(k)}) \log(1 - \hat{P}^{(k)}(d_i, t_j)), \quad (8)$$

$$= -\sum_{i,j} W_{ij}^{(k)} \left(R_{ij} \log \hat{P}_{ij}^{(k)} + (1 - R_{ij}) \log(1 - \hat{P}_{ij}^{(k)}) \right),$$

where $W_{ij}^{(k)} = W^{(k)}(d_i, t_j)$ and $\hat{P}_{ij}^{(k)} = \hat{P}^{(k)}(d_i, t_j)$.

Base Learner. Note that if $W_{ij}^{(k)} \propto 1 \, \forall i, j$ Eq. (8) is exactly the objective function employed by NRLMF, except by the constant c, controlling the relative weight of the positive examples, and the regularization terms. That means that a principled method to combine DTI filters correspond to solve re-weighted versions of NRLMF objectives at each iteration, where the weights for each drug-target pair are iteratively updated using Eq. (6). It is hence natural to adopt the probabilistic model used by NRLMF to implement $\hat{P}_{ij}^{(k)}$, that is, set $\hat{P}^{(k)}(d_i, t_j) = \sigma(u_i^k (v_j^k)^T)$ where $\{u_i^{(k)}\}_i, \{v_j^{(k)}\}_j$ correspond to new embeddings for drugs $\{d_i\}_i$ and targets $\{t_j\}_j$. An advantage of this decision is that we can rely on proven methods to fit probabilistic interaction models on DTI data. For instance, we can easily adapt the alternated gradient method employed in [9] to optimize (8). The required derivatives are exactly those employed by standard NRLMF, except that they become scaled by the weight distribution $W_{ij}^{(k)}$. We can also easily incorporate the additional components in the objective functions of NRLMF to each iteration of our boosting procedure in order to handle the high sparsity of the interaction matrices available in typical DTI applications. In practice, the regularization parameters can be tuned using model selection techniques, eventually leading to the plain objective of (8) is this setting is optimal.

Algorithm. The proposed method is summarized as Algorithm 1. As mentioned in the previous paragraph, step 4 of this method can be implemented using alternated gradient descent. Note also that step 3 can be performed recursively exploiting the additivity of $F^{(k)}$.

4   Experiments

We evaluate our method in the Yamanishi dataset collection[1], a gold standard for assessing DTI algorithms. It is composed of 4 prediction problems, namely, enzymes, ion channels (IC), g-protein coupled receptors (GPCR) and nuclear

---

[1] Yamanishi datasets are publicly available at http://web.kuicr.kyoto-u.ac.jp/supp/yoshi/drugtarget/.

Algorithm 1. Proposed Algorithm (AdaNRLMF).

---

1   Initialize the ensemble as $F^{(0)} = 0$;

2   **for** $k \leftarrow 0$ **to** $K - 1$ **do**

3   Compute the example weights as in Equation (6);

4   Implement the model $\hat{P}^{(k)}(d_i, t_j) = \sigma(u_i^k (v_j^k)^T)$ where $\{u_i^{(k)}\}, \{v_j^{(k)}\}$ are new embeddings for drugs $\{d_i\}_i$ and the targets $\{t_j\}_j$ obtained by training NRMLF with example weights $W_{ij}^{(k)}$;

5   Set $f^{(k+1)}$ as in Equation (5) and expand the ensemble $F^{(k+1)} = F^{(k)} + f^{(k+1)}$;

6   **end**

7   Return an ensemble of K DTI filters $F^{(K)}$.

---

receptors (NR) [14], corresponding to different types of proteins. We also consider an updated version of these four datasets, introduced in [7], in which more recently discovered drug-target interactions have been included. As usual, we adopt the *area under precision recall curve* (AUPR) as evaluation metric. This score is preferred over other information retrieval metrics in DTI studies as it illustrates better the differences between algorithms where there are significantly more negative than positive examples.

We compare our method[2] with NRLMF [9], a state-of-the-art method for DTI, and AdaMF [13], an ensemble algorithm for recommendations which is not specialized for DTI. In order to select the optimal parameters for NRLMF, we used a stratified cross-validation scheme. A train/test split is first obtained by randomly selecting 10% of positive and negative interactions for testing and 90% for training. Parameter selection is then performed using 10-fold stratified cross-validation on the resulting training set. That is, the training data is further split into 10 non-overlapping blocks. Each block is retained once as the validation data for evaluating the model that is trained on the remaining 9 blocks. The different results are averaged to produce a single performance estimation. We perform the optimal parameter selection in the same parameter space utilized in NRLMF. In order to speed up the parameter selection process, we adopt the Bayesian optimization method specifically devised for NRLMF in [1]. Once the best parameters for a given train/test split have been determined, the model is trained using the full training set and its output prediction is evaluated in the test set. This stratified cross-validation scheme is repeated 10 times using different train-test splits to obtain more significant results. The performance of the proposed method as well as that of AdaMF are computed on the same train-test splits used for NRLMF. However, in order to select parameters for these methods, we adopt a more simple strategy. For AdaMF, we adopt the parameters suggested by the authors in [13]. For our method, we apply simplifications. First, we train each learner in the ensemble with exactly the same parameters, since it allows to evaluate better the effect of our boosting approach (different

---

[2] Our code is available at https://gitlab.com/cw_cw/adanrlmf.

parameters may introduce additional diversity in the ensemble not due to the weight distribution adaptation). Second, since we are employing NRMLF as the base learner, we set the base learner parameters to the same values selected for this method in each train-test split. A more exhaustive parameter search may have resulted in slightly better results.

Table 1 shows the average AUPR score obtained by the different methods in each dataset. Standard deviations (computed among the 10 train-test splits) are shown in parenthesis. We can see that the proposed method improves with respect to NRLMF in 7 of 8 datasets, including all the augmented versions of the Yamanishi collection. Our worst result is obtained in the Nuclear Receptors dataset, which correspond to the DTI problem with less known annotations. This may suggest that an ensemble of DTI filters require more positive examples than a single filter to generalize well. Indeed, though the performance of our method in the augmented variants is not always better than the performance observed in the original datasets, the best relative improvements with respect to NRMLF are achieved exactly in those cases, probably because they are more dense in terms of available annotations. Our experiments show also that an ensemble of collaborative filters not specialized for DTI can obtain quite poor results in this type of task. We attribute this result to the fact that AdaMF does not employ information beyond the interaction matrix to predict drug-target interactions, while NRLMF and our method exploit specific knowledge regarding drug and protein similarities to improve their predictions.

Table 1. Average AUPR over 10 trial of 10 fold stratified CV for Yamanishi dataset and its extended version. AdaMF and AdaNRLMF were trained with 10 base learners. Best results are in bold. The last column has the relative improvement of AdaNRLMF with respect to NRLMF.

Dataset	NRLMF	AdaMF	AdaNRLMF	Relative improvement
NR	**0.774 (0.089)**	0.089 (0.025)	0.693 (0.106)	−10.47%
NR Ext.	0.613 (0.099)	0.182 (0.060)	**0.632 (0.082)**	3.09%
GPCR	0.739 (0.073)	0.112 (0.039)	**0.785 (0.035)**	6.22%
GPCR Ext.	0.800 (0.071)	0.538 (0.036)	**0.870 (0.035)**	8.75%
IC	0.899 (0.016)	0.423 (0.038)	**0.943 (0.017)**	4.89%
IC Ext.	0.889 (0.025)	0.562 (0.034)	**0.942 (0.006)**	6.92%
Enzyme	0.881 (0.013)	0.539 (0.030)	**0.909 (0.011)**	3.18%
Enzyme Ext.	0.753 (0.029)	0.488 (0.023)	**0.816 (0.012)**	8.37%

5   Conclusions

In this paper we have devised an Adaboost algorithm specialized for drug-target interaction prediction. It entails solving weighted versions of the objective function underlying NRMLF, a well-known method for this type of problems.

Our experiments show that this method outperforms a single DTI filter and an Adaboost algorithm not specialized for DTI in 7 of 8 datasets. Future work includes the use of the Adaboost as a feature selector, following a multi-kernel approach for DTI. In this variant, several base learners are trained with different similarity measures at each round, and the best predictor is added to the ensemble.

Acknowledgements. This research was partially supported by PIIC-2018 program of DGIP from the Federico Santa María Technical University.

References

1. Ban, T., Ohue, M., Akiyama, Y.: Efficient hyperparameter optimization by using Bayesian optimization for drug-target interaction prediction. In: IEEE 7th ICCABS, pp. 1–6, October 2017
2. Cobanoglu, M.C., Liu, C., Hu, F., Oltvai, Z.N., Bahar, I.: Predicting drug-target interactions using probabilistic matrix factorization. J. Chem. Inf. Model. **53**(12), 3399–3409 (2013)
3. Ding, H., Takigawa, I., Mamitsuka, H., Zhu, S.: Similarity-based machine learning methods for predicting drug-target interactions: a brief review. Briefings Bioinform. **15**(5), 734 (2014). https://doi.org/10.1093/bib/bbt056
4. Friedman, J., Hastie, T., Tibshirani, R.: Additive logistic regression: a statistical view of boosting. Ann. Stat. **38**(2), 337–407 (2000)
5. Gönen, M.: Predicting drug-target interactions from chemical and genomic kernels using bayesian matrix factorization. Bioinformatics **28**(18), 2304–2310 (2012)
6. Johnson, C.C.: Logistic matrix factorization for implicit feedback data. In: Advances in Neural Information Processing Systems 27 (2014)
7. Keum, J., Nam, H.: Self-BLM: prediction of drug-target interactions via self-training SVM. PLOS ONE **12**(2), 1–16 (2017). https://doi.org/10.1371/journal.pone.0171839
8. Li, Z., et al.: In silico prediction of drug-target interaction networks based on drug chemical structure and protein sequences. Sci. Rep. **7**(1), 11174 (2017)
9. Liu, Y., Wu, M., Miao, C., Zhao, P., Li, X.L.: Neighborhood regularized logistic matrix factorization for drug-target interaction prediction. PLOS Comput. Biol. **12**(2), 1–26 (2016). https://doi.org/10.1371/journal.pcbi.1004760
10. Rayhan, F., Ahmed, S., Shatabda, S., Farid, D.M., Mousavian, Z., Dehzangi, A., Rahman, M.S.: iDTI-ESBoost: identification of drug target interaction using evolutionary and structural features with boosting. Sci. Rep. **7**(1), 17731 (2017)
11. Smola, A.J., Schölkopf, B.: Learning with kernels, vol. 4. Citeseer (1998)
12. Tsai, C.F., Hung, C.: Cluster ensembles in collaborative filtering recommendation. Appl. Soft Comput. **12**(4), 1417–1425 (2012)
13. Wang, Y., Sun, H., Zhang, R.: AdaMF: adaptive boosting matrix factorization for recommender system. In: Li, F., Li, G., Hwang, S., Yao, B., Zhang, Z. (eds.) WAIM 2014. LNCS, vol. 8485, pp. 43–54. Springer, Cham (2014). https://doi.org/10.1007/978-3-319-08010-9_7
14. Yamanishi, Y., Araki, M., Gutteridge, A., Honda, W., Kanehisa, M.: Prediction of drug-target interaction networks from the integration of chemical and genomic spaces. Bioinformatics **24**(13), i232 (2008). https://doi.org/10.1093/bioinformatics/btn162

15. Yuan, Q., Gao, J., Wu, D., Zhang, S., Mamitsuka, H., Zhu, S.: Druge-rank: improving drugtarget interaction prediction of new candidate drugs or targets by ensemble learning to rank. Bioinformatics **32**(12), i18–i27 (2016)
16. Zheng, X., Ding, H., Mamitsuka, H., Zhu, S.: Collaborative matrix factorization with multiple similarities for predicting drug-target interactions. In: Proceedings of the 19th ACM SIGKDD, pp. 1025–1033. ACM (2013)

Fast Adapting Mixture Parameters Schemes for Probability Density Difference-Based Deformable Model

Aicha Baya Goumeidane[✉] and Nafaa Nacereddine

Research Center in Industrial Technologies CRTI, P.O. Box 64,
16014 Algiers, Algeria
{a.goumeidane,n.nacereddine}@crti.dz, ab_goumeidane@yahoo.fr

Abstract. This paper presents a new region-driven active contour using the *pdf* difference to evolve. The *pdf* estimation is done via a new and fast Gaussian mixture model (GMM) parameters updating scheme. The experiments performed on synthetic and X-ray images have shown not only an accurate contour delineation but also outstanding performance in terms of execution speed compared to the GMM estimation based on EM algorithm and to non-parametric *pdf* estimations.

Keywords: Active contour · Adaptive mixture ·
GMM parameters updates

1 Introduction

Image segmentation is of major importance in the field of computer vision. It is the process of dividing a digital image into something that is more meaningful and easier to analyze by the image analysis stages. Image segmentation can reveal to be hard for numerous reasons: Firstly, partitioning the image into non overlapping regions and extracting regions of interest require a tradeoff between the computational efficiency of the involved algorithm, its degree of automation and the accuracy of its outcomes. Secondly, image noise linked to the image acquisition, and poor contrast are very difficult to reckon with segmentation algorithms without the user interacting [2]. So, designing a robust and efficient segmentation method is still not trivial and difficult for practical applications. Among segmentation methods, the active contour is one of the most successful ones. Broadly speaking, an active contour is a curve that evolves from an initial position, under some constraints and energies to match the desired features. This curve can be edge-driven or region-driven depending on the nature of these energies. The region-driven ones tend to rely on global information to guide the contour evolution. Hence, the inner and the outer region defined by the model are considered, which leads to better handling of noise and smooth or vanished boundaries as well as sensitivity to initial conditions [8]. Global information can be established by considering the probability density function (*pdf*) of regions

© Springer Nature Switzerland AG 2019
R. Vera-Rodriguez et al. (Eds.): CIARP 2018, LNCS 11401, pp. 221–228, 2019.
https://doi.org/10.1007/978-3-030-13469-3_26

intensities and then, are based on the probability theory. Image segmentation techniques built on probability theory have been extensively used and can be considered as clustering or classification problems [5]. They must return necessary knowledge that would enable to assign a label to each pixel. Most of them merely obtain a label map that is inferior to active contours outcomes, which have smooth and regular boundaries of connected regions [5]. Many statistical modeling can be applied to distribute image features. We can cite among others, parametric modeling by mixtures. The most commonly used mixture model is the GMM [12,17]. GMMs have been extensively employed to this aim, due to their simplicity and ease of implementation. Associating statistical approaches and active contours method bring several advantages as the merits of both are combined. Unfortunately, this association leads to prohibitive computation cost [11]. That is why a particular attention should be directed to how this combination is achieved to take advantage from it by finding strategies to speed up the contour evolution. In this paper, a novel region-driven parametric active contour is proposed, whose evolution is based on the differences between the estimated *pdf* inside and outside the model curve. The *pdf* estimations are carried out by the mean of GMMs, whose parameters are computed in a new recursive scheme to alleviate the computation load and accelerate the parameters estimations.

The structure of the remainder is as follows. In Sect. 2, we introduce the mathematical foundation of active contours and the adaptive mixtures. Our method for object extraction via the new *pdf* estimation is presented in Sect. 3. The experimental results are shown in Sect. 4. We draw the main conclusions in Sect. 5.

2   Background

2.1   Active Contours

The active contour, also called "snake", is a curve $\mathbf{c}(s) = [x(s), y(s)]'$, $s = [0\ 1]$ which evolves towards image features to minimize the following energy [9]

$$E(\mathbf{c}) = \int_0^1 (E^{int}(\mathbf{c}(s)) + E^{ext}(\mathbf{c}(s)))ds \tag{1}$$

Where s is the curvilinear abscissa, E^{int} the internal energy and E^{ext} the image energy responsible for driving the contour toward edges. The minimization of Eq. (1) leads to the iterative solution of Eq. (2).

$$\begin{cases} x_t = (A + \gamma I_d)^{-1}(\gamma x_{t-1} + \nabla E_x^{ext}(x_{t-1}, y_{t-1})) \\ y_t = (A + \gamma I_d)^{-1}(\gamma y_{t-1} + \nabla E_y^{ext}(x_{t-1}, y_{t-1})) \end{cases} \tag{2}$$

If the model is made of N nodes, then, A is a $N * N$ matrix, I_d an identity matrix sized as A, γ an evolution coefficient, x_t and y_t are the model nodes coordinates at the iteration t. $\nabla E_x^{ext}(x_t, y_t)$ and $\nabla E_y^{ext}(x_t, y_t)$ are the external forces of the input image at the model nodes locations in the x and y direction respectively. In addition to the external force proposed in [9], a variety of external forces have been proposed to improve the snakes performance. They can be classified as dynamic and static [10]. The dynamic forces are those which depend on the snake position and, as a result, change as the snake deforms. In turn, the static ones are those that are computed once for all and remain unchanged.

Pressure Forces. The pressure force given by Eq. (3) [3] is an inflation/deflation dynamic force if the model is considered as a balloon.

$$F_B(\mathbf{c}(s^*)) = k_p.\mathbf{n}(\mathbf{c}(s^*)) \tag{3}$$

$\mathbf{n}(\mathbf{c}(s^*))$ is the normal unit vector to the curve at $\mathbf{c}(s^*)$ and k_p a weight. By introducing an individual pressure weight k_p for each node as done in [6] for example, the model is strengthened, regarding to the initialization issue, since some parts of it can inflate/deflate independently from the other ones [7]. The individual k_p may be released to various forms. An example is proposed in [1] (Eq. (4)), where k_p is introduced as a difference between the *pdfs* estimated inside and out side the model. This difference is evaluated at the node position grey level value.

$$k_p = p(z_{s^*}/O) - p(z_{s^*}/B) \tag{4}$$

z_{s^*} is the node position grey value, whereas $p(z_{s^*}/O)$ and $p(z_{s^*}/B)$ are the conditional *pdf* of the object (O) and the background (B) respectively. The problem here is to accurately estimate the *pdf* inside and outside the active contour to achieve a successful progression to the boundaries.

2.2 Probability Density Function Estimation

To exploit the weight of Eq. (4), one should have a good estimation of the *pdf*. To this end, the GMM is used here. Expectation Maximization (EM) algorithm is usually employed to compute the mixture parameters [4]. However, numerical procedure with EM algorithm can reveal to be very expensive [16]. That is why an adaptive updating is chosen instead of the EM one. It relies on the works of [16] and later [14] to achieve such update. The following set of recursive equations for normal components presented in [14] are used to the aim of parameters vector computation θ. For K components, θ consists of $3K$ elements (mixture proportions, means and standard deviations); $\theta_n = \{\pi_n^1, \mu_n^1, \sigma_n^1, ..., \pi_n^K, \mu_n^K, \sigma_n^K\}$.

$$\begin{cases} \beta_{(n)}^{(i)} = 1/n \\ \rho_{n+1}^{(i)} = \frac{\pi_n^{(i)} \phi^{(i)}(x_{n+1})}{F_n(x_{n+1})} \\ \pi_{n+1}^{(i)} = \pi_n^{(i)} + \beta_{(n)}^{(i)}(\rho_{n+1}^{(i)} - \pi_n^{(i)}) \\ \mu_{n+1}^{(i)} = \mu_n^{(i)} + (\pi_n^{(i)})^{-1}\beta_{(n)}^{(i)}\rho_{n+1}^{(i)}(x_{n+1} - \mu_n^{(i)}) \\ \sigma_{n+1}^{2(i)} = \sigma_n^{2(i)} + (\pi_n^{(i)})^{-1}\beta_{(n)}^{(i)}\rho_{n+1}^{(i)}((x_{n+1} - \mu_n^{(i)})^2 - \sigma_n^{2(i)}) \end{cases} \tag{5}$$

ρ denotes the membership function, x_n the nth observation, θ_n the parameters estimates after n observations, $\phi^{(i)}$ the normal distribution with parameters $\theta_n^{(i)}$

and $\hat{F}_n = \sum_{i=1}^{K} \pi_n^{(i)} \phi^{(i)}$ the estimated *pdf* after n observation. The superscript (i) indicates that the calculation is done for the ith mixture component.

3   Fast Mixture Updating Scheme for Contour Evolution

The proposed active contour uses probabilistic pressure forces as external forces, where k_p, as is [1], are computed as the differences between the estimated *pdfs* inside and outside contour curve. During the model progression, the *pdf* estimates change as the inner and the outer regions change with the deformations. When the inner region is considered, from an iteration t to $t+1$, new pixels get inside the curve while some others are left outside. The idea is to remove from the *pdf* estimate $\hat{F}_t$, represented by its parameters, the gray levels contribution of the pixels that have been left out. This is done in order to get new mixture parameters defining $\hat{F}_t^-$, the intermediate *pdf* estimate. These parameters are once again updated with the new gray levels values that have been added inside, to get $\hat{F}_{t+1}$, the new *pdf* estimate for $t+1$. In other words, if M pixels $y_j, j = 1 \ldots M$ have been left out in $t+1$, and the inner region in t consists of n pixels (n observation), $\hat{F}_t^-$ is obtained by M successive updates achieved with Eq. (6).

$$
\begin{cases}
\beta_{(n-j+1)}^{(i)} = 1/(n-j+1) \\
\rho_{n-j}^{(i)} = \dfrac{\pi_{n-j+1}^{(i)} \phi^{(i)}(y_j)}{\hat{F}_{n-j+1}(y_j)} \\
\pi_{n-j}^{(i)} = \pi_{n-j+1}^{(i)} - \beta_{(n-j+1)}^{(i)}(\rho_{n-j}^{(i)} - \pi_{n-j+1}^{(i)}) \\
\mu_{n-j}^{(i)} = \mu_{n-j+1}^{(i)} - (\pi_{n-j+1}^{(i)})^{-1}\beta_{(n-j+1)}^{(i)}\rho_{n-j}^{(i)}(y_j - \mu_{n-j+1}^{(i)}) \\
\sigma_{n-j}^{2(i)} = \sigma_{n-j+1}^{2(i)} - (\pi_{n-j+1}^{(i)})^{-1}\beta_{(n-j+1)}^{(i)}\rho_{n-j}^{(i)}((y_j - \mu_{n-j+1}^{(i)})^2 - \sigma_{n-j+1}^{2(i)})
\end{cases}
\tag{6}
$$

After the updating performed with Eq. (6) for $j = 1 \ldots M$, the recursive operations of Eq. (5) are applied then on the pixels gray level values that have been added inside the curve, beginning with $\hat{F}_t^-$ ($n \longleftarrow n - M$, $\pi_{n-M}^{(i)}$, $\mu_{n-M}^{(i)}$, $\sigma_{n-M}^{(i)}$, $i = 1 \ldots K$). Furthermore, the intersection of the two sets representing the added and the subtracted pixels gray levels values, could be not empty, which means that same gray levels are going to be processed twice, once by Eq. (6) and then by Eq. (5). This situation can be avoided by removing the set intersection to prevent unnecessary operations, as the *pdfs* are smooth-wise gray levels values counting. This can be explained by an example: if a gray level value g is found m times in the subtracted pixels and k times in the added ones, so this gray level value will be processed $m - k$ times by Eq. (5) or Eq. (6), for $k < m$ or $m < k$ respectively. Moreover, if L pixels of the same gray level value g, have to be processed in the same iteration, the updates are performed once for all the L pixels. Indeed, if we assume that for a big n, $\hat{F}$ does not significantly change when adding few gray level values, then ρ will remain utmost the same and kept unchanged in the L iterations. The same assumption is done for β. As for L iterations, β grows from $1/n$ to $1/(n+L-1)$, we choose to use the median value

$\beta_{n+(L-1)/2} = 1/(n + (L - 1)/2)$. An example of the updating development for the parameter π is given in Eq. (7) where $\beta_{n+(L-1)/2}$ is noted β

$$
\begin{cases}
\pi_{n+1}^{(i)}(1) = \pi_n^{(i)} + \beta^{(i)}(\rho_{n+1}^{(i)} - \pi_n^{(i)}) & 1^{st} \text{ pixel} \\
\pi_{n+1}^{(i)}(2) = \pi_n^{(i)} + 2\beta^{(i)}(\rho_{n+1}^{(i)} - \pi_n^{(i)}) + (\beta^{(i)})^2(\rho_{n+1}^{(i)} - \pi_n^{(i)}) & 2^{nd} \text{ pixel} \\
\pi_{n+1}^{(i)}(3) = \pi_n^{(i)} + 3\beta^{(i)}(\rho_{n+1}^{(i)} - \pi_n^{(i)}) - (\beta^{(i)})^2(\rho_{n+1}^{(i)} - \pi_n^{(i)}) - & \\
(\beta^{(i)})^3(\rho_{n+1}^{(i)} - \pi_n^{(i)}) & 3^{rd} \text{ pixel} \\
\pi_{n+1}^{(i)}(L) = \pi_n^{(i)} + L\beta^{(i)}(\rho_{n+1}^{(i)} - \pi_n^{(i)}) + O(\beta) & L^{th} \text{ pixel}
\end{cases}
\tag{7}
$$

$O(\beta)$ is a polynomial of β with degrees going from 2 to L. $O(\beta)$ is negligible as $\beta \ll 1$. The same results are obtained for the other mixtures parameters. Updates for the L pixels of the same gray level value g are then given by Eq. (8):

$$
\begin{cases}
\beta^{(i)} = 1/(n + (L - 1)/2) \\
\rho_{n+1}^{(i)} = \frac{\pi_n^{(i)}\phi^{(i)}(g)}{\hat{F}_n(g)} \\
\pi_{n+1 \to n+L}^{(i)} = \pi_n^{(i)} + L\beta^{(i)}(\rho_{n+1}^{(i)} - \pi_n^{(i)}) \\
\mu_{n+1 \to n+L}^{(i)} = \mu_n^{(i)} + L(\pi_n^{(i)})^{-1}\beta^{(i)}\rho_{n+1}^{(i)}(g - \mu_n^{(i)}) \\
\sigma_{n+1 \to n+L}^{2(i)} = \sigma_n^{2(i)} + L(\pi_n^{(i)})^{-1}\beta^{(i)}\rho_{n+1}^{(i)}((g - \mu_n^{(i)})^2 - \sigma_n^{2(i)})
\end{cases}
\tag{8}
$$

The index $n + 1 \to n + L$ means that the update is computed as a contribution of all the L pixels. Thus, updating $\hat{F}$ no longer relies on the observations number (pixels number) as suggested by Eq. (5) but only on the gray level values of the pixels involved in the computation. It is worth to note that the same procedure is applied for the background (the outer region), to update the outer *pdf* estimate. These modified recursions give a convenient way for computing quickly the mixture parameters as the model curve progresses.

Once the *pdf* estimation is performed, the contour evolution is carried out by the following iterative equations where k_p is the *pdf* estimation difference for each node position gray level value.

$$
\begin{cases}
x_t = (A + \gamma I_d)^{-1}(\gamma x_{t-1} + k_p.N_x) \\
y_t = (A + \gamma I_d)^{-1}(\gamma y_{t-1} + k_p.N_y)
\end{cases}
\tag{9}
$$

$N_x(N_y)$ is the normal unit vector components in the $x(y)$ direction.

During the active contour initialization, the first round of *pdf* estimation is performed with EM algorithm to get quickly the first *pdf* estimate. For the other rounds, the proposed updates are carried out as the active contour evolves in the image domain.

Algorithm Complexity. Assume that the number of the processed pixels in one iteration is equal to N_p represented on L_g gray levels, then, each of the *pdf* parameters ρ, π, μ and σ updates requires $L_g \times K$ operations for the proposed *pdf* parameters updating, while it requires $N_p \times K$ operations for the recursive model provided in [14]. Then, a gain of execution time with our approach is obviously obtained since $L_g \leq N_p$.

4   Experiments

As first experiment, we have compared the proposed *pdf* estimation method to
the EM-based one. As illustrated in Fig. 1, the implementation results of Eq. (9)
on a 250×250 synthetic image corrupted by a Gaussian noise with $\sigma = 20$, show
a successful contour delineation for the two methods. However, the proposed
pdf update have reduced the computation time by 50% compared with the EM
algorithm. One can note that in addition of a good performance in object contour
extraction, thanks to a good *pdf* estimation, as shown in Fig. 1, the strength of
the proposed method is related to the computation time. Indeed, for comparison
purpose, the proposed model is faster than the non-parametric *pdf* estimation-
base active contour with Parzen [13] and with the Averaged shifted histogram
ASH [15], where the execution time was reduced by 50% for *ASH*, and more
than 95% for Parzen. Another experiment shows capabilities of the proposed
active contour in boundaries extraction in very noisy images (Fig. 2).

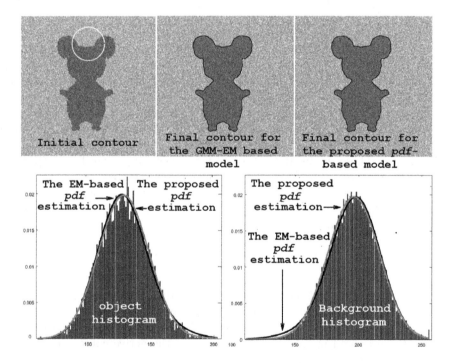

Fig. 1. Active contours results and *pdfs* estimations.

The last experiment consists in applying the proposed model on an X-ray
image shown in Fig. 3 which contains a region of interest (ROI) of welded joint
X-ray image to segment, the initial and the final contours, and the histograms of
the extracted defect and background depicted with the *pdf* estimates. The background of the weld X-ray images can be modeled by more than one component

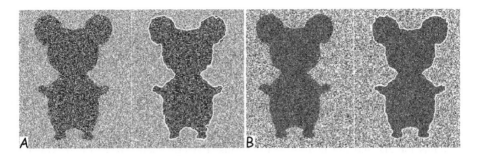

Fig. 2. Final contours on images corrupted with pronounced Gaussian noises. A: $\sigma = 30/50$ for object/background. B: $\sigma = 50/30$ for object/background

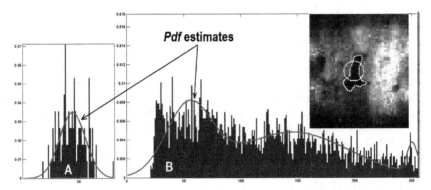

Fig. 3. The proposed model application to an X-ray image. A: Defect histogram and defect *pdf* estimate. B: Background histogram and background *pdf* estimate

because of the high illumination non-uniformity characterizing such images [11]. Here the number of background components is taken equal to 3. The bad quality of the image shown in Fig. 3 does not prevent our model to extract the weld defect indication successfully. In conclusion, the main advantage of our method consists in reducing the computation time. Indeed, applying an active model evolving with EM-based *pdf* estimate on the image of Fig. 3 has slowed the progression down 2 times compared to the proposed model progression speed.

5   Conclusion

In this paper, a new probabilistic active contour is presented. The contour progression based on a new *pdf* updating scheme of GMM parameters shows to be effective. Indeed, the contour delineation is achieved successfully despite the noise and the images bad quality. Moreover, the convergence was faster compared to others *pdf*-based methods, which ascertains the opportunity of exploiting the proposed *pdf* estimation via our new parameters updating scheme in such active contour model. For further works, we plan to extend the proposed updating to other mixtures of distributions related to normal one.

References

1. Abd-Almageed, W., Ramadan, S., Smith, C.: Kernel snakes: non-parametric active contour models. In: Proceedings of IEEE International Conference on Systems, Man and Cybernetics, pp. 1131–1147 (2003)
2. Akram, F., Jeong, H.K., Lim, H.U., Nam, C.K.: Segmentation of intensity inhomogeneous brain MR images using active contours. Comput. Math. Methods Med. **2014**, 1–14 (2014)
3. Cohen, L., Cohen, I.: Finite-element methods for active contour models and balloons for 2D and 3D images. IEEE Trans. Pattern Anal. Mach. Intell. **15**(11), 1131–1147 (1993)
4. Dempster, A., Laird, N., Rubin, D.: Maximum likelihood from incomplete data via the EM algorithm. J. R. Stat. Soc. Ser. B **39**(1), 1–38 (1977)
5. Gao, G., Wen, C., Wang, H.: Fast and robust image segmentation with active contours and student's-t mixture model. Pattern Recogn. **3**(C), 71–86 (2017)
6. Goumeidane, A.B., Khamadja, M., Odet, C.: Parametric active contour for boundary estimation of weld defects in radiographic testing. In: Proceedings of ISSPA, pp. 1–4, September 2007
7. Goumeidane, A.B., Nacereddine, N.: Spatially varying weighting function-based global and local statistical active contours. application to x-ray images. In: Blanc-Talon, J., Distante, C., Philips, W., Popescu, D., Scheunders, P. (eds.) ACIVS 2016. LNCS, vol. 10016, pp. 181–192. Springer, Cham (2016). https://doi.org/10. 1007/978-3-319-48680-2_17
8. Goumeidane, A., Nacereddine, N., Kahamdja, M.: Computer aided weld defect delination using active contours in radiographic inspection. J. X-Ray Sci. Technol. **23**(3), 289–310 (2015)
9. Kass, M., Witkin, A., Terzopoulos, A.: Snakes: active contour models. Int. J. Comput. Vis. **1**(4), 321–331 (1988)
10. Li, B., Acton, S.T.: Automatic active model initialization via Poisson inverse gradient. IEEE Trans. Image Process. **17**(8), 1406–1420 (2008)
11. Nacereddine, N., Hamami, L., Ziou, D., Goumeidane, A.B.: Adaptive B-spline model based probabilistic active contour for weld defect detection in radiographic imaging. In: Choraś, R.S. (ed.) Image Processing and Communications Challenges 2. AISC, vol. 84, pp. 289–297. Springer, Heidelberg (2010). https://doi.org/10. 1007/978-3-642-16295-4_33
12. Nishio, M., Tanaka, Y.: Heterogeneity in pulmonary emphysema: analysis of ct attenuation using Gaussian mixture model. PLoS ONE **13**(2), e0192892 (2018)
13. Parzen, E.: On the estimation of a probability density function and the mode. Ann. Math. Stat. **33**, 1065–1076 (1962)
14. Priebe, C.: Adaptive mixturesa. J. Am. Stat. Assoc. **89**, 796–806 (1994)
15. Scott, D.: Averaged shifted histogram: effective non parametric density estimators in several dimensions. Ann. Stat. **13**(3), 1024–1040 (1985)
16. Titterington, D.M.: Recursive parameter estimation using incomplete data. J. R. Stat. Soc. Ser. B **46**, 257–267 (1984)
17. Yin, S., Zhang, Y., Karim, S.: Large scale remote sensing image segmentation based on fuzzy region competition and Gaussian mixture model. IEEE Access **6** (2018)

Optimal Stochastic Excitation for Linear Flaw Detection in a Solid Material

Nesrine Houhat[1]([✉]), Sébastien Ménigot[2,3], Tarek Boutkedjirt[4],
Redouane Drai[1], and Jean-Marc Girault[2,3]

[1] Research Center in Industrial Technologies CRTI,
Chéraga, P.O. Box 64, 16014 Algiers, Algeria
{n.houhat,r.drai}@crti.dz
[2] Eseo Group, Angers, France
{sebastien.menigot,jean-marc.girault}@eseo.fr
[3] LAUM, CNRS UMR 6613, Le Mans Iniversité, Le Mans, France
[4] Physics of Ultrasound Research Team, Faculty of Physics,
USTHB, Algiers, Algeria
tboutkedjirt@usthb.dz

Abstract. The field of ultrasonic nondestructive testing has known a great development during the recent years. In order to increase the flaw detection sensitivity, many improvements have been made in the equipment and the sensors technology. In the present work, the optimal command which maximizes the flaw detection is investigated experimentally. A parametric optimization consisting of finding the optimal excitation frequency which maximizes the Euclidean distance between a reference medium and a medium with a linear flaw has been obtained automatically by using the gradient descent algorithm. Moreover, the waveform excitation optimization has been considered. A set of stochastic signals have been transmitted to the medium. A closed loop optimization process based on a genetic algorithm allowed to find the optimal excitation without a priori knowledge on the shape of the signal. This optimal excitation converged to a sinusoidal pulse with the optimal frequency found by the parametric optimization.

Keywords: Optimal command · Nondestructive testing ·
Gradient descent algorithm · Genetic algorithm · Ultrasound

1 Introduction

The ultrasound nondestructive testing (NDT) domain has known a great development during the last decade, especially by the advent of nonlinear NDT which permits the detection of microscopic damages such as cracks. Nevertheless, the introduction of the optimal command in such systems remains quite new and little-used. Fink has proposed a time reversal closed loop system which makes possible the optimization of the signal to noise ratio (SNR) for a linear behavior system [1]. Precursory works using the optimal command principle for nonlinear

© Springer Nature Switzerland AG 2019
R. Vera-Rodriguez et al. (Eds.): CIARP 2018, LNCS 11401, pp. 229–236, 2019.
https://doi.org/10.1007/978-3-030-13469-3_27

systems were initiated in [2,4–6] in the field of medical contrast imaging. The originality of this work was to search for the optimal input excitation parameter/shape without any *a priori* knowledge of the studied system, by using well known optimization algorithms. However, the definition of an efficient cost function enabling to express correctly the optimization purpose remains the main difficulty. The stochastic approach is principally devoted to be used for nonlinear systems. Indeed, it allows to find the stochastic optimal command which improves the simple frequency optimization results. The present study is an extension to the NDT domain, of previous works [2,4], in which the optimal command was applied in ultrasound medical imaging for the improvement of the image contrast. It is a preliminary work which consists in setting up an experimental closed loop platform allowing to experiment the procedure described in [2]. It constitutes a first step in the validation of the stochastic optimization approach for linear systems since our ultimate goal remains its application on nonlinear systems. The optimal excitation wave enables us the best discrimination between two media: a reference one without flaw and a medium with a linear flaw. An efficient cost function able to quantify the result of the optimization process will be defined by the Euclidean distance between the echoes emanating from the two media. A conventional ultrasound measuring system is therefore changed into a new system including a feedback. First, a parametric optimization is achieved. The parameter to be optimized is the transmitted frequency by using a gradient descent algorithm [7]. This first result constitutes a suboptimal solution. For an optimal solution, the excitation waveform optimization is considered. A set of stochastic signals is then transmitted to the investigated media and the optimal excitation can be found automatically by a genetic optimization algorithm [3]. The results obtained from the parametric optimization and the shape optimization will be compared.

2   Method and Material

2.1   Closed Loop System for Linear Flaw Detection

The principle of our method is to add a feedback to a conventional open loop ultrasound system for linear flaw detection (Fig. 1). For an iteration k, an excitation signal $x_k(t)$ is transmitted to the reference medium (switch position 1), then, to the medium with the linear flaw (switch position 2). The temporal received signal indicates the existence of a flaw by the presence of an echo positioned between the excitation and the medium back face echo. Adding a feedback to such a system permits us to optimize the flaw detection thanks to the input excitation without *a priori* information about the transducer and the medium. An Euclidean distance d_k is computed between the two media. An optimization algorithm is used to find the optimal command which discriminates to the best the two media by maximizing the Euclidean distance d_{k+1}. For the parametric optimization, $x_k(t)$ is a Gaussian modulated sinusoidal pulse with a frequency f_k and a duration of 1 μs. The power of the transmitted signal E_x is adjusted to the power of a reference one $E_{x_{ref}}$ with a transmitted frequency of 1 MHz and with an amplitude of A_0. The amplitude of the transmitted pulse is then given by:

$$A = \sqrt{\frac{A_0^2 E_{x_{ref}}}{E_x}} \tag{1}$$

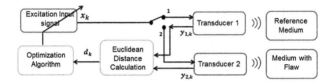

Fig. 1. Bloc diagram of the optimization closed loop system.

2.2 Cost Function

Our main goal through this study is the improvement of the flaw detection. For this, we compare two media, a reference medium without flaw and a medium with the same characteristics including a linear flaw by considering an Euclidean distance between them. The greater the distance is, the more the flaw is highlighted. The cost function to be maximized, here, is an Euclidean distance between the temporal signal power received from the reference medium and those received from the medium with a flaw. The optimization of the Euclidean distance between the two media amounts to maximize the power of the flaw echo:

$$d_k = \sqrt{(E_{1,k} - E_{2,k})^2}, \tag{2}$$

where $E_{1,k}$ is the power of the temporal signal emanating from the medium with flaw and $E_{2,k}$ is the power of the temporal signal received from the reference medium.

2.3 Algorithms

Gradient Descent Algorithm. For the parametric optimization, a gradient descent algorithm is used to find the suboptimal command. This algorithm has been chosen because the expression of the Euclidean distance as a function of frequency is unknown. The optimization is based on the selection of the best transmitted frequency f^* which maximizes the Euclidean distance between the two media d_k [7]:

$$f^* = \arg\max_f(d(f)) \tag{3}$$

The gradient descent is an iterative algorithm defined by the recurrence relation:

$$f_{k+1} = f_k + \mu_k(\nabla d(f_k)), \tag{4}$$

where f_k is the transmitted frequency at the iteration k. The coefficient μ_k governs the speed of convergence and $\nabla d(f_k)$ is the Euclidean distance gradient at the iteration k for the transmitted frequency f_k and is given by the expression:

$$\nabla d(f_k) = \frac{\partial d}{\partial f} \approx \frac{d_{k-1} - d_k}{f_{k-1} - f_k}. \tag{5}$$

The coefficient μ_k sets the speed of convergence as follows:

$$\mu_k = \begin{cases} 0 & if \ k \leq 3; \\ \varDelta f & if \ k = 4; \\ \mu_{k-1} & if \ sgn\left[\nabla(d(f_k))\right] = sgn\left[\nabla(d(f_{k-1}))\right] \\ -\frac{\mu_{k-1}}{2} & if \ sgn\left[\nabla(d(f_k))\right] \neq sgn\left[\nabla(d(f_{k-1}))\right] \end{cases} \tag{6}$$

where $\varDelta f$ was fixed to $1\,\mathrm{MHz}$. This value must be chosen in order to ensure a good compromise between the speed of convergence and the robustness. The sign function $sgn(t) = 1$ for $t > 0$, 0 for $t = 0$ and -1 for $t < 0$. For $k = \{1, 2, 3\}$, the first three frequencies must be given initially. These three values can have an influence on the speed of convergence of the algorithm under the concavity hypothesis of the algorithm.

Genetic Algorithm. For the shape optimization, the search of the optimal command w_k^* is based on the investigation of stochastic signal which maximizes the Euclidean distance by using the genetic algorithm [3] that is $w_k^* = \arg\max_{w_k}(d(f_k))$. At the first generation ($k = 0$), 12 stochastic signals are randomly chosen from a continuous uniform distribution. They constitute the initial population for the genetic optimization process. Each signal $x_k = A.w_k$ is composed from 40 samples with a time duration of $1\mu s$. In order to compare results obtained from the parametric optimization, the transmitted stochastic signal amplitude A is adjusted according to Eq. (1). For the next generation $k + 1$, the 6 best signals maximizing the cost function are kept to become parents. 6 new stochastic signals named offspring are generated by the crossover operator which mixes the best parent with one of the 5 remaining parents. A rate of 40% of the samples corresponding to the mutation rate are mutated to obtain a robust optimization. It should be noted that these settings could be reached from several tests.

3   Experimental Study

3.1   Samples Description

Two aluminium cylindrical blocs with identical dimensions $80\,\mathrm{mm} \times 80\,\mathrm{mm}$ were considered (Fig. 2). A hole of $4\,\mathrm{mm}$ diameter and $20\,\mathrm{mm}$ depth was drilled on the back side of the first sample in order to simulate a linear flaw.

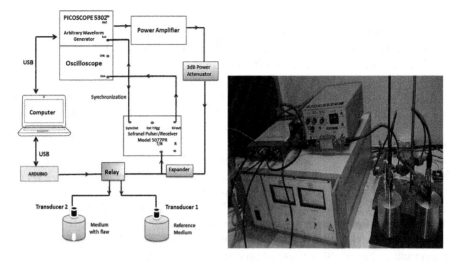

Fig. 2. Experimental setup.

3.2   Experimental Setup

The experimental setup is described in Fig. 2. The excitation signal $x_k(t)$ was generated digitally by Matlab (Mathworks, Natick, MA, USA) with a computer. It was transmitted to a PicoScope PS5203 arbitrary waveform generator (PicoTech, St Neots, UK) via USB, then amplified by 50 dB using a power amplifier (AAP-200-1-10, Adece, Veigné, France) which was protected by a 3 dB high power attenuator (HFP-5100-3/3-NM/ NF, Trilithic, Indianapolis, IN, USA). The signal was transmitted to the reference medium from a 2.25 MHz PZT single element transducer (IM-2.25-12-P, Imasonic Sas, France) with a fractional bandwidth of 72% at $-6\,\mathrm{dB}$, then, to the medium with flaw from a paired transducer. This switching was possible by a relay circuit (TQ2-5V) commanded by the computer via an Arduino Uno micro controller. The received wave from the medium was collected by the same transducer (echo mode) and transmitted to a Sofranel Squarewave Pulser/Receiver Model 5077PR (Olympus NDT Inc, Waltham, USA) via a diode bridge. For each iteration, ten acquisitions were made by an oscilloscope (PicoScope PS5203) to increase the SNR. Finally an averaged echo was transmitted and recorded by the computer.

3.3   Results

Parametric Optimization. The first step of the study a so called "empirical optimization" was to check for the existence of a global maximum of the Euclidean distance versus frequency. For this purpose, a frequency sweeping in a range between 1 MHz and 6 MHz with a step of 50 kHz was achieved. The obtained result is represented in Fig. 3 (red solid line). This first result indicates that the cost function has a global maximum localized at about $f = 3.3\,\mathrm{MHz}$.

This justifies the use of the gradient descent algorithm which operates under the convexity hypothesis of the cost function. This maximum can also be reached automatically with the gradient descent algorithm. The results of the first fifty iterations are shown in Fig. 3 (black solid line). We can note the convergence of the distance to the maximum, and that the values obtained automatically are very close to those obtained empirically by the first experiment. It can also be noticed for the gradient optimization, a little variation of the cost function value for the same frequency. This observation is directly due to the experimental conditions.

Figure 4 shows the results of the gradient descent algorithm optimization. Variations of the distance (Fig. 4a) and the transmit frequency (Fig. 4b) versus iterations for two different initializations ($f_1 = 1$ MHz, $f_2 = 1.2$ MHz, $f_3 = 1.3$ MHz and $f_1 = 6$ MHz, $f_2 = 5.8$ MHz, $f_3 = 5.5$ MHz) are presented. For both cases, after 30 iterations, the transmit frequency converges to the same value $f = 3.2$ MHz while the distance value shows weak fluctuations around an average value of 40 a.u (arbitrary unit). These fluctuations are probably due to the experimental conditions. The optimal transmit frequency can be reached automatically for the two algorithm initializations with the same speed of convergence.

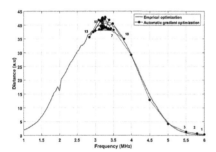

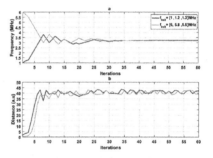

Fig. 3. Empirical optimization: Euclidean distance measurement for a transmit frequency of 1 to 6 MHz with a step of 50 kHz (red solid line) and the gradient descent automatic optimization (black line) for the 50 fifty first iterations. (Color figure online)

Fig. 4. Gradient descent algorithm optimization results for two different initializations: $f_1 = 1$ MHz, $f_2 = 1.2$ MHz, $f_3 = 1,3$ MHz and $f_1 = 6$ MHz, $f_2 = 5.8$ MHz, $f_3 = 5.6$ MHz. (a) Transmitted frequency versus iterations. (b) Euclidean distance versus iterations.

Shape Optimization. Figure 5a shows the distance as a function of generations k (solid line) and the parametric optimization result (dashed line) obtained previously. We can note that the cost function has reached an optimal value of 44 a.u after 430 generations. This value is almost identical to those obtained with the optimal transmitted frequency which was around 41 a.u. Figure 5b represents the corresponding optimal stochastic command w_k^*. For the comparison of the

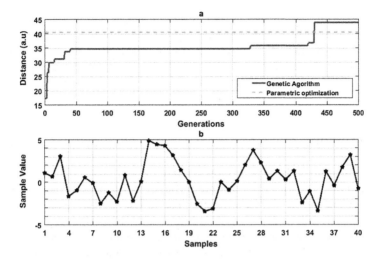

Fig. 5. (a) Genetic algorithm optimization of the Euclidean distance versus generations (blue solid line) and the parametric optimization result in dashed line, (b) Optimal transmitted stochastic signal. (Color figure online)

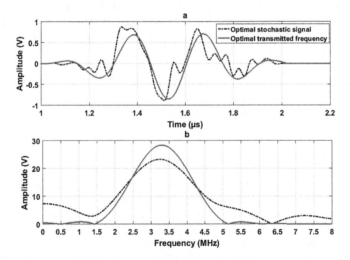

Fig. 6. Optimal stochastic signal (dashed line) and the sinusoidal pulse at the optimal transmitted frequency (red solid line) and their respective spectra. (Color figure online)

results obtained by both parametric and shape optimization, an illustration of the optimal stochastic signal and the sinusoidal pulse at the optimal frequency is given in Fig. 6a. Their respective spectra are shown in Fig. 6b. The two signals have been resampled to have the same sampling frequency of the experimental system and filtered with the same Hann window, then, rescaled in order to have the same power. The optimal stochastic signal converges to a sinusoidal pulse at the optimal frequency. We suppose that a better matching between the two results could have been reached for a greater number of generations. It can be said that for a linear flaw type, the use of stochastic signals for the shape optimization reinforces the result of the sine pulse parametric optimization. The expected optimal excitation, here, is the time reversed impulse response of the system including the transducer and the medium.

4   Conclusion

In the present study, the best excitation wave which enabled to maximize the linear flaw detection was investigated through two process types, parametric and shape optimization. An experimental closed loop system was set up to find automatically the suboptimal/ optimal command. The cost function considered was an Euclidean distance between two media: a reference one and a medium with a linear flaw. The main outcome was the performance similarity between the parametric and the stochastic approaches. Nevertheless, the stochastic approach didn't require any *a priori* knowledge nor initialization values. For a linear flaw type, the optimal stochastic command tends to the time reversal solution which is a sinusoidal pulse at a fixed frequency. The stochastic approach may be more efficient for nonlinear systems, even for cases where the cost function is no longer convex, for which the use of simple parametric optimization is compromised. This work is ongoing and will be presented in a future paper.

Acknowledgment. The authors thank Dr Jean- Marc GREGOIRE (Université Françis Rabelais, Inserm, Imagerie et Cerveau, UMR U930, France, Tours) for his realizations, helpful discussions and advices about the experimental setup.

References

1. Fink, M.: Time reversal of ultrasonic fields–Part I: basic principles. IEEE Trans. Ultraso. Ferroelectr. Freq Contr. **39**(5), 555–566 (1992)
2. Girault, J.M., Ménigot, S.: Contrast optimization by metaheuristic for inclusion detection in nonlinear ultrasound imaging. Phys. Procedia **70**, 614–617 (2015)
3. Haupt, R., Haupt, S.: Practical Genetic Algorithms (2004)
4. Ménigot, S., Geryes, M., Charara, J., Girault, J.M.: Inclusion/flaw detection in ultrasound imaging through optimization of random transmitted wave. In: Acoustics 2013, New Delhi (2013)
5. Ménigot, S., Girault, J.M.: Optimization of contrast resolution by genetic algorithm in ultrasound tissue harmonic imaging. Ultrasonics **71**, 231–244 (2016)
6. Ménigot, S., Girault, J.M., Voicu, I., Novell, A.: Optimization of contrast-to-tissue ratio by frequency adaptation in pulse inversion imaging. IEEE Trans. Ultraso. Ferroelectr. Freq Contr. **59**(11), 2431–2438 (2012)
7. Widrow, B., Stearns, S.: Adaptive Signal Processing. Prentice Hall, Englewood Cliffs (1985)

Computing Anomaly Score Threshold
with Autoencoders Pipeline

Igr Alexánder Fernández-Saúco[1]($\boxtimes$), Niusvel Acosta-Mendoza[2],
Andrés Gago-Alonso[2], and Edel Bartolo García-Reyes[2]

[1] DATYS - Technological Solutions, 5a ♯3401 e/34 and 36,
Miramar, Playa, 11300 Havana, Cuba
`alexander.fernandez@datys.cu`
[2] Advanced Technologies Application Center (CENATAV),
7a ♯21406 e/214 and 216, Siboney, Playa, 12200 Havana, Cuba
{`nacosta,agago,egarcia`}`@cenatav.co.cu`

Abstract. Autoencoders neural networks are considered an unsupervised learning algorithm which can be used for detecting anomalies on datasets. In anomaly detection systems powered by autoencoders, the evaluated samples are sorted by the reconstruction error and the anomaly score threshold is set by experts. This threshold helps to select the set of anomaly candidates. In most of the real-world scenarios, the anomaly score threshold estimation is a non-trivial task even for an expert. This paper contains a proposal for an iterative training method based on an autoencoders pipeline to automatically compute the anomaly score threshold. The proposed method achieves encouraging and consistent results collected through the experimentation over two well-known datasets. According to the network configuration, training and tuning, the estimated anomaly score threshold from the proposed method is close to the best possible for the dataset.

Keywords: Anomaly detection · Autoencoders · Deep neural networks

1 Introduction

In data mining, anomaly detection is about the identification of samples which do not share the pattern or behavior followed by most of the elements in a dataset. Anomaly detection techniques have become important tools in several real-world applications such as malicious activity detection [1], intrusion detection [2–4], fraud detection [5,6], surveillance [7,8], and others. For instance, in certain businesses, specifically in banks or telecommunication companies where customers execute financial transactions between accounts, an anomaly detection system is very useful as it alerts on unusual account behavior in a period [5,9].

    In terms of anomaly detection, one of the most successful methods is autoencoders from Deep Learning. Autoencoder networks can learn a compressed representation of the input data, providing an efficient reconstructed output by

© Springer Nature Switzerland AG 2019
R. Vera-Rodriguez et al. (Eds.): CIARP 2018, LNCS 11401, pp. 237–244, 2019.
https://doi.org/10.1007/978-3-030-13469-3_28

reducing the input dimensionality [10]. Moreover, it turns out that autoencoders are more concerned in the difference between the input and output than in the output itself. This difference is known as reconstruction error. According to autoencoder features, a high reconstruction error or score indicates the occurrence of an anomaly [10].

High score samples are highlighted as anomalies. To do so, a selection of the score threshold to compare against is required [4, 8, 10]. Usually this value is either set by a human expert or it is statistically estimated assuming a theoretical distribution. For this reason, in this paper, an iterative training method is introduced which estimates the anomaly score threshold.

This paper is organized as follows: in Sect. 2, the related works are discussed. In Sect. 3, the proposed autoencoder pipeline method is introduced. In Sect. 4, the experimental results are shown and discussed. Finally, in Sect. 5, the conclusions and future work directions are presented.

2   Related Works

Rule-based approach is one of the mainstream techniques in the field of anomaly detection including malicious activity, intrusion or fraud detection [1]. Nowadays, a common scenario requires processing a large volume of unlabeled data where rule-based approaches fail and only unsupervised algorithms are able to support anomaly detection systems. The expansion of the computational power boots up the application of Deep Learning, whose unsupervised algorithms can be used to process large volumes of unlabeled data. These algorithms include the autoencoder networks [6, 11].

2.1   Anomaly Detection with Autoencoders

Autoencoders are a good option in the absence of the ground truth. Since, the introduction of replicator neural network as outlier detection tool [12], autoencoder networks have been used to solve anomaly detection problems [6, 10, 11]. This kind of network consists of two parts: the encoder, shaped like a funnel, and the decoder that expands back out to the full input dataset size at the output layer [10].

The autoencoder structure allows the network to learn a compressed representation of datasets, obtaining a reduced representation of the input data in terms of its dimensions. The output of autoencoders is a reconstruction of the input data in the most efficient way [10]. One of the most interesting characteristics of the autoencoders, since they are a variant of feed-forward neural networks, is the presence of an extra bias that allows the network to recognize normal regions in the feature space, and to compute the reconstruction error [10, 11]. As a consequence, a high reconstruction error indicates an anomaly.

There is a probabilistic version of autoencoders, known as Variational Autoencoders (VAE) [13]. The main advantage of a VAE over an autoencoder network is a probabilistic output which means a reconstruction probability instead of a reconstruction error as an anomaly score. As stated in the literature, probabilities do not require model specific thresholds for considering an evaluated sample as an anomaly since they represent the foundations of what is happening [13]. However, setting a threshold to identify the boundaries and to judge properly what high means is required.

Searching the best anomaly score threshold for automatic anomaly recognition is not a trivial task. The common approaches include to set the anomaly score threshold by human experts or to estimate it from a heuristic (e.g. three-sigma rule [14]) assuming that the dataset fits a theoretical distribution [10].

In the literature, a method for network intrusion detection, which attempts to compute the anomaly score threshold was reported [4]. The proposed training process uses normal samples only. Therefore each autoencoder from the ensemble computes its own anomaly score threshold by selecting the maximum score from training samples.

The reviewed applications of autoencoders are focused on detecting specific dataset anomalies. For example, the classical detection of outlier digits over MNIST database [10], anomalies detection over accounting data [6], or continuous video stream [7] or network intrusion detection [15]. In all mentioned application samples, the anomaly score threshold is a parameter. The estimation of this value is an expert task.

At this point, we conclude there are no reported solutions (neither an exploration) for automatically obtaining the anomaly score threshold from the autoencoders themselves. This paper introduces Autoencoders Pipeline as a valid method to estimate the normality limits.

3   Proposed Method

The goal of the method is to compute the anomaly score threshold. The idea is to arrange and train the autoencoders in sequence, resulting in an iterative training method from which the anomaly score threshold can be obtained. This approach is called "Autoencoders Pipeline" (AEP).

3.1   Autoencoders Pipeline

AEP starts as a regular training. The dataset is split into training and evaluation set. The method consists of the training of a new autoencoder network while normal samples remain in the evaluation set. The normal sample is defined as an evaluated one with a score below the expected anomaly score threshold for the iteration. All anomalous candidate data results are reintegrated for reprocessing in upcoming iterations.

In the first iteration, the $scoreThreshold$ is initialized as follows:

$$scoreThreshold = min(score_0) \tag{1}$$

and the $scoreIncrement$ computed as follows:

$$scoreIncrement = \frac{max(score_0) - min(score_0)}{100} \tag{2}$$

where $score_0$ is the vector with the scores of each evaluated sample.

The evaluated sample score is compared with $scoreThreshold +$ $scoreIncrement$ on each iteration. Every sample with a score greater than this value is considered anomaly candidate. If anomaly candidates are collected at the end of the iteration, the $scoreThreshold$ is updated as follows:

$$scoreThreshold = scoreThreshold + scoreIncrement. \tag{3}$$

When all evaluated samples in the iteration are anomaly candidates, the stop condition of the algorithm is reached and the final $scoreThreshold$ is computed as follows:

$$scoreThreshold = \frac{scoreThreshold + min(score_l)}{2} \tag{4}$$

where l indicates the last iteration.

If the stop condition isn't reached, all anomaly candidates are merged back in the training set and split again at random to train a new autoencoder and start a new iteration. The output of this method is the best-trained autoencoder network from the first iteration and the anomaly score threshold. Figure 1 depicts an overview of how AEP works.

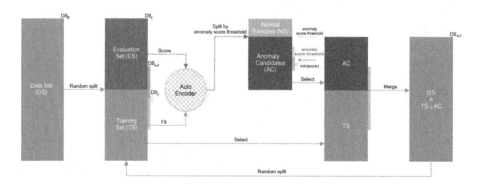

Fig. 1. Overview of AEP algorithm.

Notice that as the anomaly candidates are merged back with the previous training set, a new set with more anomaly average (less normality) is obtained. This approach downgrades smoothly the learning capacity of the new autoencoders from the new datasets until the last autoencoder which considers all evaluated samples as anomalies. When the algorithm reaches this condition the anomaly score threshold is close to the dataset normality limits.

4 Experiments

In this section, the experimental results obtained over two datasets of outliers, following the training method explained in Sect. 3 are shown. All experiments were carried out on a personal computer with an Intel(R) Core(TM) i3-2100 CPU @ 3.10GHz with 16GB of RAM. The algorithm was implemented in Java, powered by Deeplearning4j[1] and executed on Microsoft Windows 10 Professional Operating System.

The datasets used in the experiments are from the Outlier Detection DataSets Library (ODDS)[2]. The datasets were split into equal parts (50% for training and 50% for evaluating) as experiment design approach. Each experiment comprises fifteen executions of the method, looking for a tendency or similarity in the estimated anomaly score thresholds, that allows to validate its effectiveness.

For the scope of the experiments, similar network configurations for the autoencoders were used. The main hyperparameters are Stochastic Gradient Descent (SGD) as optimization algorithm, Xavier as weight initializer, Rectified linear units (ReLU) as activation function and RMSProp as the updater for each layer, and Mean squared error (MSE) as network loss function. The input and output layer sizes depend on the dataset dimensionality. The encoder reduces the dimensionality to 75% on each hidden layer reaching the bottleneck with a size close to 33% of the input size. The decoder increases the dimensionality back using the same values of the encoder in reverse order.

The experiment results are shown in a table that includes the following columns: Anomaly Score Threshold (AST), Detected Anolamies (DA), True Positives (TP), False Positives (FP), True Negatives (TN), False Negatives (FN), Accuracy (AC), Precision (P), Recall (R) and F-measure (F1). Each row of the table represents an isolated execution of the method.

The anomaly score thresholds output from every single execution are overall good estimations, with a few exceptions. From all these results, a better anomaly score threshold can be computed and, according to this value, an associated network can be selected. In the experiments results, the selection of a trained network by the proximity to the denser cluster mean is included. This cluster is an output of the Single-linkage clustering algorithm [16] alongside a heuristic to score each created cluster in the process.

4.1   Arrhythmia Dataset Experiment

"The arrhythmia dataset is a multi-class classification dataset with dimensionality 279. There are five categorical attributes which are discarded here, totalling 274 attributes. The smallest classes, i.e., 3, 4, 5, 7, 8, 9, 14, 15 are combined to form the outliers class and the rest of the classes are combined to form the inliers class"[3].

In Table 1a, the arrhythmia datasets composition used in this experiment is presented. Table 1b enumerates the input and output layer sizes of the network. Furthermore, Table 1c summarizes the results of the executions. The best anomaly score threshold is **430.6269** but the algorithm selects 409.4530 .

---

[1] Deep Learning Library for the JVM http://deeplearning4j.org.

[2] ODDS http://odds.cs.stonybrook.edu.

[3] ODDS Arrhythmia dataset http://odds.cs.stonybrook.edu/arrhythmia-dataset.

Table 1. Arrhythmia dataset experiment

(a) Datasets composition

Dataset	Records	Outliers
Original	452	66(14%)
Training	226	38(16%)
Evaluation	226	28(12%)

(b) Network layers sizes

Part	Layer	Input	Output
Encoder	0	274	205
	1	205	153
	2	153	114
	3	114	90
Decoder	4	90	114
	5	114	153
	6	153	205
	7	205	274

(c) Executions results

AST	DA	TP	FP	TN	FN	AC	P	R	F1
147.0698	215	27	188	10	1	0.16	0.13	**0.96**	0.22
332.7005	54	17	37	161	11	0.79	0.31	0.61	0.41
376.3150	36	12	24	174	16	0.82	0.33	0.43	0.38
379.9096	32	11	21	177	17	0.83	0.34	0.39	0.37
383.6539	32	11	21	177	17	0.83	0.34	0.39	0.37
389.0941	32	11	21	177	17	0.83	0.34	0.39	0.37
390.3418	31	11	20	178	17	0.84	0.35	0.39	0.37
394.6437	30	11	19	179	17	0.84	0.37	0.39	0.38
400.3525	31	12	19	179	16	0.85	0.39	0.43	0.41
403.9024	31	12	19	179	16	0.85	0.39	0.43	0.41
406.7784	31	12	19	179	16	0.85	0.39	0.43	0.41
409.4530	21	10	11	187	18	0.87	0.48	0.36	0.41
430.6269	24	11	13	185	17	0.87	0.46	0.39	**0.42**
447.6577	21	10	11	187	18	0.87	0.48	0.36	0.41
570.6298	10	6	4	194	22	**0.88**	**0.60**	0.21	0.32

This value is the closest to the mean of the cluster from 332.7005 to 570.6298. This effects the selection of the trained network associated with the selected execution.

This is a result of a very poorly tuned network. Notice values of F1 are under 0.5. As mentioned before, the algorithm is not looking for the best network configuration for the dataset, but for the best possible anomaly score threshold. The average of iterations to convergence was 62 (min:37, max:154).

4.2 Wisconsin-Breast Cancer Dataset Experiment

"The Wisconsin-Breast Cancer (Diagnostics) dataset (WBC) is a classification dataset with dimensionality 30, which records the measurements for breast cancer cases. There are two classes, benign and malignant. The malignant class of this dataset is downsampled to 21 points, which are considered as outliers, while points in the benign class are considered inliers"[4].

In Table 2a, the WBC datasets composition used in this experiment is presented. Table 2b enumerates the input and output layer sizes of the network. Furthermore, the results of the executions are listed in Table 2c. The best anomaly score threshold is **0.05666** but the unsupervised selection is 0.05697 due to its proximity to the mean of the cluster from 0.05622 to 0.05883. This selection also includes the associated network.

This is the result of a better trained network than the one presented in Sect. 4.1. The configuration and training are not the best possible but are sufficient for purpose of this paper. Values of F1 greater than 0.7 in some executions have been achieved. The average of iterations to convergence was 49 (min:28, max:101).

---

[4] ODDS WBC dataset http://odds.cs.stonybrook.edu/wbc.

Table 2. WBC dataset experiment

(a) Datasets composition

Dataset	Records	Outliers
Original	378	21(5%)
Training	189	12(6%)
Evaluation	189	9(4%)

(b) Network layers sizes

Part	Layer	Input	Output
Encoder	0	30	22
	1	22	16
	2	16	12
	3	12	9
Decoder	4	9	12
	5	12	16
	6	16	22
	7	22	30

(c) Executions results

AST	DA	TP	FP	TN	FN	AC	P	R	F1
0.02859	16	8	8	172	1	0.95	0.50	**0.89**	0.64
0.03361	21	8	13	167	1	0.93	0.38	**0.89**	0.53
0.03423	20	8	12	168	1	0.93	0.40	**0.89**	0.55
0.03563	20	8	12	168	1	0.93	0.40	**0.89**	0.55
0.03993	14	8	6	174	1	0.96	0.57	**0.89**	0.70
0.04062	15	8	7	173	1	0.96	0.53	**0.89**	0.67
0.04108	16	8	8	172	1	0.95	0.50	**0.89**	0.64
0.04628	14	8	6	174	1	0.96	0.57	**0.89**	0.70
0.04649	13	8	5	175	1	**0.97**	0.62	**0.89**	0.73
0.05622	10	6	4	176	3	0.96	0.60	0.67	0.63
0.05633	11	7	4	176	2	**0.97**	0.64	0.78	0.70
0.05659	13	8	5	175	1	**0.97**	0.62	**0.89**	0.73
0.05666	12	8	4	176	1	**0.97**	**0.67**	**0.89**	**0.76**
0.05697	13	8	5	175	1	**0.97**	0.62	**0.89**	0.73
0.05883	11	7	4	176	2	**0.97**	0.64	0.78	0.70

5   Conclusions

In this paper, the Autoencoder Pipeline as an iterative training method to find the anomaly score threshold for a dataset according to the network configuration, training and tuning was introduced. The method is evaluated over two well-known datasets.

The reliability of the method has been exposed through a couple of experiments and the results are encouraging. Based on the experiments, we conclude that is possible to automatically compute the anomaly score threshold by autoencoders themselves. In essence, an arrangement of autoencoders in a pipeline is required along with a smoothly downgrade of the normal samples from the training set.

As future work, the unsupervised selection of the best network from several executions can be improved. In an ideal case, all networks from the cluster with the best ones should work together by consolidating the anomaly criterion.

References

1. Herrera-Semenets, V., Pérez García, O.A., Gago-Alonso, A., Hernández-León, R.: Classification rule-based models for malicious activity detection. Intell. Data Anal. **21**, 1141–1154 (2017)
2. Denning, D.E.: An intrusion-detection model. IEEE Trans. Softw. Eng. **SE-13**(2), 222–232 (1987)
3. Jones, A.K., Sielken, R.S.: Computer system intrusion detection: a survey. Technical report, University of Virginia, February 2001

4. Mirsky, Y., Doitshman, T., Elovici, Y., Shabtai, A.: Kitsune: an ensemble of autoencoders for online network intrusion detection. CoRR abs/1802.09089 (2018)

5. Pumsirirat, A., Yan, L.: Credit card fraud detection using deep learning based on auto-encoder and restricted Boltzmann machine. Int. J. Adv. Comput. Sci. Appl. **9**, 18–25 (2018)

6. Schreyer, M., Sattarov, T., Borth, D., Dengel, A., Reimer, B.: Detection of anomalies in large scale accounting data using deep autoencoder networks. CoRR abs/1709.05254 (2017)

7. Narasimhan, M.G., Sowmya Kamath, S.: Dynamic video anomaly detection and localization using sparse denoising autoencoders. Multimed. Tools Appl. **77**(11), 13173–13195 (2018)

8. Xu, D., Yan, Y., Ricci, E., Sebe, N.: Detecting anomalous events in videos by learning deep representations of appearance and motion. Comput. Vis. Image Underst. **156**, 117–127 (2017). Image and Video Understanding in Big Data

9. Zheng, Y.J., Zhou, X.H., Sheng, W.G., Xue, Y., Chen, S.Y.: Generative adversarial network based telecom fraud detection at the receiving bank. Neural Networks **102**, 78–86 (2018)

10. Patterson, J., Gibson, A.: Deep Learning: A Practitioner's Approach. O'Reilly, Beijing (2017)

11. Xu, H., et al.: Unsupervised anomaly detection via variational auto-encoder for seasonal KPIs in web applications. CoRR abs/1802.03903 (2018)

12. Hawkins, S., He, H., Williams, G., Baxter, R.: Outlier detection using replicator neural networks. In: Proceedings of the Fifth International Conference and Data Warehousing and Knowledge Discovery (DaWaK02), pp. 170–180 (2002)

13. An, J., Cho, S.: Variational Autoencoder Based Anomaly Detection Using Reconstruction Probability. Seoul National University, Seoul (2015)

14. Upton, G., Cook, I.: A Dictionary of Statistics. Oxford University Press, New York (2008)

15. Yu, Y., Long, J., Cai, Z.: Network intrusion detection through stacking dilated convolutional autoencoders. Secur. Commun. Networks **2017**, 1–10 (2017)

16. Gower, J.C., Ross, G.J.S.: Minimum spanning trees and single linkage cluster analysis. J. Roy. Stat. Soc. Ser. C (Appl. Stat.) **18**(1), 54–64 (1969)

Generating Random Variates via Kernel Density Estimation and Radial Basis Function Based Neural Networks

Cristian Candia-García[1]([✉]), Manuel G. Forero[2]([✉]) [ID],
and Sergio Herrera-Rivera[2]

[1] Faculty of Engineering, Escuela Colombiana de Ingeniería Julio Garavito,
Bogotá, Colombia
cristian.candia@mail.escuelaing.edu.co
[2] Faculty of Engineering, Universidad de Ibagué, Ibagué, Colombia
{manuel.forero,sergio.herrera}@unibague.edu.co

Abstract. When modeling phenomena that cannot be studied by deterministic analytical approaches, one of the main tasks is to generate random variates. The widely-used techniques, such as the inverse transformation, convolution, and rejection-acceptance methods, involve a significant amount of statistical work and do not provide satisfactory results when the data do not conform to the known probability density functions. This study aims to propose an alternative nonparametric method for generating random variables that combines kernel density estimation (KDE), and radial basis function based neural networks (RBFBNNs). We evaluate the method's performance using Poisson, triangular, and exponential probability density distributions and assessed its utility for unknown distributions. The results show that the model's effectiveness depends substantially on selecting an appropriate bandwidth value for KDE and a certain minimum number of data points to train the algorithm. the proposed method enabled us to achieve an R^2 value between 0.91 and 0.99 for analyzed distributions.

Keywords: General regression neural network · Probabilistic neural network · Kernel density estimation · Random variable · Probability distribution

1 Introduction

Computational models are a widely-used alternative method for solving problems that cannot be studied by deterministic analytical approaches [1]. This has led to the development of a fairly small number of density functions to describe how values are distributed over the sample spaces of a large number of real phenomena. However, preparing and statistically analyzing the data to take advantage of these distributions requires significant effort, and does not produce good results when the system analyzed depends on random variables that do not follow known probability density functions, leading us to look for unconventional alternatives that can reproduce the stochasticity of real systems [2].

© Springer Nature Switzerland AG 2019
R. Vera-Rodriguez et al. (Eds.): CIARP 2018, LNCS 11401, pp. 245–252, 2019.
https://doi.org/10.1007/978-3-030-13469-3_29

Estimating random variable distributions has played an important role in several recent studies, studying monthly rainfall and water flow to determine drought indicators [3], predicting crime based on Twitter messages [4], and studying trends in the marine duck populations along the Atlantic coast of the United States [5].

For more than 40 years, nonparametric probability density estimation techniques, such as the Kolmogorov–Smirnov and chi-squared tests, have been the most widely-used density estimation methods, because they do not depend on the explicit form of the distribution or its parameter values, as parametric techniques do [6, 7]. However, these tests only suggest how to adjust the data when working with known distributions, and they are also sensitive to common errors in interpreting the p-value [8].

Since its introduction in 1956, KDE has become one of the most widely-used nonparametric density estimation methods [9, 10]. Over time, various authors have extensively modified the original technique in order to reduce its sensitivity to the choice of the kernel function and bandwidth [11]. Most recent methods suggest using maximum likelihood algorithms, with maximum entropy [12] and histogram trend filters [13]. These nonparametric techniques have proved useful for analyzing phenomena that do not conform to known distributions, such as wind speeds [14], crime prediction using social network data [4], and smart sensor-based electricity readings [15].

Once a given random variable's distribution has been established, the subsequent problem consists of generating numerical values that follow the same distribution. The most common conventional random variable generation techniques are the inverse transformation, the acceptance-rejection, and convolution methods. However, these all have issues in terms of the calculation speed, computational resources required, and effort needed to prepare and statistically analyze the data [1]. Some researchers have presented universal methods of generating random variables by means of generalized acceptance-rejection algorithms [16], multilayer neural networks [17], transforming random variables to generate continuous distribution families [18], and specialized algorithms for producing particular distributions such as geometric [19] distributions.

This paper presents a new nonparametric approach that combines KDE with RBFBNNs to generate random variable values regardless of their probability distributions and whether they are discrete or continuous variables, thus reducing the dependence on goodness of fit tests, for both data that follows a known distribution and those that are distributed atypically.

2 Kernel Density Estimation

KDE is a common nonparametric technique for estimating the probability density functions of random variables. Given a set of n independent observations $X_1, X_2, \ldots,$ X_n, represented by the same probability density function f, this model estimates the probability density function (PDF) f_n associated with these observations as follows:

$$f_n(x) = n^{-1}h^{-1} \sum_{j=1}^{n} K\{h^{-1}(x - X_j)\}. \tag{1}$$

Here, K is the kernel function, which weights the result by the proximity of x to the sampled points, and h is the bandwidth, which defines the size of the kernel function's weighting window.

KDE's accuracy depends on the kernel function K and bandwidth h used. The value of K does not significantly affect the model's statistical efficiency, but it does impact the calculation speed for large data sets [10]. In contrast, the bandwidth h is a sensitive parameter that governs the model's overall behavior, so it is essential to select an optimal value for it when estimating the PDF [10, 11].

3 Generalized Regression Neural Networks and Probabilistic Neural Networks (RBFBNNs)

GRNNs and PNNs are RBFBNNs introduced by Donald Specht between 1990 and 1991. In case of PNNs, Specht demonstrated that the Bayes–Parzen classifier can be split into many simple processes and hence implemented as a multilayer neural network [20], also showed that the GRNNs can be implemented for any regression problem in which an assumption of linearity is no justified [21]. In general, the structure for GRNNs and PNNs can be summarized as shown in Fig. 1:

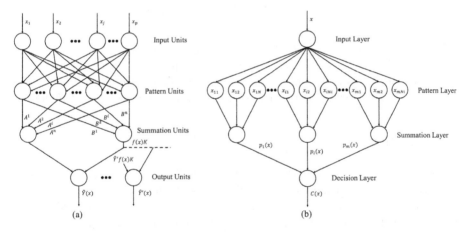

Fig. 1. Neural Networks structure for (a) GRNN (b) PNN. (Source: adapted from [20, 21])

In both cases the input layer distributes the input to the neurons of the next, or pattern, layer, when it receives a pattern x, pattern layer neuron x_{ij} calculates its output, that is later distributed in the units of sum that determine the output according to some weights or defined relation, finally the result obtained is used to estimate the classification generated in PNNs case, or the continuous value in GRNNs case [20, 21].

One important characteristic of this type of networks is that no iterative training is required; instead, the parameters are saved and used to make predictions. This makes it a computationally lightweight algorithm, which is significant when handling large amounts of data [22].

4   Combining KDE and RBFBNNs

Figure 2 gives an overview of the proposed method. It starts by estimating the shape of the sample data's PDF using KDE. Here we used the Epanechnikov weighting function and established an appropriate bandwidth for each data set using a local search procedure, starting from the reference bandwidth value proposed by Silver [10]. Once PDF's shape is estimated, we compute the CDF's shape using a numerical approximation of PDF's area under curve by trapezoidal Riemann Sum. While in the analytically case the highest probability of CDF must be equal to one, in the estimation case, the highest value of the estimated CDF is better when is closer to one.

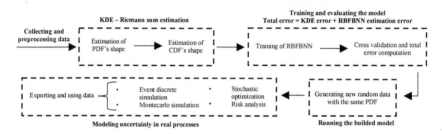

Fig. 2. Overview of the proposed method. (Source: the authors)

The computed points from CDF estimation are used to train a GRNN in case of continuous variable or a PNN in case of discrete variable. This produces a model that enables random values to be generated according to the same distribution as the sample data via an inverse transform procedure by replacing the CDF with the RBFBNN.

5   Evaluation

For this study, a computer with an Intel Core i7 2.60 GHz processor and 8 GB of RAM was used. All the calculations were carried out using Python 3.2.6.

The GRNNs and PNNs implemented using the NeuPy library, were trained on 70% of the input data set, with the remaining 30% reserved for the subsequent validation step. For this evaluation, we used the learning curve algorithm from the scikit-learn library. This method evaluates the neural network's accuracy by varying the training data set and performing repeated cross-validation, preserving the 70/30 split for each training data subset and using R^2 metric.

To evaluate the total error of our model (Eq. (2)), we used three probability distributions with known CDFs, so that their inverse transforms could be computed analytically for a given set of uniform random values, enabling us to calculate different errors between the analytic values obtained from the inverse transformations and the values generated by the RBFBNN. The mixture of normal distributions data set was used as an illustration of applicability of proposed model to generate random variates from unknown distributions.

$$\text{Total error} = \text{KDE error} + \text{Riemann sum error} + \text{RBFBNN error} \qquad (2)$$

5.1 Data Sets Used

To evaluate the proposed model, we used four different data sets, of 600 samples each, generated using SciPy Python's library. The first three data sets used the Poisson, triangular, and exponential distributions, while the fourth was a mixture of three different normal distributions, contributing 200 samples each. Table 1 lists the parameters used for each distribution, given according to SciPy's nomenclature.

Table 1. Details of the data sets used.

Distribution	Type	Parameters	Total Samples
Poisson	Discrete	mu = 10, loc = 0	600
Triangular	Continuous	c = 1, loc = 0, scale = 1	600
Exponential	Continuous	scale = 20	600
Mixture of normal	Continuous	loc 1 = 15, scale 1 = 2	600
		loc 2 = 25, scale 2 = 2	
		loc 3 = 35, scale 3 = 3	

6 Results and Discussion

6.1 PDFs and CDFs Estimations

Figure 3 shows histograms of the 600 samples from each probability distribution, together with the estimated PDFs and corresponding CDFs.

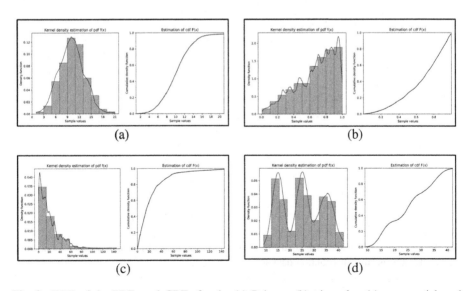

(a)   (b)

(c)   (d)

Fig. 3. KDE of the PDFs and CDFs for the (a) Poisson, (b) triangular, (c) exponential, and (d) mixed normal distribution data sets.

The bandwidth computed with the local search procedure shown in Table 2, allows good fit for PDF and CDF especially for Poisson and mixture of normal distributions, where the smoothed curves are closers to the histogram representations. In the case of triangular and exponential distributions, the KDE exhibits non-smoothed shapes in comparison with the histograms for both distributions, which is an evidence of histogram's width class sensitivity in PDF's shape estimation.

Table 2. Overall errors for the proposed method on each of known distributions.

Distribution	Kernel bandwidth	R^2	MAE	MSE	Explained variance
Poisson	1.1903	0.9824	0.1741	0.1763	0.9827
Triangular	0.0451	0.9980	0.0084	0.0001	0.9984
Exponential	2.9018	0.9118	3.6563	64.0301	0.9241

Otherwise, the learning curves shown in Fig. 4 for each data set, reflect the impact of the training data variation on the RBFBNN's R^2, allowing us to establish that, for the triangular and Poisson distributions, a training set of size approximately 150 was sufficient for good fitting, while, for the exponential distribution, the R^2 increases considerably above 300 samples, meaning that distributions with extreme values with low probability of occurrence, require a larger number of sample data for good CDF estimation.

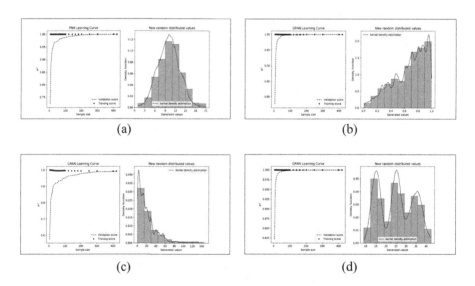

Fig. 4. Learning curves and estimated PDFs for the (a) Poisson, (b) triangular, (c) exponential, and (d) mixture normal distribution data sets.

Figure 4 also shows the histograms and estimated PDFs for 10,000 new random values generated by each of the RBFBNN models, suggesting graphically that the original and generated data follow identical distributions.

6.2 Precision of the Method

We determined the method's overall precision by considering the MSE, mean absolute error (MAE), R^2, and explained variance, calculated by comparing the analytic results with the KDE-based CDFs for each of the known probability distributions and the values generated by the RBFBNNs, as discussed in Sect. 5.

The results shown in Table 2 indicate that that the accuracy was generally good for the Poisson and triangular distributions, but the correlation and explained variance are notably reduced for the exponential distribution. This is probably due to the fact that exponential distribution includes extreme values that are unlikely to appear in the training data and therefore do not feature in the estimated PDFs and CDFs, weakening the GRNN's and PNN's ability to generate accurate results.

In case of mixture of normal distributions data set, where analytical CDF is unknown, we only analyzed KDE adjust between original data set and the histogram for 10,000 new random values generated using the proposed method, finding good fitting as shown in Fig. 4.

7 Conclusions

In this paper, we have proposed a nonparametric model for generating random variable values that has considerable advantages in terms of reducing the amount of preparatory and statistical analysis work required to represent the stochasticity of real phenomena in computer simulations. The integration of KDE and RBFBNNs enable us to replicate known and unknown random variate distributions without needed of goodness of test fit procedures, improving the model's applicability when the data do not conform to the known probability density functions as shown before in the case of mixture of normal distributions.

One of the main weaknesses of our model is the strict need to establish a suitable KDE bandwidth, to prevent errors propagating to neural networks training process and hence guarantee the CDF curves are well-adjusted, since this involves a local search procedure to stablish an adequate bandwidth value with an associated computational cost. This weakness is especially evident in distributions where unlikely values will generally not appear in the sample data, and thus will not be reflected in the KDE and the RBFBNN's prediction, meaning a greater amount of data will be needed for training.

References

1. Banks, J. (ed.): Handbook of Simulation: Principles, Methodology, Advances, Applications, and Practice, 1 edn. Wiley-Interscience, New York/Norcross (1998)
2. Krishnamoorthy, K.: Handbook of Statistical Distributions with Applications, 2nd edn. CRC Press, Boca Raton (2016)

3. Svensson, C., Hannaford, J., Prosdocimi, I.: Statistical distributions for monthly aggregations of precipitation and streamflow in drought indicator applications. Water Resour. Res. **53**(2), 999–1018 (2017)
4. Gerber, M.S.: Predicting crime using Twitter and kernel density estimation. Decis. Support Syst. **61**(Suppl. C), 115–125 (2014)
5. Zipkin, E.F., Leirness, J.B., Kinlan, B.P., O'Connell, A.F., Silverman, E.D.: Fitting statistical distributions to sea duck count data: implications for survey design and abundance estimation. Stat. Methodol. **17**(Suppl. C), 67–81 (2014)
6. Berkson, J.: Some difficulties of interpretation encountered in the application of the chi-square test. J. Am. Stat. Assoc. **33**(203), 526–536 (1938)
7. Massey, F.J.: The Kolmogorov-Smirnov test for goodness of fit. J. Am. Stat. Assoc. **46**(253), 68–78 (1951)
8. Gutiérrez, M., Agustín, P., Gómez-Restrepo, C.: Beyond p value. Rev. Colomb. Psiquiatr. **38**(3), 574–586 (2009)
9. Rosenblatt, M.: Remarks on some nonparametric estimates of a density function. Ann. Math. Stat. **27**(3), 832–837 (1956)
10. Silverman, B.W.: Algorithm AS 176: kernel density estimation using the fast fourier transform. J. R. Stat. Soc. Ser. C Appl. Stat. **31**(1), 93–99 (1982)
11. Heidenreich, N.-B., Schindler, A., Sperlich, S.: Bandwidth selection for kernel density estimation: a review of fully automatic selectors. AStA Adv. Stat. Anal. **97**(4), 403–433 (2013)
12. Agarwal, R., Chen, Z., Sarma, S.V.: A novel nonparametric maximum likelihood estimator for probability density functions. IEEE Trans. Pattern Anal. Mach. Intell. **39**(7), 1294–1308 (2017)
13. Padilla, O.H.M., Scott, J.G.: Nonparametric density estimation by histogram trend filtering. arXiv:150904348 Stat, September 2015
14. Xu, X., Yan, Z., Xu, S.: Estimating wind speed probability distribution by diffusion-based kernel density method. Electr. Power Syst. Res. **121**, 28–37 (2015)
15. Arora, S., Taylor, J.W.: Forecasting electricity smart meter data using conditional kernel density estimation. Omega **59**(Part A), 47–59 (2016)
16. Barabesi, L., Pratelli, L.: Universal methods for generating random variables with a given characteristic function. J. Stat. Comput. Simul. **85**(8), 1679–1691 (2015)
17. Magdon-Ismail, M., Atiya, A.: Density estimation and random variate generation using multilayer networks. IEEE Trans. Neural Netw. **13**(3), 497–520 (2002)
18. Alzaatreh, A., Lee, C., Famoye, F.: A new method for generating families of continuous distributions. METRON **71**(1), 63–79 (2013)
19. Bringmann, K., Friedrich, T.: Exact and efficient generation of geometric random variates and random graphs. In: Fomin, F.V., Freivalds, R., Kwiatkowska, M., Peleg, D. (eds.) ICALP 2013. LNCS, vol. 7965, pp. 267–278. Springer, Heidelberg (2013). https://doi.org/10.1007/978-3-642-39206-1_23
20. Specht, D.F.: Probabilistic neural networks. Neural Netw. **3**(1), 109–118 (1990)
21. Specht, D.F.: A general regression neural network. IEEE Trans. Neural Netw. **2**(6), 568–576 (1991)
22. Pedregosa, F., et al.: Scikit-learn: machine learning in python. J. Mach. Learn. Res. **12**, 2825–2830 (2012)

Detection of Bat Acoustics Signals Using Voice Activity Detection Techniques with Random Forests Classification

Adrian T. Ruiz[1,2]([✉]), Julian Equihua[2], Santiago Martínez[2],
Everardo Robredo[2], Günther Palm[1], and Friedhelm Schwenker[1]

[1] Institute of Neural Information Processing, Ulm University,
James-Franck-Ring, 89081 Ulm, Germany
adrian.ruiz@uni-ulm.de
[2] National Commission for the Knowledge and Use of Biodiversity (CONABIO),
Liga Periférico Sur – Insurgentes Sur No. 4903, Col. Parques del Pedregal, Tlalpan,
14010 Mexico, D.F., Mexico

Abstract. Bats are indicators for ecosystem health, and therefore the determination of bat activity and species abundance provides essential information for biodiversity research and conservation monitoring. In this study, we propose a computational method for the detection of bat echolocation calls. This method uses feature engineering and consists of a statistical model-based Voice Activity Detector combined with a Random Forests classifier (VAD+RF). Using an open-access library (www.batdetective.org), we trained and tested the performance of our method and compare it to other existing detection methods. These methods include a detector based on deep neural networks along with other commercial detection systems. To visualize the detector performance over the full range of possible class distributions and misclassification costs, we calculated the Cost Curves and F_1-measure Curves. Results show that the detecting power of VAD+RF is comparable to methods based on deep learning. Based on the results we give recommendations to improve the future designs of the bat call detector.

Keywords: Bat echolocation · Animal sound detection ·
Random forests · Voice activity detection ·
Convolutional neural networks · ROC curves

1 Introduction

Detection and recognition of animal species are among the most fundamental challenges in biodiversity research and conservation monitoring, in particular for the assessment of bioindicator species that provide valuable information on the health of the respective ecosystem. The highly diverse bats (Order Chiroptera)

Supported by CONABIO (National Commission for the Knowledge and Use of Biodiversity).

R. Vera-Rodriguez et al. (Eds.): CIARP 2018, LNCS 11401, pp. 253–261, 2019.
https://doi.org/10.1007/978-3-030-13469-3_30

are such bio-indicators and therefore the determination of bat activity and bat species abundance is an essential challenge in conservation and ecology projects [7]. An acoustic identification of bat species relies on the observation and recognition of species-specific call patterns from sonograms of ultrasonic recordings [6]. Nevertheless this "manual" identification is very time-consuming and requires a high degree of training and skills. Current bat monitoring necessities, e.g. particularly those connected to the essential monitoring of the animals around wind energy turbines, produce huge datasets that can vastly profit from computer-assisted identification methods. For identifying the bat call components in the ultrasonic frequency range, most of the current techniques work with a time-frequency representation of the audio signal. However frequent background noises (insects, footsteps, other electronic devices and power lines) and signal distortions (over-gained microphones) may hamper signal detection in recordings from the field. Moreover, other signals such as insect vocalizations or rain drops may have a frequency distribution in the ultrasonic range. For this reason, methods based on the calculation of the instantaneous dominant frequency such as zero-crossing are not suitable to apply for detection. Some studies have shown that detecting bat calls based on spectrograms is a more effective method, e.g., a spectral peak detector [12]. Nevertheless, in the case of low signal-to-noise ratio, some studies have shown that model-based detection produces fewer false positive detections than spectral peak detection [11]. Recently was proposed by Aodha et al. [8] a detection method based on deep neural networks in which a representation learning is automatically performed. The results shown that deep learning methods can perform better than other existing detection methods. Nevertheless, we consider that the metric applied is sensitive to imbalanced ratio of false and true positive detections.

In this study, we propose a method for the detection of bat echolocation calls that uses a statistical model-based Voice Activity Detector combined with an ensemble of tree classifiers using the Random Forests algorithm. We use global evaluation curves to visualize the detector performance over the full range of possible distributions of positive and false detections. Our approach aims to accurately detect a more extensive and diverse set of bat species within complex and noisy soundscapes.

2   Methods

The objective of the following techniques is to detect and locate ultrasound signals of bat echolocations calls within broad band recordings from natural environments. In the following we describe the methods that will be later compared on a performance test.

2.1   Energy-Based Detector

This detection method has been used in many studies as the baseline detector [11,12] and consists of a short-term broadband energy signal. Usually, this signal is calculated from a Time-Frequency (TF) representation X of the audio signal $x(t)$. Using the Short Time Fourier Transform (STFT), we estimate a TF representation $X(t_m, f_k)$ with discrete variables $t_m = m\Delta t$ and $f_k = k\Delta f$ with $m = 1, 2, \ldots, M$ and $k = 1, 2, \ldots, K$. Thereafter, the mean energy signal is defined as

$$EBD_{mean}(t_m) = \frac{1}{K} \sum_{f_k} |X(t_m, f_k)|^2 \tag{1}$$

Another alternative is to calculate the peak energy as follows

$$EBD_{max}(t_m) = \max_{f_k} |X(t_m, f_k)|^2 \tag{2}$$

To avoid non-relevant noises in the sonic range, the TF representation is filtered using a band-pass with cut-off frequencies of 12.5 kHz and 250 kHz. Thereafter, a time frame t_m is said to contain a bat call if the energy signal $EBD(t_m)$ is above some predefined threshold θ.

2.2   Voice Activity Detector

Here we propose a detection method based on a Voice Activity Detector (VAD) technique [10,13]. This model-based approach is often used in speech processing for detecting the presence or absence of speech. The VAD uses a Time-Frequency (TF) representation X of the audio signal $x(t)$ as explained in Sect. 2.1. The following definitions are evaluated at each time frame t_m. First, we defined a coefficient vector $\mathbf{X} = (X_1, \ldots, X_k, \ldots, X_K)$ where $X_k = X(t_m, f_k)$ is the kth component that corresponds to the frequency bin f_k. Assuming that the target signal $s(t)$ is degraded by uncorrelated additive noise $n(t)$, for each frame t_m are considered two hypothesis H_0 and H_1 for absent signal and present signal respectively, i.e.

$$H_0 : \mathbf{X} = \mathbf{N}$$
$$H_1 : \mathbf{X} = \mathbf{N} + \mathbf{S}$$

where $\mathbf{X}$, $\mathbf{N}$ and $\mathbf{S}$ are the coefficient vectors of $x(t)$, $n(t)$, and $s(t)$ with their respectively components X_k, N_k, and S_k. A gaussian statistical model is adopted such that the coefficients vectors of each process are asymptotically independent gaussian random variables [5,13]. The probability density functions conditioned on H_0 and H_1 are given by $p(\mathbf{X}|H_0) = \prod_{k=1}^{K} p(X_k|H_0)$ and $p(\mathbf{X}|H_1) = \prod_{k=1}^{K} p(X_k|H_1)$ respectively. For each frequency bin f_k a likelihood ratio Λ_k is defined as the ratio of the probability density functions $p(X_k|H_0)$ and $p(X_k|H_1)$. According to [5] the likelihood ratio Λ_k has the form

$$\Lambda_k \triangleq \frac{p(X_k|H_1)}{p(X_k|H_0)} = \frac{1}{1 + \xi_k} \exp\left(\frac{\gamma_k \xi_k}{1 + \xi_k}\right) \tag{3}$$

where $\xi_k = \lambda_S(k)/\lambda_N(k)$ and $\gamma_k = |X_k|^2/\lambda_N(k)$ are called the *a priori* and *a posteriori* signal-to-noise ratios respectively. These ratios are defined by $\lambda_N(k)$ and $\lambda_S(k)$, which denote the variances of N_k and S_k, respectively. To estimate the parameters ξ_k and γ_k it is important to estimate the noise variance $\lambda_N(k)$. According to [13], we applied a noise statistic estimation procedure based on a decision-directed method.

The decision rule to presume that a signal is *absent* or *present* is established from the likelihood ratio $LR(t_m)$ which is the geometric mean of $\Lambda_k(t_m)$ among all frequencies f_k at time t_m, this means

$$LR(t_m) \equiv \log \Lambda(t_m) = \frac{1}{K} \sum_{k=1}^{K} \log \Lambda_k(t_m) \underset{H_1}{\overset{H_0}{\gtrless}} \theta_d \qquad (4)$$

where the parameter θ_d is a given threshold value that delimitates the occurrence of hypothesis H_0 and H_1. The next process is to locate all the detections of the target signal (i.e. bat call signal). This means to estimate a time t_d and a frequency f_d for each detection event $d = 1, 2, \ldots$, such that hypothesis H_1 is true in Eq. 4. A detection event is delimited by the compact interval $\Delta T_d = [T_{onset}, T_{offset}]$ such that $LR(t_m) > \theta$ for all $t_m \in \Delta T_d$. The detection point $\mathbf{x}_d = (t_d, f_d)$ is obtained by

$$t_d = \underset{t_m}{\operatorname{argmax}} \ LR(t_m) \qquad (5a)$$

$$f_d = \underset{f_k}{\operatorname{argmax}} \ p(X(t_d, f_k)|H_1) \qquad (5b)$$

For this study, we set the STFT with a Hamming window of 2.5 ms length and an overlap of 75%. The STFT was filtered using a band-pass with cut-off frequencies of 12.5 kHz and 250 kHz. We based the VAD detector on [3], and the parameters were adapted for ultrasonic recordings and adjusted to target bat call signals. The adjustment was based on general values for call duration and pulse interval.

Table 1. Call features used for classification with Random Forests algorithm

Type	Feature	Type	Feature
VAD	Likelihood value	Image shape	Eccentricity
Call sonogram	Time length		Orientation
	Frequency interval		Solidity
	Peak frequency point		MajorAxisLength
	Power spectrum density range		MinorAxisLength
	Power spectrum density mean		Centroid
			WeightedCentroid

2.3   Voice Activity Detector with Random Forests Classification

This method (VAD+RF) combines the VAD detector described in Sect. 2.2 with an ensemble of tree classifiers based on the Random Forests [2] algorithm. We implemented a feature extraction task for every detection point $\mathbf{x}_d = (t_d, f_d)$ (see Eq. 5) based on a heuristic image segmentation technique applied on a previous study [10]. This technique separates background components from the call detection and keeps only the spectral components connected to the detection point $\mathbf{x}_d$. For the call segmentation we used a cut-off threshold $\theta_S = 12$ dB and a call area limit from 2 sHz to 200 sHz. Thereafter, we extracted a set of features of different types (see Table 1), using the filtered detection sonogram S_θ. Using this features a binary Random Forests classifier predicts whether the detection is a positive or a negative call detection. As an output of the RF classifier we obtain a posterior probability $P(+|S_\theta(\mathbf{x}_d))$ of a positive call detection $(+)$ given the detection sample S_θ located at $\mathbf{x}_d$. Contrary to the detectors described in the previous sections, this method is a supervised learning algorithm and requires a training set with positive and negative detection examples.

2.4   Evaluation Metrics

The receiver operating characteristic curve is commonly used to evaluate the performance of a detection method. This curve is created by plotting the true positive rate (tpr) against the false positive rate (fpr) at various threshold settings. In this case, these standard metrics are not suitable due the fact that in noisy soundscapes there is a significantly greater proportion of negative detections (non-bat calls) than positive examples (bat calls). Instead, we applied global evaluation curves such as the *Cost Curves* [4] and the F_1-*measure Curves* [14]. Aodha et al. [8] plotted their the results using a PR-curve of precision P against recall R, nevertheless this PR-curve is sensitive to class imbalance, given its dependence on precision [14]. Different operating conditions (skew levels) lead to different PR-curves, which makes classifier comparison difficult. *Cost Curves* [4] are an alternative metric to visualize the expected cost (EC) of classification over a range of misclassification costs and/or skew levels. Denoting $C(-|+)$ and $C(+|-)$ as the misclassification costs of positive and negative samples (usually the cost of correct classifications is zero), then the expected cost is $EC = fnr \cdot p(+) \cdot C(-|+) + fpr \cdot p(-) \cdot C(+|-)$, where fnr is the false negative rate, and $p(+)$ and $p(-) = 1 - p(+)$ are the prior probability of the positive and negative class. The Cost Curves depicts the *Normalized Expected Cost* $(NEC \in [0,1])$ as a function of $pc(+) \in [0,1]$ as follows

$$NEC = (1 - tpr - fpr)\, pc(+) + fpr \qquad (6)$$

The term $pc(+)$ is the normalized product of $p(+) \cdot C(-|+)$ and is defined as

$$pc(+) = \frac{(1/m - 1) \cdot p(+)}{(1/m - 2) \cdot p(+) + 1} \qquad (7)$$

where $m = C(+|-)/(C(+|-)+C(-|+))$. For this metric a lower curve indicates a better classification performance. Soleymani et al. [14] recently proposed an analogous metric to Cost Curves based on the F_α-*measure*. In this metric, a classifier is represented as a curve that shows its performance over all of its decision thresholds and a range of imbalance levels. In this case we give equal weights to recall and precision, this means $\alpha = 1$. The F_1-measure Curve is defined as

$$F_1 = \frac{tpr}{(1/p(+) - 1)fpr + tpr} \tag{8}$$

For this metric a higher curve implies a better classification performance.

The detection methods described in the previous sections produces as output, some detection signal $D(t)$ which value indicates the likelihood of detection at a time t. To obtain the Cost and F_1-measure Curves it is necessary to swept a determined detection threshold θ and get the fpr and the tpr as functions of θ. This task can be optimized by measuring the *prominence* of each peak d on $D(t)$. We applied the function findpeaks in MATLAB [9] to estimate the prominence $h(d)$ of each peak d. Next, we calculated the peak width at prominence height $\beta \cdot h(d)$ with $\beta = 7/8$ and we used it to determine the time interval location Δt_d of the detection d. We considered a true positive detection $tp(d)$ if any true detection t_+ were found within the interval Δt_d, i.e. $tp(d) = 1$ if any $t_+ \in \Delta t_d$, otherwise $tp(d) = 0$.

3   Experiments

We used an open-access library labeled by citizen scientists [8] that comprises ultrasonic audio collected along road-transects across Europe. The audio library includes three datasets: iBats (E. Europe), iBats (UK) and NBP (Norfolk). These datasets were chosen to represent three different realistic use cases commonly used for bat surveys and monitoring programmes. These datasets are divided in a train and a test set. We added a fourth dataset comprising all datasets together. We trained and tested the performance of our method and compared it to other existing detection methods. We included the performance test results of the BatDetective tool [8] based on deep neural networks. We included also the performance test data provided in [8] for three existing closed-source commercial detection systems. The tested detection methods are: *VAD+RF*, *VAD*, EBD_{mean}, EBD_{max}, BatDetective (Aodha et al. [8]), SonoBat (version 3.1.7p [15]), SCAN'R (version 1.7.7 [16]) and Kaleidoscope (version 4.2.0 alpha4 [1]). The Cost Curves and F_1-measure Curves from the performance tests are depicted in Figs. 1 and 2, and their respective *area under curve* are shown in Table 2. Using Cost Curves, a lower value indicates a superior detection performance and vice-versa for F_1-measure Curves. We observe that BatDetective and VAD+RF outperforms the other detection methods on all datasets. Except iBats (E.Europe), the performance of VAD+RF is comparable to the BatDetective method. Specially for iBats (UK) and using all datasets, the detection performance of

VAD+RF is the most superior for a large range of $p(+)$ and $pc(+)$, which implies a powerful detection under a large range of detection operating conditions (from quiet to noisy soundscapes). In other words, VAD+RF can perform accurately under a larger range of possible distributions of positive and negative detections. Contrary to deep neural networks, our approach method uses a model-based signal processing technique and a feature engineering to detect bat calls. One of the advantages of deep learning is that some hidden representations can be learned from the data. Based on the obtained results on this study, we suggest that a combined approach of VAD signal processing with deep neural networks may enhance the detection performance.

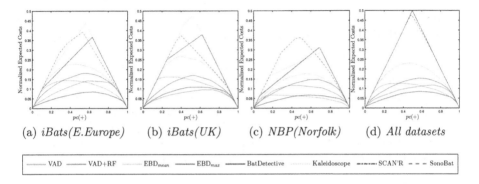

(a) *iBats(E.Europe)*   (b) *iBats(UK)*   (c) *NBP(Norfolk)*   (d) *All datasets*

Fig. 1. Comparison of the detection methods using *Cost Curves*

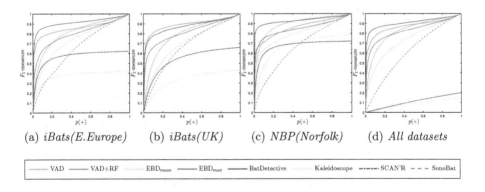

(a) *iBats(E.Europe)*   (b) *iBats(UK)*   (c) *NBP(Norfolk)*   (d) *All datasets*

Fig. 2. Comparison of the detection methods using F_1-*measure Curves*

Table 2. Area under curve of the *Cost Curves* (A_C) and area under curve of the F_1-measure Curves (A_{F_1})

Method	iBats (E.Europe)		iBats (UK)		NBP (Norfolk)		All datasets	
	A_C	A_{F_1}	A_C	A_{F_1}	A_C	A_{F_1}	A_C	A_{F_1}
EDBmean	0.159	0.735	0.177	0.708	0.121	0.803	0.157	0.738
EDBmax	0.124	0.798	0.112	0.815	0.010	0.846	0.106	0.828
VAD	0.106	0.809	0.115	0.793	0.051	0.893	0.094	0.826
VAD+RF	0.097	0.855	**0.068**	**0.891**	0.084	0.858	0.083	0.870
BatDetective	**0.058**	**0.908**	0.080	0.872	**0.047**	**0.928**	**0.060**	**0.907**

4 Conclusions

In this study, we propose a method for the detection of bat echolocation calls that uses a statistical model-based Voice Activity Detector combined with an ensemble of tree classifiers based on the Random Forests algorithm. We use global evaluation curves to visualize the detector performance over the full range of detection operating conditions. Results show that the detecting power of VAD+RF is comparable to methods based on deep learning. Based on the results, we give recommendations to improve the future designs of bat call detectors.

References

1. Wildlife Acoustics: Kaleidoscope (2012). http://www.wildlifeacoustics.com
2. Breiman, L.: Random forests. Mach. Learn. **45**(1), 5–32 (2001)
3. Brookes, M.: VOICEBOX: a speech processing toolbox for matlab (2006). http://www.ee.ic.ac.uk/...hp/staff/dmb/voicebox/voicebox
4. Drummond, C., Holte, R.C.: Cost curves: an improved method for visualizing classifier performance. Mach. Learn. **65**(1), 95–130 (2006)
5. Ephraim, Y., Malah, D.: Speech enhancement using a minimum mean-square error log-spectral amplitude estimator. IEEE Trans. Acoust. **33**(2), 443–445 (1985)
6. Fenton, M.B., Bell, G.P.: Recognition of species of insectivorous bats by their echolocation calls. J. Mammal. **62**(2), 233–243 (1981)
7. Jones, G., Jacobs, D.S., Kunz, T.H., Wilig, M.R., Racey, P.A.: Carpe noctem: the importance of bats as bioindicators. Endanger. Species Res. **8**(1–2), 93–115 (2009)
8. Mac Aodha, O., et al.: Bat detective–deep learning tools for bat acoustic signal detection. PLoS Comput. Biol. **14**(3), 1–19 (2018)
9. MATLAB: Version 8.5 (R2015a). The MathWorks Inc., Natick (2015)
10. Ruiz, A.T., Jung, K., Tschapka, M., Schwenker, F., Palm, G.: Automated identification method for detection and classification of neotropical bats. In: 8th International Conference of Pattern Recognition Systems (ICPRS 2017), pp. 1–6, July 2017
11. Skowronski, M.D., Fenton, M.B.: Model-based automated detection of echolocation calls using the link detector. J. Acoust. Soc. Am. **124**(1), 328–36 (2008)

12. Skowronski, M.D., Harris, J.G.: Acoustic detection and classification of microchiroptera using machine learning: lessons learned from automatic speech recognition. J. Acoust. Soc. Am. **119**(3), 1817–1833 (2006)
13. Sohn, J., Kim, N.S., Sung, W.: A statistical model-based voice activity detection. IEEE Signal Process. Lett. **6**(1), 1–3 (1999)
14. Soleymani, R., Granger, E., Fumera, G.: F-measure curves for visualizing classifier performance with imbalanced data. In: Pancioni, L., Schwenker, F., Trentin, E. (eds.) ANNPR 2018. LNCS (LNAI), vol. 11081, pp. 165–177. Springer, Cham (2018). https://doi.org/10.1007/978-3-319-99978-4_13
15. Szewczak, J.: Sonobat v. 3 (2010)
16. Binary Acoustic Technology: Scan'r v.1.7.7 (2014)

Space Efficient Incremental Betweenness Algorithm for Directed Graphs

Reynaldo Gil-Pons$^{(\boxtimes)}$ (ID)

CERPAMID, Santiago de Cuba, Cuba
rey@cerpamid.co.cu
https://www.cerpamid.co.cu/

Abstract. Betweenness is one of the most popular centrality measures in the analysis of social networks. Its computation has a high computational cost making it implausible for relatively large networks. The dynamic nature of many social networks opens up the possibility of developing faster algorithms for the dynamic version of the problem. In this work we propose a new incremental algorithm to compute the betweenness centrality of all nodes in directed graphs extracted from social networks. The algorithm uses linear space, making it suitable for large scale applications. Our experimental evaluation on a variety of real-world networks have shown our algorithm is faster than recalculation from scratch and competitive with recent approaches.

Keywords: Social network analysis · Betweenness centrality ·
Dynamic algorithms · Dynamic graphs

1 Introduction

Centrality is one of the most important concepts in the analysis of social networks. Among centrality measures, one of the most popular is betweenness centrality [1,6]. The betweenness of a node is a measure of the control this node has on the communication paths in the network. Therefore, it can be used to rank nodes according to their relative importance in a graph. Betweenness has been used effectively in a variety of applications, such as: design and control of communications networks [15], traffic monitoring [13], identifying key actors in terrorist networks [11], finding essential proteins [8], and many others.

Computing the betweenness of all nodes in a network has a high computational cost, so efficiency is the target of much related research. Nowadays, most graphs are inherently dynamic. When a graph suffers small changes, recomputing betweenness from scratch would be very inefficient. Therefore, dynamic algorithms capable of computing betweenness faster by using previous computations have been proposed [10,12]. None of these is better than Brandes [3] (**brandes**) in the worst case, and there is evidence that this is likely very hard to overcome [16]. Despite that, good speedups in typical instances have been achieved [2,7].

© Springer Nature Switzerland AG 2019
R. Vera-Rodriguez et al. (Eds.): CIARP 2018, LNCS 11401, pp. 262–270, 2019.
https://doi.org/10.1007/978-3-030-13469-3_31

In this work, we focus on the exact computation of betweenness centrality in incremental graphs. While not allowing edges to be deleted, incremental graphs cover some important applications, as has been pointed by several authors before [2,9,12]. Two recently proposed algorithms deal with the same problem, obtaining better performance than previous work, so we compare with them:

1. **icentral** [7] works on undirected connected graphs, and allows edges to be deleted and inserted. It only stores the betweenness of all nodes of the graph, so memory requirement is linear. First, it decomposes the graph into biconnected components, and then updates betweenness of nodes in the component affected by the update. In the article it's proven that for undirected graphs, the betweenness can change only for nodes in the affected component. Its time complexity is highly dependent on the size of the affected biconnected component.
2. **ibet** [2] works on directed graphs, and allows edges to be inserted. It stores all distances between pairs of nodes, so memory requirement is quadratic. First, it identifies efficiently all pairs of nodes which distance or number of shortest paths are affected by the update. Then it applies an optimized procedure to calculate changes in betweenness for nodes affected by the update. Experiments showed it outperforms previous approaches requiring quadratic memory.

In this paper we present a space efficient algorithm to compute the betweenness centrality of all nodes in a directed incremental network. Its space complexity is linear in the size of the input graph and its time complexity is similar to that of **icentral**. In the worst case, it's equivalent to recalculating betweenness in the biconnected component where the added edge resides, plus some linear overhead. Up to the authors knowledge it's the first algorithm calculating betweenness centrality in incremental directed graphs, showing better performance than recalculation, and at the same time, having less than quadratic space complexity. On the other hand, it works with disconnected graphs, detail usually left out by previous approaches, but important in real world applications.

In the next section we define betweenness, biconnected component and incremental algorithms. In Sect. 3 we present the proposed algorithm, prove its correctness, and determine space and time complexity. In Sect. 4 we show the experimental validation of our algorithm. At the end, the conclusions and references.

2   Preliminaries

For simplicity, we will refer to directed, simple and unweighted graphs. In the following we will refer to a graph $G = (V, E)$ with n nodes and m edges.

2.1   Betweenness

Betweenness centrality of a node is formally defined by the following formula:

$$C_B(v) = \sum_{\substack{s \neq v, t \neq v \\ s,t \in V}} \frac{\sigma_{st}(v)}{\sigma_{st}} \tag{1}$$

where $\sigma_{st}(v)$ is the number of shortest paths from s to t passing through v and σ_{st} is the number of shortest paths from s to t. A naive algorithm using this formula has $\mathcal{O}(n^3)$ complexity.

In [3] Brandes showed a more efficient way to calculate betweenness values:

$$C_B(v) = \sum_{s \neq v, s \in V} \delta_{s\cdot}(v) \tag{2}$$

where $\delta_{s\cdot}(v) = \sum_{s \neq v, t \neq v, t \in V} \frac{\sigma_{st}(v)}{\sigma_{st}}$. Using this formula betweenness values can be computed in time $\mathcal{O}(n \cdot m)$, by running a BFS (Breath First Search [4]) on each node and computing the required values (distances, σ, δ). For a complete explanation see [3].

2.2   Biconnected Components

Biconnected components were first proposed as a good heuristic for speeding up betweenness computations in [14], and more recently in the context of dynamic graphs in [7]. We will make use of the following definitions:

Definition 1. *Let G be an undirected graph. A biconnected component is a connected induced subgraph A of G, such that the removal of any node doesn't disconnect A, and is maximal.*

Definition 2. *Any node belonging to more than one biconnected component is called articulation point.*

2.3   Incremental Graphs

We call a dynamic graph incremental if edges can be inserted, but not deleted. As previously mentioned in this work we focus on incremental graphs. Computing betweenness in such context is usually done in two steps. In the first step some preprocessing is done and initial betweenness is computed. Next, after each edge insertion, betweenness is updated. The two steps could have different time complexities, so both define the time complexity of an incremental algorithm. All algorithms mentioned here have the same complexity in the first step (the same as **brandes**), so in comparisons we will only take into account the update step.

3   Algorithm

The proposed algorithm is a generalization of **icentral** to deal with directed graphs.

Definition 3. *Let G be a graph, and let G^* be the graph G after inserting a new edge (u, v). We define affected component as the biconnected component of the undirected version of G^* to which the newly inserted edge (u, v) belongs.*

The main obstacle in generalizing **icentral** is that, in directed graphs, when an edge is inserted, betweenness values of nodes outside the affected component can change as well. In the next theorem we prove a formula allowing to compute those changes efficiently.

Theorem 1. *Let x be a node outside the affected component A, and let s be the articulation point inside the component such that its removal disconnects x from A. Then after the update, the betweenness of x changes by*

$$\delta_s(x) \cdot (reach^*(s) - reach(s)) + \delta_s^r(x) \cdot (reach^{*r}(s) - reach^r(s)) \qquad (3)$$

where $reach(s)$ equals the number of nodes z such that there exists a shortest path from z to x passing through A, superscript r means the function is applied to the reversed graph, and superscript $*$ indicates the function is applied to the updated graph.

Proof. For the sake of clearness, lets rename variables in the definition of betweenness 1:

$$C_B(x) = \sum_{\substack{a \neq x, b \neq x \\ a,b \in V}} \frac{\sigma_{ab}(x)}{\sigma_{ab}} \qquad (4)$$

In the sum on the right the only terms that can change after an update are such that a and b are in different biconnected components, and such that all shortest paths from a to b pass through A. Therefore, all these paths must pass through s. Then, two cases may occur, according to the relative orders of s and x in the paths from a to b that go through x:

1. $a, s, x, b \implies \frac{\sigma_{ab}(x)}{\sigma_{ab}} = \frac{\sigma_{as}\sigma_{sx}\sigma_{xb}}{\sigma_{as}\sigma_{sb}} = \frac{\sigma_{sx}\sigma_{xb}}{\sigma_{sb}} = \frac{\sigma_{sb}(x)}{\sigma_{sb}}$
2. $a, x, s, b \implies \frac{\sigma_{ab}(x)}{\sigma_{ab}} = \frac{\sigma_{ax}\sigma_{xs}\sigma_{sb}}{\sigma_{as}\sigma_{sb}} = \frac{\sigma_{ax}\sigma_{xs}}{\sigma_{as}} = \frac{\sigma_{as}(x)}{\sigma_{as}}$

Therefore, the terms that can change equal:

$$\sum_{a,b \text{ in case } 1} \frac{\sigma_{sb}(x)}{\sigma_{sb}} + \sum_{a,b \text{ in case } 2} \frac{\sigma_{as}(x)}{\sigma_{as}} = reach(s) \cdot \delta_s(x) + reach^r(s) \cdot \delta_s^r(x) \quad (5)$$

and the theorem easily follows.

Following Theorem 1, pseudocode for the function updating betweenness outside A is shown in Algorithm 3. Then, it remains to update betweenness inside the component; this can be done as in **icentral**, and is shown in Algorithm 2. The Brandes-like function in lines 8 and 9 computes delta values in the affected component, as in **icentral**, using $reach_o^r$ values to add the contribution of nodes outside the affected component. r and $*$ have the same meaning as in Theorem 1. The pseudocode of the proposed algorithm is shown in Algorithm 1.

Algorithm 1. Update Betweenness

---

procedure UPDATE-BETWEENNESS(G, (u,v), C_B)
   $A \leftarrow$ Affected-Biconnected-Component($G, (u,v)$)
   $A^* \leftarrow A$ with edge (u,v) inserted
   update-betweenness-inside($G, A, (u,v), A^*, C_B$)
   update-betweenness-outside(G, A, A^*, C_B)
   return C_B

Algorithm 2. Update Betweenness Inside Affected Component

1: **procedure** UPDATE-BETWEENNESS-INSIDE(G, A, (u,v), A^*, C_B)
2:   $Sr \leftarrow$ Affected-Sources($A, (u,v)$)
3:   **for all** $s \in$ articulation-points(A) **do**
4:      reach$_o(s) \leftarrow$ number of nodes directly reaching s outside A
5:      reach$_o^r(s) \leftarrow$ number of nodes directly reachable from s outside A
6:   **for all** $s \in Sr$ **do**
7:      $\delta_s \leftarrow$ Brandes-like(A, s)
8:      $\delta_s^* \leftarrow$ Brandes-like(A^*, s)
9:      **for all** $x \in A$ **do**
10:         $C_B(x) \leftarrow C_B(x) + \delta_s^*(x) - \delta_s(x)$
11:      **if** s is articulation point **then**
12:         **for all** $x \in A$ **do**
13:            $C_B(x) \leftarrow C_B(x) + (\delta_s^*(x) - \delta_s(x))\cdot$reach$_o(s)$

3.1 Complexity

The overall space complexity is linear (in the size of the graph) as the algorithm only uses a constant number of arrays with linear size (C_B, the different variants of reach, A, A^*, and the different variants of δ). Only C_B and the graph itself persist across updates.

Time complexity of the proposed algorithm (Algorithm 1) equals the complexity of finding biconnected components (linear), plus the complexity of Algorithm 2, plus the one of Algorithm 3. Let n_A and m_A be the number of nodes and edges respectively in the affected component. Algorithm 2 has exactly the same complexity as **icentral**, which is $\mathcal{O}(n + m + |Sr| * (n_A + m_A))$, where Sr is the set of affected sources (as defined in [7]).

In Algorithm 3, for a given s all variants of reach (lines 3 and 7) can be computed using BFS in time $\mathcal{O}(n_A + m_A)$, as there is no need to do any computation outside A at this point. As any node outside A will have at most one corresponding articulation point s, in lines 4, 5, 6, 8, 9, and 10 each node and edge of the graph appears at most once, and so the total complexity of these is $\mathcal{O}(n + m)$. Summing up, the complexity of Algorithm 3 is $\mathcal{O}(n + m + |$articulation-points$(A)| * (n_A + m_A))$.

Overall, using that there are at most n_A articulation points in A, and also at most n_A affected sources, complexity of the proposed algorithm is proven to be $\mathcal{O}(n + m + n_A * (n_A + m_A))$, matching that of **icentral**.

Algorithm 3. Update Betweenness Outside Affected Component

1: **procedure** UPDATE-BETWEENNESS-OUTSIDE(G, A, A^*, C_B)
2:     **for all** $s \in$ articulation-points(A) **do**
3:         Compute reach(s), reach*(s) using BFS (defined in Theorem 1)
4:         $\delta_s \leftarrow \delta$ values of nodes reachable from s outside A
5:         **for all** $x \in$ nodes directly reachable from s outside A **do**
6:             $C_B(x) \leftarrow C_B(x) + \delta_s(x) \cdot (\text{reach}^*(s) - \text{reach}(s))$
7:         Compute reach^r(s), reach^{*r}(s) using BFS (defined in Theorem 1)
8:         $\delta_s^r \leftarrow \delta$ values of nodes that reach s outside A
9:         **for all** $x \in$ nodes directly reaching s outside A **do**
10:       $C_B(x) \leftarrow C_B(x) + \delta_s^r(x) \cdot (\text{reach}^{*r}(s) - \text{reach}^r(s))$

3.2 Notes

It's possible to modify slightly the proposed algorithm to work with graphs with arbitrary positive weights, by using Dijkstra algorithm [5] instead of BFS. In graphs with multiples edges, parallel edges can be substituted with the edge with smallest weight, and then obtain a simple graph with the same betweenness.

On the other hand, it's straightforward to parallelize the most time consuming part of the algorithm, the computation of the betweenness changes inside the affected component. As the δ values respect to affected sources are computed independently, this computations could be done by different nodes in a parallel environment. In this environment, good speedups are expected, similar to those in [7].

4 Experiments

We experimentally evaluate the proposed algorithm by measuring time and memory, and comparing it with **icentral**, **ibet** and **brandes**. All algorithms were implemented in pure python, and graphs were stored and manipulated using the python library NetworkX[1]. Algorithms were run on a GNU/Linux 64 bit machine, processor Intel(R) Core(TM) i3-4160 CPU @ 3.60 GHz, with 5 GBytes of main memory.

The datasets used for experimentation were taken from online sources, some of them being already referenced in [2] or [7]; p2p-Gnutella08, Wiki-Vote, and CollegeMsg, were taken from SNAP graphs collection. The description of the data is shown in Table 1.

For each graph, we randomly selected 100 edges that were not already contained in the graph, and measured the average time and maximum memory used by each algorithm to update the betweenness of all nodes when each edge is inserted. In the case of algorithms that work with directed graphs, when testing on an undirected one, each edge was transformed into two edges, one for each possible direction. Results are shown in Table 2. Note it's not possible to test **icentral** on directed graphs.

---

[1] http://networkx.github.io/.

Table 1. Statistics of graph datasets (lbc refers to largest biconnected component)

Graph dataset	# nodes	# edges	Diameter	lbc	Edge type
CollegeMsg	1893	20292	8	1498	Directed
Cagr	4158	13428	16	2651	Undirected
Epa	4253	8897	10	2163	Undirected
Eva	4475	4654	17	234	Undirected
p2p-Gnutella08	6299	20776	9	4535	Directed
Wiki-Vote	7066	103663	7	4786	Directed

Table 2. Results, time given in seconds and memory in MBytes.

Graph dataset	brandes		ibet		icentral		Ours	
	Time	Mem	Time	Mem	Time	Mem	Time	Mem
CollegeMsg	2.7	**131**	**0.7**	380	-	-	2.2	154
Cagr	31.0	**148**	**4.9**	1643	15.3	145	12.3	175
Epa	26.4	**146**	**4.2**	1851	9.0	143	8.2	167
Eva	17.1	142	6.8	1989	**0.8**	**135**	1.2	159
p2p-Gnutella08	18.1	**148**	**3.0**	3249	-	-	13.3	179
Wiki-Vote	27.6	**198**	**2.9**	3781	-	-	10.4	331

As expected, both our algorithm and **icentral** perform very similar, both in time and memory, and are consistently faster than **brandes**. This speedup is highly dependent on the size of the affected component. Best performance respect to **brandes** was obtained in dataset Eva, where the number of nodes in the largest biconnected component is relatively small. On average, our algorithm is between 2 and 3 times faster than **brandes**.

On the other hand, **ibet** is the fastest of all on most datasets, but it's memory usage is very high, making it very expensive for graphs of tens of thousands of nodes. Also note, that for datasets like Eva, **ibet** is outperformed by algorithms **icentral** and our proposal, stressing the relevance of algorithms using the biconnected components decomposition.

5   Conclusions

In this work an algorithm for computing betweenness in incremental directed graphs has been proposed. Its memory usage is linear allowing it to scale to large graphs. It's time complexity is similar to that of algorithm proposed in [7], despite of handling the more general case of directed graphs. Experiments have proven it can be a practical replacement of **brandes** for directed and undirected graphs, mostly when quadratic memory usage is not feasible due to large input.

As future work we plan to conduct experiments with a distributed and parallel implementation of the proposed algorithm. Also, we will extend the proposed algorithm to work with edge deletions. Moreover, it seems possible to apply some of the optimizations proposed in [2] to update betweenness values inside the affected biconnected component.

References

1. Anthonisse, J.M.: The Rush in a Directed Graph. Stichting Mathematisch Centrum, Mathematische Besliskunde (1971)
2. Bergamini, E., Meyerhenke, H., Ortmann, M., Slobbe, A.: Faster betweenness centrality updates in evolving networks. In: LIPIcs-Leibniz International Proceedings in Informatics, vol. 75, pp. 1–16 (2017). https://doi.org/10.4230/LIPIcs.SEA.2017. 23
3. Brandes, U.: A faster algorithm for betweenness centrality. J. Math. Soc. **25**(2), 163–177 (2001). https://doi.org/10.1080/0022250X.2001.9990249
4. Cormen, T.H., Leiserson, C.E., Rivest, R.L., Stein, C.: Introduction to Algorithms. MIT Press, Cambridge (2009)
5. Dijkstra, E.W.: A note on two problems in connexion with graphs. Numer. Math. **1**(1), 269–271 (1959). https://doi.org/10.1007/BF01386390
6. Freeman, L.C.: A set of measures of centrality based on betweenness (1977). https://doi.org/10.2307/3033543
7. Jamour, F., Skiadopoulos, S., Kalnis, P.: Parallel algorithm for incremental betweenness centrality on large graphs. IEEE Trans. Parallel Distrib. Syst. (2017). https://doi.org/10.1109/TPDS.2017.2763951
8. Joy, M.P., Brock, A., Ingber, D.E., Huang, S.: High-betweenness proteins in the yeast protein interaction network. J. Biomed. Biotechnol. **2005**(2), 96–103 (2005). https://doi.org/10.1155/JBB.2005.96
9. Kas, M., Wachs, M., Carley, K.M., Carley, L.R.: Incremental algorithm for updating betweenness centrality in dynamically growing networks. In: Proceedings of the 2013 IEEE/ACM International Conference on Advances in Social Networks Analysis and Mining - ASONAM 2013, pp. 33–40 (2013). https://doi.org/10.1145/ 2492517.2492533
10. Kourtellis, N., Morales, G.D.F., Bonchi, F.: Scalable online betweenness centrality in evolving graphs. IEEE Trans. Know. Data Eng. **27**(9), 2494–2506 (2015). https://doi.org/10.1109/TKDE.2015.2419666
11. Krebs, V.E.: Mapping networks of terrorist cells. Connections **24**(3), 43–52 (2002)
12. Nasre, M., Pontecorvi, M., Ramachandran, V.: Betweenness centrality – incremental and faster. In: Csuhaj-Varjú, E., Dietzfelbinger, M., Ésik, Z. (eds.) MFCS 2014. LNCS, vol. 8635, pp. 577–588. Springer, Heidelberg (2014). https://doi.org/ 10.1007/978-3-662-44465-8_49
13. Puzis, R., Altshuler, Y., Elovici, Y., Bekhor, S., Shiftan, Y., Pentland, A.S.: Augmented betweenness centrality for environmentally aware traffic monitoring in transportation networks. J. Intell. Transp. Syst. **17**(1), 91–105 (2013). https:// doi.org/10.1080/15472450.2012.716663

14. Puzis, R., Zilberman, P., Elovici, Y., Dolev, S., Brandes, U.: Heuristics for speeding up betweenness centrality computation. In: Proceedings - 2012 ASE/IEEE International Conference on Privacy, Security, Risk and Trust and 2012 ASE/IEEE International Conference on Social Computing, SocialCom/PASSAT 2012, pp. 302–311 (2012). https://doi.org/10.1109/SocialCom-PASSAT.2012.66
15. Tizghadam, A., Leon-Garcia, A.: Betweenness centrality and resistance distance in communication networks. IEEE Netw. **24**(6), 10–16 (2010). https://doi.org/10.1109/MNET.2010.5634437
16. Williams, V.V.: On some fine-grained questions in algorithms and complexity. In: Proceedings of the ICM (2018)

Confusion Matrix-Based Building of Hierarchical Classification

Paulo Cavalin[1(✉)] and Luiz Oliveira[2]

[1] IBM Research, Rio de Janeiro, RJ, Brazil
pcavalin@br.ibm.com
[2] Universidade Federal do Paraná (UFPR), Curitiba, PR, Brazil

Abstract. Present an evaluation of methods for automatically building hierarchical classifiers from the analysis on the confusion matrix generated with flat classification. By defining a basic framework for that, we investigate the effects of different methods for transforming the confusion matrix, for computing the similarity between classes, and the choice of base classifier. The experimental evaluation, conducted on three datasets from EMNIST with varied number of classes and samples, has shown that the choice of method can highly affect not only the overall accuracy of the system, but also the underlying hierarchical structure that is created. Among such methods, we demonstrate that the proposed penalty matrix with Pearson correlation as similarity metric might be the best option for finding confusion between the classes.

Keywords: Classification · Hierarchical classification ·
Confusion matrix

1 Introduction

Classification methods have evolved significantly in recent years, specially with advances in deep learning, and very often such methods are beating state-of-the-art benchmark results, where flat classification has been the most used type of classification [6]. With the increase popularity of Deep Learning and Representation Learning, it is expectable that instead of dealing with the N-class problem by learning a single representation for all classes, more specific representations could be learned for better dealing with inter-class confusion, so hierarchical classification could be better alternative to tailor Convolutional Neural Network (CNN) architectures [6].

Although some hierarchical approaches rely on domain knowledge to be built, the process of creating the hierarchy in automated way has been investigated. One way to do so is by exploiting the information presented by a confusion matrix [3,5,6]. That is, after a classifier has been trained, the confusion matrix produced by this classifier on a validation set could be used to find which classes present some confusion in the classification, and then a more specialised classification structure could be generated. Some works have exploited this idea, but there is

© Springer Nature Switzerland AG 2019
R. Vera-Rodriguez et al. (Eds.): CIARP 2018, LNCS 11401, pp. 271–278, 2019.
https://doi.org/10.1007/978-3-030-13469-3_32

a lack of a better investigation of the impact of the different methods that are involved in the stages of such process, from which we select three stages that we judge as relevant: (a) **the way the confusion matrix is represented and evaluated**, i.e. whether it is the raw matrix or after some transformation applied onto it [6]; (b) **the metric that is used to compute (dis-)similarity between the classes**, that could be the Euclidean distance, Pearson correlation, a cluster algorithm, and thus forth; and (c) **the impact of the base classifier itself**, whether a more or less accurate classifier can change the final generation of the hierarchical structure and the resulting accuracy.

The aim of this work is to present an investigation on different methods that could be employed to make a hierarchical classification structure, by taking into account the three aforementioned stages. By considering three character-recognition datasets from the Extended MNIST (EMNIST) repository, i.e. Digits, Letters and Balanced, we provide not only a quantitative analysis, by presenting the impact on the accuracy on the test set, but also a qualitative analysis given the easiness of associating class confusions with the shape of the characters.

2   Methodology

The main framework for hierarchical classification consists creating binary verifiers, such as the ones that proved to be efficient for handwriting recognition problems [4]. In greater detail, during the training phase, given the original N-class problem, we first train an N-class flat classifier C, using a base classifier of type B, which we apply on the validation set[1] and compute a normalised confusion matrix CM, where the columns sum up to one. Then, CM' is computed by applying a transformation T on CM, and next, the ranking R with the pairs of classes with the highest level of confusion is computed, by considering the similarity metric S. Afterwards, by making use of a base classifier of type B', we train a set of M 2-class verifiers $V = \{v_1, \ldots, v_M\}$, corresponding to the M highest positions in R, and associate then to the set of confusing classes $CC = \{cc_1, \ldots, cc_M\}$, where $cc_i = \{class_j, class_k\}$ and $j \neq k, j \leq N, k \leq N$. For the test phase, for each test sample x, the method consists of using a verifier from V whenever the top-two predictions $pred_1$ and $pred_2$ are equal to some pair of classes in CC, and the likelihood of $pred_1$ is below the confidence level θ. If that is the case, the prediction of the selected verifier v_i is used for the final prediction.

2.1   Transformations on the Confusion Matrix

We take into account three different transformations T that can be applied onto CM to generate CM'. The first one is the raw matrix itself, i.e. no transformation at all and $CM' = CM$. The other two we describe below.

---

[1] Another set could be used, such as the training set, but we make use of validation to avoid an over-fit.

The second approach is based on the transformation used in [6], to which we refer to as the distance matrix (DM). In this method, the confusion matrix is first converted to the so-called distance matrix D, where $D = 1 - CM$ and the elements in the diagonal of D are set to zero. Next, D is converted to symmetric matrix with $D = 0.5 * (D + D^T)$, where entry D_{ij} is supposed to represents how easy it is to discriminate categories i and j. In this case, $CM' = D$.

In addition, we propose a method to which we refer as the penalty matrix (PM), where the idea is to create a matrix that penalises the pairs of classes that present more inter-class errors. In greater detail, giving the normalised confusion matrix CM, we initialise the penalty matrix P with zeros. Then, for each entry CM_{ij} where $i \neq j$, i.e. an entry in CM that represents a classification mistake, we increment the entries P_{ij}, P_{ji}, P_{ii}, and P_{jj}, with CM_{ij}. We expect that the classes i and j with the highest level of confusion to generate grater values in P. Note that by incrementing both P_{ij} and P_{ji} at the same time will result in a symmetric matrix, similar to DM. And by setting P_{ii} and P_{jj} with the same values, we aim to penalise the classes with highest mistake. In the end of the day, in the ideal case we expect P_{ij}, P_{ji}, P_{ii}, and P_{jj} to have similar values.

2.2   Similarity Metrics

In order to compute the similarity of two classes, denoted class i and class j, we apply similarity metrics on the columns of the transformed confusion matrix CM'. That is, let cm'_i be the column of class i and cm'_j the column for class j, to compute the similarity sim_{ij} between classes i and j we make use of the similarity function S as:

$$sim_{ij} = S(cm'_i, cm'_j). \tag{1}$$

For implementing S, we consider two different metrics. The first one is the well-know Euclidean distance[2], defined as:

$$S(cm'_i, cm'_j) = \sqrt{\sum_{k=1}^{N}(cm'_i - cm'_{jk})^2} \tag{2}$$

Given that in the Euclidean space different pairs of points can present the same distance even if they are in completely differente locations in the space, of even at different angles, we consider the Person correlation coefficiente in order to capture a more precise correlation between each pair of cells cm'_{ik} and cm'_{jk}. In this case, the similarity metric is defined as:

$$S(cm'_i, cm'_j) = \frac{cov(cm'_i, cm'_j)}{\sigma(cm'_i)\sigma(cm'_j)}, \tag{3}$$

where $cov(cm'_i, cm'_j)$ is the covariance between populations cm'_i and cm'_j, $\sigma(cm'_i)$ is the standard deviation of cm'_i, and $\sigma(cm'_j)$ is the standard deviation of cm'_j.

---

[2] Although the Euclidean is a distance metric and not a similarity metric, we refer to as similarity for the sake of simplicity. The ranking R can be computed simply by sorting from lowest to highest values instead of being from highest to lowest.

2.3   Base Classifiers

For the base classifiers B and B' (in this work $B' = B$), we consider three different types of classifiers from the family of neural networks, ranging from less to
more complex approaches, which we expect to vary significantly in terms of accuracy in flat classification. The three methods we evaluate are Logistic Regression
(LR), Multi-Layer Perceptron (MLP) Neural Networks, and Convolution Neural
Networks (CNN).

Both the LR and the MLP classifiers are standard models, trained with
stochastic gradient descent algorithm, where for the MLP we set one hidden
layer with 1,000 neurons. For the CNN, we consider a network comprising the
following architecture: a layer with 32 convolution filters with size 3 by 3; another
layer of 64 convolution filter with size 3 by 3; a max pooling layer with size 2×2;
a dropout layer with rate set to 0.25; a dense layer with 128 neurons; another
dropout layer with rate set to 0.5; and the final activation layer with the softmax
function. Note that for all convolution and dense layers, the rectified linear unit
activation function is used.

3   Experiments

For the experimental evaluation of the proposed methodology, we consider
datasets from the extended MNIST (EMNIST) repository[3] [2]: Digits, with 10
classes, and 240,000 samples for training and 40,000 samples for test; Letters, 26
classes with 124,800 samples for training and 20,800 samples for test; Balanced,
47 classes, with 112,800 samples for training and 18,800 samples for test.

Given this protocol, the first step of our evaluations consisted of evaluating the different combinations of transformation methods for T and similarity
metrics for S. In this case, we consider four different combinations:

- ED, with $CM' = CM$ and the Euclidean distance for S;
- PC, also with $CM' = CM$ but with Pearson correlation for S;
- DM, with DM for T and Pearson correlation for S;
- PM, with the PM method for T and Pearson correlation for S.

For these experiments, we fixed the base classifier B to MLP in order to
have at the same time a simple and fast approach, compared with a CNN, but
a more accurate one, as we believed, compared with LR. In addition, M was set
to 10 for all experiments. The comparison of the different methods, in terms of
recognition accuracy on the test set, are presented in Table 1.

On Digits, the proposed hierarchical methods does not seem to improve the
recognition rates. With the exception of the ED method, the application of the
other method resulted in lower accuracies. It is curious that PC, DM and PM
performed identically in terms of accuracy, but the number of samples selected for
verification by DM was much smaller than those of PC and PM. That indicates
the DM might not be the best option to detect confusion between classes. On

---

[3] https://www.nist.gov/itl/iad/image-group/emnist-dataset.

Letters and Balanced datasets, on the other hand, improvements in accuracy were show by all methods. In this case though, ED performed slightly worse than PC and PM, but still better than DM. Overall, it seems that PM might be a better method for this problem, since it has been able to reach the highest accuracies on both Letters and Balanced.

To complement this analysis, we also present in Table 1 the result of PM*, which consists of the PM method but with the threshold θ optimized with the validation set. With such optimization, only on Digits a value below 1.00 was found. In that case, the final accuracy was a little higher than with $\theta = 1.00$, but still lower than the flat classifier.

Table 1. Accuracy of the MLP classifier with the different methods, on all datasets, where: %Flat: Accuracy with flat classifier; %Hier: Accuracy with hierarchical classifier; #Ver(%): total of verified samples, with the percentage between parentheses; %BV: accuracy on verified samples before verification, i.e. with flat classifier; %AV: accuracy on verified samples after verification, i.e. with verifiers.

	Method	%Flat	%Hier	#Ver(%)	%BV	%AV	θ
Digits	ED	99.07	99.07	9,795 (24.5)	99.04	99.01	1.00
	PC	99.07	99.04	20,168 (5.0)	99.10	99.03	1.00
	DM	99.07	99.04	3,899 (9.7)	98.61	98.26	1.00
	PM	99.07	99.04	19,445 (48.6)	99.05	98.99	1.00
	PM*	99.07	99.05 x	3,986 (9.9)	99.37	99.20	0.55
Letters	ED	90.53	90.60	2,087 (10.0)	93.15	93.82	1.00
	PC	90.53	90.80	5,231 (25.1)	84.50	85.59	1.00
	DM	90.53	90.56	556 (2.7)	86.51	87.77	1.00
	PM	90.53	90.80	5,698 (27.4)	86.26	87.26	1.00
	PM*	90.53	90.80	5,698 (27.4)	86.26	87.26	1.00
Balanced	ED	84.33	84.42	2,375 (10.0)	83.23	84.00	1.00
	PC	84.33	84.74	4,032 (21.4)	64.73	66.67	1.00
	DM	84.33	84.35	739 (4.0)	70.09	70.09	1.00
	PM	84.33	84.82	4,111 (21.9)	66.58	68.43	1.00
	PM*	84.33	84.82	4,111 (21.9)	66.57	68.84	1.00

In Table 2 we present the rankings of confusing classes generated by each method. We can observe that the PC and PM methods tend to generate the most similar rankings, with an intersection of 9 elements in Digits and 7 elements in Letters and Balanced. Qualitatively we may claim that the ranking of those two methods make a lot of sense, since the most similar classes found by the methods are characters with similar shapes, such as 4 and 9, 3 and 8, I and L, F and f, and thus forth. The ED and DM methods, on the other hand, resulted in some odd elements in the rankings, such as 0 and 1, P and T, which are characters with very different shapes.

Table 2. Ranking of confusing classes with the four methods for transformation and similarity, with multi-layer perceptron neural networks.

	Digits				Letters				Balanced			
	ED	PC	DM	PM	ED	PC	DM	PM	ED	PC	DM	PM
1	0:6	4:9	2:5	4:9	N:W	I:L	A:G	I:L	C:e	F:f	G:b	0:O
2	0:1	3:5	1:9	3:5	C:E	G:Q	M:W	G:Q	5:S	0:O	8:9	F:f
3	1:6	7:9	4:7	3:8	M:S	U:V	J:L	U:V	0:O	1:L	M:N	5:S
4	4:9	2:3	2:9	2:3	U:V	A:Q	U:Y	M:N	M:W	1:I	W:n	2:Z
5	1:7	3:8	6:9	7:9	M:N	I:J	P:T	D:O	2:Z	9:q	9:g	1:L
6	1:2	0:6	0:3	0:6	S:W	F:T	Q:S	F:T	7:T	I:L	7:t	9:q
7	5:6	5:8	5:8	5:8	C:M	D:O	H:M	C:E	K:X	g:q	I:L	1:I
8	4:6	4:6	1:2	4:7	M:P	V:Y	B:R	J:S	7:d	9:g	C:E	6:b
9	1:4	5:6	7:8	2:8	M:Z	M:N	R:X	A:Q	M:d	5:S	D:O	I:L
10	0:5	2:8	0:4	4:6	C:O	A:G	G:P	F:P	W:d	2:Z	H:n	g:q

Given that PM resulted in the highest accuracies in the previous experiments, we present the evaluation of the LR and CNN classifiers only with that approach. The results of LR, in terms of accuracy, are presented in Table 3, and those of the CNN are presented in Table 4.

With LR classifier we observe much lower accuracies with the flat classifier, compared with MLP (see Table 1). That said, it was expected that with a classifier with a higher error would benefit better from the hierarchical classification, and that was the case for both Digits and Letters. In the former the gain was of about 0.96 % points, and in the former of about 0.68 % points. The MLP classifier had a decrease of 0.02 % points and a gain of 0.27 % points in the same datasets. In the Balanced dataset, even with higher error, the use of LR classifiers did not resulted in a higher increase of accuracy, which we suspect is due to not being able to generate good verifiers for this problem. In addition, we observe that optimizing the parameter θ does not bring any gain. In fact, it resulted in lower accuracies in two datasets.

Table 3. Accuracies with the Logistic Regression classifier.

	%Flat	%Hier	#Ver.(%)	%BV	%AV	θ
Digits	93.01	93.97	17,264 (43.1)	92.63	94.85	1.00
	93.01	93.06	3,939 (9.8)	94.31	94.82	0.55
Letters	70.51	71.19	4,638 (22.3)	74.77	77.79	1.00
	70.51	71.19	3,645 (17.5)	68.78	72.62	0.70
Balanced	66.63	66.86	3,156 (16.8)	60.74	62.07	1.00
	66.63	66.85	2,532 (13.5)	54.30	55.92	0.55

With CNNs we also observe the expected behavior of reaching the highest accuracies for all problems, and the smaller impact of the verifiers in improving the flat classification. In this case, improvements can only be observed if θ is optimized. In Letters, if θ is optimized, an increase of 0.14 PP was observed. In Digits and Balanced, only a increase of 0.01% points and 0.02% points was achieved. In our opinion, this does not mean that the idea of hierarchical classification is not promising for deep learning, which might be the most robust classifier in some problems, but these approaches might need some tailoring in the CNN's architecture for better dealing with 2-class problems. Transfer learning from the flat classifier can also be a way to deal with the smaller training set generated for each verifier. Furthermore, since we observe very high accuracy rates for both CNN and MLP in Digits and the hierarchical scheme can degrade such rates, the results indicate that it might not be worth to hierarchical since flat classification works very well for the problem.

Table 4. Accuracies with Convolutional Neural Networks

	%Flat	%Hier	#Ver.(%)	%BV	%AV	θ
Digits	99.46	99.42	9,782 (24.4)	98.98	98.81	1.00
	99.46	99.47	55 (0.1)	58.18	63,64	0.80
Letters	93.63	93.54	8,337 (40.1)	91.07	90.84	1.00
	93.63	93.77	2,010 (9.6)	69.05	70.50	0.90
Balanced	87.18	87.00	5,307 (16.8)	62.73	62.31	1.00
	87.18	87.20	2,378 (28.2)	76.82	76.18	0.75

In Table 5 we present the rankings generated by the three type of base classifiers that we evaluated. By analysing the intersection of the rankings, the results show the type of base classifier can actually affect the generation of the ranking of confusing classes. However, the difference looks less pronounced when the complexity of the classification problem is higher, for instance the Balanced dataset where the methods presented an intersection of at least 7 elements in their rankings. In Digits, the intersections ranged from 4 to 7 elements only, being MLP and LR the classifier with most intersection, which is somewhat a surprising result. That is, given that MLP and CNN present a much narrow gap in accuracy than that of LR and MLP, we were expecting the results of an MLP to be more similar to those of a CNN than of an LR. Nonetheless, MLP and CNN present higher intersection than LR and CNN, indicating that the latter are the classifiers that behave the least similar to each classifiers, as expected.

4   Conclusions and Future Work

In this work we presented a deep analysis of different methods for automatically creating hierarchical classification from the confusion matrix of a flat classifier.

Table 5. Comparison of rankings generated by MLP, LR and CNN

	Digits			Letters			Balanced		
	MLP	LR	CNN	MLP	LR	CNN	MLP	LR	CNN
1	4:9	7:9	4:9	I:L	I:L	I:L	0:O	0:O	0:O
2	3:5	3:5	5:6	G:Q	G:Q	G:Q	F:f	F:f	F:f
3	3:8	4:9	0:6	U:V	M:N	U:V	5:S	5:S	5:S
4	2:3	2:8	2:8	M:N	C:E	M:N	2:Z	2:Z	2:Z
5	7:9	5:8	8:9	D:O	D:O	D:O	1:L	1:L	1:L
6	0:6	3:8	3:5	F:T	T:Y	K:X	9:q	1:I	9:q
7	5:8	0:5	4:7	C:E	J:S	C:E	1:I	9:q	1:I
8	4:7	2:3	2:3	J:S	F:P	V:Y	6:b	6:b	C:e
9	2:8	2:6	2:7	A:Q	U:V	H:N	I:L	I:L	T:t
10	4:6	1:8	1:7	F:P	U:W	F:T	g:q	9:g	4:Z

The results demonstrated that transformation and similarity metric can greatly affect the way it is computed the list of classes with the highest inter-class confusion. As future work, we intent to conduct a better investigation in optimising classifiers' architecture for both flat and hierarchical classification. In addition, we plan to conduct further evaluation on other datasets, such as the DTD dataset [1], where the inter-class confusion appears to be very challenging.

References

1. Cimpoi, M., Maji, S., Kokkinos, I., Mohamed, S., Vedaldi, A.: Describing textures in the wild. In: Proceedings of the IEEE Conference on Computer Vision and Pattern Recognition (CVPR) (2014)
2. Cohen, G., Afshar, S., Tapson, J., van Schaik, A.: EMNIST: an extension of MNIST to handwritten letters. CoRR, abs/1702.05373 (2017)
3. Godbole, S., Sarawagi, S., Chakrabarti, S.: Scaling multi-class support vector machines using inter-class confusion. In: Proceedings of the Eighth ACM SIGKDD International Conference on Knowledge Discovery and Data Mining, KDD 2002, pp. 513–518. ACM, New York (2002)
4. Oliveira, L.S., Sabourin, R., Bortolozzi, F., Suen, C.Y.: Impacts of verification on a numeral string recognition system. Pattern Recogn. Lett. **24**(7), 1023–1031 (2003)
5. Xiong, Y.: Building text hierarchical structure by using confusion matrix. In: 2012 5th International Conference on BioMedical Engineering and Informatics, pp. 1250–1254, October 2012
6. Yan, Z., et al.: HD-CNN: hierarchical deep convolutional neural networks for large scale visual recognition. In: 2015 IEEE International Conference on Computer Vision, ICCV 2015, Santiago, Chile, 7–13 December 2015, pp. 2740–2748 (2015)

Information Potential Variability for Hyperparameter Selection in the MMD Distance

Cristhian K. Valencia[1(✉)], Andrés Álvarez[1], Edgar A. Valencia[1],
Mauricio A. Álvarez[2], and Álvaro Orozco[1]

[1] Automatic Research Group, Universidad Tecnológica de Pereira, Pereira, Colombia
ckvalencia@utp.edu.co
[2] Department of Computer Science, University of Sheffield, Sheffield, UK

Abstract. Nowadays, the methodologies based on Reproducing Kernel Hilbert Space (RKHS) embeddings have been gaining importance in machine learning. In tasks such as time series classification, there is a tendency to construct classifiers based on RKHS metrics to find separability among classes, identifying an appropriate RKHS tuning characteristic kernel hyperparameters. In most applications, the characteristic kernel hyperparameter is adjusted based on cross-validation heuristic techniques. These approaches require the construction of a grid of possible values in order to evaluate the performance regarding each of these, which can lead to inaccurate values because the optimal value can not necessarily be contained in the grid. Also, this may involve a computational expense and a high computation time. We propose to use the information potential variations (IPV) from a Parzen-based probability density estimator. Specifically, we search for an RKHS by optimizing the global kernel hyperparameter which describes the IPV. Our methodology is tested on time series classification using a well-known RHKS metric called Maximum Mean Discrepancy (MMD) with a 1-NN classifier. Results show that our strategy allows estimating suitable RKHSs favoring data separability and achieving competitive results in terms of the average classification accuracy.

Keywords: RKHS · MMD · Characteristic kernel · Information potential

1 Introduction

Reproducing Kernel Hilbert Space (RKHS) embeddings are widely used in supervised and unsupervised learning [1,5,11], because probability functions (PFs) are mapped to vectors in an HS. This property allows applying basic operations over PFs, such as distances, inner products, norms, among others [8]. Accordingly, some authors [1,2,7] has developed distance measures between PFs based on the mentioned property of RHKS to construct classifiers. However, it raises the

© Springer Nature Switzerland AG 2019
R. Vera-Rodriguez et al. (Eds.): CIARP 2018, LNCS 11401, pp. 279–286, 2019.
https://doi.org/10.1007/978-3-030-13469-3_33

issue related to the suitable RKHS to use. In the RKHS context, the mapping of distributions is done by an injective operator that depends on a characteristic kernel [6]. In addition, it must be universal according to [9]. In most cases, the Gaussian kernel is chosen because it fulfills the necessary properties and is easy to use. However, this kernel depends on the bandwidth (scale) hyperparameter which must be accurately tuned for estimating an RKHS. Otherwise, a wrong bandwidth value leads to distinct not fulfilling the learning task. In most applications, the characteristic kernel hyperparameter is adjusted based on cross-validation heuristic techniques [1,2,7]. These approaches require the construction of a grid of possible values in order to evaluate the performance obtained for each one, which can lead to inaccurate values because the optimal value may not be contained in the grid. Also, the cross-validation is a procedure with high computational cost [4].

In this paper, we propose an automatic selection of the characteristic Gaussian kernel hyperparameter of the RKHS metric known as Maximum Mean Discrepancy (MMD) [6]. The main goal is to construct a suitable RKHS for time series classification. Inspired by the approach [5], we use the potential information variability (IPV) from a Parzen-based probability density estimator. IPV follow coding information quantities from data that go beyond second order statistics and making connections with RKHS [10]. Specifically, we search for an RKHS by optimizing the global kernel parameter which describes the IPV. Then, a 1-nearest neighbor classifier is trained using the MMD distance to discriminate time series. Our approach is tested on synthetic and real public datasets. Results show that our strategy allows estimating suitable RKHSs favoring data separability and achieving competitive results in terms of the average classification accuracy.

The remainder of this paper is organized as follows: Sect. 2 describes the mathematical background, Sect. 3 presents the experimental set-up, Sect. 4 shows the results and discussion, the conclusions appear in Sect. 5.

2   Materials and Methods

2.1   MMD Distance for Time Series Classification

In order to discriminate two different time series from their samples set $\{x_n\}_{n=1}^N$ and $\{y_m\}_{m=1}^M$, we introduce a RKHS embedding-based distance as follows: let $\mathcal{P}$ be the space of all probability distributions and let $X, Y \subset \mathcal{X}$ be two random variables that follow the distribution functions $\mathbb{P}$ and $\mathbb{Q}$, respectively; then $\mathbb{P}, \mathbb{Q} \in \mathcal{P}$, $x_n \in X$, and $y_m \in Y$. Let $\mu\{\cdot\}$ be a marginal embedding operator that maps a given sample $x \in X$ from a probability distribution $\mathbb{P}$ to an (RKHS) $\mathcal{H}$, as follows: $\mu(\mathbb{P}) = \mathbb{E}_X[\phi(x)] = \int_{\mathcal{X}} \phi(x)d\mathbb{P}(x)$, where $\phi : \mathcal{X} \to \mathcal{H}$. This embedding of probability distributions into RKHS allows to compute distances between them. According to [3], the RKHS-based distance over the probability measures $\mathbb{P}$ and

$\mathbb{Q}$, yields: $d_\kappa^2(\mathbb{P}, \mathbb{Q}) = \|\mu(\mathbb{P}) - \mu(\mathbb{Q})\|_{\mathcal{H}}^2$, which can be rewritten as:

$$d_\kappa^2(\mathbb{P}, \mathbb{Q}) = \left\| \int_{\mathcal{X}} \phi(x)d\mathbb{P}(x) - \int_{\mathcal{X}} \phi(y)d\mathbb{Q}(y) \right\|_{\mathcal{H}}^2.$$

Afterward, we define a function $\kappa(x, x') = \langle \phi(x), \phi(x') \rangle_{\mathcal{H}}$, $\forall x, x' \in \mathcal{X}$ as a reproducing characteristic kernel on $\mathcal{H}$. If the probability distributions $\mathbb{P}(x)$ and $\mathbb{Q}(y)$ admit density functions $p(x)$ and $q(y)$, respectively, we have $d\mathbb{P}(x) = p(x)dx$ and $d\mathbb{Q}(y) = q(y)dy$. According to [6], the distributions $\mathbb{P}$ and $\mathbb{Q}$ are assumed empirics, hence $p(x) = \frac{1}{N} \sum_{n=1}^{N} \delta(x - x_n)$ and $q(y) = \frac{1}{M} \sum_{m=1}^{M} \delta(y - y_m)$. Finally, using a Gaussian characteristic kernel $\kappa_G(\cdot, \cdot) \in \mathbb{R}^+$, the RKHS-based distance estimation $\hat{d}_\kappa^2(\mathbb{P}, \mathbb{Q})$ is given by

$$\hat{d}_\kappa^2(\mathbb{P}, \mathbb{Q}) = \frac{1}{N^2} \sum_{n,m=1} \kappa_G(x_n, x_m|\sigma) + \frac{1}{M^2} \sum_{n,m=1} \kappa_G(y_n, y_m|\sigma) - \frac{2}{NM} \sum_{n,m=1} \kappa_G(x_n, y_m|\sigma).$$

Above equation is known as Maximum Mean Discrepancy (MMD) and was introduced by authors of [6]. Note that the function distance MMD depends on the characteristic kernel parameter $\sigma \in \mathbb{R}^+$. The adequately selection of this parameter is highly relevant finding a suitable RKHS that guarantees separability between samples in tasks such as clustering and classification [5]. Usually, a heuristic method based on cross-validation (CV) is used to tune σ [1,2,7], which may affect the performance of machine learning algorithms. In this paper, we realize an estimation of MMD σ hyperparameter using an approach based on IPV.

2.2   Kernel Function Estimation from Information Potential Variability

In order to estimate the characteristic kernel σ hyperparameter of MMD, we used an automatic selection strategy based on IPV developed in [5]. The method is described as follows: let $\mathbf{\Lambda}$ a set of observable data, then a density function $p(\mathbf{\lambda}, \sigma)$ is estimated using a Gaussian Parzen-window density estimator, that is:

$$\hat{p}(\mathbf{\lambda}, \sigma) = \frac{1}{N_T} \sum_{i,j=1}^{N_T} \frac{1}{(2\pi\sigma^2)^{D/2}} \exp\left(\frac{\|\mathbf{\lambda}_i - \mathbf{\lambda}_j\|^2}{2\sigma^2} \right), \tag{1}$$

where $\mathbf{\lambda} \subset \mathbf{\Lambda}$, D is the dimensionality of the input space and N_T is the total number of samples. In this sense, $\hat{p}(\mathbf{\lambda}, \sigma)$ depends on a Gaussian kernel and can be written concerning the Euclidean distance as seen in Eq. (1). Then, we seek an RKHS maximizing the overall (IPV) respect to σ. To this end, the variability of $\hat{p}(\mathbf{\lambda}, \sigma)$ is maximized in terms of kernel bandwidth parameter as:

$$\sigma^* = \arg \max_{\sigma} \text{var}\{\hat{p}(\mathbf{\lambda}, \sigma)\}, \tag{2}$$

where $\mathrm{var}\{\hat{p}(\boldsymbol{\lambda}, \sigma)\} = \mathbf{E}\{(\hat{p}(\boldsymbol{\lambda}, \sigma) - \mathbf{E}\{\hat{p}(\boldsymbol{\lambda}, \sigma)\})^2\}$. Deriving (2) with respect to σ, the optimal parameter value can be written in terms of information potential (IP) $V(\boldsymbol{\Lambda})$ and information force (IF) $F(\boldsymbol{\lambda}_i|\boldsymbol{\lambda}_j)$ as

$$\frac{d}{d\sigma}\mathrm{var}\{\hat{p}(\boldsymbol{\lambda}, \sigma)\} = \frac{2(N_T^2 + N_T)}{\sigma}\left(\sigma^2 \sum_{i,j=1}^{N_T} F^2(\boldsymbol{\lambda}_i|\boldsymbol{\lambda}_j) - V(\boldsymbol{\Lambda})\sum_{i,j=1}^{N_T}(F(\boldsymbol{\lambda}_i|\boldsymbol{\lambda}_j))^\top(\boldsymbol{\lambda}_i - \boldsymbol{\lambda}_j)\right).$$

Finally, equaling the above equation to zero, the fixed point update rule becomes:

$$\sigma_{k+1}^2 = \frac{V_k(\boldsymbol{\Lambda})\mathbf{E}\{(F_k(\boldsymbol{\lambda}_i|\boldsymbol{\lambda}_j))^\top(\boldsymbol{\lambda}_i - \boldsymbol{\lambda}_j) : \forall i,j \in [1, N_T]\}}{\mathbf{E}\{F_k^2(\boldsymbol{\lambda}_i|\boldsymbol{\lambda}_j) : \forall i,j \in [1, N_T]\}}, \tag{3}$$

where $V_k(\boldsymbol{\Lambda})$ and $F_k(\boldsymbol{\lambda}_i|\boldsymbol{\lambda}_j)$ are the IP and conditional IF obtained when $\sigma = \sigma_k$, respectively. In this way, we obtained a scale rule as a function of the IFs, which are induced by a kernel applied over a finite sample set. This approach is named for authors as Kernel Function Estimation from Information Potential Variability (KEIPV) [5]. Notably, the optimization problem described in the Eq. (2) is non-convex, that is, the σ value may converge to a local minimum. Therefore, the performance of the optimization process may be affected unless it is initialized suitability.

3   Experimental Set-Up

We test our proposed approach on public datasets belonging to the *University of California in Riverside (UCR) time series classification* repository[1]. We used thirty-one binary datasets corresponding to synthetic and real-world problems. Each one of datasets come previously partitioned in data train and data test.

Then, we implement a 1-NN classifier from an MMD metric representation using the automatic search of bandwidth parameter σ from the characteristic kernel KEIPV among time series from all datasets from training sets. To validate our methodology, we use a 1-NN classifier tunning the σ parameter in a heuristic way: a grid is built between 1×10^{-3} and 1000, besides we implement a cross-validation methodology and we evaluate the performance in terms of σ values. Also, we illustrate KEIPV method projecting the time series to a low dimensionality space using Principals Components Analysis (PCA).

4   Results and Discussion

To show the performance of KEIPV approach for automatic selection of characteristic kernel hyperparameter, we test this method using the Wafer dataset from UCR repository. We use the training set $\boldsymbol{\Lambda} \in \mathbb{R}^{1000 \times 152}$ as input space, then we

---

[1] www.cs.ucr.edu/~eamonn/time_series_data/.

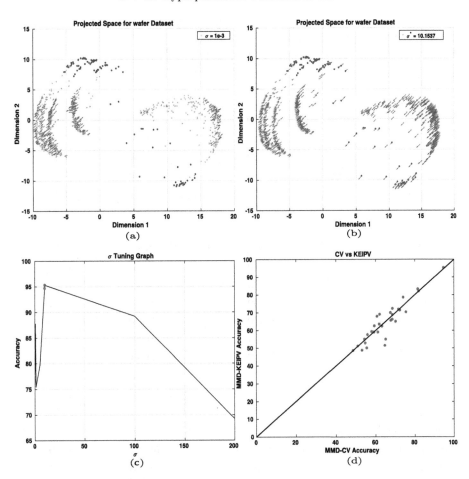

Fig. 1. (a) Illustrates the IFs when the $\sigma = 1 \times 10^{-3}$, in this case, particles tend to apart from each other and IPV is slow. (b) shows that for the selected parameter using KEIPV, IFs magnitudes change regardless of their directions. (c) shows the accuracy obtained using the CV approach, the blue point is the optimal using KEIPV methodology, and red point is the highest value obtained with CV. (d) exhibits the comparison between our approach and CV, red points shows the accuracies values from Table 1. Points above black line represent the accuracies where our method is better than CV. Points below black line vice versa. (Color figure online)

projected $\mathbf{\Lambda}$ to $\mathbf{Z} \in \mathbb{R}^{1000 \times 2}$ using Principal Components Analysis (PCA) representation. Thus, we represent time series as points in the projected space. Figure 1(a) shows that for $\sigma = 1 \times 10^{-3}$ low similarities between pair-wise of time series (particles) and low magnitude IFs are computed due to Gaussian kernel κ reduces the scaling of the Euclidean distance between particles. For this reason, particles are forced to apart from each other. In another hand, in Fig. 1(b), we can see how IFs magnitudes change regardless their directions, that

Table 1. The thirty-one binary datasets from UCR repository with the size of training and testing sets, used to compare the performance of KEIPV selection and cross-validation for characteristic kernel hyperparameter of MMD.

Dataset	Train size	Test size	MMD CV (%)	Our (%)
BeetleFly	20	20	**65.00**	55.00
BirdChicken	20	20	**70.00**	65.00
Coffee	28	28	60.71	**67.86**
Computers	250	250	68.40	**72.25**
DistalPhalanxOutlineCorrect	176	600	**59.16**	59.00
ECG200	100	100	62.00	**69.00**
ECGFiveDays	24	871	**72.24**	71.34
Earthquakes	139	322	81.98	81.98
FordA	1320	3622	**53.17**	48.73
FordB	810	3636	51.01	**51.15**
GunPoint	50	150	82.00	82.00
Ham	109	105	48.57	48.57
HandOutlines	370	1000	**67.60**	65.60
Herring	64	64	59.37	**62.50**
ItalyPowerDemand	67	1029	**54.81**	52.85
Lighting2	60	61	**75.40**	70.32
MiddlePhalanxOutlineCorrect	291	600	**63.16**	62.33
MoteStrain	20	1252	73.96	**77.15**
PhalangesOutlinesCorrect	1800	858	55.94	**57.58**
ProximalPhalanxOutlineCorrect	600	291	68.38	**68.76**
ShapeletSim	20	180	**55.55**	50.00
SonyAIBORobotSurfaceII	20	601	67.38	**69.95**
SonyAIBORobotSurfaceII	27	953	61.80	**63.45**
Strawberry	360	613	**68.35**	66.13
ToeSegmentation1	40	228	71.49	**71.78**
ToeSegmentation2	36	130	81.53	**83.15**
TwoLeadECG	22	20	54.43	**55.00**
Wine	57	1139	**61.11**	59.00
WormsTwoClass	77	54	58.01	**59.24**
Wafer	1000	6164	94.66	**95.30**
Yoga	300	3000	**64.60**	51.46
Mean accuracy (%)			**65.54**	64.95

is, close particles according to the Euclidean distance get high pairwise similarities while far ones have low similarities using the σ^* parameter obtained through

KEIPV. Therefore, KEIPV finds an RKHS where time series share widely spread IF magnitudes.

Figure 1(c) shows the accuracy in terms of σ values chosen as of cross-validation (CV) for Wafer dataset. The accuracy obtained using CV for Wafer dataset was 94.66%, similar to accuracy obtained using KEIPV methodology (95.30%). We can see that the automatic selection of σ parameter using KEIPV achieves find an optimal value (blue point) close to the one that makes the best performance using CV (red mark). Besides, Table 1 shows the results of classification for thirty-one binary datasets from UCR repository. Overall, the mean of accuracies obtained using our methodology was 64, 95%, which is lower than the MMD-based 1-NN classifier using CV. However, our approach succeeded to win for five-ten datasets, while other approaches achieve to win over four-teen datasets. Figure 1(d) exhibits the comparison between our proposal and CV; red points show the accuracies values for the thirty-one binary datasets from UCR. Points above the black line represent the accuracies where our method is better than CV. Points below black line vice versa. For GunPoint and Ham datasets, both methodologies obtained equal performance (points on the black line). In addition, our methodology achieves improve the performance of CV when the proportion between the sizes of training and validation sets is similar. Otherwise, our approach achieves low performance when the training set is small with respect to the validation set because KEIPV takes advantage of the information provided by all training set Λ according to Sect. 2.2.

In general, our methodology is competitive with respect to MMD using CV. Previous results allow us to say that our approach achieves tune hyperparameter σ suitability, allows estimating RKHSs favoring data class separability in comparison with a heuristic way (cross-validation).

5   Conclusions

We present a scheme to optimize the characteristic kernel hyperparameter of RKHS distance MMD. We test our approach on synthetic and real public datasets belonging to UCR repository. In general, our methodology is competitive with respect to MMD using cross-validation. Obtained results show that our methodology allows estimating an RKHS favoring data separability and reaching competitive results concerning the average classification accuracy. How future works, we propose to apply our approach to other metrics in RKHS and compare with others methodologies in the state-of-the-art such as classifiers based on DTW distance, Kernel Adaptive Filters, Gaussian processes and others.

Acknowledgments. The research was supported by the project 1110-744-55778, funded by Colciencias. Authors would like to thank the Master in Electrical Engineering from Universidad Tecnológica de Pereira, Colombia, for partially funding this research.

References

1. Zuluaga, C.D., Valencia, E.A., Álvarez, M.A., Orozco, Á.A.: A parzen-based distance between probability measures as an alternative of summary statistics in approximate bayesian computation. In: Murino, V., Puppo, E. (eds.) ICIAP 2015. LNCS, vol. 9279, pp. 50–61. Springer, Cham (2015). https://doi.org/10.1007/978-3-319-23231-7_5
2. Blandon, J.S., Valencia, C.K., Alvarez, A., Echeverry, J., Alvarez, M.A., Orozco, A.: Shape classification using hilbert space embeddings and kernel adaptive filtering. In: Campilho, A., Karray, F., ter Haar Romeny, B. (eds.) ICIAR 2018. LNCS, vol. 10882, pp. 245–251. Springer, Cham (2018). https://doi.org/10.1007/978-3-319-93000-8_28
3. Sriperumbudur, B.K., Gretton, A., Fukumizu, K., Schölkopf, B., Lanckriet, G.R.: Hilbert space embeddings and metrics on probability measures. J. Mach. Learn. Res. **11**, 1517–1561 (2010)
4. Moore, A.W., Lee, M.S.: Efficient algorithms for minimizing cross validation error. In: Machine Learning Proceedings 1994, pp. 190–198. Elsevier (1994)
5. Álvarez-Meza, A.M., Cárdenas-Peña, D., Castellanos-Dominguez, G.: Unsupervised kernel function building using maximization of information potential variability. In: Bayro-Corrochano, E., Hancock, E. (eds.) CIARP 2014. LNCS, vol. 8827, pp. 335–342. Springer, Cham (2014). https://doi.org/10.1007/978-3-319-12568-8_41
6. Smola, A., Gretton, A., Song, L., Schölkopf, B.: A hilbert space embedding for distributions. In: Hutter, M., Servedio, R.A., Takimoto, E. (eds.) ALT 2007. LNCS (LNAI), vol. 4754, pp. 13–31. Springer, Heidelberg (2007). https://doi.org/10.1007/978-3-540-75225-7_5
7. González-Vanegas, W., Alvarez-Meza, A., Orozco-Gutierrez, Á.: Sparse hilbert embedding-based statistical inference of stochastic ecological systems. In: Mendoza, M., Velastín, S. (eds.) CIARP 2017. LNCS, vol. 10657, pp. 255–262. Springer, Cham (2018). https://doi.org/10.1007/978-3-319-75193-1_31
8. Hein, M., Bousquet, O.: Hilbertian metrics and positive definite kernels on probability measures. In: AISTATS, pp. 136–143 (2005)
9. Steinwart, I.: On the influence of the kernel on the consistency of support vector machines. J. Mach. Learn. Res. **2**, 67–93 (2001)
10. Giraldo, L.G.S., Principe, J.C.: Information theoretic learning with infinitely divisible kernels. arXiv preprint arXiv:1301.3551 (2013)
11. Berlinet, A., Thomas-Agnan, C.: Reproducing Kernel Hilbert Spaces in Probability and Statistics. Springer Science & Business Media, New York (2011)

A Fuzzy Classifier for Data Streams with Infinitely Delayed Labels

Tiago Pinho da Silva[1]([✉]), Vinicius Mourão Alves Souza[1],
Gustavo Enrique Almeida Prado Alves Batista[1],
and Heloisa de Arruda Camargo[2]

[1] Universidade de São Paulo, São Carlos, SP 13566-590, Brazil
tpinho@usp.br, {vmasouza,gbatista}@icmc.usp.br
[2] Universidade Federal de São Carlos, São Carlos, SP 13565-905, Brazil
heloisa@dc.ufscar.br

Abstract. In data stream learning, classification is a prominent task which aims to predict the class labels of incoming examples. However, in classification, most of the approaches from literature make assumptions that limit the usefulness of the methods in real scenarios such as the supposition that the label of an example will be available right after its prediction, i.e., there is no time delay to acquiring actual labels. It is a very optimistic assumption, since labeling the entire data stream is usually not feasible. Some recent approaches overcome this limitation, considering unsupervised learning methods to deal with delayed labels. Also, some proposals explore concepts of fuzzy set theory to add more flexibility to the learning process, although restricted to data streams with no delayed labels. In this paper, we propose a fuzzy classifier for data streams with infinitely delayed labels called *FuzzMiC*. Our algorithm generates a model based on fuzzy micro-clusters that provides flexible class boundaries and allows the classification of evolving data streams. Experiments show that our approach is promising in dealing with incremental changes.

Keywords: Data streams · Classification · Delayed labels · Fuzzy

1 Introduction

Data streams generate a considerable amount of data that can be used by machine learning methods for the automatic acquisition of useful knowledge. However, real-world data streams can be potentially infinite in size and susceptible to

This study was financed in part by the Coordenação de Aperfeiçoamento de Pessoal de Nível Superior - Brazil (CAPES) - Finance Code 001, FAPESP (#2016/04986-6 and #2018/05859-3), and CNPq (306631/2016-4). This material is based upon work supported by the United States Agency for International Development under Grant No AID-OAA-F-16-00072.

© Springer Nature Switzerland AG 2019
R. Vera-Rodriguez et al. (Eds.): CIARP 2018, LNCS 11401, pp. 287–295, 2019.
https://doi.org/10.1007/978-3-030-13469-3_34

changes in their distributions [3]. Hence, traditional methods cannot deal with data streams particularities, requiring the development of online mechanisms.

Among the possible tasks under data streams, classification is the primary focus of this paper. In this task, unlabeled examples arrive continuously in an orderly fashion over time, and a classifier should predict the label of each example in real-time or at least before the arrival of the next example [3]. However, data streams present concept drifts, which can degrade the performance of a classification model over time if it is outdated to the recent changes [3]. Thus, stream classifiers require constant updates so that their performance remains stable over time in dynamic environments.

The changes may appear in different ways such as abrupt, recurring, gradual, and incremental [3]. In this paper, we deal with incremental drifts, where there are many intermediary concepts between one concept and another. This type of change allows using similarities among consecutive concepts to update the classification model and adapts in scenarios with label latency [10].

Latency is a characteristic present in many streams applications, and it is defined as the time delay between the process of classifying an example and the arrival of its respective actual label. This time can be null ($delay = 0$), intermediate ($0 < delay < \infty$), or extreme ($delay = \infty$) [8]. One of the main reasons for latency is the high cost for manual labeling by experts along with a high arrival rate. Besides, other problems related to the data generation mechanism that can also cause this delay, such as failures in the transmission of the labels [10].

In the most challenging scenario of extreme latency, the absence of actual labels makes it unfeasible to monitor performance indicators, such as accuracy, for change detection and to use labeled data for model update. Therefore, under this delay condition, it is necessary to develop methods capable of producing a stable performance, even with the presence of latency. The present work contributes with algorithms for learning under extreme latency, which is regarded as a challenging task, but also a more realistic scenario for many real applications.

To obtain more flexible learning models under evolving data stream scenarios, researchers have developed methods using concepts of the fuzzy set theory [4,7]. In this work, we propose a Fuzzy Micro-cluster Classifier (*FuzzMiC*), which uses concepts of fuzzy set theory. Our proposal adopts the Supervised Fuzzy Micro-Clusters (SFMiC) [9] as summarization structure for the classification for incoming examples. Based on the memberships values, the algorithm associates a class label with a new example. Our experimental evaluation shows that the proposed method is more robust to class overlapping and presents more stable results when compared to non-fuzzy methods.

The paper is organized as follows: Sect. 2 discusses related works concerning classification under latency and fuzzy approaches for streams. In Sect. 3 we describe the proposed method *FuzzMiC*. In Sects. 4 and 5 we discuss the experiments and analysis of the results. Conclusions are provided in Sect. 6.

2   Related Work

COMPOSE (Compacted Object Sample Extraction) [2] is a method that deals with extreme latency problem in data streams with incremental concept drifts. This method uses semi-supervised learning and computational geometry techniques to identify and adapt the classification model to incremental changes.

Similarly, the Arbitrary Sub-Populations Tracker (APT) [6] addresses the extreme latency problem by monitoring subpopulations of examples with arbitrary probability distributions. A subpopulation is defined with a function belonging to a set of examples generating functions in a multidimensional space.

SCARGC (Stream Classification Algorithm Guided by Clustering) [11] uses successive steps of clustering over time to deal with incremental changes and extreme latency. Each group found by the clustering algorithm has label information, inherited from old concepts since the initial labeled training data.

The *MClassification* algorithm [10], which is the base of our proposal, applies unsupervised learning approaches to classify new incoming examples without requiring the actual label of examples to update the classification model. The method creates an initial model composed of a supervised summarization structure called micro-clusters obtained from an initial labeled set. During the data stream classification, the algorithm checks if a new example is within a micro-cluster maximum radius. If right, the example is classified as the micro-cluster class and associated with it. If not, a new micro-cluster is created with the new example as a prototype and the class associated is from the closest micro-cluster. Besides, the algorithm searches by the two farthest micro-clusters from the predicted class to merge them.

Recently, the fuzzy set theory has emerged with promising results to deal with data streams. In [7] the authors proposed a fuzzy clustering algorithm, called *Fuzztream*, that uses a fuzzy summarization structure named *Fuzzy Micro-Clusters* (FMiC), to maintain information about the stream examples in real time. According to the authors, the application of fuzzy set theory, in the data stream clustering, presented improvement scenarios with noise data. Besides, Hashemi et al. [4] proposed a flexible decision tree (FlexDT) for stream classification, integrating the Very Fast Decision Tree (VFDT) [5] with concepts of fuzzy sets. FlexDT was able to generate a good performance in scenarios where concept change, noise, and missing values coexist.

Although showing good results, the classification fuzzy algorithms discussed consider the availability of actual labels after the example prediction. Thus, we propose in this paper a fuzzy method based on the *MClassification*, which we named *FuzzMiC*.

3   Fuzzy Micro-cluster Classifier - *FuzzMiC*

FuzzMiC is an approach for classification where extreme latency and incremental changes coexist. Our proposal is based on the *MClassification* algorithm, previously discussed, that uses micro-clusters to perform the classification task.

Therefore, our method separates the learning process into a *offline* and *online* phase. In the *offline* phase a decision model is learned from an initial labeled set of examples. Later, in the *online* phase, new unlabeled examples from the stream are incrementally classified in one of the known classes.

Seeking for better noise handling and flexibility, we propose a method that uses the Fuzzy C-Means (FCM) [1] clustering algorithm to create the initial classification decision model composed by a set of fuzzy summarization structures called SFMiC (Supervised Fuzzy Micro-Cluster) [9]. Through the *online* phase, the method makes use of these structures to classify new examples.

The SFMiC [9] is defined as the vector $(M, \overline{CF1^x}, t, class\_id)$, where M is the linear sum of the membership values of the examples in the micro-cluster, $\overline{CF1^x}$ is the linear sum of the n examples x_j weighted by their membership, t is the timestamp of the most recent example associated to the SFMiC, and $class\_id$ is the class associated to the micro-cluster.

While the MClassification algorithm associates an example from the data stream to only one micro-cluster, *FuzzMiC* considers membership degrees to associate an example for a set of SFMiCs from the same class.

Concerning the proposed method, Algorithm 1 shows the *offline* phase. In this phase are required as input the FCM parameter $m_o ff$, a multiplying factor ω concerning the number of micro-clusters by class and the initial labeled set used to calculate the first micro-clusters *init_points*.

Algorithm 1. *FuzzMiC - Offline* Phase

Require: $m_o ff, \omega, init\_points$
1: $model \leftarrow \emptyset$
2: **for each** *class* $C_i \in init\_points$ **do**
3:     $class\_clusters \leftarrow \text{FCM}(init\_points_{class=C_i}, m_o ff, \omega * d)$
4:     $class\_SFMiC \leftarrow \text{SUMMARIZE}(class\_clusters)$
5:     $model \leftarrow model \cup class\_SFMiC$
6: **end for**

In the beginning, for each class of the initial labeled data, the set of corresponding points is given as entry for the FCM clustering algorithm (Step 3) to generate $\omega * d$ clusters for each class, where d corresponds to the number of attributes in the evaluated dataset. The clusters found for a class are stored in the variable *class_cluster* and lately summarized in a supervised fuzzy micro-cluster structure in the function *summarize* (Step 4). The decision model is defined as the set of SFMICs found for all different classes (Step 5).

For the *online* phase of the algorithm, the classification is performed considering arriving examples from the data stream DS. Algorithm 2 presents the process for the *online* phase, where θ correspond to an adaptation threshold for the classification step, max_mic_class is the maximum number of SFMiCs per class, and m_{on} is the fuzzification parameter regarding the membership.

In Algorithm 2, for each example x arriving from the stream, the algorithm calculates the membership of x to all current SFMiCs (Step 3), the membership is calculated in the same way as in the FCM algorithm [1]. After, the memberships regarding SFMiCs of the same class are summed, resulting in a value of compatibility of x to each class, which we called class compatibility (Steps 5–8).

These values will be used to decide which label of an existing class, x will be assigned. This process is done by verifying the maximum compatibility of x to a class. After that, the algorithm checks if x is inside the decision boundary formed by the SFMiCs of the predicted class C_i (Step 9), by verifying if the maximum compatibility is greater or equal than a threshold parameter θ. If true, a new SFMiC is created for C_i with x as the prototype, to do so, if the maximum number of SFMiCs (max_mic_class) of C_i is reached, then the oldest SFMIC from C_i is removed based on the timestamp component t (Steps 12–13). Otherwise, x is considered an outlier and it is only updated into the SFMiCs of class C_i

This procedure ensures that SFMiCs will be created only inside the class decision boundary. Since we are dealing with incremental concept drifts, the constant creation of new SFMiCs along with updates from outliers help the SFMiCs to move in the direction of the drift. Besides, not creating SFMiCs on the class boundaries decreases misclassification when there is partial class overlapping.

Algorithm 2. *FuzzMiC - Online* Step

Require: $DS, \theta, max\_mic\_class, m_{on}$
1: **while** !ISEMPTY(DS) **do**
2:      $x \leftarrow$ NEXT(DS)
3:      $all\_membership \leftarrow$ MEMBERSHIP($x, model, m_{on}$)
4:      $all\_comp \leftarrow \emptyset$
5:      **for each** *class* $C_i \in model$ **do**
6:          $class\_compatibility \leftarrow$ SUM($all\_membership_{class=C_i}$)
7:          $all\_comp \leftarrow all\_comp \cup class\_compatibility$
8:      **end for**
9:      $(max\_class, max\_comp) \leftarrow$ MAX(all_comp)
10:      $x.class \leftarrow max\_class$
11:      **if** $max\_comp \geq \theta$ **then**
12:          CREATE_SFMIC($model, x$)
13:          **if** $|model_{class=max\_class}| > max\_mic\_class$ **then**
14:              REMOVE_OLD_SFMIC($model$)
15:          **end if**
16:      **else**
17:          UPDATE($model_{class=max\_class}, x$)
18:      **end if**
19: **end while**

---

4   Experimental Setup

We evaluated our proposed method on two real-world problems and 13 synthetic benchmark datasets proposed in [11]. In order to verify the advantages of the fuzzy-based approach proposed here, we compare the results for *FuzzMiC* against the results obtained by *MClassification*. We also consider two bounds that simulate a static supervised learning classifier *(Static)* and a classifier that is constantly updated without delay time to achieve the actual labels *(Sliding)*.

Regarding the parameters for all synthetic datasets, the initial labeled set ($init\_points$) was defined as the first 150 examples from the data stream. Concerning our proposal, the offline phase parameters m_{off} and ω had their values defined as 2. In addition, the online phase parameters m_{on}, θ and max_mic_class were defined as 2, 0.9 and $\omega * d$ respectively, where d correspond to the number of attributes from the evaluated dataset.

For the Keystroke dataset, which describes 8 sessions of 4 users typing the password ".tie5Roanl" plus the *Enter* key 400 times for each session, we consider the examples from the first session as the initial labeled set for all methods. The *FuzzMiC* offline phase parameters m_{off} and ω were defined as 2 and 4 respectively, the online phase parameters m_{on}, θ and max_mic_class were defined as 2, 0.39 and $\omega * d$ respectively.

For the NOAA dataset initial labeled set was defined as the first 30 examples for the *Static* and *Sliding* methods, as described in [10]. The *MClassification* and *FuzzMiC* methods had their initial labeled set defined as the first 10 examples from the data stream. Regarding *FuzzMiC* parameters, the offline parameters m_{off} and ω were defined as 2 and 0.25 respectively, the online phase parameters m_{on}, θ and max_mic_class were defined as 2, 0.85 and $4 * d$ respectively.

These parameter values were chosen for the *offline* and *online* phases because they have led to the best results in preliminary experiments. Concerning *MClassification*, the parameter r was defined with it default value (0.1).

5   Analysis of Results

A first assessment of the averaged accuracy (Table 1) shows that *FuzzMIC* performs slightly equally or better than *MClassification* in most of the cases. However, this average may not represent the performance of each algorithm over time. For a more thorough evaluation, we present some examples in detail (Fig. 1).

Table 1. Average accuracies over time on benchmark data

Dataset	Static	Sliding	MClassification	FuzzMiC
1CDT	97.01	99.88	**99.89**	99.88
1CHT	91.96	99.24	**99.38**	99.31
1CSurr	65.75	98.52	**85.15**	79.50
2CDT	54.38	93.47	95.23	**95.95**
2CHT	54.03	85.44	87.93	**89.07**
4CE1CF	95.81	97.15	**94.38**	92.28
4CRE-V1	26.17	97.64	90.63	**98.22**
4CRE-V2	27.11	89.37	91.59	**92.02**
5CVT	40.72	86.86	88.40	**90.37**
GEARS 2C 2D	93.62	99.86	94.73	**95.20**
UG 2C 2D	47.28	94.27	**95.28**	94.98
UG 2C 3D	60.64	92.86	94.72	**94.88**
UG 2C 5D	68.81	89.91	91.25	**91.86**
NOAA	66.19	72.01	67.54	**68.63**
KEYSTROKE	68.69	90.14	**90.62**	90.25

In Fig. 1a, we show the results considering 100 evaluation moments for the 4CRE-V1 dataset. We can note that all methods present 5 majors decays, which are related to moments of class overlapping (Fig. 2b and a). However, the proposed method had the lowest decay in most moments, achieving the best results for this dataset. This can be explained by the fact that *FuzzMiC* do not create micro-clusters nearby a classes boundaries (see Fig. 2b), which is not true for *MClassification*. Therefore, our proposal decreases the misclassification when partial class overlapping moments occur.

In GEARS 2C 2D, the decision boundaries for each class has the shape of a star that rotates in a fixed center over time (Fig. 2c and d). The outcomes are shown considering 100 evaluation moments (Fig. 1b). Concerning *FuzzMiC*, the results show that our proposal was able to generate more stable results when compared to *MClassification*. Besides, *FuzzMiC* had similar behavior as the approach with no latency (*Sliding*), while *MClassification* had a similar behavior to the *Static* approach. Indicating a certain invariance of *FuzzMiC* concerning the changes in this dataset, due to the generation of new micro-clusters nearby the stationary center of the classes (see Fig. 2c). On the other hand, *MClassification* may generate new micro-clusters on the classes boundaries, where the changes occur, causing some instabilities in their performance.

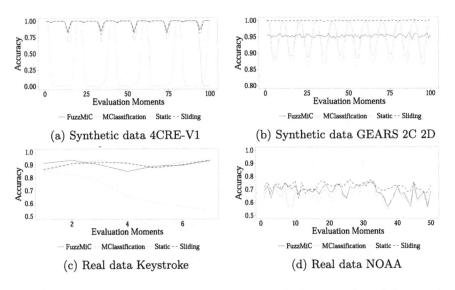

(a) Synthetic data 4CRE-V1

(b) Synthetic data GEARS 2C 2D

(c) Real data Keystroke

(d) Real data NOAA

Fig. 1. Accuracy achieved over time by the methods in 4 evaluated datasets

Concerning the real data Keystroke, the evaluation was carried considering 7 evaluation moments related to each session of data collection (Fig. 1c). In this dataset, *FuzzMiC* was able to generate better results in the first 2 sessions, when compared to the remaining approach. However, our approach presents a minor decrease in accuracy during sessions 3 and 4. Thus, increasing the chances to create micro-cluster for noise data. Nonetheless, during the sessions 5, 6 and 7, our

(a) Eval. Moment: 14(b) Eval. Moment: 15 (c) Eval. Moment: 1 (d) Eval. Moment: 2

Fig. 2. Snapshots of 4CRE-V1 (left) and GEARS 2C 2D (right). Each class is described as a different color and the micro-clusters are represented by the X shaped marks (Color figure online)

proposal was able to recover and even achieve slightly better results on sessions 5 and 7 when compared to *MClassification*. Altogether, except for the *Static*, the remaining methods presented a similar behavior as seen in Table 1, which can be observed as an advantage for methods *FuzzMiC* and *MClassification*.

The evaluation on real data NOAA was carried considering 50 time moments related to each year of weather measurements (Fig. 1d). *FuzzMiC* generated better results than *MClassification* in the initial moments while achieving similar results in the remaining. Despite the low accuracy results obtained by *FuzzMiC* and *MClassification* over time, the *Sliding* approach also achieved approximated results, which indicates the high complexity of this dataset. Thus, the results obtained by the proposed method can be seen as positive, since they provide a slight increase in accuracy when compared to *MClassification*.

In general, we can see that *FuzzMiC* presents similar or superior results than *MClassification*. It is better at handle partial overlapping classes, and presented a certain level of invariance to some concept changes, because the SFMiC structure turns possible a flexible learning process.

6   Final Considerations

This work presents a fuzzy classifier for data streams under extreme latency named *FuzzMiC*. Experiments show that *FuzzMiC* obtains promising results in the evaluated datasets. Notably, the flexibility added by the integration of fuzzy micro-clusters enables the proposed method to better deal with changes in the data stream, regarding the crisp approach *MClassification*, especially in the presence of partial class overlapping.

The experiments held in this work were made with the purpose to validate our proposal and highlight its advantages with respect to the algorithm that motivated its creation. Thus, there is still room for further investigations such as the comparison with others data stream classifiers for extreme latency scenarios and tests with different real-world datasets with incremental drifts. Another line of further research must contemplate the automatic adaptability of θ threshold.

References

1. Bezdek, J.C.: Pattern Recognition with Fuzzy Objective Function Algorithms. Springer US, New York (1981). https://doi.org/10.1007/978-1-4757-0450-1
2. Dyer, K.B., Capo, R., Polikar, R.: COMPOSE: a semisupervised learning framework for initially labeled nonstationary streaming data. TNNLS **25**(1), 12–26 (2014)
3. Gama, J., Žliobaitė, I., Bifet, A., Pechenizkiy, M., Bouchachia, A.: A survey on concept drift adaptation. CSUR **46**(4), 44 (2014)
4. Hashemi, S., Yang, Y.: Flexible decision tree for data stream classification in the presence of concept change, noise and missing values. Data Min. Knowl. Disc. **19**(1), 95–131 (2009)
5. Hulten, G., Spencer, L., Domingos, P.: Mining time-changing data streams. In: ACM SIGKDD, pp. 97–106. ACM (2001)
6. Krempl, G.: The algorithm APT to classify in concurrence of latency and drift. In: Gama, J., Bradley, E., Hollmén, J. (eds.) IDA 2011. LNCS, vol. 7014, pp. 222–233. Springer, Heidelberg (2011). https://doi.org/10.1007/978-3-642-24800-9_22
7. Lopes, P.A., Camargo, H.A.: Fuzzstream: fuzzy data stream clustering based on the online-offline framework. In: FUZZ-IEEE (2017)
8. Marrs, G.R., Hickey, R.J., Black, M.M.: The impact of latency on online classification learning with concept drift. In: Bi, Y., Williams, M.-A. (eds.) KSEM 2010. LNCS (LNAI), vol. 6291, pp. 459–469. Springer, Heidelberg (2010). https://doi.org/10.1007/978-3-642-15280-1_42
9. Silva, T.P., Urban, G.A., Lopes, P.A., Camargo, H.A.: A fuzzy variant for on-demand data stream classification. In: BRACIS, pp. 67–72 (2017)
10. Souza, V.M.A., Silva, D.F., Batista, G.E.A.P.A., Gama, J.: Classification of evolving data streams with infinitely delayed labels. In: ICMLA, pp. 214–219 (2015)
11. Souza, V.M.A., Silva, D.F., Gama, J., Batista, G.E.A.P.A.: Data stream classification guided by clustering on nonstationary environments and extreme verification latency. In: SIAM SDM, pp. 873–881 (2015)

Generalized Multitarget Linear Regression with Output Dependence Estimation

Hector Gonzalez[1], Carlos Morell[2], and Francesc J. Ferri[3(✉)]

[1] Universidad de las Ciencias Informaticas (UCI), La Habana, Cuba
`hglez@uci.cu`
[2] Universidad Central Marta Abreu (UCLV), Villa Clara, Cuba
`cmorellp@uclv.edu.cu`
[3] Dept. Informàtica, Universitat de València, Burjassot, Spain
`Francesc.Ferri@uv.es`

Abstract. Multitarget regression has recently received attention in the context of modern, large-scale problems in which finding good enough solutions in a timely manner is crucial. Different proposed alternatives use a combination of regularizers that lead to different ways of solving the problem. In this work, we introduce a general formulation with several regularizers. This leads to a biconvex minimization problem and we use an alternating procedure with accelerated proximal gradient steps to solve it. We show that our formulation is equivalent but more efficient than some previously proposed approaches. Moreover, we introduce two new variants. The experimental validation carried out, suggests that important performance gains can be obtained with the newly proposed approach in several different publicly available multitarget regression problems.

Keywords: Multitarget regression · Accelerated proximal gradient

1 Introduction

There is a recent interest in unconventional pattern recognition problems to solve modern, large-scale problems across several application domains. Among these, structured prediction problems [1] in which outputs may exhibit structure along with strong interdependences are particularly challenging. The case in which the output structure is a vector is referred to as Multitarget Regression (MTR) [2,16,17].

It is well-known that the straightforward approach of predicting multiple outputs in an independent way is not optimal. First attempts to improve this combined the independently estimated outputs using canonical correlation [4]

This work has been partially funded by FEDER and Spanish MEC through project TIN2014-59641-C2-1-P and UVEG grant INV17-01-15-03.

© Springer Nature Switzerland AG 2019
R. Vera-Rodriguez et al. (Eds.): CIARP 2018, LNCS 11401, pp. 296–304, 2019.
https://doi.org/10.1007/978-3-030-13469-3_35

or used a low-rank decomposition of the input-output covariance matrix [6]. More recently proposed approaches [8,14] take into account these dependences using different sparseness patterns in the prediction model induced by different regularizers.

Another option to promote sparseness is using random subspaces as in [12] where new variables are formed by linearly combining k outputs with random weights drawn from a normal distribution. Modern large-scale problems can be tackled if the problem is formulated using two prediction steps to introduce latent variables and convenient regularizers [5,16,17]. These composite approaches lead usually to nonconvex formulations that require particular solving strategies.

The present work proposes a general MTR model that considers several recent approaches as particular cases and introduces new variants. In what follows, the MTR problem is presented and our main contribution is introduced. An empirical evaluation using publicly available data and involving several state of the art approaches is also considered. Finally, the main conclusions along with lines of future research are outlined.

2 Multitarget Regression

Let x, y be input and output vectors, respectively, and let $\left(x^j, y^j\right) \in \mathbb{R}^p \times \mathbb{R}^q$, for $i = 1, \ldots, N$, be a given training set. The MTR problem consists of obtaining a predictor $h : \mathbb{R}^p \rightarrow \mathbb{R}^q$ in such a way that the expected deviation between true and predicted outputs is minimized for all possible input/output pairs.

The most straightforward approach consists of obtaining a univariate predictor for each one of the output variables in an independent way using any of the available methods for single-target prediction [2] which constitutes the simplest of the so-called problem transformation (also known as local) methods that consist of transforming the given MTR problem into one or more single-target ones [12]. The alternative approach to tackle MTR is through algorithm adaptation (also known as global) methods [2] which consists of adapting a particular strategy to deal directly with multiple targets. Global methods are interesting because they focus on explicitly capturing all interdependencies and internal relationships among targets.

A straightforward adaptation method for MTR is Multivariate Linear Regression with q output variables [2]. In this approach it is possible to estimate the coefficient matrix [1], $W \in \mathbb{R}^{p \times q}$, through unconstrained optimization by combining an appropriate loss function, $\mathcal{L}(W)$, and a regularizer, $\mathcal{R}(W)$, as

$$\hat{W} = \underset{W}{\operatorname{argmin}} \mathcal{L}(W) + \lambda \mathcal{R}(W) \tag{1}$$

As in most previous works on MTR, the loss function used here is the Mean Squared Error (MSE) between real outputs and predictions, $\frac{1}{2N}\|XW - Y\|_F^2$, where $\|\cdot\|_F$ designates the Frobenius norm, and $X \in \mathbb{R}^{N \times p}$ and $Y \in \mathbb{R}^{N \times q}$.

---

[1] For the sake of simplicity, we obviate here the bias terms. In general, an extra row in W along with extended input vectors should be considered.

On the other hand, the regularizer function depends on the kind of structure we want to enforce in W. For example, using the Frobenius norm, $\|.\|_F^2$, leads to multivariate ridge regression. For a sparser structure (attribute selection) we can use lasso, $\|.\|_1$, or grouped lasso, $\|.\|_{21}$ [9,15], or particular combination of these. The nuclear (or trace) norm [7], $\|.\|_*$, can also be used to enforce low rank in W.

In the above formulation, the underlying structure that establishes the conditional dependence that may exist among output variables is not specified. It has been shown in previous works [4,10] that it is possible to improve the predictive capacity of the models if these dependences are taken into account e.g. by using other output variables as inputs for predicting each output variable. In the particular case of the Curds & Wheys approach [4], this problem is modeled as a linear combination of the output variables. In other words, the final predictions of the output variables are expressed as a linear combination of the initial (independent) predictions. This approach of combining the outputs has been exploited in recent years using different ways of modeling the structures of the coefficient matrices and the dependence between the output variables [5,16,17].

3   MTR with Output Dependence Estimation

In line with previous works described above, our model consists on two prediction steps. First, a linear prediction in a latent space of the same dimension of the output is obtained for each input vector, x, as xW. Then, this latent vector is again linearly transformed into xWS using a dependence matrix, $S \in \mathbb{R}^{q \times q}$. The corresponding loss term on X can be then written as $\mathcal{L}(W, S) = \frac{1}{2N}\|XWS - Y\|_F^2$.

Note that the predictive power of the model is exactly the same as in the linear case. But by decomposing the coefficient matrix in two factors, we introduce the possibility of modelling different kind of dependencies by using separate regularizers for these matrix factors. In particular, our model will use a linear combination of regularizers, $\mathcal{R}(W, S) = \lambda_1 g_1(W) + \lambda_2 g_2(S)$.

This approach to the regularization model can be seen as a generalization with regard to previously proposed models as e.g. MTL [5], MMR [16], or MLSR [17]. In all previous cases, specific particular solution to the corresponding optimization problem have been developed through direct derivation of the corresponding subgradients. Moreover, MMR and MSLR are developed in the general case of using kernels that introduce flexibility and power but compromise scalability.

The proposed general approach for the MTR problem can be formulated using a coefficient matrix, W, and a dependence matrix, S, as

$$\min_{\{W,S\}} \frac{1}{2N}\|XWS - Y\|_F^2 + \lambda_1 g_1(W) + \lambda_2 g_2(S) \tag{2}$$

where g_1 and g_2 are any valid regularizers, usually matrix norms.

To solve problem (2) we will follow a widely used strategy which consists in breaking the global (non-convex) problem into two (convex) subproblems in an alternating way [13]. In our particular case, we fix one of the matrices and optimize the other one which leads to two simpler convex problems that can be sequentially solved in turn until convergence.

$$\min_{W} \frac{1}{2N} \|Y - XWS\|_F^2 + \lambda_1 g_1(W) \qquad \text{for a given } S \qquad (3)$$

$$\min_{S} \frac{1}{2N} \|Y - XWS\|_F^2 + \lambda_2 g_2(S) \qquad \text{for a given } W \qquad (4)$$

Each subproblem described in (3) and (4) is convex but not necessarily differentiable depending on the regularizers. But in most of the interesting cases as $\|.\|_1$, $\|.\|_{21}$, or $\|.\|_*$ the resulting function is not differentiable.

3.1 Applying the Accelerated Proximal Gradient (APG) Method

The two alternating optimization problems in (3) and (4) involve only one variable and consist of a first term which is convex and differentiable and a second term which is convex but not differentiable. Consequently, we can express any of the two problems for a wide range of regularizers as

$$\min_{A} f(A) + g(A) \qquad (5)$$

where f and g represent the differentiable and non differentiable parts, respectively. The usual gradient update for a step size s_t from a current solution, A, is the one that minimizes the quadratic approximation of the criterion around A. In our case, we can instead approximate only the differentiable part and minimize instead

$$\hat{f}_{s_t,A}(B) + g(B) = f(A) + \langle \nabla f(A), B - A \rangle + \frac{1}{2s_t}\|B - A\|_F^2 + g(B) \qquad (6)$$

The update that substitutes the usual gradient descent update for a given step size, s_t, at a particular iteration, t, is [11]

$$\mathbf{prox}_{s_t}(A - s_t \nabla f(A), g)$$

where the so-called proximal operator is defined as

$$\mathbf{prox}_s(\alpha, g) = \underset{\beta}{\operatorname{argmin}} \frac{1}{2s}\|\alpha - \beta\|_F^2 + g(\beta)$$

The step size, s_t, can be selected using the quadratic approximation of the differentiable part, $\hat{f}_{s_t,A}(B)$, to guide a linear search procedure. Convergence can be further improved by combining the above proximal gradient update with the Nesterov's acceleration scheme [11].

3.2   Using Different Regularizer Functions

In a wide range of interesting cases, the proximal operator reduces to a closed-form solution. For example, when the Euclidean norm in $\mathbb{R}^n$ is used, $g(z) = \lambda\|z\|_2$, the proximal operator is the projection onto the Euclidean unit ball which is given by

$$\mathbf{prox}_s(z, g) = (1 - \tfrac{\lambda s}{\|z\|_2})_+ z$$

where $(z)_+$ is used as a shorthand for $\max(0, z)$.

The grouped lasso regularizer for matrices, also referred to as $\ell_{2,1}$ norm, is defined as $\lambda\|A\|_{2,1} = \lambda\sum_i\|A_i\|_2$ where A_i is the i-th row in matrix A. And the corresponding proximal operator can be computed separately for each row as

$$[\mathbf{prox}_s(A, g)]_i = (1 - \tfrac{\lambda s}{\|A_i\|_2})_+ A_i$$

In the same way, the (element-wise) lasso regularizer, $\lambda\|A\|_1$, leads to

$$\mathbf{prox}_s(A, g) = \mathcal{S}_{\lambda s}(A)$$

where $\mathcal{S}_\tau$ is the soft-thresholding operator applied element-wise to matrix A,

$$[\mathcal{S}_\tau(A)]_{ij} = (A_{ij} - \tau)_+ - (-A_{ij} - \tau)_+ = \begin{cases} A_{ij} - \tau & \text{if} \quad A_{ij} > \tau \\ 0 & \text{if} \quad -\tau \leq A_{ij} \leq \tau \\ A_{ij} + \tau & \text{if} \quad A_{ij} < -\tau \end{cases}$$

The proximal update can be computed in a relatively easy way in the case of using the nuclear norm as a regularizer in terms of the soft-thresholding operation and the singular value decomposition of the corresponding matrix [16].

Using different regularizers one can obtain different optimization schemes. For example, the MMR algorithm [16] considers ridge regularizers for both W and S matrices and the spectral norm regularizer also for matrix S, and the MLSR algorithm [17] considers a rigde regularizer for S and the grouped lasso for S.

In the present work we will reproduce these two algorithms in the context of our generalized scheme along with two new particular algorithms to study and compare different sparsity patterns in the sought solutions. The first variant, $GLMR_1$, considers an element-wise lasso regularizer for both matrices W and S. And the second variant, $GLMR_2$, combines this same regularizer for the dependency matrix S with a grouped lasso regularizer for the coefficient matrix W to enforce the selection of relevant attributes. The corresponding decompositions, gradients and proximal updates for all alternatives considered are shown in Table 1, where $\mathcal{L}$ stands for $\frac{1}{2N}\|XWS - Y\|_F^2$ and its corresponding gradients are

$$\nabla_W\mathcal{L} = X^T(XWS - Y)S^T \quad \text{and} \quad \nabla_S\mathcal{L} = W^TX^T(XWS - Y).$$

The way in which the alternating optimization scheme is applied in our generalized scheme is of crucial importance. Following recommendations in [3] we propose alternating updates instead of completely solving each subproblem as in original MMR and MSLR algorithms. According to preliminary experiments, we obtain better and faster results in general.

4   Experiments and Results

The generalized scheme including two newly proposed variants and algorithms MMR and MSLR have been considered in this work. All have been implemented using the Accelerated Proximal Gradient strategy in the linear case. A set of 16 publicly available databases from [2,10] has been considered to carry out comparative experiments. As in other similar works, we use the average Relative Root Mean Squared Error (aRRMSE) as a performance measure. Given a test set, D_{test}, and a predictor, h, this measure is given as

$$aRRMSE(h; D_{test}) = \frac{1}{q} \sum_{i=1}^{q} \sqrt{\frac{\sum_{(x,y) \in D_{test}} (h(x) - y)^2}{\sum_{(x,y) \in D_{test}} (\overline{y} - y)^2}}$$

where $\overline{y}$ is the mean target value, y, and $h(x)$ is the corresponding prediction.

In all cases, the datasets were divided into training and test sets following a 80/20 proportion. The two new variants and the MLSR algorithm use two regularization parameters that were selected using a grid search with 20 logarithmically spaced values for each parameter. The MMR algorithm needs three regularization parameters and the corresponding grid search used 15 values for each. The best performing values for each algorithm and dataset were selected.

In all cases, the alternating strategy converged to relatively good solutions at a reasonable speed. Figure 1 contains representative plots illustrating the convergence of the different algorithms for databases atp1d and sf1. The aRRMSE values corresponding to all datasets are shown in Table 2. As it can be seen, the variant $GMLR_2$ is the one that performs the best in a majority of cases, 10, followed by MMR, $GMLR_1$, and MLSR. The relative goodness of each of the four variants considered can be graphically observed in Fig. 2 that corresponds to the result of the Friedman test with Shafer correction. Even though we do not have significant differences, except for the case of $GMLR_2$ with regard to MSLR, these results can be seen as very encouraging specially taking into account that we have restricted ourselves to the linear case.

Another important fact worth mentioning is that the datasets with a larger number of attributes and targets, are the ones for which the difference between $GMLR_2$ and the rest is bigger. This is not so surprising if we think that the grouped lasso regularizer is specially good to perform attribute selection.

Table 1. Differentiable and non differentiable parts, gradients and proximal updates for the different alternatives considered. $S = UDV^T$ is the SVD of matrix S.

	MLSR	MMR	$GMLR_1$	$GMLR_2$
$f(W,S)$	$\mathcal{L} + \lambda_1 \|W\|_F^2$	$\mathcal{L} + \lambda_1 \|W\|_F^2 + \lambda_2 \|S\|_F^2$	$\mathcal{L}$	
$\nabla_W f$	$\nabla_W \mathcal{L} + \lambda_1 W S S^T$		$\nabla_W \mathcal{L}$	
$\nabla_S f$	$\nabla_S \mathcal{L}$	$\nabla_S \mathcal{L} + \lambda_2 W^T W S$	$\nabla_S \mathcal{L}$	
$g(W,S)$	$\lambda_2 \|S\|_{21}$	$\lambda_3 \|S\|_*$	$\lambda_1 \|W\|_1 + \lambda_2 \|S\|_1$	$\lambda_1 \|W\|_{21} + \lambda_2 \|S\|_1$
$\mathbf{prox}_W$			$\mathcal{S}_{\lambda_1 s_t}(W)$	$(1 - \frac{\lambda_1 s_t}{\|W_i\|_2})_+ W_i$
$\mathbf{prox}_S$	$(1 - \frac{\lambda_2 s_t}{\|S_i\|_2})_+ S_i$	$U \mathcal{S}_{\lambda_3 s_t}(D) V^T$	$\mathcal{S}_{\lambda_2 s_t}(S)$	

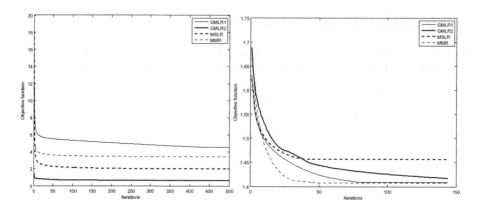

Fig. 1. Criterion values corresponding to datasets atp1d (left) and sf1 (right).

Table 2. Dataset details and performance results obtained for all considered algorithms.

Dataset	Size (N)	Attributes (p)	Targets (q)	$GMLR_1$	$GMLR_2$	MSLR	MMR
andro	49	30	6	0.696	**0.662**	0.698	0.678
edm	154	16	2	**0.792**	0.793	0.799	0.798
wq	1060	16	14	0.949	0.949	0.950	**0.948**
sf1	323	10	3	0.965	0.966	**0.964**	**0.964**
sf2	1066	10	3	**0.967**	0.977	**0.967**	**0.967**
enb	768	8	2	0.299	**0.296**	**0.296**	**0.296**
jura	359	15	3	0.599	**0.593**	0.603	0.601
slump	103	7	3	**0.701**	0.709	0.707	0.706
atp1d	337	411	6	0.558	**0.504**	0.555	0.557
atp7d	296	411	6	0.720	**0.708**	0.742	0.732
oes10	410	298	16	0.339	**0.308**	0.343	0.346
oes97	334	263	16	0.582	**0.519**	0.573	0.568
scm20d	8966	61	16	0.740	**0.736**	0.744	0.744
scm1d	9803	280	16	0.406	**0.387**	0.407	0.406
rf2	9125	576	8	0.515	**0.359**	0.507	0.486
rf1	9125	64	8	0.407	0.406	0.406	**0.405**

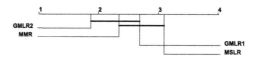

Fig. 2. Results of the Friedman test with Shafer correction: $\chi^2 = 2.8688$, $df1 = 3$, $df2 = 45$, and $p_v = 0.04683$.

5   Conclusions and Further Work

A common framework to solve large-scale MTR problems based on alternating optimization and APG methods has been presented in this work. Within this framework, we have been able to reproduce previously proposed algorithms along with two new variants. The proposed scheme is flexible and can be used in a variety of situations showing a smooth behavior leading to appropriate solutions. The experiments carried out give strong evidences that the approach can be competitive with regard to other state of the art methods. Further research is directed to consider a wide catalogue of regularizers along with extending the method to the nonlinear case using kernels.

References

1. Bakir, G.H., Hofmann, T., Schölkopf, B., Smola, A.J., Taskar, B., Vishwanathan, S.V.N.: Predicting Structured Data (Neural Information Processing). The MIT Press, Cambridge (2007)
2. Borchani, H., Varando, G., Bielza, C., Larrañaga, P.: A survey on multi-output regression. Wiley Interdisc. Rev.: Data Min. Knowl. Disc. **5**(5), 216–233 (2015)
3. Boyd, S., Vandenberghe, L.: Convex Optimization. Cambridge University Press, New York (2004)
4. Breiman, L., Friedman, J.H.: Predicting multivariate responses in multiple linear regression. J. R. Stat. Soc.: Ser. B (Stat. Methodol.) **59**(1), 3–54 (1997)
5. Chen, J., Zhou, J., Ye, J.: Integrating low-rank and group-sparse structures for robust multi-task learning. In: Proceedings of the 17th ACM SIGKDD International Conference on Knowledge Discovery and Data Mining, pp. 42–50. ACM (2011)
6. Izenman, A.J.: Reduced-rank regression for the multivariate linear model. J. Multivar. Anal. **5**(2), 248–264 (1975)
7. Recht, B., Fazel, M., Parrilo, P.A.: Guaranteed minimum-rank solutions of linear matrix equations via nuclear norm minimization. SIAM Rev. **52**(3), 471–501 (2010)
8. Rothman, A.J., Levina, E., Zhu, J.: Sparse multivariate regression with covariance estimation. J. Comput. Graph. Stat. **19**(4), 947–962 (2010)
9. Simon, N., Friedman, J., Hastie, T.: A blockwise descent algorithm for group-penalized multiresponse and multinomial regression (2013)
10. Spyromitros-Xioufis, E., Tsoumakas, G., Groves, W., Vlahavas, I.: Multi-target regression via input space expansion: treating targets as inputs. Mach. Learn. **104**(1), 55–98 (2016)
11. Tibshirani, R., Wainwright, M., Hastie, T.: Statistical Learning with Sparsity: The Lasso and Generalizations. Chapman and Hall/CRC, Boca Raton (2015)
12. Tsoumakas, G., Spyromitros-Xioufis, E., Vrekou, A., Vlahavas, I.: Multi-target regression via random linear target combinations. In: Calders, T., Esposito, F., Hüllermeier, E., Meo, R. (eds.) ECML PKDD 2014. LNCS (LNAI), vol. 8726, pp. 225–240. Springer, Heidelberg (2014). https://doi.org/10.1007/978-3-662-44845-8_15
13. Udell, M., Horn, C., Zadeh, R., Boyd, S., et al.: Generalized low rank models. Found. Trends® Mach. Learn. **9**(1), 1–118 (2016)

14. Yuan, M., Ekici, A., Zhaosong, L., Monteiro, R.: Dimension reduction and coefficient estimation in multivariate linear regression. J. R. Stat. Soc.: Ser. B (Stat. Methodol.) **69**(3), 329–346 (2007)
15. Yuan, M., Lin, Y.: Model selection and estimation in regression with grouped variables. J. R. Stat. Soc.: Ser. B **68**(1), 49–67 (2006)
16. Zhen, X., Mengyang, Y., He, X., Li, S.: Multi-target regression via robust low-rank learning. IEEE Trans. Pattern Anal. Mach. Intell. **40**(2), 497–504 (2018)
17. Zhen, X., et al.: Multitarget sparse latent regression. IEEE Trans. Neural Netw. Learn. Syst. 29(5), 1575–1586 (2018)

A New Weighted k-Nearest Neighbor Algorithm Based on Newton's Gravitational Force

Juan Aguilera[1(✉)], Luis C. González[1], Manuel Montes-y-Gómez[2], and Paolo Rosso[3]

[1] Universidad Autónoma de Chihuahua, Chihuahua, Mexico
{p271672,lcgonzalez}@uach.mx
[2] Instituto Nacional de Astrofísica, Óptica y Electrónica, Puebla, Mexico
mmontesg@inaoep.mx
[3] Universitat Politècnica de València, Valencia, Spain
prosso@dsic.upv.es

Abstract. The kNN algorithm has three main advantages that make it appealing to the community: it is easy to understand, it regularly offers competitive performance and its structure can be easily tuning to adapting to the needs of researchers to achieve better results. One of the variations is weighting the instances based on their distance. In this paper we propose a weighting based on the Newton's gravitational force, so that a mass (or relevance) has to be assigned to each instance. We evaluated this idea in the kNN context over 13 benchmark data sets used for binary and multi-class classification experiments. Results in F_1 score, statistically validated, suggest that our proposal outperforms the original version of kNN and is statistically competitive with the distance weighted kNN version as well.

1 Introduction

The k-Nearest Neighbor (kNN) classification algorithm is one of the most popular approaches used by researchers and practitioners in the areas of Pattern Recognition and Machine Learning. Altogether with the Support Vector Machine (SVM), it is considered a firm representative of the classification *by analogy* principle [4].

Generally speaking, kNN only needs one parameter to be adjusted, k, which represents how many closest neighbors are to be considered to classify an unseen object. Once this parameter is set, two main approaches are followed in order to classify an object, (i), the vote of the majority of the k neighbors, and (ii), a weighted vote of all k neighbors considering the distance from where each of them are located with respect to the object to classify. Following these two ideas, the kNN algorithm has been successfully applied in such diverse learning task such as data mining [14], image processing [6], and recommender systems [7].

For classification purposes, all kNN variants, up to now, have assumed that, independently of the voting strategy that they follow (by majority or weighted)

© Springer Nature Switzerland AG 2019
R. Vera-Rodriguez et al. (Eds.): CIARP 2018, LNCS 11401, pp. 305–313, 2019.
https://doi.org/10.1007/978-3-030-13469-3_36

all objects in the training set are equal in their classification power. For instance, if two objects from different classes are exactly at the same distance of a test object, both objects will contribute the same amount to the final decision. Another way to perceive this is by saying that the two training objects have the same relevance. In this work, we are interested in proposing some ideas to alter this behavior. Motivated by how big bodies exert and influence to proximate objects, we think of assigning a *mass* to each of the objects in the training set.

There are several scenario applications that make us hypothesize that assigning a mass to all the training objects could have positive effects in the classification performance of the kNN algorithm. Particularly, this could be of interest when some aspect or natural feature of the problem needs to be considered. For example, within the field of Natural Language Processing (NLP), for the task of news classification, capturing the temporal aspect may be relevant, i.e. more recent news could be more informative (or have more context) than older ones[1]. In this case, we could think of the more recent news to have a larger influence, thus a larger mass. Another application of this approach could be the recognition of highly heterogeneous categories. In this case it is usual that the majority of the neighbors (to the object to classify) vote for a wrong label. With objects with different masses it would be possible to overcome this decision, i.e. if the objects with the right class have proper mass.

In this work we approach these ideas by proposing two different ways to calculate a mass for a given object. We formulate the kNN algorithm to take into consideration this mass by using a voting strategy based on Newton's gravitational force. We tested our proposal in 13 benchmark data sets and contrasted the results against the regular kNN and weighted kNN algorithms.

2   Related Work

Literature has reported several ways in which the kNN algorithm could improve its performance. Naturally, finding an optimal value of k has been one of the questions that some works have attempted to solve [16,17]. Besides finding this k value, there is an open question regarding which distance metric is the more suitable to use. In this regard, some previous works have evaluated new and traditional metrics in a variety of classification problems [2,8,15].

Using a weighting scheme was firstly proposed by Dudani [5] in the 70's, this variant of kNN is called the *Distance-Weighted k-Nearest-Neighbor Rule* (DWkNN). Since then, different weighting schemes have been proposed. Among the most recent works, Tan [12] proposed the algorithm *Neighbor-Weighted k-Nearest Neighbor* (NWkNN), which applies a weighting strategy based on the distribution of classes. When working with unbalanced data sets, NWkNN gives a minor weight to objects of majority classes and more weight to objects less

---

[1] Before 2016 it would not be surprising to classify a news containing the term *Donald Trump* in the Business section, when now it would be more appropriate to assign it to the political section.

represented. For the case of text classification, Soucy and Mineau [11] proposed a weighting based on the similarity of texts (objects), measured by the cosine similarity between their bag-of-word representations. Mateos-García et al. [9] developed a technique similar to those used in Artificial Neural Networks to optimize some weights that would indicate the importance that each neighbor has with respect to the test objects. Finally, Parvinnia et al. [10] also computed a weight for each training object based on a matching strategy between the training and testing data sets.

3 Proposed Algorithm

In this section we present two approaches to calculate a mass for a given object in the training set. We then explain the complete kNN framework that exploits the concept of mass, by considering Newton's gravitational force.

3.1 Mass Assignment

Approach 1: Circled by Its Own Class (CC). This approach is based on a instance selection strategy known as Edited Nearest Neighbor (ENN) originally proposed by Wilson [13]. The rationale of ENN is to keep an instance that is surrounded (or circled) by other instances of its same class. For the CC approach, the mass of an object x is directly proportional to the number of objects from its same class that circled it. By doing this, we aim to give less importance to objects that are in regions of the feature space that are more likely to represent a different class. In other words, the idea is to penalize rare objects and, as a consequence, make the classifier more robust to outliers. To calculate the mass via CC we apply the Eq. 1.

$$m(x \in c_i) = \log_2(SN_k(x, c_i) + 2) \tag{1}$$

where x is a training object, c_i is its class and the function $SN_k()$ calculates how many out of the k closest objects to x belong to its same class. The $log_2()$ function serves as a smoothing factor; we include a constant 2 to avoid computation errors or obtaining masses equal to zero.

Approach 2: Circled by Different Classes (CD). This approach is the opposite of the CC approach. It gives more mass to objects that are surrounded by objects from different classes, that is, the mass is inversely proportional to the number of objects of the same class. CD aims to balance the discriminative power of an outlier object, since it could be relevant to classify other outlier object in the testing set. It also allows to better modeling heterogeneous classes formed by different small subgroups of objects. To assign a mass following this approach we applied the Eq. 2. The interpretation of its elements is the same as in Eq. 1.

$$m(x \in c_i) = \log_2(k - SN_k(x, c_i) + 2) \tag{2}$$

3.2 Weighted Attraction Force kNN algorithm (WAF-kNN)

The traditional weighted kNN algorithm is as follows: given a set of training objects $\{(x_1, f(x_1)), ..., (x_i, f(x_i))\}$ (being x_i an object and $f(x_i)$ its label), an unlabeled object x_q, and the set of the k closest neighbors to x_q in the training set $\{x_1, ..., x_k\}$, the class of x_q is determined by Eq. 3:

$$f(x_q) \leftarrow \arg \max_{c \in C} \sum_{i=1}^{k} weight(x_i) \times \delta(c, f(x_i)) \tag{3}$$

where C represents the set of classes, $weight(x_i)$ indicates the weight for the vote from object x_i, and $\delta(c, f(x_i))$ is a function that returns 1 if x_i belongs to class c or 0, otherwise.

Supported on this framework, our proposal, that we call *Weighted Attraction Force kNN*, or simply WAF-kNN, uses a weighting scheme based on the Law of Universal Gravitation as presented by Eq. 4.

$$weight(x_i) = G \frac{m(x_q)m(x_i)}{dist^2(x_q, x_i)} \simeq \frac{m(x_i)}{dist^2(x_q, x_i)} \tag{4}$$

where $weight(x_i)$ is the attraction force or the voting amount exerted by the training object x_i to classify the object x_q. $m(x_q)$ and $m(x_i)$ are the masses of the testing and training objects respectively, and $dist(\cdot, \cdot)$ is a distance metric between the two objects. The reader could detect that there are two constants that we could omit to simplify the original equation, since they only serve as scaling factors without affecting how the vote is computed. These two constants are G and $m(x_q)$. Note that $m(x_i)$ could be calculated by any of the two approaches, CC or CD, that we already presented in Sect. 3.1 for mass assignment.

4 Experiments and Results

4.1 Experimental Configuration

For the evaluation of the proposed approach we considered 13 different data sets from the UCI data repository[2]. All these data sets exclusively contain numeric features and do not show any missing value. These data sets are commonly used in classification tasks. Table 1 presents some statistics on these data sets such as the number of instances, features, and classes.

We applied a common experimental setting for the experiments across all the collections. Firstly, we considered three different values for k, namely, 3, 5 and 7. Then, we standardized the data by means of their z-scores. In all the experiments we used the Euclidean distance as the distance measure, and employed the F_1 score as main evaluation metric due to its appropriateness for describing results in unbalanced data sets. A 10-fold cross-validation procedure was applied to get the results. Finally, we applied the non-parametric Bayesian Signed-Rank (BSR) test [1] for analyzing the statistical significance of the obtained results.

---

[2] https://archive.ics.uci.edu/ml/datasets.html.

Table 1. Data sets characteristics.

Data sets	Instances	Features	Classes	Classes distribution
Arcene	100	10000	2	56/44
Ecoli	336	7	8	143/77/52/35/20/5/2/2
Glass	214	9	6	76/70/29/17/13/9
Haberman	306	3	2	225/81
Ionosphere	351	34	2	225/126
Iris	150	4	3	50/50/50
Landsat	6435	36	6	1533/1508/1358/707/703/626
Page blocks	5473	10	5	4913/329/115/88/28
Pima	768	8	2	500/268
Sonar	208	60	2	111/97
Thyroid	215	5	3	150/35/30
Vehicle	846	18	4	218/217/212/199
Wine	178	13	3	71/59/48

4.2 Results

Table 2 presents a first comparison of the approaches used to calculate the masses (CC and CD), each employed within the WAF-kNN algorithm. This table is organized by the three k values that were evaluated. The best results, for each k, are shown in bold face. Globally, the CD approach slightly outperforms the CC approach, being this more evident when $k = 7$; notwithstanding, there are data sets where the CC approach is better for all k values, e.g. Arcene and Ecoli. The analysis of the Ecoli data set tell us that classes are more or less well defined in homogeneous clusters. Being this the case, the CD approach gives more mass to *outliers*, causing a larger classification error than CC, which assigns less mass to objects away from their class main centroid and having the effect of reducing noise. Both approaches, CC and CD, aim to offer a better weighting scheme to improve classification performance, but which one to use will ultimately depend on the distribution of classes in the data set of interest.

To evaluate our proposal against kNN and DWkNN algorithms, we chose the CD approach given its consistent performance in the previous experiment. This new comparison is presented in Table 3, where it can be observed that our proposal outperforms the baseline methods in the majority of data sets. This behavior is consistent among the three values of k that are considered. Again, the best performance is obtained with $k = 7$.

To further analyze these results, we applied the non-parametric BSR test [3]. According to this test three possibilities do exist for a given pairwise comparison of methods A and B: (scenario 1) A outperforms B, (scenario 2) both methods show the same performance, or (scenario 3) B outperforms A. The BSR test computes the probability of occurrence of each scenario when we applied approaches

Table 2. F$_1$ scores of WAF-kNN, using the two approaches for mass assignment.

Data sets	CC	CD	CC	CD	CC	CD
	k = 3		k = 5		k = 7	
Arcene	**0.762**	0.753	**0.774**	0.758	**0.761**	0.759
Ecoli	**0.714**	0.652	**0.736**	0.706	**0.752**	0.725
Glass	0.556	**0.618**	0.560	**0.613**	0.577	**0.594**
Haberman	**0.571**	0.570	0.535	**0.549**	0.507	**0.528**
Ionosphere	0.796	**0.851**	0.793	**0.826**	0.785	**0.831**
Iris	0.954	0.954	0.954	0.954	0.954	0.954
Landsat	**0.894**	0.883	0.894	**0.895**	0.889	**0.893**
Page Blocks	**0.827**	0.808	**0.826**	0.814	0.815	**0.817**
Pima	**0.697**	0.683	**0.702**	0.692	0.694	**0.695**
Sonar	0.847	**0.863**	0.817	**0.839**	0.803	**0.839**
Thyroid	0.904	**0.933**	0.909	**0.933**	0.909	**0.916**
Vehicle	0.694	**0.707**	0.689	**0.714**	0.688	**0.720**
Wine	0.951	**0.956**	0.969	0.969	0.964	**0.969**

Table 3. Comparison of kNN, DWkNN and WAF-kNN using CD masses.

Data sets	kNN	DWkNN	WAF	kNN	DWkNN	WAF	kNN	DWkNN	WAF
	k = 3			k = 5			k = 7		
Arcene	**0.762**	**0.762**	0.753	**0.796**	**0.796**	0.758	0.736	0.736	**0.759**
Ecoli	0.688	**0.697**	0.652	0.727	**0.729**	0.706	**0.748**	0.747	0.725
Glass	0.610	0.610	**0.618**	0.597	0.604	**0.613**	0.536	0.572	**0.594**
Haberman	0.547	0.561	**0.570**	0.521	0.526	**0.549**	0.524	0.519	**0.528**
Ionosphere	0.797	0.797	**0.851**	0.811	0.813	**0.826**	0.777	0.777	**0.831**
Iris	0.954	0.954	0.954	0.946	**0.954**	0.954	0.947	**0.968**	0.954
Landsat	**0.894**	**0.894**	0.883	0.893	0.892	**0.895**	0.889	0.890	**0.893**
Page Blocks	**0.816**	0.814	0.808	0.820	**0.827**	0.814	0.787	**0.817**	0.817
Pima	**0.706**	0.703	0.683	**0.706**	0.704	0.692	0.704	**0.707**	0.695
Sonar	0.847	0.847	**0.863**	0.794	0.798	**0.839**	0.812	0.817	**0.839**
Thyroid	0.904	0.904	**0.933**	0.906	0.909	**0.933**	0.877	0.915	**0.916**
Vehicle	0.706	0.703	**0.707**	0.713	0.711	**0.714**	0.711	0.707	**0.720**
Wine	0.951	0.951	**0.956**	0.964	0.964	**0.969**	0.964	0.964	**0.969**

A and B over a given data set. Table 4 presents the probabilities of occurrence for each scenario when comparing the baseline approaches kNN and DWkNN with our proposed WAF-kNN approach, respectively.

According to the performance of the WAF algorithm in each data set (with $k = 7$), it was in Ionosphere and Ecoli, where we obtained the largest improvement and decrement with respect to the baseline methods, respectively. When

Table 4. BSR output probabilities. **A** refers to the baseline methods, kNN and DWkNN respectively, whereas **B** refers to the proposed WAF-kNN approach.

Compared algorithms	Scenarios		
	A > B	A = B	A < B
kNN vs WAF-kNN	0.0001	0.1951	**0.8048**
DWkNN vs WAF-kNN	0.0018	**0.6305**	0.3677

visualizing these data sets, it is possible to notice some data characteristics that could shed some light on details about the behavior of the method.

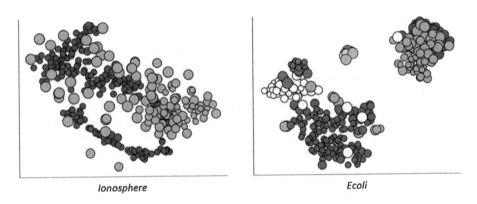

Ionosphere   Ecoli

Fig. 1. t-SNE mapping of the Ionosphere and Ecoli data sets. (Color figure online)

Figure 1 shows the distribution of objects in these two data sets using the t-distributed Stochastic Neighbor Embedding (t-SNE). The Ionosphere data set is composed by two classes. Class 1, represented in red color and grouped in two well defined clusters which are located in the upper and lower section of the space. Class 2, represented in blue color and mainly spread along the mapping space with an identifiable cluster on the right side of the figure. For this case, the CD approach favors the classification of objects of class 2 by assigning more mass to training objects that are located in the central and upper left region, which are clearly *circled by objects of class 1*, thus getting right label assignment even in regions where majority of objects belong to different class. On the other hand, in the Ecoli data set, CD gives more mass to hypothetical noisy objects located away from their normal behavior of its own class (see blue and white objects over the green cluster objects), then negatively affecting the classifier.

5 Conclusions

In this work we introduced the WAF-kNN algorithm, which is a variant of the weighted kNN algorithm but based on the attraction force that exist between two objects. We present two methods of assigning mass to training objects, i.e. *Circled by its own class* (CC) and *Circled by different classes* (CD). For testing purposes 13 known data sets were employed. Comparisons indicate that our proposal obtained better classification results than kNN and is statistically competitive with DWkNN. These results were validated with a non-parametric BSR test.

Acknowledgement. This research was partially supported by CONACYT-Mexico (project FC-2410). The work of Paolo Rosso has been partially funded by the SomEM-BED TIN2015-71147-C2-1-P MINECO research project.

References

1. Benavoli, A., Mangili, F., Corani, G., Zaffalon, M., Ruggeri, F.: A Bayesian Wilcoxon signed-rank test based on the Dirichlet process. In: Proceedings of the 31st International Conference on Machine Learning, vol. 32, p. 9 (2014)
2. Bhattacharya, G., Ghosh, K., Chowdhury, A.S.: An affinity-based new local distance function and similarity measure for kNN algorithm. Pattern Recogn. Lett. **33**(3), 356–363 (2012)
3. Carrasco, J., García, S., del Mar Rueda, M., Herrera, F.: rNPBST: an R package covering non-parametric and bayesian statistical tests. In: Martínez de Pisón, F.J., Urraca, R., Quintián, H., Corchado, E. (eds.) HAIS 2017. LNCS (LNAI), vol. 10334, pp. 281–292. Springer, Cham (2017). https://doi.org/10.1007/978-3-319-59650-1_24
4. Domingos, P.: The Master Algorithm: How the Quest for the Ultimate Learning Machine Will Remake Our World. Basic Books, New York City (2015)
5. Dudani, S.A.: The distance-weighted k-nearest-neighbor rule. IEEE Trans. Syst. Man Cybern. SMC **6**(4), 325–327 (1976)
6. Guru, D.S., Sharath, Y.H., Manjunath, S.: Texture features and KNN in classification of flower images. Int. J. Comput. Appl. **1**, 21–29 (2010)
7. Lam, S.K., Riedl, J.: Shilling recommender systems for fun and profit. In: Proceedings of the 13th International Conference on World Wide Web - WWW 2004,break p. 393 (2004)
8. López, J., Maldonado, S.: Redefining nearest neighbor classification in high-dimensional settings. Pattern Recogn. Lett. **110**, 36–43 (2018)
9. Mateos-García, D., García-Gutiérrez, J., Riquelme-Santos, J.C.: An evolutionary voting for k-nearest neighbours. Expert Syst. Appl. **43**, 9–14 (2016)
10. Parvinnia, E., Sabeti, M., Jahromi, M.Z., Boostani, R.: Classification of EEG Signals using adaptive weighted distance nearest neighbor algorithm. J. King Saud Univ. - Comput. Inf. Sci. **26**(1), 1–6 (2014)
11. Soucy, P., Mineau, G.: A simple KNN algorithm for text categorization. In: Proceedings 2001 IEEE International Conference on Data Mining, pp. 647–648 (2001)
12. Tan, S.: Neighbor-weighted K-nearest neighbor for unbalanced text corpus. Expert Syst. Appl. **28**(4), 667–671 (2005)
13. Wilson, D.L.: Asymptotic properties of nearest neighbor rules using edited data. IEEE Trans. Syst. Man Cybern. **2**(3), 408–421 (1972)
14. Wu, X., et al.: Top 10 algorithms in data mining. Knowl. Inf. Syst. **14**, 1–37 (2008)
15. Xu, Y., Zhu, Q., Fan, Z., Qiu, M., Chen, Y., Liu, H.: Coarse to fine K nearest neighbor classifier. Pattern Recogn. Lett. **34**(9), 980–986 (2013)

16. Zhang, S., Cheng, D., Deng, Z., Zong, M., Deng, X.: A novel kNN algorithm with data-driven k parameter computation. Pattern Recogn. Lett. **0**, 1–11 (2017)
17. Zhu, Q., Feng, J., Huang, J.: Natural neighbor: a self-adaptive neighborhood method without parameter K. Pattern Recogn. Lett. **80**, 30–36 (2016)

Towards Hierarchical Classification
of Data Streams

Antonio Rafael Sabino Parmezan$^{(\boxtimes)}$, Vinicius M. A. Souza,
and Gustavo E. A. P. A. Batista

Instituto de Ciências Matemáticas e de Computação, Universidade de São Paulo,
São Carlos, SP, Brazil
parmezan@usp.br, {vmasouza,gbatista}@icmc.usp.br

Abstract. In data stream mining, state-of-the-art machine learning
algorithms for the classification task associate each event with a class
belonging to a finite, devoid of structural dependencies and usually small,
set of classes. However, there are more complex dynamic problems where
the classes we want to predict make up a hierarchal structure. In this
paper, we propose an incremental method for hierarchical classification
of data streams. We experimentally show that our stream hierarchical
classifier present advantages to the traditional online setting in three
real-world problems related to entomology, ichthyology, and audio processing.

Keywords: Hierarchical classification · Data streams · Online learning

1 Introduction

Most problems in data mining involve the prominent classification task. The
purpose of this task is to find, from a significant number of examples, a function that maps the features that describe each example in its respective known
class (category). Besides establishing the relationships between features and a
category, the discovery function can predict the class of new examples [1].

Traditional supervised machine learning algorithms lead to the data categorization in a flat way, *i.e.*, they seek to associate each example with a class
belonging to a finite, devoid of structural dependencies and usually small, set of
classes. However, there are a significant number of problems whose classes can be
divided into subclasses or grouped into superclasses. This structural dependence
between classes characterizes the hierarchical classification [13].

In the hierarchical classification, supervised machine learning methods induce
a hierarchical decision model (hierarchical classifier). Such a model links the

Supported by CNPq [grants #140159/2017-7, and #306631/2016-4]; and FAPESP
[grants #16/04986-6, and #18/05859-3]. This material is based upon work supported
by the United States Agency for International Development under Grant No AID-
OAA-F-16-00072.

R. Vera-Rodriguez et al. (Eds.): CIARP 2018, LNCS 11401, pp. 314–322, 2019.
https://doi.org/10.1007/978-3-030-13469-3_37

features of the examples to a class hierarchy, usually structured as a tree or as an acyclic directed graph, with different levels of specificity and generality. The main advantage of a hierarchical classifier is that it divides the original problem into levels to reduce the complexity of the classification function and give flexibility to the process.

Current hierarchical classification algorithms work in a batch setting, *i.e.*, they assume as input a fixed-size dataset that we can fully store in memory. At this point, a challenge not yet addressed by the data mining community focuses on the proposition, or even adaptation, of hierarchical classification techniques capable of dealing with unlimited and evolving data that arrives over time called data streams [16]. Data streams require real-time responses, adaptive models, and impose memory restrictions.

In this paper, we extend the state-of-the-art proposing the first incremental method of hierarchical classification for the data stream scenario. The algorithm represents the class hierarchy as a tree and performs single path predictions. Our study has three major contributions:

- We design an incremental method based on k-Nearest Neighbors (kNN) [4] for the hierarchical classification of data streams. Our algorithm uses a fixed-size memory buffer and builds a one-class local dataset for each node of the class tree, except for the root node, using a set of positive examples that represent the current class. The classification of a new event from the stream is done top-down. Our method stands out for its simplicity in decomposing the feature space of the original problem into subproblems with a smaller number of classes. Thus, every time we go down through the levels of the class tree, the input and output spaces are reduced;
- We build three stream hierarchical datasets and make them available online. Such data are from real-world problems related to entomology, ichthyology, and audio processing;
- We experimentally compare our algorithm with an online kNN flat classifier. In this comparison, we show that in problems where the class labels naturally make up a hierarchy, hierarchical classification methods provide better results than those obtained by flat classifiers. Although other studies have evidenced this fact with static batch learning [3,13], our work is the first which considers the data stream scenario.

The remaining of this paper is structured as follows: Sect. 2 introduces the fundamentals of hierarchical classification and data streams. Section 3 describes our proposal. Section 4 specifies our experimental evaluation. Section 5 presents results and discussion. Finally, Sect. 6 reports our conclusions.

2   Background and Definitions

We provide in this section the main concepts and definitions of hierarchical classification and data streams, which are essential for understanding our proposal.

Hierarchical Classification. Flat classification differs from hierarchical one by the way domain classes are organized. In flat classification, while a portion of the problems is discerned by the non-existence of interrelationships between classes (single-label classification), the other part is characterized by non-structural relationships between labels (multi-label classification). Structural dependencies, which reflect super or subclass relations, configure hierarchical classification.

A dataset in the attribute-value format for hierarchical classification contains N pairs of examples $(\vec{x}_i, Y_i)$, where $\vec{x}_i = (x_{i_1}, x_{i_2}, \ldots, x_{i_M})$ and $Y_i \subset L = \{L, L.1, L.2, \ldots\}$. That is, each example $\vec{x}_i$ is described by M predictive features (attributes) and has a set of labels Y_i for which there are relationships that respect a previously defined hierarchical class structure. The class attribute, in turn, represents the concept to be learned and described by the built hierarchical models using supervised machine learning algorithms.

Hierarchical classification methods can be distinguished according to four main aspects [13]. The first one refers to the type of hierarchical structure – tree or Direct Acyclic Graph (DAG) –, used to represent the relationships between classes. In the tree structure (Fig. 1(a)), each node, except the root node, is associated with at most one parent node. In the DAG structure (Fig. 1(b)), each node, except the root node, can have one or more parent nodes.

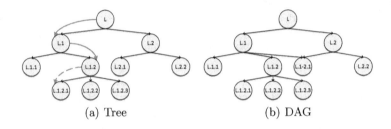

(a) Tree   (b) DAG

Fig. 1. Hierarchical class structures

The second aspect indicates whether the algorithm can predict classes in only one or several (more than one) paths in the hierarchical structure. For example, in the class hierarchy tree of Fig. 1(a), if the model can predict both class L.2.1 and L.2.2 for a given example, which equates to paths L→L.2→L.2.1 and L→L.2→L.2.2, then it is able to predict multiple paths – Multiple Path Prediction (MPP). In contrast, when this type of association is not valid, the method performs the Single Path Prediction (SPP).

The third aspect concerns the hierarchical level of the classification. An algorithm can make predictions using only classes depicted by leaf nodes – Mandatory Leaf-Node Prediction (MLNP) – or by using classes represented by any node, internal or leaf, of the hierarchical structure – Non-Mandatory Leaf-Node Prediction (NMLNP). Figure 1(a) illustrates the difference between these strategies. In this figure, the path L→L.1→L.1.2 represents the NMLNP strategy, while the path L→L.1→L.1.2→L.1.2.1 portrays the MLNP strategy. We need to emphasize that the NMLNP is especially useful in applications that opt for the freedom to conduct a more generic prediction, but with higher reliability.

The fourth and last aspect is related to the mode adopted by machine learning methods to manipulate the hierarchical structure. We can divide the approaches described in the literature into three broad groups: (i) flat approach, (ii) local approach, and (iii) global approach. Further details are available in [13].

Data Stream Mining. A data stream is a sequence of examples (or events) generated continuously over time that imposes severe processing and storage limitations [12]. The features that describe such events can undergo variations over time due to the volatility of the dynamic environment in which they are. These changes are known as concept drift [8,16]. Concept drifts impose the use of adaptive models to maintain a stable classification accuracy over time.

3   Proposed Method

We propose an incremental algorithm based on kNN to classify data streams hierarchically. Our method represents the class hierarchy as a tree and performs single path predictions using a top-down strategy. Algorithm 1 shows the pseudo-code of the proposal.

Algorithm 1. kNN for Hierarchical Classification of Data Streams

---

```
    /* Initial training set T; Unlabeled data stream DS; Number of nearest neighbors k; Reliability
       threshold δ; Size of the memory buffer η; Set of predicted labels Ŷ for each x̄ ∈ DS      */
    Input:  T, DS, k, δ, η
    Output: Ŷ
 1  begin
 2  |    H ← buildClassHierarchy(T);
 3  |    H ← oneClassLocalDatasetPerNode(H, T);
 4  |    forall the x̄ ∈ DS do
 5  |    |    node ← H;
 6  |    |    Ŷ ← {node.label};
 7  |    |    while ¬node.isLeaf do
 8  |    |    |    children ← node.children;
 9  |    |    |    d ← {};
10  |    |    |    for i ← 1 to |children| do
11  |    |    |    |    local_dataset ← node[children[i].label];
12  |    |    |    |    d ← {d, averageDistance(x̄, local_dataset, k)};
13  |    |    |    end
14  |    |    |    dists ← d/max(d);
15  |    |    |    dists ← dists − min(dists);
16  |    |    |    if |dists <= δ| > 1 then
17  |    |    |    |    break;
18  |    |    |    end
19  |    |    |    predicted_node ← children[getIndex(d == min(d))];
20  |    |    |    Ŷ ← {Ŷ, predicted_node.label};
21  |    |    |    node ← predicted_node;
22  |    |    end
23  |    |    Y ← getCorrectLabelSet(x̄);
24  |    |    H ← includeExampleLabeled(H, {x̄, Y}, η);
25  |    end
26  end
```

In the 2nd line of Algorithm 1, we build a class hierarchy $\mathcal{H}$ from the initial labeled training set $\mathcal{T}$. In the 3rd line, each node of the class hierarchy, except the root node, is associated with a one-class local dataset. We generate these one-class local datasets using the inclusive heuristic admitting only positive examples [2]. In the 7th line, we employ the top-down prediction strategy, so that to classify an example $\vec{x}$ belonging to stream $\mathcal{DS}$ the hierarchical structure $\mathcal{H}$ is traversed from the root node to an internal or leaf node depending on the value of δ ($\delta \in [0,1]$). We expanded a node when the average distance of the k examples from the local dataset nearest to $\vec{x}$ is the lowest compared to the others in the same branch and level. In the 16th line, if δ is greater than zero, we apply the NMLNP. In practical terms, we interrupt the traverse in the class hierarchy when the differences between the average distances calculated for each node of the same branch and level are less than or equal to δ. In the 24th line, we associated the current $\vec{x}$ to its set of correct labels and inserted it into the training dataset. Here, we use a fixed-size memory buffer that holds only the most recent η examples of each class.

4   Experimental Setup

We conducted our experiments using three stream hierarchical datasets related to entomology, ichthyology, and audio processing. These datasets are available online at https://goo.gl/4pxeWx and are an original contribution of this paper.

We partitioned each dataset into two sets: (i) initial training set, which covers five labeled examples per class. The class is a set of labels that represents a complete path – from the root to a leaf node – in the label hierarchy; and (ii) test set, composed of the remaining unlabeled examples of the dataset.

We apply our method considering Euclidean distance, $k = 3$, $\delta = 0$, and $\eta = 1000$. The parameter δ set to zero indicates a mandatory leaf-node prediction.

We face the proposed algorithm with an online 3NN flat classifier with Euclidean distance and $\eta = 1000$, where we consider the online flat model as a baseline method. To make a fair comparison, we retrieve from the hierarchical structure all the ancestor labels of each class predicted by the flat classifier (complete path). Thus, we can directly compare a label path predicted by the hierarchical algorithm with a label path predicted by the flat method.

We analyzed the results according to the following performance measures [9]: hierarchical Precision (hP), hierarchical Recall (hR), and hierarchical F-measure (hF). They are defined as follows:

$$\text{hP} = \frac{\sum_i |Y_i \cap \hat{Y}_i|}{\sum_i |\hat{Y}_i|} \quad (1) \quad \text{hR} = \frac{\sum_i |Y_i \cap \hat{Y}_i|}{\sum_i |Y_i|} \quad (2) \quad \text{hF} = \frac{(\beta^2 + 1) \times \text{hP} \times \text{hR}}{\beta^2 \times \text{hP} + \text{hR}} \quad (3)$$

In Eqs. 1 and 2, $\hat{Y}_i$ refers to the set of labels predicted for a test example i and Y_i denotes the set of true classes of this example. During the computation of hP and hR, we need to disregard the root node of the label hierarchy, since by definition it is common to all examples.

In Eq. 3, β belongs to $[0, \infty)$ and corresponds to the importance assigned to the hP and hR values. When $\beta = 1$, the two measures have the same weight in the calculation of the final average. With $\beta = 2$, hR receives double the weight given to hP, whereas for $\beta = 1/2$ the inverse situation occurs, $i.e$, hP receives twice the weight than hR. We use $\beta = 1$.

5   Experimental Results

In this section, we present and discuss the experimental results for each of the three datasets evaluated. Note that the sequence of our discussion accompanies the classification task complexity, which is proportional to the number of classes.

5.1   Online Hierarchical Classification of Insect Species

The first problem evaluated comprises an entomology and public health application of insect species recognition by optical sensors [14]. This task is the core of intelligent traps developed to catch only target species such as disease vectors. The hierarchical dataset built for this problem has 21,722 examples distributed in 14 different classes. To perform the classification, we extracted 33 features from the signals generated by the sensor such as the energy sum of frequency peaks and harmonic positions. Figure 2 illustrates the class hierarchy of this dataset.

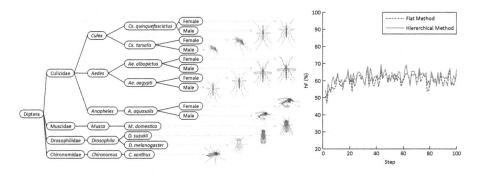

Fig. 2. Hierarchy of insects

Fig. 3. hF over time for the insects dataset

Figure 3 shows, in terms of hF, the results achieved by the online classification algorithms using the insect species dataset. In this figure, the hierarchical classifier reached a hF of 61.91% while the baseline method obtained a hF of 59.95%. Our algorithm had an average gain of 1.96% on the flat classifier. It is important to note that this difference is small because we "force" our classifier to return the complete paths for the sake of a fair comparison. However, our approach can return less specific outputs in situations with high uncertainty. We deem that a correct generic response is more useful than an incorrect specific one.

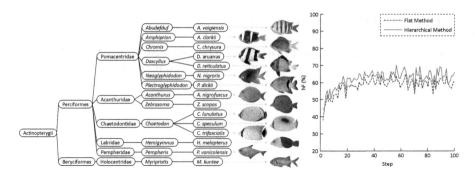

Fig. 4. Hierarchy of fish

Fig. 5. hF over time for the fish dataset

5.2 Online Hierarchical Classification of Fish Species

Our second hierarchical classification problem contemplates fish species automatic identification based on image analysis [7]. In this problem, we extracted 15 features: 14 based on Haralick descriptors [6] and one involving fractal dimension [10]. Our dataset includes 22,444 examples and 15 classes (Fig. 4).

Figure 5 exhibits the hF results obtained from the online methods employing the fish species dataset. Precisely, the hierarchical model reached a hF of 62.30% while the baseline algorithm achieved a hF of 58.35%. In general, our classifier had a gain of 3.94% over the flat setting.

5.3 Online Hierarchical Classification of Musical Instruments

The last real-world problem evaluated is related to the musical instrument classification based on the analysis of audio signals. We extracted from the signals, 30 features from the Mel Frequency Cepstral Coefficients [11]. The generated dataset has 9,419 examples distributed into 31 classes (Fig. 6).

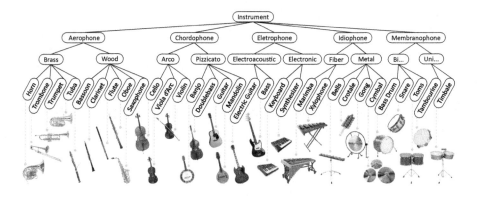

Fig. 6. Hierarchy of musical instruments

Figure 7 displays, in terms of hF, the results achieved from the online classification methods using the musical instruments dataset. In this figure, the hierarchical classifier reached a hF of 84.77% while the baseline model obtained a hF of 82.22%. Our algorithm had an average gain of 2.55% on the flat classifier.

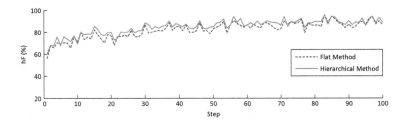

Fig. 7. hF over time for the musical instruments dataset

6   Conclusion and Future Work Prospects

In this paper, we presented an incremental method based on kNN for hierarchical classification of data streams. The algorithm expresses the class hierarchy as a tree and applies a top-down strategy to perform single path predictions. It also adopts a fixed-size memory buffer to store the most recent data and to adapt to concept drift.

To the best of our knowledge, our method is the first that benefits from local information to label events of a stream. We get that local information by decomposing the feature space of the problem into subproblems with a smaller number of classes. Thus, the process gains simplicity, flexibility, and robustness.

We have compared our method with an online kNN flat classifier. The proposed method outperformed the baseline algorithm in all datasets evaluated. This result shows that we can use the information intrinsic to the class hierarchy structure to improve the classification task. In future work, we intend to explore the use of drift detectors [5] and scenarios with delayed labels [15].

References

1. Caruana, R., Karampatziakis, N., Yessenalina, A.: An empirical evaluation of supervised learning in high dimensions. In: ICML, pp. 96–103 (2008)
2. Eisner, R., Poulin, B., Szafron, D., Lu, P., Greiner, R.: Improving protein function prediction using the hierarchical structure of the gene ontology. In: CIBCB, pp. 1–10 (2005)
3. Fagni, T., Sebastiani, F.: On the selection of negative examples for hierarchical text categorization. In: Language Technology Conference, pp. 24–28 (2007)

4. Fix, E., Hodges, J.L.: Discriminatory analysis, nonparametric discrimination, consistency properties. Technical report 4, Project 21–49-004, US Air Force School of Aerospace Medicine (1951)
5. Gonçalves Jr., P.M., Santos, S.G.T.C., Barros, R.S.M., Vieira, D.C.L.: A comparative study on concept drift detectors. Expert Syst. Appl. **41**(18), 8144–8156 (2014)
6. Haralick, R.M., Shanmugam, K., Dinstein, I.: Textural features for image classification. IEEE SMC **3**(6), 610–621 (1973)
7. Joly, A., et al.: LifeCLEF 2016: multimedia life species identification challenges. In: Fuhr, N., et al. (eds.) CLEF 2016. LNCS, vol. 9822, pp. 286–310. Springer, Cham (2016). https://doi.org/10.1007/978-3-319-44564-9_26
8. Kelly, M.G., Hand, D.J., Adams, N.M.: The impact of changing populations on classifier performance. In: SIGKDD, pp. 367–371 (1999)
9. Kiritchenko, S., Matwin, S., Famili, A.F.: Functional annotation of genes using hierarchical text categorization. In: ACL-ISMB Workshop (2005)
10. Lee, H.D., et al.: Dermoscopic assisted diagnosis in melanoma: reviewing results, optimizing methodologies and quantifying empirical guidelines. In: KBS (2018)
11. Logan, B.: Mel frequency cepstral coefficients for music modeling. ISMIR **270**, 1–11 (2000)
12. Nguyen, H.L., Woon, Y.K., Ng, W.K.: A survey on data stream clustering and classification. KAIS **45**(3), 535–569 (2015)
13. Silla, C.N., Freitas, A.A.: A survey of hierarchical classification across different application domains. DMKD **22**(1), 31–72 (2011)
14. Souza, V.M.A., Silva, D.F., Batista, G.E.A.P.A.: Classification of data streams applied to insect recognition: initial results. In: BRACIS, pp. 76–81 (2013)
15. Souza, V.M.A., Silva, D.F., Gama, J., Batista, G.E.A.P.A.: Data stream classification guided by clustering on nonstationary environments and extreme verification latency. In: SDM, pp. 873–881 (2015)
16. Widmer, G., Kubat, M.: Learning in the presence of concept drift and hidden contexts. Mach. Learn. **23**(1), 69–101 (1996)

Computer Vision

Non-parametric Contextual Relationship Learning for Semantic Video Object Segmentation

Tinghuai Wang[1] and Huiling Wang[2(✉)]

[1] Nokia Technologies, Tampere, Finland
tinghuai.wang@nokia.com
[2] Laboratory of Signal Processing, Tampere University of Technology,
Tampere, Finland
huiling.wang@tut.fi

Abstract. We propose a novel approach for modeling semantic contextual relationships in videos. This graph-based model enables the learning and propagation of higher-level spatial-temporal contexts to facilitate the semantic labeling of local regions. We introduce an exemplar-based nonparametric view of contextual cues, where the inherent relationships implied by object hypotheses are encoded on a similarity graph of regions. Contextual relationships learning and propagation are performed to estimate the pairwise contexts between all pairs of unlabeled local regions. Our algorithm integrates the learned contexts into a Conditional Random Field (CRF) in the form of pairwise potentials and infers the per-region semantic labels. We evaluate our approach on the challenging YouTube-Objects dataset which shows that the proposed contextual relationship model outperforms the state-of-the-art methods.

1 Introduction

Semantic object segmentation in videos is a challenging task which enables a wide range of higher-level applications, such as robotic vision, object tracking, video retrieval and scene understanding. Tremendous progress has been witnessed lately toward this problem via integrating higher-level semantic information and contextual cues [2,5,8,13,15,16,18,23]. However, akin to classical figure-ground video segmentation, fast motion, appearance variations, pose change, and occlusions pose significant challenges to delineate semantic objects from video sequence. Difficulty in resolving the inherent semantic ambiguities further complicates the problem.

Recently, segmentation by detection and tracking approaches have been proposed to address this challenging problem. Early work in this direction trained classifiers to incorporate scene topology and semantics into pixel-level object detection and localization [15]. Later, both object detector and tracker were employed to either impose spatio-temporal coherence [2,23] or learn an appearance model [16] for encoding the appearance variation of semantic objects.

© Springer Nature Switzerland AG 2019
R. Vera-Rodriguez et al. (Eds.): CIARP 2018, LNCS 11401, pp. 325–333, 2019.
https://doi.org/10.1007/978-3-030-13469-3_38

Lately, hierarchical graphical model has also been proposed to integrate longer-range object reasoning with superpixel labeling [18]. Despite of significant advances that have been made by the above methods, global contextual relationships between semantic video objects remain under-explored. Yet, contextual relationships are ubiquitous and provide important cues for scene understanding related tasks.

The importance of exploiting pairwise relationships between objects has been highlighted in semantic segmentation [6] and object detection [4] tasks, where the relationship is formulated in terms of co-occurrence of higher-level statistics of object class. These methods tend to favor frequently appeared objects in the training data to enforce rigid semantic label agreement. Furthermore, these conventional context models are sensitive to the number of pixels or regions that objects occupy, with one consequence being that the small objects are more likely to be omitted.

In this work, we propose a novel graphical model to thoroughly exploit contextual relationships among semantic video objects without relying on training data. Such a way of modeling spatio-temporal object contextual relationships has not been well studied. We present a novel nonparametric approach to capture the intra- and inter- category contextual relationships by considering the content of an input video. This nonparametric context model is comprised of a set of spatial-temporal context exemplars via performing higher-level video analysis, *i.e.* object detection and tracking. These context exemplars provide a novel interpretation of contextual relationships in a link view which formulates the problem of learning contextual relationships as the label propagation problem on a similarity graph. This similarity graph naturally reflects the intrinsic and extrinsic relationship between semantic objects in the spatial-temporal domain. Due to the sparsity of this similarity graph, the learning process can be very efficient.

The key contributions of this work are as follows. Firstly, we establishes a novel link prediction view of semantic contexts. In this view, the problem of learning semantic relationships is formulated as graph-based label propagation problem. Secondly, our approach is exemplar-based nonparametric model which therefore does not require additional training data to build an explicit context model. Hence, it is favorable for video semantic object segmentation, a domain where annotated data are scarce. The paper is organized as follows. We introduce the novel link prediction view of contexts in Sect. 2.3, utilizing the semantic contextual information from object trajectory hypotheses in Sect. 2.1. Link prediction algorithm is described in Sect. 2.4 and the final semantic labeling is described in Sect. 2.5.

2   The Approach

In this section, we describe our proposed exemplar-based nonparametric model and how the learned contextual relationships are integrated into semantic labeling in a principled manner.

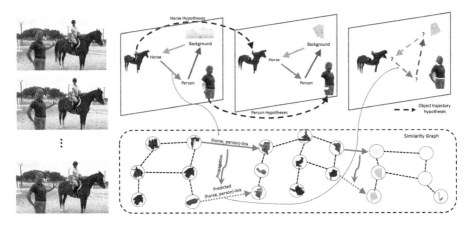

Fig. 1. Illustration of the proposed approach. Two trajectory hypotheses are extracted to provide initial annotations for 'horse' and 'person' classes, which form the context exemplars such as (horse, person)-link between the corresponding vertices on the similarity graph. Our method propagates such contextual relationship on the graph and predicts the probability of (horse, person)-link between unlabeled vertices based on similarity.

2.1 Trajectory Hypotheses

For a given video sequence with T frames, we generate a set of object trajectory hypotheses with respect to semantic categories via object detection and temporal association which characterize the long-range spatio-temporal evolution of various object features and are commonly tied to higher-level contexts such as object interactions and behaviours [7,14,17–22].

Specifically, we firstly extract generic object proposals by applying MCG [1] in each frame. Object detection is performed on this pool of object proposals by using faster R-CNN [11], which is trained on 20 PASCAL VOC classes. A set of object hypotheses $\mathbb{D}$ are formed by keeping proposals with detection confidence exceeding a threshold (0.5).

Object trajectory hypotheses $\mathbb{T}$ w.r.t. each semantic class are generated by temporally associating a cohort of object hypotheses $\mathbb{D}$ by imposing frame-to-frame spatio-temporal consistency, similar to [18]. Specifically, we utilize object tracker [9] to track object hypotheses over time to both ends of the video sequence as follows.

- Initialize an empty trajectory hypothesis $T_i \in \mathbb{T}$
- Rank remaining object hypotheses in $\mathbb{D}$ based on detection confidence
- Initialize tracker with the bounding box of the highest ranked object hypothesis and perform tracking to both directions simultaneously
- Select object hypothesis in the new frame which have a sufficient overlap, *i.e.* Intersection-over-Union (IoU) higher than a threshold (0.5), with the tracker box which is added to T_i and consequently removed from $\mathbb{D}$.

The above steps are iteratively performed until no new trajectory hypothesis containing three or more object instances can be generated from $\mathbb{D}$. Figure 1 shows exemplars of object trajectory hypotheses extracted from a video sequence. Regions [3] are extracted from each frame as the atomic data units. Let $\mathcal{R}_D$ be the set of regions constituting video object hypotheses, and $\mathcal{R}_U$ be the unlabeled regions.

2.2   Graph Construction

We firstly initialize a k-nearest neighbor similarity graph $\mathcal{G} = (\mathcal{V}, \mathcal{E})$ between all N regions from $\mathcal{R}_D \cup \mathcal{R}_U$. Each vertex $v_i \in \mathcal{V}$ of the graph is described by the L2-normalized VGG-16 Net [12] fc6 features f_i of the corresponding region. Each weight $w_{i,j} \in \mathbf{W}$ of edge $e_{i,j} \in \mathcal{E}$ is defined as the inner-product between the feature vectors of neighboring vertices, i.e., $w_{i,j} = <f_i, f_j>$.

2.3   Context Modeling

Frames containing object hypotheses are considered as annotated data to generate context exemplars, as object trajectory hypotheses normally capture essential parts of video objects. Let $\mathcal{F}$ be this set of annotated frames and $\hat{\mathcal{F}}$ be all the other frames in current video sequence. A context exemplar consists of a pair of regions and the corresponding semantic labels. The intuition behind this setting is that one region with its semantic label supports the paired region to be labeled with its corresponding semantic label. This exemplar is able to encode the global interaction and co-occurrence of semantic objects beyond local spatial adjacencies. The goal is to impose the consistency between each pair of regions from un-annotated frames and the extracted context exemplars.

Formally, given a set of semantic labels $\mathcal{C} = \{c_0, c_1, \ldots, c_{L-1}\}$ comprising all classes in the annotated data, we represent the context exemplars for each class pair (c_m, c_n) as

$$\mathbf{A}^{m,n} = \{(v_i, v_j) : C(v_i) = c_m, C(v_j) = c_n, v_i, v_j \in \mathcal{F}\}$$

where $v_i, v_j \in \mathcal{F}$ stands for two regions v_i and v_j from the annotated frame set $\mathcal{F}$ and $C(v_i)$ represents the semantic label of region v_i. Hence, all object class pairs as well as contextual relationships in the annotated frames are represented as $\mathcal{A} = \{\mathbf{A}^{0,0}, \mathbf{A}^{0,1}, \ldots, \mathbf{A}^{L-1,L-1}\}$.

We transform the above context exemplar to a context link view of contextual knowledge, where context exemplar (v_i, v_j) can be referred to as a (c_m, c_n)-type link between two vertices on the similarity graph. Let $\mathcal{P}$ denote the set of $N \times N$ matrices, where a matrix $\mathbf{P}^{m,n} \in \mathcal{P}$ is associated with all (c_m, c_n) class pair links. Each entry $[\mathbf{P}^{m,n}]_{i,j} \in \mathbf{P}^{m,n}$ indicates the confidence of (c_m, c_n)-link between two regions v_i and v_j. The confidence ranging between 0 and 1 corresponds to the probability of the existence of a link, where 1 stands for high confidence of the existence of a link and 0 indicates the absence of a link. The (c_m, c_n)-links

Algorithm 1. Context learning algorithm

1: **procedure** LINK PREDICTION
2:     $S(v_i, c_i, v_j, c_j) \leftarrow \varnothing$
3:     Graph $\mathcal{G} \leftarrow$ all *regions of video*
4:     Affinity matrix $\mathbf{W} \leftarrow$ *k-nearest neighbors*
5:     $d_i = \sum_{j=1}^{N} w_{ij}$
6:     $\mathbf{D} \leftarrow \text{diag}([d_1, \ldots, d_N])$
7:     $\mathbf{L} \leftarrow \mathbf{D}^{-\frac{1}{2}} \mathbf{W} \mathbf{D}^{-\frac{1}{2}}$
8:     $\mathcal{A} \leftarrow$ *context exemplars*
9:     $\mathcal{O} \leftarrow$ *context links* $\in \mathcal{A}$
10:    **for** each *class pair* (c_m, c_n) **do**
11:        $\mathbf{P}_r(1) \leftarrow \mathbf{0}$, $\mathbf{P}_c(1) \leftarrow \mathbf{0}$
12:        *Convergence* $\leftarrow$ **false**
13:        **while** *Convergence* is **false do**   ▷ row-wise
14:            $\mathbf{P}_r(t+1) \leftarrow \mu \mathbf{L} \mathbf{P}_r(t) + (1-\mu) \mathbf{O}^{m,n}$
15:        *Convergence* $\leftarrow$ **false**
16:        **while** *Convergence* is **false do**   ▷ column-wise
17:            $\mathbf{P}_c(t+1) \leftarrow \mu \mathbf{L} \mathbf{P}_c(t) + (1-\mu) \hat{\mathbf{P}}_r$
18:        $S(v_i, c_i = c_m, v_j, c_j = c_n) \leftarrow [\hat{\mathbf{P}}_c]_{ij}$

which have been observed within the annotated frames can be represented by another set of matrices $\mathbf{O}^{m,n} \in \mathcal{P}$ such that

$$[\mathbf{O}^{m,n}]_{i,j} = \begin{cases} 1 \text{ if} & (v_i, v_j) \in \mathbf{A}^{m,n} \\ 0 \text{ otherwise} \end{cases} \tag{1}$$

All the observed context link can be denoted as $\mathcal{O} = \{\mathbf{O}^{0,0}, \mathbf{O}^{0,1}, \ldots, \mathbf{O}^{L-1,L-1}\}$.

2.4   Context Prediction

Given the above context link view of contextual knowledge, we formulate the context prediction problem as a task of link prediction problem which determines how probable a certain link exists in a graph. To this end, we predict (c_m, c_n)-links among the pairs of vertices from $\mathcal{R}_U$ based on $\mathbf{O}^{m,n}$ consistent to the intrinsic structure of the similarity graph. Specifically, we propagate (c_m, c_n)-links in $\mathbf{O}^{m,n}$ to estimate the strength of the pairs of vertices from $\mathcal{R}_U$. We drop the m, n suffix for clarity.

Directly solving the link prediction problem is impractical for video segmentation since the complexity is as high as $O(N^4)$. Hence we propose to decompose the link propagation problem into two separate label propagation processes. As described in Algorithm 1, row-wise link predication (step 13–14) is firstly performed, followed by column-wise link prediction (step 16–17). More specifically, the j-th row $\mathbf{O}^{j,\cdot}$, *i.e.* the context exemplars associated with v_j, serves as an initial configuration of a label propagation problem [24] with respect to vertex v_j. Each row is handled separately as a binary label propagation which converges to $\hat{\mathbf{P}}_r$. It is observed that the label propagation does not apply to the rows of

O corresponding to $\mathcal{R}_U$, and thus we only perform row-wise link propagation in rows corresponding to annotated regions, which is much less than N. For the column-wise propagation, the i-th converged row $[\hat{\mathbf{P}}_r]_i$ is used to initialize the configuration. After convergence of the column-wise propagation, the probability of (c_m, c_n)-link between two vertices of $\mathcal{R}_U$ is obtained.

2.5   Inference

We formulate semantic video object segmentation as a region labeling problem, where the learned context link scores $S(v_i, c_i, v_j, c_j)$ can be incorporated while assigning labels to the set of regions $\mathcal{R}_D \cup \mathcal{R}_U$. We adopt the fully connected CRF that is proved to be effective in encoding model contextual relationships between object classes.

Consider a random field $\mathbf{x}$ defined over a set of variables $\{x_0, \ldots, x_{N-1}\}$, and the domain of each variable is a set of class labels $\mathcal{C} = \{c_0, c_1, \ldots, c_{L-1}\}$. The corresponding Gibbs energy is

$$E(\mathbf{x}) = \sum_i \psi(x_i) + \sum_{i,j} \phi(x_i, x_j). \tag{2}$$

The unary potential $\psi(x_i)$ is defined as the negative logarithm of the likelihood of assigning v_i with label x_i. To obtain $\psi(x_i)$, we learn a SVM model based on hierarchical CNN features [9] by sampling from the annotated frames.

The pairwise potential $\phi(x_i, x_j)$ encodes the contextual relationships between the regions learned via link prediction, which is defined as

$$\phi(x_i, x_j) = \exp(-\frac{S(v_i, c_i, v_j, c_j)^2}{2\beta}) \tag{3}$$

where $\beta = < S(v_i, c_i, v_j, c_j)^2 >$ is the adaptive weight and $< \cdot >$ indicates the expectation.

We adopt a combined QPBO and α-expansion inference (a.k.a fusion moves) [?] to optimize (2) and the resulting label assignment gives the semantic object segmentation of the video sequence.

3   Experiments

We evaluate our proposed approach on YouTube-Objects [10], which is the *de facto* benchmark for assessing semantic video object segmentation algorithms. The class labels of these two densely labeled datasets belong to the 20 classes of PASCAL VOC 2012. The YouTube-Objects dataset consists of videos from 10 classes with pixel-level ground truth for totally more than $20,000$ frames. These videos are very challenging and completely unconstrained, with objects of similar colour to the background, fast motion, non-rigid deformations, and fast camera motion. We compare our approach with six state-of-the-art semantic video object segmentation methods which have been reported on this dataset,

Table 1. Intersection-over-union overlap on YouTube-Objects Dataset

	Aeroplane	Bird	Boat	Car	Cat	Cow	Dog	Horse	Mbike	Train	Avg.
ODW	0.517	0.175	0.344	0.347	0.223	0.179	0.135	0.267	0.412	0.250	0.285
DSA	0.178	0.198	0.225	0.383	0.236	0.268	0.237	0.140	0.125	0.404	0.239
SOD	0.758	0.608	0.437	0.711	0.465	0.546	0.555	0.549	0.424	0.358	0.541
SDA	0.760	0.747	0.588	0.659	0.557	0.675	0.574	0.575	0.569	0.430	0.613
DTS	0.744	0.721	0.585	0.600	0.457	0.612	0.552	0.566	0.421	0.367	0.562
CGG	0.757	0.766	0.666	0.758	0.624	0.720	0.671	0.526	0.547	0.392	0.643
Ours	**0.785**	**0.772**	**0.725**	**0.766**	**0.672**	**0.731**	**0.672**	**0.607**	**0.614**	**0.407**	**0.675**

Fig. 2. Qualitative results of our algorithm on YouTube-Objects Dataset.

i.e. [10] (ODW), [13] (DSA), [23] (SOD), [16] (SDA), [2] (DTS) and [18] (CGG). Standard average IoU is used to measure the segmentation accuracy, $IoU = \frac{S \cap G}{S \cup G}$, where S is the segmentation result and G stands for the ground-truth mask.

We summarize the comparisons of our algorithm with other approaches in Table 1. Table 1 demonstrates the superior performance of our proposed algorithm which surpasses the competing methods in all classes, with a significant increase of segmentation accuracy, *i.e.* 3.2% in average over the best competing method CGG. We attribute this improvement to the capability of learning and propagating higher-level spatial-temporal contextual relationships of video objects, as opposed to imposing contextual information in local labeling (CGG) or modeling local appearance (SDA). One common limitation of these methods is that they are error-prone in separating interacting objects exhibiting similar appearance or motion, which is intractable unless the inherent contextual relationship is explored.

Our algorithm outperforms another two methods which also utilize object detection, *i.e.* DTS and SOD, with large margins of 11.3% and 13.4%. DTS shares some similarity with our approach in that it also uses faster R-CNN for the initial object detection which makes it a comparable baseline to demonstrate the effectiveness of our algorithm. By exploiting contextual relationships in a global manner, our algorithm is able to account for object evolutions in the video data to resolve both appearance and motion ambiguities. SOD performs the worst among the three as it only conducts temporal association of detected object segments without explicitly modeling either the objects or contexts. Some qualitative results of the proposed algorithm on YouTube-Objects dataset are shown in Fig. 2.

4   Conclusion

We have proposed a novel approach to modeling the semantic contextual relationships for tackling the challenging video object segmentation problem. The proposed model comprises an exemplar-based nonparametric view of contextual cues, which is formulated as link prediction problem solved by label propagation on a similarity graph of regions. The derived contextual relationships are utilized to estimate the pairwise contexts between all pairs of unlabeled local regions. The experiments demonstrated that modeling the semantic contextual relationships effectively improved segmentation robustness and accuracy which significantly advanced the state-of-the-art on challenging benchmark.

References

1. Arbeláez, P., Pont-Tuset, J., Barron, J.T., Marques, F., Malik, J.: Multiscale combinatorial grouping. In: CVPR, pp. 328–335 (2014)
2. Drayer, B., Brox, T.: Object detection, tracking, and motion segmentation for object-level video segmentation. arXiv preprint arXiv:1608.03066 (2016)
3. Felzenszwalb, P.F., Huttenlocher, D.P.: Efficient graph-based image segmentation. Int. J. Comput. Vis. **59**(2), 167–181 (2004)
4. Gidaris, S., Komodakis, N.: Object detection via a multi-region and semantic segmentation-aware CNN model. In: ICCV, pp. 1134–1142 (2015)
5. Hartmann, G., et al.: Weakly supervised learning of object segmentations from web-scale video. In: Fusiello, A., Murino, V., Cucchiara, R. (eds.) ECCV 2012. LNCS, vol. 7583, pp. 198–208. Springer, Heidelberg (2012). https://doi.org/10.1007/978-3-642-33863-2_20
6. Lin, G., Shen, C., van den Hengel, A., Reid, I.: Efficient piecewise training of deep structured models for semantic segmentation. In: CVPR, pp. 3194–3203 (2016)
7. Liu, B., He, X.: Multiclass semantic video segmentation with object-level active inference. In: CVPR, pp. 4286–4294 (2015)
8. Liu, X., Tao, D., Song, M., Ruan, Y., Chen, C., Bu, J.: Weakly supervised multiclass video segmentation. In: CVPR, pp. 57–64 (2014)
9. Ma, C., Huang, J.B., Yang, X., Yang, M.H.: Hierarchical convolutional features for visual tracking. In: ICCV, pp. 3074–3082 (2015)
10. Prest, A., Leistner, C., Civera, J., Schmid, C., Ferrari, V.: Learning object class detectors from weakly annotated video. In: CVPR, pp. 3282–3289 (2012)
11. Ren, S., He, K., Girshick, R., Sun, J.: Faster R-CNN: towards real-time object detection with region proposal networks. In: NIPS, pp. 91–99 (2015)
12. Simonyan, K., Zisserman, A.: Very deep convolutional networks for large-scale image recognition. arXiv preprint arXiv:1409.1556 (2014)
13. Tang, K.D., Sukthankar, R., Yagnik, J., Li, F.: Discriminative segment annotation in weakly labeled video. In: CVPR, pp. 2483–2490 (2013)
14. Tang, P., Wang, C., Wang, X., Liu, W., Zeng, W., Wang, J.: Object detection in videos by short and long range object linking. arXiv preprint arXiv:1801.09823 (2018)
15. Taylor, B., Ayvaci, A., Ravichandran, A., Soatto, S.: Semantic video segmentation from occlusion relations within a convex optimization framework. In: Heyden, A., Kahl, F., Olsson, C., Oskarsson, M., Tai, X.-C. (eds.) EMMCVPR 2013. LNCS, vol. 8081, pp. 195–208. Springer, Heidelberg (2013). https://doi.org/10.1007/978-3-642-40395-8_15

16. Wang, H., Raiko, T., Lensu, L., Wang, T., Karhunen, J.: Semi-supervised domain adaptation for weakly labeled semantic video object segmentation. In: Lai, S.-H., Lepetit, V., Nishino, K., Sato, Y. (eds.) ACCV 2016. LNCS, vol. 10111, pp. 163–179. Springer, Cham (2017). https://doi.org/10.1007/978-3-319-54181-5_11

17. Wang, H., Wang, T.: Primary object discovery and segmentation in videos via graph-based transductive inference. Comput. Vis. Image Underst. **143**(2), 159–172 (2016)

18. Wang, H., Wang, T., Chen, K., Kämäräinen, J.K.: Cross-granularity graph inference for semantic video object segmentation. In: IJCAI, pp. 4544–4550 (2017)

19. Wang, T.: Submodular video object proposal selection for semantic object segmentation. In: ICIP (2017)

20. Wang, T., Collomosse, J.P.: Probabilistic motion diffusion of labeling priors for coherent video segmentation. IEEE Trans. Multimed. **14**(2), 389–400 (2012)

21. Wang, T., Han, B., Collomosse, J.P.: TouchCut: fast image and video segmentation using single-touch interaction. Comput. Vis. Image Underst. **120**, 14–30 (2014)

22. Wang, T., Wang, H.: Graph transduction learning of object proposals for video object segmentation. In: Cremers, D., Reid, I., Saito, H., Yang, M.-H. (eds.) ACCV 2014. LNCS, vol. 9006, pp. 553–568. Springer, Cham (2015). https://doi.org/10.1007/978-3-319-16817-3_36

23. Zhang, Y., Chen, X., Li, J., Wang, C., Xia, C.: Semantic object segmentation via detection in weakly labeled video. In: CVPR, pp. 3641–3649 (2015)

24. Zhou, D., Bousquet, O., Lal, T.N., Weston, J., Sch, B.: Learning with local and global consistency. In: NIPS, pp. 321–328 (2004)

Superpixel Segmentation by Object-Based Iterative Spanning Forest

Felipe Belém[1(✉)], Silvio Jamil F. Guimarães[2], and Alexandre Xavier Falcão[1]

[1] University of Campinas, Campinas, SP 13083-852, Brazil
`felipedkstro@hotmail.com, afalcao@ic.unicamp.br`
[2] Computer Science Department, Pontifical Catholic University of Minas Gerais,
Belo Horizonte, MG 31980-110, Brazil
`sjamil@pucminas.br`

Abstract. Superpixel segmentation methods aim at representing image objects by the union of connected regions (superpixels). Such aim can be better approximated with a higher number of superpixels per object, which often leads to an unnecessary over-segmentation due to the absence of prior object information. In this work, we extend the *Iterative Spanning Forest* (ISF) framework to include object information and present a superpixel segmentation method based on object saliency detection. As ISF, the new framework, named *Object-based ISF* (OISF), relies on multiple executions of the *Image Foresting Transform* (IFT) algorithm for improved seed sets, such that each seed defines one connected superpixel as a spanning tree rooted at that seed. We describe an IFT-based method for object saliency detection and show that the corresponding saliency maps can improve seed estimation and connectivity function, increasing the superpixel resolution inside a given object. Experimental results on two medical image datasets demonstrate that the proposed OISF-based method outperforms the state-of-the-art in boundary adherence with higher number of superpixels inside the object.

Keywords: Superpixels · Object saliency map ·
Image Foresting Transform

1 Introduction

Image segmentation into connected regions (superpixels) has been actively investigated in order to represent image objects by the union of their superpixels [1,6,9,11,12]—a criterion that often leads to unnecessary over-segmentation of the image. For instance, content/structure-sensitive approaches may reduce the superpixel size (increase over-segmentation) in heterogeneous regions of the image, but the absence of object information makes them sensitive to the heterogeneity of the background [6,12]. Moreover, these methods cannot usually

The authors thank CNPq (302970/2014-2, 421521/2016-3, 307062/2016-3, 131000/2018-7), FAPEMIG/PPM (00006-16), and FAPESP (2014/12236-1).

© Springer Nature Switzerland AG 2019
R. Vera-Rodriguez et al. (Eds.): CIARP 2018, LNCS 11401, pp. 334–341, 2019.
https://doi.org/10.1007/978-3-030-13469-3_39

guarantee a desired number of superpixels. In many applications, however, there is an object of interest and, for a fixed number of superpixels, it should be expected higher superpixel resolution inside that object than elsewhere, except for possible parts of the background with similar image properties. At the same time, for a reduced number of superpixels, the boundaries of the object should be preserved as much as possible (Fig. 1).

In this work, we extend a superpixel segmentation framework, named *Iterative Spanning Forest* (ISF) [11], to incorporate object information from an object saliency map. ISF-based methods use multiple executions of the *Image Foresting Transform* (IFT) algorithm [4] for improved seed sets, such that each seed defines one spanning tree as a connected superpixel. An ISF-based method involves the choice of four components: (i) a seed sampling strategy to obtain the first segmentation; (ii) an adjacency relation that defines the image graph in 2D or 3D (for superpixel- or supervoxel-based representation); (iii) a connectivity function that estimates how strongly connected are the pixels to the seed set; and (iv) a seed recomputation procedure for the subsequent execution of the IFT algorithm.

We first use the IFT framework to design a method for object saliency detection. For a given image and a set of training pixels (interior and exterior scribbles) on a given object, we train a pixel classifier to estimate an *object saliency map* from any new image containing that object. We then propose a method that exploits the saliency map to make seed sampling and connectivity function more specific for that object. The new framework is termed *Object-based* ISF (OISF) and the proposed OISF-based method is shown to increase boundary adherence with more superpixels inside the object than their ISF-based counterparts and state-of-the-art methods.

The next sections present the IFT framework and related definitions (Sect. 2), its applications to object saliency detection and superpixel segmentation (Sects. 3 and 4), the proposed OISF framework and its evaluation (Sects. 5 and 6), conclusion and future work (Sect. 7).

2   Image Foresting Transform

An image is a pair $(\mathcal{I}, I)$ such that $I(t)$ assigns a set of local image features (e.g., color) to every element $t \in \mathcal{I}$. We will address only 2D images, then those elements are pixels. For a given *adjacency relation* $\mathcal{A} \subset \mathcal{I} \times \mathcal{I}$ and set $\mathcal{N} \subseteq \mathcal{I}$, one can interpret $(\mathcal{N}, \mathcal{A}, I)$ as an image graph G weighted on the nodes. Let Π_G be the set of paths in the graph, a path $\pi_t \in \Pi_G$ be a sequence $\langle t_1, t_2, \ldots, t_n = t \rangle$ of nodes with terminus t, such that $(t_i, t_{i+1}) \in \mathcal{A}$, $i = 1, 2, \ldots, n - 1$ (being trivial when $\pi_t = \langle t \rangle$), and f be a *connectivity function* that assigns a value (e.g., a cost) to any path in Π_G. A path π_t is optimum when $f(\pi_t) \leq f(\tau_t)$ for any other path $\tau_t \in \Pi_G$ irrespective to its starting node. For the sufficient conditions in [2], Dijkstra's algorithm can solve the minimization problem $C(t) = \min_{\forall \pi_t \in \Pi_G} \{ f(\pi_t) \}$ by computing an *optimum-path forest* in the graph—i.e., a predecessor map P that assigns to every node $t \in \mathcal{N}$ its predecessor $P(t) \in \mathcal{N}$

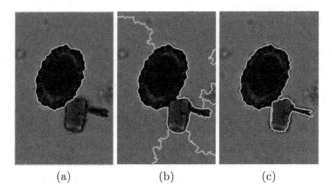

(a)   (b)   (c)

Fig. 1. (a) Original image in which the contour indicates an object of interest. For only three superpixels, (b) the result of a content-sensitive approach based on entropy [11] and (c) the result of the proposed method based on object information.

in the optimum path π_t^* or a marker $P(t) = nil \notin \mathcal{N}$ when t is a *root* of the map. Even when those conditions are not satisfied, the algorithm can output a spanning forest with properties that are useful for several applications. This framework to the design of image operators based on optimum-path forest is called *Image Foresting Transform* (IFT) [4].

In this work we are interested in two of its applications: object saliency detection based on pixel classification [8]; and superpixel segmentation [11]. The next sections illustrate IFT-based image operators with examples of adjacency relation and connectivity function for those applications.

3   IFT-based Object Saliency Detection

A map O that assigns values $O(t)$, $t \in \mathcal{I}$, proportional to the similarity between t and a given object is said *object saliency map*. We create object saliency maps by training a pixel classifier [8] from user-drawn scribbles inside and outside a given object in one training image. Of course, one can build a pixel training set from scribbles drawn on several training images as well, whenever this is required by the application. The scribbles represent a set of training pixels whose color/texture properties may be mapped onto overlapping regions in the corresponding feature space. By clustering, we first select a small set (e.g., 500 pixels) of the most representative object and background pixels to train the classifier with minimum overlapping between regions of distinct classes in the feature space. Therefore, let $\mathcal{N}$ be such selected set of training pixels and $\mathcal{A}$ be a complete adjacency relation that connects any pair of pixels $(s, t) \in \mathcal{N} \times \mathcal{N}$. A seed set $\mathcal{S} \subset \mathcal{N}$ is defined with the closest pixels from distinct classes (object or background) in G according to the Euclidean norm $\|I(t), I(s)\|$ between their colors in the CIELab color space. The set $\mathcal{S}$ is usually obtained by computing a Minimum Spanning Tree (MST) in G and selecting nodes from distinct classes that share an arc in the MST [8]. Let f_o and f_b be path-cost functions such as

$$f_x(\langle t \rangle) = \begin{cases} 0 & \text{if } t \in \mathcal{S}_x \subset \mathcal{S}, \\ +\infty & \text{otherwise,} \end{cases} \tag{1}$$

$$f_x(\pi_s \cdot \langle s, t \rangle) = \max\{f_x(\pi_s), \|I(t), I(s)\|\},$$

where $\mathcal{S}_x$ contains either object ($x = o$) or background ($x = b$) seeds, and $\pi_s \cdot \langle s, t \rangle$ indicates the extension of π_s by an arc $\langle s, t \rangle$ with the two joining instances of s merged into one. The IFT algorithm is executed for each path-cost function in order to obtain two minimum path-cost maps, which are combined into the final object saliency map O, such that $O(t) = \frac{C_b(t)}{C_o(t) + C_b(t)}$, where $C_x(t) = \min_{\forall \pi_t \in \Pi_G}\{f_x(\pi_t)\}$. For each node in $t \in \mathcal{N}$, $C_o(t)$ and $C_b(t)$ store the costs of the paths rooted at the most closely connected seeds in $\mathcal{S}_o$ and $\mathcal{S}_b$. Those seeds offer to t paths whose maximum arc weight $\|I(t), I(s)\|$ is minimum. For pixels t very similar to the object, it is expected that $C_b(t) \gg C_o(t) \implies O(t) \approx 1$.

4   Superpixel Segmentation by Iterative Spanning Forest

The *Iterative Spanning Forest* (ISF) framework consists of four components: (i) a seed sampling strategy; (ii) an adjacency relation; (iii) a connectivity function; and (iv) a seed recomputation procedure [11]. For a given choice of these components, one can design distinct superpixel segmentation methods. ISF executes the IFT algorithm multiple times for improved seed sets in order to obtain the final superpixel segmentation.

In 2D, the adjacency relation $\mathcal{A} \subset \mathcal{I} \times \mathcal{I}$ connects pairs of 4-neighboring pixels. The graph is defined as $G = (\mathcal{I}, \mathcal{A}, I)$. The connectivity function may be

$$f_1(\langle t \rangle) = \begin{cases} 0 & \text{if } t \in \mathcal{S}, \\ +\infty & \text{otherwise,} \end{cases} \tag{2}$$

$$f_1(\pi_s \cdot \langle s, t \rangle) = f_1(\pi_s) + [\alpha \|I(r_s), I(t)\|]^\beta + \|t, s\|,$$

where $\mathcal{S}$ is a set of seed pixels, r_s is the starting pixel (root) of π_s, $\alpha \geq 0$, $\beta > 1$, and $\|t, s\| = 1$ since it represents the Euclidean norm between 4-neighboring pixels. The role of α is to provide user control over the superpixel compactness and regularity—lower is α, more compact and regular they are. The β parameter controls the boundary adherence—higher is β, higher is the adherence of superpixels to the boundaries of the objects, but this reduces their shape regularity and compactness. For an initial set $\mathcal{S} \subset \mathcal{I}$, the IFT algorithm aims at finding minimum-cost paths from $\mathcal{S}$ to the remaining pixels in $\mathcal{I} \backslash \mathcal{S}$. The connectivity function may not satisfy the conditions in [2], but each seed in $\mathcal{S}$ defines one spanning tree (connected superpixel) suitable for image representation. The seed recomputation procedure aims at improving the seed set $\mathcal{S}$ for the subsequent execution of the IFT algorithm using the same connectivity function. Among the components presented in [11], the authors concluded that the ones that use f_1, as defined in Eq. 2, and recomputes one seed inside each superpixel as the closest pixel to its geometric center, were the most competitive. ISF uses a convergence criterion to select new seeds and so the spanning forest can efficiently be updated in a differential way [3].

Taking into account the seed sampling strategies in [11], *GRID* and *MIX* are the most competitive to estimate the initial set $\mathcal{S}$. GRID selects a given number of equally spaced pixels from $\mathcal{I}$ and then approximate them to the closest minimum in a gradient image. MIX seed sampling creates a two-level quad-tree, using the normalized Shannon entropy, as predicate, and performs GRID on the leaves of the tree. While GRID prioritizes a regular sampling over the image domain, MIX aims at increasing the number of seeds in heterogeneous regions, such as a content-sensitive approach, and at the same time preserving the regularity of the grid sampling.

5   Object-Based ISF for Superpixel Segmentation

In applications with a given object of interest (e.g., an organ in medical images), one can train a pixel classifier (e.g., the approach described in Sect. 3) to estimate the object saliency map O from any given image. We then propose the use of that map in ISF to increase the number of initial seeds in the image regions most similar to the object (brighter regions in the map). For a fixed number of superpixels, this should lead to higher superpixel resolution inside the object than elsewhere in comparison with other ISF-based methods. We call this approach *object-based seed sampling*. We also propose the use of an *object-based connectivity function* similar to the one proposed in [10] in order to increase the boundary adherence of the superpixels to the high-contrast regions of the saliency map. The new framework is then named *Object-based* ISF (OISF).

5.1   Object-Based Seed Sampling Strategy

A binary mask M with most object pixels is defined as $M(t) = 1$, if $O(t) \geq T$ (e.g., $T = 0.5$), or $M(t) = 0$ otherwise. The binary mask may consist of multiple components and the number of seeds in each component is proportional to its area. Our approach selects a percentage of seeds within those components and the remaining seeds in regions where $M(t) = 0$ to compose the initial set $\mathcal{S}$. This process uses *geodesic grid sampling—i.e., equally spaced seeds inside each component.*

5.2   Object-Based Connectivity Function

The authors in [10] proposed a new function f_2, derived from f_1, which takes into account the relevance of a presegmentation map (for segmentation resuming). Thus, for our proposal, f_2 can be rewritten as $f_2(\langle t \rangle) = f_1(\langle t \rangle)$ and

$$f_2(\pi_s \cdot \langle s, t \rangle) = f_2(\pi_s) + \|t, s\| + \tag{3}$$
$$\left[\alpha \| I(r_s), I(t) \| \gamma^{|O(r_s) - O(t)|} + \gamma |O(r_s) - O(t)| \right]^{\beta},$$

where $\gamma > 0$ controls the balance between boundary adherence to high-contrast regions of the image and saliency map. Figure 2 illustrates the impact of γ in the proposed OISF-based method, named *OISF-GRID* due to the geodesic grid sampling—i.e., higher is γ higher is the adherence to the object boundaries in the saliency map.

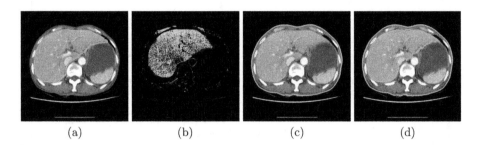

(a)   (b)   (c)   (d)

Fig. 2. (a) Original image with the contour indicating the object of interest. (b) The object saliency map using the classifier pre-trained on another image. Result for three superpixels only using OISF-GRID with (c) $\gamma = 1$ and (d) $\gamma = 10$.

6   Experimental Results

The experiments used two datasets: *Parasites*, with 77 images of *Schistosoma* Mansoni eggs, and *Liver*, with 40 CT-image slices of the liver, being the eggs and the liver their respective objects of interest. We fixed $\alpha = 0.5$ and $\beta = 12$, as suggested in [11], to prioritize boundary adherence over compactness. For γ, the best values for Liver and Parasites were $\gamma = 1.75$ and $\gamma = 1.5$, respectively, as obtained by grid search on $\approx$30% of the images. The classifier used to create object saliency maps was trained from 500 pixels of a single image (Sect. 3).

Methods for superpixel segmentation are usually assessed by two boundary adherence measures: (i) boundary recall (BR) [1] (higher is better); and (ii) under-segmentation error (UE) [7] (lower is better). Since the size of the object's boundary is usually very small as compared to its size, these measures cannot capture the ability of a method to retain more superpixels inside the object than elsewhere. Except for a low number of superpixels, they can show when a method best preserves the object's boundary due to that property. Therefore, boundary adherence with higher superpixel resolution in a given object than elsewhere is measured by $wBR = BR \cdot P$ and $wUE = \frac{UE}{P}$, where P is the percentage of superpixels inside that object. We compare OISF-GRID with four ISF-based methods [11] (ISF-GRID-MEAN, ISF-GRID-ROOT, ISF-MIX-MEAN, ISF-MIX-ROOT) and two state-of-the-art approaches, the popular SLIC [1] and a more recent one, LSC [5], according to those weighted boundary adherence measures (see Fig. 3). The performance of OISF-GRID is by far the best, mainly because the penalization for irrelevant background superpixels.

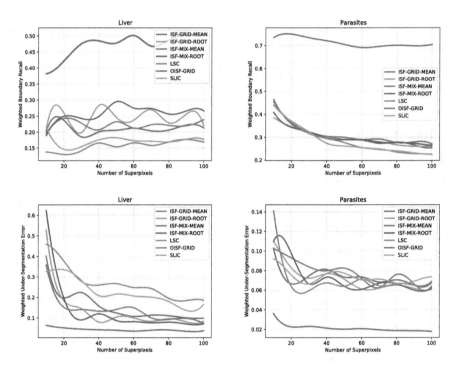

Fig. 3. OISF-GRID *versus* different superpixel-generation methods for varying number of superpixels.

Although the computation of the object saliency map is detached from the OISF-GRID algorithm, our proposal requires slightly higher processing time than ISF due to the geodesic grid sampling on each component of the map. However, the processing time of OISF is equivalent to the one of ISF in the remaining steps.

7 Conclusion

We presented the Object-based Iterative Spanning Forest framework (OISF) and an OISF-based method that considerably improves boundary adherence with higher number of superpixels inside a given object than elsewhere (thus, it reduces the quantity of irrelevant superpixels in the background). OISF incorporates object information from an object saliency map. We have shown an effective solution for saliency detection, but OISF can be used with other saliency detection methods. We intend now to investigate new OISF-based methods, evaluate them on 3D medical image datasets, and explore OISF in applications that require object delineation (i.e., semantic image segmentation).

References

1. Achanta, R., Shaji, A., Smith, K., Lucchi, A., Fua, P., Süsstrunk, S.: SLIC superpixels compared to state-of-the-art superpixel methods. IEEE Trans. Pattern Anal. Mach. Intell. **34**, 2274–2282 (2012). https://doi.org/10.1109/TPAMI.2012.120
2. Ciesielski, K.C., Falcão, A.X., Miranda, P.A.V.: Path-value functions for which Dijkstra's algorithm returns optimal mapping. J. Math. Imaging Vis. **60**, 1025–1036 (2018). https://doi.org/10.1007/s10851-018-0793-1
3. Condori, M.A.T., Cappabianco, F.A.M., Falcão, A.X., De Miranda, P.A.V.: Extending the differential image foresting transform to root-based path-cost functions with application to superpixel segmentation. In: Proceedings of 30th Conference on Graphics Pattern Images (SIBGRAPI), pp. 7–14, October 2017. https://doi.org/10.1109/SIBGRAPI.2017.8
4. Falcão, A.X., Stolfi, J., Lotufo, R.A.: The image foresting transform: theory, algorithms, and applications. IEEE Trans. Pattern Anal. Mach. Intell. **26**, 19–29 (2004). https://doi.org/10.1109/TPAMI.2004.1261076
5. Li, Z., Chen, J.: Superpixel segmentation using linear spectral clustering. In: Proceedings of 28th Conference on Computer Vision and Pattern Recognition, pp. 1356–1363, June 2015. https://doi.org/10.1109/CVPR.2015.7298741
6. Liu, Y.J., Yu, M., Li, B.J., He, Y.: Intrinsic manifold SLIC: a simple and efficient method for computing content-sensitive superpixels. IEEE Trans. Pattern Anal. Mach. Intell. **40**(3), 653–666 (2018). https://doi.org/10.1109/TPAMI.2017.2686857
7. Neubert, P., Protzel, P.: Superpixel benchmark and comparison. In: Proceedings of Forum Bildverarbeitung, vol. 6, pp. 1–12 (2012)
8. Papa, J.P., Falcão, A.X., Suzuki, C.T.: Supervised pattern classification based on optimum-path forest. Int. J. Imaging Syst. Technol. **19**(2), 120–131 (2009). https://doi.org/10.1002/ima.20188
9. Stutz, D., Hermans, A., Leibe, B.: Superpixels: an evaluation of the state-of-the-art. Computer Vis. Image Underst. **166**, 1–27 (2018). https://doi.org/10.1016/j.cviu.2017.03.007
10. Tavares, A.C.M., Miranda, P.A.V., Spina, T.V., Falcão, A.X.: A supervoxel-based solution to resume segmentation for interactive correction by differential image-foresting transforms. In: Angulo, J., Velasco-Forero, S., Meyer, F. (eds.) ISMM 2017. LNCS, vol. 10225, pp. 107–118. Springer, Cham (2017). https://doi.org/10.1007/978-3-319-57240-6_9
11. Vargas-Muñoz, J.E., Chowdhury, A.S., Alexandre, E.B., Galvão, F.L., Miranda, P.A.V., Falcão, A.X.: An iterative spanning forest framework for superpixel segmentation. IEEE Trans. Image Process (to appear 2019)
12. Wang, P., Zeng, G., Gan, R., Wang, J., Zha, H.: Structure-sensitive superpixels via geodesic distance. Int. J. Comput. Vis. **103**, 1–21 (2013). https://doi.org/10.1007/s11263-012-0588-6

Frequency Analysis of Topological Projections onto Klein Bottle for Texture Characterization

Thiago Pirola Ribeiro[1]([✉]) [ID], André L. Naves de Oliveira[2] [ID],
and Celia A. Zorzo Barcelos[2] [ID]

[1] Faculty of Computing, Federal University of Uberlândia,
Uberlândia, MG, Brazil
tpribeiro@ufu.br
[2] Faculty of Mathematics, Federal University of Uberlândia,
Uberlândia, MG, Brazil
{andrenaves,celiazb}@ufu.br

Abstract. This work presents an approach for texture based image characterization through topological projections onto the Klein Bottle of small high-contrast regions (patches) extracted from the images. Several configurations of cut-off frequency were analyzed in order to reduce the vector size of features and to increase accuracy. Experiments using the proposed method for texture classification, on several established datasets, show that the proposed method not only manages to reduce feature vector size, but also improves correct classification rates when compared to other state-of-the-art methods.

Keywords: Frequency analysis · Texture characterization · Topology · Klein Bottle

1 Introduction

The literature approaches the problem of texture characterization through several methods. To classify an image, visual attributes presented in the image need to characterize the image singularly or highlight characteristics that are found in a class of images, making them distinguishable from other classes.

According to [4], natural image statistics is an extremely important field in several areas such as computer vision, statistics, neuroscience and physiology. The authors proposed the study of the local behavior of images by analyzing a space of small high-contrast regions (patches) extracted from the images.

The authors [9] present a novel framework for estimating and representing the distribution around low dimensional submanifolds of pixel space using the Klein Bottle space.

The authors gratefully acknowledge the financial support of CNPq (National Council for Scientific and Technological Development, Brazil) (Grant #309186/2017-0), PPGCO-FACOM-UFU and PROPP-UFU.

R. Vera-Rodriguez et al. (Eds.): CIARP 2018, LNCS 11401, pp. 342–350, 2019.
https://doi.org/10.1007/978-3-030-13469-3_40

This work proposes a new approach to determine the feature vector of texture characterization via projections of patches on the topology of the Klein Bottle. A new configuration of cut-off frequency was proposed based on the definitions of [9] for projections in the Klein Bottle.

Experiments in classification show that the method is robust for texture classification and provides very high accuracy for several texture databases, outperforming other state-of-the-art descriptors, while reducing a number of dimensions on the feature vector. In Sect. (2, 2.1, 2.2), the results of Lee et al. ([8]), Carlson et al. ([4]) on the Klein Model $\mathcal{K}$ are reviewed. In Sect. (2.3), the achievement of an estimation for the probability density function of the projected space in [9] is reviewed and new configurations for generating the descriptors are presented. In Sect. (3), the results of this work are stated. Finally, in Sect. (4) the results are discussed.

2   Overview of the Multi-scale Invariant Descriptor Process

The simplified steps created to generate a multi-scale invariant descriptor are illustrated in Fig. 1. Initially the image is selected (A) and the patches are extracted (B). These patches are projected onto the space of the Klein Bottle (C). The calculation of the Estimated K-Fourier Coefficients are based on the projected patches. After choosing the cut-off frequency to construct the estimated probability function, the vector descriptor EKFC is created (D). This process is executed over all images of the Texture Bases. Following on, this set of descriptor vectors is submitted for classification in order to analyze the accuracy of the method (E).

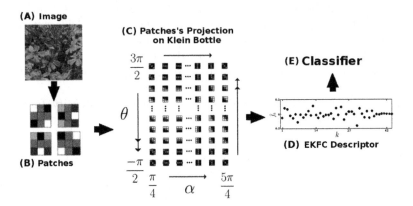

Fig. 1. Flow of processing steps.

2.1   Patches

Initially, patches (E) are extracted from the image (Fig. 1B) based on [8], in which patches with $n \times n$ pixel dimensions are extracted. Then, 5.000 patches are randomly selected.

For each one of these selected patches $E = [e_{ij}]$, the log is applied generating $A = [a_{ij}]$ with $a_{ij} = \ln(e_{ij})$ and the D-norm are calculated as $\|A\|_D^2 = \sum_{ij \sim kl}(a_{ij} - a_{kl})^2$, with $a_{ij} \sim a_{kl}$ if, and only if $|i - k| + |j - l| \leq 1$.

Only those patches with D-norm greater than or equal to a given threshold are considered (the authors [9] considered 0.01). As such, the 1.000 highest D-norm patches or the remaining patches are selected.

For each one of these patches, the average is subtracted and then normalized:

$$\mathbf{P} = \frac{A - \dfrac{1}{n^2} \sum_{j=1}^{n} \sum_{i=1}^{n} a_{ij} B}{\left\| A - \dfrac{1}{n^2} \sum_{j=1}^{n} \sum_{i=1}^{n} a_{ij} B \right\|_D} \tag{1}$$

where if B is the $n \times n$ matrix with all elements equals 1.

2.2   Projection

To create the projection (Fig. 1C), the authors herein used the Klein Bottle space $\mathcal{K}$ obtained from the rectangle $R = \left[\frac{\pi}{4}, \frac{5\pi}{4}\right] \times \left[\frac{-\pi}{2}, \frac{3\pi}{2}\right]$, where each point $\left(\alpha, \frac{-\pi}{2}\right)$ is identified with $\left(\alpha, \frac{3\pi}{2}\right)$ and each $\left(\frac{\pi}{4}, \theta\right)$ is identified with $\left(\frac{5\pi}{4}, \pi - \theta\right)$ for all $(\alpha, \theta) \in R$. So, the space $\mathcal{K}$ with the Topology of the Klein Bottle was created. Figure 1(C) exemplifies the patches projected onto the space $\mathcal{K}$.

Each patch can be parameterized by the direction $\alpha \in \left[\frac{\pi}{4}, \frac{5\pi}{4}\right)$ and by the transition of the bar/edge structure defined by the angle θ. Different pairs of (α, θ) can describe the same sample, e.g., $\left(\frac{\pi}{4}, 0\right)$ and $\left(\frac{5\pi}{4}, \pi\right)$ describe the edge steps with direction of the gradient toward the northwest.

To obtain $(\alpha, \theta) \in \mathcal{K}$, which determines a single patch, one adds $a + ib = e^{i\alpha}$ and $c + id = e^{i\theta}$.

These numbers are obtained from the fact that the intensity function is approximated by a polynomial p

$$p(x, y) = c\frac{(ax + by)}{2} + d\frac{\sqrt{3}(ax + by)^2}{4}, \quad c^2 + d^2 = 1. \tag{2}$$

We then can think the patch $E = e_{ij}$ as coming from this polynomial via the local averaging

$$e_{ij} = \int_{1 - \frac{2i}{n}}^{1 - \frac{2i-2}{n}} \int_{-1 + \frac{2j-2}{n}}^{-1 + \frac{2j}{n}} p(x, y) \, dx \, dy, \quad i, j = 1, ..., n. \tag{3}$$

and $\mathbf{P} = [p_{ij}]$ is the centered log normalization of $E = e_{ij}$.

The $\nabla I_\mathbf{P}$ (gradient intensity function) is sectionally constant and equal to the discrete gradient of $\mathbf{P}$, and through such, $\nabla I_\mathbf{P} \cong \nabla \mathbf{P}$. The centralized discretization was used.

If $2 \leq i, j \leq n - 1$ then

$$\nabla \mathbf{P}(i, j) = \frac{1}{2} \begin{bmatrix} p_{i+1,j} - p_{i-1,j} \\ p_{i,j+1} - p_{i,j-1} \end{bmatrix} \tag{4}$$

$$H\mathbf{P}(i, j) = \begin{bmatrix} p_{i+1,j} - 2p_{i,j} + p_{i-1,j} & H_{xy}\mathbf{P}(i, j) \\ H_{xy}\mathbf{P}(i, j) & p_{i,j+1} - 2p_{ij} + p_{i,j-1} \end{bmatrix} \tag{5}$$

where

$$H_{xy}\mathbf{P}(i, j) = \frac{p_{i+1,j+1} - p_{i-1,j+1} - p_{i+1,j-1} + p_{i-1,j-1}}{4}. \tag{6}$$

If $i \in \{1, n\}$ or $t \in \{1, n\}$, then there is a single $(i, j) \in \{2, ..., n-1\}^2$ that minimizes $|r - i| + |t - j|$, with

$$\nabla \mathbf{P}(r, t) = \nabla \mathbf{P}(i, j) + H\mathbf{P}(i, j) \begin{bmatrix} r - i \\ t - j \end{bmatrix} \tag{7}$$

Using the first order Taylor expansion, the approximation of $\mathbf{P}$ at a location (r, t) near (i, j) is calculated. For the gradient expansion $I_\mathbf{P}$, let $\nabla I_\mathbf{P}(x, y) = \nabla \mathbf{P}(i, j)$ if

$$\left| x - \left(-1 + \frac{2j - 1}{n} \right) \right| + \left| y - \left(1 - \frac{2i - 1}{n} \right) \right| < \frac{1}{n} \tag{8}$$

for some $(i, j) \in \{1, ..., n\}^2$, and $\mathbf{0}$ otherwise.

If the eigenvalues of $C_\mathbf{P}(i, j) = \iint_{[-1,1]^2} \frac{\partial I_\mathbf{P}}{\partial x_i} \frac{\partial I_\mathbf{P}}{\partial x_j} dx dy$ $\quad i, j = 1, 2, ..., n$. (obtained explicit from $\nabla \mathbf{P}$ through the quadratic form in Eq. (4) and discretized as in Remark 3.2 of [9]) are real and different, then $\alpha_\mathbf{P} \in [\frac{\pi}{4}, \frac{5\pi}{4})$ is defined as the direction of the eigenspace corresponding to the highest eigenvalue, or patch is discarded otherwise. a and b are so that $a + ib = \cos \alpha_\mathbf{P} + i \sin \alpha_\mathbf{P} = e^{i\alpha_\mathbf{P}}$.

Let $\langle f, g \rangle = \iint_{[-1,1]^2} \langle \nabla f(x, y), \nabla g(x, y) \rangle dx dy$ $\quad$ denote the inner product inducing the D-norm $\|.\|_D$. If $u = \frac{(ax + by)}{2}$, then the vector $\begin{bmatrix} c* \\ d* \end{bmatrix} \in S^1$ that minimizes $\Phi(c, d) = \left\| I_\mathbf{P} - (cu + d\sqrt{3}u^2) \right\|_D$, with $c^2 + d^2 = 1$ is given by

$$c^* = \frac{\langle I_\mathbf{P}, u \rangle_D}{\sqrt{\langle I_\mathbf{P}, u \rangle_D^2 + 3 \langle I_\mathbf{P}, u^2 \rangle_D^2}} \qquad d^* = \frac{\sqrt{3} \langle I_\mathbf{P}, u^2 \rangle_D}{\sqrt{\langle I_\mathbf{P}, u \rangle_D^2 + 3 \langle I_\mathbf{P}, u^2 \rangle_D^2}} \tag{9}$$

whenever

$$\varphi(I_\mathbf{P}, \alpha_\mathbf{P}) = \langle I_\mathbf{P}, u \rangle_D^2 + 3 \langle I_\mathbf{P}, u^2 \rangle_D^2 \neq 0 \tag{10}$$

and it determines a unique $\theta_{\mathbf{P}} \in \left[\frac{-\pi}{2}, \frac{3\pi}{2}\right)$ so that $c^* + id^* = \cos(\theta_{\mathbf{P}}) + i \sin \theta_{\mathbf{P}} = e^{i\theta_{\mathbf{P}}}$.

If

$$\Phi(c^*, d^*) = \left\| I_{\mathbf{P}} - (c^*u + d^*\sqrt{3}u^2) \right\|_D = \sqrt{2\left(1 - \sqrt{\varphi(I_{\mathbf{P}}, \alpha_{\mathbf{P}})}\right)}, \qquad (11)$$

then $\Phi(c^*, d^*)$ can be seen as the distance from $\mathbf{P}$ to $\mathcal{K}$ and $\Phi(c^*, d^*) \leq \sqrt{2}$. So $\varphi(I_{\mathbf{P}}, \alpha_{\mathbf{P}})$ exists in the sample $S \subset \mathcal{K}$ if $\Phi(c^*, d^*) \leq r_n$, where r_n are the set, so that $\sqrt{\varphi} \geq \frac{1}{2^{n-1}}$.

After finding a, b, c and d for a patch $\mathbf{P}$, one can obtain $a + ib = e^{i\alpha_{\mathbf{P}}}$ and $c + id = e^{i\theta_{\mathbf{P}}}$.

Using $(\alpha_{\mathbf{P}}, \theta_{\mathbf{P}})$ for each selected patch, the projection on $\mathcal{K}$ is made.

2.3   EKFC Descriptor

With these patches projected, the calculation for the Estimated K-Fourier Coefficients can be made, with the estimated $\widehat{f}$ corresponding to the probability density function $f : K \to \mathbb{R}$; $\widehat{f}(\alpha, \theta) = \sum_{k \in N_\omega} \widehat{f_k}\phi_k(\alpha, \theta)$ where $\{\phi_k\}_{k \in \mathbb{N}}$ is a trigonometric base for $L^2(K, \mathbb{R})$.

Let $\Pi_{n,m} = \frac{(1-(-1)^{n+m})\pi}{4}$ and N be the number of projected patches; then the trigonometric base $\{\phi\}$ for $L^2(K, \mathbb{R})$ is:

$$1, \quad \sqrt{2}\cos(m\theta - \Pi_{0,m}), \quad \sqrt{2}\cos(2n\alpha), \quad \sqrt{2}\sin(2n\alpha), \qquad (12)$$
$$2\cos(n\alpha)\cos(m\theta - \Pi_{n,m}), \quad 2\sin(n\alpha)\cos(m\theta - \Pi_{n,m});$$

and the Estimated K-Fourier Coefficients are:

$$\widehat{a}_m = \frac{1}{N}\sum_{k=1}^{N}\sqrt{2}\cos(m\theta_k - \Pi_{0,m}), \quad \widehat{b}_n = \frac{1}{N}\sum_{k=1}^{N}\sqrt{2}\cos(2n\alpha_k), \quad \widehat{c}_n = \frac{1}{N}\sum_{k=1}^{N}\sqrt{2}\sin(2n\alpha_k),$$

$$\widehat{d}_{n,m} = \frac{1}{N}\sum_{k=1}^{N}2\cos(n\alpha_k)\cos(m\theta_k - \Pi_{n,m}), \quad \widehat{e}_{n,m} = \frac{1}{N}\sum_{k=1}^{N}2\sin(n\alpha_k)\cos(m\theta_k - \Pi_{n,m});$$

where the summation is over all N $(\alpha_{\mathbf{P}}, \theta_{\mathbf{P}})$ selected patches.

If we order them with respect to their (total) frequencies and alphabetic placement as

$$\widehat{a}_1, \underbrace{\widehat{a}_2, \widehat{b}_1, \widehat{c}_1, \widehat{d}_{1,1}, \widehat{e}_{1,1}}_{frequency=2}, \underbrace{\widehat{a}_3, \widehat{d}_{1,2}, \widehat{d}_{2,1}, \widehat{e}_{1,2}, \widehat{e}_{2,1}}_{frequency=3}, \widehat{a}_4, \widehat{b}_2, ...$$

then we get the ordered sequence $\widehat{K\mathcal{F}}(f)$ and the parameterization $\widehat{K\mathcal{F}}_\omega(f, S)$ consists of the K-Fourier estimated coefficients of the estimated probability density function $\widehat{f}(\alpha, \theta)$ with a frequency less than or equal ω.

The presented paper proposed the investigation of different configuration, given by [9], of patch size (n) and cut-off frequencies (ω) in the estimated probability density function.

In this paper $EKFC_n = \left(\widehat{K\mathscr{F}}_\omega(f, S)\right)$ will be the Estimated K-Fourier Coefficients with frequency less than or equal to ω obtained from $n \times n$ projected *patches* and $EKFC = [EKFC_{n_1}, EKFC_{n_2}, ..., EKFC_{n_j}]$ will be the concatenated Estimated K-Fourier Coefficients of j values of n that generate the descriptors (Fig. 1D).

For more details of the equations in Sects. 2.1, 2.2 and 2.3 see [11].

3   Results and Discussion

Analyzing the equations of the previous section, the size of the patches and the cut-off frequency have a great influence on the quality and quantity of feature vectors.

The patch sizes configuration was analyzed in [11] getting great results and reducing the setting for $n = 4, 5, 6$ using the fixed cutoff frequency.

The cutoff frequency used by [9] kept the same value ($\omega = 6$) proposed by [14] to calculate the estimating function $\widehat{f}$, influencing the calculation of the Estimated K-Fourier Coefficients.

Motivated also by the lack of criteria in choosing the cutoff frequency proposed by [9], we performed experiments with 5 datasets: KTH-TIPS [6], CUReT [5], Brodatz [2], Vistex [12] and ALOT [3].

Across all experiments we used the Large Margin Nearest Neighbor (LMNN) [13], in the metric learning with the 3 nearest neighbors to acquire a global metric, as well as 20% of the training set for cross validation. For classification we used the mean and variance of the percentage of test images, which were labeled correctly, and computed in 100 random split training/test sets. We used half the images per class for the training set, in all experiments.

For the first experiment, we used configurations of patch sizes ($n = 3, 7, 11, 15, 19$) as in [9]. We vary the cutoff frequency ($\omega = 2, ..., 12$). Table 1 presents the results obtained in the first experiment.

Table 1. Comparison of classification results of different frequencies for KTH-TIPS.

Frequency	2	3	4	5	6	7	8	9	10	11	12
Descriptors	30	55	100	145	210	275	360	445	550	655	780
Greater Accuracy	67.32	77.07	85.12	88.54	90.98	93.17	96.10	96.83	71.95	97.80	**99.27**
Average Accuracy	61.85	73.53	81.35	84.07	87.37	89.91	92.25	93.39	66.86	95.66	96.57
Variance	4.0E−4	3.8E−4	3.5E−4	3.6E−4	2.1E−4	3.2E−4	2.0E−4	2.7E−4	4.9E−4	1.5E−4	1.5E−4

The results (Table 1) showed that when we increases the cutoff frequency, consequently the size of descriptor increases too and the accuracy increased too in most cases. The best results for the KTH-TIPS dataset using the cutoff frequency 12 obtained 99.27% of accuracy.

For the second experiment, we used two sets configurations of patch sizes ($n = 3, 7, 11, 15, 19$ and $n = 3, 4, 5$) and vary the cutoff frequency ($\omega = 2, ..., 12$). The second setting was set after testing with various patch configurations [11]. In this experiment, we analyzed the results of the best accuracy in all tested datasets. However, we impose a limit of 210 on the size of descriptor based on [9]. We consider this limit because we want to have better accuracy with fewer descriptors. Table 2 presents the best results obtained in the second experiment.

Table 2. Results yielded for two different sets of patches.

Datasets	[3 7 11 15 19]					[3 4 5]				
	Brodatz	CUReT	KTH-TIPS	Vistex	ALOT	Brodatz	CUReT	KTH-TIPS	Vistex	ALOT
Frequency	6	6	6	6	6	5	5	5	5	5
Descriptors	210	210	210	210	210	87	87	87	87	87
Gtr. Acc.	91.67	80.43	90.98	91.44	81.63	**94.14**	**86.78**	**93.66**	**95.14**	**82.29**
Avg. Acc.	88.98	78.70	87.37	88.27	80.75	92.48	85.56	90.16	91.65	81.16
Variance	8.5E−5	5.2E−5	2.1E−4	2.0E−4	1.7E−5	4.4E−5	2.7E−5	3.1E−4	1.8E−4	1.6E−5

The results (Table 2) shows the best accuracy of two different sets of patches for five datasets with the limited descriptor size. Comparing two sets for all datasets, an increase in accuracy with reduced frequency cutoff was observed.

Table 3. Comparison of the our approach with the methods in the literature.

Method	Number of descriptors	Success rate (%)				
		KTH-TIPS	CUReT	Brodatz	Vistex	ALOT
Wavelets	36	58.52	50.99	70.27	72.11	3.67
LBP	25	74.07	67.37	89.58	88.89	68.3
Gabor	64	80.12	82.60	82.49	91.67	61.59
[1]	108	90.37	84.32	95.27	86.76	68.85
[7]	3888	-	-	**98.55 ± 0.53**	-	**97.49 ± 0.86**
[9]	215	94.77 ± 1.3	**95.66 ± 0.45**	-	-	-
[10]	140	98.4	-	-	-	93.35
[15]	20	-	-	85.02	71.23	58.83
[16]	100	94.90 ± 1.6	-	94.90 ± 0.7	-	-
[17]	648	**98.86 ± 1.12**	94.44 ± 1.13	-	-	-
Our approach	87	93.66	86.78	94.14	**95.14**	82.29

We also performed a comparison with traditional and state of art texture analysis methods. Table 3 presents the results yielded for each method. These methods use classifiers other than LMNN, such as LDA or Neural Networks. Emphasis is given here to the fact that we were not able to implement all the approaches under comparison due to the complexity of the method or missing information in their respective papers. Thus, for methods that lack results for one or more datasets, these results correspond to those presented in their respective paper. We also compared our approach with the fixed configuration of patch sizes. For this comparison we used our results previously presented in Table 2.

The results on Table 3 indicate that our approach presents a reduced amount of descriptors and consistently high performance in across all texture datasets tested. It yielded the highest success rate in the Vistex dataset using a reduced number of descriptors.

4 Conclusions

The approach proposed in this work yields feature vectors smaller than other state of the art methods, while keeping on par with those results found in such methods, in terms of classification rates over several image databases, as shown by the experiments performed. The cutoff frequency and the size of the patches has a great influence on the computational cost and in our approach we managed to reduce the quantity and the size of the patches.

As future work, we intend to investigate the use of polynomial order greater than two or other different kinds of function, which may aid in reducing further reduce the size of the descriptor.

References

1. Backes, A.R., Casanova, D., Bruno, O.M.: Texture analysis and classification: a complex network-based approach. Inf. Sci. **219**, 168–180 (2013). https://doi.org/10.1016/j.ins.2012.07.003
2. Brodatz, P.: Textures: a photographic album for artists and designers. Dover pictorial archives, Dover Publications (1966)
3. Burghouts, G.J., Geusebroek, J.M.: Material-specific adaptation of color invariant features. Pattern Recogn. Lett. **30**, 306–313 (2009)
4. Carlsson, G., Ishkhanov, T., De Silva, V., Zomorodian, A.: On the local behavior of spaces of natural images. Int. J. Comput. Vis. **76**(1), 1–12 (2008)
5. Dana, K.J., van Ginneken, B., Nayar, S.K., Koenderink, J.J.: Reflectance and texture of real-world surfaces. ACM Trans. Graph. **18**(1), 1–34 (1999)
6. Hayman, E., Caputo, B., Fritz, M., Eklundh, J.-O.: On the significance of real-world conditions for material classification. In: Pajdla, T., Matas, J. (eds.) ECCV 2004. LNCS, vol. 3024, pp. 253–266. Springer, Heidelberg (2004). https://doi.org/10.1007/978-3-540-24673-2_21
7. Ji, L., Ren, Y., Pu, X., Liu, G.: Median local ternary patterns optimized with rotation-invariant uniform-three mapping for noisy texture classification. Pattern Recogn. **79**, 387–401 (2018)
8. Lee, A.B., Pedersen, K.S., Mumford, D.: The nonlinear statistics of high-contrast patches in natural images. Int. J. Comput. Vis. **54**(1–3), 83–103 (2003)
9. Perea, J.A., Carlsson, G.: A Klein-Bottle-based dictionary for texture representation. Int. J. Comput. Vis. **107**(1), 75–97 (2014)

10. Quan, Y., Xu, Y., Sun, Y., Luo, Y.: Lacunarity analysis on image patterns for texture classification. In: Proceedings of the IEEE Conference on Computer Vision and Pattern Recognition, pp. 160–167 (2014)

11. Ribeiro, T.P., de Oliveira, A.L.N., Barcelos, C.A.Z.: Texture characterization via projections onto a Klein Bottle topology. In: 2018 25th IEEE International Conference on Image Processing (ICIP), pp. 2097–2101, October 2018. https://doi.org/10.1109/ICIP.2018.8451120

12. VisTex: Vision Texture Database (2009)

13. Weinberger, K.Q., Saul, L.K.: Distance metric learning for large margin nearest neighbor classification. J. Mach. Learn. Res. **10**, 207–244 (2009)

14. de Wit, T.D., Floriani, E.: Estimating probability densities from short samples: a parametric maximum likelihood approach. Phys. Rev. E **58**(4), 5115–5122 (1998). https://doi.org/10.1103/PhysRevE.58.5115

15. Yang, H., Liang, L., Zhang, C., Wang, X., Niu, P., Wang, X.: Weibull statistical modeling for textured image retrieval using nonsubsampled contourlet transform. Soft Comput. (2018). https://doi.org/10.1007/s00500-018-3127-8. ISSN: 1433-7479

16. Zhang, J., Marszalek, M., Lazebnik, S., Schmid, C.: Local features and kernels for classification of texture and object categories: a comprehensive study. In: 2006 Conference on Computer Vision and Pattern Recognition Workshop, CVPRW 2006, p. 13 (2006)

17. Zhang, J., Liang, J., Zhang, C., Zhao, H.: Scale invariant texture representation based on frequency decomposition and gradient orientation. Pattern Recogn. Letters **51**, 57–62 (2015)

Singular Patterns in Optical Flows as Dynamic Texture Descriptors

Leandro N. Couto[1]($\boxtimes$) and Celia A. Z. Barcelos[2]🅳

[1] Faculdade de Computação, Universidade Federal de Uberlândia, Uberlândia, Brazil
leandronc@ufu.br
[2] Faculdade de Matemática, Universidade Federal de Uberlândia, Uberlândia, Brazil
celiazb@ufu.br

Abstract. This work introduces a novel approach to dynamic texture description. The proposed method is based on statistics from a vector field feature extractor that decomposes and describes features of distinctive local vector patterns as composites of singular patterns from a dictionary. The extractor is applied to a time-varying vector field, namely a dynamic texture's optical flow frames. An interest point pooling method statistically highlights the recurring texture patterns, generating a histogram signature that is descriptive of the temporal changes in the texture. The proposed descriptor is used as feature vector on classification experiments in a widespread dataset. The classification results demonstrate our method improves on the state of the art for dynamic textures with non-trivial motion, while employing a smaller feature vector.

Keywords: Dynamic textures · Optical flow · Singular patterns

1 Introduction

It is difficult to provide a formal definition of texture, but it can be described as a complex spatial arrangement of visual patterns that have particular properties and recurring characteristics [7]. Dynamic textures extend the concept of self-similarity and periodicity of textures to include repeating patterns in the temporal dimension, such as in videos that present periodic motion [2]. Dynamic texture recognition has been an area of recent interest in computer vision and pattern recognition. The most important step towards dynamic texture recognition is to determine a meaningful and discriminating computational description of the texture that is capable of capturing similarities between alike textures while distinguishing different textures. Many methods have been proposed with this goal in mind, which can be classified into four main categories: (i) motion based methods (often involving optical flow), (ii) filters and transform based methods, (iii) model based methods, and (iv) statistical methods [6]. Statistical methods are particularly effective because statistical analysis highlights the

The authors gratefully acknowledge the financial support of CNPq - National Council for Scientific and Technological Development, Brazil, Grant #309186/2017-0.

R. Vera-Rodriguez et al. (Eds.): CIARP 2018, LNCS 11401, pp. 351–358, 2019.
https://doi.org/10.1007/978-3-030-13469-3_41

repeating local patterns that are distinctive of textures. They are among some of the best performing texture descriptor methods today, such as LBP [18] and deterministic walks [3,6], which offer static and dynamic texture implementations. These methods describe pixel neighborhoods with efficacy and robustness to noise and changes.

Taking into account that the optical flow [14] is a suitable descriptor of motion between video frames, it has also seen extensive use as a dynamic texture descriptor [1,5]. Statistical approaches to optical flow description have achieved good results in diverse pattern recognition tasks [12].

The work of Liu and Ribeiro [11] proposed a scale and rotation invariant feature extractor for vector fields, similar to the popular SIFT feature detector [13]. The feature extractor is based on identifying points of interest in a vector field and decomposing their region into constituent elements that are matched to a dictionary of singular vector field patterns. The method has been shown to be effective in decomposing and reconstructing flows and matching points of interest in fluid motion vector fields. Optical flows are vector fields, and as such, local regions of an optical flow can be described by their component singular patterns. Describing an entire optical flow via local patterns requires pooling the information of the local patterns into a global signature. Methods for describing a whole object by its local features are not new in computer vision; the statistical grouping of visual features can be approached in a number of ways. Many of these approaches employ histograms to compile image features, and many histogram based methods fall into the bag-of-visual-words category (also called bag-of-keypoints or bag-of-features), inspired by an analogous text analysis technique [4].

This work proposes and validates a dynamic texture descriptor based on describing the texture's temporal aspect by employing as the feature vector a histogram of interest points acquired using the singular vector field patterns feature detector. Sections 2 and 3 describe known literature approaches to singular patterns detection and bag-of-features, respectively. Section 4 presents our novel approach to using singular patterns occurrence statistics as a global dynamic texture descriptor. The method has been validated on Dyntex, a widely used literature dynamic texture dataset. In Sect. 5, results are shown for the proposed method being applied to perform a classification task. In Sect. 6, we evaluate our proposed methods' viability and effectiveness in comparison to other state-of-the-art techniques.

2   Singular Vector Field Patterns Detector

Most natural vector fields present particular local characteristics and points of interest. Vector field descriptors that can recognize and describe such regions have been extensively employed in several applications [10,15]. An effective way of modeling local features of a field vector is given by Liu and Ribeiro [11]. The method is based on decomposing the vector field into singular patterns, which are components from a set of symbols, a dictionary of patterns whose linear weighted combination is an approximation of that region of the field. An important choice is which patterns compose the dictionary, since there are no clear definitions for most visible vector field patterns of interest, such as sinks and sources [9]. Rao and Jain [16], in their seminal vector field analysis work, proposed as a dictionary six distinct patterns in which the field nullifies itself (which means the resulting vector is zero). The singular patterns detector uses a wider set of patterns as dictionary. It includes the patterns in which the flow field is nullified, but also defines a complex-valued function $F(z)$. If we choose a given point z_0 as the origin, $F(z)$ can be approximated by $f(z)$, whose Taylor expansion is a linear combination of complex basis functions, as shown in Eq. 1.

$$F(z) \approx f(z) = \sum_k a_k \phi_k(z) \tag{1}$$

In this equation, $\phi_k(z)$ are the basis flows and a_k are the coefficients that weight their effect on the local pattern around the origin, and complex basis flows are chosen instead of real ones because the former model more smooth and natural flows. The a_k coefficients are computed by cross-correlation, by projecting the vector field $F(z)$ over the basis flows. Therefore, local maxima in the sum of a_k coefficients are chosen as singular pattern points. Each pattern has an energy value which denotes its relevance. The method also builds into each chosen interest point rotation and scale invariance.

3   Bag-of-Features Based Descriptors

There are several strategies for pooling sparse local features into a signature for the whole [17]. The standard bag-of-features approach begins with the extraction of a vocabulary from a training dataset. This consists in acquiring features from diverse samples of data, clustering those features using a quantization algorithm such as k-means, and defining a vocabulary of features around the centroids of those clusters. Once that is done, new data can be described by extracting its features and clustering these new points onto the previously obtained vocabulary clusters. The number of occurrences of local features belonging to each of these clusters is a discriminating statistical aspect of the whole object; these occurrences can be captured in a histogram, which can be used as a feature vector for the complete entity. The bag-of-features histogram has great descriptive potential, given its potentially small size relative to the original data [8].

4   Singular Patterns as a Global Optical Flow Descriptor

We propose to use a set of singular patterns into a descriptor for the temporal changes in a dynamic texture, with two data pooling strategies that are customized to the specific characteristics of the singular patterns feature detector.

4.1 Best Coefficient Bag-of-features

We would usually employ a training sample to create a feature vocabulary, but, conveniently, the singular patterns detector already suggests k distinctive ϕ_k basis flows. In this case, we consider the centroids $C_1, C_2, ..., C_k$ in the clustering process to be given by the basis flows, such that $C_1 = (1, 0, 0, ..., 0)$, $C_2 = (0, 1, 0, ..., 0)$ and so forth.

Consider a new, unknown optical flow F_{new}, and its detected set of singular patterns $X_{F_{new}}$. Also consider each feature $x \in X_{F_{new}}$ is described by its corresponding a_k coefficient vector $\boldsymbol{a}_x = (a_1, a_2, ..., a_k)$. For each x, its values are grouped into one of the M clusters, by the criterion of the centroid C_x closest to x. Equation 2 shows the choice of cluster for a feature x.

$$C_x = arg \min_{m | 1 \leq m \leq M} |a_x - C_m|, x \in X_{F_{new}} \tag{2}$$

Once the features are assigned to clusters, a histogram $H_{F_{new}}$ of the occurrences of features in each cluster can be built to describe the set of patterns $X_{F_{new}}$. In the histogram, each bin corresponds to a C_x, and each feature $x \in X_{F_{new}}$ increments one bin, as shown in Eq. 3.

$$H_{F_{new}}(m) = \sum_{m=1}^{M} \delta(C_x, m), \forall x \in X_{F_{new}} \tag{3}$$

Where $\delta(j, i)$ is Kronecker's delta:

$$\delta(j, i) = \begin{cases} 1, & j = i \\ 0, & j \neq i \end{cases} \tag{4}$$

Notice that due to the temporal periodicity of the dynamic texture, the method is expected to detect recurring patterns, which will be highlighted by the histogram. This pooling method is shown in Fig. 1.

4.2 Coefficient Values Histogram

Another possible approach to pooling the acquired features is to consider each coefficient in the feature's vector individually. This way it is possible to measure the presence of each singular pattern component in the optical flow. To represent the occurrence of values a_k, k histograms $H_{F,k}$ are constructed, where, for each value k, the a_k coefficients for all features $x \in X_{F_{new}}$ are evaluated and organized into bins, each representing a range of values for a_k, according to Eq. 5.

$$H_{F,k}(i) = \sum_{i=1}^{n} \mathbf{1}_A(a_x(k)), \forall x \in F, \tag{5}$$

where $\mathbf{1}_A(x)$ is the indicator function:

$$\mathbf{1}_A(x) = \begin{cases} 0, x \notin A \\ 1, x \in A \end{cases} \tag{6}$$

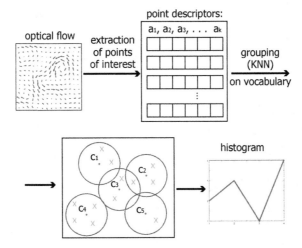

Fig. 1. Summary of the bag-of-features pooling method for vector field features.

The proposed method of pooling features components into coefficient value histograms is summarized in Fig. 2. Notice how a histogram is generated for every a_k coefficient, yielding k histograms which each describe the presence of a dictionary pattern on the composition of the optical flow.

In both methods, we append to each computed histogram its measures of energy, entropy, skewness, contrast, average, variance and kurtosis, which have been shown to significantly enhance the discriminating power of the histogram [3].

5 Experiments and Results

5.1 Experimental Parameters

The singular patterns detector employed 18 ϕ_k basis flows and pattern energy threshold in accordance with the chosen published parameters in the original work [11]. In the coefficient values histogram method, we found that 12 bins in each histogram yields good results with a reasonably sized final feature vector. One important detail is that the bins are not of equal size. We observed the coefficient value distribution resembles a Gaussian with expected value zero (coefficients can be negative) and low variance, therefore logarithmic bin sizes, with the smallest bins closest to zero, provided a much more balanced distribution of the data. Considering 18 histograms of size 12, and 7 statistics per histogram, the feature vector has 342 values.

Experiments were carried out on a challenging subset of the Dyntex dataset, with 10 different 25 frame samples (288×352 pixels) from 2 different videos for each class. Our Dyntex subset involved 79 classes, for a total 790 samples, and all classes in the dataset with non-trivial temporal variation were included.

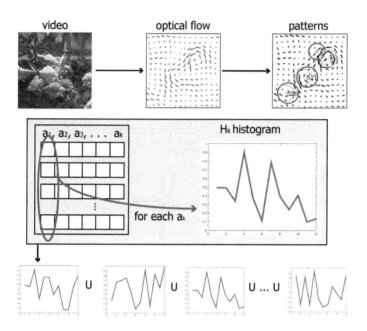

Fig. 2. Summary of the a_k coefficient values histogram generation. Here, k histograms are generated, one for each coefficient, and the feature vector is their concatenation.

Because the method has a relatively high computational cost, we also evaluated classification results after down-sampling the vector fields in half. Classification for all experiments were performed with the same parameters, using Linear Discriminant Analysis (LDA) with leave-one-out cross-validation.

5.2   Results

Table 1 presents classification results for the experiments. Results are provided with and without the inclusion of the histogram statistics metadata (referred to as *Stats* on the table), and for the statistics by themselves.

We compared our best results to the performance of LBP-TOP$_{[8,8,8]}$ [18], one of the state-of-the-art dynamic texture descriptors, on the same dataset, with the same parameters and classifier, and it can be noted our descriptor outperforms LBP-TOP while using a smaller feature vector. Results for the down-sampled vector fields were also good, considering the method is about 4 times faster to compute. The option of down-sampling gives the method flexibility depending on the application's requirements.

Table 1. Correct classification rates for singular patterns optical flow on the Dyntex dataset using both statistical pooling strategies. Spatial LBP and LBP-TOP results are also presented for comparison. Best result in bold.

Method	Dimension	Correct classifications (%)
Coefficient histogram (down-sampled)		
Stats	126	89.88
Histogram	216	84.63
Histogram + Stats	342	95.66
Coefficient histogram		
Stats	126	91.83
Histogram	216	87.80
Histogram + Stats	342	97.44
Best coefficient bag-of-features		
Stats	7	24.76
Histogram	18	44.27
Histogram + Stats	25	48.90
Coefficient hist. + bag-of-features		
Stats	133	93.17
Histogram	234	86.83
Histogram + Stats	367	**97.69**
LBP results for comparison		
Spatial LBP	256	87.32
LBP-TOP	768	95.98

6 Analysis and Conclusion

Our approach provides strong correct classification rates compared to LBP-TOP. Focusing on motion description alone it offers high correct classification rates for dynamic textures. When combined with a spatial descriptor like spatial LBP, the results are better than LBP-TOP, while maintaining a manageable descriptor size.

The best coefficient bag-of-features pooling approach did not fare well on its own. This is likely because most non-synthetic vector field patterns are a weighted combination of many basis flows; reducing each pattern to a single component risks discarding important information.

Realistically, vector fields are complex results of many forces. What separates one pattern from another are the a_k component coefficients. Therefore, the second approach based on values of histograms performed substantially better.

Optical flow is a strong descriptor for motion, but it is also high dimensionality data. Singular patterns address this problem, as powerful tools to summarize descriptive aspects of the flow in much less data. Our approach based on extracted flow field features with appropriate statistical grouping yields a powerful dynamic texture descriptor of manageable dimension for most applications.

References

1. Chao, H., Gu, Y., Napolitano, M.: A survey of optical flow techniques for robotics navigation applications. J. Intell. Rob. Syst. **73**(1–4), 361–372 (2014)
2. Chetverikov, D., Péteri, R.: A brief survey of dynamic texture description and recognition. In: Kurzyński, M., Puchała, E., Żołnierek, A. (eds.) Computer Recognition Systems, vol. 30, pp. 17–26. Springer, Heidelberg (2005). https://doi.org/10.1007/3-540-32390-2_2
3. Couto, L., Backes, A., Barcelos, C.: Texture characterization via deterministic walks' direction histogram applied to a complex network-based image transformation. Pattern Recogn. Lett. **97**, 77–83 (2017)
4. Csurka, G., Dance, C., Fan, L., Willamowski, J., Bray, C.: Visual categorization with bags of keypoints. In: Workshop on statistical learning in computer vision ECCV. vol. 1, pp. 1–2. Prague (2004)
5. Fazekas, S., Chetverikov, D.: Analysis and performance evaluation of optical flow features for dynamic texture recognition. Sig. Process. Image Commun. **22**(7–8), 680–691 (2007)
6. Gonçalves, W., Machado, B., Bruno, O.: A complex network approach for dynamic texture recognition. Neurocomputing **153**, 211–220 (2015)
7. Hájek, M.: Texture analysis for magnetic resonance imaging. Texture Analysis Magn Resona (2006)
8. Hoey, J., Little, J.: Bayesian clustering of optical flow fields, p. 1086. IEEE (2003)
9. Jiang, M., Machiraju, R., Thompson, D.: Detection and visualization of The Visualization Handbook 295 (2005)
10. Kihl, O., Tremblais, B., Augereau, B.: Multivariate orthogonal polynomials to extract singular points. In: Image Processing, 2008. ICIP 2008. 15th IEEE International Conference on. pp. 857–860. IEEE (2008)
11. Liu, W., Ribeiro, E.: Detecting singular patterns in 2d vector fields using weighted laurent polynomial. Pattern Recogn. **45**, 3912–3925 (2012)
12. Liu, Y., Zhang, J., Yan, W., Zhao, G., Fu, X.: A main directional mean optical flow feature for spontaneous micro-expression recognition. IEEE Trans. Affect. Comput. **7**(4), 299–310 (2016)
13. Lowe, D.: Distinctive image features from scale-invariant keypoints. Int. J. Comput. Vis. **60**(2), 91–110 (2004)
14. Lucas, B., Kanade, T., et al.: An iterative image registration technique with an application to stereo vision. IJCAI **81**, 674–679 (1981)
15. Mahbub, U., Imtiaz, H., Roy, T., Rahman, S., Ahad, A.: A template matching approach of one-shot-learning gesture recognition. Pattern Recogn. Lett. **34**(15), 1780–1788 (2013)
16. Rao, R., Jain, R.: Computerized flow field analysis: oriented texture fields. IEEE Trans. Pattern Anal. Mach. Intell. **14**(7), 693–709 (1992)
17. Zhang, J., Marszałek, M., Lazebnik, S., Schmid, C.: Local features and kernels for classification of texture and object categories: a comprehensive study. Int. J. Comput. Vis. **73**(2), 213–238 (2007)
18. Zhao, G., Pietikainen, M.: Dynamic texture recognition using local binary patterns with an application to facial expressions. IEEE Trans. Pattern Anal. Mach. Intell. **29**(6), 915–928 (2007)

Efficient Unsupervised Image Segmentation by Optimum Cuts in Graphs

Hans H. C. Bejar, Lucy A. C. Mansilla, and Paulo A. V. Miranda$^{(\boxtimes)}$

Department of Computer Science, Institute of Mathematics and Statistics,
University of São Paulo, Rua do Matão, 1010, São Paulo, SP 05508-090, Brazil
{hans,lucyacm,pmiranda}@vision.ime.usp.br

Abstract. In this work, a method based on optimum cuts in graphs is proposed for unsupervised image segmentation, that can be tailored to different objects, according to their boundary polarity, by extending the Oriented Image Foresting Transform (OIFT). The proposed method, named UOIFT, encompasses as a particular case the single-linkage algorithm by minimum spanning tree (MST), establishing important theoretical contributions, and gives superior segmentation results compared to other approaches commonly used in the literature, usually requiring a lower number of image partitions to isolate the desired regions of interest. The method is supported by new theoretical results involving the usage of non-monotonic-incremental cost functions in directed graphs. The results are demonstrated using a region adjacency graph of superpixels in medical and natural images.

Keywords: Unsupervised segmentation · Image Foresting Transform · Graph-cut measure

1 Introduction

Unsupervised segmentation is an important problem in computer vision, since perceptual grouping plays a powerful role in human visual perception [25]. In this context, the method must decide what are the relevant image regions without user guidance, based on color and texture similarity or local contrast.

The unsupervised over-segmentation of an image into compact regions of similar and connected pixels is commonly called *superpixels* [1, 22]. It can greatly reduce the computational time of computer vision algorithms, by replacing the rigid structure of the pixel grid [1]. In graph-based methods, it allows the fast creation of a Region Adjacency Graph (RAG), drastically reducing the number of graph elements compared to the graph at the pixel level (Figs. 1a-b).

Several graph-based methods have been proposed for unsupervised segmentation, including watersheds [3], mean cut [24], ratio cut [23], normalized cuts [4,19], and minimum spanning tree (MST) based methods [7,9–12,26].

© Springer Nature Switzerland AG 2019
R. Vera-Rodriguez et al. (Eds.): CIARP 2018, LNCS 11401, pp. 359–367, 2019.
https://doi.org/10.1007/978-3-030-13469-3_42

For instance, Felzenszwalb and Huttenlocher proposed an efficient segmentation algorithm that evaluates a predicate for measuring the evidence for a boundary between two regions, which produces segmentations satisfying global properties, although based on greedy decisions [9]. Other methods include the usage of component trees [20,21], which can also be combined with watersheds, allowing the selection of catchment basins according to their extinction values.

Seed-based methods for region-based image segmentation are known to provide satisfactory results for several applications, being usually easy to extend to multi-dimensional images. In this work, we extend a seed-based method, named *Oriented Image Foresting Transform* (OIFT) [15,17], to perform unsupervised image segmentation, leading to a new method based on optimum cuts in graphs, named UOIFT, that can be tailored to different objects, according to their boundary polarity. OIFT has been demonstrated to be an effective and efficient solution for the segmentation of a given target object based on user provided seeds, allowing the incorporation of several high-level constraints, including shape constraints [16,18] and connectivity priors [14].

The proposed method is based on the Image Foresting Transform (IFT) [8] algorithm, which has linearithmic implementations, being much faster compared to other methods based on cuts in graphs [4,19,23,24]. Differently from [13], our method exploits non-monotonic-incremental cost functions in directed graphs.

The proposed method encompasses as a particular case the single-linkage algorithm by MST, establishing important theoretical contributions, and requires a lower number of image partitions to isolate the desired regions of interest as compared to other approaches commonly used in the literature.

Figures 1c–h present the central idea of this work, which is to explore the boundary polarity in the unsupervised segmentation of images in directed graphs. Figure 1a shows a synthetic image containing dark and bright regions to be segmented in five different regions. Regular unsupervised methods, based on undirected graphs, such as watersheds, cannot distinguish the different types of boundary polarity, giving as output a mixture of bright and dark regions, as shown in Figs. 1c-d. Our proposed method can favor a particular polarity, giving the results shown in Figs. 1e-f or Figs. 1g-h.

2   Graph Concepts

We consider a weighted digraph G as a triple $\langle \mathcal{V}, \mathcal{A}, \omega \rangle$, where $\mathcal{V}$ is a nonempty set of vertices or nodes, $\mathcal{A}$ is a set of ordered pairs of distinct vertices called arcs or directed edges, and $\omega : \mathcal{A} \to \mathbb{R}$ represents the weights associated to the arcs.

An image can be interpreted as a weighted digraph $G = \langle \mathcal{V}, \mathcal{A}, \omega \rangle$, whose nodes $\mathcal{V}$ are the image pixels (or superpixels) in its image domain and whose arcs are the ordered pairs $\langle s, t \rangle \in \mathcal{A}$ of neighboring pixel (superpixels), e.g., 4-neighborhood in case of 2D images. The digraph G is symmetric if for any of its arcs $\langle s, t \rangle \in \mathcal{A}$, the pair $\langle t, s \rangle$ is also an arc of G, but we can have $\omega(\langle s, t \rangle) \neq \omega(\langle t, s \rangle)$. The transpose G^T of G is the unique weighted digraph on the same set of vertices $\mathcal{V}$ with all arcs reversed compared to the corresponding arcs in G.

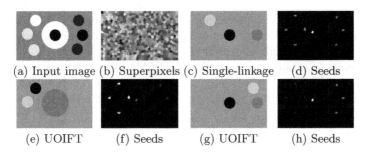

(a) Input image (b) Superpixels (c) Single-linkage   (d) Seeds

(e) UOIFT   (f) Seeds   (g) UOIFT   (h) Seeds

Fig. 1. (a) Input image with 320×200 pixels. (b) Image divided into 640 superpixels by IFT-SLIC [2]. (c) The segmentation into five regions by a single-linkage algorithm using the MST of the RAG. (d) Candidate seeds ranked by their energies by UOIFT without boundary polarity lead to the same result depicted in (c). The UOIFT results into five regions and seeds ranked by their energies, with polarity favoring transitions: (e-f) from bright to dark pixels and (g-h) from dark to bright pixels.

For a given image graph $G = \langle \mathcal{V}, \mathcal{A}, \omega \rangle$, a path $\pi = \langle t_1, t_2, \ldots, t_n \rangle$ is a sequence of adjacent nodes (i.e., $\langle t_i, t_{i+1} \rangle \in \mathcal{A}$, $i = 1, 2, \ldots, n-1$) with no repeated vertices ($t_i \neq t_j$ for $i \neq j$). A path $\pi_t = \langle t_1, t_2, \ldots, t_n = t \rangle$ is a path with terminus at a node t. When we want to explicitly indicate the origin of the path, the notation $\pi_{s \rightsquigarrow t} = \langle t_1 = s, t_2, \ldots, t_n = t \rangle$ may also be used, where s stands for the origin and t for the destination node. A path is *trivial* when $\pi_t = \langle t \rangle$. A path $\pi_t = \pi_s \cdot \langle s, t \rangle$ indicates the extension of a path π_s by an arc $\langle s, t \rangle$. To notation $\Pi(G)$ is used to indicate the set of all possible paths in a graph G.

A *predecessor map* is a function P that assigns to each node t in $\mathcal{V}$ either some other adjacent node in $\mathcal{V}$, or a distinctive marker *nil* not in $\mathcal{V}$ — in which case t is said to be a *root* of the map. A *spanning forest* is a predecessor map which contains no cycles — i.e., one which takes every node to *nil* in a finite number of iterations. For any node $t \in \mathcal{V}$, a spanning forest P defines a path π_t^P recursively as $\langle t \rangle$ if $P(t) = nil$, and $\pi_s^P \cdot \langle s, t \rangle$ if $P(t) = s \neq nil$.

A *connectivity function* $f : \Pi(G) \rightarrow \mathbb{R}$ computes a value $f(\pi_t)$ for any path π_t, usually based on arc weights. A path π_t is *optimum* if $f(\pi_t) \leq f(\tau_t)$ for any other path τ_t in G. The optimum-path value $V_{opt}(t)$ is uniquely defined by $V_{opt}(t) = \min_{\pi_t \in \Pi(G)} \{f(\pi_t)\}$. An *optimum-path forest* P is a spanning forest where all paths π_t^P for $t \in \mathcal{V}$ are optimum.

The cost of a trivial path $\pi_t = \langle t \rangle$ is usually given by a handicap value $H(t)$. For example, $H(t) = 0$ for all $t \in \mathcal{S}$ and $H(t) = \infty$ otherwise, where $\mathcal{S}$ is a seed set. The costs for non-trivial paths follow a path-extension rule. For example:

$$f_{\max}(\pi_s \cdot \langle s, t \rangle) = \max\{f_{\max}(\pi_s), \omega(\langle s, t \rangle)\} \tag{1}$$

$$f_{\Sigma}(\pi_s \cdot \langle s, t \rangle) = f_{\Sigma}(\pi_s) + \omega(\langle s, t \rangle) \tag{2}$$

$$f_{\omega}(\pi_s \cdot \langle s, t \rangle) = \omega(\langle s, t \rangle) \tag{3}$$

The max-arc path-cost function $f_{\max}$ and the additive path-cost function f_{Σ} with $\omega(\langle s, t \rangle) \geqslant 0$ are *Monotonic-Incremental* cost functions (MI), while f_{ω} indicates a non-monotonic-incremental cost function.

The *image foresting transform* (IFT) [8] (Algorithm 1) computes the path-cost map V, which is precisely V_{opt} in the case of MI functions [6]. It is also optimized in handling infinite costs, by storing in $\mathcal{Q}$ only the nodes with finite-cost path, assuming without loss of generality that $V_{opt}(t) < +\infty$ for all $t \in \mathcal{V}$.

Algorithm 1 – IFT ALGORITHM

INPUT: Image graph $G = \langle \mathcal{V}, \mathcal{A}, \omega \rangle$, initial labeling function $\lambda : \mathcal{V} \to \{1, \ldots, k\}$ and path-cost function f.

OUTPUT: Optimum-path forest P, label map $L : \mathcal{V} \to \{1, \ldots, k\}$ and the path-cost map V, which is precisely V_{opt} in the case of MI functions.

AUXILIARY: Priority queue $\mathcal{Q}$, variable tmp, and set of nodes $\mathcal{F}$.

1. **For each** $t \in \mathcal{V}$, **do**
2. | Set $P(t) \leftarrow nil$, $L(t) \leftarrow \lambda(t)$ and $V(t) \leftarrow f(\langle t \rangle)$.
3. | Set $\mathcal{F} \leftarrow \varnothing$.
4. | **If** $V(t) \neq +\infty$, **then** *insert t in* $\mathcal{Q}$.
5. **While** $\mathcal{Q} \neq \varnothing$, **do**
6. | Remove s from $\mathcal{Q}$ such that $V(s)$ is minimum.
7. | Add s to $\mathcal{F}$.
8. | **For each** node t such that $\langle s, t \rangle \in \mathcal{A}$ and $t \notin \mathcal{F}$, **do**
9. | | Compute $tmp \leftarrow f(\pi_s^P \cdot \langle s, t \rangle)$.
10. | | **If** $tmp < V(t)$, **then**
11. | | | **If** $V(t) \neq +\infty$, **then** *remove t from* $\mathcal{Q}$.
12. | | | Set $P(t) \leftarrow s$, $V(t) \leftarrow tmp$, $L(t) \leftarrow L(s)$.
13. | | | Insert t in $\mathcal{Q}$.

3 Efficient Optimum Cuts in Graphs

For a given partition of the graph nodes in two sets X and $\mathcal{V} \setminus X$, let $\mathcal{C}(X) = \{\langle s, t \rangle \in \mathcal{A} \mid s \in X \text{ and } t \notin X\}$ denote the set of arcs in its cut from X to $\mathcal{V} \setminus X$. Consider the following energy formulation:

$$E(X) = \min_{\langle s, t \rangle \in \mathcal{C}(X)} \omega(\langle s, t \rangle) \qquad (4)$$

Let $\mathcal{U}(x, y) = \{X \subset \mathcal{V} \mid x \in X \text{ and } y \in \mathcal{V} \setminus X\}$ denote the universe of all possible partitions separating the nodes x and y, where y represents the background. By using x and y as internal and external seeds, respectively, the OIFT algorithm [17] computes an optimum partition $X_{opt} \in \mathcal{U}(x, y)$ by maximizing the above energy (Eq. 4) in a symmetric directed graph, that is,

$E(\boldsymbol{X}_{opt}) = \max_{\boldsymbol{X} \in \mathcal{U}(x,y)} E(\boldsymbol{X})$. OIFT is build upon the IFT framework by considering the following path function in a symmetric digraph:

$$f^{\vec{\sigma}}(\langle t \rangle) = \begin{cases} -1 & \text{if } t \in \boldsymbol{S_1} \cup \boldsymbol{S_0} \\ +\infty & \text{otherwise} \end{cases}$$

$$f^{\vec{\sigma}}(\pi_{r \rightsquigarrow s} \cdot \langle s, t \rangle) = \begin{cases} \omega(\langle s, t \rangle) & \text{if } r \in \boldsymbol{S_1} \\ \omega(\langle t, s \rangle) & \text{otherwise} \end{cases} \tag{5}$$

where, in this work, we use $\boldsymbol{S_1} = \{x\}$ and $\boldsymbol{S_0} = \{y\}$. The set $\boldsymbol{X}_{opt} \in \mathcal{U}(x,y)$ by OIFT is defined from the forest P computed by Algorithm 1 with $f^{\vec{\sigma}}$, by taking the pixels that were conquered by paths rooted in $\boldsymbol{S_1} = \{x\}$ [15].

For the purpose of unsupervised segmentation, for a given reference point r in the background, we would like to find a node $t' \in \boldsymbol{V} \setminus \{r\}$, resulting in a partition of maximum energy among all results in $\bigcup_{t \in \boldsymbol{V} \setminus \{r\}} \mathcal{U}(t, r)$. Fortunately, t' can be efficiently obtained by taking $t' = \arg \max_{t \in \boldsymbol{V}} V(t)$, where V is the cost map by IFT using f_{max} with $\boldsymbol{S} = \{r\}$ in the transpose graph, according to Lemma 1 from [5]. This result can be equally obtained by taking as V the cost map by IFT using f_ω with $\boldsymbol{S} = \{r\}$ in the transpose graph, but this later approach has the advantage that it allows us to rank the nodes according to their non-increasing order of values, such that the next cut with maximum energy can be easily selected (Figs. 1d, f, h). In this way we can create a hierarchy of partitions according to the following proposed algorithm:

Algorithm 2 – Unsupervised OIFT Algorithm (UOIFT)

INPUT: Image graph $G = \langle \boldsymbol{V}, \boldsymbol{A}, \omega \rangle$, a background reference node r and the desired number of regions k.

OUTPUT: Graph partition into k regions.

1. *Compute $V : \boldsymbol{V} \to \mathbb{R}$ by IFT with f_w and $\boldsymbol{S} = \{r\}$ in transpose graph G^T.*
2. *Sort the nodes in a non-increasing order of costs in V, getting $\{t_1, t_2, \ldots, t_n\}$, such that $V(t_i) \geq V(t_{i+1})$, $i = 1, \ldots, n-1$, where $n = |\boldsymbol{V}|$.*
3. *For each t_i, $i = 1, \ldots, k-1$, compute the graph partition of the strongly connected component containing t_i, separating its reference node from t_i by OIFT, and mark t_i as the reference node of the new obtained partition.*

Algorithm 2 generates a hierarchical segmentation by successive binary divisions, leading at the end to a segmentation with k partitions. Each IFT execution has linearithmic complexity in the number of involved nodes. Since UOIFT is based on multiple OIFTs executions (at each iteration being applied to smaller graphs), we considered a Region Adjacency Graph (RAG), where the regions are the superpixels computed by IFT-SLIC [2, 22] of size 10×10 pixels, rather than using the pixels directly (Fig. 1b). The initial reference node for the background was taken to be the first top/left superpixel in the image. In order to exploit the boundary polarity, we consider the following arc weight assignment:

$$\omega(\langle s, t \rangle) = \begin{cases} |I(t) - I(s)| \times (1 + \alpha) & \text{if } I(s) > I(t) \\ |I(t) - I(s)| \times (1 - \alpha) & \text{if } I(s) < I(t) \\ |I(t) - I(s)| & \text{otherwise} \end{cases} \tag{6}$$

where the weights $\omega(\langle s,t \rangle)$ are a combination of an undirected dissimilarity measure $|I(t) - I(s)|$ between neighboring superpixels s and t, multiplied by an orientation factor for $\alpha \in [-1,1]$, such that $\alpha < 0$ favors the segmentation of dark objects in a brighter background (Fig. 1g) and $\alpha > 0$ favors the opposite orientation (Fig. 1e), and $I(t)$ is the mean intensity inside superpixel t.

We conducted experiments, comparing the proposed unsupervised segmentation by OIFT with other graph-base methods. In the following, MST denotes the clustering of the previously described RAG nodes, obtained by successive removals of edges of maximum weight from the minimum spanning tree, where $\omega(\langle s,t \rangle) = |I(t) - I(s)|$, which is related to the nearest-neighbor (single-linkage) algorithm. FH denotes the unsupervised approach by Felzenszwalb and Huttenlocher [9], which computes a predicate for measuring the evidence for a boundary between two regions based on the minimum spanning tree computed in the RAG graph. EF+WS indicates the IFT-based watershed transform [3], after a volume extinction filter [20] set to preserve k leaves of the Min-tree, in order to consider only the most relevant catchment basins of a morphological gradient by a disk of radius 1. We used the code for the extinction filter available in the iamxt toolbox [21]. Note that Algorithm 2 encompasses as a particular case the single-linkage algorithm (MST) for $\alpha = 0.0$, since its first step corresponds to a MST computation for $\alpha = 0.0$ and each $V(t_i)$ on its second step corresponds to an edge of maximum weight in the MST.

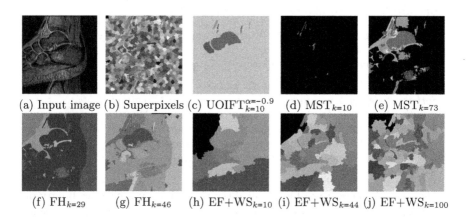

(a) Input image (b) Superpixels (c) UOIFT$_{k=10}^{\alpha=-0.9}$ (d) MST$_{k=10}$ (e) MST$_{k=73}$

(f) FH$_{k=29}$ (g) FH$_{k=46}$ (h) EF+WS$_{k=10}$ (i) EF+WS$_{k=44}$ (j) EF+WS$_{k=100}$

Fig. 2. Segmentation results for a real MR image of the foot. In order to properly segment the talus bone, MST required $k = 73$, FH $k = 46$ and EF+WS $k = 44$, while UOIFT could get it using $k = 10$ only.

We performed experiments using 40 slice images from real MR images of the foot to segment the talus bone (Fig. 2) and 40 slice images from CT cervical spine studies of 10 subjects to segment the spinal-vertebra. We computed the mean accuracy curve of all the methods for different values of k (Fig. 3). For each value of k, we computed the Dice similarity coefficient between the ground truth and

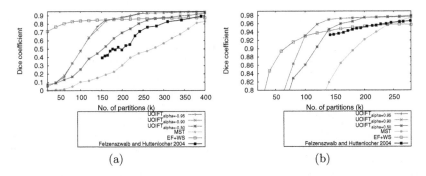

Fig. 3. The mean curves of Dice accuracy of the best union of produced regions for different values of k and methods, to segment: (a) talus bone and (b) spinal-vertebra.

the best union of segmented regions leading to the object. Since the method by Felzenszwalb and Huttenlocher only provides indirect control over the number of generated regions, in our plot, we are showing for FH the mean number of regions obtained for each value of its input parameter. The results indicate that UOIFT requires a lower value of k compared to the other approaches to generate the talus bone and the spinal-vertebra for different values of α, due to its boundary polarity information, demonstrating the robustness of UOIFT.

Regarding the computational time, for an image of 256×256 pixels, to compute 625 superpixels by IFT-SLIC takes 203.4 ms and the final clustering into 300 regions by UOIFT in the RAG takes only 13.15 ms, in an Intel Core i3-5005U CPU @ 2.00 GHz×4. As future work, we intend to extend UOIFT to consider more sophisticated predicates based on the following works [7,10–12,26].

Acknowledgements. Thanks to CNPq (308985/2015-0, 486988/2013-9, FINEP 1266/13), FAPESP (2014/12236-1, 2016/21591-5), NAP eScience and Coordenação de Aperfeiçoamento de Pessoal de Nível Superior (CAPES) - Finance Code 001 for funding.

References

1. Achanta, R., Shaji, A., Smith, K., Lucchi, A., Fua, P., Susstrunk, S.: Slic superpixels compared to state-of-the-art superpixel methods. IEEE Trans. Pattern Anal. Mach. Intell. **34**(11), 2274–2282 (2012)
2. Alexandre, E., Chowdhury, A., Falcão, A., Miranda, P.: IFT-SLIC: a general framework for superpixel generation based on simple linear iterative clustering and image foresting transform. In: 28th SIBGRAPI Conference on Graphics, Patterns and Images, pp. 337–344 (2015)
3. Audigier, R., Lotufo, R.: Seed-relative segmentation robustness of watershed and fuzzy connectedness approaches. In: Proceedings of the XX Brazilian Symposium on Computer Graphics and Image Processing, pp. 61–68, October 2007
4. Carballido-Gamio, J., Belongie, S., Majumdar, S.: Normalized cuts in 3D for spinal MRI segmentation. IEEE Trans. Med. Imaging **23**(1), 36–44 (2004)

5. Ccacyahuillca Bejar, H.H., Miranda, P.A.: Oriented relative fuzzy connectedness: theory, algorithms, and its applications in hybrid image segmentation methods. EURASIP J. Image Video Process. **2015**(1), 21 (2015)
6. Ciesielski, K.C., Falcão, A.X., Miranda, P.A.V.: Path-value functions for which dijkstra's algorithm returns optimal mapping. J. Math. Imaging Vis. **60**(7), 1025–1036 (2018)
7. Cousty, J., Najman, L., Kenmochi, Y., Guimarães, S.: Hierarchical segmentations with graphs: quasi-flat zones, minimum spanning trees, and saliency maps. J. Math. Imaging Vis. **60**(4), 479–502 (2018)
8. Falcão, A., Stolfi, J., Lotufo, R.: The image foresting transform: theory, algorithms, and applications. IEEE Trans. PAMI **26**(1), 19–29 (2004)
9. Felzenszwalb, P.F., Huttenlocher, D.P.: Efficient graph-based image segmentation. Int. J. Comput. Vis. **59**(2), 167–181 (2004)
10. Feng, W., Xiang, H., Zhu, Y.: An improved graph-based image segmentation algorithm and its GPU acceleration. In: 2011 Workshop on Digital Media and Digital Content Management, pp. 237–241, May 2011
11. Guimarães, S., Kenmochi, Y., Cousty, J., Jr., Z.P., Najman, L.: Hierarchizing graph-based image segmentation algorithms relying on region dissimilarity. Math. Morphol. Theory Appl. **2**(1), 55–75 (2017)
12. Guimarães, S.J.F., Cousty, J., Kenmochi, Y., Najman, L.: A hierarchical image segmentation algorithm based on an observation scale. In: Gimelfarb, G. et al. (eds) Structural, Syntactic, and Statistical Pattern Recognition. SSPR /SPR 2012. Lecture Notes in Computer Science, vol. 7626. Springer, Heidelberg (2012). https://doi.org/10.1007/978-3-642-34166-3_13
13. Krähenbühl, P., Koltun, V.: Geodesic object proposals. In: Fleet, D., Pajdla, T., Schiele, B., Tuytelaars, T. (eds.) ECCV 2014. LNCS, vol. 8693, pp. 725–739. Springer, Cham (2014). https://doi.org/10.1007/978-3-319-10602-1_47
14. Mansilla, L.A.C., Miranda, P.A.V., Cappabianco, F.A.M.: Oriented image foresting transform segmentation with connectivity constraints. In: 2016 IEEE International Conference on Image Processing (ICIP), pp. 2554–2558, September 2016
15. Mansilla, L., Miranda, P.: Image segmentation by oriented image foresting transform: handling ties and colored images. In: 18th International Conference on Digital Signal Processing (DSP), pp. 1–6. IEEE, Santorini, July 2013
16. Mansilla, L.A.C., Miranda, P.A.V.: Image segmentation by oriented image foresting transform with geodesic star convexity. In: Wilson, R., Hancock, E., Bors, A., Smith, W. (eds.) CAIP 2013. LNCS, vol. 8047, pp. 572–579. Springer, Heidelberg (2013). https://doi.org/10.1007/978-3-642-40261-6_69
17. Miranda, P., Mansilla, L.: Oriented image foresting transform segmentation by seed competition. IEEE Trans. Image Process. **23**(1), 389–398 (2014)
18. de Moraes Braz, C., Miranda, P.A.V.: Image segmentation by image foresting transform with geodesic band constraints. In: 2014 IEEE International Conference on Image Processing (ICIP), pp. 4333–4337, October 2014
19. Shi, J., Malik, J.: Normalized cuts and image segmentation. IEEE Trans. Pattern Anal. Mach. Intell. **22**(8), 888–905 (2000)
20. Silva, A.G., Lotufo, R.D.A.: Efficient computation of new extinction values from extended component tree. Pattern Recogn. Lett. **32**(1), 79–90 (2011)
21. Souza, R., Rittner, L., Machado, R., Lotufo, R.: iamxt: Max-tree toolbox for image processing and analysis. SoftwareX **6**, 81–84 (2017)
22. Vargas-Muñoz, J.E., Chowdhury, A.S., Barreto-Alexandre, E., Galvão, F.L., Miranda, P.A.V., Falcão, A.X.: An iterative spanning forest framework for super-pixel segmentation abs/1801.10041 (2018). http://arxiv.org/abs/1801.10041

23. Wang, S., Sinkind, J.: Image segmentation with ratio cut. IEEE Trans. Pattern Anal. Mach. Intell. **25**(6), 675–690 (2003)
24. Wang, S., Siskind, J.: Image segmentation with minimum mean cut. In: International Conference on Computer Vision (ICCV), vol. 1, pp. 517–525 (2001)
25. Wu, Z., Leahy, R.: An optimal graph theoretic approach to data clustering: theory and its applications to image segmentation. IEEE Trans. Pattern Anal. Mach. Intell. **15**(11), 1101–1113 (1993)
26. Zhang, M., Alhajj, R.: Improving the graph-based image segmentation method. In: 2006 18th IEEE International Conference on Tools with Artificial Intelligence (ICTAI 2006), pp. 617–624, November 2006

Dirichlet Series in Complex Network Modeling of Texture Images

João Batista Florindo[(✉)] [iD]

Institute of Mathematics, Statistics and Scientific Computing,
University of Campinas, Rua Sérgio Buarque de Holanda, 651,
Cidade Universitária "Zeferino Vaz" - Distr. Barão Geraldo,
Campinas, SP 13083-859, Brazil
jbflorindo@ime.unicamp.br
http://www.ime.unicamp.br

Abstract. This work investigates the use of Dirichlet series in the modeling of texture images, with application in image classification. The proposed model is based on a strategy that associates each pixel with its corresponding color (gray level in our case) to a vertex of a complex network and the gray level dissimilarity within neighbor pixels with edge weights. The degree distribution of such network is known to be very effective in providing image descriptors. Here, we propose an improvement over this technique, by working on this distribution as a Dirichlet (exponential) series and varying the exponential parameter. A family of statistical measures are extracted from the series and compose a feature vector employed here for texture image classification. In our tests, the achieved accuracy is promising when compared with other state-of-the-art approaches in different databases classically used for benchmark purposes.

Keywords: Complex networks · Dirichlet series ·
Texture image classification

1 Introduction

Texture images have been one of the most important elements in computer vision systems during the last decades, with numerous applications in material sciences [4], physics [12], medicine [16], geology [15], biology [18], and many other areas.

Even though texture image (or visual texture) is not a concept defined in rigorous terms, there exist some consensual points that such type of image is supposed to follow. One of the most important of such points is the locality, i.e., the idea that most information conveyed by a texture is confined within the limits of a local neighborhood around each pixel, i.e., in local pixel patterns.

The locality property is one of the main motivations for the modeling of texture images using complex networks, more specifically, by "small-world" models

© Springer Nature Switzerland AG 2019
R. Vera-Rodriguez et al. (Eds.): CIARP 2018, LNCS 11401, pp. 368–375, 2019.
https://doi.org/10.1007/978-3-030-13469-3_43

like those proposed in [2]. There, the image pixels are associated to vertexes in the network and the initial graph is complete (fully connected) with weighted edges. The edge weight corresponds to a normalized distance between pairs of corresponding pixels that takes into account both the spatial separation and the gray level dissimilarity. The dynamics of the image is analyzed by applying successive threshold values to the edge weight, in such a way that more and more edges are removed, making the network more and more sparse. Finally, the authors in [2] propose that the distribution of degrees in this family of networks can be used to provide texture descriptors. They apply such descriptors in image classification with great success.

Despite the accuracy achieved by the degree distribution, other measures extracted from complex networks based on histograms are more suitable to describe global information yet they are usually not sufficiently precise to represent the local picture. In this way, we propose in this study the use of Dirichlet series [7] to control the locality of the distribution by means of a carefully chosen parameter. This is a classical series where a succession of terms are powered to an exponential parameter and accumulated into a summation.

The proposed method, dubbed Dirichlet Complex Network (DCN) descriptors, employs the values in the degree histogram of the network as terms in the Dirichlet series and takes partial sums from that series to provide image descriptors. The accuracy in texture classification is tested over two benchmark databases (UIUC [9] and USPTex [3]) and compared to other state-of-the-art descriptors, namely, Local Binary Patterns (LBP) [13], LBP+VAR [13], Bouligand-Minkowski (BM) fractal descriptors [1], Local Phase Quantization (LPQ) [14], Binarized Statistical Image Features (BSIF) [8], and the original complex network (CN) descriptors in [2]. Our proposal is competitive when compared with all the other compared methods in both databases. The results confirm our expectation about the potential of Dirichlet exponentiation as a means of evidencing complex statistical relations that are not explicit in the original histogram.

2   Related Works

Most methods for texture recognition in the literature can be divided into local-based (e.g. co-occurrence matrices [6], local binary patterns [13], bag-of-visual-words [19] and their respective variations) and multiscale approaches (e.g. multifractals [20] and fractal descriptors [3], spatial pyramids [10], scale-invariant feature transform [11], and others).

Complex networks represent in this context a paradigm that allows a combination of both local and multiscale viewpoint over the image. The most well-known and successful method in this category is that presented in [2]. Despite the success of basic statistical quantifiers as those used in [2], more recently the literature have presented more advanced techniques to better express the network model. An example of such alternative analysis is the estimation of a type of fractal dimension in [17] based on the well-known Riemann zeta function.

The method proposed here is inspired in [2] and [17], even though we do not use the zeta function but rather the most general idea of Dirichlet series. Besides, we are not focusing on specific measures like the fractal dimension, but on a technique to obtaining texture descriptors as precise and generalist as possible.

3   Complex Networks Model for Texture Description

The complex networks employed here are described in details in [2] and here we only summarize the main idea. In that model, the gray-scale image I is represented by a network $G(V, E)$, where G is a set of vertexes and E a set of edges. Each pixel in I with Cartesian coordinates (x, y) is associated with a vertex $v_{xy} \in V$. The set of edges is composed by

$$E = \{e = (v_{xy}, v_{x'y'}) : \sqrt{(x - x')^2 + (y - y')^2} \leq r\}, \tag{1}$$

where r is the neighborhood radius, a predefined parameter. Each edge $e = (v_{xy}, v_{x'y'})$ is associated with a weight $w(e)$, defined by

$$w(e) = \frac{(x - x')^2 + (y - y')^2 + r^2 \frac{|I(x,y) - I(x',y')|}{L}}{2r^2}, \tag{2}$$

where L is the maximum gray level. This corresponds to a normalized Euclidean distance in a three-dimensional space where the pixels are mapped to points with coordinates $(x, y, I(x, y))$.

To analyze the evolution dynamics of the network model, the original model $G(V, E)$ gives rise to a family of subgraphs $G_t(V, E_t)$, which preserves the set of vertexes but removes a subset of edges by thresholding the corresponding weights, i.e.:

$$E_t = \{e \in E : w(e) \leq t\}. \tag{3}$$

For each vertex $g \in G_t$ we can compute its degree by

$$d_t(g) = |\{e \in E_t : v \in e\}|, \forall g \in G, \tag{4}$$

where $|\cdot|$ stands for set cardinality.

4   Proposed Method

We propose the use of Dirichlet series as a mechanism to highlight different patterns in the degree distribution. The obtained descriptors are called Dirichlet Complex Network (DCN) descriptors.

The family of Dirichlet series are characterized by the general expression

$$\sum_{n=1}^{\infty} a_n n^{-\alpha}, \tag{5}$$

where both the sequence of numbers a_n and the exponent α are complex-valued (here they are real-valued in particular). As usual in any conventional series, n are integer numbers, although in practice the same effect of a real-valued n is achieved by setting the α parameter appropriately.

Here, we use the number of vertexes with a particular degree n as the term a_n and take the partial sums of the series. Therefore given the degree vector d_t as defined in (4), we have the degree histogram

$$h_t(k) = \sum_{g \in G} \delta(d_t(g), k), \tag{6}$$

where $\delta(x, y)$ is the Kronecker delta (1 if $x = y$, 0, otherwise) and the kth term in the proposed Dirichlet series is obtained by

$$D_t^\alpha(k) = \sum_{n=1}^{k} h_t(n) n^\alpha, \tag{7}$$

where α is a parameter free to be set empirically or using any specific heuristic. The degree Dirichlet distribution is provided by

$$p_t^\alpha(k) = D_t^\alpha(k) / \sum_{k=1}^{d_{max}} D_t^\alpha(k). \tag{8}$$

The statistical measures employed to compose the descriptors are similar to those described in [2], i.e., the energy E, entropy K and contrast C:

$$E_t^\alpha = \sum_{k=1}^{d_{max}} (p_t^\alpha(k))^2 \qquad K_t^\alpha = -\sum_{k=1}^{d_{max}} p_t^\alpha(k) \log p_t^\alpha(k) \qquad C_t^\alpha = \sum_{k=1}^{d_{max}} k^2 p_t^\alpha(k) \tag{9}$$

Here, we obtained interesting performance by combining $\alpha = -9$ and $\alpha = -10$. We also employed $r = 2$ and t ranging between 0.05 and 0.53, with increments 0.015, as recommended in [2]. The dimension of the feature vector is reduced by the Karhunen-Loève (KL) transform [5], such that the final descriptors effectively correspond to

$$D = KL \left(\bigcup_{t \in [0.05, 0.53], \, \alpha \in \{-9, -10\}} \{E_t^\alpha, K_t^\alpha, C_t^\alpha\} \right), \tag{10}$$

where $KL(x)$ is the KL transform of the vector x. Figure 1 summarizes the main steps.

5 Experiments

Two benchmark data sets are employed for validation and comparisons in this work, namely, UIUC as used in [9] and USPTex [3].

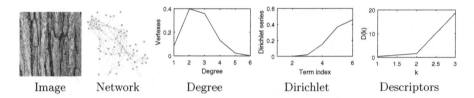

| Image | Network | Degree | Dirichlet | Descriptors |

Fig. 1. Proposed method. From left to right, the original texture, network representation, degree distribution, Dirichlet series ($\alpha = -9$) and the respective descriptors (energy, entropy and contrast).

UIUC is a database composed by 40 large gray-scale images representing landscapes, animals, materials, etc. Each image is split into 25 non-overlapping windows, each one with dimensions 256×256. This results in a database of 1000 texture images categorized into 25 groups.

The process to generate USPTex [3] is similar to that employed in UIUC. Originally, 192 large photographies (512×384) are captured under non-controlled conditions and from each one of these images we extract 12 smaller windows (128×128) without overlapping. At the end this corresponds to a collection of images with a total amount of 2292 samples divided into 191 classes. Finally, for the comparison accomplished here where only gray-scale methods are considered, these images are converted to gray levels.

The proposal here described is compared with other classical and state-of-the-art texture descriptors in the literature, to know, Local Binary Patterns (LBP) [13], LBP+VAR [13], Bouligand-Minkowski (BM) fractal descriptors [1], Local Phase Quantization (LPQ) [14], Binarized Statistical Image Features (BSIF) [8], and the original complex network (CN) descriptors in [2].

The classifier employed for the proposed descriptors is the linear discriminant analysis [5]. Testing and training sets are determined by following a randomized 5-fold scheme, which is repeated 100 times to provide the average accuracy as well as the corresponding error (standard deviation). As for the other compared methods from the literature, we adopted the parameters suggested in the respective references.

6   Results

Table 1 lists the accuracy of the proposed method (DCN) in texture classification compared with other state-of-the-art approaches. The proposed descriptors achieved the highest accuracy in both databases. Descriptors based on complex networks, i.e., that presented in [2] and the method proposed here, present relevant advantage over the other approaches, especially in USPTex. This is exactly the most challenging data set, presenting a significantly larger number of images and categories.

Figure 2 exhibits the confusion matrices for the methods providing the two highest accuracies in both data sets. We restricted USPTex matrices to the first

Table 1. Percentage of images correctly classified in UIUC and USPTex databases and respective errors.

Method	UIUC	USPTex
LBP	77.6 ± 0.8	67.9 ± 0.4
LBP+VAR	79.5 ± 0.7	69.9 ± 0.6
BM	78.6 ± 0.6	77.9 ± 0.4
LPQ	74.2 ± 0.9	76.3 ± 0.4
BSIF	78.0 ± 0.8	75.8 ± 0.4
CN	78.8 ± 0.4	86.0 ± 0.3
DCN (Proposed)	80.1 ± 0.6	87.7 ± 0.4

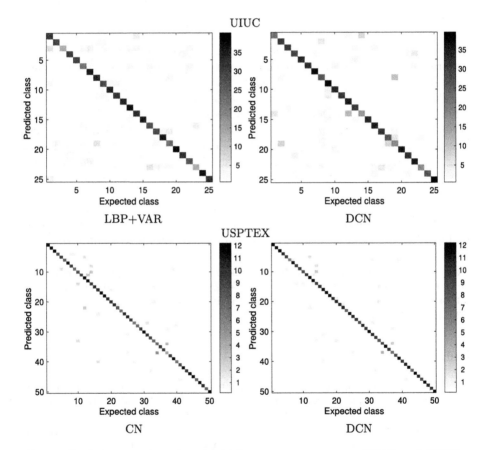

Fig. 2. Confusion matrices for the highest success rates on UIUC and USPTex databases.

50 classes to facilitate the visualization. Even though both approaches present difficulties in distinguishing complex groups as the classes 18/19 in UIUC, the

presented proposal yielded a reduced number of gray points outside the diagonal, especially in USPTex database.

Here the role of the exponentiated Dirichlet summation is to equip the histogram with a nonlinear viewpoint, which allows richer analysis of the represented texture. In particular, the negative exponents employed in our application have the ability of giving larger significance to the smaller values of the histogram. The final descriptors are in this way more balanced than the original ones and information that was originally disregarded are now taken into account in the classification process. The effectiveness of such consideration is verified and confirmed by the outstanding result obtained in such challenge task of classifying large databases of texture images.

7 Conclusions

This work proposed and investigated the use of Dirichlet series to improve the performance of histogram-based descriptors of texture images, in particular, those descriptors acquired from a complex network modeling.

The method was tested on the classification of benchmark databases and the achieved accuracy outperformed other state-of-the-art descriptors. Such great performance is explained by the nonlinearity introduced by the Dirichlet series. The partial sum used here employs negative exponents, which, by giving higher weight to the smaller histogram values, make the descriptors more balanced and preserve information that is usually discarded by the classical complex network descriptors.

The great accuracy confirmed by the tests also suggests the potential of the proposed descriptors for practical applications in a number of real-world problems where the classification of texture images plays fundamental role.

Acknowledgements. J. B. F. gratefully acknowledges the financial support of The State of São Paulo Research Foundation (FAPESP) (Proc. 2016/16060-0) and from National Council for Scientific and Technological Development, Brazil (CNPq) (Grant #301480/2016-8).

References

1. Backes, A.R., Casanova, D., Bruno, O.M.: Plant leaf identification based on volumetric fractal dimension. Int. J. Pattern Recognit. Artif. Intell. **23**(6), 1145–1160 (2009)
2. Backes, A.R., Casanova, D., Bruno, O.M.: Texture analysis and classification: a complex network-based approach. Inf. Sci. **219**, 168–180 (2013)
3. Casanova, D., Florindo, J., Falvo, M., Bruno, O.: Texture analysis using fractal descriptors estimated by the mutual interference of color channels. Inf. Sci. **346**, 58–72 (2016)
4. Chappard, D., Degasne, I., Hure, G., Legrand, E., Audran, M., Basle, M.: Image analysis measurements of roughness by texture and fractal analysis correlate with contact profilometry. Biomaterials **24**(8), 1399–1407 (2003)

5. Duda, R.O., Hart, P.E.: Pattern Classification and Scene Analysis. Wiley, New York (1973)
6. Haralick, R.M.: Statistical and structural approaches to texture. Proc. IEEE **67**(5), 786–804 (1979)
7. Hardy, G., Riesz, M.: The General Theory of Dirichlet's Series. Cambridge Tracts in Mathematics and Mathematical Physics. University Press, London (1952)
8. Kannala, J., Rahtu, E.: BSIF: binarized statistical image features. In: ICPR, pp. 1363–1366. IEEE Computer Society (2012)
9. Kilic, K., Abiyev, R.: Exploiting the synergy between fractal dimension and lacunarity for improved texture recognition. Sig. Process. **91**(10), 2332–2344 (2011)
10. Lazebnik, S., Schmid, C., Ponce, J.: Beyond bags of features: spatial pyramid matching for recognizing natural scene categories. In: Proceedings of the 2006 IEEE Computer Society Conference on Computer Vision and Pattern Recognition - Volume 2, pp. 2169–2178, CVPR 2006. IEEE Computer Society, Washington, DC (2006)
11. Lowe, D.G.: Distinctive image features from scale-invariant keypoints. Int. J. Comput. Vision **60**, 91–110 (2004)
12. Nkono, C., Féménias, O., Lesne, A., Mercier, J.C., Ngounouno, F.Y., Demaiffe, D.: Relationship between the fractal dimension of orthopyroxene distribution and the temperature in mantle xenoliths. Geol. J. **51**(5), 748–759 (2016)
13. Ojala, T., Pietikäinen, M., Mäenpää, T.: Multiresolution gray-scale and rotation invariant texture classification with local binary patterns. IEEE Trans. Pattern Anal. Mach. Intell. **24**(7), 971–987 (2002)
14. Ojansivu, V., Heikkilä, J.: Blur insensitive texture classification using local phase quantization. In: Elmoataz, A., Lezoray, O., Nouboud, F., Mammass, D. (eds.) ICISP 2008. LNCS, vol. 5099, pp. 236–243. Springer, Heidelberg (2008). https://doi.org/10.1007/978-3-540-69905-7_27
15. Plotnick, R.E.: Recurrent hierarchical patterns and the fractal distribution of fossil localities. Geology **45**(4), 295 (2017)
16. Raman, S.P., Chen, Y., Schroeder, J.L., Huang, P., Fishman, E.K.: CT texture analysis of renal masses: pilot study using random forest classification for prediction of pathology. Acad. Radiol. **21**(12), 1587–1596 (2014)
17. Shanker, O.: Graph zeta function and dimension of complex network. Mod. Phys. Lett. B **9**, 639–644 (2007)
18. da Silva, N.R., Florindo, J.B., Gómez, M.C., Rossatto, D.R., Kolb, R.M., Bruno, O.M.: Plant identification based on leaf midrib cross-section images using fractal descriptors. PLoS ONE **10**(6), 1–14 (2015)
19. Varma, M., Zisserman, A.: A statistical approach to texture classification from single images. Int. J. Comput. Vision **62**(1–2), 61–81 (2005)
20. Xu, Y., Ji, H., Fermueller, C.: Viewpoint invariant texture description using fractal analysis. Int. J. Comput. Vision **83**(1), 85–100 (2009)

Detection of Vertices in Sketched Drawings of Polyhedral Shapes

Pedro Company[1] , Peter A. C. Varley[1] , Raquel Plumed[2(✉)] ,
and Jorge D. Camba[3]

[1] Institute of New Imaging Technology, Universitat Jaume I,
Castellón de la Plana, Spain
pcompany@uji.es, varley@uji.es
[2] Department of Mechanical Engineering and Construction, UJI,
Castellón de la Plana, Spain
plumed@uji.es
[3] Department of Computer Graphics Technology, Purdue University,
West Lafayette, USA
jdorribo@purdue.edu

Abstract. We outline an artificial perception model for an algorithm that detects junctions in casual sketches. These sketches are used by skilled individuals to visually and quickly convey ideas.

The new algorithm detects junctions in 2D, before any 3D model is available. Tips of line segments are merged into 2D junctions that are assumed to depict 3D vertices. The current scope is limited to line-drawings of polyhedral objects vectorized from sketches. The process mainly uses information that is available in the neighborhood of the candidate junction. The algorithm calculates a figure of merit that estimates how likely a junction is to be perceived as such.

Keywords: Sketch-based modeling · Polyhedral shapes · Vertices · Junctions

1 Introduction

People use sketches because they convey visual information that can readily be perceived by humans (although not so readily by computers). Junctions are not necessarily contained explicitly in the original sketch or automatically obtained at the vectorization stage.

In this paper, we describe and assess an improved approach for merging tips of vectorized lines to produce 2D junctions (points where the tips of the lines meet) that depict 3D vertices (points where the edges of polyhedral shapes meet). The input for our vertex-merging approach is a set of vectorized line segments (or simply "lines") delimited by their tips. Then, vertex detection must merge dangling tips to determine junctions that depict valid vertices. The output is a *line-drawing*: a list of lines and a list of junctions, where each line connects two

© Springer Nature Switzerland AG 2019
R. Vera-Rodriguez et al. (Eds.): CIARP 2018, LNCS 11401, pp. 376–383, 2019.
https://doi.org/10.1007/978-3-030-13469-3_44

junctions. Junctions are *(x, y)* coordinate pairs of shared endpoints that likely correspond to vertices of the depicted object.

We distinguish *careful* and *casual* sketches (also called *detailed* and *quick* sketches). Examples of both types of sketches are provided in Fig. 1. Based on the classification of sketches defined by Ferguson [5], we assume that thought sketches are usually casual, while prescriptive sketches tend to be more careful.

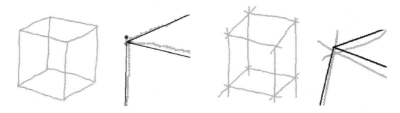

Fig. 1. Careful sketches include junctions detected by proximity (left), while casual sketches include junctions detected by closure (right).

The algorithm does not assert "this is a vertex" but "this is more or less likely to be a vertex". In this regard, we provide a candidate beautified line drawing for a subsequent global perception mechanism based on our hypothesis that a local intersection of a set of strokes which can barely be accepted as depicting a common junction when perceived separately, may be seen as a valid vertex when put into context (see, for instance, the lower left junction in example of Fig. 1, right).

2 Related Work

Approaches to drawing vectorization and beautification typically include *endpoint snapping* strategies (like the intersection detection in [7]).

Optimization based formulations [4], or machine learning techniques (such as convolutional network approaches [11]) are necessarily global approaches. Training a machine learning system with abstract drawings that do not represent any perceivable shape would be unrealistic, while using sketches that depict shapes necessarily forces the trainer to use—even unconsciously—her global perception to judge the particular junctions.

Instead, our goal is to improve the approach of determining a linearly decreasing likelihood for tip snapping based on the distance between tips [6]. A similar approach was recently proposed by Liu et al. to simplify over-traced sketches [9]. Similarly to Liu et al., we have also adopted a strategy based on proximity and continuity, but also closure.

Finally, detecting whether a user is drawing carefully or casually is feasible—see, for instance, recent efforts to use the design intent embedded in the features of the product to quantify uncertainty [3]. However, sketches may contain a mixture of casual and careful junctions. Therefore, by assuming that both junction types must be detected, a bi-fold approach was adopted.

3   Proposed Approach

Two main ideas are combined in the new approach: (1) well-known Gestalt Principles must guide the *perception* of the junctions, and (2) the strategy must manage both *careful* and *casual* sketches.

Careful sketches are based on reification: the action of perceiving the tips of two or more lines as representing one single junction. By applying the Gestalt law of proximity, two or more carefully drawn tips that are close to each other are to be reified as a single junction (Fig. 1, left). The way this rule applies is explained in detail by Hoffman's rule #2, "if the tips of two lines coincide in an image, then always interpret them as coinciding in 3D", and #4 "Interpret elements nearby in an image as nearby in 3D" [8].

For casual sketches, the driving idea is emergence, i.e., tips are presumed to be imprecise, thus junctions must emerge, not at the tips of the lines but at the intersections between the lines (or their extensions). In this case, the law of closure dominates (Fig. 1, right). As stated by Hoffman's rule #13, "if three or more curves intersect at a common point in an image interpret them as intersecting at a common point in space" [8].

The goodness of the detected junctions must be quantified by a figure of merit, which is in the range [0, 1]. 1 means that the junction is to always be perceived as such by humans; 0 means that humans will hardly ever perceive the junction.

The full source code of the algorithm is freely available at [2], including examples that demonstrate the capabilities and limitations of the approach.

3.1   Reification of Careful Vertices

The classic nearest-neighbor criterion of merging tips by determining their distances to one another is used by our approach to merge junctions that represent vertices defined by carefully drawn lines. To this end, the Delaunay triangulation of the set of tips is calculated by using an adapted version of the Dumoulin C++ implementation of the algorithm by Bourke [1]. Next, for each tip, those other tips that share at least one triangle with it are labeled as neighbors, unless they also share one line. Finally, the neighboring tips are checked to determine whether they are close enough to be merged. This strategy is fast and favors finding trihedral junctions. Some junctions of the external outline, or of higher valence, may not get completely reified (thus forcing the later emergence process to complete them). The method was improved in a number of ways.

First, we consider the perceptual principle that longer lines usually belong to main features—which are perceived first—whereas shorter lines are usually perceived as belonging to secondary details. Thus, the algorithm searches for junctions between longer lines first.

Second, errors that are acceptable in the location of the tips tend to be proportional to the total length of each line: errors in the location of the tips of longer lines are accepted to be greater in absolute value than those of shorter lines. Thus, the threshold distance between the tip and the candidate junction is defined as a percentage of the length of each line.

Third, since the sketches are assumed to depict orthographic representations of flat figures or pictorial representations of polyhedral shapes, the range between right angles and cubic corners (see [10] for a definition of cubic corners) is prioritized. To this end, an anisotropic *merging area* is defined around each tip (see Fig. 2 left, where the tip v_2 of line e_2 must be closer than v_3 to be labeled as close enough to merge with v_1). The merging area depicted in Fig. 2 left is merely illustrative, since the intersection between the lines may not necessarily be coincident with any of the tips. Therefore, the distance allowed between two lines (e_1 and e_2 in Fig. 2 right) is calculated and then compared to the actual distance between their tips. The allowed distance (r_2 in Fig. 2 right) is calculated as the product of a threshold *maxDist* (fixed at 8% of the length of the line) and an *allowance* $= 2 - cos(e_i, e_j)$. The allowed distance (*maxDist*allowance*) is at its maximum value for 90° (20%), and still high for 60° (15%). In axonometric views squared lines are commonly depicted by lines at angles close to 60°.

The allowance penalizes merging tips of collinear lines that are poorly drawn. Naturally, collinear lines are uncommon in polyhedral vertices and non collinear lines are seldom depicted as collinear (as this situation would conflict with Hoffman's rule #3 "Always interpret lines collinear in an image as collinear in 3D" [8]). By using the allowance to calculate the merits of the candidate junctions, the merging of perpendicular lines is prioritized.

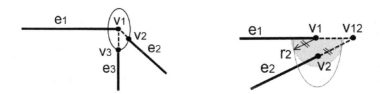

Fig. 2. The neighborhood of each tip depends on the relative angles of the lines that contain the candidate tips to merge (left), while close tips are merged at the intersection of both segments, even if the intersection falls outside the merging area (right).

If tip v_2 is sufficiently close to v_1 (this is, if $|v_1 - v_2| < |r_2|$, where $|r_2|$ depends on the relative orientation between e_1 and e_2) the intersection of the two segments is defined as the common merged tip, regardless of whether or not this new tip falls outside the merging area (Fig. 2 right). This way, lines are prevented from rotating while merging their tips.

Up to this point, our approach assumes that tips of vectorized lines are not yet connected to each other, i.e., the *valence* (number of lines that share the tip) is 1 for all the tips. However, this is not the case when the merging-vertices algorithm progresses, as tips that have already been visited may be partially merged. Therefore, the goal is to prioritize the most populated junctions. The general rules to *cluster* tips of valence other than 1 are as follows: (1) If valences are different for both tips, the tip with the highest valence remains fixed while the other is moved to the cluster, (2) If valences are equal (and different from 1) both tips are moved to the cluster into the midpoint they define. A clustering threshold is defined to prevent lines from excessive rotation. A merge is declared valid if all the lines connected to the moving tip rotate less than $maxRot$ (fixed at $10°$) when redirected to the new tip.

Therefore, the merit of reified junctions is assigned -1 if tips are separated more than the allowed distance or the maximum rotation of any line exceeds $maxRot$. Otherwise, the merit of reified junctions is in the range average-to-good, calculated as a fixed minimum reward for careful junctions RM (fixed at 0.50), plus two variable components. The first variable component, which depends on the distance merit, equals RD if both tips are coincident, and decreases linearly to 0 for tips separated by the allowed distance ($maxDist*allowance$). The second variable component depends on the rotations: it equals RR if no line rotates to merge the tips, and linearly decreases to 0 if the maximum rotation of any line equals $maxRot$. To ensure that the merits of valid junctions are in the range $[0, 1]$, RD is fixed as $(1 - RM)$, and RR is null, for lines with valence 1. For other lines, both RD and RR are fixed as $(1 - RM)/2$.

3.2 Emergence of Casual Vertices

Two rules apply to help the emergence of junctions at the intersections between casual lines (or their extensions).

First, Hoffman's rule #13 is used to prioritize trihedral junctions as follows: three dangling lines that intersect close to each other, and close to their tips, define a new junction (Fig. 1 left). The maximum allowed distance between intersections is $maxDistTriplets$ (set to 10% of the length of the longest line in the triplet). The distance from the intersection to the tips must fit in a *valid range*. It may not be longer than $inTol$ (50%) of the average length of the three candidate lines for intersections inside the segment, and no longer than $outTol$ (25%) of the average length of the three candidate lines for intersections in the extension of the segment. Assigning an asymmetric range ($inTol > outTol$) prioritizes intersections inside the segments, which was experimentally determined to be the common perceptual behavior.

The intersections must be the closest to the tips in order to prevent false merges such as the one illustrated in Fig. 3, left. In this case, semi-line e_1 could be incorrectly merged with semi-lines e_0 and e_2 if they were processed from longer to shorter. The three semi-lines that intersect close to each other are connected to a common junction located at the centroid of the three intersection points (Fig. 3, middle). The merit of the emerged triple junction is in the range $[0, ETM]$, since it is assigned as $ETM * (1 - distCentroid/maxDistTriplets)$, where $distCentroid$ is the distance between the centroid and the most distant intersection point. In our implementation, ETM is fixed as 0.5, to ensure that the merits of emerged junctions are in the average-to-poor range. Next, a relaxed search is performed after removing the condition that intersections must be the closest ones to the tips. This provides a second chance for detecting those casual triplets that are close to each other and include long lines (which are parsed first) that are more casual than the short ones.

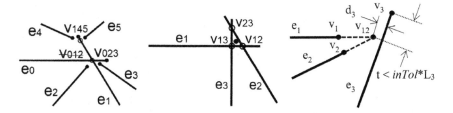

Fig. 3. Triplets should only merge semi-lines that intersect closer to the tips (left), while the centroid of the intersections between three dangling lines emerges as a junction (middle), and a line that needs excessive rotation to merge to the original neighboring tips can merge when relaxing rotation (right).

Second, emergence is also considered by clustering dangling lines to nearby junctions, i.e., a dangling line that passes closely to a junction of valence two or higher must be clustered to it. "Passing closely" implies that the distance between the line and the junction (such as d_3 in Fig. 3 right) is less than *maxDist-Dangling*, which is set to a percentage (10%) of the length of the dangling line. An allowed distance (*maxDistDangling*allowance*) is used where the *allowance* is calculated between the dangling line and its most collinear line in the junction (i.e. lowest allowance between the dangling line and each of the lines in the junction). It also implies that the point of perpendicular projection of the junction on the semi-line must fit in the *valid range*: *inTol* of its length from the tip of the semi-line if it is inside the segment (t in Fig. 3 right), or *outTol* if it is in the extension of the segment.

The merit for dangling lines merged to junctions (*EDM*) is calculated as the minimum of two components: first, merit is 1 for dangling lines passing over the junction, and decreases down to 0 for lines passing at a distance of *maxDistDangling*. Second, merit is 1 for dangling lines where the closest point to the junction is the tip of the dangling line, and decreases linearly for lines whose closest point to the junction is at the limit of the *valid range*. Dangling lines with negative merit are not merged. As a result, the new merit assigned to the junction where a dangling line is merged is the minimum between the current merit of the junction and the merit of merging the dangling line to the junction.

4 Validation

A total of 91 subjects (17 from Spain, 61 from the US, and 13 from Italy) were interviewed. Most subjects had an engineering background (18 were engineering educators and 73 engineering students). Participants were asked to casually sketch the models shown in Fig. 4.

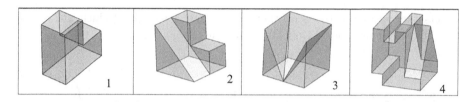

Fig. 4. Transparent models, built with SolidWorks, used in the experiment.

Incorrect sketches included: (a) missing strokes, (b) dashed hidden lines, (c) ignored short beautification strokes and (d) overtraced sketches. We discarded 44 sketches from model 1, 25 from model 2, 24 from model 3 and 43 from model 4 (all from engineering students). Model 4 frequently included missing lines, most likely because of its complexity, while missing lines in Model 1 where possibly due to its viewpoint or orientation.

The participants' sketches were vectorized by the authors and the line drawings parsed against the "ground truth" of the vertices of the models. Since the subjects were asked to replicate four particular models, we assume they tried to replicate the junctions of the model. Our algorithm was used to calculate which of those junctions were more or less frequently detected. From the analysis of the frequencies with which vertices of each model were recognized correctly, we can conclude that:

- The algorithm does not fail in recognizing all "carefully" drawn vertices.
- The algorithm always assigns merits greater than 0.5 to careful vertices.
- For imperfect vertices, the assigned merits are in the range [0, 0.5].
- The algorithm tends to leave lines without converging to a vertex (dangling lines) before making false convergences. In borderline cases of particular points of view (such as Model 1) the algorithm becomes more sensitive to casual vertices.
- When the drawing contains strokes of very different lengths (Model 4), the algorithm finds it difficult to group the short vertices correctly.
- The algorithm is not susceptible to the direction in which the strokes are drawn. The general metrics we used eliminate the possible bias that could be introduced by drawing with the right or left hand.

5   Conclusions

Our hypothesis that carefully sketched vertices must be reified, while casually sketched vertices must emerge, was indirectly validated, as it guided the design and implementation of an algorithm that improves on previous vectorization techniques, which were based exclusively on reification strategies.

The perceptual essence of the algorithm combined with sequential detection provides efficiency. The algorithm detects and fixes the best defined junctions, and only applies more complex calculations to poorly defined vertices.

Our approach quickly and correctly detects vertices in line drawings of polyhedral objects that have been vectorized from hand-drawn sketches. Vertices of polyhedral shapes depicted by highly casual sketches can still be detected provided that the sketch does not contain extremely close junctions. In addition, our tests suggest that our method, if re-tuned, may also be useful for other sketched shapes.

We are confident that the set of metrics based on relevant geometric features derived from studies on human perception, along with the required global scene information, may feed a future machine learning approach to further improves the current success ratio of our approach. However, since the approach still relies on an excessively large set of parameters, further studies are needed to determine whether a reduced set of independent parameters can be defined.

References

1. Bourke, P.: Triangulate: efficient triangulation; algorithm suitable for terrain modelling. In: Pan Pacific Computer Conference (1989). http://paulbourke.net/papers/triangulate/. Accessed June 2018
2. Company, P., Plumed, R., Varley, P., Camba, J.: Finding vertices in 2D line-drawings of polyhedral shapes (2018). http://www.regeo.uji.es/FindingVertices.htm, geometric Reconstruction Group, http://www.regeo.uji.es
3. Ekwaro-Osire, S., Cruz-Lozano, R., Endeshaw, H., Dias, J.: Uncertainty in communication with a sketch. J. Integr. Des. Process. Sci. **20**(4), 43–60 (2016)
4. Favreau, J., Lafarge, F., Bousseau, A.: Fidelity vs. simplicity: a global approach to line drawing vectorization. ACM Trans. Graph. **35**(4) (2016). Article No. 120
5. Ferguson, E.: Engineering and the Mind's Eye. The MIT Press, Cambridge (1992)
6. Fišer, J., Asente, P., Schiller, S., Sýkora, D.: Advanced drawing beautification with shipshape. Comput. Graph. **2**(56), 46–58 (2016)
7. Governi, L., Furferi, R., Palai, M., Volpe, Y.: 3D geometry reconstruction from orthographic views: a method based on 3D image processing and data fitting. Comput. Ind. **2**(64), 1290–1300 (2013)
8. Hoffman, D.: Visual Intelligence: How We Create What We See. W.W. Norton & Company, New York (1998)
9. Liu, X., Wong, T., Heng, P.: Closure-aware sketch simplification. ACM Trans. Graph. **34**(6) (2015). Article No. 168
10. Perkins, D.: Cubic Corners, Oblique Views of Pictures, the Perception of Line Drawings of Simple Space Forms. Geometry and the Perception of Pictures: Three Studies. Technical report, Harvard University, Cambridge, Mass. Graduate School of Education (1972). files.eric.ed.gov/fulltext/ED114328.pdf
11. Simo-Serra, E., Iizuka, S., Sasaki, K., Ishikawa, H.: Learning to simplify: fully convolutional networks for rough sketch cleanup. ACM Trans. Graph. **35**(4) (2016)

A Note on the Phase Congruence Method in Image Analysis

Carlos A. Jacanamejoy[1,2] and Manuel G. Forero[1(✉)]

[1] Facultad de Ingeniería, Universidad de Ibagué, Ibagué, Colombia
{carlos.jacanamejoy,manuel.forero}@unibague.edu.co
[2] Facultad de Ciencias Naturales y Matemáticas,
Universidad de Ibagué, Ibagué, Colombia

Abstract. Phase congruence technique developed by Kovesi allows the detection of edges in images by analyzing the phases of their frequency components. A limitation of this technique is that it does not allow the detection of closely spaced edges that have different intensities. However, this situation occurs frequently in images, which therefore limits the use of this method. This study aims to propose a method that can overcome this limitation. Unlike the original technique, the proposed study uses a high degree of overlap between different frequency components to allow the detection of contiguous edges of low intensity. To avoid the problems that arise from high overlap, we modify the sensitivity of the phase congruence, allowing us to detect weak edges while discarding the noise associated with the proposed changes. We present our results and compare them with the results obtained using the existing technique.

Keywords: Phase congruency · Edge detection · Image processing · Segmentation

1 Introduction

Segmentation is one of the most important techniques in image processing as it allows the separation of regions of interest from the image background. There are various methods for conducting segmentation. Phase-congruence method, which was proposed by Kovesi [2], is based on a perception model that uses the local energy of the image, postulating that its most important characteristics occur where its frequency components maximize the phase coincidence. Unlike most popular segmentation techniques, this method uses the frequency spectrum, which makes it unattractive due to its high computational cost and high sensitivity to noise. With recent changes introduced by Kovesi in the definition of phase congruence coupled with the use of more powerful computers, this technique has taken on new significance. An important disadvantage of the original method is that it does not allow the detection of closely spaced edges of variable intensity. Nevertheless, this technique has been used by a number of researchers because it is invariant to changes in illumination and contrast [4–10].

© Springer Nature Switzerland AG 2019
R. Vera-Rodriguez et al. (Eds.): CIARP 2018, LNCS 11401, pp. 384–391, 2019.
https://doi.org/10.1007/978-3-030-13469-3_45

In order to overcome this deficiency in edge detection, in the proposed study, we analyzed the original technique proposed by Kovesi, and contrary to what he established, we adjusted the parameters of the banks of wavelet filters, allowing the spectra of each filter to overlap. This overcomes the limitation of the original technique. To overcome the generation of false edges that this overlapping produces, we have reinterpreted the concept of phase congruence to reduce its sensitivity to false edges.

This article is organized as follows. In Sect. 2, we first present a brief description of phase congruence proposed by Kovesi, highlighting the above mentioned problem. In Sect. 3, we discuss our proposed solution, and in Sect. 4 we present the results obtained from synthetic and real images. Finally, we present our conclusions in Sect. 5.

2   Phase Congruency

Kovesi [2] describes phase congruency in the following way:

For a one-dimensional signal, the phase congruence (PC) function at a point x is defined as the local energy function $E(x)$ divided by the sum of the different Fourier components A_n, Eq. (1). Figure 1 shows a vector scheme of the concept.

$$PC(x) = \frac{E(x)}{\sum_{n=1}^{N} A_n(x)}. \tag{1}$$

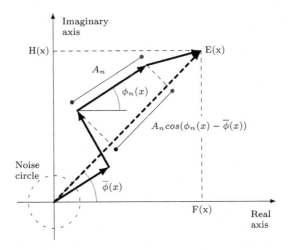

Fig. 1. The relation between phase congruency, local energy, and the sum of the Fourier amplitudes, adapted from [2].

Bandpass quadrature filters are often used to extract information such as energy from images [1]. In phase congruency, Kovesi used log-Gabor (log-normal) quadrature filters. The responses of pairs of quadrature filters are treated as the real and imaginary components of a complex number. In Eq. (2), we present the pair of responses in vector form, where I is the signal, M_n^e the even-symmetry wavelet, M_n^o is the odd-symmetry wavelet, both for the scale n, and $e_n(x)$ and $o_n(x)$ are the respective results:

$$[e_n(x), o_n(x)] = [I(x) * M_n^e, I(x) * M_n^o]. \tag{2}$$

In Eq. (3), these pairs of responses are used to obtain the amplitude A_n for the nth scale, which can be conveniently approximated as the nth Fourier component of Eq. (1).

$$A_n(x) = \sqrt{e_n(x)^2 + o_n(x)^2}, \tag{3}$$

and the phase is obtained using Eq. (4):

$$\phi_n(x) = atan2(e_n(x), o_n(x)). \tag{4}$$

To reduce the problems that occur when the components are of small magnitude, Kovesi added a positive constant ε to the denominator in Eq. (1). The effect of noise is also quite important. To reduce this problem, he considered a noise circle of radius T; any value less than or equal to T is not considered and set equal to zero.

Smoothing reduces the high-frequency components of the signal, i.e., it reduces the span of the frequency spectrum. In an extreme case, where the locally whispered signal is practically a pure signal, i.e., where it has a single frequency component, the PC will be maximal throughout the entire signal. To solve this problem, Kovesi weighted the PC using Eq. (5):

$$s(x) = \frac{1}{N} \left(\frac{\sum_{n=1}^{N} A_n(x)}{\varepsilon + A_{max}(x)} \right), \tag{5}$$

$s(x)$ is a measure of the frequency distribution, it takes on values between 0 and 1, and it is used in the weight function in Eq. (6):

$$W(x) = \frac{1}{1 + e^{\gamma(c - s(x))}}, \tag{6}$$

where c is the cut-off value for $s(x)$, which penalizes PC when the signal is formed by only a few frequency components, and γ is a gain factor that controls the sharpness of the cut-off.

To increase the sensitivity of PC, Kovesi redefines the way in which the phase difference ϕ_n at each scale influences the weighted average phase $\overline{\phi}$. Kovesi originally used a cosine function (see Fig. 1), but this has a problem in edge detect that a significant difference is required between $\phi(x)_n$ and $\overline{\phi}(x)$ in order for the value to decrease appreciably. He therefore proposes Eq. (7):

$$\Delta\Phi_n(x) = \cos(\phi_n(x) - \overline{\phi}(x)) - \left|\sin(\phi_n(x) - \overline{\phi}(x))\right|. \tag{7}$$

The improvements introduced by Kovesi to the phase congruence calculation are reflected in the Eq. (8), where the effect due to noise is reduced and sensitivity is increased, even when there are signals with a certain level of smoothing. The operator $\lfloor x \rfloor$ indicates that x is positive if $x > 0$, and zero if $x \leq 0$.

$$PC(x) = \frac{\sum_{n=1}^{N} W(x) \lfloor A_n(x) \Delta \Phi_n(x) - T \rfloor}{\sum_{n=1}^{N} A_n(x) + \varepsilon}. \tag{8}$$

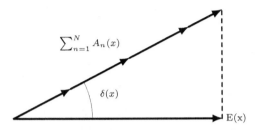

Fig. 2. Phase congruence such as the cosine of an angle δ

To use the Eq. (8) in images, the same transfer function is assumed for filters in all directions. However, the obtained phase congruence results do not allow the precise location of the edges. For this reason, Kovesi uses additional steps to improve the results, which consist of the adaptation in the space of phase congruence of Canny's techniques for localization of local maxima and the suppression of false edges by hysteresis. However, some additional improvements, which have not been published in articles, were introduced by the same author in the code available on his website [3]. The most striking change affects the very definition of phase congruence. In the initial definition according to the Eq. (1), the phase congruence can be understood as the cosine of an angle δ, which arises from the right triangle, which hypotenuse sums the magnitudes of each component, and as an adjacent leg the magnitude of the signal energy (see Fig. 2). The change in the definition of phase congruence consists of going from $\cos(\delta(x))$ to being $1 - |\delta(x)|$. With the new adjustment, introducing the previous improvements, and adding a gain α to the phase deviation $(\delta(x))$ we have the Eq. (9).

$$PC(x) = W(x) \lfloor 1 - \alpha |\delta(x)| \rfloor \frac{\lfloor E(x) - T \rfloor}{E(x) + \varepsilon}. \tag{9}$$

In the implementation of the Eq. (9), several parameters can be modified to apply the filter. Those of special interest in this work correspond to σ_o and α. The value of σ_o directly influences the transfer function of the filter bank (see Eq. 10), it is related to the bandwidth [1], and α, helps to better discriminate phase congruence. It should be added that in order to apply phase congruence to images, monogenic filters are used for the present study.

$$G(\omega) = exp\left(\frac{-(\log(\omega/\omega_0))^2}{2(\log(\sigma_o))^2}\right). \tag{10}$$

It is important to mention that in order to model the effect of noise in the calculation of phase congruence, three premises are required: (I) the noise is an additive character, (II) the noise power is constant and (III) they are close together. This latter restriction limits proper edge detection in images. As illustrated by the example in Fig. 3b.

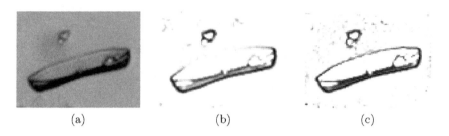

(a)   (b)   (c)

Fig. 3. Phase Congruency at microscopy image of a real case. (a) Diatom image. (b) With default parameters. (c) Parameters: σ_o at 0.3, α at 3.5

3   Analysis of nearby edges

Phase congruence has difficulties in detecting nearby edges with different width and intensity, as illustrated by the Fig. 4, where two parallel edges appear, one high and one low intensity. If phase congruence is used following the recommendations suggested by Kovesi the result obtained does not allow to differentiate the low intensity edge (see Fig. 4c). However, if the image consists only of the low intensity line, this edge is correctly identified.

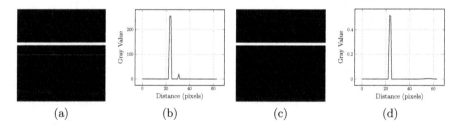

(a)   (b)   (c)   (d)

Fig. 4. Synthetic image filtered at phase congruency with default parameters. (a) Image with near edges at 255 and 20 intensity. (b) Vertical profile of (a). (c) Image filtered at phase congruency with default parameters. (d) Vertical profile of (c).

In phase congruence, the frequency spectrum of the edges to be identified is quite important, which, following the definitions given by Kovesi, conforms to a power distribution of a square signal [2]. In this way, each wavelet is associated with a Gabor filter, and the overlap of all filters covers the entire spectrum (see Fig. 5).

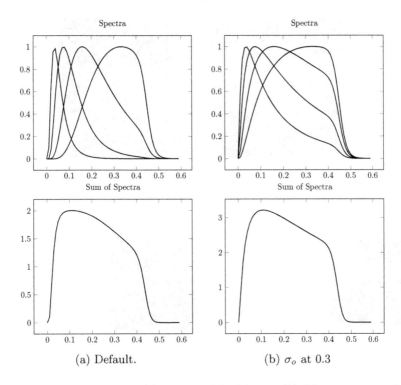

Fig. 5. Spectrum of wavelets. (a) Suggested by Kovesi. (b) The new proposal. The upper panel displays the individual wavelets, while the lower panel shows the sum of the spectra

In Fig. 4a, the different intensities of the signals produced by the edges overlap in frequency space, hiding the smaller one. This problem disappears, to a certain extent, if the signal intensities are similar, but there is a delocalization of the edges, due precisely to this overlap. To solve the problem of the detection of closely spaced edges, we propose to increase the bandwidths of the filters in such a way that the attenuation of the weaker signal can be reduced. This can be achieved by reducing the value of σ_o, beyond the range recommended by Kovesi. The disadvantage of increasing the filter bandwidths is that false edges appear due to the high degree of overlap (see Fig. 7a). Figure 6a shows the result of varying σ_o in the range from 0.55 down to 0.3 (From left to right in the Figure), which is below the theoretical range of 0.55–0.85 established by Kovesi.

To solve this overlap problem, which arises due to the increases in the bandwidths of the filters ($\sigma_o = 0.3$), it is necessary to increase the sensitivity of the PC by adjusting the gain α. In this way, it is possible to reduce the noise generated by the frequency overlap of the different filters. In Fig. 6b we show the result obtained by varying α from 1.5 to 3.5 (from left to right in the Figure).

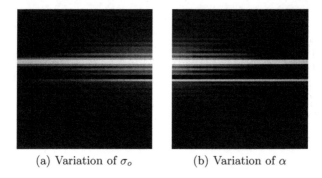

(a) Variation of σ_o (b) Variation of α

Fig. 6. Changes from Phase congruency when vary σ_o and α.

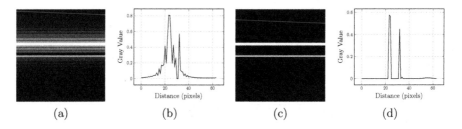

(a)   (b)   (c)   (d)

Fig. 7. Synthetic image filtered at phase congruency, (a) $\sigma_o = 0.3$, (b) vertical profile of (a), (c) σ_o at 0.3 and α at 3.5, and (d) is a vertical profile of (c).

4 Results for Synthetic and Real Images

From our synthetic images, we have found heuristically that the appropriate values of σ_o and α, which are necessary to obtain a PC that allows the detection of low intensity edges that appear close to high intensity edges are $\sigma_o = 0.3$, and $\alpha = 3.5$. As shown in Fig. 7c, applying PC to the Fig. 4a with these values allows to detection of both edges.

The distribution of the frequency spectrum after this adjustment of the filter band passes is shown in Fig. 5b.

5 Conclusions

One of the limitations of phase congruence is its inability to detect closely spaced edges. In this work we have presented a solution based on allowing the overlap of the Gabor filter responses through which it is possible to reinforce the responses to weak signals. This solution leads to the generation of spurious signals, but we have eliminated them by readjusting the sensitivity of the PC. The results obtained from synthetic and real images have allowed us to verify the quality of this solution.

References

1. Boukerroui, D., Noble, J.A., Brady, M.: On the choice of band-pass quadrature filters. J. Math. Imaging Vis. **21**(1–2), 53–80 (2004)
2. Kovesi, P.: Image features from phase congruency. Videre J. Comput. Vis. Res. **1**(3), 1–26 (1999)
3. Kovesi, P.: MATLAB and Octave Functions for Computer Vision and Image Processing (2013). http://www.peterkovesi.com/matlabfns/#phasecong
4. Liu, Z., Laganiere, R.: On the use of phase congruency to evaluate image similarity. In: 2006 IEEE International Conference on Acoustics, Speech and Signal Processing, ICASSP 2006 Proceedings, vol. 2, pp. 937–940. IEEE (2006)
5. Patil, R., Jondhale, K.: Edge based technique to estimate number of clusters in k-means color image segmentation. In: 2010 3rd IEEE International Conference on Computer Science and Information Technology (ICCSIT), vol. 2, pp. 117–121. IEEE (2010)
6. Pinto, C.H.V., Ferrari, R.J.: Initialization of deformable models in 3d magnetic resonance images guided by automatically detected phase congruency point landmarks. Pattern Recognit. Lett. **79**, 1–7 (2016)
7. Sosik, H.M., Olson, R.J.: Automated taxonomic classification of phytoplankton sampled with imaging-in-flow cytometry. Limnol. Ocean Methods **5**(6), 204–216 (2007)
8. Wong, A., Bishop, W.: Efficient least squares fusion of MRI and CT images using a phase congruency model. Pattern Recognit. Lett. **29**(3), 173–180 (2008)
9. Yuan, X., Shi, P.: Iris feature extraction using 2D phase congruency. In: Third International Conference on Information Technology and Applications, ICITA 2005, vol. 2, pp. 437–441. IEEE (2005)
10. Zhang, L., Zhang, L., Zhang, D., Guo, Z.: Phase congruency induced local features for finger-knuckle-print recognition. Pattern Recognit. **45**(7), 2522–2531 (2012)

An Efficient CBIR System for High Resolution Remote Sensing Images

Samia Bouteldja and Assia Kourgli[✉]

USTHB, FEI, LTIR, Bab-Ezzouar, Alger, Algérie
assiakourgli@gmail.com

Abstract. High resolution satellite images (HRSI), contain a great range of objects and spatial patterns appearing with a large variation of scale, rotation and illumination. In this paper, we propose a Content Based Image Retrieval (CBIR) system for HRSI by employing SURF features and boost them through the addition of color, texture and structural information around key points; and by learning a category-specific dictionary for each image class. An extensive experimental evaluation on the well- known UC Merced dataset has been performed and compared with other feature extraction methods including Convolutional Neural Networks. It is demonstrated that our method is quite competitive in terms of performance.

Keywords: CBIR · Retrieval · SURF · BOVW ·
High resolution satellite images

1 Introduction

Recently, both the quantity and quality of remote sensing (RS) images are growing at a rapid rate. These images are used to help solve plenty of important problems. In order to make full use of remote sensing big data, there is an insistent need of efficient information management, mining and interpretation methods. Therefore, significant efforts have been made in developing efficient retrieval methods to search data of interest from large RS databases. Newer generations of high resolution satellite imagery (HRSI) are of increasingly importance for earth observation because they allow to recognize a big range of objects. Considerable amount of literatures has made efforts to extract discriminating features for HRSI retrieval. Feature extraction methods can be divided into three categories. The first category includes methods based on global features, which describe an image as a whole in terms of color [1], texture [2], and shape distributions [3]. Several studies have employed multi-resolution features to index HRSI, such as the Discrete Wavelet Transform (DWT) [4], Gabor filter [5], and Steerable pyramids [6]. The drawback of global features is losing the image detail information. The second category comprises local approaches, which have shown a better performance than global approaches as they possess significant invariance capacities [7, 8]. The local raw features are encoded using bag-of-visual-words (BoVW), Fisher vector (FV) or vector locally aggregated descriptors (VLAD). The third category consists of deep learning methods like Convolutional Neural Networks (CNN), which have provided impressive results in object recognition [9, 10]. However,

© Springer Nature Switzerland AG 2019
R. Vera-Rodriguez et al. (Eds.): CIARP 2018, LNCS 11401, pp. 392–400, 2019.
https://doi.org/10.1007/978-3-030-13469-3_46

despite their outstanding efficiency, various factors are likely to limit the performance of deep learning methods. First, they require a large amount of labeled data, and second, they are extremely computationally expensive to train. In this work, we propose an efficient CBIR system for HRSI based on boosted SURF features through the addition of local color, texture and structural content around key points and by using a category specific strategy for dictionary creation. In the rest of the paper, we provide in Sect. 2, a description of the feature extraction method. In Sect. 3, we present the experimental setup. The obtained results and comparison with state of the art references are presented in Sect. 4, and finally we draw conclusions.

2 Feature Extraction

Feature extraction is accomplished by using the Speeded Up Robust Features algorithm (SURF) [11]. It is a scale and rotation-invariant interest point detector and descriptor and is computationally very fast, factors that make it suitable for our retrieval system. The SURF descriptor is boosted by adding color, texture and structural content around the key points as described below:

(a) Color features: color information plays a vitally important role. SURF descriptor being designed mainly for gray images, it is then difficult for it to distinct color regions that appear very similar in the corresponding gray images when the color is omitted. Many variations on SURF were developed when considering the use of color data, like color histograms around the key point or the concatenation of the SURF descriptors computed separately for three RGB channels, yielding a 64×3-dimensional feature vector. In this work, the problem of the color is addressed in a simple manner, the RGB values of the key point are taken as the color feature. The conducted evaluation shows that using the key point color is better than using the color histogram around that point.

(b) Texture features: are based on the assumption that a great amount of the information around a key point is coded in its local variance (LV) distribution, which is in its turn, illumination and rotation invariant. We compute LV around each key point for each color channel. The quantization of local variance into bins requires a priori knowledge of the maximum variance of our dataset. Yet, in the presence of noise, LV becomes sensitive in such a way that noise will induce a significant increase of LV value. To surmount this limitation, we propose to compute the LV on a smoothed neighborhood. Smoothing is obtained through the use of an anisotropic diffusion filter. Anisotropic diffusion, also called Perona–Malik diffusion, is a technique aiming at reducing image noise without removing significant parts of the image content, typically edges, lines or other details that are important for the interpretation of the image. Smoothed local variance histograms are computed over a given neighborhood. The size of the analysis window has an important impact on the ability to represent the textural information. For this investigation, several neighborhood sizes ranging from 3×3 pixels up to 13×13 pixels were tried. The local variance technique performed better at 5×5 window size.

(c) Structural features: they are extracted using the Local Binary Pattern (LBP) operator, which was first introduced in 1994 by Ojala et al. [12]. Originally, it operated with 3×3 rectangular neighborhood using the center pixel as a threshold. The LBP code associated with the central pixel is calculated by multiplying thresholded values by weights given by the power of two and adding the results. An improved uniform gray-scale and rotation invariant operator denoted $LBP_{P,R}^{riu2}$ operator consists of a histogram of P + 2 bins, each bin codifies the occurrence of a given shape primitive present in the image. Shape primitives include different types of edges, spots, flat areas, line ends, corners, etc. The drawback of the LBP operator is that a small change in the input image would cause a change in the output. LBP may not work properly for noisy images. In order to make it more robust, we propose to compute it on the smoothed image obtained by the anisotropic diffusion. In this work, the $LBP_{8,1}^{riu2}$ was used and the smoothed LBP histograms for the three color channels are computed over a 5×5 neighborhood around the key point and then, concatenated. The number of local features for each image may be immense. Wherefore, the model of Bag of Visual Words (BoVW) is proposed as an approach to solve this problem by quantizing descriptors into "visual words". After assigning each image a set of local descriptors, these will be used to generate, with the K-means algorithm, a dictionary of visual words. Afterward, a histogram is computed by counting how many descriptors are assigned to each visual word. Nevertheless, there are two disadvantages of the traditionally visual vocabulary strategy. Firstly, the computational burden of performing clustering on a large pool of feature vectors is heavy in terms of memory and computational time. Secondly, since the clustering algorithm is performed on the whole image set, it cannot guarantee a visual vocabulary with a good discriminative ability for image retrieval. In order to generate more discriminative visual words and reduce the memory demand, we propose to use a category specific visual word creation. It consists of performing k-means clustering of just one category at a time and then grouping the small codebooks together into a single codebook. The feature extraction process is illustrated in Fig. 1.

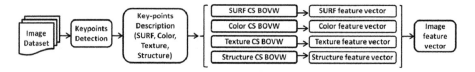

Fig. 1. Feature extraction process.

3 Experimental Setup

The database used in this study, illustrated in Fig. 2, is a land use/land cover UC Merced dataset (UCMD) [8]. It contains 21 categories of high resolution satellite images. Each category contains 100 images of size $(256 \times 256 \times 3)$, and a spatial resolution of 30 cm, corresponding to different regions of the earth: agricultural, airplane, baseball diamond, beach, buildings, chaparral, dense residential, forest, freeway, golf course, harbor, intersection, medium density residential, mobile home park, overpass, parking lot, river, runway, sparse residential, storage tanks, and tennis courts. In the indexing phase, our system extracts SURF, color, texture and LBP descriptors for all the images of the dataset. These are used to generate color, texture and LBP codebooks by adopting traditional clustering once, and a category specific clustering another time, and then, a histogram for each description is computed. As a result, we end up with boosted features consisting of four histograms representing each image in the dataset. In the query phase, the feature vectors are extracted from the query image and the retrieval is performed with the chi-square similarity measure. Coefficients are added to weight each description. The experiments indicate that the best precision is obtained when giving more importance to SURF feature and almost equal weights to the added features ($k_{surf} = 0.8$, $k_{color} = 0.15$, $k_{texture} = 0.15$, $k_{LBP} = 0.2$). Retrieval performance has been assessed by the most commonly used evaluation measures: Precision (Pr), Recall (Re), Mean Average Precision (MAP), and the Average Normalized Modified Retrieval Rank (ANMRR).

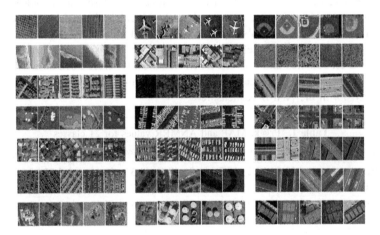

Fig. 2. Land use dataset samples.

4 Results and Discussion

In this section, we present experimental results for retrieval on the 21 image class dataset, as well as, on a reduced dataset containing only eight classes: agricultural, airplane, beach, buildings, and chaparral, dense residential, forest and harbor, and this is mainly for comparison purposes.

The experimental evaluation was initiated by evaluating the performance of SURF features in indexing HRSI. We have noticed that SURF features perform very well for some classes like chaparral, forest, harbor, medium residential, and parking lot, but, it is less efficient for the other classes. This is due to the confusion between classes having similar local characteristics. The most notable confusions were noticed between buildings and intersection, dense residential and mobile home park, freeway and overpass, golf course and sparse residential, river and sparse residential, storage and airplane, as well as between tennis court and mobile home park. Visual similarity of these classes is high even for human observers. We have also, noticed that each image class prefers a different codebook size. However, in terms of the global accuracy, the maximum was obtained for 420 codebook size. We, therefore, chose this size for subsequent tests, to get the compromise time/accuracy. The preliminary results justify the requirement of introducing other visual features, like color and texture that can discriminate similar classes, and the need for generating specific dictionaries for each image class to produce more discriminative visual words. Table 1 illustrates the obtained results for 21 classes, in terms of different percentages of relevant images over the retrieved. Many observations can be made. First, using the category-specific (CS) learned dictionaries leads to a an improvement of 3% in the average precision and 3.6% in MAP measure and a decrease of 0.04 in the ANMRR measure for conventional SURF features. An improvement of 7.89 in the average precision, a gain of 8.22 in MAP measure, and a decrease of 0.02 in the ANMRR measure were obtained for boosted SURF features. Second, boosting SURF features clearly increases the average precision by 14.27 and MAP measure by 14.38, it also decreases the ANMRR value by 0.18 for general codebook creation. An increase of 19.16 in the average precision, and of 19 in the MAP measure is obtained, as well as, a decrease of 0.16 in the ANMRR value for category specific codebook creation. Finally, by using the category-specific (CS) learned dictionaries and boosted SURF features, we have been able to achieve a total improvement in the average precision by 22.16, and 22.6 in MAP measure, and a decrease by 0.2 in the ANMRR measure.

Table 1. Pr@k, MAP and ANMRR values for 21 classes

	10%	20%	40%	60%	80%	100%	Average	MAP	ANMRR
SURF	68.6	62.2	55.7	51.2	47.1	43.3	53.46	45.13	0.46
CS SURF	70.6	64.5	58.5	54.4	50.7	46.7	56.46	48.73	0.42
Boosted SURF	84.2	78.0	70.5	65.4	60.7	55.5	67.73	59.51	0.28
CS Boosted SURF	90.6	85.6	79.0	73.7	68.5	62.7	75.62	67.73	0.26

We performed in Table 2 a comparative evaluation of the proposed approach against several state-of-the-art retrieval methods [8, 9, 13, 14], according to the metrics Pr@10, Pr@50, Pr@100, average precision, MAP, and ANMRR. As can be seen from Table 2, the global descriptors: simple statistics, Gabor texture features and HLS Color histogram have the lowest performance among all the mentioned descriptors. Simple statistics are the least efficient ones. Steerable pyramids, local features as well as global and local morphological descriptors present better performance, with ANMRR values ranging from 0.460 to 0.591. In fact, global methods represent each image by capturing information from the whole scene, without paying attention to the constituents of the image, and by taking into account only a single aspect, such as texture or color, which justifies their poor performance. In the other hand, Dense Sift and Sift local features show less performance than the proposed approach, because they take into account the gradient information around key-points and ignore the other features. The CNN-based descriptors present a best MAP value of 61.85, and a best ANMRR value of 0.316. Our proposed method achieves a MAP value of 67.73, which is higher of about 5.88% to that of CNN based descriptors, and an ANMRR value of 0.26 which is lower of about 0.056 to that of CNN based descriptors. By observing the behavior of the different precision levels Pr@k, the Pr@10 equals 90.60 which is approximately equivalent to that of CNN descriptors, it starts performing better afterwards, ending at Pr@100 which is higher of about 6.04%. These results confirm that when having a small image set, traditional methods become more adequate than deep learning solutions. The algorithm complexity of the proposed approach is similar to most of the local and global approaches. The proposed method requires a small processing power and a small training set, which makes it fast and simple to implement. Few minutes were required to train the whole UC-Merced dataset on an i5 CPU (2.2 Ghz, 8GO Ram). It requires less parameters to set and therefore less memory is needed for storing the image features. On the contrary, a CNN requires GPU's that most people cannot afford, and millions of labeled images to train it, which makes the training process very time consuming. It also, needs a lot of memory to store the weights of the network, and experience to make design decisions.

Table 2. Retrieval feature evaluation for 21 image classes

Features	P@10	P@50	P@100	Average	MAP	ANMRR
CS Boosted SURF	90.60	76.45	62.70	75.62	67.73	0.260
Vgg M [9]	91.13	70.93	56.64		61.85	0.316
Vgg M 2048 [9]	91.20	71.58	56.66		61.76	0.316
Dense SIFT (VLAD) [9]						0.460
Global morphological descriptors [13]						0.575
Local morphological descriptors [13]						0.585
Pyramid LPS-augmentation [14]					0.472	0.437
Simple statistics [8]						0.807
Gabor texture features [8]						0.630
HLS Color histogram [8]						0.735
Sift Local features [8]						0.591

For the reduced set, we present in Table 3, the obtained results in terms of MAP measure and in terms of different percentages of relevant images over the retrieved images. We notice an increase in the average precision of 11.95, and 12.59 in MAP measure. Comparison with many state of the art methods [1, 6, 15], shown in Fig. 3. demonstrates that our approach is consistently better.

The Precision/Recall curves are plotted to make comparisons with references [1, 6,

Table 3. Pr@k, MAP values for 8 classes

	10%	20%	40%	60%	80%	100%	Average	MAP
SURF	89.48	86.43	82.52	79.14	75.11	70.00	79.75	75.41
CS Boosted SURF	98.31	96.93	94.73	92.11	88.18	81.54	91.70	88.00

8, 9] for 21 class dataset in Fig. 4, and with [1, 6, 15] for 8 class dataset in Fig. 5. Obviously, the proposed image representation which combines SURF, color, texture and structure features around key-points, and the category specific codebook creation have enabled to obtain a complete description of key points, and to generate highly discriminative visual words, which led to the best performance among the state of the art methods.

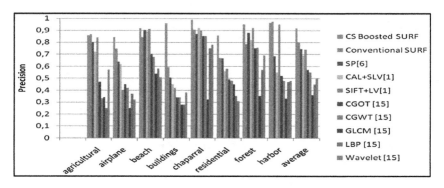

Fig. 3. Retrieval feature evaluation for 8 image classes

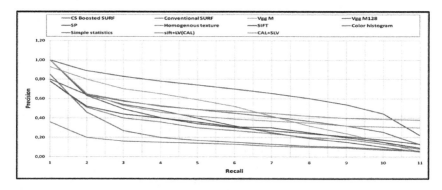

Fig. 4. Pr/Re curves for 21 classes

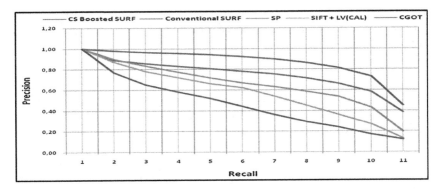

Fig. 5. Pr/Re curves for 8 classes

5 Conclusion

In this paper, an effective image representation method for high resolution remote sensing image retrieval was proposed. The proposed method consists of boosting SURF features through the addition of color, texture and structural content around key points and also, by adopting the strategy of category specific codebook generation, which enabled us to produce more discriminative visual words. The experimental results obtained on UC-Merced dataset outperform many local and global techniques and even deep Neural Networks. The powerful ability of the proposed method for HRSI description makes it suitable to achieve retrieval and classification of color natural images. In a future work, it would be interesting to explore other descriptors to provide complementary information especially for those categories with high interclass correlation such as buildings and dense residential, freeway and runway.

References

1. Sebai, H., Kourgli, A.: Improving high resolution satellite images retrieval using color component features. In: Murino, V., Puppo, E. (eds.) ICIAP 2015. LNCS, vol. 9280, pp. 264–275. Springer, Cham (2015). https://doi.org/10.1007/978-3-319-23234-8_25
2. Zhang, X., et al.: A study for texture feature extraction of high-resolution satellite images based on a direction measure and gray level co-occurrence matrix fusion algorithm. Sensors (Switzerland) **17**(7), 1474 (2017)
3. Shi, Z., et al.: Ship detection in high-resolution optical imagery based on anomaly detector and local shape feature. IEEE Trans. Geosci. Rem. Sens. **52**, 4511–4523 (2014)
4. Yang, X., Wen, G.: Road extraction from high-resolution remote sensing images using wavelet transform and hough transform. In: 5th International Congress on Image and Signal Processing, China (2012)
5. Chen, C., et al.: Gabor-filtering-based completed local binary patterns for land-use scene classification. In: IEEE International Conference on Multimedia Big Data (BigMM), China (2015)

6. Bouteldja, S., Kourgli, A.: Multiscale texture features for the retrieval of high resolution satellite images. In: International Conference on Systems, Signal and Image Processing (IWSSIP), London (2015)

7. Pham, M.T., et al.: Texture retrieval from VHR optical remote sensed images using the local extrema descriptor with application to vineyard parcel detection (2016). https://hal.archives-ouvertes.fr/hal-01311993

8. Yang, Y., Newsam, S.: Geographic image retrieval using local invariant features. IEEE Trans. Geosci. Rem. Sens. **51**(2), 818–832 (2013)

9. Napoletano, P.: Visual descriptors for content-based retrieval of remote sensing image. Int. J. Rem. Sens. **39**(5), 1343–1376 (2018). https://doi.org/10.1080/01431161.2017.1399472

10. Cheng, G., et al.: Learning rotation-invariant convolutional neural networks for object detection in VHR optical remote sensing images. IEEE Trans. Geosci. Rem. Sens. **54**(12), 7405–7415 (2016)

11. Bay, H., Tuytelaars, T., Van Gool, L.: SURF: speeded up robust features. In: Leonardis, A., Bischof, H., Pinz, A. (eds.) ECCV 2006. LNCS, vol. 3951, pp. 404–417. Springer, Heidelberg (2006). https://doi.org/10.1007/11744023_32

12. Ojala, T., et al.: Multiresolution gray-scale and rotation invariant texture classification with local binary patterns. IEEE Trans. Pattern Anal. Mach. Intell. **24**, 971–987 (2002)

13. Erchan, A.: Bag of morphological words for content-based geographical retrieval. In: Proceedings of the International Workshop on Content-Based Multimedia Indexing, Austria, pp. 1–5 (2014). https://doi.org/10.1109/cbmi.2014.6849837

14. Petra, B., et al.: Retrieval of remote sensing images with pattern spectra descriptors. ISPRS Int. J. Geo-Inf. **5**(12), 228 (2016). https://doi.org/10.3390/ijgi5120228

15. Zhenfeng, S., et al.: Improved color texture descriptors for remote sensing image retrieval. J. Appl. Rem. Sens. **8**(1), 083584 (2014)

Experimental Analysis of Measurements Fusion for Pose Estimation Using PMD Sensor

Ksenia Klionovska$^{(\boxtimes)}$, Heike Benninghoff, Eicke-Alexander Risse, and Felix Huber

German Space Operations Center, Muenchener Str. 20, 82234 Wessling, Germany
{ksenia.klionovska,heike.benninghoff
eicke-alexander.risse,felix.huber}@dlr.de

Abstract. This article presents the experimental investigation of the fusion concept of two relative position and orientation (pose) estimates of the rotating target using single Photonic Mixer Device (PMD) sensor for the frame-to-frame tracking. For each frame PMD depth sensor provides co-registered depth and amplitude images of the scene. We propose to use two different pose estimation techniques for each of the data channel with a further fusion of its measured state vectors. The fusion architecture of the state measurements is based on a low complexity weighted average algorithm. The weights for the fusion operator are calculated experimentally with the real data from PMD sensor mounted on DLR's European Proximity Operations Simulator. The fused state vector obtained with experimental results outperforms the accuracy of the two incoming pose measurements. This allows us to ensure robust pose estimation of a rotating target for the whole tracking.

Keywords: PMD sensor · Data fusion · Pose estimation · Optical navigation

1 Introduction

Computer vision refers to the discipline where the combination of the theory and technology of the artificial systems aims to extract, analyze and understand necessary information from digital image or video. Computer vision is used in different application fields, e.g. in medical computer vision or medical image processing, in industry, for military purposes, for the autonomous land based and aerial vehicles [1]. Currently the scope of our work is directed to computer vision in space applications, namely, visual pose estimation of the target spacecraft during the rendezvous phase for On-Orbit Servicing (OOS) missions. Main duties of OOS mission include, e.g. refuel, repairs/upgrades of some parts of satellite and also deorbiting of no more usable spacecraft. The problem can be addressed as follow: the chaser spacecraft should autonomously navigate to the target by estimating relative position and orientation of the target spacecraft using visual sensor and extracting information from an image or sequence of images.

© Springer Nature Switzerland AG 2019
R. Vera-Rodriguez et al. (Eds.): CIARP 2018, LNCS 11401, pp. 401–409, 2019.
https://doi.org/10.1007/978-3-030-13469-3_47

Different types of visual sensors have been considered and tested for the pose estimation during the rendezvous phase. These are LiDAR [2], monocular and stereo cameras [3] and also time-of-flight sensors based on Photonic Mixer Device (PMD) [4,5] technology. Since the PMD camera has never been used in space so far, we continue investigating it as one possible candidate for visual navigation in space. In this paper we provide an experimental research on the fusion of the state vectors estimated using PMD sensor and suitable algorithms.

Having a look into a recent state-of-the-art techniques for the sensor data fusion in other different areas of computer vision, one can mention the work of Schramm et al. [6], where the authors present an approach to fuse the data from stereo, depth and thermal cameras for robust self-localization. The resulting position is obtained through the Extenden Kalman Filter (EKF). The Kim et al. [7] show how to fuse the radar and visual images for the advanced driver assistance system via extrinsic calibration process. Deilamsalehy et al. [8] propose to fuse data from LiDAR, camera and Inertial Measurement Unit (IMU) using EKF for pose estimation. Instead of using mentioned EKF or any other filter for the data fusion, we create a distributed system with a weighted average algorithm, where one state vector is calculated with a depth image, whereas the other one independently with an amplitude image. The weighted average approach for the state vector fusion is simple to implement, and moreover, its suitable for any application, since it doesn't require to know a system dynamics.

All experiments presented in this paper were tested in the European Proximity Operations Simulator (EPOS 2.0) [9] at the German Aerospace Center (DLR), which allows real-time simulation of close range proximity operations under realistic space illumination conditions.

2   Visual Navigation with PMD Sensor

2.1   Problem Statement

The problem addressed in this paper is to accurately estimate position and orientation of the target spacecraft with measurements from a time-of-light PMD sensor. In this work we provide experiments with DLR-Argos 3D-P320 Camera prototype (Fig. 1, left up) released by Bluetechnix company with technical characteristic presented in the Table 1.

The depth measurement principle of the PMD technologies is based on the calculation of the phase shift between the emitted NIR signal by the LED's of camera and reflected signal from the target. Co-registered amplitude information of the reflected signal is calculated simultaneously. An example of depth and amplitude images acquired by the DLR-Argos 3D-P320 Camera in DLR's EPOS is presented in Fig. 1 (left and right down images). The images illustrate target mockup (see Fig. 1, right up) used for the further test simulation for this paper. In the next section we provide experimentally justified fusion technique of two pose estimates from different sources in order to get one accurate pose for every frame.

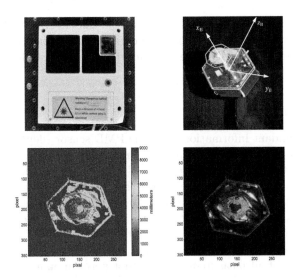

Fig. 1. Left up: DLR-Argos 3D-P320 Camera. Right up: The mockup in EPOS laboratory. Left down: Depth image. Right down: Amplitude image.

Table 1. Technical data of the PMD sensor inside the DLR-Argos 3D-P320 camera.

Field of view	28.91 × 23.45 deg
Resolution of the chip	352 × 287 pixels
Integration time	24 ms
Frames per second	45
Modulated frequencies	5.004 MHz, 7.5 MHz, 10.007 MHz, 15 MHz, 20.013 MHz, 25.016 MHz, 30 MHz
Mass/Power consumption	2 kg/<25.5 W

2.2 Pose Estimation Techniques

Two completely different tracking methods are suggested for model-based pose estimation techniques of the target spacecraft. Model-based techniques refer to the knowledge of the 3D model of the target object throughout the entire tracking period. The modified version of state-of-the-art Iterative Closest Point (ICP) [10] algorithm with "reverse-calibration" method [11] for the nearest-neighbor search is proposed for the estimation of the state vector with depth images. Pose estimation technique for the amplitude images based on finding feature correspondences between 3D known model and detected features in the 2D gray scaled image. Throughout variety of the solvers here we propose to take a Gauss-Newton solver [12] based on a least square minimization problem in order to estimate position of the target related to the camera frame. Please, refer to the work of Klionovska et al. [5] for the detailed description of the pose estimation technique for the depth images and for the feature identification from amplitude images.

2.3   Fusion of Measurements

Due to the redundant information from the PMD sensor (depth and amplitude channels) it is a good chance to increase the reliability of the system and enhance the accuracy of the calculated state vector during the approach by fusion of two estimated measurements. Moreover, with the redundant state information the tracking of the target can still be provided even when one of the pose estimation techniques gives incorrect information. One of the simplest ways for the combination of measurements is to take a weighted average [13] of the pose vectors which is obtained after two different pose estimation techniques. The simple arithmetic mean of all measurements does not perform enough, since one measurement can be more reliable than other [14]. Taking in account this fact, it is better to assign more importance and greater weight to an observation y_i from one output channel that is more reliable, whereas a less accurate observation from the other output channel will receive minor weights. The weighted average for the fused estimate of n different measurements y_i with non-negative weights ω_i looks as

$$y_{fused} = \frac{\sum_{i=1}^{n} \omega_i y_i}{\sum_{i=1}^{n} \omega_i}. \tag{1}$$

We can simplify an Eq. 1 when the weights are normalized and sum up to 1:

$$y_{fused} = \sum_{i=1}^{n} \omega_i' y_i, \sum_{i=1}^{n} \omega_i' = 1. \tag{2}$$

From the mathematical point of view the weights ω_i for every single member of the pose vector can be assigned as estimated variance of the measurement error σ_i^2 occurred during pose estimation with one of the suggested methods

$$\omega_i = \frac{1}{\sigma_i^2}. \tag{3}$$

In the work of Elmenreich [15] the author shows that the variance of the fusion result y_{fused} is minimized and always smaller than the input variances

$$\sigma_{fused}^2 = \sum_{i=1}^{n} \omega_i^2 \sigma_i^2 = \sum_{i=1}^{n} \frac{1}{\sigma_i^2}. \tag{4}$$

3   Experimental Scenarios and Performance Analysis

In order to find correct weights for fusion of both estimates, firstly we propose to run both algorithms separately. The offline test presents a straight frontal approach scenario, which starts at approximately distance 8 m between chaser and the target. The termination point is situated at the distance a bit less than 5 m. These both distances are chosen due to the characteristics of the DLR-Argos 3D-P320 sensor. Namely, the starting point of the simulation is chosen with relation to the resolution of the current PMD sensor. Since the resolution of the PMD sensor is small in compare with existent CCD sensors, the features of the imaged object become not to be clearly observable and it leads to the big errors in pose estimation. Moreover, the current illumination unit of the camera is suitable for the close range simulations (<10 m) and not for the long one. The final point is limited because of the field of view of the current camera. When the distance is less than 5 m the whole target is no more observable and pose estimation is not possible. In this test the target (Fig. 1, right up) is rotating around its principal axis of inertia at a rate of 2 deg/s. Overall the data set consists of 170 images. According to the number of image, the distance range is configured as following: from image 1 to 67 corresponds to the approach from 8 to 7 m; from image 68 to 118 is a range from 7 to 6 m (e.g. Fig. 2, images at the first row); and starting from image 119 to 170 the distance decreases from 6 to 4.9 m (e.g. Fig. 2, images at the second row). The ground truth for every logged image is provided by EPOS. The experimental scenarios, which we consider in this paper, are follows. Test scenario 1 presents frame-to-frame pose estimation technique using depth image and ICP with reverse calibration technique. Test scenario 2 concludes the result of the pose estimation algorithm with aforementioned image processing of amplitude images. Test scenario 3 shows the results of the fusion technique with calculated weights. What is special here is that in the Test scenario 3 the fusion technique is applied for the translational part, whereas the rotation is completely taken from the pose vector estimated with the amplitude image. This is so, because the algorithm with the amplitude images is less sensitive for the estimation of the orientation and usually provides better results. The camera coordinate frame is used in order to evaluate the results, where Z-axis is taken along the optical axis of the camera.

3.1   Test Cases 1 and 2: Pose Estimation Using Depth and Amplitude Images Separately

We run separately the algorithms for the depth images and amplitude images using provided dataset. In Fig. 3 we present the plots of the errors for rotation and translation components of the estimated pose for every frame in the Test case 1 (left up and down images) for the Test case 2 (right up and down images). The mean errors for the both cases are presented in the Table 2. From the results depicted in Fig. 3 and collected in Table 2 after offline simulation of the proposed estimation techniques explained in the Sect. 2.2, one can observe that estimation of the rotational components with the 2D technique using amplitude image dominates over the 3D pose estimation pipeline. It is due to the fact that the errors in the angles calculated with 3D pose estimation algorithm have a tendency to accumulate. This is caused by the nature of the algorithm - since the previous estimate for a new frame strong diverges from the real one, the follow calculated orientation (sometimes also position vector) within a next new frame has also big measurement errors. However, position of the target during the tracking was defined more accurate using the depth images, especially the distance component (position along Z axis).

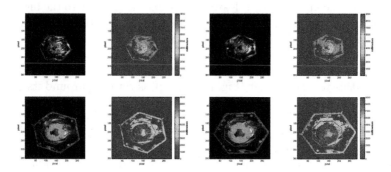

Fig. 2. Depth and amplitude images within distance 7 to 6 m (first row) and within distance 6 to 5 m (second row).

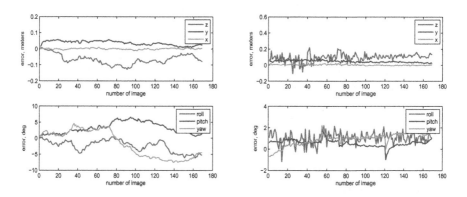

Fig. 3. Translation and rotation errors for the Test cases 1 (left up and down) and 2 (right up and down).

In order to apply the fusion technique described in the Sect. 2.3, there is a prerequisite to define weights. According to the Eq. 3, it is necessary to define the variances. Table 2 presents the result of the standard deviations for three rotation angles and for Z, Y, X components of the position vector.

Table 2. Standard deviations and mean errors.

σ	Test case 1	Test case 2	μ	Test case 1	Test case 2	Test case 3
σ_{roll}, deg	1.75	0.47	μ_{roll}, deg	2.41	1.04	0.96
σ_{pitch}, deg	1.74	0.27	μ_{pitch}, deg	3.19	0.57	0.62
σ_{yaw}, deg	2.18	0.43	μ_{yaw}, deg	3.91	0.98	1.10
σ_z, m	0.0306	0.0415	μ_z, m	0.0654	0.1004	0.0392
σ_y, m	0.0129	0.0129	μ_y, m	0.0366	0.0472	0.0405
σ_x, m	0.0024	0.0058	μ_x, m	0.0034	0.0065	0.0038

Table 3. Weights for the translation components.

Weight	Depth estimate	Amplitude estimate
ω_z	0.65	0.35
ω_y	0.54	0.46
ω_x	0.85	0.15

3.2   Test Cases 3: Fusion of Pose Vectors with Weights

Taking into account revealed tendency after test cases 1 and 2, we propose to make simulations of the pose estimation during the approach for the same dataset and by using the weighted average technique for the translation components. We apply weights for the Z, Y and X coordinates presented in the Table 3. In Fig. 4 we plot the results of the angular and position measurement errors after conducted Test case 3.

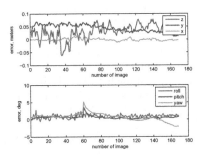

Fig. 4. Translation and rotation errors for the Test cases 3.

In fact, as we expected, the fused technique with its measurements errors presented in Fig. 4 overcomes the drawbacks of both pose estimation techniques. The mean errors for Test case 3 are shown in the last column of Table 2. It means that the attitude of the target has almost the same mean errors as in the Test case 2, whereas the mean errors for the position are more similar with the Test case 1. The peaks for the pitch and yaw angles presented in Fig. 4 don't corrupt or abrupt the tracking process, allowing reliably continue pose estimation of the target.

4 Discussion

With this paper we proved experimentally that the fusion technique guarantee accurate calculation of the position and orientation of the target using PMD sensor. Here for every frame the weighted average method fuses two estimates, which were calculated with depth and amplitude images independently. By different test simulations we have shown the main advantage of the fusion - decrease of the measured errors for the attitude and for the position of the target. Moreover, having a fused estimate we ensure stable frame-to-frame tracking during the approach. The proposed concept of the data fusion for pose estimation and tracking based on PMD sensor technologies can be used not only for space applications. For example, independent redundant information from one PMD visual sensor can be used in the field of (semi)autonomous driving and also driver assistance systems. This approach together with PMD sensor helps to reduce the number of visual sensors, but at the same time ensures increase of the accuracy and reliability of the visual system.

References

1. Examples of Applications for Computer Vision. http://www.idc-online.com/technical_references/pdfs/electronic_engineering/Examples_of_applications_for_computer_vision.pdf
2. Opromolla, R., Fasano, G., Rufino, G., Grassi, M.: Uncooperative pose estimation with a LIDAR-based system. Acta Astronautica **110**, 287–297 (2015)
3. Oumer, N.W.: Visual Tracking and Motion Estimation for an On-Orbit Servicing of a Satellite (2016)
4. Ringbeck, T., Hagebeuker, B.: A 3D Time of Flight Camera for object detection. Optical 3D Measurement Technologies (2007)
5. Klionovska, K., Ventura, J., Benninghoff, H., Huber, F.: Close Range Tracking of an Uncooperative Target in a Sequence of Photonic Mixer Device (PMD) Images (2018). https://doi.org/10.3390/robotics7010005
6. Schramm, S., Rangel, J., Kroll, A.: Data fusion for 3D thermal imaging using depth and stereo camera for robust self-localization. In: IEEE Sensors Applications Symposium (SAS) (2018)
7. Kim, J., Han, D.S., Senouci, B.: Radar and vision sensor fusion for object detection in autonomous vehicle surroundings. In: Tenth International Conference on Ubiquitous and Future Networks (2018)
8. Deilamsalehy, H., Havens, T.C.: Sensor fused three-dimensional localization using IMU, camera and LiDAR. IEEE Sensors (2016)
9. Benninghoff, H., Rems, F., Risse, E.-A., Mietner, C.: European Proximity Operations Simulator 2.0. (EPOS)- a robotic-based rendezvous and docking simulator. J. Large Scale Res. Facil. **3**, A107 (2017)

10. Mckay, N., Besl, P.: A method for registration of 3d shapes. IEEE Trans. Pattern Anal. Mach. Intell. **14**, 239–256 (1992)
11. Blais, G., Levine, M.: Registering multiview range data to create 3D computer objects. IEEE Trans. Pattern Anal. Mach. Intell. **17**, 820–824 (1995)
12. Nocedal, J., Wright, S.: Numerical Optimization. Springer, New York (2006). https://doi.org/10.1007/978-0-387-40065-5
13. Grossman, J., Grossman, M., Katz, R.: The First Systems of Weighted Differential and Integral Calculus. Archimedes Foundation, Rockport (1980)
14. Schrgendorfer, A., Elmenreich, W.: Extended confidence-weighted averaging in sensor fusion. In: Proceedings of the Junior Scientist Conference (2006)
15. Elmenreich, W.: Fusion of continuous-valued sensor measurements using confidence-weighted averaging. J. Vib. Control. **13**, 1303–1312 (2007)

Automated Colony Counter for Single Plate Serial Dilution Spotting

Dimitria Theophanis Boukouvalas[1(✉)] ⓘ, Peterson Belan[1] ⓘ,
Cintia Raquel Lima Leal[2] ⓘ, Renato Araújo Prates[2] ⓘ,
and Sidnei Alves de Araújo[1] ⓘ

[1] Informatics and Knowledge Management Graduate Program,
Universidade Nove de Julho – UNINOVE, Rua Vergueiro, 235/249 – 12º Andar,
Liberdade, São Paulo, SP 01504-001, Brazil
dtbouk@uninove.edu.br
[2] Postgraduate Program in Biophotonics Applied to Health Sciences,
Universidade Nove de Julho – UNINOVE, Rua Vergueiro, 235/249 – 12º Andar,
Liberdade, São Paulo, SP 01504-001, Brazil

Abstract. This paper discusses the automated visual identification and quantification of colony forming units (CFU) in Single Plate Serial Dilution Spotting (SP-SDS) through correlation-based granulometry under uncontrolled lighting conditions. There are many different approaches in the literature based on images captured under controlled conditions, which is not the real life situation of laboratories that present high variation in illuminating conditions resulting in low contrast between bacterial colonies and background, background noise, and in addition, high variation in CFU features. Furthermore, SP-SDS has been widely used due to its reduction in the use of resources, but most of previous approaches are not capable of counting separately the number of CFU present in each dilution zone. In that sense, our study focuses on analyzing real images taken at laboratory day-to-day conditions and proposes an approach suitable for real laboratory practice with high accuracies.

Keywords: Colony counter · Correlation-based granulometry · Serial dilution

1 Introduction

A common practice in bio laboratories, counting of colony forming units (CFU) of microorganisms in Petri dishes is a time-consuming routine. Although different solutions are found in the literature, the automation of this procedure is still not common, except in large laboratories that use commercially available high-cost tools.

There are a number of approaches that focus on presenting better solutions than previously investigated ones, we can mention [1–5], presenting comparisons between proposed solutions predominantly regarding the technique used for CFU agglomerates segmentation, which are CFU that grow very close superposing each other, one of the most challenging problems [1–11].

In addition, the standard spread plate technique for microorganism culture, Fig. 1a, involves a large amount of resources, materials, time and labor. An alternative for this technique is single plate serial dilution spotting (SP-SDS) [12], Fig. 1b, which has been

© Springer Nature Switzerland AG 2019
R. Vera-Rodriguez et al. (Eds.): CIARP 2018, LNCS 11401, pp. 410–418, 2019.
https://doi.org/10.1007/978-3-030-13469-3_48

widely used in laboratories, however, approaches for automatic count found in the literature focus on the standard spread plate technique.

Furthermore, images used in these studies were obtained in controlled environments, eliminating several elements present in images obtained by laboratory operators with minimum control of conditions such as shadows, reflections, and insufficient illumination. Thus, when using the solutions developed to deal with images acquired in more realistic laboratory conditions, the limitations of such approaches can be perceived.

With this in view, this work aimed to investigate the techniques used for automatic CFU counting in the literature and to develop an approach for automatic CFU counting in images acquired in real-life situations of laboratories using SP-SDS. In addition, a database of images was created and is available for other researchers.

2   Theoretical Background

2.1   Single Plate Serial Dilution Spotting (SP-SDS)

In the standard spread plate technique, Fig. 1a, spreading of culture media is prepared at various dilutions, generally between 10^{-1} and 10^{-7}, from a suspension of microorganisms. Colony growth means the development of a population from a single CFU and, according to the golden rule, the dilution that will allow counting must have between 30 and 300 CFUs that are isolated enough to be counted [13]. Thus, it is necessary to produce one plate for each dilution and three replicates for each experiment, totaling 21 plates per experiment.

SP-SDS, Fig. 1b, has been used instead of the standard technique since it allows determining which dilution will produce the amount of CFU to be considered for counting and counting itself, producing only 3 plates per experiment, thus resulting in economy of time, labor and materials [12].

In this work, we created seven stripes using a multichannel pipette with 10 μL per dilution, evidenced in Fig. 1b by numerated rectangles.

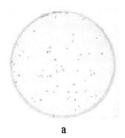
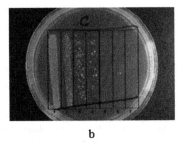

a   b

Fig. 1. Dilution schemes (a) Single dilution (Source: [5]) (b) Serial dilution

For CFU counting according to the golden rule it should be considered the number of CFU that can be counted by the naked eye located between the upper and lower blue lines included by the operator as limits. Thus, in Fig. 1b stripes valid for counting are 3, 4, 5, 6 and 7.

2.2   Related Works

In the last five years, many researchers have developed approaches for CFU automatic count including imaging devices and algorithms. Methods used and results obtained in works of this period are presented briefly in Table 1 which contains authors, approach proposed (alg: algorithm; ap: image capturing apparatus; auto: automatic; semi: semiautomatic; HT: Hough transform), accuracy and techniques employed for segmentation and counting of CFU. It is important to notice that accuracy comparisons are unfair since the approaches do not use the same dataset.

In [2, 4, 11], image acquisition devices were developed to improve contrast between CFU and background, aiming to reduce the presence of noise such as reflections and shadows, and to delimit the region of interest in order to reduce the preprocessing of images and to improve the accuracy rate of the developed algorithms. Authors [6, 10, 14] proposed applications for smartphones with image acquisition and processing but poor quality of images acquired by the cameras of the devices led do inferior results when compared to other authors' results.

Table 1. Published works from 2013 to 2017

Work	Approach		Accuracy	Techniques	
				CFU detection	Segmentation of agglomerates
[7]	alg	auto	99.5	Exhaustive search of local maxima	Nearest neighbor search
[1]	alg	semi	99.0	Correlation-based granulometry and maximally stable extremal regions	k-means
[9]	alg	auto	92.8	Convolutional neural networks	Convolutional neural networks
[8]	alg	semi	99.0	Connected components	Morphological opening
[2]	ap	auto	98.2	Distance transform	Distance transform
[10]	alg	auto	86.8	Classification algorithm	HT
[11]	ap	auto	97.0	HT	HT
[3]	alg	semi	98.8	HT and template matching	HT and template matching
[4]	ap	auto	99.0	Template matching	Watershed
[5]	alg	semi	97.4	Connected components	Watershed
[6]	alg	semi	90.3	Not informed	Watershed
[14]	alg	auto	74.0	Connected components	-
[15]	alg	auto	99.4	Connected components	-
[16]	alg	auto	75.7	Shape descriptor	-

The remaining studies used images obtained under controlled conditions from Petri dishes or images from databases available on the Internet, also obtained under controlled conditions. E.g., [1, 3, 15] used images acquired and made available by [5].

Some authors, such as [1, 3, 5, 6, 8] have chosen to add manual steps to the algorithm in order to assist the segmentation and counting steps. In addition, many authors such as [3, 5, 6, 7, 11, 16] invested in filtering processes in the preprocessing stage, aiming at improving segmentation and counting steps.

The techniques most used for segmentation of agglomerates were watershed transform (WT) [4, 5, 6] and Hough transform (HT) [3, 10, 11], probably due to the ease of its implementations, although WT is known for leading to super segmentation.

It should be emphasized that all works listed in Table 1 considered CFU counting in Petri dishes with a single dilution, making them not suitable for SP-SDS since they do not distinguish any segmentation that may exist within the area of the Petri dish. An alternative would be to manually separate the stripes and analyze them individually, but only solutions [3, 5] allow that.

3 Materials and Methods

Images were acquired with dishes on black background using a Canon EOS DIGITAL REBEL XS, mounted on a pedestal, focal length of 48 mm, without flash. In addition to ambient lighting, a circular LED lamp (50 mm) was placed at 50 mm on the right. Differently from most of the previously cited studies, there was no control over the acquired images. In this way, we have obtained real images of daily-life laboratory tests, which includes shadows, reflexes, bubbles and contaminations in agar, and experiments with failed or unexpected results.

To conduct the experiments from which the image base was obtained, it was used a *Streptococcus mutans* strain cultured aerobically in BHI (brain heart infusion) culture medium, incubated at 37 °C for a period of 48 h and suspended in sterile buffered saline solution (PBS) at pH 7.2. Six (6) experiments were performed on *Streptococcus mutans* with methylene blue and three replicates for each experiment, divided into control (C), blue light (FS), 5 min LED (L), 5 min 3 s LED (0.3 s) LED 6 min (1), and LED 7 min (2), in a total of 18 Petri dishes. Each experiment was prepared according to the SP-SDS technique containing seven (7) dilutions. The results of manual counting of CFU are presented in Table 2. Dilutions 1 and 2 exhibited more than 300 CFU therefore were not accounted for as determined by the golden rule.

Table 2. Manual counting per dilution (Dil) per plate (image)

	Image	Dil 3	Dil 4	Dil 5	Dil 6	Dil 7		Image	Dil 3	Dil 4	Dil 5	Dil 6	Dil 7
C	img_0801	81	4	1	0	0	0.3 s	img_0810	116	55	36	12	35
	img_0802	84	13	0	1	1		img_0811	120	49	25	30	15
	img_0803	75	6	5	3	0		img_0812	121	47	26	22	29
FS	img_0804	84	15	3	3	5	1	img_0813	113	23	12	3	6
	img_0805	92	14	4	3	2		img_0814	135	33	5	7	15
	img_0806	67	17	2	1	2		img_0815	71	22	13	11	8
L	img_0807	235	68	36	34	20	2	img_0816	68	14	5	2	8
	img_0808	227	40	28	27	22		img_0817	83	25	5	3	2
	img_0809	218	60	27	32	23		img_0818	121	20	14	5	5

The proposed approach was implemented in C/C++ language, using DevC++ compiler and OpenCV library [17] and its performance was analyzed through the measure of accuracy. The composed database of images is available at www.saraujo. pro.br/cfu.

4   Proposed Approach

The developed algorithm consists of two main steps: (i) image processing to obtain the regions of interest (ROI) corresponding to the stripes of dilutions, and (ii) segmentation and counting for each dilution using cross-correlation granulometry technique.

4.1   First Step – ROI Segmentation

Given a colored image with $X \times Y$ pixels, similar to that shown in Fig. 1b, denoted by $I_{RGB} = (I_R, I_G, I_B)$, where I_R, I_G, I_B are bands red, green and blue, initially I_{RGB} is converted to gray levels generating image $I_{gray}(x, y) = [I_R(x, y) + I_G(x, y) + I_B(x, y)]/3$.

For reducing noise, we apply a median filter on I_{gray} using a 5×5 window. In the sequence, to obtain only the inner area of the dish, the circular area is detected through HT [18] and the algorithm creates a mask for removal of the unwanted area, Fig. 2a.

Following, as there are different lighting conditions in different areas, we perform Gaussian adaptive thresholding using a 7×7 window with $c = 4$ and $\sigma = 1.4$, resulting in image I_{bin}, Fig. 2b. Parameters for thresholding were determined experimentally.

To align the stripes at a 90° angle, the histogram of vertical projections of I_{bin} is analyzed by varying its rotation angle from $-15°$ to $+15°$, the highest peak determines the alignment angle generating I_{rot} shown in Fig. 2c. Undesirable regions of I_{rot} are removed, results observed on Fig. 2d. Finally, the histogram of vertical projections of I_{rot} is analyzed and ROIs (R_1–R_7) relative to dilutions are segmented, Fig. 2e.

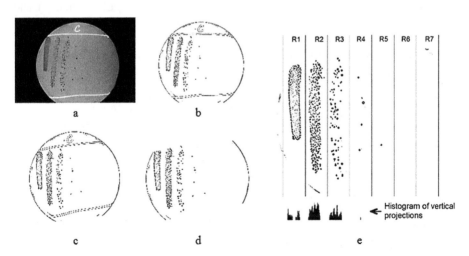

Fig. 2. ROI segmentation steps. (a) Inner area of the dish (b) Binarization after borders and exterior removal (c) Stripes alignment (d) Noise removal (e) ROI segmentation

4.2   Second Step – Segmentation and Counting of CFU

For determination of the amount of CFU in each dilution, it was applied cross correlation-based granulometry as proposed by Maruta et al. [19] for characterizing porous silicon nanomaterials, which, unlike WT, does not incur in super segmentation.

The discrete cross correlation between an image R_i and a template τ, Eq. 1, is used to find the template τ inside image R_i through template matching operation, which computes the mean-corrected image $\tilde{\tau} = \tau - \bar{\tau}$ by subtracting the mean grayscale $\bar{\tau}$ from each pixel of image τ and computes the cross correlation $c(x,y) = \tau(x,y) \circ R_i(x,y)$ where the peaks of image c correspond to the occurrences of τ in R_i.

$$\tau(x,y) \circ R_i = \sum_m \sum_n \tau(m,n) R_i(x+m, y+n) \tag{1}$$

Our approach computes cross correlations using as templates five circular kernels $(\tau_1, \ldots, \tau_5)$, Fig. 3, of different radii varying in geometric progression according to a median radius (r) in pixels defined by the mean radius of the connected components present in R_i. In our experiments, τ varies from $r - 2$ to $r + 2$ pixels.

Fig. 3. Kernel used in granulometry (τ). Black pixels have negative values, white pixels have positive and gray have zero. In each kernel the sum of black pixels is -0.5, the sum of white pixels is $+0.5$. As gray pixels vary from 0 to 1, the result image from correlation will vary from -1 to $+1$ [19].

Correlation peaks are sorted in decreasing order and a peak is discarded when intersecting with other peak with intersect rate (I) larger than $I = 95\%$ (experimentally defined) of the circular area of τ, allowing the detection of partially intersecting CFU. The value of I is constant for R_i. A minimum correlation (c) was determined experimentally for each R_i depending on r and on the number of connected components (n) present in R_i as follows: for $r \leq 2$, $c = 13$; for $r = 3$ and $n \geq 50$, $c = 18$; and for $r \geq 3$ and $n < 50$, $c = 25$.

5   Results and Discussion

Results in Table 3 were obtained considering manual count and automatic count. Presence of CFUs very close to the edges prevent the complete removal of edges, as well as upper and lower boundary lines in several images, resulting in noise that could be interpreted as CFU during correlation, since some CFU have very small areas.

Dilution 3 was the most complex concerning segmentation and counting of CFU, reducing accuracy due to the presence of large amounts of CFU, a large variation in the mean radius and many agglomerates of small CFU.

The presence of large and small CFUs in similar amounts in the same ROI led to a detection error, since when small CFUs were counted, large CFUs were erroneously segmented. This influenced the determination of c and r used in correlation.

Also, r shows wide variation in the same dilution, which should be considered in the determination of c for each dilution in each image individually.

Likewise, the adequate c avoided detection of foreign objects in agar, such as bubbles, as if they were CFUs.

Table 3. Analysis of accuracy (%) for each experiment separated by dilution (Dil)

	Image	Dil3	Dil4	Dil5	Dil6	Dil7		Image	Dil3	Dil4	Dil5	Dil6	Dil7
C	img_0801	100	100	100	100	100	0.3 s	img_0810	100	98.2	100	91.7	97.2
	img_0802	100	100	100	100	100		img_0811	92.5	93.9	96.0	93.3	93.3
	img_0803	100	100	100	100	100		img_0812	83.5	93.6	100	100	96.6
FS	img_0804	100	100	100	100	100	1	img_0813	93.8	73.9	100	100	83.3
	img_0805	98.9	100	100	100	100		img_0814	97.8	90.9	100	100	80.0
	img_0806	100	94.1	100	100	100		img_0815	98.6	95.5	92.3	100	100
L	img_0807	99.1	100	100	94.1	100	2	img_0816	100	100	100	100	100
	img_0808	97.4	97.5	100	100	100		img_0817	97.6	100	100	100	100
	img_0809	100	98.3	100	100	100		img_0818	96.7	95.0	92.9	100	100

6   Conclusions

We have shown that it is possible to automatically count CFU in real laboratory images for SP-SDS, without great control on image acquisition and without manual interference, with accuracy above 80% for dilutions where there is presence of CFU with r between 1.5 and 2.5 pixels, and close to 100% when CFUs have $r > 2.5$ pixels with low variation. The presence of noise in images can generate false positives, when noise is interpreted as CFUs, or false negatives, when the proper segmentation of agglomerates does not occur. The use of additional filters for noise removal can jeopardize the count of very small CFU. Thus, it is evident that the simultaneous presence of very small CFUs and noises directly influence accuracy, even when considered for the determination of c and I parameters, showing that a careful evaluation of CFU median radius in each dilution is crucial. Future work could evaluate other methods of agglomerates segmentation, as well as other microorganisms and other culture media.

References

1. Junior, J.M.S., Balian, S.C., Kim, H.Y.: MSGRANUL: Granulometria baseada em Correlação e MSER aplicada a contagem de colônias de bactérias. In: Congresso Brasileiro de Automática, pp. 2151–2156 (2016)
2. Martinez-Espinosa, J.C., et al.: Nondestructive technique for bacterial count based on image processing. Biol. Eng. Med. **1**, 1–6 (2016). https://doi.org/10.15761/BEM.1000103
3. Siqueira, A.A., de Carvalho, P.G.S.: MicroCount: free software for automated microorganism colony counting by computer. IEEE Lat. Am. Trans. **15**, 2006–2011 (2017). https://doi.org/10.1109/TLA.2017.8071248
4. Chiang, P.J., Tseng, M.J., He, Z.S., Li, C.H.: Automated counting of bacterial colonies by image analysis. J. Microbiol. Methods **108**, 74–82 (2015). https://doi.org/10.1016/j.mimet.2014.11.009
5. Geissmann, Q.: OpenCFU, a new free and open-source software to count cell colonies and other circular objects. PLoS ONE **8**, 1–10 (2013). https://doi.org/10.1371/journal.pone.0054072
6. Wong, C.-F., Yeo, J.Y., Gan, S.K.: APD colony counter app : using watershed algorithm for improved colony counting. Nat. Methods Appl. Notes. 1–3 (2016). https://doi.org/10.1038/an9774
7. Yoon, S.C., Lawrence, K.C., Park, B.: Automatic counting and classification of bacterial colonies using hyperspectral imaging. Food Bioprocess Technol. **8**, 2047–2065 (2015). https://doi.org/10.1007/s11947-015-1555-3
8. Barbedo, J.G.A.: An algorithm for counting microorganisms in digital images. Vii Work. Da Rede Nanotecnologia Apl. Ao Agronegócio **11**, 1354–1359 (2013)
9. Ferrari, A., Lombardi, S., Signoroni, A.: Bacterial colony counting with convolutional neural networks in digital microbiology imaging. Pattern Recognit. **61**, 629–640 (2017). https://doi.org/10.1016/j.patcog.2016.07.016
10. Austerjost, J., et al.: A smart device application for the automated determination of E. coli colonies on agar plates. Eng. Life Sci. **17**, 959–966 (2017). https://doi.org/10.1002/elsc.201700056
11. Matić, T., Vidović, I., Siladi, E., Tkalec, F.: Semi-automatic prototype system for bacterial colony counting. In: Proceedings of 2016 International Conference on Smart Systems and Technologies, SST 2016, pp. 205–210 (2016)
12. Thomas, P., Sekhar, A.C., Upreti, R., Mujawar, M.M., Pasha, S.S.: Optimization of single plate-serial dilution spotting (SP-SDS) with sample anchoring as an assured method for bacterial and yeast cfu enumeration and single colony isolation from diverse samples. Biotechnol. Rep. **8**, 45–55 (2015). https://doi.org/10.1016/j.btre.2015.08.003
13. Sutton, S.: Accuracy of plate counts. J. Valid. Technol. **17**, 42–46 (2011). https://doi.org/10.1016/j.fm.2005.01.010
14. Sánchez-femat, E., et al.: Mobile application for automatic counting of bacterial colonies. Trends Appl. Softw. Eng. Adv. Intell. Syst. Comput. **537**, 221–230 (2017). https://doi.org/10.1007/978-3-319-48523-2
15. Boukouvalas, D.T., De Araújo, S.A.: Contagem de Unidades Formadoras de Colônias de Microrganismos Através de Visão Computacional. In: SETII - Seminário em Tecnologia da Informação Inteligente, pp. 87–93. UNINOVE, São Paulo (2017)
16. Maretić, Igor S., Lacković, I.: Automated colony counting based on histogram modeling using gaussian mixture models. CMBEBIH 2017. IP, vol. 62, pp. 548–553. Springer, Singapore (2017). https://doi.org/10.1007/978-981-10-4166-2_83

17. Bradski, G.: The OpenCV library. Dr Dobbs J. Softw. Tools. **25** (2000). https://doi.org/10.1111/0023-8333.50.s1.10
18. Shapiro, L., Stockman, G.: Computer Vision. Comput. Vis. 9 (2001)
19. Maruta, R.H., Kim, H.Y., Huanca, D.R., Salcedo, W.J.: A new correlation-based granulometry algorithm with application in characterizing porous silicon nanomaterials. ECS Trans. **31**, 273–280 (2010)

Image Inpainting Based on Local Patch Search Supported by Image Segmentation

Sarah Almeida Carneiro[1,2], Helio Pedrini[2],
and Silvio Jamil Ferzoli Guimarães[1(✉)]

[1] Computer Science Department, Pontifical Catholic University of Minas Gerais,
Belo Horizonte, MG, Brazil
sjamil@pucminas.br
[2] Institute of Computing, University of Campinas, Campinas, SP, Brazil

Abstract. Image inpainting can be defined as a restoration process in which damaged or selected regions are repaired by taking into account the image content. In this work, we employ a local-based strategy instead of a global one to identify the best existing patch with information to replace the damaged/selected patch. In order to properly identify the most representative patches, we propose a method based on the (i) creation of a local graph using a similarity of patches in the original image and (ii) partition of the image into regions according to hierarchical image segmentation to support the local patch identification. The experimental results demonstrate that our local search outperformed the results of image inpainting in terms of both qualitative and quantitative aspects, when compared to global search of patches.

Keywords: Image inpainting · Hierarchical image segmentation · Patch graph

1 Introduction

Image inpainting, also known as image restoration, is the term used to describe the restoration process in order to repair a damaged or selected region of a given image [9,10,18,19]. According to Bertalmio et al. [3], most of the inpainting approaches are either based on the extraction of fractions of the image, known as patch interpolation, or partial differential equation (PDE) approaches.

In the patch-based category, techniques for texture expansion by recursively filling pixel by pixel of the masked region of the image were performed by Efros and Leung [8]. Unfortunately, the size of the neighborhood and, in some cases, the tendency of reproducing incoherent textures are two problems related to their method. Another similar approach was proposed by taking into account

This work received funding from CAPES, FAPESP (17/12646-3), FAPEMIG (PPM 00006-16), and CNPq (Universal 421521/2016-3, PQ 307062/2016-3 and PQ 305169/2015-7).

changes in the filling order by (i) prioritizing border pixels without information and (ii) copying entire image patches to cover the flaws, making it possible to work with linear structures [6]. In this sense, this method aims to be able to remove large objects from the image by considering the principles of patch priority, propagating texture and structure information, and updating the values of the filled patches. A disadvantage of the method proposed by Criminisi [6] is the difficulty in working with images in perspective.

In the non-local patch graph category, some methods have been proposed in the literature [4,7,11–13,17]. Partial differential equation (PDE) [16] approaches have also been conducted through the construction of a Gaussian pyramid based on convolutions and samples of the original image [13]. Therefore, a region selected for inpainting can be filled by linear interpolation using samples from the Gaussian pyramid. Other studies have been developed by interpolating gray scale images, thus extending the lines of constant intensity [12]. On the other hand, studies to reproduce the technique used by manual painting restorers have been accomplished in order to propagate information of the areas near the flaws along the border [4]. One of the drawbacks related to this technique is the difficulty in producing content for regions with large failures. Extensions of the study have used the idea of dynamic fluid propagation in order to scatter the padding information from the external regions towards the fault [2].

Fig. 1. Example of image inpainting. From left to right, we illustrate the original image, the image mask, the result obtained with the method described in [6], and the result obtained with our approach by taking into account local constraints. (Color figure online)

To deal with some problems in images with perspectives and some kind of texture, mainly due to the computation of patch priority, we propose an image inpainting method by considering patch locality in conjunction to hierarchical image segmentation since we look for patches close to the missing patch to be restored. In Fig. 1, we illustrate an example of inpainting in which the selected region represented by the green mask is restored by the method developed by Criminisi et al. [6] and our local-based approach. As we can observe, the result obtained in [6] when applied to the original image presents some problems, such as texture garbage and discontinuities. On the other hand, our local patch search strategy better reconstructed some parts of the original image, as illustrated in the rightmost image. It is worth observing that, compared to [6], the main difference is related to the local patch search which is supported by an image segmentation and, of course, this new local search will affect the patch priority computation. Considering that, in this work, our main assumption is that the probability of similar patches to the blank patch is higher if the patch with information belongs to a closer region to the mask, we propose (i) the creation of a local graph using a similarity of patches in the original image and (ii) the partition of the image into regions according to a hierarchical image segmentation to support the local patch identification.

Due to the use of a local patch graph and image partitions, our main contributions are two-folds: (i) possibility of controlling the size of the patch search space preserving the homogeneous region properties; and (ii) only patches completely inside the patch search space are considered and consequently patches with texture due to different regions are ignored.

This work is organized as follows. In Sect. 2, we define some important concepts and we describe two methods graph-based image inpainting to be studied and compared. In Sect. 3, we describe our method for coping with image inpainting. In Sect. 4, some experimental results are presented and analyzed. We have showed that the proposed method outperformed, in terms of PSNR and MSE values, the compared approaches. Some final remarks and directions for future work are outlined in Sect. 5.

2   Theoretical Background

In this section, we define some important concepts and we present the two inpainting methods that will be explored.

2.1   Patch Graph

Let I be an image. We define a patch extraction operator R who returns the pixels into the squared $\sqrt{d} \times \sqrt{d}$ around a pixel location x, thus $R(x) = (I(x_1), \cdots, I(x_d))$, in which d is the number of pixels of the patch. Let x and y be two pixel locations, given two patches centered at x and y, we define the distance between them as the usual squared Euclidean distance. According to [7], the visual similarity between two patches normalized in $[0,1]$ can be computed given the distance between them by a simple exponential filtering defined as $w(x,y) = e^{-\frac{d(x,y)}{h^2}}$, where $d(x,y)$ is the squared Euclidean distance between x and y, and the parameter h controls the decay of the exponential function.

Let $G = (V, E)$ be a patch graph which models the relationship between the patches extracted from the image I, in which V is the set of pixels of the image I and E is the set of edges. (G, W) be a weighted patch graph in which W is a weight function that assigns a positive weight to each edge. Each pixel at location x of the image I is represented by a vertex u whose data is given by the patch $R(x)$. Each pair of vertices u and v, that represents the pixels at locations x and y, is connected by an edge (u, v) whose weight is computed by the similarity function $w(x, y)$. This weight is positive and tends to zero when patches are highly dissimilar. In practice, we only connect the K nearest neighbors (KNN) to reduce the number of edges. As discussed in [7], similar patches should be well connected together while weakly connected to the others, while the patches located at the transition between textures are ideally mildly connected to both clusters. Vertices representing patches who contain unknown pixels are not connected to any other vertex during the patch graph construction, thus this graph is initially disconnected and will ultimately be fully connected as these vertices are sequentially inserted.

2.2   Image Inpainting

The following subsections briefly describe two image inpainting approaches used for comparison purpose in this work.

Defferrard's Method. The method proposed by Defferrard [7] could be defined as follows. A non-local patch graph from the known patches of the source region defined as the entire image minus the damaged/selected region. Thus, for computing the graph G, all pixels can be considered for computing the weight edges. Unknown patches are completely disconnected. Thus, the method is a sequential process with the following steps: (i) those among the disconnected patches who possess a sufficient amount of information (*i.e.*, some fraction of the pixels they represent have a value) are compared against all known; and (ii) connected patches are inserted into the graph with appropriate weights. The graph is thus sequentially completed, while no pixels have actually been inpainted. To allow further graph completion, we must indeed inpaint unknown pixels to recover enough information about a patch to compare it to the others.

Criminisi et al.'s Method. The method proposed in [6] is an exemplar-based image inpainting defined as follows. The original image is decomposed into two components: (i) one of which is processed by inpainting; and (ii) the other by texture synthesis. The result is the sum of the two processed components. Let I be the image to be inpainted. As in the Defferrard's method, the source region may be defined as the entire image minus the damaged/selected region to be inpainted. Next, as with all exemplar-based texture synthesis, the size of the patch must be specified. In this method, each pixel maintains a colour value (or "empty", if the pixel is unfilled) and a confidence value, which reflects our confidence in the pixel value, and which is frozen once a pixel has been filled. During the course of the algorithm, patches along the fill front are also given a temporary priority value, which determines the order in which they are filled. Then, the algorithm iterates the following three steps until all pixels have been filled: (i) computing patch priorities; (ii) propagating texture and structure information; and (iii) updating confidence values.

3   Local-Based Strategy for Image Inpainting

Instead of computing patch similarity taking into account the entire image as in the original method [6,7], we reduce the patch search space by using segmentation strategy for maintaining homogeneous patches in that search. This kind of strategy will influentiate the patch priority computation. Thus, our assumption is that the probability of similar patches to the blank patch is higher if the patch with information belongs to a closer region to the mask. Closer regions are obtained through a hierarchical segmentation algorithm. Further details about this method can be found in [5,14].

Algorithm 1. Image inpainting algorithm based on local patch graph.

Input: Original image f
Input: Image mask m
Parameter : Radius r
Parameter : Method $method$
Output: Inpainted image

1 $segImage \leftarrow$ Watershed (m);
2 $adjList \leftarrow$ Neighborhood $(segImage, r)$;
3 $(G, W) \leftarrow$ CreatePatchGraph $(m, method, adjList)$;
4 $patches \leftarrow$ ComputeBlankPatches $(method, m)$;
5 **while** $patches$ is not $empty$ **do**
       // Identify patches with high filling priority
6      $p \leftarrow$ PatchPriority $(method, patches)$;
7   Inpaint the missing patch p;
8      $patches \leftarrow patches \setminus \{p\}$;
9   Update $(G, W, method)$;
10 **end**

The main steps of the proposed method for image inpainting is illustrated in Algorithm 1. The main goal of our work is to study the behavior of different inpainting methods, for instance, Criminisi et al. [6] and Defferrard [7], when we limit the patch search space for nearest regions to the blanked patches to be restored. Instead of partitioning the images in fixed regions, we have applied a watershed method (Line 1) to produce a set of regions. Considering that the watershed by area will compute a hierarchy of partitions, an ideal cut could be identified by Mumford-Shah energy [1]. After that, we compute the neighboring regions (Line 2) of the blanked patches that are at most r regions farther. Lines 3, 4 and 6 depend on the method in which we are interested to improve. In our proposal, function CreatePatchGraph is the most important one since it will compute the patch graph based on the two studied inpainting methods taking into account our local-based search strategy, in which only the patches inside the r regions farther are considered as candidates to restore the blanked patch. At the end (Line 9), the patch graph G must be updated. It is worth observing that if the adjacency list has all image patches, instead of local one, the result is the same as the original method.

4   Experiments

In order to analyze the results achieved with our approach compared to the original ones, we will illustrate some examples to show the quality of our results. Moreover, we present some quantitative values in terms of peak signal-noise ratio (PSNR) and mean square error (MSE). Here, we compare the following methods: Defferrard [7], local-based Defferrard, Criminisi et al. [6], and local-based Criminisi et al.

4.1   Qualitative Analysis

For a qualitative analysis, we illustrate some examples in which the restoration process is done through the compared methods. It is worth observing that, when dealing with homogeneous colors, such as water and sky, the Defferrard method [7] presents some disagreements when compared to homogeneity and texture. Such problems have been solved when local-based analysis is applied (for instance, the water is better restored in the Boat image). The local-based approach in conjunction with the method by Criminisi et al. [6] clearly exhibited a better construction compared to the original. For instance, the horse in Fig. 2 is properly removed through our inpainting method.

4.2   Quantitative Analysis

For a quantitative analysis, we compute the most widely used measure for image inpainting according to [15], the peak signal-noise ratio (PSNR) and mean square error (MSE). The PSNR is used to measure the quality of the reconstructed compressed data, whereas the MSE is a liability function. Higher PSNR values usually correspond to the composition with better quality, whereas smaller MSE values mean that the restoration is superior.

Since, to the best of our knowledge, there is no benchmark dataset for image inpainting, we decide to use a set of images commonly employed in this type of application. According to our experiments (illustrated in Fig. 2), the MSE values for Defferrard [7], local-based Defferrard, Criminisi et al. [6] and local-based Criminisi et al. approaches are 43.41, 31.19, 54.38 and 33.24, respectively, whereas the PSNR values are 34.43, 35.87, 35.09 and 36.56, respectively. As we can observe from these results, our inpainting method based on local strategy has improved both measures. More specifically, the MSE for Criminisi et al. [6] is 54.38, while the value for our local-based proposed method is 33.24.

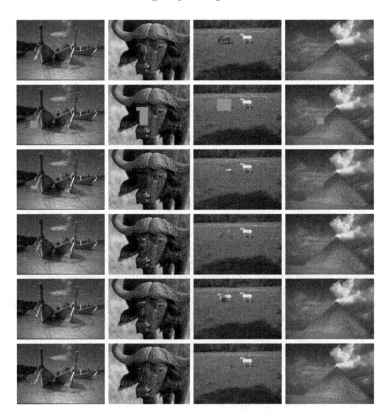

Fig. 2. Some results obtained with inpainting methods, more specifically, with the original methods Defferrard [7] and Criminisi et al. [6], and our proposed methods, local-based Defferrard and local-based Criminisi et al., based on these original ones in which we modified the search strategy in order to take into account the nearest regions to the one to be restored. Results for the compared methods are shown from top to bottom: original image; image mask; (third row) Defferrard [7]; (fourth row) local-based Defferrard; (fifth row) Criminisi et al. [6]; and (sixth) row local-based Criminisi et al. In terms of quantitative results, the MSE values are 43.41, 31.19, 54.38 and 33.24, respectively, whereas the PSNR values are 34.43, 35.87, 35.09 and 36.56, respectively.

5   Conclusions

Image inpainting could be defined as a restoration process in which damaged or selected regions are repaired taking into account the image content. In this paper, we have used local-based strategy instead of a global one to identify the best existing patch with information to replace the damaged/selected patches. Considering that our main assumption is that the probability of similar patches to the blank patch is higher if the patch with information belongs to a closer region to the mask, the (i) creation of a local graph using a similarity of patches in the original image and (ii) the partition of the image into regions according to hierarchical image segmentation to support the local patch identification could be considered as our main contributions.

In order to properly identify the most representative patches, we proposed a method based on a partition of the image into regions according to hierarchical image segmentation to help in the identification of the local patches. According to our experiments, the local patch analysis have contributed to improve the quality of the results in both qualitative and quantitative assessment.

As directions for future work, we intend to investigate the use of a learning structure based on predetermined image data sets. Moreover, we will consider more sophisticated measure for evaluating image inpainting methods, some examples of these measures are summarized in [15].

References

1. Ambrosio, L., Fusco, N., Hutchinson, J.E.: Higher integrability of the gradient and dimension of the singular set for minimisers of the Mumford-Shah functional. Calc. Var. Partial. Differ. Equ. **16**(2), 187–215 (2003)
2. Bertalmio, M., Bertozzi, A.L., Sapiro, G.: Navier-stokes, fluid dynamics, and image and video inpainting. In: IEEE Computer Society Conference on Computer Vision and Pattern Recognition, vol. 1. IEEE (2001)
3. Bertalmio, M., Caselles, V., Masnou, S., Sapiro, G.: Inpainting. Technical report, Duke University (2011)
4. Bertalmio, M., Sapiro, G., Caselles, V., Ballester, C.: Image inpainting. In: 27th Annual Conference on Computer Graphics and Interactive Techniques, pp. 417–424. ACM Press/Addison-Wesley Publishing Co. (2000)
5. Cousty, J., Najman, L., Kenmochi, Y., Guimarães, S.: Hierarchical segmentations with graphs: quasi-flat zones, minimum spanning trees, and saliency maps. J. Math. Imaging Vis. **60**, 479–502 (2017)
6. Criminisi, A., Pérez, P., Toyama, K.: Region filling and object removal by exemplar-based image inpainting. IEEE Trans. Image Process. **13**(9), 1200–1212 (2004)
7. Defferrard, M.: Graph-based image inpainting. Technical report, École Polytechnique Fédérale de Lausanne (EFPL) (2014)
8. Efros, A., Leung, T.: Texture synthesis by non-parametric sampling. In: Seventh IEEE International Conference on Computer Vision, p. 1033. IEEE, September 1999
9. Fan, Q., Zhang, L.: A novel patch matching algorithm for exemplar-based image inpainting. Multimedia Tools Appl. **77**, 1–15 (2017)
10. Guillemot, C., Le Meur, O.: Image inpainting: overview and recent advances. IEEE Signal Process. Mag. **31**(1), 127–144 (2014)
11. Karaca, E., Tunga, M.A.: An interpolation-based texture and pattern preserving algorithm for inpainting color image. Expert Syst. Appl. **91**, 223–234 (2018)
12. Masnou, S., Morel, J.-M.: Level Lines based disocclusion. In: International Conference on Image Processing, pp. 259–263. IEEE (1998)
13. Ogden, J.M., Adelson, E.H., Bergen, J.R., Burt, P.J.: Pyramid-based computer graphics. RCA Eng. **30**(5), 4–15 (1985)
14. Perret, B., Cousty, J., Guimarães, S.J.F., Maia, D.S.: Evaluation of hierarchical watersheds. IEEE Trans. Image Process. **27**(4), 1676–1688 (2018)

15. Qureshi, M.A., Deriche, M., Beghdadi, A., Amin, A.: A critical survey of state-of-the-art image inpainting quality assessment metrics. J. Vis. Commun. Image Represent. **49**, 177–191 (2017)
16. Roubívcek, T.: Nonlinear Partial Differential Equations with Applications, vol. 153. Springer, Basel (2013). https://doi.org/10.1007/978-3-0348-0513-1
17. Wang, H., Jiang, L., Liang, R., Li, X.-X.: Exemplar-based image inpainting using structure consistent patch matching. Neurocomputing **269**, 90–96 (2017)
18. Yang, C., Lu, X., Lin, Z., Shechtman, E., Wang, O., Li, H.: High-resolution image inpainting using multi-scale neural patch synthesis. In: IEEE Conference on Computer Vision and Pattern Recognition, vol. 1, p. 3 (2017)
19. Zhao, G., Liu, J., Jiang, J., Wang, W.: A deep cascade of neural networks for image inpainting, deblurring and denoising. Multimed. Tools Appl. **77**, 1–16 (2017)

Bio-Inspired Perception Sensor (BIPS) Concept Analysis for Embedded Applications

Louise Sarrabezolles[1,2]([✉])[ID], Antoine Manzanera[2][ID], and Nicolas Hueber[1][ID]

[1] French-German Research Institute of Saint-Louis, 68300 Saint-Louis, France
louise.sarrabezolles@isl.eu
[2] ENSTA ParisTech, 91120 Palaiseau, France

Abstract. The Bio-inspired Perception Sensor (BIPS) component is a small and low power bio-inspired on-chip device which has been used in different computer vision applications (traffic analysis, driving assistance, object tracking). It caught the attention of the embedded vision community, since its specifications could help overcoming the time, size, weight and energy bottlenecks that still limits the current development of computer vision systems. For a long time, the lack of mathematical and algorithmic models of the component has prevented it to spread among the research community. But the recent formalization of BIPS basic functions and mechanisms has allowed to develop numerical models and simulators, in order to better evaluate the advantages and limitations of the concept. In this paper, we experimentally address the generalization capability of the BIPS concept, by evaluating it on the road lane detection application. This allows to illustrate how its parameters can be adapted for a specific vision task. This approach permits to automatically instantiate the main parameters, which stabilizes the system output and improves its performance. The obtained results reach the level of the *caltech-lanes* reference.

Keywords: Bio-inspired · Embedded vision · Road lane detection

1 Introduction

The detection and recognition applications in embedded computer vision systems for robots, autonomous vehicles, security cameras or drones, are limited by the constraints on their execution time, size, weight and power consumption. Building efficient, versatile and evolving algorithms in such context is one of today's challenges of Computer Vision. The current best algorithms according to the academic datasets and challenges (e.g. [5,8]) are based on deep learning methods, which imply huge learning databases and off-line training. Most of these algorithms are tested on multi-GPU environment: for example the KITTI challenge best algorithms were all tested on CPU/GPU platforms and yet, few

© Springer Nature Switzerland AG 2019
R. Vera-Rodriguez et al. (Eds.): CIARP 2018, LNCS 11401, pp. 428–435, 2019.
https://doi.org/10.1007/978-3-030-13469-3_50

of them are real-time [5]. There are several attempts to integrate deep networks on low power system-on-chip but they have to reduce the size of the network and they are not processing the training phase [10]. As Ehsan et al. proposed for the UAVs application [4], we believe that a new strategy must be followed in the design of computer vision algorithms, based on fully hardware or hybrid solutions.

The bio-inspired computer vision community follows this strategy and proposed several interesting methods inspired by the human vision and leveraging the properties of electronic components. Among those, one particular component caught our attention: the Bio-inspired Perception Sensor (BIPS). This component is small and low power: $50\,mm^2$, $2\,W$ [12]. It has been used and showed interesting results in different industrial computer vision applications such as traffic analysis, driving assistance and object tracking. For a long time, the concept of the BIPS has remained unknown to the community and the communication about its principles limited to some patents and a few general public articles [11,12]. Recently, through the study of Sarrabezolles et al. [14], a mathematical formalization has been established, allowing to evaluate the method on different practical applications.

In this paper, we present the results obtained using this method on the road lane detection application. The formalization and models recalled on Sect. 2 allow to adapt the method to road lane detection, as explained on Sect. 3. Using the *caltech-lanes* database [1], we were able to compare the performance of the method in this application and to illustrate the influence of its internal parameters on Sect. 4. The promising results consolidate the focusing of our research on this method and its possible improvements, as well as its potential adaptation to different computer vision applications, as discussed in Sect. 5.

2   The BIPS Concept

The Bio-Inspired Perception Sensor (BIPS) component has been developed by Pirim [11] based on bio-inspired electronic designs. Its experimental development did not provide a true formalization of the concept behind, thus impeding its use for academic researches. The recent study by Sarrabezolles et al. [14] provides the basic functions underlying the BIPS concept, that can be decomposed into two parts: an extraction of local features, and an original region of interest detection and description process.

The extraction part is inspired from the retinal and first layer of the visual cortex processes [6]. Its current implementation computes on the fly different kinds of local features: the tonal features luminance, saturation and hue; the structural features gradient and curvature; and the temporal features temporal variation and optical flow. Each feature can be represented by an application F defined on the pixel set $[\![0; W]\!] \times [\![0; H]\!]$, where W and H are the dimensions of the input images. A more detailed description of the local features used in the BIPS is given in [14].

The detection part is addressed by an original method called "dynamic attractor" (DA) by its inventor P. Pirim. It consists of the joint computation of feature histograms and the sequential detection of the histograms principal mode(s). The original component works on three features: one descriptive (i.e. tonal, structural or temporal), and two spatial ones (i.e. the coordinates X and Y), but the formalization shows that the number of features could be extended [14]. This process is inspired by the visual cortex processing model, which shows plasticity [13] and combines two information streams, namely the dorsal and the ventral streams, semantically related to the "what" and the "where", respectively [7]. The DA process allows to find a bounding in the feature space, which selects a set of pixels representative of an object. This process is iterative and can be summarized by the following equations:

Initialization $k = 0$

$$\forall m \in [\![1, M]\!], \ A_m^0 = \min(\Omega_m) \text{ and } B_m^0 = \max(\Omega_m). \tag{1}$$

Iteration for $k = 1$ **to** K_{steps}

Histogram Computation
$\forall n \in [\![1, M]\!]$,

$$H_n^k(f) = \mathbf{card} \left\{ p \in \mathbb{I} \times \mathbb{J} \ \middle/ \ \begin{array}{l} val(p) = 1, F_n(p) = f \text{ and} \\ \forall m \in [\![1, M]\!], \ A_m^k \leq F_m(p) \leq B_m^k \end{array} \right\}. \tag{2}$$

which gives $q_{\max} = \max_{f \in \Omega}(H(f))$ and $f_{\max} = \arg \max_{f \in \Omega}(H(f))$ the histogram maximums and associated features, and where Ω_m is the feature space of the mth feature; $\mathbb{I} = [\![0; W]\!]$ et $\mathbb{J} = [\![0; H]\!]$ are the input images dimensions; A_m^k and B_m^k are the boundaries applied to the mth feature; and val is a binary validation map that comes either from thresholds on the input images or from another DA.

These histogram computations are computed on the fly and provide the detection outputs: $(q_{\max}^{n,k}, f_{\max}^{n,k})_{n \in [\![1,M]\!]}$ the histogram modes; $(A_n^k, B_n^k)_{n \in [\![1,M]\!]}$ the feature boundaries; and N_k the number of selected pixels.

Boundaries Update
The boundaries update is the most important part of the process, allowing and defining the convergence of the "dynamic attractor" (DA). Two kinds of update are possible, the first one concentrates on a unique histogram maximum which is the mode, while the second may encompass several maxima. This update is done on one single feature at each step of the DA iteration (Fig. 1).

At each k, $\exists! \, n \in [\![1, M]\!]$, such that $k = qM + n, q \in \mathbb{R}_+$,

Mode 1: *Concentrate on a unique maximum*

$$A_n^{k+1} = \min \left\{ f \in \Omega_n, f \leq f_{\max}^{n,k} \ \middle/ \ \forall f' \in [f; f_{\max}^{n,k}], H_n^k(f') > \tau_n^k \right\},$$
$$B_n^{k+1} = \max \left\{ f \in \Omega_n, f \geq f_{\max}^{n,k} \ \middle/ \ \forall f' \in [f_{\max}^{n,k}; f], H_n^k(f') > \tau_n^k \right\}, \tag{3}$$

Mode 2: *Encompass several maxima*

$$A_n^{k+1} = \max \left\{ f \in \Omega_n \ \middle/ \ \forall f' \in [\min(\Omega_n); f[, H_n^k(f') \leq \tau_n^k \right\},$$
$$B_n^{k+1} = \min \left\{ f \in \Omega_n \ \middle/ \ f' \in]f; \max(\Omega_n)], H_n^k(f') \leq \tau_n^k \right\}, \tag{4}$$

where τ_n^k is the threshold and must be strictly inferior to $q_{max}^{n,k}$ to ensure the convergence. And $\forall\, m \in [\![1, M]\!], m \neq n, A_m^{k+1} = A_m^k$ and $B_m^{k+1} = B_m^k$.

In order to limit the processing time, a criterion on the size of the sought objects is used to define a threshold for stopping the convergence of the DA if its selected pixels are too few to correspond to such objects.

The DAs can be processed in parallel in different regions of the feature space, or even on different feature spaces. However, their convergence can only be formally proven in the general case when they are processed sequentially.

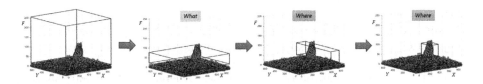

Fig. 1. Convergence steps of a "dynamic attractor" (DA) in the feature space. Example in the case of the detection of a tennis ball, using the hue and spatial coordinates.

This formalization brings forward several parameters that determine the detection process: the chosen feature space; the DA architecture; the size of the sought objects; the update mode; the detection threshold of each feature. Neither the choice of these parameters for a practical application nor their level of influence on the whole concept is made explicit by the inventor. Thus, in order to illustrate the behavior of the method and the possible influence of its parameters, we chose to apply it to a specific computer vision application.

3   Behavior Analysis Method

The road lane application is appropriate for the demonstration of the BIPS concept behavior, since the lanes are distinguished by their gradient angle and their position in the image. It is usually applied for autonomous driving, the existing solutions are based on edge detectors, Hough transform or RANSAC method [2,3,9]. For the BIPS concept, it allows to fix the architecture of the DAs, i.e. the choice of the input features with their order and the interaction mechanism between DAs through the binary validation map (Eq. 2), and to focus on the main parameters.

Each road lane can be described by its border lines which almost have (up to the perspective) the same gradient angle and are spatially close to each other. Thus, one lane can be detected by a DA working on the gradient angle feature and two spatial coordinates. The gradient angle is computed using the derivative Gaussian kernels. The chosen Gaussian kernel G has a standard deviation of 1.5 and a corresponding width of 9 pixels, to smooth the image and then to regularize the histograms. The polar transformation gives the gradient module and angle. A threshold is applied in order to validate only the pixels with a strong

Fig. 2. On the left: the extracted gradient angle within $[0; 180]$, only the strong gradients are visualized. On the right: example of the rotated coordinates for the central road lane detection.

gradient. Then the two spatial coordinates can be rotated to obtain a narrower bounding of the lane. This choice implies a change in the DA formalization: the computation of the spatial features evolves during the iteration process. The rotation angle α_k is computed dynamically to better suit the direction of the detected lane. The chosen rotation put the axis Y along the lines and the axis X at $90°$ counterclockwise (Fig. 2). In that feature space, a line corresponds to one gradient angle and one position X, which can be detected using the mode 1 on these two features. Along the axis Y, the line will then be represented by a flat and low histogram, a strict threshold at zero is enough to detect this line.

A series of DAs as constructed here allows then to detect all the lines in the frame. However, in the context of road lane detection, we can use several assumptions to reduce the detected lines to only the road lanes.

1. The dashed lanes can be represented by one lane using the mode 2 on Y.
2. A lane is represented by two lines close to each other. The first detection can be used to obstruct the second using an extension of its borders.

The chosen architecture leaves several parameters free: the number of DAs n_{DA}; the threshold on the size (in pixels) of the sought lines τ_N; the threshold on the angle mode detection τ_{ang} and the threshold on the X mode detection τ_X. The two first parameters are somehow linked. In fact, the number of DAs needed corresponds to the number of objects sought, and the threshold on the size of the sought object determines this number. The first step of our experiment will be to find the relation between those two parameters. The mode detection thresholds τ_{ang} and τ_X can be chosen proportionally to the maximum of the computed histogram. The choice of a too low percentage brings noise to the selected mode, but the choice of a too high percentage may loose relevant information describing the lines. For the first experiments, we choose to set $\tau_{ang} = 30\%$ and $\tau_X = 50\%$.

4   Results on Road Lane Detection

The experiments have been run on the *caltech-lanes* dataset. This dataset has been developed by the team of Aly [1]. It is composed of four sets of videos taken from a car. The clip contains several difficulties: curvatures, writing on the street, sun facing, strong shadows, passing cars, etc. Moreover, the ground truth concentrates only on visible road lanes from the car and provides a 3rd degree Bezier spline description of them, which may lead the BIPS detector to generate many false alarms (Fig. 3). To evaluate the output of the BIPS method, we compute the 1st degree spline s corresponding to the DA output and based on the two points: (X_{max}, A_Y) and (X_{max}, B_Y). We use the same metric as Aly [1], i.e. the distance between the detected spline s and one ground truth spline s_{GT}.

$$d_{mean} = \min\left(\underset{p \in s}{\text{mean}}\left(dist(p, s_{GT})\right), \underset{p \in s_{GT}}{\text{mean}}\left(dist(p, s)\right) \right)$$

$$d_{median} = \min\left(\underset{p \in s}{\text{median}}\left(dist(p, s_{GT})\right), \underset{p \in s_{GT}}{\text{median}}\left(dist(p, s)\right) \right)$$

(5)

The validation of the detection corresponds to $d_{mean} < 20$ and $d_{median} < 15$. Only one DA can validate the detection (the first one that converges). The others are considered as false positives.

Fig. 3. Challenging images from the caltech-lanes dataset and their ground truth.

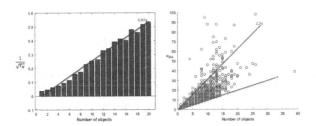

Fig. 4. On the left, linear regression made on the observation of $\frac{1}{\sqrt{\tau_N}}$ and the number of sought objects. On the right, observation of the necessary number of DAs compared to the number of sought objects.

Firstly, we run 100 DAs on each image of the dataset with a zero threshold on the size of the objects. The overall trend shows that the first engaged DAs are converging to the bigger objects whereas the following ones converge to smaller objects up to the noise level. The number of DAs necessary to detect all the sought object is then proportional to the number of objects. The study of this value on the four sets shows that the proportion is between 1 and 2.5 (Fig. 4-right). In parallel, we can use the set of observation to estimate the relation between the number of objects and the threshold τ_N. The four image sets give the same relation founded by linear regression (Fig. 4-left). The final relation between the number of DAs necessary and the threshold τ_N is:

$$n_{DA} = \frac{2.5}{0.02\sqrt{\tau_N}}$$

(6)

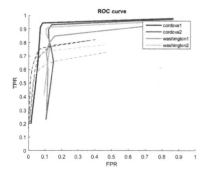

Clip	correct rate		false pos. rate	
	[Aly]	[BIPS]	[Aly]	[BIPS]
cordova1	91,62%	91,06%	5,66%	6,99%
cordova2	85,5%	89,55%	40,64%	11,95%
washington1	92,78%	79,89%	13,11%	12,35%
washington2	93,66%	89,86%	8,59%	10,42%

Fig. 5. On the left: ROC curves obtained with the four datasets using the variation of the threshold τ_N. The plain curves are computed with the DA number automation (Eq. 6); the dashed curves are computed with a fixed number of DAs. On the right: performance comparison with the *caltech-lanes* reference.

The ROC curve Fig. 5 is established using different values of the threshold τ_N. The use of the established relation (Eq. 6) allows to increase the area under the curve for each video. The inflexion point of the curve is for $\tau_N = 10$ and $n_{DA} = 39$; using these values we obtain results that are at the level of the reference.

5   Discussion and Conclusive Remarks

In order to assess the potential and the generalization capability of the BIPS concept, we have chosen to apply it on the road lane detection application. In this specific context indeed, the architecture of the DA can be fixed allowing to focus this study to its main internal parameters. We have established the relation between the needed number of DAs and the size of the sought road lanes on the basis of the *caltech-lanes* dataset.

This relation both automates the parametrization and significantly improves the obtained results on the *caltech-lanes* database, which are at the level of the reference. It optimizes the number of DAs engaged, thus minimizing the computation time and resources. Furthermore it stabilizes the rate of false positives, that remains however high due to the ground truth. In fact, the centered two lanes are considered as only one lane, but are mostly detected by two DAs, and the curved lines cannot be entirely detected by this DA configuration. The method used by M.Aly exploits several pre- and post-processings, whereas this study relies entirely on the BIPS method.

Now both the quality and the efficiency should be improved by integrating a prediction mechanism inside the dynamical process. This should be the main focus of our future work. We will also investigate the possibility of modifying the DA architecture in order to address a wider range of applications.

Acknowledgement. We would like to thank P. Pirim for his help in the understanding of the BIPS component and its extended possibilities, and for sharing his valuable knowledge.

References

1. Aly, M.: Real time detection of lane markers in urban streets. In: 2008 IEEE Intelligent Vehicles Symposium, pp. 7–12, June 2008
2. Bar Hillel, A., Lerner, R., Levi, D., Raz, G.: Recent progress in road and lane detection: a survey. Mach. Vis. Appl. **25**, 727–745 (2014)
3. Borkar, A., Hayes, M., Smith, M.T.: Robust lane detection and tracking with RANSAC and Kalman filter. In: 2009 16th IEEE International Conference on Image Processing (ICIP), pp. 3261–3264, November 2009
4. Ehsan, S., McDonald-Maier, K.D.: On-board vision processing for small UAVs: time to rethink strategy. In: NASA/ESA Conference on Adaptive Hardware and Systems, pp. 75–81, July 2009
5. Geiger, A., Lenz, P., Urtasun, R.: Are we ready for autonomous driving? the KITTI vision benchmark suite. In: Conference on Computer Vision and Pattern Recognition (CVPR), pp. 3354–3361. IEEE Computer Society, Washington, DC, June 2012
6. Hubel, D.H.: Eye, Brain, and Vision (Scientific American Library, No 22), 2nd edn. W. H. Freeman, New York (1995)
7. Jiongjiong, W., et al.: Relationship between ventral stream for object vision and dorsal stream for spatial vision: an fMRI+ERP study. Hum. Brain Mapp. **8**(4), 170–181 (1999)
8. Lin, T.-Y., et al.: Microsoft COCO: common objects in context. In: Fleet, D., Pajdla, T., Schiele, B., Tuytelaars, T. (eds.) ECCV 2014. LNCS, vol. 8693, pp. 740–755. Springer, Cham (2014). https://doi.org/10.1007/978-3-319-10602-1_48
9. Nieto, M., Salgado, L., Jaureguizar, F., Arrospide, J.: Robust multiple lane road modeling based on perspective analysis. In: IEEE International Conference on Image Processing, pp. 2396–2399, October 2008
10. Ota, K., Dao, M.S., Mezaris, V., de Natale, F.G.B.: Deep learning for mobile multimedia: a survey. ACM Trans. Multimed. Comput. Commun. Appl. **13**, 34:1–34:22 (2017)
11. Pirim, P.: Processeur de perception bio-inspiré : une approche neuromorphique. Techniques de l'ingénieur - Innovations en électronique et optoélectronique (May 2015)
12. Pirim, P.: Perceptive invariance and associative memory between perception and semantic representation USER a Universal SEmantic Representation implemented in a System on Chip (SoC). In: Lepora, N.F.F., Mura, A., Mangan, M., Verschure, P.F.M.J.F.M.J., Desmulliez, M., Prescott, T.J.J. (eds.) Living Machines 2016. LNCS (LNAI), vol. 9793, pp. 275–287. Springer, Cham (2016). https://doi.org/10.1007/978-3-319-42417-0_25
13. Bach-y Rita, P., Tyler, M.E., Kaczmarek, K.A.: Seeing with the Brain. Int. J. Hum. Comput. Interact. **15**(2), 285–295 (2003)
14. Sarrabezolles, L., Manzanera, A., Hueber, N., Perrot, M., Raymond, P.: Dual field combination for unmanned video surveillance. In: SPIE Defense and Commercial Sensing, Real-Time Image and Video Processing, vol. 10223. International Society for Optics and Photonics, Anaheim, May 2017

Deterministic Partially Self-avoiding Walks on Networks for Natural Shapes Classification

Lucas C. Ribas[1,2(✉)] and Odemir M. Bruno[1]

[1] Institute of Mathematics and Computer Science, University of São Paulo - USP,
Avenida Trabalhador são-carlense, 400, São Carlos, SP 13566-590, Brazil
`lucascorreiaribas@gmail.com, bruno@ifsc.usp.br`
[2] São Carlos Institute of Physics, University of São Paulo - USP,
PO Box 369, São Carlos, SP 13560-970, Brazil

Abstract. Shape is an important characteristic used by different classification tasks in computer vision. In particular, shape is useful in many biological problems (e.g. plant species recognition and fish otolith classification), which are challenging due to the diversity found in nature. This paper proposes a novel method for shape analysis and classification based on deterministic partially self-avoiding walks (DPSWs) on networks. First, a shape contour is modeled as a network by mapping each contour pixel as a vertex. Then, deterministic partially self-avoiding walks are performed on the network and a robust shape signature is obtained using statistics of the trajectories of the DPSWs. We evaluate this feature vector in a classification experiment using two different natural shape databases: USPLeaves and Otolith. The experimental results demonstrate a high classification accuracy of the method when compared to the other methods. This suggests that our method is a promising option for the classification task in biological problems.

Keywords: Deterministic walk · Networks · Shape analysis

1 Introduction

Shape is a classical attribute used in different tasks of computer vision. It is one of the most important features for object recognition with first studies dated from the 60's [1]. Furthermore, one of the interests in this feature is inspired by biological problems where shape characteristics are necessary [6].

Many methods for shape classification have been proposed in the literature. These methods can be divided into three main categories [14]: skeleton-based, region-based and contour-based techniques. The category of a method is related to the process used to extract the features from the shape. In this sense, skeleton-based methods use the medial axes of the shape for characterization and have as advantage the robustness for shapes with occlusion (e.g. [2,5]). On the other hand, region-based techniques use the whole image to characterize the shapes.

© Springer Nature Switzerland AG 2019
R. Vera-Rodriguez et al. (Eds.): CIARP 2018, LNCS 11401, pp. 436–443, 2019.
https://doi.org/10.1007/978-3-030-13469-3_51

Examples of this category are Zernike moments [23] and Hu moments-based methods [12]. The last category, uses contour information of the shape for characterization (e.g. Fourier descriptors [21], Curvature Scale Space [15] and multi-scale fractal dimension [20]). However, many methods of this category suffer when the silhouette is degraded. Recently, methods based on complex networks have been proposed to analyze shapes [3,18,19] and to deal with non-perfect contours that are often found in biological problems.

In this paper, we proposed a novel method for shape analysis based on the deterministic partially self-avoiding walk (DPSW) on networks. To accomplish this task, the shape contour is modeled as a network, including the information about the distribution of the contour pixels in the image. Then, we apply the DPSW on the network and use statistical measurements about the trajectories to obtain a shape signature, which can be used to distinguish different classes of shapes. The proposed method was applied on biological shape classification, which is a changeling problem, due to the diversity found in nature. Experiments results on the two natural databases showed the effectiveness of the proposed method compared to other shape methods.

This paper is organized as follows. Section 2 describes the proposed method to obtain a shape signature. Then, Sect. 3 presents the results obtained by the proposed method and others. Finally, in Sect. 4, the conclusions of the work are drawn.

2   Proposed Method

2.1   Modeling Contour as Network

Different approaches have been proposed to model contour as network [3,19]. Based on this, we model the contour as follows. Let a network represented by a set of vertices $V = \{v_1, v_2, ..., v_n\}$ and a set of edges E where each edge e_{v_i,v_j} connects two vertices v_i and v_j. The neighbors of a vertex are given by $\nu(v)$. Now, consider a set of pixels S of size N that belong to the contour C of a shape. Each pixel $s_i \in S$ is represented by discrete numerical values $s_i = (x_i, y_i)$ representing its Cartesian coordinates. To build a network, each point of the contour $s_i \in S$ is mapped into a vertex $v_i \in V$ of the network. Then, we connected each pair of vertices with a non-directed edge. For each edge e_{v_i,v_j} is attributed a weight $w(e_{v_i,v_j})$ according to the Euclidean distance considering the coordinates of the pixels s_i and s_j represented by the vertices v_i and v_j, $w(e_{v_i,v_j}) = \sqrt{(x_i - x_j)^2 + (y_i - y_j)^2}$. The edges weights are normalized by the largest distance between all pixels w_{max} of the contour, $w(e_{v_i,v_j}) = \frac{w(e_{v_i,v_j})}{w_{max}}$. This normalization aims to keep the edges weights in the interval $[0, 1]$ and invariant to scale of the shape.

At the moment, the network presents a regular behavior, i.e., all vertices have the same degree. Thus, it is necessary to apply a procedure to transform the network and to reveal important characteristics [17]. To accomplish this task, a simple and widely used approach is to apply a threshold t to remove edges. In this approach, a new network $G_t = (V_t, E_t)$ is obtained for each value of threshold t (Fig. 1(a)). Therefore, the transformed network G_t is obtained removing all edges of E whose the weight is equal or smaller than t, $E_t = \{e_{v_i,v_j} \in E | w(e_{v_i,v_j}) \leq t\}$.

Each value of t highlights different patterns of the network topology. In this way, we use different threshold values to achieve a richer set of measurements that describe the network dynamics [7,9]. Thus, the network characterization is performed using a set of thresholds T, which is defined by an initial threshold t_0, an incremental threshold t_i and a final threshold t_f.

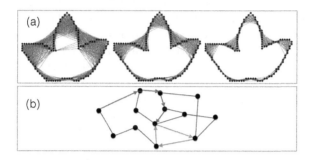

Fig. 1. (a) Example of the application of different values of threshold in a contour network. (b) Illustration of a DPSW on a network using the $r = max$, $\mu = 1$ and the vertex degree as criterion of distance. The edges in red represent the movements of the tourist until find the attractor (edges in green). (Color figure online)

2.2   Deterministic Partially Self-avoiding Walk on Network

Recently, DPSW has emerged as a promising approach for pattern recognition, obtaining great results in different problems such as texture analysis [4], dynamic texture analysis [8] and synthetic complex networks classification [9]. A DPSW on the network can be interpreted as a tourist that visit N vertices of the network. The tourist starts the walk from a pre-defined vertex v_i and the rule of movement r to visit the next vertex v_j is: go to the neighboring vertex that minimizes the distance $d(v_i, v_j)$ and has not been visited in the previous μ steps. In this rule, named as $r = min$, the tourist moves by minimizing the distances between vertices. On the other hand, in the rule $r = max$, the tourist maximize the distances between vertices. On networks, it is necessary to define the distance $d(v_i, v_j)$ between two vertices v_i and v_j. In this way, we consider two different criterion of distance c: the degree of the neighboring vertex $d(v_i, v_j) = k_{v_j}$ and the edge weight $d(v_i, v_j) = w(e_{v_i,v_j})$. It can occur of two neighboring vertices have the same distance, in this case, we consider as tiebreaker: the edge weight for the criterion of degree and the vertex degree for the criterion of the edge weight.

The memory $(\mu - 1)$ is the window in which the tourist performs a deterministic walk partially self-repulsive. In other words, the tourist will consider a visited vertex attractive again after having traveled μ vertices. The rule of movement is based on the neighborhood of the vertex $\nu(v)$ and a short memory μ, which although simple, can generate DPSW of great complexity [4,7]. The tourist walk can be divided into two parts: transient and attractor. The transient is the initial part of the walk that has size τ, and the attractor is the final part of the walk, consisting of a cycle of period $\rho \geq (\mu + 1)$ in which the attractor gets trapped. The attractor is a cycle of vertices of period ρ that will always be visited by the tourist, i.e when entering an attractor the tourist cannot escape. Therefore, the transient is the route of the tourist until finding an attractor, where its size τ is the number of vertices traveled by the tourist from the initial vertex to the first vertex of the attractor. Figure 1(b) illustrates a trajectory performed by a DPSW. In some cases, depending on the topology of neighboring vertices and the size of memory μ, it can occur that the tourist does not find an attractor. In this case, the trajectory is considered only by the transient time τ.

Each vertex of the network is considered as an initial condition to perform a walk. Thus, given a network composed of N vertices, we obtain a set of N trajectories. To measure this set of trajectories performed on the network, a transient time and attractor period joint distribution $S_{\mu,r}(\tau, \rho)$ is used. This distribution combines the transient time τ and the attractor period ρ, storing in each position of the distribution the frequency of trajectories with transient τ and attractor ρ [4,7],

$$S_{\mu,r}^t(\tau, \rho) = \frac{1}{N} \sum_{i=1}^{N} \begin{cases} 1, & \text{if } \tau_i = \tau \text{ and } \rho_i = \rho \\ 0, & \text{otherwise} \end{cases} \tag{1}$$

where i is the vertex where the walk was started and t is the value of the threshold applied in the network.

In the last years, several approaches have used features obtained from the joint distribution for classification [4,7]. In this sense, the histogram $h_{\mu,r}^t(l)$ proved to achieve better results in classification tasks. This histogram computes the number of trajectories with size $l = \tau + \rho$ in a joint distribution calculated with memory size μ, rule of movement r, value of threshold t and criterion of distance c according to $h_{\mu,r}^{t,c}(l) = \sum_{b=0}^{l-1} S_{\mu,r}^k(b, l - b)$.

In order to construct a feature vector to characterize a shape, we use the n first descriptors of the histogram $h_{\mu,r}^{t,c}(l)$. In this work, we define empirically $n = 4$. The first position of the histogram is $(\mu + 1)$ since there is no attractor smaller than $(\mu + 1)$. Thus, the feature vector $\Psi(\mu, r)_t^c$ is given by $\Psi(\mu, r)_t^c = [h_{\mu,r}^t(\mu + 1), h_{\mu,r}^t(\mu + 2), ..., h_{\mu,r}^t(\mu + n)]$. Each rule of movement extracts different properties from the network [9]. Therefore, we combine the feature vector $\Psi(\mu, r)_t^c$ for the two rule of movement. To obtain a robust feature vector, we also concatenate the feature vector $\Psi(\mu, r)_t^c$ for the two criterion of distance (degree and edge weight). Thus, a combined feature vector Υ_μ^t is given by $\Upsilon_\mu^t = [\Psi(\mu, min)_t^k, \Psi(\mu, max)_t^k, \Psi(\mu, min)_t^w, \Psi(\mu, max)_t^w]$, where k is the criterion of distance based on degree and w is the criterion of distance based on edges weights.

Earlier works [2,3,19] have demonstrated that characteristics of the network dynamic evolution using different values of threshold significantly improves the network topology analysis. In this way, a combined feature vector Φ_μ that considers information of networks transformed by different values of t and uses memory size μ is given by: $\Phi_\mu = [\Upsilon_\mu^{t_0}, \Upsilon_\mu^{t_1}, ..., \Upsilon_\mu^{t_f}]$. Finally, the feature vector Ω is given by concatenating feature vectors Φ_μ for different values of memory size μ, starting from 0 to the maximum value of memory size M_μ. This final feature vector is defined as $\Omega = [\Phi_0, \Phi_1, ..., \Phi_{M_\mu}]$.

3   Results and Discussion

3.1   Experimental Setup

The proposed method and others were applied on two databases: USPLeaves and Otolith. The USPLeaves [3] database contains images of different species of plants. The classification of this database is a challenging task since that different species of plants have similar shapes and in the digitalization step of the images, overlaps can occur in the adjacency of the objects. This database is composed of 30 leaf species with 20 samples each. The Otolith database is composed of the fish natural database for fish recognition. The database was provided by AFORO [13], which is an open online catalog of otolith images. This database contains 180 different otolith images with 20 different species each.

The literature methods considered for this experiment are: CN Degree [3], Fourier descriptors [16], Curvature descriptors [22], Zernike Moments [23], Multi-Scale Fractal Dimension [20], Segment Analysis [11] and Angular Descriptors of Complex Networks (ADCN) [19]. In order to evaluate the proposed method and other methods, we perform a classification task over its feature vectors using a 10-fold cross-validation scheme and ten repetitions. We use the SVM classifier [10] with a linear kernel, a well-known supervised method.

3.2   Parameter Evaluation

The evaluated parameters of the proposed method are the set of threshold T and the values of memory size μ. The set of threshold T is defined by an initial threshold t_0, an incremental threshold t_i and a final threshold t_f. Table 1 presents the classification results for different configurations of t_0, t_i and t_f. Firstly, we consider $t_0 = 0.025$ and $t_i = 0.025$ for different values of final threshold t_f. Note that the best accuracy was obtained for $t_f = 0.95$. We also note that low values of t_i provided better accuracies. Thus, we define the values $t_0 = 0.025$, $t_i = 0.025$ and $t_f = 0.950$ as the default parameters of the proposed method, since these values obtained good results on the two databases.

The values of memory size are evaluated in function of the maximum value of memory size M_u in Table 2. Note that the accuracies tend to decrease or oscillate very little as we increase the value of M_μ. Also, as we increase the values of M_μ the number of features increases as well. In this way, the value $M_\mu = 2$ presents a good tradeoff between performance and number of features on the two databases. Therefore, the final feature vector is given by $\Omega = [\Phi_0, \Phi_1, \Phi_2]$.

Table 1. Accuracies obtained for different set of thresholds.

Thresholds			Accuracy (%)	
t_0	t_i	t_f	USPLeaves	Otolith
0.025	0.025	0.650	87.25 (0.11)	63.33 (0.78)
0.025	0.025	0.800	87.42 (0.35)	65.83 (0.39)
0.025	**0.025**	**0.950**	**88.00 (0.11)**	**68.88 (0.11)**
0.025	0.050	0.625	85.16 (0.94)	61.94 (1.17)
0.025	0.050	0.775	85.66 (0.47)	64.44 (1.57)
0.025	0.050	0.925	85.00 (0.23)	67.50 (0.39)
0.050	0.025	0.950	88.25 (0.35)	68.33 (0.33)
0.075	0.025	0.950	88.00 (0.47)	68.33 (0.78)
0.100	0.025	0.950	87.66 (0.47)	68.61 (0.39)

Table 2. Accuracies for different values of maximum memory M_μ.

M_μ	Accuracy (%)	
	USPLeaves	Otolith
2	**88.58 ($\pm$0.82)**	**70.55 ($\pm$0.39)**
3	88.66 ($\pm$0.23)	68.88 ($\pm$0.16)
4	87.92 ($\pm$0.35)	66.94 ($\pm$1.18)
5	88.25 ($\pm$0.58)	66.11 ($\pm$1.57)
6	88.50 ($\pm$0.47)	65.83 ($\pm$0.39)

3.3   Comparison with Other Methods

This section presents a comparison experiment between the proposed method and others (cited in Sect. 3.1). Table 3 shows the accuracies achieved for each shape method evaluated on the two shape databases. For the proposed method, we used the best parameter setting evaluated in Sect. 3.2. For the literature methods, we considered the default parameters defined by the authors. The results showed that the proposed method presents the highest accuracy for both USPLeaves and Otolith databases. On the USPLeaves database, the performance of the proposed method is 3.42% superior to the second best method (C.N. Degree). On the other hand, the proposed method significantly improves the accuracy on the Otolith database when compared to the second best method (Segment Analysis), e.g. from 63.47% to 70.55%. The Otolith database is a much harder classification database due to the presence of little inter-class variability.

Concerning the method based on networks, the proposed method also achieved the highest accuracy on the two databases. On the USPLeaves database, the proposed method improves the accuracy compared to the C.N. Degree and ADCN methods in 3.42% and 9.75%, respectively. On the Otolith database, the proposed method significantly improves correct classification rate compared to the network-based methods, e.g. from 48.08% to 70.55% (C.N. Degree) and from 36.32% to 70.55% (ADCN). These results indicate that the DPSW obtains more significant characteristics of the network for the classification task than other measures.

Table 3. Classification performance of various shape methods on the two databases.

Methods	Accuracy (%)	
	USPLeaves	Otolith
C.N. degree	85.16 (±3.63)	48.08 (±1.07)
Fourier	83.16 (±4.61)	50.35 (±0.72)
Curvature	81.66 (±3.33)	49.93 (±1.31)
Zernike	76.33 (±5.07)	20.04 (±1.44)
M.S. Fractal	73.66 (±5.81)	46.89 (±0.91)
Segment analysis	83.50 (±4.26)	63.47 (±0.77)
ADCN	78.83 (±3.68)	36.32 (±0.71)
Proposed method	**88.58 (±0.82)**	**70.55 (±0.39)**

4   Conclusion

In this paper, we proposed a novel method for shape classification based on DPSW on networks. After network modeling, DPSWs are performed on networks and statistical measures of the trajectories are used as a signature. These statistical measurements proved to be powerful for shapes classification. In the classification experiments on biological shapes, the proposed method provided better results when compared to other methods. Furthermore, the proposed method outperformed the other network-based methods.

Acknowledgments. Lucas Correia Ribas gratefully acknowledges the financial support grant #2016/23763-8, São Paulo Research Foundation (FAPESP). Odemir M. Bruno thanks the financial support of CNPq (Grant # 307797/2014-7) and FAPESP (Grant #s 14/08026-1 and 16/18809-9).

References

1. Ataer-Cansizoglu, E., Bas, E., Kalpathy-Cramer, J., Sharp, G.C., Erdogmus, D.: Contour-based shape representation using principal curves. Pattern Recogn. **46**(4), 1140–1150 (2013)
2. Backes, A.R., Bruno, O.M.: Shape skeleton classification using graph and multiscale fractal dimension. In: Elmoataz, A., Lezoray, O., Nouboud, F., Mammass, D., Meunier, J. (eds.) ICISP 2010. LNCS, vol. 6134, pp. 448–455. Springer, Heidelberg (2010). https://doi.org/10.1007/978-3-642-13681-8_52
3. Backes, A.R., Casanova, D., Bruno, O.M.: A complex network-based approach for boundary shape analysis. Pattern Recogn. **42**(1), 54–67 (2009)

4. Backes, A.R., Gonçalves, W.N., Martinez, A.S., Bruno, O.M.: Texture analysis and classification using deterministic tourist walk. Pattern Recogn. **43**(3), 685–694 (2010)
5. Bai, X., Latecki, L.J.: Path similarity skeleton graph matching. IEEE Trans. Pattern Anal. Mach. Intell. **30**(7), 1282–1292 (2008)
6. da Fona Costa, L., Cesar Jr, R.M.: Shape Analysis and Classification: Theory and Practice. CRC Press, Inc., Boca Raton (2000)
7. Gonçalves, W.N., Backes, A.R., Martinez, A.S., Bruno, O.M.: Texture descriptor based on partially self-avoiding deterministic walker on networks. Expert Syst. Appl. **39**(15), 11818–11829 (2012)
8. Gonçalves, W.N., Bruno, O.M.: Dynamic texture segmentation based on deterministic partially self-avoiding walks. Comput. Vis. Image Underst. **117**(9), 1163–1174 (2013)
9. Gonçalves, W.N., Martinez, A.S., Bruno, O.M.: Complex network classification using partially self-avoiding deterministic walks. Chaos Interdisc. J. Nonlinear Sci. **22**(3), 033139 (2012)
10. Hearst, M.A., Dumais, S.T., Osuna, E., Platt, J., Scholkopf, B.: Support vector machines. IEEE Intell. Syst. Appl. **13**(4), 18–28 (1998)
11. de Joaci, J., Junior, M.S., Backes, A.R.: Shape classification using line segment statistics. Inf. Sci. **305**, 349–356 (2015)
12. Liao, S.X., Pawlak, M.: On image analysis by moments. IEEE Trans. Pattern Anal. Mach. Intell. **18**(3), 254–266 (1996)
13. Lombarte, A., Chic, Ò., Parisi-Baradad, V., Olivella, R., Piera, J., García-Ladona, E.: A web-based environment for shape analysis of fish otoliths. The aforo database. Sci. Mar. **70**(1), 147–152 (2006)
14. Loncaric, S.: A survey of shape analysis techniques. Pattern Recogn. **31**(8), 983–1001 (1998)
15. Mokhtarian, F., Bober, M.: Curvature Scale Space Representation: Theory, Applications, and MPEG-7 Standardization, vol. 25. Springer Science & Business Media, Berlin (2013)
16. Osowski, S., et al.: Fourier and wavelet descriptors for shape recognition using neural networks—a comparative study. Pattern Recogn. **35**(9), 1949–1957 (2002)
17. Ribas, L.C., Junior, J.J., Scabini, L.F., Bruno, O.M.: Fusion of complex networks and randomized neural networks for texture analysis. arXiv preprint arXiv:1806.09170 (2018)
18. Ribas, L.C., Neiva, M.B., Bruno, O.M.: Distance transform network for shape analysis. Inf. Sci. **470**, 28–42 (2019)
19. Scabini, L.F., Fistarol, D.O., Cantero, S.V., Gonçalves, W.N., Machado, B.B., Rodrigues Jr., J.F.: Angular descriptors of complex networks: a novel approach for boundary shape analysis. Expert Syst. Appl. **89**, 362–373 (2017)
20. da Silva Torres, R., Falcao, A.X., da F. Costa, L.: A graph-based approach for multiscale shape analysis. Pattern Recogn. **37**(6), 1163–1174 (2004)
21. Wallace, T.P., Wintz, P.A.: An efficient three-dimensional aircraft recognition algorithm using normalized fourier descriptors. Comput. Graph. Image Process. **13**(2), 99–126 (1980)
22. Wu, W.Y., Wang, M.J.J.: Detecting the dominant points by the curvature-based polygonal approximation. CVGIP Graph. Models Image Process. **55**(2), 79–88 (1993)
23. Zhenjiang, M.: Zernike moment-based image shape analysis and its application. Pattern Recogn. Lett. **21**(2), 169–177 (2000)

Hierarchy-Based Salient Regions: A Region Detector Based on Hierarchies of Partitions

Karla Otiniano-Rodríguez[1,2(✉)], Arnaldo de A. Araújo[1,2],
Guillermo Cámara-Chávez[3], Jean Cousty[1], Silvio Jamil F. Guimarães[1,4],
and Benjamin Perret[1]

[1] University Paris-Est, LIGM, A3SI, ESIEE, Paris, France
karlaotiniano@gmail.com
[2] Federal University of Minas Gerais, Computer Science Department,
Belo Horizonte, Brazil
[3] Federal University of Ouro Preto, Computer Science Department,
Ouro Preto, Brazil
[4] Pontifical Catholic University of Minas Gerais, Computer Science Department,
Belo Horizonte, MG, Brazil

Abstract. This article introduces a novel region detector based on hierarchies of partitions, so-called Hierarchy-Based Salient Regions (HBSR). This approach enables to combine the clues given by a high quality contour detector with a custom salient region detection procedure. The evaluation of the proposed method HBSR with a standard feature detection assessment framework shows that HBSR outperforms the state-of-the-art methods, in average. These promising results may lead to improvements in many computer vision tasks.

Keywords: Region detector · Mathematical morphology ·
Hierarchy of partitions · Computer vision

1 Introduction

The extraction of local image features is a conventional approach for providing compact image descriptors that can be used to solve many computer vision tasks, like image stitching, tracking, reconstruction, image retrieval. Some examples of local features are edges, corners, ridges and blobs. The desirable qualities of image features (*e.g.*, repeatability, distinctiveness, accuracy) [13] are tightly linked to the invariance properties of the detector (*e.g.*, invariance to viewpoint, to luminosity, and to compression). Some of the best-known feature detectors are SIFT [5], SURF [1], ORB [12], MSER [6], Harris-Affine and Hessian-Affine [9]. In this article, we present a local region detector based on hierarchies of partitions.

This work received funding from FONDECYT-CONCYTEC (contract number 004-2016-FONDECYT), CAPES (PVE 125000/2014-00), FAPEMIG (PPM 00006-16), and CNPq (Universal 421521/2016-3 and PQ 307062/2016-3).

© Springer Nature Switzerland AG 2019
R. Vera-Rodriguez et al. (Eds.): CIARP 2018, LNCS 11401, pp. 444–452, 2019.
https://doi.org/10.1007/978-3-030-13469-3_52

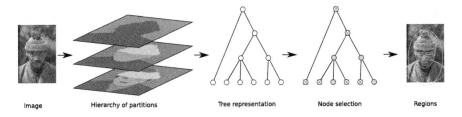

Fig. 1. Main steps of the proposed region detector HBSR.

Existing feature detection methods based on hierarchies, like MSER [6], TBMR [14], or TOS-MSER [2], rely on component trees (min-tree, max-tree, and level-line tree) and thus on the study of the lightness of the image, seen as a topographical relief. Here, we propose to replace the use of component trees by hierarchies of partitions whose construction rely on the gradient of the image. Actually, this approach allows us to take advantage of machine learning based contour detectors to obtain a high-quality multiscale representation of the image from which we select salient nodes. The evaluation of the proposed method, called *Hierarchy-based Salient Regions* (HBSR), with a standard feature detection assessment framework shows that the proposed method outperforms the current state-of-the-art on average.

This article is organized as follows. Section 2 presents the proposed method and the fundamentals of hierarchy of partitions. Section 3 describes the evaluation framework used in Sect. 4 for the comparison with the state-of-the-art methods. Finally, conclusions and future works are drawn in Sect. 5.

2   The Novel Region Detector

Ideally, in a hierarchy of partitions of an image, the scene is iteratively refined in its objects, parts of the objects, parts of the parts, and so on. Thus, each region (also called node) of the hierarchy should represent a *salient* element of the scene. However, in practice, hierarchical representations are not perfect and generally contain artifacts (regions that do not correspond to any meaningful element of the scene) and redundancy (several nodes representing the same region with slight variations). The proposed method aims at selecting nodes from a hierarchy of partitions of an image by determining the *salient nodes* of the hierarchy and then filtering redundancy among them (see Fig. 1). Finally, each selected node of the hierarchy is represented by its best fitting ellipse.

2.1   Preliminary Definitions

In the sequel of this article, the *graph* $\mathcal{G}$ is defined as a pair (V, E) where V is a finite set and E is composed of pairs of distinct elements in V, *i.e.*, E is a subset of $\{\{x, y\} \subseteq V \mid x \neq y\}$. Each element of V is called a *vertex or a pixel* (of $\mathcal{G}$), and each element of E is called an *edge* (of $\mathcal{G}$). The graph $\mathcal{G}$ provides a structure to the image spatial domain, *i.e.*, V is the regular 2D grid of pixels, and E is the 4- or 8-adjacency relation. We denote by W a function from E to $\mathbb{R}$ that weights the edges of $\mathcal{G}$. Therefore, the pair $(\mathcal{G}, W)$ is an *edge-weighted graph*, and, for any $u \in E$, the value $W(u)$ is the *weight of u*.

A *hierarchy* (or *dendrogram*) $\mathcal{H}$ of $\mathcal{G}$ is a family of subsets of V such that any two elements A and B of $\mathcal{T}$ are either nested or disjoint: *i.e.*, $A \cap B \in \{\emptyset, A, B\}$. Any element of $\mathcal{H}$ is called a *node* or *region* of $\mathcal{H}$. The minimal elements of $\mathcal{H}$ are called the *leaves*. The parent of a node $N \neq V$ of $\mathcal{H}$, denoted by $Parent(N)$, is the smallest node N' of $\mathcal{H}$ that is strictly larger than N. Conversely, we say that a node N is a child of its parent $Parent(N)$. When the leaves, *i.e.*, the nodes without any child, of the hierarchy $\mathcal{H}$ forms a partition of V, then the hierarchy can be represented as a sequence of nested partitions (see Fig. 1).

2.2 Selection of Salient Regions

We aim at selecting the salient regions from a hierarchy $\mathcal{H}$ obtained from the weighted graph $(\mathcal{G}, W)$. The result of this selection process is a new hierarchy $\mathcal{H}'$ whose nodes are the selected regions of $\mathcal{H}$. Salient regions are identified based on three local features: size, contrast, and geometrical complexity. In the following of this section, R denotes a region of the hierarchy $\mathcal{H}$.

Size Criterion. The *area* of the region R, denoted by $A(R)$, is defined as the number of vertices in R (*i.e.*, $A(R) = |R|$). We assume that a salient region is neither too small nor too large, leading to the following selection criterion: $A_{min} \leq A(R) \leq A_{max}$, with A_{min} and A_{max} two real parameters representing respectively the minimum and maximum area of a salient region.

Contrast Criterion. We consider that the edge-weights of the graph represent gradient values between pixels. The contrast being a relative measure of difference between the region and its surroundings, we use the gradient inside the parent of the given region to estimate it. We define the *depth* of the region R, denoted by $D(R)$, as the maximal weight of the edges linking two vertices of the parent region of R (*i.e.*, $D(R) = \max\{W(e), e \in E \mid e \subseteq Parent(R)\}$). We assume that a salient region should have a significant contrast leading to the following criterion: $D_{min} \leq D(R)$, with D_{min} a real parameter representing the minimum depth of a salient region.

Shape Complexity Criterion. The ellipse is a common shape used to represent a region in an image [15], and a way to measure the geometric complexity of a region is to quantify the difference between the real shape and its best fitting ellipse. We define the *shape complexity* of R, denoted $C(R)$, as the ratio of the area of the best fitting ellipse of R (estimated with second ordered moments), denoted by $A(E_R)$, with the area of R (*i.e.*, $C(R) = A(E_R)/A(R)$). We assume that a salient region should have a low shape complexity leading to the following criterion: $C(R) \leq C_{max}$, with C_{max} a real parameter representing the maximum shape complexity of a salient region.

Thus, we use these criteria for identifying candidate regions on a given hierarchy of partitions $\mathcal{H}$. The result is a new hierarchy $\mathcal{H}_1$ composed of the regions of $\mathcal{H}$ identified as salient:

$$\mathcal{H}_1 = \{R \in \mathcal{H} \mid A_{min} \leq A(R) \leq A_{max}, D_{min} \leq D(R), \text{ and } C(R) \leq C_{max}\}.$$

2.3   Filtering of Redundant Regions

The new hierarchy $\mathcal{H}_1$ composed by the salient regions of $\mathcal{H}$ may still contain redundant regions, *i.e.*, very similar nodes. The aim of the filtering procedure presented in this section is to select a representative node from similar ones. Thus, we propose a two-step procedure to perform this selection:

- Similarly to [14], we identify topological changes in the hierarchy as regions having at least two children. Indeed, when a region of the hierarchy has a single child, it cannot be viewed as the decomposition of an object into its parts. Therefore, the single child of this region is discarded. Formally, this process leads to a new hierarchy $\mathcal{H}_2$ defined by:

$$\mathcal{H}_2 = \{R \in \mathcal{H}_1 \mid Ch(Parent(R)) \geq 2\},$$

  where $Ch(Parent(R))$ is the number of children of the parent region of R.
- Then, we discard a node when its shape is similar to the one of its parent. The dissimilarity between the shapes of two regions is evaluated by computing the relative difference of the area of their best fitting ellipses. This leads to a final hierarchy $\mathcal{H}_3$:

$$\mathcal{H}_3 = \left\{R \in \mathcal{H}_2 \mid \frac{|A(E_R) - A(E_{Parent(R)})|}{A(E_{Parent(R)})} \geq DS_{min}\right\},$$

  where DS_{min} is a real parameter representing the minimum dissimilarity between a region and its parent.

The final set of detected regions is composed of the best fitting ellipses of the regions of $\mathcal{H}_3$. Regarding the computational cost, the detection of salient regions and the filtering of the redundant regions can be computed in linear time with respect to the number of vertices in the graph $\mathcal{G}$.

3   Evaluation Framework

We rely on the framework of Mikolajczyk et al. [8] to provide an objective assessment of the proposed method. The framework is associated with a dataset of eight image sequences, with six images each. The dataset includes five types of transformations: viewpoint changes (a) & (b); scale changes (c) & (d); image blur (e) & (f); JPEG compression (g); and illumination (h) (see Fig. 2).

Fig. 2. Some examples for each sequence of the dataset. (a) Graffiti, (b) Wall, (c) Boat, (d) Bark, (e) Bikes, (f) Trees, (g) UBC and (h) Leuven.

For each image sequence of the dataset, the framework compares the regions provided by the detectors on the first image of the sequence with the ones obtained on the other images of the sequence. Two measures are used as follows:

1. the *repeatability score* which evaluates the theoretical performance of the detector by calculating the ratio of the number of correspondences between regions of the two images and the number of proposed regions. Given two regions, we say that there is a correspondence if the overlap error between their best fitting ellipses is small; and
2. the *matching score* which evaluates the practical performance of the detector by calculating the ratio of the number of correct matches in the feature space and the number of proposed regions. A match between two regions is considered correct if they are nearest neighbours in the feature space, and if they have the smallest overlap error.

4   Experimental Analysis

In this section, we discuss the experimental results showing some illustrations of our region detector and the quantitative comparison between the proposed method HBSR and the state-of-the-art methods.

4.1   Experimental Setup

In the following experiments, an image is represented as a 4-adjacency graph from which a *Quasi-Flat Zones (QFZ) hierarchy* [7] is computed. QFZ hierarchies are naturally invariant to photometric changes and geometric changes (up to quantization effects). A quasi-flat zone of the weighted graph $(\mathcal{G}, W)$ at level $\lambda \in \mathbb{R}$ is a maximal set of vertices such that, between any two of its vertices, there exists a path along which the maximal weight is λ. The set of quasi-flat zones of the weighted graph at all levels λ forms the *quasi-flat zones hierarchy* of the weighted graph. According to [11], we chose to use the Structured Edge Detector (SED) [4] in order to weight the edges of the graph: indeed this detector offers good performances in combination with quasi-flat zones hierarchies on natural images while being fast to compute. To further improve the invariance of the salient region detection process (in particular, the definition of the depth of a region), we propose to perform a histogram normalization of the gradient produced by SED. Note that, the QFZ hierarchy can be efficiently computed in (quasi) linear time from the graph weighted by SED [3,10].

The proposed region detector has five parameters, which were optimized to maximize the average of the repeatability and matching scores on the evaluation dataset: the minimum area ($A_{min} = 0.08$), the maximum area ($A_{max} = 0.25$), the minimal depth ($D_{min} = 22$), the maximal shape complexity ($C_{max} = 1.1$), and the minimum dissimilarity ($DS_{min} = 20\%$). Note that the area parameter are expressed as a percentage of the total image size.

4.2   Quantitative Assessment

In this section, we assess the proposed method HBSR within Mikolajczyk et al. framework [8]. We provide quantitative results and a discussion about the invariance of our method, against geometric and photometric changes, by analyzing the results of each sequence of the dataset separately. The proposed method is compared to four state-of-the-art region detectors: Harris-Affine [9], Hessian-Affine [9], Maximally Stable Extremal Region (MSER) [6], and Tree-Based Morse Regions (TBMR) [14]. The Harris-Affine and the Hessian-Affine are two related methods which detect interest points in scale-space based on the Laplacian operator. The MSER and TBMR detectors both operate on hierarchical representations of the images called min- and max-trees that represent the minima (respectively maxima) of the image and their merging order as the brightness increases (respectively decreases). While MSER looks for long branches of the hierarchy with small area variations, TBMR searches for topological changes (critical points of the lightness function) in the hierarchy. Figure 3 shows the regions provided by our detector on some images of the evaluation dataset. We can see that the proposed detector produces a reasonable number of regions corresponding to well identified shapes of the scene.

Table 1 shows the results of repeatability and matching scores. The results obtained on each sequence are presented separately in order to analyze the results of each geometrical or photometrical change. We can observe that HBSR is

Fig. 3. Detected regions (yellow ellipses) by HBSR, the proposed region detector, on images from the *Boat* and the *Wall* sequences. (Color figure online)

Table 1. Repeatability and matching scores. Each value represents the average repeatability of the five results of each detector for each sequence.

	Sequence	Harris	Hessian	MSER	TBMR	HBSR
Repeatability	Graffiti	39.69	47.10	**64.48**	52.07	41.13
	Wall	44.63	49.17	55.13	53.63	**64.42**
	Boat	49.28	**59.21**	50.69	42.04	49.73
	Bark	60.94	**75.98**	48.73	63.03	30.00
	Bikes	56.52	73.25	57.12	50.46	**87.35**
	Trees	50.25	55.39	39.61	40.24	**70.00**
	UBC	80.37	**86.12**	50.01	45.69	71.11
	Leuven	56.27	67.50	**77.85**	68.50	76.78
	Average	54.74	**64.22**	55.46	51.96	61.32
Matching	Graffiti	16.26	20.45	**48.31**	36.96	28.50
	Wall	19.33	26.63	37.90	34.35	**42.08**
	Boat	24.68	31.04	35.49	27.83	**41.89**
	Bark	33.38	**45.67**	26.16	38.43	30.00
	Bikes	30.62	38.29	42.27	28.09	**82.46**
	Trees	9.02	12.78	17.11	11.55	**70.00**
	UBC	64.10	**70.44**	41.28	27.91	66.67
	Leuven	30.55	34.93	**65.59**	52.83	64.50
	Average	28.49	35.03	39.27	32.24	**53.26**
Average score		41.62	49.63	47.37	42.10	**57.29**

particularly robust to blurring (*Bikes* and *Trees* sequences) where it obtains best repeatability and matching scores. Luminosity changes (*Leuven* sequence) and JPEG compression artifacts (*UBC* sequence) are also very well handled with repeatability and matching scores very close to the ones. The proposed method also manages to deal with moderate viewpoint change on highly textured images (*Wall* sequence) very well (first on both scores). Significant viewpoint changes (*Graffiti* and *Boat* sequences) are however moderately well handled with average scores. Finally, the main weakness of the proposed method appears with large viewpoint changes combined with smooth surfaces (*Bark* sequence) where the SED contour detector fails to detect any meaningful contour, hence leading to the absence of meaningful regions. Furthermore, Table 1 also shows aggregated repeatability and matching scores in terms of average on the eight sequences. We can see that our method obtains the best average score, with an average repeatability very close to the best method and with an average matching score significantly higher than all other methods.

5   Conclusion

We presented HBSR, a local region detector based on hierarchies of partitions, that allows us to take advantage of high-quality contour detectors. We proposed several heuristics to select and filter redundant regions from a hierarchy of partitions to obtain robust, relevant and multi-scale regions of an image. Our experiments show promising results, with better average results than state-of-the-art methods. In future works, we plan to improve the node selection method further, to experiment with other hierarchies of partitions, and to apply the proposed method to various computer vision tasks.

References

1. Bay, H., Ess, A., Tuytelaars, T., Gool, L.V.: Speeded-up robust features (SURF). CVIU **110**(3), 346–359 (2008)
2. Bosilj, P., Kijak, E., Lefèvre, S.: Beyond MSER: Maximally Stable Regions using Tree of Shapes. In: BMVC. Swansea, United Kingdom (2015)
3. Cousty, J., Najman, L., Perret, B.: Constructive Links between some morphological hierarchies on edge-weighted graphs. In: Hendriks, C.L.L., Borgefors, G., Strand, R. (eds.) ISMM 2013. LNCS, vol. 7883, pp. 86–97. Springer, Heidelberg (2013). https://doi.org/10.1007/978-3-642-38294-9_8
4. Dollár, P., Zitnick, C.L.: Fast edge detection using structured forests. IEEE TPAMI **37**(8), 1558–1570 (2015)
5. Lowe, D.G.: Object recognition from local scale-invariant features. In: ICCV, pp. 1150–1157 (1999)
6. Matas, J., Chum, O., Urban, M., Pajdla, T.: Robust wide-baseline stereo from maximally stable extremal regions. IVC **22**(10), 761–767 (2004)
7. Meyer, F., Maragos, P.: Morphological scale-space representation with levelings. In: Nielsen, M., Johansen, P., Olsen, O.F., Weickert, J. (eds.) Scale-Space 1999. LNCS, vol. 1682, pp. 187–198. Springer, Heidelberg (1999). https://doi.org/10.1007/3-540-48236-9_17

8. Mikolajczyk, K., et al.: A comparison of affine region detectors. IJCV **65**(1), 43–72 (2005)
9. Mikolajczyk, K., Schmid, C.: Scale & affine invariant interest point detectors. IJCV **60**(1), 63–86 (2004)
10. Najman, L., Cousty, J., Perret, B.: Playing with Kruskal: algorithms for morphological trees in edge-weighted graphs. In: Hendriks, C.L.L., Borgefors, G., Strand, R. (eds.) ISMM 2013. LNCS, vol. 7883, pp. 135–146. Springer, Heidelberg (2013). https://doi.org/10.1007/978-3-642-38294-9_12
11. Perret, B., Cousty, J., Guimarães, S.J., Maia, D.S.: Evaluation of hierarchical watersheds. IEEE TIP **27**(4), 1676–1688 (2018)
12. Rublee, E., Rabaud, V., Konolige, K., Bradski, G.R.: ORB: an efficient alternative to SIFT or SURF. In: ICCV, pp. 2564–2571. IEEE Computer Society (2011)
13. Tuytelaars, T., Mikolajczyk, K.: Local invariant feature detectors: a survey. Found. Trends Comput. Graph. Vis. **3**(3), 177–280 (2008)
14. Xu, Y., Monasse, P., Géraud, T., Najman, L.: Tree-based morse regions: a topological approach to local feature detection. IEEE TIP **23**(12), 5612–5625 (2014)
15. Zhang, D., Lu, G.: Review of shape representation and description techniques. PR **37**(1), 1–19 (2004)

Logarithmic Mathematical Morphology: A New Framework Adaptive to Illumination Changes

Guillaume Noyel[1,2]([envelope]) [iD]

[1] University of Strathclyde Institute of Global Public Health, Ecully, France
guillaume.noyel@i-pri.org
[2] International Prevention Research Institute, iPRI, Lyon, France

Abstract. A new set of mathematical morphology (MM) operators adaptive to illumination changes caused by variation of exposure time or light intensity is defined thanks to the Logarithmic Image Processing (LIP) model. This model based on the physics of acquisition is consistent with human vision. The fundamental operators, the logarithmic-dilation and the logarithmic-erosion, are defined with the LIP-addition of a structuring function. The combination of these two adjunct operators gives morphological filters, namely the logarithmic-opening and closing, useful for pattern recognition. The mathematical relation existing between "classical" dilation and erosion and their logarithmic-versions is established facilitating their implementation. Results on simulated and real images show that logarithmic-MM is more efficient on low-contrasted information than "classical" MM.

Keywords: Mathematical morphology · Contrast variations ·
Illumination changes · Logarithmic Image Processing ·
Pattern recognition

1 Introduction

Images are functions whose values are bounded between 0 and M (e.g. 256 for 8 bits images) and depend of the illumination conditions. During the acquisition, some parts of the image may be underexposed to light with dark values close to 0, whereas other parts may be overexposed to light with bright values close to M. Therefore, the processing should not be the same in the bright and in the dark parts. When processing grey-level images by Mathematical Morphology (MM) [3,8,17], dark parts and bright parts are processed in the same way and in some cases the transformed image may have values that exceed the upper limit M.

The aim of this paper is to overcome this issue by defining morphological operators adaptive to lighting variations thanks to an appropriate model, the Logarithmic Image Processing (LIP) one [4,5] which allows to brighten or darken images in a way compatible with the physics of acquisition and with the human

© Springer Nature Switzerland AG 2019
R. Vera-Rodriguez et al. (Eds.): CIARP 2018, LNCS 11401, pp. 453–461, 2019.
https://doi.org/10.1007/978-3-030-13469-3_53

visual system [2]. Previously, a morphological transform, the LIP-top-hat, was defined with the LIP model in [4]. A model, the Symmetric Logarithmic Image Processing (SLIP) one [12] was combined with wavelets in [11]. Homomorphic models [12,14] and retinex algorithms [9] were also used with convolution. However, these models, interesting from a mathematical point of view, are not related to the physics of acquisition.

This paper constitutes the first attempt to define morphological operators adaptive to lighting variations - without any pre-processing. Such a property makes the definition of Logarithmic-Mathematical Morphology of the utmost importance for many applications where the acquisition depends on the illumination (e.g. industry, outdoor scenes, forensics, medical images etc.) [7,13,15,18]. The paper is organised as follows: (i) after a reminder about MM and the LIP model, (ii) MM will be defined in the logarithmic-additive framework. The morphological properties of the operators will be verified and (iii) the Logarithmic-MM will be illustrated and compared to the classical MM.

2 Prerequisites

2.1 Mathematical Morphology

Definition 1. Complete lattice. *Given a set $\mathscr{L}$ and a partial order $\leq$ on $\mathscr{L}$, $\mathscr{L}$ is a complete lattice if every subset $\mathscr{X}$ of $\mathscr{L}$ has an infimum (a greatest lower bound), $\wedge\mathscr{X}$, and a supremum (a least upper bound), $\vee\mathscr{X}$.*

MM [8,10,17] is defined on complete lattices [1,3]. The least element O and the greatest element I are two important elements of the lattice $\mathscr{L}$. A grey-level image is a function $f: D \subset \mathbb{R}^n \to [O, M[$, with $M \in \mathbb{R}$. The space of images is denoted $\mathcal{I} = [O, M[^D$. The (bounded) set of images $\overline{\mathcal{I}} = [0, M]^D$ and the set of functions $\overline{\mathbb{R}}^D$, $\overline{\mathbb{R}} = \mathbb{R} \cup \{-\infty, +\infty\}$ are complete lattices with the order $\leq$. For $\overline{\mathcal{I}}$, the least and greatest elements are the constant functions equal to zero, f_0, and M, f_M. The supremum and infimum are respectively, for any $\mathscr{X} \subset \overline{\mathcal{I}}$: $(\wedge_{\overline{\mathcal{I}}}\mathscr{X})(x) = \wedge_{[0,M]}\{f(x) : f \in \mathscr{X}, x \in D\}$ and $(\vee_{\overline{\mathcal{I}}}\mathscr{X})(x) = \vee_{[0,M]}\{f(x) : f \in \mathscr{X}, x \in D\}$.

Definition 2. Erosion, dilation [1,16]. *Given $\mathscr{L}_1$ and $\mathscr{L}_2$ two complete lattices, a mapping $\psi \in \mathscr{L}_2^{\mathscr{L}_1}$ is: (i) an erosion ε: iff $\forall \mathscr{X} \subset \mathscr{L}_1$, $\psi(\wedge\mathscr{X}) = \wedge\psi(\mathscr{X})$ or (ii) a dilation δ: iff $\forall \mathscr{X} \subset \mathscr{L}_1$, $\psi(\vee\mathscr{X}) = \vee\psi(\mathscr{X})$.*

As the definitions of these mappings apply even to the empty subset of $\mathscr{L}_1$, we have: $\varepsilon(I) = I$ and $\delta(O) = O$.

Definition 3. Adjunction [3]. *Let $\varepsilon \in \mathscr{L}_2^{\mathscr{L}_1}$ and $\delta \in \mathscr{L}_1^{\mathscr{L}_2}$ be operators between complete lattices $\mathscr{L}_1$ and $\mathscr{L}_2$; the pair (ε, δ) is called an adjunction between $\mathscr{L}_1$ and $\mathscr{L}_2$ if for all $X \in \mathscr{L}_1$, $Y \in \mathscr{L}_2$ there is $\delta(Y) \leq X \Leftrightarrow Y \leq \varepsilon(X)$.*

Proposition 1. *In an adjunction (ε, δ), ε is an erosion and δ a dilation [3].*

When using an additive structuring function $b \in [O, M]^{D_b}$, $D_b \subset D$, invariant under translation (in D), the previously defined dilation δ and erosion ε in the lattice $(\overline{\mathbb{R}}^D, \leq)$, can be expressed as [3, 16]:

$$\delta_b(f)(x) = \vee \{f(x - h) + b(h), h \in D_b\} = (f \oplus b)(x) \tag{1}$$

$$\varepsilon_b(f)(x) = \wedge \{f(x + h) - b(h), h \in D_b\} = (f \ominus b)(x). \tag{2}$$

$\oplus$ and $\ominus$ are the extension to functions of Minkowski operations on sets [17].

Definition 4. Opening, closing [3, 17]. An operator $\psi \in \mathscr{L}^{\mathscr{L}}$ on the complete lattice $\mathscr{L}$ is called:

– an opening if ψ is increasing ($\forall X, Y \in \mathscr{L}$, if $X \leq Y$ then $\psi(X) \leq \psi(Y)$), anti-extensive ($\forall X \in \mathscr{L}$, $\psi(X) \leq X$) and idempotent ($\psi \circ \psi = \psi$),
– a closing if ψ is increasing, extensive ($\forall X \in \mathscr{L}$, $X \leq \psi(X)$) and idempotent.

Proposition 2. Let $(\varepsilon, \delta) \in \mathscr{L}_2^{\mathscr{L}_1} \times \mathscr{L}_1^{\mathscr{L}_2}$ be an adjunction between $\mathscr{L}_1$ and $\mathscr{L}_2$, then $\delta\varepsilon$ is an opening on $\mathscr{L}_1$ and $\varepsilon\delta$ is a closing on $\mathscr{L}_2$ [3].

2.2 Logarithmic Image Processing

The LIP model, introduced by Jourlin et al. [4,5], is a mathematical framework for image processing based on the physical law of transmittances. Its consistency with the human visual model [2] makes it suitable not only for images acquired with transmitted light but also for images acquired with reflected light. Due to the relation, $T_f = 1 - f/M$, between the transmittance $T_f(x)$ at point x and the grey level $f(x)$, the grey scale is inverted in the LIP-model: 0 corresponds to the white extremity, when no obstacle is placed between the light source and the sensor, whereas M corresponds to the black value, when the source cannot be transmitted through the obstacle. The addition of two images corresponds to the superposition of two obstacles generating the images f and g:

$$f \mathbin{\triangle} g = f + g - fg/M. \tag{3}$$

The multiplication of an image f by a real number λ is deduced from the Eq. 3, $\lambda \mathbin{\triangle} f = M - M(1 - f/M)^\lambda$, and corresponds to a variation of thickness (or opacity) of the object. The opposite function $\mathbin{\triangle} f$ of f and the difference between two grey level functions f and g are expressed by:

$$\mathbin{\triangle} f = (-f)/(1 - f/M) \qquad \text{and} \qquad f \mathbin{\triangle} g = (f - g)(1 - g/M). \tag{4}$$

Let us note that $\mathbin{\triangle} f$ is not an image (as it takes negative values) and $f \mathbin{\triangle} g$ is an image if and only if $f \geq g$.

Property 1 (A strong physical property). The negative values $\mathbin{\triangle} f$, with $f \geq 0$, are light intensifiers that can be used to compensate the light attenuation due a variation of exposure-time (or light intensity) [5].

Property 2 (Mathematical properties). Let $\mathcal{F} =]-\infty, M[^D$ be the space of functions with values in $]-\infty, M[$. The space $(\mathcal{F}, \mathbin{\triangle}, \mathbin{\triangle})$ is a real *vector space* and $(\mathcal{I}, \mathbin{\triangle}, \mathbin{\triangle})$ represents the positive cone of this vector space [4,5]. $\mathcal{F}$ and $\mathcal{I}$ are both ordered by the usual order $\leq$ [4].

3   Logarithmic-Mathematical Morphology

MM is defined on the lattice of functions with real values $\overline{\mathbb{R}}^D$. When performing a dilation by a (non-flat) structuring function, the dilated function may have values which exceed the range $[0, M[$. In order to solve this issue and to perform operations adaptive to light variations, let us extend MM with Logarithmic-MM, on the lattice of functions $\overline{\mathcal{F}} = [-\infty, M]^D$ with values in $[-\infty, M]$. First of all, the fundamental operators of erosion and dilation are needed:

Proposition 3. *Let $f \in \overline{\mathcal{F}}$ be a function and $b \in]-\infty, M[^{D_b}$ a structuring function, the mappings in $\overline{\mathcal{F}}$ defined by*

$$\delta_b^{\triangle}(f)(x) = \vee \{f(x - h) \,\triangle\, b(h), h \in D_b\} \tag{5}$$

$$\varepsilon_b^{\triangle}(f)(x) = \wedge \{f(x + h) \,\triangle\, b(h), h \in D_b\} \tag{6}$$

form an adjunction $(\varepsilon_b^{\triangle}, \delta_b^{\triangle})$, with $\varepsilon_b^{\triangle}$ an erosion and $\delta_b^{\triangle}$ a dilation. $\varepsilon_b^{\triangle}$ is called a logarithmic-erosion and $\delta_b^{\triangle}$ a logarithmic-dilation.

Proof. of Proposition 3.

- $\delta_b^{\triangle}$ is a dilation (Definition 2). As the operation $\triangle$ preserves the order $\leq$ [4], we have $\forall f, g \in \overline{\mathcal{F}}, \forall x \in D, \delta_b^{\triangle}(f \vee g)(x) = \vee_{h \in D_b} \{((f \vee g)(x - h)) \,\triangle\, b(h)\}$
  $= \vee_{h \in D_b} \{(f(x - h) \,\triangle\, b(h)) \vee (g(x - h) \,\triangle\, b(h))\} = [\vee_{h \in D_b} \{f(x - h) \,\triangle\, b(h)\}] \vee [\vee_{h \in D_b} \{g(x - h) \,\triangle\, b(h)\}] = \delta_b^{\triangle}(f)(x) \vee \delta_b^{\triangle}(g)(x)$.
  In addition, with $b(h) \in]-\infty, M[$, we have: $\delta_b^{\triangle}(O)(x) = \delta_b^{\triangle}(f_{-\infty})(x) = \vee_{h \in D_b} \{(-\infty(x - h) \triangle b(h))\} = \vee_{h \in D_b} \{-\infty(1 - b(h)/M) + b(h)\} = -\infty = O(x)$.
- Similarly, $\forall f, g \in \overline{\mathcal{F}}, \varepsilon_b^{\triangle}(f \wedge g) = \varepsilon_b^{\triangle}(f) \wedge \varepsilon_b^{\triangle}(g)$ and $\varepsilon_b^{\triangle}(I) = \varepsilon_b^{\triangle}(f_M) = M = I$. Therefore, $\varepsilon_b^{\triangle}$ is an erosion.
- $(\varepsilon_b^{\triangle}, \delta_b^{\triangle})$ is an adjunction because: $\delta_b^{\triangle}(f) \leq g \Leftrightarrow \forall x \in D, \vee_{h \in D_b} \{f(x - h) \,\triangle\, b(h)\} \leq g(x) \Leftrightarrow \forall x \in D, \forall h, f(x - h) \,\triangle\, b(h) \leq g(x) \Leftrightarrow \forall y \in D, \forall h, f(y) \leq g(y + h) \,\triangle\, b(h) \Leftrightarrow \forall y \in D, f(y) \leq \wedge_{h \in D_b} \{g(y + h) \,\triangle\, b(h)\} \Leftrightarrow f \leq \varepsilon_b^{\triangle}(g)$.

Let us verify that the new operations are dual by their *negative function*.

Proposition 4. *The negative function [3] is $f^*(x) = \triangle f(x)$.*

Proposition 5. *Let $\bar{b}(x) = b(-x)$ be the reflection of the structuring function b, the logarithmic-erosion $\varepsilon_b^{\triangle}$ and dilation $\delta_b^{\triangle}$ are dual by their negative function:*

$$(\delta_b^{\triangle}(f^*))^* = \varepsilon_{\bar{b}}^{\triangle}(f) \quad and \quad (\varepsilon_b^{\triangle}(f^*))^* = \delta_{\bar{b}}^{\triangle}(f). \tag{7}$$

Proof. $(\delta_b^{\triangle}(f^*))^*(x) = \triangle(\vee_{h \in D_b} \{\triangle f(x - h) \triangle b(h)\}) = \wedge_{h \in D_b} \{f(x - h) \triangle b(h)\} = \wedge_{h \in D_{\bar{b}}} \{f(x + h) \,\triangle\, \bar{b}(h)\} = \varepsilon_{\bar{b}}^{\triangle}(f)(x)$. Similarly, we have $(\varepsilon_b^{\triangle}(f^*))^* = \delta_{\bar{b}}^{\triangle}(f)$.

As $(\varepsilon_b^{\triangle}, \delta_b^{\triangle})$ is an adjunction, an opening and a closing can be defined [3].

Proposition 6. *Given an adjunction* $(\varepsilon_b^{\triangle}, \delta_b^{\triangle})$, *the operator* $\gamma_b^{\triangle} = \delta_b^{\triangle} \varepsilon_b^{\triangle}$ *is an opening and* $\varphi_b^{\triangle} = \varepsilon_b^{\triangle} \delta_b^{\triangle}$ *is a closing (by adjunction).* $\gamma_b^{\triangle}$ *is called a logarithmic-opening and* $\varphi_b^{\triangle}$ *a logarithmic-closing.*

A relation between the logarithmic operations and the "classical" ones exists. This facilitates the implementation of the logarithmic operations, as the "classical" ones are available in many image analysis toolboxes.

Proposition 7. *Let* $f \in \overline{\mathcal{F}}$ *be a function and* $b \in]-\infty, M[^{D_b}$ *a structuring function, the logarithmic-dilation* $\delta_b^{\triangle}$ *and the logarithmic-erosion* $\varepsilon_b^{\triangle}$ *are related to the dilation* δ_b *and erosion* ε_b *by:*

$$\delta_b^{\triangle} f = M(1 - \exp\left(-\delta_b(\acute{f})\right)) \quad and \quad \varepsilon_b^{\triangle} f = M(1 - \exp\left(-\varepsilon_b(\acute{f})\right)) \quad (8)$$

with $\acute{f} = -\ln\left(1 - f/M\right), \acute{f} \in \mathbb{R}.$

Proof. The dilation δ_b and the erosion ε_b are mappings of the lattice $\overline{\mathbb{R}}^D$, whereas the logarithmic-dilation $\delta_b^{\triangle}$ and erosion $\varepsilon_b^{\triangle}$ are mappings of the lattice $[-\infty, M]^D$. In order to link these operations, a bijective mapping (i.e. an isomorphism) is needed between these two lattices. Such an isomorphism $\xi : \overline{\mathbb{R}}^D \to [-\infty, M]^D$ and its inverse ξ^{-1} are both defined in [6] by $[\xi(f)](x) = M(1 - \exp\left(-f/M\right))$ and $\left[\xi^{-1}(f)\right](x) = -M\ln\left(1 - f/M\right)$. As increasing bijections, ξ ans ξ^{-1} distribute over infima and suprema. Therefore, the dilation $\delta_b^{\triangle}$ can be expressed by: $\delta_b^{\triangle} f(x) = \xi \circ \xi^{-1}(\vee_{h \in D_b} \{f(x - h) \triangle b(h)\}) = \vee_{h \in D_b} \{M(1 - e^{\ln\left(1 - \frac{f(x-h)\triangle b(h)}{M}\right)})\} = M(1 - e^{\wedge_{h \in D_b} \ln\left((1 - \frac{f(x-h)}{M})(1 - \frac{b(h)}{M})\right)}) = M(1 - e^{-\vee_{h \in D_b} \{-\ln\left(1 - \frac{f(x-h)}{M}\right) - \ln\left(1 - \frac{b(h)}{M}\right)\}}) = M(1 - e^{-\delta_b(\acute{f})})$. Similarly, we have $\varepsilon_b^{\triangle} = M(1 - e^{-\varepsilon_b(\acute{f})})$.

4   Results

In the Fig. 1, the "classical" operations of MM and those of Logarithmic-MM are compared on a simulated signal. For each operation of Logarithmic-MM, the amplitude of the structuring function (sf) changes according to the values of the image because of the LIP-laws, $\triangle$ or $\underline{\triangle}$, used in their definition (Eqs. 5 and 6), whereas for the operations of "classical" MM the amplitude of the sf remains the same. In the Fig. 1b, the values of the logarithmic-dilation $\delta_b^{\triangle}(f)$ always remain below the upper limit $M = 256$, whereas for the "classical" dilation $\delta_b(f)$, some grey-levels may exceed the limit M. Such a property is due to the LIP addition law $\triangle$. In the Fig. 1a, the lowest values of both erosions $\varepsilon_b^{\triangle}(f)$ and $\varepsilon_b(f)$ are negative because of the laws $\underline{\triangle}$ and $-$ used in Eqs. 6 and 2. For real value functions $\overline{\mathbb{R}}^D$, the negative values have no physical justification, whereas in the LIP model they correspond to light intensifiers [5]. In the Fig. 1c (resp. Fig. 1d), the disparity between the openings $\gamma_b(f)$ and $\gamma_b^{\triangle}(f)$ (resp. closings $\varphi_b(f)$ and $\varphi_b^{\triangle}(f)$) is greater for the grey-levels close to M than for those close to zero. Indeed, the LIP difference $\underline{\triangle}$ is non linear along the grey-level axis.

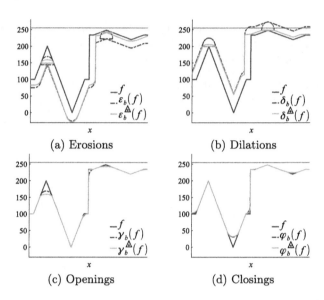

Fig. 1. Comparison between the operations of "classical" MM and Logarithmic-MM: (a) erosions $\varepsilon_b(f)$, $\varepsilon_b^{\triangle}(f)$, (b) dilations $\delta_b(f)$, $\delta_b^{\triangle}(f)$, (c) openings $\gamma_b(f)$, $\gamma_b^{\triangle}(f)$ and (d) closings $\varphi_b(f)$, $\varphi_b^{\triangle}(f)$. (a), (b) The structuring function is represented for both peaks and for all the operations $\varepsilon_b(f)$, $\varepsilon_b^{\triangle}(f)$, $\delta_b(f)$ and $\delta_b^{\triangle}(f)$.

In the Fig. 2, two images of the same scene are acquired at two different exposure time (i.e. shutter speed): a bright image f (Fig. 2a) and a dark image f^d (Fig. 2d). Both images f and f^d are complemented ($f^c = M - 1 - f$) before computing a morphological gradient $\varrho_b(f^c) = \delta_b(f^c) - \varepsilon_b(f^c)$ [16] (Fig. 2b, e) and its logarithmic version $\varrho_b^{\triangle}(f^c) = \delta_b^{\triangle}(f^c) \triangle \varepsilon_b^{\triangle}(f^c)$ (Fig. 2c, f). For comparison purpose, the amplitudes of each gradient are scaled between 0 and 255. The logarithmic-gradient of the dark image $\varrho_b^{\triangle}((f^d)^c)$ (Fig. 2f) finds much more contours than the "classical" one $\varrho_b((f^d)^c)$ (Fig. 2e). Even on the bright image f, the logarithmic-gradient $\varrho_b^{\triangle}(f^c)$ (Fig. 2c) finds more contours than the "classical" one $\varrho_b^{\triangle}(f)$, especially on the darkest parts (Fig. 2b). The logarithmic-gradient is also few sensitive to lighting variations (Fig. 2c and f).

In the Fig. 3, an opening $(\gamma_b((f^d)^c))^c$, a closing $(\varphi_b((f^d)^c))^c$, a logarithmic-opening $(\gamma_b^{\triangle}((f^d)^c))^c$ and a logarithmic-closing $(\varphi_b^{\triangle}((f^d)^c))^c$ are compared on the complement of the dark image f^d (Fig. 2b), using an hemisphere of radius 15 pixels as structuring function. For comparison purpose, the amplitudes of each filtered image are scaled between 0 and 255. The "classical" opening and closing (Fig. 3a, c) have a limited effect in terms of transformation whereas the logarithmic-opening and closing have a more important effect (Fig. 3b, d). E.g. on the body of the soft toy monster, the words are removed with the logarithmic-opening and closing and not with the "classical" opening and closing.

Those examples illustrate the property of the logarithmic-MM to adapt to important contrast variations caused by varying illumination conditions.

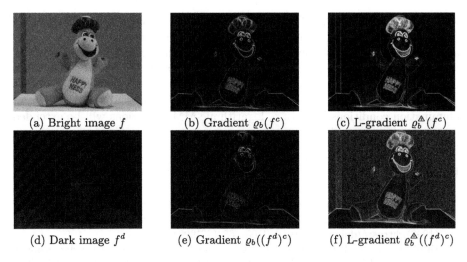

(a) Bright image f (b) Gradient $\varrho_b(f^c)$ (c) L-gradient $\varrho_b^{\triangle}(f^c)$

(d) Dark image f^d (e) Gradient $\varrho_b((f^d)^c)$ (f) L-gradient $\varrho_b^{\triangle}((f^d)^c)$

Fig. 2. Comparison between the gradient ϱ_b (b, e) and the Logarithmic-gradient $\varrho_b^{\triangle}$ (c, f) on a bright image f (a) (acquired with an exposure time of $1/40$ s) and on a dark image of the same scene (d) (exposure time of $1/800$ s). The sf b is an hemisphere of radius 2 pixels.

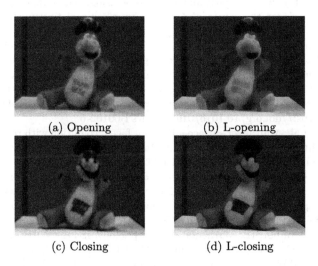

(a) Opening   (b) L-opening

(c) Closing   (d) L-closing

Fig. 3. (a) Opening $(\gamma_b((f^d)^c))^c$ and (b) logarithmic-opening $(\gamma_b^{\triangle}((f^d)^c))^c$ on the dark image f^d. (c) Closing $(\varphi_b((f^d)^c))^c$ and (d) logarithmic-closing $(\varphi_b^{\triangle}((f^d)^c))^c$. The sf b is an hemisphere of radius 15 pixels.

5   Conclusion and Perspectives

Logarithmic-mathematical morphology is introduced in this paper. The fundamental operators of logarithmic-dilation $\delta_b^{\triangle}$ and erosion $\varepsilon_b^{\triangle}$ are defined for a structuring function thanks to the LIP-addition law $\triangle$. Their expressions are related to the "classical" dilation δ_b and ε_b facilitating their implementation. As both operators form an adjunction, a logarithmic-opening and closing are defined. The logarithmic-MM is compared to the "classical" MM based on an additive structuring function through several examples. Results show that Logarithmic-MM operators are particularly efficient to detect contrast variations in the dark parts (and also in the bright parts) of images caused by different illumination conditions. In future, logarithmic-MM operations will be extended to colour and multivariate images.

References

1. Banon, G.J.F., Barrera, J.: Decomposition of mappings between complete lattices by mathematical morphology, part i. general lattices. Sig. Process. **30**(3), 299–327 (1993). https://doi.org/10.1016/0165-1684(93)90015-3
2. Brailean, J., et al.: Evaluating the EM algorithm for image processing using a human visual fidelity criterion. In: ICASSP-91, vol. 4, pp. 2957–2960, April 1991. https://doi.org/10.1109/ICASSP.1991.151023
3. Heijmans, H.: Morphological Image Operators. Advances in Electronics and Electron Physics: Supplement, vol. 25. Academic Press, New York (1994)
4. Jourlin, M., Pinoli, J.: Logarithmic image processing: the mathematical and physical framework for the representation and processing of transmitted images. In: Hawkes, P.W. (ed.) Advances in Imaging and Electron Physics, vol. 115, pp. 129–196. Elsevier (2001). https://doi.org/10.1016/S1076-5670(01)80095-1
5. Jourlin, M.: Logarithmic Image Processing: Theory and Applications. Advances in Imaging and Electron Physics, vol. 195. Elsevier Science, New York (2016)
6. Jourlin, M., Pinoli, J.C.: Image dynamic range enhancement and stabilization in the context of the logarithmic image processing model. Sig. Process. **41**(2), 225–237 (1995). https://doi.org/10.1016/0165-1684(94)00102-6
7. Lai, Z.R., et al.: Multilayer surface albedo for face recognition with reference images in bad lighting conditions. IEEE Trans. Image Process. **23**(11), 4709–4723 (2014). https://doi.org/10.1109/TIP.2014.2356292
8. Matheron, G.: Eléments pour une théorie des milieux poreux. Masson, Paris (1967)
9. Meylan, L., Susstrunk, S.: High dynamic range image rendering with a retinex-based adaptive filter. IEEE Trans. Image Process. **15**(9), 2820–2830 (2006). https://doi.org/10.1109/TIP.2006.877312
10. Najman, L., Talbot, H.: Mathematical Morphology. ISTE , Wiley (2013)
11. Navarro, L., Courbebaisse, G., Jourlin, M.: Chapter two - logarithmic wavelets. In: Hawkes, P.W. (ed.) Advances in Imaging and Electron Physics, vol. 183, pp. 41–98. Elsevier (2014). https://doi.org/10.1016/B978-0-12-800265-0.00002-3
12. Navarro, L., Deng, G., Courbebaisse, G.: The symmetric logarithmic image processing model. Digit. Sig. Process. **23**(5), 1337–1343 (2013). https://doi.org/10.1016/j.dsp.2013.07.001
13. Noyel, G., et al.: Superimposition of eye fundus images for longitudinal analysis from large public health databases. Biomed. Phys. Eng. Express **3**(4), 045015 (2017). https://doi.org/10.1088/2057-1976/aa7d16
14. Oppenheim, A.V., et al.: Nonlinear filtering of multiplied and convolved signals. Proc. IEEE **56**(8), 1264–1291 (1968). https://doi.org/10.1109/PROC.1968.6570

15. Peng, Y.T., Cosman, P.C.: Underwater image restoration based on image blurri-ness and light absorption. IEEE Trans. Image Process. **26**(4), 1579–1594 (2017). https://doi.org/10.1109/TIP.2017.2663846
16. Serra, J.: Image Analysis and Mathematical Morphology: Theoretical Advances, vol. 2. Academic Press, London (1988)
17. Serra, J., Cressie, N.: Image Analysis and Mathematical Morphology, vol. 1. Aca-demic Press, London (1982)
18. Sugimura, D., et al.: Enhancing color images of extremely low light scenes based on RGB/NIR images acquisition with different exposure times. IEEE Trans. Image Process. **24**(11), 3586–3597 (2015). https://doi.org/10.1109/TIP.2015.2448356

FqSD: Full-Quaternion Saliency Detection in Images

Reynolds León Guerra$^{(\boxtimes)}$, Edel B. García Reyes,
Annette M. González Quevedo, and Heydi Méndez Vázquez

Advanced Technologies Application Center (CENATAV), Havana, Cuba
rleon@cenatav.co.cu

Abstract. Saliency detection aims to segment in two groups the pixels of an image, in important or less important visual information. Important information can be used to detect objects with some semantics for tasks in computer vision. In this paper, we develop a saliency detection method using full-quaternion. The proposed method makes a combination between local and global approaches. Local features are obtained at patches level using a Module Local Binary Patterns and the comparison between feature vectors (module and phase). The salient object is obtained by a weighted combination of salient maps where a function of center-bias and refinement is applied. To verify the effectiveness of our method, this is validated using the mean absolute error metric in the ECSSD-1000 and DUT-OMRON datasets and compared with others state of the art algorithms. A statistical analysis is applied to the results to obtain the statistical significance among color spaces with the method of Wilcoxon signed test. The results show that the HSV color space is better in effectiveness than others.

Keywords: Full-quaternion · Salient map · Color · Feature · Object

1 Introduction

Saliency detection task aims to detect objects in images that are visually salient for persons [1]. When a person looks at a scene it has the tendency to focus on relevant information and reject the redundant information [2]. This can be useful to make different tasks in computer vision, for example, visual classification [3], image retrieval [4], person re-identification [5] and so on. In general, there are two approaches to search salient objects in images, **bottom up** and **top down**. The baseline in the first approach is to get the features less frequent in the scene and consider them as salient regions. **Top down** is used to look for salient regions with some prior knowledge about the objects.

In recent years, different saliency detection methods have been developed. Erdem and Erdem [6] use region covariance descriptor with features of color, orientation and spatial information, extracted at patches level to compare among

© Springer Nature Switzerland AG 2019
R. Vera-Rodriguez et al. (Eds.): CIARP 2018, LNCS 11401, pp. 462–469, 2019.
https://doi.org/10.1007/978-3-030-13469-3_54

themselves. Hu et al. [7] proposed a method where local and global features are combined in a final map and all pixels are weighted according to their distance to center of the image. Liu and Hu [8] make a combination among maps obtained using Quaternion Fast Fourier Transform (QFFT) to look for the optimum. Yu et al. [9] proposed to use the global contrast of color to obtain a salient map grouping the background pixels, considering that these are similar. Wang et al. [10] based their work on two neural networks to learn local and global features to obtain the salient maps and later these are combined in a single map. Rajankar and Kolekar [11] applied a scale reduction using interpolation of the Fourier coefficients in quaternion space getting the salient map.

Colors and contrasts are features very important to obtain salient maps. However, in the works using this features the correlation among them is not considered at different levels with different approaches. To solve this, we propose a saliency detection method **FqSD** where unlike other works, we link the spatial and frequency information using quaternions preserving the correlation among colors and contrast. Contributions of this paper are summarized as follows: First, a combination of local and global features in quaternion space at different scales is done. Second, a comparative study is developed where we obtain the best color space to use the proposed method.

This paper is organized as follows. In Sect. 2 we explain our approach. In Sect. 3 experimental results are presented and analyzed. Finally the conclusions are set out in Sect. 4.

2   Our Approach

The data input to method **FqSD** is an image represented in any color space. In step 2, a Gaussian pyramid reduction is applied to get several images with different resolutions where a lot of less important information is eliminated. After, in step 3 each image is processed to build salient maps using local and global approaches in the spatial and frequency domain using full-quaternions (combining values of contrast and color channels). Also previous images are merged into a single image per method. As there are three salient maps, another merge step is required (step 4), which is done by means of a weighted sum of maps. In step 5, two functions (center-bias and refinement) are applied to finally obtain the salient object (output).

2.1   Multiple Resolution

Generally, salient objects are invariant when a scale transformation is applied to the image. But, the information of not-salient objects is lost during the change of resolution e.g. background information in the image. As explained before, we used a Gaussian pyramid by reduction [12] in step 2, where four images are obtained and we preserve the original image. As original images have different sizes, these are normalized to get a standard size.

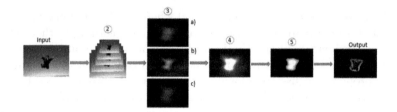

Fig. 1. Show the different steps in the proposed method **FqSD**.

2.2 Local and Global Salient Maps

After obtaining the images in step 2, these are transformed from original space to full-quaternion space, where the image has four channels. First channel is the clear-dark contrast effect (for more detail see [13]) and the other channels are values of a color space, for example, Red-Green-Blue **(RGB)**. We develop three approaches to obtain the salient maps (Local Salient Map **(LSM)**, Module Local Binary Pattern Salient Map **(MLBP)** and Quaternion Fast Fourier Transform to global Salient Map **(QFFT)**).

For a better understanding of the proposed method, firstly several properties of quaternion algebras are explained. Quaternion is a hypecomplex number given by Hamilton [14] and is denoted with letter $\mathcal{H}$. If $q \in \mathcal{H}$, this is represented as follows:

$$\{q = t + xi + yj + zk | (t, x, y, z) \in \mathcal{R}\} \tag{1}$$

Where the complex operators $\mathbf{i}, \mathbf{j}, \mathbf{k}$ have the next rules $\{i^2 = j^2 = k^2 = ijk = -1, ij = k = -ji, ki = j = -ik, jk = i = -kj\}$. It is clear that the multiplication between quaternions is not commutative. If $t = 0$, is a pure quaternion and $q = xi + yj + zk$, if $t \neq 0$ is a full-quaternion. The module and the phase are:

$$|q| = (t^2 + x^2 + y^2 + z^2)^{1/2} \tag{2}$$

$$\phi = \tan^{-1}(\frac{(x^2 + y^2 + z^2)^{1/2}}{t}) \tag{3}$$

LSM: Images are divided in little patches and in each one of them two feature vector are obtained. The first vector is associated to each full-quaternion in the patch and their elements are the module and phase (see Eqs. (2) and (3)). The second feature vector has the average of the module and phase of all the full-quaternions in the patch. To obtain a salient map in each patch an euclidean distance is applied between the first and second feature vector. The full-quaternions with high value have the highest probability to be different from their neighbors (see Fig. 1, 3.(a)).

MLBP: In this approach, each full-quaternion is codified using Local Binary Pattern (LBP). We extend the LBP to the full-quaternion using the module because is sensitive to the color changes. See following equation:

$$mLBP_{S_i} \sum_{j=0}^{p-1} h(s_j - s_i)2^j, h(r) = \begin{cases} 0 \text{ if } r \geq 0 \\ 1 \text{ if } r < 0 \end{cases} \quad (4)$$

Where S is a 3×3 windows, $p \in S$, s_i and s_j module of full-quaternion analysis and its neighborhood respectively. Here, the salient map is obtained equal that the **LSM** method, but using the value of the modules (see Fig. 1, 3.(c)).

QFFT: Quaternion Fast Fourier Transform is used to build salient map in a global way [8]. Spectral module is modified using a low-pass filter, where a stable color region is obtained with the Inverse Fourier Transform as follows.

$$F(p, s) = S \sum_{m=0}^{m-1} \sum_{n=0}^{n-1} e^{-\mu 2\pi(\frac{pm}{M}) + (\frac{sn}{N})} f(m, n) \quad (5)$$

$$f(m, n) = |S \sum_{p=0}^{p-1} \sum_{s=0}^{s-1} e^{\mu 2\pi(\frac{pm}{M}) + (\frac{sn}{N})} (exp(\Upsilon + (\Lambda(p, s) \circ \Gamma)))|^2 \quad (6)$$

$$\Lambda = \frac{Vq}{|Vq|}, \Lambda \in F(p, s) \quad (7)$$

Where, $S = \sqrt{\frac{1}{MN}}$, the Eqs. (5) and (6) are the direct and inverse Quaternion Fourier Transforms, μ is a unit pure quaternion (module is aqual to 1), p y s are frequency coefficients, m y n are spatial coordinates of the image. Λ y Γ are the eigenaxis and phase, Υ is the spectral module modified to the filter and $\circ$ is the Hadamard product (see Fig. 1, 3.(b)).

2.3 Image Fusion

To show the salient map obtained in step 3, it is necessary to make a fusion among the images obtained by each level in the Gaussian pyramid and process these images (as explained in the Sect. 2.2). Finally, a single image is obtained by each method. We developed the Eq. (8) taking into account that in level 2 there is a trend to keep high values of salient points. Nonetheless, in other levels the values are high or low according to the scene.

$$SM = max(Map_0, Map_1, Map_3, Map_4) + Map_2 \quad (8)$$

Where, SM, may be LSM, mLBP-SM or QFFT-SM. $Map\{.\}$ is the map obtained in different levels. The next step is to fuse the three salient maps obtained previously with a weight value to each map as follow:

$$MSsingle = \alpha(\psi * LSM) + \beta log((\psi * MLBP) + 1) + \delta(\psi * QFFT) \quad (9)$$

Where, ψ is a radial filter, $\{\alpha, \beta, \delta\}$ are parameters of weight for the maps and $\{*\}$ convolution product (see Fig. 1, image 4).

2.4   Refinement

A refinement step is needed to improve the salient map obtained in the last step. Center-bias here is used to give a weight to each element of a salient map [15]. Theory of center-bias is based on the way that images are captured, in general the salient object is localized in the center of the image. Hence, Eq. 10 is used to weight the values according to the distance of a pixel to the center of the image.

$$MS_{cb} = MSsingle_{(m,n)}(1 - d), d = \sqrt{(m - v)^2 + (n - \rho)^2}/(v^2 + \rho^2) \quad (10)$$

Where, v and ρ are the center coordinates of the image.

Generally speaking, in practical tasks we only need to know the values associated with salient objects. To solve this, unlike other works, an adaptive threshold is applied to eliminate values that are far from the interest objects as follows.

$$MS_{threshold} = \begin{cases} 0 \text{ if } r \leq 0 \\ \omega \text{ if } r > 0 \end{cases} \quad (11)$$

Where, ω is the value of the $MS_{cb}(m, n)$, r is the threshold (sum of the average with the standard deviation in MS_{cb}).

Other interesting detail of salient maps is that a salient object can have different parts with several probability of be observed. Therefore, it is done a refinement as follow:

$$MS_{final} = log(|MS_{threshold}| + 1) \quad (12)$$

3   Experimental Results

Our aim is to validate the performance of the developed method using different color spaces and performing a comparison with other state-of-the-art methods. The datasets used are ECSSD-1000 and DUT-OMROM. ECSSD-1000 [16]: has 1000 images (with their salient mask respectively) where there are from 1 to n salient objects. Salient objects have been labeled by five persons to obtain the mask or ground truth (GT). DUT-OMROM [17]: contains 5168 images with complex scene and their masks respectively. We performed experiments using 4 color spaces: RGB, HSV (Hue-Saturation-Value), Lab (lightness, color opponents green-red and blue-yellow) and Ycbcr (Y is the Luma component and CB and CR are the blue-difference and red-difference chroma components). Our best parameter configuration is: $\delta = 1.4$, $\beta = 1.3$, $\delta = 0.3$, $\mu = (i, j, k)/\sqrt{3}$. As metric of evaluation we used Mean Absolute Error (MAE), see Eq. 13. The Wilcoxon signed test is used to know the statistical significance than there are among the result obtained in the different color spaces. In this test, a value of 1 means significance (the results are not casual), if the value is 0 the results are doubtful.

$$MAE = \frac{1}{MN} \sum_{n=1}^{N} \sum_{m=1}^{M} |MS_{final}(m, n) - GT(m, n)| \quad (13)$$

Table 1. Different results among FqSD and other methods in terms of MAE.

Methods	ECSSD-1000	DUT-OMROM
FqSD(HSV)	**0.2002**	**0.1551**
FqSD(RGB)	0.2102	0.1718
FqSD(Lab)	0.2198	0.1551
FqSD(Ycbcr)	0.2241	0.1552
IT (1998) [18]	0.2730	0.1980
Wco (2014) [19]	0.2250	-
LPS (2015) [20]	0.2370	-
Jiang (2017)[21]	0.2430	-
BL (2015) [22]	0.2620	0.2390
CPMC-GBVS (2014) [23]	-	0.2345
HDCT (2014) [24]	-	0.1669
BSCA (2015) [25]	-	0.1910
XIA (2017) [26]	-	0.1632
BSP (2018) [27]	0.2200	-

Table 2. Statistical significance among the different color space vs HSV.

Color spaces	ECSSD-1000	DUT-OMROM
RGB	1	1
Lab	1	0
Ycbcr	1	0

We can observe in Table 1 that our method using the HSV color space got the best results in both datasets (see Fig. 2). However, the results with Wilcoxon signed test show difference in the dataset. For the images analyzed in ECSSD-1000 represented in other color spaces different than HSV there is statistical significance (see Table 2) and the results are better than the algorithms of state of the art. On the other hand, the results in the DUT-OMROM dataset have zero value in the Wilcoxon signed test. This result is associated with the characteristic present in dataset, where the patterns in different images are repeated with high frequency along the dataset (the variance among image data is small).

The advantage of HSV color space over Lab, Ycbcr and RGB, is because there is a correlation among different features represented by full-quaternions, where the four features (Hue, Saturation, Value, Clear-Dark Contrast) are combined linearly and processed as a single element. Moreover, the combination between local and global features allows highlighting regions of interest that could be ignored with a simple analysis (local or global). Center-bias and refinement act as a function of adjustment delineating better the contour of the salient objects.

Fig. 2. Different salient objects with the proposed method **FqSD(HSV)** in ECSSD-1000 and DUT-OMROM dataset. From top to bottom the rows are, original image, ground truth and salient objects respectively.

4 Conclusions

Experimental results show good performance using the HSV color represented by means of full-quaternions. The integration of the local and global salient maps to look for features that are less frequent in images allows improving the results analyzed with the Mean Absolute Error. The Wilcoxon signed test showed that little variety in the images in a dataset can give untrustworthy results. In future works, we plan to develop a deep learning-based method with neural network using full-quaternions to learn parameters in front of the complexity of different scenes that appear in the real world.

References

1. Wang, X., et al.: Edge preserving and multi-scale contextual neural network for salient object detection. IEEE Trans. Image Process. **27**(1), 121–134 (2018)
2. Aytekin, C., Iosifidis, A., Gabbouj, M.: Probabilistic saliency estimation. Pattern Recognit. **74**, 359–372 (2018)
3. Murabito, F., et al.: Top-down saliency detection driven by visual classification. arXiv preprint arXiv:1709.05307 (2017)
4. Li, S., Mathews, P.: Can image retrieval help visual saliency detection? arXiv preprint arXiv:1709.08172 (2017)
5. Zhu, F., et al.: A novel two-stream saliency image fusion CNN architecture for person re-identification. Multimed. Syst., 1–14 (2017)
6. Erdem, E., Erdem, A.: Visual saliency estimation by nonlinearly integrating features using region covariances. J. Vis. **13**(4), 11–11 (2013)
7. Hu, D., et al.: Saliency region detection via local and global (2015)
8. Liu, S., Hu, J.: Visual saliency based on frequency domain analysis and spatial information. Multimed. Tools Appl. **75**(23), 16699–16711 (2016)
9. Yu, C., Zhang, W., Wang, C.: A saliency detection method based on global contrast. Int. J. Signal Process. Image Process. Pattern Recognit. **8**(7), 111–122 (2015)
10. Wang, L., et al.: Deep networks for saliency detection via local estimation and global search. In: 2015 IEEE Conference on Computer Vision and Pattern Recognition (CVPR), pp. 3183–3192. IEEE (2015)
11. Rajankar, O.S., Kolekar, U.D.: Scale space reduction with interpolation to speed up visual saliency detection. Int. J. Image Graph. Signal Process. **7**(8), 58 (2015)

12. Burt, P.J., Adelson, E.H.: The Laplacian pyramid as a compact image code. In: Readings in Computer Vision, pp. 671–679 (1987)
13. Guerra, R.L., García Reyes, E.B., Mata, F.J.S.: Full-quaternion color correction in images for person re-identification. In: Mendoza, M., Velastín, S. (eds.) CIARP 2017. LNCS, vol. 10657, pp. 339–346. Springer, Cham (2018). https://doi.org/10.1007/978-3-319-75193-1_41
14. Morais, J.P., Georgiev, S., Sprößig, W.: Real Quaternionic Calculus Handbook. Springer, Basel (2014). https://doi.org/10.1007/978-3-0348-0622-0
15. Buso, V., Benois-Pineau, J., Domenger, J.-P.: Geometrical cues in visual saliency models for active object recognition in egocentric videos. Multimed. Tools Appl. **74**(22), 10077–10095 (2015)
16. Yan, Q., et al.: Hierarchical saliency detection. In: 2013 IEEE Conference on Computer Vision and Pattern Recognition (CVPR), pp. 1155–1162. IEEE (2013)
17. Yang, C., et al.: Saliency detection via graph-based manifold ranking. In: 2013 IEEE Conference on Computer Vision and Pattern Recognition (CVPR), pp. 3166–3173. IEEE (2013)
18. Itti, L., Koch, C., Niebur, E.: A model of saliency-based visual attention for rapid scene analysis. IEEE Trans. Pattern Anal. Mach. Intell. **20**(11), 1254–1259 (1998)
19. Zhu, W., et al.: Saliency optimization from robust background detection. In: Proceedings of the IEEE Conference on Computer Vision and Pattern Recognition, pp. 2814–2821 (2014)
20. Li, H., et al.: Inner and inter label propagation: salient object detection in the wild. IEEE Trans. Image Process. **24**, 3176–3186 (2015)
21. Jiang, L., Zhong, H., Lin, X.: Saliency detection via boundary prior and center prior. Int. Robot. Autom. J. **2**(4), 00027 (2017). https://doi.org/10.15406/iratj.2017.02.00027
22. Tong, N., et al.: Salient object detection via bootstrap learning. In: 2015 IEEE Conference on Computer Vision and Pattern Recognition (CVPR), pp. 1884–1892. IEEE (2015)
23. Li, Y., et al.: The secrets of salient object segmentation. In: 2014 IEEE Conference on Computer Vision and Pattern Recognition (CVPR), pp. 280–287. IEEE (2014)
24. Kim, J., et al.: Salient region detection via high-dimensional color transform. In: Proceedings of the IEEE Conference on Computer Vision and Pattern Recognition, pp. 883–890 (2014)
25. Qin, Y., et al.: Saliency detection via cellular automata. In: 2015 IEEE Conference on Computer Vision and Pattern Recognition (CVPR), pp. 110–119. IEEE (2015)
26. Xia, C., Zhang, H., Gao, X.: Saliency detection by aggregating complementary background template with optimization framework. arXiv preprint arXiv:1706.04285 (2017)
27. Wang, H., et al.: Saliency region detection method based on background and spatial position. Int. J. Pattern Recognit. Artif. Intell. **32**(07), 1850024 (2018)

Graph-Based Image Segmentation Using Dynamic Trees

Jordão Bragantini[(✉)], Samuel Botter Martins, Cesar Castelo-Fernandez,
and Alexandre Xavier Falcão

Laboratory of Image Data Science, University of Campinas, Campinas, Brazil
{jordao.bragantini,samuel,cesar.castelo,afalcao}@lids.ic.unicamp.br
https://lids.ic.unicamp.br

Abstract. Image segmentation methods have been actively investigated, being the graph-based approaches among the most popular for object delineation from seed nodes. In this context, one can design segmentation methods by distinct choices of the image graph and *connectivity function*—i.e., a function that measures how strongly connected are seed and node through a given path. The framework is known as *Image Foresting Transform* (IFT) and it can define by seed competition each object as one *optimum-path forest* rooted in its internal seeds. In this work, we extend the general IFT algorithm to extract object information as the trees evolve from the seed set and use that information to estimate arc weights, positively affecting the connectivity function, during segmentation. The new framework is named *Dynamic IFT* (DynIFT) and it can make object delineation more effective by exploiting color, texture, and shape information from those dynamic trees. In comparison with other graph-based approaches from the state-of-the-art, the experimental results on natural images show that DynIFT-based object delineation methods can be significantly more accurate.

Keywords: Image Foresting Transform · Multiple object delineation ·
Graph Cut · Image segmentation by seed competition

1 Introduction

Image segmentation is a challenging task that often requires user's assistance for corrections [11]. Deep neural networks can provide impressive object approximations [10], but object delineation is still not accurate, even when the user provides careful object localization [12] (Fig. 1). On the other hand, the combination of interactive object localization and graph-based object delineation may solve the problem in a few iterations of corrections with simple user effort (Fig. 1c).

The authors thank CNPq (302970/2014-2 grant), FAPESP (2014/12236-1, 2017/03940-5 and 2018/08951-8 grants) and the Department of Statistics of the University of Campinas for the financial support.

R. Vera-Rodriguez et al. (Eds.): CIARP 2018, LNCS 11401, pp. 470–478, 2019.
https://doi.org/10.1007/978-3-030-13469-3_55

Among many interesting approaches, graph-based object delineation has become quite popular with methods based on Random Walks [8], Graph Cuts [2], Watershed Cuts [6], and Image Foresting Transform (IFT) [7]. These frameworks interpret an image as a graph and, often from some hard constraints (e.g., seed nodes that were chosen by the user to locate the objects), the methods delineate the objects by optimizing some energy function [3,13].

In this work, we explore the optimum-path trees that dynamically evolve from seed nodes during the IFT algorithm for more effective object delineation. This defines a new framework, named *Dynamic* IFT (DynIFT), with methods that can estimate the arc weights in the graph during object delineation by exploiting the object knowledge that increases at each moment. The methods are compared with state-of-the-art graph-based delineation approaches [2,3,6] using a natural image dataset with two types of seed sets provided by users. The experimental results using color information only already show considerable effectiveness gains in object delineation using the DynIFT algorithm.

The next sections present the proposed framework, with algorithm and examples of dynamic arc-weight estimation methods, the experimental results, discussion, and conclusion.

(a)   (b)   (c)

Fig. 1. (a) Original image with four extreme points (magenta) for the method in [12] and orange and green markers for the proposed algorithm. (b) Result of the method in [12] with errors and (c) the desired segmentation using the proposed algorithm. (Color figure online)

2 Dynamic Image Foresting Transform

A 2D image is a pair $(D_I, \mathbf{I})$ in which $\mathbf{I}(p)$ assigns a set of local image features (e.g., color components) to each pixel $p \in D_I \subset \mathcal{Z}^2$. An image may be interpreted as a graph $(\mathcal{N}, \mathcal{A})$ in various distinct ways by defining the nodes in $\mathcal{N} \subseteq D_I$, for example, as pixels, superpixels, or pixel vertices, and using some *adjacency relation* $\mathcal{A} \subset \mathcal{N} \times \mathcal{N}$ in the image domain and/or feature space to define the arcs. For the sake of simplicity, we focus on pixels as nodes ($\mathcal{N} = D_I$), with $\mathbf{I}(\mathbf{p})$ being the CIELab color components of pixel p, and the 4-neighborhood relation to define the arcs.

For a given seed set $\mathcal{S}$—e.g., labeled scribbles (markers) drawn by the user in each object (including background) for object localization and/or segmentation correction—we wish to partition the image into objects such that each

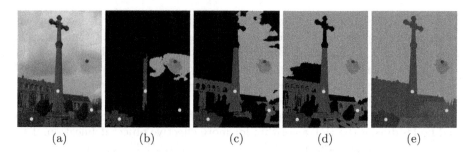

(a)   (b)   (c)   (d)   (e)

Fig. 2. (a) Original image with markers (yellow and blue circles) drawn by the user. (b–e) Dynamic tree evolution in some iterations (each color being one different tree). Notice that each marker has multiple trees (one for each root pixel), but some roots may conquer most pixels in the region dominated by the marker. (Color figure online)

object consists of the pixels more closely connected to its internal seeds than to any other. Each seed $p \in \mathcal{S}$ is then uniquely identified as belonging to one among c objects by a labeling function $\lambda_O(p) \in \{0, 1, 2, \ldots, c\}$, being 0 the background. Similarly, one can also identify the marker $\lambda_M(p) \in \{1, 2, \ldots, m\}$ among m markers that contains the seed p. This can be used, for instance, to control marker deletion and addition during segmentation correction. Therefore, a *connectivity function* f measures how closely connected are seed and node through any given path in the image graph from the former to the latter. A path $\pi_q = \langle p_1, p_2, \ldots, p_n = q \rangle$ with terminus q is a sequence of nodes, such that $(p_i, p_{i+1}) \in \mathcal{A}$, $i = 1, 2, \ldots, n-1$, being trivial when $\pi_q = \langle q \rangle$. A path π_q is *optimum* when $f(\pi_q) \leq f(\tau_q)$ for any other path τ_q, irrespective to its starting node. Defining Π as the set of all possible paths in the graph, the Image Foresting Transform (IFT) algorithm [7] minimizes a path cost map C,

$$C(q) = \min_{\forall \pi_q \in \Pi} \{f(\pi_q)\}, \tag{1}$$

by computing an *optimum-path forest* P—i.e., an acyclic predecessor map that assigns to every node q its predecessor $P(q) \in D_I$ in the optimum path π_q^P with terminus q or a marker $P(q) = nil \notin D_I$, when q is a *root* (starting node) of the map (i.e., $\pi_q^P = \langle q \rangle$ is optimum). The algorithm can also propagate to every node $p \in D_I$, the root $R(p) \in \mathcal{S}$ in the optimum-path forest, the object label map $L(p) = \lambda_O(R(p)) \in \{0, 1, 2, \ldots, c\}$ (resulting segmentation), and the marker label map $M(p) = \lambda_M(R(p))$. The roots of the map are drawn from $\mathcal{S}$, such that each object is defined by the optimum-path forest rooted in its internal seeds. Connectivity functions may be defined in different ways, which do not always guarantee the optimum cost mapping conditions [4], but can produce effective object delineation [14]. In this work, we explore the connectivity function

$$f_{\max}(\langle q \rangle) = \begin{cases} 0 & \text{if } q \in \mathcal{S}, \\ +\infty & \text{otherwise}, \end{cases}$$

$$f_{\max}(\pi_p \cdot \langle p, q \rangle) = \max\{f_{\max}(\pi_p), w(p, q)\}, \tag{2}$$

where $\pi_p \cdot \langle p, q \rangle$ indicates the extension of path π_p by an arc $\langle p, q \rangle$ and $w(p,q)$ is an arc weight usually estimated from $\mathbf{I}$ (e.g., $w(p,q) = \|\mathbf{I}(q) - \mathbf{I}(p)\|$). The IFT algorithm with $f_{\max}$ computes optimum paths from $\mathcal{S}$ to the remaining nodes by growing one optimum-path tree $\mathcal{T}_r$ for each seed $r \in \mathcal{S}$.

The *dynamic* IFT essentially exploits the sets $\mathcal{T}_r$ to estimate the arc weights $w(p,q)$ as the costs of including q, through $\pi_p \cdot \langle p, q \rangle$, as part of the same object that contains p at the time the optimum path π_p is found (Fig. 2).

2.1 DynIFT Algorithm for $f_{\max}$

The dynamic IFT algorithm for $f_{\max}$ is a variant of the IFT algorithm, which maintains the dynamic trees $\mathcal{T}_r$, for all $r \in \mathcal{S}$, object label map L, path cost map C, marker label map M, predecessor map P, and root map R for possible use during the segmentation process, especially for arc weight estimation.

Algorithm 1. DYNAMIC IFT FOR $f_{\max}$

INPUT:　　　Image $(D_I, \mathbf{I})$, adjacency relation $\mathcal{A}$, and seed set $\mathcal{S}$ with labeling functions λ_O and λ_M.

OUTPUT:　　Object label map L.

AUXILIARY: Priority queue $Q = \emptyset$, dynamic sets $\mathcal{T}_r = \emptyset$, $\forall r \in \mathcal{S}$, maps C, R, P, and M, and variable *tmp*.

1.　**For each** $p \in D_I$
2.　　　$C(p) \leftarrow +\infty$, $R(p) \leftarrow p$, and $P(p) \leftarrow nil$
3.　　　**If** $p \in \mathcal{S}$
4.　　　　　$C(p) \leftarrow 0$, $L(p) \leftarrow \lambda_O(p)$, and $M(p) \leftarrow \lambda_M(p)$
5.　　　Insert p in Q
6.　**While** $Q \neq \emptyset$
7.　　　Remove p from Q, such that $p = \arg\min_{\forall q \in Q}\{C(q)\}$
　　　　and $\mathcal{T}_{R(p)} \leftarrow \mathcal{T}_{R(p)} \cup \{p\}$
8.　　　**For each** $(p,q) \in \mathcal{A} \mid q \in Q$
9.　　　　　Estimate $w(p,q)$ as described in Section 2.2
10.　　　　$tmp \leftarrow \max\{C(p), w(p,q)\}$
11.　　　　**If** $tmp < C(q)$
12.　　　　　　$C(q) \leftarrow tmp$, $R(q) \leftarrow R(p)$
13.　　　　　　$L(q) \leftarrow L(p)$, $M(q) \leftarrow M(p)$, and $P(q) \leftarrow p$

Lines 1–5 of the DynIFT algorithm initialize the maps, being all pixels $p \in D_I$ defined as trivial paths $\langle p \rangle$ in P and inserted in Q. The main loop (Lines 6–13) computes in P optimum paths from the minima of the cost map (i.e., the seeds in $\mathcal{S}$) to the remaining pixels in $D_I \setminus \mathcal{S}$. When a pixel p is removed from Q in Line 7, the current path π_p^P, that can be obtained backward in P, is optimum and p is inserted in the dynamic tree $\mathcal{T}_{R(p)}$ of the root of p. The internal loop (Lines 8–13) considers only the adjacent pixels $q \in Q$ that does not belong to any dynamic set yet. It can estimate the arc weight $w(p,q)$ by extracting object information from the maps and dynamic sets (Sect. 2.2). The remaining lines compute the cost of the extended path $\pi_p^P \cdot \langle p, q \rangle$ and if this cost is lower than the current path cost $C(q)$, it updates the maps and the path π_q^P becomes $\pi_p^P \cdot \langle p, q \rangle$ in P.

Next we explore simple and yet effective ways to estimate the arc weights.

2.2 Dynamic Arc Weight Estimation

Algorithm 1 executes in $|D_I|$ iterations of the main loop. By the time a pixel p is removed from Q in Line 7, the tree $\mathcal{T}_{R(p)}$ contains information about the region conquered by the root $R(p) \in \mathcal{S}$ (which includes p), the map P contains the optimum path π_p^P, the map M contains the union $\bigcup_{\forall r \in \mathcal{S} | M(r) = M(p)} \mathcal{T}_r$ of trees rooted in each marker $M(p) \in \{1, 2, \ldots, m\}$, and the map L contains the union $\bigcup_{\forall r \in \mathcal{S} | L(r) = L(p)} \mathcal{T}_r$ of trees rooted in each object $L(p) \in \{1, 2, \ldots, c\}$. Therefore, color, texture, and shape information about the object or its regions can be explored for dynamic arc weight estimation—i.e., to estimate the cost of including q as part of the object that contains p. We then evaluate the following dynamic arc weight functions based on the tree mean color $\mu_{\mathbf{R(p)}}$ of the pixels $p \in \mathcal{T}_{R(p)}$ and the object mean color $\mu_{\mathbf{L(p)}}$ of the pixels $p \in \bigcup_{\forall r \in \mathcal{S} | L(r) = L(p)} \mathcal{T}_r$.

$$w_1(p, q) = \|\mu_{\mathbf{R(p)}} - \mathbf{I(q)}\|, \tag{3}$$

$$w_2(p, q) = \min_{\forall r \in \mathcal{S} | L(r) = L(p)} \{\|\mu_{\mathbf{r}} - \mathbf{I(q)}\|\}, \tag{4}$$

$$w_3(p, q) = \|\mu_{\mathbf{L(p)}} - \mathbf{I(q)}\|, \tag{5}$$

$$w_4(p, q) = w_1(p, q) + \|\mathbf{I(q)} - \mathbf{I(p)}\|, \tag{6}$$

$$w_5(p, q) = w_2(p, q) + \|\mathbf{I(q)} - \mathbf{I(p)}\|, \tag{7}$$

$$w_6(p, q) = w_3(p, q) + \|\mathbf{I(q)} - \mathbf{I(p)}\|. \tag{8}$$

DynIFT with w_1 assumes that the mean color of the region of the object that contains p (i.e., the dynamic tree $\mathcal{T}_{R(p)}$) is more representative than $\mathbf{I(p)}$. However, it also assumes that each seed can only conquer pixels q whose color is similar to the mean color of that region. The purpose of w_2 is to relax this criterion by considering the closest mean color of all dynamic trees rooted in the same object. This allows, for instance, to delineate object regions not necessarily connected to their most similar seeds (Fig. 3). Function w_3 extends the concept of w_1 for the entire object, which should not be a good idea since the object may be represented by different parts. The remaining functions essentially add the local arc weight $\|\mathbf{I(q)} - \mathbf{I(p)}\|$ to the previous ones in order to evaluate the importance of the local contrast between regions.

3   Experimental Results

For comparison, we use the *power watershed* $(PW_{q=2})$ algorithm [5] (i.e., image segmentation based on minimum spanning forest and random walk), the IFT algorithm for $f_{\max}$ with arc weight function $w(p, q) = \|\mathbf{I(q)} - \mathbf{I(p)}\|$ (i.e., a

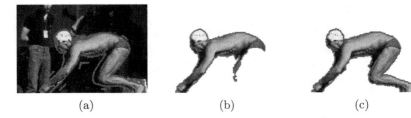

(a)   (b)   (c)

Fig. 3. (a) Original image with markers (red and blue) and ground-truth delineation (magenta). Segmentation results using arc weight functions (b) w_4 and (c) w_5. Even without object markers on the swimmer's legs, w_5 is still able to delineate it, because of the global similar tree search. (Color figure online)

watershed transform [7]), and the min-cut/max-flow algorithm [2,15]. The IFT-based watershed transform provides a cut in the graph given hard constraints (seed set) such that the lowest arc weight in the cut is maximum (i.e., it is an energy maximizer, $GC_{\max}$, as defined in [3] or a watershed cut as defined in [6]). Its counterpart is the energy minimizer, GC_{sum}, as defined in [3], which uses the min-cut/max-flow algorithm [2,15] and obtains a cut in the graph given the seed set such that the sum of the arc weights in the cut is minimum. For that, one can simply use the normalized complementary arc weight function $\bar{w}(p,q) = |\frac{w_{\max}-w(p,q)}{w_{\max}}|^\alpha$, where $\alpha \geq 1$ and $w_{\max}$ is the maximum value of $w(p,q)$ in the graph, in the min-cut/max-flow algorithm with source and sink connected to the seed set.

As proposed by Andrade and Carrera [1], our experiments run on two prede-fined sets of markers to avoid bias of prior knowledge of the process of segmenting with each algorithm. The first is the dataset from [9], in which about four mark-

Table 1. Experimental results.

Method	Gulshan's markers dataset		Andrade's markers dataset	
	Dice Acc. (%)	Time (secs)	Dice Acc. (%)	Time (secs)
GC_{sum}	76.2 ± 1.6	0.230 ± 0.167	90.6 ± 0.08	0.123 ± 0.075
$GC_{\max}$	75.6 ± 1.6	0.038 ± 0.012	89.5 ± 0.09	0.039 ± 0.012
$PW_{q=2}$	72.3 ± 1.7	0.966 ± 0.300	89.9 ± 0.08	1.015 ± 0.299
DynIFT w_1	84.0 ± 1.3	0.042 ± 0.016	92.1 ± 0.08	0.046 ± 0.018
DynIFT w_2	81.9 ± 1.8	4.633 ± 2.573	$\mathbf{95.4 \pm 0.04}$	8.460 ± 3.802
DynIFT w_3	74.7 ± 2.2	0.035 ± 0.012	82.8 ± 0.16	0.036 ± 0.013
DynIFT w_4	83.1 ± 1.4	0.047 ± 0.017	91.7 ± 0.08	0.048 ± 0.017
DynIFT w_5	$\mathbf{84.3 \pm 1.7}$	4.538 ± 2.484	95.3 ± 0.04	8.030 ± 3.485
DynIFT w_6	74.4 ± 2.1	0.039 ± 0.013	82.9 ± 0.16	0.037 ± 0.013

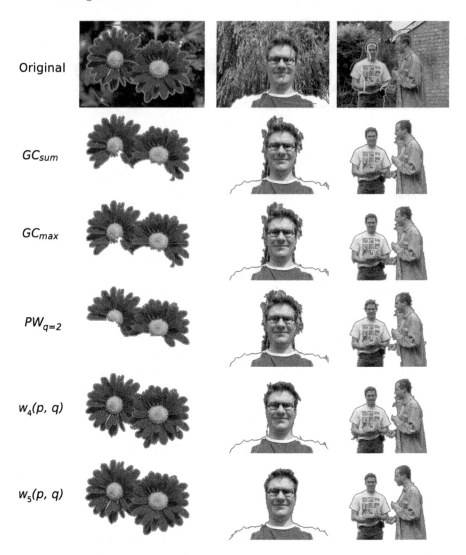

Fig. 4. Examples of segmentation results using DynIFT and the baselines. First row shows the images with the chosen markers for the objects (blue and yellow) and background (red), and the borders of the ground-truth segmentations (magenta and green). The remaining rows show the segmentations from the considered methods for the chosen markers. Note that GC_{sum} is only able to produce binary segmentations. (Color figure online)

ers cover a small area of both the background and foreground on each image. The second dataset contains a more carefully selected set of scribbles [1].

Table 1 shows the mean and standard deviation of the results over the 50 images of the *GrabCut* dataset and their respective markers, two baselines (with

$\alpha = 100$ for the GC_{sum} algorithm), and the six proposed arc weight functions. Computations were performed on an Intel Core i7-7700 CPU 3.60 GHz.

In all cases, except for w_3 and w_6, as predicted, the DynIFT-based methods can considerably improve the accuracy of object delineation in comparison with the baselines. Note that the relaxed versions, represented by w_2 and w_5, can obtain better results than using the local mean color only of the tree $\mathcal{T}_{R(p)}$, represented by w_1 and w_4. Figure 4 illustrates these results on a few examples.

4   Conclusion

In this paper, we present a new framework, named *Dynamic* IFT (DynIFT), that explores the object knowledge from the evolution of optimum-path trees during the IFT algorithm for more effective object delineation. We evaluated the DynIFT with some arc-weight estimation methods using color information. Experimental results show that DynIFT attains considerable accuracy gains in object delineation when compared to three well-established baselines. As future work, we intend to explore the dynamic proprieties of the optimum-path forest and its combination with pattern recognition algorithms to better understand how image delineation can be improved.

References

1. Andrade, F., Carrera, E.V.: Supervised evaluation of seed-based interactive image segmentation algorithms. In: Symposium on Signal Processing, Images and Computer Vision, pp. 1–7 (2015)
2. Boykov, Y., Veksler, O., Zabih, R.: Fast approximate energy minimization via graph cuts. IEEE Trans. Pattern Anal. Mach. Intell. **23**(11), 1222–1239 (2001)
3. Ciesielski, K.C., et al.: Joint graph cut and relative fuzzy connectedness image segmentation algorithm. Med. Image Anal. **17**(8), 1046–1057 (2013)
4. Ciesielski, K.C., et al.: Path-value functions for which Dijkstra's algorithm returns optimal mapping. J. Math. Imaging Vis., 1–12 (2018)
5. Couprie, C., Grady, L., Najman, L., Talbot, H.: Power watershed: a unifying graph-based optimization framework. IEEE Trans. Pattern Anal. Mach. Intell. **33**(7), 1384–1399 (2011)
6. Cousty, J., Bertrand, G., Najman, L., Couprie, M.: Watershed cuts: thinnings, shortest path forests, and topological watersheds. IEEE Trans. Pattern Anal. Mach. Intell. **32**(5), 925–939 (2010)
7. Falcão, A.X., Stolfi, J., de Lotufo, R.A.: The image foresting transform: theory, algorithms, and applications. IEEE Trans. Pattern Anal. Mach. Intell. **26**(1), 19–29 (2004)
8. Grady, L.: Random walks for image segmentation. IEEE Trans. Pattern Anal. Mach. Intell. **28**(11), 1768–1783 (2006)
9. Gulshan, V., et al.: Geodesic star convexity for interactive image segmentation. In: IEEE Conference on Computer Vision and Pattern Recognition, pp. 3129–3136 (2010)
10. Guo, Y., et al.: A review of semantic segmentation using deep neural networks. Int. J. Multimed. Inf. Retr. **7**(2), 87–93 (2018)

11. Kronman, A., Joskowicz, L.: Image segmentation errors correction by mesh segmentation and deformation. In: Mori, K., Sakuma, I., Sato, Y., Barillot, C., Navab, N. (eds.) MICCAI 2013. LNCS, vol. 8150, pp. 206–213. Springer, Heidelberg (2013). https://doi.org/10.1007/978-3-642-40763-5_26
12. Maninis, K.K., et. al: Deep extreme cut: from extreme points to object segmentation. In: IEEE Conference on Computer Vision and Pattern Recognition (2018)
13. Miranda, P.A.V., Falcão, A.X.: Elucidating the relations among seeded image segmentation methods and their possible extensions. In: Conference on Graphics, Patterns and Images (SIBGRAPI), pp. 289–296 (2011)
14. Miranda, P.A.V., Mansilla, L.A.C.: Oriented image foresting transform segmentation by seed competition. IEEE Trans. Image Process. **23**(1), 389–398 (2014)
15. Rother, C., Kolmogorov, V., Blake, A.: GrabCut: interactive foreground extraction using iterated graph cuts. In: ACM Transactions on Graphics, vol. 23, pp. 309–314 (2004)

Radial Textures: A New Approach to Analyze Meat Quality by Using MRI

Daniel Caballero[1,2]([⊠])(iD), Andrés Caro[1](iD), José Manuel Amigo[2](iD), Mar Ávila[1], Teresa Antequera[3](iD), and Trinidad Pérez-Palacios[3](iD)

[1] Computer Science Department, Research Institute of Meat and Meat Product, University of Extremadura, Av. Ciencias S/N, 10003 Cáceres, Spain
{dcaballero,andresc,mmavila}@unex.es
[2] Chemometrics and Analytical Technology, Department of Food Science, University of Copenhagen, Rolighedsvej 26, 1958 Frederiksberg C, Denmark
{caballero,jmar}@food.ku.dk
[3] Food Technology Department, Research Institute of Meat and Meat Product, University of Extremadura, Av. Ciencias S/N, 10003 Cáceres, Spain
{tantero,triny}@unex.es

Abstract. Traditionally, the quality traits of meat products have been determined by means of physico-chemical methods. As an alternative, computer vision algorithms applied on MRI have been proposed, mainly, because of the non-destructive, non-ionizing and innocuous nature of MRI. Usually, the computer vision algorithms developed to analyze meat quality are based in classical textures. In this paper, a new texture algorithm (called RTA, Radial Texture Algorithm) based on the radial distribution of the images and second order statistics is proposed. The results obtained by RTA were compared to the obtained by means of three well known classical texture algorithms: GLCM (Gray Level Co-occurrence Matrix), GLRLM (Gray Level Run Length Matrix) and NGLDM (Neighbouring Gray Level Dependence Matrix) and correlated to the results obtained by means of physico-chemical methods. GLRLM and NGLDM achieved correlation coefficients between 0.50 and 0.75 whereas RTA and GLCM reached very good to excellent relationship (R > 0.75) for the quality parameters of loins. RTA achieved the best results (0.988 for moisture, 0.883 for lipid content and 0.992 for salt content). These high correlation coefficients confirm the new algorithm as a firm alternative to the classical computational approaches in order to compute the quality traits of meat products in a non-destructive and efficient way.

Keywords: MRI · Algorithms · Texture · Quality traits · Iberian loin

Daniel Caballero thanks the "Junta de Extremadura" for the post-doctoral grant (PO17017). The authors wish to acknowledge the funding received for this research from both the "Junta de Extremadura" (Regional Goverment Board - Research Project (IB16089) and economic support for research group (GRU15173 and GRU15113)). We also thank the funding received from the FEDER-MICCIN Infrastructure Research Project (UNEX-10-1E-402). We also wish to thank the Animal Foodstuffs Innovation Service (SiPA, Cáceres, Spain) from the University of Extremadura.

R. Vera-Rodriguez et al. (Eds.): CIARP 2018, LNCS 11401, pp. 479–486, 2019.
https://doi.org/10.1007/978-3-030-13469-3_56

1   Introduction

Computer vision algorithms have been successfully applied in several industrial processes, such as robotics, industrial image processing, food processing, and other fields [1]. Quickness, possibilities for non-destructive evaluation, easy procedures for application, and quantum of output per unit time are some advantages that promote the application of computer vision algorithms to food engineering [2]. Several methods to extract features from images are based on statistical approach. The most powerful computer vision algorithms to evaluate features described the textures from the images by co-occurrence matrix, differences of neighbourhoods matrix and run-length matrix [3]. However, as our knowledge, there are not algorithm to evaluate the texture distribution of the images in a radial way.

Magnetic Resonance Imaging (MRI) is a non-destructive, non-invasive, non-intrusive, non-ionizing and innocuous technique to acquire images. This makes MRI an alternative for determining physico-chemical attributes of meat and meat products, since the traditional methods of analysis are laborious, time and organic solvent consuming and require the destruction of the piece. Several studies were carried out to determine quality parameters of dry-cured products by MRI, allow monitoring the ripening process of Iberian [4], Parma [5] and San Daniele hams [6].

The extraction of textural information is very common to explore parameters related to meat quality. Caballero et al. [7] applied texture features for monitoring the diffusion of salt in Iberian ham. Pérez-Palacios et al. [8] predicted some physico-chemical characteristics in Iberian loin. Texture features algorithms were applied to study the marbling of beef [9], to predict the tenderness of cooked beef from images of fresh beef [10]. The efficiency of the computational texture features algorithms to solve problems related to meat products, in fresh and dry-cured products, have been tested previously [11,12].

In this paper, a new computer vision algorithm based on radial distribution of the image is proposed, in order to determine quality characteristics of the meat products in a non-destructive way.

This paper is organized as follows: Sect. 2 presents the materials used in this work. Section 3 shows the methods applied in this work. Section 4 describes the obtained results and their discussion. Section 5 draws the main conclusions and their implications.

2   Materials

MRI images from twenty Iberian loins (ten fresh loins and ten dry-cured loins) were acquired at the Animal Source Foodstuffs Innovation Services (SiPA, Cáceres, Spain). A low-field MRI scanner (ESAOTE VET-MR E-SCAN XQ 0.18 T) was used with a hand/wrist coil, with nine different configurations on echo time (TE) and repetition time (TR). Sequences of Spin Echo (SE) weighted on T1 were applied with a field of view (FOV) of $150 \times 150\,mm^2$, slice thickness of 4 mm, a matrix size of 256×204 and 29 slices per sample were obtained. Five thousand two hundred and twenty MRI images were obtained.

All images were acquired in DICOM format, with a 512×512 resolution and 256 gray levels. The MRI acquisition was performed at $23\,°C$.

In addition, the quality parameters of fresh and dry-cured loins were determined by means of traditional physico-chemical techniques in order to obtain values for moisture [13], salt [13] and lipids content [14].

3   Methods

3.1   Classical Texture Algorithms

Three classical texture algorithms were applied in this study. Gray level co-occurrence matrix (GLCM), gray level run length matrix (GLRLM) and neighbouring gray level dependence matrix (NGLDM). These algorithms require a previous step, the selection of largest area rectangle inscribed on the image closed contour [15]. These areas, Region of Interest (ROI), need to be rectangular for the algorithms applied in this study [3].

GLCM [16] was computed by counting the number of times that each pair of gray levels occurred at a given distance "d" in all directions. In this matrix, each item "p(i, j)" denotes the number of times that two neighbouring pixels separated by distance "d" (d = 1 in this case) occur on the image, one with gray level "i" and the other pixel with gray level "j". Ten computational texture features were obtained from which all the textural features are extracted [16]: Energy (ENE), Entropy (ENT), Correlation (COR), Haralick's correlation (HC), Inverse Difference Moment (IDM), Inertia (INE), Cluster shade (CS), Cluster Prominence (CP), Contrast (CON) and Dissimilarity (DIS).

GLRLM [17] includes runs into the image, i.e., a set of consecutive pixels in the image with the same gray level value. The runs with the same gray level were computed in four different directions: 0°, 45°, 90° and 135°. Eleven computational texture features were obtained from this method [17]: Short run emphasis (SRE), long run emphasis (LRE), gray level non-uniformity (GLNU), run length non-uniformity (RLNU), run percentage (RPC), low gray-level run emphasis (LGRE), high gray-level run emphasis (HGRE), short run low gray-level emphasis (SRLGE), long run low gray-level emphasis (LRLGE), short run high gray-level emphasis (SRHGE) and long run high gray-level emphasis (LRHGE).

NGLDM uses angular independent features by considering the relationship between an element and all its neighbouring elements at one time rather than one direction at a time [18]. This process eliminates the angular dependency while simultaneously reducing the calculations required to process an image. It is based on the assumption that the gray level spatial dependence matrix of an image can adequately specify this texture information. Five computational texture features were obtained by using this method [18]: small number emphasis (SNE), large number emphasis (LNE), number non-uniformity (NNU), second moment (SM) and entropy (ENT).

3.2   Radial Texture Algorithm (RTA)

Our proposal, Radial Texture Algorithm (RTA), was studied as the fourth algorithm. Figure 1 summarizes the flow chart of this algorithm.

A   B   C   D   E

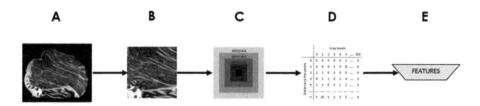

Fig. 1. The flow chart of the proposed computational texture algorithm (RTA). (A) Input Image. (B) Largest area square inside of loin contour. (C) Selecting ratios. (D) Input grey level values in the matrix. (E) Computing features.

First, the image acquisition process obtained sets of MRI, in a high resolution (Fig. 1A). Once the images were acquired, the largest area square inscribed in the contour of the loin was selected as ROIs (Fig. 1B) [15]. Then, the center of the ROIs was calculated, and the grey levels for each pixels in each ratio (distance from the pixels to the center of the ROI) were gathered (Fig. 1C). After that, these grey level values were gathered in a matrix (Fig. 1D). Thus, the pixels with the same grey values and the same distance to the center of the ROI were assigned to the same cell, where the grey value is the column of the matrix and the distance to the center of ROI is the row of the matrix (Fig. 1E).

Finally, seven texture features were computed on each ROI (Fig. 1E), based on second order statistics [19]: Uniformity (UNI), Entropy (ENT), Correlation (COR), Homogeneity (HOM), Inertia (INE), Contrast (CON) and Efficiency (EFI). Table 1 shows the equations to calculate each feature from the values of the previous matrix. Algorithm 1 shows the pseudocode of the RTA algorithm.

The selection of the largest area square from the image ensure that our algorithm is invariant to translation. Thus, Fig. 2 shows the invariant rotation. Figure 2A shows an example image of the ROI and another one image with the selection of the center of the ROI with three pixels at a different distances from the center of the ROI. Figure 2B shows the image rotated 90° to right. In this figure, the center of the ROI is the same that the example image, and also, the distance from the pixels to the center of the ROI. Therefore the matrix to compute the features is the same. This process avoid the rotation dependence. If the images were 90° rotated to left, the result would be the same, as the matrix to compute the feature would be the same. Therefore, the RTA algorithm is invariant to rotation. This process also reduces the calculations required to process an image.

Algorithm 1. Main method of RTA

Input: img: image
Output: featurevector: vector
1: Begin
2: /* Obtain largest area square inside contour of meat piece */
3: $roi \leftarrow$ obtain ROI(img)
4: $(height, width) \leftarrow$ obtain dimensions (roi)
5: $ratio \leftarrow$ height/2
6: $columns \leftarrow 256$
7: $rows \leftarrow$ ratio
8: /* Initially value of the matrix cells are equal to 0 */
9: $mat \leftarrow$ create matrix (rows,columns)
10: **for** $i = 0$ to $i <= ratio - 1$ increment: $i + +$ **do**
11:    **for** $j = ratio - i$ to $j <= ratio + i$ increment: $j + +$ **do**
12:       **for** $k = ratio - i$ to $k <= ratio + i$ increment: $k + +$ **do**
13:          $gray \leftarrow$ obtain gray level(roi,j,k)
14:          $cont \leftarrow$ obtain value(mat,i,gray)
15:          /* Update matrix with the new counter value */
16:          update matrix (mat,i,gray,cont+1)
17:       **end for**
18:    **end for**
19: **end for**
20: /* Computing equations from Table 1 */
21: compute features(mat,featurevector)
22: End

Table 1. Texture features equations of RTA

	Equation	
Uniformity (UNI)	$\sum_i \sum_j P(i,j)^2$	(1)
Entropy (ENT)	$\sum_i \sum_j P(i,j) * log_{10}(P(i,j))$	(2)
Correlation (COR)	$\dfrac{\sum_i \sum_j \mu_x * \mu_y * P(i,j)}{\sigma_x/\sigma_y}$	(3)
Homogeneity (HOM)	$\dfrac{\sum_i \sum_j P(i,j)}{1 + (i-j)^2}$	(4)
Inertia (INE)	$\sum_i \sum_j P(i,j) * (i-j)^2$	(5)
Contrast (CON)	$\sum_i \sum_j P(i,j)^2 * (i-j)^2$	(6)
Efficency (EFI)	$\dfrac{\sigma_x}{\mu_x} + \dfrac{\sigma_y}{\mu_y}$	(7)

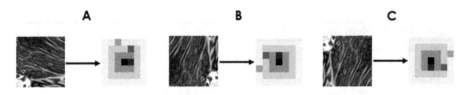

Fig. 2. Invariant rotation of the RTA algorithm. (A) Example image. (B) Rotate 90° to right. (C) Rotate 90° to left.

3.3   Prediction Analysis

The prediction of physico-chemical parameters was made as a function of computer vision features from GLCM, GLRLM, NGLDM and RTA algorithms. For achieving the prediction, data mining techniques were carried out, specifically, Multiple Linear Regression (MLR) [20]. MLR models the linear relationship between a target variable and more independent prediction variables, to produce a linear regression equation that can be used to predict future values. For this purpose, the free software WEKA was used (http://www.cs.waikato.ac.nz/ml/weka - last accessed June 2018). The M5 method was applied to select attributes and a ridge value of 1.0×10^{-4} was applied in the linear regression.

4   Results and Discussion

The predicted values based on the three classical texture algorithms and RTA were correlated to the real values obtained by physico-chemical analysis. Thus, the correlation coefficient (R) of equations were calculated (Table 2), and was used to evaluate the accuracy in the predictions. These results were analyzed taking into account the rules given by Colton [21], who considered the correlation values between 0 and 0.25 as little degree of relationship, from 0.25 to 0.50 as a fair degree of relationship, from 0.50 to 0.75 as moderate to good relationship and between 0.75 and 1 as very good to excellent relationship.

As can be seen in Table 2, according Colton [21], for physico-chemical parameters, all texture algorithms achieved very good to excellent correlations. RTA obtained slightly higher R values, for all physico-chemical attributes, than the remaining texture algorithms (0.988 for moisture, 0.883 for lipid content and 0.992 for salt content). In addition, the texture algorithms were previously validated in order to predict some physico-chemical parameters of loin [8]. Therefore, this fact could validate the use of RTA in order to predict quality traits from the loins.

Table 3 shows the prediction equations of quality parameters of loin as a function of features obtained from RTA. As can be seen, there are six independent variables of the prediction equations for the RTA. In addition, only seven features were computed by RTA algorithm, while GLCM with slightly lower values of R, need to compute ten features. All these facts point out the suitability of RTA for MRI analysis in order to predict some quality traits of loin.

Table 2. Correlation coefficients between some physico-chemical traits and texture algorithms

	GLCM	GLRLM	NGLDM	RTA
Moisture (%)	0.948	0.905	0.914	**0.988**
Lipid (%)	0.791	0.689	0.683	**0.883**
Salt (%)	0.949	0.908	0.907	**0.992**

Table 3. Prediction equations obtained applying OPFTA algorithm

	Equation
Moisture (%) =	39.179 * ENT - 53.834 * COR - 7.821 * HOM
	- 7.904 * INE + 60.550 * CON - 83.599 * EFI + 38.444
Lipid (%) =	46.579 * UNI - 23.620 * COR - 18.581 * HOM
	+ 8.276 * INE - 27.439 * CON - 31.222 * EFI + 17.575
Salt (%) =	- 3.913 * ENT + 2.950 * COR + 0.911 * HOM
	+ 0.645 * INE - 4.852 * CON + 7.344 * EFI + 2.481

5   Conclusions

In this study, a new texture algorithm based on radial distribution and second order statistics has been proposed, developed and validated. The prediction of moisture, lipid and salt content of loins by applying the proposed algorithm on MRI have also been tested. Therefore, the use of this approach could be suitable for the meat industries in order to characterize meat products in a non-destructive, effective, efficient and accurate way.

References

1. Mahendran, R., Jayashree, G.C., Alagusundaram, K.: Application of computer vision techniques on sorting and grading of fruits and vegetables. J. Food Process. Technol. S1-001 **10**, 2157–7110 (2012)
2. Brosnan, T., Sun, D.W.: Improving quality inspection of food products by computer vision - a review. J. Food Eng. **61**, 3–16 (2004)
3. Caballero, D., et al.: Comparison of different image analysis algorithms on MRI to predict physico-chemical and sensory attributes of loin. Chemometr. Intell. Lab. Syst. **180**, 54–63 (2018)
4. Antequera, T., Caro, A., Rodríguez, P.G., Pérez-Palacios, T.: Monitoring the ripening process of Iberian ham by Computer Vision on Magnetic Resonance Imaging. Meat Sci. **76**, 561–567 (2007)
5. Fantazzini, P., Gombia, M., Schembri, M., Simoncini, N., Virgili, R.: Use of Magnetic Resonance Imaging for monitoring Parma dry-cured ham processing. Meat Sci. **82**, 219–227 (2009)

6. Manzoco, L., Anese, M., Marzona, S., Innocente, N., Lazagio, C., Nicoli, M.C.: Monitoring dry-curing of San Daniele ham by Magnetic Resonance Imaging. Food Chem. **141**, 2246–2252 (2013)
7. Caballero, D., et al.: Modeling salt diffusion in Iberian ham by applying MRI and data mining. J. Food Eng. **189**, 115–122 (2016)
8. Pérez-Palacios, T., Caballero, D., Antequera, T., Durán, M.L., Ávila, M.M., Caro, A.: Optimization of MRI acquisition and texture analysis to predict physico-chemical parameters of loins by data mining. Food Bioprocess Technol. **10**, 750–758 (2017)
9. Shiramita, K., Miyajima, T., Takiyama, R.: Determination of meat quality by texture analysis. Pattern Recogn. Lett. **19**, 1319–1324 (1998)
10. Li, J., Tan, J., Martz, F.A., Heymann, H.: Image texture features as indicators of beef tenderness. Meat Sci. **53**, 17–22 (1999)
11. Jackman, P., Sun, D.W.: Recent advances in the use of computer vision technology in the quality assessment of fresh meat. Trends Food Sci. Technol. **22**(4), 185–197 (2011)
12. Jackman, P., Sun, D.W.: Recent advances in image processing using image texture features for food quality assessment. Trends Food Sci. Technol. **19**, 35–43 (2013)
13. Association of Official Analytical Chemists (AOAC): Official method of analysis of AOAC international. 17th edn. AOAC International. Gaithersburg, Maryland, USA
14. Pérez-Palacios, T., Ruiz, J., Martín, D., Muriel, E., Antequera, T.: Comparison of different methods for total lipid quantification. Food Chem. **110**, 1025–1029 (2008)
15. Molano, R., Rodríguez, P.G., Caro, A., Durán, M.L.: Finding the largest area rectangle of arbitrary orientation in a closed contour. Appl. Math. Comput. **218**(19), 9866–9874 (2012)
16. Haralick, R.M., Shanmugam, K., Dinstein, I.: Textural features for image classification. IEEE Trans. Man Cybern. **3**(6), 610–621 (1973)
17. Galloway, M.M.: Texture classification using gray level dependence matrix. Comput. Vis. Image Process. **4**, 172–179 (1975)
18. Sun, C., Wee, G.: Neighbouring gray level dependence matrix. Comput. Vis. Image Process. **23**, 341–352 (1982)
19. Peckinpaugh, S.: An improved method for computing gray-level co-occurrence matrix based texture measured. Comput. Vis. Graph. Image Process. **53**, 574–580 (1991)
20. Witten, I.H., Frank, E.: Data Mining: Practical Machine Learning Tools and Techniques with Java Implementations. Morgan-Kauffmann, San Francisco (2005)
21. Colton, T.: Statistics in Medicine. Little Brown and Co., New York (1974)

An Enhanced Sequential Search Feature Selection Based on mRMR to Support FCD Localization

J. Castañeda-Gonzalez[✉], A. Alvarez-Meza, and A. Orozco-Gutierrez

Automatics Research Group, Universidad Tecnológica de Pereira, Pereira, Colombia
jhojaicastaneda@utp.edu.co

Abstract. One of the most common abnormalities that create a disorder in brain activity is the Focal Cortical Dysplasia (FCD), which can cause pharmacoresistant epilepsy. Patients with this kind of pathology can be treated surgically to remove the lesioned zone of the brain. However, the location of these lesions depends on the specialist expertise. Then, suitable support regarding the FCD analysis is required to minimize the localization subjectivity, primarily, for imbalance scenarios, e.g., few pathological regions are provided. In this work, we propose a new image processing approach to support FCD localization using a minimal redundancy maximal relevance-based feature selection stage that relies on a mutual information cost function to deal with imbalance problems. Then, our proposal finds a feature space through sequential searching aiming to highlight significant relationships between FCD labels and structural-based parameters from magnetic resonance brain images. Achieved results show a more significant improvement in terms of classifications statistics compared to state-of-the-art works.

Keywords: Image processing · Imbalance classification · Feature selection

1 Introduction

Focal Cortical Dysplasias (FCDs) are one of the most common abnormalities that produce a disorder in the electrical functioning of the brain, which is related to epilepsy. FCD can be caused by genetic factors, lack of oxygen during brain development, parasites among others [7]. Patients with pharmacoresistant epilepsy can be treated surgically. Nevertheless, it is necessary to identify with high precision the location of the FCDs. Currently, invasive electrophysiological tests are performed to locate these abnormalities. However, due to these test are invasive, they are uncomfortable and even dangerous for the patient. In this sense, it is necessary to develop non-invasive tools for locating FCD based on medical images [10]. Commonly, to localize FCDs a radiologist (or a group of specialists) performs a visual analysis over magnetic resonance images (MRIs), assessing a set of radiological features related to FCD [10]. Moreover, the diagnosis of these

© Springer Nature Switzerland AG 2019
R. Vera-Rodriguez et al. (Eds.): CIARP 2018, LNCS 11401, pp. 487–495, 2019.
https://doi.org/10.1007/978-3-030-13469-3_57

features depends almost entirely on the radiologist expertise, which causes that the localization of a FCD be a subjective process [1]. Therefore, systems that can locate FCD automatically get high importance in terms of avoiding possible wrong when the specialist is locating these abnormalities.

Among the systems that have been developed to locate automatically FCD, we can recognize that they are mainly focused on a binary classification problem. Authors in [1] characterize MRI images by establishing structural markers of FCD like cortical thickness, intensity contrast at the gray-white matter boundary, and fluid attenuation inversion recovery (FLAIR) signal intensity. Besides, they create a "doughnut" method which calculates the difference between an area of cortex and its surrounding annulus at each vertex (points of brain surface). Also, intrinsic curvature and local cortical deformation (LCD) are computed to encourage the FCD localization robustness regarding the scale and cortical shape. Finally, these features are used to train a Neuronal Network (NN) to classify cortical regions into lesional and non-lesional vertex. Nevertheless, a remarkable issue in this type of approach is that it does not take into account the imbalance between lesional and non-lesional examples. Consequently, imbalanced data can compromise the performance of most standard learning algorithms, which assume balanced classes or equal misclassification costs, yielding to biased results towards the majority class (non-lesional) [4]. To address this drawback, authors in [2] used a random bagging approach to built a set of "base-level" classifiers, each trained using a logistic regression approach. Otherwise, the approach in [5] proposes to randomly select non-lesional vertex, with the aim of balancing the number of samples in both classes. But this may cause that the remaining non-lesional examples be redundant to discriminate both classes conducing to spurious results. Recently, [6] proposed a novel technique for assessing the predictive performance using a Cluster-based Under-sampling NN with bagging, as an alternative to address the class imbalance in FCD classification. Although state-of-the-art works tend to deal with the imbalance problem in FCD trough sub sampling-based techniques, the contribution of each provided input feature are not revealed. The latter can be helpful to enhance the localization performance while favoring the classification training stage and the data interpretability.

In this work, we present image processing approach to support FCD localization based on a sequential search feature selection strategy that employs as cost function a minimal redundancy maximal relevance (mRMR) criterion [8]. Indeed, mRMR relies on a mutual information measure to reveal discriminative input features concerning the target labels (lesional and non-lesional vertex). So, mRMR relaxes the imbalance issue in FCD leveraging a probability functional representation within a supervised feature selection technique. Indeed, we built an input feature set of structural markers from MRIs and then an ensemble classifier with RUSBoost algorithm using a decision tree as base learner, is trained based on a sequential searching scheme based on the mRMR function. Attained results on a public available dataset for FCD localization with 22 patients with confirmed FCD, demonstrate that our methodology, named mRMR sequential search (mRMR-SS), achieves higher results in term on locating the FCD by finding a suitable set of feature that can explain the most the target labels.

The remainder of this paper is organized as follows: Sect. 2 explains the introduce feature selection approach based on mRMR. Section 2 (Sequential Search Based on mRMR Criterion) explain the RUSBoost algorithm for classification with ensemble. Section 3 presents the experimental setup. Section 4 contains the results and discussions and Sect. 5 the concluding remarks.

2   Feature Selection Based on mRMR

Let $\{\mathbf{x}_i, y_i\}_{i=1}^N$ be a set holding N vertex examples $\mathbf{x}_i \in \mathbb{R}^P$, the full input matrix is defined as $\mathbf{X} = \{\boldsymbol{\zeta}_1, \ldots, \boldsymbol{\zeta}_j\}$, where $\boldsymbol{\zeta}_j \in \mathbb{R}^N$ ($j \in \{1, \ldots, P\}$) is the j-th column vector of features of $\mathbf{X}$, and output labels $y_i \in \{1, 0\}$ concerning to lesional and non-lesional vertex. Due to the high imbalance present in data, we introduce a mRMR-based feature selection that can deal with it, and supports the FCD localization.

mRMR-Based Cost Function: In order to select feature with the imbalance present in FCD data, we employ the criterion proposed by Peng et al. [8], called *minimal-redundancy-maximal-relevance* (mRMR), which is a combination of Max-Relevance (d) and min-Redundancy criteria (r). mRMR finds a set $\tilde{\mathbf{X}} \in \mathbb{R}^{N \times L}$ with $L \leq P$, which contains the best features $m = \{1, \ldots, P\}$, corresponding to the most relevant features, which jointly achieves the highest explanation for the target class $\mathbf{y}$. mRMR is obtained by maximizing $\Phi(\mathrm{d}, \mathrm{r})$, where Φ is defined as:

$$\Phi(\mathrm{d}, \mathrm{r}) = \mathrm{d} - \mathrm{r} = \frac{1}{\left|\tilde{\mathbf{X}}\right|} \sum_{\boldsymbol{\zeta}_m \in \tilde{\mathbf{X}}} I(\boldsymbol{\zeta}_m; \mathbf{y}) - \frac{1}{\left|\tilde{\mathbf{X}}\right|^2} \sum_{\boldsymbol{\zeta}_m, \boldsymbol{\zeta}_k \in \tilde{\mathbf{X}}} I(\boldsymbol{\zeta}_m; \boldsymbol{\zeta}_k), \qquad (1)$$

where d is *Max-Relevance* and r *minimal-Redundancy* where $|\tilde{\mathbf{X}}|$ represents the cardinality of $\mathbf{s}$, and $I(\cdot; \cdot)$ is the mutual information is defined as following:

$$I(\boldsymbol{\zeta}_m; \mathbf{y}) = \int \int p(\boldsymbol{\zeta}_m, \mathbf{y}) \log \frac{p(\boldsymbol{\zeta}_m, \mathbf{y})}{p(\boldsymbol{\zeta}_m) p(\mathbf{y})} d\boldsymbol{\zeta}_m d\mathbf{y}. \qquad (2)$$

It is important to remark that mutual information is a measure of dependence between the two distribution, in this sense, this measure is based on the probability distributions, which avoids the imbalance and can find the features that explain the best the vector class. In order to find the best subset of feature, the enhanced sequential searches are defined with the following algorithm:

Sequential Search Algorithm
Given the set $\mathbf{X} = \{\boldsymbol{\zeta}_1, \ldots, \boldsymbol{\zeta}_j\}$ ($j \in \{1, \ldots, P\}$) find a solution set $\tilde{\mathbf{X}} = \{\boldsymbol{\zeta}_1, \ldots, \boldsymbol{\zeta}_e\}$ ($e \in \{1, \ldots, L\}$), where $L \leq P$ that minimizes an objective function $J(\cdot)$.
Do While ($j \leq P$)

1. (**BE**) Start with the full set $\mathbf{X}_0 = \mathbf{X}$
   (**FS**) Start with the empty set $\mathbf{X}_0 = \{\emptyset\}$
2. (**BE**) Remove the worst feature $\zeta' = \arg\max_{\zeta_j \in \mathbf{X}_e} J(\mathbf{X}_e - \zeta_j)$
   (**FS**) Select the next best feature $\zeta' = \arg\max_{\zeta_j \in \mathbf{X}_e} J(\mathbf{X}_e + \zeta_j)$
3. (**BE**) Update $\mathbf{X}_{e+1} = \mathbf{X}_e - \zeta'$, $e = e + 1$
   (**FS**) Update $\mathbf{X}_{e+1} = \mathbf{X}_e + \zeta'$, $e = e + 1$
4. (**BE/FS**) If $J_e > J_{e-1}$ repeat since step (2). If don't stop algorithm.

The objective function J for this case, will be the mRMR criterion described in paragraph "mRMR-Based Cost Function" in Sect. 2.

Sequential Search Based on mRMR Criterion: Given an unbalanced training data $\{\tilde{\mathbf{X}}, \mathbf{y}\}$, the RUSBoost algorithm proposed by Seiffert et al. [9] is a combination of tow components: Random Under-sampling and Adaptive Boosting (AdaBoost), both use for imbalance classification. Firstly, data sampling techniques attempt to alleviate the problem of class imbalance by adjusting the class distribution of the training data set. This can be accomplished by removing examples from the majority class at random until a desired class distribution is achieved [9]. Finally the main idea of boosting is to iteratively create an ensemble of weak hypothesis, which are combined to predict the class of unlabeled examples. Initially, all examples in the training dataset are assigned with equal weights. During the iterations of AdaBoost, a weak hypothesis is formed by the base learner. The error associated with the hypothesis is calculated, and the weight of each example is adjusted such that misclassified examples have their weights increased while correctly classified examples have their weights decreased. Therefore, subsequent iterations of boosting will generate hypothesis that are more likely to correctly classify the previously mislabeled examples. After all iterations are completed, a weighted vote of all hypothesis is used to assign a class to the unlabeled examples. Since boosting assigns higher weights to misclassified examples and minority class examples are those most likely to be misclassified. The above is the reason for which minority class examples will receive higher weights during the boosting process, making it similar in many ways to cost-sensitive classification [3].

3   Experimental Setup

The aim of our work is to build an automatic framework to locate FCDs in MRI studies, which takes into account the problem of unbalance (see Fig. 1). The scheme of our proposal begins with the unbalanced data, this data is the characterizations proposed by Adler et al. [1] over the MRI images of 22 patients (more information below). Due to the high amount of samples, it necessary to perform a stage of features selection, every of the 28 features in this dataset, has about 3 million of samples, then if it is possible to reduce at least 1 of them, the algorithm does not need to deal with 3 million less of values, which considerably may reduce the computational cost. Finally, the classification stage is focus in

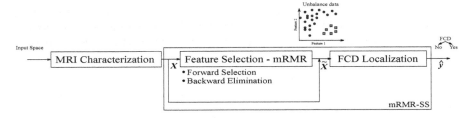

Fig. 1. Scheme of the proposed methodology for locating FCDs.

dealing with the actual unbalanced in the data with has relation of 1:49 samples from non-lesional vertex over the lesional ones.

Dataset: This proposal is tested in a public FCDs dataset[1] used by Adler et al. [1]. This dataset was generated originally with 27 patient with radiologically FCD (mean age = 11.57 ± 3.97, range = 3.79 − 16.21 years, 10 females) who underwent 3D T1 and FLAIR imaging following permission by the Great Ormond Street Hospital ethical review board. To generate this structural features, FreeSurfer Software v5.3 was used and 5 patients were excluded due to severe motion artifacts. For the 22 included patients the lesion masks were created manually on axial slices of volumetric scan, these were identified combining information from T1 and FLAIR images, previous radiological reports, report from multi-disciplinary team meeting, as well as oversight from a consultant pediatric neurologist. These identified lesion were then registered onto the cortical surface reconstruction with FreeSurfer. It is important to say that for this dataset $\mathbf{X} \in \mathbb{R}^{P \times N}$ with $P = 28$ and $N = 3307529$, $\mathbf{y} = \{y_1, \ldots, y_N\} \in \mathbb{R}^N$ as the labels vector, the imbalance class order is 97.71% for non-lesional vertex (0) and the remaining 2.29% for the lesional vertex (1). From MRI reconstructed with FreeSurfer the features generated were: the cortical thickness, define as the mean minimum distance between each vertex on the pial and white matter surfaces, the grey-white matter intensity contrast calculated as the ratio of the gray matter to the white matter signal intensity, the FLAIR intensity was sampled at the grey-white matter boundary as well as at 25%, 50% and 75% depths of the cortical thickness and at −0.5 mm and −1 mm below the grey-white matter boundary, the mean curvature was measured at the grey-white matter boundary as the inverse of the radius, where the radious is an inscribed circle and is equal to the mean of the principal curvatures, and finally, the sulcal depth as the dot product of the movement vector of the cortical surface during inflation.

mRMR-SS Training: To increase the predictive performance of the ensemble classifier using the RUSBoost technique, a feature selection method based on mutual information with the common sequential searches was performed, to give more stability to the classifier for identification of FCDs with unbalanced data. The relevant features were selected using a threshold in the normalized

---

[1] Available online in https://doi.org/10.17863/CAM.6923.

explanation scoring for the features, allowing to keep those feature which jointly achieve the set threshold. The *WeakLearn* used for this ensemble was *decision tree*, and the following statistics were computed to compare the estimate performance of the method class-by-class: G-mean, which is the root of the product of class-wise sensitivity, sensitivity that quantifies the ability to avoid false negatives, and specificity that quantifies the ability to avoid false positives. A hold out validation was implemented, the data was split into 70% for training and 30% for validation. The first 70% of the data was split again into 70%–30% (train-test) 10 times. Then a nested cross-validation was employed for each of the 10 repetitions to determinate the optimal parameters of the classifier (Percentage of total instances represented by the minority class (M), number of iterations (T) and learning rate (Lr)). The grid for this nested cross-validation goes for M from 10% to 100%, for T from 100 to 1000 iterations, and for the learning rate of the ensemble from 0.1 to 1. Once all the results were obtained, the best configurations of parameters was selected and a the initial 30% of data for validation were used to test the model trained model.

Comparison Methods: We compare our results with the methodologies to address the class imbalance oriented to automatic detection of FCD proposed: Cluster-based under-sampling (CBUS) and CBUS with Baggin [6], without under-sampling (WUS) [1], random under-sampling (RUS) [5] and bagging approach [2] on five random samples of majority class, each one of equal size of the minority class. Similar to [6] we test all those mentioned schemes with Neural Network classifiers (NN), trained using surface based measures from samples selected by each method. A single hidden layer neural network is chosen as the classifier because it can be rapidly trained on large datasets [1]. The number of hidden neurons in the network is determined through a principal component analysis applied to the input features, using the number of components that explained over 99% of the variance. In our case, we fit an ensemble with a grid of ten values for each parameter, only was reported the optimal parameter configuration.

4   Results and Discussion

For every feature Fig. 2 shows the explanation score calculated using the sequential search based on mRMR criterion between these features and the target class. Even these scores are for every single feature, due to the nature of the FS and BE searches, the scores of subsequence features depend on the previous. The number of relevant features for both searches were established by computing the cumulative explanation score, and cutting when this decrease from previous stages. In this case, for FS the amount of features were 15, and 14 for BE, the top ranking of feature of this two, are nearly the same features, they have 13 features in common, this exhibit that our feature selection stage is stable. Is important to note, that those best feature in both cases belongs to asymmetry between both hemispheres of the brain, and the features related to the contrast between gray and white matter in the FLAIR images.

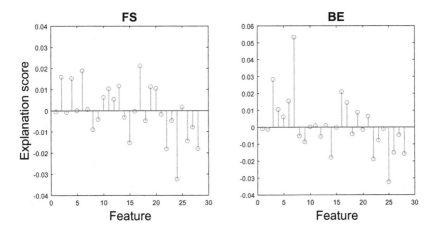

Fig. 2. Explanation score of every single feature selected either searches, FS and BE using the mRMR criterion.

As we mention in Sect. 3, the RUSBoost ensemble has three free parameters to be tuned, implementing the nested cross-validation scheme we determinate the best set of parameters for the classification problem, obtaining for $T = 100$ iterations, $Lr = 0.1$ and $M = 60\%$, latter results shown in Table 1 were obtained using this parameters configuration. Table 1 shows the results obtained for the state art methods; Without under-sampling (WUS), Random under-sampling (RUS), random bagging, Cluster-based under-sampling (CBUS) and the combination of CBUS and bagging, All those under-sampling methods were used on a Neuronal Network classifier. Without under-sampling the classifier achieves a high specificity (99.7%), nevertheless the sensitivity is low (49.8%). This happens because the classifier is biased towards the healthy class due to the high class imbalance. When input data is randomly under-sampled the sensitivity results increases, but the specificity decreases. However, the G-mean value, which encompasses sensitivity and specificity information, increases significantly. The bagging approach improves the G-mean value, with respect to the two previews methods. Besides of the state of art methods here implemented, shown equivalent results for the RUSBoost classifier, for the database with no selected features (NFS). But it is important to note that after using out mRMR-SS stage, the ensemble with the same parameters and same base learner improve significantly in terms of G-mean, specificity and sensitivity the FCD localization.

It is clearly shown a high performance and stability for RUSBoost classifier over the NN, in addition, the selected features under mRMR-SS exhibit more stability than all the set of features. The RUSBoost technique probe to be a solid alternative for unbalance data classification like FCDs datasets. Even when result with all the features shows more efficient than other methods, the mRMR-SS feature selection strategy can provide more stability to the classifier by selecting an optimal set of feature that satisfactory explain the target labels, even when dealing the imbalance data, in this case FCD data.

Table 1. Comparative results in term of G-mean, sensitivity and specificity, for our scheme and the state-of-art works.

Method(# features)	G-mean (%)	Sensitivity (%)	Specificity (%)
NN+WUS(28)	70.46 ± 1.34	49.8 ± 1.22	99.7 ± 1.28
LDA+RUS(28)	86.19 ± 2.28	84.1 ± 2.36	88.4 ± 1.82
NN+Bagging(28)	89.46 ± 0.71	88.95 ± 0.78	89.98 ± 0.85
NN+CBUS(28)	92.19 ± 1.18	92.6 ± 1.92	91.8 ± 2.17
NN+CBUS-Bagging(28)	94.15 ± 0.21	95.11 ± 0.49	93.2 ± 0.33
RUSBoost+NSF(28)	**97.25 ± 0.01**	**98.25 ± 0.03**	**96.19 ± 0.01**
RUSBoost+FS-Q(15)	**99.99 ± 7 × 0.00**	**100 ± 0.00**	**99.7 ± 0.00**
RUSBoost+BE-Q(14)	**99.97 ± 0.00**	**99.99 ± 0.00**	**98.87 ± 0.00**

5   Conclusion and Future Work

We proposed a classification approach to locate FCD by using a mRMR sequential search for feature selection that avoids biased results due to imbalance issue, and provides stability to the classification stage, doing a efficient complement with the ensemble classifier with RUSBoost algorithm for this task, the results shows high performance in FCD localization in terms of G-mean, specificity and sensitivity. Thus, we conclude this approach probe to be more stable and gets better results than other proposed in literature by applying an efficient feature selection stage. Also, the mRMR-SS proved to be a solid and suitable feature selection strategy for selecting feature that explain the best a target label, because of it uses the probability distribution which obviate the imbalance, instead of variability that may be comprised for the number of examples making this kind of strategy to bias to majority class. We propose as future work, to reduce the computational cost by implementing this methodology in parallel. Other proposal is to implement the COBRA strategy for feature selection proposed by Naghibi et al. [11], and complement this feature selection stage with a posterior feature extraction stage, which also, relays on mutual information measures. In terms of classification we propose to prove other weak learners, which may present similarly results to the decision tree, but improve the computational time, or even, which may have less free parameters to be tuned.

Acknowledgments. Under grants provided by the project "Desarrollo de un sistema de apoyo al diagnóstico no invasivo de pacientes con epilepsia farmacoresistente asociada a displasias corticales cerebrales: método costo efectivo basado en procesamiento de imágenes de resonancia magnética" with code 111074455778 funded by COLCIENCIAS. J. Castañeda is partially funded by "Metodología para la segmentación automática de la corteza cerebral sobre imágenes MRI con base en características volumétricas usadas en técnicas de renderizado tridimensional por funciones de transferencia" by the Vicerrectoria de Investigación and the Maestría en ingeniría eléctrica program, both from the Universidad Tecnológica de Pereira.

References

1. Adler, S., Wagstyl, K., Gunny, R., et al.: Novel surface features for automated detection of focal cortical dysplasias in paediatric epilepsy. NeuroImage Clin. **14**, 18–27 (2017)
2. Ahmed, B., et al.: Cortical feature analysis and machine learning improves detection of "MRI-negative" focal cortical dysplasia. Epilepsy Behav. **48**, 21–28 (2015)
3. Elkan, C.: The foundations of cost-sensitive learning. In: International Joint Conference on Artificial Intelligence, vol. 17, pp. 973–978. Lawrence Erlbaum Associates Ltd. (2001)
4. He, H.: Imbalanced learning. In: Self-Adaptive Systems for Machine Intelligence, pp. 44–107 (2013)
5. Hong, S.-J., Kim, H., Schrader, D., Bernasconi, N., Bernhardt, B.C., Bernasconi, A.: Automated detection of cortical dysplasia type II in MRI-negative epilepsy. Neurology **83**(1), 48–55 (2014)
6. Hoyos-Osorio, K., Álvarez, A.M., Orozco, Á.A., Rios, J.I., Daza-Santacoloma, G.: Clustering-based undersampling to support automatic detection of focal cortical dysplasias. In: Mendoza, M., Velastín, S. (eds.) CIARP 2017. LNCS, vol. 10657, pp. 298–305. Springer, Cham (2018). https://doi.org/10.1007/978-3-319-75193-1_36
7. Najm, I.M., Tassi, L., Sarnat, H.B., Holthausen, H., Russo, G.L.: Epilepsies associated with Focal Cortical Dysplasias (FCDs). Acta Neuropathol. **128**(1), 5–19 (2014)
8. Peng, H., Long, F., Ding, C.: Feature selection based on mutual information criteria of max-dependency, max-relevance, and min-redundancy. IEEE Trans. Pattern Analy. Mach. Intell. **27**(8), 1226–1238 (2005)
9. Seiffert, C., Khoshgoftaar, T.M., Van Hulse, J., Napolitano, A.: Rusboost: a hybrid approach to alleviating class imbalance. IEEE Trans. Syst. Man Cybern. Part A Syst. Hum. **40**(1), 185–197 (2010)
10. Wiwattanadittakul, N., et al.: Location, size of focal cortical dysplasia, and age of seizure onset in children who underwent epilepsy surgery. In: EPILEPSIA, NJ, USA, vol. 58 (2017)
11. Naghibi, T., Hoffmann, S., Pfister, B.: A semidefinite programming based search strategy for feature selection with mutual information measure. IEEE Trans. Pattern Anal. Mach. Intell. **37**(8), 1529–1541 (2015)

Automated Identification and Classification of Diatoms from Water Resources

Jose Libreros[1]([⊠]) (iD), Gloria Bueno[2] (iD), Maria Trujillo[1]([⊠]) (iD), and Maria Ospina[3] (iD)

[1] Multimedia and Computer Vision Group, Universidad del Valle, Cali, Colombia
{jose.libreros,maria.trujillo}@correounivalle.edu.co
[2] Grupo de Visión y Sistemas Inteligentes, Universidad de Castilla La Mancha, Ciudad Real, Spain
gloria.bueno@uclm.es
[3] Grupo de Investigación en Biología de Plantas y Microorganismos, Universidad del Valle, Cali, Colombia
maria.ospina.gonzalez@correounivalle.edu.co

Abstract. The quantity of certain types of diatoms is used for determining water quality. Currently, a precise identification of species present in a water sample is conducted by diatomists. However, different points of view of diatomists along with different sizes and shapes that diatoms may have in samples makes diatoms identification difficult, which is required to classify them into genera to which they belong to. Additionally, chemical processes, that are applied to eliminate unwanted elements in water samples (debris, flocs, etc.) are insufficient. Thus, diatoms have to be differentiated from those structures before classifying them into a genus. In fact, researchers have a special interest on looking for different ways to perform an automated identification and classification of diatoms. In spite of applications, an automatic identification of diatom has a high level of difficulty, due to the present of unwanted elements in water samples. After diatoms have been identified, diatoms classification into genera is an additional problem.

In this paper, an automatic method for identification and classification diatoms from images is presented. The method is based on the combination of Scale and Curvature Invariant Ridge Detector (SCIRD-TS), following by a post processing method, and the use of a nested Convolutional Neural Networks (CNN). Whilst the identification approach is able to identify well-defined ridge structures, the nested CNN is able to classify a diatom into the genus to which it belongs to.

Keywords: Diatoms · Handcraft filters · Nested CNN · Paleo-environmental studies · Water quality monitoring

© Springer Nature Switzerland AG 2019
R. Vera-Rodriguez et al. (Eds.): CIARP 2018, LNCS 11401, pp. 496–503, 2019.
https://doi.org/10.1007/978-3-030-13469-3_58

1   Introduction and Related Work

Diatoms are a type of microscopic algae or plankton called phytoplankton, divided into more than twenty thousand species. They are used as paleoenvironmental indicators since the presence of certain diatom's genres indicates water purity or contamination, along with the presence of fecal matter, among others. Additionally, diatoms may be used to make historical environmental estimates of water sources, through the abundance or scarcity of some diatom individuals in water sources, such as studying of fossil deposits in lake sediments. Also, environmental variables that have been affected or dominated in the past can be tracked and estimated by identifying the present of diatoms in the source to be analysed [1]. Variations in temperature, pH or conductivity over centuries may be estimated by studying diatoms in sediments, allowing to know how climate has affected a studied area, along with to state baseline conditions from which it is possible to define a set of criteria to determine quality of water, and establish parameters by environmental regulatory bodies of some governments.

Currently, diatomists visually identify those microscopical structures from a given sample in a microscope. Visual identification of diatoms is a task mainly based on subjective with limited repeatability and requires inter-observer agreements [3,4]. However, images of different sections of water samples can be obtained connecting a camera to a microscope. Different methods for diatom identification have been studied. Identification methods based on coherent optics and holography have been also proposed. However, these methods have a high computational cost and have not been adopted as an alternative to support biologists. The use of operators invariant to translation, rotation and scale, as well as Legendre Polynomials and Principal Component Analysis have been used to identify specific genera of diatoms [6,7]. Rojas Camacho et al. [5] studied the use of a tuning method to set up the best parameters iteratively, as an optimisation problem, comparing the current result with the last result, and then validated them with Canny edge detector and a binarisation technique.

Although segmentation of structures, like diatoms, is the first step in any investigation, computer science applied to the diatoms field is focused on the classification of species. The Automatic Diatom Identification and Classification (ADIAC) project is a reference in the investigation of diatoms analysis systems [8]. In ADIAC, 171 features were used for diatom classification, using features to describe symmetry, shape, geometry and texture by the means of different descriptors. Dimitrovski et al. argue that, in ADIAC image data set, the SIFT descriptors have better results that the use of Support Vector Machines (SVM). The best results, up to 97.97% accuracy, have been obtained with 38 classes using Fourier and SIFT descriptors with a random forest classifier. Alvarez et al. [11] proposed a method to classify diatoms using Learning Vector Quantization (LVQ) neural network. According with Hawickhorst et al. [12], the use of LVQ allows lower training time that networks based on a training with backpropagation. However, if it is necessary to include more hidden units, the LVQ network will take more time. Approaches as [3,4] are based on hand-crafted or "hand-designed" methods where a set of fixed features is used. However, hand-crafted methods present limited results as in [9], where 14 classes were classified with SVMs, 10 fcv, using 44 GLCM features that describe geometric and morphological properties. They obtained an accuracy of 94.7%.

In this paper, an automated method for identification and classification of diatom from images is presented. The proposed method is based on the combination of Scale and Curvature Invariant Ridge Detector (henceforth SCIRD-TS) [2] followed by a post processing, and the use of nested Convolutional Neural Networks (CNN). An experimental evaluation is conducted using the F-Score for assessing results, using a ground truth images set. Our approach is able to segment well-defined ridge structures or Regions of Interest (henceforth, RoIs) and the nested CNN is able to classify those RoIs that have been previously segmented in an image of a water sample. The first CNN allows to discard those RoIs from well-defined structures, but which correspond to undesired elements (debris, flocs, etc.), and a second CNN classifies those RoIs containing diatoms into genera to which they belong to.

2   Identification and Classification of Diatoms

The diatoms identification method has two phases: the first phase is focused on segmentation of objects present in images, called RoIs, and the second phase is focused on identification of diatoms by classifying those RoIs depending on whether a RoI corresponds to diatom or not. Whilst the classification is done using identified RoIs as diatoms for classifying them into genera.

2.1   RoIs Segmentation

The segmentation of RoIs is based on SCIRD-TS, which is presented as a filter bank in the application domain of retinal images and it is able to identify thin structures [2]. SCIRD-TS filter bank is adapted and tests on a set of diatom images, using the implementation available at the author's web-page. SCIRD-TS filter bank, by Annunziata [2], is defined as:

$$F(x; \sigma; k) = \frac{1}{\sigma_2^2} \left[\frac{(x_2 + kx_1^2)^2}{\sigma_2^2} - 1 \right] exp \left[-\frac{x_1^2}{2\sigma_1^2} - \frac{(x_2 + kx_1^2)^2}{2\sigma_2^2} \right], \quad (1)$$

where (x_1, x_2) represents a point in the image coordinate system, k is a shape parameter and $\sigma = (\sigma_1, \sigma_2)$ corresponds to standard deviations in the Gaussian distribution, in each coordinate direction, and k, σ_1 and σ_2 are parameters provided by a user. Since quality of water sample images may vary, two segmentation methods are presented: **Method 1:** it is proposed for images with high luminosity, large diatoms size, fluorescence conditions, debris concentration of large size and low noise levels, along with diatoms have high relief. It is based on the application of SCIRD-TS with the following parameters: $\sigma_1 = [1, 2]$ with step 1, $\sigma_2 = [1, 2]$ with step 1; $k = [-0.1, 0.1]$ with step 0.1 and $\theta_{step} = 15$ and a post-processing with fixed threshold, morphological operations and filtering based on area, under the assumption that flocs are of small size, due to low noise levels. **Method 2:** it is proposed for images with high noise levels—caused by large load of particles, fragments and flocs of organic matter—, and low signal-to-noise ratio. It is based on a difference of Gaussians that is calculated by subtracting a resulted image after a single application of SCIRD-TS and a resulted image after a double application of SCIRD-TS. The first image is obtained using the set of parameters: $\sigma_1 = [1, 2]$ with step 1, $\sigma_2 = [1, 2]$ with step 1; $k = [-0.1, 0.1]$ with step 0.05 and $\theta_{step} = 15$; and the second image is obtained using the set of parameters—with a variation on σ_2—: $\sigma_1 = [1, 2]$ with step 1, $\sigma_2 = [1, 11]$ with step 3; $k = [-0.1, 0.1]$ with step 0.05 and $\theta_{step} = 15$. Since images have high presence of fluff and dust, the first image has higher intensities than the second one. Subtracting two Gaussian blurs allows to keep the spatial information conserved in the two blurred images, which is assumed to be the desired information [10]. That means to purge dust and fluff. After the difference of Gaussians, an adaptative threshold is applied following by morphological operations and filtering objects by area. Figure 1 illustrates results obtained during the different steps of the two methods.

2.2 Classification of Diatoms

After segmented RoIs, three nested Convolutional Neural Networks (henceforth, CNNs) are used to classify them into diatom and non-diatom. AlexNet, GoogLeNet and ResNet are the best known, commonly used for recognition of objects, such as animals, people and equipment, or for recognition of specialised objects through transfer learning techniques. Using a fine-tuning technique, a pre-trained CNN model is taken and modified some layers to recalculate parameters in order to learn about training images in the problem that is addressed. A nested CNN consists of a first network that allows discarding those unwanted elements that have been segmented in the segmentation phase (background and debris). RoIs classified as diatoms are taken into a second network, where they are classified according to genera to which they belong. Figure 2 shows the classification results obtained using three nested CNN models.

3   Experimental Results

The experimental evaluation is performed using two groups of images, according to the previously defined methods. Hence, the first group is composed of 96 images, obtained with a microscope Nikon Eclipse Ni-U90 and the second one is composed of 269 images, obtained with a microscope Nikon E200. The ground truth consists of the 365 images of the two groups aforementioned, with labelled regions indicating the specimens, by experts. CNN models are trained using 16,000 segmented RoIs that contain diatoms, background and debris are used. CNNs are trained with MATLAB©Deep Learning Toolbox^{TM}. The performance of the proposed segmentation methods is evaluated using two levels of quantitative strategies: pixel and diatom identification, and measure with F-Score. Table 1 shows the results in terms of pixels correctly identified and at the

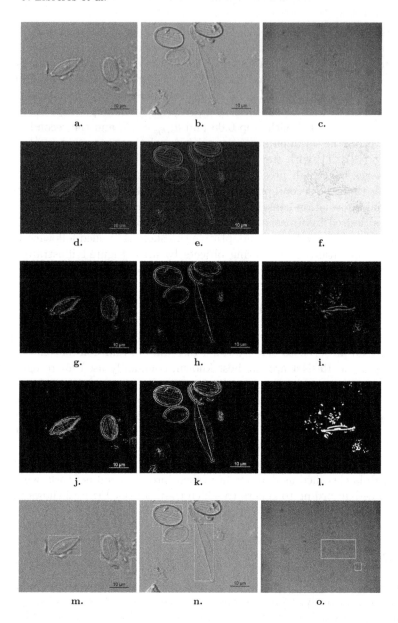

Fig. 1. Illustration of the two proposed methods: images, in the first and the second columns, have characteristics for using the *Method 1*; and the image, in the third column, has characteristics for using the *Method 2*. Up to down: The first row illustrates obtained results after applying SCIRD-TS, **e.**. The second row illustrates the difference of two Gaussians using SCIRD-TS. The third row presents obtained results after applying the threshold to SCIRD-TS images using the *Method 1* (images **g.** and **h.**) with a fixed threshold and the *Method 2* (image i) with local adaptive thresholds. The fourth row shows obtained results from morphological operations, the size of the structural elements vary between the two methods. The fifth row shows identified diatoms.

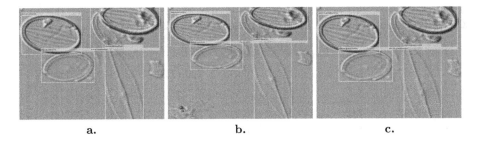

a.   b.   c.

Fig. 2. Illustration of classification results using three nested CNN models, from left to right and from top to bottom, respectively: **a. Alexnet**: *diatom, nitzscia*; *diatom, noidentified*; *diatom, nitzscia*; *diatom, noidentified*. **b. GoogLeNet**: *diatom, cocconeis*; *diatom, noint*; *diatom, cocconeis*; *diatom, nitzscia*. **c. ResNet**: *diatom, goomphonema*; *diatom, goomphonema*; *diatom, goomphonema*; *diatom, goomphonema*.

Table 1. Error analysis of segmentation results using G1 and G2, that symbolise the group 1 and the group 2 of images.

Method	Method 1 using G1		Method 2 using G2	
Level	Pixel	Diatom	Pixel	Diatom
Precision	0,74	0,77	0,56	0,58
Recall	0,78	0,94	0,71	0,89
Accuracy	0,95	0,73	0,97	0,55
F1-Score	0,75	0,84	0,62	0,70

diatom identification level. The experimental results indicate that the *Method 1* yields higher F-Scores at pixel and at diatom levels than the *Method 2*, whist the *Method 2* has higher accuracy than the *Method 1* at pixel level.

Classification tests using three nested CNN models were done using as input the RoIs obtained in the segmentation phase. Table 2 shows the architecture per network with the respective error analysis. Among the three nested CNN, AlexNet shown the best performance.

4 Final Remarks

We proposed a method for automatically identify and classify diatoms. The method combines SCIRD-TS hand-crafted filter banks with a post-processing, in two different ways depending on specific image characteristics, in order to identify RoIs. We reckon that combining detection of structures and a post-processing strategy to detect potential regions of interest, may lead to a substantial speed-up of diatom segmentation, since a post-processing allows filtering unwanted elements. Although, morphological operations and filters remove flocs of small sizes, there remain regions with flocs of large size. Those flocs cannot

Table 2. Classification error analysis at the diatom identification level using the three CNNs. G1 and G2 symbolise the group 1 and the group 2 of images.

Parameter	GoogLeNet		ResNet		AlexNet	
Nested CNN	1st CNN	2nd CNN	1st CNN	2nd CNN	1st CNN	2nd CNN
Layers	22		177		25	
Iterations	90	15	66	18	10556	8060
Epochs	1		1		4	
Valid accuracy	0,92	0,22	0,89	0,32	0,99	0,74
d_prec G1	0,84	0,04	0,60	0,03	0,84	0,48
d_recall G1	0,98	0,04	0,67	0,03	0,95	0,48
d_F1 Score G1	0,90	0,04	0,63	0,03	0,89	0,48
d_prec G2	0,76	0,04	0,74	0,01	0,77	0,53
d_recall G2	0,96	0,04	0,81	0,01	0,92	0,53
d_F1 Score G2	0,84	0,04	0,77	0,01	0,83	0,53

be removed by the above mentioned operations, because wanted structures, such as diatoms, may be affected and they may have even smaller size of unwanted structures.

Well-known CNN models were tested for classifying RoIs into diatoms and unwanted elements, such as debris or flocs. Once diatoms are identified from RoIs, a second CNN is used for classifying those diatoms into genera. AlexNet has shown the best performance among the three evaluated networks. In general, the first network, in the nested CNN models, has had a good performance which can be improved in a future work. This indicates that the proposal meets with the objective of discarding those RoIs that are not desired. It is possible that some of those RoIs have no justification in being discarded, which contributes to false negatives. We notice that the performance of second network, used to classify identified diatoms into different genera, goes down. This allows to set a horizon of improvement of the networks. It appears to be very important to maintain a balance among training images by class. While the first network has an acceptable level of balance (more than 16,000 diatom training images), the imbalance of the second network's classes is large. This is due to a scarce image bank, which makes it necessary to have a larger set of images per genus, especially with those genera with a limited number of individuals. In addition, there is a lot of work in trying other ways to increase the data, enhancing different characteristics to be learned by a network.

Acknowledgments. The first author thanks to Santander Bank for the financial support for his mobility to *Universidad de Castilla-La Mancha*, Ciudad Real, Spain.

Gloria Bueno acknowledges financial support of the Spanish Government under the Aqualitas-retos project (Ref. CTM2014-51907-C2-2-R-MINECO).

The authors acknowledge the contribution to this work of Dr. E. Peña from *Universidad del Valle*. The authors are also grateful to the anonymous reviewers for their valuable comments, suggestions and remarks, which contributed to improve the paper.

References

1. Smol, J.P., Stoermer, E.F. (eds.): The Diatoms: Applications for the Environmental and Earth Sciences, vol. 17, pp. 283–284. Cambridge University Press, Cambridge (2010)
2. Annunziata, R., Trucco, E.: Accelerating convolutional sparse coding for curvilinear structures segmentation by refining SCIRD-TS filter banks. IEEE Trans. Med. Imag. **35**, 2381–2392 (2016)
3. Bueno, G., et al.: Automated diatom classification (Part A): handcrafted feature approaches. Appl. Sci. **7**, 753 (2017)
4. Pedraza, A., Bueno, G., Deniz, O., Cristóbal, G., Blanco, S., Borrego-Ramos, M.: Automated diatom classification (Part B): a deep learning approach. Appl. Sci. **7**, 460 (2017)
5. Rojas Camacho, O., Forero, M., Menéndez, J.: A tuning method for diatom segmentation techniques. Appl. Sci. **7**, 762 (2017)
6. Pech-Pacheco, J.L., Alvarez-Borrego, J.: Optical-digital system applied to the identification of five phytoplankton species. Mar. Biol. **132**, 357–365 (1998)
7. Pappas, J.L., Stoermer, E.F.: Legendre shape descriptors and shape group determination of specimens in the Cymbella cistula species complex. Phycologia **42**, 90–97 (2003)
8. Du Buf, H., et al.: Diatom identification: a double challenge called ADIAC. In: 10th International Conference on Image Analysis and Processing, pp. 734–739 (1999)
9. Lai, Q.T.K., Lee, K.C.M., Tang, A.H.L., Wong, K.K.Y., So, H.K.H., Tsia, K.K.: High-throughput time-stretch imaging flow cytometry for multi-class classification of phytoplankton. Opt. Soc. Am. **24**, 28170–28184 (2016)
10. Davidson, M.W., Abramowitz, M.: Molecular expressions microscopy primer: digital image processing-difference of gaussians edge enhancement algorithm. Olympus America Inc., and Florida State University (2006)
11. Alvarez, T., et al.: Classification of microorganisms using image processing techniques. In: 2001 International Conference on Image Processing (Cat. No. 01CH37205), Thessaloniki, vol. 1, pp. 329–332. IEEE Conferences (2001)
12. Hawickhorst, B.A., Zahorian, S.A., Rajagopal, R.: A comparison of three neural network architectures for automatic speech recognition. In: Intelligent Engineering Systems Through Artificial Neural Networks, vol. 5, pp. 221 (1995). In: Advances in Neural Information Processing Systems. Neural Information Processing Systems Foundation Inc., La Jolla, CA, USA, pp. 1097–1105 (2012)

Novel Scene Recognition Using TrainDetector

Sebastien Mambou[(✉)] and Ondrej Krejcar

Center for Basic and Applied Research, Faculty of Informatics and Management,
University of Hradec Kralove, Rokitanskeho 62,
500 03 Hradec Kralove, Czech Republic
{jean.mambou, ondrej.krejcar}@uhk.cz

Abstract. Our ability to process the image keeps improving day by day, since the introduction of deep learning. Lastly, this contributed to the advance of object recognition through a Convolutional neural network and Place recognition, which is our concern in this paper. Through this research, it was observed a complexity in the extraction of the correct and relevant features for scene recognition. To address this issue, we extracted at the pixel level several sub-areas which contain more color intensity than other parts, and we went through each image once to build the feature representation of it. We also noticed that several available models based on Convolution Neural Network requires a Graphics Processing Units (GPU) for their implementation and are difficult to train. We propose in this paper, a novel Scene Recognition method using Single-Shot-Detector (SSD), Multi-modal Local-Receptive-Field (MM-LRF) and Extreme-Learning-Machine (ELM) that we named TrainDetector. It outperforms the state-of-the-art techniques when we apply it to three well-known scene recognition Datasets.

Keywords: SSD · MM-LRF · ELM · TrainDetector

1 Introduction

Computer vision comes with several challenges, like Place recognition and Scene recognition which are often confusing. During the past few years, we saw in several Scene recognition publications [1–3], the need to resolve in the better manner Scene classification and Scene representation. One of the distinctions between these two is that: Scene classification draws effective classifiers, and Scene representation comes with the goal of extracting discriminative features. Also, they can be divided into two main categories: learning-based features as mentioned in [4, 5] and hand-crafted elements [6]. Although, Hand-crafted methods contend census transform histogram (CENTRIST), generalized search trees (GIST) and oriented texture curves (OTC) [7]. In addition, their components investigate low-level visual information such as textual and structural information in scene images. Despite the quality of those features, they are not sufficient for more complex scene images. Moreover, some discriminating objects can be found in a scene with high probability and sometimes appear in other scenes; whereas, multiple objects may appear in separate Scenes with a similar chance. Our goal is to give as input to our finetune TrainDetector model a patch of images containing relevant features. Thus, this research proposes, a compelling semantic

© Springer Nature Switzerland AG 2019
R. Vera-Rodriguez et al. (Eds.): CIARP 2018, LNCS 11401, pp. 504–512, 2019.
https://doi.org/10.1007/978-3-030-13469-3_59

descriptor based on Single-Shot-Detector (SSD), Multi-modal Local-Receptive-Field (MM-LRF) and Extreme-Learning-Machine (ELM) that we baptized TrainDetector for scene recognition. The subsequent section of this paper is as follow: Sect. 2 introduces the related studies; Sect. 3 reveals the design proposed model; Sect. 4 presents and will discuss the experimental results; while Sect. 5 gives an adequate conclusion to our work.

2   Related Studies

In this part, a brief review is provided for three main points in our research, such as ELM, scene classification, and scene representation.

Extreme-Learning-Machine. The following model (see Fig. 1), known as Extreme Learning Machine (ELM), was first introduced in [8] with single hidden feedforward neural networks and achieves great performance in image processing.

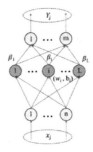

Fig. 1. The basic model of an ELM [8]

Let say; we want to learn N different samples $\{X, T\} = \{X_j, t_j\}_{j=1}^{N}$ where $X_j \in R^n$ and $t_j \in R^m$, with the activation function g(x) and we want to train a single-hidden layer feedforward neural networks (SLFNs) by having K hidden neurons. Instead of assigning values as input for hidden biases and weights, they are randomly generated in ELM. As a result, this process allows converting the nonlinear system to a linear system

$$Y_j = \sum_{i=1}^{L} \beta_i g_i(X_j) = \sum_{i=1}^{L} \beta_i g_i(X_j W_i^T + b_j) = t_j, j = 1, 2, \ldots . M \tag{1}$$

Where $X_i \in R^n$ defines the input weight vector acting as a connector between inputs nodes and i^{th} hidden neuron; and $Y_j \in R^m$ defines the output vector of jth training sample. Furthermore, g(.) represents the nonlinear activation functions; as connector between the ith hidden neuron and output neurons, we have the $\beta_i = (\beta_{i1}, \beta_{i2}, \ldots, \beta_{im})^T$ weight vector. So then, we can rewrite the previous equations as:

$$H\beta = T \tag{2}$$

Where T is the target matrix, and H can be explicitly defined as:

$$H = \begin{bmatrix} g\left(X_1 W_1^T + b_1\right) & \cdots & g\left(X_1 W_L^T + b_L\right) \\ \vdots & \cdots & \vdots \\ g\left(X_1 W_L^T + b_1\right) & \cdots & g\left(X_N W_L^T + b_L\right) \end{bmatrix} \tag{3}$$

$$\beta = \begin{bmatrix} \beta_1^T \\ \vdots \\ \beta_L^T \end{bmatrix}, \quad T = \begin{bmatrix} t_1^T \\ \vdots \\ t_N^T \end{bmatrix} \tag{4}$$

Hence, we can see that compute the value of Y (the output vector) is like finding the least-square (LS) solution to the given linear system. Considering (1), LS will be:

$$\hat{\beta} = H^{-1} \tag{5}$$

Where H^{-1} is the Moore–Penrose (MP) generalized inverse of matrix H. As mentioned by Huang, et al., we can see a great generalization performance and a considerable increase in the learning speed for ELM using such MP inverse methods.

3 Local Features and Discriminative Objects

To design a TrainDetector, in such a way that we can easily distinguish the area responsible for the extraction of local features and the one responsible for the extraction of global features. As shown (see Fig. 2), the multi-model training architecture presented in this study, goes through three main procedures: unsupervised feature representation which deals with each modality; feature fusion representation with output a feature H obtains after the combination of each features Matrix H_i where $i \in [1, 2]$; supervised featured classification performs by a Single Shot Model.

Object Detection. As mentioned before, each modality (RGB and Depth) is handled separately. Furthermore, we submit them simultaneously to a single LRF-ELM net layer, which allows us to deform to some extent a part of an object and permits to get low-level features as edges. Moreover, the output can be easily computed to provide the output of each LRF-ELM net layer (H_1^c and H_1^d) as $K \times N \cdot (1 - r + d)^2$, where K corresponds to the number of feature maps. N is the input samples, r represents the size of the receptive field and d is the input size H_1^c and H_1^d are both features matrices which are combined into a single one H as follow:

$$H = \left[H_1^c; H_1^d\right]^T \tag{6}$$

This combine matrix H of features will be submitted to our last component (SSD) which will give as out a precise batch of objects detected with high precision.

Unsupervised Feature Representations. The local receptive fields of this research framework are based on ELM, and it allows us to extract important features. As illustrated (see Fig. 3), we explained the process of learning representation which is obtained after the processing features of each modality. Our LRF-ELM can be divided into two main operations: Firstly, we randomly generate the initial Weight Matrix $\left(\hat{W}^c_{init} \text{ and } \hat{W}^d_{init}\right)$ with the open field r^2, the input size d^2. Hence, we obtain a feature map of size $(1 - r + d) \times (1 - r + d)$.

$$\hat{w}^c_{init}, \hat{w}^d_{init} \in R^{r^2}, \ \hat{W}^c_{init}, \hat{W}^d_{init} \in R^{r^2 \times t}, \ t = 1, 2, 3, \ldots T \tag{7}$$

Thus, through Singular Value Decomposition (SVD), we orthogonalize $\hat{W}^c_{init}$ and $\hat{W}^d_{init}$. Secondly, we generate the combinatorial node as follow: we assume the size of the feature map equal to the pooling map, p being the pooling size which is the distance between the edge of the pooling area and the center. Furthermore, $w^c_{p,q,t}$, $w^d_{p,q,t}$, $C^c_{i,j,t}$ and $C^d_{i,j,t}$ are respectively the combinatorial node (p, q) obtains in k^{th} pooling map and The node (i, j) obtains in the kth feature map as shown below:

$$\begin{cases} w^c_{p,q,t} = \sqrt{\sum_{i=p-e}^{p+e} \sum_{j=q-e}^{q+e} C^{2c}_{i,j,t}} \\ w^d_{p,q,t} = \sqrt{\sum_{i=p-e}^{p+e} \sum_{j=q-e}^{q+e} C^{2d}_{i,j,t}} \end{cases} \tag{8}$$

Where p, q $= 1 \ldots (1 - r + d)$ and $C^c_{i,j,t}, C^d_{i,j,t} = 0$.

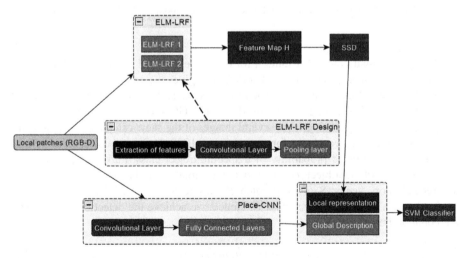

Fig. 2. The pipeline of the proposed TrainDetector approach for scene representation. We process as follow: firstly, we compute the features map by extracting relevant part of the images. Secondly, we passed our features map through our SSD to extract object score vectors, discriminative objects, and local representation. Thirdly, through a Place–CNN, we retrieve general feature and global description. Not the least, we classified our Scene.

Supervised Featured Classification. Taking as input, the combined feature obtained from the previous step, we have sufficient parameters to process the third step (SSD) which receives data directly to its convolution classifiers layers. It consists of the featured classification so that we obtain a set of score vectors at SoftMax layer.

Discriminative Objects. Obtaining Objects of an image is just one step in the process. The next step was to select among those objects the one with high discriminative factor, but before we elaborate on that, there is the need for the reader to understand what Discriminative objects means.

For this study therefore, Discriminative objects is defined as: objects that appear with a high probability of occurrence in one class but has a low probability of occurrence in other classes of the dataset. An example can be the objects marked with (+) (see Fig. 3).

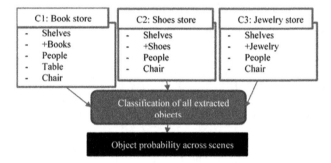

Fig. 3. The similar global layout on three different scenes which contains common objects (e.g., shelves and people) and some discriminative objects (e.g., books in the Bookstore and shoes in Shoe store).

The multinomial object distribution for each category is derived from object score vectors at the softmax layer of our network, and it gives the probability statistics of all object classes in a scene category. To be more precise, at the training time, we supplied to an ImageNet-CNN (e.g., the well-known VGGNet) a set of patches $P = [p_1, p_2, \ldots, p_i, \ldots, p_N]$ coming from several images of the same category (e.g., kitchen). At the softmax layer, we obtain for each patch a 1000-dimensional score vector representing the occurrence probability of a specific object class. Furthermore, to detect the occurrence of an object O_i in a patch of images, it is essential to compute beforehand score vector S of each patch P_i, where $S = [S_1, \ldots, S_i, \ldots S_N]$, and we randomly set a confidence level σ for S. Hence, we achieve the detection by applying the equation below:

$$\delta(x|\sigma) = h[S_i(x) - \sigma] \tag{9}$$

Where $h(x) = 1$, $x \geq 0$ and $h(x) = 0$, $x < 0$. To avoid to miss some infrequent classes, we apply the function f_O on a batch of images I and to detect the occurrence object O_i without the need of the confidence level as follows:

$$f_O(x) = \sum_{P_i \in I} S_i \tag{10}$$

Where P_i is a patch of the images I and S_i is the score vector of the patch P_i.

Considering a set of images $I_C \in ClassC$, we can compute the maximum possibility of an Object O on class C as:

$$p(O|C) = \frac{1}{N_{I_c}} \sum_{X_i \in I_C} f_O(X_i) \tag{11}$$

We set in this paper, $p(O|C)$ as the object multinomial distribution of C. (see Fig. 4) shows various objects distributions and the results after computation of $p(O|C)$ on different classes. Furthermore, we can now compute the posterior probability of scene classes by taking in account the observation of all objects and by applying the Bayes rule, we can obtain:

$$P(C_j|O_i) = \frac{p(O|C_j)p(C_j)}{\sum_j p(O|C_j)p(C_j)} \tag{12}$$

Where $p(O|C_j)$ is similar to Eq. (11) given the scene class C_j and $p(C_j)$ is a prior scene class probability.

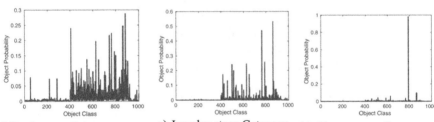

a) Book store Category   c) Jewelry store Category   b) Shoes store Category

Fig. 4. Considerable variation in object multinomial distribution in different scene categories. (a) shows that our model can get with less confidence (<0.5) a book as a discriminative object in bookstore Category, whereas in (b) the model detects shoes (shoes Store) easily and in (c) several other objects can be detected, but jewelry has the highest probability (>0.5).

4   Experiments and Comparison Table with the State-of-the-Art Methods

As mentioned in the introduction, we applied our method on three well know dataset including Scene 15 [9], the MIT Indoor 67 [10] and SUN 397 [11]. Also, to better address indoor and outdoor scene, the scene dataset SUN 397 and Scene 15 are used.

Also, MIT indoor 67 datasets are used to confirm the accuracy of our method. The following parts describe the experiment performed with those datasets.

- Scene 15 Dataset [9] which offers relevant images for indoor and outdoor scene contains 4485 gray pictures of 15 different scenes. However, it does not include a training set and a testing set, reason why we choose to compute the mean of the classification performance across splits base on five random splits. Furthermore, we use 100 training images for each category, and we use the remaining image for the test.
- MIT indoor 67 Dataset [10] is a considerable dataset which contains 15 620 color images and 15 scene categories. It offers an essential variation among groups with at least 100 images per category. As per as the process described in [10], we apply our method to 80 images from each category for training.
- Sun 397 Dataset [11] is a massive dataset which offers at least 100 images per categories and 397 scenes categories. As per as the protocol defines in [11], we trained our model on 50 training images and 50 test images.

From the above explanation, several approaches have been proposed and applied on SUN 397, MIT Indoor 67, and Scene 15. However, we are comparing those methods with our proposed method as shown in Tables 1, 2 and 3.

Table 1. Comparison of our approach with other Scene 15 dataset.

CNN based methods	Accuracy (%)
BoW [9]	74.80
LDA [9]	59.0
SMN [12]	71.7
ObjectBank [13]	80.9
SPMSM [14]	82.5
SR-LSR [13]	85.7
EMFS [62]	85.7
OUR	89.3

Table 2. Comparison of our approach with other CNN based approach on MIT Indoor 67

CNN based methods	Accuracy (%)
HybridNet [15]	70.80
PlaceNet [15]	68.24
CNNaug-SVM [17]	69.00
DSFL+CNN [16]	76.23
CFV(VGG-19) [18]	81.00
CS(VGG-19) [18]	82.24
VSAD [9]	86.20
OUR	86.79

Table 3. Comparison of our approach with another approach on SUN 397 dataset

CNN based methods	Accuracy (%)
HybridNet [15]	53.86
Places-CNN [15]	54.23
CNNaug-SVM [12]	69.00
VSAD [9]	73.00
OUR	81.1

5 Conclusion

In this paper, we have proposed a novel semantic descriptor TrainDetector framework for scene recognition, in which information of each modality has its extracted feature independently of others, and they have been combined to get the discriminative objects, local and global representation across scenes. We experimented with our framework, three benchmark scene datasets, and we demonstrated the efficiency of our approach.

Acknowledgement. The work and the contribution were supported by the SPEV project "Smart Solutions in Ubiquitous Computing Environments 2018", University of Hradec Kralove, Faculty of Informatics and Management, Czech Republic.

References

1. Luo, J., Boutell, M.: Natural scene classification using overcomplete ICA. Pattern Recognit. **38**(10), 1507–1519 (2005)
2. Mundhenk, T., Flores, A., Hoffman, H.: Classification and segmentation of orbital space based objects against terrestrial distractors for the purpose of finding holes in Shape from Motion 3D reconstruction. In: Proceedings of SPIE, vol. 9025 (2014)
3. Wang, Q., Chen, L., Shen, D.: Group-wise registration of large image dataset by hierarchical clustering and alignment. In: Proceedings of SPIE, vol. 7259, no. 35 (2009)
4. Newsam, S., Kamath, C.: Comparing shape and texture features for pattern recognition in simulation data. Electron. Imaging **5672**, 106–117 (2005)
5. Kunter, M., Knorr, S., Krutz, A., Sikora, T.: Unsupervised object segmentation for 2D to 3D conversion. In: Proceedings of SPIE, vol. 7237 (2009)
6. Yu, K., Lin, Y., Lafferty, J.: Learning image representations from the pixel level via hierarchical sparse coding. http://dblp.uni-trier.de/db/conf/cvpr/cvpr2011.html. Accessed 2011
7. Asif, U., Bennamoun, M., Sohel, F.: Efficient RGB-D object categorization using cascaded ensembles of randomized decision trees. http://dblp.uni-trier.de/db/conf/icra/icra2015.html. Accessed 2015
8. Huang, G.-B., Zhu, Q.-Y., Siew, C.-K.: Extreme learning machine: a new learning scheme of feedforward neural networks. http://ieeexplore.ieee.org/document/1380068. Accessed 2004
9. Lazebnik, S., Schmid, C., Ponce, J.: 2006 IEEE Computer Society Conference on Computer Vision and Pattern Recognition - Volume 2, CVPR 2006 (2006)
10. Quattoni, A., Torralba, A.: Recognizing indoor scenes. http://people.csail.mit.edu/torralba/publications/indoor.pdf. Accessed 2009

11. Xiao, J., Hays, J., Ehinger, K., Oliva, A., Torralba, A.: SUN database: Large-scale scene recognition from abbey to zoo. http://ieeexplore.ieee.org/document/5539970. Accessed 2010
12. Huang, G.-B., Bai, Z., Kasun, L., Vong, C.: Local receptive fields based extreme learning machine. IEEE Comput. Intell. Mag. **10**(2), 18–29 (2015)
13. Preim, B., Botha, C.: Image analysis for medical visualization. https://sciencedirect.com/science/article/pii/b9780124158733000043. Accessed 2014
14. Razavian, A., Azizpour, H., Sullivan, J., Carlsson, S.: CNN features off-the-shelf: an astounding baseline for recognition. In: Computer Vision and Pattern Recognition, pp. 512–519 (2014)
15. Zhou, B., Lapedriza, À., Xiao, J., Torralba, A., Oliva, A.: learning deep features for scene recognition using places database. https://papers.nips.cc/paper/5349-learning-deep-features-for-scene-recognition-using-places-database. Accessed 2014
16. Cimpoi, M., Maji, S., Vedaldi, A.: Deep filter banks for texture recognition and segmentation. http://dblp.uni-trier.de/db/conf/cvpr/cvpr2015.html. Accessed 2015
17. Zuo, Z., Wang, G., Shuai, B., Zhao, L., Yang, Q., Jiang, X.: Learning discriminative and shareable features for scene classification. https://link.springer.com/chapter/10.1007/978-3-319-10590-1_36. Accessed 2014
18. Xie, G.-S., Zhang, X.-Y., Yan, S., Liu, C.-L.: Hybrid CNN and dictionary-based models for scene recognition and domain adaptation. IEEE Trans. Circuits Syst. Video Technol. **27**, 1263–1274 (2016)

PointNet Evaluation for On-Road Object Detection Using a Multi-resolution Conditioning

Jose Pamplona[1(✉)], Carlos Madrigal[1], and Arturo de la Escalera[2]

[1] Artificial Vision and Photonics Lab, Instituto Tecnológico Metropolitano,
Calle 54 A #30-01, Medellín, Colombia
josepamplona212620@correo.itm.edu.co
[2] Intelligent Systems Lab, Universidad Carlos III de Madrid,
Avda. de la Universidad 30, 28911 Leganés, Spain
http://www.itm.edu.co, http://portal.uc3m.es

Abstract. On-road object detection is one of the main topics in the development of autonomous vehicles. Factors related to the diversity of classes, pose changes, occlusions, and low resolution make object detection challenging. Most of the object detection techniques which have been based on RGB images, have limitations because of the influence of environmental lighting conditions. Consequently, other sources of information have become interesting for undertaking this task. This paper proposes an on-road object detection method, which uses 3D information acquired by a LiDAR HD sensor. We evaluate a neural network architecture based on PointNet for multi-resolution 3D objects. To carry this out, a multi-resolution conditioning stage is proposed in order to optimize the performance of the PointNet architecture applied over LiDAR data. Both the training and evaluation processes are performed by using the KITTI dataset. Our approach uses low computational cost algorithms, which are based on occupancy grid maps for on-road object segmentation. The experiments show that the proposed method achieves better results than PointNet evaluated on a single resolution.

Keywords: Pedestrian detection · LiDAR · Deep learning · Resolution conditioning

1 Introduction

Traffic accidents are the first preventable death cause worldwide [8]. An emerging approach to solve this problem is autonomous driving [3]. In recent years, there has been an increasing interest in autonomous vehicles. Based on Scopus database, in 2017 more than 3,500 published papers show the interest of the researching community.

One of the greatest challenges on autonomous driving is object detection, which is needed to take driving decisions. Therefore, the autonomous vehicles have integrated diverse devices to sense their environment. Commonly, an

© Springer Nature Switzerland AG 2019
R. Vera-Rodriguez et al. (Eds.): CIARP 2018, LNCS 11401, pp. 513–520, 2019.
https://doi.org/10.1007/978-3-030-13469-3_60

autonomous vehicle has GPS, encoders, inertial measurement units, cameras, and LiDAR sensors [5]. The last two comprise an artificial vision system used for object detection applications.

Since 2010, autonomous vehicles have incorporated 3D vision systems. Those that stand out the most are LiDAR-based sensors, which reconstruct their surrounding environment in three dimensions by using a point cloud representation. Some studies examined LiDAR as an option for object detection in an autonomous driving environment by using a 2D LiDAR device [7,16]. Due to the low resolution of 2D LiDAR sensors, most of these papers use this device as a part of a sensor fusion scheme for object detection, where the main sensor is an RGB camera. This scheme is limited by hard environmental light conditions. Despite the 2D LiDAR low resolution, the papers that only use this device, achieve good results on vehicle detection, but the information is limited for detecting small objects. With the inclusion of a high definition LiDAR [14] in autonomous driving platforms, there is a growing number of researchers, who have exclusively used 3D information for on-road object detection tasks [1,6,17].

An early approach to the object detection on LiDAR data focused on hand-crafted features. Those features are extracted by using different techniques [6]. However, as it is evident from object detection tasks based on RGB images, in recent years, Deep Learning started to dominate 3D data object detection, too.

Based on a KITTI 3D object detection benchmark [], there have been a number of studies, which involve Deep Learning that has reported the best performance on different street object detection. Some methods listed in the benchmark still use RGB images, even if these are only used for 3D region proposals [9]. However, there are explorations which exclusively use LiDAR data for object detection. One of the outstanding methods is VoxelNet. This method applies voxelization of the entire point cloud in order to use it as an organized representation on a Deep Net Architecture [17]. An approach more recently presented implements a multilayer bird's eye view representation of the 3D point cloud to use it into a convolutional network [1]. Despite its results, the representations used may lose information in the transformation process, which can be essential on object detection tasks.

A novel approach for point cloud object classification and segmentation has been proposed by Qi et al. in two architectures: PointNet [10] and Point-Net++ [12], which exclusively and directly use raw point clouds. This architecture is mainly based on a symmetric function to transform the point cloud into an orderly invariant space. The PointNet architecture has shown good results on object classification in benchmarks, such as ModelNet [15]. However, this architecture has a limitation as for the number of points to be processed. This architecture uses a fixed number for input points, which makes inefficient its use on data with variable resolution. The data captured by a LIDAR sensor have different resolution for different distances to object. This entails the necessity to improve the PointNet architecture to use it in autonomous vehicle applications.

In this paper, a PointNet evaluation for on-road object detection is presented, which uses LiDAR data. Our work has 3 main blocks. The first one, a 3D object generator, which segments a LIDAR point cloud scene into 3D on-road objects. The second one, a multi-resolution conditioning stage, which adjusts each object point cloud to a specific-resolution. And the third one, six PointNet models at six different resolutions were trained.

This paper is structured as follows: Sect. 2 describes the methodology used to design our method. And Sect. 3 contains the experimental results and conclusions.

2 Framework Overview

Figure 1 represents the global architecture of our approach. Here, block 1 presents the segmentation process, block 2 represents a resolution conditioning process, and block 3 represents a multiresolution approach based on PointNet.

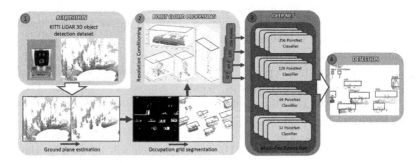

Fig. 1. General scheme of our traffic detection method by using a multi-resolution PointNet architecture.

In the following sub-sections, each block on the Fig. 1 and some tools and techniques needed for the process will be explained.

2.1 Segmentation

The elimination of the ground points is a necessary step for non-ground element segmentation. For this purpose, a modeling of ground plane is done by an algorithm named Random Sample Consensus (RANSAC) [13], which meets the model of the plane that has the higher number of points into a defined distance. The RANSAC algorithm is restricted by 3° from the plane defined by the Z axes and the sensor position height. The result of applying the algorithm is presented in Fig. 2b.

The occupation grid is an approach in 2 dimensions, which has been efficiently used on pedestrian detection [6]. Starting with the point cloud without the ground plane points, a mesh over the XY plane is established. The mesh is defined by 20 cm by 20 cm^2, taking 20 cm as a prudent distance in order to

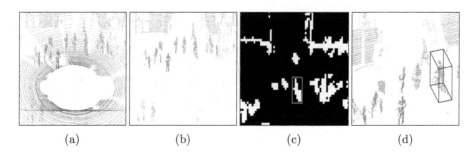

(a)   (b)   (c)   (d)

Fig. 2. Segmentation process. (a) Original LiDAR point cloud frame. (b) LiDAR point cloud frame after ground extraction. (c) Occupation grid representation with an object bounding box. (d) 3D bounding box from occupation grid.

establish two point clouds as different objects. All the points on each square of the mesh are projected into a single plane in order to use the number of points into each square as input of the occupation array. To ignore very low resolution elements, squares with less than 4 points are removed.

Figure 2c shows an occupation array where the white points represent 20 by 20 squares with more than 3 points. This array is treated by a connected region algorithm to determine those groups, which compose an object [2]. From the connected regions, the bounding boxes are extracted and these are transformed into 3D bounding boxes giving an extra margin to avoid the loss of points as it is shown in the Fig. 2d. The point cloud into each 3D bounding box is stored with the label information, into an H5 format, which will be used by the Deep Net architecture.

2.2   Resolution Conditioning

In order to take advantage of the parallel computing, the Deep Net architectures use groups of information to compute it simultaneously by reducing the processing time. This batch should be made up of information of the same size or shape. By the nature of the point cloud 3D representation, each object in a given point cloud has a different quantity of points and a group of different objects, which will have a variable shape, for that reason, a resolution conditioning is required to unify a batch size for a Deep Net training.

As our approach is based on multi-resolution, the data prepared to train our method should be separated depending on the number of points, which compose each object. As it will be explained on the deep architecture subsection, our approach uses 6 different resolutions (16, 32, 64, 128, 256, and 512 points). For objects with more than 512 points, a sub-group of 512 points is randomly selected. For objects with points between 256 and 512, 256 points randomly selected and the same is true for the rest of ranges except for objects that have less than 16 points. In this case, points are aggregated to achieve the 16 points resolution, which is made up by the most simple up-sampling procedure. This is performed repeating the existing points in the object until the desired number of points is reached. Since the objective of this paper is to evaluate the performance of the PointNet architecture, it is unwanted to improve the data, which is used in it.

2.3 PointNet Architecture for Multiple Resolution Objects

Due to the multi-resolution of the objects represented by a LiDAR point cloud, a method which can handle a highly variable point quantity is required. For this purpose, a parallel architecture of point nets, which process separately point clouds with six ranges of resolutions is established. This architecture learns specific features for each resolution, which takes advantage of the available information on each object. Besides, this approach avoids the excessive down-sampling or up-sampling, which is required by a single resolution PointNet.

The evaluation approach is made up of six PointNets, where each one will be trained with different batch shapes. Finally, in the evaluation process, the trained model will be selected depending on the quantity of points, which represents the object to be classified. This ensures that the evaluation process will not have more computation cost than a single resolution PointNet.

3   Experiments

3.1   Dataset

The data that is used on our approach was obtained from the KITTI vision benchmark suite. The dataset has 22 sequences of LiDAR data, which represents 39.2 Km in diverse autonomous driving environments. From all the data on the dataset, the 3D object detection benchmark selected 12,000 frames of tridimensional information, which was acquired by an HD LiDAR sensor [4]. From these 29 Gb of LiDAR data, over 40,000 individual objects are extracted and stored in an H5 format with its respective labels.

More than 30,000 objects in the dataset are small vehicles, which are labeled as Car-Van. This implies a highly unbalanced database, which can hinder training process. To improve this issue, new examples from the existent data were generated. It was performed by a sub-sampling process in order to simulate different acquisition distances for the same object.

The existent examples, which have enough points, are randomly sub-sampled in order to generate new objects simulating acquisitions distances of up to 70 m. This process is performed on pedestrians, cyclists, and miscellaneous elements. These classes have a low number of examples compared to the vehicles on the dataset. At the end of the process, the data set is made up of 58,566 objects on multiple resolutions. The dataset is divided in order to get 80% for the training process and 20% for the evaluation.

3.2   Training Process

The model, which is described in Subsect. 2.3, is trained in 6 stages and defined by resolution groups. In order to individually establish the models, which would process each resolution of point clouds, the training process was done by each PointNet architecture separately. The 46,853 objects in the training dataset were conditioned following the procedure described in Sect. 3.2. Since there are some objects, which appear with an extremely low resolution, a threshold of eight points was defined to leave out of the training process, that is to say, those elements with less than eight points. To increase the training data, some of the shelf methods to generate new point clouds from the existent data are applied [11]. From each training object, a new object was created through a random angle rotation over its Z axis, and other were created through adding a random level of noise moving their points from 1 cm to 4 cm. The random noise added to the new objects also gives some robustness in environments like mild frog or rainy conditions. As our approach uses 6 PointNets, the training time increases compared to a single resolution PointNet. The training time of our proposal was near to the double of a single resolution PointNet trained with 512 points, about 45 h in a basic computer with a single GTX650Ti GPU.

3.3   Evaluation Process

To assess the performance of the proposed multi-resolution approach, the Point-Net with all the testing dataset, in a single resolution architecture, was tested. In order to keep the original information of the objects with a resolution under the architecture defined, an up-sampling process by using repeated points was applied. The evaluation process of the single resolution PointNet was performed in six different resolutions, separately, in order to see the behavior of the detection across of each resolution. The results are presented in the first six rows of Table 1. As it can be seen, the low resolution objects negatively affect the performance of the PointNet object detector when it is used with 512 and 256 points. Nevertheless, the performance of this architecture is outstanding for the data used for training and evaluation. Interestingly, the results shown in Table 1 indicate that the resolution where each class achieves the better results are not the same. This means that if a model with a specific resolution is chosen, some classes would decrease their score. As far as the experimental evaluation of the multi-resolution architecture, the last row of Table 1 illustrates the performance of the proposed method.

Taken together, these results show that even when the single resolution Point-Net can have lightly better results on certain classes, our multi-resolution adaption improves the general performance in 3.5% over the 32 points resolution single PointNet, which is the best result for the single-resolution architecture.

To illustrate the performance over the KITTI dataset, in the Fig. 3 two frames are shown with the detection results.

Table 1. Classification results of PointNet on KITTI 3D object detection data set

Resolution\classes	Average precision					
	Pedestrian	Cyclist	Car-van	Truck-Tram	Misc	General
512 points	0,718	0,156	0,888	0,631	0,186	0,717
256 points	0,887	0,447	0,862	0,632	0,413	0,797
128 points	0,949	0,517	0,828	**0,828**	0,438	0,811
64 points	0,988	0,624	0,884	0,73	**0,441**	0,861
32 points	**0,993**	0,623	**0,965**	0,519	0,146	0,881
16 points	0,987	0,643	0,94	0,63	0,153	0,872
Multiple Res.	0,9899	**0,7563**	0,9507	0,7958	0,3742	**0,9068**

Fig. 3. Performance over KITTI 3D object detection dataset. Green boxes contain the good predictions (Color figure online)

4 Conclusions

The PointNet architecture was evaluated on the detection of on-road 3D objects using multiple resolutions of point cloud data, but without using any RGB information. A proposed resolution conditioning of 3D objects allowed us to use the point clouds representations of these objects on multiple specific resolution nets. This proposed approach using multiple resolutions on PointNet architecture yielded an improvement of 3.5% in general AP compared with the best performance of a single resolution approach. On the pedestrian class, the average precision of detection was 99%, but it is worth to note that this class is easily differentiable from the other objects because of its size characteristics. Future work will entail labeling process in order to increase the number of classes of the dataset, for example including classes like road signs and trees. With this, we attempt to find a more robust detector over the most common on-road objects. The labeling process should also have a data balancing purpose in order to improve the training process.

References

1. Beltran, J., Guindel, C., Moreno, F.M., Cruzado, D., Garcia, F., de la Escalera, A.: Birdnet: a 3D object detection framework from LiDAR information. arXiv preprint arXiv:1805.01195 (2018)
2. Carson, C., Belongie, S., Greenspan, H., Malik, J.: Blobworld: image segmentation using expectation-maximization and its application to image querying. IEEE Trans. Pattern Anal. Mach. Intell. **24**(8), 1026–1038 (2002)
3. Fagnant, D.J., Kockelman, K.: Preparing a nation for autonomous vehicles: opportunities, barriers and policy recommendations. Transp. Res. Part A Policy Pract. **77**, 167–181 (2015)
4. Geiger, A., Lenz, P., Urtasun, R.: Are we ready for autonomous driving? The kitti vision benchmark suite. In: 2012 IEEE Conference on Computer Vision and Pattern Recognition (CVPR), pp. 3354–3361. IEEE (2012)
5. Hwang, S., Kim, N., Choi, Y., Lee, S., Kweon, I.S.: Fast multiple objects detection and tracking fusing color camera and 3D LiDAR for intelligent vehicles. In: 2016 13th International Conference on Ubiquitous Robots and Ambient Intelligence (URAI), pp. 234–239. IEEE (2016)
6. Kidono, K., Miyasaka, T., Watanabe, A., Naito, T., Miura, J.: Pedestrian recognition using high-definition LiDAR. In: 2011 IEEE Intelligent Vehicles Symposium (IV), pp. 405–410. IEEE (2011)
7. Lin, B.Z., Lin, C.C.: Pedestrian detection by fusing 3D points and color images. In: 2016 IEEE/ACIS 15th International Conference on Computer and Information Science (ICIS), pp. 1–5. IEEE (2016)
8. Global status report on road safety 2015. World Health Organization (2015)
9. Qi, C.R., Liu, W., Wu, C., Su, H., Guibas, L.J.: Frustum pointnets for 3D object detection from RGB-D data. arXiv preprint arXiv:1711.08488 (2017)
10. Qi, C.R., Su, H., Mo, K., Guibas, L.J.: Pointnet: deep learning on point sets for 3D classification and segmentation. In: Proceedings of the Computer Vision and Pattern Recognition (CVPR), vol. 1, no. 2, p. 4. IEEE (2017)
11. Qi, C.R., Su, H., Nießner, M., Dai, A., Yan, M., Guibas, L.J.: Volumetric and multi-view CNNs for object classification on 3D data. In: Proceedings of the IEEE Conference on Computer Vision and Pattern Recognition, pp. 5648–5656 (2016)
12. Qi, C.R., Yi, L., Su, H., Guibas, L.J.: Pointnet++: deep hierarchical feature learning on point sets in a metric space. In: Advances in Neural Information Processing Systems, pp. 5099–5108 (2017)
13. Raguram, R., Frahm, J.-M., Pollefeys, M.: A comparative analysis of RANSAC techniques leading to adaptive real-time random sample consensus. In: Forsyth, D., Torr, P., Zisserman, A. (eds.) ECCV 2008. LNCS, vol. 5303, pp. 500–513. Springer, Heidelberg (2008). https://doi.org/10.1007/978-3-540-88688-4_37
14. Schwarz, B.: LiDAR: mapping the world in 3D. Nat. Photonics **4**(7), 429 (2010)
15. Wu, Z., et al.: 3D shapenets: a deep representation for volumetric shape modeling. In: CVPR, vol. 1, p. 3 (2015)
16. Xue, J.r., Wang, D., Du, S.y., Cui, D.x., Huang, Y., Zheng, N.n.: A vision-centered multi-sensor fusing approach to self-localization and obstacle perception for robotic cars. Front. Inf. Technol. Electron. Eng. **18**(1), 122–138 (2017)
17. Zhou, Y., Tuzel, O.: Voxelnet: end-to-end learning for point cloud based 3D object detection. arXiv preprint arXiv:1711.06396 (2017)

Multimodal Object Recognition Using Deep Learning Representations Extracted from Images and Smartphone Sensors

Javier Ortega Bastida, Antonio-Javier Gallego$^{(\boxtimes)}$, and Antonio Pertusa

Department of Software and Computing Systems, University of Alicante,
03690 San Vicente del Raspeig, Alicante, Spain
job5@alu.ua.es, {jgallego,pertusa}@dlsi.ua.es

Abstract. In this work, we present a multimodal approach to perform object recognition from photographs taken using smartphones. The proposed method extracts neural codes from the input image using a Convolutional Neural Network (CNN), and combines them with a series of metadata gathered from the smartphone sensors when the picture was taken. These metadata complement the visual contents and they can provide additional information in order to determine the target class. We add feature selection and metadata pre-processing, by encoding textual features, such as the kind of place where a picture was taken, using Doc2Vec in order to maintain the semantics. The deep representations extracted from images and metadata are combined with early fusion to classify samples using different machine learning methods (k-Nearest Neighbors, Random Forests and Support Vector Machines). Results show that metadata preprocessing is beneficial, SVM outperforms kNN when using neural codes on the visual information, and the combination of neural codes and metadata only improves the results slightly when the images are classified into very general categories.

Keywords: Multimodality · Object recognition · Metadata · Learning representations

1 Introduction

Object recognition is a field of computer vision that aims to identify objects or entities in images or videos. This is a highly active topic which can be particularly useful for mobile devices [7] as regards retrieving information about objects on the fly. Using supervised learning techniques such as Convolutional Neural Networks (CNN), we can build models to recognize the objects present in an image.

In order to achieve a better prediction, some recognition methods use additional information to help identify the predominant objects in images. In some cases, metadata such as the GPS location [15] are included. This leads to multimodal methods which use different information sources. Some previous

© Springer Nature Switzerland AG 2019
R. Vera-Rodriguez et al. (Eds.): CIARP 2018, LNCS 11401, pp. 521–529, 2019.
https://doi.org/10.1007/978-3-030-13469-3_61

approaches successfully combined visual descriptors with textual information [3], and also with features such as the camera metadata [2] in order to facilitate object identification. Multimodality in deep learning has also been studied for the creation of complex networks which can detect the most relevant characteristics of the different data sources. An example is the Multimodal Convolutional Neural Network [10] for matching images and sentences, or the Image-Text Multimodal Representation Learning by Adversarial Backpropagation [13].

In this work, we use the MirBot [15] dataset which contains images taken from smartphones along with their associated metadata. MirBot[1] is a collaborative object recognition system which allows users to take a photograph and select a rectangular region of interest (ROI) in which a target object is located. The image, the ROI coordinates and a series of associated metadata are sent to a server, which performs a similarity search and returns the class (a WordNet [4] synset such as chair, dog, laptop, etc.) of the most likely image in the training set. The app users can validate the system response in order to improve the classification results for future queries, and this feedback allows the database to grow continuously with new labeled images.

The metadata of the Mirbot dataset are extracted from the smartphone sensors (angle with regard to the horizontal, gyroscope, flash, GPS, etc.), reverse geocoding information (type of place, country, closest points of interest, etc.) and EXIF camera data (aperture, brightness, ISO, etc.). The gathered metadata can be used to reduce the search space. For instance, if a user takes a photograph of an elephant, it is more likely that it will be in a zoo rather than on a beach, that the angle respect to the horizontal will be close to 90°, and that the flash will be off [15].

In the present work, we extend the multimodal method from [15], and use a supervised learning classifier to perform early-fusion on the learned deep representations of both images and metadata.

The remainder of this paper is organized as follows. Section 2 describes the dataset and Sect. 3 the methodology used for multimodal classification. The evaluation results are detailed in Sect. 4. Finally, Sect. 5 addresses our conclusions and future work.

2   Dataset

As the MirBot data is dynamic and user-driven, statistics change over time. In the following, experiments refer to the dataset from October 23, 2016 for a direct comparison with the results given in [15]. On this date, 3,431 users had added 25,292 images distributed in 1,808 classes. Some objects appear more frequently than others and the classes are, therefore, highly unbalanced. Most images are categorized as objects (18,685), followed by animals (4,928), food/drinks (1,113), and plants (546).

---

[1] http://www.mirbot.com.

2.1   Metadata

Device Metadata. 29 metadata are obtained from the smartphone sensors for each image as described in [14]. These metadata correspond to the device information (model, version, etc.), geolocation data (latitude, longitude, altitude, locality, sublocality, PC, country, etc.), activation of the camera flash, and the sensor values (accelerometer, gyroscope, network status, etc.).

Gisgraphy Features. In addition, given a latitude and a longitude, reverse geocoding is performed in the server with Gisgraphy[2], which uses the GeoNames geographical database. This allows to obtain valuable data such as the feature class and code [1] that provide information about the kind of place (for example, University, Park, Restaurant, Zoo, etc). The list of the 17 Gisgraphy features can be seen in [14].

EXIF Metadata. The camera parameters of the pictures are also stored. The exchangeable image file format (EXIF) information sent to the server includes 23 parameters such as the focal length, aperture value, brightness, ISO speed, white balance, etc.

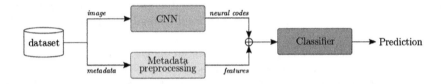

Fig. 1. Overall architecture of the proposed method.

3   Methodology

The proposed architecture for classification is summarized in Fig. 1. On the one hand, we send the input image to a CNN to generate the neural codes that represent the visual information. On the other hand, we use a series of metadata, which can either be numerical values (such as pitch, sharpness, etc.) or textual (such as country, gis feature code, gis feature class, etc.). Then, we concatenate the neural codes to the metadata features to be used as input for classification.

3.1   Neural Codes Extraction

Color images are resized to 224×224 pixels and given to a ResNet50 [6] CNN pre-trained with ImageNet and fine-tuned with the MirBot dataset. The visual features correspond to the neural codes (vectors of dimension 1,256) extracted from the last hidden layer of the CNN and normalized using ℓ_2. The details to get these visual descriptors are given in [15].

---

[2] http://www.gisgraphy.com/.

3.2   Metadata Preprocessing

MirBot metadata include numerical values, categorical data and text strings which have to be presented as sequential values to a classifier. In this work, like in [15], the features *osversion* and *model* are first removed, along with all the information related to an specific user such as its identifier.

Those metadata containing numerical values (such as pitch, sharpness, focal length, etc.) are normalized into the interval $[0, 1]$. In [15], textual metadata (such as country, gis feature code, gis feature class, etc.) were codified in a one-hot manner as they have not any specific ordering. This way, the distance between two categorical features can only be 1 if they are different or 0 if they match.

In this work, we pre-process the textual features. For example, there are some strings (such as the address) in many different languages. All these strings were translated into English. To automate this process we used the Google Translator API.

In addition, the problem of using a one-hot vector for representing textual data is that semantics are lost. In order to address this issue, differently from [15], in this work we propose to encode the categorical values using Doc2Vec [9], which is an extension of Word2Vec [12]. As its name suggests, Doc2Vec extracts a vector that represents the paragraphs and sentences, considering the context of the words in the paragraph. Doc2Vec is used instead Word2Vec because the textual strings are composed by sentences.

We used a Doc2Vec model [8] implemented in Gensim, a Python library for vector space modeling. This library includes two pre-trained models: *English Wikipedia DBOW* and *Associated Press New DBOW*. Initially, we tested the two models on our metadata with the default parameters, and the best accuracy was obtained using the Wikipedia model, consistently with the results given in [8].

Some of the metadata returned by the mobile device are codes instead of words (such as UK for United Kingdom in the country data or SCH for School in the feature code). In these cases, we determined that it was more effective to use the full name represented by the codes. In order to encode the feature codes (type of place where the picture was taken), we created a sentence by concatenating the name with its corresponding description given in [1]. For example, the code "SCH" is converted into *"School, building where instruction in one or more branches of knowledge takes place"* to be used as input for the Doc2Vec model.

With this pre-trained model, we transformed the following text features: name, locality, sublocality, admin-area, thoroughfare, gis-name, gis-adm1-name, gis-adm2-name, gis-adm3-name, country, gis-feature-code and gis-feature-class into vector embeddings. Figure 2 shows an example of the Doc2Vec processing with our dataset using t-Distributed Stochastic Neighbor Embedding (t-SNE [11]). It can be seen that similar concepts are grouped together. For example, country values of South America, Africa or Europe are close.

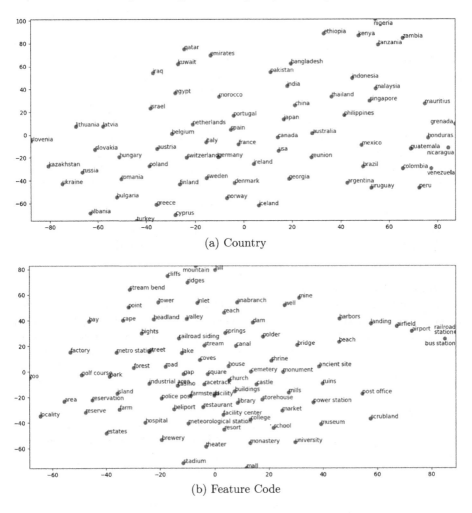

(a) Country

(b) Feature Code

Fig. 2. Document embeddings projection into a reduced space for country and feature codes using t-SNE [11].

3.3 Classification

Once the visual and metadata features are extracted, different classifiers can be used for this task. In particular, we evaluate k-Nearest Neighbors (kNN), Support Vector Machines (SVM) and Random Forests (RF). In the case of multimodal experiments, metadata features are appended to the neural codes to serve as input for the classifiers.

Different parameters for the classifiers were evaluated: kNN with $k \in [1, 100]$; SVM with $C \in [1, 1000]$; and RF with the number of trees within the range $[5, 1000]$.

4 Experiments

In this section, we evaluate the accuracy improvements offered by the new approaches presented in this paper with respect to the previous version of Mirbot [15]. We compare the results using metadata with one-hot encoding and with the preprocessed Doc2Vec model, the results with the visual features, and the combination of visual and metadata features.

Experiments were performed using a 5-fold cross validation. Only the images belonging to the classes with more than one prototype were used for evaluation (24, 794 images from 1, 180 classes). The accuracy is provided using the top-1 evaluation metric, where a true positive is considered when the class of the closest prototype matches the query class. The classification was done at three levels: Root level (with the 5 main categories: animals, food and drink, man-made objects, natural objects, and plants), the second level of the WordNet hierarchy (with 92 classes), and the leaf level (with the 1,180 classes).

Evaluation Using Metadata. Attribute selection was first performed in order to rank and select the best subset of metadata features. For this, we applied several selection methods [5]: Best First, Genetic search, Greedy Stepwise, Linear Forward Selection, Random Search, Scatter Search V1, Subset Size Forward Selection, and InfoGain. After testing all these selection techniques, we applied a voting scheme to select the best attributes, which are shown in Table 1. The rest of the attributes were ignored for the following stages.

Table 1. Selected metadata using different attribute selection methods with a voting scheme. All features are numerical values except by those pre-processed using Doc2Vec, which are marked with (*).

Sensors	Location	EXIF
pitch	reliable location	sharpness
selected area	country (*)	focal length
wifi	ocean	brightness value
flash	gis feature code (*)	color space
	gis feature class (*)	subject area

As expected, one of the most representative metadata is the feature code [1], which stores the kind of place: Zoo, Mall, University, Beach, etc.

Table 2 shows the best results for each classifier. The best results with kNN were obtained with a very low neighbor value ($k = 1$). When using RF, the highest accuracy was obtained with 150–300 trees, and SVM did not improved the accuracy with values of C larger than 10. The results obtained for the first levels of the hierarchy are surprisingly good considering that the classification is performed without any visual information and there are 1, 180 classes. An explanation for this is that the dataset is highly unbalanced. We checked the confusion matrices in order to assess that the yielded classes are varied and there is no overfitting.

Table 2. Comparison of the best results for each classifier using the metadata without preprocessing and with preprocessing.

Method	Without preprocessing			With preprocessing		
	Root	2nd level	Class	Root	2nd level	Class
kNN	73.67	51.73	7.31	75.52	52.08	**27.37**
RF	67.80	35.31	9.94	**76.96**	52.77	20.01
SVM	73.70	52.01	6.29	76.09	**54.88**	15.51

Evaluation Using Visual Features. Results using Neural Codes (NC) are shown in Table 3. The kNN classifier was already evaluated in [15], but in the present work we include RF and SVM accuracy. As can be seen, RF outperforms the results from kNN given in [15] at the class level, although SVM obtains the best results at the root level.

Table 3. Comparison of the best results for each classifier using only the NC and the multimodal data (the combination of NC and metadata).

Method	Neural codes			Multimodal data		
	Root	2nd level	Class	Root	2nd level	Class
kNN	93.72	83.60	77.70	94.36	82.19	58.28
RF	90.24	**84.24**	**78.68**	90.60	80.11	51.94
SVM	94.81	84.02	76.93	**94.98**	82.02	52.33

Evaluation Combining Metadata and Visual Features. Although the main source of information is given by the image features, metadata could complement this information. In [15], metadata were only used when the confidence was low, that is when the difference of the distances between the first and second class returned by the visual classifier was small. Here, we perform early fusion for comparison, and the results show that multimodal data is more adequate than using only the visual features at the root level (particularly using SVM), although in the other levels results clearly decrease.

5 Conclusions and Future Work

In this work, we use visual features and metadata for object recognition. Feature selection was performed to get the most suitable metadata features, and we show that encoding textual features using Doc2Vec outperforms a one-hot representation, as similar locations are also close in the vector space. In addition, we combine metadata with visual features in a early-fusion approach, although results only outperformed visual features at the root level.

Results obtained preprocessing metadata with Doc2Vec show a considerable accuracy improvement compared to the one-hot encoding used in [15]. We also show that SVM outperforms the results obtained in [15] with kNN.

It should be noted that the combination of metadata with the neural codes slightly increases the results at the root level but significantly decreases with finer levels. This may be because the metadata contains very general information that only helps identifying the highest hierarchy level.

As future work, we plan to evaluate multimodal neural networks for learning more complex relationships between data in order to improve classification at the class level.

Acknowledgment. This work was supported by the Pattern Recognition and Artificial Intelligence Group (PRAIg) from the University of Alicante, Spain.

References

1. Geonames feature codes. http://www.geonames.org/export/codes.html. Accessed 14 June 2018
2. Boutell, M., Luo, J.: Beyond pixels: exploiting camera metadata for photo classification. Pattern Recognit. **38**(6), 935–946 (2005)
3. Dinakaran, B., Annapurna, J., Kumar, C.A.: Interactive image retrieval using text and image content. Cybern. Inf. Technol. **10**(3), 20–30 (2010)
4. Fellbaum, C.: WordNet: an electronic lexical database (1998). https://doi.org/10.1139/h11-025
5. Hall, M., Frank, E., Holmes, G., Pfahringer, B., Reutemann, P., Witten, I.H.: The WEKA data mining software: an update. SIGKDD Explor. Newsl. **11**(1), 10–18 (2009)
6. He, K., Zhang, X., Ren, S., Sun, J.: Deep residual learning for image recognition. arXiv preprint arXiv:1512.03385 (2015)
7. Howard, A.G., et al.: MobileNets: Efficient Convolutional Neural Networks for Mobile Vision Applications. CoRR (2017)
8. Lau, J.H., Baldwin, T.: An empirical evaluation of doc2vec with practical insights into document embedding generation. CoRR abs/1607.05368 (2016)
9. Le, Q.V., Mikolov, T.: Distributed representations of sentences and documents. CoRR abs/1405.4053 (2014). http://arxiv.org/abs/1405.4053
10. Ma, L., Lu, Z., Shang, L., Li, H.: Multimodal convolutional neural networks for matching image and sentence. In: IEEE International Conference on Computer Vision (ICCV) (2015)
11. van der Maaten, L., Hinton, G.: Visualizing high-dimensional data using t-SNE. J. Mach. Learn. Res. **9**, 2579–2605 (2008)

12. Mikolov, T., Sutskever, I., Chen, K., Corrado, G., Dean, J.: Distributed representations of words and phrases and their compositionality. CoRR abs/1310.4546 (2013). http://arxiv.org/abs/1310.4546
13. Park, G., Im, W.: Image-text multi-modal representation learning by adversarial backpropagation. CoRR abs/1612.08354 (2016)
14. Pertusa, A., Gallego, A.-J., Bernabeu, M.: MirBot: a multimodal interactive image retrieval system. In: Sanches, J.M., Micó, L., Cardoso, J.S. (eds.) IbPRIA 2013. LNCS, vol. 7887, pp. 197–204. Springer, Heidelberg (2013). https://doi.org/10. 1007/978-3-642-38628-2_23
15. Pertusa, A., Gallego, A.J., Bernabeu, M.: MirBot: a collaborative object recognition system for smartphones using convolutional neural networks. Neurocomputing **293**, 87–99 (2018)

Object Detection on Base of Modified Convolutional Network

Alexey Alexeev[1]([✉]) [iD], Yuriy Matveev[1] [iD], and Georgy Kukharev[2] [iD]

[1] ITMO University, Saint-Petersburg, Russia
aaalexeev@corp.ifmo.ru, matveev@speechpro.com
[2] West Pomeranian University of Technology, Szczecin, Poland
gkukharev@wi.zut.edu.pl

Abstract. The work involves a new object detector using a convolutional network with a kernel of type NiN (Network in Network). Detection refers to the simultaneous localization of objects on an image and their recognition. The operation of the detector is possible on images of arbitrary size. To learn the network images 100×100 pixels are used. The proposed method has a high computational efficiency, so processing time of HD frame on a single CPU core is about 300 ms. As will be seen from the paper, a high degree of uniformity of network operations creates conditions for streaming parallel processing of data on the GPU, with an estimated operating time of less than 10 ms. Our method is resistant to small overlaps, the average quality of images of detected objects and represents the end-to-end learner model, the output of which is delimited by the boundaries and classes of objects throughout the image. In work, an open dataset of images obtained from car recorders is used to evaluate the algorithm for detecting objects. A similar approach can be used to detect and count other types of objects, for example people's faces. This method is not limited to the use of one type of objects, it is possible to simultaneously detect a mixture of objects. The algorithm of the detector was tested on our own a3net framework, without using third-party neural network programs.

Keywords: Object detection · Region proposal · CNN · NiN

1 Introduction

Recent advances in the detection of objects in images are due to the use of convolutional CNN networks in localization and recognition problems. Gradually, it was possible to significantly reduce the computational capacity of algorithms and simultaneously improve the quality of the systems. Some works divide the tasks of localization and recognition by constructing cascade systems [1], others are so-called end-to-end learning systems that allow a complete picture of

This work was financially supported by the Government of the Russian Federation (Grant 08-08).

© Springer Nature Switzerland AG 2019
R. Vera-Rodriguez et al. (Eds.): CIARP 2018, LNCS 11401, pp. 530–537, 2019.
https://doi.org/10.1007/978-3-030-13469-3_62

the detected objects in one run at the output [2]. A number of algorithms provide work with a fixed resolution of the input image or lead the latter to a predetermined size [2]. Other algorithms that do not have this limitation use a fixed number of candidates for detectable objects in each detector area [1]. Recently, the computationally costly semantic segmentation [3,4] has become popular, which allows you to select objects of interest per pixel. With known forms of objects, it is possible to superimpose the form of the object as a priori information taking into account the calculated position of the object [5]. Most algorithms work with color images. All these approaches have advantages and disadvantages. Either qualitative detection, but the presence of some limitations and low speed of work, or vice versa. The purpose of our work was to find a compromise by creating a fast end-to-end detector of a certain set of objects on images of arbitrary size running on the CPU and providing acceptable quality and speed. In this article, we describe the algorithmic refinement, which consists of the combination of NiN [6–8] as well as the significant repeatability of operations, which ultimately gives an elegant solution that allows the use of parallel stream processing. Using a non-linear convolution kernel in the form of a fully connected network allows you to provide a large stride and to abandon the pooling. Also we refused to take color into account, going to work with luminous images. The offered approaches allowed to achieve high speed of processing, comparable or exceeding speed state-of-the-art algorithms.

2   Related Work

Today, there are many methods for solving the task of detecting objects in images. A brief mention is made in the works [1,2,4,9]. To solve many of them, deep neural networks are used. In these works described the next algorithms: Fast R-CNN, Faster-CNN, YOLO, Mask R-CNN, which are using NN and which are currently the most popular algorithms in the tasks of object detection.

2.1   A Combination of Region Proposals and Object Classification

In [1] (Faster R-CNN method) two levels of CNN and one intermediate Region Proposal Network (RPN) are used. The first performs the role of calculating visual features on the last layer. The intermediate level regression over a set of 9 anchors forms a rectangle of the area and calculates the probability of the presence of objects. The third level provides a classification. This method does not require a fixed image size. In [2] (YOLO method), the emphasis is on combining all tasks to perform a one-pass detection. This is achieved using CNN, which eventually gets a set of areas and their confidence with the subsequent use of non-max suppression to filter and merge them. This allowed the authors to get high FPS on the GPU. The algorithm requires image scaling. The values of the domain detection errors do not depend on the size of the objects, which affects the quality of the definition of small objects. The method is inferior in recognition quality to the Faster R-CNN method, but has a lower false detection value. The Mask R-CNN method [4] is based on Faster R-CNN, but an instance segmentation is added. It allow make pixel presize segmentation.

2.2   CNN and Convolution via Full Connect Net

The basis of modern network methods is convolutional (CNN) networks. The standard CNN uses a set of standard linear filters with the kernel $k \in \mathbb{R}^{M,M}$. With a large stride, there are interlacing effects, which adversely affects the quality of the network. The proposed architecture uses non linear classifiers such as NiN [6–8]. At first the idea came to us on its own, later we saw a similar architecture in the works mentioned. Our differences from NiN consist in changing the last level and refusing to use the global average pooling. Instead, it uses the same convolutional NiN layer, the number of which will be determined by the size of the image. Also below is the developed algorithm of backpropagation for the entire network, since nowhere else in the works devoted to NiN did we see its description.

3   A3Net

The human visual system consists of two main subsystems - the primary V1 cortex, and then in the secondary V2 cortex [10]. Formally, our architecture follows this principle, without losing the properties of the end-to-end architecture.

3.1   Network Architecture

The neural network architecture is presented in Fig. 1a. An example of a neural network pyramid is shown in Fig. 1b.

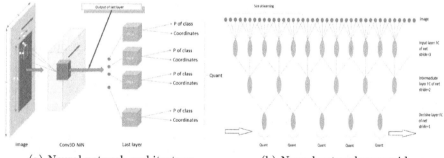

(a) Neural network architecture   (b) Neural network pyramid

Fig. 1. (a) Output classifiers are independent of each other and therefore can simultaneously display several classes of images. (b) An example of a three-layer FC neural network pyramid in one of the projections. The number of quants is proportional to the size of the image.

3.2 Working Algorithms

Network Training. Training takes place on images of fixed resolution NxN pixels. When choosing the number of layers, stride and window size, it is desirable to fully cover the NxN area to get maximum recognition efficiency. To do this, it is desirable that the fractional part of the expression be minimal ($Image_{size}$ − $kernel_{size}$ + $2padding$)/$stride$. During the training, the parameters {P, x0, y0, w, h} were calculated.

3.3 The Algorithm Backpropagation

Direct sequential pass through all layers of images (features set) by a fully connected (FC) network

$$Z_{xy}^{n+1} = FC_{w,b}^n(Z_{s*x,s*y}^n) \tag{1}$$

where Z is the input or output of FC network, n is the convolution layer, s-stride, xy-coordinates, wb-weighting coefficients of the network.

Direct passage through layers inside the FC

$$FC_{w,b}^l => FC : A \rightarrow B = a^{l+1} = \sigma(w^{l+1}a^l + b^{l+1}) \tag{2}$$

where l is the layer of a fully connected FC network.

Calculating the delta for the last layer

$$\delta^L = \nabla_a C \odot \sigma'(z^L) \tag{3}$$

where C is the cost function, $\odot$-Hadamard product, σ-non linear activation function

Calculation of delta for subsequent layers

$$\delta^l = ((w^{l+1})^T \delta^{l+1}) \odot \sigma'(z^l) \tag{4}$$

Calculating the delta for the zero layer (for use by the last layer of the next parent convolutional layer)

$$\delta^0 = ((w^1)^T \delta^1) \tag{5}$$

Accumulation of delta for the zero layer (for use by the last layer of the next parent convolutional layer)

$$\delta_n^L(sx, sy)\big|_{x=1,y=1}^{X,Y} = \delta_n^L(sx, sy) + \delta_{n+1}^0(x, y) \tag{6}$$

where XY-dimensions of the image area at the output FC_{n+1}, s-stride.

The error derivatives with respect to the weights b and w are standard.

3.4 Network Features

Optimization of Convergence. To speed up learning, is used the ADAM optimizer [11].

Initializing the Weights. The initial initialization of the weights is carried out through

$$w_{ij} = \sqrt[2]{\frac{2}{N_{l-1}}} \mathcal{N}(\mu, \sigma^2) \tag{7}$$

where N_{l-1} is the number of neurons at layer before.

Activation Functions. Standard LRELU function with $0.01x$ at the negative part. This reduces the effect of the vanishing gradient problem, in addition, the derivative of the function is not computationally resource-intensive. On the last layer of the last FC, the sin(x) activation function is selected.

Cost Function. Standard Error Function MSE (Mean squared error).

Network Settings. The problem with large batch values is poor convergence [12]. So we chose batch = 10. We also consider this low value in the low learning rate parameter value = 0.00001.

Network Regularization. The well-known dropout $r_j^l \sim Bernoulli(p)$ algorithm was not used, since it is not effective for small networks. To ensure a good generalizing ability, augmentation of images of objects was carried out during training. In particular, the center of the object was displaced within a certain window by specifying the parameters {a, b} with respect to the x and y coordinates through the uniform distribution $r_j^l \sim P(i|a, b)$. The parameters {a, b} are chosen equal to the final step of the network, $\{a, b\} = \prod_i stride(i)$.

Stop Network Training. The network stopping during training occurred with the long absence of the accuracy parameter reduction on the validation sample, the size of which was taken 2000 objects images dataset. Recognition results on a testing sample of 2,000 images dataset coincided with the results on a validation dataset.

3.5   Filtering and Merging Areas

To eliminate false detections after regression calculation of regions, their filtration occurs. The value of IoU should exceed 0.6, and the number of areas from different detections should be at least 3. The resulting zone is selected as the average area of all zones with an average central coordinate.

4   Experiments

The testing of algorithms and software took place on a PC with an x64 processor Intel (R) Core (TM) i5-2500 CPU @ 3.30 GHz, with a memory of 12 GB. The software in terms of matrix calculations was optimized, including taking into account the hardware capabilities of SSE2, but the work was done only on one core of the CPU.

4.1   Recognition

The experiments were based on the a3net framework and two datasets - MNIST and RTSD. The standard MNIST dataset was used to check the quality of the classification and the overall quality of the framework. The RTSD dataset includes 104,000 HD and FullHD images with resolution from 18 to 120 pixels. We selected only 30 types of traffic signs with limited size in the range from 30 to 85 pixels. The final size of the dataset became 28,000 traffic signs. Recognition results for MNIST and RTSD datasets showed 99.45% and 97.3% respectively.

4.2   Detection

When the object detector was working on images, the percentage of false detections was 3%. This is not so much, given that the work on improving the detector will continue.

(a) Fragment of image be-   (b) Fragment of image after   (c) Fragment image after fil-
fore localization   localization   tering areas

Fig. 2. Localization of objects in the image taken by the authors on a Nokia3 phone.

5   Conclusions

As a result of the work carried out, a new fast neural network detector of objects working on images of arbitrary size is presented. The high speed of the detector is achieved due to the use of a neural network pyramid with a high stride size. Standard CNN can not afford a big step because of the interleasing effects associated with the fact that the task of filters is to simply correlate the weight coefficients with the luminance values of the image pixels. In our architecture, a large step is possible, since the neural network components are invariant to displacements. From the shortcomings of the work of our algorithms, it is worth noting the presence of false detections (Fig. 2b), the number of which we plan to significantly reduce in the future by including one class classification algorithms, for example [13]. Also, we want to abandon the use of real images for learning and move on to using model objects, which we think give us the capsule approach [14,15], which allows to dynamically calculate the links between layers and thereby cut off the background from the zone of interest along the course of the detector. We also plan to further develop our neural network framework, include batch-normalization, softmax and crossentropy. The development of our own project helps us better understand the work of the neural network components, and also contributes to the generation of our own ideas.

A   Detailed Network Architecture

Net consists of three convolutional layers which are represented by an FC network. The actual network composition used in the work is given in the Table 1. At the output of the network, there are 150 outputs for 30 classes of RTSD dataset objects, since each class is represented by five components {p, x0, y0, width, height}. The neurons of each last FC layer with the next shift of the convolution kernel window form a column on a rectangular area. The number of such columns is determined by the number of window shifts on this convolutional network layer. The connection of these FC columns to the input of the next conv layer occurs via a fully connection between them (Fig. 3).

Table 1. Network composition

Network composition		
Conv3D 1, 10x10, stride 5	Conv3D 2, 5x5, stride 3	Conv3D 3, 5x5, stride 1
1	FC 1, 64, lrelu	FC 1, 64, lrelu	FC 1, 64, lrelu
2	FC 2, 64, lrelu	FC 2, 64, lrelu	FC 2, 64, lrelu
3	FC 3, 64, lrelu	FC 3, 64, lrelu	FC 3, 64, lrelu
4			FC 4, 150, sin

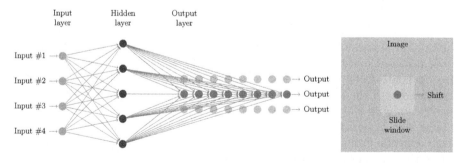

Fig. 3. Showing one of the FC networks, as well as its outputs, represented by a column. The window of the next convolutional layer is shown at the right image. Convolution is in three-dimensional space.

References

1. Ren, S., He, K., Girshick, R., Sun, J.: Faster R-CNN: towards real-time object detection with region proposal networks. ArXiv e-prints, June 2015
2. Redmon, J., Divvala, S.K., Girshick, R.B., Farhadi, A.: You only look once: unified, real-time object detection. CoRR, abs/1506.02640 (2015)
3. Long, J., Shelhamer, E., Darrell, T.: Fully convolutional networks for semantic segmentation. CoRR, abs/1411.4038 (2014)
4. He, K., Gkioxari, G., Dollár, P., Girshick, R.B.: Mask R-CNN. CoRR, abs/1703.06870 (2017)
5. Lee, H.S., Kim, K.: Simultaneous traffic sign detection and boundary estimation using convolutional neural network. CoRR, abs/1802.10019 (2018)
6. Lin, M., Chen, Q., Yan, S.: Network in network. CoRR, abs/1312.4400 (2013)
7. Pang, Y., Sun, M., Jiang, X., Li, X.: Convolution in convolution for network in network. CoRR, abs/1603.06759 (2016)
8. Chang, J., Chen, Y.: Batch-normalized maxout network in network. CoRR, abs/1511.02583 (2015)
9. Girshick, R.B.: Fast R-CNN. CoRR, abs/1504.08083 (2015)
10. Laskar, M.N.U., Giraldo, L.G.S., Schwartz, O.: Correspondence of deep neural networks and the brain for visual textures. ArXiv e-prints, June 2018
11. Kingma, D.P., Ba, J.: Adam: a method for stochastic optimization. CoRR, abs/1412.6980 (2014)
12. Keskar, N.S., Mudigere, D., Nocedal, J., Smelyanskiy, M., Tang, P.T.P.: On large-batch training for deep learning: generalization gap and sharp minima. CoRR, abs/1609.04836 (2016)
13. Perera, P., Patel, V.M.: Learning deep features for one-class classification. CoRR, abs/1801.05365 (2018)
14. Sabour, S., Frosst, N., Hinton, G.E.: Dynamic routing between capsules. CoRR, abs/1710.09829 (2017)
15. Frosst, N., Hinton, G.E., Sabour, S.: Matrix capsules with EM routing. In: International Conference on Learning Representations (2018)

Robust Fourier-Based Checkerboard Corner Detection for Camera Calibration

Benjamin Spitschan$^{(\boxtimes)}$ and Jörn Ostermann

Institut für Informationsverarbeitung (TNT), Leibniz Universität Hannover,
Appelstr. 9A, 30167 Hannover, Germany
spitschan@tnt.uni-hannover.de

Abstract. Precise localization of reference markers is crucial for the accuracy of target-based camera calibration. State-of-the art detectors, however, are sensitive to optical blur corrupting the image in many practical calibration scenarios. We propose a novel method for the sub-pixel refinement stage of common checkerboard target detectors. It uses the symmetry of checkerboard crossings and exploits the periodicity in the angular frequency domain when the origin of a polar coordinate system is centered at the crossing. The detector estimates the crossing center's sub-pixel position by minimizing spurious frequency components that occur increasingly at ever larger distances from the crossing center.

An average localization error of 0.08 px is achieved in noisy and artificially blurred synthetic images, surpassing the state of the art by 65 %. In addition, we evaluated the detector in real-world camera calibration using a public data set, achieving an reprojection error of 0.11 px compared to 0.27 px for the state of the art.

Keywords: Optical blur · Camera calibration ·
Checkerboard detection

1 Introduction

1.1 Motivation

Fiducial markers with distinct appearance properties are widely used in many computer vision tasks. Accurate localization of these markers within an image determines the performance of applications such as camera calibration, photogrammetry, or augmented reality. For calibration, checkerboard crossings, or x-corners, are superior to other markers [1] and are therefore predominantly used.

Since accurate marker localization is crucial for subsequent estimation tasks, research on their robust detection is of ongoing interest. An important aspect that has been widely ignored, though, is the influence of the focussing behavior of real lenses, i. e. optical systems not observing the pin-hole camera model. Common algorithms for calibration target detection rely on images exhibiting sharp high-contrast edges. In contrast, we imagine a scenario in which a camera focussed to far distances needs to be calibrated. In this setting, the calibration

© Springer Nature Switzerland AG 2019
R. Vera-Rodriguez et al. (Eds.): CIARP 2018, LNCS 11401, pp. 538–546, 2019.
https://doi.org/10.1007/978-3-030-13469-3_63

would usually be carried out with targets in near-range, the camera being refocussed to obtain focussed images of the target. However, the geometric imaging properties, i. e. the calibration parameters, change when the focus is moved. It is therefore desirable to accurately detect markers in unfocussed, blurred images as well.

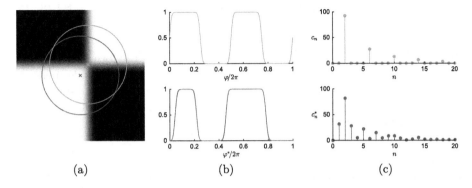

(a)   (b)   (c)

Fig. 1. (a) Decentered and blurred x-corner, (b) signal intensities along local polar angles φ (red) and φ^* (blue), and (c) corresponding magnitudes c_n and c_n^* of complex Fourier series coefficients. (Color figure online)

1.2 Related Work

Commonly, the detection of checkerboard calibration targets in images is carried out in a two-stage hierarchical fashion. First, a coarse detection is typically implemented by Harris-type corner detection [2], or by detecting crossing lines.

In the second step, the coarse localization is refined to sub-pixel accuracy. Frequently, sub-pixel x-corner locations are estimated by fitting a polynomial surface and computing the saddle point [3,4]. For edge approximation, gradient-based methods are used [5], or blurred step responses are fitted to the image [6]. Donné et al. [7] use a convolutional neural network (CNN) to train a single-step detector under different viewing angles. Previous approaches, however, often suffer from reduced precision in the presence of strong optical blur.

In [8,9] circular symmetry is used for crossing detection, which in part spurred the development of the proposed method. Further inspiration was drawn from [10] in which angular steerable filters are used as a matching template.

1.3 Contributions

To enable accurate checkerboard-crossing detection even in severely blurred images, we propose a new specialized detector comprising the following advancements:

- We restate that the projective transformation of a single checkerboard crossing is affine and derive the resulting angles at which it is perspectively distorted;

- We provide a Fourier analysis of the intensity signal of perspectively distorted x-corners subject to Gaussian blur given in polar coordinates;
- We formulate an optimization problem in the frequency domain for locating the center of an x-corner, exploiting angular periodicities;
- And we present comparative experimental results for the localization error on a set of *synthetic* images, and for reprojection errors and estimation variances of state-of-the-art camera calibration on a set of *real* images.

Structure. This paper is organized as follows: Following the formulation of the checkerboard pattern in Sect. 2, we derive its geometric distortion under perspective transformation and its blurred intensity signal. In Sect. 3, the crossing-center detection is discussed. We present a twofold experimental evaluation in Sect. 4 using synthetic images and by applying the method to camera calibration, and conclude with a discussion (Sect. 5).

2   Image Formation

We assume the calibration target plane to be centered in the xy-plane of a 3-D world coordinate system, i.e. $z = 0$, aligned with the x- and y-axes. Let intensity values $\{0, 1\}$ represent black and white, respectively. The 2-D intensity signal $s(x, y)$ of a single black/white crossing centered at the origin is given by

$$s(x, y) = \tfrac{1}{2} + \tfrac{1}{2} \operatorname{sgn}(x) \operatorname{sgn}(y), \tag{1}$$

where $\operatorname{sgn}(\cdot)$ denotes the signum function. In 3-D homogeneous coordinates, its geometry is given by two orthogonal lines

$$\boldsymbol{L}_1 \equiv (\tau_1, 0, 0, 1)^{\mathsf{T}} \quad \text{and} \quad \boldsymbol{L}_2 \equiv (0, \tau_2, 0, 1)^{\mathsf{T}}, \quad \tau_1, \tau_2 \in \mathbb{R}. \tag{2}$$

2.1   Geometric Projection

Subsequently, the common model of a projective pin-hole camera is adopted, neglecting non-linear lens distortions. Here, a projective camera is assumed with rotation $\boldsymbol{R} \equiv (r_{ij}) \in \mathbb{R}^{3 \times 3}$ and translation $\boldsymbol{T} \equiv (t_x, t_y, t_z)^{\mathsf{T}}$ (extrinsic parameters), and camera calibration matrix $\boldsymbol{K} \in \mathbb{R}^{3 \times 3}$ (intrinsic parameters). We employ a simplified calibration matrix with focal length f, vanishing skew coefficient, and a centered principal point. Hence, the projections of $\boldsymbol{L}_1$ and $\boldsymbol{L}_2$ by a projection matrix $\boldsymbol{P} \equiv \boldsymbol{K} \left[\boldsymbol{R} \,|\, \boldsymbol{T} \right]$ are

$$l_1 = \boldsymbol{P} \boldsymbol{L}_1 = \begin{pmatrix} fr_{11}\tau_1 + ft_x \\ fr_{21}\tau_1 + ft_y \\ r_{31}\tau_1 + t_z \end{pmatrix} \quad \text{and} \quad l_2 = \boldsymbol{P} \boldsymbol{L}_2 = \begin{pmatrix} fr_{12}\tau_2 + ft_x \\ fr_{22}\tau_2 + ft_y \\ r_{32}\tau_2 + t_z \end{pmatrix}, \tag{3}$$

or, after normalization to Euclidean 2-D coordinates of the image plane,

$$\hat{l}_1 = \frac{1}{r_{31}\tau_1 + t_z} \begin{pmatrix} fr_{11}\tau_1 + ft_x \\ fr_{21}\tau_1 + ft_y \end{pmatrix} \quad \text{and} \quad \hat{l}_2 = \frac{1}{r_{32}\tau_2 + t_z} \begin{pmatrix} fr_{12}\tau_2 + ft_x \\ fr_{22}\tau_2 + ft_y \end{pmatrix}. \tag{4}$$

Applying the re-parametrizations

$$\tau_1' = -\left(\frac{t_z^2}{r_{31}\tau_1} + t_z\right)^{-1} \quad \text{and} \quad \tau_2' = -\left(\frac{t_z^2}{r_{32}\tau_2} + t_z\right)^{-1} \tag{5}$$

to $\hat{l}_1$ and $\hat{l}_2$, respectively, we obtain

$$\hat{l}_1 = \begin{pmatrix} f\left(t_x - \frac{r_{11}}{r_{31}}t_z\right)\tau_1' + f\frac{t_x}{t_z} \\ f\left(t_y - \frac{r_{21}}{r_{31}}t_z\right)\tau_1' + f\frac{t_y}{t_z} \end{pmatrix} \quad \text{and} \quad \hat{l}_2 = \begin{pmatrix} f\left(t_x - \frac{r_{12}}{r_{32}}t_z\right)\tau_2' + f\frac{t_x}{t_z} \\ f\left(t_y - \frac{r_{22}}{r_{32}}t_z\right)\tau_2' + f\frac{t_y}{t_z} \end{pmatrix}, \tag{6}$$

which is a 2-D affine transformation of the straight lines

$$\boldsymbol{L}_1' \equiv (\tau_1', 0, 1)^\mathsf{T} \quad \text{and} \quad \boldsymbol{L}_2' \equiv (0, \tau_2', 1)^\mathsf{T} \tag{7}$$

in the image plane. We see that for the pair of orthogonal lines $\boldsymbol{L}_1$ and $\boldsymbol{L}_2$, the projective transform reduces to an affine one.

Using Eq. (6) we can calculate the angles β_1 and β_2 at which the projections $\hat{l}_1$ and $\hat{l}_2$, respectively, intersect the x-axis of the image plane, as

$$\beta_1 = \arctan\frac{r_{31}t_y - r_{21}t_z}{r_{31}t_x - r_{11}t_z} \quad \text{and} \quad \beta_2 = \arctan\frac{r_{32}t_y - r_{22}t_z}{r_{32}t_x - r_{12}t_z}, \tag{8}$$

and see that both lines intersect with the angle $\beta = \beta_2 - \beta_1$, $0 < \beta < \pi$, at $\boldsymbol{x}_0 \equiv (x_0, y_0)^\mathsf{T}$. Note that throughout this paper, the quadrant-aware arc tangent is used. The projected intensity at $\hat{\boldsymbol{x}} \equiv (\hat{x}, \hat{y}, 1)^\mathsf{T} = \boldsymbol{A}(x, y, 1)^\mathsf{T}$ is then

$$\hat{s}(x, y) = s(\hat{x}, \hat{y}) \tag{9}$$

or, using the backprojection $\boldsymbol{A}^{-1}\hat{\boldsymbol{x}}$ and the substitutions Eq. (8),

$$\hat{s}(x, y) = \tfrac{1}{2} + \tfrac{1}{2}\,\mathrm{sgn}\left((x - x_0)\sin\beta_2 - (y - y_0)\cos\beta_2\right) \\ \times \mathrm{sgn}\left(-(x - x_0)\sin\beta_1 + (y - y_0)\cos\beta_1\right). \tag{10}$$

We can simplify $\hat{s}(x, y)$ further by dropping the translation $\boldsymbol{x}_0$ and rotating by $-\beta_1$ such that $\hat{l}_1$ coincides with the x-axis, and obtain the aligned intensity signal

$$\hat{s}(x, y) = \tfrac{1}{2} + \tfrac{1}{2}\,\mathrm{sgn}(x - y\cot\beta)\,\mathrm{sgn}(y). \tag{11}$$

2.2   Optical Blur

The blur introduced by the optical system is commonly assumed to be Gaussian, i. e. the projected 2-D image intensity signal $\hat{s}(x, y)$ is subject to a convolution

$$\hat{s}_{\mathrm{blur}}(x, y) = \hat{s}(x, y) * g(x, y) \tag{12}$$

with a separable isotropic Gaussian blur kernel

$$g(x, y) = \frac{1}{2\sigma^2\pi}\,e^{-\frac{x^2 + y^2}{2\sigma^2}}. \tag{13}$$

Case 1: X-corner without projective transformation ($\beta = 90°$). First, we consider a simple undistorted checkerboard crossing at the origin (Eq. (1)). Carrying out the convolution yields the 2-D step response of the Gaussian kernel

$$s_{\text{blur}}(x, y) = \tfrac{1}{2} + \tfrac{1}{2} \operatorname{erf}\left(\frac{x}{\sqrt{2}\sigma}\right) \operatorname{erf}\left(\frac{y}{\sqrt{2}\sigma}\right), \tag{14}$$

where $\operatorname{erf}(\cdot)$ is the Gaussian error function [11, Eq. (7.2.1)]. We change to polar coordinates (r, φ) with $x = r\cos\varphi$, $y = r\sin\varphi$ according to

$$s_{\text{blur}}(r, \varphi) = \tfrac{1}{2} + \tfrac{1}{2} \operatorname{erf}\left(\frac{r\cos\varphi}{\sqrt{2}\sigma}\right) \operatorname{erf}\left(\frac{r\sin\varphi}{\sqrt{2}\sigma}\right) \tag{15}$$

and develop the Fourier series expansion

$$s_{\text{blur}}(r, \varphi) = \frac{a_0}{2} + \sum_{n=1}^{\infty} (a_n \cos n\varphi + b_n \sin n\varphi). \tag{16}$$

Apart from the constant offset, Eq. (15) is odd in φ, hence we immediately find $a_n = 0$ for $n = 1, 2, 3, \ldots$, and $a_0 = 1$.

Since $s_{\text{blur}}(r, \varphi)$ is π-periodic with respect to φ (cf. Fig. 1(b), top panel), its Fourier expansion is non-zero only for the doubled odd n, i.e. $n = 2, 6, 10, \ldots = 2(2k+1)$, $k \in \mathbb{N}_0$, and equals $b_n = 0$ otherwise (cf. Fig. 1(c), top panel).

Case 2: X-corner subject to projective transformation ($0 < \beta < 180°$). For $\beta \neq 90°$, $\hat{s}_{\text{blur}}(r, \varphi)$ is not odd any more, cf. Fig. 1(b), bottom panel. Due to the signal nevertheless being π-periodic, all odd coefficients still vanish, i.e. $a_n, b_n = 0$ for $n = 2k + 1$. However, the even cosine coefficients differ from zero in this case, i.e. $a_n \neq 0, n = 2k$ (cf. Fig. 1(c), bottom panel).

3   Corner Detection

Now we assume the origin of the local polar coordinate system be offset by $\boldsymbol{x}_0$ (cf. Fig. 1(a)). Using the decentered polar coordinates

$$r^*(x, y) \equiv r(x - x_0, y - y_0) = \sqrt{(x - x_0)^2 + (y - y_0)^2} \tag{17}$$

and

$$\varphi^*(x, y) \equiv \varphi(x - x_0, y - y_0) = \arctan\frac{y - y_0}{x - x_0}, \tag{18}$$

we obtain the complex Fourier coefficients

$$a_n^* + j\,b_n^* = \frac{1}{2\pi} \int_0^{2\pi} \hat{s}_{\text{blur}}(r^*, \varphi^*)\, e^{jn\varphi^*}\, d\varphi^*. \tag{19}$$

Since we saw that the Fourier components c_n are non-zero only for even n due to the π-periodicity of $\hat{s}_{\text{blur}}$, the task of localizing the center of the X-corner, viz. the estimation of the offset $\boldsymbol{x}_0 = (x_0, y_0)^{\mathsf{T}}$, is simply the problem of minimizing the magnitudes $c_n^* = |a_n^* + \mathrm{j}b_n^*|$, $n = 2k + 1$, of the odd components along the offset polar angle φ^* with respect to $\boldsymbol{x}_0$. This can be expressed as the non-linear least-squares minimization problem

$$\boldsymbol{x}_0^{\text{est}} \equiv (x_0^{\text{est}}, y_0^{\text{est}})^{\mathsf{T}} = \arg\min_{x_0, y_0} \sum_{k=0}^{\infty} \left| a_{2k+1}^* + \mathrm{j}b_{2k+1}^* \right|^2, \tag{20}$$

or, inserting Eq. (19),

$$\boldsymbol{x}_0^{\text{est}} = \arg\min_{x_0, y_0} \sum_{k=0}^{\infty} \left| \frac{1}{2\pi} \int_0^{2\pi} \hat{s}_{\text{blur}}(r^*, \varphi^*) \, \mathrm{e}^{\mathrm{j}(2k+1)\varphi^*} \, \mathrm{d}\varphi^* \right|^2 \tag{21}$$

for a particular radius r^*. To exploit image information at all radii, we integrate along r^*, wherein we account for the Jacobian determinant r^* of polar coordinates. Moreover, we introduce a weighting term $r^* \exp\left(-\frac{r^{*2}}{2\alpha^2}\right)$ such that the influence at very small ($r \ll \alpha$) and large radii ($r > \alpha$) is attenuated for improved robustness, and obtain an improved second estimate $\boldsymbol{x}_0^{\text{est2}} \equiv (x_0^{\text{est2}}, y_0^{\text{est2}})^{\mathsf{T}}$ as

$$\boldsymbol{x}_0^{\text{est2}} = \arg\min_{x_0, y_0} \sum_{k=0}^{\infty} \left| \frac{1}{2\pi} \int_0^{2\pi} \int_0^{\infty} r^{*2} \exp\left(-\frac{r^{*2}}{2\alpha^2}\right) \hat{s}_{\text{blur}}(r^*, \varphi^*) \, \mathrm{e}^{\mathrm{j}(2k+1)\varphi^*} \, \mathrm{d}r^* \, \mathrm{d}\varphi^* \right|^2. \tag{22}$$

Since the signal $\hat{s}_{\text{blur}}$ is only given on a Cartesian sampling grid, we now change to discrete positions (i, j) in a finite window of interest W of size $N \times N$ and find

$$\boldsymbol{x}_0^{\text{est2}} = \arg\min_{x_0, y_0} \sum_{k=0}^{\infty} \left| \sum_{(i,j) \in W} \frac{r^*(i,j)}{N^2} \exp\left(-\frac{r^{*2}(i,j)}{2\alpha^2}\right) \hat{s}_{\text{blur}}(i,j) \, \mathrm{e}^{\mathrm{j}(2k+1)\varphi^*(i,j)} \right|^2 \tag{23}$$

with $r^*(i,j) = \sqrt{(i - x_0)^2 + (j - y_0)^2}$ and $\varphi^*(i,j) = \arctan\frac{j - y_0}{i - x_0}$. By computing the Jacobian which is omitted here, it can be seen that Eq. (23) is locally convex within the sub-pixel search range $\|\boldsymbol{x}_0\| \leq 1/\sqrt{2}$ px.

4   Experimental Results

4.1   Synthetic Images

Grayscale images of blurred and perspectively distorted X-corners for varying blur parameter σ, distortion angle β, and sub-pixel offset (x_0, y_0) were generated. They were subsequently corrupted by additive Gaussian noise of reasonable variance $\sigma_n^2 = 25$ (w. r. t. an intensity value range of $0 \dots 255$), corresponding to a

PSNR of 34.1 dB, and quantized to 8 bit. Experiments were repeated 20× with different realizations of random noise in each iteration, with the results averaged.

In all experiments, we assumed that the first coarse localization with integer-pixel accuracy has already been done, and only evaluated the sub-pixel detection stage. The proposed method Eq. (23) was realized using MATLAB's lsqnonlin(), which implements the trust-region reflective algorithm. The analytically derived Jacobian was provided as input. An offset of $x_0 = (0, 0)$ was used as initialization, and the lower and upper bounds $\xi_l = (-0.5, -0.5)$ and $\xi_u = (0.5, 0.5)$, respectively, were imposed. A window size of $N = 81$ was used to accommodate for high blur levels. Average execution times of 0.42 s were measured on a 3.5 GHz CPU.

We benchmarked against OpenCV v3.4.1's cornerSubPix() [5] based upon Bouguet's CALTECH toolbox [3], and detectCheckerboardPoints() from MATLAB's CV System Toolbox (v8.1, R2018a) based upon Geiger et al. [12].

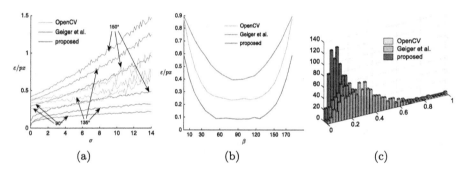

(a)   (b)   (c)

Fig. 2. *Synthetic x-corners:* Absolute localization error (a) w.r.t. blur parameter σ, and (b) w.r.t. distortion angle β at a typical blur level of $\sigma = 6$ px. (c) *Real images:* Distribution of reprojection errors e_{repr} after camera calibration.

For distortion angles $\beta = 90°, (90 \pm 45)°$, and $(90 \pm 60)°$, the absolute localization error ε averaged over all sub-pixel offsets is depicted in Fig. 2(a) as a function of the blur parameter σ. We can see that the proposed method outperforms the state of the art increasingly with the amount of blur. It was noted that the detector still performs well in blur ranges of $\sigma > 15$ px where the state-of-the-art methods fail to return meaningful results.

For $\sigma = 6$ px which was empirically determined from the Dima data set (cf. Sect. 4.2 and [13]) as a typical value for real-world applications, we varied the distortion angle β in a range from 10° to 170° (Fig. 2(b)). We find that the localization error of our method is invariant for distortions between 50° and 130°.

4.2 Application: Calibration with Checkerboard Targets

To evaluate the proposed detector for practical applications, we applied it to camera calibration with checkerboard calibration rigs. For that purpose, we chose the CALTECH Camera Calibration Toolbox for MATLAB [3], which implements the popular method by Zhang [14], and substituted the three aforementioned sub-pixel detectors for the toolbox-native one. We used the data set by Dima *et al.* [13], comprising 18-Mpx images of a target taken with a DSLR at 17 viewpoints.

In this setup, no ground truth data were available. We therefore followed the common approach to assess the detector by analysing the parameter estimation variances. The key results are presented in Table 1. It can be seen that the enhanced accuracy demonstrated in Sect. 4.1 significantly reduced the standard deviation of the estimated camera parameters in most of the cases compared to the state of the art, and reduced the mean absolute reprojection error e_{repr} by 58 %. Histograms of e_{repr} are depicted in Fig. 2(c).

Table 1. *Real images.* Impact of detection method on calibration accuracy.

Method	OpenCV [5]	Geiger *et al.* [12]	Proposed
Position/mm (SD)	5.73	11.21	**4.21**
Principal point/px (SD)	8.87	12.15	**7.09**
Radial coeff. κ_1 (SD)	0.014	**0.004**	0.005
e_{repr}/px (MAE±SD)	0.301 ± 0.215	0.265 ± 0.190	**0.112 ± 0.060**

5 Conclusions

In this paper, we presented a novel method for sub-pixel accurate estimation of the position of checkerboard crossings in images. It exploits the π-periodicity of their intensity signal in local polar coordinates, which are analyzed in the frequency domain to derive a non-linear cost function for least-squares optimization. To this end, we restated the transformation of X-corners under perspective projection.

The proposed detector was evaluated with synthetic images of blurred checkerboard crossings and compared against two widely-used state-of-the-art methods. The results show an improvement of the localization error by 65 % at minimum.

In addition, in order to demonstrate its practical advantages, our method was used as a drop-in replacement in a common checkerboard-based camera calibration toolchain, and again evaluated against both state-of-the-art detectors using a real calibration image set. We found better or—in one case—comparable results for the estimation variance, and a 58 % lower reprojection error over all experiments. We conclude that our method for detecting checkerboard crossings with very high sub-pixel accuracy will be greatly beneficial for real-world applications.

References

1. Mallon, J., Whelan, P.F.: Which pattern? Biasing aspects of planar calibration patterns and detection methods. PRL **28**(8), 921–930 (2007)
2. Harris, C., Stephens, M.J.: A combined corner and edge detector. In: Proceedings of the Alvey Vision Conference, pp. 147–151 (1988)
3. Bouguet, J.-Y.: Camera Calibration Toolbox for Matlab (2017). http://www.vision. caltech.edu/bouguetj/calib_doc
4. Fürsattel, P., et al.: OCPAD – occluded checkerboard pattern detector. In: Proceedings of the WACV. IEEE, March 2016
5. Opencv, Open Source Computer Vision library, version 3.4.1 (2018). http:// opencv.org/
6. Ha, H., et al.: Accurate camera calibration robust to defocus using a smartphone. In: Proceedings of the ICCV. IEEE (2015)
7. Donné, S., et al.: MATE: machine learning for adaptive calibration template detection. Sensors **16**(11), 1858 (2016)
8. Bennett, S., Lasenby, J.: ChESS – quick and robust detection of chess-board features. Comput. Vis. Image Underst. **118**, 197–210 (2014)
9. Bok, Y., et al.: Automated checkerboard detection and indexing using circular boundaries. PRL **71**, 66–72 (2016)
10. Mühlich, M., et al.: Design and implementation of multisteerable matched filters. IEEE Trans. Patt. Anal. Mach. Intell. **34**(2), 279–291 (2012)
11. NIST. Handbook of Mathematical Functions. Cambridge University Press, Cambridge (2010)
12. Geiger, A., et al.: Automatic camera and range sensor calibration using a single shot. In: Proceedings of the ICRA. IEEE, May 2012
13. Dima, E., et al.: Assessment of multi-camera calibration algorithms for two-dimensional camera arrays relative to ground truth position and direction. In: Proceedings of the 3DTV-Conference. IEEE, July 2016
14. Zhang, Z.: A flexible new technique for camera calibration. IEEE Trans. Pattern Anal. Mach. Intell. **22**(11), 1330–1334 (2000)

Spatiotemporal CNNs for Pornography Detection in Videos

Murilo Varges da Silva[1,2(✉)] ⓘ and Aparecido Nilceu Marana[3] ⓘ

[1] UFSCar - Federal University of Sao Carlos, Sao Carlos, SP, Brazil
[2] IFSP - Federal Institute of Education of Sao Paulo, Birigui, SP, Brazil
murilo.varges@ifsp.edu.br
[3] UNESP - Sao Paulo State University, Bauru, SP, Brazil
nilceu.marana@unesp.br

Abstract. With the increasing use of social networks and mobile devices, the number of videos posted on the Internet is growing exponentially. Among the inappropriate contents published on the Internet, pornography is one of the most worrying as it can be accessed by teens and children. Two spatiotemporal CNNs, VGG-C3D CNN and ResNet R(2+1)D CNN, were assessed for pornography detection in videos in the present study. Experimental results using the Pornography-800 dataset showed that these spatiotemporal CNNs performed better than some state-of-the-art methods based on bag of visual words and are competitive with other CNN-based approaches, reaching accuracy of 95.1%.

Keywords: Pornography detection · Spatiotemporal CNN · 3D CNN · Video classification

1 Introduction

With the increasing use of social networks and mobile devices, the number of videos posted on the Internet is growing exponentially. Thus, the recognition of videos with unwanted content (e.g. pornography, violence, scenes with blood, etc.) becomes essential. Pornography is probably the type of unwanted content that causes most problems because it is inappropriate for some ages, inappropriate for some environments (e.g. public places, schools, workplace), and unwanted by some people who do not like to be exposed to this material. Another important aspect is that some of this content might be prohibited by law from being produced and disseminated, as in the case of child pornography, which is considered a crime in several countries.

Video understanding is a challenging task in the fields of Computer Vision and Pattern Recognition and has been studied for many decades. Much of the research developed in these areas are focused on creating spatiotemporal descriptors for video understanding. The most relevant studies that deal with hand-crafted feature extraction from videos include those based on spatiotemporal interest points: STIPs (HARRIS3D) [12], SIFT-3D [17], HOG3D [10], MBH [6]

© Springer Nature Switzerland AG 2019
R. Vera-Rodriguez et al. (Eds.): CIARP 2018, LNCS 11401, pp. 547–555, 2019.
https://doi.org/10.1007/978-3-030-13469-3_64

and Cuboids [7]. These efforts are based on 2D image descriptors and use different encoding schemes based in pyramids and histograms. In addition to these, another very important state-of-the-art method is the improved Dense Trajectories (iDT) [24], which presents good performance in tasks related to video understanding.

The great development of methodologies that use deep learning in still-image recognition tasks, driven by the development of the AlexNet network [11], increased the interest in research using deep learning techniques applied to videos. Some approaches proposed to apply trained CNN in images to extract features from individual video frames and then fuse these features into a descriptor with fixed size using pooling and high-dimensional encoding. Another alternative is to use 3D spatiotemporal CNNs. Ji et al. [8], for instance, proposed 3D CNN spatiotemporal convolutions to recognize human actions in videos. Simonyan and Zisserman [18] introduced a new influential two-stream framework approach based on CNNs, in which deep motion features extracted from the optical flow are fused with traditional CNN activations computed from RGB input. In [16] the authors use this two-stream framework approach based on CNNs to detect pornography in videos.

Two spatiotemporal-based CNNs proposed in literature, VGG-C3D CNN [21] and ResNet R(2+1)D CNN [22], were used in the present study for pornography detection in videos. To the best of our knowledge, this is the first study to use 3D CNN to detect pornography in videos.

2   VGG C3D CNN

In [21] the authors realized that a homogeneous setting with convolution kernels of $3 \times 3 \times 3$ is the best option for 3D CNNs. This is similar to the 2D CNNs proposed in [19], which are also known as VGG. By using a dataset with a huge amount of data, it is possible to train a 3D CNN with $3 \times 3 \times 3$ kernel as deep as possible, due to the amount of memory available in current GPUs. The authors designed the 3D CNN to have 8 convolution layers, 5 pooling layers, followed by two fully connected layers, and a softmax output layer. Figure 1 shows the 3D Spatiotemporal CNN proposed in [21] (called VGG-C3D in this paper). The 3D convolution filters of VGG-C3D are of dimension $3 \times 3 \times 3$ with stride $1 \times 1 \times 1$. In turn, the 3D pooling layers are $2 \times 2 \times 2$ with stride also of $2 \times 2 \times 2$, except for pool1 which presents kernel size of $1 \times 2 \times 2$ and stride $1 \times 2 \times 2$ with the intention of preserving the temporal information at the early phase. Each fully connected layer has 4,096 output units.

The model provided by the authors [21], which was trained on the Sports-1M dataset in train split, was used in the present study. Sports-1M was created by Google Research and Stanford Computer Science Department and contains 1,133,158 videos of 487 sports classes. Since Sports-1M has many long videos, five 2-seconds long clips were randomly extracted from every training video. The clips were then resized to have a frame size of 128×171. During the training phase, the clips were randomly cropped into $16 \times 112 \times 112$ crops for spatial and

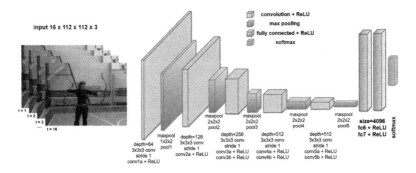

Fig. 1. VGG-C3D architecture based in VGG-11 [19] proposed by [21].

temporal jittering, and horizontally flipped with 50% probability. The training was done by Stochastic Gradient Descent (SGD) with a minibatch size of 30 examples. The initial learning rate was of 0.003 and was divided by 2 every 150 K iterations. The optimization was stopped at 1.9 M iterations (about 13 epochs).

After training, the VGG-C3D may be used as feature extractor. In order to extract features, a video needs to be split into clips with 16 frames in length. For the present study, clips with an 8-frame overlap between two consecutive clips were used. After that, the clips were submitted to the VGG-C3D to extract **fc6** activations. Each video may have an arbitrary number of clips, so to generate only one descriptor for each video the **fc6** activations were averaged to form a 4,096-sized descriptor, followed by L2-normalization.

To evaluate the VGG-C3D features extracted from the Pornography-800 dataset [2], fc6 features were extracted from all clips and then projected to 2D spacing using the t-SNE [13] (Fig. 2a) and PCA (Fig. 2b). It is worth noting that no fine-tuning was conducted to verify if the model showed good generalization capability across the datasets. Figure 2 illustrates that the VGG-C3D features are semantically separable, although samples of pornography and difficult non-pornography presented some overlapping.

3   ResNet R(2 + 1)D CNN

Recent studies have indicated that replacing 3D convolutions by two operations, a 2D spatial convolution and a 1D temporal convolution, can improve the efficiency of 3D CNN models. In [22], the authors designed a new spatiotemporal convolutional block, R(2 + 1)D, that explicitly factorizes 3D convolution into two separate and successive operations, a 2D spatial convolution and a 1D temporal convolution. Using this architecture, we can add nonlinear rectification like ReLU between 2D and 1D convolution. This would double the number of nonlinearities compared to a 3D CNN, but with the same number of parameters to optimize, allowing the model to represent more complex functions. Moreover,

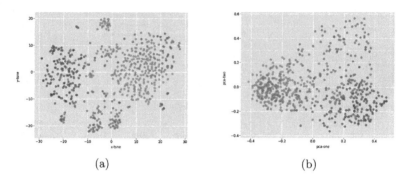

(a)   (b)

Fig. 2. Feature embedding visualizations of VGG-C3D on samples from Pornography-800 dataset: pornography (blue), easy non-pornography (red) and difficult non-pornography (green). (a) Using t-SNE and (b) Using PCA. (Color figure online)

the decomposition into two convolutions makes the optimization process easier, producing in practice less training loss and less test loss.

Another method proposed by [25] showed that replacing 3D convolutions with spatiotemporal-separable 3D convolutions makes the model 1.5× more computationally efficient (in terms of FLOPS) than 3D convolutions.

Experiments performed in [22] demonstrated that ResNets adopting homogeneous $(2 + 1)$D blocks in all layers, achieved state-of-the-art performance on both Kinetics and Sports-1M datasets.

Spatiotemporal decomposition can be applied to any 3D convolutional layer. An illustration of this decomposition is given in Fig. 3 for the simplified setting, where the input tensor contains a single channel.

(a)   (b)

Fig. 3. 3D convolution *vs* $(2 + 1)$D convolution. (a) Full 3D convolution using a filter of the size $t \times d \times d$, where t denotes the temporal extent and d is the spatial width and height. (b) A $(2 + 1)$D convolutional block, where a spatial 2D convolution is followed by a temporal 1D convolution. Adapted from [22].

The architecture proposed in [22] was applied in the present study. This relatively simple structure was based on deep residual networks, which have shown good performance. Table 1 presents the architecture details of R$(2 + 1)$D.

Table 1. R(2 + 1)D architecture [22] used in the present study.

Layer name	Output size	34-layer
conv1	$L \times 5 \times 56$	$3 \times 7 \times 7, 64$, stride $1 \times 2 \times 2$
conv2	$L \times 56 \times 56$	$\begin{bmatrix} 3 \times 3 \times 3, 64 \\ 3 \times 3 \times 3, 64 \end{bmatrix} \times 3$
conv3	$\frac{L}{2} \times 28 \times 28$	$\begin{bmatrix} 3 \times 3 \times 3, 128 \\ 3 \times 3 \times 3, 128 \end{bmatrix} \times 4$
conv4	$\frac{L}{4} \times 14 \times 14$	$\begin{bmatrix} 3 \times 3 \times 3, 256 \\ 3 \times 3 \times 3, 256 \end{bmatrix} \times 6$
conv5	$\frac{L}{8} \times 7 \times 7$	$\begin{bmatrix} 3 \times 3 \times 3, 512 \\ 3 \times 3 \times 3, 512 \end{bmatrix} \times 3$
	$1 \times 1 \times 1$	Spatiotemporal pooling, fc layer with softmax

Experiments were conducted using a model that had been pre-trained on Kinetics dataset. A transfer learning technique was applied to fine-tune the model on the Pornography-800 dataset. The R(2 + 1)D network used had 34 layers and videos frames were resized to 128 × 171, with each clip generated by randomly cropping 112×112 windows. A total of 32 consecutive frames were randomly sampled from each video applying temporal jittering during the process of fine-tuning.

Although Pornography-800 has only about 640 training videos in each split, epoch size was set at 2,560 for temporal jittering considering 4 clips for each training video per epoch. This setup was chosen to optimize the training time since the videos have different sizes.

Batch normalization was applied to all convolutional layers and mini-batch size was set to 4 clips due to GPU memory limitations. The initial learning rate was set to 0.0001 and divided by 10 every 2 epochs, while the process of fine-tuning was conducted in 8 epochs. In the classification phase, the videos were split into 32-frame long clips. ResNet R(2 + 1)D CNN was used on clips with 16 frames that overlap between two consecutive clips to extract features and for softmax classification. Each video can have an arbitrary number of clips, so average pooling on softmax probabilities was conducted to aggregate predictions over clips to obtain video-level prediction.

4 Experiments and Results

The Pornography-800 dataset [2] was chosen to evaluate the 3D CNNs used in the present study. This dataset contains 800 videos, representing a total of 80 h, which encompass 400 pornography videos and 400 non-pornography videos. Figure 4 shows some selected frames from a small sample of this dataset, illustrating the diversity and challenges posed.

Fig. 4. Pornography-800 dataset [2]. Top row: pornographic videos. Middle row: challenging cases of non-pornographic videos. Bottom row: easy cases of non-pornographic videos.

The VGG-C3D network evaluated in the present study was developed using Caffe [9] and the ResNet R(2+1)D architecture was developed using Caffe2[1]. All experiments were run on a computer with an Intel Xeon E5-2630 v3 2.40 GHz processor, 32 GB RAM and a NVIDIA Titan XP GPU with 12 GB of memory. The results presented are the mean value obtained from the 5 splits of the Pornography-800 dataset using 5-fold-cross-validation protocol (640 videos in training set and 160 in the test set on each fold, which is the same protocol proposed in [2]).

Table 2 shows the accuracy of both approaches: VGG-C3D with a Linear SVM classifier and ResNet R(2 + 1)D CNN with softmax classifier. The VGG-C3D architecture with a linear SVM classifier achieved a better performance, with accuracy of 95.1%, while with the ResNet R(2 + 1)D architecture using the softmax classifier achieved accuracy of 91.8%.

Table 2. Results achieved by VGG-C3D (Sect. 2) and ResNet R(2 + 1)D (Sect. 3) on the Pornography-800 dataset.

Approach	Accuracy (%)
VGG-C3D + Linear SVM	**95.1 ± 1.7**
ResNet R(2 + 1)D CNN + Softmax	91.8 ± 2.1

Table 3 presents some results reported in the literature obtained applying other methods to the Pornography-800 database. As observed in Tables 2 and 3 the CNN-based methods outperform all methods based on bag of visual words.

---

[1] https://caffe2.ai/.

Table 3. Results obtained by state-of-the-art methods for pornography video detection on the Pornography-800 dataset.

Approach	Reference	Year	Accuracy (%)
BoVW-Based	Avila et al. [1]	2011	87.1% ± 2.0
	Valle et al. [23]	2011	91.9% ± NA
	Souza et al. [20]	2012	91.0% ± NA
	Avila et al. [2]	2013	89.5% ± 1.0
	Caetano et al. [3]	2014	90.9% ± 1.0
	Caetano et al. [4]	2016	92.4% ± 2.0
	Moreira et al. [14]	2016	95.0 % ± 1.3
2D CNN RGB	Moustafa [15]	2015	94.1% ± 2.0
	Perez et al. [16]	2017	97.0% ± 2.0
2D CNN OF	Perez et al. [16]	2017	95.8% ± 2.0
Two Stream CNN	Perez et al. [16]	2017	**97.9% ± 1.5**

5   Conclusion and Future Work

The experimental results obtained in the present study on the Pornography-800 dataset showed that the spatiotemporal CNNs adopted (VGG-C3D and ResNet R(2 + 1)D) performed better than all methods based on bag of visual words compared. Moreover, these spatiotemporal CNNs were competitive with other CNN-based approaches observed, reaching accuracy of 95.1%.

With recent creation and availability of large video databases, along with the evolution of GPUs, we believe that 3D CNNs will be able to achieve a state-of-the-art level in video understanding tasks, similar to what happened with the launch of AlexNet. The proof of this is that a 3D CNN (I3D) [5] has recently reached the best result in the Kinetics database.

Future research is expected to: apply VGG-C3D and ResNet R(2+1)D CNNs to larger databases; fuse VGG-C3D features with the iDT; to evaluate the behavior of the 3D CNNs using the Optical Flow and the fusion with the RGB; and use the ResNet R(2 + 1)D CNN as feature extractor.

Acknowledgments. We thank NVIDIA Corporation for the donation of the GPU used in this study. This study was financed in part by CAPES - Brazil (Finance Code 001).

References

1. Avila, S., Thome, N., Cord, M., Valle, E., Araújo, A.D.A.: Bossa: extended bow formalism for image classification. In: 18th IEEE ICIP, pp. 2909–2912 (2011)
2. Avila, S., Thome, N., Cord, M., Valle, E., Araújo, A.D.A.: Pooling in image representation: the visual codeword point of view. Comput. Vis. Image Underst. **117**(5), 453–465 (2013)
3. Caetano, C., Avila, S., Guimarães, S., Araújo, A.D.A.: Pornography detection using BossaNova video descriptor. In: 2014 22nd (EUSIPCO), pp. 1681–1685 (2014)
4. Caetano, C., Avila, S., Schwartz, W.R., Guimarães, S.J.F., Araújo, A.D.A.: A mid-level video representation based on binary descriptors: a case study for pornography detection. CoRR abs/1605.03804 (2016)
5. Carreira, J., Zisserman, A.: Quo vadis, action recognition? A new model and the kinetics dataset. CoRR abs/1705.07750 (2017)
6. Dalal, N., Triggs, B., Schmid, C.: Human detection using oriented histograms of flow and appearance. In: Leonardis, A., Bischof, H., Pinz, A. (eds.) ECCV 2006. LNCS, vol. 3952, pp. 428–441. Springer, Heidelberg (2006). https://doi.org/10.1007/11744047_33
7. Dollar, P., Rabaud, V., Cottrell, G., Belongie, S.: Behavior recognition via sparse spatio-temporal features. In: 2005 IEEE International Workshop on Visual Surveillance and Performance Evaluation of Tracking and Surveillance, pp. 65–72 (2005)
8. Ji, S., Xu, W., Yang, M., Yu, K.: 3D convolutional neural networks for human action recognition. IEEE Trans. Pattern Anal. Mach. Intell. **35**(1), 221–231 (2013)
9. Jia, Y., et al.: Caffe: convolutional architecture for fast feature embedding. arXiv preprint arXiv:1408.5093 (2014)
10. Klaser, A., Marszalek, M., Schmid, C.: A spatio-temporal descriptor based on 3D-gradients. In: Everingham, M., Needham, C., Fraile, R. (eds.) BMVC 2008–19th British Machine Vision Conference, pp. 275:1–10. British Machine Vision Association, Leeds, United Kingdom (2008)
11. Krizhevsky, A., Sutskever, I., Hinton, G.E.: Imagenet classification with deep convolutional neural networks. In: Proceedings of the 25th International Conference on Neural Information Processing Systems - Volume 1, NIPS 2012, pp. 1097–1105. Curran Associates Inc., USA (2012)
12. Laptev, I., Lindeberg, T.: Space-time interest points. In: Proceedings Ninth IEEE International Conference on Computer Vision, vol. 1, pp. 432–439 (2003)
13. van der Maaten, L., Hinton, G.: Visualizing data using t-SNE. J. Mach. Learn. Res. **9**, 2579–2605 (2008)
14. Moreira, D., et al.: Pornography classification: the hidden clues invideo spacetime. Forensic Sci. Int. **268**, 46–61 (2016)
15. Moustafa, M.: Applying deep learning to classify pornographic images and videos. CoRR abs/1511.08899 (2015)
16. Perez, M., et al.: Video pornography detection through deep learning techniques and motion information. Neurocomputing **230**, 279–293 (2017)
17. Scovanner, P., Ali, S., Shah, M.: A 3-dimensional sift descriptor and its application to action recognition. In: Proceedings of the 15th ACM International Conference on Multimedia, MM 2007, pp. 357–360. ACM, New York (2007)
18. Simonyan, K., Zisserman, A.: Two-stream convolutional networks for action recognition in videos. In: Ghahramani, Z., Welling, M., Cortes, C., Lawrence, N.D., Weinberger, K.Q. (eds.) Advances in Neural Information Processing Systems 27, pp. 568–576. Curran Associates, Inc. (2014)

19. Simonyan, K., Zisserman, A.: Very deep convolutional networks for large-scale image recognition. CoRR abs/1409.1556 (2014)
20. de Souza, F.D.M., Valle, E., Cámara-Chávez, G., Araújo, A.: An evaluation on color invariant based local spatiotemporal features for action recognition. In: IEEE SIBGRAPI (2012)
21. Tran, D., Bourdev, L., Fergus, R., Torresani, L., Paluri, M.: Learning spatiotemporal features with 3d convolutional networks. In: IEEE ICCV, pp. 4489–4497. Washington, DC, USA (2015)
22. Tran, D., Wang, H., Torresani, L., Ray, J., LeCun, Y., Paluri, M.: A closer look at spatiotemporal convolutions for action recognition. CoRR abs/1711.11248 (2017)
23. Valle, E., de Avila, S., da Luz Jr., A., de Souza, F., Coelho, M., Araújo, A.: Content-based filtering for video sharing social networks. CoRR abs/1101.2427 (2011)
24. Wang, H., Schmid, C.: Action recognition with improved trajectories. In: 2013 IEEE International Conference on Computer Vision, pp. 3551–3558 (2013)
25. Xie, S., Sun, C., Huang, J., Tu, Z., Murphy, K.: Rethinking spatiotemporal feature learning for video understanding. CoRR abs/1712.04851 (2017)

Nose Based Rigid Face Tracking

Luan P. e Silva$^{(\boxtimes)}$, Flávio H. de B. Zavan , Olga R. P. Bellon ,
and Luciano Silva

Universidade Federal do Paraná, Curitiba, Paraná, Brazil
{luan.porfirio,flavio,olga,luciano}@ufpr.br

Abstract. Face detection is one of the first stages of face recognition
systems. Thanks to advances in deep neural networks, success has been
achieved on many similar image recognition tasks. When videos are available, temporal information can be used for determining the position of
the face, avoiding having to detect faces for all frames. Such techniques
can be applied in in-the-wild environments where current face detection
methods fail to perform robustly. To address these limitations, this work
explores an original approach, tracking the nose region initialized based
on face quality analysis. A quality score is calculated for assisting the nose
tracking initialization, avoiding depending on the first frame, in which
may contain degraded data. The nose region, rather than the entire face
was chosen due to it being unlikely to be occluded, being mostly invariant to facial expressions, and being visible in a long range of head poses.
Experiments performed on the 300 Videos in the Wild and Point and
Shoot Challenge datasets indicate nose tracking is a useful approach for
in-the-wild scenarios.

1 Introduction

According to Jain *et al.* [4], facial recognition is one of the fundamental problems
in computer vision. For this reason, robust and efficient face detection needs to be
performed for almost all face processing tasks. When working with videos, face
tracker can make use of the temporal information, avoiding constant detection.
The most common approaches to this are landmark-based [15,16] unfortunately,
they tend to not be robust for in-the-wild scenarios, including profile head poses
where half of the landmarks are occluded by the face [11]. At the same time,
generic object trackers have been successfully applied to predicting the location of a large range of objects, including faces [7,8], treating its targets as a
rectangular bounding box.

Existing generic tracking methods can be based on the principal component
analysis (PCA) [10], sparse representations [5], Haar-like features [18], correlation filters [13], and convolutional neural networks [3]. However, they tend to
have poor performance in uncontrolled environments, where deformations, partial occlusions and changes in illumination are common. To this end, Nam and
Han [7] proposed MDNet (Multi-Domain Network), designed to learn shared

© Springer Nature Switzerland AG 2019
R. Vera-Rodriguez et al. (Eds.): CIARP 2018, LNCS 11401, pp. 556–563, 2019.
https://doi.org/10.1007/978-3-030-13469-3_65

features and classifiers specific to different tracking sequences, achieving state-of-the-art results on the Visual Object Tracking Challenge [6] and the Object Tracking Benchmark [14]. All these approaches rely on accurate bounding box initialization in the first frame.

This paper proposes combining Nam and Han's generic tracker [7] with a robust initialization step based on a customized face quality score, using the nose region for performing face tracking in unconstrained environments. While the nose composes a smaller region, it has been shown efficient for biometrics [2,17], it is visible even on profile faces, not easily deformed by facial expression and, due to its nature, also unlikely to be occluded by accessories.

The initialization step selects the best starting frame by maximizing a face quality score. This method allows the tracker to overcome a common limitation in which the reference region may be of poor quality or include large variations in illumination or occlusion, negatively affecting its performance. This work expands on a preliminary study [12] that has evaluated the possibility of this approach. While the initial results were positive, indicating the potential of the selection step, tracking was initialized using ground-truth annotations. This paper explores a completely automated approach, simulating real life scenarios when no ground-truth data is available.

Experiments are performed on the 300VW dataset [11], which includes numerous videos categorized into difficulty levels. Additionally, 100 videos from the PaSC dataset [1] were annotated and used for testing and comparing against face tracking.

2   Nose Tracking in the Wild

This work proposes tracking faces in in-the-wild scenarios solely using the nose region as target. To this end, face quality assessment is adopted for estimating the best frame as reference to initialize tracking. Due to the first frame not necessarily being used for initializing, the nose region needs to be tracked twice: forwards and backwards in time. When the tracker finishes, the frame sequence is reordered.

The adopted face quality assessment method [12] has five main steps: (1) the face region is first detected using Faster-RCNN [9]; (2) face quality is then estimated based on Abaza et al.'s method: the geometric mean of the contrast, brightness, focus, sharpness, and illumination; (3) nose detection is performed using Faster-RCNN [9]; (4) the yaw head pose angle is estimated using a support vector machine classifier [17], predicting the pose into five classes $(-90, -45, 0, 45, 90°)$; and (5) facial quality score is then combined with head pose estimation preferring near frontal faces and best face quality for tracking initialization. Frames with no detected face or nose are skipped when assessing the quality and estimating the pose.

After face quality estimation, MDNet [7] is used for tracking and locating the nose region on other frames. It uses a convolutional neural network with five hidden layers and two fully connected layers, sharing all common features during the training phase. MDNet also has multiple specific-domain layers, one for each video used for training, enabling binary classification between foreground and background to be performed.

At the test stage, MDNet [7] fine-tunes the pre-trained weights and replaces the specific-domain layers into a single one by using 500 positives and 5,000 negatives samples around the first frame ground truth. Hard negative mining strategy and bounding box regression are also adopted making the predictions more robust to different views, scale, drift and illumination changes. Note that MDNet [7] by itself does not perform the initial detection, it depends on manual initialization. The nose tracking pipeline is shown in Fig. 1, outlining the face quality analysis and visual tracking integration.

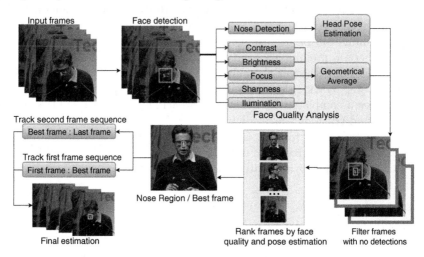

Fig. 1. Image quality and nose tracker diagram. Red and green lines are the detected and tracker predicted regions, respectively. (Color figure online)

2.1   Experimental Results

Experiments were performed on the 300 Videos in the Wild (300VW) [11] and Point and Shoot Challenge (PaSC) [1] datasets, comparing the nose tracking approach with face tracking. For the latter, the pre-trained MDNet method of Nam and Han [7] was used. In this case, traditional first frame ground-truth initialization was used. This difference allows for comparing the nose tracking strategy with using the entire face region.

Visual tracking performance is evaluated frame by frame using two metrics, the intersection coefficient, also called success rate [6,14], and precision [6], which measures the distance between the final estimation and the respective ground-truth.

300VW Dataset. The 300VW dataset [11] has 50 training videos and 64 test videos with approximately one minute of duration each, containing 68 annotated landmarks at each frame. This allows for extracting the nose and face regions to be used for evaluating tracking performance. The test videos are subdivided into three degrees of difficulty, containing 31, 19 and 14 videos.

For nose tracking, the nose region of 300VW's training subset was used in the training stage. Two evaluations were performed when tracking the nose: initializing with the automatic detection and initializing with the manually annotated nose (ground truth), both cases starting the process using the best quality frame. The latter was adopted for allowing a fair comparison against face tracking.

Results obtained in the 64 test videos show nose tracking achieving great accuracy (Fig. 2a), reaching 90.61% when started from the automatic nose detection, and 97.67% of precision when starting from the ground truth nose. Face tracking reached 96.68% precision. The threshold was 20 pixels for all cases, as it is by the visual object tracking challenge [6].

Following a stricter evaluation protocol, the error threshold is reduced to ten pixels. Nose tracking achieves 82.30% when it is started from the automatic nose detection, and 92.09% precision when it is initialized from the ground truth annotation. Face tracking performance decrease to 76.20% precision, showing a better results with the nose when under a strict protocol.

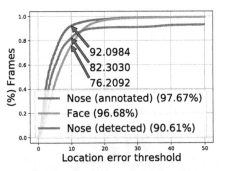 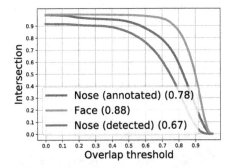

(a) Precision metric. In parenthesis: value at 20 pixels error. Arrows point to the ten pixels threshold.

(b) Success metric. In parenthesis: the area under the curve

Fig. 2. Results on the 300VW dataset.

Despite the superior precision using nose tracking, its intersection coefficient is, in general, inferior when compared to face tracking, as demonstrated in Fig. 2b. Visual analysis indicates the lower rates was caused by the nose tracking prediction being slightly larger than the ground truth annotations, as it is not trivial to separate the nose region from the background, the face. When performing face tracking, the background can be easily discriminated from the target, favoring a correct scale estimation.

When considering the different testing subsets, nose and face tracking achieved similar precision on easy and medium difficulty videos, as shown in the Table 1 (categories 1 and 2). These subsets include variations in illumination and facial expressions, but no occlusion and rarely any head pose changes. Nose tracking initialized from the detection suffers degraded performance when the initial estimation is not perfect, affecting the subsequent tracking step.

Table 1. Precision results obtained on each 300VW testing subset using a threshold of 20 pixels.

Methods	Cat. 1 (Easy)	Cat. 2 (Medium)	Cat. 3 (Hard)
Nose tracking (annotated)	97.94	97.44	97.32
Face (annotated)	98.57	97.45	91.47
Nose tracking (detected)	90.81	88.44	92.75

The third category contains completely unrestricted environments including occlusion, illumination changes, large head pose variations, and facial expressions. In this scenario nose tracking is superior to the face, reaching 92.75% accuracy when started with the automatic detection, and .97.32% when it uses the ground truth region. The face achieves 91.47% of precision, showing that the proposed approach outperforms face tracking in the most challenging scenarios. These results are summarized on the last column of Table 1.

Figure 3 demonstrates samples of the tracked nose and face regions initialized from the ground-truth annotations and detections. Then the head pose changes, face tracking is lost, but the discriminating features of the nose allow the tracker to locate it.

Fig. 3. Results obtained on the most challenging 300VW subset. The blue and green boxes were located by the nose tracker, detected and manually annotated, respectively. Face tracking results are in red. Frames were cropped to aid visualization. (Color figure online)

PaSC Dataset. The Point and Shoot Challenge (PaSC) dataset [1] consists of in-the-wild images and videos with varying degrees of degradation. However, it does not include face or nose region annotations, therefore 100 videos were randomly selected, and every frame was manually annotated to be used for testing. The same 300VW trained model was used for performing the nose tracking experiments on PaSC. Because the nose detection step necessary for face quality analysis failed on most frames, the nose tracker was only initialized using the manual annotations.

In some cases, nose tracking performs visually better than when the face is used, as can be seen in Fig. 4. Favorable nose tracking results are seen, as face tracking does not take account variations in scale and fails to predict the correct size.

Fig. 4. Results on a low quality video with variations in scale obtained from PaSC. The blue and red boxes were located by performing nose and face tracking respectively. Frames were cropped to aid visualization. (Color figure online)

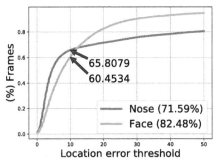
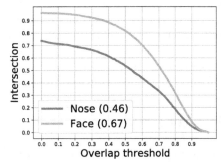

(a) Precision plot: Parenthesis and arrows indicate the values at the 20 and 10 pixels thresholds respectively.

(b) Success plot: The area under the curve is shown in parenthesis.

Fig. 5. Results on the PaSCdataset

In general, face tracking achieved better results compared to the nose PaSC. This is due to the following reasons: The dataset has many low-resolution videos and large variations in scale, which drastically reduces the size of the nose region, rendering nose tracking harder compared to the whole face.

Taking into account the ten pixels error threshold, nose tracking reaches better precision rates (65.30% for the nose and 60.45% for the face). However, this relationship is not preserved as the threshold increases, as shown in Fig. 5a. When measuring the intersection coefficient, face tracking shows greater consistency in such scenarios, as demonstrated the Fig. 5b.

3   Final Remarks

In this work, a nose tracking approach was proposed as an alternative to face tracking in unconstrained environments. In addition, a quality assessment step was integrated into tracking initialization, avoiding depending on starting it using the first frame, which may contain poor illumination, occlusion or extreme head poses. The method was benchmarked on two datasets 300VW [11] and PaSC [1]. Experiments included nose tracking with automatic nose detection and ground truth annotations, comparing the results against face tracking.

It was shown that nose tracking achieves similar precision compared to using the whole face on common scenarios. On difficult, in-the-wild situations the proposed method achieves better precision against the face. Reaching 97.32% when the face reaches 91.47% on the most challenging 300VW [11] subset. These results promote nose tracking as a viable option when head pose variations, occlusions and illumination changes are present. Experiments also indicate that it is not trivial to precisely fit the nose region when tracking, given the similarity of the nose with the background (face) pixels, decreasing the accuracy when there are changes in scale. Experiments performed on 100 manually annotated videos from the PaSC dataset [1] show the difficulty found by nose tracking in videos with large scale variations where the target region is reduced. As future work, a nose detection correction step can be integrated into nose tracking pipeline, reducing the error when large scale variations are present.

Acknowledgements. This study was financed in part by the Coordenação de Aperfeiçoamento de Pessoal de Nível Superior - Brasil (CAPES) - Finance Code 001.

References

1. Beveridge, J.R., et al.: The challenge of face recognition from digital point-and-shoot cameras. In: IEEE BTAS (2013)
2. Chang, K.I., Bowyer, K.W., Flynn, P.J.: Multiple nose region matching for 3D face recognition under varying facial expression. IEEE Trans. Pattern Anal. Mach. Intell. (TPAMI) **28**, 1695 (2006)
3. Guo, Q., Feng, W., Zhou, C., Huang, R., Wan, L., Wang, S.: Learning dynamic siamese network for visual object tracking. In: International Conference on Computer Vision (ICCV). IEEE (2017)
4. Jain, A.K., Flynn, P., Ross, A.A.: Handbook of Biometrics. Springer, Heidelberg (2007). https://doi.org/10.1007/978-0-387-71041-9
5. Jia, X., Lu, H., Yang, M.H.: Visual tracking via adaptive structural local sparse appearance model. In: Computer Vision and Pattern Recognition (CVPR). IEEE (2012)
6. Kristan, M., et al.: The visual object tracking vot2015 challenge results. In: Proceedings of the IEEE International Conference on Computer Vision Workshops (CVPR Workshops) (2015)
7. Nam, H., Han, B.: Learning multi-domain convolutional neural networks for visual tracking. In: Proceedings of the IEEE Conference on Computer Vision and Pattern Recognition (CVPR) (2016)

8. Ranftl, A., Alonso-Fernandez, F., Karlsson, S., Bigun, J.: Real-time AdaBoost cascade face tracker based on likelihood map and optical flow. IET Biometrics **6**, 468 (2017)
9. Ren, S., He, K., Girshick, R., Sun, J.: Faster R-CNN: towards real-time object detection with region proposal networks. In: Advances in Neural Information Processing Systems (NIPS) (2015)
10. Ross, D.A., Lim, J., Lin, R.S., Yang, M.H.: Incremental learning for robust visual tracking. Int. J. Comput. Vis. (IJCV) **77**, 125 (2008)
11. Shen, J., Zafeiriou, S., Chrysos, G.G., Kossaifi, J., Tzimiropoulos, G., Pantic, M.: The first facial landmark tracking in-the-wild challenge: benchmark and results. In: International Conference on Computer Vision Workshop (ICCV Workshops). IEEE (2015)
12. Silva, L., Zavan, F., Silva, L., Bellon, O.: Follow that nose: tracking faces based on the nose region and image quality feedback. In: Conference on Graphics, Patterns and Images (SIBGRAPI) (2016)
13. Valmadre, J., Bertinetto, L., Henriques, J., Vedaldi, A., Torr, P.H.: End-to-end representation learning for correlation filter based tracking. In: Computer Vision and Pattern Recognition (CVPR). IEEE (2017)
14. Wu, Y., Lim, J., Yang, M.H.: Object tracking benchmark. IEEE Trans. Pattern Anal. Mach. Intell. (TPAMI) **37**, 1834 (2015)
15. Xiao, S., Yan, S., Kassim, A.A.: Facial landmark detection via progressive initialization. In: Proceedings of the IEEE International Conference on Computer Vision Workshops (CVPR Workshops) (2015)
16. Yang, J., Deng, J., Zhang, K., Liu, Q.: Facial shape tracking via spatio-temporal cascade shape regression. In: Proceedings of the IEEE International Conference on Computer Vision Workshops (CVPR Workshops) (2015)
17. Zavan, F., Nascimento, A., Silva, L., Bellon, O.: Nosepose: a competitive, landmark-free methodology for head pose estimation in-the-wild. In: Conference on Graphics, Patterns and Images (SIBGRAPI) (2016)
18. Zhang, K., Zhang, L., Yang, M.-H.: Real-time compressive tracking. In: Fitzgibbon, A., Lazebnik, S., Perona, P., Sato, Y., Schmid, C. (eds.) ECCV 2012. LNCS, vol. 7574, pp. 864–877. Springer, Heidelberg (2012). https://doi.org/10.1007/978-3-642-33712-3_62

Biometrics

On Combining Face Local Appearance and Geometrical Features for Race Classification

Fabiola Becerra-Riera[1]([✉]), Nelson Méndez Llanes[1],
Annette Morales-González[1], Heydi Méndez-Vázquez[1], and Massimo Tistarelli[2]

[1] Advanced Technologies Application Center (CENATAV),
7A #21406 Siboney, Playa, 12200 Havana, Cuba
{fbecerra,nllanes,amorales,hmendez}@cenatav.co.cu
[2] Computer Vision Laboratory PolComing, University of Sassari,
Viale Mancini 5, 07100 Sassari, Italy
tista@uniss.it

Abstract. In the field of demographic attribute classification, race estimation is perhaps the least studied topic in the literature. CNN-based approaches report the best results to the day, but they are computational expensive for practical applications. We propose a simpler approach by combining local appearance and geometrical features to describe face images, and to exploit the race information from different face parts by means of a component-based methodology. Experimental results obtained in the FERET subset from EGA database, with traditional but effective classifiers like Random Forest and Support Vector Machines, are very close to those achieved with a recent deep learning proposal.

Keywords: Soft-biometrics · Race classification ·
Face appearance representation · Face anthropometric representation

1 Introduction

Visual attributes are one of the most intuitive and natural ways of describing a face. They can range from soft biometrics, which include demographic information (gender, age, race), facial marks and certain physical characteristics of the face; to other environmental related aspects. The estimation of visual attributes has been an active research topic in recent years because of their multiple applications in domains such as biometric authentication, access control, video surveillance and security systems. Soft biometrics can be useful in different ways: to perform recognition by means of a bag of attributes, to reduce the search space of a hard biometric system by restricting comparisons to those matching a certain soft biometric profile, and to complement the evidence from hard biometric traits [9].

Among the demographic attributes, race (ethnicity) is perhaps the least studied soft biometric in the literature. In particular, in the recognition of race, the

© Springer Nature Switzerland AG 2019
R. Vera-Rodriguez et al. (Eds.): CIARP 2018, LNCS 11401, pp. 567–574, 2019.
https://doi.org/10.1007/978-3-030-13469-3_66

somatic traits of some populations are not well defined; within the same population, people may exhibit certain characteristics to a greater or lesser extent [5]: in the case of Caucasians, for example, the skin tone and the geometry of some facial features can vary from one individual to another. Taking these factors into account, it is clear that the accuracy of a race classifier is intrinsically linked to the robustness in the estimation of other attributes that characterize it by definition, such as skin color and face shape.

Different approaches have been proposed for race classification [7]. They range from using global [13] to local features [12], as well as other visual information such as skin and lips color, and forehead area [16]. The combination of local descriptors have also shown to be effective [4,17], despite recently the best state-of-the-art results in this topic have been achieved using Convolutional Neural Networks (CNN) [2,20]. However, deep learning approaches continue to be extremely demanding in terms of computing time and memory consuming during training and deployment, among different aspects that remains to be addressed to make them practical [6].

In this work we propose a simple but accurate method to race estimation. We first exploit the effectiveness of component-based approaches for attribute classification [11] and analyze the influence of different face regions for the specific problem of race estimation. Besides, we incorporate anthropometric information directly linked to the race definition itself [8]. We then evaluate different strategies for the fusion of both local appearance descriptors and geometrical features. Traditional classifiers are employed to obtain the best feature combination for the final prediction. The rest of this paper is organized as follows. Section 2 introduces the proposal. Section 3 presents the evaluation protocol and Sect. 4 the experimental analysis. Finally, Sect. 5 concludes the paper.

2   Proposed Approach

Since the definition of race from face includes the consideration of intrinsic attributes such as skin color and shape of the facial features, we base our face representation on both appearance and geometric characteristics. We analyze the impact of using color and texture features, and anthropometric measures separately and explore the best way of combining them in a more robust descriptor through the use of two different classifiers: Support Vector Machine (SVM) and Random Forest (RF). In the following subsections we explain in details how the face image is represented taking into account this two different features and the strategies used to combine them.

2.1   Appearance Features

The texton-like features [18] incorporate 17 filters (filterbank) to extract color and texture information that we exploit to obtain an appearance-based face representation for the estimation of race.

We subdivided a face image into 10 interest regions (see Fig. 1) to explore its influence separately for race estimation. We follow the procedure defined in [3] for extracting the regions and we include hair and contour components since visual information surrounding the face has proven to be important for attribute classification in the literature [1]. The filterbank features were employed to codify the face parts because of their good results for the classification of irregular regions [10]. For each region we consider only a set of sparse points to avoid redundant and expensive calculations, and extract color and texture information for each of them. The appearance representation of a single region is a 34-component descriptor where the mean and variance of the extracted filterbank features are concatenated; SVM and RF classifiers are used to find the best combination of regions in such a way that information provided by each one complements the others. The final representation of a face image is conceived as the concatenation of the best region feature vectors, which can result in a 340-component descriptor (34 region descriptor $*$ 10 regions) if the complete set of regions is used.

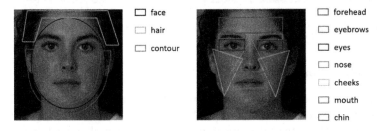

Fig. 1. Face image subdivision into 10 regions of interest: face, hair, contour, forehead, eyebrows, eyes, nose, cheeks, mouth and chin.

2.2   Geometrical Features

Anthropometric or shape-based methodologies have been widely used in literature to tackle race estimation problem [7]. Most of these approaches use 3D anthropometric statistics for race categorization. Hence, they recover the facial geometrical structure by using 3D face models. Obtaining these 3D models can be computational costly, so we have decided to use some distances between landmark points in 2D images that can be seen as geometric invariants in 3D models. This geometric representation was inspired in the work of [14], that explored multiple 2D/3D geometric invariants for face recognition.

We use 68 landmark points (control points) distributed around the face in the following way: 17 points for face contour, 12 for the eyes, 10 for the eyebrows, 9 corresponding to the nose and 20 to the mouth. Following the 2D/3D invariant measures described in [14] for the case of 2D images, we computed the ratio of distances of all possible combination of four and five non-coplanar or collinear control points. This led us to a high-dimensional vector that is reduced applying Principal Components Analysis (PCA). It is evident that some configurations (distances or ratios) are more significant than others, and some of them can be redundant, so this allows us to obtain the best invariants for our problem. Some of the selected distances are illustrated in Fig. 2.

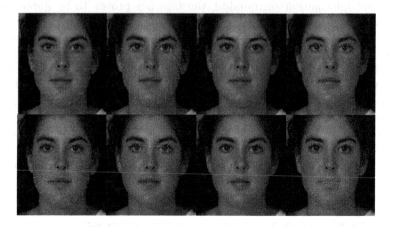

Fig. 2. Invariant distances for geometric face representation

2.3   Combination Strategies

Two different strategies for feature combination were explored as well as the influence of the selected classifiers (SVM, RF) in the final accuracy results. By means of the first strategy we concatenate appearance and geometric features in a single descriptor and validate its effectiveness in the estimation of race. The second strategy was inspired in the work of [19], in which different late fusion procedures were analyzed. In particular, we employed the geometric mean of the probabilistic outputs, that showed the best performance results in [19], outperforming even the more sophisticated fusion techniques. This second strategy has the additional advantage that different classifiers can be used for different features, therefore allowing the combination of their best performance individually.

3   Evaluation Protocol

Although there are several works in this topic, there is not a direct comparison among different approaches with a fixed protocol or database. Most researches use commonly accepted representative databases for face recognition, such as FERET [2]. However, these databases are usually race ill-balanced. For that reason we have decided to use the EGA database [15] which integrates different single race datasets to create a more heterogeneous and representative collection for race recognition (see Fig. 3).

The EGA dataset contains 2 345 images taken from CASIA-Face V5, FEI, FERET, FRGC, JAFFE and Indian Face Database. Images are labeled in terms of gender, 3 age groups (young, adult and middle age people) and 5 racial groups

(African-American, Asian, Caucasian, Indian, and Latin). Most of the images are frontal and they do not present illumination problems, nor occlusions (except for some cases using eyeglasses) nor facial expression variation. Since this dataset does not have a standard protocol for attribute classification, we designed our own. We split the total images into 5 folds balanced in terms of age, gender and race and performed a 5-fold cross validation. In the next section we explain in detail how the experiments were conducted.

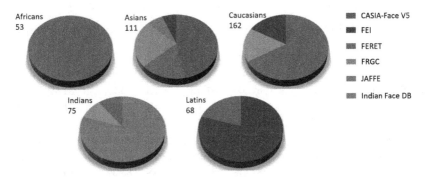

Fig. 3. Contribution (number of subjects) by race of each source dataset to EGA.

4   Results and Discussion

With the aim of showing the effectiveness of the proposed descriptors for race estimation, we performed several experiments in the EGA dataset.

First, we evaluated multiple region combinations codified with filterbank features, to find the subset that contributes in a most significant way for race estimation. Our experiments showed that the eyes-cheeks-chin-face-hair combination (using a 170-dimensional vector after the concatenation) achieved the best general performance with a good balance between classes. In Table 1, each reported result that use the appearance filterbank features was obtained with this best region combination.

Before exploring feature combination strategies, we evaluated the appearance and geometric features separately for the race estimation task. In the case of geometric features we selected 150 components after applying PCA, in order to be similar in dimension to the appearance-based descriptor. As can be seen in Table 1, filterbank features showed the higher accuracy by means of a RF classifier (row 1), while in the case of the geometric measures SVM achieved a better separation between classes (row 4). In general, the best results with individual features was obtained with the SVM classifier (83.7% for geometrics).

We conducted a second group of experiments taking into account the different strategies to combine the face feature representations. Although the SVM classifier achieved superior results with single features, its general performance taking into account both appearance and geometric descriptors was similar to the one obtained with the RF classifier which, in the correct classification of Latin people, was more accurate in all the experiments. This previous result reinforce the fact that, by using the first combination strategy, denoted as FB + Geom in Table 1, RF classifier obtained the most accurate race estimation (83.1%), with a better balance between the 5 classes, and the highest results in the classification of Latins (80.2%), which makes a great difference in relation to the 66.8% achieved by SVM.

Table 1. Race classification accuracy on EGA dataset

Features	Classifier	Accuracy					
		General	African	Asian	Caucasian	Indian	Latin
filterbank (FB)	RF	82.9%	87.9%	78.7%	85.2%	84.3%	77.9%
filterbank (FB)	SVM	75.6%	74.7%	77.1%	78.4%	81.3%	60.6%
geometrics (Geom)	RF	75.8%	78.1%	69.7%	81.9%	75.5%	69.7%
geometrics (Geom)	SVM	83.7%	89.8%	85.7%	89.1%	82.9%	63.8%
FB + Geom	RF	83.1%	87.9%	78.1%	84.6%	85.9%	**80.2%**
FB + Geom	SVM	81.4%	84.5%	78.9%	85.3%	86.7%	66.8%
gMean FB + Geom	RF + SVM	**87%**	**90.9%**	**87.5%**	**90.4%**	**87.5%**	74.7%

With the second strategy we fused appearance and anthropometric measures by employing the geometric mean (gMean) of their probabilistic results. We used RF classifier with the filterbank representation and SVM with geometric features, according to the results obtained in the first set of experiments. This late fusion strategy reported the best results in Table 1, achieving a general performance of 87% of accuracy; with around 91% of effectiveness in the estimation of Africans and Caucasians and an improvement to 87.5% in the case of Asians and Indians.

We also compared our proposal with a recent CNN approach based on the VGG-architecture [2], in the FERET subset from the EGA dataset. In this case, similar to previous works, we focused on the estimation of only 3 classes: Black, Asian and White people. In Table 2 we show our results by employing single descriptors and their combinations.

It can be seen that the 93.7% of accuracy achieved by using our late fusion of local descriptors is very close to the 94% obtained with the Anwar and Islam deep learning solution, with only 0.3% of average accuracy difference. However, our individual classification of Black and White people is superior to the one reported for the network: 1.3% more accurate in the case of Whites and almost 8% for Black people. Asian estimation is, according to the overall obtained results, the weak-spot of our proposal. Once again the geometric mean of appearance and geometric features achieved superior results compared to single descriptors and their concatenation.

Table 2. Race classification accuracy on FERET subset from the EGA database

Features	Classifier	Accuracy			
		General	Black	Asian	White
filterbank (FB)	RF	85.6%	87.2%	20.9%	97.3%
geometrics (Geom)	SVM	92.9%	92.5%	74.3%	96.9%
FB + Geom	SVM	87.8%	91.3%	43.8%	94.5%
gMean FB + Geom	RF + SVM	93.7%	**93.9%**	68.6%	**98.5%**
Anwar and Islam CNN [2]	-	**94%**	86%	**94.3%**	97.8%

5   Conclusions

In this work we tackle the race estimation problem by means of a component-based approach and geometric descriptors. We exploit the information provided by different face regions, and codify them with both appearance and geometric characteristics to achieved a description of attributes that distinguish race by definition, such skin color and shape of the facial features. We explore two different feature combination strategies and employ traditional classifiers like SVM and RF to obtain a final race prediction. Our late fusion strategy, based on the geometric mean of both appearance and anthropometric probabilistic results, achieved accuracy values very close to those obtained by a recent deep learning proposal (only 0.3% less accurate than the CNN approach), in the FERET subset from EGA database. These results show that there are still some promising alternatives to the use of expensive CNN approaches for the estimation of attributes.

Acknowledgment. This research work has been partially supported by a grant from the European Commission (H2020 MSCA RISE 690907 "IDENTITY") and by a grant of the Italian Ministry of Research (PRIN 2015).

References

1. Afifi, M., Abdelhamed, A.: Afif4: Deep gender classification based on adaboost-based fusion of isolated facial features and foggy faces. arXiv preprint arXiv:1706.04277 (2017)
2. Anwar, I., Islam, N.U.: Learned features are better for ethnicity classification. Cybern. Inf. Technol. **17**(3), 152–164 (2017)
3. Becerra-Riera, F., Méndez-Vázquez, H., Morales-González, A., Tistarelli, M.: Age and gender classification using local appearance descriptors from facial components. In: International Joint Conference on Biometrics (IJCB), pp. 799–804 (2017)
4. Bekhouche, S.E., Ouafi, A., Dornaika, F., Taleb-Ahmed, A., Hadid, A.: Pyramid multi-level features for facial demographic estimation. Expert. Syst. Appl. **80**(C), 297–310 (2017)
5. Carcagnì, P., Coco, M.D., Cazzato, D., Leo, M., Distante, C.: A study on different experimental configurations for age, race, and gender estimation problems. EURASIP J. Image Video Process. **2015**(1), 37 (2015)

6. Cheng, J., Wang, P., Li, G., Hu, Q., Lu, H.: Recent advances in efficient computation of deep convolutional neural networks. Front. Inf. Technol. Electron. Eng. **19**(1), 64–77 (2018)
7. Fu, S., He, H., Hou, Z.G.: Learning race from face: a survey. Trans. Pattern Anal. Mach. Intell. (TPAMI) **36**(12), 2483–2509 (2014)
8. Gill, G., Hughes, S., Bennett, S., Miles Gilbert, B.: Racial identification from the midfacial skeleton with special reference to american indians and whites. J. Forensic Sci. **33**(1), 92–99 (1988)
9. González-Sosa, E., Fiérrez, J., Vera-Rodríguez, R., Alonso-Fernández, F.: Facial soft biometrics for recognition in the wild: recent works, annotation and cots evaluation. IEEE Trans. Inf. Forensics Secur. **13**(7), 2001–2014 (2018)
10. Gould, S., Fulton, R., Koller, D.: Decomposing a scene into geometric and semantically consistent regions. In: Proceedings of the IEEE International Conference on Computer Vision and Pattern Recognition (CVPR), pp. 1–8, September 2009
11. Kumar, N., Berg, A.C., Belhumeur, P.N., Nayar, S.K.: Describable visual attributes for face verification and image search. Trans. Pattern Anal. Mach. Intell. (TPAMI) **33**(10), 1962–1977 (2011)
12. Manesh, F.S., Ghahramani, M., Tan, Y.P.: Facial part displacement effect on template-based gender and ethnicity classification. In: 11th International Conference on Control Automation Robotics Vision, pp. 1644–1649. IEEE (2010)
13. Ou, Y., Wu, X., Qian, H., Xu, Y.: A real time race classification system. In: International Conference on Information Acquisition. IEEE (2005)
14. Riccio, D., Dugelay, J.L.: Geometric invariants for 2D/3D face recognition. Pattern Recognit. Lett. **28**(14), 1907–1914 (2007)
15. Riccio, D., Tortora, G., Marsico, M.D., Wechsler, H.: EGA - ethnicity, gender and age, a pre-annotated face database. In: Workshop on Biometric Measurements and Systems for Security and Medical Applications (BIOMS), pp. 1–8. IEEE (2012)
16. Roomi, S.M.M., Virasundarii, S.L., Selvamegala, S., Jeevanandhame, S., Hariharasudhan, D.: Race classification based on facial features. In: 3rd National Conference on Computer Vision, Pattern Recognition, Image Processing and Graphics (NCVPRIPG), pp. 54–57. IEEE (2011)
17. Salah, S.H., Du, H., Al-Jawad, N.: Fusing local binary patterns with wavelet features for ethnicity identification. Int. J. Comput. Inf. Syst. Control. Eng. **7**, 330–336 (2013)
18. Shotton, J., Winn, J., Rother, C., Criminisi, A.: *TextonBoost*: joint appearance, shape and context modeling for multi-class object recognition and segmentation. In: Leonardis, A., Bischof, H., Pinz, A. (eds.) ECCV 2006. LNCS, vol. 3951, pp. 1–15. Springer, Heidelberg (2006). https://doi.org/10.1007/11744023_1
19. Tamrakar, A., et al.: Evaluation of low-level features and their combinations for complex event detection in open source videos. In: IEEE Conference on Computer Vision and Pattern Recognition (CVPR), pp. 3681–3688 (2012)
20. Wang, W., He, F., Zhao, Q.: Facial ethnicity classification with deep convolutional neural networks. In: You, Z., et al. (eds.) CCBR 2016. LNCS, vol. 9967, pp. 176–185. Springer, Cham (2016). https://doi.org/10.1007/978-3-319-46654-5_20

Facial Landmarks Detection Using a Cascade of Recombinator Networks

Pedro Diego López, Roberto Valle$^{(\boxtimes)}$, and Luis Baumela

Univ. Politécnica Madrid, Madrid, Spain
diego.lopez.maroto@alumnos.upm.es, {rvalle,lbaumela}@fi.upm.es

Abstract. Nowadays, Convolutional Neural Nets (CNNs) have become the reference technology for many computer vision problems, including facial landmarks detection. Although CNNs are very robust, they still lack accuracy because they cannot enforce the estimated landmarks to represent a valid face shape.

In this paper we investigate the use of a cascade of CNN regressors to make the set of estimated landmarks lie closer to a valid face shape. To this end, we introduce CRN, a facial landmarks detection algorithm based on a Cascade of Recombinator Networks. The proposed approach not only improves the baseline model, but also achieves state-of-the-art results in 300W, COFW and AFLW that are widely considered the most challenging public data sets.

Keywords: Face alignment · Cascaded shape regression · Convolutional neural networks

1 Introduction

Facial landmarks detection is a fundamental problem in computer vision with applications in many real-world tasks such as attributes and pose estimation [1], facial verification [8], etc. Current state-of-the-art methods are based on deep Convolutional Neural Nets (CNNs). Lv *et al.*'s [7] approach uses CNNs to set up a global and a set of local face parts regressors for fine-grained facial deformation estimation. Xiao *et al.* [10] is one of the first approaches that fuse the feature extraction and regression steps into a recurrent neural network trained end-to-end. Kowalski *et al.* [5] and Yang *et al.* [11] are among the top performers in the Menpo competition [12]. Both use global similarity transform to normalize landmark locations followed by a VGG-based and a Stacked Hourglass network respectively to regress the final shape.

CNN approaches are very robust to face deformations and pose changes due to the large receptive fields of deep nets. However, they lack accuracy because of two factors. First, the loss of feature maps resolution in the concatenation of many convolutional and pooling layers. Second, the difficulty in imposing a valid face shape on the set of estimated landmark positions.

© Springer Nature Switzerland AG 2019
R. Vera-Rodriguez et al. (Eds.): CIARP 2018, LNCS 11401, pp. 575–583, 2019.
https://doi.org/10.1007/978-3-030-13469-3_67

The Recombinator Network addresses the first factor by combining features computed at different scales [3]. This is achieved by processing the image in a set of branches at different resolutions. Finer and deeper branches pass information to the coarser ones allowing for the net to combine the information at different levels of abstraction and scales.

In this paper we address the issue of making the set of estimated landmarks look like a valid face. To this end we present a method called Cascade of Recombinator Networks (CRN) that uses cascade of deep models to enforce valid face shapes on the set of estimated landmark positions. We also introduce a new loss function robust to missing landmarks and an aggressive data augmentation approach to improve Honari *et al.*'s [3] baseline system.

2   Cascade of Recombinator Networks

In this section we present the Cascade of Recombinator Networks (CRN) (see Fig. 1). It is composed of S stages where each stage represents a network that combines features across multiple branches B based on Honari *et al.*'s [3] architecture. The output of each stage is a probability map per each landmark providing information about the position of the L landmarks in the input image. The maximum of each probability map determines the landmarks positions.

The key idea behind our proposal is to employ a cascade of regressors that incrementally refine the location of the set of landmarks. The input for each regressor is the set of probability maps produced by the previous stage of the cascade. Between each cascade stage, we introduce a *map dropout* layer that deletes, with probability p, the map of a landmark (see red-crossed map in Fig. 1). In this way we force the net to learn the structure of the face, since it must predict the position of some landmarks using the location of its neighbors. This idea of ensemble of regressors has been extensively used within the so-called Cascade Shape Regressor (CSR) framework [4,5,11].

In our implementation we use a loss function that is able to handle missing landmarks. In this way we can use data augmentation with large face rotations, translations and scalings, labeling landmarks falling outside of the bounding box as missing. It also enables us to train with data sets where some landmarks are not annotated, such as AFLW.

Our loss function, $\mathcal{L}$, is given by

$$\mathcal{L} = \sum_{i=1}^{N} \left(-\frac{1}{||\mathbf{w}_i^g||_1} \sum_{l=1}^{L} (\mathbf{w}_i^g(l) \cdot \mathbf{m}_i^g(l) \cdot \log(\mathbf{m}_i(l))) \right), \tag{1}$$

where $\mathbf{m}_i(l)$ and $\mathbf{m}_i^g(l)$ represent the predicted probability map and the ground truth respectively, $\mathbf{w}_i^g(l)$ the labeled mask indicator variable (takes value "1" when a landmark is annotated, "0" otherwise), N the number of training images and L the number of landmarks.

We have further improved the accuracy of the Recombinator Network baseline by replacing max-pooling layers with convolutional layers with stride 2.

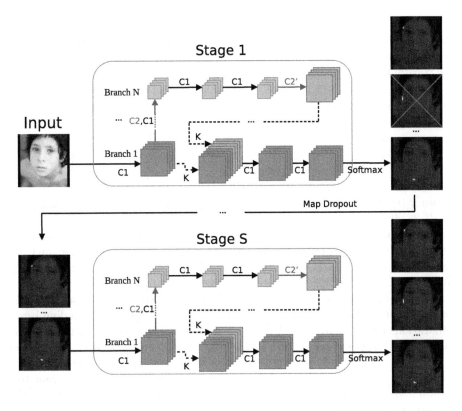

Fig. 1. CRN framework architecture diagram. Each stage is a RCN [3] where $C1$, $C2$ and $C2'$ represent a stride 1 conv layer, stride 2 conv layer and a transpose convolution with stride 2 respectively. The output of each stage is the input to the next one. Between each stage we introduce a *map dropout* layer. (Color figure online)

Finally, we found that locating each landmark at the position with maximum probability is very sensitive to noise. We propose to apply a Gaussian smoothing filter to each probability map to improve the robustness of the predictions. Thus, large areas are favored with respect to single pixels with high probability.

3   Experiments

We perform experiments using 300W, COFW and AFLW that are considered the most challenging public face alignment data sets. To train our algorithm we shuffle each training subset and split it into 90% train-set and 10% validation-set.

We use common evaluation metrics to measure the shape estimation error. We employ the normalized mean error (NME), the average euclidean distance between the ground-truth and estimated landmark positions normalized with the constant d_i. Depending on the database we report our results using different values of d_i: the distance between the eye centers (*pupils*), the distance between the outer eye corners (*corners*) and the bounding box size (*height*). The NME is given by

$$NME = \frac{100}{N} \sum_{i=1}^{N} \left(\frac{1}{||\mathbf{w}_i^g||_1} \sum_{l=1}^{L} \left(\frac{\mathbf{w}_i^g(l) \cdot ||\mathbf{x}_i(l) - \mathbf{x}_i^g(l)||}{d_i} \right) \right), \tag{2}$$

where $\mathbf{x}_i(l)$ and $\mathbf{x}_i^g(l)$ denote respectively the predicted and ground truth landmarks positions.

In addition, we also use a second group of metrics based on the Cumulative Error Distribution (CED) curve. We calculate AUC_ε as the area under the CED curve for faces with NME smaller than ε and FR_ε as the failure rate representing the percentage of testing faces with error greater than ε.

For our experiments we train the CRN stage by stage, selecting the model parameters with lower validation error. We crop faces using the bounding boxes annotations enlarged by 30%. We augment the data in each epoch by applying random rotations between $\pm30°$, scaling by $\pm15\%$ and translating by $\pm5\%$ of bounding box size, randomly flipping images horizontally and generating random rectangular occlusions. We use Adam stochastic optimization with parameters $\beta_1 = 0.9$, $\beta_2 = 0.999$ and $\epsilon = 1e^{-8}$. We train each stage until convergence. Initial learning rate is $\alpha = 0.001$. When the validation error levels out for 10 epochs, we multiply the learning rate by 0.05. The cropped input face is reduced from 160×160 to 1×1 pixels gradually halving their size across $B = 8$ branches applying a stride 2 convolution with kernel size 2×2[1]. All layers contain 68 filters to describe the required landmarks features. We apply a Gaussian filter with $\sigma = 31$ to the output probability maps to reduce the noise effect. Finally, we set the number of stages $S = 2$ since more stages report a poor improvement. Training using AFLW takes 24 h using a NVidia GeForce GTX 1080Ti GPU (11 GB) with a batch size of 32 images.

At run-time our method requires on average 40 ms to process a detected face, a rate of 25 FPS. This processing speed could be halved reducing the number of CNN stages, at the expense of a slight reduction in accuracy (see CRN ($S\!=\!1$) at Tables 1, 2, 3 and 4).

We compare our model with the top algorithms in the literature. We show in Tables 1, 2, 3 and 4 the results reported in their papers. We have also trained DAN [5], RCN [3], and GPRT [6] with the same settings, including same training, validation and bounding boxes. In Fig. 2 we plot the CED curves. In the legend we provide the AUC_8 and FR_8 values for each algorithm.

---

[1] 5×5 images are reduced to 2×2 pixels applying a kernel size of 3×3.

From the results in Tables 1 and 2 we can conclude that in the 300W data set our approach provides results with an accuracy comparable to the best in the literature. However, we notice that Yang *et al.* [11] takes several seconds to process one image, whereas ours runs in real-time. In COFW we report the best result in the literature (see Table 3). Similarly, in the largest and most challenging data set, AFLW, we claim to report the best result, since TSR [7] ignores the two landmarks attached to the ears, which are the ones with largest error (see Table 4).

If we consider the CED metrics in Fig. 2, we can see that our approach, CRN, is the one with highest AUC values and smallest FR. In all experiments our CED

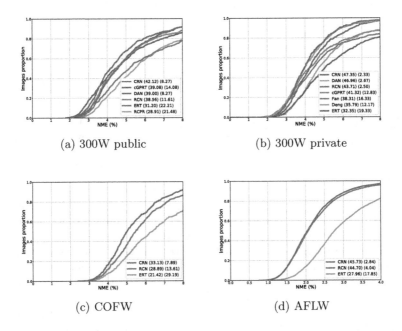

(a) 300W public   (b) 300W private

(c) COFW   (d) AFLW

Fig. 2. Cumulative error distributions sorted by AUC for each data set.

Table 1. Error of face alignment methods on the 300W public test set.

Method	Common		Challenging		Full			
	Pupils NME	Corners NME	Pupils NME	Corners NME	Pupils NME	Corners		
						NME	AUC_8	FR_8
RCN [3]	4.70	-	9.00	-	5.54	-	-	-
RCN+DKM [3]	4.67	-	8.44	-	5.41	-	-	-
DAN [5]	4.42	3.19	7.57	5.24	5.03	3.59	55.33	1.16
TSR [7]	4.36	-	7.56	-	4.99	-	-	-
RAR [10]	4.12	-	8.35	-	4.94	-	-	-
SHN [11]	4.12	-	7.00	4.90	-	-	-	-
CRN ($S = 1$)	4.26	3.07	8.69	6.01	5.09	3.62	55.62	2.75
CRN ($S = 2$)	4.12	2.97	7.90	5.47	4.83	3.44	57.44	1.88

Table 2. Error of face alignment methods on the 300W private test set.

Method	Indoor corners			Outdoor corners			Full corners		
	NME	AUC_8	FR_8	NME	AUC_8	FR_8	NME	AUC_8	FR_8
DAN [5]	-	-	-	-	-	-	4.30	47.00	2.67
SHN [11]	4.10	-	-	4.00	-	-	4.05	-	-
CRN $(S=1)$	4.42	45.91	1.66	4.45	45.25	2.66	4.43	45.59	2.16
CRN $(S=2)$	4.28	47.36	2.66	4.25	47.32	2.00	4.26	47.35	2.33

Table 3. COFW results.

Method	Pupils		
	NME	AUC_8	FR_8
RAR [10]	6.03	-	-
Wu *et al.* [9]	5.93	-	-
SHN [11]	5.6	-	-
CRN $(S=1)$	5.75	30.91	11.04
CRN $(S=2)$	5.49	33.13	7.88

Table 4. AFLW results.

Method	Height
	NME
Bulat *et al.* [2]	2.85
CCL [13]	2.72
TSR [7]	2.17
CRN $(S=1)$	2.29
CRN $(S=2)$	2.21

curve is consistently above the rest except for the cGPRT [6] algorithm in the 300W public data set. In this case, cGPRT reports better results in "easy" faces, with NME below 3.5, and we are much better in the difficult cases, with higher NMEs, and in the final FR_8 and global AUC_8.

We have also compared CRN with the original RCN baseline model and its denoising key-point model approach (RCN+DKM) [3]. Our modifications to the basic net together with the cascade have boosted the result to the top of the state-of-the-art.

Finally, in Fig. 3, we report qualitative results for all data sets. Here we have also included the recent Menpo competition [12] images whose test annotations have not been released.

(a) 300W public

(b) 300W private

(c) COFW

(d) AFLW

(e) Menpo

Fig. 3. Representative results using CRN in 300W, COFW, AFLW and Menpo testing subsets. The first three faces and the following three ones show respectively successful and failure cases. Blue and green colors represent ground truth and shape predictions. (Color figure online)

4   Conclusions

In this paper we have introduced CRN, a facial landmarks detection algorithm that exploits the benefits of a cascade of CNN regressors to make the set of estimated landmark positions lie closer to the valid shape of a human face.

We have proved experimentally that our improvements to the basic Recombinator model together with the cascade approach and the data augmentation boost the performance to achieve state-of-the-art results in the 300W data set and the best reported results in COFW and AFLW.

The analysis of the CED curves show that our approach is consistently above all its competitors except for the easy/frontal images in the 300W public set, for which cGPRT [6] has better results. This proves that CNN approaches are more robust in challenging situations, but a standard cascade of regressors with handcrafted local features such as cGPRT may achieve better results when it is properly initialized. To facilitate the reproduction of our results we will release our implementation after publication.

Acknowledgments. Authors acknowledge funding from the Spanish Ministry of Economy and Competitiveness under project TIN2016-75982-C2-2-R.

References

1. Amador, E., Valle, R., Buenaposada, J.M., Baumela, L.: Benchmarking head pose estimation in-the-wild. In: Proceedings of Iberoamerican Congress on Pattern Recognition (CIARP) (2017)
2. Bulat, A., Tzimiropoulos, G.: Binarized convolutional landmark localizers for human pose estimation and face alignment with limited resources. In: Proceedings of International Conference on Computer Vision (ICCV) (2017)
3. Honari, S., Yosinski, J., Vincent, P., Pal, C.J.: Recombinator networks: learning coarse-to-fine feature aggregation. In: Proceedings of IEEE Conference on Computer Vision and Pattern Recognition (CVPR) (2016)
4. Kazemi, V., Sullivan, J.: One millisecond face alignment with an ensemble of regression trees. In: Proceedings of IEEE Conference on Computer Vision and Pattern Recognition (CVPR) (2014)
5. Kowalski, M., Naruniec, J., Trzcinski, T.: Deep alignment network: a convolutional neural network for robust face alignment. In: Proceedings of IEEE Conference on Computer Vision and Pattern Recognition Workshops (CVPRW) (2017)
6. Lee, D., Park, H., Yoo, C.D.: Face alignment using cascade Gaussian process regression trees. In: Proceedings of IEEE Conference on Computer Vision and Pattern Recognition (CVPR) (2015)
7. Lv, J., Shao, X., Xing, J., Cheng, C., Zhou, X.: A deep regression architecture with two-stage re-initialization for high performance facial landmark detection. In: Proceedings of IEEE Conference on Computer Vision and Pattern Recognition (CVPR) (2017)
8. Sun, Y., Wang, X., Tang, X.: Hybrid deep learning for face verification. IEEE Trans. Pattern Anal. Mach. Intell. (TPAMI) **38**, 1997–2009 (2016)
9. Wu, Y., Ji, Q.: Robust facial landmark detection under significant head poses and occlusion. In: Proceedings of International Conference on Computer Vision (ICCV) (2015)
10. Xiao, S., Feng, J., Xing, J., Lai, H., Yan, S., Kassim, A.: Robust facial landmark detection via recurrent attentive-refinement networks. In: Leibe, B., Matas, J., Sebe, N., Welling, M. (eds.) ECCV 2016. LNCS, vol. 9905, pp. 57–72. Springer, Cham (2016). https://doi.org/10.1007/978-3-319-46448-0_4
11. Yang, J., Liu, Q., Zhang, K.: Stacked hourglass network for robust facial landmark localisation. In: Proceedings of IEEE Conference on Computer Vision and Pattern Recognition Workshops (CVPRW) (2017)

12. Zafeiriou, S., Trigeorgis, G., Chrysos, G., Deng, J., Shen, J.: The menpo facial landmark localisation challenge: a step towards the solution. In: Proceedings of IEEE Conference on Computer Vision and Pattern Recognition Workshops (CVPRW) (2017)
13. Zhu, S., Li, C., Change, C., Tang, X.: Unconstrained face alignment via cascaded compositional learning. In: Proceedings of IEEE Conference on Computer Vision and Pattern Recognition (CVPR) (2016)

Measuring the Gender and Ethnicity Bias in Deep Models for Face Recognition

Alejandro Acien[✉], Aythami Morales[✉],
Ruben Vera-Rodriguez[✉], Ivan Bartolome[✉], and Julian Fierrez[✉]

Biometrics and Data Pattern Analytics (BiDA) Lab, EPS, Universidad Autonoma
de Madrid, C/Francisco Tomas y Valiente 11, 28049 Madrid, Spain
{alejandro.acien, aythami.morales, ruben.vera,
bartolome.gonzalez, julian.fierrez}@uam.es

Abstract. We explore the importance of gender and ethnic attributes in the decision-making of face recognition technologies. Our work is in part motivated by the new European regulation for personal data protection, which forces data controllers to avoid discriminative hazards while managing sensitive data like biometric data. The experiments in this paper are aimed to study what extent sensitive data like gender or ethnic origin attributes are present in the most common face recognition networks. For this, our experiments include two popular pre-trained networks: VGGFace and Resnet50. Both pre-trained models are able to classify gender and ethnicity easily (over 95% of performance) even suppressing 80% of the neurons in their embedding layers. The experimentation is conducted on a publicly available database known as Labeled Faces in the Wild with more than 13000 images of faces with a huge range of poses, ages, races and nationalities.

Keywords: Face recognition · Human attributes · Gender · Ethnic · Discrimination

1 Introduction

Face recognitions systems have become popular due to good performance in human recognition, which has led this technology to take on a leading role in the last years. For example, common devices such as smartphones or laptops are applying face recognition for authentication and verification improving traditional recognition technologies based on passwords or swipe patterns. Advanced video surveillance also apply face recognition for continuous monitoring or intrusion detection with good results [1, 2]. Additionally, various applications of face recognition are beyond identity management. The capacity to collect personal data has given advertisers the possibility to individualize marketing campaigns [3]. User profiling based on face images is a technology that brings the opportunity to collect gender, age and ethnicity from a picture of the face.

The performance of face recognition technology has been boosted by deep convolutional neuronal networks that have drastically reduced the error rates in the last decade [4]. These developments have resulted in a large variety of networks available for the research community and industry. Among the most popular stand out VGGFace [5],

© Springer Nature Switzerland AG 2019
R. Vera-Rodriguez et al. (Eds.): CIARP 2018, LNCS 11401, pp. 584–593, 2019.
https://doi.org/10.1007/978-3-030-13469-3_68

Resnet50 [6] and FaceNet [7]. These neuronal networks architectures are able to identify people with a face image with more than 97% of accuracy in the public dataset Labeled Face in the Wild [8], furthermore the pre-trained models (both architecture and weights) of these networks are totally available and the use of them by research groups and commercial applications is growing continuously. As example of the impact of these pre-trained models, VGGFace, Resnet50 and FaceNet references [5–7] have achieved more than 12900 citations during the last 3 years according to Google Scholar.

A face image reveals information not only about who we are but also about what we are. During last decade, researchers have proposed to exploit auxiliary data of the users to improve face recognition [9, 10]. Most of these auxiliary data, such as gender, ethnicity, age and behavior among others, can be easily inferred from a face picture. These auxiliary data are known as soft biometrics, which refer to those biometrics that can distinguish different groups of people but do not provide enough information to uniquely identify a person. Those attributes can be extracted with high accuracy (over 95%) using just one face picture [11].

Biometric technology and privacy of users have been confronting each other for a long time [12]. There is a never-ending trade-off between security of citizens and their privacy. Citizens and governments around the world are very conscious about data protection and personal information on the Big Data era. As a prove of this, in April 2016 the European Parliament adopted a set of laws aimed to regularize the collection, storage and use of personal information, the General Data Protection Regulation (GDPR) [13]. Biometric data is defined as sensitive data in this new GDPR due to its capacity to *"uniquely identifying a natural person"*. This regulation is a step forward with respect to previous national and European laws and establishes the foundations of what anyone can do with data in this new era. Is biometric technology complying with this new regulation? According to paragraph 71 of GDPR, data controllers who process sensitive data have to *"implement appropriate technical and organizational measures..."* that *"...prevent, inter alia, discriminatory effects"*. The discrimination is the unjust or prejudicial treatment of different categories of people, especially on the grounds of race, age, religion or gender. According to this definition, face images belong to this group of sensitive data regulated by the GDPR [14]. Facial attributes revealing the gender, age or ethnic have the potential to discriminate citizens based on the group to which that person belongs. It is important to note that we do not argue that face technology is discriminatory but rather, the hazard exists in case of unethical usages.

The aim of this paper is to study to what extent discriminative attributes such as gender or race can be obtained from feature vectors generated by state-of-the-art face recognition algorithms. This information is part of the decision making of any application based on these algorithms even if we use high-dimensional feature spaces trained for a different task. Our experiments include two popular pre-trained models: VGGFace and Resnet50. These models are able to classify gender and race easily with high performance (up to 95%) just adding a classification layer to the pre-trained model. Furthermore, suppressing most of the features from the features vector, they still classify gender and race quite well, showing the discriminative power of these attributes in VGGFace and Resnet50 pre-trained models. For our experiments, we use face images from the publicly available database LFW (Labeled Faces in the Wild). This database comprises over 13000 face images with high variety of races, poses, ages and nationalities. We have chosen LFW database because many state-of-the-art face recognition algorithms use it as a benchmark for comparisons.

The rest of this paper is organized as follows: Sect. 2 explains the method proposed to achieve our goals. Section 3 describes the database and the experimental protocol. Section 4 presents the results and Sect. 5 summarizes the conclusions.

2   Proposed Method

Our objective is to measure to what extent gender and ethnicity information is present in the feature vectors generated by two of the most popular state-of-the-art face recognition models: VGGFace and Resnet50. To do this, we will follow two approaches:

Fixed Classification: we employ the pre-trained models to extract the feature vector from each face image by removing the last classification layer from both models [5]. Then, we add a fully connected layer and train this layer in order to classify attributes. Finally, we will gradually suppress the most relevant features from the embedding layer (i.e., the layer that extracts the feature vectors) and test the networks for attribute classification and for identity verification as well. The idea is to test whether it is possible to keep a high performance in the verification task while suppressing the embedding features related to gender or ethnicity.

Retrained Classification: the second approach studies what happens if we retrain the attribute classification layer after the suppression of these embedding features. To do this, in each iteration we suppress features and retrain the attribute classification layer using the remaining features.

3   Experiments

3.1   Database

The experiments are conducted in the LFW database (Labeled Faced in the Wild) [8]. LFW is one of the most popular datasets used in face recognition with more than 13000 face images of famous people collected from the web. We have used the aligned dataset where each image was aligned with funneling techniques [15] and labeled according to the gender, age and ethnicity among others (see [16] for details). The database was split into training and test set according to the "*View 1*" protocol [8]. This protocol employs up to 4038 face images for training and 1711 for testing. The database is highly biased, the statistics related to gender and ethnicity attributes are summarized in Table 1. We can observe that both gender and ethnicity distributions are unbalanced, as most of the images belong to Caucasian male. An unbalanced dataset could yield a drop of performance for classes with less samples, but as we will see in the next section the performance is stable across classes despite of the unbalanced dataset. We have decided to use the public protocol in order to allow a fair comparison with existing benchmarks.

Table 1. Distribution of gender and ethnicity in the considered LFW dataset.

	Gender (male)	Ethnicity (Caucasian/Black/Asian)
Train	74.2%	79.8%/6.3%/13.9%
Test	74.4%	81.5%/6.2%/12.3%

3.2 Face Recognition Pre-trained Models

We use two popular CNNs which have recently achieved some of the best state-of-the-art performance in face recognition tasks: VGGFace, proposed in [5], and ResNet50, proposed in [6].

VGGFace is a CNN with a VGG16 architecture (see [5] for details) trained from scratch with a dataset that contains more than 2,6 million images of 2622 celebrities (different from LFW). The architecture comprises 8 blocks of convolutional layers followed by activation layers like ReLU or maxpooling, and 3 blocks of fully connected layers with ReLU activations. VGGFace has an overall of 145,002,878 parameters split in 16 trainable layers (convolutional and fully connected layers). The results obtained testing VGGFace for verification with LFW and YFD (Youtube Face Dataset) datasets were 97.27% and 92.8% of accuracy respectively.

ResNet50 is another CNN based on Residual Neuronal Network architecture. This network is inspired in VGG nets, but with fewer filters and lower complexity. The key of this network is to insert shortcut connections among blocks which turn the network into a residual network version. ResNet50 has a total of 41,192,951 parameters split in 34 residual layers for training. In [17], they trained from scratch a ResNet50 network with VGGface2 dataset. VGGface2 contains up to 3,331 million images of 9,321 subjects and was collected with a huge range of pose, age and ethnicity. This Resnet50 model is aimed to improve the recognition performance over age and pose, achieving 98.0% of accuracy in verification testing with the IJB-A dataset [18] according to [17].

3.3 Experimental Protocol

We employ the pre-trained models of VGGFace and ResNet50 provided in [19]. These model were tested using the *"unrestricted"* and *"outside training data"* protocols proposed in [8], due to both pre-trained models were trained with other databases, namely: [5] for VGGFace, and VGGFace2 [17] for Resnet50 respectively. The protocol includes 6000 one-to-one comparisons composed by 3000 genuine pairs (pairs of images from the same person) and 3000 impostor pairs (pairs of images belonging to different persons).

Identity Verification: The feature vectors for each face image are extracted removing the last classification layer from both models. The number of features extracted is $L = 4096$ and $L = 2048$ for VGGFace and ResNet50 respectively. The distance between two face embeddings is obtained as the L2-distance for one-to-one comparisons in the verification task.

VGGFace achieves 92.3% of verification accuracy and Resnet50 84.1%. Note that performance on VGGFace is slightly worse as the one reported in [5]. This is due to different preprocessing of the data.

Gender and Ethnicity Classification: We add a fully connected layer with one unit in order to classify attributes (see Fig. 1) and freeze all remaining layers. Then, we train two separate layers for gender and ethnicity. About training details: the learning rate was $\alpha = 10^{-4}$, Adam optimizer was used with $\beta_1 = 0.9, \beta_2 = 0.999$ and $\varepsilon = 10^{-8}$ respectively, 50 epochs for VGGFace and 30 epochs for ResNet50 without minibatches. The activation function of the classification layer was sigmoid for gender (only one neuron for gender classification) and softmax for ethnicity (three neurons to classify among Black, Asian and Caucasian people). The performance will be reported in terms of correct classification accuracy.

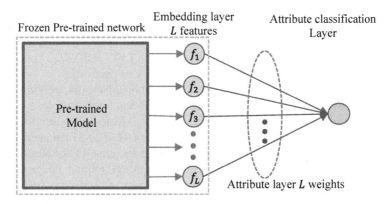

Fig. 1. Architecture of the VGGFace network trained for gender classification. Only the $L = 4096$ weights from the attribute classification layer were trained from scratch, the remaining weights are equal to the pre-trained VGGFace model.

4   Results

The performance achieved by both CNNs trained for classification of gender and ethnicity are summarized in Table 2. The best results are obtained with VGGFace network in both tasks.

Table 2. Accuracy (%) of VGGFace and ResNet50 trained for gender and ethnicity classification.

	VGGFace	ResNet50
Gender	94.8	89.01
Ethnicity	90.1	80.05

Figure 2 shows the distribution of weights obtained for the attribute-classification layer of VGGFace. We can observe similar normal distributions for both attributes with a high percentage of weights close to zero. There are two possible reasons for these weights: (A) some features do not include information about these attributes and therefore to their contribution is minimized during the attribute classification training or; (B) there is a high level of redundancy in the features and some features are minimized during training.

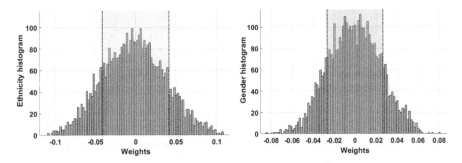

Fig. 2. Histograms of weights on the classification layer of VGGFace. The grey area contains 70% of the weights.

To measure the presence of gender or ethnicity information in the identity verification task, we will evaluate the verification performance decay by suppressing features from the embedding layer gradually in accordance of it gender/ethnicity importance. For that purpose, we suppress a feature by forcing the value of its weight in the classification layer to zero, starting from the weights with highest absolute values to lower ones. At the same time, we test the network for identity verification trying to keep a high performance in verification while we suppress the neurons related to gender or ethnicity discrimination.

Figure 3 shows the performance decay for gender classification and identity verification tasks related to the percentage of suppressed features (from highest to lowest importance in gender classification). We can observe that both models are able to achieve almost 80% of accuracy for gender recognition with 50% of the features of the classification layer suppressed. Even though VGGFace achieves better gender classification performance, its performance drops faster than ResNet50, which is able to classify up to 75% of accuracy with 65% of weights suppressed. Regarding the verification task, it was surprising to find out that the performance keeps stable while we gradually suppress neurons from the embedding layer. In fact, VGGFace is able to verify with only 10% of the neurons (less than 400 neurons) from its embedding layer without performance decay. Regarding ResNet50, the performance starts to drop when 70% of neurons are suppressed. This behavior shows there is a very high redundancy of neurons in these networks in their embedding layer for identity verification. Finally, suppressing 80%, the two networks are still able to verify the identity of the users with a similar performance as using all their original embeddings.

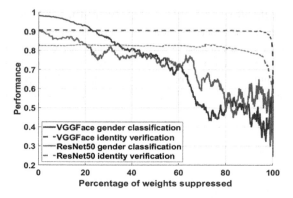

Fig. 3. Classification and verification performance of both VGGFace and ResNet50 models according to the percentage of weights suppressed for gender classification.

In ethnicity classification, our experiments include three classes: Caucasian, Asian and Black. The classification accuracy was calculated for each class according to a one-vs-all protocol. In this case, the classification layer has $3 \times L$ weights (L weights for each class) and we add all three weights vectors in order to have only one vector of L weights to sort [20]. The idea is to sort the weights according to the most relevant weights for all classes (ethnicities).

Figure 4 shows the performance decay for ethnicity classification in both models related to the number of weights suppressed (from highest to lowest importance in ethnicity classification). It is remarkable how well both networks classify Black with 90% of accuracy even if the training dataset was highly unbalanced. Regarding Caucasian and Asian, ResNet50 achieves worse performance and decays faster than VGGFace.

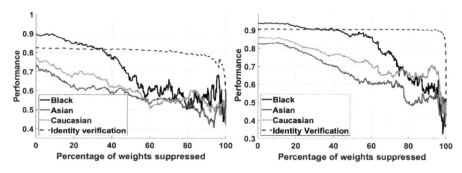

Fig. 4. Classification and verification performance of ResNet50 (left) and VGGFace (right) according to percentage of weights suppressed for ethnicity classification.

Regarding identity verification, we can see again that performance is not affected by the neurons suppressed until we suppress almost all of them. These experiments suggest that we can suppress features in order to reduce the gender and ethnicity bias while keeping the verification performance of the face recognition algorithms. However, the results showed in Figs. 3 and 4 were obtained on the basis of a training phase including all the embedding features. What if we retrain the attribute classification layer after the suppression of these features? To do this, in each itineration we suppress again the most "relevant" feature (the one with the highest absolute weight value) of the embedding layer and we retrain the attribute classification model using the remaining features, always freezing the network up to the embedding layer. Figure 5 depicts the performance for VGGFace. As we expected, the model is able to keep almost the same performance until 50% of features are suppressed. This demonstrates that gender and ethnicity attributes are latent in almost all features of the embedding layer for both pre-trained networks. Even with 85% of the features suppressed they are still able to classify quite well, revealing the discriminative power of these models.

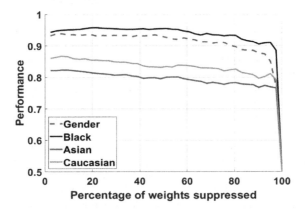

Fig. 5. Performance of VGGFace for gender and ethnicity classification retraining the classification layer in each iteration.

5 Conclusions

In this paper, we have studied the importance of gender and ethnicity attributes in the decision-making of the most popular face recognition technologies. Although these attributes are useful for recognition, the risk using them for unethical purpose is tacit.

Firstly, we have explored how well VGGFace and Resnet50 pre-trained models classify gender and ethnicity by training a classification layer connected to the embedding layer of these models. The results suggest that these networks are able to discriminate among gender and ethnicity without performance decay suppressing almost 50% of the neurons of their embedding layer.

We have then studied the impact in identity verification of removing features related to gender and ethnicity. For the considered deep models, we have shown that removing up to 90% of the embedding features most related to gender and ethnicity does not affect much their performance in identity verification.

As future work, we are interested in more advanced methods for improving privacy in biometrics data processing, both at the learning stage [21] or by incorporating cryptographic constructions [22].

Acknowledgments. This work was funded by the project CogniMetrics (TEC2015-70627-R) and Bio-Guard (Ayudas Fundación BBVA a Equipos de Investigación Científica 2017).

References

1. Neves, J., Narducci, F., Barra, S., Proença, H.: Biometric recognition in surveillance scenarios: a survey. Artif. Intell. Rev. **46**(4), 515–541 (2016)
2. Gonzalez-Sosa, E., Vera-Rodriguez, R., Fierrez, J., Ortega-Garcia, J.: Exploring facial regions in unconstrained scenarios: experience on ICB-RW. IEEE Intell. Syst. **33**(3), 60–63 (2018)
3. Selinger, E., Polonetsky, J., Tene, O.: The Cambridge Handbook of Consumer Privacy, 1st edn. Cambridge University Press, Cambridge (2018)
4. Ranjan, R., et al.: Deep learning for understanding faces: machines may be just as good, or better, than humans. IEEE Signal Process. Mag. **35**, 66–83 (2018)
5. Parkhi, O.M., Vedaldi, A., Zisserman, A.: Deep face recognition. Proc. Br. Mach. Vis. **1**(3), 6 (2015)
6. He, K., Zhang, X., Ren, S., Sun, J.: Deep residual learning for image recognition. In: CVPR, pp. 770–778 (2016)
7. Schroff, F., Kalenichenko, D., Philbin., J.: FaceNet: a unified embedding for face recognition and clustering. In: Proceedings of CVPR (2015)
8. LFW Homepage. http://vis-www.cs.umass.edu/lfw/. Accessed 15 June 2018
9. Tome, P., Fierrez, J., Vera-Rodriguez, R., Nixon, M.: Soft biometrics and their application in person recognition at a distance. IEEE Trans. Inf. Forensics Secur. **9**(3), 464–475 (2014)
10. Tome, P., Vera-Rodriguez, R., Fierrez, J., Ortega-Garcia, J.: Facial soft biometric features for forensic face recognition. In: Forensic Science International, vol. 257, pp. 171–284, December 2015
11. Dantcheva, A., Elia, P., Ross, A.: What else does your biometric data reveal? A survey on soft biometrics. IEEE Trans. Inf. Forensics Secur. **11**(3), 441–467 (2016)
12. Prabhakar, S., Pankanti, S., Jain, A.K.: Biometric recognition: Security and privacy concerns. IEEE Secur. Priv. Mag. **1**(2), 33–42 (2003)
13. EU 2016/679 (General Data Protection Regulation). https://gdpr-info.eu/. Accessed 17 Oct 2018
14. Goodman, B., Flaxman, F.: European Union regulations on algorithmic decision-making and a "right to explanation". AI Mag. **38**(3), 50–57 (2016)
15. Huang, G.B., Mattar, M., Lee, H., Learned-Miller, E.: Learning to Align from the scratch. In: Advances in Neural Information Processing Systems NIPS (2012)
16. Gonzalez-Sosa, E., Fierrez, J., Vera-Rodriguez, R., Alonso-Fernandez, F.: Facial Soft biometrics for recognition in the wild: recent works, annotation and COTS evaluation. IEEE Trans. Inf. Forensics Secur. **13**(7), 2001–2014 (2018)
17. Cao, Q., Shen, L., Xie, W., M. Parkhi, O., Zisserman, A.: VGGFace2: a dataset for recognising faces across pose and age. arXiv:1710.08092 (2017)
18. Klare, B., et al.: Pushing the frontiers of unconstrained face detection and recognition: IARPA Janus benchmark A. In: CVPR, pp. 1931–1939 (2015)

19. Malli, R.C.: Github Homepage. https://github.com/rcmalli/keras-vggface. Accessed 15 June 2018
20. Fierrez, J., Morales, A., Vera-Rodriguez, R., Camacho, D.: Multiple classifiers in biometrics. Part 1: fundamentals and review. Inf. Fusion **44**, 57–64 (2018)
21. Mirjalili, V., Raschka, S., Namboodiri, A., Ross, A.: Semi-adversarial networks: convolutional autoencoders for imparting privacy to face images. In: Proceedings of 11th IAPR International Conference on Biometrics, Australia, February 2018
22. Gomez-Barrero, M., Maiorana, E., Galbally, J., Campisi, P., Fierrez, J.: Multi-biometric template protection based on homomorphic encryption. Pattern Recogn. **67**, 149–163 (2017)

3D Face Recognition with Reconstructed Faces from a Collection of 2D Images

João Baptista Cardia Neto[1(✉)] and Aparecido Nilceu Marana[2]

[1] São Carlos Federal University - UFSCAR, São Carlos, SP 13565-905, Brazil
joao.cardia@fatec.sp.gov.br
[2] UNESP - São Paulo State University, Bauru, SP 17033-360, Brazil
nilceu@fc.unesp.br

Abstract. Nowadays, there is an increasing need for systems that can accurately and quickly identify a person. Traditional identification methods utilize something a person knows or something a person has. This kind of methods has several drawbacks, being the main one the fact that it is impossible to detect an imposter who uses genuine credentials to pass as a genuine person. One way to solve these kinds of problems is to utilize biometric identification. The face is one of the biometric features that best suits the covert identification. However, in general, biometric systems based on 2D face recognition perform very poorly in unconstrained environments, common in covert identification scenarios, since the input images present variations in pose, illumination, and facial expressions. One way to mitigate this problem is to use 3D face data, but the current 3D scanners are expensive and require a lot of cooperation from people being identified. Therefore, in this work, we propose an approach based on local descriptors for 3D Face Recognition based on 3D face models reconstructed from collections of 2D images. Initial results show 95% in a subset of the LFW Face dataset.

Keywords: Biometrics · 3D face recognition · 3DLBP ·
Face reconstruction

1 Introduction

The several drawbacks of the traditional methods have stimulated the research on biometric identification methods, which are based on biological or behavioral traits of the individuals. Because biometric identification systems use something that persons are, they are more difficult to circumvent [11].

In surveillance systems, the utilization of biometric characteristics can drastically improve the system performance and, among several other characteristics, face has several advantages [9]. Face is the biometric feature that best suits the covert identification, since the current technology is able to provide high resolution 2D face images captured by low cost cameras, in a secret way, at a distance and without cooperation from the people being identified [9]. However,

© Springer Nature Switzerland AG 2019
R. Vera-Rodriguez et al. (Eds.): CIARP 2018, LNCS 11401, pp. 594–601, 2019.
https://doi.org/10.1007/978-3-030-13469-3_69

in general, biometric systems based on 2D face recognition perform very poorly in unconstrained environments, common in covert identification scenarios, since the input images present variations in pose, illumination and facial expressions.

One way to increase the automated facial recognition system accuracy is to utilize sensing devices such as 3D scanners [5]. However, it would be impossible to utilize such scanners in unconstrained environments for covert identification, since they need cooperation from the people being identified, in order to capture the 3D face models.

One alternative for obtaining 3D facial data from a person, without collaboration, in unconstrained scenarios, would be to reconstruct a 3D face model from a gallery of 2D face images of such a person. The reconstruction method proposed by [13] can be utilized to such end.

In this work we intend to develop a new approach based on 3D face models obtained from collections of 2D face images, in order to identify people in unconstrained or very harsh environments.

2   Unconstrained 3D Face Reconstruction

The method proposed by [13] has the following three main steps (for more details refer to the original work):

First step: Given a collection of unconstrained face images, the method performs 2D landmark estimation and enhances a 3D template by deforming a generic 3D face template such that the projection of its 3D landmarks are consistent with the estimated 2D landmarks;

Second step: The method estimates the person-specific face normals via photometric stereo. It takes 2D face images at all poses and project them onto the enhanced 3D face template to establish a dense correspondence across the images. Then, it jointly estimates the lighting and surface normals via SVD (Singular-Value Decomposition);

Third step: The method deforms the 3D shape so that its updated surface normals become similar to the estimated ones, under the landmark constrain and an additional boundary constraint. This process iterates until convergence.

Figure 1 illustrates the result of the 3D face model reconstruction of a person from a collection of 2D faces from this person by using the method proposed in [13].

3   3D Local Binary Pattern

In [4] the 3D Local Binary Patterns (3DLBP) was proposed. This variation of the original operator considers not only the signal of the difference, but also the absolute depth difference. In the original work was stated that, for face, more than 93% of all depth differences (DD) with $R = 2$ are smaller than 7. Due to this property the absolute value of the DD is stored in three binary units ($i_2 i_3 i_4$). Therefore, it is possible to affirm:

$$|DD| = i_2 \cdot 2^2 + i_3 \cdot 2^1 + i_4 \cdot 2^0 \tag{1}$$

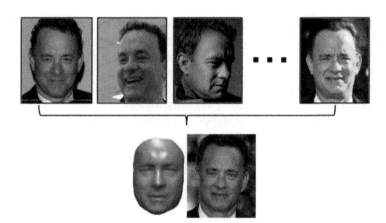

Fig. 1. Example of the 3D face model reconstructed by using the method in [13]. Adapted from: http://cvlab.cse.msu.edu/project-face-recon.html

There is also i_1, a binary unit defined by:

$$i_1 = \begin{cases} 1 \text{ if DD } \geq 0; \\ 0 \text{ if DD } < 0. \end{cases} \tag{2}$$

Those four binary units are divided into four layers and, for each of those layers, four decimal numbers are obtained: P_1, P_2, P_3, P_4. The value of the P_1 has the same value as the original LBP. For matching, the histograms of the local regions (P_1, P_2, P_3, P_4) are concatenated. The Fig. 3 shows the process for the generation of the 3DLBP, given an image (Fig. 2).

4   Proposed Method

Our method receives a collection of 2D face images and, utilizing the reconstruction method [13], builds a 3D face model. After constructing the model our method extracts a cloud point and utilizes it as input to the 3DLBP module.

The 3DLBP module was inspired in [2] but, after the construction of the new depth maps, the 3DLBP is applied in 64 micro regions and the histograms of each of those regions are concatenated. The final image descriptor is the concatenation of the histograms from each region. Figure 3 shows a block diagram of our proposed method for 3D face recognition with reconstructed faces from a collection of 2D images.

The pre-processing steps are the following:

Symmetric Filling: The Symmetric Filling technique, proposed in [7], utilizes the left side of the face to increase point density by including the set of mirrored points from the right side of the face, and vice-versa. However, not all the mirrored points are useful because the goal is to fill only in the missing

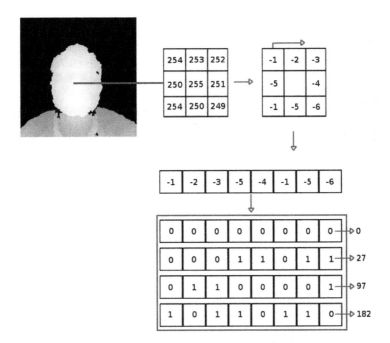

Fig. 2. The process of the 3DLBP proposed by [4]. Each of the differences is encoded into the layers (layer 2, 3 and 4) and the signal into the layer 1.

data (occluded regions, for instance). Likewise in [7], the strategy to be used in our method is to add the mirrored point only if there is no neighboring point at that location. During this process, if the Euclidean distance from a mirrored point to its neighbors in the original point cloud is greater than a threshold value δ, then that point will be added to the original face data.

Iterative Closest Point: The Iterative Closest Point (ICP) [1], is a very well known solution for the problem of registration. It tries to find a rigid transformation that minimizes the least-square distance between two points. Given two 3D point set (A and B), ICP performs the following three basic steps:

1. Pair each point of A to the closest point in B;
2. Compute the motion that gives the lowest Mean Squared Error (MSE) between the points;
3. Apply the motion to the point set A and update the MSE.

The three aforementioned steps are performed until the MSE is lower than a threshold τ. A complete description of this method can be found in [1,3].

Savitzky-Golay Filter: The Savitzky-Golay filter is a lowpass filter based on least-squares polynomial approximation [15]. The Savitzky-Golay filter tries to find filter coefficients c_n that preserves the higher moments of the filtered data. It utilizes the idea of a window moving through the function data and approximate it by a polynomial of higher order, quadratic or quartic [12]. More details about this filter can be found in [14,15].

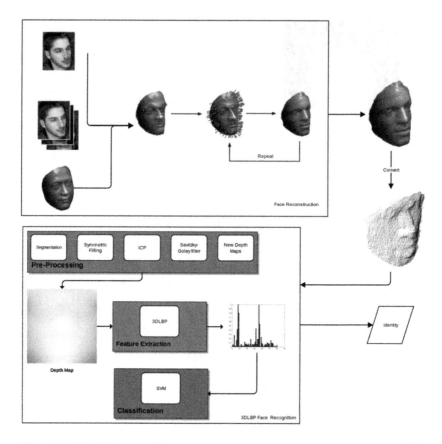

Fig. 3. A block diagram that describes the proposed method. Inspired in [2].

Generation of Depth Map: In the proposed method, depth maps from cloud points must be generated. Cloud points will be obtained from the reconstructed 3D face models. In order to generate depth maps from cloud points, a circular region with radius R is cropped centered at the nose tip. Then, the cropped image goes through the symmetric filling process. Finally, the resulting face image is fitted to a smooth surface using an approximation method, implemented by an open source code[1] written in Matlab. The result of this process is a 100×100 matrix, as illustrated in Fig. 3.

5   Databases

For evaluating the performance of the proposed approach we utilized the Labeled Faces in the Wild (LFW).

---

[1] http://mathworks.com/matlabcentral/fileexchange/8998-surface-fitting-using-gridfit.

The Labeled Faces in the Wild [6] is a dataset composed of 13,000 images collected on the Web, to serve as means for studying the problem of unconstrained face recognition. The dataset contains 1,680 subjects with a varying quantity of images, each folder of a subject is labeled with its name. The Fig. 4 shows some examples of the LFW face dataset.

Fig. 4. Examples from a set of images from the LFW Face Database [6].

As it is possible to see the base can be quite challenging and, utilizing the face reconstruction, can help to attenuate pose and illumination problem.

6   Experiments

For the LFW databases the experiments were made following the protocol:

- A subset with thirty subjects were separated in order to be possible to get subjects with at least twelve face images;
- For each subject two 3D face model with half the images were created and;
- For each 3D face model, they were rotated from −30 to 30° in the Y and X axis;
- The classification results were evaluated with a 10-fold cross-validation.

The results achieved a Rank 1 of 94.74% of recognition rate, Fig. 5 shows them average Cumulative Match Characteristics (CMC) curve obtained in the aforementioned experiments on part of the LFW database. Comparing this result with the results of the literature one can observe, currently, the recognition rate from most of them have around 97% to 99% Rank 1 in their hardest cases [8,10, 16–19]. But it is not a fair comparison since the protocols are different and the current work is in progress so, it is expected, to improve the recognition rate, utilizing CNNs and more appropriate fusion strategies of characteristics.

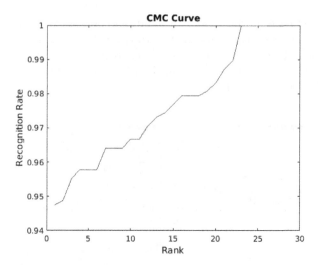

Fig. 5. Average CMC curve obtained on part of LFW Face Database.

7   Conclusion

With the obtained so far it is already possible to conclude that 3D Face Recognition can be done utilizing reconstructed 3D models, this can be applied to several scenarios, such as surveillance systems. It is possible to improve the recognition rate, for instance, by using a CNN for subject classification and fusing the decision of other methods.

For the LFW database, it is needed to increase the number of face images for some subjects, this can be done by developing a web-crawler which can search the internet for more faces for particular subjects.

All those improvements are being considered as future work.

Acknowledgement. This study was financed in part by the Coordenação de Aperfeiçoamento de Pessoal de Nível Superior - Brasil (CAPES). This study utilizes a GPU granted by the NVIDIA Grant Program.

References

1. Besl, P.J., McKay, N.D.: A method for registration of 3-D shapes. IEEE Trans. Pattern Anal. Mach. Intell. **14**(2), 239–256 (1992). https://doi.org/10.1109/34.121791
2. Cardia Neto, J.B., Marana, A.N.: Utilizing deep learning and 3DLBP for 3D face recognition. In: Mendoza, M., Velastín, S. (eds.) CIARP 2017. LNCS, vol. 10657, pp. 135–142. Springer, Cham (2018). https://doi.org/10.1007/978-3-319-75193-1_17
3. Chetverikov, D., Stepanov, D., Krsek, P.: Robust Euclidean alignment of 3D point sets: the trimmed iterative closest point algorithm. Image Vis. Comput. **23**(3), 299–309 (2005). https://doi.org/10.1016/j.imavis.2004.05.007. http://www.sciencedirect.com/science/article/pii/S0262885604001179

4. Huang, Y., Wang, Y., Tan, T.: Combining statistics of geometrical and correlative features for 3D face recognition. In: Proceedings of the British Machine Vision Conference, pp. 90.1–90.10. BMVA Press (2006). https://doi.org/10.5244/C.20.90
5. Kakadiaris, I.A., et al.: Three-dimensional face recognition in the presence of facial expressions: an annotated deformable model approach. IEEE Trans. Pattern Anal. Mach. Intell. **29**(4), 640–649 (2007). https://doi.org/10.1109/TPAMI.2007.1017
6. Learned-Miller, E., Huang, G.B., RoyChowdhury, A., Li, H., Hua, G.: Labeled faces in the wild: a survey. In: Kawulok, M., Celebi, M.E., Smolka, B. (eds.) Advances in Face Detection and Facial Image Analysis, pp. 189–248. Springer, Cham (2016). https://doi.org/10.1007/978-3-319-25958-1_8
7. Li, B., Mian, A., Liu, W., Krishna, A.: Using kinect for face recognition under varying poses, expressions, illumination and disguise. In: 2013 IEEE Workshop on Applications of Computer Vision (WACV), pp. 186–192 (2013). https://doi.org/10.1109/WACV.2013.6475017
8. Liu, J., Deng, Y., Bai, T., Huang, C.: Targeting ultimate accuracy: face recognition via deep embedding. CoRR abs/1506.07310 (2015). http://arxiv.org/abs/1506.07310
9. Nguyen, V., Do, T., Nguyen, V.-T., Ngo, T.D., Duong, D.A.: How to choose deep face models for surveillance system? In: Sieminski, A., Kozierkiewicz, A., Nunez, M., Ha, Q.T. (eds.) Modern Approaches for Intelligent Information and Database Systems. SCI, vol. 769, pp. 367–376. Springer, Cham (2018). https://doi.org/10.1007/978-3-319-76081-0_31
10. Parkhi, O.M., Vedaldi, A., Zisserman, A., et al.: Deep face recognition. In: BMVC, vol. 1, p. 6 (2015)
11. Prabhakar, S., Pankanti, S., Jain, A.: Biometric recognition: security and privacy concerns. IEEE Secur. Priv. **1**, 33–42 (2003). https://doi.org/10.1109/MSECP.2003.1193209
12. Press, W.H., Teukolsky, S.A., Vetterling, W.T., Flannery, B.P.: Numerical Recipes 3rd Edition: The Art of Scientific Computing, 3rd edn. Cambridge University Press, New York (2007)
13. Roth, J., Tong, Y., Liu, X.: Unconstrained 3D face reconstruction. In: Proceedings of the IEEE Conference on Computer Vision and Pattern Recognition (CVPR), June 2015
14. Savitzky, A., Golay, M.J.E.: Smoothing and differentiation of data by simplified least squares procedures. Anal. Chem. **36**(8), 1627–1639 (1964). https://doi.org/10.1021/ac60214a047
15. Schafer, R.W.: What is a savitzky-golay filter? [lecture notes]. IEEE Signal Process. Mag. **28**(4), 111–117 (2011). https://doi.org/10.1109/MSP.2011.941097
16. Schroff, F., Kalenichenko, D., Philbin, J.: FaceNet: a unified embedding for face recognition and clustering. In: Proceedings of the IEEE Conference on Computer Vision and Pattern Recognition (CVPR), June 2015
17. Sun, Y., Wang, X., Tang, X.: Deeply learned face representations are sparse, selective, and robust. In: Proceedings of the IEEE Conference on Computer Vision and Pattern Recognition (CVPR), June 2015
18. Wen, G., Chen, H., Cai, D., He, X.: Improving face recognition with domain adaptation. Neurocomputing **287**, 45–51 (2018). https://doi.org/10.1016/j.neucom.2018.01.079. http://www.sciencedirect.com/science/article/pii/S0925231218301127
19. Wen, Y., Zhang, K., Li, Z., Qiao, Y.: A discriminative feature learning approach for deep face recognition. In: Leibe, B., Matas, J., Sebe, N., Welling, M. (eds.) ECCV 2016. LNCS, vol. 9911, pp. 499–515. Springer, Cham (2016). https://doi.org/10.1007/978-3-319-46478-7_31

Comparison of Angle and Size Features with Deep Learning for Emotion Recognition

Patrick Dunau[1,5(✉)], Marco F. Huber[2,3], and Jürgen Beyerer[4,5]

[1] USU Software AG, Rüppurer Str. 1, 76131 Karlsruhe, Germany
p.dunau@usu.de
[2] Institute of Industrial Manufacturing and Management (IFF),
University of Stuttgart, Stuttgart, Germany
[3] Fraunhofer IPA, Stuttgart, Germany
[4] Fraunhofer IOSB, Karlsruhe, Germany
[5] Karlsruhe Institute of Technology (KIT), Karlsruhe, Germany

Abstract. The robust recognition of a person's emotion from images is an important task in human-machine interaction. This task can be considered a classification problem, for which a plethora of methods exists. In this paper, the emotion recognition performance of two fundamentally different approaches is compared: classification based on hand-crafted features against deep learning. This comparison is conducted by means of well-established datasets and highlights the benefits and drawbacks of each approach.

Keywords: Emotion recognition · Classification · Deep learning

1 Introduction

The human face provides a rich display of emotions via facial expressions. The ability to read the sentiment from facial expressions significantly enhances communication, especially in the context of human machine interaction. To allow for a computer to recognise the emotion from a facial expression, it is necessary to classify the sentiment given an image of a human's face.

The field of classifying static images provides a broad variety of methods. This paper presents a comparison of two specific methodologies: the Angle and Size Featureset (ASF) in [3] and deep convolutional neural networks (CNN). The ASF represents the class of feature engineering, while the CNN is a representative of deep learning. While ASF concentrates on specific hand-crafted features to retrieve a high amount of coded information, the CNN automatically mines hidden features. This paper aims for comparing the feature extraction and decision ability of both approaches.

The remainder of this paper organises as follows: the next section formally defines the classification problem. Then each method is described thoroughly in the following Section. In Sect. 4, both classification approaches are compared by means of well-known benchmark datasets. Section 5 concludes this paper.

© Springer Nature Switzerland AG 2019
R. Vera-Rodriguez et al. (Eds.): CIARP 2018, LNCS 11401, pp. 602–610, 2019.
https://doi.org/10.1007/978-3-030-13469-3_70

2   Problem Statement

In general, the classification problem consists of four vital parts: an observation, feature extraction, a classifier, and a prediction. In case of emotion recognition, the observation corresponds to the image of an emotional facial expression. Figure 1 displays the six facial expressions from the Cohn-Kanade+ (CK) dataset for the basic emotion classes *anger*, *disgust*, *fear*, *happiness*, *sadness*, and *surprise* provided by Ekman in [4].

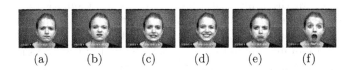

(a)   (b)   (c)   (d)   (e)   (f)

Fig. 1. Figures (a)–(f) show the basic emotion classes anger, disgust, fear, happiness, sadness, and surprise of subject S055 from the CK dataset (©Jeffrey Cohn).

In the feature extraction step structural information is gathered that allows for classifying the emotional class. The process' output corresponds to the class estimate given in terms of a vector containing class probabilities. The whole process is depicted in Fig. 2.

Fig. 2. Process flow of the classification problem.

3   Considered Approaches

In the following, the ASF is compared to the CNN approach. First, the properties and techniques used in the ASF are described. Second, a brief introduction to the CNN is given.

3.1   Angle and Size Featureset (ASF)

ASF is described in detail in Dunau et al. [3]. The feature set constitutes on geometric and local properties. The extraction process is done in four steps: (1) face localisation, (2) facial landmark extraction, (3) estimation of ellipses for sizes computations, and (4) line constructions for angle evaluations. The face is located using a deep neural network provided by the OpenCV library. The facial landmarks are retrieved using the landmark extractor by Qu et al. [6], which yields a landmark model comprising 68 points. Based on this model, the contours of the eyes and the mouth can be retrieved reliably. For the size evaluation, ellipses are fitted to the eyes and the mouth. The size is computed from the ratio of the major and minor semi-axes of the ellipses. The next step constructs lines from selected pairs of points and computes angles between pairs of lines.

In contrast to the original paper [3], we apply the following modifications: First, the multi-layered perception is replaced by XGBoost classifier [12], which is based on gradient boosted random forests. The XGBoost classifier turned out to be more stable given the problem at hand compared to the MLP classifier. Furthermore, the classifier is not prone to overfitting, given a small amount of data. Also, the experiments showed, that the classifier was able to separate the classes quite well. Second, the implementation of the facial landmark extraction process has been improved. In the original implementation, the computation of the similarity transformation to back-project the landmarks to the facial image was done inversely in an intermediate step, which resulted in low performance and a random choice of alignment positions. The correction of the back-projection stabilised the landmark extraction process and resulted in a significantly improved emotion recognition performance.

3.2 Convolutional Neural Network (CNN)

Deep learning poses a distinct path in machine learning. It is based on artificial neural networks and aims at problems that are easily solved by humans, e.g., emotion recognition given facial expressions. Particularly for image data, so-called deep CNNs as depicted in Fig. 3 have proofed to perform similar or even better compared to humans in some recognition tasks. These networks comprise an input and an output layer as well as several intermediate hidden layers, which can also be convolutional layers.

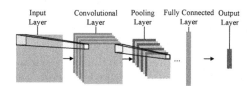

Fig. 3. An example CNN architecture from Peng et al. [14].

The layers represent so called filters. They are used to extract features from the input data to perform the classification task. In the training procedure, the weights of the connections between the layer's nodes are optimized. Additionally, each node has an activation function, which determines the output of the nodes. The activation function used for the network at hand is a Rectified Linear Unit (ReLU) activation function, which is $R(z) = \max(0, z)$.

A deep CNN comprises a vast number of nodes. Consequently, a high number of weights has to be trained, which requires a large number of training data to train the network from scratch. There is also the possibility to use a pre-trained network. As we are concentrating on the recognition of the emotional class given input images, the training effort can be reduced by using pre-trained models from the imagenet dataset [7]. These nets were trained to discriminate 1000 classes. Given these weights also small datasets like the Cohn-Kanade+ (CK) [1] and the Oulu-Casia (OC) [2] datasets can be utilized. In doing so, training the network becomes rather a fine-tuning of the last 10 layers' and the output layer's weights.

In the literature examples of specially trained CNNs for the classification of emotional facial expressions exist: Lopes et al. [8] present a CNN with seven layers. The images were preprocessed by correcting the face orientation with the alignment of the eye centres to the horizontal axis. Then the face was cropped to eliminate background information from the images to only retrieve information being relevant to expressions. The intensity of the images was normalised to overcome lighting variations, and the images were downsampled to 32 by 32 pixels. Furthermore, data augmentation by image rotation and geometric distortions was applied to increase the dataset. In doing so, a high accuracy of 96.76 % for the CK dataset was achieved. Another example of a seven-layered CNN is presented in Liu et al. [9]. They adapted a 3D CNN to learn a deformable action parts model for dynamic facial expression analysis. Furthermore, they incorporated action parts learning to detect special facial action parts under structured spatial constraints to obtain deformable part detection maps for expression classification. As input n consecutive frames from expression videos were extracted and normalized to 64 by 64 pixels. On the CK dataset, Liu et al. reported accuracy rates up to 92 %. Mollahosseine et al. [10] approximated a sparse neural network by using inception layers for this task. The inception layers were used to incorporate another network into the main network. For preprocessing, the facial images were registered by means of aligning landmarks to an average face. Furthermore, the images were downsized to 48 by 48 pixels and data augmentation based on image cropping and flipping was applied. The resulting network achieved an accuracy of 93.2 %.

In this paper, preprocessing is kept at a minimum on purpose, as the idea of deep learning is to allow end-to-end learning, i.e., images are processed directly. Thus, we merely cropped and resized the images. No further preprocessing is performed.

4   Experiments

For the comparison, we used a VGG-16 network by Simonyan and Zisserman [11] from the Keras library for Python with the TensorFlow backend. As described earlier the network was pre-trained given the imagenet weights. For the problem at hand, the output layer of the network was truncated and replaced by a softmax layer with six output nodes. To avoid overfitting, we equipped a dropout layer before the output layer. A validation set containing 10 percent of the training data was used to regularize the neural network. The ASF was used with the XGBoost classifier. The preprocessing for both models consists of cropping the facial region and resizing to 224 by 224 pixels. Additionally, the brightness was altered by applying an exponent of 0.5 to the gray values to brighten dark regions of the face.

The six emotional classes given by Ekman [4] were used, as defined in Sect. 2. The data for the experiments was retrieved from the CK and the OC datasets. The CK dataset consists of image sequences ranging from the neutral facial expression to the full emotional expression. The OC dataset is constructed similarly, but the image resolution is lower. From both datasets the last three images of each subject and emotion were used, as these images show the full emotional expression. This increased the number of training samples. For CK this resulted in 1329 and for OC in 1440 images. For the combined test we mixed the images from both datasets and added the neutral images from each participant of the datasets. This resulted in 2769 input images.

We used a computer powered by an Intel Core i7 CPU with 16 GB of RAM, equipped with a NVIDIA Quadro 1000 GPU with four GB of video RAM. For comparison, we computed the metrics recall, precision, f_1-score, and accuracy. A cross-validation scheme with 10 folds was applied to compute the class individual metrics. First, we present the experiment on each dataset individually. Second, we discuss the results on the combined dataset.

4.1   Experiment 1: Cohn-Kanade+ Dataset

In Table 1 the results for the CK dataset are listed, where the tolerances correspond to one-sigma values. The results retrieved by the VGG-16 network are already good, but compared to Lopes et al., Liu et al., Mollahosseini et al., and Liu et al. [8–10,13] superior accuracies on this dataset can be achieved for CNNs. Their improvements in performance result from significantly higher efforts spend on image preprocessing as stated above. The results given from the ASF are significantly higher compared to the VGG-16 and comparable to the state of the art. Also, compared to [3] the improved accuracies obtained by the ASF can be explained from an updated version of the landmark detector by Qu et al. [6] as well as by replacing the MLP classifier with XGBoost.

4.2   Experiment 2: Oulu-Casia Dataset

The experiment on the OC dataset is conducted similarly to the previous one. Table 2 shows the corresponding results, which in case of the VGG-16 network are lower compared to the first experiment. This can be explained by the lower resolution of the pictures contained in the OC dataset. Furthermore, the data is corrupted by high noise, which leads to vanishing facial features. Nevertheless, the ASF performs better compared to VGG-16.

4.3   Experiment 3: Compound Test

The final experiment stacks all pictures from both datasets, i.e., the images showing full emotions from the CK and OC datasets. Table 3 gives the results

Table 1. Experimental results for the CK dataset.

Emotion	VGG-16			ASF		
	Recall	Precision	F_1-Score	Recall	Precision	F_1-Score
Anger	0.51 ± 0.09	0.98 ± 0.04	0.66 ± 0.08	0.97 ± 0.04	0.96 ± 0.05	0.97 ± 0.04
Disgust	0.88 ± 0.07	0.95 ± 0.06	0.91 ± 0.03	0.99 ± 0.02	0.97 ± 0.04	0.98 ± 0.02
Fear	0.98 ± 0.02	0.77 ± 0.02	0.86 ± 0.02	0.98 ± 0.03	0.97 ± 0.03	0.97 ± 0.02
Happiness	0.92 ± 0.04	0.97 ± 0.03	0.94 ± 0.03	0.99 ± 0.02	1.00 ± 0.01	0.99 ± 0.01
Sadness	0.98 ± 0.02	0.79 ± 0.02	0.87 ± 0.01	0.94 ± 0.04	0.96 ± 0.03	0.95 ± 0.03
Surprise	0.98 ± 0.02	0.97 ± 0.02	0.97 ± 0.01	0.97 ± 0.02	0.99 ± 0.02	0.98 ± 0.02
Average	0.88 ± 0.18	0.90 ± 0.10	0.87 ± 0.11	0.97 ± 0.02	0.97 ± 0.02	0.97 ± 0.01

Table 2. Experimental results on the OC dataset.

Emotion	VGG-16			ASF		
	Recall	Precision	F_1-Score	Recall	Precision	F_1-Score
Anger	0.23 ± 0.19	0.87 ± 0.17	0.31 ± 0.17	0.71 ± 0.11	0.81 ± 0.20	0.72 ± 0.08
Disgust	0.65 ± 0.11	0.49 ± 0.07	0.55 ± 0.04	0.79 ± 0.16	0.61 ± 0.26	0.63 ± 0.09
Fear	0.52 ± 0.05	0.43 ± 0.12	0.46 ± 0.08	0.68 ± 0.06	0.92 ± 0.03	0.78 ± 0.04
Happiness	0.50 ± 0.11	0.58 ± 0.18	0.51 ± 0.06	0.74 ± 0.06	0.95 ± 0.03	0.83 ± 0.04
Sadness	0.10 ± 0.10	0.48 ± 0.26	0.16 ± 0.15	0.77 ± 0.12	0.82 ± 0.19	0.76 ± 0.09
Surprise	0.96 ± 0.31	0.57 ± 0.18	0.69 ± 0.13	0.71 ± 0.04	0.96 ± 0.03	0.82 ± 0.03
Average	0.49 ± 0.31	0.57 ± 0.16	0.45 ± 0.19	0.73 ± 0.04	0.84 ± 0.12	0.76 ± 0.07

Table 3. Experimental results on the mixed dataset.

Emotion	VGG-16			ASF		
	Recall	Precision	F_1-Score	Recall	Precision	F_1-Score
Anger	0.33 ± 0.11	0.82 ± 0.10	0.46 ± 0.10	0.78 ± 0.07	0.76 ± 0.12	0.76 ± 0.05
Disgust	0.67 ± 0.11	0.74 ± 0.11	0.69 ± 0.06	0.83 ± 0.06	0.69 ± 0.17	0.74 ± 0.08
Fear	0.38 ± 0.10	0.75 ± 0.06	0.49 ± 0.08	0.75 ± 0.06	0.89 ± 0.15	0.76 ± 0.07
Happiness	0.70 ± 0.10	0.87 ± 0.03	0.77 ± 0.06	0.85 ± 0.02	0.93 ± 0.03	0.89 ± 0.02
Sadness	0.83 ± 0.06	0.76 ± 0.06	0.79 ± 0.04	0.79 ± 0.03	0.88 ± 0.03	0.83 ± 0.03
Surprise	1.00 ± 0.00	0.49 ± 0.09	0.66 ± 0.07	0.83 ± 0.03	0.96 ± 0.02	0.89 ± 0.01
Average	0.65 ± 0.26	0.74 ± 0.13	0.64 ± 0.14	0.81 ± 0.03	0.84 ± 0.10	0.81 ± 0.06

on the mixed dataset. Again ASF outperforms VGG-16 significantly. The results show a high capability of generalization for the ASF model. Furthermore, the higher amount of training data stabilizes the VGG-16 model. This implies that an even higher amount of training data would improve the CNNs performance.

4.4 Experiments Summary

Table 4 lists the accuracies obtained for all three experiments using the ASF with a XGBoost model and the VGG-16 CNN model. Additionally, the results on the CK dataset reported by Lopes et al., Liu et al., Mollahosseini et al., and Liu et al. [8–10,13] are provided. Liu et al. [13] also gives results on the OC dataset. The results obtained by the ASF are close to or even better than the state of the art.

Table 4. Accuracy results for all tests on the CK and OC datasets.

Model	CK	OC	CK and OC
ASF	0.97 ± 0.01	0.73 ± 0.03	0.81 ± 0.01
VGG16	0.89 ± 0.02	0.49 ± 0.06	0.66 ± 0.05
Lopes et al. [8]	0.97	–	–
Liu et al. [9]	0.92	–	–
Mollahosseini et al. [10]	0.93	–	–
Liu et al. [13]	0.95	0.79	–

With regard to practical applications, it is neccessary to also discuss the runtime of both methods. According to Table 5, the training of a CNN consumes a very high amount of time, while a standard classifier can be trained in a glimpse compared to that. The total runtime comprises the times spent on preprocessing, feature extraction, and prediction. Preprocessing is similar for both methods, but the runtime performing the prediction deviates significantly. Feature extraction in a CNN is performed implicitly by traversing the network and thus, contributes to the prediction time. For XGBoost instead, the actual prediction is very fast, but a lot of time has to be spent for explicit feature extraction. However, it is worth mentioning that VGG-16 benefits from GPU support for all processing steps but preprocessing, while ASF merely runs on CPU. This explains the high runtime for feature extraction, which relies on a CNN for face detection. Thus, the ASF would benefit from a GPU. Furthermore, the high runtime for feature extraction is also caused by the facial feature point detector, as it is repeatedly extracting SIFT features from the input image for every internal regression step.

Table 5. Processing times for the ASF with an XGBoost model and the VGG-16 model. Preprocessing, Feature Extraction, and Prediction correspond to Classification.

Model	Training	Preproc	Feat. Extraction	Prediction	Classification (Total)
VGG-16	1987.8 ms	34.8 ms	–	25.3 ms	60.1 ms
ASF	40 ms	37.8 ms	121 ms	0.08 ms	158.88 ms

5   Conclusions

This paper compares deep learning, represented by the VGG16 model, against the ASF feature set for the emotion recognition problem from facial images. The state of the art indicates that deep learning is capable of reaching high recognition performances similar to ASF, but this paper shows that pure end-to-end learning obtains mediocre results. Very good results can be obtained with very high effort spent on image preprocessing, resulting in a high demand for computational resources as well as a high amount of training data. Contrarily, the ASF is a much more simple model compared to a CNN. This fact provides several advantages: First, the ASF provides an interpretable model. Second, significantly fewer data is needed. Consequently, the ASF has significantly lower computational demands for training. The currently high computational demand for feature extraction can be reduced by utilizing GPUs and by replacing the facial feature point detector.

Currently, the ASF offers a robust feature set for emotion classification based on static imagery. In the future, the model will be extended to handle dynamic data. The explicit exploitation of crafted features efficiently enables the tracking of changes in facial expressions. From that, dynamic analysis and detection of facial expressions can be performed.

References

1. Lucey, P., Cohn, J.F., Kanade, T., Saragih, J., Ambadar, Z., Matthews, I.: The extended cohn-kanade dataset (CK+): a complete dataset for action unit and emotion-specified expression. In: 2010 IEEE Computer Society Conference on Computer Vision and Pattern Recognition - Workshop Proceedings, pp. 94–101, San Francisco, USA (2010)
2. Zhao, G., Huang, X., Taini, M., Li, S.Z., Pietikäinen, M.: Facial expression recognition from near-infrared videos. Image Vis. Comput. **29**, 607–619 (2011)
3. Dunau, P., Bonny, M., Huber, M.F., Beyerer, J.: Reduced feature set for emotion recognition based on angle and size information. In: Strand, M., Dillmann, R., Menegatti, E., Ghidoni, S. (eds.) IAS 2018. AISC, vol. 867, pp. 585–596. Springer, Cham (2019). https://doi.org/10.1007/978-3-030-01370-7_46
4. Ekman, P.: Basic emotions. In: Handbook of Cognition and Emotion, pp. 45–60. Wiley (1999)
5. King, D.E.: Dlib-ml: a machine learning toolkit. J. Mach. Learn. Res. **10**, 1755–1758 (2009)
6. Qu, C., Gao, H., Monari, E., Beyerer, J., Thiran, J.P.: Towards robust cascaded regression for face alignment in the wild. In: Proceedings of the 2015 IEEE Conference on Computer Vision and Pattern Recognition Workshops (CVPRW), pp. 1–9 (2015)
7. Deng, J., Dong, W., Socher, R., Li, L.J., Li, K., Fei-Fei, L.: ImageNet: a large-scale hierarchical image database. In: Proceedings of the 2009 IEEE Conference on Computer Vision and Pattern Recognition (2009)
8. Lopes, A.T., de Aguiar, E., De Souza, A.F., Oliveira-Santos, T.: Facial expression recognition with convolutional neural networks: coping with few data and the training sample order. Pattern Recognit. **61**, 610–628 (2017)

9. Liu, M., Li, S., Shan, S., Wang, R., Chen, X.: Deeply learning deformable facial action parts model for dynamic expression analysis. In: Cremers, D., Reid, I., Saito, H., Yang, M.-H. (eds.) ACCV 2014. LNCS, vol. 9006, pp. 143–157. Springer, Cham (2015). https://doi.org/10.1007/978-3-319-16817-3_10

10. Mollahosseini, A., Chan, D., Mahoor, M.H.: Going deeper in facial expression recognition using deep neural networks. In: Proceedings of the 2016 IEEE Winter Conference on Applications of Computer Vision (WACV), pp. 1–10 (2016)

11. Simonyan, K., Zisserman, A.: Very deep convolutional networks for large-scale image recognition. CoRR, Volume abs/1409.1556, arXiv (2014)

12. Chen, T., Guestrin, C.: XGBoost: a scalable tree boosting system. CoRR, Volume abs/1603.02754, arXiv (2016)

13. Liu, M., Shan, S., Wang, R., Chen, X.: Learning expressionlets via universal manifold model for dynamic facial. CoRR, Volume abs/1511.05204, arXiv (2015)

14. Peng, M., Wang, C., Chen, T., Liu, G.: NIRFaceNet: a convolutional neural network for near-infrared face identification. Information 7(4), Article no. 61 (2016)

Fast and Accurate Person Re-identification with Xception Conv-Net and C2F

Arthur van Rooijen[1,2]([✉]), Henri Bouma[1], and Fons Verbeek[2]

[1] TNO, Oude Waalsdorperweg 63, 2597 AK The Hague, Netherlands
arthur.vanrooijen@tno.nl
[2] Leiden University, Niels Bohrweg 1, 2333 CA Leiden, Netherlands

Abstract. Person re-identification (re-id) is the task of identifying a person of interest across disjoint camera views in a multi-camera system. This is a challenging problem due to the different poses, viewpoints and lighting conditions. Deeply learned systems have become prevalent in the person re-identification field as they are capable to deal with the these obstacles. Conv-Net using a coarse-to-fine search framework (Conv-Net+C2F) is such a deeply learned system, which has been developed with both a high-retrieval accuracy as a fast query time in mind. We propose three contributions to improve Conv-Net+C2F: (1) training with an improved optimizer, (2) constructing Conv-Net using a different Convolutional Neural Network (CNN) not yet used for person re-id and (3) coarse descriptors having fewer dimensions for improved speed as well as increased accuracy. With these adaptations Xception Conv-Net+C2F achieves state-of-the-art results on Market-1501 (single-query, 72.4% mAP) and the new, challenging data split of CUHK03 (detected, 42.6% mAP).

Keywords: Person re-identification · Large-scale person retrieval · Convolutional neural networks · Image retrieval · Feature extraction

1 Introduction

Person re-identification (re-id) is the task of finding the same person in multiple (surveillance) video resources. This is relevant, because a manual search for individuals in these resources is too laborious and is infeasible for real-world camera networks. In recent years the field of person re-identification has seen an improvement in the accuracy on challenging datasets like Market-1501 [23] (see Table 5). However, most research focuses just on accuracy without taking retrieval time into account. As a consequence, such research is less usable in practice.

Exception to this is the work of Yao et al. [21] who combine a high accuracy with a fast retrieval time. They demonstrate state-of-the-art Rank-1 accuracy of

© Springer Nature Switzerland AG 2019
R. Vera-Rodriguez et al. (Eds.): CIARP 2018, LNCS 11401, pp. 611–619, 2019.
https://doi.org/10.1007/978-3-030-13469-3_71

75.13% on CUHK03, 84.64% (single-query) on Market-1501 and 64.58% (single-query) on the extended version of Market-1501 containing 520k images. For the latter, an average query time of 180 ms is obtained. They employ Conv-Net with a coarse-to-fine retrieval framework (Conv-Net+C2F). The C2F retrieval framework uses coarse descriptors to narrow down the search space, this enables fast searching. Subsequently fine descriptors are used to find matches in the reduced gallery which results in the high accuracy.

We have investigated an improved Conv-Net+C2F which advances the state-of-the-art w.r.t. accuracy and retrieval time on Market-1501 and CUHK03. To this end three modifications to Conv-Net+C2F are proposed: (1) For increased accuracy Adadelta [22] is used instead of Stochastic Gradient Descent [13] (SGD) as optimizer for training Conv-Net. (2) Constructing Conv-Net using Xception [2] instead of GoogLeNet [17] further improves this accuracy. (3) Decreasing the dimensionality of the coarse descriptor to 8 instead of 128 reduces both the average query time and increases the accuracy.

This paper is organized as follows: Related work (Sect. 2), Method (Sect. 3), Experimental setup (Sect. 4), Results (Sect. 5) and Conclusion (Sect. 6).

2   Related Work

Our research leads to direct improvement of the Conv-Net with the coarse-to-fine (C2F) retrieval framework proposed by Yao et al. [21]. Having an understanding of this Conv-Net+C2F is therefore crucial. Conv-Net is created by replacing the fully connected layers in GoogLeNet with a classifier block. This classifier block consists of a convolutional layer with C kernels, thereby producing a single feature map of $H \times W$ for every class in the training dataset. The values in each feature map are combined into a single average score per feature map (representing confidence) using Global Average Pooling (GAP). After training the model using SGD, this added classifier block is discarded entirely and the output of the current last convolutional layer of Conv-Net is used to produce image descriptors.

The coarse-to-fine (C2F) retrieval framework enables the fast ranking of the gallery image descriptors w.r.t. a query image descriptor. Distances between descriptors are calculated by taking the Euclidean distance after L2 normalizing each descriptor. The C2F retrieval framework makes a trade-off between accuracy and speed by using two different descriptors: a coarse descriptor and a fine descriptor. The small coarse descriptor is created by applying GAP to the filters in the last convolutional layer of Conv-Net. This results in a K-dimensional vector with K equal to the number of filters in the last layer. This is then reduced to 128 using PCA. The large fine descriptor is created by applying GAP to four equal-sized, non-overlapping, horizontal bands on every filter, thereby creating a $4 \times K$-dimensional fine descriptor. The coarse descriptors are used to rapidly reduce the search space to $M = 500$ images, after which re-ranking is performed using the fine descriptors. Since both the descriptors are computed using the same activation function, the network needs to be used only once in order to construct both. This is described in detail by Yao et al. [21].

3   Proposed Approach

We propose three additions to Conv-Net+C2F in order to increase performance speed and accuracy. The first adaptation is to use an improved optimizer for training. Conv-Net is originally trained using SGD, which uses a learning-rate scheme that is experimentally found to work well by Yao et al. [21]. We wish to move away from the manual tuning of the optimizer and therefore suggest the use of the Adadelta [22] optimizer. Besides automatically tuning the learning rate, this also improves the accuracy of the model.

The second improvement to the original Conv-Net is using an improved base-model. A model is transformed into its Conv-Net variant by removing all dense layers present in the network. Next a classifier block is appended to this reduced model during training; similar to the original Conv-Net based on GoogLeNet. In the testing phase this classifier block is removed and the output of the current last convolutional layer is used to create a descriptor. We propose to use this procedure for the Xception [2] model. Compared to GoogLeNet (InceptionV1), Xception uses improved Inception modules. This leads to an improved performance on the ImageNet [14] challenge. We refer to this new network as Xception Conv-Net. This Xception Conv-Net has $K = 2048$ filters in its last layer, thus yielding 2048-dimensional fine descriptors. Furthermore, with an input size of 512×256 these filters have a dimensionality of 16×8.

Third, we propose to improve the coarse descriptors. These are key in the C2F retrieval framework, as they enable the fast querying of the gallery. A further improvement can be accomplished by dimension reduction. We propose a dimensionality of 8. In this manner the average query time is reduced through a lower number of comparisons. Furthermore, as the PCA removes noise from the descriptors, an increase in quality is accomplished. This results in an enhanced accuracy and system performance.

4   Experimental Setup

Models are trained on the train subsets of the Market-1501 [23] and CUHK03 (detected) [10] datasets, results are reported on the respective test sets.

Market-1501 [23] consists of 32,668 images with 1501 labeled identities. These are split into a train set containing 12,936 images with 751 identities and a test set containing 19,732 with 750 identities. Additionally 500,000 gallery distractor images are available to construct an extended test set with a size of 520k.

CUHK03 (detected) [10] contains 13,164 automatically detected images of 1360 pedestrians. These are subdivided into train and test subsets. Previously, a common approach was to select 100 identities for the test set and using the remaining identities for the train set. However, we use the more realistic and significantly more difficult approach proposed by Zhong et al. [25]. With this approach the detected subset contains 7365 training images, 1400 query images and 5332 gallery images.

As evaluation metric we report the Cumulative Matching Characteristic (CMC) Rank-r and the mean of average precisions (mAP). The Rank-r indicates the probability that at least one matching image is in the first r positions of the ranked gallery. We mainly use the Rank-1. The mAP is calculated by taking the mean value of the average precisions for all of the performed queries.

The models in the experiments are initialized with ImageNet pre-trained weights without freezing any layers. For such networks it is a common practice to normalize images by subtracting the standard values $104, 117, 123$ from the red, blue and green channels respectively. Furthermore, data augmentation is done by flipping the images in training data sets with a chance of 50%.

5   Experiments and Results

For the experiments, a machine was used with an Nvidia Titan X GPU and an Intel Core i7-4790 CPU. All models were implemented in Keras [1].

5.1   Automatic Optimizers

In order to increase the accuracy of the net as well as allowing automated adjustment of the learning rate during the training, we propose to use the Adadelta optimizer. To demonstrate the effectiveness of Adadelta the ResNet50 [6] model is trained for 50 epochs on Market-1501 using various optimizers with their default settings [1]. Images are resized to 224×224, the standard image size for ImageNet. These are fed to the network in batches of 16. This batch size was experimentally shown to yield a higher accuracy than batches with 8 images. However, our system did not permit a larger batch size than 16. Note that ConvNet and/or the C2F framework is not used. Results are presented in Table 1.

From our experiment in which 7 optimizers are tested Adadelta achieves the highest accuracy, both scores are with an absolute difference of 12.7% (mAP) and 8.7% (Rank-1) considerably higher than those of runner up AdaMax. Moreover, Adadelta exceeds the 51.48% mAP of ResNet50 trained using SGD as presented by Yao et al. [21], which is trained with better than default settings.

Table 1. Performance of ResNet50, trained with various optimizers on Market-1501

Optimizer	mAP	Rank-1	Rank-20	Optimizer	mAP	Rank-1	Rank-20
RMSprop [20]	29.8%	58.5%	90.0%	SGD [13]	46.4%	70.5%	93.9%
Adam [9]	31.3%	57.1%	87.6%	AdaMax [9]	46.5%	72.0%	94.1%
Nadam [3]	36.1%	63.6%	90.9%	Adadelta [22]	59.2%	80.7%	96.6%
Adagrad [4]	36.7%	62.0%	91.5%				

5.2   Base-Models for Conv-Net

Constructing Conv-Net+C2F using Xception instead of GoogLeNet improves its accuracy. The coarse dimensionality of the descriptors is reduced with PCA to 128 as suggested by Yao et al. [21]. Training is performed for 75 epochs on Market-1501 using a batch size of 16 and Adadelta as optimizer.

The input image size determines the dimensionality of the final output filters. An image size of 512×256 is used as much as possible for training these Conv-Net variants; this was suggested by Yao et al. This results in a final Conv-Net output of 16×8 for most models. This ensures that the models are tested on the same image sizes and at the same time supports in the construction of the descriptors. Especially the construction of the fine descriptor depends on the fact that the number of rows of the final output filters is evenly divisible by 4.

Unfortunately, this approach is not suitable for InceptionV3 and Inception-ResNetV2, since these setting would yield a final output of 14×6. To alleviate this problem, the image size is set to 586×299 for these two networks, which does result in a final output of 16×8 while respecting the $2 : 1$ height-width ratio as much as possible. Note that changing this size either violates the aspect ratio even more or results in a different sized final output. Moreover, MobileNet [8] requires its inputs to be square and no larger than 224×224. Results are presented in Table 2. Using Xception as a basis-network for constructing Conv-Net ('Xception Conv-Net') shows improved performance.

Table 2. Performance of various models as a basis for Conv-Net+C2F

Base-model	mAP	Rank-1	Base-model	mAP	Rank-1
GoogLeNet [21]	64.6%	84.6%	InceptionV3 [19]	61.4%	82.1%
VGG19 [15]	32.0%	53.5%	InceptionResNetV2 [18]	63.3%	84.4%
VGG16 [15]	34.0%	55.3%	ResNet50 [6]	64.8%	86.4%
MobileNet [8]	54.4%	81.1%	Xception [2]	66.5%	85.8%

5.3   Coarse Descriptor Dimensionality Reduction

Using PCA to reduce the dimensionality of the coarse descriptors improves the accuracy of Xception Conv-Net+C2F. To demonstrate this, the performance of the model on Market-1501 and CUHK03 (detected) is measured with a coarse descriptor dimensionality range of 2^x with $1 \leq x \leq 8$. Training on the respective datasets is performed using Adadelta with a batch size of 16 for 75 epochs. Results are listed in Table 3.

The results clearly illustrate that 8-dimensional coarse descriptors offer the best mAP performance on Market-1501 and 4-dimensional coarse descriptors perform best on the smaller CUHK03 (cf. Table 3). The former settings are recommended for large gallery sizes where a high mAP is of importance. Furthermore, the mAP/Rank-1 scores with 8 (or 4) dimensions outperforms the state-of-the-art method of Sun et al. [16] (37.83%/41.50%). This indicates that our approach generalizes to multiple datasets. Note that the new training/testing protocol for CUHK03 is used here. Using the old protocol Sun et al. obtained a mAP of 81.8% and Rank-1 of 84.8%. These accuracies are state-of-the-art as they outdo most other published works [16]. Our method outperforms theirs on the CUHK03 with the new protocol and by the principle of transitivity it is therefore acceptable to assume that our method would achieve state-of-the-art on the old protocol as well.

Table 3. Effect of coarse PCA descriptor dimensionality for Xception Conv-Net+C2F

	Market-1501		CUHK03	
dim	mAP	Rank-1	mAP	Rank-1
256	67.7%	86.6%	41.3%	41.9%
128	67.7%	86.6%	41.3%	41.9%
64	67.8%	86.6%	41.3%	41.9%
32	68.3%	86.6%	41.5%	41.9%
16	69.7%	86.5%	42.0%	41.8%
8	72.4%	85.7%	42.6%	41.9%
4	72.2%	81.6%	43.0%	41.6%
2	61.8%	64.6%	40.9%	38.4%

5.4   Market-1501 Extended Test Data

Xception Conv-Net+C2F obtains both a high accuracy and a fast retrieval speed on a dataset with a large gallery containing many imperfections such as misaligned bounding-boxes and false-positives. The in Sect. 5.2 trained Xception Conv-Net is applied to the 520k Market-1501 images, results are listed in Table 4. Xception Conv-Net with 8-dimensional coarse descriptors improves on the mAP of Yao et al. [21] and also reduces the average query time by half. Furthermore, compared to only using GoogLeNet it is a factor 12 times faster.

5.5   Xception Conv-Net+C2F Component-Wise Contribution

What is the influence of Xception Conv-Net and coarse-to-fine search on the obtained accuracy? And how does this compare to the state-of-the-art? To test this three different configurations are used. A baseline Xception network is compared to the Xception Conv-Net variant without C2F, with C2F using 128 coarse descriptors and another using 8-dimensional coarse descriptors.

Table 4. Performance of Xception Conv-Net+C2F (Our method) on extended Market

Model	Coarse dim	mAP	Rank-1	Query time (ms)
GoogLeNet (Yao [2])	N/A	36.38%	56.05%	960
GoogLeNet Conv-Net+C2F (Yao [2])	128	46.74%	64.58%	180
Xception Conv-Net+C2F (Ours)	128	58.0%	79.4%	152
Xception Conv-Net+C2F (Ours)	32	61.7%	79.2%	102
Xception Conv-Net+C2F (Ours)	8	63.8%	67.9%	81

The baseline Xception model is trained on the Market-1501 dataset for 75 epochs using Adadelta. Its descriptors are created by applying GAP to the 2048 filters of the last convolutional layer during testing, consequently these are 2048-dimensional. Xception Conv-Net is used in similar fashion as is done in Sect. 5.2 for the other models. For the variant without the C2F framework, only the coarse descriptors are used and PCA is not applied. Results for Conv-Net+C2F, with coarse descriptors having 128 or 8 dimensions, are taken from Sect. 5.3. Results are presented in Table 5.

Table 5. Xception Conv-Net+C2F (ours) component-wise single-query results on Market-1501 compared to the state-of-the-art

Model (coarse dim)	mAP	Rank-1	Model (coarse dim)	mAP	Rank-1
Sun [16]	62.1%	82.3%	Zheng [24]	66.07%	83.97%
Zhong [25]	63.63%	77.11%	Hermans [7]	69.14%	84.92%
Yao [21]	64.6%	84.6%	Xception	57.5%	79.0%
Lin [12]	64.67%	84.29%	Xception Conv-Net	64.2%	83.8%
Li [11]	65.5%	85.1%	Xception Conv-Net +C2F (128)	67.7%	86.6%
Geng [5]	65.60%	83.75%	Xception Conv-Net +C2F (8)	72.4%	85.7%

The results show that all components of Xception Conv-Net+C2F improve its performance. The use of the Xception Conv-Net design instead of plain Xception contributes the most, with an absolute increase in mAP of 6.7% and in Rank-1 of 4.8%. Moreover, the use of the C2F framework increases the performance compared to using just Xception Conv-Net. This amounts to a further increase in mAP of 3.5% and in Rank-1 of 2.8%. Finally, using 8-dimensional coarse descriptors gives the best performance, this amounts to an absolute increase of the mAP with 4.7%. These results indicate that all components are necessary to achieve the reported state-of-the-art accuracy on Market-1501 (Table 5).

6 Conclusion

For fast and accurate person re-id we propose to train Xception Conv-Net+C2F using Adadelta as optimizer with a batch size of at least 16. Furthermore, it is recommended to create coarse descriptors with a dimensionality of 8. Results on Market-1501 (single-query 72.4% mAP), its extended version (single-query 63.8% mAP) and CUHK03 with the new protocol (detected 42.6% mAP) show that this results in higher accuracy, lower retrieval time (only 81 ms for 520k images) and faster experimentation (no manual tuning of optimizer needed).

References

1. Chollet, F., et al.: Keras (2017). https://github.com/fchollet/keras
2. Chollet, F.: Xception: deep learning with depthwise separable convolutions. arXiv:1610.02357 (2016)
3. Dozat, T.: Incorporating Nesterov momentum into Adam. openreview (2016)
4. Duchi, J., Hazan, E., Singer, Y.: Adaptive subgradient methods for online learning and stochastic optimization. JMLR **12**, 2121–2159 (2011)
5. Geng, M., Wang, Y., Xiang, T., Tian, Y.: Deep transfer learning for person re-identification. arXiv:1611.05244 (2016)
6. He, K., Zhang, X., Ren, S., Sun, J.: Deep residual learning for image recognition. In: IEEE CVPR, pp. 770–778 (2016)
7. Hermans, A., Beyer, L., Leibe, B.: In defense of the triplet loss for person re-identification. arXiv:1703.07737 (2017)
8. Howard, A., Zhu, M., Chen, B., et al.: Mobilenets: efficient convolutional neural networks for mobile vision applications. arXiv:1704.04861 (2017)
9. Kingma, D., Ba, J.: Adam: a method for stochastic optimization. arXiv (2014)
10. Li, W., Zhao, R., Xiao, T., Wang, X.: Deepreid: deep filter pairing neural network for person re-identification. In: IEEE CVPR, pp. 152–159 (2014)
11. Li, W., Zhu, X., Gong, S.: Person re-identification by deep joint learning of multi-loss classification. arXiv:1705.04724 (2017)
12. Lin, Y., Zheng, L., Zheng, Z., Wu, Y., Yang, Y.: Improving person re-identification by attribute and identity learning. arXiv:1703.07220 (2017)
13. Robbins, H., Monro, S.: A stochastic approximation method. Ann. Math. Stat. **22**(3), 400–407 (1951)
14. Russakovsky, O., Deng, J., Su, H., et al.: ImageNet large scale visual recognition challenge. IJCV **115**(3), 211–252 (2015)
15. Simonyan, K., Zisserman, A.: Very deep convolutional networks for large-scale image recognition. arXiv:1409.1556 (2014)
16. Sun, Y., et al.: SVDNet for pedestrian retrieval. arXiv (2017)
17. Szegedy, C., et al.: Going deeper with convolutions. In: IEEE CVPR (2015)
18. Szegedy, C., Ioffe, S., Vanhoucke, V.: Inception-v4, Inception-ResNet and the Impact of Residual Connections on Learning. arxiv:1602.07261 (2016)
19. Szegedy, C., Vanhoucke, V., Ioffe, S., Shlens, J., Wojna, Z.: Rethinking the inception architecture for computer vision. In: IEEE CVPR, pp. 2818–2826 (2016)
20. Tieleman, T., Hinton, G.: RMSprop Gradient Optimization. Neural Networks for Machine Learning (2015). http://www.cs.toronto.edu/
21. Yao, H., et al.: Large-scale person re-identification as retrieval. In: ICME (2017)

22. Zeiler, M.D.: Adadelta: an adaptive learning rate method. arXiv:1212.5701 (2012)
23. Zheng, L., Shen, L., Tian, L., et al.: Scalable person re-identification: A benchmark. In: IEEE ICCV, pp. 1116–1124 (2015)
24. Zheng, Z., Zheng, L., Yang, Y.: Unlabeled samples generated by GAN improve the person re-identification baseline in vitro. In: ICCV (2017)
25. Zhong, Z., Zheng, L., Cao, D., Li, S.: Re-ranking person re-identification with k-reciprocal encoding. arXiv:1701.08398 (2017)

A Novel Multi-purpose Deep Architecture for Facial Attribute and Emotion Understanding

Ankit Sharma[(⊠)], Pooyan Balouchian[(⊠)], and Hassan Foroosh[(⊠)]

Department of Computer Science, University of Central Florida, Orlando, FL, USA
{ankit.sharma285,pooyan}@knights.ucf.edu, foroosh@cs.ucf.edu

Abstract. Facial expression estimation has for years been studied benefiting a wide array of application areas ranging from information retrieval
and sentiment analysis to video surveillance and emotion analysis. Methods have been proposed to tackle the problem of facial attribute recognition using deep architectures yielding high accuracies, however less
efforts exist to focus on the performance of these architectures. Here in
this work, we make use of Squeeze-Net [6] for the first time in the literature to perform facial emotion recognition benchmarked on *Celeb-A*
and *AffectNet* datasets. Here we extend Squeeze-Net by introducing a
new 5×5 convolution kernel after the last fully-connected layer offered
by Squeeze-Net, merging the 1×1 and 3×3 outputs from the last fully-
connected layers, to perform a more domain-specific feature extraction.
We run extensive experiments using widely-used datasets; i.e. *Celeb-A*
and *AffectNet*, using AlexNet and Squeeze-Net in addition to our proposed architecture. Our proposed architecture, an extension to Squeeze-
Net, yields results inline with state of the art while offering a simple architecture involving less complexity compared to state of the art, reporting
accuracies of 90.47% and 56.38% compared to 90.94% and 52.36%, in
Attribute Prediction and *Expression Prediction* respectively.

Keywords: Attribute prediction · Emotion recognition ·
Convolutional neural network

1 Introduction

For the past decade, Facial expression estimation has been a subject of attention
in the literature due to large array of application areas it can serve. A wide range of
salient information is traceable in a human face, including but not limited to age,
gender, race, emotion triggered, etc. Application areas include *social media mining,
face search and retrieval systems* as well as *video surveillance*, to name a few.

Many conventional methods used for feature extraction in the context of
computer vision problems have been replaced by convolutional neural networks
[8]. CNNs have proved their effectiveness in attribute classification, hence justi-
fying such replacement. However, CNNs have introduced their own challenges,

© Springer Nature Switzerland AG 2019
R. Vera-Rodriguez et al. (Eds.): CIARP 2018, LNCS 11401, pp. 620–627, 2019.
https://doi.org/10.1007/978-3-030-13469-3_72

such as the constant need for relatively large-scale and reliable labeled training samples as well as the complexity involved in modifying the default functionality of different layers in a given network in an attempt to take advantage of transfer learning.

Most works in the literature focus on improving the classification accuracy by introducing highly complex architectures. To address this problem [6] offers a smaller CNN architecture that achieves AlexNet-level accuracy on ImageNet with 50x fewer parameters. Less works in this area, however, have made use of SqueezeNet's architecture specifically to perform Facial Attribute Estimation. Here in this work, not only we make such use of Squeeze-Net, but we also introduce a completely new convolutional layer at the end of the network with a larger kernel size. Benchmarks run on SqueezeNet compared to our proposed architecture, equipped with our newly introduced layer, suggests a high accuracy inline with state of the art, while keeping the micro-architecture a lot simpler than the traditional CNNs performing feature extraction.

The remainder of this paper is organized as follows. Section 2 provides information on the most recent efforts in the literature on the subject of facial attribute estimation and understanding. Next, we discuss our proposed method in Sect. 3 providing details on *Face Attribute Expression* as well as *Face Expression Recognition*. Moreover, we dig into the experimental setup of our proposed micro-architecture in Sect. 4, providing details on the configuration of the proposed CNN and experiments run. Finally, Sect. 5 provides a thorough analysis of the results of experiments, comparing our work against state of the art. Section 6 concludes the paper and provides potential future work directions.

2   Related Works

There exist considerable amount of research on Attribute Estimation taking advantage of different CNN architectures and multi-label classification. The most popular open source packages available for training and testing of deep CNNs include, but are not limited to Caffe [7], TensorFlow [1] and Keras [3]. Deep-Face applied both siamese deep CNN and a classification CNN in order to maximize the distance between impostors and minimize the distance between true matches. Efforts in the field of Face Recognition mainly focus on developing deeper and more complex architectures, yielding relatively higher accuracies at the cost of higher complexity introduced to the architectures.

[5] takes advantage of the discriminative power of CNNs to learn semantic attribute classifiers as a mid-level representation for subsequent use in recognition and verification systems. In a close work to ours, [4] presents a Deep Multi-Task Learning approach to jointly estimate multiple heterogeneous attributes from a single face image. They tackle attribute correlation and heterogeneity with convolutional neural networks (CNNs) consisting of shared feature learning for all the attributes, and category-specific feature learning for heterogeneous attributes. [4] reports an average accuracy of 86.1% for smile and gender classification.

Approaches using hand-crafted and deep learning features can be grouped into two categories: (i) single-task learning of per attribute classifier; and (ii) multi-task learning of a joint attribute classifier. A known caveat with single-task learning is lack of attention to the correlation between the tasks, hence estimating each task separately. Here in this work, however, we propose a multi-task approach where multiple models are learned for multi-attribute estimation using a shared representation. This approach can also be observed in [2] tackling human attribute prediction problem.

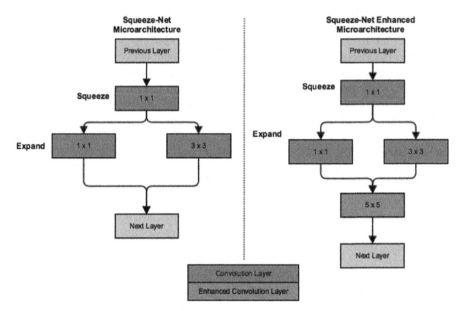

Fig. 1. Microarchitectural view: organization of convolution filters in the **Fire module**. The microarchitecture depicted on the left shows default organization of Squeeze-Net. The microarchitecture depicted on the right shows Squeeze-Net enhanced with the proposed 5×5 convolution layer.

3   Our Proposed Method

The goal in this work is to demonstrate that our proposed architecture, for feature extraction, depicted in Fig. 2, outperforms Alex-Net as well as Squeeze-Net architectures specifically when dealing with Face Attribute Estimation. Towards this aim, here we extend the microarchitecture offered by Squeeze-Net as depicted in Fig. 1. Squeeze-Net begins with a standalone convolution layer (conv1), followed by 8 fire modules (fire2–9), ending with a final convolution layer (conv10). The number of filters per fire module increases gradually from the beginning to the end of the network. Squeeze-Net performs max-pooling with a stride of 2 after layers conv1, fire4, fire8, and conv10. A Fire module is comprised of a squeeze convolution layer (only 1×1 filters), feeding into an expand

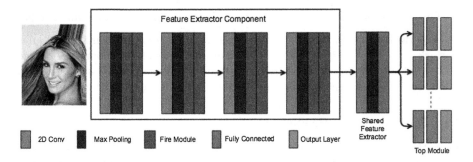

Fig. 2. System architecture depicting 4 blocks, each containing a 2D convolutional layer, two fire modules and max pooling layer, a shared feature extractor, followed by the top module

layer that has a mix of 1×1 and 3×3 convolution filters. The output of the fire-module is the concatenated outputs of the *expand* layer.

In our proposed micro-architecture, we (i) add a batch normalization layer after the squeeze convolution layer, and (ii) introduce dropout layers after the *expand* layers as depicted in Fig. 1. The result of our experiments further discussed in Sect. 5 demonstrate that our proposed microarchitecture yields a higher generalization ability compared to state of the art.

It is worth mentioning that in fine-grained tasks, such as Face Attribute Prediction and Face Expression Recognition, the objective is to find features that are capable of capturing the subtle highly localized intra-class variations. Therefore, here, we inject our newly developed convolution layer of 5×5 filters into our microarchitecture after every few fire modules. We borrow our intuition from the fact that a convolution layer with a larger kernel size provides us with better discriminative features after a sequence of convolution layers with 1×1 and 3×3 filters.

As depicted in Fig. 1, our microarchitecture begins with a block of two fire modules (squeeze filters, expand filters), followed by a convolution layer of 5×5 of expand filters, further followed by a max-pooling layer of size 3 with stride 2. Our experiments, further explained in Sect. 4 are run on the proposed architecture depicted in Fig. 2.

The proposed feature extractor, as part of our proposed architecture, benefits from the following setup:

- A convolution layer of 7×7 kernel of 96 filters
- A micro-architecture with (squeeze filters = 16, expand filters = 64)
- A micro-architecture with (squeeze filters = 32, expand filters = 128)
- A micro-architecture with (squeeze filters = 48, expand filters = 192)
- A micro-architecture with (squeeze filters = 64, expand filters = 256)
- A fully-connected layer of size 1024

This feature extractor is attached to a top-network that is domain-specific:

- To perform Face Attribute Prediction, as a multi-label problem, our top network consists of multiple independent sub-networks of fully connected layers.
- To perform Face Expression Recognition, as a multi-classification problem, our top network consists of up of 2 fully connected layers with dropouts.

3.1 Face Attribute Prediction

Face Attribute Prediction is a multi-label classification problem that aims at determining if a given face matches attributes among a set of binary attributes. The *CelebA* [9] dataset benefits from 40 attributes, such as eyeglasses, wearing hat etc. Excerpts from *CelebA* dataset are shown in Fig. 3. In this work, the architecture designed for Face Attribute Prediction makes use of the proposed feature extractor with the top network consisting of 40 independent sub-networks; i.e. the same number as the number of attributes supported by *CelebA* dataset. Each sub-network consists of a fully-connected layer of size 512, followed by a fully-connected layer of size 256 and a final output layer with sigmoid activation.

3.2 Face Expression Recognition

Face Expression Recognition, a multi-classification problem, is a well-studied problem in computer vision. We use a subset of *AffectNet* [10] as our dataset to run experiments for Face Expression Recognition. Here we sub-sampled the dataset in an attempt to avoid the class imbalance problem posed by the original *AffectNet*. Our sub-sampled dataset offers 8 categories with each category containing a maximum of 5,000 images. For the Face Expression Recognition, our proposed architecture makes use of the feature extractor with a top network of fully connected layers of sizes [512,512] and a final layer of size 8 with softmax activation.

Table 1. Experiments table showing benchmarked datasets, number of epochs, number of classes as well as the batch size used

Dataset	No. of epoch	No. of classes	Batch size
CelebA	20	-	64
Affect-Net	50	8	64

4 Experimental Setup

All experiments pointed out in this work are run on a AWS p2.x Large instance with a memory of 61 GiB. The implementation is done using the Keras Python Deep Learning Library. Table 1 shows the number of epochs, batch size and number of classes for each task.

I2 regularization value of 0.0001 is used for the convolution layers for both implementations. Bath size is set to 64 and the learning rate is configured to 0.001. Adam Optimizer was used to perform optimization.

Fig. 3. Excerpts from *AffectNet* and *CelebA* datasets.

Table 2. Attribute estimation accuracies across multiple methodologies benchmarked on *AffectNet* and *CelebA*. AffectNet* refers to the sub-sampled balanced dataset to avoid class imbalance problem.

Problem	Dataset	Method	Accuracy
Attribute prediction	CelebA	PANDA [12]	85%
Attribute prediction	CelebA	Zhong [13]	89.8%
Attribute prediction	CelebA	MOON [11]	90.94%
Attribute prediction	CelebA	SqueezeNet [6]	82.14%
Attribute prediction	CelebA	SqueezeNet-Enhanced	**90.47%**
Attribute prediction	CelebA	Hand [5]	91.26%
Attribute prediction	CelebA	Han [4]	93%
Expression prediction	AffectNet*	AlexNet [8]	52.36%
Expression prediction	AffectNet*	SqueezeNet [6]	48.16%
Expression prediction	AffectNet*	SqueezeNet-Enhanced	**56.38%**

5   Results and Analysis

In this section, we analyze the results reported by state of the art as well as our proposed architecture, depicted in Fig. 2.

5.1   Attribute Prediction Results

As shown in Table 2, our proposed architecture outperforms state of the art in Expression Prediction and yields almost the same accuracy compared to state of the art when tackling Attribute Prediction, while avoiding the complexities introduced in [12,13] and [11]. [4] proposes a method for inferring human attributes, such as gender, hair style, etc., from images of people under large variation of viewpoint pose, appearance, articulation and occlusion, hence offering a part-based model. This method, while yielding reasonable accuracy, requires more training as well as labeled data when compared to our method proposed here. [13], on the other hand, considers mid-level CNN features as an alternative to the high-level ones for attribute prediction. Their intuition is based on the observation that the mid-level deep representations outperform the prediction accuracy achieved by the fine-tuned high level abstractions. This work requires transfer learning as opposed to our proposed methodology, where all features are learned from the beginning of the network from scratch, eliminating the need to perform transfer learning, while not sacrificing the achieved accuracy. In [11], the focus is addressing the multi-label imbalance problem by introducing a novel mixed objective optimization network (MOON) with a loss function that mixes multiple task objectives with domain adaptive re-weighting of propagated loss. This work yields an accuracy of 90.94%, which is closest to the accuracy reported here in this work; i.e. 90.47%. The marginal difference in the accuracy reported by MOON compared to the accuracy reported by our method can be attributed to the fact that MOON's loss function implementation is more complex than our loss function; i.e. standard cross entropy.

5.2   Expression Prediction Results

In order to demonstrate the effectiveness of our proposed method in other application areas, here we run experiments for Expression Prediction on a sub-sampled balanced version of *AffectNet*. As reported in Table 2, our proposed method offers an accuracy of 56.38%, beating accuracies yielded by AlexNet and SqueezeNet, reported as 52.36% and 48.16% respectively. Here the observation is that the standard AlexNet and SqueezeNet implementations are more challenged to extract localized information compared to our proposed architecture, equipped with our 5×5 convolution filter, as part of its Fire Module.

6   Conclusion

In this work, we propose a novel CNN architecture, an enhanced version of Squeeze-Net, which extends Squeeze-Net's fire module by adding a 5×5 convolution kernel to perform a more accurate feature extraction. To demonstrate the effectiveness of our proposed architecture, we ran experiments on two wildly-used datasets; i.e. *CelebA* and *AffectNet*, across two separate problem domains; i.e. Face Attribute Prediction and Face Expression Recognition. Our results provide proof that while inline with accuracies reported by state of the art; i.e. beating state of the art in Expression Prediction and reporting a very close accuracy in Attribute Prediction, less complexity is involved in the proposed architecture. In the Attribute Prediction and Expression Prediction domains, our system yields accuracies of 90.47% and 56.38% respectively, compared to best accuracies reported by the state-of-the-art methods; i.e. 90.94% and 52.36% on the mentioned domains. Work is currently in progress to run similar experiments with a slightly different architecture; i.e. adding a 7×7 convolution kernel instead of the proposed 5×5 kernel currently in use and analyze the architecture's effectiveness accordingly.

References

1. Abadi, M., et al.: Tensorflow: a system for large-scale machine learning. In: OSDI, vol. 16, pp. 265–283 (2016)
2. Abdulnabi, A.H., Wang, G., Lu, J., Jia, K.: Multi-task CNN model for attribute prediction. IEEE Trans. Multimedia **17**(11), 1949–1959 (2015)
3. Chollet, F., et al.: Keras: deep learning library for theano and tensorflow, vol. 7(8) (2015). https://keras.io/k
4. Han, H., Jain, A.K., Shan, S., Chen, X.: Heterogeneous face attribute estimation: a deep multi-task learning approach. IEEE Trans. Pattern Anal. Mach. Intell. **40**(11), 2597–2609 (2017)
5. Hand, E.M., Chellappa, R.: Attributes for improved attributes: a multi-task network utilizing implicit and explicit relationships for facial attribute classification. In: AAAI, pp. 4068–4074 (2017)
6. Iandola, F.N., Han, S., Moskewicz, M.W., Ashraf, K., Dally, W.J., Keutzer, K.: Squeezenet: alexnet-level accuracy with 50x fewer parameters and < 0.5 mb model size. arXiv preprint arXiv:1602.07360 (2016)
7. Jia, Y., et al.: Caffe: convolutional architecture for fast feature embedding. In: Proceedings of the 22nd ACM International Conference on Multimedia, pp. 675–678. ACM (2014)
8. Krizhevsky, A., Sutskever, I., Hinton, G.E.: Imagenet classification with deep convolutional neural networks. In: Advances in Neural Information Processing Systems, pp. 1097–1105 (2012)
9. Liu, Z., Luo, P., Wang, X., Tang, X.: Deep learning face attributes in the wild. In: Proceedings of the IEEE International Conference on Computer Vision, pp. 3730–3738 (2015)
10. Mollahosseini, A., Hasani, B., Mahoor, M.H.: Affectnet: a database for facial expression, valence, and arousal computing in the wild. arXiv preprint arXiv:1708.03985 (2017)
11. Rudd, E.M., Günther, M., Boult, T.E.: MOON: a mixed objective optimization network for the recognition of facial attributes. In: Leibe, B., Matas, J., Sebe, N., Welling, M. (eds.) ECCV 2016. LNCS, vol. 9909, pp. 19–35. Springer, Cham (2016). https://doi.org/10.1007/978-3-319-46454-1_2
12. Zhang, N., Paluri, M., Ranzato, M., Darrell, T., Bourdev, L.: Panda: pose aligned networks for deep attribute modeling. In: Proceedings of the IEEE Conference on Computer Vision and Pattern Recognition, pp. 1637–1644 (2014)
13. Zhong, Y., Sullivan, J., Li, H.: Leveraging mid-level deep representations for predicting face attributes in the wild. In: 2016 IEEE International Conference on Image Processing (ICIP), pp. 3239–3243. IEEE (2016)

Are Deep Learning Methods Ready for Prime Time in Fingerprints Minutiae Extraction?

Ana Rebelo$^{(\boxtimes)}$ ⓘ, Tiago Oliveira ⓘ, Manual E. Correia ⓘ,
and Jaime S. Cardoso ⓘ

INESC TEC Science and Technology, Porto, Portugal
arebelo@inesctec.pt

Abstract. Currently the breakthroughs in most computer vision problems have been achieved by applying deep learning methods. The traditional methodologies that used to successfully discriminate the data features appear to be overwhelmed by the capabilities of learning of the deep network architectures. Nevertheless, many recent works choose to integrate the old handcrafted features into the deep convolutional networks to increase even more their impressive performance. In fingerprint recognition, the minutiae are specific points used to identify individuals and their extraction is a crucial module in a fingerprint recognition system. This can only be emphasized by the fact that the US Federal Bureau of Investigation (FBI) sets as a threshold for a positive identification a number of 8 common minutiae. Deep neural networks have been used to learn possible representations of fingerprint minutiae but, however surprisingly, in this paper it is shown that for now the best choice for an automatic minutiae extraction system is still the traditional road map. A comparison study was conducted with state-of-the-art methods and the best results were achieved by handcraft features.

Keywords: Biometrics · Handcraft features · Deep learning ·
Convolutional neural networks · Fingerprint verification ·
Image processing

1 Introduction

An increasing number of biometrics have been deployed in real-world applications and its use is becoming a daily life practice for an ever growing number of

This work is financed by the ERDF – European Regional Development Fund through the Operational Programme for Competitiveness and Internationalisation - COMPETE 2020 Programme within project POCI-01-0145-FEDER-006961, and by National Funds through the Portuguese funding agency, FCT - Fundação para a Ciência e a Tecnologia as part of project UID/EEA/50014/2013. The authors would also like to thank the Portuguese Mint and Official Printing Office (INCM) for its collaboration and support.

© Springer Nature Switzerland AG 2019
R. Vera-Rodriguez et al. (Eds.): CIARP 2018, LNCS 11401, pp. 628–636, 2019.
https://doi.org/10.1007/978-3-030-13469-3_73

people around the world. In consequence, a high level of reliability and robustness is required for sensitive applications such as border control, access control to military or laboratory facilities, as well as access to personal accounts for mobile on-line banking. Biometric traits can provide this automatic recognition measuring unique physical or behavioral characteristics.

Notwithstanding face has been preferred in a number of biometric applications (such as border control e-gates, on-line banking apps, CCTV surveillance identification, selfie-based authentication on smartphones, among others), fingerprint is still one of the most used biometric traits principally because of its social acceptance and stability.

Portugal was the pioneer with the "Match-on-Card" (MoC) fingerprint matching algorithm implemented in the national eID card. This technique brought very significant changes in this state: (1) modernization, (2) simplification and (3) technical evolution. The Portuguese National Printing Office – INCM (Imprensa Nacional Casa da Moeda SA) –, responsible for the creation of the method, provided to the Portuguese Government an innovative way of fingerprint matching in the microprocessor of the card without any contact to a central biometric database. The biometric information and the technology inserted in the Citizen Card allows an high security authentication.

In this context, a national fingerprint recognition algorithm (fingerIDAlg) capable of MoC was developed by a Portuguese R&D institute in partnership with INCM. The main contributions of this work were: (1) an algorithm with better accuracy than the previous solution; (2) an extremely competitive time processing MoC algorithm; and (3) an independent proprietary sensor solution. The proposed solution opens an opportunity to study the integration of deep neural networks in the enrollment phase of a fingerprint verification system. Thereby, in this paper we present a comparison study between handcraft and machine learnt minutiae extraction methods. The novelty of this work is in the way how the final results are demonstrated. To the best of our knowledge, most of the related works only evaluate the robustness of their frameworks by the precision, recall and F1 score of the minutiae detection which do not reflect the impact of the behaviour of the biometric system in a real scenario. Most of the state-of-the-art methods using deep learning are only capable of detecting minutiae positions making very difficult or even impossible (without an extra minutiae orientation algorithm) to show the outcome of their fingerprint recognition system through the most common used metric Equal-Error-Rate. The two related papers that compute this metric use only 1600 fingerprint images.

The following study can open new lines of research such as end-to-end fingerprint verification framework and new environment setups and conditions in order to integrate Convolutional Neural Networks (CNN's) in the recognition process.

2   Learned vs. Handcrafted Features for Minutiae Extraction

A typical fingerprint recognition system as the one represented in Fig. 1, where handcraft minutiae features are extracted, can include several modules.

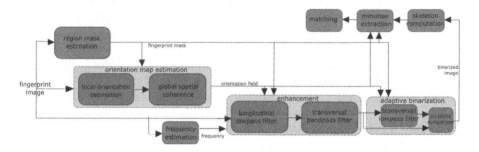

Fig. 1. Traditional fingerprint recognition architecture.

The region mask estimation consists on the identification of the region in the image containing the ridge structures and serves two purposes, on the one hand allows to restrict the processing to the foreground region, speeding up the following tasks, on the other hand allows to remove from the matching process minutiae close to the foreground boundaries and therefore more likely to be unreliable or "false minutiae". A threshold based on the average magnitude in each image block was proposed in [16]. Since the fingerprint area is rich in edges due to the ridge/valley alternation, the gradient response is high in the fingerprint area and small in the background. In [7] the authors measure the local energy in the Fourier spectrum. Ridges and valleys locally exhibit a sinusoidal-shaped plane wave with a well-defined frequency and orientation, whereas background regions are characterized by very little structure and hence very little energy. Ferreira et al. [10] proposed a method which followed the morphological fingerprint segmentation algorithm presented by Fahmy et al. [9] and is implemented in the $fingerIDAlg$. The authors introduced a robust binarization process based on a fuzzy C-means clustering algorithm.

The ridge orientation map estimation represents the local direction of the ridge-valley structure. Typically, the ridge orientation is estimated following one of two approaches: (a) correlation with a bank of templates (sine waves) of different frequencies and phases [27]; (b) computation of the orientation of the gradient [22] or Short Time Fourier Transform (STFT) analysis [7]. In the $fingerIDAlg$ both approaches are chosen. The frequency estimation is used to estimate the inter-ridge separation in different regions of the fingerprint image. In [14], the same procedure integrated in $fingerIDAlg$, the local ridge frequency is computed by accumulating, for each column x, the gray-levels of the corresponding pixels in the oriented window.

The directional enhancement is commonly used since fingerprint images are typically low-pass filtered along the orientation of the ridges-valleys and an isotropic smoothing would destroy that structure. Therefore, a Gabor filter [12] is the most applied technique. Other methods decompose the image into different frequency bands to compensate different noise components at different scales [6,11]. The $fingerIDAlg$ algorithm follows the most usual practice based on Gabor filters.

The binarization is the last step before skeletonization. Usually, the contrast is not uniform in the image, varying with the pressure made during the acquisition. In [27] a pixel is assigned a binary value based on the ridge flow direction associated with the block centered on the pixel. An extension of this adaptive method is implemented in $fingerIDAlg$.

The skeletonization is performed in order to thin the binarized image to facilitate the minutiae extraction. Shin et al. [23] encode thick binary ridges with Run Length Code (RLC) and extract minutiae by searching for the termination or bifurcation points of ridges in the RLC. In [21] the Learning Vector Quantizer algorithm is used to discriminate between minutiae and non-minutiae. The $fingerIDAlg$ has it owns skeleton method with specific heuristics to detect minutiae.

The enrollment phase of a fingerprint recognition system ends with the creation of minutiae templates composed by xy positions, angle and type (bifurcation, ending or unknown). Some works can also add the quality of the minutiae. The matching step consists in the comparison of two of those given templates. The output could be a degree of similarity or a binary decision. Benhammadi et al. [1] matches fingerprints based on texture information and [3] uses a Minutia Cylinder-Code (MCC) algorithm. The procedure implemented in $fingerIDAlg$ is an extension of this last algorithm.

2.1 Learned Features

Recent works propose an alternative to the previous pipeline through deep learning methods. The output is a probability map of minutiae positions in the image. Some authors [19,25] use the domain knowledge combined with CNN's to guide the structure design and the weight initialization and others prefer to learn from scratch a neural network [8,13,20,24]. These deep learning methods can also be used to design specific architectures for each module of the enrollment phase [2,13]. At the end, after a post-processing step to precise the minutiae locations and orientation, a matching algorithm, as described before, is applied.

3 Experimental Evaluation

3.1 Datasets

The Synthetic FINgerprint GEnerator (SFinGe) [18] was used to test the minutia extraction algorithms. In total, 56000 images with a dimension of 260×264

and a resolution of 500 *dpi* were generated in SFinGe. Fingerprint images with background noise, pores, scars and cuts were generated. Different orientations were also included. The ground truth information obtained comprises the minutia positions, their angle, their type and also the quality information.

Experiments were also conducted using the FVC databases: FVC2000 [17], FVC2002 [15], FVC2004 [4] and FVC2006 [5]. Each FVC database is composed of 4 subsets (DB1_A, DB2_A, DB3_A and DB4_A). Since we also generate synthetic images with SFinge, we only considered the real subsets. The first 3 sets have a total of 800 images, acquired from 100 fingers with 8 samples per finger. FVC2006 comprises 1680 fingerprints images acquired from 140 fingers with 12 samples per finger. In total, 12240 fingerprints are available for testing the algorithms. The images have a resolution ranging from 250 to 569 *dpi*. The dimensions vary from 96 to 640 pixels in width, and 96 to 480 pixels in height.

3.2   Goal-Directed Evaluation

A goal-directed performance evaluation is directly associated with the ultimate goal of the system. The results of this benchmark are expressed in terms of Equal-Error Rate (*EER*) which denotes the error rate at the threshold t for which both False Match Rate and False Non-Match Rate are identical: $FMR(t) = FNMR(t)$. The FMR and $FNMR$ scores were computed, using the FVC Fingerprint Verification Protocol[1]. The commercial minutiae extraction algorithm by INCM was denoted by *fingerIDAlg*. In order to have a fair comparison, all the state-of-the-art methods were tested having as the matching algorithm the same commercial SDK of INCM. Moreover, this matcher was submitted to MINEX[2] in order to eliminate the possibility of dependency between extractor and matcher.

In Tables 1 and 2 are presented the results of the comparison of the fingerprint verification systems, respectively, for the synthetic and the real databases in terms of EER (%). The rationale behind the choice of the deep learning method *FingerNet* [25] was due to the fact it outperforms its state-of-the-art sibling methods.

As the results show the hand-crafted feature extraction methods have a better performance than the learned features. Moreover, the minutiae extraction module from *fingerIDAlg* overcome the other algorithms.

It is important to state that the study was not extended to independent identities such as MINEX[3] or FVC ongoing[4] since it is not available yet some hardware conditions to run a CNN module such as GPU.

---

[1] https://biolab.csr.unibo.it/FVCOnGoing/UI/Form/BenchmarkAreas/
BenchmarkAreaFV.aspx.

[2] https://www.nist.gov/itl/iad/image-group/minutiae-interoperability-exchange-
minex-iii.

[3] https://www.nist.gov/itl/iad/image-group/minutiae-interoperability-exchange-
minex-iii.

[4] https://biolab.csr.unibo.it/FvcOnGoing/UI/Form/Home.aspx.

Table 1. Comparison of fingerprint verification systems in terms of EER (%) for the synthetic database. Numbers in boldface are the best results.

	FVC2007				FVC2008			
	DB1	DB2	DB3	DB4	DB1	DB2	DB3	DB4
$NBIS$ [27]	0.04	0.10	0.06	0.08	0.70	2.07	0.81	2.31
$FingerNet$ [25]	0.00	0.00	0.00	0.00	11.23	11.23	11.24	12.19
$fingerIDAlg$	**0.00**	**0.00**	**0.00**	**0.00**	**0.09**	**0.32**	**0.08**	**0.16**
$Verifinger$ [26]	3.90	3.86	3.93	3.92	2.54	3.86	2.29	3.49
	FVC2009				FVC2005		FVC2006	
	DB1	DB2	DB3	DB4	DB1		DB1	
$NBIS$ [27]	2.51	1.87	1.71	1.80	2.81		11.19	
$FingerNet$ [25]	11.50	11.65	11.62	12.46	1.23		17.43	
$fingerIDAlg$	**0.31**	**0.15**	**0.30**	**0.30**	**1.23**		**6.46**	
$Verifinger$ [26]	5.06	3.81	3.42	4.37	2.79		13.11	

Table 2. Comparison of fingerprint verification systems in terms of EER (%) for the real database. Numbers in boldface are the best results.

	FVC2000			FVC2002		
	DB1	DB2	DB3	DB1	DB2	DB3
$NBIS$ [27]	2.79	2.40	7.23	1.56	1.86	6.79
$FingerNet$ [25]	1.88	2.79	5.98	18.44	18.12	17.23
$fingerIDAlg$	**1.11**	**0.55**	**2.18**	0.87	**0.44**	2.63
$Verifinger$ [26]	3.01	1.09	4.18	**0.69**	0.77	**1.84**
	FVC2004			FVC2006		
	DB1	DB2	DB3	DB1	DB2	DB3
$NBIS$ [27]	7.15	8.75	6.04	17.02	0.78	5.95
$FingerNet$ [25]	15.23	17.09	2.93	22.43	1.04	4.58
$fingerIDAlg$	4.0	**3.23**	**3.23**	10.63	**0.33**	4.15
$Verifinger$ [26]	**3.72**	5.29	3.25	18.72	0.63	**4.10**

3.3 Ground-Truth Based Evaluation

Two different error metrics were considered: the percentage of minutiae falsely detected and the percentage of minutiae missed to detect. In order to perform this evaluation the average Euclidean distance between each reference minutiae (x and y position in the image) and each detected minutiae were computed. The matching problem on the resulting bipartite graph was computed by minimizing the distance. A radius of 10 pixels was chosen to assume a correct matched. The other unmatched pairs were assumed to be from a false positive minutiae being matched to an undetected true minutiae. As the number of unmatched detected

Table 3. Detection performance on synthetic database in percentage: average (standard deviation).

	False detection rate	Miss detection rate
NBIS [27]	57.40% (27.22)	29.05% (14.04)
FingerNet [25]	12.23% (10.06)	28.29% (11.72)
fingerIDAlg	17.01% (12.89)	**12.62% (12.62)**
Verifinger [26]	**7.00% (7.81)**	25.30% (12.19)

Table 4. Detection performance on real database in percentage: average (standard deviation).

	False detection rate	Miss detection rate
NBIS [27]	115.51% (78.28)	**13.62% (9.46)**
FingerNet [25]	30.02% (17.96)	15.85% (11.00)
fingerIDAlg	60.82% (72.68)	14.15% (10.12)
Verifinger [26]	**25.82% (26.87)**	30.09% (12.06)

minutiae results the false positive and as the number of unmatched reference minutiae results the missed to detect.

When we compare the results from Tables 1 and 2 with the results from Tables 3 and 4 we definitely see a robustness of the commercial matching algorithm of INCM to false positives. The excess of missed minutiae consistent in both synthetic and real databases in deep network approach is related to the needed final filtering to eliminate redundant detections.

4 Conclusions and Future Work

Nowadays it seems the computer vision problems have been solved by deep learning methods. The traditional methodologies for capturing the best features in the data appear to be overfilled with extensive experimental testing to obtain the best design for the network architecture. The work presented in this paper focuses on the performance of a complete fingerprint recognition system when using different methods for the minutiae extraction. Even being already learnt a possible representation of a minutiae through a deep neural network in this paper we demonstrate that the best choice for this specific biometric problem is still the traditional road map.

References

1. Benhammadi, F., Amirouche, M., Hentous, H., Beghdad Bey, K., Aissani, M.: Fingerprint matching from minutiae texture maps. Pattern Recogn. **40**, 189–197 (2007)
2. Cao, K., Jain, A.K.: Latent orientation field estimation via convolutional neural network. In: 2015 International Conference on Biometrics (ICB), pp. 349–356 (2015)
3. Cappelli, R., Ferrara, M., Maltoni, D.: Minutia cylinder-code: a new representation and matching technique for fingerprint recognition. IEEE Trans. Pattern Anal. Mach. Intell. **32**(12), 2128–2141 (2010)
4. Cappelli, R., Maio, D., Maltoni, D., Wayman, J., Jain, A.: Performance evaluation of fingerprint verification systems. IEEE Trans. Pattern Anal. Mach. Intell. **28**(1), 3–18 (2006)
5. Cappelli, R., Ferrara, M., Franco, A., Maltoni, D.: Fingerprint verification competition 2006. Biometric Technol. Today **15**(7), 7–9 (2007)
6. Cheng, J., Tian, J., Zhang, T.: Fingerprint enhancement with dyadic scale-space. In: ICPR (2002)
7. Chikkerur, S., Cartwright, A.N., Govindaraju, V.: Fingerprint enhancement using stft analysis. Pattern Recogn. **40**(1), 198–211 (2007)
8. Darlow, L.N., Rosman, B.: Fingerprint minutiae extraction using deep learning. In: IEEE International Joint Conference on Biometrics (IJCB), pp. 22–30 (2017)
9. Fahmy, M.F., Thabet, M.A.: A fingerprint segmentation technique based on morphological processing. In: IEEE International Symposium on Signal Processing and Information Technology, pp. 000215–000220 (2013)
10. Ferreira, P.M., Sequeira, A.F., Rebelo, A.: A fuzzy c-means algorithm for fingerprint segmentation. In: Paredes, R., Cardoso, J.S., Pardo, X.M. (eds.) IbPRIA 2015. LNCS, vol. 9117, pp. 245–252. Springer, Cham (2015). https://doi.org/10.1007/978-3-319-19390-8_28
11. Fronthaler, H., Kollreider, K., Bigun, J.: Local features for enhancement and minutiae extraction in fingerprints. IEEE Trans. Image Process. **17**, 354–63 (2008)
12. Gao, X., Chen, X., Cao, J., Deng, Z., Liu, C., Feng, J.: A novel method of fingerprint minutiae extraction based on gabor phase. In: IEEE International Conference on Image Processing, pp. 3077–3080 (2010)
13. Jiang, L., Zhao, T., Bai, C., Yong, A., Wu, M.: A direct fingerprint minutiae extraction approach based on convolutional neural networks. In: International Joint Conference on Neural Networks (IJCNN), pp. 571–578 (2016)
14. Jiang, X.: Fingerprint image ridge frequency estimation by higher order spectrum. In: International Conference on Image Processing (ICIP), vol. 1, pp. 462–465 (2000)
15. Maio, D., Maltoni, D., Cappelli, R., Wayman, J., Jain, A.: FVC 2002: second fingerprint verification competition. In: International Conference on Pattern Recognition, vol. 3, 811–814 (2002)
16. Maio, D., Maltoni, D.: Direct gray-scale minutiae detection in fingerprints. IEEE Trans. Pattern Anal. Mach. Intell. **19**, 27–40 (1997)
17. Maio, D., Maltoni, D., Cappelli, R., Wayman, J.L., Jain, A.K.: FVC 2000: fingerprint verification competition. IEEE Trans. Pattern Anal. Mach. Intell. **24**(3), 402–412 (2002)
18. Maltoni, D., Maio, D., Jain, A.K., Prabhakar, S.: Handbook of Fingerprint Recognition. Springer Professional Computing. Springer, London (2009). https://doi.org/10.1007/978-1-84882-254-2

19. Nguyen, D.L., Cao, K., Jain, A.K.: Robust minutiae extractor: integrating deep networks and fingerprint domain knowledge. In: 2018 International Conference on Biometrics (ICB), pp. 9–16 (2018)
20. Pinetz, T., Huber-Mörk, R., Soukop, D., Sablatnig, R.: Using a u-shaped neural network for minutiae extraction trained from refined, synthetic fingerprints. In: Proceedings of the OAGM&ARW Joint Workshop: Vision, Automation and Robotics, May 2017
21. Prabhakar, S., Jain, A.K., Pankanti, S.: Learning fingerprint minutiae location and type. Pattern Recogn. **36**, 1847–1857 (2003)
22. Ratha, N.K., Chen, S., Jain, A.K.: Adaptive flow orientation-based feature extraction in fingerprint images. Pattern Recogn. **28**(11), 1657–1672 (1995)
23. Shin, J.H., Hwang, H.Y., Chien, S.I.: Detecting fingerprint minutiae by run length encoding scheme. Pattern Recogn. **39**, 1140–1154 (2006)
24. Tang, Y., Gao, F., Feng, J.: Latent fingerprint minutia extraction using fully convolutional network. In: IEEE International Joint Conference on Biometrics (IJCB), pp. 117–123 (2017)
25. Tang, Y., Gao, F., Feng, J., Liu, Y.: Fingernet: an unified deep network for fingerprint minutiae extraction. In: IEEE International Joint Conference on Biometrics (IJCB), pp. 108–116 (2017)
26. Verifinger: Neuro-technology (2010)
27. Watson, C.I., et al.: User's guide to NIST biometric image software (NBIS) (2007)

Fingerprint Image Quality Assessment Based on Oriented Pattern Analysis

Raimundo Claudio da Silva Vasconcelos[1,2](✉) and Helio Pedrini[2](✉)

[1] Federal Institute of Brasília, Taguatinga, DF 72146-050, Brazil
[2] Institute of Computing, University of Campinas, Campinas, SP 13083-852, Brazil
r.claudio@gmail.com, helio@ic.unicamp.br

Abstract. Decision based on fingerprint image quality is crucial for automatic fingerprint classification and recognition tasks. Quality is challenging due to a variety of noise types that may exist in an image. Researches have been conducted to propose suitable combination of techniques for assessing fingerprint quality, however, it is difficult to achieve a generic solution for different data sets. This work proposes a fingerprint image quality indicator based on directional information inherent in fingerprint ridges and evaluates a metric for quality assessment. Experimental results on Fingerprint Verification Competition (FVC) data sets demonstrate the usability of the proposed index.

Keywords: Fingerprint images · Quality · Directional information

1 Introduction

Identification systems based on fingerprints became the most used among all biometric systems due to certain characteristics [12,18]: (i) fingerprint patterns are stable and invariant, satisfying the requirement of uniqueness; (ii) the use of fingerprint is more acceptable to people in comparison to other kinds of biometric modalities.

Fingerprints are oriented texture patterns created by interleaved *ridge* and *valley* information present on the fingertip surface. There are different possible ways to obtain an image representation from these patterns. The traditional technique consists in rolling an inked finger surface on a paper and then scanning the produced impression. Nowadays, due to the advances in sensor technology, a variety of fingerprint sensors can also be used on online acquisition [12,18]. Figure 1 illustrates some images acquired with different techniques.

Automatic recognition depends on accurate extraction of features derived from a fingerprint pattern. These features are roughly categorized in the literature into three levels [5,12]. Level 1 refers to *singular points*, where the ridge orientation is discontinuous or changes abruptly [21]. Level 2 corresponds to local

This work was partially supported by CAPES, FAPESP (17/12646-3) and CNPq (305169/2015-7).

Fig. 1. Visual differences among fingerprint acquisition techniques.

discontinuities in the ridges, known as *minutiae* [5,17]. Level 3 corresponds to fine intra-ridge details, such as fingertip *pores* [7].

The performance of fingerprint systems depends substantially on the reliability of features extracted from the sensed fingerprint image. Thus, depending on this quality information, a significant number of spurious features may be created and a percentage of genuine ones may be ignored [2]. Some approaches attempt to improve the reliability of the detected features via postprocessing [17] or to improve the quality of fingerprint images through enhancement or other preprocessing approaches.

Fingerprint quality is usually defined as the ease in extracting relevant characteristics for identification, such as minutiae, nucleus and deltas. It can also be considered as a measure for ridge and valley clarity. Therefore, it is desirable that ridges and valleys are well characterized and have well-defined guidelines [1,20]. More generally, we can define quality using extrinsic and intrinsic fingerprint factors [9]. Intrinsic factor refers to quality degradation caused by inaccurate parameter estimation during the image processing, whereas extrinsic factor is related to the fingerprint acquisition process, which is affected by physical skin injuries, inconsistent contact, residues on sensor surface, among others.

This work presents a novel image quality index to assist Automated Fingerprint Identification Systems (AFIS) in the decision-making process when a fingerprint image sample must be discarded and a new one is required. Our index, referred here as neighborhood strengthness homogeneity (NSH), can be computed by considering a multiscale directional operator.

In terms of directional field estimation, the proposed operator is less noise sensitive than some classical gradient approaches. Such performance analysis should not only evaluate extrinsic, but also intrinsic factors and can be used to assess the estimated ridge orientation. In addition, despite the emphasis on the fingerprint domain, the quality index is fairly general and can be used to measure the significance of many other methods related to directional information.

The remainder of this paper is organized as follows. Section 2 introduces our operator for extracting anisotropic quality information from fingerprint images. Experimental results are presented in Sect. 3, as well as the fingerprint database, Griaule AFIS used for fingerprint matching, and a result discussion. Concluding remarks are provided in Sect. 4.

2   Directional Information Operator

In this work, we are particularly interested in a measure of the distance between ridge and valley information in fingerprint images. A systematic way to compute such distance is initially considered within a given neighborhood. Then, we define a specific fingerprint quality index.

Consider Γ as a sliding window of size $M \times N$ (usually, $M = N = (2l+1), l \in \mathbb{Z}$) of an image $f(x, y), f : (x, y) \in \mathcal{D}_f \subset \mathbb{Z}^2 \mapsto \mathbb{Z}$. Let D be the number of considered directions in Γ, and n the corresponding number of pixels in a given direction. In order to represent all D directions in a two-dimensional grid, n has a minimum bound, that is, it can be defined up to $(2n - 2)$ directions, for any $n \geq 2$. Thus, coordinates (x, y) of the n points, in a given direction α, can be computed as: $x = x_{center} + p \cdot \cos(\alpha)$ and $y = y_{center} - p \cdot \sin(\alpha)$, for all p such that $-n/2 \leq p \leq n/2$. x_{center} and y_{center} are the coordinates of the point containing the sliding window Γ centered in this location.

Finally, this neighborhood can be defined as a set S_i^n of D test points with length n and discrete direction i, which can easily be computed by repeating the above procedure for all D directions ($i \in \{0, 1, ...D-1\}$), by respectively changing the value of α accordingly ($\alpha = 0, 1 \cdot 180/D, 2 \cdot 180/D, ..., (D - 1) \cdot 180/D$).

In this approach, it is assumed that, in the aforementioned neighborhood, the physics of the image acquisition imposes certain arrangements on the image gray levels. This is the case, for example, when image points are associated with two distinct regions: one which is parallel and the other perpendicular to the flow orientation contained in an intensity pattern created by some anisotropic process [8].

Algorithm 1. Algorithm for Directional Information Operator

1: Input: fingerprint image I; neighborhood S; the number of directions D

2: Output: quality index R

3: **for all** pixel $(x, y) \in \mathcal{D}_f$ centered in S **do**

1. Compute an information parameter (for instance, mean, standard deviation, moments of higher orders, morphological measures, among others) on $S_i(x, y)$ for each of the D directions. In terms of implementation issues, these data can be stored into an array $A[i]$, where $i \in \{0, 1 \ldots D - 1\}$.

2. The information associated with each direction i is compared to the one obtained from another direction j, $i \neq j$. Once perpendicular direction pairs are sufficient to characterize oriented patterns, the value of $A[i]$ is compared to $A[i + \frac{D}{2}]$, where $i \in \{0, 1, \ldots, \frac{D}{2} - 1\}$, and $i + \frac{D}{2}$ is the corresponding perpendicular direction.

3. The pair of directions i and j exhibiting the highest information contrast ($\text{argmax}_i \mid A[i] - A[i + \frac{D}{2}] \mid$), in a given pixel, defines the local orientation image O.

4. Neighborhood strengthness homogeneity (NSH) quality indicator is obtained as an average of this directional information in a given neighborhood and expresses the strength of the estimated anisotropic information in any region R.

For the sake of simplification, this work adapts the formalism presented by Oliveira and Leite [13], whose approach employed oriented information to reconnect broken ridges. Here, it is used to measure quality. Therefore, the abstract idea behind this quality index consists in analyzing samples drawn from these two image regions in order to quantify the difference that makes the anisotropy distinguishable.

A high-level description of our operator is presented in Algorithm 1. Different amounts of test points and directions can be set up in accordance with a certain scale and resolution for a given image. Similarly, several quality and information criteria can be considered to express separability (or contrast), variability, homogeneity, completeness, entropy, among others.

In this work, we consider fingerprint pattern as a regular anisotropic texture, that is, there is a certain regularity on the ridge and valley information. Despite the gradual changes on ridge and valley gray levels, there is a certain homogeneity of the pixels along their parallel orientations. The operator expresses the strength of information along certain oriented pattern. Based on this information, it is possible to extract two types of information: one based on the strength of direction - its absolute value - and another based on the direction of its neighbors. The latter was considered promising and used as an indicator of image quality.

3   Experiments

The main purpose of these experiments is to compare the behavior of quality measures by assessing their utility when, based on them, certain images are rejected. In this study, Griaule AFIS [6] was used to represent and match fingerprints as minutiae. Minutiae matching is certainly the most well-known and widely used method for fingerprint correspondence, as an analogy with the way forensic experts compare fingerprint images and their acceptance as a proof of identity in court [12].

3.1   Fingerprint Database

The Fingerprint Verification Competition (FVC) took place in 2000, 2002, 2004 and 2006, as an initiative to compare fingerprint matching algorithms. This competition was organized by the Biometric System Laboratory of the University of Bologna [16], as well as Pattern Recognition and Image Processing Laboratory of the Michigan State University, Biometric Test Center of San Jose State University and, in the last year, Biometrics Research Laboratory of the Universidad Autonoma de Madrid. In this work, 2004 and 2006 data sets were used in our experiments to validate the proposed directional information operator.

3.2   Griaule AFIS

The Griaule fingerprint recognition framework [6] won the Open Category, section "average results over all databases" of the Fingerprint Verification Contest 2006 [16], achieving the best average equal error rate (EER).

Regarding the fingerprint matching algorithm, we can highlight: (i) fingerprint images are acquired by a fingerprint scanner; (ii) images are enhanced through better contrast and distinctness; (iii) noise and defects are eliminated; (iv) fingerprint features are detected and analyzed; and (v) minutiae are identified.

Fingerprint search on the database is made based on some measures, for instance, polygons are determined by connecting three minutiae. Thus, internal angles, sides and each minutiae angle are computed. These measures are invariant to rotation and translation. This method allows that a desired fingerprint can be localized on the database even with position variation (displacement and rotation) in relation to the found fingerprint.

3.3 Experiment Design

In our experiments, we compare the performance of the verification process before and after the removal of the worse quality fingerprints based on the proposed index. The protocols employed in the comparison are the same as those used for the performance of FVC 2004/2006 verification algorithms. Griaule AFIS was used to compare all of the images to each other, following the protocol described in the FCV competition.

This work compared our quality indicator with eight of the others available in the literature:

- OCL (Orientation Certainty Level) [10]: is a measure of the energy concentration strength along the dominant ridge flow orientation. The feature operates in a block-wise manner.
- LCS (Local Clarity Score) [3]: computes the block-wise clarity of ridge and valleys by applying linear regression to determine a gray-level threshold, classifying pixels as ridge or valley. A ratio of misclassified pixels is determined by comparing with the normalized ridge and valley width of that block.
- OFL (Orientation Flow) [3]: is a measure of ridge flow continuity based on the absolute orientation difference between a block and its neighboring blocks.
- RPS (Radial Power Spectrum) [4]: is a measure of maximal signal power in a defined frequency band of the global radial Fourier spectrum. Ridges can be locally approximated by means of a single sine wave, hence high energy concentration in a narrow frequency band corresponds to consistent ridge structures.
- FDA (Frequency Domain Analysis) [11]: operates in a block-wise manner. A one-dimensional signature of the ridge-valley structure is extracted and a discrete Fourier transform is computed on the signature to determine the frequency of the sinusoid following the ridge-valley structure.
- RVU (Ridge Valley Uniformity) [10]: is a measure of the consistency of the ridge and valley widths. The expectation for a finger image with clear ridge and valley separation is that the ratio between ridge and valley widths remains fairly constant and thus the standard deviation of ratios is used as an indication of the sample quality.

- GAB (Gabor Quality Feature) [14]: operates on a per-pixel basis by calculating the standard deviation of the Gabor filter bank responses.
- GSH (Gabor Shen) [19]: is a Gabor-based feature to separate blocks into two classes: good and bad. The scalar quality is the ratio between number of foreground blocks and number of foreground blocks marked as poor.

In this work, we used an implementation of these measures provided by Olsen [15], which were compared to our quality operator.

3.4   Discussion

Each FVC data set has its own features: distinct dimensions, different sensors were used to capture (thermal, optical, electric) in such way that noise types and other eventual injuries are also distinct. Criteria for evaluation and weighting should also be distinct, reflecting the ridge and valley patterns.

Furthermore, other issues should be taken into account when defining the weighting: (i) absolute position (first, second and third position) achieved by the index when compared to the others; and (ii) experiments consisted in removing the worst quality fingerprint images according to the index. In each experiment, a distinct percentage of images is removed (1, 5, 10, 15 and 20%).

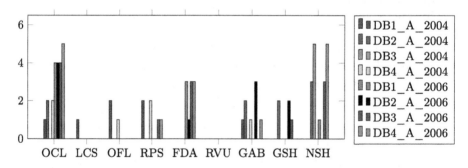

Fig. 2. Average number of times in which the indices were ranked among the top-3 according to AUC value.

Twelve different combinations of weights related to the image removal were performed in each dataset. Experiments were summarized and counted how many times each indicator occurred in the first three positions, considered here as a simple average. The evaluations were based on the calculation of area under the curve (AUC) and equal error rate (EER).

Our approach requires the configuration of several parameters: percentage of samples to be removed, weights relative to such removal, weights related to the absolute position in the precision. It can be observed from Fig. 2 that our indicator (NSH) has a suitable response on DB2_A_2004, DB3_A_2004, DB3_A_2006 and DB4_A_2006 data sets with respect to AUC. Considering EER (Fig. 3), our proposal also has satisfactory results on DB2_A_2004, DB3_A_2004 and DB4_A_2006 data sets.

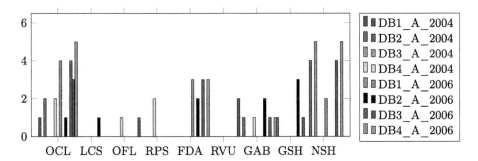

Fig. 3. Average number of times in which the indices were ranked among the top-3 according to EER value.

4   Conclusions and Future Work

Fingerprint image quality plays an important role in biometric systems. For quality evaluation, it is necessary to use specific metrics for each data set due to their inherent characteristics. This makes the task of selecting a subset of features and their weights more challenging, however, more suitable for a combined quality metric.

In this work, we presented a fingerprint quality index based on directional information through a multiscale directional operator. This operator demonstrate to be less noise sensitive than classical gradient approaches. Despite its application in the fingerprint domain, our quality index could be used to assess the significance of many other methods related to directional information.

As directions for future research, we intend to combine different quality features in a way that minimizes the dependence on individual features while maintaining a sufficient predictive behavior with respect to the biometric performance. We also plan to develop an adaptive system that takes into account the characteristics of the sensor to determine the quality of the acquired images.

References

1. Alonso-Fernandez, F., et al.: A comparative study of fingerprint image-quality estimation methods. IEEE Trans. Inf. Forensics Secur. **2**(4), 734–743 (2007)
2. Bazen, A.M., Gerez, S.H.: Systematic methods for the computation of the directional fields and singular points of fingerprints. IEEE Trans. Pattern Anal. Mach. Intell. **24**(7), 905–919 (2002)
3. Chen, T., Jiang, X., Yau, W.: Fingerprint image quality analysis. In: IEEE International Conference on Image Processing, pp. 1253–1256 (2004)
4. Chen, Y., Dass, S., Jain, A.: Fingerprint quality indices for predicting authentication performance. In: International Conference on Audio-and Video-Based Biometric Person Authentication, pp. 160–170 (2005)
5. Feng, J., Jain, A.K.: Fingerprint reconstruction: from minutiae to phase. IEEE Trans. Pattern Anal. Mach. Intell. **33**, 209–223 (2011)

6. Griaule Biometrics. Griaule Big Data Biometrics (2018). http://www.griaulebiometrics.com/new/
7. Jain, A.K., Chen, Y., Demirkus, M.: Pores and ridges: fingerprint matching using level 3 features. IEEE Trans. Pattern Anal. Mach. Intell. **29**, 15–27 (2007)
8. Kass, M., Witkin, A.: Analyzing oriented patterns. Comput. Vis. Graphics Image Process. **37**(3), 362–385 (1987)
9. Lee, S., Choi, H., Choi, K., Kim, J.: Fingerprint-quality index using gradient components. IEEE Trans. Inf. Forensics Secur. **3**(4), 792–800 (2008)
10. Lim, E., Jiang, X., Yau, W.: Fingerprint quality and validity analysis. In: IEEE International Conference on Image Processing, vol. 1, 469–472 (2002)
11. Lim, E., Toh, K.-A., Suganthan, P., Jiang, X., Yau, W.-Y.: Fingerprint image quality analysis. In: IEEE International Conference on Image Processing, pp. 1241–1244 (2004)
12. Maltoni, D., Maio, D., Jain, A.K., Prabhakar, S.: Handbook of Fingerprint Recognition, 2nd edn. Springer, London (2009). https://doi.org/10.1007/978-1-84882-254-2
13. Oliveira, M.A., Leite, N.J.: A multiscale directional operator and morphological tools for reconnecting broken ridges in fingerprint images. Pattern Recogn. **41**(1), 367–377 (2008)
14. Olsen, M., Xu, H., Busch, C.: Gabor filters as candidate quality measure for NFIQ 2.0. In: 5th IAPR International Conference on Biometrics, pp. 158–163 (2012)
15. Olsen, M.A., Smida, V., Busch, C.: Fingerprint Quality Assessment Algorithms (2015). http://www.nislab.no, https://www.dasec.h-da.de
16. Cappelli, A.F.R., Ferrara, M., Maltoni, D.: Fingerprint verification competition 2006. Biometric Technol. Today **15**(7–8), 7–9 (2007)
17. Ratha, N.K., Chen, S., Jain, A.K.: Adaptive flow orientation based feature extraction in fingerprint images. Pattern Recogn. **28**, 1657–1672 (1995)
18. Ross, A., Nadgir, R.: A thin-plate spline calibration model for fingerprint sensor interoperability. IEEE Trans. Knowl. Data Eng. **20**, 1097–1110 (2008)
19. Shen, L., Kot, A.C., Koo, W.M.: Quality measures of fingerprint images. In: 3rd International Conference on Audio- and Video-Based Biometric Person Authentication, pp. 266–271 (2001)
20. Yun, E.-K., Cho, S.-B.: Adaptive fingerprint enhancement with fingerprint image quality analysis. Image Vis. Comput. **24**, 101–110 (2006)
21. Zhou, J., Chen, F., Gu, J.: A novel algorithm for detecting singular points from fingerprint images. IEEE Trans. Pattern Anal. Mach. Intell. **31**, 1239–1250 (2009)

Towards End-to-End DNN-Based Identification of Individual Manta Rays from Sparse Imagery

Tuana Celik[1]([✉]), Benjamin Hughes[2,3], and Tilo Burghardt[1]

[1] University of Bristol, Bristol BS8 1UB, UK
tc13007@bristol.ac.uk, tilo@cs.bris.ac.uk
[2] Save Our Seas Foundation, Geneva, Switzerland
ben@saveourseas.com
[3] The Manta Trust, Corscombe, Dorchester DT2 0NT, UK

Abstract. This paper presents an end-to-end deep learning approach for the fine-grained identification of individual manta rays (*Manta alfredi*) based on characteristic ventral coat patterns where training is restricted to sparse photographic sets of <10 ventral images per individual. The dataset is captured by divers in underwater habitats. Its content is challenging due to non-linear deformations (of the rays), perspective pattern distortions, partial occlusions, as well as lighting and noise-related acquisition issues. We show how a combination of data augmentation, encounter fusion, and transfer learning techniques can address the sparsity and noise challenges at hand so that deep learning pipelines can operate effectively in this uncompromising data environment. We demonstrate that using the proposed approach with an adapted InceptionV3 deep neural network (DNN) architecture significantly outperforms tested baselines including the Manta Matcher approach, the so-far best performing traditional, widely used method published for the application at hand.

1 Introduction

Visual detection and subsequent identification of members of a species by recognition of characteristic coat patterns – ideally to the fine-grained granularity of an individual – is a subdiscipline of computational animal biometrics [1]. It is an effective and potentially non-invasive approach to gain knowledge about aspects of a population of interest: be that to estimate presence, abundance, dynamics, or changes in behavior or social networks over time and space [1].

In order to enable modern deep learning approaches to operate successfully in the animal biometrics domain, large datasets that represent the individuals to be identified would appear to be of paramount importance. Yet, there are significant challenges associated with acquiring high quality visuals at scale, particularly in scenarios where species are rare, move unpredictably across vast areas, or live in habitats that are difficult to monitor (e.g. remote jungle or underwater).

© Springer Nature Switzerland AG 2019
R. Vera-Rodriguez et al. (Eds.): CIARP 2018, LNCS 11401, pp. 645–653, 2019.
https://doi.org/10.1007/978-3-030-13469-3_75

This paper focusses on *Manta alfredi*, a species whose members carry individually characteristic blob patterns on their highly flexible ventral body surface (see Fig. 1). These markings have been exploited in the past, both via manual and semi-automated methodologies [2] using traditional computer vision in order to derive individual animal identities based on photographic evidence.

The objective of this paper is to show that a deep learning approach can be highly effective in our particular problem scenario of individual manta ray identification given sparse ventral pattern imagery. Our approach is depicted in Fig. 2 and combines data augmentation, encounter fusion, and transfer learning techniques to address the sparsity and noise issues at hand – all with the ultimate objective of enabling recent deep learning pipelines to operate successfully in this domain.

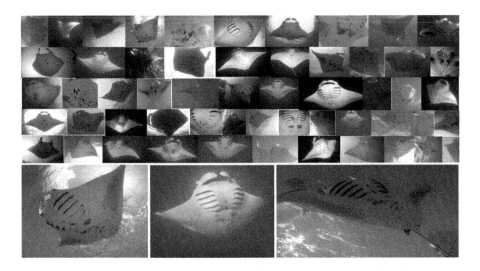

Fig. 1. Ventral Manta Ray Imagery. *(top)* Representative samples from the utilized 'Manta2018' data provided by The Manta Trust (see Footnote 2). Note the various non-linear deformations of animals, perspective distortions, partial occlusions, as well as lighting and noise-related challenges. *(bottom)* Three sample images showing the same individual under different lighting, pose, and acquisition conditions.

The remainder of the thesis is structured as follows. Section 2 briefly reviews most relevant methodologies and prior work. Section 3 describes the dataset, test architectures, experiments and recorded performance. Section 4 presents results and benchmarks them against those obtained from our re-implementation of the best performing manta identification method published to date [2]. Finally, Sect. 5 provides conclusions and closing remarks.

2 Related Work

For more than a decade now, computational animal biometrics have provided support for non-intrusive, often visual alternatives to traditional invasive tagging and marking methodologies, fueling ecological applications: camera-trapping, visual drone censuses, and colony counts via satellite provide a few commonly used examples [1]. Yet, whilst applicable across a wide range of species and semi-automated application scenarios [1–4], computerized visual identification of individuals widely relied on the use of *hand-crafted features* such as Scale-Invariant Feature Transform (*SIFT*) [5] or related extraction techniques [6].

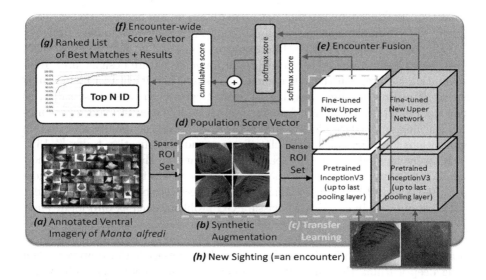

Fig. 2. Overview of Approach. *(a)* Field imagery with Region of Interest (ROI) and identity annotations covering a manta ray population of interest is used as system input. *(b)* A large pool of visual data is synthesized to enable network training based on domain-specific, geometric data augmentation. *(c)* Fine-tuning of a pre-trained InceptionV3-like architecture yields an inference network that can map from entire images to *(d)* a score vector over all individuals or, *(e)* for optional encounter fusion, two such vectors summed to produce *(f)* a score over all individuals produced for an entire encounter set. *(g)* A ranked list of best manta matches is then inferred for *(h)* new sightings in red. (Color figure online)

In particular, Town et al. in [2] describe a system to identify individual manta rays, one which semi-automatically produces a ranked list of known rays that best match a single provided query image. The system as published requires users to correct for in-plane image rotation and select a rectangular Region of Interest (ROI) aligned with the animal. After noise removal and adaptive contrast equalization, SIFT features are extracted and matched by computing all possible pairings between the feature vectors representing the query image I and every entry J in the feature database. A similarity score between I and J is then computed via all N_{F_i, F_j} matches as:

$$score(I, J) = \frac{\sum_{n=1}^{N_{F_i, F_j}} w_n}{max(|F_i|, |F_j|)} \tag{1}$$

resulting in a score between 0 and 1, where F_i and F_j are the sets of SIFT features of images I and J, respectively, and each matched feature pair is weighted via w_n based on the *significance* and the *strength* of the match as given in [2]. Finally, a similarity score between image I and Manta m is established:

$$Score(I, Manta_m) = mean(score(I, J_m)) \tag{2}$$

where J_m are labeled images that belong to Manta m. For benchmarks, we interpreted [2] to re-implement the pipeline – confirming their results (see Table 1).

Over the past decade or so, limitations of hand-crafted feature approaches have emerged due to inherently suboptimal, *manual* feature designs [5,6]. Representation learning, on the other hand, has established itself as a viable alternative: it utilizes machine learning to evolve features to those best suited to map from inputs to the target domain. Such data-driven end-to-end representation learning, applied via deep neural networks (DNNs), dominates mainstream applications for object detection, classification and identification today [7–13].

In order to apply such deep learning techniques to the task at hand, individual manta ray identification may be understood as a fine-grained classification (FGC) task [14] aiming at differentiating effectively between highly similar classes or objects. In contrast to classic FGC problems such as bird [8] or plant [9] species recognition, we are interested in an intra-species classification of conspecifics here, conceptually in line with recent work for the individual identification of great white sharks [4], gorillas [10] or chimpanzees [3,15]. However, when using deep learning the supervised training of required networks is often crucially dependent on the availability of large, representative, manually annotated training data[1]. If this is not available then an effective application of deep FGC techniques to complex identification tasks is, mainly hampered by overfitting, not straight forward despite the application of regularization, dropout etc.

Yet, large annotated datasets such as ImageNet [17] have led to the training of deep convolutional neural networks (CNNs) such as AlexNet [11], VGG [12] or Inception [13] capable of effectively disambiguating a wide range of visual classes relevant to real imagery. Assuming that visual knowledge encoded in network weights can be 'shared' between related tasks – and visual tasks are indeed related – then starting new optimizations from pre-trained weight settings is potentially beneficial for avoiding narrow generalization. We will explore the use of an InceptionV3-like architecture [13] as basis for late layer fine-tuning (see Sect. 3.2). Note that this network has a reduced footprint on the GPU (i.e. $5M$ compared to the $60M$ of AlexNet [11]) due to extensive kernel factorization.

---

[1] Consider that in [10], for instance, $12,765$ images covering 147 individuals are used for training, that is on average 86.8 images per animal. Holstein Friesian cattle identification by Andrew et al. [16] utilizes $46,430$ frames describing only 23 individuals.

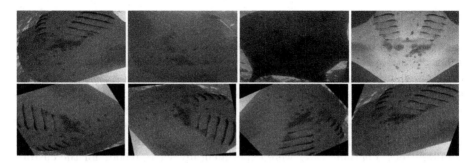

Fig. 3. ROIs and Augmentation. *(top row)* Four examples of ROIs of the same individual as used for training re-scaled to 512^2 or 299^2 pixels. *(bottom row)* Four representative examples of synthesized training images all from one source image (given at the top left). Shear and rotation produce 60 training images for each input image, overall synthesizing $47,520$ training samples from 792 source images. Since ROIs are provided, scale or shift are not augmented.

3   Methodology

3.1   Dataset and Augmentation

Our initial sparse 'Manta2018' dataset of ventral *Manta alfredi* digital photographs is provided by The Manta Trust[2]. Figure 1 depicts a representative subset of the overall 990 class-labeled images with ROIs belonging to 99 individuals – covering exactly 10 images per individual. As exemplified in Fig. 3, provided ROIs contain at most one full single manta instance, potentially less. The data is captured by divers in natural, often murky and poorly lit underwater habitats. Non-linear deformations (of the rays), perspective pattern distortions, partial occlusions, as well as lighting and noise-related acquisition image degradation are prominent in the dataset. All patches given by ROIs are reshaped to fit the network inputs. Each individual's data are split into 8 patches for training and 2 (withheld) for testing. This yields 792 training and 198 testing instances.

Synthetic generation of a 60-times increased training base consists of 50 rotations of patches randomly sampled from a uniform distribution between -180 to $180°$, plus a shear transform using a uniform distribution from -30 to $30°$, plus 8 cases where we combine a fully random rotation and shear transforms. Together with the original, we thus produce 60 representations of the same image, resulting in each class now having 480 examples in its training pool. Overall, this yields $47,520$ training patches – see Fig. 3 (bottom) for samples.

---

[2] **Acknowledgments:** The dataset has been provided by The Manta Trust, Catemwood House, Corscombe Dorchester, Dorset DT2 0NT, UK. The Manta Trust holds copyrights of all data. Please contact The Manta Trust directly to obtain the dataset.

3.2   Implementation

We compare and experiment with three architectures: (1) the current domain-specific state-of-the-art Manta Matcher pipeline detailed in [2], (2) a custom deep baseline network specified in Fig. 4a, and (3) our InceptionV3-like fine-tuning architecture either used as a single network as detailed Fig. 4b, or as a subnet integrated into an encounter-fusion architecture as explained in Fig. 2.

All deep models were trained on Nvidia P100 GPU nodes with batch sizes of 32 using Adaptive Moment Estimation (Adam) as optimizer over up to $240,000$ training steps. Learning rates were experimentally set to 0.0001 for the custom baseline network and to 0.1 for InceptionV3 fine-tuning. We initialize all (non-pre-trained) weights over a random uniform distribution within $(-0.05, 0.05)$ where the custom baseline network is fully trained from scratch. For InceptionV3 fine-tuning, we use pre-trained weights from ImageNet up to the final pooling layer of the network (see Fig. 4b). Transferring layer weights directly, we then train a newly formed fully connected and a final softmax-loss layer with our data. Figure 5 (right) depicts a representative training run with test results in red.

Assuming a user has access to two or more samples of the same manta ray, e.g. acquired during the same dive, we also tested an encounter fusion architecture where we feed all inputs through the fine-tuned subnet in turn, as shown in Fig. 2, before summing output scores over all streams into one output vector.

type	kernel size/stride	filters	activation	input size
conv + BN	3x3	32	Relu	512x512x3
MaxPool	3x3/2	–	–	512x512x32
conv + BN	5x5	32	Relu	256x256x32
MaxPool	3x3/2	–	–	256x256x32
conv + BN	5x5	64	Relu	128x128x32
MaxPool	3x3/2	–	–	128x128x64
conv + BN	3x3	64	Relu	64x64x64
MaxPool	3x3/2	–	–	64x64x64
conv + D1 + BN	3x3	64	Relu	32x32x64
MaxPool	3x3/2	–	–	32x32x64
conv + BN	3x3	64	Relu	16x16x64
MaxPool	3x3/2	–	–	16x16x64
conv + D2	3x3	128	Relu	8x8x64
FC1	1x1	8192	Relu	8x8x128
FC2	1x1	99	–	8192
softmax – loss	–	99	–	99

(a) Custom deep net

type	patch size/stride or remarks	input size
conv	3x3/2	299x299x3
conv	3x3/1	149x149x32
conv	3x3/1	147x147x32
pool	3x3/2	147x147x64
conv	3x3/1	73x73x64
conv	3x3/2	71x71x80
conv	3x3/1	35x35x192
3xInception		35x35x288
5xInception		17x17x768
2xInception		8x8x1280
pool	8x8	8x8x2048
linear	logits	1x1x2048
softmax	classifier	1x1x99

(b) InceptionV3-like net

Fig. 4. Deep Net Architectures. The overview provides details on the layer types used, the sizes of kernel and their stride, as well as the layer dimensions.

4   Results

Individual identification results are presented in Table 1. As shown in magenta there, we first confirm that the Manta Matcher approach performs similarly on our dataset as on the one reported in [2] with classification accuracy above 46%.

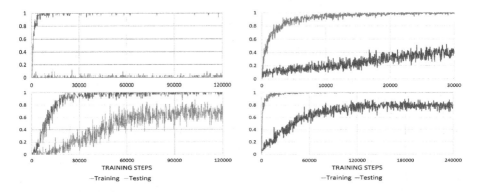

Fig. 5. Accuracy Evolution During Optimization. Graphs depict the development of accuracy (y-axis) along network training steps (x-axis) for our custom model (left) and during InceptionV3 transfer learning (right). *(top left)* Custom network optimized without augmentation is unable to generalize training performance (blue) towards testing performance (orange) and overfits the data. *(bottom left)* The same network is able to learn more effectively when provided with augmented data. *(top right)* Early performance of fine-tuned InceptionV3-like model using the same augmented data, and *(bottom right)* long-term learning of this approach. The latter yields competitive benchmarks (also see Table 1). (Color figure online)

Table 1. Top-N accuracy results

Model (and Dataset)	Top-1 accuracy	Top-10 accuracy
Manta Matcher (their 581)	46.82%	65.06%
Manta Matcher (our 198)	46.46%	65.15%
Custom DNN (our 198)	69.69%	79.29%
Fine-tuned InceptionV3 (our 198)	**79.29%**	87.88%
Fine-tuned + Encounter Fusion	78.79%	**91.92%**

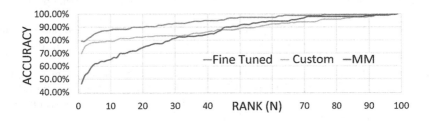

Fig. 6. Top-N accuracy for single image ID on our 198 test samples.

In our case, however, the sparsity of the original training data causes deep learning without augmentation to fail completely w.r.t. generalization, overfitting on the training samples (see Fig. 5, top left). However, augmentation addresses this problem effectively (see Fig. 5, bottom left) yielding a *classification accuracy* just above 69% as shown in ochre in Table 1 and Fig. 6. Our fine-tuned InceptionV3-like model trained over long term (see Fig. 5, bottom right) outperformed both approaches with a classification accuracy above 79% as shown in blue in Table 1 and Fig. 6. Practical applications with a human in the loop can, however, tolerate some ranking error – confirming a match against a dozen or so candidates is practically feasible. Thus, accuracy within the *Top 10 interval predictions* (see Table 1, column three) made by a model is also of interest. Whilst the described encounter fusion gives no gain of the Top-1 accuracy, we observe accuracy improvements in the Top-10 statistics from 87.88% to 91.92%.

5   Conclusion and Future Work

We have shown that, for the problem of photo-based recognition of individual manta rays, a combination of augmentation, transfer learning, and encounter-wide fusion techniques can address sparsity and noise challenges to enable deep learning to operate effectively – potentially assisting field work beyond previous capabilities. We demonstrated that an InceptionV3-like network trained on augmented data and fusing multiple encounter images outperforms the so-far best traditional approach published. Overall, this indicates that deep learning techniques in conjunction with augmentation and regularisation approaches have a role to play in advancing the performance of animal biometrics systems for visual manta ray identification. Future work will target fully automated processing of imagery as well as deep learning extensions that allow for open set identification, that is to avoid retraining of models whenever new individuals are encountered.

References

1. Kühl, H., Burghardt, T.: Animal biometrics: quantifying and detecting phenotypic appearance. Trends Ecol. Evol. **28**, 432–441 (2013)
2. Town, C., Marshall, A., Sethasathien, N.: Manta matcher: automated photographic identification of manta rays using keypoint features. Ecol. Evol. **3**, 1902–1914 (2013)
3. Loos, A., Ernst, A.: An automated chimpanzee identification system using face detection and recognition. EURASIP Image Video Process. **2013**(1), 49 (2013)
4. Hughes, B., Burghardt, T.: Automated visual fin identification of individual great white sharks. IJCV **122**(3), 542–557 (2017)
5. Lowe, D.G.: Object recognition from local scale-invariant features. In: IEEE International Conference on Computer Vision, vol. 2, pp. 1150–1157 (1999)
6. Bay, H., Tuytelaars, T., Van Gool, L.: SURF: Speeded Up Robust Features. In: Leonardis, A., Bischof, H., Pinz, A. (eds.) ECCV 2006. LNCS, vol. 3951, pp. 404–417. Springer, Heidelberg (2006). https://doi.org/10.1007/11744023_32

7. Redmon, J., Divvala, S., Girshick, R., Farhadi, A.: You only look once: unified, real-time object detection. In: Proceedings of IEEE CVPR, pp. 779–788 (2016)
8. Branson, S., Van Horn, G., Belongie, S., Perona, P.: Bird species categorization using pose normalized deep convolutional nets. arXiv:1406.2952 (2014)
9. Kumar, N., et al.: Leafsnap: a computer vision system for automatic plant species identification. In: Fitzgibbon, A., Lazebnik, S., Perona, P., Sato, Y., Schmid, C. (eds.) ECCV 2012. LNCS, pp. 502–516. Springer, Heidelberg (2012). https://doi.org/10.1007/978-3-642-33709-3_36
10. Brust, C.-A., et al.: Towards automated visual monitoring of individual gorillas in the wild. In: Proceedings of IEEE CVPR, pp. 2820–2830 (2017)
11. Krizhevsky, A., Sutskever, I., Hinton, G.E.: ImageNet classification with deep convolutional neural networks. In: Pereira, F., Burges, C.J.C., Bottou, L., Weinberger, K.Q. (eds.) Advances in Neural Information Processing Systems, vol. 25, pp. 1097–1105. Curran Associates Inc. (2012)
12. Simonyan, K., Zisserman, A.: Very deep convolutional networks for large-scale image recognition. arXiv:1409.1556, pp. 1929–1958 (2014)
13. Szegedy, C., Vanhoucke, V., Ioffe, S., Shlens, J., Wojna, Z.: Rethinking the inception architecture for computer vision. In: Proceedings of IEEE CVPR, pp. 2818–2826 (2016)
14. Freytag, A., Rodner, E., Darrell, T., Denzler, J.: Exemplar-specific patch features for fine-grained recognition. In: Jiang, X., Hornegger, J., Koch, R. (eds.) Pattern Recognition, pp. 144–156. Springer, Cham (2014)
15. Freytag, A., Rodner, E., Simon, M., Loos, A., Kühl, H.S., Denzler, J.: Chimpanzee faces in the wild: log-euclidean CNNs for predicting identities and attributes of primates. In: Rosenhahn, B., Andres, B. (eds.) GCPR 2016. LNCS, vol. 9796, pp. 51–63. Springer, Cham (2016). https://doi.org/10.1007/978-3-319-45886-1_5
16. Andrew, W., Greatwood, C., Burghardt, T.: Visual localisation and individual identification of Holstein Friesian cattle via deep learning. In: IEEE International Conference on Computer Vision Workshop, pp. 2850–2859 (2017)
17. Deng, J., Dong, W., Socher, R., Li, L.J., Li, K., Fei-Fei, L.: ImageNet: a large-scale hierarchical image database. In: Proceedings of IEEE CVPR, pp. 248–255, June 2009

Two Stream Deep CNN-RNN Attentive Pooling Architecture for Video-Based Person Re-identification

W. Ansar[1(✉)], M. M. Fraz[1,2,3,5], M. Shahzad[1,5], I. Gohar[1], S. Javed[2], and S. K. Jung[4]

[1] School of Electrical Engineering and Computer Science,
National University of Sciences and Technology, Islamabad, Pakistan
`wansar.mscs16seecs@seecs.edu.pk`
[2] Department of Computer Science, University of Warwick, Coventry, UK
[3] The Alan Turing Institute, British Library, London NW1 2DB, UK
[4] Kyungpook National University, Daegu, Republic of Korea
`skjung@knu.ac.kr`
[5] Deep Learning Laboratory, National Center of Artificial Intelligence (NCAI),
Islamabad, Pakistan

Abstract. Person re-identification (re-ID), is the task of associating the relationship among the images of a person captured from different cameras with non-overlapping field of view. Fundamental and yet an open issue in re-ID is extraction of powerful features in low resolution surveillance videos. In order to solve this, a novel Two Stream Convolutional Recurrent model with Attentive pooling mechanism is presented for person re-ID in videos. Each stream of the model is a Siamese network which is aimed at extracting and matching most differentiated feature maps. Attentive pooling is used to select most informative video frames. The output of two streams is fused to formulate one combined feature map, which helps to deal with major challenges of re-ID e.g. pose and illumination variation, clutter background and occlusion. The proposed technique is evaluated on three challenging datasets: MARS, PRID-2011 and iLIDS-VID. Experimental evaluation shows that the proposed technique performs better than existing state-of-the-art supervised video based person re-ID models. The implementation is available at https://github.com/re-identification/Person_RE-ID.git.

Keywords: Person re-identification · Spatial stream · Temporal stream

1 Introduction

Person re-ID is a task to recognize an individual in the images/videos captured from the cameras of disjoint non over-lapping field of view. It has its application areas in action recognition, people tracking, and surveillance videos at public places (like airport, museums, train stations, shopping mall, roads, universities etc.) [1]. An automated surveillance system is required, when images/video data in enormous amount is produced by the surveillance camera network which is difficult to be monitored manually. Person re-ID is a non-trivial task because of the challenges associated with it, which

© Springer Nature Switzerland AG 2019
R. Vera-Rodriguez et al. (Eds.): CIARP 2018, LNCS 11401, pp. 654–661, 2019.
https://doi.org/10.1007/978-3-030-13469-3_76

includes change in body posture, variation in light, cluttered background, occlusion and low resolution images [2]. Person re-ID can be classified in two categories: image-based re-iD and video-based re-ID. Nowadays, multiple cameras are used for surveillance and produced massive amount of data. Therefore, image-based models cannot perform efficiently on large datasets [3, 4]. In contrast, video-based methods boost performance of person re-ID task due to multiples frames provide rich information, which involves temporal information associated to person motion. Still in video-based re-ID, some issues are not solved: Most of the methods [5] use a single stream convolutional neural network (CNN) to acquire temporal and spatial features through concatenation of RGB and optical flow, which limits the network capability to acquire the spatial and temporal data adequately. In this architecture, max-pooling is used for down sampling of features, which only focus on features with maximum value, so this model misses visual cues e.g. shoes and handbags. However, in order to deal with inter-class variations these small scale attributes are very beneficial. Thus single stream models seems not at optimal choice for features learning in low resolution videos. Secondly, different kind of cameras are used to capture videos sequences and produce low resolution video sequences. It's difficult to capture spatial features from low resolution images. So far, person re-ID methods are single stream CNN, which first extract spatial features and then fed these to recurrent unit to extract temporal information. These model cannot perform well in this situations and unable to learn gait feature independently e.g. arm and leg motion which remain same even in low resolution videos frames. Thirdly, consecutive video frames contain redundant information, thus it's so time taking and memory consuming process to see and remember each video frames.

To solve the issues mentioned above, we present novel two stream convolutional recurrent model with attentive pooling mechanism, using RGB frames and optical flow separately parallel as input to the network. The first stream named as spatial-net, which handle RGB video frames to capture useful spatial features representations like intensity gradient and color for each person in the video frames. The second stream named as temporal-net, handle the optical flows as input and learn gait features even in low resolution video frames. This solve second issue mentioned above. To solve third problem, the attentive pooling is used which selectively focus on discriminative video frames contain human being and ignore non informative frames. The fusion of spatial-net and temporal-net is done using a weighted objective function to give more weight to temporal features, which is based on both data and model fusion to utilize learned features maps. Finally, Siamese model is deployed on attention vectors, to judge the extent of matching.

Remaining paper is structured as follow: In Sect. 2 related work for video-based re-ID will be discussed. Our novel proposed architecture will be discussed in Sect. 3. The result of proposed model on PRID-2011 [6], MARS [7] and iLIDS-VID [8] will be discussed and compared with other models in Sect. 4. At last conclusion will be discussed in Sect. 5.

2   Related Work

In literature, researchers have explored various deep neural network (DNN) for video-based re-ID, to handle large data volume [4, 9–13]. The DNN models for re-ID can be further classified into two aspects: (i) the methods focused on spatial image-level representations e.g. person appearance such as color, style and shape of clothes [8], However, these techniques are generally build dense and complicated networks. For instance, Zheng et al. [7] attempts to train a classification network, in which a single feature vector represents each single image. A deeper and complex hierarchy is inevitable to establish in their models. (ii) The models which are paying more focus to temporal sequence-level representations e.g. person movement such as arm swinging and gait information [14]. Recently video-based re-ID models have explored the use of both temporal and spatial information [5, 9]. Yi et al. [9] presented the first Siamese-based CNN (S-CNN) architecture, which leveraged S-CNN model to the covered parts of the individual picture. To extract temporal information optical flows are computed, and then simply concatenated with person image as input of model to assemble the spatio-temporal features. McLaughlin et al. [5] proposed another model combination of CNN and recurrent neural network (RNN), which is also capable of learning features representation from multiple frames. In their model CNN extracts spatial information and fed features to RNN to effectively learn temporal information between different time frames. However, these methods used single stream to extract spatial and temporal information simultaneously, which limited capacity to fully obtained and combined temporal and spatial information. Chung et al. [15], used CNNs only to extract both spatial and short term temporal information, without taking into account the long term temporal information.

On the other hand, when we look at a picture, the one part of the picture is the focal point of our attention and perception. Even though the rest of the picture is still in eyes, we pay less attention to them. In context of computer vision, this mechanism is called attention model. A wide range of applications use attention models, such as action recognition task, image caption generation and questioning-answering models. To the best of our knowledge, just a few techniques [14, 16] utilized attention algorithms for person re-ID. However, these methods only use either spatial or temporal attention in single stream model. At present, there is no method for re-ID which utilized both temporal attention and spatial attention simultaneously to examine individual re-ID. Therefore, use of both spatial and temporal information are equally supportive to fully express a person in videos frames.

To address aforementioned issues, we proposed an end-to-end two stream CNN-RNN model with attentive pooling. In this model, both streams learn different feature maps, and finally merge output of two stream to obtain union of characteristics. This model can act as efficient features extractor for video-based re-ID, as well as it produces hidden unit representations for measuring similarity score for time series input.

3   The Proposed Model

This paper presents an end-to-end two stream convolutional-recurrent model with attentive pooling for video based person re-ID. To capture local effective contextual information spatial stream is used with RGB images as input and to obtain motion information temporal stream is used with optical flow as input, shown in Fig. 1. Each stream is Siamese based and output of CNN in each stream is images level representation, which then fed into recurrent neural network to extract temporal information of video sequence over long time. Following subsections will discuss two stream model and attentive pooling in more detail.

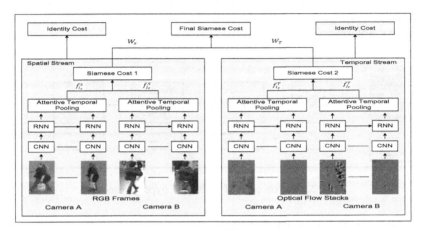

Fig. 1. The proposed two stream CNN-RNN architecture with attentive pooling

3.1   Two-Stream CNN-RNN

We express the input video sequence as V_s, s belongs to a, b used for camera A and camera B respectively. Input for first stream of our model are RGB frames: $V_s = \left(R^{(1)}...R^{(L)}\right)$ and for second stream optical flow images are used, $V_s = \left(T^{(1)} \cdots T^{(L)}\right)$. L is sequence length, since we have the gallery and probe sequences are of different size, so for training and testing we fixed the length of each person sequence to 16 and 128 respectively fairness of experimentations. Lucas-Kanade [17] technique is used to compute optical flows. Then by utilizing the convolutional network depict in Fig. 2; we obtain feature maps set $C_s = \left(C^{(1)}...C^{(L)}\right)$ and $C_T = \left(O^{(1)}...O^{(L)}\right)$ for RGB frames and Optical flow respectively. Unlike max pooling (only focus on maximum valued features) we used multiple convolutional layers in CNN for directly down sampling with stride of 2, it focuses on learned feature maps with fixed position and give us better performance. Output of CNN are then fed to RNN, recurrent layer is formulized by Eq. (1):

$$o^t = Ur^t + Ws^{t-1}, \quad s^t = tanh(o^t) \tag{1}$$

Where r^t is input of recurrent layer for time t, s^{t-1} is the hidden state which contain information for prior time step, and o^t is the output. Through matrix U recurrent layer implants high dimensional feature vector into low dimensional feature vector and $W \in R^{N \times N}$ which project s^{t-1} from R^1 to R^N. For first time step hidden state (s^0) is set to zero; tanh activation function is used to pass hidden state between different time steps. In the proposed model each stream helps other stream to learn multiple different aspect of feature maps, which is not possible in single stream models. Each batch of training images contains same number of positive and negative examples. We set the margin to 4 and learning rate to $2e^{-3}$ with stepwise decay for training the Siamese network. After training phase, we have stored the features vectors for all gallery sequences. During inference, the new sequence of probe persons is passed through the model to yield a feature vector. Afterwards, the probe feature vector is matched with the gallery features using a single matrix vector product.

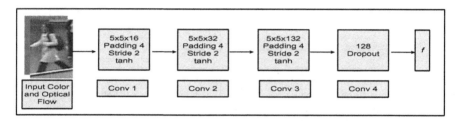

Fig. 2. The structure of CNN with hyper parameters.

3.2   Attentive Temporal Pooling Layer

There is many redundant information in consecutive video frames such as clothes and cluttered background. To tackle with this problem, we presented attentive temporal pooling for re-ID; which only focus on useful information. Attentive pooling layer is placed between RNN and distance measuring layer. By convolution and recurrent layer we obtained image and sequence level features, which are stored in P and G matrices for probe and gallery respectively; whose i^{th} row denotes output in the ith time step of the recurrent. Then attention matrix A is computed by Eq. (2):

$$A = tanh(PUG^t) \qquad (2)$$

In Eq. (2), both P and $Q \in R^{T \times N}$, $U \in R^{N \times T}$ and $A \in R^{T \times T}$. Matrix U is learned by network and intent for information sharing. Attention matrix calculates weight scores in temporal dimension and it is capable to have vision on both probe (t_p) and gallery (t_g) sequence features. Finally, in each stream, soft-max function is applied on temporal weight vectors. It transform the ith weight $[t_p]_i$ and $[t_g]_i$ to the attention ratio $[a_p]_i$ and $[a_g]_i$ using the following Eq. (3):

$$[a_p]_i = \frac{e^{[t_p]_i}}{\sum_{j=1}^{T} e^{[t_p]_j}} \qquad (3)$$

Where Eq. 4 applies to both two stream CNN-RNN similarly with changed sort of input. To acquire the sequence-level representation v_p and v_g, we applied dot product among the feature matrices P, G and attention vectors a_p as shown in Eq. (4):

$$v_p = P^T a_p, \quad v_g = G^T a_g \tag{4}$$

At last, we use a Siamese network for both two streams, which tries to decrease the distance between positive pairs and endeavor the separation between negative pairs during training, as shown in Fig. 1. From each stream we have two Siamese cost functions. Thusly, we characterize the joined cost function as Eq. (5):

$$D\left(V_p, V_g\right) = \omega_s E\left(f_{i_{S_c}}^-, f_{j_{S_c}}^-\right) + \omega_T E\left(f_{i_{T_c}}^-, J_{j_{T_c}}^-\right) \tag{5}$$

ω_s, ω_T are the weights for Spatial-Net and Temporal-Net, E denote Euclidean distance and $f_{i_{S_c}}^-$ $and f_{j_{S_c}}^-$ are the attentive pooled feature vectors for person i and j separately. We utilized the unique weights for each stream to have the capacity to underline the spatial features when contrasted with the optical features for re-ID. Despite the fact that motions features include discriminative capacity to the accuracy even with low resolution image. Hence, we set the weights observationally with the condition $\omega_T \geq \omega_s$. Our ultimate training goal is grouping of Siamese and identity loss $L\left(V_p, V_g\right) = D\left(V_p, V_g\right) + I\left(V_p\right) + I\left(V_g\right)$.

4 Experimental Evaluation

The proposed model is evaluated on three publically available datasets: PRID-2011 [6], MARS [7] and iLIDS-VID [8].

4.1 Datasets

The PRID-2011 [6] dataset comprises of 749 persons, taken by two disjoint cameras. The dimension of frames differs from 5 to 675 for each person image sequence. It has simple backgrounds and less occlusions as compared with the iLIDS-VID dataset. We utilized only first 200 individuals captured by both cameras. MARS [7] is considered as the largest dataset for video-based person re-ID. It contains 1261 different persons, captured by 2 to 6 cameras and on average each person has 13 sequences. The iLIDS-VID [8] dataset consist of 300 persons, where every single individual is represented by two sequences taken at arrival hall of airport via two separate cameras. Size of sequences differs from 23 to 192 frames. It is very challenging dataset, because of dress resemblances for different persons, change in illumination, viewpoint deviations and arbitrary occlusions. For all three datasets, experiments were repeated 10 times with altered test and train splits to ensure constant results.

4.2   Quantitative Results and Comparison with Other Methods

In this section, we compared the results of our proposed architecture with state-of-the-art models for video-based re-ID. The proposed model achieves better performance than other methods on iLIDS-VID, PRID-2011 and MARS datasets in terms of Rank-1 (R1), Rank-5 (R5), Rank-10 (R10) and Rank-20 (R20) accuracies. The quantitative results are compared with other models in Table 1. The proposed model achieved matching rate of R1 = 72.6%, 84% and 56% on iLIDS-VID PRID-2011 and MARS dataset respectively, which is higher than other methods.

Table 1. Quantitative performance measures and comparison with other methods

Method	Dataset											
	iLIDS-VID				PRID-2011				MARS			
	R1	R5	R10	R20	R1	R5	R10	R20	R 1	R5	R 10	R20
Liu et al. [16]	44.3	71.7	83.7	91.7	64.1	87.3	89.9	92.0	–	–	–	–
Karanam et al. [18]	24.9	44.5	55.6	66.2	35.1	59.4	69.8	79.7	–	–	–	–
McLaughlin et al. [5]	58.0	84.0	91.0	96.0	70.0	90.0	95.0	97.0	40.0	64.0	70.0	77.0
Xu et al. [14]	62.0	86.0	94.0	98.0	77.0	95.0	99.0	99.0	44.0	70.0	74.0	81.0
Yu et al. [4]	66.5	89.5	96.6	98.2	79.2	97.4	99.5	100	45.6	**72.4**	75.4	82.6
Boin et al. [3]	76.4	**95.3**	**98.0**	99.1	58.0	87.5	93.7	97.5	–	–	–	–
Ouyang et al. [19]	64.8	90.7	96.4	98.3	78.3	96.7	99.3	99.7	–	–	–	–
Proposed Model	**76.6**	90.8	96.6	**99.7**	**84.0**	**97.6**	**99.8**	**100**	**56**	67	77	90

5   Conclusion

In this paper, we have presented an end-to-end two streams CNN-RNN architecture with attentive pooling. The model uses two separate streams for the RGB frames and the optical flows to learn feature maps with different aspects. Only informative frames over full sequence are selected through attentive pooling followed by the concatenation of features. Quantitative results show that proposed model achieve greater performance to the existing state-of-the-art supervised re-ID models on PRID-2011, iLIDS-VID and MARS datasets. The proposed method performs better because the two streams emphasis on different feature maps and incorporate the temporal information for re-identification. The proposed architecture is simple to implement and generate best features even with low resolution input frames. In future we aim to extend the model using LSTM for solving the Open-world re-ID in real time.

Acknowledgements. This research was supported by development project of leading technology for future vehicle of the business of Daegu metropolitan city (No. 20180910). We are also thankful to NVIDIA Corporation for donating the TitanX GPU which is used in this research.

References

1. Karanam, S., et al.: A systematic evaluation and benchmark for person re-identification: features, metrics, and datasets. IEEE Trans. Pattern Anal. Mach. Intell. **41**(3), 523–536 (2018)
2. Perwaiz, N., Fraz, M.M., Shahzad, M.: Person re-identification using hybrid representation reinforced by metric learning. IEEE Access **6**, 77334–77349 (2018)
3. Boin, J.-B., Araujo, A., Girod, B.: Recurrent neural networks for person re-identification revisited. arXiv preprint arXiv:1804.03281 (2018)
4. Yu, Z., et al.: Three-stream convolutional networks for video-based person re-identification. arXiv preprint arXiv:1712.01652 (2017)
5. McLaughlin, N., Martinez del Rincon, J., Miller, P.: Recurrent convolutional network for video-based person re-identification. In: Proceedings of the IEEE Conference on Computer Vision and Pattern Recognition (2016)
6. Hirzer, M., Beleznai, C., Roth, P.M., Bischof, H.: Person re-identification by descriptive and discriminative classification. In: Heyden, A., Kahl, F. (eds.) SCIA 2011. LNCS, vol. 6688, pp. 91–102. Springer, Heidelberg (2011). https://doi.org/10.1007/978-3-642-21227-7_9
7. Zheng, L., et al.: MARS: a video benchmark for large-scale person re-identification. In: Leibe, B., Matas, J., Sebe, N., Welling, M. (eds.) ECCV 2016. LNCS, vol. 9910, pp. 868–884. Springer, Cham (2016). https://doi.org/10.1007/978-3-319-46466-4_52
8. Wang, T., Gong, S., Zhu, X., Wang, S.: Person re-identification by video ranking. In: Fleet, D., Pajdla, T., Schiele, B., Tuytelaars, T. (eds.) ECCV 2014. LNCS, vol. 8692, pp. 688–703. Springer, Cham (2014). https://doi.org/10.1007/978-3-319-10593-2_45
9. Yi, D., et al.: Deep metric learning for person re-identification. In: 22nd International Conference on Pattern Recognition (ICPR). IEEE (2014)
10. Mumtaz, S., et al.: Weighted hybrid features for person re-identification. In: 7th International Conference on Image Processing Theory Tools and Applications, Montreal (2017)
11. Mubariz, N., et al.: Optimization of person re-identification through visual descriptors. In: 13th International Joint Conference on Computer Vision, Imaging and Computer Graphics Theory and Applications, Funchal, Madeira, Portugal, pp. 348–355 (2018)
12. Khurram, I., Fraz, M.M., Shahzad, M.: Detailed sentence generation architecture for image semantics description. In: Bebis, G., et al. (eds.) ISVC 2018. LNCS, vol. 11241, pp. 423–432. Springer, Cham (2018). https://doi.org/10.1007/978-3-030-03801-4_37
13. Bashir, R.M.S., Shahzad, M., Fraz, M.M.: DUPL-VR: deep unsupervised progressive learning for vehicle re-identification. In: Bebis, G., et al. (eds.) ISVC 2018. LNCS, vol. 11241, pp. 286–295. Springer, Cham (2018). https://doi.org/10.1007/978-3-030-03801-4_26
14. Xu, S., et al.: Jointly attentive spatial-temporal pooling networks for video-based person re-identification. arXiv preprint arXiv:1708.02286 (2017)
15. Chung, D., Tahboub, K., Delp, E.J.: A two stream siamese convolutional neural network for person re-identification. In: The IEEE International Conference on Computer Vision (ICCV) (2017)
16. Liu, K., et al.: A spatio-temporal appearance representation for viceo-based pedestrian re-identification. In: Proceedings of the IEEE International Conference on Computer Vision (2015)
17. Lucas, B.D., Kanade, T.: An iterative image registration technique with an application to stereo vision (1981)
18. Karanam, S., Li, Y., Radke, R.J.: Sparse re-id: block sparsity for person re-identification. In: Proceedings of the IEEE Conference on Computer Vision and Pattern Recognition Workshops (2015)
19. Ouyang, D., Zhang, Y., Shao, J.: Video-based person re-identification via spatio-temporal attentional and two-stream fusion convolutional networks. Pattern Recogn. Lett. **117**, 153–160 (2018)

Medical Applications and Brain Signals

Recognition of Genetic Disorders Based on Deep Features and Geometric Representation

Jadisha Yarif Ramírez Cornejo[✉] and Helio Pedrini[✉]

Institute of Computing, University of Campinas, Campinas, SP 13083-852, Brazil
jadisha@gmail.br, helio@ic.unicamp.br

Abstract. In this work, we analyze facial abnormalities in people diagnosed with different genetic disorders through deep features and anthropometric measurements. Based on the assumption that patients with distinct genetic conditions present significant differences in facial morphology, we conjecture that such facial patterns and geometric distances could help in the detection of certain syndromes. Experiments conducted on an available dataset demonstrate the effectiveness of the proposed recognition methodology.

Keywords: Genetic disorders · Syndrome recognition ·
Deep features · Geometric features · Facial patterns

1 Introduction

There is currently a notable population of near 8% of people with genetic disorders due to mutations in genes, which can affect any part of the body and its functionality. Approximately a third of people with genetic disorders present more serious symptoms that compromise their physical and mental well-being. About 3 to 6% of babies will be born with a genetic disease or a birth disability. In addition, 1 to 3% of people worldwide have an intellectual disability. More than 20% of infant deaths are caused by genetic conditions or congenital defects. Therefore, genetic disorders can be lethal or require major medical care. Genetic conditions affect people of all ages, genders and ethnic groups [6].

Furthermore, 30 to 40% of genetic syndromes present facial and cranial abnormalities, which help physicians diagnose certain disorders, such as Angelman syndrome, Down syndrome, Williams syndrome, among others. Although there are more than 6,000 known genetic disorders, only a few people with a suspected syndrome receive a clinical diagnosis [6]. In this work, we propose and evaluate a strategy for recognizing patterns of facial abnormalities associated with different genetic disorders.

This work was partially supported by CAPES, FAPESP (17/12646-3) and CNPq (305169/2015-7).

© Springer Nature Switzerland AG 2019
R. Vera-Rodriguez et al. (Eds.): CIARP 2018, LNCS 11401, pp. 665–672, 2019.
https://doi.org/10.1007/978-3-030-13469-3_77

Several studies have been conducted in the literature to investigate facial abnormalities in images of patients with genetic disorders. Loos et al. [16] presented a computer-based recognition of dysmorphic faces to describe facial patterns among five types of syndromes. Their method extracted a set of features through Gabor wavelet transformations. Similarly, Boehringer et al. [1] applied a set of Gabor wavelet filters at facial landmarks to identify facial abnormalities of ten types of syndromes. Vollmar et al. [19] presented an analysis to determine the impact on recognition accuracy when increasing the number of syndromes. They also described the improvements in the use of geometric features and their combination with texture features in accuracy rates. Ferry et al. [12] proposed an approach to extracting phenotype information using a combination of shape and texture features to recognize eight syndromes. They performed syndrome recognition through supervised and unsupervised learning methods.

The remainder of the paper is organized as follows. Section 2 describes the methodology proposed in this work, composed of preprocessing, feature extraction, feature reduction and classification stages. Section 3 presents and evaluates the experimental results. Section 4 concludes the paper with final remarks.

2 Methodology

The proposed methodology for genetic syndrome recognition is composed of four main stages: preprocessing, feature extraction, feature reduction, and classification. These steps are illustrated in Fig. 1 and explained as follows.

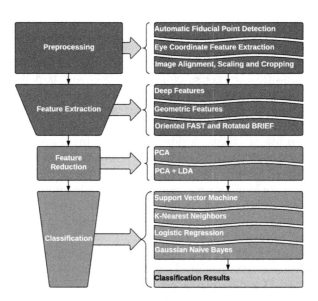

Fig. 1. Main steps of the genetic syndrome recognition methodology.

2.1 Preprocessing

The image preprocessing procedure is crucial for the genetic syndrome recognition task, whose primary purpose is to provide aligned and cropped faces. This preprocessing stage consists of the following five steps: (i) automatic landmark detection by Dlib library [15]; (ii) eye coordinate feature extraction; (iii) face alignment due to eye coordinates; (iv) cropping the face region applying a fitting bounding rectangle; and (v) and scaling the images to 224 × 224 pixels.

2.2 Feature Extraction

Three feature extraction techniques – Deep Features, Geometric Representation and Oriented FAST and Rotated BRIEF (ORB) [18] – were extracted and fused for genetic syndrome recognition.

We employed a Deep Convolutional Neural Network (CNN) architecture based on the very deep network with the triplet loss function [17], which was trained on 2622 identities of 2.6 million images. The CNN model receives images with size of 224 × 224 pixels as input. The model consists of 3 × 3 convolution kernels with stride 1, which are followed by non-linear rectification layers (ReLU), and 3 fully connected layers. This model does not use local contrast normalization. Then, the deep features are extracted from the cropped facial images through this CNN model, forming a feature vector of length 2622.

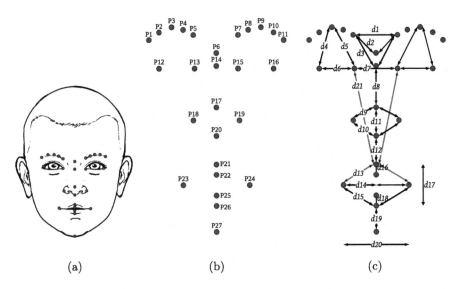

Fig. 2. Feature extraction. (a)–(b) twenty seven facial fiducial points detected; (c) twenty one distances extracted from the twenty seven landmarks.

A geometric representation is created from the detected facial fiducial points. The geometric descriptor employs twenty seven 2D facial landmarks: two points for the outer corner eyebrows (P_1, P_2), two points for the inner corner eyebrows (P_5, P_7), six points for the middle of the eyebrows $(P_2, P_3, P_4, P_8, P_9, P_{10})$, one point for the glabella (P_6), four points for the inner and outer corner of the eyes $(P_{12}, P_{13}, P_{15}, P_{16})$, one point for the root of nose (P_{14}), one point for the supratip (P_{17}), two points for the alars sidewalls (P_{18}, P_{19}), one point for the subnasale (P_{20}), two points for the mouth corners (P_{23}, P_{24}), two points for the top and bottom of the upper lip (P_{21}, P_{22}), two points for the top and bottom of the lower lip (P_{25}, P_{26}), and one point for the gnathion (bottom of chin) (P_{27}). Figure 2 (a)–(b) shows the localization of the twenty-seven facial landmarks.

Thirty one geometric features are extracted from the specified twenty seven fiducial points. From these thirty one geometric features, we calculated twenty one distances, as illustrated in Fig. 2(c), which are normalized to the face width in order to ensure the features to be scale invariant. The eleven distances d_2, d_3, d_4, d_5, d_6, d_9, d_{10}, d_{13}, d_{14}, d_{15} and d_{21} represent the average values of the two mirrored distances on the left and right sides of the face. The distance d_{14} is computed using the intersection point of the line between the points on the top of the upper lip and bottom of the lower lip, and the line between the left and right corners of the mouth. From the upper lip thickness d_{16} and the lower lip thickness d_{18}, we calculated the ratio between them $(R_{lips} = d_{16}/d_{18})$.

We also computed the curvature from the fiducial points of both eyebrows $(P_1, P_2, P_3, P_4, P_5, P_7, P_8, P_9, P_{10}, P_{11})$. For each eyebrow, we obtained three coefficients and their discriminant curve value, forming eight geometric features. Moreover, we calculated the subnasale angle $\alpha_{subnasale}$, generated by three points (P_{18}, P_{20}, P_{19}), where P_{20} is the central point, and P_{18} and P_{19} are the extreme points of the angle. Therefore, we form a geometric feature vector of total length 31.

Individuals with Cornelia de Lange syndrome frequently present a long philtrum, that is, the distance between the subnasale and the upper lip. Distance d_{12} represents this feature. They also have thin lips, which are described by the distance d_{16} and the ratio R_{lips} [8]. They usually exhibit a short upturned nose that is captured by the angle $\alpha_{subnasale}$ and nose distances d_9 to d_{11}. On the other hand, in the case of people with Progeria syndrome, they show a beak-shaped nose, which is also described by the previously mentioned nose features. Another common symptom of Progeria syndrome is a shrunken chin, being represented by the distance d_{19} [14].

People with Down syndrome often feature telecanthus, referring to the increased intercanthal distance, that is, the space between the inner corners of the eyes. The distance d_7 can represent this symptom. Another frequent symptom is a flattened nose, whose characteristic is covered by the subnasale angle and nose distances. Another common sign is a small mouth, which is described using the mouth distances d_{13}, d_{14}, d_{15}, d_{17} and d_{20}. The presence of upslanting palpebral fissures, that is, the distance between the lateral and medial canthus of the eyes, is also a symptom captured by the distance d_6 [5,10].

For Treacher Collins syndrome recognition, it is essential to consider the chin length d_{19}. The most common clinical feature is the presence of a small lower jaw and chin. Another typical characteristic is a small upper jaw, which is represented by the philtrum distance d_{12}. Moreover, as well as Down syndrome symptom, a Treacher Collins symptom is the presence of short and down-slanting palpebral fissures (d_6) [3]. This symptom also characterizes Apert syndrome. Individuals with this syndrome also present a broad and short nose with a bulbous tip, which can be described using the subnasale angle and nose distances [4].

People with Angelman syndrome have a prominent chin, whose feature is captured by the distance d_{19}. They also have a wide mouth, featured by the mouth distances [2]. People with Williams syndrome also present a wide mouth. However, they show a small chin. Another Williams syndrome feature is a short nose with broad nasal tip, which can be represented by the nose distances. As Cornelia de Lange syndrome, William syndrome features a long philtrum (d_{12}) [11]. Moreover, regarding Fragile X syndrome, people with this syndrome have a prominent forehead, a long and thin face, and a large jaw [13], which are covered by several facial distances.

ORB is a feature descriptor based on Features from Accelerated Segment Test (FAST) keypoint detector and Robust Independent Elementary Features (BRIEF) descriptor, which appeared as a fast and efficient alternative to Scale Invariant Feature Transform (SIFT), Speed up Robust Feature (SURF) in computation cost and matching performance. For generating ORB features, we selected fifteen facial keypoints previously detected: two points for the middle of the eyebrows (P_1, P_2), four points for the inner and outer corner of the eyes (P_3, P_4, P_6, P_7), one point for the root of nose (P_5), one point for the supratip (P_8), two points for the alars sidewalls (P_9, P_{10}), one point for the columella (P_{11}), two points for the mouth corners (P_{13}, P_{14}), two points for the top of the upper lip and bottom of the lower lip (P_{12}, P_{15}), and one point for the bottom of chin (P_{16}). Figure 2(a)–(b) show the localization of the sixteen facial points. Then, an ORB feature vector is computed for each keypoint. The resulting ORB descriptor is formed by the concatenation of the generated vector for each keypoint.

For several computational problems, it has been demonstrated that recognition accuracy can enhance by fusing feature descriptors [20]. After extracting the deep, geometric and ORB features, the combined feature vector is set to 3069 features and then scaled.

2.3   Feature Reduction and Classification

We followed two approaches, PCA and PCA+LDA, for performing feature reduction. Firstly, Principal Component Analysis (PCA) was employed over the resulting feature vector set, obtaining the principal feature vectors. Finally, Linear Discriminant Analysis (LDA) was applied over the PCA reduced feature vector, forming a new reduced feature space.

For the classification stage, we used Support Vector Machines (SVM), K-Nearest Neighbors (K-NN), Logistic Regression (LR) and Gaussian Naïve Bayes (GNB) classifiers to compare the accuracy rates for the genetic syndrome recognition. After performing dimensionality reduction, the classifiers are trained with reduced feature vectors. We applied the same validation protocol as the one used in the syndrome dataset from Ferry et al. [12], splitting the training and testing sets with a 4:1 ratio and obtaining a classification average from 10 repeats.

3   Experimental Results

The proposed methodology was tested on the Diagnostically Relevant Facial Gestalt Information from Ordinary Photos Database, collected by Ferry et al. [12]. This dataset is composed of 1499 ordinary and spontaneous photographs of different patients diagnosed into one of eight genetic syndromes: Angelman (205), Apert (200), Cornelia de Lange (250), Down (197), Fragile X (163), Progeria (150), Treacher Collins (103), and Williams-Beuren (231). This dataset comprises facial pose variations, illumination deviations, low-resolution photographs, different backgrounds, and occlusions, such as glasses, hair, scarves, hand gestures, among others. The subjects present in this dataset are of different ethnicities, genders, and ages, including children, adolescents, and adults.

For obtaining images of healthy controls, we employ the Dartmouth Database of Children's Faces [7]. This dataset contains 40 male and 40 female children between 6 and 16 years of age. Models were photographed from different angles and lighting conditions, and also performing eight facial expressions: anger, contempt, disgust, fear, happiness, neutral, sadness, and surprise. From this image collection, we randomly selected 187 images, that is, the average number of images per genetic syndrome class, considering females and males who exhibit distinct pose deviations, facial expressions, and illumination variations. It is worth mentioning that we made this decision due the fact that children present the same facial musculature as adults [9].

Therefore, our dataset is composed of $1686(= 1499 + 187)$ images in total to verify our recognition method. Then, we conducted experiments using our geometric representation, deep features, ORB features and the fusion of both features through the following approaches: PCA+K-NN, PCA+LDA+K-NN, PCA+SVM, PCA+LDA+SVM, PCA+LR, PCA+LDA+LR, PCA+GNB, and PCA+LDA+GNB.

We validated our methodology following the same protocol used in the Diagnostically Relevant Facial Gestalt Information from Ordinary Photos Database [12], that is, we randomly select 80% of samples of each class for the training set and the remaining 20% for the testing set. The results are reported in Table 1, whose values represent the average recognition accuracy rates obtained through the execution of ten repeats.

From our experiments, we can observe that the fusion of deep features with the geometric and ORB representation provides a high accuracy rate for genetic syndrome recognition. We can also notice that the individual use of deep features enables reaching an accuracy of about 85%, which is much superior to just using geometric or ORB representation independently. It is also shown that following a PCA+LDA approach provides increasing recognition rates. Table 2 shows the best detection accuracy rates achieved with the fusion feature set proposed in

Table 1. Average accuracy (%) using our geometric, ORB and deep features, and the fusion between them on the evaluated dataset.

Recognition method	Geometric (%)	ORB (%)	Deep features (%)	Geometric + ORB + Deep features (%)
K-NN	50.62	46.86	71.76	73.20
PCA+K-NN	50.78	48.43	72.81	74.87
PCA+LDA+K-NN	58.33	62.65	85.10	**88.33**
SVM	64.48	65.23	85.42	88.69
PCA+SVM	64.57	66.34	85.62	88.56
PCA+LDA+SVM	65.03	66.24	85.65	**89.08**
LR	65.23	62.97	84.18	88.53
PCA+LR	65.52	65.03	85.95	89.80
PCA+LDA+LR	64.87	67.29	86.31	**90.16**
GNB	51.73	54.44	63.01	62.97
PCA+GNB	57.94	53.66	45.75	46.76
PCA+LDA+GNB	65.82	67.29	86.86	**90.29**

Table 2. Comparison of average accuracy rates (%) for genetic syndrome recognition.

Recognition method	Strategy	Accuracy (%)
Our method	Deep, geometric and ORB representation + PCA+LDA+GNB	90.29
Ferry et al. [12]	Appearance and shape descriptors + SVM	93.10

our approach and the methodology developed by Ferry et al. [12]. The accuracy rates were obtained using the validation protocol by Ferry et al. [12]. We can see that the proposed approach reaches competitive results.

4   Conclusions

Experimental results demonstrated that the use of geometric and ORB representation allowed to enhance the discriminative power of the deep features. Our approach also proved to be robust for recognizing genetic syndromes in ordinary photographs in the presence of different occlusions, for instance, facial expressions, glasses, facial pose deviations, among others. Although the geometric and ORB representation did not provide a higher recognition rate individually, their fusion achieved a higher accuracy rate with deep features. Furthermore, PCA and LDA approaches, as well as the reduction and selection of discriminative features, allowed to increase the recognition rates significantly.

References

1. Boehringer, S., et al.: Syndrom identification based on 2D analysis software. Eur. J. Hum. Genet. **14**(10), 1082 (2006)
2. Clayton-Smith, J., Laan, L.: Angelman syndrome: a review of the clinical and genetic aspects. J. Med. Genet. **40**(2), 87–95 (2003)
3. Cobb, A.R., et al.: The surgical management of treacher collins syndrome. Br. J. Oral Maxillofac. Surg. **52**(7), 581–589 (2014)
4. Cohen, M.M., Kreiborg, S.: A clinical study of the craniofacial features in apert syndrome. Int. J. Oral Maxillofac. Surg. **25**(1), 45–53 (1996)
5. Cornejo, J.Y.R., Pedrini, H., Machado-Lima, A., Nunes, F.L.S.: Down syndrome detection based on facial features using a geometric descriptor. J. Med. Imaging **4**(4), 044008 (2017)
6. Correa, A., et al.: Reporting birth defects surveillance data 1968-2003. Birth Defects Res. Part A Clin. Mol. Teratol. **79**(2), 65 (2007)
7. Dalrymple, K.A., Gomez, J., Duchaine, B.: The dartmouth database of childrens̓ faces: acquisition and validation of a new face stimulus set. PloS One **8**(11), e79131 (2013)
8. Deardorff, M.A., Noon, S.E., Krantz, I.D.: Cornelia de Lange Syndrome (2016)
9. Ekman, P., Oster, H.: Facial expressions of emotion. Annu. Rev. Psychol. **30**(1), 527–554 (1979)
10. Epstein, C.J., et al.: Protocols to establish genotype-phenotype correlations in down syndrome. Am. J. Hum. Genet. **49**(1), 207–235 (1991)
11. Ewart, A.K., et al.: Hemizygosity at the elastin locus in a developmental disorder Williams syndrome. Nat. Genet. **5**(1), 11 (1993)
12. Ferry, Q., et al.: Diagnostically relevant facial gestalt information from ordinary photos. Elife **3**, 1–22 (2014)
13. Garber, K.B., Visootsak, J., Warren, S.T.: Fragile X syndrome. Eur. J. Hum. Genet. **16**(6), 666 (2008)
14. Hennekam, R.: Hutchinson–Gilford progeria syndrome: review of the phenotype. Am. J. Med. Genet. Part A **140**(23), 2603–2624 (2006)
15. King, D.E.: Dlib-ML: a machine learning toolkit. J. Mach. Learn. Res. **10**(July), 1755–1758 (2009)
16. Loos, H.S., Wieczorek, D., Würtz, R.P., von der Malsburg, C., Horsthemke, B.: Computer-based recognition of dysmorphic faces. Eur. J. Hum. Genet. **11**(8), 555 (2003)
17. Parkhi, O.M., Vedaldi, A., Zisserman, A.: Deep face recognition. In: British Machine Vision Conference (2015)
18. Rublee, E., Rabaud, V., Konolige, K., Bradski, G.: ORB: an efficient alternative to SIFT or SURF. In: International Conference on Computer Vision, pp. 2564–2571, November 2011
19. Vollmar, T., et al.: Impact of geometry and viewing angle on classification accuracy of 2D based analysis of dysmorphic faces. Eur. J. Med. Genet. **51**(1), 44–53 (2008)
20. Zhang, Z., Lyons, M., Schuster, M., Akamatsu, S.: Comparison between geometry-based and gabor-wavelets-based facial expression recognition using multi-layer perceptron. In: Third IEEE International Conference on Automatic Face and Gesture Recognition, pp. 454–459. IEEE (1998)

Circular Non-uniform Sampling Patch Inputs for CNN Applied to Multiple Sclerosis Lesion Segmentation

Gustavo Ulloa[1]([✉]), Rodrigo Naranjo[1], Héctor Allende-Cid[2], Steren Chabert[3], and Héctor Allende[1]

[1] Universidad Técnica Federico Santa María, Av. España 1680, Valparaíso, Chile
gustavo.ulloa@gmail.com
[2] Pontificia Universidad Católica de Valparaíso, Av. Brasil 2950, Valparaíso, Chile
[3] CINGS, Universidad de Valparaíso, Blanco 951, Valparaíso, Chile

Abstract. Convolutional Neural Networks (CNN) have been obtaining successful results in the task of image segmentation in recent years. These methods use as input the sampling obtained using square uniform patches centered on each voxel of the image, which could not be the optimal approach since there is a very limited use of global context. In this work we present a new construction method for the patches by means of a circular non-uniform sampling of the neighborhood of the voxels. This allows a greater global context with a radial extension with respect to the central voxel. This approach was applied on the 2015 Longitudinal MS Lesion Segmentation Challenge dataset, obtaining better results than approaches using square uniform and non-uniform patches with the same computational cost of the CNN models.

Keywords: Convolutional Neural Networks · Image segmentation ·
Multiple sclerosis lesions · Magnetic resonance imaging ·
Non-uniform patch

1 Introduction

Magnetic resonance imaging (MRI) of the brain has become an important tool in the medical practice due to its favourable features like the use of non-ionizant radiation, high spatial resolution, high contrast of soft tissues and the possibility to get different channels of acquisition of the same tissue. The segmentation of different tissues and structures of the brain is very useful for clinical analysis due to the fact that it allows a quantitative measurement of features present in certain diseases [6]. There is a special interest in the clinical practice of Multiple Sclerosis (MS) lesions segmentation because it allows to assist the disease diagnosis and to monitor the number and volume of the lesions [4]. The automatization of this task decreases the segmentation time considerably and could solve in part the intra and inter expert variability present in the segmentation provided by different medical practitioners.

© Springer Nature Switzerland AG 2019
R. Vera-Rodriguez et al. (Eds.): CIARP 2018, LNCS 11401, pp. 673–680, 2019.
https://doi.org/10.1007/978-3-030-13469-3_78

A variety of methods have been applied to MS lesion segmentation on 3D MR images. In the last years, CNN have obtained state-of-the-art results in most of visual recognition tasks; in particular in image classification and object detection, where the input corresponds to the full image. The usual way to extend the image classification process using CNNs for a segmentation problem is using as input a patch surrounding the interest voxel to classify in one of the defined classes. The patches correspond to an intensity sampling of the neighbourhood around each voxel of the image by means of square uniform patches, where the central coordinate samples the intensity of the voxel of interest. A 33 × 33 square uniform patch is illustrated in Fig. 1(a). The size of the patch is an important parameter in the image segmentation task. On one hand, a very small patch only captures local spatial dependencies between the central voxel and the surrounding voxels, and on the other hand, the larger the patch size, the larger the context that is caught by the patch and the global spatial dependency that is taken into account at the moment of classifying the central voxel. It is important to note that increasing the patch size entails a greater computational cost, which not always ensures a considerable increment on the segmentation quality. The use of a square uniform patch implies the implicit assumption that there is not redundant information specially in the furthest voxels from the central voxel.

In the last years several methods based on CNNs for the task to MS lesion segmentation on MR images with square uniform patches [1,2,9] have been proposed. In [10] a cubic uniform patch was proposed as inputs. In [5] a non-uniform patch with a greater global context as input to a CNN was proposed, which resulted in an approach that outperforms the results obtained using square uniform patch as input in the same CNN architecture. The methodology for obtaining these patches is by multiplying the vectors corresponding to the coordinates of the patch by a exponential function which has its minimum point equal to 1 positioned in the center of the patch. Although this non-uniform way of expanding the patches obtain better results, the sampling of the peripheral coordinates is done with a marked asymmetry in the coordinates close to the corners, which entails that in those very distant sampling points from the central voxel, there is less significant contribution to the contextual information, since there is less spatial dependence between the voxel of interest and the more distant points. The aforementioned effect can be seen in Fig. 1(b). In this work, a new type of CNN input patches is presented, which performs a circular non-uniform sampling, that is, radially to the central voxel coordinate. This patch has two parameters to adjust, the radius of extension of the sampling and the sampling density coefficient of the local neighborhood to the coordinate of the central voxel.

The paper is organized as follows: In the Sect. 2 we present the proposed circular non-uniform patch, then in Sect. 3 the methodology details are discussed. In Sect. 4 we show comparative results on the 2015 Longitudinal MS Lesion Segmentation Challenge dataset. Finally, we present some concluding remarks and discuss future work.

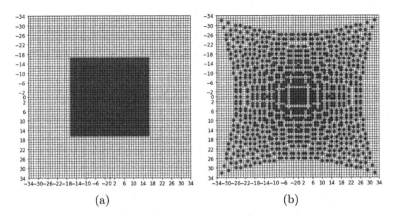

(a)   (b)

Fig. 1. (a) Square uniform patch and (b) Non-uniform patch proposed in [5].

2 Circular Non-uniform Patch

In [5] the authors propose to sample a non-uniform patch around an interest voxel, by performing a multiplication of its coordinates by an exponential function of its euclidean distance (isotropic transformation). We can see this as a transformation $T_{NU}(\cdot)$ in Eq. (1), where the subindex NU corresponds to Non-Uniform,

$$T_{NU}(P) = \begin{bmatrix} P_r \\ P_c \end{bmatrix} \cdot e^{\gamma \cdot \|P\|_2}, \tag{1}$$

where P correspond to a point in the square uniform patch Fig. 1(a), with P_r and P_c coordinates, $\|\cdot\|_2$ is the 2-norm or euclidean distance and the only setting parameter correspond to the expansion parameter γ. This approach applies an isotropic transformation to the sampling points with respect to the central coordinate, which leads to the fact that the sampling coordinates obtained in the furthest places or corners are greatly expanded. This implies that the sampling points of the periphery capture information with different resolution according to the angle with respect to the central voxel of the patch, which is the point of interest to classify.

In this work we propose a circular non-uniform sampling patch, which applies an anisotropic transformation to the points of the square uniform patch, generating a patch capable of extracting context in an isotropic way around the central voxel of interest. The transformation $T_{CNU}(\cdot)$ of the coordinates is expressed in Eq. (2), where the subindex CNU corresponds to Circular Non-Uniform,

$$T_{CNU}(P) = \begin{bmatrix} P_r \\ P_c \end{bmatrix} \cdot \left[1 + \left[\frac{r}{D(\theta_P)} - 1 \right] \cdot \left(\frac{\|P\|_2}{D(\theta_P)} \right)^{\alpha} \right], \tag{2}$$

where θ_P is the angle of the point P. $D(\cdot)$ is a function that returns the distance of the point belonging to the contour of the square uniform patch with the same angle, r is the parameter corresponding to the radius of the circular patch and α is the parameter that determines the sampling density of the points near the center. In this way, when the point to expand corresponds to a point in the contour of the square uniform patch we will have $\left(\frac{\|P\|_2}{D(\theta_P)}\right)^{\alpha} = 1$ and $\left\|\begin{bmatrix} P_r \\ P_c \end{bmatrix} \cdot \frac{r}{D(\theta_P)}\right\|_2 = r$. It can be noticed that the rest of the interior points of the square uniform patch will be multiplied by values belonging to the interval $\left[1, \frac{r}{D(\theta_P)}\right)$ increasing according to a power function of the parameter α. In Fig. 2 two patches with different values of its two parameters, radius and density coefficient are depicted.

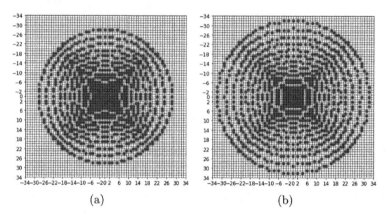

(a)   (b)

Fig. 2. Circular non-uniform patches with parameters: (a) $r = 28$, $\alpha = 2.2$ and (b) $r = 32$, $\alpha = 1.6$.

3   Methods

The proposed and the state-of-the-art approach were evaluated on the data set of the 2015 Longitudinal MS Lesion Segmentation Challenge [2]. The data set consist of longitudinal multi-channel MR images from 19 different patients, where the training set is conformed by the MR images from five patients (segmented data set) and the test set from fourteen patients. Since in the testing set we do not have the segmentation done by experts we used only the training data set. 4.4 average time points were acquired by patient (4, 5 or 6 time points by patient) in the training and testing data sets on a 3.0 Tesla MRI scanner, where four channels were available for each patient, corresponding to T1-weighted, T2-weighted, PD-weighted and FLAIR. Each MR image has a $1[mm]$ cubic voxel resolution. The training data includes a binary mask with manual lesion segmentation performed by an expert.

3.1   Preprocessing

The preprocessing procedure is the previous step applied to each multi-channel MR images of the patients before to the extraction of the patch data set used as input to the CNN in the training. We can identify two preprocessing stages applied to each multi-channel MR images of the patients. The first stage corresponds to the preprocessing made by the organization on the available data set of the 2015 Longitudinal MS Lesion Segmentation Challenge [2]. This process had the following steps: (1a) Inhomogeneity bias correction, (1b) skull-stripping, (1c) dura mater stripping, (1d) a second inhomogeneity correction and (1e) rigid registration to a $1[mm]$ isotropic MNI template. The second stage corresponds to the following steps similar to the preprocessing made in [1]: (2a) Intensity normalization by histogram matching each MR image to a single reference case, which corresponded to the first FLAIR MR channel of the patient 1, (2b) the intensity was truncated to the percentiles in the range $[0.01, 0.99]$, (2c) the intensity values were scaled to $[0, 1]$, (2d) register the FLAIR image to the ICBM452 probabilistic atlas [8], (2e) the last step correspond to candidate extraction of a subset of image voxels which is performed by intersecting the sets obtained by exceeding two thresholds: (1) the intensity of FLAIR image because of the MS lesions appear as hyper-intense regions in FLAIR images [4], and (2) the probability that it belongs to the white matter due to the MS lesions are mostly located in the white matter [7].

3.2 CNN Architecture

Each convolutional block includes a convolutional layer with a specific number and size of filters and a max pooling layer of 2×2. All convolutional and fully connected layers use a Leaky ReLU activation function with a negative slope coefficient $\beta = 0.3$.

The architecture used is called Single-View Multi-Channel (SVMC), which is presented in Fig. 3. This architecture has an input layer that receives four patches of 33×33 coming from the axial view, where the patches correspond to T1-weighted, T2-weighted, PD-weighted and FLAIR channels. This patch size was chosen, due to the fact that it was the size that obtained the best results in [1]. After the third convolutional block there is a fully connected layer of sixteen nodes and as output layer a fully connected layer of two nodes with softmax activation function, which yield two output probabilities for non-lesion and lesion classes by the center voxel of the patches. This architecture is based on the structure of the V-Net CNN presented in [1].

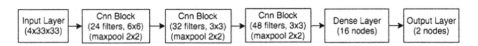

Fig. 3. Architecture of the SVMC.

3.3 Evaluation Metrics

To compare our approach with the state-of-the-art, we use three metrics: the True Positive Rate (TPR), Positive Predictive Value (PPV) and Dice Similarity Coefficient (Dice). TPR indicates the rate of voxels correctly segmented as lesions (Eq. (3)), PPV indicates the rate of segmented voxels from ones estimated as lesions (Eq. 4) and the Dice similarity coefficient (or F1-score, Eq. (5)) which is commonly used metric for imbalanced binary classification problems. This is an overlap measure between two binary label masks which value are in the range $[0, 1]$, where 0 indicates no agreement and 1 means that the two masks are identical. The $\mathcal{M_R}$ mask correspond to the lesion segmentation performed by the human rater and $\mathcal{M_A}$ is the generated mask by the algorithm, TP, FN and FP correspond to the amount of true positive values, false negative values and false positive values.

$$\mathrm{TPR}(\mathcal{M_R}, \mathcal{M_A}) = \frac{|\mathcal{M_R} \cap \mathcal{M_A}|}{|\mathcal{M_R} \cap \mathcal{M_A^C}|} = \frac{TP}{TP+FN}, \tag{3}$$

$$\mathrm{PPV}(\mathcal{M_R}, \mathcal{M_A}) = \frac{|\mathcal{M_R} \cap \mathcal{M_A}|}{|\mathcal{M_R^C} \cap \mathcal{M_A}|} = \frac{TP}{TP+FP}, \tag{4}$$

$$\mathrm{Dice}(\mathcal{M_R}, \mathcal{M_A}) = \frac{1}{\frac{1}{\mathrm{TPR}(\mathcal{M_R},\mathcal{M_A})} + \frac{1}{\mathrm{PPV}(\mathcal{M_R},\mathcal{M_A})}} = \frac{2TP}{2TP+FN+FP}. \tag{5}$$

3.4 Training Details

The weights were updated with the stochastic gradient descent and the loss function used was the categorical cross entropy function. As regularization method we used dropout with probability of 0.25 after each layer. The data set for the training was labeled into two classes, non-lesion tissue and lesion tissue. Since the voxels belonging to the non-lesion tissue are larger in quantity, it is a imbalanced classification problem. To handle this, we generated augmented data from the lesion class which balanced the data set and obtained even better results than the approach of down-sampling the majority class. The augmentation process consisted mainly in creating rotated images from angles drawn from a $N(0, 5)$. To compare the segmentation performance of our approach and the state-of-the-art approaches, we implemented a cross patient validation where five identical models were trained, corresponding to the 5 available patients in the dataset. So, each model was trained with patches from 4 patients and was tested on the remaining 5th patient. In the training process, 80% of the patches were used to estimate the parameters and the remaining 20% were used for validation purposes (to avoid overfitting). The number of patches used for training and validation for the 5 models are: 422654, 289610, 517798, 561768 and 539002.

The implementation and trainning of the CNN was carried out using Keras Deep Neural Network Library [3] with TensorFlow as backend numerical engine. The model was trained using a NVIDIA GeForce GTX 1080TI Graphic Card.

4   Results

The cross-validation results are shown in Table 1, which corresponds to the average and standard deviation of the three metrics considered after ten cross-validations experiments on the labeled dataset, where each cross-validation experiment took around five hours. The three methods implemented and evaluated correspond to the square uniform patch (UP), the current state-of-the-art corresponding to the non-uniform patch (NUP) [5], and the proposed circular non-uniform patch (CNUP). It can be observed that the NUP with $\gamma = 0.04$ obtained the best results in the TPR metric, instead the proposed CNUP obtained the best results in PPV metric by $r = 30$ and $\alpha = 2.4$ and also by the combined Dice metric with $r = 30$ and $\alpha = 2.6$, outperforms the current state-of-the-art method corresponding to the NUP method with parameter $\gamma = 0.02$, which is the same obtained in [5]. It is important to emphasize that the Dice metric is the most used metric for the comparison of image segmentation methods.

Table 1. Comparison of types of patches with different parameters.

Method	γ	radio	α	TPR (s.d.)	PPV (s.d.)	Dice (s.d.)
UP	-	-	-	0.6880(0.0231)	0.6546(0.0174)	0.6556(0.0070)
NUP	0.01	-	-	0.6838(0.0247)	0.6647(0.0274)	0.6579(0.0095)
NUP	0.02	-	-	0.6888(0.0273)	0.6689(0.0234)	0.6657(0.0130)
NUP	0.03	-	-	0.6895(0.0211)	0.6633(0.0179)	0.6643(0.0092)
NUP	0.04	-	-	0.7808(0.0208)	0.5457(0.0248)	0.6242(0.0133)
CNUP	-	30	2.4	0.6853(0.0189)	0.6713(0.0242)	0.6661(0.0072)
CNUP	-	30	2.6	0.7029(0.0251)	0.6620(0.0244)	0.6710(0.0112)
CNUP	-	30	2.8	0.6885(0.0164)	0.6674(0.0230)	0.6649(0.0103)

5   Conclusions

This work shows that the quality of the context information captured by a patch depends on the manner in which the sampling of the intensity of the voxels is performed around the voxel of interest; where a non-uniform sampling with a higher sampling density near the center and with a global context sampling radially or circularly in the periphery, produces better results than current state-of-the-art proposals while preserving the same computational cost. These results can be attributable to the fact that the circular patch samples in a radial way the neighborhood of the voxel of interest, which is more similar to the spherical/ovoid shape of the lesions and the capacity of this sampling patch allows to set its extension and the density of sampling.

As future work, we will propose the possibility of extending this approach of non-uniform circular patches to non-uniform spherical patches and will analyze the option of using the temporary information present in the data set used in this work. Also we will explore the use of this approach to other medical and Synthetic Aperture Radar (SAR) images.

Acknowledgments. This work was supported by the Fondecyt Grant 1170123 and in part by Fondecyt Grant FB0821. Héctor Allende-Cid is supported by project Fondecyt Initiation into Research 11150248. Steren Chabert is supported by Centro de Investigación y Desarrollo en Ingeniería en Salud (CINGS).

The research of Gustavo Ulloa is also supported by the Incentive program for scientific initiation (PIIC) of the Universidad Técnica Federico Santa María DGIIP.

References

1. Birenbaum, A., Greenspan, H.: Multi-view longitudinal CNN for multiple sclerosis lesion segmentation. Eng. Appl. Artif. Intell. **65**, 111–118 (2017)
2. Carass, A., et al.: Longitudinal multiple sclerosis lesion segmentation: resource and challenge. NeuroImage **148**, 77–102 (2017)
3. Chollet, F., et al.: Keras (2015). https://keras.io
4. García-Lorenzo, D., Francis, S., Narayanan, S., Arnold, D.L., Collins, D.L.: Review of automatic segmentation methods of multiple sclerosis white matter lesions on conventional magnetic resonance imaging. Med. Image Anal. **17**(1), 1–18 (2013)
5. Ghafoorian, M., et al.: Non-uniform patch sampling with deep convolutional neural networks for white matter hyperintensity segmentation. In: 2016 IEEE 13th International Symposium on Biomedical Imaging (ISBI), pp. 1414–1417, April 2016
6. González-Villà, S., Oliver, A., Valverde, S., Wang, L., Zwiggelaar, R., Lladó, X.: A review on brain structures segmentation in magnetic resonance imaging. Artif. Intell. Med. **73**, 45–69 (2016)
7. Inglese, M., Oesingmann, N., Casaccia, P., Fleysher, L.: Progressive multiple sclerosis and gray matter pathology: an MRI perspective. Mt. Sinai J. Med.: J. Transl. Personalized Med. **78**(2), 258–267 (2011)
8. Mazziotta, J., et al.: A probabilistic atlas and reference system for the human brain: International consortium for brain mapping (ICBM). Philos. Trans. Royal Soc. London B: Biol. Sci. **356**(1412), 1293–1322 (2001)
9. Roy, S., Butman, J.A., Reich, D.S., Calabresi, P.A., Pham, D.L.: Multiple sclerosis lesion segmentation from brain MRI via fully convolutional neural networks. CoRR abs/1803.09172 (2018)
10. Valverde, S., et al.: Improving automated multiple sclerosis lesion segmentation with a cascaded 3D convolutional neural network approach. NeuroImage **155**, 159–168 (2017)

End-to-End Ovarian Structures Segmentation

Diego S. Wanderley[1,2(✉)], Catarina B. Carvalho[2], Ana Domingues[2],
Carla Peixoto[3], Duarte Pignatelli[3,4], Jorge Beires[3], Jorge Silva[1,2],
and Aurélio Campilho[1,2]

[1] Faculdade de Engenharia da Universidade do Porto, Porto, Portugal
diego.wanderley@fe.up.pt
[2] INESC TEC, Porto, Portugal
[3] Centro Hospitalar de São João, Porto, Portugal
[4] Faculdade de Medicina da Universidade do Porto, Porto, Portugal

Abstract. The segmentation and characterization of the ovarian structures are important tasks in gynecological and reproductive medicine. Ultrasound imaging is typically used for the medical diagnosis within this field but the understanding of the images can be difficult due to their characteristics. Furthermore, the complexity of ultrasound data may lead to a heavy image processing, which makes the application of classical methods of computer vision difficult. This work presents the first supervised fully convolutional neural network (fCNN) for the automatic segmentation of ovarian structures in B-mode ultrasound images. Due to the small dataset available, only 57 images were used for training. In order to overcome this limitation, several regularization techniques were used and are discussed in this paper. The experiments show the ability of the fCNN to learn features to distinguish ovarian structures, achieving a Dice similarity coefficient (DSC) of 0.855 for the segmentation of the stroma and a DSC of 0.955 for the follicles. When compared with a semi-automatic commercial application for follicle segmentation, the proposed fCNN achieved an average improvement of 19%.

Keywords: Ovarian structures segmentation · Ultrasound imaging ·
Convolutional neural network (CNN)

1 Introduction

Diseases of the female reproductive system can cause pain and discomfort, hormonal dysfunctions, infertility and even death, representing around 16% of all the cancers diagnosed in women worldwide and affecting annually more than 1.85 million women [10]. Due to the difficulty of distinguishing between benign and malignant tumors and to a high interobserver variability, ovarian malignant tumors result in a 68% fatality rate in the European Union [10]. A better characterization of the ovarian structures can have an important role in the early

© Springer Nature Switzerland AG 2019
R. Vera-Rodriguez et al. (Eds.): CIARP 2018, LNCS 11401, pp. 681–689, 2019.
https://doi.org/10.1007/978-3-030-13469-3_79

detection of pathologies (e.g ovarian cyst, polycystic ovarian syndrome or even ovarian cancer), while it can also help the monitoring of follicle growth and distribution, important features for assisted reproductive treatments.

The brightness mode (B-mode) ultrasound imaging is commonly used in the gynecological clinical practice because it allows a visualization of the ovary and its structures. In B-mode images, follicles are represented as hypo-echogenic elliptical structures, while the stroma of the ovary exhibits a slight variation in texture relative to its surrounding tissue and has partially hyper-echogenic boundaries. Figure 1 shows an example of a gynecological B-mode image containing an ovary with three follicles, and their manual segmentation.

Image segmentation methods are often used to automatically extract objects from images, reducing the time of analysis and also diagnostic errors. However, ultrasound image segmentation is not easy due to the presence of several image artifacts and noise [6]. According to the latest review in follicles detection [7], the methods used to segment ovarian structures can only detect and measure large follicles. To the best of our knowledge, the segmentation of the stroma has not received enough attention, being only used to reduce the search space for follicle detection [1].

Neural network techniques have been achieving impressive results in visual recognition systems. Among them, fully convolutional neural networks (fCNN) are specially good at learning image features from training data and have proved to be a powerful tool for segmentation of biomedical images [8]. The herein presented research aims to explore the use of fCNNs for the segmentation of the ovarian structures, namely stroma and follicles, in a single process.

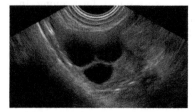   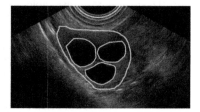

(a) B-mode ultrasound image   (b) Ovary and three follicles

Fig. 1. B-mode image of an ovary and three follicles, and their segmentation.

2 Methodology

This section presents the methods implemented in this work to segment the ovarian structures in B-mode images. In the following subsections, the proposed system, its fCNN architecture and loss functions used are detailed.

2.1 Architecture

An overview of the proposed system is shown in Fig. 2. Switches S_1 and S_2 can be triggered to change the input data of the network and the tasks to be trained, respectively. These changes can work as regularization of the fCNN.

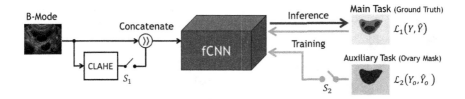

Fig. 2. Overview of the proposed system with multiple tasks.

When switch S_1 is turned on, the B-mode image is preprocessed by a contrast limited adaptive histogram equalization (CLAHE) [11] in order to enhance local contrast and improve the visualization of the ovarian structures. Both CLAHE and original images can be used as input data, as represented in Fig. 2, left side.

For the training, the switch S_2 can be used to activate the multi-task learning, which consists of using the same network to simultaneously solve multiple tasks. In this work, a mask of the ovary is used as ground truth of an auxiliary task in order to prevent the network to classify elements outside the ovary as follicles or from classifying pixels inside of the ovary as background. The auxiliary task acts as regularization during the training of the network [9], and can help the network to focus the attention on difficult cases [3].

The fCNN architecture used in this work (Fig. 3) is based on the U-net [8]. This architecture consists of a downsampling stream (left side) followed by a symmetric upsampling stream (right side). Data from downsampling stream are skip connected to the corresponding layer in the upsampling stream. The convolutional layers are followed by a batch normalization layer and ReLu activation layer; also a dropout layer is inserted between them, when pooling or concatenating operations are performed. The last layer is a 1×1 convolution followed by a softmax, which produces a pixel-wise discrete probability distribution of the three classes of interest (follicle, stroma of the ovary or background).

2.2 Loss Function

The proposed loss function can be decomposed into the main and the auxiliary tasks. Also, weight maps can be applied as regularization, in order to penalize wrong classifications. The details of each step are explained below.

The average Dice Similarity Coefficient (DSC) of each class, as proposed in [5], is the main component of the loss function. The average DSC can be defined as $\overline{\text{DSC}}(Y, \hat{Y}) = 0.5[\text{DSC}(Y_f, \hat{Y}_f) + \text{DSC}(Y_s, \hat{Y}_s)]$, where Y represents the predictions and $\hat{Y}$ represents the ground truth (GT); the indexes f and s represent the follicles and the stroma, respectively. The background was not considered in the loss function because it is the largest region in the image and, so, the results can be heavily influenced by it.

In addition, two weight maps were computed to be applied with the DSC. The first one (W_f) intends to penalize wrong classifications between nearby follicles, as in $w(x)$, defined by U-net [8]. The value of $W_f(i)$ is calculated using

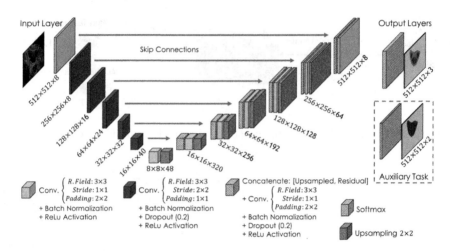

Fig. 3. Architecture of the implemented fCNN.

the distance between the ith pixel and the borders of the two nearest follicles. The second one (W_o) is applied to penalize false detections of ovarian structures in the background region, and is defined for each pixel as:

$$W_o(i) = \begin{cases} 0 & \text{if } i \text{ is inside the ovary} \\ 1 & \text{if } \Delta_o(i) > \ln(10)\sigma^2 \\ 0.1 \cdot \exp(\frac{\Delta_o(i)}{\sigma^2}) & \text{otherwise,} \end{cases} \quad (1)$$

where $\Delta_o(i)$ is the distance from pixel i to the nearest pixel of the ovary, and σ is a constant that controls the distribution of the weights around the ovary.

Then, the loss function of the main task is computed as:

$$\mathcal{L}_1(Y,\hat{Y}) = 1 - \lambda_1 \overline{\text{DSC}}(Y,\hat{Y}) + \lambda_2 \frac{\sum_i Y_f(i)W_f(i)}{\sum_i Y_f(i)} + \lambda_3 \frac{\sum_i Y_s(i)W_o(i)}{\sum_i Y_s(i)}, \quad (2)$$

where $\lambda_{1,2,3} \in \mathbb{R}^+$ are constants used to adjust the influence of each weight map.

The loss function of the auxiliary task is given by:

$$\mathcal{L}_2(Y_o,\hat{Y}_o) = 1 - \text{DSC}(Y_o,\hat{Y}_o), \quad (3)$$

where $\hat{Y}_o$ is the GT mask of the ovary and Y_o is the predicted ovary.

Finally, the total loss function is defined as:

$$\mathcal{L}(Y,\hat{Y}) = \alpha_1 \mathcal{L}_1(Y,\hat{Y}) + \alpha_2 \mathcal{L}_2(Y_o,\hat{Y}_o) \qquad \forall \alpha_{1,2} \in \mathbb{R}^+ | \alpha_1 + \alpha_2 = 1, \quad (4)$$

where $\alpha_{1,2}$ are constants used to adjust the influence of each component.

2.3   Implementation Steps

The proposed system was evaluated using six variations. The input data of the fCNN (Fig. 2) is changed by the switch S_1; and the switch S_2 controls the multi-task learning. When S_2 is "off", the Eq. (4) is written with $\alpha_1 = 1$ and $\alpha_2 = 0$, otherwise $\alpha_1 = 0.75$ and $\alpha_2 = 0.25$. Finally, the values of λ_2 and λ_3, in Eq. (2), determine if the weight maps are added or not to the loss function. For all these experiments $\lambda_2 = \lambda_3 \in [0, 1]$, and $\lambda_1 = 1$. The values of α, λ and σ were defined empirically and were not changed during each train.

All original B-mode images were converted to gray-scale and cropped to 512×512 pixel. Aside from the batch normalization layers, no regularization or normalization to zero mean and unit variance were applied to the input images. To increase the training set, a data augmentation process using random linear transformations such as rotation, translation, flip and zoom was applied in each iteration of the training. Each iteration was performed with a batch of 4 images.

The network was trained using Adam (Adaptive Moment Estimation) optimizer [4] with an initial learning rate of 10^{-2}. In this state-of-the-art stochastic optimization method, there is a learning rate for each weight of the network, and the learning rates are adapted during the training. To reduce the probability of overtraining, an early stopping callback is set to stop the training if the improvement of the validation loss is less than 10^{-3}, during 50 epochs. This work was implemented in Python 2.7 using Keras 1.2.2 framework with TensorFlow 1.0.0 as backend.

3   Results

This section presents the dataset, the evaluation methodologies and the obtained results.

3.1   Dataset

The dataset consists of 87 B-mode images. Each image contains one ovary of a woman in childbearing age with at least one follicle. The images were acquired with an Ultrasonix SonixTouch Q+. During acquisition, the medical doctor performed semi-automatic segmentations using the Ultrasonix Auto Follicle segmentation (AF) tool [2]. It must be noted that not all of the follicles were segmented by the doctor, leading to, for instance one ovary with 4 follicles and only one semi-automatic segmentation. Posteriorly, a medical expert manually segmented each ovary and each follicle to produce the GT. The images were randomly divided as: 57 for training, 15 for validation and 15 for testing.

3.2   Evaluation

The quantitative evaluation of the results was divided into two different validation methodologies. First, the DSC between the GT and the predicted segmentations, obtained by the different trained networks, are presented. Secondly, a single follicle evaluation (SFE) was performed and then compared with the AF segmentation, mentioned in Sect. 3.1.

The motivation for SFE lays on the fact that a GT mask may have more segmented follicles than the ones annotated by the doctor using the AF tool during the acquisition. For example, while the GT of the test set has 44 follicles manually segmented, only 25 follicles were annotated with the AF tool. The SFE verifies if a follicle segmented by the AF has a corresponding follicle in the GT and in the fCNN segmentations. Then, for each follicle present in the AF data, the DSC of GT vs AF and GT vs fCNN are computed.

In Fig. 4 two scenarios of SFE are illustrated. Figure 4(a) represents a SFE with a larger overlay while Fig. 4(b) represents an incorrect segmentation. In this case, the fCNN and the AF segmented a large single follicle which merged the existing two follicles into one, leading to an inaccurate detection.

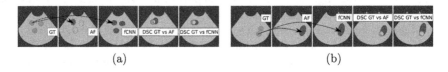

(a)   (b)

Fig. 4. Illustration of SFE for GT (green) vs AF/fCNN (red); yellow represents the agreement with GT. The correspondences between the GT and the predictions are represented by the arrows. (a) Successful case where a single follicle in GT corresponds to a single follicle segmented by AF and fCNN; (b) an incorrect segmentation since two follicles were merged. (Color figure online)

3.3   Results

The overall DSC results for the six trained networks are shown in Table 1. The fCNNs #1 and #4 show the best overall DSC for the follicles and the stroma. In Fig. 5, four examples of the segmentation performed by the developed fCNNs are shown. The highest DSC achieved for follicles was 0.955, with the fCNN #1 – Fig. 5(a), and for the stroma was 0.855, with the fCNN #3 – Fig. 5(b). Also, a standard case and the image with the worst segmentations are presented in Fig. 5(c) and (d), respectively.

Table 1. Overview of DSC for the predicted segmentations of the fCNN trained.

Architecture				Follicle DSC			Stroma of ovary DSC		
#	S_1	S_2	W. Maps	Median	Mean	Std.	Median	Mean	Std.
1	Off	Off	$\lambda_{2,3} = 0$	0.839	0.757	0.207	**0.695**	0.657	0.138
2	Off	On	$\lambda_{2,3} = 0$	**0.844**	0.691	0.331	0.651	0.525	0.251
3	Off	On	$\lambda_{2,3} = 1$	0.779	0.739	0.221	0.678	0.624	0.195
4	On	Off	$\lambda_{2,3} = 0$	0.826	**0.784**	0.197	0.687	**0.677**	0.085
5	On	On	$\lambda_{2,3} = 0$	0.809	0.765	0.172	0.612	0.632	0.088
6	On	On	$\lambda_{2,3} = 1$	0.783	0.763	0.111	0.623	0.619	0.107

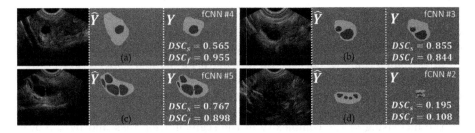

Fig. 5. Examples of segmentation results: (a) the best follicle DSC, (b) the best stroma DSC, (c) a standard case, (d) the worst image.

In a qualitative analysis, the application of multi-task learning prevented follicles for being classified outside the ovary. This approach obtained a fast convergence in training and the smallest validation errors. However, for three test images with low contrast – e.g. Fig. 5(d), the ovarian structures were poorly or not detected, which impaired the overall results. The application of CLAHE improved the results and the use of the weight map W_o solved the problem of false positive ovaries. However, weight map W_f did not significantly reduce misclassification of the pixels between too close follicles; in addition, it produced the wrong classification of the outer boundary of the follicles as background.

The results of the SFE are presented in Table 2. The AF was overcome by all architectures except the fCNN #2. The best overall results for the SFE were obtained with the simplest architecture. Although the CLAHE improved the contrast in boundary regions, the SFE did not improve when CLAHE was used.

Table 2. Overview of DSC for single follice evaluation (SFE).

Method	Median	Mean	Std.	Max.
fCNN #1	**0.823**	**0.735**	0.206	0.961
fCNN #2	0.575	0.556	0.321	**0.972**
fCNN #3	0.817	0.723	0.237	0.952
fCNN #4	0.755	0.659	0.299	**0.972**
fCNN #5	0.775	0.691	0.237	0.971
fCNN #6	0.773	0.729	0.176	0.927
Auto Follicle (AF)	0.712	0.615	0.271	0.948

4 Conclusions

In this paper, the first supervised fCNN for the segmentation of the stroma and follicles of ovaries in B-mode images, in an end-to-end fashion, was presented. Despite being trained with a small dataset, the developed method does not depend on heavy preprocessing or post-processing strategies. The visual results show that a fCNN can learn features that allow to distinguish the ovarian structures in B-mode images. This functionality could allow a better characterization of the overlooked stroma region. Also, the proposed method proved to be more accurate than a commercialized semi-automatic method for follicle segmentation.

Despite presenting slightly better results in the validation set, the proposed regularization techniques show worse overall DSC results for the test set, when comparing with the simplest fCNNs (#1 and #4). This may have been caused by the increasing of the complexity of the segmentation task and by the overwhelming of the data information by the regularization terms. An improvement of the proposed regularizations should be investigated to yield better results.

For future steps of this investigation, the proposed fCNN will be extended to a deeper architecture, increasing the number of learnable features. Due to the scarcity of data, a k-fold cross-validation should be applied to better evaluate the consistency of each architecture. Also, a more efficient loss function will be elaborated in order to force the network to learn the boundaries of the follicles. Finally, the increasing of the dataset is fundamental to improve the variability of the training set.

Acknowledgments. This work is financed by the ERDF – European Regional Development Fund through the Operational Programme for Competitiveness and Internationalisation - COMPETE 2020 Programme within project "POCI-01-0145-FEDER-006961", and by National Funds through the Portuguese funding agency, FCT - Fundação para a Ciência e a Tecnologia as part of project "UID/EEA/50 014/2013".

References

1. Chen, T., Zhang, W., Good, S., Zhou, K.S., Comaniciu, D.: Automatic ovarian follicle quantification from 3D ultrasound data using global/local context with database guided segmentation. In: IEEE 12th ICCV, pp. 795–802 (2009)
2. Eskandari, H., Azar, R.Z., Pendziwol, L.: Ovarian follicle segmentation in ultrasound images. US Patent 9,679,375 (2017)
3. Ferreira, F.T., Sousa, P., Galdran, A., Sousa, M.R., Campilho, A.: End-to-end supervised lung lobe segmentation. In: 2018 IJCNN, pp. 1–8 (2018)
4. Kingma, D.P., Ba, J.: Adam: a method for stochastic optimization. CoRR (2014). http://arxiv.org/abs/1412.6980
5. Milletari, F., Navab, N., Ahmadi, S.A.: V-net: fully convolutional neural networks for volumetric medical image segmentation. In: 4th International Conference on 3DV, pp. 565–571 (2016)
6. Noble, J.A., Boukerroui, D.: Ultrasound image segmentation: a survey. IEEE Trans. Med. Imaging **25**(8), 987–1010 (2006)
7. Potočnik, B., Cigale, B., Zazula, D.: Computerized detection and recognition of follicles in ovarian ultrasound images: a review. Med. Biol. Eng. Comput. **50**(12), 1201–1212 (2012)
8. Ronneberger, O., Fischer, P., Brox, T.: U-Net: convolutional networks for biomedical image segmentation. In: Navab, N., Hornegger, J., Wells, W.M., Frangi, A.F. (eds.) MICCAI 2015. LNCS, vol. 9351, pp. 234–241. Springer, Cham (2015). https://doi.org/10.1007/978-3-319-24574-4_28

9. Ruder, S.: An overview of multi-task learning in deep neural networks. arXiv (2017). http://arxiv.org/1706.05098
10. Stewart, B.W., Wild, C.P.: IARC World Cancer Report 2014. International Agency for Research on Cancer, Lyon (2014)
11. Zuiderveld, K.: Contrast limited adaptive histogram equalization. In: Heckbert, P.S. (ed.) Graphics Gems IV, pp. 474–485. Academic Press Professional Inc, USA (1994)

Exploring Deep-Based Approaches for Semantic Segmentation of Mammographic Images

Hugo Neves de Oliveira[1]([✉]), Claudio Saliba de Avelar[2],
Alexei Manso Corrêa Machado[3,4], Arnaldo de Albuquerque Araujo[1],
and Jefersson Alex dos Santos[1]

[1] Computer Science Department, Universidade Federal de Minas Gerais,
Belo Horizonte, Brazil
{oliveirahugo,arnaldo,jefersson}@dcc.ufmg.br
[2] Clinical Hospital, Universidade Federal de Minas Gerais, Belo Horizonte, Brazil
claudiosaliba.rad@gmail.com
[3] School of Medicine, Universidade Federal de Minas Gerais, Belo Horizonte, Brazil
[4] Computer Science Department, PUC Minas, Belo Horizonte, Brazil
alexei@pucminas.br

Abstract. Pectoral muscle and background elimination are common steps for automated software in mammographic image preprocessing. We investigate FCNs, U-nets and SegNets in the task of mammogram segmentation, addressing three subtasks: pectoral muscle, background and breast region segmentation. The MIAS and INbreast datasets were used for evaluating Deep Neural Networks on the segmentation of these regions. Several objective evaluation metrics were used in order to compare our results with the ones available in the literature. State-of-the-art results were observed in most comparisons, significantly surpassing the baselines in most metrics. Best Jaccard values (in %) for Deep Learning algorithms were 89.7 ± 2.5, 98.4 ± 0.1 and 97.0 ± 0.4 for pectoral muscle, background and breast region segmentation, respectively, in the MIAS dataset. For INbreast, the best Jaccard value achieved for pectoral muscle segmentation was 90.8 ± 2.5.

Keywords: Pectoral muscle segmentation · Breast segmentation · Mammography · Deep Learning

1 Introduction

Pectoral muscle segmentation has been used as a preprocessing step for breast cancer analysis in Computer-Aided Detection/Diagnosis (CAD) systems. Due to density similarities with potentially cancerous breast tissue, the rate of False Positive results in detection tasks tends to increase [2,3,8,14]. The Medio-Lateral Oblique (MLO) view of mammograms is the most affected by the presence of pectoral muscles. Depending on anatomy and patient positioning during image

© Springer Nature Switzerland AG 2019
R. Vera-Rodriguez et al. (Eds.): CIARP 2018, LNCS 11401, pp. 690–698, 2019.
https://doi.org/10.1007/978-3-030-13469-3_80

acquisition, the pectoral muscle could occupy as much as half of the breast region, or as little as a few percent of it. Pectoral muscles can appear concave, convex or have irregular shapes in mammograms, possibly with homogeneous boundaries between it and the breast tissue. Thus, pectoral muscle segmentation is a computationally demanding task, requiring the algorithm to be able to discriminate between different shapes, sizes and breast density variations. Other important preprocessing steps in mammogram analysis are background and breast region segmentation, which present challenges due to artifacts in the background of Screen Film Mammograms (SFMs), the low-contrast of the skin-air boundary region, and to large amounts of noise, mainly present in digitized SFMs [14].

Despite their success in many Computer Vision tasks, Machine Learning methods have been noticeably absent in the mammogram segmentation body of research. As shown by Ganesan *et al.* [4], preprocessing tasks rely mostly on low-level techniques or simple statistical modelling, which may suffer from generalization/stability problems. Due to advances in high-performance parallelism, Deep Learning-based methods have evolved to comprise the state-of-the-art of most Computer Vision tasks and, recently, in Biomedical Image tasks [9].

The most recent survey [4] divides the methods used for pectoral muscle segmentation into five categories: intensity-based methods, line detection, statistical techniques, wavelet methods and active contour [3]. Further explanations of these methods is out of the scope of this paper and, therefore, readers should refer to Ganesan *et al.* [4] for a more detailed analysis of the state-of-the-art of mammogram segmentation. Several factors hamper the comparison among methods in the mammogram segmentation field. The main one is that there is not one standard set of metrics for comparison, so most of the literature uses only subjective evaluation metrics for the segmentation results, such as non-standardized specialist assessments of segmentation quality. This problem is aggravated by the lack of standardized datasets and ground truths, leading to the use of private data, severely hampering the reproducibility of most results. The most recent attempt to standardize the area was presented by Rampun *et al.* [14], which used only objective segmentation metrics and publicly available datasets, as well as ground truths obtainable upon email request. This work used active contour for modeling both the background and pectoral muscle boundary layers. It also comprised the state-of-the-art for the researched tasks, therefore it will be used as the main baseline throughout this paper.

Ganesan *et al.* [4] argues that there is not one specific method which works perfectly well for the problem of pectoral muscle segmentation. Therefore, following recent advances in Semantic Segmentation [1,10,15], the main contribution of this work is to evaluate Deep Learning-based approaches for mammogram segmentation. Secondary contributions include: (i) State-of-the-art results in pectoral muscle, background and breast region segmentation; (ii) Assessment of the superiority in stability of Deep Learning methods compared to classical approaches; (iii) Segmentation predictions and pretrained models are publicly available online for future academic use and reproducibility.

2   Deep Semantic Segmentation Approaches

Most Deep Neural Networks (DNNs) for image analysis has been based on convolution operations. Vanilla implementations of Convolutional Neural Networks (CNNs) [7] are essentially stackings of three types of layers: convolutional layers, pooling layers and fully connected layers. Convolutional and pooling layers are often stacked in the beginning of these networks and serve as learnable feature extractors, while fully connected layers play the role of the classifier at the end of the network, as can be seen in Fig. 1. In the following paragraphs we introduce the DNNs used in our experimental setup.

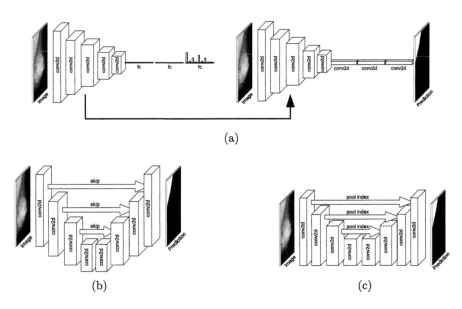

Fig. 1. Architecture examples for (a) FCNs [10]. (b) U-nets [15]. (c) SegNets [1].

Fully Convolutional Networks (FCNs). The most basic architectures [10], they can be understood as a patchwise approach, wherein each pixel in an image is a sample (Fig. 1a). Whole image fully convolutional training is identical to patchwise training where each batch consists of all the pixels in a set of images. Replacing fully connected layers by convolutional layers and adding a spatial loss produces an efficient machine for end-to-end dense learning [10].

U-Nets. Ever since FCNs, several attempts to mitigate the vanishing gradient problem have been proposed, most relying on alternative paths for information flow [6]. Skip connections are the most common way to create alternative paths, serving as highways for backpropagation to reach earlier layers in the network without passing through all the layers in front of them. U-nets [15] take advantage of skip connections to map higher-level contextual information to low-level pixel information. These networks are Encoder-Decoder architectures wherein the downsampling half (Encoder) is symmetrical to the upsampling half (Decoder), as shown in Fig. 1b. There is also a larger amount of feature channels in the upsampling layers compared to FCNs, which allows for more information to be propagated to higher resolution layers [15].

SegNets. SegNets [1], like U-nets, are Encoder-Decoder architectures for segmentation with symmetric layers. The Encoder half of the network is composed of VGG-like [16] convolutional layers. The construction of the Decoder network is accomplished by simply mirroring the Encoder layers and replacing the pooling layers for upsampling components (Fig. 1c). One main advantage of SegNet is the use of the pooling indices in the upsampling processes. SegNet uses the max pooling indices to upsample (without learning) the feature maps and convolves with a trainable decoder filter bank [1].

3   Methodology

Mammographic Datasets. Following the experimental procedure described by Rampun et al. [14], this paper's experiments were performed only on publicly available datasets. The main publicly available datasets are the Mammographic Image Analysis Society (MIAS[1]) dataset [17], the Digital Database for Screening Mammography (DDSM) [5], the Breast Cancer Digital Repository (BCDR) [11] and the INbreast[2] dataset [12]. Despite several attempts, we could not contact the BCDR team for access to their dataset, therefore it was not possible to run tests on these data. Also, to our knowledge, there are no publicly available ground truths to DDSM images, which were also removed from the analysis. The ground truths for the MIAS dataset were provided by Oliver et al. [13].

While DDSM, MIAS and BCDR are all SFM datasets, INbreast [12] is the only one acquired with the Full-Field Digital Mammography (FFDM) technique, rendering it the best dataset regarding image quality. This dataset contains accurate pixelwise annotations for the lesions and pectoral muscle regions. A total of 200 MLO images (from the 208 in the dataset) from INbreast were used in our tests. The 8 remaining MLO mammograms were not used due to problems with decoding the ground truths. All 322 images in MIAS were used in our experiments. Our experimental procedure was performed on the three tasks using MIAS and one task using INbreast (pectoral muscle segmentation). There is no need for breast region nor background segmentation on INbreast images, as the background can be easily segmented with a thresholding operation.

Experimental Procedure. We resized the mammograms and ground truths to 256×256 pixels and slightly changed the U-net architecture (setting the padding to 1) to receive these sizes of images. As the predictions of the DNNs match the 256×256 pixel size, after forwarding the images through the networks,

---

[1] https://www.repository.cam.ac.uk/handle/1810/250394.
[2] http://medicalresearch.inescporto.pt/breastresearch/index.php/
Get_INbreast_Database.

we upsampled the images to their original sizes again. Results were obtained using a 5-fold cross-validation methodology over the datasets. In order to avoid artificially high results due to the similarities in breast structures of a subject, fold division was done per subject, assuring that all images of a patient are placed in the same fold. For each test fold, one of the other 4 training folds was not used in training and served as a second validation step in order to select the epoch with the best results. Details regarding the implementation and hyperparameters of the DNNs can be found in the supplementary material. Preprocessing was comprised only by the rescaling, normalization by mean and standard deviation and by horizontally flipping some mammograms in order for all images to have the same orientation. A simple post-processing of keeping only the largest contiguous white region and filling the gaps on the DNNs' binary predictions was also applied and was observed to consistently improve the results.

Evaluation Metrics. Based on previous works, we used several different segmentation metrics for validating the results. Rampun et al. [14] used Jaccard ($\ddot{J}$), Dice ($\ddot{D}$), Accuracy ($\ddot{A}$), Sensitivity ($\ddot{S}$), Specificity ($\bar{S}$) and Correctness ($\ddot{C}$). Other works [2,3,8] rely mostly on FP and FN metrics. In order to compare with all these works, we provide the values of all previously mentioned metrics for FCNs, U-nets and SegNets in our results (Sect. 4).

4   Results and Discussion

Due to its thorough methodology and state-of-the-art results, the main baseline used for comparison is the work of Rampun et al. [14]. The values for all metrics are presented in percentages (%) for easier comparisons, as some metrics (mainly FP and FN) yielded tiny proportional values, hampering the readability of the results. For assessing the statistical significance of the results compared with the baseline, we performed z-score hypothesis tests, as the number of samples is relatively large (322 images for MIAS and 200 for INbreast). Full numerical values for all metrics can be found in tables in the complementary material. In order to improve reproducibility, the best pretrained models used in our experimental procedure – as well as other complementary materials such as a script for running the pretrained models on other sets of images and additional results – are publicly available on our team's website[3].

Comparison with the Main Baseline. Figure 2 shows Confidence Intervals (CIs) with $p \leq 0.05$ for the $\ddot{J}$ and $\ddot{D}$ metrics in both INbreast and MIAS using both DNNs and Rampun et al.'s [14] method. One can see that in all cases the deep strategies obtained state-of-the-art results with $\ddot{D}$ and $\ddot{J}$ values close to 90% for pectoral muscle segmentation and accuracies for all tasks above 98%. Background segmentation proved to be the easiest task, with $\ddot{J}$ values over 98% and $\ddot{D}$ over 99%, configuring almost perfect background eliminations. One could argue that breast region segmentation is the most important task of all three, as most CADs are interested only on the breast region area, ignoring both the

---

[3] http://www.patreo.dcc.ufmg.br/deep-mammography-segmentation/.

background and pectoral data in the images. The best $\ddot{J}$ and $\ddot{D}$ values for this task were of 97.01% and 98.46%, respectively, again yielding highly precise segmentation predictions.

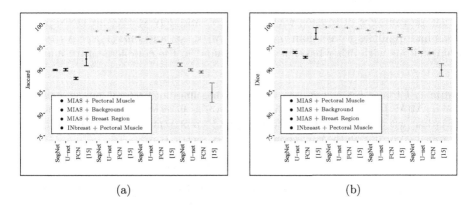

(a)   (b)

Fig. 2. CIs for the MIAS dataset [17] in the pectoral muscle segmentation, breast region segmentation and background segmentation tasks and INbreast [12] in pectoral muscle segmentation. Vertical axis represents (a) $\ddot{J}$ and (b) $\ddot{D}$ metrics for $p \leq 0.05$. The lower end of the plot was trimmed at 75% to improve visualization of the CIs.

SegNet [1] and U-net [15] achieved similar results in most tasks and metrics, suggesting that both DNNs are good choices for these kinds of biomedical image segmentation tasks. The FCN architecture with a VGG16 basis achieved slightly lower results, but still was found to be significantly better than shallow approaches in most metrics and tasks.

Standard deviation values for DNNs were typically around one order of magnitude lower than the baseline, rendering deep segmentation schemes more reliable alternatives for fully automatic segmentation of mammograms. The only case where Rampun et al. [14] surpassed the deep architectures in the $\ddot{J}$ and $\ddot{D}$ metrics was in pectoral muscle segmentation, even though the standard deviations are considerably higher for the baseline. Results for the INbreast dataset [12] showed similar trends to the ones for the MIAS dataset [17]. DNNs outperformed the baseline for almost all metrics, but Specificity, reaching significantly better results than Rampun et al. [14] for all other metrics.

Comparisons with Other Baselines. It is hard to perform thorough comparisons between most papers in the area of mammographic image segmentation mainly due to the different evaluation metrics and the different datasets and subsets of images selected for most papers [14]. Many works use either a combination of FP and FN or custom metrics. One can see in Table 1 that deep methods achieved state-of-the-art-results also in FP and FN results, surpassing all methods in the FN metric with significantly better results. U-nets reached significantly better FP values compared to the best baseline (Ferrari et al. [3]), with the advantage of not compromising the FN metric, while SegNets and FCNs achieved comparable results in FP and vastly better results in FN. Also, while other methods in the state-of-the-art achieved $FP < 5\%$ and $FN < 5\%$ in between 50% and 60% of cases, FCNs, U-nets and SegNets reached this level of accuracy in 97.8%, 98.1% and 98.4% of images, respectively. Besides vastly larger percentages of images with $FP < 5\%$ and $FN < 5\%$, no DNN predictions had qualities worse than $min(FP, FN) < 5\%$ and $max(FP, FN) > 10\%$. Comparisons with other baselines can be found in the complementary material.

Table 1. FP and FN comparison with other baselines for pectoral muscle segmentation on MIAS [17]. FP and FN values are shown as percentages followed by standard deviation, when available. Values followed by % represent the percentage of images stratified according to the corresponding quality metric (row).

Metrics	FCN	U-net	SegNet	[2]	[3]	[8]
FP	0.68 ± 0.25	$\mathbf{0.53 \pm 0.16}$	0.62 ± 0.13	0.64	0.58	1.45
FN	0.39 ± 0.12	0.38 ± 0.12	$\mathbf{0.30 \pm 0.9}$	5.58	5.77	5.52
$FP < 5\%$ & $FN < 5\%$	97.8%	98.1%	98.4%	51.2%	53.6%	57.1%
$min(FP, FN) < 5\%$ & $5\% < max(FP, FN) < 10\%$	1.2%	1.2%	0.6%	22.6%	0%	33.3%
$min(FP, FN) < 5\%$ & $max(FP, FN) > 10\%$	0.9%	0.6%	0.9%	26.2%	0%	8.3%
$5\% < FP < 10\%$ & $5\% < FN < 10\%$	0%	0%	0%	0%	26.2%	0%
$5\% < min(FP, FN) < 0.10\%$ & $max(FP, FN) > 10\%$	0%	0%	0%	0%	0%	1.2%
$FP > 10\%$ & $FN > 10\%$	0%	0%	0%	0%	20.2%	0%

5   Conclusion

As far as the authors are aware, this paper reported the first use of Deep Learning for the segmentation of breast regions. We performed exhaustive tests using three DNN architectures for semantic segmentation and compared the results with state-of-the-art methods in the literature using several metrics and two publicly available datasets. In an effort to improve reproducibility and standardize the area, we only used objective evaluation metrics and provided a website containing several supplementary materials, including segmentation predictions, pretrained models and code for researchers to test the pretrained models in their own datasets. Even though the amount of data used in our experiments was suboptimal for deep methods, our experimental evaluation found that DNNs significantly surpassed the baselines in most cases and presented much better stability, that is, lower standard deviations. Data Augmentation techniques should improve DNN performance even further, as these methods tend to better converge with large sets of data. Most methods previously shown in the literature rely mostly on simple image processing filtering and segmentation and often stack several preprocessing and post-processing modules to the methodology. Despite their expensive training procedure, DNNs have a more plug-and-play nature, achieving state-of-the-art results with minimal pre and post-processing. Also the cost of forwarding images in pretrained DNNs is very computationally inexpensive, even without GPUs.

Future work includes a post-processing for shape regularization. Experimental evaluation also revealed that errors in distinct DNNs occurred in different places, therefore a late fusion scheme should improve the results.

Acknowledgments. Authors would like to thank NVIDIA for their support with GPUs; CAPES, CNPq and FAPEMIG (APQ-00449-17) for their financial support and Drs. Andrik Rampun and Arnau Oliver for the MIAS ground truths.

References

1. Badrinarayanan, V., Kendall, A., Cipolla, R.: SegNet: a deep convolutional encoder-decoder architecture for image segmentation. TPAMI **39**(12), 2481–2495 (2017)
2. Camilus, K.S., Govindan, V., Sathidevi, P.: Pectoral muscle identification in mammograms. J. Appl. Clin. Med. Phys. **12**(3), 215–230 (2011)
3. Ferrari, R., Frere, A., Rangayyan, R., Desautels, J., Borges, R.: Identification of the breast boundary in mammograms using active contour models. Med. Biol. Eng. Comput. **42**(2), 201–208 (2004)
4. Ganesan, K., Acharya, U.R., Chua, K.C., Min, L.C., Abraham, K.T.: Pectoral muscle segmentation: a review. CMPB **110**(1), 48–57 (2013)
5. Heath, M., Bowyer, K., Kopans, D., Moore, R., Kegelmeyer, P.: The digital database for screening mammography. In: Digital Mammography, pp. 431–434 (2000)
6. Huang, G., Liu, Z., Weinberger, K.Q., van der Maaten, L.: Densely connected convolutional networks. In: CVPR, vol. 1, p. 3 (2017)
7. Krizhevsky, A., Sutskever, I., Hinton, G.E.: Imagenet classification with deep convolutional neural networks. In: Pereira, F., Burges, C.J.C., Bottou, L., Weinberger, K.Q. (eds.) NIPS, pp. 1097–1105. Curran Associates, Inc., New York (2012)
8. Li, Y., Chen, H., Yang, Y., Yang, N.: Pectoral muscle segmentation in mammograms based on homogenous texture and intensity deviation. Pattern Recogn. **46**(3), 681–691 (2013)
9. Litjens, G., et al.: A survey on deep learning in medical image analysis. Med. Image Anal. **42**, 60–88 (2017)
10. Long, J., Shelhamer, E., Darrell, T.: Fully convolutional networks for semantic segmentation. In: CVPR, pp. 3431–3440, June 2015
11. Lopez, M.G., et al.: BCDR: a breast cancer digital repository. In: ICEM (2012)
12. Moreira, I.C., Amaral, I., Domingues, I., Cardoso, A., Cardoso, M.J., Cardoso, J.S.: INbreast: toward a full-field digital mammographic database. Acad. Radiol. **19**(2), 236–248 (2012)

13. Oliver, A., Lladó, X., Torrent, A., Martí, J.: One-shot segmentation of breast, pectoral muscle, and background in digitised mammograms. In: ICIP (2014)
14. Rampun, A., Morrow, P.J., Scotney, B.W., Winder, J.: Fully automated breast boundary and pectoral muscle segmentation in mammograms. Artif. Intell. Med. **79**, 28–41 (2017)
15. Ronneberger, O., Fischer, P., Brox, T.: U-Net: convolutional networks for biomedical image segmentation. In: Navab, N., Hornegger, J., Wells, W.M., Frangi, A.F. (eds.) MICCAI 2015. LNCS, vol. 9351, pp. 234–241. Springer, Cham (2015). https://doi.org/10.1007/978-3-319-24574-4_28
16. Simonyan, K., Zisserman, A.: Very deep convolutional networks for large-scale image recognition. arXiv preprint arXiv:1409.1556 (2014)
17. Suckling, J., et al.: The mammographic image analysis society digital mammogram database. In: Exerpta Medica. International Congress Series, vol. 1069, pp. 375–378 (1994)

Short Time EEG Connectivity Features to Support Interpretability of MI Discrimination

V. Gómez[1]([✉]), A. Álvarez[1], P. Herrera[2], G. Castellanos[3], and A. Orozco[1]

[1] Automatic Research Group, Faculty of Engineerings,
Universidad Tecnológica de Pereira, Pereira, Colombia
{vigomez,andres.alvarez1,aaog}@utp.edu.co
[2] Psychiatry, Neuroscience, and Community Group, School of Medicine,
Universidad Tecnológica de Pereira, Pereira, Colombia
p.herrera@utp.edu.co
[3] Signal Proccesing and Recognition Group,
Universidad Nacional de Colombia, Manizales, Colombia
cgcastellanosd@unal.edu.co

Abstract. Brain connectivity analysis during motor imagery (MI) tasks has evolved as an essential and promising tool for its use in brain-computer interfaces (BCI). Many approaches devoted to BCI systems focus on the distinction between different MI tasks from electroencephalogram (EEG) signals. However, given the non-stationarity of the brain activity, the MI discrimination yields to different classification performances between subjects. Here, we introduced an MI discrimination system from EEG signals to reveal relevant brain connectivity patterns associated with a specific MI protocol. Indeed, we employ a windowed-based feature representation using the well-known Common Spatial Pattern (CSP) technique. Then, the classification performance along temporal windows is related to a Phase Locking Value (PLV)-based connectivity measure. Obtained results show a remarkable relationship between high classification performances and the subject coupling with the acquisition protocol concerning the windows that present the MI stimulus.

Keywords: Electroencephalogram · Motor Imagery · Brain connectivity

1 Introduction

Motor imagery (MI) is the cognitive process of thinking about an action without motor execution. The characterization of MI tasks by mapping the brain activity has aroused growing interest over the past few years due to its high potential in brain-computer interfaces (BCI) applications, such as physical therapy, rehabilitation, and assistive technologies [2]. Thus, the main cortical brain

© Springer Nature Switzerland AG 2019
R. Vera-Rodriguez et al. (Eds.): CIARP 2018, LNCS 11401, pp. 699–706, 2019.
https://doi.org/10.1007/978-3-030-13469-3_81

imaging techniques employed to measure brain activity are electroencephalogram (EEG), magnetoencephalogram (MEG), and functional magnetic resonance imaging (fMRI). Nevertheless, EEG is the most widely used technique in BCI due to its advantages: non-invasive, low cost, and high temporal resolution. Besides, EEG allows observing brain electrical activity changes associated with specific stimuli. However, the development of BCI systems from EEG requires to minimize its poor spatial resolution, which leads to the volume conductor problem and the non-stationary behavior of the brain activity [6]. In particular, such non-stationary yields to performance variability regarding the studied subjects.

Most of the state-of-the-art approaches employ feature extraction techniques based on spectral representation to code significant EEG patterns. Particularity, frequency bands ranging from 8–30 Hz are used in MI tasks due to the relationship of the μ and β rhythms in sensorimotor tasks [6,10]. Also, data projections are employed to support MI discrimination, including Principal Component Analysis (PCA), Independent Component Analysis (ICA), Filter Bank Common Spectral Pattern (FBCSP), Common Spatial Pattern (CSP) [1,3]. Moreover, connectivity representations like Phase Locking Value (PLV), Coherence, and Granger Causality (GC) [6], are used to discriminate MI classes from brain connectivity maps [5]. Next, given the feature space, classification algorithms have been used for distinguishing between MI tasks, such as Linear Discrimination Analysis (LDA), Neural Network (NN), Bayesian approaches, and Support Vector Machines (SVMs) [8,11]. Besides, some methods face the non-stationarity in MI by choosing a predefined segment of the EEG signal. Although these approaches obtain acceptable classification results, high variability in performance among subjects persists. Moreover, there is a lack of quantitative relationships between a satisfactory MI classification, the recorded stimuli, and brain patterns with strong activity. That is, there is no clear evidence of the differences between the performance of the subjects to the coupling with the protocol and its stimuli in MI paradigms.

Here, we introduce an MI discrimination system to enhance the identification of relevant brain connectivity patterns and their relationships to the coupling of the subjects with the MI protocol and its stimuli. In particular, our approach comprises two main stages: (i) A CSP-based feature extraction to discriminate from different EEG window segments, and (ii) a PLV-based connectivity analysis to reveal significant dependencies among brain hemispheres concerning the most discriminative window segments. Specifically, our proposal allows finding a relationship between the classification performance of the subject and its coupling with the MI protocol. The obtained results show that subjects exhibiting acceptable classification rates achieve the highest discrimination within the temporal windows associated with the MI stimulus. Besides, in the mentioned segments, these subjects present consistent connectivity patterns in the contralateral hemisphere that seems to be related to the task under study. Otherwise, subjects with low classification performances do not show connectivity patterns according to the specific task; therefore, quantitatively it is demonstrated that their brain connectivity patterns are not in agreement with the MI protocol.

2   Materials and Methods

Let $\{\boldsymbol{X}_l \in \mathbb{R}^{C \times T}\}_{l=1}^{L}$ be an EEG signal set holding L trials with C channels at T time instants. Moreover, each trial can be related to a given MI condition through the label vector $\boldsymbol{y} \in \{-1, +1\}^L$. With the aim to code short-time discriminative patterns, a windowing process is carried out to divide each EEG trial $\boldsymbol{X}_l$ into V segments of size R. So, at the l-th trial we built the following set: $\{\boldsymbol{Z}_{l,v} \in \mathbb{R}^{C \times R}\}_{v=1}^{V}$. In turn, to reveal relevant brain patterns related to the studied MI paradigm, our EEG processing approach comprises two main stages: (i) MI discrimination from EEG-based short-time features, and (ii) EEG connectivity analysis in line with the MI acquisition protocol.

MI discrimination from EEG-Based Short-Time Features. Given the v-th segment at the l-trial, we compute a supervised linear mapping based on the well-known Common Spatial Patterns (CSP) algorithm. Namely, the CSP technique rotates the EEG channels through the matrix $\boldsymbol{W}_v \in \mathbb{R}^{C \times C}$ to avoid linear dependencies among EEG channels while enhancing the separability between MI classes. Thereby, the projection matrix at the v-th temporal window can be computed by solving the following eigenvalue problem: $\boldsymbol{\vartheta}_v^+ \boldsymbol{W}_v = \boldsymbol{\Delta}_v (\boldsymbol{\vartheta}_v^- + \boldsymbol{\vartheta}_v^+) \boldsymbol{W}_v$, where $\boldsymbol{\Delta}_v = \mathrm{diag}(\lambda_1, \lambda_2, \ldots, \lambda_C)$ is a diagonal matrix holding the eigenvalues $(\lambda_1 \geq \lambda_2 \geq \cdots \geq \lambda_C)$, and $\boldsymbol{\vartheta}_v^+, \boldsymbol{\vartheta}_v^- \in \mathbb{R}^{C \times C}$ are the covariance matrices of the input space for EEG trials belonging to the class $+1$ and -1, respectively. Afterward, a feature matrix $\boldsymbol{H}_v \in \mathbb{R}^{L \times 2M}$ is build for each temporal window, holding row vectors $\boldsymbol{h}_{l,v} \in \mathbb{R}^{2M}$ as the log variance of the projected EEG channels:

$$\boldsymbol{h}_{v,l} = \log \left(\frac{\mathrm{diag}\left(\tilde{\boldsymbol{W}}_v^\top \boldsymbol{Z}_{l,v} \boldsymbol{Z}_{l,v}^\top \tilde{\boldsymbol{W}}_v \right)}{\mathrm{Tr}\left(\tilde{\boldsymbol{W}}_v^\top \boldsymbol{Z}_{l,v} \boldsymbol{Z}_{l,v}^\top \tilde{\boldsymbol{W}}_v \right)} \right) \tag{1}$$

where $\tilde{\boldsymbol{W}}_v \in \mathbb{R}^{L \times 2M}$ contains the first and the last M eigenvectors of $\boldsymbol{W}$, $\mathrm{diag}(\cdot)$, and $\mathrm{Tr}(\cdot)$ stand to the diagonal elements and trace functions, respectively [3]. Further, an SVM classifier is trained to estimate the MI condition from the v-th EEG window as follows: $\hat{y}_l = \sum_{\boldsymbol{h}_{j,v} \in \Omega_v} \alpha_j y_j \kappa_\sigma(\boldsymbol{h}_{l,v}, \boldsymbol{h}_{j,v}) + b$, where $\alpha_j \in \mathbb{R}$ is the weight for the sample $\boldsymbol{h}_{j,v} \in \Omega_v$, Ω_v is a set holding the support vectors, $b \in \mathbb{R}$ is a bias term, and $\kappa_\sigma : \mathbb{R}^{2M} \times \mathbb{R}^{2M} \to \mathbb{R}^+$ is a Gaussian kernel function with bandwidth $\sigma \in \mathbb{R}^+$.

EEG Connectivity Analysis to Code the MI Protocol Coupling. We use a measure based on brain connectivity, knows as Phase Locking Value (PLV), to assess the interaction between different brain regions by means of phase synchronization, that allows a straight comparison between the instantaneous phases of two EEG signals. In particular, this step allows to highlight the relationships between the classification performance of the subject and its coupling with the MI protocol concerning the brain connectivity patterns within each temporal segment. So, given a pair of input channels at the v-th window for the l-th trial $\boldsymbol{z}, \boldsymbol{z}' \in \boldsymbol{Z}_{l,v}$; the instantaneous phase vectors $\boldsymbol{\phi}, \boldsymbol{\varphi} \in \mathbb{R}^R$ are computed as: $\phi_t = \arctan\left(\mathcal{H}\{z_t\}/z_t\right)$, being $\mathcal{H}$ the Hilbert transform function (analogously for

φ_t) [12]. In turn, a PLV-based connectivity matrix $\boldsymbol{K} \in \mathbb{R}^{C \times C}$ can be computed as follows:

$$k_{c,c'} = \left| \frac{1}{R} \sum_{t=1}^{R} e^{i(\phi_t - \varphi_t)} \right|. \tag{2}$$

Lastly, to quantify the phase synchronization strength between EEG-channels along the trials associated with an MI condition, the overall brain connectivity matrices $\boldsymbol{\Psi}_v^+, \boldsymbol{\Psi}_v^- \in \mathbb{R}^{C \times C}$ can be computed as follows: $\boldsymbol{\Psi}_v^\xi = \mathbb{E}\left\{ \boldsymbol{K}_{l,v} : \forall y_l = \xi \right\}$, where $\xi \in \{+1, -1\}$.

3   Experimental Set-Up

For concrete testing, the proposed EEG processing approach is used to highlight relevant spatiotemporal patterns from an MI discrimination task. In particular, the publicly available BCI Competition IV dataset 2a is employed.[1] This database is provided by the Institute for Knowledge Discovery (Laboratory of Brain-Computer Interfaces) at Graz University of Technology and consists of the recorded EEG data from 9 healthy subjects performing the MI task during one trial. Each trial begins with a fixed cross on the computer screen accompanied by a beep. At second 2, an arrow pointing left, right, down or up (MI of the left hand, right hand, both feet, and tongue, respectively) is shown as a visual stimulus on the screen during 1.25 s. Then, at second 3, the subject is petitioned to perform the MI task until the fixed cross disappeared from the screen at second 6. A short break of 1 s follows, where the screen is blank (see Fig. 1(a)). EEG signals are recorded from 22 Ag/AgCl electrodes positioned according to the international 10/20 placement system. The signals are bandpass-filtered between 0.5–100 Hz and sampled at 250 Hz. Besides, a 50 Hz Notch filter is used. In this work, we select only the first two MI tasks of the experimental paradigm (left and right hands). Afterward, the EEG signals per each trial are down-sampled at 128 Hz and filtered between 8–30 Hz using a 5th order Butterworth bandpass filter to highlight the α (8–12 Hz) and β (12–30 Hz) frequency bands avoiding the influence of muscle noise [6,10]. Next, we segment each EEG trial into six-time windows of 2 s with a 50% overlapping through a Hamming window. Namely, the EEG data is divided into six segments of equal length: 0–2 s, 1–3 s, ..., 5–7 s.

Further, the CSP-based representation is carried out on every window. We fix the number of eigenvectors in the CSP algorithm to $M = 4$ [11]. Then, we train a SVM classifier under a nested 10-folds cross-validation scheme, where 90% of the trials per subject are used as training set and the remaining 10% as testing. The kernel bandwidth value is searched from the set $[0.5\sigma_o, 1.0\sigma_o]$, where $\sigma_o \in \mathbb{R}^+$ holds the median of the Euclidean distances of the input space. Moreover, to evaluate the propagation of neural activity recorded in each trial, the PLV is computed as described in Sect. 2. Besides, we perform a statistical test to determine if there are statistically significant differences between the accumulated electrical activity estimated (regarding the PLV connectivity values) from

---

[1] http://www.bbci.de/competition/iv/desc_2a.pdf.

the left and the right cerebral hemispheres. We test the null hypothesis, that the two data samples are from populations with equal means, assuming a Student's t distribution with a significance level of 5% (p-value < 0.05).

4   Results and Discussion

Table 1 summarizes the classification results in terms of the accuracy and Cohen's kappa coefficient. Note that significant state-of-the-art works are shown for comparison purposes [3,4,8,9,11]. Concerning the introduced approach, we also display the number of the temporal window with the highest classification performance and the p-value measuring the statistical differences of the PLV-based connectivities between the left and the right hemispheres. As seen, our strategy obtains the highest accuracy in average in comparison to the Elasuty et al., Liang et al. and Li et al. methodologies. Moreover, in these approaches, the MI discrimination based on feature extraction is calculated for the specific time segment associated with the stimulus. Now, our MI discrimination system achieves mean classification values along subjects between 62.53% to 93.19% for accuracy, and 0.29 to 0.86 for the kappa coefficient.

Table 1. MI discrimination results for the BCI Competition IV dataset 2a. The accuracy and kappa coefficients are presented. Also, the window related to the achieved classification is displayed for our approach. The p-value quantifies the statistical difference of the PLV-based connectivity between the left and right hemispheres (the lower p-value the higher the brain connectivity differences).

Subject	p-value	Accuracy (%)					Kappa coefficient (κ)			
		Our approach	(win)	Elasuty et al. [4]	Liang et al. [9]	Li et al. [8]	Our approach	Ang et al. [3]	Nicolas-Alonso et al. [11]	Abbas et al. [1]
S01	0.117	87.75 ± 6.69	(4)	76	62.13	88.19	0.76 ± 0.13	0.78 ± 0.02	0.82	0.70
S02	0.838	62.53 ± 11.57	(6)	45	67.86	64.58	0.29 ± 0.17	0.45 ± 0.03	0.39	0.45
S03	2.003e−5	89.12 ± 7.63	(4)	92	75.71	**94.44**	0.78 ± 0.15	**0.86 ± 0.01**	0.92	0.71
S04	0.860	73.72 ± 10.24	(4)	77	72.14	65.97	0.47 ± 0.21	0.47 ± 0.02	0.51	0.96
S05	0.040	86.79 ± 6.40	(3)	64	67.46	76.39	0.74 ± 0.13	0.63 ± 0.02	0.89	0.60
S06	0.035	67.42 ± 13.35	(3)	70	66.67	67.39	0.36 ± 0.24	0.32 ± 0.03	0.49	0.43
S07	0.004	83.34 ± 7.85	(5)	59	71.43	75.00	0.67 ± 0.16	0.85 ± 0.01	**0.96**	0.55
S08	8.464e−9	**93.19 ± 5.66**	(4)	**98**	**78.57**	88.19	**0.86 ± 0.11**	0.79 ± 0.02	**0.96**	0.61
S09	0.052	88.86 ± 7.99	(3)	80	70.00	88.89	0.77 ± 0.16	0.78 ± 0.01	0.81	0.57
AVG	—	**81.41 ± 8.60**	(4)	73.44	70.22	78.78 ± 11.41	0.63 ± 0.16	0.66 ± 0.02	**0.75**	0.62

As a comparative evaluation of the approach proposed in Fig. 1 are showed the statistical and connectivity analysis carried out for the best (S08) and the worst (S02) subject, according to the classification results for the task left hand MI per window. Remarkably, the lowest and highest performances are related to the subjects 02 and 08, respectively. In fact, as seen in Fig. 1(b), the classification performance along windows for the S08 evidence the expected behavior concerning to the MI protocol, having its best result in the window (4) where the stimulus appeared. Otherwise, the performance curve for the S02 shows an

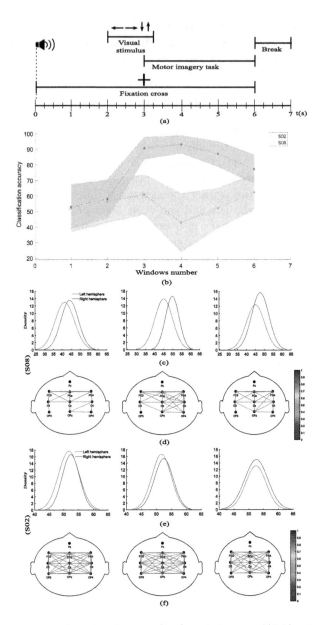

Fig. 1. Connectivity analysis for the best (S08) and the worst (S02) subject based on classification results, in the left hand MI task discrimination. (a) MI protocol. (b) Visualization of variability in classification performance throughout the temporal windows. (c) Probability density function of the electrical activity associated with each cerebral hemisphere from PLV-based connectivity values and (d) Connectivity maps showing interactions between EEG channels for the windows 1, 4 and 6 for the best subject, and analogously for (e) and (f) the worst subject. The dots of the plots (d) and (f) represent the spatial distribution of the EEG electrodes on the sensorimotor area.

indiscriminate behavior, having its worst value in this window. In this sense, these results demonstrate that there is a direct relationship between the subject coupling with MI protocol and the classification performance. Figure 1(c) allow us to see the probability density function of the accumulated connectivity strength linked to each hemisphere in the windows 1, 4, and 6. We noted that the distributions for the S08 are significantly different, while the S02 ones do not reveal discriminative connectivity between brain hemispheres (see Fig. 1(e)). Figure 1(d) and Fig. 1(f) display the connectivity maps for both subjects respectively. The connectivity maps viewed are based on visualization function of the Matlab toolbox HERMES.[2] Notably, the connectivity distribution for the sensorimotor area shown in Fig. 1(d) and Fig. 1(f) corresponds to the following EEG channels: FC3, C3, and CP3 in the left hemisphere; FCz, Cz, and CPz in the middle, and FC4, C4, and CP4 in the right hemisphere. The observed behavior of the networks generated by PLV for MI task, left hand, per subject varies slightly due to the trials average activity recorded for the segments shown. After visual inspection of the connectivity maps, per window, it is possible to observe the different patterns of dynamic changes in the brain that are generated in subjects 08 and 02 in the states of concentration, execution of the MI task and resting, respectively. The patterns exhibited by the graphs in the middle, for both subjects, represent the average activity measured for the segment between 3–5 s where the brain activity associated with the MI task is mainly recorded. In this sense, the best subject presents more activity in the contralateral hemisphere to the task under study, that is, there is a greater representation of the connection between the nodes of the right hemisphere [7], which does not happen with the worst subject allowing us to interpret with greater clarity the classification results.

5   Conclusions

In this study, we employed an MI discrimination system to enhance the identification of relevant brain connectivity patterns. Although different methodologies based on feature extraction have been used for the distinction between MI tasks, including connectivity analysis, it is not known why those classification systems exhibit differences concerning their accuracy per subject. Our EEG analysis strategy first makes a windows representation of the temporal information of the signal. Then, consistent spatial patterns for MI discrimination are extracted using CSP. Next, the spatiotemporal features are used as inputs to an SVM classifier. Finally, we use a PLV analysis based characterization of the segmented EEG signals to reveal relevant brain connectivity patterns. Our approach focuses on discriminating the spatiotemporal features associated with each MI task for its subsequent visual interpretation employing brain connectivity estimators and a statistical test. According to our results, subjects with higher classification performances exhibited stronger activity in the contralateral hemisphere for the MI task studied. As future work, we plan to test the proposed approach with

---

[2] http://hermes.ctb.upm.es/.

effective connectivity measures, e.g., Granger Causality, which not only indicate activity between electrodes but also describe the influence that one signal exerts over another. Moreover, to better code brain dynamics we propose employing variants of Canonical Correlation Analysis (CCA) based on kernels [13]. This type of analysis allows improving the robustness of classification systems and provides greater flexibility through the use of non-linear relationships between EEG signals.

Acknowledgments. This study was supported by the projects 1110-744-55778 and 6-18-1 funded by Colciencias and Universidad Tecnológica de Pereira, respectively. V. Gómez-Orozco was supported by the program "Doctorado Nacional en Empresa - Convoctoria 758 de 2016", funded by Colciencias. A. Orozco was supported by the Master in Electrical Engineering from Universidad Tecnológica de Pereira.

References

1. Abbas, W., et al.: A discriminative spectral-temporal feature set for motor imagery classification. In: 2017 IEEE International Workshop on Signal Processing Systems (SiPS), pp. 1–6 (2017)
2. Abdulkader, S.N., et al.: Brain computer interfacing: applications and challenges. Egypt. Inform. J. **16**(2), 213–230 (2015)
3. Ang, K.K., et al.: Filter bank common spatial pattern algorithm on BCI competition IV datasets 2a and 2b. Front. Neurosci **6**, 39 (2012)
4. Elasuty, B., et al.: Dynamic Bayesian networks for EEG motor imagery feature extraction. In: 2015 7th International IEEE/EMBS Conference on Neural Engineering (NER), pp. 170–173 (2015)
5. Ghosh, P., et al.: Functional connectivity analysis of motor imagery EEG signal for brain-computer interfacing application. In: 2015 7th International IEEE/EMBS Conference on Neural Engineering (NER), pp. 210–213 (2015)
6. Hamedi, M., et al.: Electroencephalographic motor imagery brain connectivity analysis for BCI: a review. Neural Comput. **28**, 999–1041 (2016)
7. Kelly, R., et al.: Distinctive laterality of neural networks supporting action understanding in left-and right-handed individuals: an EEG coherence study. Neuropsychologia **75**, 20–29 (2015)
8. Li, D., et al.: A self-adaptive frequency selection common spatial pattern and least squares twin support vector machine for motor imagery electroencephalography recognition. Biomed. Signal Process. Control. **41**, 222–232 (2018)
9. Liang, S., et al.: Discrimination of motor imagery tasks via information flow pattern of brain connectivity. Technol. Health Care **24**(s2), S795–S801 (2016)
10. Loboda, A., et al.: Discrimination of EEG-based motor imagery tasks by means of a simple phase information method. Int. J. Adv. Res. Artif. Intell. **3**(10), 11–15 (2014)
11. Nicolas-Alonso, L.F., et al.: Adaptive stacked generalization for multiclass motor imagery-based brain computer interfaces. IEEE Trans. Neural Syst. Rehabil. Eng. **23**(4), 702–712 (2015)
12. Sakkalis, V.: Review of advanced techniques for the estimation of brain connectivity measured with EEG/MEG. Comput. Biol. Med. **41**(12), 1110–1117 (2011)
13. Uurtio, V., et al.: A tutorial on canonical correlation methods. ACM Comput. Surv. (CSUR) **50**(6), 95 (2017)

Improving Ensemble Averaging by Epoch Detrending in Evoked Potentials

Idileisy Torres-Rodríguez[1] , Carlos A. Ferrer[1,2(✉)] ,
Ernesto Velarde-Reyes[3] , and Alberto Taboada-Crispi[1]

[1] Informatics Research Center, Universidad Central
"Marta Abreu" de Las Villas, 54830 Santa Clara, Cuba
{itrodriguez, cferrer, ataboada}@uclv.edu.cu
[2] Pattern Recognition Lab, Friedrich Alexander University
Erlangen-Nuremberg, 91054 Erlangen, Germany
[3] Electronics Department, Cuban Neurosciences Center, CNEURO,
11600 Havana, Cuba
evelarde1980@gmail.com

Abstract. The objective of this work is to evaluate different detrending methods in the quality of auditory evoked responses. We compared the average responses obtained by simply removing the DC level and the linear trend, and also the estimated trends using polynomials and Fourier models up to the 8th order. Two quality measures were used to compare the results: the standard deviation ratio, as a measure of the signal-to-noise ratio, and the correlation coefficient between consecutive responses obtained under the same experimental conditions. The best results were obtained using a polynomial model of order 7.

Keywords: Detrending · Ensemble averages · Evoked potential · CCR · SDR

1 Introduction

1.1 Evoked Potentials

The Evoked Potentials are signals that appear embedded in the electroencephalographic signal (EEG) after a given stimulus is presented to the subject, being of very weak amplitudes (in the order of 0.1–100 μV) [1]. The EEG signal is considered the main source of noise [1, 2], but other interferences and noise can also be found that contaminate this signal and make difficult to detect them, such as artifacts inside the body, the environment, sensors and electrodes. Specifically, the sources related to the electrodes and sensors used for the registration have a special attention [3]. In the case where the recording is done using a single channel, these interferences cannot be suppressed using linear combinations of channels as in ICA or other linear techniques.

To recover these low-amplitude evoked potentials, the most common technique performs a Coherent Average (described in more detail in next section) of a large number or responses to the stimulus. The EEG signal includes slow derivatives [3–5] from the electrode-gel-skin interfaces. These drifts can affect the result of the Coherent Average inducing a reproducible pattern that does not exist. Generally, these drifts can

R. Vera-Rodriguez et al. (Eds.): CIARP 2018, LNCS 11401, pp. 707–714, 2019.
https://doi.org/10.1007/978-3-030-13469-3_82

be treated with high-pass filters, but these in turn include the introduction of other types of artifacts. New morphological forms appear that depend on the cutoff frequency, the order, and the type of filter used. Another problem is the size of the signal analysis window: for very small sizes some trends cannot be eliminated even if high-pass filters are used.

1.2   Coherent Average

The Coherent Average can be computed from the ensemble matrix P that is formed with the set of evoked responses [6–11], as shown in Eq. (1):

$$P_{ij} = \begin{bmatrix} p_{11} & \cdots & p_{1N} \\ \vdots & \ddots & \vdots \\ p_{M1} & \cdots & p_{MN} \end{bmatrix}, \ 1 \leq i \leq M, \ 1 \leq j \leq N \tag{1}$$

Here, the response p_{ij} to the i-th stimulus is assumed to be the sum of the deterministic (constant) component of the signal or evoked response s plus a random noise r_i which is asynchronous with the stimulus. The model for each of the M responses is given by Eq. (2).

$$p_i = s + r_i \tag{2}$$

where the deterministic component s is given by Eq. (3):

$$s = s(n), \ 1 < n < N \tag{3}$$

and the noise r_i is given by Eq. (4):

$$r_i = [\Gamma_i(1)\Gamma_i(2)\ldots\Gamma_i(N)] \tag{4}$$

In the model given by Eqs. (1)–(4), N is the number of samples that compose the epoch, and $\Gamma(n)$ (the current noise) is assumed to be stationary and normal, with zero mean [12–19]. Consequently, the variance of noise must be fixed and equal in all potentials. The CA average, or arithmetic mean as it is also known, is a simple and direct method to estimate the deterministic component s and produce an estimate of it, which we will call $\hat{s}$ (Eq. 5):

$$\hat{s} = \frac{1}{M} \sum_{i=1}^{M} p_i(n) \tag{5}$$

In some Coherent Averaging applications, this $\hat{s}$ can be then used to extract, from each p_i, the noise part and obtain an estimate of the signal-to-noise ratio of the ensemble, from which the possible biases produced by the number of responses M and amplitude variability in s has been removed [20, 21].

If the individual responses r_i present marked tendencies, the estimated signal $\hat{s}$ can show changes in its morphology (given the very low amplitude of the s component), and important values in the diagnosis, like the amplitudes of the individual components of the evoked potential, can be distorted.

1.3   Detrending

One solution to the problems caused by high-pass filtering is to perform detrending. Detrending consist in removing means, offsets, or linear trends from regularly sampled time-domain input-output data signals. Detrending can be developed using a smoothing function, for example a low-order polynomial that fits the data [3, 22–25], and subtracting it from the data, in order to eliminate fluctuations. Other models can be used for the same purpose [3, 4, 26].

The detrending assumes a model of the signal that must be flexible to the adjustment of the existing trend, if it is inextricable it does not absorb fluctuations of interest. Choosing the parameters (e.g. the polynomial order) is a critical step. Simple trends are easily removed with low-order polynomials, or the first terms of a Fourier series. It can be conceived that the unwanted tendency contains fewer oscillations than the waveform of the evoked potentials, and this, in turn, contains fewer oscillations than the noise, so a general concept could be that the order of the detrending is low enough so it does not adjust to the signal of interest.

In this paper, we propose to select the model and the order that best fits brainstem evoked potentials to eliminate present tendencies and thereby improve the quality of the coherent average. Quality measures commonly used to validate the estimate in Eq. (5) were chosen to evaluate the results.

2   Methods

2.1   Data

The database used in this study consists of Transient Auditory Evoked Potentials registered in 39 neonatal patients between 1–3 months of age born in Hospital Materno Ramón González Coro, in Havana, Cuba [27]. The signals were recorded with an AUDIX electro-audiometer. A click stimulus with duration 0.1 ms was provided at different intensities (100, 80, 70, 60, 30 dBnHL and 0 dBpSPL) via inserted earphones (EarTone3A) [28, 29]. Ag/AgCl dry electrodes were used, which were fixed with electrolytic paste on the forehead (positive), ipsilateral mastoids (negative) and contralateral mastoids (earth). The impedance values were maintained below 5 kΩ. The sampling frequency used was 13.3 kHz, and the analysis windows to form the ensemble matrix P (Eq. 5) and calculate the coherent average were of approximately 15 ms, that is about 200 samples per window ($N = 200$). From this database, only records obtained at 100 dBnHL (78 signals) were used, where it was confirmed by specialists that a response was present. These signals were used in order to guarantee the maximum values of the quality measures for this database. The signal was analogically filtered with a band-pass filter with cut-off frequencies of 20 and 2000 Hz. Although it has been said previously that filtering can produce trends, it is necessary in this type of signals (EEG). The limitation in this case, being the size of the analysis window (15 ms), persists, which is much lower than the minimum analysis period of the filter, equal to 1/20 Hz (50 ms).

According to [30], there are up to 8 oscillations with clinical value in the first 15 ms of the auditory evoked potentials, an aspect of relevance when choosing the order of the detrending model.

2.2   Models for Detrending Considered

Polynomial Model
Polynomial models for curves are given by Eq. (6).

$$y = \sum_{i=1}^{n+1} p_i x^{n+1-i} \tag{6}$$

where $n + 1$ is the *order* of the polynomial, n is the *degree* of the polynomial. The order gives the number of coefficients fit, and the degree gives the highest power of the predictor variable. For instance, a third-degree (cubic) polynomial is given by:

$$y = p_1 x^3 + p_2 x^2 + p_3 x + p_4 \tag{7}$$

Polynomials are often used when a simple empirical model is required. The main advantages of polynomial fits include reasonable flexibility for data that is not too complicated, and they are linear, which means the fitting process is simple. The main disadvantage is that high-degree fits can become unstable. Additionally, polynomials of any degree can provide a good fit within the data range, but can diverge wildly outside that range. Therefore, caution must be exercised when extrapolating with polynomials.

Polynomials of order n can adapt to trends showing up to $n - 1$ local extremes, which in turn implies a maximum of $(n - 1)/2$ full oscillations in the trend. As mentioned, there are up to 8 oscillations of clinical relevance for the considered duration of the auditory evoked potentials. To limit the maximum number of oscillations detrended to be less than half of these useful oscillations, we evaluated polynomial models from order 0 to 8. The zero order corresponds to the classical procedure of eliminating the DC level, while the 1st order polynomial corresponds to a linear detrending.

Fourier Series Models
The Fourier series is a sum of sine and cosine functions that describes a periodic signal. It is represented in either the trigonometric or the exponential form:

$$y = a_0 + \sum_{i=1}^{n} a_i \cos(iwx) + b_i \sin(iwx) \tag{8}$$

where a_0 models a constant (intercept) term in the data and is associated with the $i = 0$ cosine term, w is the fundamental frequency of the signal, and n is the number of terms (harmonics) in the series. In this case, we evaluated Fourier models up to n = 8, to keep up with the number of polynomial models considered, even if the number of oscillations modeled can match the ones with clinical interest.

2.3   Quality Measures Used

Correlation Coefficient Ratio

The correlation coefficient ratio (CCR) is a statistic that reflects the replicability between two sub-averages, computed as follows:

$$CCR = \frac{\sum_{i=1}^{NM} (\hat{s}_1 \hat{s}_2)}{\sqrt{\sum_{i=1}^{NM} (\hat{s}_1) \sum_{i=1}^{NM} (\hat{s}_2)}} \tag{9}$$

According to the Audiology Assessment Protocol in [31], for a window of interest of 10 ms the value of CCR must be greater than 0.7 between two sub-averages obtained with 2000 epochs each.

Standard Deviation Rate

The standard deviation rate is a signal-to-noise ratio,

$$SDR = \mathrm{var}(\hat{s})/\mathrm{var}(\theta) \tag{10}$$

where $\mathrm{var}(\hat{s})$ is the variance of the estimated signal and $\mathrm{var}(\theta)$ is the residual noise variance. The residual noise is estimated as the difference between the even sub-average and the odd sub-average.

$$\theta = \hat{s}_1 - \hat{s}_2 \tag{11}$$

The standards [31], suggest values of SDR > 1 to guarantee the presence of response.

3   Results

To evaluate the results obtained, a Friedman test was performed where the average values of each of the adjustment models for each of the quality measures used in the 78 signals were evaluated. In all cases, the test resulted in a value of $p < 0.05$, which suggests that there are significant differences between at least two models. In order to identify the models in which the differences existed, a post-hoc test was developed using the Bonferroni method. Figure 1 shows the results obtained for both quality measures, CCR in the left and SDR in the right panels, respectively. Non-overlapping segments are those that show significant differences. There is a consistent performance of Poly 7 as the best method across both measures, with Poly 5 also consistently ranking second in both measures.

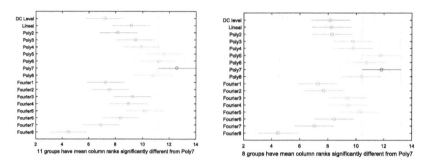

Fig. 1. Differences between the average ranks of the different models evaluating: the CCR (left) and SDR (right). Grayed-out models have rank confidence intervals overlapping with the best model (Poly 7)

There is an obvious tendency for deterioration in Fourier models as they approach the 8th order, which could be explained by the reduction in the amplitude of the recovered response due to an increase in its ability to match $\hat{s}$. In Fig. 2, an example of the recovered $\hat{s}$ using the evaluated methods for one of the 78 subjects is shown.

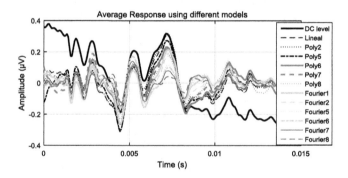

Fig. 2. Auditory evoked potentials recovered using the detrending methods for one subject.

Figure 2 shows the result of the average potential obtained for a subject using the different detrending models, where most Polynomial and Fourier models improves the resulting signal compared to the subtraction of the DC level (standard procedure), in correspondence with results shown in Fig. 1. The smaller amplitudes of $\hat{s}$ for the higher order Fourier approaches are also visible.

4   Conclusions

An adequate detrending can improve the detection of auditory evoked potentials according to recommended quality measures. It allows obtaining individual responses better suited to perform the coherent averaging. Although the best results were obtained here for a polynomial model of order 7, the use of a smaller order (i.e. 5) can be considered as an option given the interest in avoiding a fit to the oscillations of clinical interest. In future works an analysis of the variance of the remaining noise by subtracting the trends should be considered.

Acknowledgements. This work was partially supported by the Cuban National Program of Creation of an R+D Platform in Neuro-technology and by an Alexander von Humboldt Foundation Fellowship granted to C. A. Ferrer-Riesgo (Ref 3.2-1164728-CUB-GF-E).

References

1. Sörnmo, L., Laguna, P.: Bioelectrical Signal Processing in Cardiac and Neural Applications. Academic Press, London (2005)
2. Paulraj, M.P., et al.: Auditory evoked potential response and hearing loss: a review. Open Biomed. Eng. J. **9**, 17–24 (2015)
3. de Cheveigné, A., Arzounian, D.: Robust detrending, rereferencing, outlier detection, and inpainting for multichannel data. NeuroImage **172**(2018), 903–912 (2018)
4. Kugiumtzis, D., Tsimpiris, A.: Measures of Analysis of Time Series (MATS): a MATLAB toolkit for computation of multiple measures on time series data bases. J. Stat. Softw. **33**(i.5) (2010)
5. Casula, E.P., et al.: TMS-evoked long-lasting artefacts: a new adaptive algorithm for EEG signal correction. Clin. Neurophysiol. **128**(9), 1563–1574 (2017)
6. Taboada-Crispi, A., Lorenzo-Ginori, J.V., Lovely, D.F.: Adaptive line enhancing plus modified signal averaging for ventricular late potential detection. Electron. Lett. **35**(16), 1293–1295 (1999)
7. Taboada-Crispi, A.: Improving ventricular late potentials detection effectiveness. Doctoral dissertation, Ph.D. thesis, University of New Brunswick, Canada (2002)
8. Laguna, P., Sörnmo, L.: Sampling rate and the estimation of ensemble variability for repetitive signals. Med. Biol. Eng. Comput. **38**(5), 540–546 (2000)
9. Kotas, M., Pander, T., Leski, J.M.: Averaging of nonlinearly aligned signal cycles for noise suppression. Biomed. Signal Process. Control **21**, 157–168 (2015)
10. ACNS: Guideline 9C: guidelines on short-latency auditory evoked potentials. Am. Clin. Neurophysiology Soc. Guidel. **46**(3), 275–286 (2006)
11. Ireland, K.H.: Can the auditory late response indicate audibility of speech sounds from hearing aids with different digital processing strategies. Doctoral dissertation, Ph.D. thesis, University of Southampton, United Kingdom (2014)
12. Rasheed, H.: A maximum likelihood method to estimate EEG evoked potentials. Doctoral dissertation, Ph.D. thesis, McGill University, Canada (1985)
13. Effern, A., Lehnertz, K., Schreiber, T., Grunwald, T., David, P., Elger, C.E.: Nonlinear denoising of transient signals with application to event related potentials. Physica D **140**(3–4), 257–266 (2000)
14. Davila, C.E., Mobin, M.S.: Weighted averaging of evoked potentials. IEEE Trans. Biomed. Eng. **39**(4), 338–345 (1992)
15. Khashei, M., Bijari, M.: A new class of hybrid models for time series forecasting. Expert Syst. Appl. **39**(4), 4344–4357 (2012)
16. Pander, T., Przybyla, T., Czabanski, R.: An application of the L P-norm in robust weighted averaging of biomedical signals. J. Med. Informatics Technol. **22**(2), 1–8 (2013)

17. de Weerd, J.P.C.M.: Estimation of evoked potentials: a study of a posteriori 'Wiener' filtering and its time varying generalization. Doctoral dissertation, Ph.D. thesis, Catholic University of Nijmegen, The Netherlands (1981)
18. Ting, C.M., Salleh, S.H., Zainuddin, Z.M., Bahar, A.: Artifact removal from single-trial ERPs using non-Gaussian stochastic volatility models and particle filter. IEEE Signal Process. Lett. **21**(8), 923–927 (2014)
19. Silva, I.: Estimation of postaverage SNR from evoked responses under nonstationary noise. IEEE Trans. Biomed. Eng. **56**(8), 2123–2130 (2009)
20. Ferrer, C.A., González, E., Hernández-Díaz, M.E.: Correcting the use of ensemble averages in the calculation of harmonics to noise ratios in voice signals. J. Acoust. Soc. Am. **118**(2), 605–607 (2005)
21. Ferrer, C., González, E., Hernández-Díaz, M.E., Torrer, D., del Toro, A.: Removing the influence of shimmer in the calculation of harmonics-to-noise ratios using ensemble-averages in voice signals. EURASIP J. Adv. Signal Process. **2009**, 1–7 (2009)
22. Gopinath, K.S.: Reduction of noise due to task correlated motion in event related overt word generation functional magnetic resonance imaging paradigms, University of Florida (2003)
23. Ozaki, T.: Time Series Modeling of Neuroscience Data. CRC Press, Boca Raton (2012)
24. Davé, R.N., Krishnapuram, R.: Robust clustering methods: a unified view. IEEE Trans. Fuzzy Syst. **5**(2), 270–293 (1997)
25. Tarvainen, M.P., Ranta-aho, P.O., Karjalainen, P.A.: An advanced detrending method with application to HRV analysis. EEE Trans. Biom. Eng. **49**(2), 172–175 (2002)
26. Gharieb, R.R., Cichocki, A.: Noise reduction in brain evoked potentials based on third-order correlations. IEEE Trans. Biomed. Eng. **48**(5), 501–512 (2001)
27. Cabana-Pérez, I.M., Velarde-Reyes, E., Torres-Fortuny, A., Eimil-Suarez, E., García-Giró, A.: Automatic ABR detection at near-threshold intensities combining template-based approach and energy analysis. In: Torres, I., Bustamante, J., Sierra, D. (eds.) VII Latin American Congress on Biomedical Engineering CLAIB 2016, Bucaramanga, Santander, Colombia, October 26th -28th, 2016. IP, vol. 60, pp. 122–125. Springer, Singapore (2017). https://doi.org/10.1007/978-981-10-4086-3_31
28. Doubell, T.P., et al.: The effect of interaural timing on the posterior auricular muscle reflex in normal adult volunteers. PLoS ONE **13**(4), e0194965 (2018)
29. Gregory, L., Rosa, R.F.M., Zen, P.R.G., Sleifer, P.: Auditory evoked potentials in children and adolescents with down syndrome. Am. J. Med. Genet. Part A **176**(1), 68–74 (2018)
30. Picton, T.W., Hillyard, S.A., Krausz, H.I., Galambos, R.: Human auditory evoked potentials. I: evaluation of components. Electroencephalogr. Clin. Neurophysiol. **36**, 79–190 (1974)
31. British Columbia Early Hearing Programme: Audiology Assessment Protocol. V. 4.1 (2012). http://www.phsa.ca/Documents/bcehpaudiologyassessmentprotocol.pdf. Accessed 10 May 2018

Color Features Extraction and Classification of Digital Images of Erythrocytes Infected by *Plasmodium berghei*

Juan V. Lorenzo-Ginori[1]([✉]) ⓘ, Lyanett Chinea-Valdés[1],
Yanela IzquierdoTorres[1], Rubén Orozco-Morales[1] ⓘ,
Niurka Mollineda-Diogo[2], Sergio Sifontes-Rodríguez[2],
and Alfredo Meneses-Marcel[2]

[1] Universidad Central Marta Abreu de Las Villas,
54830 Santa Clara, Villa Clara, Cuba
juanl@uclv.edu.cu
[2] Centro de Bioactivos Químicos, 54830 Santa Clara, Villa Clara, Cuba

Abstract. The development of antimalarial drugs requires performing laboratory experiments that include the analysis of blood smears infected with *Plasmodium berghei*. Analyzing visually the resulting microscopy images is usually a slow and tedious task prone to errors due to fatigue and subjectivity of the analysts. These facts motivated the creation of digital image processing systems to automate the aforementioned analysis. We present in this work a computer vision solution which processes microscopy images of blood smears. This system performs tasks like illumination correction, color compensation, image segmentation including separation of clumped objects and the extraction and selection of color features. Then a set of classifiers was tested to find the best one in terms of classification results. Here a new feature named pixels fraction was introduced and a number of other color features were extracted, from which a subset was selected for the classification of the cells into either normal or infected. The classifiers tested for this application were: support vector machines (SVM), K-nearest neighbors (KNN), J48, Random Forest (RF), Naïve Bayes and linear discriminant analysis (LDA). All of them were evaluated in terms of their performance expressed as correct classification rate, sensitivity, specificity, F-measure and area under Receiver Operating Characteristic (ROC) curve (AUC). The usefulness of the pixels fraction as a new and effective feature was demonstrated by the experimental results. In regard of classifiers, J48 and Random Forest showed the best results.

Keywords: Malaria · Image processing · Computer vision · Feature extraction · Classifiers

1 Introduction

Malaria is an infectious disease showing high degrees of morbidity and mortality, for which the World Health Organization estimated 215 million of infected persons and 445000 deaths in 2016 [1]. This serious health problem claims for new diagnose tools

© Springer Nature Switzerland AG 2019
R. Vera-Rodriguez et al. (Eds.): CIARP 2018, LNCS 11401, pp. 715–722, 2019.
https://doi.org/10.1007/978-3-030-13469-3_83

and anti-malarial drugs. Microscope analysis of large amounts of blood smears in order to detect the presence of the *Plasmodium* parasite is a problem of primary importance both to diagnose the disease in humans and to determine the infection rate in laboratory mice during the process of developing anti-malarial drugs. This analysis, when made by human experts is a slow and tedious process whose results are prone to errors due to tiredness, subjectivity and to the probable low rate of positive cases (infected erythrocytes). This has motivated developing digital image processing (DIP) - computer vision (CV) solutions for this process, which is the topic addressed in this work.

There are various published works on this problem, usually implementing diverse image processing procedures to obtain appropriate image features and afterwards performing the classification of the erythrocytes, examples of which can be found in [2–5]. These procedures include tasks such as image conditioning through non-uniform illumination correction, filtering and color normalization. Image segmentation of the microscope digital images of blood smears is essential to separate erythrocytes from other blood components and artifacts, as well as to appropriately separate clumped (touching and overlapping) erythrocytes. After this, there have been different approaches to obtain appropriate features from segmented erythrocytes, to ensure an effective classification. Finally, testing and selecting effective classifying algorithms complete the design of the system. Examples of this can be found in [6–9]. Classifiers like linear discriminant analysis (LDA), K-nearest neighbors (KNN), support vector machines (SVM) and others have been used for this purpose.

The contribution of this paper consists in finding new color features with high discriminating capabilities, combined with a study of their best possible combination with appropriate classifier algorithms. The system is oriented towards applications to anti-malarial drug development, in which the analysis of blood smears from laboratory mice demands a low rate of false positives.

2 Materials and Methods

2.1 Sample Images

The images used in this research were taken from Giemsa-stained blood smear slides from mice experimentally infected with *Plasmodium berghei*, kindly donated by Dr. José Antonio Escario García Trevijano from the Faculty of Pharmacy, Universidad Complutense de Madrid. A Zuzi 122/148 tri-ocular microscope was used, equipped with a Microscopy 319 CU digital camera with 3.2 MP resolution and 8-bit RGB output without compression, producing a 2048 × 1536 pixels matrix, with pixel size 3.2 × 3.2 μm, signal to noise ratio 43 dB and optical magnification 50×. The digital images were saved in .tiff (tagged image file) format. An annotated database was created with the aid of two expert analysts from CBQ. This database is intended to perform all the DIP-CV procedures to obtain the features, training the classifiers and realizing tests to assess the effectiveness of classification. A total of 211 images were obtained, from which a set of 600 images of independent segmented erythrocytes was formed, comprising 400 un-infected and 200 *Plasmodium*-infected cells, for which examples are shown in Fig. 1. Notice the reddish-purple spots inside individual erythrocytes that harbor the parasites.

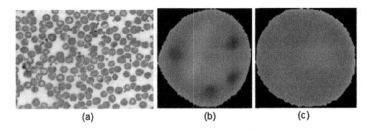

(a)   (b)   (c)

Fig. 1. Microscopy images employed. (a) image of a blood smear showing multiple erythrocytes, (b) segmented, infected erythrocyte and (c) segmented, normal erythrocyte.

The size of the sample set was determined following [10] as a minimum necessary to obtain a reasonable error when evaluating the correct classification rate CCR, when it is expected to be above 0.95 for the classifiers evaluated. These numbers attempted also to cope with a possible class-imbalance. The image sizes of individual cells depend on their physical size, which can exhibit certain natural variability and can also be affected by the presence or not of the parasite.

2.2   Image Conditioning

All the images were initially acquired in the RGB color space with 8 bpp/channel and the intensity of the color components was normalized to the interval [0, 1]. They were converted afterwards to the HSI color space. Other pre-processing steps applied were [3 × 3] median filtering to the intensity component and a morphological *top hat* with an appropriate structuring element to compensate any possible illumination imbalance. Conversion of the images to the La*b* space was made also after segmentation to allow obtaining more features. Information on color spaces is given in [11].

2.3   Segmentation

Segmentation of erythrocytes was performed in two steps. Firstly, the Otsu's algorithm as used in [2] was applied in this case adaptively to intensity component of the image by dividing it into 16 patches that were segmented independently. This coarse segmentation binarized the image into foreground objects (cells, including clumps) and background. Then the cell clumps were separated (fine segmentation) employing a modification of the algorithm described in [12], using weighted outer distance and marker-controlled watershed transforms, with the regional maxima of the distance transform as internal markers. This process proved to be effective in accurately detecting and splitting the cell clumps. Other components of the blood smears like leukocytes and platelets were eliminated using the procedure described in [6] and other artifacts were suppressed as well by morphological area opening, using a threshold derived from the median size of the erythrocytes.

2.4 Color Normalization

Color-based features obtained from the images are essential here for the classification process. In microscopy images, color can be altered due to changes in the illumination source and to the procedure of preparing the samples. This led to the necessity of color normalization by means of DIP techniques. Here the method described in [4] was used for this purpose and the results are illustrated in Fig. 2.

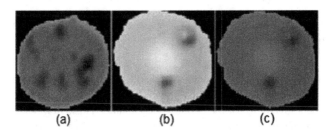

     (a)   (b)   (c)

Fig. 2. Color normalization: (a) reference, (b) target and (c) color-corrected images.

2.5 Feature Extraction and Pixels Fraction

As we stated previously, the classification process was performed here on the basis of color features solely. A total of 13 features were obtained for each of the RGB, HSI and La*b* color spaces. These were, for each color component: mean, variance and skewness as described in [13], as well as kurtosis and a new feature whose introduction is the main contribution of this work: the pixels fraction. Considering the three color spaces this led to a total of 39 features.

The pixels fraction is defined here based in the relative coincidence of the pixel values of the target and a reference, in the planes corresponding to the three color channels, for a specific color space. A small set of regions of interest (ROI) located inside the reddish-purple colored region characteristic of the parasites in a color-normalized erythrocyte were taken as a reference, as shown in Fig. 3. For this set of regions, the mean μ_c and standard deviation σ_c of the intensity in each color channel are determined, where C can take the values R (red), G (green) or B (blue). To illustrate the calculation of the pixels fraction in the RGB color space, consider a cell being analyzed. Then the number of pixels is determined for it, whose intensities imC corresponding to the three color components satisfy simultaneously the condition

$$\mu_c - 2\sigma_c < imC < \mu_c + 2\sigma_c \tag{1}$$

In Eq. 1, the factor 2 multiplying σ_c widens the acceptance intervals for the color components of a given pixel and was determined heuristically. The pixels fraction p_f is finally determined for the image of an erythrocyte in a specific color space by dividing the number of pixels n_f satisfying the condition 1 by the total number N of pixels in the image.

$$p_f = \frac{n_f}{N} \tag{2}$$

The value of p_f was determined analogously in the HSI and La*b* color spaces.

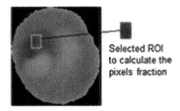

Fig. 3. Illustrating the procedure used to calculate the pixels fraction.

2.6 Feature Selection and Classification

In this step Weka 3.9 [14] facilities were used. Firstly, a selection from the erythrocyte features previously described, by means of filtering (*CfsSubsetEval* with a greedy stepwise search method) was used. This selected seven features. Then, a ranking alternative (*InfoGainAttributeEva*) allowed using the first 20 ranked features as well as the first 7 (to match the number selected through filtering) for classification, as well as all the features. Then the effectiveness of these alternatives were compared.

Classification was then made comparing the following algorithms: SVM, KNN, J48, Random Forest (RF), Naïve Bayes (NB) and Linear Discriminant Analysis (LDA). In the case of SVM and KNN various alternatives in their parameters (polynomial and PUK kernels in SVM, K = 1, 3, 5, 7 for KNN) were tested and those with the best results were used in the comparison to the rest of the classifiers.

The comparison among the various classifiers was performed by ten-fold cross-validation and 1/3−2/3% split. The indexes of effectiveness used were the correct classification rate (CCR), sensitivity (Se), specificity (Sp), F-measure and AUC. Finally a more realistic experiment was performed considering the possibility of defining visually dubious cases as a third class, a situation often encountered in practice due to spurious colored pixels. In this case the results were expressed in terms of confusion matrices. All the features were previously normalized.

3   Results and Discussion

All the steps described in Sect. 2 were performed for the dataset composed of 600 erythrocytes that was mentioned earlier. Special attention was paid to building the (600 × 39) feature matrix of this dataset.

3.1   Feature Selection

Results of feature selection by using the two methods (filter and ranking) are shown in Table 1. Notice that despite in general the seven first features ranked by the Info-GainAttributeEva method differ from those selected by CfsSubsetEval, in both cases the pixels fraction in the three color spaces used were the first ones in the list, which confirms their usefulness.

Table 1. Results of the feature selection process.

CfsSubsetEval method		InfoGainAttributeEva, first 20 ranked features,			
1	Pixels fraction HSI	1	Pixels fraction HSI	11	Variance, H
2	Pixels fraction La*b*	2	Pixels fraction RGB	12	Variance, R
3	Pixels fraction RGB	3	Pixels fraction La*b*	13	Skewness, R
4	Variance, G	4	Skewness, G	14	Skewness, L
5	Skewness, R	5	Skewness, a*	15	Skewness, H
6	Skewness, B	6	Skewness, S	16	Kurtosis, H
7	Mean, R	7	Variance, S	17	Kurtosis, R
8		8	Variance, a*	18	Kurtosis, L
9		9	Variance, G	19	Skewness, B
10		10	Variance, L	20	Skewness, b

3.2 Classification

Classification results by using 7 features obtained through ranking and filtering, are shown in Tables 2 and 3, respectively. In this case the performance measures used in a 10-fold cross-validation experiment were CCR, Se, Sp, F-measure and AUC. Classification results using the whole set of features or the first 20 in the ranking list, not shown due to space limitations, were inferior to those shown in the tables. This suggests that there is some degree of noisy behavior in the discarded features whose deletion improved the classification results. Some variants of SVM and KNN were disregarded previously in favor of those included in the tables, which exhibited better behavior. Notice that the best performance was obtained by the J48 and Random Forest classifiers, which yielded results close to 100%.

Table 2. Results of classification with features selected through InfoGainAttributeEva ranker, using the 7 best ranked features and ten-fold cross-validation.

Classifier	CCR	Sp	Se	F-measure	AUC
SVM	95.13	0.85	0.99	0.97	0.93
RF	99.95	1.00	1.00	1.00	1.00
J48	100.00	1.00	1.00	1.00	1.00
LDA	94.27	0.84	0.99	0.96	0.96
KNN, K = 1	96.20	0.91	0.97	0.97	0.95
KNN, K = 3	96.18	0.90	0.98	0.97	0.96
NB	98.50	0.95	0.98	0.99	0.99

Notice that the pixels fraction should be theoretically zero for a normal erythrocyte. This could lead to the idea that classification of a cell is a trivial task. However, in practice some spurious colored pixels could appear and provoke an erroneous classification. This motivated here to employ a larger set of color-based features that could provide classification improvements in these cases, as well as introducing a third "dubious" class. Table 4 shows the confusion matrix obtained in the classification process when considering this third class. This is important because, differently to malaria diagnose in humans, when determining the infection rate in laboratory mice through microscopy analysis, which is the target of this work, dubious cells are usually disregarded by human analysts. Following the same procedure as before, in this case only four features (pixels fraction among them) were chosen by the filter selector. When using the J48 and RF classifiers, almost all dubious cases were correctly classified, all normal cells were still classified as normal and a small proportion of infected erythrocytes were classified as dubious.

Table 3. Results of classification, features selected by CfsSubsetEval (Greedy Stepwise), 10-fold cross-validation.

Classifier	CCR	Sp	Se	F-measure	AUC
SMO, con Puk	94.78	0.84	1.00	0.96	0.92
Random Forest	99.93	1.00	1.00	1.00	1.00
J48	100.00	1.00	1.00	1.00	1.00
LDA	91.45	0.74	1.00	0.94	0.97
KNN, K = 1	93.80	0.87	0.97	0.95	0.92
KNN, K = 3	94.82	0.86	0.99	0.96	0.95
Naive Bayes	98.67	0.96	1.00	0.99	0.99

Table 4. Confusion matrices from the classification results, considering a third class (dubious cases), J48 and RF classifiers.

J48, %CCR = 98.667					Random Forest, %CCR = 98,5		
Classified as →		a	b	c		a	b	c
Normal	a	400	0	0	a	400	0	0
Infected	b	0	159	7	b	0	159	7
Dubious	c	0	1	33	c	0	2	32

4   Conclusion

Automated classification of erythrocytes to detect the presence of *Plasmodium berghei* parasites is a very important task in anti-malarial drug development. This is currently an open area of research and this work presents two contributions in this area. The first one has been an improvement of the use of color information in the classification process by means of the definition of a new feature, called the *pixels fraction*, whose effectiveness was proved by two facts. Firstly, its values for the three color spaces involved in this study (RGB, HSI and La*b*) were selected among the most important features by both the filter and the ranker feature selectors used. Secondly, the classification results using the pixels fraction were remarkable. Several classifier algorithms were tested among which J48 and RF exhibited the best results in terms of the evaluated measures of performance. The second contribution was linking a set of image processing steps with the classifiers, to complete a computationally efficient way to classify erythrocytes in malaria studies. Future work will address an evaluation of the effectiveness of Convolutional Neural Networks classifiers for the application studied in this work.

Acknowledgment. The authors acknowledge the VLIR-UOS Project Cuba ICT Network for the financial support provided to this work.

References

1. World Health Organization. World Malaria Report (2017)
2. Arco, J.E., Górriz, J.M., Ramírez, J., et al.: Digital image analysis for automatic enumeration of malaria parasites using morphological operations. Expert Syst. Appl. **42**, 3041–3047 (2015). https://doi.org/10.1016/j.eswa.2014.11.037
3. Abdul-Nasir, A.S., Mashor, M.Y., Mohamed, Z.: Colour image segmentation approach for detection of malaria parasites using various colour models and k-means clustering. WSEAS Trans. Biol. Biomed. **10**(1), 41–55 (2013)
4. Tek, F.B., Dempster, A.G., Kale, I.: Parasite detection and identification for automated thin blood film malaria diagnosis. Comput. Vis. Image Underst. **114**, 21–32 (2010). https://doi.org/10.1016/j.cviu.2009.08.003
5. Das, D.K., Maiti, A.K., Chakraborty, C.: Automated system for characterization and classification of malaria-infected stages using light microscopic images of thin blood smears. J. Microsc. **257**, 238–252 (2015). https://doi.org/10.1111/jmi.12206
6. Di Ruberto, C., Dempster, A., Khan, S., Jarra, B.: Analysis of infected blood cell images using morphological operators. Image Vis. Comput. **20**, 133–146 (2002). https://doi.org/10.1016/S0262-8856(01)00092-0
7. Ajala, F.: Comparative analysis of different types of malaria diseases using first order features. Int. J. Appl. **8**, 20–26 (2015). https://doi.org/10.5120/ijais15-451297
8. Loddo, A., Di Ruberto, C., Kocher, M.: Recent advances of malaria parasites detection systems based on mathematical morphology. Sensors **18**(2), 513 (2018). https://doi.org/10.3390/s18020513
9. Chavan, S., Nagmode, M.: Malaria disease identification and analysis using image processing. Int. J. Latest Trends Eng. Technol. **3**(3), 218–223 (2014)
10. Walpole, R.E., Myers, R.H., Myers, S.L., Keying, E.Y.: Probability and Statistics for Engineers and Scientists: Pearson New International Edition. Pearson Higher Education, Upper Saddle River (2013)
11. Gonzalez, R.C., Woods, R.E.: Digital Image Processing, 3rd edn. Pearson Prentice Hall, Upper Saddle River (2008)
12. Jierong, C., Rajapakse, J.C.: Segmentation of clustered nuclei with shape markers and marking function. IEEE Trans. Biomed. Eng. **56**(3), 741–748 (2009). https://doi.org/10.1109/TBME.2008.2008635
13. Saikrishna, T.V., Yesubabu, A., Anandarao, A., Rani, T.S.: A novel image retrieval method using segmentation and color moments. Adv. Comput. **3**(1), 75–80 (2012). https://doi.org/10.5121/acij.2012.3106
14. Bouckaert, R., Frank, E., Hall, M., et al.: WEKA Manual for Version 3-6-13. CreateSpace Independent Publishing Platform (2015)

Automated Pneumothorax Diagnosis Using Deep Neural Networks

Tony Lindsey[1,2]($\boxtimes$), Rebecca Lee[2], Ronald Grisell[3],
Saul Vega[3], and Sena Veazey[3]

[1] Department of Biomedical Informatics, Stanford University, Palo Alto, CA, USA
[2] NASA Ames Research Center, Mountain View, CA, USA
{antonia.e.lindsey,rebecca.l.lee-1}@nasa.gov
[3] US Army Institute of Surgical Research, San Antonio, TX, USA
{ronald.d.grisell2.ctr,saul.j.vega.ctr,sena.r.veazey.ctr}@mail.mil

Abstract. Thoracic ultrasound can provide information leading to rapid diagnosis of pneumothorax with improved accuracy over the standard physical examination and with higher sensitivity than anteroposterior chest radiography. However, the clinical interpretation of a patient medical image is highly operator dependent. Furthermore, remote environments, such as the battlefield or deep-space exploration, may lack expertise for diagnosing certain pathologies. We have developed an automated image interpretation pipeline for the analysis of thoracic ultrasound data and the classification of pneumothorax events to provide decision support in such situations. Our pipeline consists of image preprocessing, data augmentation, and deep learning architectures for medical diagnosis. In this work, we demonstrate that robust, accurate interpretation of chest images and video can be achieved using deep neural networks. A number of novel image processing techniques were employed to achieve this result. Affine transformations were applied for data augmentation. Hyperparameters were optimized for learning rate, dropout regularization, batch size, and epoch iteration by a sequential model-based Bayesian approach. In addition, we utilized pretrained architectures, applying transfer learning and fine-tuning techniques to fully connected layers. Our pipeline yielded binary classification validation accuracies of 98.3% for M-mode images and 99.8% with B-mode video frames.

Keywords: Deep learning · Pneumothorax classification ·
Ultrasound · Transfer learning · Bayesian optimization

1 Motivation

Thoracic ultrasound is a noninvasive, readily-available imaging modality that supplements clinical examination in the evaluation of chest pathologies involving the pleural cavity [6]. In particular, radiologists have identified multiple sonographic

Supported by the Space Technology Mission Directorate.

© Springer Nature Switzerland AG 2019
R. Vera-Rodriguez et al. (Eds.): CIARP 2018, LNCS 11401, pp. 723–731, 2019.
https://doi.org/10.1007/978-3-030-13469-3_84

artifacts indicative of pneumothorax (PTX), such as sliding lung absence, reverberation, bar code pattern and transition point presence [1,7]. The expertise available for diagnosis and treatment of PTX may be curtailed in austere or remote locations, such as the battlefield or aboard a deep space exploration vehicle. Due to the limited resources in these environments, artificial intelligence can potentially play a significant role in augmenting clinically-relevant and interpretable medical patient diagnosis. A common occurrence on the battlefield is penetrating or blunt force thoracic injury that impairs the airways and may induce collapsed lung. Although PTX pathology is rare among astronauts, acute hypobaric decompression exposure is a plausible risk factor in microgravity and would present a significant challenge in both diagnosis and immediate treatment. Therefore, reliable interpretation capability for this life threatening condition is imperative for celeritous intervention. We hypothesized that machine learning is efficacious for accurate, early diagnosis of PTX in traumatic injuries, and accordingly developed an ultrasound medical imaging platform for thoracic pulmonary injury diagnosis. The objective of this study was to build and assess an automated computer model that provides near real-time binary PTX diagnosis of porcine pulmonary ultrasound images. The model's effectiveness was quantified by analyzing performance metrics on the train, validation and test sets.

An intelligent clinical decision support system is a powerful tool that aids clinical management of patient care and treatment for potentially life-threatening injuries as well as evaluating affected areas following medical procedures. Machine learning algorithms trained to distinguish pulmonary feature signs indicative of PTX were developed and examined. These algorithms, when applied to previously unseen test images, exhibited relatively high statistical performance metrics of sensitivity, specificity and positive predictive value. Our foremost algorithm is equipped to work with sonographic M-mode images and B-mode video frames of normal and pathological pulmonary function.

2 Dataset

Porcine clinical ultrasound data sources of pulmonary health were supplied by the US Army Institute of Surgical Research. Ground truth categorical binary labels for PTX pathology associated with 404 M-mode (209 bmp, 195 jpg) images and 420 B-mode mp4 video clips were provided to build automated medical diagnosis models. Baseline classification accuracy statistics as computed by the iFAST computerized assistant were 97.5% for M-mode images and 84.7% for B-mode video [8]. A Sonosite M-Turbo ultrasound machine captured all images and video loops. Cine-videos were 5 seconds in duration with a frequency of 40 frames per second. The associated linear transducer monitored 2nd intercostal space for each subject and acquired images utilizing settings: mechanical index 0.7, probe depth 4 cm, and soft tissue thermal index 0.1.

3   Methods

In recent years, deep learning has become a topic of much discussion and research due to its impressive pattern recognition discernment on large multi-class data sets, such as ImageNet. Transfer learning has mitigated computation time, improved accuracy and enhanced development of robust deep learning models. Consequently, computer-aided diagnosis via deep learning is now feasible, despite a lack of large medical database prevalence. We have developed a complete software pipeline for the medical diagnosis of PTX cases from ultrasound image products using convolutional neural networks. In addition to transfer learning, we have utilized various image preprocessing techniques, data augmentation, fine-tuning, and Bayesian optimization.

3.1   Data Retrieval

A total of 420 B-mode videos and 404 M-mode still images from eight female Yorkshire porcine models (*Sus scrofa*) with and without PTX, used in a previous study [8], were acquired for our experiments. The images were then split into 80% train and 20% test sets.

3.2   Preprocessing

Ultrasound images and videos contain artifacts, such as text, lines, tick marks and granular speckle noise. Such manifestations are detrimental for accurate image classification; thus, we developed a digital image processing module to filter such uninformative structures from the ultrasound data prior to developing a learning model. Figure 1 illustrates steps taken to properly clean the medical images.

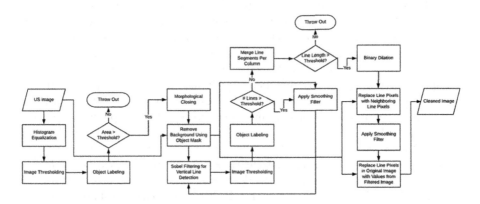

Fig. 1. Image preprocessing pipeline module component.

The initial step involved removing image frame background structures. This was accomplished by thresholding the image after histogram equalization was performed. The threshold was determined based on the histogram of intensity values taken from the histogram equalized image. Subsequently, morphological opening, closing, and hole-filling were employed in order to separate neighboring structures and to ensure complete capture of relevant structures. After this was accomplished, we sought to blend vertical line artifacts into the data. Vertical lines were localized using the x-direction Sobel filter. The line pixels were then replaced with neighboring image pixels and finally smoothed with a Gaussian filter.

3.3 Data Augmentation

The data augmentation module increased the number of images using affine transformations to improve network localization capability and generalized modeling. Augmentation of images that preserve collinearity and distance ratios was performed prior to model training. Each transform resulted in one additional output generated per image with arguments determining type of augmentation. Flips (horizontal, vertical), angled rotations, translational pixel shifts, regional zoom, random Gaussian noise and blurring by various amounts were implemented. Categorical parity was achieved by supplementing with a 3:1 ratio of negative to positive M-mode generated images. Our module extracted a 1.7:1 ratio of negative to positive frames from B-mode video to reach label parity. Finally, contrast-limited adaptive histogram equalization was applied to all images and frames for enhanced detection of subtle features.

3.4 CNN Architecture

Pretrained convolutional neural networks (CNN) are models that have been trained using a large dataset, e.g. ImageNet contains one million images with over a thousand categories. The resulting weighted connections from such a pretrained CNN were utilized to accelerate and transfer learned features with activations available in the penultimate fully connected layer. This particular layer was trained with our porcine dataset for the canonical case. Several deep neural network models were examined to determine optimal architecture for our application. A 16-layers deep model developed by Oxford University's Visual Geometry Group (VGG16) consistently recorded higher diagnostic accuracy than alternative architectures examined. The network consists of 3×3 convolutional layers stacked in increasing depth while reducing volume size by max pooling. Then two fully connected layers, each with 4,096 nodes, are followed by a softmax classifier. Increased convolution layers and improved utilization of internal network computing resources allow the network to learn deeper features. For example, the first layer might learn only edges while the deepest layer learns to interpret transition patterns differentiating movement at the pleural lines, such as seashore sign, a normal lung feature. The network contains convolution blocks with activation on the top layer that defines complex functional mappings between inputs and response variables, followed by batch normalization after each convolutional layer.

The max pooling sample-based discretization process was performed with kernel size 3×3 and stride 2. The network was then flattened to one dimension after the final convolutional block. Dropout of network layers was performed until reaching the dense five node output layer, which uses a softmax activation function to compute the probability of classification labels. Exponential and leaky rectified linear unit activation was applied with gradient value 0.01 to mitigate dead neuron bottlenecks during back-propagation. The network also used convolutional layer L_2 regularization to reduce model overfitting, binary cross-entropy computed error loss, and the Xavier method for initializing weights so that neuron activation functions begin in unsaturated regions. The inclusion of batch normalization improved validation set PTX classification accuracy on average 1.6% across both model modes.

3.5 Transfer Learning

Transfer learning based approaches were executed using VGG19, ResNet50 and VGG16 architectures pretrained with weights updated based on ImageNet visual database training. In order to achieve the transfer learning scenario, the last fully connected layer was removed followed by treating the remaining network components as a fixed feature extractor for the new train dataset [5]. The technique retains initial pretrained model weights and extracts image features via a final network layer. Additionally, further "fine-tuning" experiments were performed by extending backpropagation to the last four layers. Due to overfitting concerns, only four higher-level layer dimensions of the network were fine-tuned. Our experiments revealed that fine-tuning yielded improved performance over transfer learning alone.

3.6 Bayesian Optimization

A deep neural network's effectiveness is influenced by "higher-level" prior distribution properties of the model, such as complexity and learning rate. The optimal selection of these hyperparameters can be framed as a model validation loss minimization problem. Bayesian optimization is a probabilistic model-based approach for finding the minimum of any objective function that returns a real-value metric, such as CNN validation error with respect to hundreds of model architectures and hyperparameter choices. The approach has been applied to feed-forward computer vision models with greater efficiency than manual, random, or grid search in terms of better overall test set performance and decreased optimization time [3]. In our experiments, we optimized dropout rate, learning rate, decay rate, batch size, training epochs, and decay step size hyperparameters using the GPyOpt Python open-source library package [2].

After defining a search space for the optimization process, a posterior distribution function that best describes the objective function to optimize was constructed. As the number of observations grows, the posterior distribution improves and the algorithm becomes more certain of which regions in parameter space are worth exploring (see Fig. 2). A Gaussian process model with integrated expected improvement acquisition was used and initially explored 10 random points for the first model fit. This number was double the default value, but

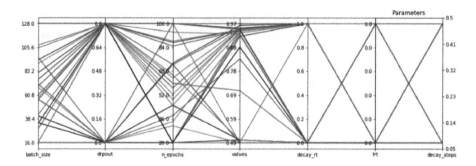

Fig. 2. Parallel coordinate multivariate visualization example across 7 dimensions for VGG16 model. Optimized configuration occurs at data cluster points: batch_size = 71, drpout = 0.0, n_epochs = 100, (accuracy) values = 0.97, decay_rt = 1.0, lrt = 1e-05, decay_steps = 0.05.

necessary since we are explored a complex and noisy 7 dimensional hyperparameter space. Consequently, the Gaussian process model fit required more time using CPU resources to complete than building and optimizing the neural network with a single GPU. Moreover, preliminary sampling of many random data points decreases risk of becoming trapped in local minima. The model explored a maximum of 100 points following the initial parameter sampling results (see Table 1).

Table 1. Gaussian process Bayesian optimization results for 3 evaluated models. Dataset labels were negative (normal lung) and positive (PTX). VGG16 models with stochastic gradient descent solvers (yellow highlight) produced the highest optimized accuracy.

M-mode Gaussian Process Hyperparameter Optimization									B-mode Gaussian Process Hyperparameter Optimization								
Pretrained Model	Dropout	Learning Rate	Decay Rate	Batch Size	Epochs	Loss	Accuracy	Solver	Pretrained Model	Dropout	Learning Rate	Decay Rate	Batch Size	Epochs	Loss	Accuracy	Solver
VGG16	0.2825	1.00e-03	0.9500	16	100	0.0886	0.9700	SGD	VGG16	0.3335	5.56e-04	0.4474	16	30	0.4450	0.8057	SGD
VGG16	0.2455	9.13e-04	0.8507	32	50	0.0534	0.9743	Adam	VGG16	0.2708	2.14e-04	0.9431	64	20	0.0313	0.9903	Adam
VGG16	0.3819	3.27e-04	0.6191	16	30	0.0654	0.9764	RMSProp	VGG16	0.5313	1.73e-04	0.9474	32	20	0.0437	0.9844	RMSProp
VGG19	0.1370	1.00e-03	0.9250	16	20	0.1486	0.9422	SGD	VGG19	0.0000	9.72e-04	1.0000	32	50	0.1861	0.9296	SGD
VGG19	0.0933	2.04e-04	0.5969	16	20	0.1045	0.9672	Adam	VGG19	0.0492	1.60e-04	0.7151	16	20	0.0717	0.9778	Adam
VGG19	0.5960	7.50e-04	0.8100	16	100	0.1106	0.9759	RMSProp	VGG19	0.4488	2.47e-04	0.9895	64	20	0.0588	0.9749	RMSProp
ResNet50	0.2790	9.89e-04	0.9782	32	100	0.4837	0.7195	SGD	ResNet50	0.5427	1.00e-03	0.7377	64	20	0.6706	0.6311	SGD
ResNet50	0.0640	1.00e-03	0.8750	128	50	0.3077	0.8608	Adam	ResNet50	0.7102	2.70e-04	0.9366	64	100	0.4778	0.7464	Adam
ReaNet50	0.5789	6.59e-04	0.8640	16	50	0.3790	0.8051	RMSProp	ResNet50	0.6979	2.22e-04	0.9591	32	30	0.4743	0.7561	RMSProp

4 Experiments and Results

4.1 Model Generation

The acquired medical imaging data products were partitioned into train, validation and test sets based using manifest supplied ground truth information. Train and validation sets were augmented using affine transformations that created synthetic images. The M-mode data partitioning resulted in 1,868 train images, 467 validation images, and 81 images for test. B-mode video was partitioned as 16, 212 train frames, 4, 053 validation frames, and 1, 013 images for test. The held-out test subsets were disjoint and analyzed only once by the trained models. The images were cropped to area size 224 × 224 and used as input data by a VGG16 architecture previously trained for generic classification tasks on Imagenet visual database. The model was then implemented with a high-level neural network API called Keras, running on the TensorFlow library backend for numerical computation using data flow graphs. An NVIDIA Tesla K80 accelerator hardware device with 12 GiB of GPU memory powered the training and a form of early stopping influenced estimation of optimal test set model epoch. Successive iterations guided construction of more complex model architectures fine-tuned for improved diagnostic interpretation of our pulmonary sonographic datasets.

4.2 Binary Model Classification

Three candidate model architectures were evaluated as binary diagnostic classifiers using porcine PTX medical images. The model validation performance was compared with baseline iFAST logistic regression classifier statistics. The VGG16 model achieved the best overall prediction accuracy. iFAST baseline statistical parameter results were outperformed for both M-mode images and B-mode video frames. Previously discussed image preprocessing, data augmentation, hyperparameter optimization and transfer learning techniques were used as a pipeline process for model generation. The results successfully achieved published state-of-the-art accuracy levels (see Table 2).

Table 2. B-mode: 4053 frames, 2028 true positives, 2 false negatives, 7 false positives, 2016 true negatives. M-mode: 467 images, 232 true positives, 1 false negative, 7 false positives, 227 true negatives.

Validation Data Set Statistics								
Modality	Model	Accuracy	95% CI	Sensitivity	Specificity	PPV	NPV	Kappa
B-mode	VGG16	0.9978	(0.9958, 0.9999)	0.9990	0.9965	0.9966	0.9990	0.9956
B-mode	iFAST	0.8465	(0.8076, 0.8803)	0.8566	0.8258	0.9102	0.7365	0.6617
M-mode	VGG16	0.9829	(0.9665, 0.9926)	0.9957	0.9701	0.9707	0.9956	0.9657
M-mode	iFAST	0.9753	(0.9551, 0.9881)	0.9818	0.9618	0.9818	0.9618	0.9436

5 Discussion and Future Directions

The VGG16 CNN models recorded a higher ratio of false positives to false negatives for both ultrasound modalities. Lichtenstein found that absence of lung sliding alone is very sensitive for PTX, but not specific in ICU patients due to large numbers of false positives [4]. Porcine subjects that are critically ill or exhibiting pulmonary contusions may cause similar interference and plausibly explain the observation.

There are multiple directions that can be pursued to bolster diagnostic results. Currently, several image processing techniques for contrast enhancement are being evaluated with the intent of improving precision and medical imaging feature discrimination. The model training dataset was class imbalanced, a property that negatively affects CNN classifier accuracy. Consequently, we plan to assess generative adversarial networks as an augmentation tool for restoring categorical parity and supplying images of superior quality. Our classifiers achieved 100% accuracy on test set images for both ultrasound modalities. However, more rigorous analysis of the models with larger datasets including human pulmonary structures is necessary and scheduled as a future activity.

6   Conclusion

In this paper we presented a fully automatic processing pipeline of thoracic ultrasound for PTX pathology classification. Data retrieval and preprocessing modules acquired ultrasound image products, removed artifacts and employed adaptive histogram equalization for improved image contrast. An initial sparse dataset was synthetically enhanced with pathology-preserving affine image transformations. Pretrained model weight utilization together with retraining selected fully connected layers improved generalizability and accelerated training time for PTX feature learning. Error analysis revealed that learning rate, optimizer type and image preprocessing were the greatest contributors to overall improved pipeline processing element performance. Bayesian optimization determined an optimal hyperparameter model configuration which outperformed random search according to our experiments.

Acknowledgements. We acknowledge Jose Salinas, PhD, chief of the Clinical Decision Support and Automation research at the US Army Institute of Surgical Research, which provided laboratory and biomedical device equipment support. We also acknowledge Maria Serio-Melvin, MSN, and Army Col. Shawn Nessen, DO, FACS, for their invaluable trauma patient clinical insights.

References

1. Alrajhi, K., Woo, M., Vaillancourt, C.: Test characteristics of ultrasonography for the detection of pneumothorax: a systematic review and meta-analysis. CHEST J. **141**, 703–708 (2012)
2. Authors, T.G.: GPyOpt: a Bayesian optimization framework in python (2016). http://github.com/SheffieldML/GPyOpt
3. Bergstra, J., Yamins, D., Cox, D.D.: Making a science of model search: hyperparameter optimization in hundreds of dimensions for vision architectures. In: Proceedings of the 30th International Conference on Machine Learning, vol. 28, no. 1, pp. 115–123, June 2013
4. Lichtenstein, D., Menu, Y.: A bedside ultrasound sign ruling out pneumothorax in the critically ill: lung sliding. Chest **108**(5), 1345–8 (1995)

5. Oquab, M., Bottou, L., Laptev, I., Sivic, J.: Learning and transferring mid-level image representations using convolutional neural networks. In: Proceedings of the IEEE Conference on Computer Vision and Pattern Recognition, pp. 1717–1724 (2014)
6. Qureshi, N., Rahman, N., Gleeson, F.: Thoracic ultrasound in the diagnosis of malignant pleural effusion. Thorax J. **64**, 139–143 (2009)
7. Stone, M.B.: Ultrasound diagnosis of traumatic pneumothorax. J. Emerg. Trauma Shock **1**(1), 19–20 (2008)
8. Summers, S.M., et al.: Diagnostic accuracy of a novel software technology for detecting pneumothorax in a porcine model. Am. J. Emerg. Med. **35**(9), 1285–1290 (2017)

Classification of Melanoma Images with Fisher Vectors and Deep Learning

Gastón Liberman[1,2], Daniel Acevedo[1,2(✉)], and Marta Mejail[1,2]

[1] Facultad de Ciencias Exactas y Naturales, Departamento de Computación,
Universidad de Buenos Aires, Buenos Aires, Argentina
`dacevedo@dc.uba.ar`
[2] Instituto de Investigación en Ciencias de la Computación (ICC),
CONICET-Universidad de Buenos Aires, Buenos Aires, Argentina

Abstract. The present work corresponds to the application of techniques of data mining and deep training of neural networks (deep learning) with the objective of classifying images of moles in 'Melanomas' or 'No Melanomas'. For this purpose an ensemble of three classifiers will be created. The first corresponds to a convolutional network VGG-16, the other two correspond to two hybrid models. Each hybrid model is composed of a VGG-16 input network and a Support Vector Machine (SVM) as a classifier. These models will be trained with Fisher Vectors (FVs) calculated with the descriptors that are the output of the convolutional network aforementioned. The difference between these two last classifiers lies in the fact that one has segmented images as input of the VGG-16 network, while the other uses non-segmented images. Segmentation is done by means of an U-NET network. Finally, we will analyze the performance of the hybrid models: the VGG-16 network and the ensemble that incorporates the three classifiers.

Keywords: Melanoma classification · Deep learning · Fisher vectors

1 Introduction

Melanoma corresponds to skin cancer that causes 75% of the deaths of all cutaneous cancer diseases. It is estimated that there are 160000 new cases of melanomas and 48000 deaths per year according to the World Health Organization. Dermatologists perform a biopsy in order to confirm the presence or not of a melanoma. This procedure increases its complexity when the person has a large number of suspicious moles, since it turns out to be an invasive process. In addition, the detection of melanoma is totally conditioned to the training of the dermatologist. Therefore it is important to have a tool that allows to classify the presence of a melanoma without invading the human body and whose effectiveness of classification is superior to the average of the dermatologists, reducing the subjectivity of human vision.

During the last years the use of automatic processes in image classification has increased notably and the classification of melanoma is not the exception.

© Springer Nature Switzerland AG 2019
R. Vera-Rodriguez et al. (Eds.): CIARP 2018, LNCS 11401, pp. 732–739, 2019.
https://doi.org/10.1007/978-3-030-13469-3_85

One of the first works corresponds to the use of the ABCD rule [1]; it is a formula computed from a combination of different characteristics of the mole: asymmetry, edges, color and diameter of the lunar. Depending on the score that is obtained, the injury is classified. Subsequently, the method of Menzies [2] has a set of characteristics related to a benign mole and another that are strictly related to a melanoma. Therefore, depending on the characteristics found in the lesion, it will be considered a malignant or benign mole. Another technique considers seven points (ELM7) [3] in which seven fundamental characteristics of the moles are evaluated. Regarding the segmentation of the lesion the Otsu method was mainly used [4]. Given these three methods and the Otsu method, different automatic melanoma detection systems were developed as can be seen in Table 1. The neural networks were used at first, and then migrated to other data mining techniques. However, from 2012/2013, with the increase in hardware speed, neural networks begin to be used again but this time with more layers. Then deep convolutional networks emerge, with a very good performance in the classification of images; today they determine the state-of-the-art in this field. In addition, papers were published independently in terms of classification and segmentation. Table 2 lists the most important works in this field.

The paper is organized as follows. Section 2 describes the methodology. Section 3 presents the experimental setup and results, and finally concluding remarks are given in Sect. 4.

Table 1. Previous background to the use of deep learning methods

References	Method	Segmentation	Classification
H Iyatomi et al. 2005. [5]	ABCD roule	Growing regions	Neural Networks
G. Capdehourat et al. 2009. [6]	ABCD roule and Argenziano method	Otsu method	Decision trees
J. F. et al. 2009. [7]	ABCD roule	Otsu method	Fusion of decision trees and bayesian networks
G. Leo et al. 2010. [8]	Argenziano method	Otsu method	Decision trees
D. Ruiz et al.2011. [9]	ABCD roule	Otsu method	Multilayer perceptron, bayesian classifier, KNN
G. Capdehourat et al. 2011 [10]	Clinic support	Otsu method	Adaboost of decision trees

2   Models Description

In the present work, images from the Buenos Aires Italian Hospital[1], ISIC Archive[2] and Dermnet[3] were used. The automatic classification of melanoma

---

[1] We thank Victoria Kowalckzuc MD from the Buenos Aires Italian Hospital for her medical advice and providing the mole images.

[2] https://isic-archive.com/.

[3] http://www.dermnet.com/images/Malignant-Melanoma.

Table 2. Reference works using deep learning methods

References	Type	Method
Xie, et al. 2016. [11]	Classification	SGNN + GA
O. Ronneberger, P. Fischer, and T. Brox et al. 2015. [12]	Segmentation	Convolution and UpSampling (UNET)
N. Codella, J. Cai, M. Abedini, R. Garnavi, A. Halpern, and J. R. Smith, et al. 2015. [13]	Classification	CNN, Sparse Coding and SVM as ensembler
Demyanov, et al. 2016. [14]	Classification	CNN 8 layers
J. Kawahara, et al. 2016. [15]	Classification	CNN converting fully connected layers into convolutional layers to extract features
A. Esteva, B. Kuprel, R. A. Novoa, J. Ko, S. M. Swetter, H. M. Blau, and S. Thrun et al. 2017. [16]	Classification	CNN - Inception V3
Zhen Yu et al. 2017. [17]	**Classification**	**Fisher Vectors, CNN and SVM as classifier**

using convolutional networks (CNNs) was investigated by Lecun et al. [18]. Even though they have a very good performance in the classification of the images, they have the disadvantage of being sensitive to the invariance of transformations: rotations, change of scale and orientation. One of the ways to solve this problem is to combine CNN (local descriptors) with Fisher vectors [19]. In this work we propose an ensemble of the hybrid system introduced by Yu et al. [17] with that of a CNN network to improve the performance of the resulting classifier. Our model includes an image preprocessing, a segmentation, and classification modules. In the preprocessing module the images were rescaled and Max-Constancy was applied [20]. Max-Constancy is a technique used to filter the effects of the light source that can produce a distortion in the image (similar to the filter that automatically performs the human being). The segmentation was performed by the UNET network [12]. In order to train the network that segments the lesion, only the images that come from the ISIC Archive source are used since they have the respective masks. The classification was solved by means of the VGG-16 network [21] trained on Imagenet[4]. In addition, heat maps were visualized on the classified images to evaluate the performance in the training phase of the VGG-16 network. The heat maps correspond to the areas that CNN uses to perform the aforementioned classification. The method that will be used to obtain these heat maps is GRAD-CAM [22].

For the CNN model, once the dataset was created data augmentation was carried out to increase the number of images in the training set. That is, they

---

[4] http://www.image-net.org.

were rotated at 0, 90 and 180∘, and zoomed at the same time, producing different versions of each image.

Fine-Tuning was performed for both the CNN model and the hybrid model. That is, the Fully-Connected layers were first removed and the images were passed through the convolutional layers. The output of the network will be called "Deep Features". Then with these descriptors a mini network formed by the last block of the CNN network and the Fully-Connected layers was trained. On the other hand, for the hybrid model, the descriptors of CNN were encoded in the Fisher vectors, which are the inputs of a SVM with the aim of training it and generating the hybrid classifier. The final classifier is an ensemble of the two hybrid models and a CNN model (VGG-16): the final class probability is estimated by the average of the probabilities provided by each model.

The **Classifier 1** is the simplest model. It is composed of a VGG-16 network pre-trained in IMAGENET, in which the weights of the last block of the network and of the last fully connected layer are changed based on the use of training and validation datasets. The Hybrid Model [17] (**Classifier 2**) takes as input the deep features which are reduced in dimentionality by Principal Component Analysis (PCA). A Gaussian mixture model (GMM) is first learned by sampled images from training set, and the Fisher Vector representation is calculated for each image. The number of PCA and GMM components are learned with the objective of maximizing the ROC curve in the Validation dataset. It should be noted that the input of this classifier corresponds to the descriptors that are the product of passing the images to the last convolutional layer of Classifier 1. This model is shown in Fig. 1. Then we have **Classifier 3** (see top chart in Fig. 3) that takes as input the descriptors of the segmented images for which we train a U-NET network with the objective of segmenting the images. Figure 2 shows an example of the application of the segmenter to an image; the grayscale area is not considered as part of the lesion for the segmenter. It should be noted that **Classifier 3** is similar to **Classifier 2** but the descriptors are obtained from the segmented images instead of the original images. Our proposed model, built by the **Ensemble** of the three classifiers, can be seen at the bottom of Fig. 3.

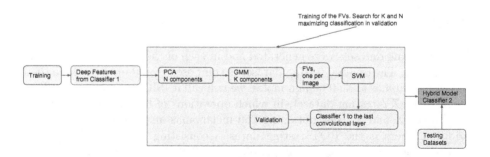

Fig. 1. Scheme of hybrid models

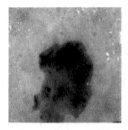

Fig. 2. Segmented melanoma with a gray scale outside the lesion

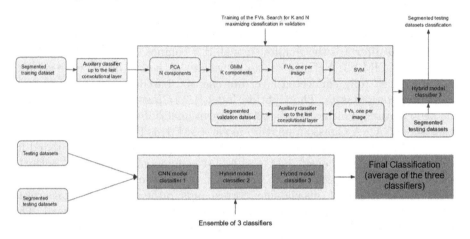

Fig. 3. Hybrid model and the ensemble of three classifiers

Finally, the **Ensemble** of classifiers is applied to the testing dataset (constituted by the original images as segmented). The segmentation in the testing file is necessary to obtain the input of **Classifier 3**, while the input of classifiers 1 and 2 are the original images.

3   Results

Several testing datasets were generated and in each of them the proposed model was applied. The original testing dataset is composed of 100 images where there are 50 melanomas and 50 benign moles, we will call it ISIC testing dataset. Then there is the XY testing dataset, in which operations of translations are carried out on the X and Y axes, obtaining 250 melanomas and 250 benign moles. In addition, there is the ROT testing dataset, consisting of rotation operations and reflection of the original images, obtaining 250 melanomas and 250 benign moles. Finally, we have the testing dataset of the Italian Hospital (HI) with lower quality images in relation to those used in the training and the ISIC, ROT and XY test dataset. As mentioned in the Sect. 2, Max-Constancy was applied to all the images. Experiments were executed on a machine with core-i7 6700 HQ microprocessor, 16 GB of memory and with a GTX 950m GPU.

The parameters that achieve an optimal performance in each model are shown in Table 3.

Table 3. Training parameters for each model.

Model	Deep learning								FV		SVM(RBF)	
	Optim. U-NET	Batch Size U-NET	Epochs U-NET	Learning Rate U-NET	Optim. VGG-16	Batch Size VGG-16	Epochs VGG-16	Learning Rate VGG-16	PCA (N)	GMM (K)	Cost (C)	Gamma
Classifier 1 (VGG-16)					SGD	16	100	10^{-5}				
Classifier 2 (Hybrid)					SGD	16	100	10^{-5}	40	20	100	$\frac{1}{\#\text{feat.}}$
Classifier 3 (Hybrid)	Adam	4	220	10^{-5}	SGD	16	100	10^{-5}	40	6	100	0.1

It should be noted that in the training of the VGG-16 network the learning rate is reduced (to half its value) if the same ROC value is obtained during 5 epochs. The binary cross-entropy is used as loss function while in the U-NET network, the Jaccard coefficient was used to measure the error between the predicted mask and the real mask.

Although with the Hybrid model the lowest performance is obtained, it is observed that when combined with Classifier 1, the best performance is obtained. The latter is visualized in Fig. 4 (a) in relation to (b) and (c) that represent Classifier 1 and the Hybrid model without segmentation (Classifier 2), respectively.

4   Conclusions

In this work we develop techniques of data mining and deep training of neural networks (deep learning) with the objective of classifying images of moles in 'Melanomas' or 'No Melanomas'. An ensemble of three classifiers is utilized for this purpose. The classifiers include a convolutional neural network (VGG-16), Fisher vector encoding, and image segmentation by means of a U-NET network. It was found that when the testing dataset is composed of images that are originated through translation operations on the X and Y axes of the original images, the performance in the CNN network decreases more rapidly than with the hybrid model. This is because the data augmentation performed in the training dataset, used in the training of the network, does not include the translation operation on the axes. We conclude that the CNN network is less invariant than the hybrid model for this type of operation, that was not applied in the data augmentation in the training dataset.

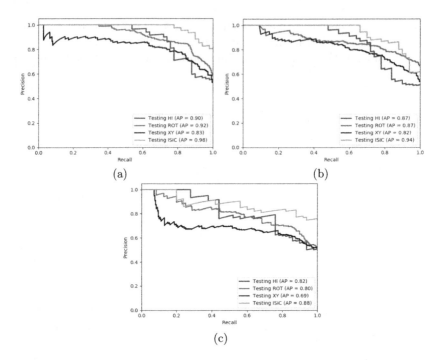

Fig. 4. (a): PR curves in the testing datasets (Ensemble model), (b): PR curves in testing datasets (Classifier 1) and (c): PR curves in testing datasets (Classifier 2).

References

1. Stolz, W., et al.: ABCD rule of dermatoscopy: a new practical method for early recognition of malignant melanoma. Eur. J. Dermatol. **4**, 521–527 (1994)
2. Menzies, S.W., Ingvar, C., Crotty, K.A., McCarthy, W.H.: Frequency and morphologic characteristics of invasive melanoma lacking specific surface microscopic features. Arch. Dermatol. **132**, 1178–1182 (1996)
3. Argenziano, G., Fabbrocini, G., Carli, P., De Giorgi, V., Sammarco, E., Delfino, M.: Epiluminescence microscopy for the diagnosis of doubtful melanocytic skin lesions comparison of the ABCD rule of dermatoscopy and a new 7-point checklist based on pattern analysis. Arch Dermatol. **134**, 1563–1570 (1998)
4. Otsu, N.: A threshold selection method from gray-level histograms. IEEE Trans. Syst. Man Cybern. **9**(1), 62–66 (1979)
5. Iyatomi, H., Oka, H., Hashimoto, M., Tanaka, M., Ogawa., K.: An internet based melanoma diagnostic system Toward the practical application. In: Proceedings of the 2005 IEEE Symposium on Computational Intelligence in Bioinformatics and Comp. Biology, pp. 1–4 (2005)
6. Capdehourat, G., Corez, A., Bazzano, A., Musé, P.: Pigmented skin lesions classification using dermatoscopic images. In: Bayro-Corrochano, E., Eklundh, J.-O. (eds.) CIARP 2009. LNCS, vol. 5856, pp. 537–544. Springer, Heidelberg (2009). https://doi.org/10.1007/978-3-642-10268-4_63

7. Alcon, J.F., et al.: Automatic imaging system with decision support for inspection of pigmented skin lesions and melanoma diagnosis. IEEE J. Sel. Top. Signal Process. **3**, 14–25 (2009)

8. Leo, G.D., Paolillo, A., Sommella, P., Fabbrocini, G.: Automatic diagnosis of melanoma: a software system based on the 7-point check-list. In: HICSS (2010)

9. Ruiz, D., et al.: A decision support system for the diagnosis of melanoma: a comparative approach. Expert. Syst. Appl. **38**, 15217–15223 (2011)

10. Capdehourat, G., et al.: Toward a combined tool to assist dermatologists in melanoma detection from dermoscopic images of pigmented skin lesions. Pattern Recognit. Lett. **32**, 1–10 (2011)

11. Xie, F., Fan, H., Yang, L., Jiang, Z., Meng, R., Bovik, A.: Melanoma classification on dermoscopy images using a neural network ensemble model. IEEE Trans. Med. Imaging **36**, 849–858 (2016)

12. Ronneberger, O., Fischer, P., Brox, T.: U-net: convolutional networks for biomedical image segmentation arXiv:1505.04597 (2015)

13. Codella, N., Cai, J., Abedini, M., Garnavi, R., Halpern, A., Smith, J.R.: Deep learning, sparse coding, and SVM for melanoma recognition in dermoscopy images. In: Zhou, L., Wang, L., Wang, Q., Shi, Y. (eds.) MLMI 2015. LNCS, vol. 9352, pp. 118–126. Springer, Cham (2015). https://doi.org/10.1007/978-3-319-24888-2_15

14. Demyanov, S., et al.: Classification of dermoscopy patterns using deep convolutional neural networks. In: IEEE 13th ISBI (2016)

15. Kawahara, J., et al.: Deep features to classify skin lesions. In: ISBI, pp. 1397–1400 (2016)

16. Esteva, A., et al.: Dermatologist-level classification of skin cancer with deep neural networks. Nature **542**(7639), 115 (2017)

17. Yu, Z., et al.: Hybrid dermoscopy image classification framework based on deep CNN and Fisher vector. In: 14th IEEE ISBI, Melbourne, Australia (2017)

18. Lecun, Y., et al.: Gradient-based learning applied to document recognition. Proc. IEEE **86**(11), 2278–2324 (1998)

19. Sanchez, J., et al.: Image classification with the fisher vector: theory and practice. IJCV **105**, 222–245 (2013)

20. Gijsenij, A., et al.: Computational color constancy: survey and experiments. IEEE Trans. Image Process. **20**, 2475–2489 (2011)

21. Simonyan, K., Zisserman, A.: Very deep convolutional networks for large-scale image recognition. arXiv 1409.1556 (2014)

22. Selvaraju, R., et al.: Grad-CAM: why did you say that? Visual explanations from deep networks via gradient-based localization (2016)

Automatic Identification of DBS Parameters from the Volume of Tissue Activated (VTA) Using Support Vector Machines

Robinson Aguilar[1], Hernán Darío Vargas-Cardona[1(✉)], Andrés M. Álvarez[1], Álvaro A. Orozco[1], and Piedad Navarro[2]

[1] Department of Electric Engineering, Universidad Tecnológica de Pereira, Pereira, Colombia
{hernan.vargas,malvarez,aaog}@utp.edu.co
[2] Corporación Instituto de Administración y Finanzas (CIAF), Pereira, Colombia
investigacion@ciaf.edu.co

Abstract. Deep brain stimulation (DBS) is a neurosurgical method to treat symptoms of Parkinson' disease. Several computational models, mostly based on finite element method (FEM) have been employed to describe the interaction of electromagnetic waves in brain tissues during DBS. Also, for planning the DBS, it is necessary to estimate with precision the neural response generated by electrodes in the stimulated region, what it is known as volume of tissue activated (VTA). However, this estimation should consider the intrinsic properties of each patient, therefore DBS parameters must be adjusted individually. In this work, we propose a 3D interaction module for estimating the DBS parameters (amplitude, contacts, among others) from a desired VTA using support vector machines (inverse problem). Also, we developed an interactive application for analyzing the VTA generated by DBS in the subthalamic nucleus (STN) combining medical imaging and non-rigid deformation models. This module is a part of the NEURONAV software, previously developed for clinical support during postoperative therapy of neuromodulation performed in Colombian PD patients. Outcomes show that it is possible to estimate with high accuracy the DBS parameters for different subjects.

1 Introduction

Deep brain stimulation (DBS) is a well-established treatment for Parkinson's disease, dystonia and essential tremor [1]. To investigate the therapeutic effects and undesirable side effects, it is necessary to estimate the neural response of brain tissue during DBS, known as volume of tissue activated (VTA) [2]. Currently, DBS devices operate in an open loop, where the stimulation parameters are configured in the surgical planning. For this reason, patients are stimulated with fixed values of amplitude, frequency and other stimulation parameters previously

© Springer Nature Switzerland AG 2019
R. Vera-Rodriguez et al. (Eds.): CIARP 2018, LNCS 11401, pp. 740–747, 2019.
https://doi.org/10.1007/978-3-030-13469-3_86

set by neurosurgeon [3]. Therefore, the selection of DBS-parameters performed by the neurosurgeon is an empirical and complex process that requires great skill and clinical experience, and for some cases the therapeutic results are not optimal [4,5].

Nowadays, the methodology for programming the DBS device is based on changing the amplitude and frequency until some symptoms disappear. However, this procedure may cause side effects and a rapid deterioration of device batteries [6,7]. To avoid side effects, it is necessary to make a good adjustment of DBS-parameters and determine the VTA previously defined by the neurosurgeon [8]. Some procedures have been proposed in literature to deal with this issue. For example, in [9], a methodology is proposed to clarify the mechanism of DBS by using computer simulations and finite element method (FEM). This first attempt allowed to relate the VTA with therapeutic results in PD patients. Nevertheless, it did not resolve the inverse problem: to find optimal parameters from a desired VTA. Then, the authors of [10] developed an interesting approach to find optimal parameters of DBS through detailed models of electrode-tissue interface, achieving interesting clinical outcomes and proving that optimal parameters can be found by analyzing the VTA. On the other hand, due to technological advances, it is possible to collate information on electrode positions with clinical effects, providing a visual representation of the electrical field related to the stimulated nucleus. It allows to incorporate patient-specific computer models to customize DBS parameter settings for each patient. Any examples include frameworks closed-source such as: the Boston Scientific Guide DBS system, Medtronic Optimise system and Renishaw NeuroInspire system [5,11], and frameworks open-source such as: DBSproc [12]. However, these systems do not identify with acceptable accuracy the parameters of neuromodulation in the treatment of Parkinson's disease. For this reason, the VTA analysis and optimal parameters of DBS are research topics with considerable gaps, because there are not significant studies regarding the inverse problem of the DBS.

The proposed methodology is performed from initial settings of the DBS, coupled with medical images obtained in the surgical procedure and brain atlas established in a previous work within the Research Group in Automatics of the Universidad Tecnológica Pereira, called NEURONAV [1]. The main objective is to estimate configuration parameters in the DBS device during postoperative therapy of PD patients. To do this, WE DEVELOPED A GRAPHICAL MODEL WITH DEFORMABLE REGISTRATION OF MEDICAL IMAGES, WHERE THE NEURO-SURGEON CAN SET THE DESIRED VTA to achieve good therapeutic results and minimal side effects in patients with PD. Then, the proposed system based on a support vector machine (SVM) defines a configuration of the DBS device that adjusts the desired electrical propagation. This proposal focuses on the solution of the inverse problem, which consists of estimating and setting the stimulation parameters for DBS electrodes (voltage/current, electrode impedance, frequency, pulse widths, and contacts), given a previous VTA set by the neurosurgeon.

2   Materials and Methods

2.1   Toolboxes

To build the graphic module, we use open source tools written in c++. To achieve an interactive tool where the neurosurgeon can identify, visualize and manipulate the VTA, we employed the visualization tool kit VTK[1]. To build a graphical user interface compatible with VTK and 3D graphics support via OpenGL, we used FLTK[2] toolkit that incorporates a GLUT emulation. Finally, to simulate the geometric variations of the VTA, we use the GetFEM[3] tool, which offers a framework for solving potentially coupled systems of linear and nonlinear partial differential equations with the finite element method (FEM). GetFEM is interconnected with languages such as python and allows to solve problems in 1D, 2D and 3D.

2.2   Surface Reconstruction

The 3D representation of VTA is done with tetrahedral mesh elements using the Delaunay method. This technique connects polygons to plot the surface of the VTA previously estimated with a GetFEM. In the bipolar configuration, it is necessary to take into account the electrode dimensions to decide which are the points corresponding to the active contacts that interact with the VTA surface. Figure 1 illustrates the pipeline of surface reconstruction inside the graphical module. The data objects (source) represent and provide access to data, and the process objects (filter) operate over data objects. Here, the connections are made using the methods setInput()/getOutput(). Once the model is built, the execution of the pipeline must be carefully controlled. In this regard, VTK uses a process of implicit distributed update.

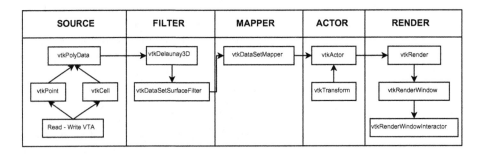

Fig. 1. Pipeline for the reconstruction of a VTA previously estimated with GetFEM.

---

[1] http://www.vtk.org/.

[2] http://www.fltk.org/.

[3] http://download.gna.org/getfem/html/homepage/.

2.3 Geometric Variations

The typical procedure to represent a point in a 3D environment is through cartesian vectors of three elements, $\mathbf{p} = (x, y, z)$. The geometric transformations are represented in homogeneous coordinates by a 4×4 transformation matrix denominated $\mathbf{T}$, such that homogeneous coordinates of a point $\mathbf{P} = (x, y, z, 1)$, becomes geometrically at point $\mathbf{P}' = (x', y', z', 1)$ with the following operation $\mathbf{P}' = \mathbf{T} \times \mathbf{P}$, known as affine transformation:

$$\begin{bmatrix} x' \\ y' \\ z' \\ 1 \end{bmatrix} = \begin{bmatrix} x & yx & zx & 1 \\ xy & y & zy & 1 \\ xz & yz & z & 1 \\ 0 & 0 & 0 & 1 \end{bmatrix} \begin{bmatrix} x \\ y \\ z \\ 1 \end{bmatrix}$$

To find the area of stimulation expected within the STN region, we apply the affine transformation to the actor object for simulating the neural activation desired by the neurosurgeon. Accordingly, we perform a transformation operation (vtkTransform) over the object (vtkActor). To apply a scaling matrix on the actor object, we center the object in the coordinates (0, 0, 0) of the render window.

2.4 Parameters Estimation with Machine Learning

We train a set of machine learning algorithms using 1000 isotropic VTA models validated by the medical team of *The institute of epilepsy and Parkinson of the eje cafetero-Neurocentro, Colombia*. Specifically, we train a SVM-regressor for the amplitude and pulse width. For active contacts $(C_0 - C_3)$ we employ SVM classifiers. In this context, the labels $\mathbf{y}$ are the parameter values. While, the numeric flag of VTA (0 refers to non-VTA and 1 is VTA positive) concatenated with the spatial coordinates correspond to the training features $\mathbf{X}$.

2.5 Experimental Setup

For the graphical module of VTA analysis, we use the Universidad Tecnologica de Pereira (DB-UTP) database. It contains recordings of MRI studies (T1 and T2 sequences with $1 \times 1 \times 1$ mm^3 voxel size) from four patients with Parkinson's disease. The STN region in MRI studies was labeled for specialists of *Neurocentro*. We use the DBS electrodes 3387 and 3389 manufactured by Medtronic[4] (Medtronic, Inc. USA). Both electrodes consist of four contacts with a length of 1.5 mm separated by 1.5 mm (3387) and 0.5 mm (3389). The diameter is 1.27 mm and the contact area has 6 mm^2. Each contact can be used as anode or cathode in bipolar electrode configuration or as cathode in monopolar stimulation setting [13]. The electric field was simulated in the neighboring of STN, with an electric potential in a range of 0.5 V to 10.5 V with steps of 0.5 V, and pulse width of

---

[4] http://professional.medtronic.com/pt/neuro/dbs-md/prod.

$60\,\mu s$ to $450\,\mu s$ (steps of $30\,\mu s$). Active contacts are C_0, C_1, C_2, C_3. GetFEM is used to solve specific VTA models for each patient.

Figure 2 shows the flow diagram to run experiments with isotropic models. First, it is performed the data acquisition: medical imaging, VTA points, and the database for training the learning algorithms (to identify the stimulation parameters for a new geometric variation of the VTA). Second, we observe the processes performed to modify interactively the VTA: reconstruction of the surface and affine transformation used for the deformation of the VTA. Finally, we have the output data (desired VTA) and the corresponding parameter values given by the SVMs.

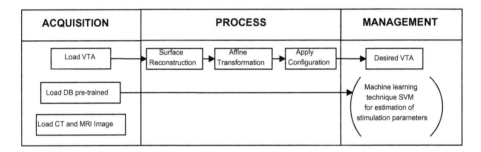

Fig. 2. Flow diagram for identifying DBS parameters given a desired VTA (inverse problem solution).

3   Experimental Results and Discussion

3.1   Parameters Estimation

In Table 1, we show accuracy results for the DBS parameters estimated with the SVM. The dataset for training the SVM has 1000 VTA models. We employ a hold-out validation scheme, where 70% of data is used for training, and 30% is kept for validation. We repeat the experiment 100 times, with a random selection of training and validation samples. These results show high accuracy to identify the parameters for a desired VTA. Therefore, the inverse solution problem can be solved with machine learning techniques.

In Fig. 3, we observe a simulated monopolar VTA given a geometric variation desired by a neurosurgeon. This procedure allows to control and visualize the neural activation, reducing side effects and minimizing the battery consumption of the implanted pulse generator. The electrode is located within the subthalamic region and the first contact is active and it stimulates a large section of the STN.

Table 1. Table of results of the accuracy in estimating the parameters.

Parameter	Accuracy
Amplitude	95,3 ± 4,1 %
Pulse width	96,9 ± 3,1 %
C_0	88,13 ± 1,95 %
C_1	84,67 ± 2,11 %
C_2	88,20 ± 1,99 %
C_3	89,13 ± 1,73 %

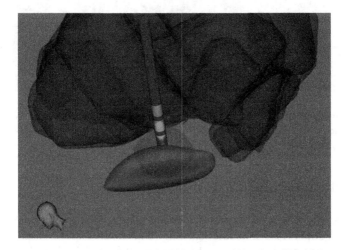

Fig. 3. VTA monopolar within the STN for a desired configuration. The blue cylinder is the stimulating electrode (Medtronic-3387) with four contacts (green areas), the VTA corresponds to the red surface and the STN is the cyan colored structure. (Color figure online)

3.2 Surface Reconstruction and Geometric Variations

Best computational performance of the module with an affine transformation to the vtkActor in the render window. We can see in Fig. 4 the points cloud which returns the GetFEM software, which constitutes a discrete estimation of VTA. For a simulation neural response generated by DBS in the brain, the Laplace equation describes the mathematical model. For this reason, a partial differential equation must be solved with finite element method. Once, the VTA points (spatially distributed) are estimated with GetFEM, we transform them in a surface depending of the type of stimulation (monopolar or bipolar).

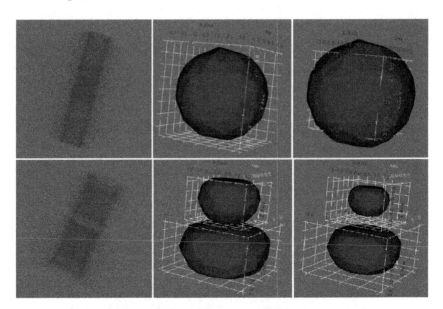

Fig. 4. Monopolar and bipolar VTA, (A) Point cloud, which returns GetFEM. (B) Reconstruction delaunay as from the point cloud. (C) Geometric variations on applying affine transformation vtkActor.

4   Conclusions and Future Work

In this work, we presented an interactive module for DBS parameters identification through supervised machine learning. The estimation of these parameters depends on a geometric variation of isotropic VTA models given by a neurosurgeon. This is known as the inverse problem of DBS. This module is integrated to the previously developed software: NEURONAV [1].

Results demonstrated that inverse problem can be successfully solved using machine learning methods. Also, the geometric variations allows to estimate monopolar and bipolar configurations of parameters. In addition, The module allows to visualize the variations of VTA without considerable delays. This property could be used in DBS therapy for controlling therapeutic outcomes and side effects in PD patients.

Three main tasks are established as future works: First, the proposed scheme can be used with anisotropic models studies using diffusion tensor imaging (DTI) of each patient. Second, to apply volume reduction techniques for generating representative models instead of a manual manipulation of the VTA. Third, to use codifications of GPU through the API of CUDA for improving processing times.

Acknowledgments. Authors thank to the *Corporación Instituto de Administración y Finanzas (CIAF)* for funding this research.

References

1. Padilla, J.B., et al.: NEURONAV: a tool for image-guided surgery - application to Parkinson's disease. In: Bebis, G., et al. (eds.) ISVC 2015. LNCS, vol. 9474, pp. 349–358. Springer, Cham (2015). https://doi.org/10.1007/978-3-319-27857-5_32
2. Schmidt, C., Flisgen, T., van Rienen, U.: Efficient computation of the neural activation during deep brain stimulation for dispersive electrical properties of brain tissue. IEEE Trans. Magn. **52**, 1 (2015)
3. Volkmann, J., Moro, E., Pahwa, R.: Basic algorithms for the programming of deep brain stimulation in Parkinson's disease. Mov. Disord. **21**, S284–S289 (2006)
4. Mikos, A., et al.: Patient-specific analysis of the relationship between the volume of tissue activated during DBS and verbal fluency. Neuroimage **54**, S238–S246 (2011)
5. Green, A.L., Aziz, T.Z.: Steering technology for deep brain stimulation. Brain **137**, 1854–1856 (2014)
6. Maks, C.B., Butson, C.R., Walter, B.L., Vitek, J.L., McIntyre, C.C.: Deep brain stimulation activation volumes and their association with neurophysiological mapping and therapeutic outcomes. J. Neurol. Neurosurg. Psychiatry **80**, 659–666 (2009)
7. Benabid, A.L., et al.: Chronic electrical stimulation of the ventralis intermedius nucleus of the thalamus as a treatment of movement disorders. J. Neurosurg. **84**, 203–214 (1996)
8. Butson, C.R., McIntyre, C.C.: Tissue and electrode capacitance reduce neural activation volumes during deep brain stimulation. Clin. Neurophysiol. **116**, 2490–2500 (2005)
9. Åström, M., Johansson, J.D., Wardell, K.: Modeling and simulation of electric fields generated by brain stimulation electrodes: the effect of cystic cavities in the basal ganglia. In: Proceedings of the 2nd International IEEE EMBS Conference on on Neural Engineering, pp. 198–201. IEEE (2005)
10. McIntyre, C.C., Butson, C.R., Maks, C.B., Noecker, A.M.: Optimizing deep brain stimulation parameter selection with detailed models of the electrode-tissue interface. In: 28th Annual International Conference of the IEEE Engineering in Medicine and Biology Society, EMBS 2006, pp. 893–895. IEEE (2006)
11. Shamir, R.R., Dolber, T., Noecker, A.M., Frankemolle, A.M., Walter, B.L., McIntyre, C.C.: A method for predicting the outcomes of combined pharmacologic and deep brain stimulation therapy for Parkinson's disease. In: Golland, P., Hata, N., Barillot, C., Hornegger, J., Howe, R. (eds.) MICCAI 2014. LNCS, vol. 8674, pp. 188–195. Springer, Cham (2014). https://doi.org/10.1007/978-3-319-10470-6_24
12. Lauro, P.M., et al.: DBSproc: an open source process for DBS electrode localization and tractographic analysis. Hum. Brain Mapp. **37**, 422–433 (2016)
13. Åström, M.: Modeling, simulation, and visualization of deep brain stimulation (2011)

Interactive Border Contour with Automatic Tracking Algorithm Selection for Medical Images

André V. Leinio, Lucas Lellis$^{(\boxtimes)}$, and Fábio A. M. Cappabianco

GIBIS, Universidade Federal de São Paulo, São José dos Campos, SP, Brazil
lellis@unifesp.br

Abstract. Contour tracking methods such as Live Wire and Riverbed have been widely used for several medical imaging applications such as tissue and tumor segmentation. Several variations of these methods have been proposed, but none of them is better than the others for all kind of tasks and image modalities. In this paper, we propose an interactive framework for medical image segmentation with four different contour tracking methods with an intuitive interface for visualizing and choosing the best option for each contour segment. The framework also includes a classifier which indicates the most appropriated method in both automatically and semi-automatically fashions. Our experiments employ a robot user which simulates the human behavior and was able to indicate the correct method for 67% of the segments.

Keywords: Contour tracking · Machine learning · Image processing

1 Introduction

Image segmentation consists of recognizing and delineating the edges of a particular object contained in an image. Several approaches accomplish this task employing distinct strategies such as region-growing or clustering algorithms [10]. Human interaction during the segmentation or database training are often required in order to achieve better results.

Within the medical area, image segmentation is key to an efficient diagnosis and treatment of diseases [14,15]. It may be used to isolate or highlight objects contained in an image of interest such as organs, tissues, and tumors. For that purpose, it is mandatory to provide an user-friendly interface that enables the specialist to visualize desired information without understanding unnecessary technical concepts employed by image processing and analysis techniques.

This work presents an implementation of a user-friendly framework with an interface in which a specialist may perform segmentations using four different kinds of contour tracking methods: Live-wire, Riverbed, Lazywalk, and straight lines. It runs all implemented methods simultaneously, allowing the user to select the most suitable for each segment. A classifier suggests the best method as the default, based on the contour segment features. Quantitative validation of the proposed framework employs a robot user which simulates human interaction.

© Springer Nature Switzerland AG 2019
R. Vera-Rodriguez et al. (Eds.): CIARP 2018, LNCS 11401, pp. 748–756, 2019.
https://doi.org/10.1007/978-3-030-13469-3_87

2   Technical Background

2.1   Image Foresting Transform - IFT

The Image Foresting Transform (IFT) [8] is a methodology extensively used for implementing several image processing operators including image segmentation [4–7]. In its context, the image is defined as a weighted graph $\mathcal{G} \in \{V, E, w\}$ where V is a set of vertexes composed by each pixel, and E is an edge set defined based on a binary adjacency relation A between pairs of pixels. $w : E \to \Re$ is a function which assigns a weight value for each edge $e \in E$. The goal is to compute an optimum path forest from $\mathcal{G}$ by apply a generalized version of Dijkstra algorithm [3] with multiple source vertexes defined by a set of seeds $S \subset V$ and a smooth path propagation function $f(\pi)$ for all paths $\pi = \{v_0, v_1, ..., v_n\} \in \Pi$, $v_i \in V$, with $e_{ij} = \langle v_i, v_{i+1} \rangle \in E$. This way, seeds compete among themselves for the most connected pixels in the entire image domain according to a greed path-propagation function.

The most commonly used adjacency relations are symmetric defining edges for small neighborhoods around each vertex in the image domain, so that $e_{ij}, e_{ji} \in E$ if and L2 distance function $d(v_i, v_j) \le \alpha$, for a small value of constant α.

The path propagation function has two components: an initial value for trivial paths of only a single vertex and a propagation value for extended paths during the algorithm computation. Equations 1 and 2 contain two commonly used functions for several image processing problems. In these equations, δ is an initial value assigned to a trivial path $\{v\}$, $\pi \cdot v$ is the concatenation of a vertex v to the end of a path π.

$$f_{sum}(\langle v \rangle) = \delta$$
$$f_{sum}(\pi \cdot v_j) = f_{sum}(\pi) + w(\langle v_i, v_j \rangle) \tag{1}$$

$$f_{max}(\langle v \rangle) = \delta$$
$$f_{max}(\pi \cdot v_j) = max\{f_{max}(\pi),\ w(\langle v_i, v_j \rangle)\} \tag{2}$$

Algorithm 1 describes IFT execution. The inputs are an image I, an adjacency relation A, a path propagation function f, and a seed set S. The outputs are a predecessor expressed as a function of the vertexes $P : V \to V, nil$ and a value map given by function $C : V \to \Re$. The predecessor map stores the predecessor of each vertex in the optimum forest, that is, if $P(v_i) = v_j$, v_j is the predecessor of v_i, and if $P(v_i) = nil$, v_i is a root of the forest. The value map contains the optimum value of the path arriving at each vertex. The auxiliary structures are a priority queue Q that sorts the path values in non-decreasing order and the temporary variables $prop\_val$, $status$, v_i, and v_j.

In line 1, the initial graph is constructed based on the image dimension and the adjacency relation. Then, in the first loop (lines 2–8) the seeds are distinguished from the other vertexes. $\delta = 0$ is assigned to all seed vertex values (line 4) and $\delta = +\infty$ for the others (line 8). Also, all seeds are inserted into the priority queue (line 5) and their predecessor function is set to nil (line 6). Finally, in the second loop (lines 19–17), the paths are propagated and the optimum-path forest generated. The loop ends when the priority queue is empty, meaning that all vertexes have been processed (line 9). A vertex v_i with minimal value is removed from the queue (line 10) and propagates its path to each adjacent v_j (line 11). The path is only propagated if the proposed value (computed in line 12) is lower than its current value (line 13). In this case, the path value and predecessor of v_j are updated (lines 16 and 17) and the conquered pixel is inserted into the queue (line 15) if it was not there yet (test in line 14).

Algorithm 1 – IFT algorithm

INPUT: Image I; adjacency rel. A; seed set S; path prop. function f.
OUTPUT: Predecessor function P; Path Value function C.
AUXILIARY: Priority queue Q; variables $prop\_val$, $status$, v_i, v_j.

1. *Generate graph* $\mathcal{G} = (V, E)$ *from* I, A
2. **For each** $v_i \in V$
3. | **If** $v_i \in S$ **then**
4. | | $C(v_i) \leftarrow 0$
5. | | $Q.insert(v_i)$
6. | | $P(v_i) = nil$
7. | **Else**
8. | | $C(v_i) \leftarrow +\infty$
9. **While** $Q! = \emptyset$
10. | $v_i \leftarrow Q.remove\_minimum()$
11. | **For each** v_j $A(v)$
12. | | $prop\_val = f(\pi_{v_i} \cdot \langle v_i, v_j \rangle)$
13. | | **If** $prop\_val < C(v_j)$ **then**
14. | | | **If** $C(v_j) == \infty$ **then**
15. | | | | $Q.insert(v_j)$
16. | | | $P(v_j) = v_i$
17. | | | $V(v_j) = prop\_val$

2.2   Contour Tracking Algorithms

Live Wire (LW) is a contour tracking technique which is most commonly used in a semi-automatic fashion [9]. It may be implemented using the IFT algorithm by utilizing the path-propagation function f_sum in Eq. 1. The edge weight function w is defined by the complement of the gradient (e.g. Sobel, Canny) of the image. The seed set consists of vertexes (or pixels) on the contour to be delineated. Finally, the adjacency relation is normally symmetric with $d(v_i, v_j) \leq \sqrt{2}$. After running the IFT algorithm, the contour is given by walking path vertexes backwards using the predecessor map P. The same strategy is also employed by Riverbed (RB) contour tracking technique [12], which simulates the water flow going down a riverbed. The only difference of RB with respect to LW is the usage of f_{l_max} in Eq. 3 as the path-propagation function.

Because of the summation in f_sum function, LW is robust to the presence of weak contours with small discontinuities and it tends to favor shorter tracks.

RB, on the other hand, will follow paths with local maximal value despite of its origins. As a result, RB is capable of following strong contours with unlimited length, but it does not have a good behavior in the presence of small gaps or high-frequency noise.

$$f_{l\_max}(\langle v \rangle) = \delta$$
$$f_{l\_max}(\pi \cdot v_j) = f_{max}(\pi) \tag{3}$$

Lazywalk (LZ) algorithm was proposed to estimate the level of water bodies in Remote Sensing Images [1]. It employs the path propagation function f_{max} in Eq. 2. The idea of this method is to overcome the weakness of both the LW and the RB. Nevertheless, LZ fails to follow paths with several discontinuities.

Most of the times, the contour detected by these algorithms is not acceptable to a variety of applications. The solution used since the first implementation of LW was to track sections of the contour running the algorithm more than once. The final pixel of the first execution is the seed of the second. In this context, seeds are called anchors. Figure 1 shows an example of the execution of LW, RB, and LZ to track the external contour of the brain in a magnetic resonance image.

2.3   Supervised Classifiers

Descriptors. Image descriptors are used in machine learning algorithms for a series of distinct tasks such as image classification and content based image retrieval [11]. Descriptors summarize important information related to color, texture, intensity, and shape from images allowing a faster and more comprehensive evaluation of their content. As medical images such as computed tomography, ultrasound, and magnetic resonance only have one color channel, the focus of this paper will be on intensity, texture and shape descriptors.

Quantized image histogram is an intensity descriptor which removes all spatial distribution information and summarizes the frequency in which intensities appear in the image. A vector bin stores the quantity of pixels in intensity ranges. If the histogram is normalized, each bin contains the probability of the intensity range for a pixel chosen randomly.

Texture based descriptors may be derived from statistics by computing the moments of the histogram given by Eq. 4, where L is the number of bins of the histogram, z_i is the intensity of the pixel, $p(z_i)$ is the probability of intensity z_i, and n is the number of the moment. For instance, with $n = 1$ Eq. 4 computes the average of intensities and for $n = 2$ it denotes their variance.

$$\mu_n = \sum_{i=0}^{L-1} (z_i - m)^n p(z_i) \tag{4}$$

$$m = \sum_{i=0}^{L-1} z_i p(z_i)$$

The Local Binary Pattern (LBP) is another texture descriptor [13]. It employs a sliding window over the image setting to 1 the pixels with intensity greater than or equal to the central pixel and setting to 0 the others. Then, each pixel is multiplied by a power of two given by its position inside the window. The sum of these multiplications is the LBP descriptor for the central pixel of the window. Histogram, statistical moments, and LBP may be used as global descriptors, extracted from the entire image, or as a local descriptor from a limited area.

An example of a local shape descriptor is the eccentricity of a region. It consists of the ratio between the longest and the shortest axises of an object. The longest axis is the largest distance between any two points of the object and the shortest axis is the smallest distance between any two points in its boundary, perpendicular to the longest axis.

A border segment of an object may also be described by its curvature: the ratio between the diameter and the distance between its initial and final points.

Support Vector Machine. Support Vector Machine (SVM) [2] is a methodology applied for data classification, regression, and outlier identification. Given data belonging to two distinct classes, linear SVM classifier tries to locate the best hyper plan which separates the samples of the classes maintaining a small margin between them. The algorithm may also be modified to allow a few outliers to lay inside the margin or in the opposite side of its class. There are also variations of non-linear SVM which separates classes using more complicated geometries than hyper planes [16].

There are some solutions for multi-class problem using classification including the one-vs-one with $N(N-1)/2$ classifiers, given N distinct classes, and the one-vs-all with only N classifiers. In the later case, the classifier which outputs the highest confidence is selected as indicating the correct class.

3   Proposed Framework

An environment was firstly implemented for interactive contour tracking in C++ using Qt Graphical Toolkit. 2D and 3D images may be loaded and presented in canvasses. Then, the user clicks on the desirable contour inserting anchors through out the track. Figure 1 shows an example of the usage of the interface on a sagittal slice of a human brain in which green circles represent anchors and the contours in different colors represent distinct path of: LW in green; RB in red; LZ in cyan; and a straight line in yellow. The purple contours are consolidated tracks of previous iterations.

At each iteration the user moves the mouse over the contour in order to find the longest correctly tracked segment by at least one of the methods. When such segment is found, the right mouse button switches among the methods and the left mouse button establishes the anchor. The straight line is useful for segments with low contrast and high noise in which all other methods behave poorly.

The next step was to automatically suggest the best contour tracking method as the default option to the user, reducing the number of clicks and consequently,

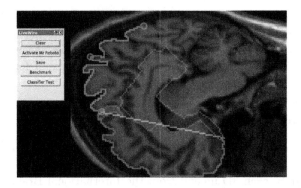

Fig. 1. Contour tracking interface: green circles: anchor points; and segments: pink: previous iterations; yellow: straight line; red: RB; green: LW; and cyan: LZ. (Color figure online)

the execution time. It employs a SVM classifier over descriptors extracted from segments computed by each method and the minimum rectangular region encompassing them. This procedure reduces the number of user interactions since the software suggests the best method most of times. The following descriptors are extracted from the paths given by each method and then concatenated into a single descriptor:

(1) Perimeter; (2) Euclidean distance between anchors; (3) Curvature; (4) 1st moment of contour segment; (5) 2nd moment of the contour segment; (6) 3nd moment of the contour segment; (7) 4nd moment of the contour segment; (8) LBP descriptor of the contour segment; (9) Global histogram of the minimum rectangular region quantized in four bins; (10) Histogram of the intensities of the contour segment pixels, quantized in four bins; and (11) Histogram of the path values of the contour segment pixels, quantized in four bins.

SVM was trained and validated utilizing two separated sets of brain image slices with ground-truth segmentation of the human brain. From a random initial contour pixel, the best method is selected, being the one that outputs the longest correct contour. The concatenated descriptor of all methods is extracted and

Table 1. Best results among feature combinations

		Linear SVM	
Features	Feature set	Accuracy	(R^2)
1	6	0.625	0.054
2	6, 10	0.64	0.008
6	4, 6, 7, 8, 10, 11	0.707	−0.001
10	**1, 3, 4, 5, 6, 7, 8, 9, 10, 11**	**0.735**	**0.03**
11	All	0.731	0.04

used for training and validation. Sets containing any number from one to all descriptors were used to investigate their relevance. The mean accuracy and the correlation coefficient R^2 were computed and the best generated results are shown in Table 1. It shows that only descriptor 2 is irrelevant for classifying the best method for tracking a given contour.

4   Experiments

The dataset used in our experiments consists of 360 2D slices extracted from 18 3D magnetic resonance images of human brains (6 sagittal, 6 axial, and 8 coronal slices from each 3D image) from the International Brain Segmentation Repository (IBSR)[1]. The slices used for this experiment were different from the ones used for descriptor evaluation. Figure 2 shows a sample axial slice and its corresponding segmented brain mask.

Fig. 2. (Left) Original MRI T1 axial slice. (Right) Binary segmentation brain mask.

To verify the efficiency of the framework, we implemented a robot user which simulates the human behavior for the problem. The task is to segment the human brain using the contour tracking tool. It selects a random initial pixel and then increases the size of the contour while at least one of the methods is following the correct contour according to the ground-truth. Note that the ground-truth is just used to select the segment length. After that, the descriptors from the segment of all methods are extracted, concatenated, and classified by SVM classifier using the leave-one-out method. For each round of the experiment, the segments of 17 images are used for training leaving the segments of the other image for test. If SVM outputs the correct method, this counts as a hit. Table 2 shows the amount of hits over the total amount of segments. In total, we used 7048 test segments.

Table 2. Accuracy results of experiments with robot user. $\overline{X}$ is the average value.

Test img	1	2	3	4	5	6	7	8	9	10	11	12	13	14	15	16	17	18	$\overline{X}$
Linear SVM	.67	.62	.60	.77	.57	.63	.71	.75	.65	.68	.71	.71	.71	.62	.64	.64	.71	.69	.67
RBF SVM	.67	.62	.59	.77	.57	.63	.71	.75	.65	.68	.71	.70	.70	.62	.63	.64	.69	.69	.67

---

[1] Their images and manual segmentations are provided by the Center for Morphometric Analysis at Massachusetts General Hospital (http://www.cma.mgh.harvard.edu/ibsr/).

5   Conclusion

In this paper, we propose a novel interactive framework for contour tracking which allows a more precise execution based on three techniques that complement each another. The user may choose the most accurate method for each segment of the contour by pressing a mouse button. Also, we developed an automated classifier which suggests the best technique with more than 67% of accuracy. Future works include testing other classifiers and descriptors.

Acknowledgment. The authors would like to thank FAPESP (2016/21591-5) for funding.

References

1. Barreto, T., Almeida, J., Cappabianco, F.: Estimating accurate water levels for rivers and reservoirs by using sar products: a multitemporal analysis. Pattern Recogn. Lett. **83**, 224–233 (2016)
2. Cortes, C., Vapnik, V.: Support-vector networks. Mach. Learn. **20**(3), 273–297 (1995)
3. Dijkstra, E.: A note on two problems in connexion with graphs. Numerische Mathematik **1**, 269–271 (1959)
4. Falcão, A.X., da Cunha, B.S.: Multiscale shape representation by the image foresting transform. In: Proceedings of SPIE, vol. 4322, pp. 1091–1100 (2001)
5. Falcão, A., Bergo, F.: Interactive volume segmentation with differential image foresting transforms. IEEE Trans. Med. Imaging **23**(9), 1100–1108 (2004)
6. Falcão, A., Costa, L., da Cunha, B.: Multiscale skeletons by image foresting transform and its applications to neuromorphometry. Pattern Recogn. **35**(7), 1571–1582 (2002)
7. Falcão, A., Cunha, B., Lotufo, R.: Design of connected operators using the image foresting transform. In: Proceedings of SPIE, vol. 4322, pp. 468–479 (2001)
8. Falcão, A., Stolfi, J., de Lotufo, R.: The image foresting transform: theory, algorithms, and applications. IEEE Trans. Pattern Anal. Mach. Intell. **26**(1), 19–29 (2004)
9. Falcão, A., Udupa, J., Samarasekera, S., Sharma, S., Hirsch, B., Lotufo, R.: User-steered image segmentation paradigms: live wire and live lane. Graph. Models Image Process. **60**(4), 233–260 (1998)
10. Haralick, R., Shapiro, L.: Image segmentation techniques. Comput. Vis. Graph. Image Process. **27**(3), 389 (1984)
11. Liu, Y., Zhang, D., Lu, G., Ma, W.: A survey of content-based image retrieval with high-level semantics. Pattern Recogn. **40**(1), 262–282 (2007)
12. Miranda, P., Falcao, A., Spina, T.: Riverbed: a novel user-steered image segmentation method based on optimum boundary tracking. IEEE Trans. Image Process. **21**(6), 3042–3052 (2012)
13. Takala, V., Ahonen, T., Pietikäinen, M.: Block-based methods for image retrieval using local binary patterns. In: Kalviainen, H., Parkkinen, J., Kaarna, A. (eds.) SCIA 2005. LNCS, vol. 3540, pp. 882–891. Springer, Heidelberg (2005). https://doi.org/10.1007/11499145_89
14. Vernooij, M., Ikram, M., et al.: Incidental findings on brain MRI in the general population. New Engl. J. Med. **357**(18), 1821–1828 (2007)

15. Visser, E., Keuken, M., et al.: Automatic segmentation of the striatum and globus pallidus using MIST: multimodal image segmentation tool. NeuroImage **125**, 479–497 (2016)
16. Wenzel, F., Galy-Fajou, T., Deutsch, M., Kloft, M.: Bayesian nonlinear support vector machines for big data. In: Ceci, M., Hollmén, J., Todorovski, L., Vens, C., Džeroski, S. (eds.) ECML PKDD 2017. LNCS (LNAI), vol. 10534, pp. 307–322. Springer, Cham (2017). https://doi.org/10.1007/978-3-319-71249-9_19

Learning to Recognize Abnormalities in Chest X-Rays with Location-Aware Dense Networks

Sebastian Gündel[1,2]([✉]), Sasa Grbic[1], Bogdan Georgescu[1], Siqi Liu[1],
Andreas Maier[1], and Dorin Comaniciu[1]

[1] Siemens Imaging Technologies, Siemens Healthineers, Princeton, NJ, USA
[2] Pattern Recognition Lab, Friedrich-Alexander-Universität, Erlangen, Germany
sebastian.guendel@fau.de

Abstract. Chest X-ray is the most common medical imaging exam used to assess multiple pathologies. Automated algorithms and tools have the potential to support the reading workflow, improve efficiency, and reduce reading errors. With the availability of large scale data sets, several methods have been proposed to classify pathologies on chest X-ray images. However, most methods report performance based on random image based splitting, ignoring the high probability of the same patient appearing in both training and test set. In addition, most methods fail to explicitly incorporate the spatial information of abnormalities or utilize the high resolution images. We propose a novel approach based on location aware Dense Networks (DNetLoc), whereby we incorporate both high-resolution image data and spatial information for abnormality classification. We evaluate our method on the largest data set reported in the community, containing a total of 86,876 patients and 297,541 chest X-ray images. We achieve (i) the best average AUC score for published training and test splits on the single benchmarking data set (ChestX-Ray14 [1]), and (ii) improved AUC scores when the pathology location information is explicitly used. To foster future research we demonstrate the limitations of the current benchmarking setup [1] and provide new reference patient-wise splits for the used data sets. This could support consistent and meaningful benchmarking of future methods on the largest publicly available data sets.

1 Introduction

Chest X-ray is the most common medical imaging exam with over 35 million taken every year in the US alone [2]. They allow for inexpensive screening of several pathologies including masses, pulmonary nodules, effusions, cardiac abnormalities and pneumothorax. Due to increasing workload pressures, many radiologists today have to read more than 100 X-ray studies daily. Therefore, automated tools trained to predict the risk of specific abnormalities given a particular X-ray image have the potential to support the reading workflow of the radiologist. Such a system could be used to enhance the confidence of the radiologist or prioritize the reading list where critical cases would be read first.

© Springer Nature Switzerland AG 2019
R. Vera-Rodriguez et al. (Eds.): CIARP 2018, LNCS 11401, pp. 757–765, 2019.
https://doi.org/10.1007/978-3-030-13469-3_88

Due to the recent availability of a large scale data set [1], several works have been proposed to automatically detect abnormalities in chest X-rays. The only peer-reviewed published work is by Wang et al. [1] which evaluated the performance using four standard Convolutional Neural Networks (CNN) architectures (AlexNet, VGGNet, GoogLeNet and ResNet [3]). The following not peer-reviewed papers can be found on arXiv. In [4], a slightly modified DenseNet architecture was used. Yao et al. [5] utilized a variant of DenseNet and Long-short Term Memory Networks (LSTM) to exploit the dependencies between abnormalities. In [6], Guan et al. proposed an attention guided CNN whereby disease specific regions are first estimated before focusing the classification task on a reduced field of view. However most of the current work on arXiv shows results by splitting the data randomly for training, validation and testing [5,6] which is problematic as the average image count per patient for the ChestX-Ray14 [1] data set is 3.6. Thus the same patient is likely to appear in both training and test set. Additionally there is a significant variability in the classification performance between splits due to the class imbalance, thus making performance comparisons problematic. The solely prior work containing publicly released patient-wise splits is the work by Wang et al. [1].

In this paper, we propose a location aware Dense Network (DNetLoc) to detect pathologies in chest X-ray images. We incorporate the spatial information of chest X-ray pathologies and exploit high resolution X-ray data effectively by utilizing high-resolution images during training and testing. Moreover, we benchmark our method on the largest data set reported in the community with 86,876 patients and about 297,541 images, utilizing both the ChestX-Ray14 [1] and PLCO [7] data sets. In addition we propose a new benchmarking set-up on this data set, including published patient-wise training and test splits, supporting the ability to effectively compare future algorithm performance on the largest public chest X-ray data set. We achieve the best performance reported on the existing ChestX-Ray14 benchmarking data set where both patient-wise train and test splits are published.

2   Datasets

The ChestX-Ray14 data set [1] contains 30,805 patients and 112,120 chest X-ray images. The size of each image is 1024×1024 with 8 bits gray-scale values. The corresponding report includes 14 pathology classes.

In the PLCO data set [7], there are 185,421 images from 56,071 patients. The original size of each image is 2500×2100 with 16 bit gray-scale values. We choose 12 most prevalent pathology labels, among which 5 pathology labels contain also the spatial information. The details of such spatial information are described in Sect. 3.3.

Across both data sets, there are 6 labels which share the same name. However, in our experiment, we avoid combining the images of similar labels as we cannot guarantee the same label definition. Additionally we assume there is no patient overlap between these two datasets.

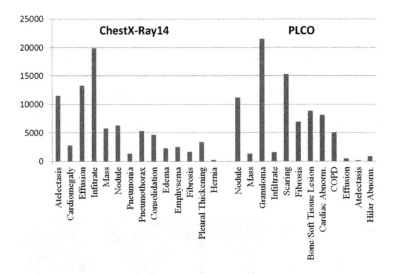

Fig. 1. Representation of the image numbers of the 2 datasets. The chart excludes the number of images where none of these pathologies appear.

The pathology labels are highly imbalanced. This is clearly illustrated in Fig. 1, which displays the total number of images across all pathologies in the 2 data sets. This poses a challenge to any learning algorithm.

3   Method

3.1   Multi-label Setup

We use a variant of DenseNet with 121 layers [8]. Each output is normalized with a sigmoid function to [0, 1]. The network is initialized with the pre-trained ImageNet model [9]. At first we focus on the ChestX-Ray14 dataset. The labels consist of a C dimensional vector $[l_1, l_2 \ldots l_C]$ where $C = 14$ with binary values, representing either the absence (0) or the presence (1) of a pathology. As a multi-label problem, we treat all labels during the classification independently by defining C binary cross entropy loss functions. As the data set is highly imbalanced, we incorporate additional weights within the loss functions, based on the label frequency within each batch:

$$\mathcal{L}(X, l_n) = -(w_P * l_n \log(p) + w_N * (1 - l_n) log(1 - p)), \tag{1}$$

where $w_P = \frac{P_n + N_n}{P_n}$ and $w_N = \frac{P_n + N_n}{N_n}$, with P_n and N_n indicating the number of presence and absence samples, respectively.

During training, we use a batch size of 128. Larger batch sizes increase the probability to contain samples of each class and increase the weight scale of w_P and w_N. The original images are normalized based on the ImageNet pre-trained model [9] with 3 input channels. We increase the global average pooling layer before the final layer to 8×8. The Adam optimizer [10] ($\beta_1 = 0.9$, $\beta_2 = 0.999$, $\epsilon = 10^{-8}$) is used with an adaptive learning rate: The learning rate is initialized with 10^{-3} and reduced 10x when the validation loss plateaus.

3.2 Leveraging High-Resolution Images and Spatial Knowledge

Two strided convolutional layers with 3 filters of 3×3 and a stride of 2 are added as the first layers to effectively exploit the high-resolution chest X-ray images. The filter weights of both layers are initialized equal to a Gaussian down-sampling operation. We use an image size of 1024×1024 as input to our network.

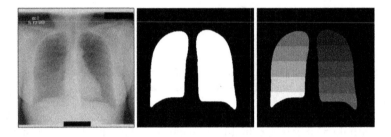

Fig. 2. Spatial Ground Truth Labels: *Left:* Chest X-ray image, *Middle:* Lung side (information whether disease is in the left lung, right lung or neither), *Right:* Splitting of the lung in fifth (more detailed information where disease is located)

Contrary to the ChestX-Ray14 [1] data set the PLCO data set [7] includes consistent spatial location labels for many pathologies. We include 12 pathology labels of the PLCO data set in our experiments (see Fig. 1, right side). The location information is available for 5 pathologies. The location information contains the information about the side (right lung, left lung), finer localization in each lung (divided in equal fifth), including an additional label for diffuse disease. The exact position information of multiple and diffused diseases is not provided.

Therefore, we create 9 additional classes: 6 are responsible for the lobe position (equally split in five parts and a "wildcard" label for multiple diseases: E.g. if the image contains nodules in multiple lung parts, only this label is present), 2 for the lung side (left and right), and 1 for diffused diseases over multiple lung parts. Figure 2 illustrates the label definition based on spatial information.

The spatial location labels are trained as binary and independent classes with cross entropy functions. The number of present class labels depend on the number of diseases that contain location information.

3.3   Dataset Pooling

We combine the ChestX-Ray14 and the PLCO datasets. The training and validation set includes images from both data sets. Several classes share similar class labels. However, we do not know if both data sets are created based on the same label definition. Due to this fact, we treat the labels independently and create different classes. We normalize brightness and contrast of the PLCO dataset images by applying histogram normalization. All images are normalized based on the mean and the standard deviation to match the ImageNet definition. Each batch contains images from both data sets.

Combining both datasets ($C = 35$), we compute the loss function

$$\mathcal{L}(X) = -\frac{1}{C} \sum_{n=1}^{C} w(w_P * l_n \log(p) + w_N * (1 - l_n)log(1 - p)), \tag{2}$$

where w is either 0 or 1, depending which dataset the image is coming from and whether the spatial information exists.

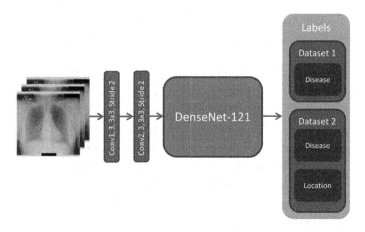

Fig. 3. Architecture of the proposed network (DNetLoc): the current image is provided in 3 channels, followed by 2 strided convolutional layer and the DenseNet-121. Then, the classes are triggered depending on the data set the current sample originates from.

3.4   Global Architecture

Overall, we create a local aware Dense Network that adaptively deals with label availability during training. The final network consists of 35 labels, 14 from the ChestX-Ray14 dataset, and 21 from PLCO dataset. Figure 3 illustrates the architecture of the network (DNetLoc).

4   Experimental Results

The ChestX-Ray14 dataset contains an average of 3.6 images per patient and PLCO 3.3 images per patient. Thus, there is a high probability the same patient appears in all 3 subsets if a random image-split is used. This paper uses only patient-wise splits. For all experiments we separate the data as follows: 70% for training, 10% for validation, and 20% for testing.

Below we present our experimental results. First, we show the state-of-the-art results on the ChestX-Ray14 dataset, following the official patient-wise split. Then, we present the results on the PLCO data set, illustrating the value of using location information and data pooling.

Table 1. We demonstrate improved AUC scores using our method on the official ChestX-Ray14 test set. Right column shows our method on a more representative random patient split where the mean AUC score increases to 0.841.

Method	Wang et al. [1]	Our DNet	Our DNet
Official Split	Yes	Yes	No
Atelectasis	0.7003	0.767	0.826
Cardiomegaly	0.8100	0.883	0.911
Effusion	0.7585	0.828	0.885
Infiltration	0.6614	0.709	0.716
Mass	0.6933	0.821	0.854
Nodule	0.6687	0.758	0.774
Pneumonia	0.6580	0.731	0.765
Pneumothorax	0.7993	0.846	0.872
Consolidation	0.7032	0.745	0.806
Edema	0.8052	0.835	0.892
Emphysema	0.8330	0.895	0.925
Fibrosis	0.7859	0.818	0.820
Pleural Thick	0.6835	0.761	0.785
Hernia	0.8717	0.896	0.941
Mean	0.7451	0.807	0.841

Table 1 shows the best AUC scores obtained on the ChestX-Ray dataset using the official test set. Our network increases the mean AUC score by over 5% compared to the previous work. We observed several limitations with the official split where training and test data sets have different characteristics. This can be either the large label inconsistency or the fact that there are on average 3 times more images per patient in the test set compared with the training set. Thus we computed several random patient-splits each leading better performance with average 0.831 AUC with 0.019 standard deviation. Detailed performance for the novel benchmarking patient-wise split is shown in Table 1 and in Fig. 4 left).

Overall, significant label variance of the follow-up exams are noticeable across the ChestX-Ray14 data set. This might be due to the circumstance that many follow-ups are generated with a specific question, e.g. did the Pneumothorax disappear. Thus repeated and consistent labeling of other abnormalities in follow-up studies varies. As the ChestX-Ray14 labels are generated from reports this would introduce incomplete labeling for many follow-ups.

Table 2. Test results on the PLCO data set: DNetLoc achieves the best AUC scores on the PLCO dataset. Both DNet and DNetLoc networks were trained on the combined ChestX-Ray14 and PLCO dataset. DNetLoc uses spatial information of 5 pathologies. The bold values in this table are pathologies which are supported by spatial knowledge.

Method	Our DNet	Our DNetLoc
Nodule	**0.817**	**0.831**
Mass	**0.845**	**0.878**
Granuloma	0.888	0.888
Infiltrate	**0.875**	**0.880**
Scaring	0.841	0.850
Fibrosis	0.873	0.875
Bone/Soft Tissue Lesion	0.853	0.845
Cardiac Abnormality	0.927	0.926
COPD	0.881	0.882
Effusion	0.933	0.926
Atelectasis	**0.831**	**0.867**
Hilar Abnormality	**0.812**	**0.841**
Mean (Location)	**0.836**	**0.859**
Mean	0.865	0.874

Finally we evaluate our method on the PLCO data. The results in Table 2 show that location information and leveraging high resolution images improve the classification accuracy for most pathologies. For a subset of pathologies where location information is provided (marked in bold), the performance increases by an average of 2.3%. Moreover, the training time was reduced by a factor of 2 when location information is used. For the PLCO data set we reach a final mean AUC score of 87.4%. Figure 4 shows the performance of our method for both the ChestX-Ray14 and the PLCO test set.

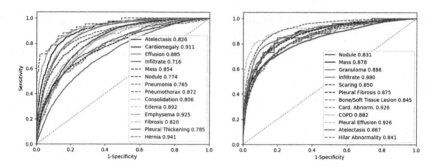

Fig. 4. The Area under Curve (AUC) scores for chest X-ray pathologies: *Left:* Results corresponding to Table 1 right column on the ChestX-Ray14 dataset using DNet, *Right:* Results corresponding to Table 2 right column on the PLCO dataset using DNetLoc.

5   Conclusion

We presented a novel method based on location aware Dense Networks to classify pathologies in chest X-ray images, effectively exploiting high-resolution data and incorporating spatial information of pathologies to improve the classification accuracy. We showed that for pathologies where the location information is present the classification accuracy improved significantly. The algorithm is trained and validated on the largest chest X-ray data set containing 86,876 patients and 297,541 images. Our system has the potential to support the current high throughput reading workflow of the radiologist by enabling him to gain more confidence by asking an AI system for a second opinion or flag "critical" patients for closer examination. In addition we have shown the limitations in the validation strategy of previous works and propose a novel setup using the largest public data set and provide patient-wise splits which will facilitate a principled benchmark for future methods in the space of abnormality detection on chest X-ray imaging.

Disclaimer: This feature is based on research, and is not commercially available. Due to regulatory reasons, its future availability cannot be guaranteed.

References

1. Wang, X., Peng, Y., Lu, L., Lu, Z., Bagheri, M., Summers, R.: Chestx-ray8: hospital-scale chest x-ray database and benchmarks on weakly-supervised classification and localization of common thorax diseases. In: Proceedings of CVPR, pp. 3462–3471 (2017)
2. Kamel, S.I., Levin, D.C., Parker, L., Rao, V.M.: Utilization trends in noncardiac thoracic imaging, 2002–2014. JACR **14**(3), 337–42 (2017)
3. He, K., Zhang, X., Ren, S., Sun, J.: Deep residual learning for image recognition. In: Proceedings of CVPR, pp. 770–778 (2016)
4. Rajpurkar, P., et al.: CheXNet: radiologist-level pneumonia detection on chest X-rays with deep learning. arXiv:1711.05225 (2017)

5. Yao, L., Poblenz, E., Dagunts, D., Covington, B., Bernard, D., Lyman, K.: Learning to diagnose from scratch by exploiting dependencies among labels. arXiv:1710.10501 (2017)
6. Guan, Q., Huang, Y., Zhong, Z., Zheng, Z., Zheng, L., Yang, Y.: Diagnose like a Radiologist: Attention Guided Convolutional Neural Network for Thorax Disease Classification. ArXiv e-prints, January 2016
7. Gohagan, J.K., Prorok, P.C., Hayes, R.B., Kramer, B.S.: The prostate, lung, colorectal and ovarian (PLCO) cancer screening trial of the national cancer institute: history, organization, and status. Control. Clin. Trials **21**(6), 251S–272S (2000)
8. Huang, G., Zhang, L., van der Maaten, L., Weinberger, K.Q.: Densely Connected Convolutional Networks. ArXiv e-prints, August 2016
9. Russakovsky, O., et al.: ImageNet large scale visual recognition challenge. IJCV **115**(3), 211–252 (2015)
10. Kingma, D.P., Ba, J.: Adam: a method for stochastic optimization. ArXiv e-prints, December 2014

An Automatic Brain Tumor Segmentation Approach Based on Affinity Clustering

C. Ramirez$^{(\boxtimes)}$, V. Gomez, I. De la Pava, A. Alvarez,
J. Echeverry, J. Rios, and A. Orozco

Automatic Research Group, Faculty of Engineerings,
Universidad Tecnológica de Pereira, Pereira, Colombia
{carartramirez,vigomez,ide,andres.alvarez1,jde,jirios,aaog}@utp.edu.co

Abstract. The computational methods for tumor segmentation from Magnetic Resonance Images (MRI) are useful tools that aim to support medical specialists in tumor detection. High-grade brain tumors present extremely heterogeneous properties and are associated with elevated mortality rates. Therefore, their segmentation constitutes a challenging and relevant research task. However, most unsupervised methodologies for brain tumor segmentation rely on adequate parameter initialization by the user to achieve satisfactory results. Here, we propose a novel automatic brain tumor core segmentation methodology based on affinity clustering that overcomes that shortcoming. Obtained results in a public database show that our approach is competitive with the state-of-the-art regarding the Dice scores between the segmented tumors and their corresponding Ground Truth images.

Keywords: Affinity Propagation · Brain tumor ·
Automatic segmentation

1 Introduction

Brain tumors are abnormal growths of brain tissue. Their malign variants are one of the most common types of cancer and present high mortality rates [8]. Automatic brain tumor segmentation methods aim to assist clinical specialists in the task of preliminary brain tumor diagnosis and localization, and to serve as a supporting tool in surgery preparation. The segmentation problem consists in separating the tumor tissues such as edema and tumor core (TC) from other brain tissues such as gray and white matter. However, brain tumor shapes, appearances, and locations are very heterogeneous, which renders the brain tumor segmentation task challenging [5].

Most conventional and automated brain tumor segmentation strategies rely on the analysis of Magnetic Resonance Images (MRI) because of their sensitivity to contrast [3]. MRI images can be acquired following several protocols that generate images with different properties, such as T1, T1 contrast, T2, and FLAIR.

© Springer Nature Switzerland AG 2019
R. Vera-Rodriguez et al. (Eds.): CIARP 2018, LNCS 11401, pp. 766–773, 2019.
https://doi.org/10.1007/978-3-030-13469-3_89

Regarding the automatic methods for brain tumor segmentation, they are classified in supervised and unsupervised methods [8]. Supervised techniques require large datasets of MRI images, and their respective Ground Truths (tumors manually segmented by a specialist), to build a segmentation model. Nonetheless, manual tumor segmentation and labeling is time-consuming and depends on the expertise of the specialist. On the other hand, unsupervised methods do not rely on any training dataset, can be applied to datasets of different imaging protocols, and reduce computational complexity without loss of segmentation accuracy compared with supervised methods [2].

Unsupervised methods for segmenting brain tumors include Fuzzy-C-Means (FCM) [7], Gaussian Mixture Model (GMM) [13], k-means [11] and spectral clustering-based methods [2]. However, these methods present numerous shortcomings. Both FCM and GMM require the adequate selection of several parameters to produce satisfactory results [4]. Particularly, for GMM the former is true in the case of parameter optimization for the Gaussian mixture by the expectation-maximization algorithm. In the same line, k-means and spectral clustering require setting the number of clusters a priori. Furthermore, k-means can change the seed points during the clustering task, which makes it a non-deterministic method better suited for course region identification than for fine tumor segmentation [5].

In this work, we propose a novel automatic brain tumor core segmentation methodology, based on affinity clustering, that minimizes the need for parameter iniftialization and user intervention. Given a set of T1 contrast MR images, our approach consists of three main stages: (i) background subtraction by superpixel averaging and k-means clustering, (ii) ROI identification through Affinity Propagation (AP), and (iii) Simple Linear Iterative Clustering (SLIC) superpixels averaging on the ROI and final tumor segmentation using Affinity Propagation. Moreover, we always fixed as 2 the number of groups to be found for both (i) and (iii). Our methodology exploits the pixel intensities to segment the tumor, owing to the fact that brain tumors present high-level contrast with respect to those of other brain tissues; and the stability of AP. We tested our proposal on the publicly available BRATS 2012 challenge database and compared its results with those obtained from FCM, GMM, k-means and spectral clustering. Our results are competitive with the state-of-the-art and show that we successfully segments the tumors while avoiding the need for parameter selection.

The rest of the paper proceeds as follows: Sect. 2 introduces the materials and methods, Sect. 3 describes the experimental setup, Sect. 4 contains the obtained results and their discussion, and Sect. 5 presents the conclusions.

2   Materials and Methods

2.1   Background Substraction

Let $\{\mathbf{X}_k \in \mathbb{R}^P\}_{k=1}^K$ be an MRI dataset holding K samples with $P = N \times M \times L$ voxels, where L is the number of slices in each sample, and N and M are the dimensions of each slice. For the l-th slice of sample k, the image is partitioned into set blocks or superpixels $\{\mathbf{B}_i \in \mathbb{R}^{H \times W}\}_{i=1}^{I}$, where i denotes the number of blocks of dimensions $H < N$ and $W < M$. Moreover, each block has a set of pixel intensity values $\{p^i\}_{j=1}^{J}$ where j is the number of pixels per block, and $J = H \times W$. Then, we characterize the blocks through a Central Tendency Value (CTV) approach [1,2], in which each block $\mathbf{B}_i$ is represented by its mean value $\mu_i = \mathbb{E}\{\mathbf{B}_i\} = (1/J) \sum_{j=1}^{J} p_j^i$. The result is an averaged image $\mathbf{Y} \in \mathbb{R}^{N/H \times M/W}$ per slice. Afterward, we vectorize $\mathbf{Y}$ to obtain a feature vector $\mathbf{y} \in \mathbb{R}^{O}$, where $O = N/H \times M/W$ is the number of pixels of the averaged image. Next, we use k-means on vector $\mathbf{y}$ to separate the pixels belonging to the brain from those of the background. Then, we assign the label *brain* to the group with the smallest number of pixels, noted $\mathbf{z} \in \mathbb{R}^{Q}$, $Q < O$.

2.2 Affinity Propagation to Find the ROI

We employ Affinity Propagation on vector $\mathbf{z} \in \mathbb{R}^{Q}$ to find the tumor ROI as:

$$c_q^* = \underset{r}{\mathrm{argmax}}\ r(q, u) + a(u, q) \tag{1}$$

where c_q^* indicates the group assigned to the element $z_q \in \mathbf{z}$, $q = 1, \ldots, Q$, $r(q, u) = s(q, u) - \max_{t:t \neq u}(a(t, q) + s(q, t))$ is the responsibility update, $a(u, q) = \min\left(0, r(q, q) + \sum_{t:t \notin \{u, q\}} \max\{0, r(t, u)\}\right)$ is the availability update, u denotes the exemplar points, and $s(q, u) = \exp(-\|z_q - z_u\|^2 / 2\sigma^2)$ is the function that measures the similarity between pixels z_q and z_u [6]. The pixels belonging to the group with the smallest number of elements are labeled as *tumor*, and are used to find the ROI by means of a Bounding Box. Once the ROI has been defined on the averaged image it is mapped back to the original image space, obtaining for each slice a matrix $\mathbf{\Lambda} \in \mathbb{R}^{D \times G}$, with $D < N$ and $G < M$.

2.3 Tumor Segmentation from the ROI

We perform the segmentation of the tumor from the ROI by means of SLIC superpixels and AP. SLIC is an adaptation of k-means for superpixel generation that consists of a weighted distance measure that combines color and spatial proximity, while simultaneously providing control over the size and compactness of the superpixels [1]. Given the ROI matrix $\mathbf{\Lambda}$ of the l-th slice, we apply SLIC clustering to obtain a set of irregular superpixels $\{\mathbf{\Psi}_\delta\}_{\delta=1}^{\Delta}$, such that $\cup_{\delta=1}^{\Delta} \mathbf{\Psi}_\delta = \mathbf{\Lambda}$. Then, we characterize each superpixel through CTV. Afterward, we use AP on the image resulting from the averaged superpixels to segment the tumor. Because of irregular form of superpixels, we can find superpixels segmented with forms similar to the tumour. Finally, we select as *tumor* the pixels belonging to the group with the smallest number of elements, and mapped them back to original image. Figure 1 summarizes our proposed methodology for brain tumor segmentation.

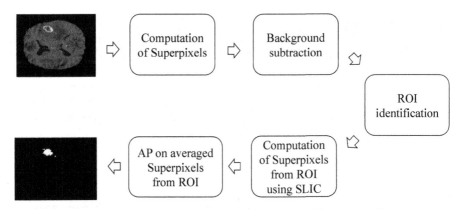

Fig. 1. Flow diagram of the proposed brain tumor segmentation methodology.

3   Experimental Setup

In this work, we use the well-known public BRATS 2012 challenge database [9]. This database contains 80 patient MRI samples: 50 synthetic samples and 30 are real ones. For the synthetic data, 25 are high-grade tumor, and 25 are low-grade tumor. While for the real samples, 20 are high-grade tumor and 10 are low-grade tumor. Each sample has four MRI modalities, T1, T1 contrast, T2, FLAIR, and its respective Ground Truth, as shown in Fig. 2.

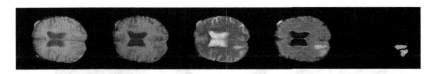

Fig. 2. From left to right: T1 image, T1 contrast image, T2 image, FLAIR image and Ground Truth image.

In order to test the proposed methodology, we select 10 real MRI samples of high-grade tumor, from which they was preprocessed using skull-stripping algorithms such as BET (Brain Extraction Tool). Later, we further select the T1 contrast images to perform tumor segmentation. This process is carried out independently for each slice. First, we partition each slice into blocks of size 8×8 pixels known as superpixels, and average them. Then, we subtract the background as described in Sect. 2.1. Once we have selected the pixels corresponding to the brain, we build a similarity matrix using a k-nearest neighbor approach based on a Gaussian kernel. The number of neighbors is set to 20, and the kernel bandwidth is selected from the range $\sigma_1 = \{0.3 : 0.1 : 1\}$. Then, we input the similarity matrix to the AP algorithm to obtain the ROI (see Sect. 2.2). Next, to enhance the tumor segmentation we use a SLIC superpixels algorithm over the ROI, average each superpixel, build a new Gaussian similarity matrix with a kernel bandwidth $\sigma_2 = 0.3$, and apply the AP algorithm again (see Sect. 2.3). The tumor segmented in the averaged image is then mapped back to the original image. Finally, to evaluate the performance of our methodology, we compute the Dice score between the segmented tumors (TC) per slice and the corresponding Ground Truth images. The performance evaluation is restricted to the slices whose Ground Truth images contain at least 300 pixels labeled as tumor, which translates into an average of 81% of the slices selected.

4   Results and Discussion

Figure 3 shows an example of the results obtained at the different stages of the proposed methodology for a single slice from one data sample. Figure 3(a) presents the image generated after performing superpixel averaging (CTV). The averaging is performed to reduce computational cost. Then, k-means is applied to the averaged image to discern between background and foreground (brain), as shown in Fig. 3(b), and background subtraction is performed. Next, AP is applied to the region labeled as brain in order to identify the tumor ROI (Fig. 3(c)). Afterward, the ROI is mapped back to the original image space (Fig. 3(d)), and SLIC superpixel averaging is carried out (Fig. 3(e)). We chose the SLIC algorithm for this stage because it allows a better characterization of irregular morphologies. Then, AP is performed on the averaged image (Fig. 3(e)) to obtain the final tumor segmentation. Lastly, the pixels labeled as tumor in the preceding stage are mapped to the original image space (Fig. 3(f)).

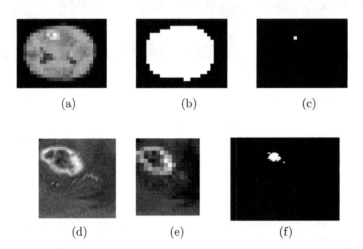

Fig. 3. (a) Averaged image, (b) Background and foreground (brain), (c) Pixels labeled as tumor by AP (ROI), (d) ROI mapped to the original image space, (e) Averaged image using SLIC, (f) final tumor segmented by AP mapped to the original image space.

In the final result of process (Fig. 3(f)), the tumor segmented is pixeled because of SLIC algorithm used in (Fig. 3(f)). The idea with this is modelling the irregular form of tumor. The results could improve, if we use more superpixels. However, it increase the burden computational in the moment of compute the similarity matrix from ROI.

The key step to ensure adequate performance of our method, from the above-described methodological stages, is the selection of the kernel bandwidth (σ_1) used to obtain the Gaussian similarity function that inputs the AP analysis during the ROI identification. For each slice, we estimate σ_1 from a set of possible values through an automatic cross-validation scheme based on the Dice score. Figures 4(a) and (b) display the influence of σ_1 in our methodology's performance for one particular MRI sample. The surface relating the kernel bandwidth used with the slices shows that, in general, a single σ_1 value cannot be employed for all slices of the volume. This can be explained by the variations in the tumor-associated pixel intensities information present in the different slices, that is, the tumor does not appear equally in all slices. In Figs. 4(a) and (b) we observe that the Dice score values are more stable in the central section slices, as opposed to those of the slices belonging to more dorsal and ventral axial views. Figure 4(c) presents a slice (112) for which little variation is observed in the Dice score as a function of σ_1, such stability facilitates tumor segmentation, allowing our methodology to attain satisfactory results (Fig. 4(d)).

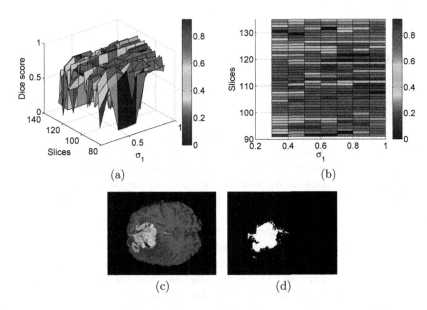

Fig. 4. (a–b) Dice score values as a function of σ_1 and the slice number. (c) Slice with stable Dice scores independently of the value of σ_1. (d) Tumor core segmented from the slice in (c).

Finally, for the selected 10 real MRI samples of high-grade tumor (T1 contrast images), the proposed AP-based automatic tumor core segmentation strategy achieved average Dice scores of 0.59 ± 0.14. As shown in Table 1 this figure is competitive with those of conventional unsupervised methods of the state-of-the-art tested on the BRATS 2012 challenge database. As mentioned before, unlike competing approaches our proposal automatically identifies the tumor ROI and performs tumor core segmentation, without needing user defined seeds or manual parameter initialization. However, since AP clustering exploits pixel intensities for data grouping the performance of our approach depends on the tumor contrast level, with degrading results for lower tumor contrast or in the presence non-tumoral tissue with high contrast levels.

Table 1. Dice score values obtained with the proposed methodology and with conventional unsupervised clustering methods.

Method	Dice score (TC)
k-means [2]	0.21
FCM [2]	0.29
GMM [2, 13]	0.30
Spectral-clustering [2]	0.58
Our approach	**0.59**

5   Conclusions

In this work, we develop a methodology for automatic brain tumor core segmentation from MR images through Affinity Propagation. The proposed methodology consists of several stages, namely: *(i)* background subtraction by superpixel averaging and k-means clustering; *(ii)* ROI identification through Affinity Propagation, using a Gaussian similarity function with an adaptive kernel bandwidth; and *(iii)* SLIC superpixels averaging on the ROI and final tumor segmentation using Affinity Propagation. We test our approach in the BRATS 2012 challenge database on 10 real patients with high-grade tumor, and evaluate our results in terms of the Dice score. Obtained results show that our proposal is competitive with other state-of-the-art methods for unsupervised brain tumor segmentation. Besides, our automatic segmentation methodology does not require any parameter initialization or manual user intervention. As future work, we will add more features, such as texture and shape, to construct the similarity matrix, which could potentially improve the tumor ROI identification. Moreover, we will compare with other automatic segmentation algorithms of the state of the art such as [12] and [10]. The first is a hybrid approach using clustering and optimization techniques. The second is based in texture and contour algorithms. We will also aim to adapt our methodology for the search of multiple tumor ROIs in slices where the tumor volume might be divided into several areas.

Acknowledgements. Under grants provided by the project 1110-744-55860, funded by Colciencias. C. Ramirez was funded under the project E6-18-10 funded by the VIIE and by the Master in Electrical Engineering-Universidad Tecnológica de Pereira. V. Gomez and I. de la Pava was supported by the program "Doctorado Nacional en Empresa - Convoctoria 758 de 2016", funded by Colciencias. Also, J. Echeverry is supported by the project Metodología para el reconocimiento y la traducción de señas aisladas en la Lengua de Señas Colombiana utilizando técnicas de visión por computador-6-16-4, funded by the VIIE-Universidad Tecnologica de Pereira.

References

1. Achanta, R., et al.: Slic superpixels compared to state-of-the-art superpixel methods. IEEE Trans. Pattern Anal. Mach. Intell. **34**(11), 2274–2282 (2012)
2. Angulakshmi, M., Priya, G.L.: Brain tumour segmentation from MRI using superpixels based spectral clustering. J. King Saud Univ.-Comput. Inf. Sci. (2018)
3. Bauer, S., Wiest, R., Nolte, L.P., Reyes, M.: A survey of mri-based medical image analysis for brain tumor studies. Phys. Med. Biol. **58**(13), R97 (2013)
4. Bezdek, J., Hall, L., Clark, M., Goldgof, D.B., Clarke, L.: Medical image analysis with fuzzy models. Stat. Method Med. Res. **6**(3), 191–214 (1997)
5. Boughattas, N., Berar, M., Hamrouni, K., Ruan, S.: Feature selection and classification using multiple kernel learning for brain tumor segmentation. In: 2018 4th International Conference on Advanced Technologies for Signal and Image Processing (ATSIP), pp. 1–5. IEEE (2018)
6. Dueck, D., Frey, B.J.: Non-metric affinity propagation for unsupervised image categorization. In: 2007 IEEE 11th International Conference on Computer Vision, ICCV 2007, pp. 1–8. IEEE (2007)
7. Emblem, K.E., Nedregaard, B., Hald, J.K., Nome, T., Due-Tonnessen, P., Bjornerud, A.: Automatic glioma characterization from dynamic susceptibility contrast imaging: brain tumor segmentation using knowledge-based fuzzy clustering. J. Magn. Reson. Imaging **30**(1), 1–10 (2009)
8. Gordillo, N., Montseny, E., Sobrevilla, P.: State of the art survey on MRI brain tumor segmentation. Magn. Reson. Imaging **31**(8), 1426–1438 (2013)
9. Menze, B., et al.: The multimodal brain tumor image segmentation benchmark (BRATS). IEEE Trans. Med. Imaging, 33 (2014). https://hal.inria.fr/hal-00935640
10. Nabizadeh, N., Kubat, M.: Automatic tumor segmentation in single-spectral MRI using a texture-based and contour-based algorithm. Expert Syst. Appl. **77**, 1–10 (2017)
11. Paul, T.U., Bandhyopadhyay, S.K.: Segmentation of brain tumor from brain MRI images reintroducing k-means with advanced dual localization method. Int. J. Eng. Res. Appl. **2**(3), 226–231 (2012)
12. Vishnuvarthanan, A., Rajasekaran, M.P., Govindaraj, V., Zhang, Y., Thiyagarajan, A.: An automated hybrid approach using clustering and nature inspired optimization technique for improved tumor and tissue segmentation in magnetic resonance brain images. Appl. Soft Comput. **57**, 399–426 (2017)
13. Zhao, L., Wu, W., Corso, J.J.: Brain tumor segmentation based on GMM and active contour method with a model-aware edge map. In: BRATS MICCAI, pp. 19–23 (2012)

Enhanced Graph Cuts for Brain Tumor Segmentation Using Bayesian Optimization

Mauricio Castaño[1(✉)], Hernán F. García[1,2,3(✉)], Gloria L. Porras-Hurtado[2(✉)], Álvaro A. Orozco[3(✉)], and Jorge I. Marin-Hurtado[4(✉)]

[1] GAMMA Research Group, Universidad del Quindío, Armenia, Colombia
mcastanoa@uqvirtual.edu.co

[2] Grupo de Investigación Salud Comfamiliar, Comfamiliar Risaralda,
Pereira, Colombia
gporras@comfamiliar.com

[3] Grupo de Investigación en Automática, Universidad Tecnológica de Pereira,
Pereira, Colombia
{hernan.garcia,aaog}@utp.edu.co

[4] GDSPROC Research Group, Universidad del Quindío,
Armenia, Colombia
jorgemarin@uniquindio.edu.co

Abstract. Brain tumor segmentation is a difficult task, due to the shape variability that malignancy brain structures exhibit between patients. The main problem in this process is that the tumor contour is usually computed from parametric models that need to be well-tuned to perform an accurate segmentation. In this paper, we propose an enhanced Graph cut on which the model parameters are selected through a probabilistic approach. Here, we use Bayesian optimization to find the optimal hyperparameters that segment the tumor volume accurately. The experimental results show that by using Bayesian optimization, the graph cut model performs an accurate segmentation over brain volumes in comparison with common segmentation methods in the state-of-the-art.

Keywords: Bayesian optimization · Graph cuts · Gaussian processes
Brain tumor segmentation

1 Introduction

Brain malignancies are the most dangerous pathologies in neurological diseases. These malignancies present different degrees of aggressiveness, different prognosis and heterogeneous histological sub-regions (i.e., peritumoral edema, necrotic core, enhancing and non-enhancing tumor core). This variability (due to intrinsic heterogeneities of gliomas) poses a challenging task in which the imaging phenotype is described by varying appearance and shape profiles across multimodal MRI scans, reflecting varying tumor tissue properties. This variability

© Springer Nature Switzerland AG 2019
R. Vera-Rodriguez et al. (Eds.): CIARP 2018, LNCS 11401, pp. 774–782, 2019.
https://doi.org/10.1007/978-3-030-13469-3_90

poses a challenging task in which the imaging phenotype is described by varying appearance and shape biological descriptors across neurological scans, reflecting varying tumor tissue properties [12].

Localizing tumor areas is a crucial procedure for brain surgery planing. One of the main problems in this case is in fact the time, in practice, radiation oncologists spend a substantial portion of their time performing the segmentation manually using segmentation and visualization tools. Besides, in the literature survey, several techniques are proposed to overcome the challenges of brain tumor segmentation. Specifically, brain tumor segmentation algorithms based on convolutional neural networks (CNNs) have been shown to be at least as effective as other automated tumor segmentation methods [8].

In recent years, the researchers focused on exploring the entire field related to neural networks, a fully automatic pipeline that involves chaining together several unique 3D U-Net, a type of 3D patch-based convolutional neural network [1]. In general, state of the art focuses on models that initiate a process of forced learning given by iterations that cause specific weights to vary until an acceptable result is reached (i.e., to find a plausible tumor contour) [12]. The main problem of these approaches is that although the results are relevant, it is difficult to extract clinical information from these learning processes (i.e., to capture tissue properties from hidden layers as in CNNs) [9].

Patch-based methods make use of energy functions to define a given contour that matches plausible shape structures (i.e., tumor contour) [10]. These energy functions allow us to define the tumor contour from appearance and shape constraints based on the tumor properties [3]. However, the resulting performance of these approaches depends on the correct selection of the model parameters (i.e., graph cuts (GC) for image segmentation) [6]. Global optimization is an essential task in any complex problem where design and choice of model parameters play a key role. In the machine learning field, such problems are found in the tuning of hyperparameters [15] and experimental design [7].

Bayesian optimization (BO) [7,15], proves to outperform state of the art for global optimization algorithms on many challenging optimization benchmark functions [11]. In this context, Bayesian optimization assumes that the objective function is sampled from a Gaussian process, maintaining the posterior distribution for this function as observations (by running learning algorithm experiments with different hyperparameters are observed). In this paper, we propose an enhanced Graph cut on which the model parameters are selected through a probabilistic approach. Here, we use Bayesian optimization to find the optimal hyperparameters that segment the tumor volume accurately. Our contribution is based on the Bayesian optimization process that finds the model parameters for controlling the energy function of the graph cut in a probabilistic way. The rest of the paper proceeds as follows. Section 2 provides a detailed discussion of materials and methods. Section 3 presents the experimental results and some discussions about the proposed method. The paper concludes in Sect. 4, with a summary and some ideas for future research.

2   Materials and Methods

2.1   Database

In this work we used the Brain Tumor Image Segmentation Challenge (Brats) 2015 [12]. This Database contains high-grade tumors, Low-grade tumors and labels maps made by experts based on landmarks. The tumors of this database are located in different brain regions. The label map showed in Fig. 1, have four different labels 1- for Necrosis (Green), 2- for the Edema (Yellow), 3- for Non-enhancing tumor (Red) and 4- for Enhancing tumor (Blue). We used the MRI T1 images with resolution of 240 × 240 pixels and 1 mm × 1 mm × 1 mm voxel size.

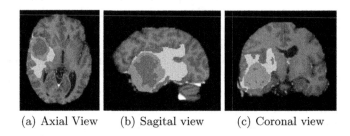

(a) Axial View   (b) Sagital view   (c) Coronal view

Fig. 1. Sample of a given abnormal tissue for the Brast2015 Database. (Color figure online)

2.2   Graph Cuts

We use a fast approximate energy minimization approach with label costs, that uses the *alpha*-expansion algorithm [5]. This algorithm is commonly used to minimize energies that involve unary, pairwise, and specialized higher-order terms that describes given appearance contour [3]. The segmented image can be modeled as an energy minimization that finds a labeling f (i.e., estimated contour) as,

$$E(f) = E_{\text{smooth}}(f) + E_{\text{data}}(f) + E_{\text{label}}(f), \tag{1}$$

where, $E_{\text{smooth}}(f)$ is a measure of the smoothness by parts of the labeling f, and $E_{\text{data}}(f)$ measures the discrepancy between f and the observed data. As in [5], the term $E_{\text{data}}(f)$ is computed as,

$$E_{data}(f) = \sum_{p \epsilon P} D_p(f_p), \tag{2}$$

where D_p measures how well the label f_p fits the pixel p. Generally, this is evaluated using a quadratic standard, which can be given by $(f_p - i_p)^2$ where

i_p is the original intensity of the pixel. The smoothness cost $E_{\text{smooth}}(f)$, is a standard regularizer which can be modeled as,

$$E_{\text{smooth}}(f) = \sum_{p,q \epsilon \mathcal{N}} V_{p,q}(f_p, f_q), \tag{3}$$

where each $V_{p,q}$ weights all $f_p \neq f_q$. A simple use of this function can be given by $V_{p,q}(f_p, f_q) = K \cdot |f_p - f_q|$ (with K being an arbitrary constant). Hence, if each $V_{p,q}$ define a metric, then the minimization of the Eq. (1) it is known as the problem of metric labeling and can be effectively optimized with the *alpha-expansion* algorithm [5]. The label cost penalize each unique label that appears in f as $E_{\text{label}}(f) = \sum_{L \subseteq \mathcal{L}} h_L \cdot \delta_L(f)$, where h_L is the non-negative label cost of labels L and the indicator function $\delta_L(.)$ is defined on a label subset L as,

$$\delta_L(f) \stackrel{\text{def}}{=} \begin{cases} 1 & \exists p : f_p \in L \\ 0 & otherwise \end{cases} \tag{4}$$

2.3   Bayesian Optimization with Gaussian Process Priors

Since we want to compute the graph cuts hyperparameters in a probabilistic way, our goal is to find the minimum of a cost function $f(\mathbf{x})$ (i.e., the performance index between the ground truth labels and the segmented tumor) on some bounded set $\mathcal{X}$ that controls the model parameters. To this end, Bayesian optimization builds a probabilistic framework for $f(\mathbf{x})$ with the aim to exploit this model to make predictions of the model parameters $\mathcal{X}$ evaluated in the cost function [15]. The main components of the Bayesian optimization framework are the prior of the function to optimize, as well as the acquisition function that will allow us to determine the next point to evaluate the cost function [13]. In this work, we use a Gaussian process prior, due to its flexibility and tractability. A Gaussian Process (GP) is an infinite collection of scalar random variables indexed by an input space such that for any finite set of inputs $\mathbf{X} = \{\mathbf{x}_1, \mathbf{x}_2, \cdots, \mathbf{x}_n\}$, the random variables $\mathbf{f} \stackrel{\Delta}{=} [f(\mathbf{x}_1), f(\mathbf{x}_2), \cdots, f(\mathbf{x}_n)]$ are distributed according to a multivariate Gaussian distribution $\mathbf{f}(\mathbf{X}) = \mathcal{GP}(m(\mathbf{x}), k(\mathbf{x}, \mathbf{x}'))$. A GP is completely specified by a mean function $m(\mathbf{x}) = \mathbb{E}[f(\mathbf{x})]$ (usually defined as the zero function) and a positive definite covariance function given by $k(\mathbf{x}, \mathbf{x}') = \mathbb{E}\left[(f(\mathbf{x}) - m(\mathbf{x}))(f(\mathbf{x}') - m(\mathbf{x}')^T)\right]$ (see [15] for further details).

Let us assume that $f(\mathbf{x})$ is drawn from a Gaussian process prior and that our observations are set as $\{\mathbf{x}_n, y_n\}_{n=1}^N$, where $y_n \sim \mathcal{N}(f(\mathbf{x}_n), \nu)$ and ν is the noise variance. The acquisition function is denoted by $a : \mathcal{X} \to \mathbb{R}^+$ and establishes the point in $\mathcal{X}$ that is evaluated in the optimization process as $x_{\text{next}} = \arg\max_{\mathbf{x}} a(\mathbf{x})$. Since the acquisition function depends on the GP hyperparameters, θ, and the predictive mean function $\mu(\mathbf{x}; \{\mathbf{x}_n, \mathbf{y}_n\}, \theta)$ (as well as the predictive variance function), the best current value is then $x_{\text{best}} = \arg\min_{\mathbf{x}_n} f(\mathbf{x}_n)$.

2.4   Enhanced Graph Cuts with Bayesian Optimization

Our approach is based on the Bayesian optimization process for estimating the model parameters of the graph cut model that segments a given brain tumor accurately in a probabilistic way. In this work, we choose to optimize the foreground seed, $\Omega_1 = \{x_f, y_f, z_f\}$, the background seed $\Omega_2 = \{x_b, y_b, z_b\}$, and the α-parameter of the swap algorithm $\Omega_3 = \alpha$ [5]. For the graph cuts implementation we use the *imcut*[1] toolbox. Besides, as for the Bayesian optimization process, we use as a cost function, the Euclidean distance between the labels of the segmented tumor and the ground truth labels. We use the $GPyOpt$[2] toolbox for python, developed by the Machine Learning group of the University of Sheffield. In this work, we report results for the expected improvement (EI), and the probability of improvement (PI) and some other relevant acquisition functions [15]. Figure 2 shows the block diagram of the proposed model used in this work.

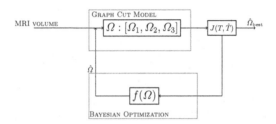

Fig. 2. Block diagram of the proposed approach for the enhanced graph cuts with Bayesian optimization

3   Results and Discussions

In this section, we show the results of our framework for optimizing the graph cuts hyperparameters. We show a comparison between a given manual tuning and an automatic tuning using Bayesian optimization. Besides, we report a comparison of the different segmentation performances of the acquisition functions, as well as some qualitative and quantitative results compared with relevant works in the state-of-art.

---

[1]   *imcut* is a Segmentation tool based on the graph cut algorithm available at https://github.com/mjirik/imcut.

[2]   *Gpyopt* is a Bayesian optimization framework in python available at http://github.com/SheffieldML/GPyOpt.

As we can see in Fig. 3, Bayesian optimization can eliminate certain inconveniences that arise for manual tunning of the graph cuts. The figure shows that the optimal parameters allow us to segment the tumor contour more appropriately (i.e., avoiding false negatives derived from the segmentation process).

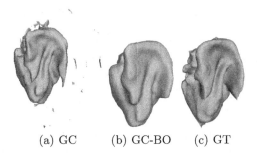

(a) GC   (b) GC-BO   (c) GT

Fig. 3. Comparison between Bayesian optimization (middle) and manual adjustment, of graph cuts hyperparameters (left). The figure shows that the manual tuning of the graph cut model (left) derived in more false negatives in comparison with ground truth tumor (GT right).

Figure 4 shows the convergence of each acquisition function of the BO process. The red plots show the distance between the hyperparameters on each iteration. As a result, we can differentiate the stages of exploration and exploitation of the hyperparameters. Here, the more variation found between each consecutive hyper-parameter indicates the stage of exploration and small distances between consecutive hyperparameters indicates the stage of exploitation. The figures outlined in blue indicate the error convergence of each method. Furthermore, the results also show that the acquisition functions: integrated lower confidence bound and integrated probability improvement perform the tumor segmentation more accurately (see bottom row of Fig. 4).

Figure 5 shows the curvature computed for three different tumors: ground truth volumes (left) and segmented tumors with BO (right). The results show that regions with high saliency (red areas in the tumor volumes), matches the segmented tumors with the optimal hyperparameters (the segmentation process preserves the relative curvature of the original tumor). Finally, Table 1 shows a comparison of different approaches reported in the state-of-the-art (BraTS 2017 challenge [12]). The results show that our approach outperforms some relevant methods in the state-of-art, which are based on deep learning approaches. Hence, since our approach performs the segmentation in an unsupervised manner, the probabilistic tuning of the model parameters sets an important result for these image segmentation approaches.

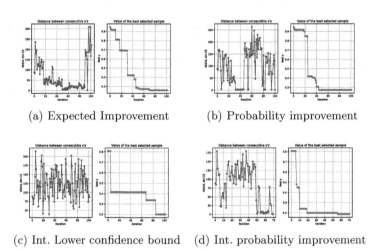

(a) Expected Improvement   (b) Probability improvement

(c) Int. Lower confidence bound   (d) Int. probability improvement

Fig. 4. Convergence of the Bayesian optimization process for different acquisition functions. The figure shows the distance between values of x selected consecutively (red plots), and the minimum value of the performance index obtained in each iteration (blue plots). (Color figure online)

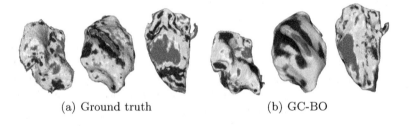

(a) Ground truth   (b) GC-BO

Fig. 5. Curvature comparison of three different subjects (left to right). The bottom row shows the curvature obtained from the segmented tumors with GC-BO. The figure shows the curvature obtained from the ground truth volumes. The figure shows that regions with high saliency (i.e., red colors) match the ground truth data. (Color figure online)

Table 1. Comparison with different methods proposed in [12] for brain tumor segmentation. We report the results as in the BRATS challenge: Dice coefficient, Hausdorff distance, sensitivity, and specificity (Some articles do not report some metrics, so they are assigned to N.R).

Method	Dice	Hausdorff	Sensitivity	Specificity
3D U-Net [12]	0.9111	19.8741	N.R	N.R
Tensor based feature extraction [2]	0.833	N.R	0.815	N.R
Volumetric Multi-modality Neural Network [4]	0.87	21.32	0.87	0.99
Label Distribution Learning [14]	0.86771	N.R	0.88816	0.99208
3D-SegNet architecture [12]	0.79767	23.64621	0.91027	0.97916
Our approach	0.88664	33.73749	0.88765	0.99849

4 Conclusions and Future Work

In this paper, we propose a Bayesian optimization framework for tuning the model parameters of a graph cuts method. Our method seeks to find the best parameters that segment a given tumor contour in a probabilistic way. The experimental results show that our approach derives in more accurate contours than a given classical procedure in image segmentation with graph cuts. Besides, since the model parameters are optimized, the resulting curvature of the segmented tumor preserves main saliency regions that match the ground truth data. Finally, our approach outperforms some important methods in the state-of-art that use deep learning frameworks.

As for the future works, we plan to extend the classical Energy minimization problem of the region growing approaches to propose a new function that can be optimized with probability black-box functions.

Acknowledgments. This research is developed under the project financed by COL-CIENCIAS with code 111074455860. H.F. García is funded by Colciencias under the program: *Formación de alto nivel para la ciencia, la tecnología y la innovación - Convocatoria 617 de 2013.*

References

1. Beers, A., et al.: Sequential 3D U-Nets for biologically-informed brain tumor segmentation. CoRR abs/1709.02967 (2017)
2. Bharath, H.N., Colleman, S., Sima, D.M., Van Huffel, S.: Tumor segmentation from multi-parametric MRI using random forest with superpixel and tensor based feature extraction. In: Brats Challenge 2017 (2017)
3. Boykov, Y., Funka-Lea, G.: Graph cuts and efficient N-D image segmentation. Int. J. Comput. Vis. **70**, 109–131 (2006)
4. Castillo, L.S., Daza, L.A., Rivera, L.C., Arbeláez, P.: Volumetric multimodality neural network for brain tumor segmentation (2017)
5. Delong, A., Osokin, A., Isack, H.N., Boykov, Y.: Fast approximate energy minimization with label costs. Int. J. Comput. Vis. **96**(1), 1–27 (2012)
6. Dogra, J., Jain, S., Sood, M.: Segmentation of MR images using hybrid kmean-graph cut technique. Proc. Comput. Sci. **132**, 775–784 (2018). International Conference on Computational Intelligence and Data Science
7. Gonzalez, J., Longworth, J., James, D., Lawrence, N.: Bayesian optimisation for synthetic gene design. In: NIPS Workshop on Bayesian Optimization in Academia and Industry (2014)
8. Havaei, M., et al.: Brain tumor segmentation with deep neural networks. Med. Image Anal. **35**, 18–31 (2017)
9. Isin, A., Direkoglu, C., Sah, M.: Review of MRI-based brain tumor image segmentation using deep learning methods. Proc. Comput. Sci. **102**, 317–324 (2016). 12th International Conference on Application of Fuzzy Systems and Soft Computing, ICAFS 2016, 29–30 August 2016, Vienna, Austria
10. Jiřík, M., Lukes, V., Svobodova, M., Železný, M.: Image segmentation in medical imaging via graph-cuts (2013)

11. Jones, D.R.: A taxonomy of global optimization methods based on response surfaces. J. Glob. Optim. **21**(4), 345–383 (2001)
12. Menze, B.H., Jakab, A., Bauer, S., Kalpathy-Cramer, J., et al.: The multimodal brain tumor image segmentation benchmark (brats). IEEE Trans. Med. Imaging **34**(10), 1993–2024 (2015)
13. Rasmussen, C.E., Williams, C.K.I.: Gaussian Processes for Machine Learning (Adaptive Computation and Machine Learning). The MIT Press (2005)
14. Shengcong Chen, C.D., Zhou, C.: Brain tumor segmentation with label distribution learning and multi-level feature representation. In: Brats Challenge 2017 (2017)
15. Snoek, J., Larochelle, H., Adams, R.P.: Practical Bayesian optimization of machine learning algorithms. In: Pereira, F., Burges, C.J.C., Bottou, L., Weinberger, K.Q. (eds.) Advances in Neural Information Processing Systems, vol. 25, pp. 2951–2959. Curran Associates, Inc. (2012)

Convolutional Neural Network Architectures for Texture Classification of Pulmonary Nodules

Carlos A. Ferreira[1]([📧]) [ID], António Cunha[2,3] [ID], Ana Maria Mendonça[1,3] [ID], and Aurélio Campilho[1,3] [ID]

[1] INESC-TEC - Institute for Systems and Computer Engineering, Technology and Science, Porto, Portugal
carlos.a.ferreira@inesctec.pt
[2] University of Trás-os-Montes e Alto Douro, Vila Real, Portugal
[3] Faculty of Engineering, University of Porto, Porto, Portugal

Abstract. Lung cancer is one of the most common causes of death in the world. The early detection of lung nodules allows an appropriate follow-up, timely treatment and potentially can avoid greater damage in the patient health. The texture is one of the nodule characteristics that is correlated with the malignancy. We developed convolutional neural network architectures to classify automatically the texture of nodules into the non-solid, part-solid and solid classes. The different architectures were tested to determine if the context, the number of slices considered as input and the relation between slices influence on the texture classification performance. The architecture that obtained better performance took into account different scales, different rotations and the context of the nodule, obtaining an accuracy of 0.833 ± 0.041.

Keywords: Texture classification · Lung nodule · 2.5D · Deep learning

1 Introduction

Cancer is a disease with great number of deaths worldwide. Recently, estimates indicate that cancer deaths may have exceeded by a narrow margin the deaths from coronary heart disease and strokes [5]. In 2018, 1,735,350 new cancer cases and 609,640 cancer deaths are projected to occur in the United States of America (USA). Lung cancer represents approximately 13% of new cancer occurrences and 26% of cancer deaths, being the leading cause of cancer deaths in the USA for both sexes. The 5-year survival rate of late-stage cancers is approximately 15%, improving with early detection [9]. It is urgent to find new methods to improve the detection, allowing a timely treatment to reduce the current high mortality.

Computerized Tomography (CT) has been the usual imaging modality for monitoring lung cancer due to the good image quality and level of detail. From

© Springer Nature Switzerland AG 2019
R. Vera-Rodriguez et al. (Eds.): CIARP 2018, LNCS 11401, pp. 783–791, 2019.
https://doi.org/10.1007/978-3-030-13469-3_91

CT acquisition to the patient's diagnosis, the steps performed are nodule detection, nodule segmentation, nodule characterization and nodule classification. Nodule detection allows to find the nodule centroid or a bounding box surrounding the nodule region. The estimation of the bounding box facilitates the next steps because the region of interest to analyze is smaller. Since characterization and classification are generally dependent on segmentation, it should be as accurate as possible. The characterization tends to extract data such as volume, Hounsfield units (HU) measures, shape, etc. For classifying the nodule, relevant characteristics are calcification, texture, spiculation, sphericity and margin. Some of these are more easily perceived and are directly related to malignancy, that can be only fully confirmed with biopsy. Lung nodule detection and classification by radiologists only based on the visualization of CT images is a tedious process. Computed-Aided Diagnosis (CAD) systems can help the decision, speeding up the analysis and contributing as a second opinion.

Texture is clearly related to malignancy. The texture classification of lung nodules reflects its internal density and can be labelled unitarily within the interval [1–5]. The solid (S) nodules, those that completely obscure the entire parenchyma, have scores 4 or 5, corresponding to structures clearer than the dark parenchyma. The non-solid/ground glass opacity (GGO) nodules are masses with non-uniformity and intensity similar to parenchyma. They are scored 1 or 2. Part solid nodules (PS) has a score of 3 and consist of a ground-glass with an area of homogeneous soft-tissue attenuation, a solid core [10]. Non-Solid, part-solid and solid have respectively 18%, 63% and 7% of being malignant nodules [6]. This information is also relatively deducible with LungRADS [8]. Figure 1 shows the middle slice of the axial view of nodules with different textures. The red contour represents the expert manual segmentation of the nodule.

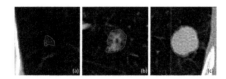

Fig. 1. Nodule Textures: (a) GGO, (b) part-solid and (c) solid.

Some studies have been carried out on the automatic classification of lung nodule texture. In Tu *et al.* [10], the images correspond to regions of interest (ROI) based on the nodule contours of ground-truth with the expanding offsets of 10 pixels. The images pass through a contourlet transform and a convolutional network with two convolution, two pooling, one fully connected layer and one softmax activation layers. With LIDC dataset, results show concordance with expert opinions and significant performance improvement over histogram analysis. Ciompi *et al.* [3] implemented a deep learning system based on multi-stream multi-scale convolutional neural network (CNN), which classified nodule as solid, part-solid, non-solid, calcified, perifissural and spiculated. The database was obtained from the Danish Lung Cancer Screening Trial. Due to class imbalance and in order to have data augmentation, the 3D volume was submitted to different number of rotations. The input data was processed by four series of convolutional and pooling layers merging in a final fully-connect layer, before the prediction. The work achieved a classification performance that outperforms the classical methods and is within the inter-observer variability among experts. In the method of Jacobs *et al.* [7], a KNN classifier was applied to a nodule descriptor constructed based on information of volume, mass and intensity of the segmented nodule. The dataset was from the Dutch-Belgian NELSON lung cancer screening trial. The pairwise agreement between this CAD system and each of expert had a performance in the same range as the interobserver. Cirujeda *et al.* [4] did a method to classify 3D textured volumes in CT scans as solid, ground-glass opacity and healthy. The 3D descriptor was a covariance-based descriptor with Riesz-wavelet features. The classification model was a "Bag of Covariance Descriptors". The dataset consists of a private data. The classification performance is computed in terms of sensitivity and specificity with average values of 82.2% and 86.2% respectively.

We develop different CNN architectures to classify the texture of lung nodules. The goal of this work was to infer if the surrounding context of the nodule, the number of slices of the 3D volume considered as input for classification and the relation between the slices have influence on the classification.

2   Material

The used dataset was the Lung Image Dataset Consortium (LIDC-IDRI) [1]. The acquired CTs are composed of parallel axial slices with resolution of 512×512 pixels ranged with spacing of 0.542 to 0.750 mm between pixels. The number of slices varies from 100 to 600 and the thickness from 0.6 to 5 mm. The CTs were analyzed by 4 radiologists, not always the same ones, among the twelve who participated in the study. Table 1 lists the number of nodules per class, number of annotations, and standard deviation of radiologists' opinion. If more than one radiologist rated the same nodule, it is taken the average of the scores. As the procedure did not require consensus among radiologists, the database contains only 907 (34.0%) nodules are marked from four radiologists. Moreover, the Table 1 shows, on one hand, a large unbalance of classes, on the other hand, that there are 27.1% of cases where the standard deviation is greater or equal than 0.5.

Figure 2 shows an example of the middle axial slice of a nodule and the segmentation defined by different radiologists (Fig. 2(b)–(d)). The attributed scores was, respectively, 3 (part-solid), 4 (solid) and 2 (non-solid). There are only three representations because one radiologist did not consider it as a nodule.

Since in the LIDC-IDRI there are different spacings between the acquired voxels, the CTs were resized. The CTs were transformed so that there is a spacing of 0.70 mm between pixels, the most common spacing in the database. The 3D volumes were centered on the nodule and have size of $64 \times 64 \times 64$ pixels

Table 1. Nodule variability in the dataset.

σ	<0.5	<0.5	≥0.5 & <1	≥1	<0.5	≥0.5 & <1	≥1	<0.5	≥0.5 & <1	≥1	Total
Annotators	1	2			3			4			
GGO class	133	38	9	9	27	5	14	10	20	8	273
PS class	64	6	21	44	7	5	24	1	7	20	199
S class	585	261	72	36	334	54	13	691	116	34	2196
Total	782	496			483			907			2668

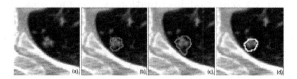

Fig. 2. Example of a nodule with different segmentations and classifications by radiologists: (a) original image, (b) doctor A, (c) doctor B and (d) doctor C.

to contain the largest nodule. The intensities were also rescaled for the $[-1000$ HU, 400 HU] range, which is the range of interest of nodules intensities.

3   Methods

The architectures were designed with the aim of understanding the influence of the context, the number of used slices and the relationship between the slices as CNN input for the texture classification. It is often converted into a classification problem in three classes rather than regression in some works since these labels are most often adopted by radiologists [2]. Figure 3 shows these CNN architectures. The number of input slices can be one (Fig. 3A–B), three (Fig. 3C–D) or even nine (Fig. 3E–F). The architectures of C, E and D, F have, respectively, the same bottom layers of A and B. However, the training is processed independently. The low number of layers, the low number of filters in the convolutional layers and the dropout were strategies used to avoid overfitting. The three slices situation correspond to the three middle slices of the cube. In case of using nine slices, the diagonals of the cube can be used in addition to the middle slices. A scheme representing the extracted slices is shown in Fig. 4.

In what concerns the context importance, CNNs were optimized with input of nodules with and without surrounding context. In the first case, the input are slices extracted directly from the 3D volume while in the second one, the slices of the 3D volume still undergo cropping and resizing so that the borders of the nodule correspond to the limit of the image. This last case was resize to 32 × 32 pixels since the database has 94.2% nodules with less than 32 pixels in diameter and the input windows with small nodules are not strongly interpolated. The nodule boundaries were defined by the LIDC-IDRI manual markings. The mask consists of the set of pixels in which there is, at least, 50% of the segmentation agreement between radiologists. In Fig. 5, these two inputs with 64 × 64 pixels and with 32 × 32 pixels (expanded in the example) are represented.

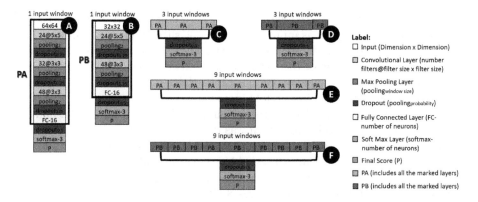

Fig. 3. Different used CNN architectures.

Fig. 4. Representation of used planes: (a) the middle slices and (b) the diagonal slices.

Fig. 5. Different used input images: (a) without rescaling; (b) with rescaling.

To deal with data imbalance, two strategies were used. In the first, the cube was rotated different number of times per class in the training set (no rotation of solid nodules, 14 rotations of part-solid nodules and 10 rotations of GGO nodules). This also serves as data augmentation. In validation and testing the number of rotations is the same with 8 rotations of 11.25° for all classes. The second strategy relies on class weights, that impose a cost dependent on the number of samples per class. These penalties are set in the loss function, which is categorical cross entropy (Eq. 1).

$$loss = -\frac{1}{N}\sum_{i=1}^{N}\sum_{j=1}^{M}\alpha_j y_{i,j} log(p_{i,j}) \ with \ \alpha_j = \frac{N}{MN_j} \ and \ N = \sum_{j=1}^{M} N_j \quad (1)$$

where N is the total data size, M is the number of classes, i is the sample number, j is the class number, α_j is the class weight of a class, $y_{i,j}$ is the one-hot-encoder ground-truth, $p_{i,j}$ is the softmax output of the CNN and N_j is the data size of the class.

Thirteen tests (seven with context and six without context) were performed to take conclusions regarding the proposed goals (Table 2). The 7th hypothesis has, as input, middle slices at different scales (1/3, 2/3, 1 relative to the original) to infer if the multi-scale strategy is able to learn better the features of the small nodules being thus only tested with inputs of 64 × 64 pixels. A 2.5D approach is called when CNN receives as input more than one slice and it takes into account the relationship between different cube views. For 2D, the class was determined by computed the average of the scores from the used slices.

There was random selection of the LIDC-IDRI database for the training, test and validation sets. 5-times 8-fold cross-validation was used with 20 nodules per class for validation and test. Table 3 shows information about the nodules present in the test set. The algorithm was developed in Keras-TensorFlow. The convergence occurred approximately after 150 epochs. The parameters of the network were optimized using the ADAM algorithm and the learning rate was 0.001. The processor used was Intel (R) Core TM i7-5829K CPU @ 3.30 GHz, the RAM was 32 GB and the GPU was 8 GB.

Table 2. Hypotheses verified with CNN architectures.

Hypotheses			1	2	3	4	5	6	7
Dimension			2D	2D	2D	2.5D	2.5D	2.5D	2.5D
Extracted slices			Middle	Middle + Diagonal	Middle	Middle	Middle + Diagonal	Middle	Middle (on three scales)
Balancing strategy			Class weights	Class weights	Different number of cube rotations	Class weights	Class weights	Different number of cube rotations	Different number of cube rotations
Used architecture	Image size (pixels)	64 × 64	A	A	A	C	E	C	E
		32 × 32	B	B	B	D	F	D	✗

Table 3. Informations about the nodules present in the test set.

	Mean diameter of the nodule				Number of annotations				σ of radiologists classification		
	<10	≥10 & <20	≥20 & <30	≥30	1	2	3	4	<0.5	≥0.5 & <1	≥1
GGO	7	10	1	2	12	3	2	3	1	6	1
PS	5	11	13	1	4	8	5	3	1	6	9
S	5	13	2	0	7	2	1	10	11	2	0

4 Results

The performance of the method was evaluated using the accuracy. Table 4 shows the results for the different hypothesis previously specified in Table 2.

The results are better when the input is not fitted to the nodule size. As the masks of manual markings were used and they do not fully agree, important information may be lost when the borders of the nodule are fully adjusted to the images limits. On the other hand, it may corroborate the idea that nodule surroundings are important to texture classification. The intensity of the nodule is important but the intensity attenuation at the border and the intensity relative to the background can also be relevant. Probably, 2.5D approaches have better results because the relationships between different views are better understood by the CNN. The best performance happened when the middle slices at different scales were used. The classification probably improved with the use of different scales because of the details in smaller scales, which have less anatomical elements. In general a larger number of slices tend to help to improve nodule classification. This was confirmed by the results of hypothesis 1 and 2. Probably the results have not improved in 3 because it reached a learning plateau in which the increase of number of slices does not improve the accuracy.

Table 4. Accuracy obtained for different architectures.

Hypotheses	1	2	3	4	5	6	7
Image size (pixels)	64 × 64	0.712 ± 0.033	0.722 ± 0.027	0.719 ± 0.052	0.751 ± 0.035	0.765 ± 0.037	0.772 ± 0.034	0.833 ± 0.041
	32 × 32	0.661 ± 0.021	0.673 ± 0.018	0.674 ± 0.035	0.691 ± 0.013	0.710 ± 0.020	0.722 ± 0.031	✗

Figure 6 shows the axial view of the best and the worst results of some nodules for the test set obtained and Table 5 shows accuracy results by class both with the hypothesis 7. The misclassified occurrences correspond to part-solid nodules with a shorter attenuation border and in little situations where there are anatomical elements surrounding the nodule. The solid nodules are not often classified as GGO and vice versa, because they are classes with quite different characteristics.

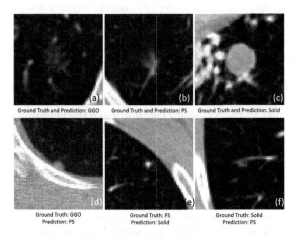

Fig. 6. Classification results: (a–c) best results, (d–f) worst results.

Table 5. Accuracy obtained for different classes with the architecture that produced better results.

		Prediction		
		GGO	PS	S
Ground Truth	GGO	0.828 ± 0.041	0.172 ± 0.041	0 ± 0
	PS	0.093 ± 0.028	0.779 ± 0.051	0.128 ± 0.044
	S	0.020 ± 0.041	0.108 ± 0.052	0.872 ± 0.030

Although the dataset is the same, this work can not be compared with the Tu *et al.* [10] because the tested nodules were not available and the ROI were different. In Tu *et al.* [10], the classification is the average of the score predictions produced for each plane by the 2D CNN. In our proposal the performance of each architecture is measured by a single final score derived from the concatenation of features inside the CNN. Also, the inter-observer calculation could not be done because there were different radiologists in the annotation process. In our opinion, the results and the conclusions that were presented are valid. We believe that the concatenation of features from different slices and a good surrounding context can be a strong contribution to an accurate classification.

5   Conclusion

This work aimed at classifying the texture of lung nodules using different CNN architectures. We were able to conclude that: (1) a larger number of slices extracted from the 3D volume helps to improve the classification; (2) the 2.5D approaches are preferable to 2D because they take into account the relationship between different views of the nodule; (3) context helps a lot in texture characterization; (4) the best performance was verified when different scales were also taken into account. For the future, a 3D approach will be developed and the implemented architectures will be used to solve malignancy classification.

Acknowledgments. This work is financed by the ERDF - European Regional Development Fund through the Operational Programme for Competitiveness - COMPETE 2020 Programme and by the National Fundus through the Portuguese funding agency, FCT - Fundação para a Ciência e Tecnologia within project POCI-01-0145-FEDER-016673.

References

1. Armato, S.G., et al.: The lung image database consortium (LIDC) and image database resource initiative (IDRI): a completed reference database of lung nodules on CT scans. Med. Phys. **38**(2), 915–931 (2011)
2. Callister, M.E.J., et al.: British thoracic society guidelines for the investigation and management of pulmonary nodules. Thorax **70**(Suppl. 2), ii1–ii54 (2015)

3. Ciompi, F., et al.: Towards automatic pulmonary nodule management in lung cancer screening with deep learning. Sci. Rep. **7**, 46479 (2017)
4. Cirujeda, P., et al.: 3d Riesz-wavelet based covariance descriptors for texture classification of lung nodule tissue in CT. In: 2015 37th Annual International Conference of the IEEE Engineering in Medicine and Biology Society (EMBC), pp. 7909–7912. IEEE (2015)
5. Ferlay, J., et al.: Cancer incidence and mortality worldwide: sources, methods and major patterns in GLOBOCAN 2012. Int. J. Cancer **136**(5), E359–E386 (2015)
6. Henschke, C.I., et al.: Early lung cancer action project: overall design and findings from baseline screening. Lancet **354**(9173), 99–105 (1999)
7. Jacobs, C., et al.: Solid, part-solid, or non-solid? Classification of pulmonary nodules in low-dose chest computed tomography by a computer-aided diagnosis system. Invest. Radiol. **50**(3), 168–173 (2015)
8. McKee, B.J., Regis, S.M., McKee, A.B., Flacke, S., Wald, C.: Performance of ACR lung-RADS in a clinical ct lung screening program. J. Am. Coll. Radiol. **12**(3), 273–276 (2015)
9. Siegel, R.L., Miller, K.D., Jemal, A.: Cancer statistics, 2018. CA: Cancer J. Clin. **68**(1), 7–30 (2018)
10. Tu, X., et al.: Automatic categorization and scoring of solid, part-solid and non-solid pulmonary nodules in CT images with convolutional neural network. Sci. Rep. **7**(1), 8533 (2017)

Reconstructed Phase Space and Convolutional Neural Networks for Classifying Voice Pathologies

João Vilian de Moraes Lima Marinus[1]([⊠]),
Joseana Macedo Fechine Regis de Araújo[2], and Herman Martins Gomes[2]

[1] Federal Institute of Alagoas, Batalha, Alagoas, Brazil
joao.marinus@ifal.edu.br
[2] Federal University of Campina Grande, Campina Grande, Brazil

Abstract. In this paper, we present a new method for classifying voice pathologies. Reconstructed Phase Space (RPS) images are employed to represent the nonlinear dynamics of the signals, and a Convolutional Neural Network (CNN) is designed to automatically learn spatial features and a classification decision from the RPS images. Due to the large parameter space of the CNN, we augmented the Massachusetts Eye and Ear Infirmary (MEEI) database with synthetic training data obtained by slowing down or speeding up the audio signal. The proposed method was evaluated in the pairwise classification of 5 voice pathologies: paralysis, edema, nodule, polyp and keratosis. Experiments were also carried out on a broader pathology class, called benign lesion, consisting of nodule, polyp and cyst signals. Accuracies similar to state-of-the-art approaches support the relevance of the method. Best accuracy was achieved in the polyp vs. nodule classification. Data augmentation was beneficial to most of the classification experiments.

Keywords: Reconstruction Phase Space ·
Convolutional Neural Network · Voice pathology

1 Introduction

The human voice is produced from an air flow passing through the various constrictions in the vocal tract structures: the vocal folds, the larynx shape, the mouth, the nose etc. As a result, voice signals embed a very unique information that may be used to identify individuals in biometric systems. Moreover, voice signals may also be used as input for systems designed to detect and classify anomalies on those structures, being a valuable tool in healthcare. Currently, about 25% of the world population work in a profession that requires excessive vocalization [1], such as teachers, lawyers, singers, and others. The size of the risk group emphasizes the importance of research in the classification of voice pathologies. The diagnosis of voice pathologies can be performed in a subjective

© Springer Nature Switzerland AG 2019
R. Vera-Rodriguez et al. (Eds.): CIARP 2018, LNCS 11401, pp. 792–801, 2019.
https://doi.org/10.1007/978-3-030-13469-3_92

way, consisting of listening to the patient's voice and deciding whether there is pathology or not, and objectively with laboratory tests which are usually more precise but highly invasive, causing discomfort to the patient.

Several researches in the area of digital processing of voice signals have been carried out with the purpose of evaluating the quality of the patient's voice and assisting a specialist in the diagnosis of voice pathologies. Acoustic analysis of voice can be an efficient tool for supporting the diagnosis of pathologies and has the advantage of not being invasive. For feature extraction, several methods based on linear acoustic theory have been used to identify voice pathologies, such as jitter and shimmer [2], cepstral coefficients [3], mel-frequency cepstral coefficients [4] and others. These methods may not be suitable to the problem, because airflow propagation through the vocal tract is more likely to follow the fluid dynamic rules, which lead to nonlinear models [5]. In recent years, researchers have proposed the use of chaos theory to identify voice pathologies. Features obtained from Reconstructed Phase Space (RPS), such as Lyapunov exponents and correlation dimension, were adopted as a nonlinear model of the speech signal [6–8]. The Reconstructed Phase Space consists of a set of m-dimensional vectors. When m = 2, it is possible to generate a 2D image from the phase space trajectory.

Convolutional Neural Networks (CNN) are widely used for image classification. Voice signals can be segmented into multiple frames, which can, in turn, be used to train a CNN. However, it is necessary to use a great amount of input samples to properly train a CNN, and usually there is a small amount of available signals of specific pathologies. For example, the well-know Massachusets Ear and Eye Infirmary database (MEEI) [9] contains only 19 signals with vocal fold nodule and 20 with vocal fold polyp. To overcome this difficulty, the speech signal may be segmented into small frames, and feature extraction is performed in each of them, so there will be more data to train the CNN. In addition, data augmentation may be employed to artificially increase the training set size.

The main goal of this work is to propose and experimentally investigate a new method for voice pathology classification that trains a CNN with RPS trajectories images. This work is organized as follows: In the next section we introduce relevant related work in this area. In Sect. 3, we present some theoretical fundamentals for the research. Section 4 contains a description of the experimental setup. Results and discussion are given in Sect. 5. Finally, Sect. 6 contains the conclusions and proposals of future work.

2   Related Work

Recent interest on the use of chaos theory for voice pathology analysis focused in obtaining a feature vector from the Reconstructed Phase Space (RPS) and presenting it as input to a classifier. Costa et al. [6] generated recurrence plots from the RPS, and extracted 7 features from the plots. They used Linear Discriminant Analysis (LDA) for classification purposes. Ghasemzadeh et al. [7] calculated the Lyapunov Spectrum from the RPS and obtained a 49-dimensional feature vector. As classifier, they used Support Vector Machines (SVM). Travieso et al. [8] obtained 10 features from the RFS to train a combined HMM-SVM classifier. Fang et al. [10] used 3 different features from the RPS to construct a 10-dimensional feature vector that was fed into a SVM classifier.

Only recently deep learning has been applied to classify voice pathologies. Frid et al. [11] used a CNN to discriminate between normal versus Parkinson's Disease voices. Fang et al. [12] used Mel-cepstral coefficients as feature vectors to train a fully connected deep learning to classify normal versus pathology. Harar et al. [13] used a CNN with a Time Distributed Layer in a similar problem.

Additional details about the related work is summarized in Table 1. Most of the works using chaos theory adopted SVM as classifier. Proprietary databases were used in 5 of the reviewed work. In the remaining papers, the publicly available datasets MEEI [9] or SVD databases [14] were used, but the signals used were different from each other. Because of these, it was not possible to perform a direct comparison between those work and ours.

Table 1. Best results of the related works.

Ref.	Database	Feature vector	Classifier	Accuracy
[6]	MEEI (53 Normal, 45 Edema)	RPS (n = 7)	LDA	88.89%
[6]	MEEI (53 Normal, 55 Paralysis)	RPS (n = 7)	LDA	100.00%
[7]	MEEI (53 Normal, 240 Pathologies)	RPS (n = 49)	SVM	98.40%
[8]	Proprietary (54 Normal, 65 Cleft Lip and Palate)	RPS (n = 10)	HMM+SVM	100.00%
[8]	MEEI (36 Normal, 36 Laryngeal Pathologies)	RPS (n = 10)	HMM+SVM	99.97%
[8]	Proprietary (50 Normal, 50 Parkinson's Disease)	RPS (n = 10)	HMM+SVM	99.94%
[10]	Proprietary (725 Intelligible Voice, 922 Non-intelligible Voice)	RPS (n = 12)	SVM	57.91%
[10]	SVD (632 Normal, 862 Pathologies)	RPS (n = 12)	SVM	60.15%
[11]	Proprietary (9 Normal, 43 Parkinson's Disease)	Raw signal (20 ms)	CNN	80.50%
[12]	Proprietary (16 Normal, 189 Pathology)	Mel-cepstral coeff. + Delta (n = 13)	DNN	94.26%
[13]	SVD (687 Normal, 1281 Pathology)	Raw signal	CNN	68.08%

3   Theoretical Review

In this section, we present a brief explanation about data augmentation methods, Reconstructed Phase Space and Convolutional Neural Networks.

3.1   Data Augmentation

Data Augmentation is a widely used strategy for increasing the amount of training data. It consists of applying one or more deformations to the original signal that results in a new synthetic signal [15]. These deformations are typically applied to signals that only belongs to the training set of a classifier. A key concept of data augmentation is that deformations applied to labeled signals will not modify the semantic meaning of the labels [16]. For the use in voice signals with some pathology, the challenge is to assure that the deformation will preserve the characteristics of the pathology. For example, a pitch variation occurs in the presence of a polyp and a deformation that changes the pitch of the signal may affect the characteristics of the polyp signal. To perform data augmentation in this paper, we used the Time Stretching (TS) method. The TS method consist in slowing down or speeding up the audio signal. Given an audio signal $x(t)$, applying a factor α yields the synthetic signal $x(\alpha t)$.

3.2 Reconstructed Phase Space

Phase space is an abstract space that represents the evolution of a dynamic system whose dimensions are state variables. The sequence of states constitutes the trajectory of the phase space. To analyze the phase space associated with a time series, such as a voice signal, it is first necessary to reconstruct the phase space of an appropriate size [18]. The most used method in the literature for phase space reconstruction is the time delay method [19] (Eq. 1).

$$\xi_t = \{x(t), x(t + \tau), ..., x(t + (m - 1)\tau)\} \tag{1}$$

where $x(t)$ is the time series, m represents the embedding dimension, τ is the optimum time delay and ξ_t represents the state in the time t.

The behavior of the trajectory in the phase space reconstruction represents the vocal dynamics. The more regular the reconstructed phase space, the more periodicity the signal has. The time delay (τ) calculation is based on the Information Theory, in which the mutual information curve of the signal is estimated [20]. The value of τ is the first minimum of the curve. Average mutual information provides the same information that the correlation function provides for linear systems [21].

3.3 Convolutional Neural Networks

A CNN has two types of layers: convolutional and pooling. It is usually organized with an input layer, one or more pairs of convolutional and pooling layers, and one or more full layers connected at the end of the network to perform the actual classification of the inputs. CNN combines three ideas to ensure some level of shift and distortion invariance: local receptive fields, shared weights, and spatial subsampling [22]. Each neuron of the convolutional layer takes inputs from a small rectangular section of the previous layer and applies a filter. Filters are replicated along with the entire input space to perform some sort of local feature extraction. The parameters of this layer are the size of the rectangular section (kernel size), number of filters (number of feature maps), stride and padding. Stride indicates the amount by which filter shifts, and padding consists in enlarging the image around its border with zero valued pixels [22]. The pooling layer is designed to achieve spatial invariance by reducing the resolution of the feature maps. This layer takes inputs from the previous convolutional layer and generates a lower resolution version by typically taking the maximum filter activation from a small rectangular region The parameters of the so called max-pooling layer are the size of the region, the stride and padding [15].

4 Experiment

In this section, we describe the experimental setup of this work. Subsection 4.1 contains a description of the database. In Subsect. 4.2, we present the methodology of the feature extraction. The used CNN Architecture are presented in Subsect. 4.3. Finally, Subsect. 4.4 contains the experimental setup.

4.1 Database

The Massachusets Eye and Ear Infirmary (MEEI) database [9] consists of 710 sustained /a/ vowel voice signals and 715 voice signals from the first 12 s of the Rainbow Passage, obtained from 777 subjects. Signals were acquired with low noise level, constant microphone distance, 16-bit resolution, sampling rate of 25.000 Hz for voice pathology signals and 50.000 Hz for normal voice signals. Altogether, 53 signals of the sustained vowel /a/ and 53 signals of the Rainbow Passage are normal voice and the remainder is voice pathologies affected by various pathologies, ranging from vocal folds pathologies such as Nodules and Cysts to neurological pathologies, such as Parkinson's disease and Stuttering. In the present work, we used normal signals (53), voice pathology signals (168), signals affected by vocal fold paralysis (67 signals), vocal fold edema (44), vocal fold keratosis (26), vocal fold nodule (19) and vocal fold polyp (20). We also group nodules and polyps signals with cyst signals (04) in a class denominated **Focal Benign Lesion of the Lamina Propria** (43), according to [17]. For conciseness, we called this class **Lesion**.

4.2 Feature Extraction

Firstly, we augmented the dataset using the approach described in Sect. 3.1. We used $\alpha = 0.8, 0.9, 1.1, 1.2$ to TS. After that, we segmented the signals using two different sizes of frame: 20 ms and 10 cycles of pitch, both of them with 50% overlap. Then, we obtained the reconstructed phase space for each frame using $m = 2$ (see Eq. 1). In Table 2 we show the total of images per class, without data augmentation. The total with data augmentation is 5× more. Next, we generate an image for each frame using the phase space trajectory (see Fig. 1). In Figs. 1 and 2, gray levels are inverted for better visualization. For dimensionality reduction, each image was divided in a box of size $N \times N$ pixels without overlapping. Each box was assigned to the count of pixels of the original image within that box. We then generate a gray scale image where the pixel intensities represent the counts obtained within each of the boxes. In this work, we used boxes with $N = 10$ and 15 (Fig. 1).

Table 2. Total of images per class.

Frame	Normal	Pathology	Paralysis	Edema	Keratosis	Polyp	Nodule	Lesion
10 Cycles	6219	5250	2249	1396	593	489	705	1289
20 ms	15608	16691	6519	4330	2462	1980	1894	4330

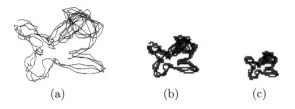

(a)   (b)   (c)

Fig. 1. (a) Reconstructed Phase Space Trajectory of the first 20 ms of an Edema voice (CAC10AN) from MEEI database and image after dimensionality reduction using (b) N = 10, and (c) N = 15.

4.3   CNN Architecture

The network is designed with 9 layers, as follows: *input ⇒ convolution (16 kernels, stride 3) ⇒ max-pooling (size 2) ⇒ convolution (32 kernels, stride 3) ⇒ max-pooling (size 2) ⇒ convolution (64 kernels, stride 3) ⇒ max-pooling (size 2) ⇒ dense RELU (1000 neurons) ⇒ dense Softmax (2 neurons)*. Three convolutional layers were used to describe the input vectors into a set local features, that become more abstract as the network depth increases. A pooling layer was used between each of the convolutional layers to reduce dimensionality. As the last component of our network, there is a stack of 2 fully connected layers ended with Softmax layer with 2 neurons (one neuron for each class) for the final classification. For the convolutional layers, we used 16, 32 and 64 kernels of size 3, and Rectified linear unit (Relu) as activation function. Other designs have been empirically evaluated, but with poorer results.

4.4   Experimental Setup

We opted to perform pairwise classifications experiments for the chosen pathologies, since this is a common approach to deal with imbalanced datasets, which is the case of MEEI. A final classification can be obtained from multiple pairwise classifiers via a majority vote scheme, but this is not within the scope of this paper. For each classification, the amount of signals used in the training set corresponded to 50% of the class with the least amount of signals. For the validation set, the amount of signals used corresponded to 10% of the class with the least amount of signals, and the remainder of the signals were used for the test set. For example, in the Paralysis versus Polyp classification, 10 signals of each class were used for training, 2 for validation, 55 of Paralysis and 8 of polyp for testing. This procedure was performed to balance the amount of signals of each class in the neural network training. The signals from each set were chosen randomly each time and it was ensured that no signal has segments in more than one of the sets. Each classification was performed 10 times and the average of the results was obtained. We used the stochastic gradient descent with momentum function during training of our proposed model, with learning rate of 0.01 and momentum of 0.9. The batch size was $K/10$, where K is the total amount of images in the training set. Training ended when there was no progress in validation loss for 5 epochs.

5   Results and Discussion

In a visual analysis of the RPS images, the trajectory of a normal voice (Fig. 2(a)) is more regular than the trajectory in voice pathologies (Figs. 2(b) to (f)). It is because normal voices are more periodicals than voice pathologies. We can see that there are differences between the pathological classes, but there are visual differences between signals from the same pathology but different subject (Figs. 1 and 2(b)). CNN classifier has been trained to extract features from the images to identify the pathology. Only frames of the whole input signal were used for training. For experimental evaluation purposes, we created a meta classification rule that outputs the most frequent class label among all classified frames for a particular signal.

The best results with and without using data augmentation are presented in the Table 3. The results were evaluated according to sensibility (SE), specificity (SP) and accuracy (ACC). N is the size of box. We can see that in most of the classifications the best results occurred with 10 cycles of pitch frame. Also, in most of cases the best results occurred when using data augmentation. Another highlight is the result of the polyp versus nodule classification. The accuracy was above 90%, with 100% of specificity.

As in the previous case (without data augmentation), most of the best results obtained when using data augmentation were obtained for 10 cycles of pitch frame. In most cases the results were better than those obtained without data augmentation. This is a good indicator that the augmentation strategy was beneficial to the CNN classifier. However, there is an exception: results involving the polyp class did not improve with data augmentation. The correct polyp-versus-edema and polyp-versus-keratosis classification rates got worse. Moreover, polyp-versus-paralysis and polyp-versus-nodule results did not significantly change. We suspect the time stretching used for data augmentation is modifying discriminative characteristics of the polyp signal. An investigation of this aspect is left as future work.

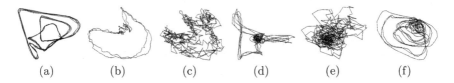

(a)   (b)   (c)   (d)   (e)   (f)

Fig. 2. Reconstructed Phase Space Trajectory of the first 20 ms of (a) a Normal voice (AXH1NAL), (b) an Edema voice (CAK25AN), (c) a Paralysis voice (RAN30AN), (d) a Nodule voice (MXN24AN), (e) a Polyp voice (MPB23AN) and (f) a Keratosis voice (EMP27AN).

Table 3. Best results without and with data augmentation.

C1	C2	Without data augmentation					With data augmentation				
		N	Frame Segments	SE (%)	SP (%)	ACC (%)	N	Frame Segments	SE (%)	SP (%)	ACC (%)
Nr	Pt	10	10 Cycles	100.0(0.0)	100.0(0.0)	100.0(0.0)	10	10 Cycles	100.0(0.0)	100.0(0.0)	100.0(0.0)
Ed	Ls	15	20 ms	58.2(8.9)	62.0(9.6)	60.0(4.0)	15	20 ms	54.6(10.6)	64.0(9.1)	59.1(5.2)
Ed	Nd	15	10 Cycles	66.2(5.4)	75.0(15.3)	67.3(4.2)	15	10 Cycles	72.4(5.5)	75.0(10.5)	72.7(3.8)
Ed	Pl	15	10 Cycles	87.6(6.0)	84.0(8.4)	87.1(4.2)	10	10 Cycles	77.9(4.5)	80.0(10.0)	78.2(3.5)
Ed	Kr	15	10 Cycles	83.2(3.8)	77.1(8.1)	81.9(3.9)	10	10 Cycles	88.0(5.3)	74.3(14.3)	85.0(4.4)
Pr	Ed	10	20 ms	82.9(5.1)	67.3(10.5)	79.1(2.4)	15	10 Cycles	83.5(6.4)	69.1(5.0)	80.0(3.7)
Pr	Ls	15	10 Cycles	77.7(7.2)	58.2(6.9)	73.0(4.6)	10	10 Cycles	81.14(8.7)	63.6(8.5)	77.0(5.4)
Pr	Nd	10	20 ms	94.0(1.7)	76.0(11.0)	92.4(1.4)	10	10 Cycles	95.9(3.2)	80.0(4.5)	94.5(2.9)
Pr	Pl	10	10 Cycles	83.9(5.7)	72.0(11.4)	82.8(4.4)	15	10 Cycles	85.4(6.6)	72.0(11.4)	84.2(5.4)
Pr	Kr	15	10 Cycles	77.9(5.5)	77.1(10.8)	77.8(4.2)	15	10 Cycles	79.2(4.3)	82.9(7.8)	79.6(2.8)
Pl	Nd	10	20 ms	93.3(4.6)	100.0(0.0)	96.4(2.5)	10	10 Cycles	93.3(4.6)	92.0(5.5)	92.7(3.8)
Kr	Ls	10	10 Cycles	90.0(4.6)	70.4(3.9)	74.5(2.3)	15	10 Cycles	83.3(8.3)	77.4(6.4)	78.6(3.5)
Kr	Nd	15	10 Cycles	80.0(7.6)	100.0(0.0)	85.9(5.3)	10	10 Cycles	83.3(3.5)	100.0(0.0)	88.2(2.5)
Kr	Pl	15	10 Cycles	70.9(9.9)	84.0(11.0)	75.0(6.6)	15	10 Cycles	81.8(7.2)	76.0(13.0)	80.0(6.0)

Legend: C1 - Class 1, C2 - Class 2, Nr - Normal, Pt - Pathology, Ed - Edema, Ls - Lesion, Nd - Nodule, Pr - Paralysis, Pl - Polyp, Kr - Keratosis

6   Conclusions and Future Work

In this paper, we proposed a novel method for the classification of voices affected by pathologies, based on RFS images and CNN. In general, when using a variable frame (10 cycles of pitch) to generate the RFS images yielded better results than using a fixed frame (20 ms). Data Augmentation turned out to be a promising method to increase correct classification rates of voice pathologies, but the chosen method affected the classifications involving the polyp class. As future work, we will analyze signals with polyp to know how the time stretching method affected them, propose additional data augmentation methods that do not affect the characteristics of the pathologies.

References

1. Al-Nasheri, A., Muhammad, G., Alsulaiman, M., Ali, Z.: Investigation of voice pathology detection and classification on different frequency regions using correlation functions. J. Voice **31**(1), 3–15 (2016)
2. Cordeiro, H.T., Fonseca, J.M., Ribeiro, C.M.: Reinke's Edema and Nodules identification in vowels using spectral features and pitch jitter. Procedia Technol. **17**, 202–208 (2014)
3. Ali, Z., Elamvazuthi, I., Alsulaiman, M., Muhammad, G.: Automatic voice pathology detection with running speech by using estimation of auditory spectrum and cepstral coefficients based on the all-pole model. J. Voice **30**(6), 757.e7–757.e19 (2016)
4. Salma, C., Asma, B., Aicha, B., Noureddine, E.: Recognition of pathological voices. In: IEEE International Multi-Conference on Systems, Signals & Devices (SSD14), Barcelona, pp. 1–6 (2014)
5. Teager, H.M., Teager, S.M.: Evidence for nonlinear sound production mechanisms in the vocal tract. In: Hardcastle, W.J., Marchal, A. (eds.) Speech Production and Speech Modelling. NATO ASI Series (Series D: Behavioural and Social Sciences), vol. 55, pp. 241–261. Springer, Dordrecht (1990). https://doi.org/10.1007/978-94-009-2037-8_10
6. Costa, W.C.A., Assis, F.M., Neto, B.G.A., Costa, S.C., Vieira, V.J.D.: Pathological voice assessment by recurrence quantification analysis. In: ISSNIP Biosignals and Biorobotics Conference (BRC), pp. 1–6 (2012)
7. Ghasemzadeh, H., Khass, M.T., Arjmandi, M.K., Pooyan, M.: Detection of vocal disorders based on phase space parameters and Lyapunov spectrum. Biomed. Signal Process. Control **22**, 135–145 (2015)
8. Travieso, C.M., Alonso, J.B., Orozco-Arroyave, J.R., Vargas-Bonilla, J.F., Nöth, E., Ravelo-García, A.G.: Detection of different voice diseases based on the nonlinear characterization of speech signals. Expert Syst. Appl. **82**, 184–195 (2017)
9. Kay Elemetrics Corp.: Disordered Voice Database, Version 1.03 (CDROM). MEEI, Voice and Speech Lab, Boston, MA, October 1994
10. Fang, C., Li, H., Ma, L., Zhang, M.: Intelligibility evaluation of pathological speech through multigranularity feature extraction and optimization. Comput. Math. Methods Med. **2017**, 1–8 (2017). https://www.hindawi.com/journals/cmmm/2017/2431573/cta/
11. Frid, A., Kantor, A., Svechin, D., Manevitz, L.M.: Diagnosis of Parkinson's disease from continuous speech using deep convolutional networks without manual selection of features. In: IEEE International Conference on the Science of Electrical Engineering (ICSEE), pp. 1–4 (2016)
12. Fang, S., et al.: Detection of pathological voice using cepstrum vectors: a deep learning approach. J. Voice (2018). https://www.sciencedirect.com/science/article/pii/S089219971730509X
13. Harar, P., Alonso-Hernandezy, J.B., Mekyska, J., Galaz, Z., Burget, Z., Smekal, Z.: Voice pathology detection using deep learning: a preliminary study. In: International Conference and Workshop on Bioinspired Intelligence (IWOBI), pp. 1–4 (2017)
14. Barry, W.J., Pützer, M.: Saarbrucken voice database. Institute of Phonetics, University of Saarland (2016). http://www.stimmdatenbank.coli.uni-saarland.de/
15. Krizhevsky, A., Sutskever, I., Hinton, G.: ImageNet classification with deep convolutional neural networks. In: Advances in Neural Information Processing Systems (NIPS), pp. 1097–1105 (2012)

16. Salamon, J., Bello, J.P.: Deep convolutional neural networks and data augmentation for environmental sound classification. IEEE Signal Process. Lett. **24**(3), 279–283 (2017)
17. Verdolini, K., Rosen, C.A., Rosen, C.A., Branski, R.C.: Classification Manual for Voice Disorders-I. Psychology Press, Oxon (2014)
18. Takens, F.: Detecting strange attractors in turbulence. In: Rand, D., Young, L.-S. (eds.) Dynamical Systems and Turbulence, Warwick 1980. LNM, vol. 898, pp. 366–381. Springer, Heidelberg (1981). https://doi.org/10.1007/BFb0091924
19. Packard, N.H.: Geometry from a time series. Phys. Rev. Lett. **45**(9), 712 (1980)
20. Fraser, A., Swinney, H.: Independent coordinates for strange attractors from mutual information. Phys. Rev. A **33**(2), 1134 (1986)
21. Li, W.: Mutual information functions versus correlation functions. J. Stat. Phys. **60**(5–6), 823–837 (1990)
22. Goodfellow, I., Bengio, Y., Courville, A.: Deep Learning. MIT Press, Cambridge (2016)

QRS Detection in ECG Signal with Convolutional Network

Pedro Silva[1], Eduardo Luz[1], Elizabeth Wanner[3], David Menotti[2], and Gladston Moreira[1](✉) ⓘ

[1] Universidade Federal de Ouro Preto, Ouro Preto, Brazil
gladston@ufop.edu.br
[2] Universidade Federal do Paraná, Curitiba, Brazil
[3] EAS, Aston University, Birmingham, UK

Abstract. The QRS complex is a very important part of a heartbeat in the electrocardiogram signal, and it provides useful information for physicians to diagnose heart diseases. Accurately detecting the fiducial points that compose the QRS complex is a challenging task. Another issue concerning the QRS detection is its computational costs since the algorithm should have a fast and real-time response. In this context, there is a trade-off between computational cost and precision. Convolutional networks are a deep learning approach, and it has achieved impressive results in several computer vision and pattern recognition problems. Nowadays there is hardware that fully embeds convolutional network models, significantly reducing computational cost for real-world and real-time applications. In this direction, this work proposes a deep learning approach, based on convolutional network, aiming to detect heartbeat pattern. We tested two different architectures with two different proposes, one very deep and that has small receptive fields, and the other that has larger receptive fields. Preliminary experiments on the MIT-BIH arrhythmia database showed that the studied convolutional network presents promising results for QRS detection which are comparable with state-of-the-art methods.

Keywords: Deep learning · Signal process · Pattern recognition

1 Introduction

The QRS complex is the main pattern of the electrocardiogram (ECG) waveform [5] and it is composed of three time-sequenced fiducial points, i.e., Q, R, and S points. This structure reflects the electrical activity of the heart during the ventricular contraction, the time of its occurrence, as well as its shape, providing much information regarding the health of an individual. Due to its peculiar rhythm and shape, the QRS complex is used as the basis for automatic determination of the heart rate, and as an entry point for classification schemes of the cardiac cycles. In that sense, QRS detection provides the fundamentals for almost all automated ECG analysis algorithms [10].

© Springer Nature Switzerland AG 2019
R. Vera-Rodriguez et al. (Eds.): CIARP 2018, LNCS 11401, pp. 802–809, 2019.
https://doi.org/10.1007/978-3-030-13469-3_93

Detecting the QRS complex is useful in various scenarios such as diagnosing arrhythmia, identifying tachycardia and also for biometrics purposes [1,9]. However, the QRS complex detection (or simply QRS detection) is a difficult task, not only due to physiological variability of the ECG wave but also due to several types of noise that can be present in the signal [12]. Noise sources include muscle noise, artifacts due to electrode displacement, power-line interference, baseline wander, and harmonic interference (T waves with a similar frequency) [12].

Deep learning is a hot topic in machine learning field nowadays and since 2012, several outstanding results have been reported in different tasks [7–9]. In a similar way, in [2] arrhythmia classification is done using CNN as a promising tool to recognize patterns in ECG signals. In [9], the authors have reported state-of-the-art results using convolutional network for biometric task through the cardiac signal. In this work, a CNN-based approach is proposed in order to detect the so-called QRS complex.

Preliminary experiments in the MIT-BIH arrhythmia database have shown that CNN is a promising tool for QRS detection, yielding figures comparable to the state-of-the-art methods. This approach could be used together with traditional QRS detectors algorithms to decrease the number of false positives and making detection more reliable. Together with the new deep learning hardware technology in development today, such as the Tensor Processing Unit (TPU) proposed by Google, FPGA base deep learning accelerators [18], or NVIDIA TX1[1], approaches based on deep learning will be the natural choice for embedding future mobile and wearable medical equipment.

The remainder of this work is organized as follows. We present and describe the related works in Sect. 2. The proposed approach and benchmark dataset is described in Sect. 3. Experimental results are described and discussed in Sect. 4. Finally, conclusions and future work are outlined in Sect. 5.

2   Related

In this section, some related works regarding QRS detection problem are described. All works described here reported state-of-the-art results and their experiments are performed on MIT-BIH database which has been widely used in literature. Several techniques have been employed.

The work proposed by Poli et al. [14] is a combination of linear-nonlinear polynomial filters and genetic algorithm to detect the QRS complex in MIT-BIH database. The first one is used to improve the quality of the signal, and the second to minimize detections errors.

Zhang and Lian [19] also used the MIT-BIH Arrhythmia Database, reaching expressive results, 99.81% sensitivity and 99.80% positive prediction. The goal is to create a method to be used in wearable ECG devices. The authors applied two strategies to improve the signal quality softening the impulsive noise and removing the baseline drift.

---

[1] http://www.nvidia.com/.

The focus of the work proposed by Chen et al. [4] is to perform a real-time QRS detection. For enhancing the accuracy and attenuating the noise, the authors introduced a wavelet-based procedure in line with a moving average-based computing method. This approach achieved about 99.5% of detection rate. According to the authors, their approach is trustworthy even when the signal quality is not the best.

Nallanthambi et al. [11] proposed a different approach. First, they changed the ECG analog input data to pulse. After that, they encoded the signal with the time-based Integrate and Fire approach, which allowed them to implement a logical decision rule for QRS detection. They highlighted how fast the process is and how it can be combined with logical hardware to reduce the power consumption.

3 Approach

This work presents an approach to detect QRS complexes from ECG signals with the well known CNN. To allow comparison with the literature, MIT-BIH Arrhythmia Database [10] is chosen since it is the most popular benchmark for ECG QRS detection and it is also the one recommended by the Association for the Advancement of Medical Instrumentation (AAMI) and described in ANSI/AAMI EC57:1998/(R)2008 (ANSI/AAMI) [3].

3.1 MIT-BIH Arrhythmia Database

MIT-BIH database provides annotations for all the recorded heartbeats, which includes patient conditions and fiducial points (read Q, R, S, T points and amplitude values) used as labels. This information is essential to train and evaluate the machine learning models.

The database was acquired using a Holter, that printed the results in tapes. Furthermore, it was digitized and the annotations were included on it by trained physicians. The frequency rate (360 samples per second per channel) was chosen to accommodate the use of simple digital notch filters to remove 60 Hz (powerline frequency) interference.

Total of 48 half-hour ECG recordings obtained from 47 individuals studied by the BIH Arrhythmia Laboratory between 1975 and 1979 was selected to compose the database. Of these 48 records, 23 (the "100 series") were chosen at random from a collection of over 4000 Holter tapes, and the other 25 (the "200 series") were selected to include examples of uncommon but clinically important arrhythmias that would not be well represented in a small random sample. The individuals included 25 men, aged 32 to 89 years, and 22 women, aged 23 to 89 years [10].

3.2 Method

In this section, we present our approach based on the convolutional network. The proposed model is considered a deep learning approach since it contains

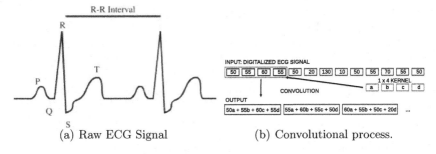

(a) Raw ECG Signal   (b) Convolutional process.

Fig. 1. One dimensional convolution process for ECG signals. The Figure illustrates a convolution process between a raw ECG and a kernel size of 1×4.

several layers and can learn representations automatically by means of supervised learning. Convolutional networks have four basic operations: convolution, activation (ReLu), pooling and normalization and all these operations are well described in the literature [7].

In our specific case, the ECG signal has a length of 833 ms (300 samples) and several kernels orders of magnitude smaller, four as shown in Fig. 1. The data is feed into the network in the raw state, without any filtering or pre-processing.

Two different network architectures are evaluated. The first is very deep and have small receptive fields, i.e., small filter kernels on the first layer, while the second uses larger filter kernels. Both architectures are inspired by [16] and [6], respectively. An example of architecture with large receptive fields is illustrated in Fig. 2.

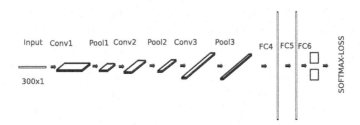

Fig. 2. CNN architecture with large receptive fields three convolutional, pooling and fully connected layers.

The QRS detection problem designed here is a binary classification problem: QRS is detected (positive class) or not (negative class). Thus, positive and negative samples must be defined. Aiming that, for each heartbeat of MIT-BIH database, three positive samples are extracted: centralized heartbeat signal, heartbeat signal shifted by $+5$ samples, heartbeat signal shifted by -5 samples. And eight negative samples are also extracted from each MIT-BIH database heartbeat: heartbeat shifted by $[\pm 30, \pm 50, \pm 80, \pm 120]$. Examples of generated samples are shown in Fig. 3.

Positive samples are defined as a signal where the QRS complex is centered on the 800 ms (or 300 samples) window, while the negative ones are based on the same signal shifted in order to intentionally misaligned the QRS complex. This way the CNN can learn to detect centralized QRS complex as a positive sample.

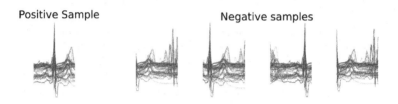

Fig. 3. Positive and negative samples from MIT-BIH records.

For training, network weights are optimized using gradient descend and the cost function used is softmax-loss. Since the generated data is large in size, the dropout is used to avoid over-fitting.

4   Experimental Results and Discussion

The computational resources used here includes an Intel (R) Core i7-5820K CPU @ 3.30 GHz 12 core, 64 GB of DDR4 RAM and a GeForce GTX TITAN X GPU. In this work, we use the MatConvNet toolbox [17] linked with NVIDIA CuDNN.

For the experiments, a total of 1280 heartbeats per record (total of 44 records of MIT-BIH) are extracted (excluding peacemaker patient records). Among those heartbeats, 480 heartbeats per record are selected for the training phase (400 for training and 80 for validation) and 800 heartbeats per record are reserved for the final evaluation. A total of 63360 samples are used as positive samples and 168960 as negative. This class imbalance is intentional in order to keep the detection window narrowed ($[+5, -5]$ samples from the center).

For CNN weights optimization, stochastic gradient descent is used on batches of size 100, momentum coefficient of 0.9 trained for 10 epochs. We have used 10% dropout after two fully connected layers and weight decay with coefficients value of 5×10^{-4}. The initial learning rate is 10^{-2}, decreasing by a factor of 10 when accuracy stagnates on validation.

The heartbeats used came from two different groups on the database: normal and arrhythmic. Between the normal ones, there are heartbeats of three types: Normal, Left and Right bundle branch block. Among the arrhythmic, heartbeats of three types are considered: Atrial premature beat, Aberrated atrial premature beat and Nodal (junctional) premature beat and Fusion of normal ventricular and normal beat. The architecture that obtained better accuracy on validation

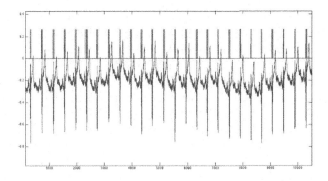

Fig. 4. Algorithm applied - 10 to 10 ms. Register 114 from MIT-BIH.

data is composed by four conv layer $[96(1 \times 49)|128(1 \times 25)|256(1 \times 9)|512(1 \times 9)]$, four pooling layer $[(1 \times 2)$ with stride 2], three fully connected $[4096(1 \times 29)|4096(1 \times 1)|2(1 \times 1)]$, dropout of 50% and softmax cost function.

When both architectures are compared, we found that the deepest network does not achieve the best result, the opposite of what is expected. This same situation can be found on a similar work [15], in which a deeper architecture does not result in the best response. Very deep networks bring instability to the training when using the gradient descent method to optimizing weights [13] and this may explain the performance of the deepest architecture. To overcome this problem, some authors segment the networks and perform the training in parts. That is, the weights are initialized from scratch only in the first stage of training [13].

Table 1. Comparison of the QRS detection with other published algorithms on the MIT-BIH arrhythmia database.

Reference	Method	Se(%)	+P(%)
Proposed method	Convolutional network	99.35	97.29
Chen et al. [4]	Wavelet de-noising	99.55	99.49
Nallathambi and Principe [11]	Pulse train	99.58	99.55
Poli et al. [14]	Genetic algorithm	99.60	99.51
Zhang and Lian [19]	Multiscale morphology	99.81	99.80

The data evaluation is created from a continuous set of 800 heartbeats for each record. A window of 300 samples is shifted by 20 samples (56 ms) and the generated signal is presented to the CNN model. With this approach, 96000 true events (QRS) and 160000 negative events (non-QRS) were generated. Results for best CNN model was 95376 True Positives (TP) and 624 False Negatives (FN), 2661 False Positives (FP) and 157339 True Negatives (TN). The total accuracy was 98.72%. Table 1 compares the proposed method with other works in the literature. To evaluate the performance, the sensitivity (Se), positive prediction (+P) were used, and are given by following equations, respectively: $Se(\%) = TP/(TP + FN)$, and $+P(\%) = TP/(TP + FP)$.

These metrics ($Se(\%)$ and $+P(\%)$) are widely used in the literature and are also the metrics recommended by AAMI [3], which means that these metrics are officially recommended for certification of algorithms/techniques embedded in medical equipment.

A practical application of the method can be seen in Fig. 4, where a 300 samples window of one MIT-BIH recording is shifted 10 to 10 ms, in a sliding window fashion. The red pulse indicates when a QRS complex is detected.

In this type of application, the occurrence of false positives is a major problem since the false positive often leads to heart rate miscalculation and thus causing unnecessary alarm for the medical staff. In real scenarios, physicians tend to lose confidence when they perceive excessive false positive events. The method proposed here, based on CNN, could be used in medical equipment, along with traditional methods that already embed those devices, to help reduce false positives.

5   Conclusions

In this paper, a QRS detection method in electrocardiogram based on convolutional network is presented. To the best of our knowledge, this is the first time that CNN is used for such aim. Experiments have shown that the proposed method is comparable to state-of-the-art methods in the literature (See Table 1) and could be a promising research path. It is worth noting that, although the results of the methods presented in Table 1 used the same database, the evaluation protocol is different, regarding the number of instances for training and testing.

Despite no pre-processing technique was considered in the present methodology, a filtering stage could impact on final results. This is a promising research direction to increase the accuracy of CNN-based QRS-detectors.

It is worthwhile noting that improvements can also be achieved by investigating other CNN architectures and other techniques for allowing training more deeper networks, such as the ones employed in [13]. For future works, CNN-based QRS detectors could be merged to traditional QRS-detector methods aiming to reduce the false positive rate and increase final accuracy.

Acknowledgements. The authors thank UFOP, UFPR and funding Brazilian agencies CNPq, Fapemig and CAPES. We gratefully acknowledge the support of NVIDIA Corporation with the donation of a Titan X Pascal GPU used for this research.

References

1. Acharya, U.R., Fujita, H., Lih, O.S., Hagiwara, Y., Tan, J.H., Adam, M.: Automated detection of arrhythmias using different intervals of tachycardia ECG segments with convolutional neural network. Inf. Sci. **405**, 81–90 (2017)

2. Al Rahhal, M., Bazi, Y., AlHichri, H., Alajlan, N., Melgani, F., Yager, R.: Deep learning approach for active classification of electrocardiogram signals. Inf. Sci. **345**, 340–354 (2016)
3. ANSI/AAMI: Testing and reporting performance results of cardiac rhythm and ST segment measurement algorithms. American National Standards Institute, Inc. (ANSI), Association for the Advancement of Medical Instrumentation (AAMI), ANSI/AAMI/ISO EC57, 1998-(R)2008 (2008)
4. Chen, S.W., Chen, H.C., Chan, H.L.: A real-time QRS detection method based on moving-averaging incorporating with wavelet denoising. Comput. Methods Programs Biomed. **82**(3), 187–195 (2006)
5. Kohler, B.U., Hennig, C., Orglmeister, R.: The principles of software QRS detection. IEEE Eng. Med. Biol. Mag. **21**(1), 42–57 (2002)
6. Krizhevsky, A., Sutskever, I., Hinton, G.E.: ImageNet classification with deep convolutional neural networks. In: Advances in Neural Information Processing Systems, pp. 1097–1105 (2012)
7. LeCun, Y., Bengio, Y., Hinton, G.: Deep learning. Nature **521**(7553), 436–444 (2015)
8. Liu, W., et al.: SSD: single shot MultiBox detector. In: Leibe, B., Matas, J., Sebe, N., Welling, M. (eds.) ECCV 2016. LNCS, vol. 9905, pp. 21–37. Springer, Cham (2016). https://doi.org/10.1007/978-3-319-46448-0_2
9. Luz, E., Moreira, G., Oliveira, L.S., Schwartz, W.R., Menotti, D.: Learning deep off-the-person heart biometrics representations. IEEE Trans. Inf. Forensics Secur. **13**, 1258–1270 (2018)
10. Luz, E.J.S., Schwartz, W.R., Cámara-Chávez, G., Menotti, D.: ECG-based heartbeat classification for arrhythmia detection: a survey. Comput. Methods Programs Biomed. **127**, 144–164 (2016)
11. Nallathambi, G., Principe, J.C.: Integrate and fire pulse train automaton for QRS detection. IEEE Trans. Biomed. Eng. **61**(2), 317–326 (2014)
12. Pan, J., Tompkins, W.J.: A real-time QRS detection algorithm. IEEE Trans. Biomed. Eng. **BME–32**(3), 230–236 (1985)
13. Parkhi, O.M., Vedaldi, A., Zisserman, A.: Deep face recognition. In: British Machine Vision Conference, vol. 1, p. 6 (2015)
14. Poli, R., Cagnoni, S., Valli, G.: Genetic design of optimum linear and nonlinear QRS detectors. IEEE Trans. Biomed. Eng. **42**(11), 1137–1141 (1995)
15. Schons, T., Moreira, G.J.P., Silva, P.H.L., Coelho, V.N., Luz, E.J.S.: Convolutional network for EEG-based biometric. In: Mendoza, M., Velastín, S. (eds.) CIARP 2017. LNCS, vol. 10657, pp. 601–608. Springer, Cham (2018). https://doi.org/10.1007/978-3-319-75193-1_72
16. Simonyan, K., Zisserman, A.: Very deep convolutional networks for large-scale image recognition. arXiv preprint arXiv:1409.1556 (2014)
17. Vedaldi, A., Lenc, K.: MatConvNet: convolutional neural networks for MATLAB. In: Proceedings of the 23rd ACM International Conference on Multimedia, pp. 689–692. ACM (2015)
18. Zhang, C., Li, P., Sun, G., Guan, Y., Xiao, B., Cong, J.: Optimizing FPGA-based accelerator design for deep convolutional neural networks. In: Proceedings of the 2015 ACM/SIGDA International Symposium on Field-Programmable Gate Arrays, pp. 161–170. ACM (2015)
19. Zhang, F., Lian, Y.: QRS detection based on multiscale mathematical morphology for wearable ECG devices in body area networks. IEEE Trans. Biomed. Circuits Syst. **3**(4), 220–228 (2009)

Gender Effects on an EEG-Based Emotion Level Classification System

I. De La Pava[1(✉)], A. Álvarez[1], P. Herrera[2], G. Castellanos-Dominguez[3], and A. Orozco[1]

[1] Automatic Research Group, Faculty of Engineerings,
Universidad Tecnológica de Pereira, Pereira, Colombia
{ide,andres.alvarez1,aaog}@utp.edu.co
[2] Psychiatry, Neuroscience and Community Group, School of Medicine,
Universidad Tecnológica de Pereira, Pereira, Colombia
p.herrera@utp.edu.co
[3] Signal Processing and Recognition Group, Department of Electrical
and Electronic Engineering, Universidad Nacional de Colombia, Manizales, Colombia
cgcastellanosd@unal.edu.co

Abstract. Emotion level classification systems based on features extracted from physiological signals have promising applications in human-computer interfaces. Moreover, there is increasing evidence that points to gender differences in the processing of emotional stimuli. However, such differences are commonly overlooked during the assessment and development of the systems in question. Here, we study gender differences in the performance of an emotion level classification system and its constituting elements, namely features extracted from electroencephalography (EEG) signals, and emotion level ratings in the Arousal/Valence (AV) dimensional space elicited from audiovisual stimuli. Obtained results show differences in the physiological and expressive responses of men and women, and in overall classification performance for the valence dimension.

Keywords: Emotion assessment · Electroencephalography · Gender differences

1 Introduction

The development of automatic systems for emotional response recognition arouses considerable interest because of their potential impact on the field of human-computer interfaces [9]. These systems aim to predict a subject's emotional response to a stimulus from audiovisual or physiological data. The emotional responses are coded using either a discrete representation (specific emotions such as happiness, fear, sadness, or anger) or a dimensional representation, that is, latent dimensions whose combination give rise to specific emotions. The most common dimensional representation being the Arousal/Valence (AV) emotional space, in which the arousal dimension places emotions in a range varying

© Springer Nature Switzerland AG 2019
R. Vera-Rodriguez et al. (Eds.): CIARP 2018, LNCS 11401, pp. 810–819, 2019.
https://doi.org/10.1007/978-3-030-13469-3_94

from inactive or calm to active or excited, while the valence dimension does so in a range varying from negative or unpleasant to positive or pleasant [7]. Regarding the data needed to infer the emotional response, EEG has received increasing attention from affective computing researchers since it is a non-invasive, fast and relatively inexpensive neuroimaging technique with well-established connections to cognitive processes [1]. However, due to the complexity of the spectral and spatiotemporal relationships between EEG signals and emotional responses that need to be deciphered, the performance of EEG-based systems remains relatively low, especially when complex stimuli (e.g., music videos) are used for emotion elicitation. These hurdles have led to many feature extraction, feature selection and classification methods being explored to improve the performance of such systems [5,9,11].

Moreover, little attention has been paid to demographic characteristics that could impact the performance of emotional response recognition systems, such as gender or age. There is a growing body of evidence suggesting differences in the way men and women process emotional stimuli: men may rely more on the recall of past emotional experiences to evaluate new ones than women [1], unpleasant and high arousing stimuli may evoke greater electrophysiological responses in women relative to men [8], and reports on EEG patterns have shown stronger group coherence among women compared with men during emotion [12]. Despite this, a recent survey gathering research about emotion recognition from EEG signals over the past 9 years, highlights important concerns: 24% of the analyzed works do not specify the participants' gender and 68% are based on unbalanced samples in regard to the men-women ratio, being men overrepresented [1]. Therefore, it is relevant to study how gender differences affect the constituting components of emotional response recognition systems based on EEG, as well as their impact on those systems' overall performance.

In this work, we study the gender differences present in an EEG-based emotion level classification system. We do so at the level of the physiological responses measured by EEG and at the level of the subjective experience and/or expressive response associated with a provided stimulus. We also study whether these differences are reflected in the overall classification performance. To those ends, the EEG data is characterized through a differential entropy (DE) analysis, which has been shown to outperform other EEG characterization strategies in emotion level classification tasks [11]; while the expressive responses are coded as ratings in independent scales for valence and arousal. These features, along with gender class vectors, are used as inputs to simple K-nearest neighbor classifiers. The analyses are carried out on the publicly available Database for Emotion Analysis Using Physiological Signals (DEAP) [7]. Obtained results show a gender difference for the valence dimension in terms of classification performance. They also show that it is feasible to classify the subjects' gender from the DE features and from ratings in the AV emotional space.

2   Materials and Methods

Database. We use EEG and subjective data obtained from the Database for Emotion Analysis Using Physiological Signals (DEAP) [7]. This database holds EEG recordings obtained from 32 healthy subjects (15 females and 17 males of average age 25.4 years and 28.3 years, respectively) while performing 40 trials of an emotion elicitation experiment. In each experiment, the subjects were exposed to 1-min long music videos. Afterward, the participants rated the music videos on discrete 9-point scales for valence and arousal; where 1 and 9 represented the lowest and highest level of emotional elicitation in either dimension. The EEG data were acquired at a sampling rate of 512 Hz using a 32 channel BioSemi ActiveTwo system. The dataset underwent eye blink artifact removal via independent component analysis, frequency down-sampling to 128 Hz, and bandpass filtering from 4–45 Hz. Besides, the data were averaged to the common reference and segmented into trials lasting 63 s.

EEG Feature Extraction. We compute the differential entropy (DE) as follows: given the EEG data recorded from each subject $\{X_n \in \mathbb{R}^{C \times M}\}_{n=1}^{N}$, where $C = 32$ is the number of channels, $M = 8064$ is the number of samples registered for each channel, and $N = 40$ is the number of trials or videos; we segment the last 10 s of each signal using a square window of 1280 points. This segmentation is performed under the premise that the subject's emotional response to the 1-min long music video should be more evident towards the end of the stimulus due to emotional reverberation [3]. Then, we compute the average power spectral density over each EEG rhythm (θ: 4–7 Hz, α: 8–13 Hz, β: 14–30 Hz, and γ: 31–45 Hz) using the Fast Fourier Transform of the segmented data $X_n' \in \mathbb{R}^{C \times L}$, with $L = 1280$. The features are restricted to 4–45 Hz since the pre-processed version of the DEAP dataset is bandpass-filtered in that frequency range. Finally, we compute the DE as the logarithm of the power spectral density [11], obtaining for each subject a set of DE matrices $\{\zeta_n \in \mathbb{R}^{C \times 4}\}_{n=1}^{N}$.

Gender Differences from DE Feature Sets. We concatenate the DE feature set so that the matrices ζ_n are transformed into vectors $\zeta_n' \in \mathbb{R}^{1 \times (C \times 4)}$. Then, we stack the $N = 40$ row vectors ζ_n', corresponding to each video to form a matrix $\Lambda_i \in \mathbb{R}^{N \times (C \times 4)}$ that contains all DE features extracted from the ith subject. For each matrix Λ_i, we assign a vector of gender labels $l_i \in \{0, 1\}^N$ (label "0" is assigned to men and "1" to women). Next, we set up a subject independent classification system with the aim of estimating the gender labels l_i from the DE features. We train a Euclidean distance-based K-nearest neighbor classifier using a 32-fold cross-validation setup. For the jth fold the features from subject jth, $\Lambda_{i=j}$, are used as the testing set and the features from all other subjects, $\Lambda_{i \neq j}$, are used as the training set. The classification is performed for all DE features, and for subsets of different EEG rhythms (θ, α, β, and γ) and cortical areas (frontal: Fp1, Fp2, AF3, AF4, F3, F4, F7, F8; central: FC1, FC2, FC5, FC6, C3, C4, CP1, CP2, CP5, CP6; parietal: P3, P4, P7, P8, PO3, PO4; temporal: T7, T8; and occipital: O1, O2) by selecting the appropriate columns of Λ_i.

Gender Differences from AV Rating Scales. For each emotion dimension, we build a matrix containing the ratings (in a 1 to 9 scale) given by the subjects to each video: $Y \in \mathbb{R}^{S \times N}$, where $S = 32$ is the number of subjects. Then, a gender label is assigned to each row of Y, obtaining a labels vector $\xi \in \{0, 1\}^S$ (0 for men and 1 for women). Next, we employ a Euclidean distance-based K-nearest neighbor classifier to estimate the gender labels from Y, following a leave-one-out cross-validation scheme. The gender classification is performed independently for valence and arousal.

Subject-Dependent Emotion Level Classification. We devise the emotion level assessment task as two binary classification problems, one for each dimension of the AV space. The rating scales for variance and arousal are divided into low (1 to 5) and high (5 to 9) levels, and given class labels -1 and 1, respectively. Thus, for each subject we have a set of matrices $\{\zeta_n \in \mathbb{R}^{C \times 4}\}_{n=1}^N$ containing the DE features, and two labels vectors $\lambda \in \{-1, 1\}^N$ (one for valence and one for arousal). Afterward, for each subject we train two Euclidean distance-based K-nearest neighbor classifiers, one for each emotional dimension, to estimate the emotion level labels from the DE features. We do so, following a leave-one-out cross-validation scheme.

For each of the above-described experiments, the number of nearest neighbors K of the classifier is selected through nested cross-validation from the set $K = \{1, 3, 5, 7, 9, 11\}$.

3   Results and Discussion

Gender Differences from DE Feature Sets: Table 1 shows the gender classification accuracy [%] per sample (video) discriminated by EEG band and cortical area. The highest accuracies are obtained for the parietal region across all frequency bands. Figure 1(a) presents the confusion matrix for classification from all frequency bands in the parietal region. Overall, the classification system is more apt at identifying male subjects than the female subjects. Figure 1(b) shows the confusion matrix obtained after estimating the subject's gender, not for each sample, but as the mode of its predicted sample labels, that is, the mode of the predicted labels of the $N = 40$ videos for each subject. The trends observed in Fig. 1(a) remain unchanged in Fig. 1(b), implying that the differences in classification performance between genders, probably cannot be attributed to variations in the recorded brain activity in response to specific stimuli (videos), but to more general differences among subjects. These differences are the result of larger variability in women's DE features as compared with men's. Figure 2(a) shows a Principal Component Analysis (PCA) based projection of the DE features (parietal region, all bands) into a 3D space. The projected features for men and women are represented as blue and red dots, respectively. Men's projected features are clustered together, while women's are more spread out, which translates into a higher variability in women's original DE features. As a consequence, the area where both groups overlap counts with a higher density of features belonging to men, which sheds light into the most common type of

Table 1. Average accuracy [%] per sample for gender classification from DE features.

	θ	α	β	γ	All
Frontal	60.6	45.7	41.9	48.1	50.2
Central	49.5	32.2	30.6	49.6	40.6
Parietal	76.9	68.9	69.6	61.3	75.1
Temporal	66.8	53.4	52.5	57.3	60.9
Occipital	56.3	59.6	55.8	52.4	61.2
All	65.0	44.0	55.0	52.3	61.4

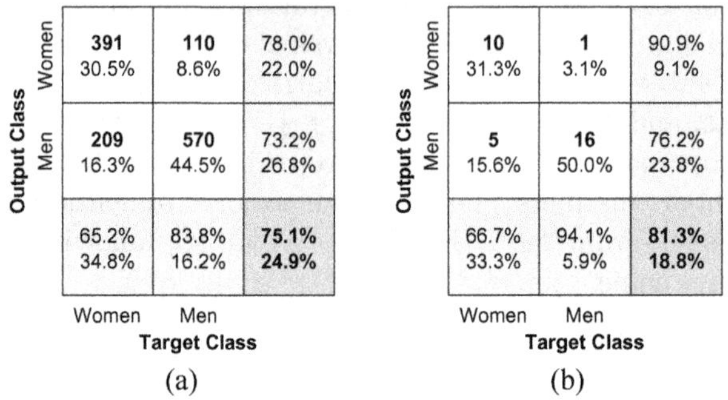

Fig. 1. Confusion matrices for gender classification from parietal DE features: (a) for each sample, (b) for each subject (mode of each subject's predicted sample labels).

classification error obtained (female subjects wrongly classified as males). This result seems to contradict previous evidence showing that women share more similar EEG patterns among them when emotions are evoked than men [12].

Figure 2(b) shows the normalized difference of the average DE between male and female subjects. As expected, the larger differences are found in the parietal and temporoparietal region, especially in the right hemisphere. It is this difference in the DE, and thus in EEG power in those regions, which accounts for the ability of the proposed classifier to discriminate between male and female subjects. These results are in agreement with previous studies that identified gender differences in parietal, temporoparietal and occipital regions in the δ, θ and β bands [4,6]. However, the cited studies found those differences during simple visual stimulation and meditation tasks. Which implies that the gender differences observed here may not be related to the emotional response to the audiovisual stimuli, but be an epiphenomenon of intrinsic gender differences such us thicker cortical gray matter and increased neural process in women, or skull thicknesses variability [6]. To determine if the performance of our DE-based gender classification system depends on an emotional response, we evaluated the average classification performance for each video and contrasted those results against the distribution of the videos in the AV dimensional space generated by the DEAP subjects' ratings shown in Fig. 2(c). The results of the carried out analysis are presented graphically in Fig. 2(d). We did not find any significant differences in gender classification when the subject was exposed to stimuli of different emotional content, according to the four quadrants of the AV space. Therefore, the results discussed in this section point to the existence of gender differences in the DE features extracted from EEG data. However, we fail to directly link those differences with the subjects' emotional response to the audiovisual stimuli.

Gender Differences from AV Rating Scales: Figure 2(e) shows the distribution of the average AV ratings discriminated by gender. A simple visual inspection reveals gender differences in the self-reported emotional estates elicited by each video, implying that besides the gender differences in the subject's physiological responses, there are differences in the subjective experience and/or expressive response associated with the stimuli. In the following, we attempt to analyze these differences independently for each emotional dimension and exploit them to identify a subject's gender from his/her ratings. Figure 3(a) presents the results of performing gender classification from the self-reported

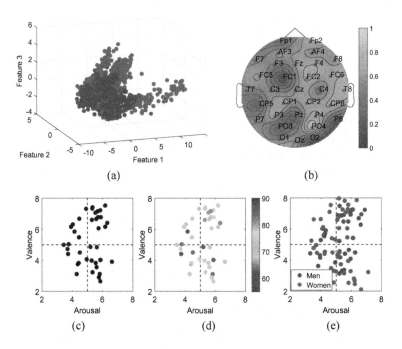

Fig. 2. (a) Gender differences in a space generated by PCA analysis over the DE features (parietal region, all bands; men - blue dots, women - red dots). (b) Normalized difference of the average DE between male and female subjects. (c) Average ratings for each video in the AV space for all subjects. (d) Gender classification accuracy for each video distributed on the AV space according to the subject ratings. (e) Average ratings for each video in the AV space discriminated by gender. (Color figure online)

valence ratings. Unlike the results obtained using the DE features, the classification system is more apt at identifying women than men, with class accuracies of 80.0% and 64.7%, respectively. The possibility of identifying a subject's gender from the valence ratings is accounted for by gender differences in psychological responses to low and high valence stimuli [10], which are at least partly observable in Fig. 2(e). Figure 3(b) shows the Euclidean distance between the valence scale self-reported ratings for all subjects ordered by gender. The distances among women's valence ratings are smaller than among men's, which is reflected in an area of small distances and little variability at the bottom right corner of the plot, explaining the results shown in Fig. 3(a). Figure 3(c) presents the confusion matrix resulting of performing gender classification from the self-reported arousal ratings. Contrary to the valence ratings, the arousal ratings do not allow to carry out gender classification successfully. At this point, it is worth noting the opposing trends described so far, regarding the intra-gender variability exhibited by the valence ratings and the DE features computed from the EEG signals. Men's DE features have less variability than women's, while for the valence ratings the opposite is true. This result poses a challenge to emotion level classification systems based on that information because the features from which the emotional responses are being inferred present large variability in similar emotional responses and vice-versa.

Subject-Dependent Emotion Level Classification: Given the gender differences in the EEG patterns and in the valence ratings found in the previous sections, it follows that the algorithms of emotion level classification should perform differently in the valence dimension for male and female subjects. For our subject-dependent binary emotional dimension level set-up, we obtain average classification accuracies of $60.0 \pm 9.7\%$ and $61.1 \pm 12.5\%$ for valence and arousal, respectively. These accuracies are in the same range as those of recent works that deal with the problem of emotion assessment from EEG and test their methods

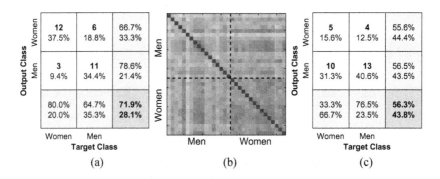

(a)   (b)   (c)

Fig. 3. (a) Confusion matrix for gender classification using the valence ratings. (b) Euclidean distance between the valence scale self-assessment ratings for all subjects ordered by gender. (c) Confusion matrix for gender classification using the arousal ratings.

in the DEAP database. A comparison with such methods is presented in Table 2. However, it has been noted that for emotional level discrimination in the DEAP database the classification accuracy can be misleading [9] because of the class imbalances in the valence and arousal ratings. The area under the Receiver Operating Characteristic (ROC) curve is a fairer way of assessing the performance of the classifier. Figure 4(a) shows the average accuracies and areas under the ROC curve per subject for valence classification. All subjects with high areas under the ROC curve also have high classification accuracies, while the contrary is not true. Finally, Fig. 4(b) shows the boxplots, displaying with the distribution of the areas under the ROC curve for all subjects, discriminated by gender for valence. As seen, there is a difference in classification performance between men and women in the valence emotional dimension, with women displaying an average area ROC of 0.58 ± 0.11 versus men's 0.52 ± 0.11. For arousal, average areas ROC of 0.50 ± 0.06 for women and 0.52 ± 0.10 for men are observed.

Table 2. Emotion level classification accuracy [%] for all subjects in DEAP.

Approach	Arousal	Valence
Koelstra et al. [7]	62.0	57.6
Gupta et al. [5]	65.0	60.0
Padilla-Buritica et al. [9]	52.8	58.6
Arnau-González et al. [2]	67.7	69.6
This work	**61.1**	**60.0**

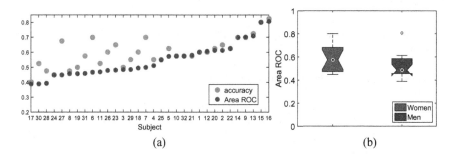

(a)   (b)

Fig. 4. (a) Average accuracies and areas under the ROC curve per subject for valence classification. The subjects are ordered according to increasing area ROC. (b) Area under the ROC curve for all subjects discriminated by gender for the valence dimension.

4   Conclusions

In this work, we study the differences between male and female subjects during an emotion elicitation experiment using EEG and behavioral measures. We assess the effects of such differences on an emotion level classification system and its components. We have adopted two different perspectives: regarding the subject's physiological responses, as measured by EEG, and their subjective experiences, as measured by rating scales in the AV dimensional space. Our results show differences between men and women in DE features extracted from EEG signals of the parietal region across all frequency bands, higher DE feature variability among female subjects, and higher variability in male subjects' ratings in the valence dimension. Our results also show a gender difference for the valence dimension in the overall performance of our emotion level classifier. Therefore, gender is a relevant factor to take into account during the development and assessment of systems that aim to automatically classify emotional responses, at least those elicited by audiovisual stimuli. Our future work will focus on the development of emotional response recognition strategies based on EEG that integrate demographic information. In particular, subject-independent emotion level classification systems that exploit gender differences to improve classification performance.

Acknowledgments. This work was supported by projects 1110-744-55778 and 6-18-1 funded by Colciencias and Universidad Tecnológica de Pereira, respectively. Author I. De La Pava was supported by the program "Doctorado Nacional en Empresa - Convoctoria 758 de 2016", also funded by Colciencias.

References

1. Alarcao, S.M., et al.: Emotions recognition using EEG signals: a survey. IEEE Trans. Affect. Comput. (2017)
2. Arnau-González, P., et al.: Fusing highly dimensional energy and connectivity features to identify affective states from EEG signals. Neurocomputing **244**, 81–89 (2017)
3. Droit-Volet, S., et al.: Emotion and time perception: effects of film-induced mood. Front. Integr. Neurosci. **5**, 33 (2011)
4. Güntekin, B., et al.: Brain oscillations are highly influenced by gender differences. Int. J. Psychophysiol. **65**(3), 294–299 (2007)
5. Gupta, R., et al.: Relevance vector classifier decision fusion and EEG graph-theoretic features for automatic affective state characterization. Neurocomputing **174**, 875–884 (2016)
6. Hashemi, A., et al.: Characterizing population EEG dynamics throughout adulthood. ENeuro **3**(6), ENEURO-0275 (2016)
7. Koelstra, S., et al.: DEAP: a database for emotion analysis; using physiological signals. IEEE Trans. Affect. Comput. **3**(1), 18–31 (2012)
8. Lithari, C., et al.: Are females more responsive to emotional stimuli? A neurophysiological study across arousal and valence dimensions. Brain Topogr. **23**(1), 27–40 (2010)

9. Padilla-Buritica, J.I., et al.: Emotion discrimination using spatially compact regions of interest extracted from imaging EEG activity. Front. Comput. Neurosci. **10**, 55 (2016)
10. Rukavina, S., et al.: Affective computing and the impact of gender and age. PloS one **11**(3), e0150584 (2016)
11. Zheng, W.L., et al.: Identifying stable patterns over time for emotion recognition from EEG. IEEE Trans. Affect. Comput. (2017)
12. Zhu, J.-Y., Zheng, W.-L., Lu, B.-L.: Cross-subject and cross-gender emotion classification from EEG. In: Jaffray, D.A. (ed.) World Congress on Medical Physics and Biomedical Engineering, June 7-12, 2015, Toronto, Canada. IP, vol. 51, pp. 1188–1191. Springer, Cham (2015). https://doi.org/10.1007/978-3-319-19387-8_288

EEG Channel Relevance Analysis Using Maximum Mean Discrepancy on BCI Systems

D. F. Luna-Naranjo[1], J. V. Hurtado-Rincon[1], D. Cárdenas-Peña[1(✉)],
V. H. Castro[2], H. F. Torres[2], and G. Castellanos-Dominguez[1]

[1] Signal Processing and Recognition Group, Universidad Nacional de Colombia,
Km 9 Vía al Aeropuerto la Nubia, Manizales, Colombia
{dflunan,jvhurtador,dcardenasp,cgcastellanosd}@unal.edu.co
[2] Universidad de Caldas, Manizales, Colombia
victorhcastrolondon@gmail.com, hector.torres_c@ucaldas.edu.co

Abstract. Brain-Computer Interfaces bridge the communication between brains and devices. Channel selection as a stage for developing BCI systems allows reducing costs and improve the overall performance. This paper proposes a relevance analysis based on the maximum mean discrepancy as the distance function between a pair of single-channel trials, termed rMMD. The proposed rMMD starts with a trial embedding that highlights temporal dynamics, and ends with a channel ranking according to a designed relevance function. The function relies on the within and between class distances to quantify the discrimination capability of each channel. We evaluate the rMMD on a bi-class motor-imagery (MI) dataset holding 64 channels and more than 40 subjects. In comparison with no channel selection and a heuristic approach, our proposed relevance analysis statistically improves the classification of MI tasks with a reduced set of channels.

Keywords: Channel selection · Time-series relevance analysis ·
Brain computer interface

1 Introduction

Brain-computer interface (BCI) systems provide a communication bridge between a brain and a computer with applications ranging from gaming to clinical. Typical BCI systems are trained using, voluntary or evoked, electroencephalographic (EEG) signals from subjects performing specific mental tasks or under particular conditions [8]. The preference of EEG signals relies on its low recording risk, low implementation cost, and high potential for practical applications as device control [10]. From the voluntary approaches, the motor-imagery (MI) paradigm relies on decoding imagination, not execution, of motor tasks that produces event-related de/synchronization (ERDS) along the brain motor

© Springer Nature Switzerland AG 2019
R. Vera-Rodriguez et al. (Eds.): CIARP 2018, LNCS 11401, pp. 820–828, 2019.
https://doi.org/10.1007/978-3-030-13469-3_95

homunculus [5]. Fed by EEG, an MI-BCI framework usually holds four stages: signal pre-processing, feature extraction, channel selection, and classification.

This work is particularly interested in the third stage as removing noisy and redundant channels improves the overall system performance, while reducing implementation costs and setup times [1]. The most explored channel selection approaches employ evolutionary and heuristic algorithms, from which the following are worth mentioning: The Glow Swarm Optimization algorithm followed by a naïve Bayes classifier [6], the Sequential Floating Forward Selection by locally grouping EEG channels [11], the Non-dominated Sorting Genetic Algorithm II for multi-objective optimization [9], and the backtracking search optimization algorithm by the binary encoding the selected channels [4]. Such kind of methods tend to outperform the accuracy rates of the full EEG montage. Nonetheless, the large set of hyperparameters to be tuned makes the heuristic and evolutionary algorithms heavily depend on the initialization. In addition, those kind of algorithms are well-known for its high computational cost in the training stage, constraining their use subject-dependent applications. Other channel selection approaches rely on information measures that are less costly and more accessible to optimize in comparison to above methods. For instance, ranking channels according to the mutual information between trial label and the Laplacian of the average channel power enhanced a BCI system that carried out the feature extraction by common spatial patterns (CSP) [12].

This paper introduces a distance-based channel relevance analysis that compare trials trough the Maximum Mean Discrepancy, termed rMMD. The proposed analysis firstly embeds each single channel to highlight the temporal dynamics of the trials. Then, we assume that each embedded trial follows its own distribution to measure the pair-wise trial distance at the channel level from their means on a Reproduced Kernel Hilbert Space. Thanks to such an assumption, we obtain a single distance value for each pair of time series. Finally, we designed a relevance measure as a function of the within and between class distances. As a result, our measure allows ranking channels according its discrimination capabilities. To evaluate our proposed relevance analysis, we include it as the channel selection stage of a typical BCI system, and compare it against no channel selection and the heuristical SFFS. Results on a dataset of more than 40 subjects evidence the benefit of the rMMD-based channel selection with a significant difference with respect to the compared approaches.

2 Methods

2.1 Single-Channel Trial-Wise Distance

Let a set of N labeled multi-channel EEG trials $\{\boldsymbol{X}_n, l_n\}_{n=1}^N$, where $\boldsymbol{X}_n = \{\boldsymbol{x}_n^c \in \mathbb{R}^T : c \in [1, C]\}$ corresponds to the n-th trial with label $l_n \in \{-, +\}$ that holds C channels recorded for T time instants. BCI systems attempt to classify unlabeled EEG trials into $-$ or $+$ depending on features extracted from its multiple channels. Here, we measure the distance at channel level between a pair of trials as the distance between the means of their approximate distributions mapped into a Reproduced Kernel Hilbert Space (RHKS), termed the Maximum Mean Discrepancy (MMD) [7]. To this end, the Hankel transform of window length L embeds each channel and trial into a time series with L time-lagged components, $\mathbb{R}^T \rightarrow \mathbb{R}^{L \times (T-L)}; \boldsymbol{x}_n^c \mapsto \{\boldsymbol{y}_{nt}^c\}_{t=1}^{(T-L)}$. Assuming that samples from an embedded trial follows the unknown distribution $\boldsymbol{y}_n^c \sim P_n^c(\boldsymbol{y}) \in [0,1]$, the MMD statistic compares two trials at the c-th channel as:

$$d(\boldsymbol{x}_n^c, \boldsymbol{x}_m^c) := D(P_n^c, P_m^c, \Phi) = \|\mu_n^c - \mu_m^c\|_{\mathcal{H}}^2$$
$$d(\boldsymbol{x}_n^c, \boldsymbol{x}_m^c) = \mathbb{E}_{t,t'} \left\{ \Phi(\boldsymbol{y}_{nt}^c)^\top \Phi(\boldsymbol{y}_{nt'}^c) \right\} - 2\mathbb{E}_{t,t'} \left\{ \Phi(\boldsymbol{y}_{mt}^c)^\top \Phi(\boldsymbol{y}_{mt'}^c) \right\} \tag{1}$$
$$+ \mathbb{E}_{t,t'} \left\{ \Phi(\boldsymbol{y}_{mt}^c)^\top \Phi(\boldsymbol{y}_{mt'}^c) \right\}$$

where $\mu_n^c \in \mathcal{H}$ stands for the mean of the distribution P_n^c in the RHKS, and $\mathbb{E}_{t,t'} \{\cdot\}$ defines the averaging operator along the time instants of two trials, and function $\Phi : \mathbb{R}^L \rightarrow \mathcal{H}$ maps from the time embedding into the RHKS. In practice, the kernel trick allows computing inner products as $\Phi(\boldsymbol{y}_{nt}^c)^\top \Phi(\boldsymbol{y}_{mt'}^c)$ by the function $\kappa(\boldsymbol{y}_{nt}^c, \boldsymbol{y}_{mt'}^c) \in \mathbb{R}^+$. Therefore, the MMD statistic results in an inherent comparison of temporal dynamics that are encoded by the probabilistic distribution of embedded trials.

2.2   Distance-Based Supervised Relevance Analysis

The purpose of a supervised relevance analysis is to quantify the discrimination capability of features so that the noisy and redundant ones are removed to improve the overall system performance. In this work, we propose to assess the relevance of each EEG channel to discriminate two conditions $\{-, +\}$ aiming to reduce the EEG montage size from the start, to easen feature extraction stage, and to improve the classification performance of the whole BCI system. In this sense, we design a relevance measure that looks for the relation between trials and their labels. Besides, the measure must determine how discriminant a channel is according its MMD statistics, so that distances between opposite classes must be very large and within class are expected to be small. Taking the above hypothesis into account, we define the relevance measure as the following ratio:

$$\rho(c) = \frac{\frac{2}{N^+ + N^-} \sum_{n \in +, m \in -} d_{nm}^c}{\frac{1}{2N^+} \sum_{n,m \in +} d_{nm}^c + \frac{1}{2N^-} \sum_{n,m \in -} d_{nm}^c} \tag{2}$$

being $d_{nm}^c = d(\boldsymbol{x}_n^c, \boldsymbol{x}_m^c)$ the simplified distance notation. The numerator and denominator of Eq. (2) account for the between and within class distances, respectively. Therefore, the larger the numerator and the smaller the denominator - the larger the relevance measure $\rho(c) \in \mathbb{R}^+$. Particularly, $\rho(c) > 1$ corresponds to a discriminant channel, while noisy channels attain $\rho(c) < 1$. In this way, our relevance measure based on the MMD statistic, termed rMMD, ranks each EEG channel according its discrimination capability fed by the trial distances computed in a RKHS.

3 Experimental Setup

3.1 EEG Dataset

We evaluate the proposed channel selection approach on the subjects from the EEG dataset for motor imagery brain-computer interface [3]. EEG data was recorded using 64 Ag/AgCl electrodes located over the scalp following a 10-10 montage and sampled at 512 Hz. For each subject, the BCI2000 recording system registered the EEG data of five or six runs splitted into 40 trials (20 per class). In turn, each trial is split into ready, instruction, and resting periods. The first period presents a black screen with a fixation cross from the trial strart ($t = 0$) to $t = 2$ s. The second one randomly instructs one of two MI tasks ("left hand" or "right hand") during $t \in [2,5]$ s. The last one displays a blank screen from $t = 5$ during a random break of 2.1–2.8 s. Trials are further labeled as *bad_trial* following criteria as the voltage magnitude, correlation with electromyographic activity, and subject comments. Given that this work avoids the bad trials, we validate our approach on the 45 subjects that remain with most of their trials.

3.2 EEG Processing and Parameter Setup

To assess the performance of the proposed relevance analysis, we introduce the rMMD into a subject-dependent BCI framework with the following stages: *(i)* preprocessing, that filters between [8–30] Hz and downsamples at 100 Hz each trial using a fifth order Butterworth filter; *(ii)* channel selection relying on the proposed distance-based supervised relevance analysis; *(iii)* feature extraction, carried out by the Common Spatial Patterns as a popular algorithm for extracting discriminative patterns from MI; *(iv)* and classification using the well-known Linear Discriminat Analysis. It is worth noting that the considered framework only processes the period of [2.5–4.5] s of each trial to focus on the learning part of the MI instruction.

Regarding the parameter setup, the rMMD relevance analysis depends on the embedding dimension. Since L constrains the minimum frequency to be analyzed, we fixed $L = 0.25$ s aiming to account for frequencies as low as 8 Hz. In addition, the computation of the MMD statistic in Eq. (1) demands the selection of a kernel function. In this respect, we use the well-known RBF with bandwith parameter tuned by maximization of the information potential variability [2]. The resulting rMMD setup allows computing the relevance function $\rho(c)$ in Eq. (2) to rank EEG channels. Figure 1 illustrates the attained accuracy along the number of the most relevant channels for each subject within the dataset. Note that subjects were sorted according its performance at 64 channels in order to highlight the benefit of the channel selection.

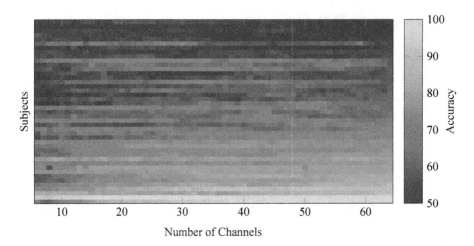

Fig. 1. Five-fold averaged accuracy along the number of selected channels for each subject using rMMD. Subjects sorted according their CSP performance. Color encodes the accuracy.

4   Results and Discussion

Aiming to compare the performance of the proposed rMMD-based relevance analysis, we also compute the classification rates of two baseline approaches, namely, the standard Common Spatial Patterns (CSP) and sequential floating forward selection (SFFS). The former corresponds to the widely accepted feature extraction approach for motor imagery tasks, computed from the 64 channels. The latter consists in a sequential heuristical search for the highest training accuracy with respect to a subset of EEG channels [11]. Figure 2 presents the performance attained by considered approaches for each subject. We ordered the subjects according the CSP accuracy to highlight the accuracy gain. In general, selecting channels based on the proposed relevance analysis outperforms the classification rate of CSP and SFFS. Particularly, rMMD achieves the highest accuracy rate on 18 subjects, while SFFS on ten of them. Accuracy on the remaining subjects is similar for both channel selection approaches. Nonetheless, SFFS underperforms CSP on nine subjects, evidencing algorithmic issues on the iterative selection; whereas rMMD only performs as CSP on five subjects that attain the highest accuracy at the full channel set. Moreover, the introduced channel selection largely increases the performance of subjects with the lowest accuracy rates up to 13% points, as the case of #17, #24, and #52. Regarding the selection performance, SFFS usually select less channels than rMMD. Particularly, seven out of ten subjects where SFFS reaches the highest accuracy requires less channels than rMMD. However, SFFS may result in a less accurate channel subset than the full EEG, as the case of seven subjects that reduce its performance up to 7% points. Such an issue is due to the suboptimal nature of SFFS. On the contrary, rMMD reduces less channels without compromising

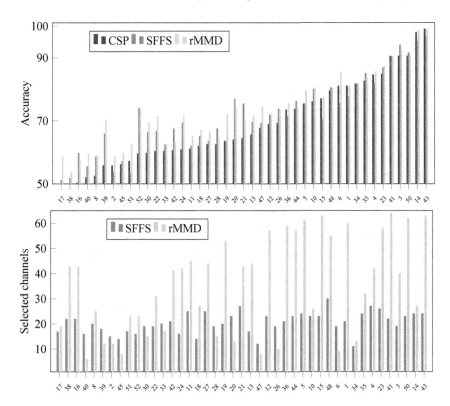

Fig. 2. Subject-wise performance of the considered approaches. Top: Average classification accuracy of five folds. Bottom: Median number of selected channels.

the classification rate. For instance, rMMD holds the 64 channels of subjects #1 and #43 to reach the highest performance. Consequently, comparing temporal dynamics among trials by means of rMMD highlights the discrimination capabilities of each EEG channel, so that a reduced EEG montage provides an enhanced classification accuracy and benefits the setup time of the MI-BCI system.

We summarize the performance attained by each compared approach in Table 1. In general, rMMD evidences an accuracy increment of 5% and 2% points regarding CSP and SFFS, respectively, with the benefit of reducing the confidence interval (CI). The further statistical means t-test with paired folds of the proposed relevance analysis against both baselines proves an overall significant accuracy increment with p-values smaller than 0.1%. Lastly, the median selected channels for rMMD corresponds to near two thirds of the full EEG montage but doubles SFFS subset. Therefore, the significative difference between the proposed rMMD-based relevance analysis and the baseline approaches proves that accounting for the channel-wise discriminative capability enhances class separability and reduces the montage setup without compromising the overall performance.

Table 1. Overall performance of the considered approaches.

	CSP	SFFS	rMMD
Accuracy	68.9 ± 13.7	71.7 ± 12.0	73.6 ± 11.3
5% CI	$(64.8, 73.0)$	$(68.1, 75.2)$	$(70.2, 77.0)$
p-value	$<0.1\%$	$<0.1\%$	-
Selected channels	64	21	40

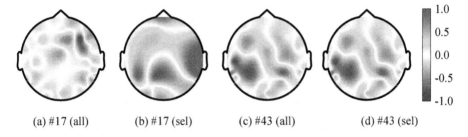

(a) #17 (all)   (b) #17 (sel)   (c) #43 (all)   (d) #43 (sel)

Fig. 3. Resulting spatial patterns for the best and worst performing subjects computed from all and selected channels.

For illustrating the influence of the relevance analysis on the feature extraction stage, Fig. 3 depicts the spatial patterns computed from all and selected channels on subjects #17 and #43 where CSP achieves the worst and best accuracy, respectively. Note that on subject #43 the both patterns are similar because achieving the highest accuracy demands the full channel set. On the contrary, the proposed relevance analysis requires only 19 out of 64 channels to increase the performance by 13% points with respect to conventional CSP on subject #17, which yields a smoother spatial pattern. As a result, the introduced relevance analysis will never underperform the standard pipeline that lacks a channel selection stage.

5   Concluding Remarks

This work proposes relevance analysis based on the maximum mean discrepancy criterion to select the most discriminative channels on large EEG montages. Our approach takes advantage of the dynamics embedded into the MMD statistic that allows comparing a pair of time series, in this case, two EEG trials on the same channel. Then, such a pair-wise similarity feeds a supervised clustering measure that allows ranking the channels according its discrimination capabilities. According to the achieved accuracy rates on a dataset holding more than 40 subjects, the discriminative relevance criterion provides a channel subset with enhanced classification rates of MI tasks.

Since the studied task is devoted to training and developing BCI systems for mass consumption, we split our future work into two research directions. Firstly, we will extend for rMMD to feature selection approaches relying on weighting coefficients (linear models) or on feature importance criteria (tree search) aiming to improve the channel selection rate. Secondly, we plan to develop a methodology for channel-wise relevance analysis on large cohorts, aiming at a single low-density EEG montage that suitably performs for a population. Lastly, we will study the subject characteristics that increase its performance with a particular channel subset, so that adaptive montages and pre-trained processing stages spread out the usage of BCI on real world applications.

Acknowledgment. This research was supported by the research project 36706 "BrainScore: Sistema compositivo, gráfico y sonoro creado a partir del comportamiento frecuencial de las señales cerebrales", funded by Universidad de Caldas and Universidad Nacional de Colombia.

References

1. Alotaiby, T., El-Samie, F.E.A., Alshebeili, S.A., Ahmad, I.: A review of channel selection algorithms for EEG signal processing. EURASIP J. Adv. Signal Process. **2015**(1), 66 (2015). https://doi.org/10.1186/s13634-015-0251-9
2. Álvarez-Meza, A.M., Cárdenas-Peña, D., Castellanos-Dominguez, G.: Unsupervised kernel function building using maximization of information potential variability. In: Bayro-Corrochano, E., Hancock, E. (eds.) CIARP 2014. LNCS, vol. 8827, pp. 335–342. Springer, Cham (2014). https://doi.org/10.1007/978-3-319-12568-8_41
3. Cho, H., Ahn, M., Ahn, S., Kwon, M., Jun, S.C.: EEG datasets for motor imagery brain-computer interface. GigaScience **6**(7), 1–8 (2017). https://doi.org/10.1093/gigascience/gix034
4. Dai, S., Wei, Q.: Electrode channel selection based on backtracking search optimization in motor imagery brain-computer interfaces. J. Integr. Neurosci. **16**(3), 241–254 (2017). https://doi.org/10.3233/JIN-170017
5. Edelman, B.J., Baxter, B., He, B.: EEG source imaging enhances the decoding of complex right-hand motor imagery tasks. IEEE Trans. Biomed. Eng. **63**(1), 4–14 (2016). https://doi.org/10.1109/TBME.2015.2467312
6. Franklin Alex Joseph, A., Govindaraju, C.: Channel selection using glow swarm optimization and its application in line of sight secure communication. Clust. Comput., 1–8 (2017). https://doi.org/10.1007/s10586-017-1177-9
7. Gretton, A., Borgwardt, K., Rasch, M.J., Scholkopf, B., Smola, A.J.: A kernel method for the two-sample problem, May 2008
8. Handiru, V.S., Prasad, V.A.: Optimized bi-objective EEG channel selection and cross-subject generalization with brain-computer interfaces. IEEE Trans. Hum. Mach. Syst. **46**(6), 777–786 (2016). https://doi.org/10.1109/THMS.2016.2573827
9. Kee, C.Y., Ponnambalam, S.G., Loo, C.K.: Multi-objective genetic algorithm as channel selection method for P300 and motor imagery data set. Neurocomputing **161**, 120–131 (2015). https://doi.org/10.1016/j.neucom.2015.02.057
10. Meng, J., Zhang, S., Bekyo, A., Olsoe, J., Baxter, B., He, B.: Noninvasive electroencephalogram based control of a robotic arm for reach and grasp tasks. Sci. Rep. **6**(1), 38565 (2016). https://doi.org/10.1038/srep38565

11. Qiu, Z., Jin, J., Lam, H.K., Zhang, Y., Wang, X., Cichocki, A.: Improved SFFS method for channel selection in motor imagery based BCI. Neurocomputing **207**, 519–527 (2016). https://doi.org/10.1016/j.neucom.2016.05.035
12. Yang, H., Guan, C., Wang, C.C., Ang, K.K.: Maximum dependency and minimum redundancy-based channel selection for motor imagery of walking EEG signal detection. In: ICASSP, IEEE International Conference on Acoustics, Speech and Signal Processing - Proceedings, pp. 1187–1191. IEEE, May 2013. https://doi.org/10.1109/ICASSP.2013.6637838

Forward Modelling Complexity Influence in EEG Source Localization Using Real EEG Data

Ernesto Cuartas Morales[1], Yohan Ricardo Céspedes Villar[2(✉)],
Carlos Daniel Acosta[1], and German Castellanos-Dominguez[1]

[1] Signal Processing and Recognition Group, Universidad Nacional de Colombia,
Km 9 Vía al Aeropuerto la Nubia, Manizales, Colombia
{ecuartasmo,cdacostam,cgcastellanosd}@unal.edu.co
[2] Centro de Bioinformática y Biología Computacional de Colombia - BIOS,
Manizales, Colombia
yohan.cespedes@bios.co

Abstract. The synergetic effects connecting spatial and functional techniques allows reduction of the weakness for single method analysis. Specifically, EEG Source Imaging (ESI) relating structural head models and distributed source localization techniques improves the time and spatial resolution of single MRI or EEG analysis. However, despite the knowing fact that the forward modelling significantly influences the accuracy of the ESI task, there is not a direct measure indicating how good a head model is considering realistic EEG data. We present a framework using volumetric forward modelling and analyzing the influence of the forward modelling complexity in the ESI task using Bayesian model selection for group studies. Our results show strong evidence in favour of most complex/realistic forward modelling fo the ESI task.

Keywords: Forward modeling · Finite differences ·
EEG Source Imaging

1 Introduction

The synergetic effects connecting spatial and functional neuroimage techniques allows reduction of the weakness for single method analysis. Specifically, EEG Source Imaging (ESI) relating structural head models and distributed source localization techniques improves the time and spatial resolution of single MRI or EEG analysis [3]. ESI information is used for diagnosis and preoperative stages

This work was supported by MINTIC for the execution of the "Plan de acción BIOS 2018". This work was also carried out under grants: *Programa Nacional de Formación de Investigadores Generación del Bicentenario, 2012*, Convocatoria 528.

© Springer Nature Switzerland AG 2019
R. Vera-Rodriguez et al. (Eds.): CIARP 2018, LNCS 11401, pp. 829–836, 2019.
https://doi.org/10.1007/978-3-030-13469-3_96

of brain surgery being, in most cases, the only suitable analysis tools because of the high risk of surgical interventions [5].

ESI techniques allow the estimation of neuronal activity from electrical potentials measured over the scalp (EEG). In particular, ESI solution needs real EEG signals, a method for mapping of the measured activity from electrodes to the sources (EEG inverse problem solution), and a correct modeling of the potentials conduction and morphology of the head, meaning, a forward solution. In this regard, the accuracy of ESI solutions directly depends on the capabilities of the forward model to adequately describe the information from sources to sensors [12].

In this regard, a more realistic representation of head volumes may be of benefit. In practice, a realistic head volume can be obtained from neuroimages such as MRI or CT containing a large number of slices in a series of two-dimensional images. Every slice must be registered in the same coordinate system to obtain a coherent three-dimensional volume. After the registration stage, the volume contains the information of head tissues codified in intensity values, that can be segmented to generate a labeling map holding compartments for specific tissues. In particular, the scalp (where the EEG electrodes are placed), the skull, the cerebrum spinal fluid, the gray matter, and the white matter are the most commonly considered tissues in the forward modeling. Due to the direct impact of the forward modeling on EEG source localization, we build a patient-specific and realistic head model holding five tissues, and anisotropic skull and white matter modeling in a $1 \, mm^3$ volumetric segmentation. Further, we use the FDM technique to calculate patient-specific head models, analyzing model complexity (number of tissue compartments) and anisotropic modeling [2] for two different ESI prior techniques, namely, Loreta-like priors (LOR) and empirical bayesian beamformer priors (EBB). Finally, we use Bayesian model selection for group studies to analyze the influence of the forward modeling in the considered distributed ESI solutions.

2   Methods

2.1   EEG Forward Problem

The EEG forward problem involves the calculation of potentials $\phi(r)$ induced by a primary current density $J(r)$ in a head volume $\Omega \in \mathbb{R}^3$ with $\partial \Omega \in \mathbb{R}^2$ boundary, holding inhomogeneous and anisotropic conductivity $\Sigma(r) \in \mathbb{R}^{3 \times 3}$. The quasi-static approximation of Maxwell's equations can be formulated, leading to the Poisson's equation as follows [7]:

$$\nabla \cdot (\Sigma(r) \nabla \phi(r)) = -\nabla \cdot J(r), \ \forall r \in \Omega \tag{1a}$$

$$\phi(r)|_{\Gamma_l}^+ = \phi(r)|_{\Gamma_l}^- \ \text{on} \ \Gamma_l, \ \forall l = 1, \ldots, N \tag{1b}$$

$$(\Sigma(r) \nabla \phi(r)) \cdot \hat{n}(r)|_{\Gamma_l}^+ = (\Sigma(r) \nabla \phi(r)) \cdot \hat{n}(r)|_{\Gamma_l}^-, \ \text{on} \ \Gamma_l \tag{1c}$$

$$(\Sigma(r) \nabla \phi(r)) \cdot \hat{n}(r)|_{\partial \Omega} = 0, \ \text{on boundary} \ \partial \Omega \tag{1d}$$

where r is a specific head volume position, N is the number of interfaces Γ_l (i.e., head layers), $\hat{n}(r) \in \mathbb{R}^3$ is a unit vector normal to Γ_l at r, and $g(r)|_{\Gamma_l}^{\pm}$ stands for the trace of function $g(r)$ from both sides of the l-th interface Γ_l. Furthermore, the solution of Eq. (1a) requires establishing proper boundary conditions between adjacent compartments having different conductivities. Thus, Eqs. (1b) and (1c) stand for the Dirichlet and Neumann flux conditions respectively, while Eq. (1d) (or non-flux homogeneous Neumann condition) implies that no current can flow out through the human head interface $\partial\Omega$ into the air.

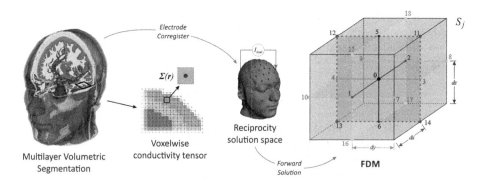

Fig. 1. Realistic head modeling methodology pipeline.

Figure 1 shows the realistic head modeling methodology pipeline, for which we define 5 different tissue conductivities for an MRI based tissue-labeling segmentation in a $1\,\text{mm}^3$ space as in [11]. The segmentation allows a voxelwise conductivity distribution for the FDM taking known conductivity parameters from the literature. In addition we define a reciprocity solution for the EEG sensors space, that is solved using the FDM technique.

2.2 Distributed Inverse Solutions

For a EEG dataset $Y \in \mathbb{R}^{N_C \times T}$ of N_C sensors, T time samples, and a given *lead-field* matrix $L_m \in \mathbb{R}^{N_C \times N_D}$, the magnitude of the neural activity $J \in \mathbb{R}^{N_D \times T}$ for N_D current dipoles distributed in the GM, is generally represented by the general linear model [3]:

$$Y = L_m J + \Xi \qquad (2)$$

where $\Xi \in \mathbb{R}^{N_C \times T}$, is an additive white noise matrix with covariance $\text{cov}(\Xi) = \exp(\lambda_0) I_C$, where $I_{N_C} \in \mathbb{R}^{N_C \times N_C}$ is an identity matrix, and $\lambda_0 \in \mathbb{R}^+$ an hyperparameter modulating the sensor noise variance. Further, solving Eq. (2) to estimate J becomes a optimization problem of the following form:

$$\tilde{J} = Q L_m^\top (Q_\Xi + L_m Q L_m^\top)^{-1} Y \qquad (3)$$

requiring prior information about the source covariance matrix Q.

Loreta-Like (LOR) Priors: Considering that sources vary smoothly over space using a Green's function $Q_G = \exp(\sigma G_M)$, with $Q_G \in \mathbb{R}^{N_D \times N_D}$, where $G_M \in \mathbb{R}^{N_D \times N_D}$ is a graph Laplacian that comprises inter-dipole connectivity information about all neighboring dipoles, and $\sigma \in \mathbb{R}^+$ rules the spatial expansion of the activated areas. Consequently, the source prior is computed as:

$$Q = \exp(\lambda_1)Q_G \tag{4}$$

with $\lambda_1 \in \mathbb{R}^+$ and hyperparameter to be estimated.

Empirical Bayesian Beamformer (EBB) Priors: Assuming one global prior for the source covariance main diagonal, where the off-diagonal elements are zeros, i.e., no correlations assumed. Thus, the d-th position of the source covariance matrix main diagonal is calculated as [1]:

$$Q = diag\left(\exp(\lambda_1)(l_{md}^\top C_Y^{-1} l_{md})\right) \tag{5}$$

where $l_{md} \in \mathbb{R}^{N_D \times 1}$ is the d-th column of the lead field matrix, and $C_Y \in \mathbb{R}^{N_C \times N_C}$ is the EEG data covariance matrix.

Further, to estimate the hyperparameter set $\{\lambda_\Xi, \lambda_P\}$, we use the verisimilitude function known as *free-energy* [14]. In this regard, for a given EEG recording and a certain forward model m, the free energy can be expressed as [6]:

$$F(m) = accuracy(\lambda) - complexity(\lambda), \tag{6}$$

Free Energy can be maximized using standard variational schemes [14]. To perform this optimization scheme, we use a greedy search (GS) algorithm. Further, the set of GS hyperparameters were tuned through the Restricted Maximum Likelihood (ReML) algorithm as given in [1].

3   Experimental Setup of the FDM-Based Forward Solution

The solution of the Poisson Eq. (1a) for realistic patient-specific head volumes is only possible using numerical approximations. In particular, individual magnetic resonance (MR) and/or computed tomography (CT) images can be segmented into different tissue types, such as white and grey matter (WM/GM), cerebrospinal fluid (CSF), skull, skin, among others.

We build a realistic, high-resolution $1\,\text{mm}^3$, patient-specific volume conductor model from neuroimages, including anisotropic skull and white matter modeling and considering five different tissue compartment segmentation as in [11], considering the following isotropic conductivity values: 0.33 (scalp), 0.0105 (skull), 1.79 (CSF), 0.33 (GM), and 0.14 (white matter) as in [12]. Further, we use T1, IDEAL T2 and diffusion-weighted imaging (DWI) MR scans acquired from a healthy 32-years-old male in the Rey Juan Carlos University, Medicine Faculty, Medical Image Analysis and Biometry Lab, Madrid, Spain. Further, based on the proposed methodology, we define three different forward model setups with increasing complexity (number of tissues). Moreover, We build three isotropic models, beginning with the simplest model M1 including only three tissues, namely skin, skull, and brain, then, for the model M2, we add the CSF, and for the model M3, we divide the brain area into GM and WM.

Furthermore, we use the multi-subject, multi-modal human neuroimaging dataset including visual event-related potentials (ERP's) (among other neuroimaging data) [13], selecting 15 patients, 8 males, and 7 females, with an age range 23–37 years, all Caucasian with European origins. An evoked potential visual experiment is carried out using face images stimuli, including two sets of 300 greyscale photographs, half of famous people and the other half of nonfamous people (unknown to participants). In the data set, half of the faces were male, half female, leaving 3 trial-types (conditions): Familiar Faces (Famous), Unfamiliar Faces (Nonfamous) and Scrambled Faces. Stimuli were projected onto a screen approximately 1.3 mts in front of the participant, and visual markers were projected to synchronize the stimuli apparition. A 70 channel Easycap EEG cap was used to record the EEG data simultaneously, with electrode layout conforming to the extended 10–10 system. EEG data were acquired at an 1100 Hz sampling rate with a low-pass filter at 350 Hz and no high-pass filter, including processing stages for automatic detection of wrong channels throughout the run, notch-filtering of the 50 Hz line-noise and its harmonics and a trial rejecting stage. Finally, an averaging the remaining trials for each of the three conditions was made to calculate ERP's for 1 s time windows.

Finally, we used Bayesian model selection based on *free-energy* in order to study the head model influence in the studied group [8]. To this end, we calculate *free-energy* factors to the full ERP time window (1 s) using the LOR and EBB techniques for the 15 considered patients, the three different visual stimuli and the 3 proposed head models for a total of 900 test. Then we group the *free-energy* of three reconstructions over stimulus conditions for each ESI technique to apply a random effects analysis at the group level, where the log group Bayes factor can be obtained summing over the 15 subjects [9].

4   Results

The Fig. 2 show the expected posterior model frequency for both ESI considered techniques, EBB (right) and LOR (left) and the three considered isotropic head models. Moreover, we include separate results for the different visual stimulus, Famous (blue), Unfamiliar (green), and Scrambled (red), showing the Bayesian omnibus risk (BOR) values in the button part of the charts. The results show strong evidence in favor of the most complex model M3 for both considerer inverse priors, namely, LOR and EBB, with an appreciable increment of the exceedance probability between the most straightforward model M1 and the model M2. All test have low BOR values indicating strong evidence in favor of the obtained results.

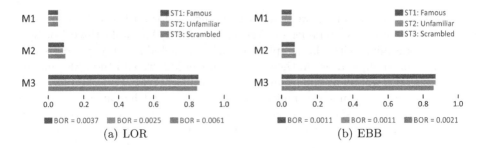

(a) LOR   (b) EBB

Fig. 2. Random fixed analysis showing expected posterior model frequency, and Bayesian omnibus risk (BOR) for the considered stimuli. (Color figure online)

4.1   Complexity Modeling of ESI Tasks

We analyze the model complexity influence in the source localization using both, the LOR and the EBB technique for the three considered models. This test shows the effect of increasing the number of tissues (M1 to M2) and also the effect of include anisotropy in both, WM and skull areas (M2 to M3). Figure 3 shows a normalized maximum intensity projection for the considered models, where it can be appreciated that the energy is more spread in model M1 compared to model M2. Moreover, the inclusion of anisotropic skull and WM for the model M3 show not only a concentrated activation area, but also possible spatial separation for individual activations in the visual cortex that appears as a mixed and single activation in the models M1 and M2. We used red squares to show the source

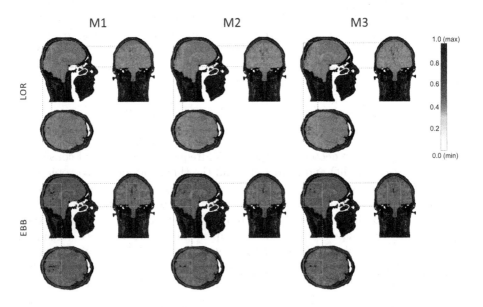

Fig. 3. Model complexity.

activation zone for the model M1, and green squares in the concentrated area of activation in the model M3, additionally, we used blue squares to show the source energy separation between two different sources that are very near one to each other. Moreover, the energy separation for more complex head models is consistent with similar analysis results [4].

4.2 Results for Visual Stimulus

Finally, we analyze the stimulus-response for the most complex model M3 using EBB and LOR source priors for a single subject (S9). Figure 4 shows the maximum intensity projection maps for the three considered stimuli namely, Famous, Unfamiliar and Scrambled, illustrating appreciable differences in the energy distribution for the different considered stimulus, with less intensity in the Thalamus area for the Unfamiliar stimulus compared to the Famous stimulus.

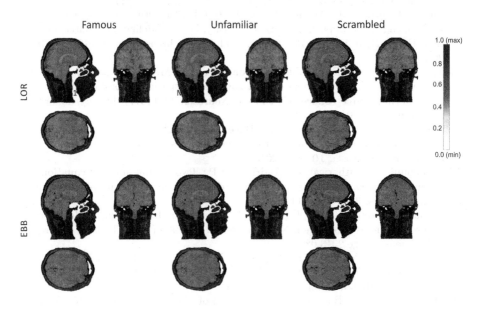

Fig. 4. Stimulus response.

5   Concluding Remark

We analyze the forward modeling complexity influence in the ESI task using a patient-specific realistic head model and real EEG data. We calculate FDM solutions in a reciprocity setup for the 70 electrodes configuration given in the multi-modal, multi-subject database [13]. Bayesian model selection for group studies using random effect analysis results, Fig. 2 shows concluding evidence in favor of most complex head models, with a high posterior model frequency probability for the two considered prior methods and visual stimulus. Results are similar to the reported in [10], where only analyze CSF inclusion. Based on our results, we suggest that at least 5-layer tissue compartments segmentation are needed to use head models for distributed ESI techniques; this result is similar to the suggested by [10].

References

1. Belardinelli, P., Ortiz, E., et al.: Source reconstruction accuracy of MEG and EEG bayesian inversion approaches. PloS One **7**(12), e51985 (2012)
2. Cuartas-Morales, E., Daniel-Acosta, C., Castellanos-Dominguez, G.: iLU preconditioning of the anisotropic-finite-difference based solution for the EEG forward problem. In: Ferrández Vicente, J.M., Álvarez-Sánchez, J.R., de la Paz López, F., Toledo-Moreo, F.J., Adeli, H. (eds.) IWINAC 2015. LNCS, vol. 9107, pp. 408–418. Springer, Cham (2015). https://doi.org/10.1007/978-3-319-18914-7_43
3. Grech, R., et al.: Review on solving the inverse problem in EEG source analysis. J. Neuroeng. Rehabil. **5**, 25 (2008). https://doi.org/10.1186/1743-0003-5-25
4. Liu, Q., Ganzetti, M., Wenderoth, N., Mantini, D.: Detecting large-scale brain networks using EEG: impact of electrode density, head modeling and source localization. Front. Neuroinform. **12**(March), 1–11 (2018). https://doi.org/10.3389/fninf.2018.00004
5. Martinez Vargas, J.D., Strobbe, G., Vonck, K., van Mierlo, P., Castellanos, D.G.: Improved localization of seizure onset zones using spatiotemporal constraints and time-varying source connectivity. Front. Neurosci. **11** (2017). https://doi.org/10.3389/fnins.2017.00156
6. Martínez-Vargas, J.D., López, J.D., Baker, A., Castellanos-Dominguez, G., Woolrich, M.W., Barnes, G.: Non-linear parameter estimates from non-stationary MEG data. Front. Neurosci. **10**, 366 (2016)
7. Rahmouni, L., Mitharwal, R., Andriulli, F.P.: Two volume integral equations for the inhomogeneous and anisotropic forward problem in electroencephalography. J. Comput. Phys. **348**, 732–743 (2017)
8. Rigoux, L., Stephan, K.E., Friston, K.J., Daunizeau, J.: Bayesian model selection for group studies - Revisited. NeuroImage **84**, 971–985 (2014). https://doi.org/10.1016/j.neuroimage.2013.08.065
9. Stephan, K.E., Penny, W.D., Daunizeau, J., Moran, R.J., Friston, K.J.: Bayesian model selection for group studies. NeuroImage **46**(4), 1004–1017 (2009). https://doi.org/10.1016/j.neuroimage.2009.03.025
10. Strobbe, G., et al.: Bayesian model selection of template forward models for EEG source reconstruction. NeuroImage **93**(Pt 1), 11–22 (2014). https://doi.org/10.1016/j.neuroimage.2014.02.022
11. Torrado, C.A.H.T.J., et al.: High-field MRI planing patient-specific tissue model segmentation in MRI. In: ISMRM 2014 (2014)
12. Vorwerk, J., Cho, J.H., Rampp, S., Hamer, H., Knösche, T.R., Wolters, C.H.: A guideline for head volume conductor modeling in EEG and MEG. NeuroImage **100**, 590–607 (2014)
13. Wakeman, D.G., Henson, R.N., et al.: A multi-subject, multi-modal human neuroimaging dataset. Sci. Data **2**, 150001 (2015). https://doi.org/10.1038/sdata.2015.1
14. Wipf, D.P., Owen, J.P., et al.: Robust Bayesian estimation of the location, orientation, and time course of multiple correlated neural sources using meg. NeuroImage **49**(1), 641–655 (2010)

Emotion Recognition with Ensemble Using mRMR-Based Feature Selection

A. Valencia-Alzate[1], J. Castañeda-Gonzalez[1(✉)], J. Hoyos-Osorio[1],
G. Daza-Santacoloma[2], and A. Orozco-Gutierrez[1]

[1] Automatics Research Group, Universidad Tecnológica de Pereira,
Pereira, Colombia
jhojaicastaneda@utp.edu.co
[2] Applied Neuroscience, Intituto de Epilepsia y Parkinsón del Eje Cafetero,
Pereira, Colombia

Abstract. Emotions play an important role in common life, understanding them can improve relationships between humans and even machines. Emotion is a mental state and a reaction caused by an event based on subjective experience and can be conditioned by environment, as well as factors due to the subject itself. This fact could make recognizing emotions a difficult task because the subject can fake their reactions. Therefore, the methodologies that allow detecting the real emotions of people become a significant advance in this field. The EEG is an electrical signal that comes from the brain, and can code the internal process of a human, even the emotions, and cannot be cheated or faked. However, find patterns in this signal is a difficult task for researchers. In this work, our goal is to present a methodology for recognizing emotions, by measuring two essential scales that usually code the typical emotions, Arousal, and Valence scales. Achieved results in emotions classification show an efficient performance in this task.

Keywords: Emotions recognition · Ensemble classification ·
Feature selection

1 Introduction

Emotion recognition systems is an increasingly important research subject in communication between humans and machines for the development of technologies that allow a more natural interaction. Emotions are fundamental in the daily life of human beings as they play an essential role in human cognition, rational decision-making, perception, human interaction, and human intelligence [3].

Emotion is a mental state and an affective reaction caused by an event based on subjective experience. However, there is an explicit separation between the physiological arousal, the behavioral expression (affect), and the conscious expression of emotion (feeling) [10,11]. Emotions play an important role in human communication and can be expressed either verbally through emotional

© Springer Nature Switzerland AG 2019
R. Vera-Rodriguez et al. (Eds.): CIARP 2018, LNCS 11401, pp. 837–845, 2019.
https://doi.org/10.1007/978-3-030-13469-3_97

vocabulary or by expressing nonverbal cues. However, behavioral expression as facial expressions and gestures can always be controlled voluntarily. Thus they are easy to fake or change providing unreliable information. It differs from using physiological signals such as electrocardiography (ECG), electromyography (EMG), galvanic skin response (GSR), respiration rate (RR) and, particularly, electroencephalography (EEG).

Over the last years, EEG signals analysis is the most preferred technique to analyzing the physiological expressions, due to the information that it contains, which allows differentiating emotional states, which helps researchers to a better understanding of human brain physiology and psychology [8]. Also, the analysis of these signals allows a more effective recognition of emotions because the subject under test cannot alter it. Several applications have been developed in deferents areas such as entertainment, e-learning, virtual worlds, or e-healthcare [1]

However, EEG characterization is a remaining issue depending on the application. In this case to recognize emotion requires to generate a feature set, which contains the most relevant information to recognize emotion, specifically the binary problem for arousal and Valence models. Authors in [1] propose a scheme for emotion recognition based on audio-visual stimulus and using as classifier an SVM. In [7], it was performed a scheme of feature selection and extraction, over features computed from EEG in time, frequency and time-frequency domains, and then use a quadratic discriminant analysis (QDA) as classifier. In this paper, we propose a methodology for emotion recognition algorithm using EEG signals based on Valence-arousal emotion model. The spectral and temporal features have been derived using the fast Fourier transform (FFT) over four different frequency bands theta (4–8 Hz), alpha (8–16 Hz), beta (16–32 Hz) and gamma (32–64 Hz). Mutual information with forward selection and backward elimination has been used for feature selection stage. Support vector machine has been used for classification stage and different binary classification problems were proposed: the classification of low/high arousal, low/high Valence. The ratings for each of these scales are thresholded into two classes (low and high). On the 9-point rating scales, the threshold was merely placed in the middle. The classifier was trained with user-independent data.

2   Model of Emotion

An emotion is a complex psychological state that involves three distinct components: a subjective experience, a physiological response, and a behavioral or expressive response [6]. Various discrete categorizations of emotion have been proposed. One of them is the discrete emotion model, according to Plutchik [13], there are eight basic emotions as acceptance, anger, anticipation, disgust, fear, joy, sadness and surprise. Ekman [4] exposed the relationship between facial expressions and emotions. In his theory proposes six emotions: anger, disgust, fear, happiness, sadness, and surprise. Later he expands the basic emotion by adding amusement, contempt, contentment, embarrassment, excitement, guilt, pride, relief, satisfaction, sensory pleasure and shame.

Other is the bi-dimensional emotion model by Russell [14], which is the most widely used from the dimensional perspective. This model is used to represent emotional states on a multidimensional scale spanned by Valence and arousal that can be subdivided into four quadrants, namely, low arousal/low Valence (LALV), low arousal/high Valence (LAHV), high arousal/low Valence (HALV), and high arousal/high Valence (HAHV). Valence represents the quality of emotion, can range from unpleasant (e.g., sad, stressed) to pleasant (e.g., happy, elated), whereas arousal denotes the quantitative activation level, ranges from inactive (e.g., uninterested, bored) to active (e.g., alert, excited). In this model, besides the arousal and Valence dimensions, an additional dimension called dominance is added. It ranges from a feeling of being in control during an emotional experience to a feeling of being controlled by the emotion.

3   Experimental Setup

3.1   Database

The dataset for emotion analysis using EEG, physiological and video signal, DEAP, was used in this research [9]. 32 participants took part in the experiment and their EEG and peripheral physiological signals such as electromyography (EMG), electrooculography (EOG), skin temperature, respiration pattern, blood volume pressure, and GSR, were recorded as they watched the 40 selected music videos. The 40 video clips were carefully pre-selected so that their intended arousal and Valence values span as large as possible in an area of the arousal/Valence space. Each participant watched a one-minute long music video as the visual stimuli to elicit different emotions. After each trial/video, each participant performs self-assessment and then to give continuous marks from 1 to 9 of their level of arousal, Valence, like/dislike, and dominance. Self-assessment manikins were used to visualize the scales. EEG and peripheral signals were recorded at a sampling rate of 512 Hz, but then the data was downsampled to 128 Hz, eye artifacts were removed and a high-pass filter was applied from 4–45 Hz. For further information, interested readers can refer to [9].

3.2   Feature Generation

In the design of an emotion recognition system, selection of effective features is an important step. Coan et al. [2] showed that positive emotions are associated with left frontal brain activity, whereas negative emotions are associated with right frontal brain activity. They also revealed that the decrease in activity in other brain regions such as the central, temporal and mid-frontal was less than the case in the frontal region. Therefore, only ten channels of the EEG record have been selected: F3, F4, F7, F8, FC1, FC2, FC5, FC6, FP1, and FP2.

Time Domain Features. Time domain features are computed as the natural representation of the EEG. So, we consider the time descriptor in Table 1.

Table 1. Time domain features

Time domain features	
Feature	Definition
Power	$P_\xi = \frac{1}{T} \sum_{-\infty}^{\infty} |\xi(t)|^2$
Mean	$\mu_\xi = \frac{1}{T} \sum_{t=1}^{T} \xi(t)$
Standard deviation	$\sigma_\xi = \sqrt{\frac{1}{T} \sum_{t=1}^{T} (\xi(t) - \mu_\xi)^2}$
1st difference	$\delta_\xi = \frac{1}{T-1} \sum_{t=1}^{T-1} |\xi(t+1) - \xi(t)|$
Normalized 1st difference	$\bar{\delta}_\xi = \frac{\delta_\xi}{\sigma_\xi}$
2nd difference	$\gamma_\xi = \frac{1}{T-2} \sum_{t=1}^{T-2} |\xi(t+2) - \xi(t)|$
Normalized 2nd difference	$\bar{\gamma}_\xi = \frac{\gamma_\xi}{\sigma_\xi}$
Activity	$A_\xi = \frac{\sum_{t=1}^{T} (\xi(t) - \mu)^2}{T}$
Mobility	$M_\xi = \sqrt{\frac{var(\dot{\xi}(t))}{var(\xi(t))}}$
Complexity	$C_\xi = \frac{M(\dot{\xi}(t))}{M(\xi(t))}$
Non-stationary index	$\sqrt{\frac{1}{l} \sum_{l=1}^{L} (\frac{\mu_\xi}{L})^2}$
Fractal dimension	$L_m(k) = \frac{T-1}{\left[\frac{T-m}{k}\right]k^2} \sum_{i=1}^{\left[\frac{T-m}{k}\right]} |\xi(m+ik) - \xi(m+(i-1)k)|$

Frequency Domain Features. Some of the time-frequency features are computed based on the well-known fast Fourier transform (FFT) to discriminate harmonic patterns. Here, we call a spectrum vector as $\Xi(f) \in \mathbb{R}^H$, $\Lambda \in \mathbb{R}^H$ a frequency index vector $\lambda_h = hF/2H$, and $F \in \mathbb{R}$ the sampling frequency. The features computed based on FFT are consigned in Table 2.

Table 2. Frequency domain features based on FFT

Frequency domain features	
Feature	Definition
Mean	$\mu_\Xi = \sum_{h=1}^{H} \frac{\Xi_h}{H}$
Central frequency	$\hat{\Xi} = \sum_{h=1}^{H} \frac{\lambda_h \Xi_h}{H\mu_\Lambda}$
Root mean square frequency	$\hat{\Xi}^{1/2}$
Standard deviation	$\left(\sum_{h=1}^{H} \frac{(\lambda_h - \hat{\Xi})^2 \Xi_h}{H\mu_\Lambda} \right)$
Kurtosis	$\sum_{h=1}^{H} \frac{\Xi_h^4}{H\mu_\Xi^2}$

Time-Frequency Domain Features. To find an informative representation of the EEG signal that could relate the time domain events with the frequency ones, we compute the Hilbert-Huang Spectrum (HHS) for each signal, which is done via empirical mode decomposition to arrive at intrinsic mode functions (IMFs) to represent the original signal. Also, the Discrete Wavelet Transform, which decomposes the signals in different approximation and detail levels corresponding to different frequency ranges, while conserving the time information of the signal.

Electrode Combination-Based Features. Considering the relations between the channels of the EEG, we calculated the magnitude coherence estimate as: $C_{ij} = \frac{|P_{ij}|^2}{P_i(f)P_j(f)}$, where the P_{ij} is the cross-power a pair of electrodes i, j and the differential asymmetry as follows: $\Delta\xi = \xi_l - \xi_r$ for l and r electrodes on the left/right hemisphere of the scalp, which measures these channels relations.

4   Feature Selection Based on Mutual Information

Let $\{\mathbf{x}_i, y_i\}_{i=1}^N$ be the training data set of a multi-class classification problem, where $\mathbf{x}_i$ is a $P-$dimensional feature vector corresponding to the instance i, and $y_i \in \{1, \dots, C\}$ is the label for the instance $\mathbf{x}_i$. For compactness, we define the input matrix $\mathbf{X} = \{\mathbf{x}_i\}_{i=1}^N \in \mathbb{R}^{N \times P}$, and $\mathbf{y} = \{y_1, \dots, y_N\} \in \mathbb{R}^N$ as the labels vector. Similarly, let $\boldsymbol{\zeta}_j \in \mathbb{R}^N$ be the column $j = \{1, \dots, P\}$ of the matrix $\mathbf{X}$. We use the criterion proposed by Peng et al. [12], called *minimal-redundancy-maximal-relevance* (mRMR), which is a combination of Max-Relevance (D) and min-Redundancy criteria (R). mRMR finds a set $\mathbf{s} \in \mathbb{R}^L$ with $L \leq P$, which contains the index $j = \{1, \dots, P\}$ corresponding to the most relevant features, which jointly achieves the highest explanation for the target class $\mathbf{y}$. mRMR is obtained by maximizing $\Phi(\mathrm{D}, \mathrm{R})$, where Φ is defined as $\Phi(\mathrm{D}, \mathrm{R}) = \mathrm{D} - \mathrm{R}$. Now, the *Max-Relevance* D, and the *minimal-Redundancy* R criteria are defined as follows

$$\mathrm{D}(\mathbf{s}, \mathbf{y}) = \frac{1}{|\mathbf{s}|_\#} \sum_{j \in \mathbf{s}} \mathrm{I}(\boldsymbol{\zeta}_j; \mathbf{y}), \qquad \mathrm{R}(\mathbf{s}) = \frac{1}{|\mathbf{s}|_\#^2} \sum_{j,k \in \mathbf{s}} \mathrm{I}(x_j; x_k),$$

where $|\mathbf{s}|_\#$ represents the cardinality of $\mathbf{s}$, and $\mathrm{I}(\mathbf{a}; \mathbf{b})$ is the mutual information of $\mathbf{a}$ and $\mathbf{b}$. A remaining issue is how to determine the optimal number of features L. The algorithm used for this task are based on two searches: forward selection (FS) and backward elimination (BE) over the matrix $\mathbf{Q} \in \mathbb{R}^{P \times P}$, where the element j, k are defined as $Q_{j,k} = \mathrm{I}(\boldsymbol{\zeta}_j, \boldsymbol{\zeta}_k; \mathbf{y})$.

5   RUSBoost Ensemble

Given an unbalanced training data $\{\mathbf{X}, \mathbf{y}\}$, the RUSBoost algorithm proposed by Seiffert et al. [15] is a combination of two components: Random Under-sampling and Adaptive Boosting (AdaBoost), both used for imbalance classification. Here, we introduce a brief description of both techniques random under-sampling and AdaBoost, in order to describe RUSboost algorithm.

Random Under-Sampling: Data sampling techniques attempt to alleviate the problem of class imbalance by adjusting the class distribution of the training data set. This can be accomplished by either removing examples from the majority class.

AdaBoost: Boosting is a meta-learning technique designed to improve the classification performance of weak learners. The main idea of boosting is to iteratively create an ensemble of weak hypotheses, which are combined to predict the class of unlabeled examples. Initially, all examples in the training dataset are assigned with equal weights. During the iterations of AdaBoost, a weak hypothesis is formed by the base learner. The error associated with the hypothesis is calculated, and the wight of each example is adjusted such that misclassified examples have their wights increased while correctly classified examples have their weights decreased. Therefore, subsequent iterations of boosting will generate hypotheses that are more likely to classify the previously mislabeled examples correctly. Once all the iterations are completed, a weighted vote of all hypothesis is used to assign a class to the unlabeled examples. Since boosting assigns higher weights to misclassified examples and minority class examples are those most likely to be misclassified. The above is the reason for which minority class examples will receive higher weights during the boosting process, making it similar in many ways to cost-sensitive classification [5].

6   Results

Both sequential searches (FS and BE), show for Arousal and Valence targets, that they tow use more 1200 features, where almost entirely belong to the frequency domain and some of them to time-frequency (Fig. 1).

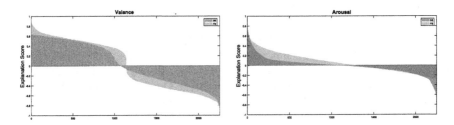

Fig. 1. Scores for every feature in both class targets, sub-figure (a) represent the score found by sequential searches in Valence class, and sub-figure (b) represent the same score for Arousal class.

The Tables 3 and 4 show the performance obtained with the base learners using all the set of features (NSF), the features selected with FS and the features selected with BE. These results were obtained with a hold-out cross-validation with 70% for training and 30% for testing.

Decision Tree was the base learner who gets the highest accuracy in the classification: NSF, FS, and BE. The SVM also reach results similar to the decision tree for both, Arousal and Valence targets. However, the SVM is more unstable than the decision tree. It is important to note that both selections improved the

Table 3. Table of comparative results between the base learners used for the ensemble in terms of accuracy, sensitivity and specificity for Arousal.

Base learner		Decision tree	Linear	Quadratic	K-NN (5)	SVM
NFS	Accuracy (%)	**65.02 ± 1.23**	36.56 ± 5.18	52.78 ± 0.93	57.00 ± 2.12	60.32 ± 3.04
	Sensitivity (%)	52.63 ± 0.56	42.12 ± 3.40	50.63 ± 1.23	49.72 ± 2.64	**63.16 ± 2.78**
	Specificity (%)	49.52 ± 0.98	30.10 ± 4.62	48.23 ± 1.84	54.46 ± 1.23	**58.00 ± 1.48**
FS	Accuracy (%)	75.32 ± 0.85	38.78 ± 3.12	72.56 ± 0.24	59.43 ± 1.35	**75.89 ± 1.53**
	Sensitivity (%)	57.94 ± 1.22	43.00 ± 2.53	50.18 ± 3.24	53.54 ± 1.79	**73.08 ± 1.08**
	Specificity (%)	**63.45 ± 0.49**	36.73 ± 2.95	62.63 ± 2.06	56.36 ± 0.87	63.02 ± 1.03
BE	Accuracy (%)	**79.24 ± 1.63**	37.68 ± 4.53	71.19 ± 1.06	57.69 ± 2.97	74.65 ± 2.01
	Sensitivity (%)	**73.42 ± 2.35**	39.48 ± 6.34	64.49 ± 2.18	50.19 ± 2.47	72.64 ± 1.49
	Specificity (%)	**74.04 ± 1.63**	32.84 ± 4.03	67.64 ± 3.48	49.23 ± 1.72	73.28 ± 1.63

classification considerably in the tree statistics (accuracy, sensitivity, and specificity). This highlight indicates that there are several features, which indeed may confuse a classifier. A possible reason for this the redundancy added from many of them, or maybe some of these features do not offer any information about the interest state.

Table 4. Table of comparative results between the base learners used for the ensemble in terms of accuracy, sensitivity and specificity for Valence.

Base learner		Decision tree	Linear	Quadratic	K-NN (5)	SVM
NFS	Accuracy (%)	59.18 ± 0.97	42.63 ± 3.26	58.57 ± 3.93	53.53 ± 2.18	**67.53 ± 1.75**
	Sensitivity (%)	**61.21 ± 1.01**	38.97 ± 1.64	57.34 ± 2.34	52.08 ± 1.63	60.74 ± 1.26
	Specificity (%)	57.36 ± 0.87	37.36 ± 2.58	51.56. ± 2.05	54.87 ± 2.01	**66.28 ± 0.93**
FS	Accuracy (%)	72.62 ± 1.36	49.42 ± 1.37	69.53 ± 1.18	58.18 ± 1.49	**72.89 ± 0.85**
	Sensitivity (%)	**71.57 ± 0.64**	50.63 ± 1.79	64.53 ± 1.13	57.63 ± 0.76	70.84 ± 1.67
	Specificity (%)	**72.50 ± 1.23**	53.36 ± 1.63	59.28 ± 1.67	53.79. ± 1.23	71.51 ± 0.97
BE	Accuracy (%)	**74.19 ± 1.42**	51.05 ± 1.45	70.18 ± 0.98	57.73 ± 1.58	72.76 ± 1.12
	Sensitivity (%)	71.36 ± 0.53	48.39 ± 2.21	71.66 ± 1.02	54.36 ± 1.31	**72.08 ± 0.87**
	Specificity (%)	72.24 ± 1.49	49.87. ± 1.58	70.23 ± 1.32	55.12 ± 2.11	**74.36 ± 2.12**

From the table of results, we can conclude that Valence target is more difficult to detect than Arousal, this could be for the features computed, or even, the selected channels may not be enough for Valence recognition. Nevertheless, with the ensembles is possible to obtain results of classification above 70% of accuracy, sensitivity, and specificity. Even though, we do not perform a parameters tuning for some of the base learners, these result probes that is possible to achieve results more efficient, demonstrating that ensemble classifiers could be stronger than single classifiers.

It is important to remark, that our data only has 22 patients with more balance between classes for both scales, Arousal and Valence. Besides, we test with all the patient mixed, instead of leaving one out and training with him.

7 Conclusions

We have presented an effective strategy to classify emotions that achieves an accuracy over 70% with a feature selection stage that efficiently finds the best set of features that explains the best the target label for scales. Nevertheless, our data employment is not the standard of state-of-art methods that train with some patient and test with the remaining, our methodology proves to be an alternative, and as future work, we propose to use the same training/test structure as the state-of-art methods.

Acknowledgments. We thank to the master degree program in electrical engineering at the Universidad Tecnológica de Pereira for the support and commitment with this research.

References

1. Ali, M., Mosa, A.H., Al Machot, F., Kyamakya, K.: EEG-based emotion recognition approach for e-healthcare applications. In: 2016 Eighth International Conference on Ubiquitous and Future Networks (ICUFN), pp. 946–950. IEEE (2016)
2. Coan, J.A., Allen, J.J.B., Harmon-Jones, E.: Voluntary facial expression and hemispheric asymmetry over the frontal cortex. Psychophysiology **38**(6), 912–925 (2001)
3. Damasio, A.R., Sutherland, S.: Descartes' error: emotion, reason and the human brain. Nature **372**(6503), 287–287 (1994)
4. Ekmanm, P.: Basic Emotions. Handbook of Cognition and Emotion, pp. 45–60. Wiley, Hoboken (1999)
5. Elkan, C.: The foundations of cost-sensitive learning. In: International Joint Conference on Artificial Intelligence, vol. 17, pp. 973–978. Lawrence Erlbaum Associates Ltd. (2001)
6. Hockenbury, D.H., Hockenbury, S.E.: Discovering Psychology. Macmillan, London (2010)
7. Jenke, R., Peer, A., Buss, M.: Feature extraction and selection for emotion recognition from EEG. IEEE Trans. Affect. Comput. **5**(3), 327–339 (2014)
8. Kim, M.-K., Kim, M., Oh, E., Kim, S.-P.: A review on the computational methods for emotional state estimation from the human EEG. Comput. Math. Methods Med. **2013**, 13 pages (2013)
9. Koelstra, S., et al.: Deap: a database for emotion analysis; using physiological signals. IEEE Trans. Affect. Comput. **3**(1), 18–31 (2012)
10. Mauss, I.B., Robinson, M.D.: Measures of emotion: a review. Cogn. Emot. **23**(2), 209–237 (2009)
11. Nivedha, R., Brinda, M., Vasanth, D., Anvitha, M., Suma, K.V.: EEG based emotion recognition using SVM and PSO. In: 2017 International Conference on Intelligent Computing, Instrumentation and Control Technologies (ICICICT), pp. 1597–1600. IEEE (2017)
12. Peng, H., Long, F., Ding, C.: Feature selection based on mutual information criteria of max-dependency, max-relevance, and min-redundancy. IEEE Trans. Pattern Anal. Mach. Intell. **27**(8), 1226–1238 (2005)
13. Plutchik, R.: The nature of emotions: human emotions have deep evolutionary roots, a fact that may explain their complexity and provide tools for clinical practice. Am. Sci. **89**(4), 344–350 (2001)

14. Russell, J.A.: A circumplex model of affect. J. Pers. Soc. Psychol. **39**(6), 1161 (1980)
15. Seiffert, C., Khoshgoftaar, T.M., Van Hulse, J., Napolitano, A.: RUSBoost: a hybrid approach to alleviating class imbalance. IEEE Trans. Syst. Man Cybernet. Part A Syst. Hum. **40**(1), 185–197 (2010)

Text and Characters Analysis

Regularization for Graph-Based Transfer Learning Text Classification

Cristián Serpell[1](✉), Héctor Allende[1], and Carlos Valle[2]

[1] Universidad Técnica Federico Santa María, Valparaíso, Chile
cserpell@alumnos.inf.utfsm.cl, hallende@inf.utfsm.cl
[2] Universidad De Playa Ancha, Valparaíso, Chile
carlos.valle@upla.cl

Abstract. In machine learning classification problems, it is common to assume train and test sets follow a similar underlying distribution. When this is not true, this can be seen as a transfer learning problem. Sometimes, there is a set of already trained source classification models available. This work focuses on how to best use these models as an ensemble of classifiers on data from a new, but related domain, assuming train data used to train those models is not available. This scenario is common in distributed systems, where sharing all data is technically difficult or there are privacy concerns. Most current solutions are graph-based methods that propagate labels given by the models into new domain data. We propose a regularization method for one of best current solutions, OAC^3, that shows improvements on accuracy on several text classification datasets.

Keywords: Graph-based methods · Ensembles · Text classification · Transfer learning · Regularization

1 Introduction

A common assumption in machine learning is that labelled data used to train or test a model is representative of the task being tackled. It is assumed that train and test sets follow the same underlying distribution. For many real tasks, it is difficult to collect enough labelled data for the task, even when getting unlabelled data is relatively easy. Because of this, an active research area is *transfer learning*. It focuses on how to make the most from data and models obtained for related, but not exactly the same task, called source tasks, together with unlabelled data for the new task, called target task.

For example, consider document classification performed on web pages of an institution, using a classifier trained with labelled data from those pages. The same classifier is applied into a new web site that has no labelled data, and pages have a different data distribution. It is required to adapt the source classifier according to the change in distribution [4]. Another example is sentiment classification applied to reviews of products, where train data has been labelled

© Springer Nature Switzerland AG 2019
R. Vera-Rodriguez et al. (Eds.): CIARP 2018, LNCS 11401, pp. 849–856, 2019.
https://doi.org/10.1007/978-3-030-13469-3_98

for one kind of products, such as books. It is desired to classify reviews of other kind of products, electronics. How users express regarding book features is different, so a new train set would be required. Instead, transfer learning is used to consider train data from book reviews, and a set of labelled and unlabelled electronics reviews [2]. Sometimes, data used to train source models has been lost, or it is difficult to get, due to technical difficulties or privacy issues, as in distributed intrusion detection systems.

In the classification scenario, most current transfer learning approaches assume relationships among observations from the unlabelled data, generally modelling them as connections in graphs. Then, constraints are added so probability estimates for each label for two observations are close, when the observations are close in the graph. Also, it is assumed that either all source tasks are equally valid, or belief levels are assigned to different source tasks.

In this work, we focus on text classification, when there is only unlabelled data for the target domain. We propose a regularization step for one of the current solutions, OAC^3, successfully reducing hypothesis space and improving its accuracy. The document is structured as follows: Sect. 2 states the concepts and problem tackled, Sect. 3 makes a short review of current approaches, Sect. 4 explains our proposal, Sect. 5 shows experiments performed to validate the proposal and Sect. 6 summarize our results.

2   Problem Setting

To describe a classification task, we assume observations come from a set $\mathcal{X}$, while labels are from a set $\mathcal{Y}$. It is assumed an underlying joint distribution $P(X = x, Y = y)$, where $x \in \mathcal{X}$, $y \in \mathcal{Y}$, and X, Y are random variables. If $\mathcal{X}$ is not discrete, a probability density function is used. The task with its underlying distribution is called *domain*, and it is written as $\mathcal{D} = (\mathcal{X}, \mathcal{Y}, P)$.

In our case, we assume m source domains, each with its own distribution, represented by $\{\mathcal{D}_i = (\mathcal{X}, \mathcal{Y}, P_i) \mid i \in \{1, \ldots, m\}\}$. For each domain, there is an already trained model h_i that assigns, for an element $x \in \mathcal{X}$, a probability vector for each class $h_i(x) \in [0, 1]^k$, with $k = |\mathcal{Y}|$ and $\sum_{l=1}^{k} h_{il}(x) = 1$. In other words, component l of $h_i(x)$ estimates conditional probability $P_i(Y = y_l \mid X = x)$ for $y_l \in \mathcal{Y}$. Note that even knowing the conditional probability, the underlying distribution $P_i(X = x, Y = y)$ is unknown.

Finally, we assume we have a data set $D \subseteq \mathcal{X}$ from domain $\mathcal{D}$, of size $n = |D|$, that we want to classify. Each $x \in D$ was obtained from marginal distribution $P(X = x)$. We separate D in two sets: $D = D_U \uplus D_L$, where D_U is unlabelled data we want to classify, and D_L is labelled data. In general, $|D_L|$ is much smaller than $|D_U|$. We focus in solutions that accept $|D_L| = 0$.

Based on source classifiers h_i and data D, the objective is to develop a classifier in target domain $\mathcal{D}$ that, for each observation $x \in \mathcal{X}$, estimates membership probabilities $P(Y = y \mid X = x)$ for each class $y \in \mathcal{Y}$. For simplicity, we use a vector u_x to denote $P(Y = y \mid X = x)$ throughout this document. To illustrate the situation, we show in Fig. 1 an example of classification using two models that were trained from different training distributions.

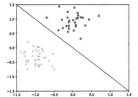 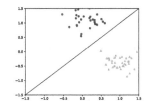 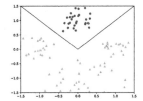

Fig. 1. Left and center figures show two linear models and data used for training them. Right figure shows that if they are used for this new domain, both agree in upper and lower part of the space, and they disagree in left and right part. Figure is based on [5].

3   Related Work

Some authors, like [11], have adapted multi task learning solutions to distributed scenarios. All models are trained together, each having access only to local data. Other recent work, like [10], train source models as part of the learning procedure. We are focused, instead, in solutions that consider source models already trained.

A group of solutions assume a Bayesian model, conditioning on models, as

$$u_x = \sum_{i=1}^{m} P\left(Y = y \mid X = x, h_i\right) P\left(h_i \mid X = x\right) = \sum_{i=1}^{m} h_i\left(x\right) P\left(h_i \mid X = x\right).$$

Writing $w_{ix} = P\left(h_i \mid X = x\right)$, this can be seen as a linear model of source models with weights w_{ix} that can be different for each model h_i and observation x:

$$u_x = \sum_{i=1}^{m} w_{ix} h_i\left(x\right).$$

Each solution differs on how to assign weights w_{ix}. *Locally Weighted Ensemble* [5] creates a graph connecting nodes in same cluster by a clustering algorithm, and a graph for each h_i model that connects nodes having same label by h_i. Weights are proportional to similarity of neighbourhoods in all graphs. If a small labelled data set D_L is available, it is extended in [7].

Other group, instead of a linear model, estimate u_x propagating source model estimates $h_i\left(x\right)$ in a graph. Nodes that are close in the graph will get a similar u_x. For example, the algorithm described in [3] builds a graph linking observation nodes with nodes associated to features and labels. To give more weight to labelled data, other graph linking unlabelled with labelled data has been proposed by [9]. *Graph-based Consensus Maximization* (GCM) [6] creates a graph with observation nodes, nodes associated to labels from each source model, and nodes associated to clusters from clustering algorithms, both with estimates q_{il}. Then, it uses an EM algorithm that iterates on u_x and q_{il} estimates to minimize

$$\min_{u_x, q_{il} \in [0,1]^k} \sum_{i=1}^{m+m_c} \sum_{l=1}^{k} \sum_{x \in \mathcal{X}} a_{ilx} \|u_x - q_{il}\|^2 + \alpha \sum_{i=1}^{m} \sum_{l=1}^{k} \|q_{il} - e_l\|^2,$$

where $e_l = (0, \ldots, 0, 1, 0, \ldots, 0) \in [0,1]^k$ is the indicator vector of class l. a_{ilx} takes value 1 when $h_i(x) = e_l$ or x is in cluster l of algorithm i, and 0 otherwise. q_{il} is estimate for node associated to model i and class l. α is a parameter that assign belief on initial labels. It assumes $h_i(x)$ assigns hard labels, with no probability estimate. This allows to treat clustering algorithms the same way. *Regularized Consensus Maximization* (RCM) [12] extends this, adding a regularization term. They propose to make the correlation matrix among classes being as diagonal as possible. Due to the regularization, computation time explodes, so the idea is simplified into a simple update that separates most correlated classes after each algorithm iteration. *Optimization Algorithm for Combining Classifiers and Clusterers* (OAC^3) [1] may be seen as a graph of nodes associated to observations, all connected, but with connection weights according to a similarity matrix $S = (s_{ij})$. It searches estimates u_x that minimize the objective function

$$\min_{u_x^r, u_x^l \in [0,1]^k} \sum_{x \in \mathcal{X}} d_\phi \left(\frac{\sum_{i=1}^m h_i(x)}{m}, u_x^r \right) + \alpha \sum_{x \in \mathcal{X}} \sum_{x' \in \mathcal{X}} s_{xx'} d_\phi \left(u_x^l, u_{x'}^r \right)$$
$$+ \lambda \sum_{x \in \mathcal{X}} d_\phi \left(u_x^l, u_x^r \right),$$

where d_ϕ is any Bregman divergence loss function,[1] and α and λ parameters. The first term links source models estimates with u_x, and the second term links observations according to the similarity matrix. The algorithm duplicates estimates u_x into u_x^l and u_x^r in order to find the optimum using an EM algorithm, so last term is added, to keep u_x^l and u_x^r close. It does not assign hard labels. Mathematically, it is possible to show that GCM is a particular case of OAC^3. More flexibility allows OAC^3 to have better accuracy in the same test datasets. In both solutions, a term may be added to the objective function when labelled data is available, to associate given labels with observations estimates u_x. Finally, authors of [8] extend GCM and OAC^3 to online classification problems.

4   Proposal

In the case of having only unlabelled data of target domain, we have seen that OAC^3 has more flexibility in label assignments, due to increased number of edges in the graph. This flexibility, though, comes with the price of increasing hypothesis space, making harder to reach good solutions. To tackle this issue, we propose a simple regularization procedure, similar to what RCM [12] does. We can see that the algorithms are estimating the following matrix U, composed by estimates for each observation and each class:

---

[1] A Bregman divergence is a function $d_\phi : S \times S \longrightarrow [0, \infty)$ defined by $d_\phi(x_1, x_2) = \phi(x_1) - \phi(x_2) - \langle x_1 - x_2, \nabla\phi(x_2) \rangle$, for any strictly convex differentiable function $\phi : S \longrightarrow \mathbb{R}$, with convex domain $S \subseteq \mathcal{X}$.

$$U = \begin{bmatrix} u_{x_1} \cdots u_{x_n} \end{bmatrix} = \begin{bmatrix} u_{x_1}^1 & \cdots & u_{x_n}^1 \\ & \ddots & \\ u_{x_1}^k & \cdots & u_{x_n}^k \end{bmatrix}, \text{ where } u_{x_i}^l \text{ estimates } P\left(Y = y_l \mid X = x_i\right).$$

The idea is to make estimates for each class, as uncorrelated as possible. In other words, make columns of U uncorrelated. The correlations between classes can be obtained using the variance-covariance matrix, estimated from data as

$$\Sigma = \frac{UU^T}{n} - \frac{U\mathbf{1}\mathbf{1}^T U^T}{n^2}, \text{ where } \mathbf{1} = \begin{bmatrix} 1 \cdots 1 \end{bmatrix}^T.$$

To achieve the objective, we would like Σ to be as diagonal as possible. So, to keep Σ as similar to a diagonal matrix Λ as possible, we would add a regularizer term to the objective function of OAC^3, such as one of $\|\Sigma - \Lambda\|_F$, where $\|\cdot\|_F$ is the Frobenius norm, or $\sum_{l=1}^{k} \sum_{l'=1}^{k} \Sigma_{ll'} \log\left(\frac{\Sigma_{ll'}}{\Lambda_{ll'}}\right)$. Unfortunately, these regularization terms add complexity to the algorithm equations, not being able to solve the EM steps easily anymore. Also, the matrix Λ would be a new set of parameters of the algorithm. Then, the idea is simplified, adding the following update on u_x estimates, after each iteration:

$$u_x^l \leftarrow u_x^l - \eta_t \left(u_x^{d_l} - u_x^l\right), \quad \text{where} \quad d_l = \arg\min_{l' \neq l} \|u_{\cdot}^{l'} - u_{\cdot}^l\|.$$

Here, d_l is the closest class, considering vectors $u_{\cdot}^l$ of estimates for class l for all observations. $\eta_t = \frac{\eta}{\sqrt{t}}$ is a learning rate. After each iteration, estimates are projected into the feasible region $\|u\|_1 = 1$. What this step does is to separate closest classes, so estimates of different classes are as far as possible. A similar procedure would be obtained adding $\sum_{l=1}^{k} \|u_{\cdot}^l - u_{\cdot}^{d_l}\|^2$ as a regularization term in the objective function, but we don't know d_l beforehand.

5 Experiments

5.1 Data and Tasks

We compared our proposal with OAC^3 in 23 tasks, based on text classification datasets, described below. For each task, we measure accuracy, defined as the proportion of well classified data $\frac{\text{TP}+\text{TN}}{|D|}$. To select best parameters for each task, we considered all combinations from Table 1, performing 5 runs of the algorithm, considering 90% of available data on each run. We considered squared euclidean ($\phi(p) = \|p\|^2$) and generalized I ($\phi(p) = \sum_l p_l \log(p_l)$) divergences. Source code of the experiments can be found at https://gitlab.com/cserpell/rgbtltc.

We use the same set of source models used to show results by our related work, including Logistic Regression, SVM and Winnow, for supervised models, and K-means and min-cut as unsupervised models. For more details, see [1,5,6].

Email and Spam Filtering. ECML/PKDD 2006 challenge dataset is used. 4000 labelled messages are used as sources train set. Three sets of 2500 messages, associated each to a different user, are used as target domain tasks.

Table 1. Parameters explored for each task, algorithm and divergence.

Parameter	Values
α	0.0001, 0.0003, 0.001, 0.003, 0.01, 0.03, 0.1, 0.3, 1
λ	0.0001, 0.001, 0.01, 0.1, 1
η	0.01, 0.03, 0.1, 0.3

Document Classification. We used 20 Newsgroups set, consisting in 20000 documents classified in categories and subcategories. Six subcategories classification tasks are generated using source classifiers trained for base categories, Six more tasks are created using the same categories in source and target classifiers. In this case, underlying distribution should not change much. Finally, three tasks are created using Reuters-21758 dataset, similarly to those from 20 Newsgroups.

Publication Classification. Four tasks are generated from Cora research publications dataset, for different research topics.

DBLP. One task is created using this dataset, composed of 4000 authors classified by research area. Classifiers of conference topics are used as source domains.

5.2   Results

In Table 2 we show average accuracy obtained for both divergences. We can see that our proposal slightly increased the accuracy on all tasks, except those of 20 Newsgroup dataset from [5], and one from Reuters-21758 dataset, where the original approach does not have good accuracy either. This is emphasized in Table 3. It is important to note that tasks from [6] (lower part of the tables) were designed for transfer learning, having more distant source and target distributions, compared with tasks from [5]. Our results show that our proposal, in these transfer learning tasks, increases the accuracy, except in two tasks of a total of 12: one with equal accuracy, and the already mentioned from Reuters-21758.

Execution times were similar for both algorithms, not reported due to space. Regarding divergences, when considering only squared euclidean divergence, our proposal worked better, probably due to the nature of considered tasks data.

6   Conclusions and Future Work

We proposed a regularized version of OAC³ algorithm that increased accuracy in text classification tasks, specially in those where source and target distributions of data and labels are related, but not the same. Our proposal was born with the idea of restricting hypothesis space, and it was effective. More complex regularization mechanisms can now be explored, specially those mentioned, without simplifications. For them, we will have to consider also execution time and effects on convergence of the algorithm, that in our proposal are still similar.

Table 2. Average accuracy and standard deviation after 100 iterations, using best set of parameters, for two divergences. Highest value for each task is highlighted.

Set	Task	Generalized I divergence		Squared euclidean divergence	
		OAC^3	+Regul.	OAC^3	+Regul.
Cora [5]	1	89.53 (±0.16)	89.80 (±0.16)	89.60 (±0.19)	**89.83** (±0.19)
	2	92.29 (±0.25)	92.22 (±0.39)	92.26 (±0.34)	**92.35** (±0.34)
	3	91.57 (±0.22)	**91.72** (±0.40)	91.46 (±0.11)	91.63 (±0.19)
	4	91.81 (±0.22)	91.77 (±0.40)	91.65 (±0.40)	**91.86** (±0.34)
DBLP [5]	1	94.27 (±0.22)	94.01 (±0.11)	94.47 (±0.32)	**94.49** (±0.43)
20 Newsgroup [5]	1	**85.29** (±0.19)	84.81 (±0.34)	84.81 (±0.11)	84.79 (±0.39)
	2	**94.08** (±0.16)	94.02 (±0.11)	93.94 (±0.54)	94.02 (±0.19)
	3	**90.71** (±0.58)	90.54 (±0.22)	90.49 (±0.35)	90.39 (±0.27)
	4	**94.07** (±0.42)	93.80 (±0.25)	93.39 (±0.35)	93.48 (±0.40)
	5	92.10 (±0.39)	**92.39** (±0.40)	92.34 (±0.30)	**92.39** (±0.30)
	6	92.31 (±0.22)	**92.41** (±0.30)	92.24 (±0.27)	92.37 (±0.11)
20 Newsgroup [6]	1	95.85 (±0.11)	95.83 (±0.11)	95.87 (±0.25)	**95.91** (±0.11)
	2	98.69 (±0.11)	**98.73** (±0.19)	98.69 (±0.11)	98.72 (±0.11)
	3	71.03 (±0.37)	71.00 (±0.35)	71.23 (±0.34)	**71.30** (±0.30)
	4	**96.80** (±0.19)	96.75 (±0.16)	96.75 (±0.19)	**96.80** (±0.19)
	5	96.88 (±0.11)	**96.90** (±0.19)	96.88 (±0.11)	**96.90** (±0.00)
	6	97.70 (±0.22)	**97.76** (±0.16)	97.70 (±0.16)	97.74 (±0.11)
Reuters-21758 [6]	1	78.05 (±0.25)	78.05 (±0.30)	78.15 (±0.57)	**78.24** (±0.27)
	2	65.63 (±0.30)	65.84 (±0.42)	65.25 (±0.30)	**66.25** (±0.75)
	3	**58.29** (±0.62)	58.25 (±0.45)	57.94 (±0.70)	58.05 (±0.72)
Spam [6]	1	82.14 (±0.43)	**82.44** (±0.25)	82.15 (±0.11)	82.42 (±0.19)
	2	83.05 (±0.32)	**83.17** (±0.30)	82.98 (±0.19)	83.01 (±0.39)
	3	83.91 (±0.11)	83.68 (±0.25)	85.06 (±0.22)	**85.15** (±0.25)

Table 3. Number of dataset tasks, where each algorithm obtains best average accuracy.

Set	OAC^3	+Regul.	Both
Cora [5]	0	4	0
DBLP [5]	0	1	0
20 Newsgroup [5]	4	2	0
20 Newsgroup [6]	0	5	1
Reuters-21758 [6]	1	2	0
Spam [6]	0	3	0

In the future, we can explore adding more flexibility to the algorithm. For example, adding weights to source models, allowing the algorithm to choose best models, instead of considering all equally valid, even those that are completely irrelevant for the task.

Acknowledgments. This work was supported in part by Conicyt doctoral scholarship 21170109, Fondecyt Grant 1170123, and Basal Project FB0821.

References

1. Acharya, A., Hruschka, E.R., Ghosh, J., Acharyya, S.: An optimization framework for combining ensembles of classifiers and clusterers with applications to non-transductive semi-supervised learning and transfer learning. ACM Trans. Knowl. Discov. Data **9**(1), 1 (2014)
2. Blitzer, J., Dredze, M., Pereira, F.: Biographies, bollywood, boom-boxes and blenders: domain adaptation for sentiment classification. In: Proceedings of the 45th Annual Meeting of the Association of Computational Linguistics, pp. 440–447. Association for Computational Linguistics (2007)
3. Dai, W., Jin, O., Xue, G.R., Yang, Q., Yu, Y.: EigenTransfer: a unified framework for transfer learning. In: Proceedings of the 26th Annual International Conference on Machine Learning, ICML 2009, pp. 193–200. ACM, New York (2009)
4. Dai, W., Yang, Q., Xue, G.R., Yu, Y.: Boosting for transfer learning. In: Proceedings of the 24th International Conference on Machine Learning, ICML 2007, pp. 193–200. ACM, New York (2007)
5. Gao, J., Fan, W., Jiang, J., Han, J.: Knowledge transfer via multiple model local structure mapping. In: Proceedings of the 14th ACM SIGKDD International Conference on Knowledge Discovery and Data Mining, KDD 2008, pp. 283–291. ACM, New York (2008)
6. Gao, J., Liang, F., Fan, W., Sun, Y., Han, J.: A graph-based consensus maximization approach for combining multiple supervised and unsupervised models. IEEE Trans. Knowl. Data Eng. **25**(1), 15–28 (2013)
7. Ge, L., Gao, J., Ngo, H., Li, K., Zhang, A.: On handling negative transfer and imbalanced distributions in multiple source transfer learning. Stat. Anal. Data Min. **7**(4), 254–271 (2014)
8. Ge, L., Gao, J., Zhang, A.: OMS-TL: a framework of online multiple source transfer learning. In: Proceedings of the 22nd ACM International Conference on Information & Knowledge Management, CIKM 2013, pp. 2423–2428. ACM, New York (2013)
9. He, J., Liu, Y., Lawrence, R.: Graph-based transfer learning. In: Proceedings of the 18th ACM Conference on Information and Knowledge Management, CIKM 2009, pp. 937–946. ACM, New York (2009)
10. Liu, X., Liu, Z., Wang, G., Cai, Z., Zhang, H.: Ensemble transfer learning algorithm. IEEE Access **6**, 2389–2396 (2018)
11. Luo, P., Zhuang, F., Hui, X., Xiong, Y., He, Q.: Transfer learning from multiple source domains via consensus regularization. In: Proceedings of the 17th ACM Conference on Information and Knowledge Management, CIKM 2008, pp. 103–112. ACM, New York (2008)
12. Xie, S., Gao, J., Fan, W., Turaga, D., Yu, P.S.: Class-distribution regularized consensus maximization for alleviating overfitting in model combination. In: Proceedings of the 20th ACM SIGKDD International Conference on Knowledge Discovery and Data Mining, KDD 2014, pp. 303–312. ACM, New York (2014)

Math Formula Script and Type Identification and Recognition

Kawther Khazri$^{(\boxtimes)}$ and Afef Kacem Echi

ENSIT-LaTICE, University of Tunis,
5 Avenue Taha Hussein, BP 56 Bab mnara, 1008 Tunis, Tunisia
kawther.khazri@yahoo.fr, afef.kacem@ensit.rnu.tn

Abstract. In this work, we propose a system for math formula script and type identification based on Convolutional Neural Network, to automatically discriminate between Printed/Handwritten and Arabic/Latin formulas before their recognition by the appropriate recognizer. An identification rate of 94.6% is reached, tested on 320 formulas. For formula recognition, we focused on Arabic machine-printed formulas and we proposed a syntax-directed system, based on symbols recognition and their arrangement analysis. To recognize symbols, we combined some statistical features and a Bayes network classifier. A rate of 96.56% for symbol recognition is achieved. For formula structure analysis, the system proceeds by top-down and bottom-up parsing scheme based on operator dominance. A set of replacement rules is defined. Formula parsing consists in applying, from the dominant operator and its context, the appropriate rule to divide the formulas into sub-formulas which will be recursively analyzed by the same way. The parser used for the formula structure analysis has shown its efficiency with a recognition rate 97.63%.

Keywords: Script and type identification · Symbol recognition · Formula's structure analysis

1 Introduction

Research on script and type identification aims to create systems able to discriminate automatically between the different forms in which a document is presented, including the language and the way it is written in machine-printed or handwritten, to select the appropriate recognition system to a given document. The state of the art on the script identification shows that no work deals with math formulas. Existent works treat this problem for text. Also, few systems are interested at the same time in Arabic/Latin and Printed/Handwritten script identification. In this context, we present a new approach dealing with the problem of identification of the script: Arabic or Latin and the type: handwritten or machine-printed of math formulas. This work comes as a part of our research on off-line recognition of arabic math formulas. The rest of the paper is organized as follow. Section gives a synthesis of the existing systems for script

© Springer Nature Switzerland AG 2019
R. Vera-Rodriguez et al. (Eds.): CIARP 2018, LNCS 11401, pp. 857–864, 2019.
https://doi.org/10.1007/978-3-030-13469-3_99

identification and math formulas recognition. Sections 3 and 4 present the proposed identification and recognition system. Experiments are reported in Sect. 5. Finally, conclusion and future works are drawn in Sect. 6.

2   State of the Art

For Script identification, most researches focus principally in text document. As far as we know, no work handled with math documents. Script and type identification problems depend on the granularity of data sample: text-bloc, text-line, word or connected component level, the number of scripts out of which the system classifies and the way the text data is presented: handwritten or machine-printed. Based on a survey done by [1] about script and type identification, we summarized some related works (Table 1).

Table 1. Script and type identification

Script	Type	Level	System	Accuracy (%)	Ref.
Arabic English	Machine-printed	text-line word	Projection profile features, Run length and moments, etc. MLP	99.7% test on 1976 text-lines, 98.6% tested on 8320 words	[2]
Arabic Latin	Machine-printed	word	Arabic character recognition using template matching	100% tested on 478 words	[3]
Arabic Latin	Machine-printed, handwritten	text-line	Projection profile and Fractal based features, K-NN, RBF	tested on 2400 text-lines, 96.64% K-NN and 98.72% RBF	[4]
Arabic Latin	Machine-Printed, handwritten	word	Steerable pyramid transform, etc., K-NN	97.5% tested on 800 words	[5]
Arabic Latin	Machine-printed, handwritten	bloc, text-line Ccx	Morphological analysis for text-bloc and geometrical analysis for line and Ccx., K-NN	88.5% tested on 200 images and 92% tested on 113 images	[6]
Arabic Latin	Machine-printed, handwritten	word	HOG, Bayes classifier	98.4% tested on 1320 words	[7]

For math formula recognition, many researches deal with this problem, especially in Latin language [8–13]. In recent years, researches dealing with Arabic formulas have emerged. In [14], Smirnova and Watt proposed to adapt their prior system for Latin formula recognition [13], to online Arabic context. They used elastic matching for symbol recognition and geometrical structure analyzer for formula recognition. Their system was tested on a database of 227 symbols and achieved a recognition rate of 91.9%. Unless the good results achieved by the symbol recognizer, the use of the elastic matching can be a big limitation for the overall approach since it is strongly affected by the size of the used vocabulary. To recognize the structure of the formula, authors proposed to identify relations between symbols but they did not consider the inclusion relation which make their system unable to recognize roots. In [15], El-Sheikh proposed a system for the online recognition of one-dimensional Arabic math formulas. For symbol recognition, some statistical features are computed. Author developed a precedence grammar based on left to right scanning scheme for the syntactic recognition of math formula. The proposed system recognized 16 isolated letters, 10 digits and 11 symbols. A recognition rate of 99% was achieved. Another system for the recognition of one-dimensional Arabic math formulas was proposed by Khalifa and Bing Ru in [16] which handle with segmentation and recognition of only simple math equations. For symbol recognition, they discriminated connected components according to their proximity properties and they used a two-level neural network as classifier. They achieved a recognition rate of 89.7% for handwritten formulas and 95.2% for printed formulas. Their proposed system do not treat complex level of math formulas. In this work, we are interested by the system proposed by Belaïd et al. [8] for the online interpretation of 2D math Latin formulas. For symbol recognition, authors used morphological features and a decision tree. To interpret formulas, they proposed a syntactic parser based on a context-free grammar. It is a top-down and a bottom-up parser based on a start character which is used to select the appropriate rule and to divide the formula into sub-formulas until the whole formula recognition. A recognition rate of 93% was achieved. Authors proved the importance of contextual information to overcome the shortcoming of the symbol recognizer. Their solution for treating ambiguities, if accompanied by a robust symbol recognizer, will certainly improve the overall system. Also the efficiency of their system will be more convenient if tested on various types of formulas. Convinced by Belaïd's approach, we propose to extend and adapt this approach for Arabic in off-line context.

3   Proposed Identification System

As the content of a math formula being variable, we use a decision at connected component level. For that, we extracted then classified connected components, using a Convolutional Neural Network (CNN). An overview of the proposed CNN is given in Fig. 1. Image symbol is of size 100×100, used as input of the network. The CNN's structure is characterized by the alternation between convolution and sub sampling layers. The convolution serves to extract features from the input image and to output, using a linear filter the feature map. We used a ReLU operation after every convolution operation, to introduce non-linearity in the CNN. We then used a spatial pooling to reduce the dimensionality of each feature map but retains the most important information.

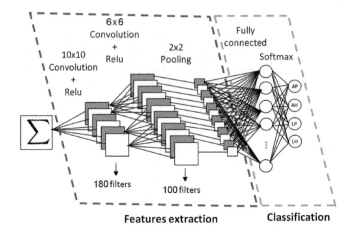

Fig. 1. CNN based system for symbol script and type identification

Once the connected components are classified, we refer to a majority vote on the decision taken for each of them to identify the script and type of the whole formula. In Fig. 2, the proposed CNN returns five Arabic Handwritten (AH) components and only one Latin Handwritten (LH) component. Thus, the formula is classified as AH. Notice that, some components are not identified, either because they are not discriminative or can be confused with other symbols. In Fig. 2, the dot above the function's name is not identified because it can be confused with the Arabic digit zero.

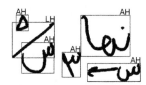

Fig. 2. Formula identification standing on CNN symbol classification.

4 Proposed Formula Recognition System

Two main stages are followed as explained in the next subsections.

4.1 Symbol Recognition

To represent symbols, we extracted 120 statistical features: Hu and Zernike moments, run-length, bi-level co-occurrence, white pixel portion and HOG, are extracted and a Bayes network classifier is used. The proposed symbol recognizer is able to identify 50 symbol classes. To select the appropriate features, we used best first algorithm, which reduced the number from 120 to 87 features to 96.86% and the run time is decreased from 0.19 s to 0.15 s in average.

Although the symbol recognizer achieved a good accuracy, its failure to distinguish certain symbols would be bothersome. In fact, some distinct symbols are in close resemblance such as the horizontal fraction bar and the minus sign. Also mirrored symbols, such as the opening and the closing parenthesis, can cause recognition problems because some used features are invariant to rotation. Observing the event of confusion, we consider some of the misrecognition cases to be too difficult to resolve without considering the context and we keep resolving some of them during the formula structure analysis.

4.2 Formula Structure Analysis

This step consists of lexical, geometrical and syntactical analysis as it will be explained below.

Lexical Analysis: It attributes a lexical unit, a label which is the syntactic category to each symbol or group of symbols. For example, the label *SS* for the literal and mirrored sum symbol. For multi-part symbols ($=, \leq$, etc.), Arabic letters, having diacritic such as (أ, ب, etc.) and function names (نه, ظَنَا, etc.), vertical regroupment is required. Horizontally adjacent digits should compose an unsigned integers. Unsigned floats consist of unsigned integers separated by a decimal point.

Geometrical Analysis: To describe spatial structure of the formula, we defined 10 spatial relations: Left, Right, Above, Below, Left and Right Superscript, Left and Right subscript, Inside and Delimited by small or great delimiters. These spatial relations, in conjunction with context, are used here to remove some confusions between symbols with similar morphologies. For example, in order for a symbol to be considered as a fraction bar, it should have no empty parts above and below.

Syntactical Analysis: The proposed parser starts by selecting the dominant operator which can be explicit, represented by a symbol like an arithmetic operator, a fraction bar, an integral, a root, a summation, a product, a new function name like ق(س), a trigonometric function such as the sinus function جَ. It can be also implicit such as subscript or a superscript or implicit multiplication. Note that Belaïd et al. [8] defined a similar concept: the starting character which is chosen based on its ability to correctly divide the formula into sub-formulas (according to the grammar) and on its priority when different characters can be used for that purpose. Thus, a priority order was defined to choose the starting character and when more than one character have the same priority, extra treatment were done to determine the best one that gives the maximum information to divide the formula and simplify its parsing. But, they only considered explicit operators. In this work, we propose to include more complex symbols such as sums, products, integrals, roots, etc. and implicit operators: subscripts, superscripts and implicit multiplication in the choice of the start operator. We compute operator dominance in conjunction with its precedence to handle with formulas that contain many operators which are not lined up. To define dominance between two operators O_1 and O_2, we consider that O_1 dominates O_2 if O_2 lies in the range of O_1. The range of an operator is the possible emplacement of its operands. After finding the dominant operator, a top-down and a bottom-up parsing algorithm is applied to analyze the formula structure. The bottom-up parser begins by looking for the dominant operator, as explained above. Then, it chooses the corresponding rule in the grammar, considering the operator contexts. This rule provides instructions to the top-down parser to partition the formula into sub-formulas which are analyzed by the same way and so on until analyzing the whole of the formula. More details can be found in our previous works [17–19].

5   Experimental Results

To train and evaluate our systems, we used for Latin script the InftyMDB-1 [20], a database of printed math formulas and CROHME [21], a database of handwritten math formulas. View the absence of standard database of Arabic math formulas, we used our database of printed formulas scanned form math books of several Arabic countries, and of handwritten formulas written by five different writers. To evaluate the identification system, we trained our CNN using a database of 4000 samples (1000 per class, 4 classes: AH, AP, LH, LP). For the tests, we used a 1400 connected components (350 instances per class). Table 2 displays the obtained results. We also built a database of 320 formulas (80 per class, 4 classes: AH, AP, LH, LP) using the previously cited databases. Table 2 shows the obtained results. To evaluate the formula recognition system, we tested the symbol recognizer on 1016 ones extracted from 100 test formulas. 930 were correctly recognized and 86 were not recognized which means a recognition rate of 91.5% which is better than the result obtained with the same test formulas in our previous work 89.9% [17]. Some of the encountered confusions were treated during the lexical analysis guided by the characteristics of the Arabic math notation which involves diacritic and multi-parts symbols. For example, the presence of the Hamza above a letter Alef, approves its identity as letter Alef and its absence guides our system to choose the second result of the symbol recognizer. Some other encountered confusion cases have been solved during syntactical analysis guided by the conventional syntax of formulas. For example, greater than or less than signs can not just before or after an equal sign, parenthesis or bracket, an arithmetic sign. When finding these symbols, our system corrects them, referring to the alternative candidates from the symbol recognizer. When considering spatial relationships, the symbol recognition rate has grown from 95.77% to 96.56% [17].

The proposed syntax directed system was tested on a database of 161 formulas (see Table 3). Formulas of order 0 are those where operators are aligned in the same line without superscripts nor subscripts. Formulas of order 1 enclose

Table 2. Identification rate of the CNN based system.

Class	Symbol classification (%)	Formula classification (%)
AH	93	100
AP	95	97.5
LH	92.6	93.75
LP	92.9	87.5
Average	93.4	94.6

subscripts, superscripts and roots. Formulas of order 2 allow operator below and above the horizontal fraction bar and formulas of order 3 include integrals, summations, etc.

Table 3. Parsing results.

Order0	Order1	Order2	Order3	Average
98% (99 form.)	95.76% (42 form.)	99.62% (8 form.)	100% (12 form.)	97.63%

6 Conclusion and Future Work

In this work, the focus was on the problem of math formula script and type identification and recognition. We firstly proposed an identification system able to automatically discriminate between printed and handwritten, Arabic and Latin math symbols based on CNN, then exploited the obtained result to identify the script and type of the whole formula before employing a particular recognizer. We then addressed the problem of formula recognition. The proposed recognition system was tested on complex math formulas containing implicit multiplication, subscripts and superscripts and gives satisfactory results. We also explained how our system offers the possibility to detect and correct some symbol recognition errors during the different steps of formula's structure analysis. Adding more features, testing other feature selection algorithms and choosing faster classifier should enhance the performance of the proposed system. Based on our experimentations, we showed that the CNN-based identification system results were promising with 94.6% identification rate. Also we argue the robustness of the recognition system, carrying tests on a reasonable number of practical math formulas. In fact, our system proves its efficiency with a recognition rate of 97.63%. In future work, we plan to work on improving the performance of the proposed CNN-based system working on the CNN's filters and architecture.

References

1. Ubul, K., Tursun, G., Aysa, A., Impedovo, D., Pirlo, G., Yibulayin, T.: Script identification of multi-script documents: a survey. IEEE ACCESS **5**, 6546–6559 (2017)
2. Elgammal, A.M., Ismail, M.A.: Techniques for language identification for hybrid Arabic-English document images. In: ICDAR, pp. 1100–1104 (2001)
3. Moalla, I., Elbaati, A., Alimi, A.A., Benhamadou, A.: Extraction of Arabic text from multilingual documents. In: ICSMC (2002)
4. Moussa, S.B., Zahour, A., Benabdelhafid, A., Alimi, A.M.: Fractal-based system for Arabic/Latin, printed/handwritten script identification. In: ICPR (2011)
5. Benjelil, M., Mullot, R., Alimi, A.: Language and script identification based on Steerable Pyramid Features. In: ICFHR (2012)
6. Kanoun, S., Ennaji, A., Lecourtier, Y., Alimi, A.M.: Script and nature differentiation for Arabic and Latin text images. In: IWFHR, pp. 309–313 (2002)
7. Saïdani, A., Kacem, A.: Arabic/Latin and machine-printed/handwritten word discrimination using HOG-based shape descriptor. In: ELCVIA (2015)
8. Belaïd, A., Haton, J.P.: A syntactic approach of handwritten mathematical formula recognition. PAMI **6**(1), 105–111 (1984)
9. Stria, J., Prusa, D., Hlavac, V.: Combining structural and statistical approach to online recognition of handwritten mathematical formulas. In: CVWW (2014)
10. Celik, M., Yanikoglu, B.: Probabilistic mathematical formula recognition using a 2D context-free graph grammar. In: ICDAR (2011)
11. Tian, X., Wang, F., Liu, X.: An improved method of formula structural analysis. In: ICDAR, pp. 161–166 (2011)
12. Awal, A., Mouchere, H., Gaudin, C.: Towards handwritten mathematical expression recognition. In: ICDAR, pp. 1046–1050 (2009)
13. Wan, B., Watt, S.: An interactive mathematical handwriting recognizer for the pocket PC. In: MathML International Conference (2002)
14. Smirnova, E., Watt, S.: Aspect of mathematical expression analysis in Arabic handwriting. In: ICDAR, vol. 2, pp. 1183–1187 (2007)
15. El-Sheikh, T.S.: Recognition of handwritten Arabic mathematical formulas. In: UK IT Conference, pp. 344–351 (1990)
16. Khalifa, M., Bing Ru, Y.: A hybrid segmentation system of offline Arabic mathematical expression recognition. CJIPCV **2**(4), 30–35 (2011)
17. Ayeb, K.K., Echi, A.K., Belaïd, A.: A syntax directed system for the recognition of printed Arabic mathematical formulas, In: ICDAR, pp. 186–190 (2015)
18. Kacem, A., Khazri, K., Belaïd, A.: Reconnaissance de formules mathématiques arabes par une approche dirigée syntaxe. In: CIFED (2010)
19. Khazri, K., Kacem, A., Belaïd, A.: Recognition of machine-printed Arabic mathematical formulas. In: ICTIA (2014)
20. Infty Project Homepage. http://www.inftyproject.org/en/database.html. Accessed 15 Oct 2018
21. CROHME Homepage. http://www.isical.ac.in/~crohme/. Accessed 15 Oct 2018

Evaluating AdaBoost for Plagiarism Detection

Thiago V. Reginaldo, Magali R. G. Meireles,
and Zenilton K. G. Patrocínio Jr.$^{(\boxtimes)}$

Pontifical Catholic University of Minas Gerais, Belo Horizonte, MG, Brazil
thiagopesquisa42@gmail.com, {magali,zenilton}@pucminas.br

Abstract. Plagiarism is a current problem with serious consequences. Recently, many research efforts have addressed plagiarism detection task. This problem is more difficult, when some obfuscation strategy is used. This work proposes and evaluates the adoption of AdaBoost for classifying suspicious text passages as plagiarism or not. We also present a simple post-processing heuristic for improving results granularity. Comparative analysis with other classification methods were conducted and experimental results have shown that Adaboost reached a F-measure of 0.93 and the best granularity score using the proposed post-processing heuristic. The assessment of three distinct obfuscation strategies pointed out that Adaboost is able to detected all of them, but it had problems in differentiating among them, which could to be related to a poor feature selection.

Keywords: Plagiarism detection · Text alignment · AdaBoost

1 Introduction

Plagiarism could be defined as the act to copy and to take as yours the work of someone else [9]. Detecting plagiarism in a huge collection of documents, such as articles, thesis, laws, news and others artifacts is not manually viable. In practice, reviewers need to use automated systems that help them checking similarity in order to detect eventual citation lack during the process of analysis of the submitted works [2]. In this way, the plagiarism detection task naturally comes to a context of automated plagiarism detectors, a specialized software to this task.

In order to contribute to plagiarism detection, this work proposes and evaluates the adoption of AdaBoost as a tool for classifying suspicious text passages

The authors thank the financial support of the Pontifical Catholic University of Minas Gerais (PUC Minas), the National Council for Scientific and Technological Development (CNPq, grant 429144/2016-4) and the Foundation for Research Support of the State of Minas Gerais (FAPEMIG, grant APQ 01454-17).

© Springer Nature Switzerland AG 2019
R. Vera-Rodriguez et al. (Eds.): CIARP 2018, LNCS 11401, pp. 865–873, 2019.
https://doi.org/10.1007/978-3-030-13469-3_100

as plagiarism or not, even when some obfuscation strategy is used. Additionally, a simple post-processing heuristic for improving results granularity is also presented. The contributions of this work are two-fold: (i) impact analysis of a boosting-based approach on plagiarism detection; and (ii) evaluation of a simple post-processing heuristic to reduce granularity of detection results.

The rest of this paper is organized as follows. Section 2 presents basic concepts and works related to plagiarism detection. In Sect. 3, our proposed approach is fully described, while in Sect. 4 experimental results are presented and analyzed. Finally, in Sect. 5, we draw some conclusions and point out possible future research directions.

2   Basic Concepts and Related Works

The task of plagiarism detection in text documents can be divided into two distinct approaches [6]: (i) external; and (ii) intrinsic. In external plagiarism detection, given a set of suspicious documents and a set of potential source documents, the task is to find all plagiarized passages in the suspicious documents and their corresponding source passages in the source documents. However, in an intrinsic approach, given the same set of suspicious documents, the task is to extract all plagiarized passages without comparing them to any potential source documents.

The external detection consists of two main steps: (i) source retrieval that queries the external world and selects source candidates; and (ii) text alignment which compares pairs of documents to find all the plagiarism occurrences between the suspicious and source documents. According to [6], the challenge in text alignment is to identify passages of text that have been obfuscated. At the end, additional steps (such as filtering) could be used to post-processing the results [6].

In this work, we used a boosting algorithm. Boosting is a method to combine a number of weak classifiers (possibly generated by the same algorithm) into a single classifier with higher performance. Thus, it is a way for a low performance classifier become a high performance one [7].

One of its most successful versions is Adaptive Boosting (AdaBoost) [3]. AdaBoost works by using resampling and reweighting of the data set. Its main features are the capacity of using data set reweighting in a way that samples with poor performance receive more attention of the next classifiers, and the use of resampling to improve the diversity of each classifier. At the end of AdaBoost iterations, many classifiers are generated and then, a single classifier can be simulated by a voting among all the classifiers created.

Since 2007, there is a series of scientific events and shared tasks on digital text forensics and stylometry, named Plagiarism analysis, Authorship identification, and Near-duplicate detection (PAN)[1]. In [8], the authors used TF-IDF to identify the words' frequency. And then, using this with some heuristics, they got to the top of PAN competitors ranking in plagiarism detection.

---

[1] https://pan.webis.de.

In [4], machine learning was used to train some classifiers to cope with plagiarism detection. A series of features were extracted from the words' occurrences on the text to train the classifiers that were inspired by the best methodologies among PAN competitors, such as the 2014 winner [8]. The author of [4] used *Decision Tree* and *Naive Bayes* classifiers; and also explores the adoption of *Random Forest*. Compared to top approaches in PAN, results obtained by learning methods proposed by [4] were very competitive, specially for *Decision Tree* and *Random Forest*.

Multiple types of n-grams were used to ensemble a system for plagiarism detection in [5]. Another work used semantic and syntactic features to feed a fuzzy logic based plagiarism detector [1].

3   Approach for Plagiarism Detection

3.1   Preprocessing and Seeding

Analogously to [4, 8], for each document, tokenization, stemming, and removal of stop-words were applied to each sentence. And, after that, a Bag-of-Words (BoW) model was generated for each of those preprocessed sentences.

According to [8], the seeding step is used to construct a large set of plagiarism candidates called *seeds*. In our case, the seeds are generated by the mapping every sentence from a source document to all sentences belonging to a suspicious document. Therefore, after seeding a large number of seeds is obtained for each pair of suspicious and source documents.

3.2   Feature Extraction and Seed Classification

In order to apply a machine learning approach to seed classification, a set of features are needed to describe each seed. We have adopted the same 13 features used by [4], which are based on *cosine* and *dice* dissimilarities computed over the BoWs representing the suspicious and the source sentences for each seed. Table 1 shows the list of those features with a brief description.

Due to the generation process and even to the problem nature, most of obtained seeds does not represent a plagiarism case, causing a significant imbalance that can hinder a machine learning approach. To cope with that, we adopted a under-sampling strategy to rebalance class distribution.

Then, training data were used to generate a classifier which is evaluated using a distinct testing subset with several metrics. In this work, we investigate the adoption of boosting for plagiarism detection; choosing to use Adaboost because it has been successfully applied to several different tasks. We have also selected *decision tree* as its base classifier, since it presented a high performance in [4].

3.3   Post-processing

After seed classification, the detected cases of plagiarism are usually fragmented into sentences. To reduce this fragmentation, improving the granularity of plagiarism detection, several distinct strategies have been proposed [4, 8].

Table 1. Features from [4] used to describe *seeds* (or plagiarism candidates).

Feature	Type	Description
Cosine	Float	BoW similarity measurement (frequency dependent)
Dice coefficient	Float	BoW similarity measurement (frequency invariant)
IsMaxCos and IsMaxDice	Boolean	TRUE if it is source fragment with the highest, respectively, Cos or Dice value for that suspicous fragment
MaxDiffCos and MaxDiffDice	Float	Difference between the current source fragment and the source fragment with the highest maximum similarity value of the same type for that suspicious fragment
MeanDiffCos and MeanDiffDice	Float	Difference between the current source fragment and the document mean maximum values of the same type for that suspicious fragment
MaxNeighbourCos and MaxNeighbourDice	Float	The highest value of the given similarity type for immediate suspicious fragment neighbors
VerticalMaxDistCos and VerticalMaxDistDice	Integer	Distance in fragments between the current source fragment and the fragment with the highest similarity value of the given type
SrcSuspLenRatio	Float	Length ratio between source and suspicious passages

In this work, we proposed a simple heuristic to join adjacent seeds. As shown in Fig. 1, seed union occurs in three steps: (i) seeds are sorted by their positions of occurrence in suspicious and source documents (see Fig. 1b); (ii) union of adjacent seeds with respect to the source document for the same suspicious fragments, *i.e.*, horizontal union (see Fig. 1c); and, finally, (iii) union of adjacent seeds with respect to the suspicious fragments in the same interval, *i.e.*, vertical union (see Fig. 1d).

4   Experimental Results

In order to evaluate the adoption of Adaboost for plagiarism detection, we used the PAN 2013 Plagiarism Corpus, named here PAN-PC-13 [6]. The corpus contains in total 3,653 suspicious documents and 4,774 source documents. The training set consists of 5,000 distinct cases: 3,000 of obfuscated plagiarism (i.e., 1,000 for each obfuscation strategy mentioned ahead), 1,000 of non-obfuscated plagiarism, and 1,000 without any plagiarism. The test set presents the same amount of document pairs with the same case distribution. Due to memory and computation power limitations, our experiments used only 20% of training document

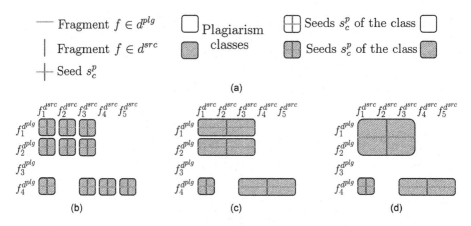

Fig. 1. Example of seed union heuristic: (a) legend of elements used; (b) sorting of seeds by their positions; (c) horizontal union; and (d) vertical union.

pairs (1,036 pairs) with 656 suspicious documents and 894 source documents. Each document in the suspicious set is related with a source document. In the collection, there are three strategies of obfuscation: random obfuscation, translation obfuscation, and summary obfuscation [6].

As seed classification metrics, we adopted the traditional precision (P) and recall (R) measures – the first measures the correctness of the classification and the second measures how many of the target classes were classified as it; and also used F-measure (F) – the harmonic mean of precision and recall. All three metrics show the best results at one (1) and the worst at zero (0). To evaluate plagiarism detection, we use the following metrics defined in [6]: detection precision ($Prec$), detection recall (Rec), detection granularity ($Gran$) and overall detection score ($PlagDet$). Those are different from the traditional classification metrics because they check the results between detections generated and the actual cases at corpus, instead of assessing seeds classes prediction. With exception of $Gran$, these metrics show the best results at one (1) and the worst at zero (0); while $Gran$ shows the best results at one (1), but it will get worse if its value is greater than one (1). The results presented are the mean and the standard deviation obtained from 30 iterations of the experiments.

Along with Adaboost, we also trained and tested other two methods: Decision Tree and Random Forest – which presented competitive results in [4]. First, we performed a binary classification experiment: *Non plagiarism × Plagiarism*. Table 2 presents classification results for the binary experiment. One can easily see that AdaBoost and Random Forest are the ones with best performances (with minor differences in their scores). Table 3 presents plagiarism detection results for the same experiment. In this case, Random Forest had the best overall performance ($PlagDet$), while AdaBoost and Random Forest obtained the best $Gran$ value, but this can be explained by the decrease of $Prec$. Before seed union, all classifiers had obtained a great performance in terms of $Prec$ and Rec, despite the high values of *Gran*. But, for all three classifiers, the value of *Prec* decreased after seed union, showing that by joining seeds, the plagiarism cases become larger and errors (*false positives*) also become more meaningful. Another possibility is that small equivocated detections, diffused by the document, are causing errors, once they become more evident after seeds union.

Table 2. Classification results for binary experiment with 20% of PAN-PC-13.

Classifier	Class	P	R	F	Seeds in test set
Decision tree	*Non plagiarism*	.88 ± .00	.94 ± .00	.91 ± .00	25854
	Plagiarism	.93 ± .00	.87 ± .00	.90 ± .00	25855
Random forest	*Non plagiarism*	.89 ± .00	**.96 ± .00**	**.93 ± .00**	25854
	Plagiarism	**.96 ± .00**	.89 ± .00	**.92 ± .00**	25855
AdaBoost	*Non plagiarism*	**.92 ± .01**	.93 ± .00	.92 ± .00	25854
	Plagiarism	.93 ± .00	**.92 ± .01**	**.92 ± .00**	25855

Table 3. Detection results for binary experiment with 20% of PAN-PC-13.

Classifier	Post-processing	*PlagDet*	*Prec*	*Rec*	*Gran*	# Detections
Decision tree	No	.19 ± .00	.93 ± .00	.92 ± .00	29.02 ± .07	24022 ± 55
	Yes	.31 ± .00	.70 ± .00	**.93 ± .00**	4.95 ± .05	5380 ± 44
Random forest	No	.19 ± .00	**.95 ± .00**	.92 ± .00	29.72 ± .10	24029 ± 93
	Yes	**.37 ± .00**	.70 ± .01	**.93 ± .00**	**3.40 ± .08**	3681 ± 60
AdaBoost	No	.18 ± .00	.92 ± .00	**.93 ± .00**	30.68 ± .25	25606 ± 280
	Yes	.33 ± .00	.59 ± .02	**.93 ± .00**	**3.56 ± .12**	4613 ± 122

All tested classifiers presented some loss. So, in order to investigate more deeply this fact, we analyze the impact in results from different obfuscation strategies. Actually, we considered five distinct classes: "Direct" or non-obfuscated, "Random obfuscation", "Translation obfucation", "Summary obfuscation", and "Non plagiarism". The same three classifiers were tested without showing any distinguishable difference among their performance. So, as an analysis reference, we only present the results for Adaboost using 5% of the corpus.

Table 4 presents classification results for the multiclass experiment, while Table 5 shows plagiarism detection results for the same experiment. One should notice that "Direct" and "Non plagiarism" classes are the easiest ones to detect, while the other three obfuscated classes presented poor results with many scores below 0.5. This behavior could be related to the selected features to describe seeds. All selected features are strongly related to statistical information coded in BoW-models. But for obfuscated cases, they usually are neither very equal neither very different, making them fuzzy in some sense. This may hinder the classifier capacity of distinguishing different obfuscation strategies. One possible

Table 4. Classification results for multiclass experiment with 5% of PAN-PC-13.

Class	P	R	F	Seeds in test set
Non plagiarism	.82 ± .04	.83 ± .02	.83 ± .02	692
Direct	**.89 ± .01**	**.91 ± .02**	**.90 ± .01**	692
Random obfuscation	.37 ± .03	.42 ± .04	.39 ± .03	692
Summary obfuscation	.52 ± .05	.41 ± .09	.45 ± .07	692
Translation obfuscation	.46 ± .03	.46 ± .05	.46 ± .03	692

Table 5. Detection results for multiclass experiment with 5% of PAN-PC-13.

Class	Post-processing	*PlagDet*	*Prec*	*Rec*	*Gran*	# Detections
Direct	No	.20 ± .00	.88 ± .01	.68 ± .01	13.55 ± .25	711 ± 17
	Yes	**.29 ± .00**	.78 ± .02	.68 ± .01	4.60 ± .11	269 ± 8
Random obfuscation	No	.16 ± .01	.36 ± .03	.69 ± .05	6.91 ± .58	812 ± 91
	Yes	.19 ± .01	.30 ± .02	.70 ± .04	**3.46 ± .26**	497 ± 42
Summary obfuscation	No	.10 ± .00	.54 ± .04	.76 ± .09	78.96 ± 10.74	582 ± 73
	Yes	.10 ± .01	.41 ± .04	.74 ± .11	34.81 ± 4.86	342 ± 42
Translation obfuscation	No	.18 ± .01	.46 ± .02	.43 ± .04	4.82 ± .49	659 ± 80
	Yes	.22 ± .01	.51 ± .02	.46 ± .04	**3.47 ± .22**	444 ± 35
Plagiarism	No	.23 ± .00	**.95 ± .01**	.83 ± .00	14.10 ± .14	2764 ± 34
	Yes	.28 ± .00	.91 ± .01	**.84 ± .00**	7.64 ± .16	1552 ± 41

solution could be the use of semantic and syntactical attributes to enrich data giving to classifiers. The values for *Gran* were worse than in binary experiment. One possible explanation is that, as data space are more fragmented (by using five classes), the seeds became more diffused in the documents, rarely forming large segments (or forming areas with a great number of gaps). The proposed seed union heuristic is not able to deal with gaps. If they occur, seed union does not work well, keeping the granularity at a high level.

We have also analyzed the detection of any plagiarism case (regardless of obfuscation strategy) by the multiclass classifier. The results are presented under class name entry "Plagiarism" at Table 5; and they present good scores values for *Prec* and *Rec*. One possible reason for this is that many missed cases in multiclass classification would be actually a hit if obfuscation strategy were ignored. In this case, AdaBoost was able to correctly detect most of the plagiarism cases with a high value of *Prec*; nonetheless, it had problems in differentiating among them, which could to be related to a poor feature selection as mentioned before.

Finally, we have conducted an experiment to assess the maximum possible performance that could be achieved by the proposed seed union heuristic. In this test, we assumed that all seeds were correctly classified (by an ideal classifier).

Table 6 shows the detection results with a maximum *Prec* value of 0.98 without the use of seed union and 0.96 when it is used. The value of *Gran* shows the effect of seed union heuristic (reducing from 20.94 to 1.63). The distance from the ideal score (which is 1 for *Gran*) shows that our proposal for reducing fragmentation could also be improved in future.

Table 6. Detection performance for a ideal classifier with 5% of PAN-PC-13.

Post-processing	*PlagDet*	*Prec*	*Rec*	*Gran*	# Detections
No	0.21	**0.98**	0.93	20.94	4104
Yes	**0.68**	0.96	0.93	**1.63**	319

5   Conclusion

Detecting plagiarism in a huge collection of documents is not manually viable. This problem is more difficult, when some obfuscation strategy is used. In this work, we have proposed and evaluated the use of AdaBoost, together with a decision tree as base classifier, for classifying suspicious text passages as plagiarism or not. Additionally, a simple post-processing heuristic for improving results granularity is also presented.

Comparative analysis with other classification methods were conducted and experimental results have shown that Adaboost reached an F-measure of 0.92 and, together with Random Forest, the best granularity score using the proposed post-processing heuristic. The assessment of three distinct obfuscation strategies pointed out that Adaboost is able to detected all of them, but it had problems in differentiating among them, which could to be related to a poor feature selection.

As future research lines, we plan to explore: (i) the use of 5-fold distribution optimally balanced stratified cross-validation (DOB-SCV); (ii) the use of statistical tests to validate the classification results; (iii) the construction of multiple specialized ensembles models for the detection of obfuscated plagiarism cases and a comparison among these multiple models; (iv) the use of other base classifiers; and (v) the use of semantic and syntactic features to obtain a more discriminating representation.

References

1. Alzahrani, S.M., Salim, N., Palade, V.: Uncovering highly obfuscated plagiarism cases using fuzzy semantic-based similarity model. J. King Saud Univ. Comput. Inform. Sci. **27**(3), 248–268 (2015)
2. Blum, S.D.: My Word!: Plagiarism and College Culture. Cornell University Press, London (2009)
3. Freund, Y., Schapire, R.E.: A decision-theoretic generalization of on-line learning and an application to boosting. J. Comput. Syst. Sci. **55**(1), 119–139 (1997)
4. Kalleberg, R.B.: Towards detecting textual plagiarism using machine learning methods. Master's thesis, University of Agder (2015)

5. Palkovskii, Y., Belov, A.: Developing high-resolution universal multi-type N-gram plagiarism detector. In: Cappellato, L., Ferro, N., Halvey, M., Kraaij, W. (eds.) CLEF 2014 Evaluation Labs and Workshop, Sheffield, UK (2014). CEUR-WS.org
6. Potthast, M., et al.: Overview of the 5th international competition on plagiarism detection. In: Forner, P., Navigli, R., Tufis, D. (eds.) Working Notes Papers of the CLEF 2013 Evaluation Labs, CLEF (2013)
7. Russell, S., Norvig, P.: Artificial Intelligence: A Modern Approach, 3rd edn. Prentice Hall Press, Upper Saddle River (2009)
8. Sanchez-Perez, M., Sidorov, G., Gelbukh, A.: A winning approach to text alignment for text reuse detection at PAN 2014. In: CLEF 2014 Working Notes, pp. 1004–1011 (2014)
9. Stevenson, A. (ed.): Oxford Dictionary of English, 3rd edn. Oxford University Press, Hardcover (2010)

Predicting Academic-Challenge Success

Dante López[⊠], Luis Villaseñor, Manuel Montes-y-Gómez, Eduardo Morales,
and Hugo Jair Escalante

Instituto Nacional de Astrofísica Óptica y Electrónica (INAOE),
Sta. María Tonantzintla, 72840 Puebla, Mexico
{danterss,villasen,emorales,hugojair}@inaoep.mx

Abstract. Academic competitions and challenges comprise an effective
mechanism for rapidly advancing the state of the art in diverse research
fields and for solving practical problems arising in industry. In fact, academic competitions are increasingly becoming an essential component of
academic events, like conferences. With the proliferation of challenges, it
is becoming more and more relevant to distinguish potentially successful challenges before they are launched. This in order to better allocate
resources, time slots, sponsorship and even to have a better estimate of
expected participation. This paper presents a first study in this direction: we collected a data set from Kaggle and aim to predict challenge
success by using information that is available before a competition starts.
We characterize competition proposals by textual information and meta-
features derived from information provided by organizers, and use these
features to predict challenge success (estimated by the number of participants and submissions). We show that both, text and meta-features
convey predictive information that can be used to estimate the success
of an academic challenge.

Keywords: Prediction of challenge success · Academic competitions ·
Challenge proposals

1 Introduction

Academic challenges dealing with data analysis represent an increasingly popular means for solving applied problems and advancing the state of the art in
a number of fields. Challenge organizers set a relevant problem, and provide
data, an evaluation protocol, rules and incentives. Then, the crowd aims to solve
the problem by making use of every skill and resource, provided they do not
harm challenge rules. Challenge campaigns and evaluation forums have a long
history within academia (e.g., DARPA programs[1], TREC [1] and ChaLearn challenges [2]) and industry (e.g., the Netflix prize [3]) and together have pushed the
boundaries of science and succeeding in practical solutions relevant to indus-
try/society problems.

---

[1] https://www.darpa.mil/our-research.

© Springer Nature Switzerland AG 2019
R. Vera-Rodriguez et al. (Eds.): CIARP 2018, LNCS 11401, pp. 874–883, 2019.
https://doi.org/10.1007/978-3-030-13469-3_101

With the availability of massive amounts of heterogeneous data being generated constantly, data analysis tasks have diversified and increased their reach in terms of societal and economical impact. This has caused a proliferation of challenges being organized and running at the same time. Since challenges are often collocated with academic events (e.g., conferences, workshops, etc.), proposing an academic challenge is getting more and more competitive: many challenge proposals and limited resources (e.g., time slots, sponsorship and even participants). Because of this, automatic ways of determining the success of challenge proposals would be extremely helpful for conference chairs, sponsors and challenge organizers themselves.

This paper explores the feasibility of predicting challenge success from information available before a challenge starts (e.g, from a challenge proposal). We build a novel data set with challenge proposals taken from Kaggle[2] (the most popular platform for challenge organization) with the aim of exploring the feasibility of the task. We define a set of meta-features that combined with textual information are used as predictive features for estimating the success of a challenge (measured as the number of participants and submissions). We analyze the performance of regressors and classifiers and show that the features convey useful information that allows us to predict the variables of interest. In addition, we analyze the most discriminative features, which can give insights for organizers. To the best of our knowledge this is the first effort in such direction.

The remainder of this paper is organized as follows. Section 2 describes the collected data set. Section 3 formulates the problem and introduces the meta-features and textual information considered for our study, also we describe the adopted supervised learning framework. Section 4 reports experimental results. Finally, Sect. 5 outlines conclusions and future work directions.

2   The Kaggle Data Set

For building the associated data set we relied on the most popular platform for challenge hosting: Kaggle. It was founded in 2010 and it was recently acquired by Google. The focus of Kaggle is on predictive analytics challenges. We postpone for future work experiments and evaluation on other popular platforms (e.g., CodaLab[3]).

We considered all of the finished competitions up to April first 2018. Completed competitions were required to built the corpus because we needed to have a way to determine the extend of success of each competition. In total 270 of Kaggle competitions were considered for the study. Figure 1 shows a snapshot of a typical Kaggle challenge website. We aimed to collect for each competition most of the information available, with emphasis on potentially discriminative information. Textual information was gathered form the overview description, evaluation, and data sections. Additional information comprising duration, prizes, number of registered teams, and tags was also compiled. Finally, we also stored

---

[2] http://kaggle.com/.
[3] http://codalab.org/.

Fig. 1. Snapshot of a typical Kaggle challenge.

information on the scores from the top ranked participants. The next section explains the set of meta-features extracted form the corpus to be used by the predictive models and the criteria we used to determine whether a challenge was successful or not.

3   Predicting Challenge Success

We focus in the problem of predicting a variable related with the success of challenges starting from information derived available before the challenge starts. Success of challenges can be measured in a number of ways: e.g., by determining how close the winning solution was from the optimal performance, by determining whether the winning solution was acquired by the organizer (e.g., a company), by the number of participants or teams involved, by the average performance of participants etc. Among these options, we opted to associate the success of a challenge with the number of registered teams and the number of submissions made by the top ranked participants. Our choices are based on the intuition that:

1. *A challenge is successful if it is attractive to people (measured by the number of participants)*;
2. *The number of submissions by top-ranked teams reflects the engagement of participants in the competition (measured by number of submissions among the top ranked participants).*

Therefore, we aim to estimate both of these variables that are directly related to challenge success. Please note that we do not opted for predicting the "successful vs. non-successful" variable[4] because it may be arguable how many participants/submissions make a competition successful. Instead we aim to estimate the number of participants and submissions, which can be a more useful variable

---

[4] Although we report some results by discretizing the output variables, see Sect. 4.

(i.e., in addition to measure the success of a challenge, these predictions can be helpful to allocate resources for competitions).

3.1 Features

The features that were used to build predictors were extracted from information that is available before a competition starts. This is motivated by the fact that challenge organizers often prepare challenge proposals that are analyzed, judged and selected by conference chairs and sponsors (see e.g., [4]). We think our model could be used by people that decide on the collocation/sponsorship of challenges as an additional support tool. Hence, we used information that is commonly available in a challenge proposal. The set of derived features is presented in Table 1.

Table 1. Features considered in this study.

Name	Type	Description
Meta-features		
Category	Type of competition: research, recruitment, novices, experts	Categorical
Tags	Associated keywords	Categorical
Type	Type of submission: code, prediction, recreation	Categorical
Prize	Amount of offered prize	Numerical
Currency	Currency of offered prize: USD, Euro, Other	Categorical
Images	Binary variable: is an image included in the description?	Binary
Duration	Challenge duration	Numerical
Data type	Text, image, numerical, other	Categorical
Winners	Number of offered prizes	Numerical
Score	Score obtained by the baseline of the competition	Numerical
Metric	Evaluation measure: RMSE, Accuracy, Log loss, etc.	Categorical
Members	Maximum number of participants per team allowed	Numerical
Submissions	Maximum number of submissions per day	Numerical
Solutions	Maximum number of final models per team	Numerical
Textual-features		
Description-text	All text used in the description of the competition	Bag of words
Evaluation-text	All text used in the description of the evaluation section	Bag of words
Data-text	All text used in the description of the Data	Bag of words

We distinguish two types of features/information: textual features, extracted from the text in the challenge site (see Fig. 1) and features derived from the challenge website (we called these meta-features to make clear the distinction from textual features). The 14 considered meta-features capture information that is, intuitively, engaging and could be related with challenge success. For instance, the amount of offered prize, the inclusion of images in the description, the number of allowed submissions, models, etc. On the other hand, textual information was considered because we wanted to study whether what organizers say may be correlated with the success of the challenge. Text was represented using a bag of words with TFIDF weighting scheme. Stop words and punctuation marks were removed, all text was converted to lower case before indexing. We performed experiments using the whole corpus vocabulary and reducing the number of dimensions by using mutual information [5] (below, the best results are described). As described below, we performed extensive experiments merging feature representations and normalizing the outputs.

3.2   Predictive Modeling

As previously mentioned, we approached the problem of predicting the number of teams registered to a competition and the average number of submission made by the top ranked participants (top-10 were used). Accordingly, popular regression methods were considered to approach the problem. In preliminary experiments we discarded several models because they were showing very low performance (e.g., linear regression, Gaussian processes and support vector regression). At the end we used random forest regression as the predictive model. Implementations in the popular Sci-kit learn library were used for all of our experiments [6].

In addition to addressing the regression problem, we formulated the problem as one of classification. Our aim was to study the feasibility of the task when trying to estimate categories instead of raw values. Artificial classes were defined by dividing the numerical outputs into three categories for each predictive variable. The generation of intervals was done manually and aiming to keep balanced classes. The induced artificial classes are shown in Table 2.

Table 2. Artificial classes per variable. The number of samples in each class is shown between parentheses.

Variable	Class 1	Class 2	Class 3
Number of participants	≤200 (97)	>200, ≤700 (88)	>700 (85)
Number of submissions	≤30 (114)	>30, ≤70 (83)	>70 (73)

Please note that the generation of these artificial classes was simply done to study whether classifiers perform better than regressors. Our goal was not to determine thresholds on the variables to distinguish successful challenges. For approaching the classification problem we considered the following classifiers: support vector machines, naïve Bayes, and j48 decision tree.

4   Experiments and Results

This section reports experimental results on the estimation of challenge success from competition proposals. As previously mentioned the generated corpus comprises 270 samples, for experimentation we adopted a cross validation strategy: we report average 5-fold cross validation performance (the same folds were used for every experiment reported herein). Regression performance was evaluated with the root-mean-squared-error (RMSE, the lower the better) and the determination coefficient (R^2 the higher the better). Classification performance was evaluated with the average of f_1 measure across classes.

4.1   Challenge Success Prediction as Regression

This section reports experimental results when predicting the number of participants and submissions directly. The problem is approached as one of regression. We tried two configurations, in the first one we predict raw values as extracted from the data set. In a second experiment we normalize the outputs to the range $[0, 1]$ and aim to predict this normalized outputs. We evaluated normalized outputs because the ranges of values in the raw values were rather large, which caused the regressors to be unstable for some samples (see below). Also, intuitively having a predictor that provides estimates as a bounded real number would be more helpful if one want to assess the successfulness of challenges in relative terms (the perfect challenge would get 1 and the worst 0). Table 3 shows the performance obtained when using meta-features, textual information and a combination of both types of features (early fusion scheme), and Fig. 2 shows plots of ground truth values vs. predictions for the different configurations.

Table 3. Challenge success prediction performance.

Configuration	Raw		Normalized	
	RMSE	R^2	RMSE	R^2
Participants				
Meta-features	1005.41	0.11	0.10	0.12
Text-features	939.36	0.27	0.09	0.29
Meta-Text-features	923.48	0.29	0.09	0.32
Submissions				
Meta-features	51.81	0.21	0.21	−0.27
Text-features	55.71	0.07	0.19	0.07
Meta-Text-features	51.94	0.19	0.19	0.05

From Table 3 it can be seen that error in raw estimations is somewhat large, mostly when estimating the number of submissions. This is decreased when estimating the normalized values. Large error values are partly due to the great variability in the range of values that such variable can take. This can be graphically seen in the left plot of Fig. 2, where an outlier is affecting the performance of all methods. From the same plot, it can be seen that, in general, the predictions from the three regression methods are rather conservative (they underestimate the number of participants). Interestingly, when predicting the number of participants, textual information reported better performance than meta-features, and the combination obtained the best overall performance. In fact, the improvement offered by textual features is considerable: about 9% in absolute RMSE and much more in terms of R^2 score. This is a very interesting result, as it suggest that the words that are used by challenge organizers to describe their competition indeed affect the number of potential participants.

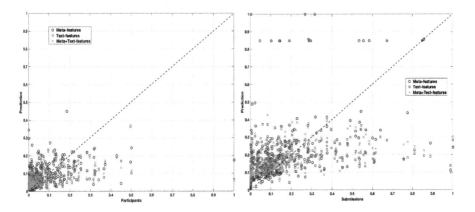

Fig. 2. Ground truth vs. predicted values. Left: predicting the number of participants. Right: predicting the number of submissions.

Regarding the prediction of the number of submissions it can be seen from Table 3 that the best performance is obtained when using meta-features only. This time adding text does not help to improve the performance. Graphically, from the right plot of Fig. 2, the predictions using meta-features are slightly closer to the ideal line (although optimistic/large values are predicted for some challenges). The variants including text are more spread and this causes a larger error.

4.2 Challenge Success Prediction as Classification

As previously mentioned, we also performed experiments by generating an artificial classification problem by thresholding raw values on the number of participants and submissions. Our hypothesis was that by discretizing the outputs would lead to satisfactory performance when predicting challenge success. Experimental results are shown in Table 4.

From this table it can be seen that performance is low in general, in fact, several configurations perform lower than a trivial baseline like predicting the

Table 4. Challenge success prediction performance as classification.

Configuration	SVM	N. Bayes	j48
Participants			
Meta-features	0.33	0.27	0.55
Text-features	0.17	0.46	0.49
Meta-Text-features	0.43	0.22	0.52
Submissions			
Meta-features	0.25	0.26	0.49
Text-features	0.20	0.40	0.40
Meta-Text-features	0.51	0.26	0.5

majority class (35% and 42% for participants and submissions, respectively). Among the considered classifiers, the best performance was obtained by the decision tree. In terms of features, both performed similarly, not clearly showing a tendency. Results from this experiment seem to indicate that the way we discretized the outputs may not be the best, in addition, since the range of values of the outputs are large, approaching the problem as one of classification may not be a good choice. Yet, being optimistic we think the results are promising, further research is needed in order to obtain satisfactory results.

Figure 3 shows the first nodes of the decision tree when using meta features for predicting participants (top) and submissions (bottom). It is somewhat expected that the root node is the *prize* feature. Interestingly, for discriminating class 2/3 samples (high number of participants), it is important if the competition category is either text or images; whereas a small number of submissions is mostly associated with class 1 samples. Regarding the number of submissions, the performance of the baseline causes a low number of submissions (class 1), whereas, a small number of daily submissions is associated with challenges having a large number of submissions.

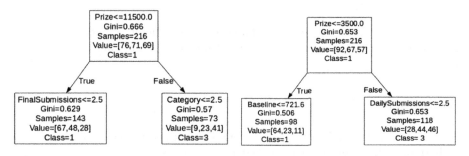

Fig. 3. Snapshot of the root of decision trees when using meta-features for predicting participants (left) and submissions (right).

Regarding textual features the most discriminative words for high participation were: *faq, mode, prepared, mitigate, properly, organization, effects*, while for low participation the following words were more important: *depending, enforce, shall, not, breaks*. We leave the reader to draw their own conclusions regarding the importance of this features. Finally, when mixed features were considered, words dominated the earlier levels of the tree for both variables participants and submissions. Interestingly, new words emerged that were associated to class 3 like: Alex, Deep, Deeper, etc.

5   Conclusions

Academic competitions are becoming increasingly popular among scientist and practitioners of data science. With this overwhelming number of challenges being organized it is becoming more and more relevant to anticipate the success of challenges, so that organizers can allocate resources, sponsorship, and number of potential participants attending academic venues. This paper comprises a first step in this direction: we introduced a novel data set comprising both textual and meta features, and deployed and analyzed predictive models for estimating challenge success (via number of participants and submissions). The following conclusions are derived from this work:

- Experimental results reveal that the considered features convey useful information for predicting challenge success in terms of the two considered variables.
- Textual information is more more helpful for estimating the number of participants than meta-features, whereas the latter were more helpful for predicting the number of submissions.
- Approaching the problem as one of classification shows the problem is quite complicated and that the performed discretization may not be the best.
- The analysis of features revealed that the *prize* meta feature was the most discriminative, and among text, words with negative connotation (e.g., *not, enforce, breaks, depending, etc.*) were negatively correlated with challenge success prediction.

Future work includes extending the data set by including information from other competition platforms, and performing a complete linguistic analysis of textual features.

References

1. Voorhees, E.M., Harman, D.K.: TREC: Experiment and Evaluation in Information Retrieval. MIT Press, Cambridge (2005)
2. Escalera, S., Baró, X., Escalante, H.J., Guyon, I.: ChaLearn looking at people: a review of events and resources. In: International Joint Conference on Neural Networks, pp. 1594–1601 (2017)

3. Bell, R.M., Koren, Y.: Lessons from the Netflix prize challenge. SIGKDD Explor. Newsl. **9**(2), 75–79 (2007)
4. ChaLearn: Chalearn procedures for organizing events and awarding prizes and travel grants (2013). http://chalearn.org
5. Yang, Y., Pedersen, J.O.: A comparative study on feature selection in text categorization. In: ICML, pp. 412–420. Morgan Kaufmann Publishers Inc., San Francisco (1997)
6. Pedregosa, F., et al.: Scikit-learn: machine learning in Python. JMLR **12**, 2825–2830 (2011)

Visual Semantic Re-ranker
for Text Spotting

Ahmed Sabir[1], Francesc Moreno-Noguer[2], and Lluís Padró[1(✉)]

[1] TALP Research Center, Universitat Politècnica de Catalunya, Barcelona, Spain
{asabir,padro}@cs.upc.edu
[2] Institut de Robòtica i Informàtica Industrial (CSIC-UPC), Barcelona, Spain
fmoreno@iri.upc.edu

Abstract. Many current state-of-the-art methods for text recognition are based on purely local information and ignore the semantic correlation between text and its surrounding visual context. In this paper, we propose a post-processing approach to improve the accuracy of text spotting by using the semantic relation between the text and the scene. We initially rely on an off-the-shelf deep neural network that provides a series of text hypotheses for each input image. These text hypotheses are then re-ranked using the semantic relatedness with the object in the image. As a result of this combination, the performance of the original network is boosted with a very low computational cost. The proposed framework can be used as a drop-in complement for any text-spotting algorithm that outputs a ranking of word hypotheses. We validate our approach on ICDAR'17 shared task dataset.

Keywords: Text spotting · Deep learning · Semantic visual context

1 Introduction

Machine reading has shown a remarkable progress in Optical Character Recognition systems (OCR). However, the success of most OCR systems is restricted to simple-background and properly aligned documents. However, text in many real images is affected by a number of artifacts including partial occlusion, distorted perspective and complex backgrounds. For this reason, OCR systems able to read text in the wild are required, problem referred to as *Text Spotting*. However, while state-of-the-art computer vision algorithms have shown remarkable results in recognizing object instances in these images, understanding and recognizing the included text in a robust manner is far from being considered a solved problem.

Text spotting pipelines address the end-to-end problem of detecting and recognizing text in unrestricted images (traffic signs, advertisements, brands in clothing, etc.). The problem is usually split in two stages: (1) *text detection stage*, to estimate the bounding box around the candidate word in the image and (2) *text recognition stage*, to identify the text inside the bounding boxes.

© Springer Nature Switzerland AG 2019
R. Vera-Rodriguez et al. (Eds.): CIARP 2018, LNCS 11401, pp. 884–892, 2019.
https://doi.org/10.1007/978-3-030-13469-3_102

In this paper we focus on the second stage, by means of a simple but efficient post-processing approach built upon Natural Language Processing (NLP) techniques.

There exist two main approaches to perform text recognition in the wild. First, lexicon-based methods, where the system learns to recognize words in a pre-defined dictionary [1,8,16]. Second, lexicon free, unconstrained recognition methods, that aim at predicting character sequences [2,5,12].

Most recent state-of-the arts systems are deep learning based approaches [2,5,8,12], which however, have some limitations: Lexicon-based approaches need a large dictionary to perform the final recognition. Thus, their accuracy will depend on the quality and coverage of this lexicon, which makes this approach unpractical for real world applications where the domain may be different to that the system was trained on. On the other hand, lexicon-free recognition methods rely on sequence models to predict character sequences, and thus they may generate likely sentences that do not correspond to actual language words. In both cases, these techniques rely on the availability of large datasets to train and validate, which may not be always available for the target domain.

In this work we propose a post-processing approach via a *visual context re-ranker* to overcome these limitations. Our approach uses visual prior to re-rank the candidate words based on the semantic relation between the scene text and its environmental *visual* context. Thus, the visual re-ranker can be applied to any of both methods, the huge dictionary in case there is a lexicon, or unconstrained recognition such as character prediction sequence, to re-rank most probable word biased by its visual information.

The work of [11] also uses visual prior information to improve text spotting results, through a new lexicon built with Latent Dirichlet Allocation (LDA) [3]. The topic modeling learns the relation between text and images. However, this approach relies on captions describing the images rather than using the main keywords semantically related to the images to generate the lexicon re-ranking. Thus, the lexicon generation can be inaccurate in some cases due to the short length of captions. In this work we consider a direct semantic relation between scene text and its visual information. Also, unlike [11] that only uses visual information over word frequency count to re-rank the most probable word, our approach combines both methods by leveraging also on a frequency count based language model.

Our main contributions therefore include several post-processing methods based on NLP techniques such as word frequencies and semantic relatedness which are typically used in pure NLP problems but less common in computer vision. We show that by introducing a candidate re-ranker based on word frequencies and semantic distances between candidate words and objects in the image, we can improve the performance of an off-the-shelf deep neural network without the need to perform additional training or tuning. In addition, thanks to the inclusion of the unigram probabilities, we overcome the baseline limitation of false detection of short words of [5,8].

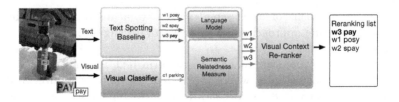

Fig. 1. Scheme of the proposed visual context information pipeline integration into the text spotting system. Our approach uses the language model and a semantic relatedness measure to re-rank the word hypotheses. In this example, the re-ranked word *pay* is semantically related with the visual *parking*.

The rest of the paper is organized as follows: Sect. 2 describes our proposed pipeline. Section 3 introduces the external prior knowledge we use, namely a visual context information. Section 4 presents experimental validation of our approach on a variety of publicly available standard datasets. Finally, Sect. 5 summarizes the work and discusses specifies future work.

2   General Approach and Baseline System

There exist two main classes of recognition approaches: (1) character based methods that rely on a single character classifier plus some kind of sequence modeling (e.g. n-gram models or LSTMs), and (2) lexicon-based approaches that aim to classify the image as a whole word.

In both cases, the system can be configured to predict the k most likely words given the input image. Our approach focuses on re-ranking that list using semantic relatedness with objects in the image (or `visual context`) in which the text was located.

We used two different off-the-shelf baseline models: First, a CNN [8] with fixed lexicon based recognition. It uses a fixed dictionary of around 90 K words. Second, we considered a LSTM architecture with a visual attention model [5]. The LSTM generates the final output words as character sequences, without relying on any lexicon. Both models are trained on a synthetic dataset [7]. The output of both models is a vector of softmax probabilities for candidate words. We next describe in more detail these components.

Let us denote the initial probabilities of the k most likely words w produced by each of the *baselines* (BL) [5,8] by:

$$P_0(w) = p(w|\text{BL}) \tag{1}$$

We introduce a Unigram Language Model (ULM) as preliminary stage for the visual re-ranker. The probabilities of the unigram model are estimated on the *Opensubtitles*[1] [14] and *Google book n-gram*[2] text corpora. The main goal of

---

[1] https://www.opensubtitles.org.
[2] https://books.google.com/ngrams.

ULM is to increase the probability of the most common words proposed by the baseline. The output of this re-ranker is then used as input for a second re-ranker based on visual context information. The ULM should be useful to (1) enhance the baseline recognition output (2) and to ensure each output is a valid word before performing the visual semantic re-ranking stage.

3   Visual Context Information

The main source of semantic information we use to re-rank the BL output is the visual context information, i.e. the semantic relation between the candidate words and the objects in the image. We use a pre-trained object classifier to detect the objects in the image and we devise a strategy to reward candidate words that are semantically related to them. As shown in Fig. 1 the top position of the re-ranking yields *pay* as the most semantically related with the object detected in the image *parking*. Next, we describe two different schemes to compute this relatedness.

3.1   Visual Classifier

In order to exploit and extract the image context information we use state-of-the-art object classifiers. We considered two pre-trained CNN classifiers: ResNet [6] and GoogLeNet [13]. The output of these classifiers is a 1000-dimensional vector with the probabilities of 1000 object instances. In this work we only consider the most likely object of the context. We set a threshold to filter out the probability predictions when the object classifier is not confident enough.

3.2   Semantic Relatedness with Word Embedding (SWE)

Once the objects in the image have been detected, we compute their semantic relatedness with the candidate words based on their word-embeddings [10]. Specifically, let us denote by $\boldsymbol{w}$ and $\boldsymbol{c}$ the word-embeddings of a candidate word w and the most likely object c detected in the image. We then compute their similarity using the cosine of the embeddings:

$$sim(w, c) = \frac{\boldsymbol{w} \cdot \boldsymbol{c}}{|\boldsymbol{w}| \cdot |\boldsymbol{c}|} \tag{2}$$

We next convert the similarity score to a probability value, in order to integrate it into our re-ranking model. Following [4], we compute the conditional probability from similarity as:

$$P_{SWE}(w|c) = P(w)^{\alpha} \quad \text{where } \alpha = \left(\frac{1 - sim(w,c)}{1 + sim(w,c)} \right)^{1 - P(c)} \tag{3}$$

$P(w)$ is the probability of the word in general language (obtained from the unigram model), and $P(c)$ is the probability of the context object (obtained from the object classifier).

Once we have the probability of a candidate word conditioned to the visual context objects, we can define $P(w|\text{SWE}) = P_{SWE}(w|c)$ and use it to re-rank the output of the BL:

$$P_1(w) = P(w|\text{BL}) \times P(w|\text{SWE}) \tag{4}$$

Note that the frequency information from the ULM is already included in $P(w|\text{SWE})$, so this step will rely on the output of the language model.

3.3 Estimating Relatedness from Training Data Probabilities (TDP)

A second possibility to compute semantic relatedness is to estimate it from training data. This should overcome the word embedding limitation when the candidate word and the image objects are not semantically related in general text, but occurred in the real world. For instance, a tennis sponsor (watch brand) *rolex* and the object *racket*, have no semantic relation according to the word embedding model, but they are found paired multiple times in the training dataset, which implies they do have a relation. To encode this relation, we use training data to estimate the conditional probability of a word w given that object c appears in the image:

$$P_{TDP}(w|c) = \frac{count(w, c)}{count(c)} \tag{5}$$

where $count(w, c)$ is the number of training images where w appears as the gold standard annotation for recognized text, and the object classifier detects object c in the image. Similarly, $count(c)$ is the number of training images where the object classifier detects object c.

We combined this re-ranker with SWE as:

$$P_2(w) = P(w|\text{BL}) \times P(w|\text{SWE}) \times P(w|\text{TDP}) \tag{6}$$

3.4 Semantic Relatedness with Word Embedding (Revisited) (TWE)

This re-ranker builds upon a word embedding, as the SWE re-ranker above, but the embeddings are learnt from the training dataset (considering two-word "sentences": the target word and the object in the image). The embeddings can be computed from scratch, using only the training dataset information (TWE).

In this case, we convert the similarity produced by the embeddings to probabilities using:

$$P_{TWE}(w|c) = \frac{\tanh(sim(w, c)) + 1}{2P(c)} \tag{7}$$

Note that this re-ranker does not take into account word frequency information as in the case of the SWE re-ranker. Also, we add this re-ranker as:

$$P_3(w) = P(w|\text{BL}) \times P(w|\text{TWE}) \times P(w|\text{TDP}) \tag{8}$$

4   Experiments and Results

In this section we evaluate the performance of the proposed approaches on the **ICDAR-2017-Task3 (end-to-end)** dataset [15]. This dataset is based on Microsoft COCO [9] (Common Objects in Context), which consists of 63,686 images, and 173,589 text instances (annotations of the images). COCO-text was not collected with text recognition in mind, therefore, not all images contain textual annotations. The *ICDAR-2017 Task3* aims for end-to-end text spotting (i.e. both detection and recognition). Thus, this dataset includes full images, and the texts in them may appear rotated, distorted, or partially occluded. Since we focus only on text recognition, we use the ground truth detection as a golden detector to extract the bounding boxes from the full image. The dataset consists of 43,686 full images with 145,859 text instances for training, and 10,000 images with 27,550 text instances for validation.

4.1   Preliminaries

For evaluation, we used a more restrictive protocol than the standard proposed by [16] and adopted in most state-of-the-art benchmarks, which does not consider words with less than three characters or with non-alphanumerical characters. This protocol was introduced to overcome the false positives on short words that most current state-of-the-art struggle with, including our Baseline. However, we overcome this limitation by adopting a language model before the visual re-ranker. Thus, we consider all cases in the dataset, and words with less than three characters are also evaluated.

In all cases, we use two pre-trained deep models, CNN [8] and LSTM [5] as a baseline (BL) to extract the initial list of word hypotheses. Since these BLs need to be fed with the cropped words, when evaluating on the ICDAR-2017-Task3 dataset we will use the ground truth bounding boxes of the words.

4.2   Experiment with Visual Context Information

The main contribution of this paper consists in re-ranking the k most likely hypotheses using the visual context information. Thus, we use ICDAR-2017-Task3 dataset to evaluate our approach, re-ranking the baseline output using the semantic relation between the spotted text in the image and its visual context.

We extract the $k = 5..9$ most likely words –and their probabilities– from the baselines. The first baseline is a CNN [8] with fixed-lexicon recognition, which is not able to recognize any word outside its dictionary. We present three different accuracy metrics: (1) *full* columns correspond to the accuracy on the whole dataset, (2) *dict* columns correspond to the accuracy over the cases where the target word is among the 90K-words of the CNN dictionary (which correspond to 43.3% of the whole dataset) and finally (3) *list* shows the accuracy over the cases where the right word was in the k-best list output by the baseline. The second baseline we consider is an LSTM [5] with visual soft-attention mechanism, using unconstrained text recognition approach without relying on a lexicon.

Both baselines work on cropped words, we do not evaluate the whole end-to-end system but only the influence of adding external knowledge. We used ground-truth bounding boxes as input to the BL. Thus, the whole image is used as input to the object classifier.

In order to extract the visual context information we considered two different pre-trained state-of-the-art object classifiers: ResNet [6] and GoogLeNet [13], both able to detect pre-defined list of 1,000 object classes. In this experiment we re-rank the baseline k-best hypotheses based on their relatedness with the objects in the image. We try two approaches for that: (1) semantic similarity computed using word embeddings [10] and (2) correlation based on co-occurrence of text and image object in the training data.

Table 1. Results of re-ranking the k-best ($k = 5, 9$) hypotheses of the baselines on ICDAR-2017-Task3 dataset (%)

Model	CNN						LSTM			
	$k = 5$			$k = 9$			$k = 5$		$k = 9$	
	full	dict	list	full	dict	list	full	list	full	list
Baseline	full: 21.1 dict: 58.6						full: 18.7			
SWE	22.5	62.5	80.6	22.6	62.8	70.4	19.5	70.1	19.9	62.3
SWE+TDP	22.7	63.1	81.6	21.4	59.5	66.6	19.5	70.1	20.0	62.6
TDP+TWE	22.9	63.8	82.2	**23.0**	**64.0**	**71.6**	20.0	73.0	**20.8**	**65.2**
SWE+TDP+TWE	22.6	62.9	81.0	22.5	62.5	70.0	20.1	72.3	20.3	63.6

First, we re-rank the words based on their embedding-based semantic relatedness with the image visual context (SWE). For instance, the semantic similarity between a visual *street* and text *way* in a signboard.

Secondly, we use the training dataset to compute the conditional probabilities between text image and object in the image happen together (TDP). As shown in Table 1 the LSTM accuracy improved up to 1.3%, and the fixed-lexicon CNN accuracy is boosted up to 1.6% on *full* dataset and 2.5% *dictionary*.

Finally, we trained a word embedding model using the training dataset (TWE). Due to the dataset is too small, we use skip-gram model with one window, and without any word filtering. In addition, we initialized the model weight with the baseline (SWE) that trained on general text. The result is 300-dimension vector for about 10 K words. The result in Table 1 shows that (TWE) outperform the accuracy of SWE model that trained on general text. The result in Table 1 shows that the combination model TDP+TWE also significantly boost the accuracy up to 5.4% *dictionary* and 1.9% *all*. Also, the second baseline LSTM accuracy boosted up to 2.1%. Not to mention that TDP+TWE model only rely on the visual context information, computed by Eq. 7.

5 Conclusion

In this paper, we have proposed a simple visual context re-ranker as post-processing approach to a text spotting system. We have shown that the accuracy of two different architecture state-of-the-art, lexicon based and lexicon free, deep networks can be improved to 2 points on standard benchmark. In the future work, we plan to explore more visual context such as multiple objects and information from the scene.

Acknowledgments. This work was supported by the KASP Scholarship Program and by the MINECO project HuMoUR TIN2017-90086-R.

References

1. Almazán, J., Gordo, A., Fornés, A., Valveny, E.: Word spotting and recognition with embedded attributes. IEEE Trans. Pattern Anal. Mach. Intell. (2014)
2. Bissacco, A., Cummins, M., Netzer, Y., Neven, H.: PhotoOCR: reading text in uncontrolled conditions. In: Proceedings of the IEEE International Conference on Computer Vision (2013)
3. Blei, D.M., Ng, A.Y., Jordan, M.I.: Latent dirichlet allocation. J. Mach. Learn. Res. (2003)
4. Blok, S., Medin, D., Osherson, D.: Probability from similarity. In: AAAI Spring Symposium on Logical Formalization of Commonsense Reasoning (2003)
5. Ghosh, S.K., Valveny, E., Bagdanov, A.D.: Visual attention models for scene text recognition. arXiv preprint arXiv:1706.01487 (2017)
6. He, K., Zhang, X., Ren, S., Sun, J.: Deep residual learning for image recognition. arXiv preprint arXiv:1512.03385 (2015)
7. Jaderberg, M., Simonyan, K., Vedaldi, A., Zisserman, A.: Synthetic data and artificial neural networks for natural scene text recognition. arXiv preprint arXiv:1406.2227 (2014)
8. Jaderberg, M., Simonyan, K., Vedaldi, A., Zisserman, A.: Reading text in the wild with convolutional neural networks. Int. J. Comput. Vis. (2016)
9. Lin, T.-Y., et al.: Microsoft COCO: common objects in context. In: Fleet, D., Pajdla, T., Schiele, B., Tuytelaars, T. (eds.) ECCV 2014. LNCS, vol. 8693, pp. 740–755. Springer, Cham (2014). https://doi.org/10.1007/978-3-319-10602-1_48
10. Mikolov, T., Sutskever, I., Chen, K., Corrado, G.S., Dean, J.: Distributed representations of words and phrases and their compositionality. In: Advances in Neural Information Processing Systems (2013)
11. Patel, Y., Gomez, L., Rusiñol, M., Karatzas, D.: Dynamic lexicon generation for natural scene images. In: Hua, G., Jégou, H. (eds.) ECCV 2016. LNCS, vol. 9913, pp. 395–410. Springer, Cham (2016). https://doi.org/10.1007/978-3-319-46604-0_29
12. Shi, B., Bai, X., Yao, C.: An end-to-end trainable neural network for image-based sequence recognition and its application to scene text recognition. IEEE Trans. Pattern Anal. Mach. Intell. (2017)
13. Szegedy, C., et al.: Going deeper with convolutions. In: Proceedings of the IEEE Conference on Computer Vision and Pattern Recognition (2015)
14. Tiedemann, J.: News from opus-a collection of multilingual parallel corpora with tools and interfaces. In: Recent Advances in Natural Language Processing (2009)

15. Veit, A., Matera, T., Neumann, L., Matas, J., Belongie, S.: COCO-text: dataset and benchmark for text detection and recognition in natural images. arXiv preprint arXiv:1601.07140 (2016)
16. Wang, K., Babenko, B., Belongie, S.: End-to-end scene text recognition. In: 2011 IEEE International Conference on Computer Vision (ICCV). IEEE (2011)

A Hybrid Feature Extraction Method for Offline Handwritten Math Symbol Recognition

Carlos Ramírez-Piña[1], Josep Salvador Sánchez[2(✉)],
Rosa M. Valdovinos-Rosas[1], and José A. Hernández-Servín[1(✉)]

[1] School of Engineering, Universidad Autónoma del Estado de México,
Toluca, Mexico
xoseahernandez@uaemex.mx
[2] Institute of New Imaging Technologies,
Department Computer Languages and Systems,
Universitat Jaume I, Castelló de la Plana, Spain
sanchez@uji.es

Abstract. This paper introduces a feature extraction scheme for offline handwritten math symbol recognition. It is a hybrid model that involves the basic ideas of the wavelet and zoning techniques so as to define the feature vectors with both statistical and geometrical properties of the symbols, with the aim of overcoming some limitations of the individual algorithms used. Experiments over a medium-sized database of isolated math symbols investigate the performance of the new hybrid technique in comparison to other algorithms. The results show that the new model performs significantly better than the rest of algorithms tested, independently of the symbol category.

Keywords: Feature extraction · Handwritten math symbol recognition

1 Introduction

Recognition of handwritten mathematical expressions allows to transform formulas in scientific documents into an electronic representation. Although it might appear that the mathematical expression recognition is equivalent to the recognition of plain text, there exist differences that make it unrealistic to apply standard solutions of handwritten character recognition to mathematical notation. First, a line of text is one-dimensional and discrete, whereas symbols in mathematical expressions are spatially arranged into complex two-dimensional structures. Second, symbol recognition is a nontrivial problem because the vocabulary is very large (digits, Latin and Greek letters, operator symbols, relation symbols, etc.) with a variety of typefaces (regular, bold, italic, calligraphic) and several font sizes (subscripts, superscripts, limit expressions) [2]. Third, mathematical

© Springer Nature Switzerland AG 2019
R. Vera-Rodriguez et al. (Eds.): CIARP 2018, LNCS 11401, pp. 893–901, 2019.
https://doi.org/10.1007/978-3-030-13469-3_103

handwriting may involve large operators such as matrix brackets, fraction bars or square roots.

Recognition of a mathematical expression comprises two main steps [5]: symbol recognition and structural analysis. The recognition stage translates the input image into a set of mathematical symbols present in the expression, being as task of most relevance. In general, symbol recognition comprises a set of processes that are applied to the input image: pre-processing, segmentation to isolate symbols, feature extraction, and classification. On the other hand, the objective of structural analysis is to determine the relations among the symbols recognized in the previous stage in order to build a complete structure that represents the mathematical expression.

The scope of this paper focuses on the field of isolated math symbol recognition, which is deemed to be a hard problem [8]. From the different operations included in this stage, feature extraction is one of the most critical elements of a mathematical recognition system because it provides the set of features used to describe each symbol precisely.

This work presents a feature extraction algorithm for offline handwritten math symbol recognition. It combines the wavelet and zoning techniques to obtain a feature vector with both statistical and geometrical properties of the symbols, thus overcoming some limitations of those individual feature extraction algorithms. The performance of the new hybrid method is compared against that of four feature extraction techniques when applied to a medium-sized database of isolated math symbols.

2   Some Feature Extraction Techniques

Feature extraction methods can be classified into two major groups: statistical and structural [2]. In the statistical approach, a character image is represented by a set of d features that are derived from the statistical distributions of pixels and can be considered as a point in d-dimensional feature space. In the structural category, various local and global properties of the character can be represented by geometrical and topological characteristics. Note that structural and statistical features are deemed to be complementary in the sense that they emphasize different properties of the characters.

2.1   The FKI Algorithm

Given a binary image I of size $M \times N$, the FKI algorithm [9] computes a set of nine geometrical values for each image column y, obtaining 9-dimensional vectors $v(y) = [v_1(y), \ldots, v_9(y)]$. The algorithm uses a sliding window of size 1, moving from the very left of the image to the very right, to calculate a set of geometrical values.

2.2   The Wavelet Method

Wavelet transform is a multi-resolution signal decomposition tool that provides a representation of an image at different levels of resolution. This work utilizes 3-level Daubechies discrete wavelet transform (DWT) [7], which recursively decomposes an input image I of size $M \times N$ into one low-frequency component (a thumbnail of the input image) and three high-frequency components for each level of decomposition j. The contour of the image is in the low-frequency sub-band and contains the approximation or scale coefficients (A_j), whereas the high-frequency sub-band includes the so-called detail coefficients H_j (horizontal), V_j (vertical) and D_j (diagonal).

The input image is fed into two filters h and g, which produce the approximation coefficient A_j and the three detail coefficients H_j, V_j and D_j, which are all down-sampled by a factor of 2. Since images are two-dimensional structures, filtering and sub-sampling are first applied along the rows of the image and then along the columns of the transformed image. The result of these operations is a transformed image with four distinct bands: the upper left band corresponds to a down-sampled version of the original image that has been, the bottom left band tends to preserve localized horizontal features, the upper right band tends to preserve localized vertical features, and the bottom right band tends to isolate localized high-frequency point features in the image. Additional levels of decomposition can be applied only to the upper left band of the transformed image at the previous level in order to extract lower frequency features in the image.

Frequency domain analysis is the background of representation of the feature vector (with a size of $\frac{M}{2} \frac{N}{2}$), but a total of 54 textural and statistical values are also computed to enhance the feature vector [10]. In particular, entropy, mean and standard deviation are computed on the gray-scale, binary and twelve sub-band images. Analogously, the Shannon entropy, the 'log energy' entropy, the threshold entropy, the sure entropy and the norm entropy are also calculated on the approximation coefficient sub-band.

2.3   The Zoning Technique

The zone-based feature extraction algorithm [3] used in this paper follows the foundations of the procedure proposed by Ashoka et al. [1]. It splits a binary image I of size $M \times N$ into a number of squared, non-overlapping zones or patches of a predefined size $m \times n$. For each zone Z_i, two values are calculated to build up the feature vector: one is the density of black pixels and the second corresponds to the normalized coordinate distance of black pixels.

Firstly, a grid L of size $M \times N$ is superimposed on the image, where the (x, y)-th element of L will be assigned to 1 if the pixel $I(x, y)$ is black and 0 otherwise. Then the density of black pixels in a zone Z_i can be computed as

$$v_1(Z_i) = \frac{1}{mn} \sum_{l(x,y) \in L} l(x, y) \tag{1}$$

where mn is the total number of pixels in Z_i and $l(x, y)$ denotes the value of the (x, y)-th element of L.

For the second value, consider the bottom left corner of each grid as the absolute origin $(0, 0)$ and compute the coordinate distance $\delta_j(Z_i)$ of the j-th pixel in zone Z_i at location (x, y). Then the normalized coordinate distance of black pixels can be obtained by dividing the sum of coordinate distances of black pixels (i.e., elements of the grid L whose value is equal to 1) by the sum of coordinate distances of all pixels in zone Z_i:

$$v_2(Z_i) = \frac{\sum\limits_{j \in Black(Z_i)} \delta_j(Z_i)}{\sum\limits_{j=1}^{mn} \delta_j(Z_i)} \tag{2}$$

where $Black(Z_i)$ denotes the set of black pixels in zone Z_i.

2.4 The Binarization Algorithm

The binarization technique for feature extraction aims to minimize the useless information that can be present in an image [6]. Accordingly, it is assumed that a binary image I has black pixels, which correspond to the characters, and white pixels for the background. Thus, it is possible to represent the image by a matrix $\mathbf{W} = [\mathbf{w_{xy}}]_{M \times N}$ where the (x, y)-th component of $\mathbf{W}$ will be assigned to 1 if the pixel $I(x, y)$ is black, and to 0 for a white pixel. This matrix $\mathbf{W}$ can be then reshaped in a row first manner to a column vector of size $M \times N \times 1$.

3 Methodology

This section presents the proposed methodology, which follows the phases of a standard image recognition system. Apart from describing the specific tasks performed at each stage, we will also introduce a new algorithm for feature extraction, which is the result of hybridizing the foundations of the DWT and zoning methods presented in the previous section.

3.1 Image Acquisition, Binarization and Segmentation

A total of 185 gray-scale images of size 4160×1200 were obtained by scanning notes and documents handwritten by a pool of writers. The documents consisted not only of mathematical expressions, but also of plain text, diagrams and graphics. With the purpose of discarding useless information and handling an image formed only by a set of mathematical symbols, the region of interest with the handwritten mathematical expression or formula was selected manually.

Then the gray-scale images were converted into binary using the Otsu's thresholding method [11], which assumes that the distribution of the pixel intensities is bi-modal: dark pixel intensities (corresponding to the object or character) can be separated from light pixel intensities (the background) in the gray-level histogram. The central idea of this method is to find the threshold that maximizes the between-class variance.

For the segmentation of the binary images, we chose a technique based on labeling connected regions (which correspond to symbols). The algorithm starts from the first foreground pixel found and then, it propagates to any of the pixel's 4-neighbors. Each already visited pixel cannot be explored again; after the entire connected region has been labeled, a region number is assigned to its pixels. Afterwards, each connected region, which has been labeled with a region number, is enclosed by a bounding box.

The coordinates of these bounding boxes allow to describe the relationships between the input symbols and distinguish single symbols from those symbols that are composed of two or more strokes. To check whether or not two or more bounding boxes correspond to the same symbol, we analyzed some characteristics of the boxes: length, height, distance between boxes, and size. Boxes complying with these characteristics were re-labeled, indicating that they belong to the same symbol. Finally, each symbol image was resized to a fixed size of 120×120.

3.2   Combining Wavelets and Zoning for Feature Extraction

We introduce a new method, hereafter called c-WZ, to extract discriminant features from the binary image and build up a feature vector by combining the bases of the DWT and zoning techniques with the aim of using both statistical and geometrical characteristics of the image.

Firstly, the 3-level Daubechies DWT decomposes the binary image I of size $M \times N$ ($M = N = 120$) in order to obtain the coefficients of the third block, which correspond to those with the most representative geometrical characteristics of the image. The approximation coefficient A_2 represents a thumbnail of I, whereas the detail coefficients H_2, V_2 and D_2 contain characteristics related to the contour of the symbol. Each of these coefficients is of size $\frac{M}{m_w} \frac{N}{n_w}$ with $m_w = n_w = 8$, leading to a total of 900 features. Next, the mean, the standard deviation and the entropy for the coefficients A_2, H_2, V_2 and D_2 are also calculated. In addition, the Shannon entropy, the 'log energy' entropy, the threshold entropy, the sure entropy and the norm entropy are calculated for the approximation coefficient A_2. Thus the wavelet-based stage of the c-WZ algorithm produces a feature vector with 917 textural and statistical values as a result of the frequency domain analysis.

Then, the zoning-based stage of c-WZ divides the image I into squared zones of size $m_z \times n_z$, and two values are calculated for each zone Z_i: the total number of black pixels (instead of the density of black pixels as done in the standard zoning technique) and the normalized coordinate distance of black pixels. This produces a feature vector of size $2(\frac{M}{m_z} \frac{N}{n_z})$ with $m_z = n_z = 15$, which gives a total of 128 values. Finally, the feature vectors that result from wavelet and zoning stages are concatenated to build up the feature vector of the c-WZ algorithm.

4   Experiments

The aim of the experiments is to compare the c-WZ method against FKI, wavelet, zoning and binarization. Six standard classifiers were applied to the sets of samples generated by the feature extraction algorithms using 10-fold cross-validation: the nearest neighbor (1-NN) rule with the Euclidean distance, the naive Bayes classifier (NBC), a Bayesian network (BN), a multi-layer perceptron (MLP) with one hidden layer, a support vector machine (SVM) with a linear kerne ($C = 1.0$), and the C4.5 decision tree with pruning by the subtree raising approach.

The empirical analysis was performed over the English database generated by Campos et al. [4], which includes digits (10 classes) with 527 samples, the uppercase Latin letters (upLatin) with 26 classes and 1402 samples, and the lowercase Latin letters (lowLatin) with 26 classes and 1321 samples. In addition, by means of the methodology described in Sect. 3.1, we also incorporated the uppercase and lowercase Greek letters (upGreek and lowGreek, respectively) with 24 classes each, and a miscellany of mathematical symbols (24 classes), all of them with 1320 samples. Putting these sets (types) of characters all together leads to a database with a total of 7210 samples of isolated math symbols that belong to 134 different classes.

Although images were resized to a fixed size of 120×120 pixels, the dimension of the feature vectors depends on each feature extraction algorithm (see Table 1).

Table 1. Dimension of the feature vectors

	Dimensionality	Size
FKI	$9N$	1080
DWT	$(\frac{M}{2}\frac{N}{2}) + 54$	3654
Zoning	$2(\frac{M}{m}\frac{N}{n})$	1152
Binar.	$M \times N$	14400
c-WZ	$4(\frac{M}{m_w}\frac{N}{n_w}) + 17 + 2(\frac{M}{m_z}\frac{N}{n_z})$	1045

5   Results

Table 2 reports the accuracy rates when using the feature extraction methods with each classifier over the whole data set (7210 samples). The values for the best performing algorithm with each classifier are highlighted in bold face. As can be seen, the proposed c-WZ method achieved the highest rates when using SVM, MLP and C4.5, whereas its accuracy were not too far from that of the best technique for the rest of classifiers. To assess the statistical significance of these results, the Friedman's average rank for each algorithm was also calculated (note that the one with the lowest average rank corresponds to the best strategy), showing that the recognition rates using the c-WZ technique were better than those obtained with any other feature extraction method.

Table 2. Accuracy rate and Friedman's rank over the whole data set

	BN	NBC	SVM	MLP	1-NN	C4.5	Rank
FKI	91.82	87.22	93.71	92.04	90.20	82.26	4.00
DWT	**92.65**	86.85	95.97	94.17	85.43	81.58	3.16
Zoning	91.50	88.05	95.76	94.14	**94.38**	83.35	2.66
Binarization	90.58	**89.99**	95.60	93.87	93.34	81.18	3.50
c-WZ	92.51	89.20	**96.54**	**94.90**	93.15	**83.83**	**1.66**

Table 3. Accuracy rate and Friedman's rank for each set of characters

		BN	NBC	SVM	MLP	1-NN	C4.5	Rank
Digits	FKI	85.85	78.02	<u>91.06</u>	89.16	84.05	72.80	4.83
	DWT	**89.31**	79.46	<u>95.47</u>	93.87	83.01	73.94	3.66
	Zoning	88.85	84.32	<u>96.31</u>	93.95	93.11	**82.18**	2.33
	Binarization	88.43	**84.35**	<u>96.33</u>	94.87	**94.24**	78.73	**2.00**
	c-WZ	89.06	83.21	**<u>96.56</u>**	**94.91**	91.89	77.39	2.16
upLatin	FKI	91.44	85.37	<u>92.32</u>	89.22	85.40	80.36	3.83
	DWT	91.75	83.37	<u>95.68</u>	94.01	75.90	79.18	3.50
	Zoning	90.50	83.47	<u>94.89</u>	93.80	94.27	**81.70**	3.00
	Binarization	88.07	**87.47**	<u>94.93</u>	93.37	**94.48**	80.33	3.00
	c-WZ	**91.89**	85.77	**<u>95.77</u>**	94.40	90.39	81.21	**1.66**
lowLatin	FKI	79.24	74.10	<u>83.10</u>	82.29	80.74	62.06	3.50
	DWT	**79.96**	69.36	<u>87.64</u>	83.97	71.81	54.82	3.33
	Zoning	76.50	73.98	<u>86.99</u>	83.42	**86.07**	**62.25**	3.00
	Binarization	76.89	**77.83**	<u>87.02</u>	83.04	84.77	60.67	2.83
	c-WZ	78.66	75.19	**<u>89.58</u>**	84.63	82.55	60.47	**2.33**
upGreek	FKI	98.87	97.61	<u>99.08</u>	97.95	98.14	95.92	3.33
	DWT	98.57	98.15	**<u>99.29</u>**	98.52	95.37	96.80	2.66
	Zoning	98.54	**99.09**	<u>99.25</u>	98.48	**98.56**	93.92	2.66
	Binarization	97.36	97.46	<u>98.81</u>	97.50	96.00	91.63	4.83
	c-WZ	**99.05**	98.46	<u>99.26</u>	**98.60**	98.25	**97.36**	1.50
lowGreek	FKI	**99.72**	88.77	96.76	93.64	93.10	82.68	3.66
	DWT	96.39	90.89	<u>97.79</u>	94.97	86.70	84.82	2.83
	Zoning	94.86	87.61	<u>97.20</u>	95.38	94.28	80.46	3.33
	Binarization	94.17	**93.53**	96.58	94.85	90.79	76.13	4.00
	c-WZ	96.45	92.68	**<u>98.11</u>**	97.05	**95.79**	**86.57**	1.66
Math	FKI	99.81	99.47	**99.97**	<u>100</u>	99.81	99.79	2.83
	DWT	**99.95**	99.92	**<u>99.97</u>**	99.72	99.81	**99.97**	2.50
	Zoning	99.75	99.83	99.95	99.85	<u>100</u>	99.61	3.33
	Binarization	98.57	99.33	<u>99.95</u>	99.62	99.81	99.61	4.66
	c-WZ	**99.95**	**99.93**	**99.97**	99.85	<u>100</u>	**99.97**	1.66

After evaluating the performance when all the characters were put into a unique data set, one might wonder whether the feature extraction algorithms would show the same behavior irrespective of the set of characters being analyzed or on the contrary, they would perform differently with each set. To outline an answer to these question, Table 3 provides the accuracy rates and the Friedman's average ranks when the feature extraction algorithms were applied to each set of characters. Bold-faced values highlight the best feature extraction algorithm for each classifier and each data set, whereas underlined values indicate the best performing classifier for each feature extraction method and each set of symbols.

The only case in which the c-WZ algorithm did not received the best Friedman's rank corresponds to the set of digits, although it was very close to the lowest ranking assigned to binarization. For the remaining data sets, c-WZ showed the best overall behavior (the lowest Friedman's average rank). In general, FKI and binarization were the techniques with the poorest performance: FKI took the highest average rank when applied to digits, uppercase Latin letters and lowercase Latin letters, and binarization overuppercase Greek letters, lowercase Greek letters and math symbols. On the other hand, the results in Table 3 also reflect that SVM was the model with the highest recognition rate independently of the feature extraction method and the set of characters.

6   Conclusions

A hybrid feature extraction method for offline handwritten math symbol recognition has been introduced. The bases of this model relies on statistical and geometrical characteristics of the symbol images, which have been obtained from the combined application of an extended version of DWT and a zoning technique.

Experiments have revealed that the hybrid method performs better than other standard feature extraction algorithms, both over the whole database with 7210 samples from 134 different classes and over almost each set of characters. Besides, we have observed that SVM and MLP can be deemed as the most appropriate classifiers to be used with the new technique. Another point of interest refers to the fact that the c-WZ method has led to feature vectors of size smaller than those given by any of the remaining feature extraction algorithms, which supposes some computational advantages for the subsequent recognition tasks.

Acknowledgement. Partially supported by the Mexican CONACYT through the Student Support Program [CVU 702528], the Generalitat Valenciana [PROME-TEOII/2014/062], and the Universitat Jaume I [P1-1B2015-74].

References

1. Ashoka, H., Manjaiah, D., Bera, R.: Feature extraction technique for neural network based pattern recognition. Int. J. Comput. Sci. Eng. **4**(3), 331–339 (2012)
2. Blostein, D., Zanibbi, R.: Processing mathematical notation. In: Doermann, D., Tombre, K. (eds.) Handbook of Document Image Processing and Recognition, pp. 679–702. Springer, London (2014). https://doi.org/10.1007/978-0-85729-859-1_21
3. Bokser, M.: Omnidocument technologies. Proc. IEEE **80**(7), 1066–1078 (1992)
4. Campos, T.E., Babu, B.R., Varma, M.: Character recognition in natural images. In: Proceedings of the International Conference on Computer Vision Theory and Applications, Lisbon, Portugal, pp. 273–280 (2009)
5. Chan, K.F., Yeung, D.Y.: Mathematical expression recognition: a survey. Int. J. Doc. Anal. Recog. **1**, 3–15 (2000)
6. Choudhary, A., Rishi, R., Ahlawat, S.: Off-line handwritten character recognition using features extracted from binarization technique. AASRI Procedia **4**, 306–312 (2013)
7. Daubechies, I.: The wavelet transform, time-frequency localization and signal analysis. IEEE Trans. Inform. Theory **36**(5), 961–1005 (1990)
8. Koerich, A.L., Sabourin, R., Suen, C.Y.: Large vocabulary off-line handwriting recognition: a survey. Pattern Anal. Appl. **6**(2), 97–121 (2003)
9. Marti, U.V., Bunke, H.: Using a statistical language model to improve the performance of an HMM-based cursive handwriting recognition system. Int. J. Pattern Recogn. **15**(1), 65–90 (2001)
10. Obaidullah, S.M., Halder, C., Das, N., Roy, K.: Numeral script identification from handwritten document images. Procedia Comput. Sci. **54**, 585–594 (2015)
11. Otsu, N.: A threshold selection method from gray-level histograms. IEEE Ttans. Syst. Man Cyb. **9**(1), 62–66 (1979)

Improving Handwritten Character Recognition by Using a Ranking-Based Feature Selection Approach

N. D. Cilia, C. De Stefano, F. Fontanella$^{(\boxtimes)}$, and A. Scotto di Freca

Università di Cassino e del Lazio meridionale, Cassino, Italy
{nicoledalia.cilia,destefano,fontanella,a.scotto}@unicas.it

Abstract. In handwriting recognition, because of the large variability of the writers, the selection of a suitable set of features is a challenging task. This has led to the development of a large variety of feature sets, which, in many cases, contain a large number of attributes, causing performance problems in terms of classification results and computational costs. In this paper, we considered a widely used set of features in handwriting recognition, to verify if it is possible to improve the classification results for handwriting recognition by using a reduced set of features. To this aim, we adopted a feature ranking based approach and tested several univariate measures. The experiments, performed on two real-world databases, confirmed the effectiveness of our proposal.

1 Introduction

In handwriting recognition, the choice of the features used for representing letters and digits is crucial for achieving satisfactory performances. The aim is to address the problem of diversity in style, size, and shape, which can be found in handwriting produced by different writers [12]. This has led to the development of a large variety of feature sets, which are becoming increasingly larger in terms of number of attributes [11,13]. Unfortunately, feature representations involving too many features may cause performance problems, especially in presence of noisy or redundant features. The former causing unsatisfactory classification performances, and the latter increasing the computational cost of the classification process of unknown samples. As for this cost, it may be problematic in handwriting recognition applications where time constraints are very strict, such as, for example, postal sorting systems. For these reasons, feature selection techniques, which select a subset of relevant features from the available ones, have been widely used to improve the performance of handwriting recognition systems [1–5]. Feature selection problems are characterized by a large search space, since the total number of possible solutions is 2^n for problems involving n features. As a consequence, the exhaustive search for the optimal subset is impracticable in most of the cases. For this reason, many search techniques have been applied to feature selection, such as heuristic or greedy algorithms [14].

© Springer Nature Switzerland AG 2019
R. Vera-Rodriguez et al. (Eds.): CIARP 2018, LNCS 11401, pp. 902–910, 2019.
https://doi.org/10.1007/978-3-030-13469-3_104

Such algorithms typically require both a search strategy for selecting feature subsets, and an evaluation function to measure the effectiveness of each selected feature subset. As for the evaluation functions, they can be divided into two broad classes *filter* and *wrapper* [14]. Wrapper approaches use the performance of a given classifier as evaluation function; this leads to high computational costs when a large number of evaluations is required, especially when large datasets are involved. Filter evaluation functions, instead, are independent of any classification algorithm and, in most cases, are faster and more general than wrapper ones.

Less computationally expensive approaches, adopt evaluation functions that measure the effectiveness of each single feature in discriminating samples belonging to different classes. Once the available features have been evaluated, the subset search procedure is straightforward: the features are ranked according to their merit and the best M features, where M must be set by the user, are selected. These approaches are typically very fast but cannot take into account the interactions that may occur between two or more features.

In this context, the aim of our work was twofold: on one hand, we tried to overcome some of the above mentioned drawbacks by adopting a feature ranking based technique for choosing the feature subset able to provide the best classification results. On the other hand, we considered one of the most effective and widely used set of features in handwriting recognition [11], to verify if it is possible to improve the classification results for handwriting recognition by using a reduced set of features. We also characterized the features that exhibit higher discriminant power among the three feature groups defined in the above feature set, namely the concavity, the contour information and the character surface. In our experiments, performed on two real-world datasets, we found that, in the large majority of cases, the character surface features were included in the best subsets.

As regards the feature ranking, we considered different univariate measures, each producing a different ranking according to a criterion that evaluates the effectiveness of a single feature in discriminating samples belonging to different classes. In the experiments we have also compared the performance of our method with that achieved by other effective and widely used search strategy: the results confirmed the effectiveness of our approach.

The remainder of the paper is organized as follows: in Sect. 2 we will illustrate the considered features sets, in Sect. 3 we will describe the feature evaluation methods, while the experimental results will be illustrated in Sect. 4. Conclusions will be eventually left to Sect. 5.

2   The Considered Feature Set

The feature set taken into account measures three properties of a segmented image representing an input sample, related to the concavity, to the contour and to the character surface [11]. The image is divided into 6 zones arranged on three rows and two columns. For each zone, 13 concavity measurements are computed using the 4-Freeman directions as well as other 4 auxiliary directions, totaling 78 concavity features (13 measurements × 6 zones), normalized between 0 and 1.

Then, in each zone, 8 contour features are extracted from a histogram of contour direction obtained by grouping the contour line segments between neighboring pixels based on the 8-Freeman direction. Therefore, there are 48 contour features for each image, normalized between 0 and 1. Finally, the last part of the feature vector is related to the character surface, where the number of black pixels in each zone is counted and normalized between 0 and 1, thus obtaining 6 values for each image. Summarizing, the total number of feature is $78 + 48 + 6 = 132$.

3   Feature Evaluation

As anticipated in the introduction, our method requires an univariate measure to rank the features. In this study, we have considered five standard univariate measures, namely Chi-square [10], Relief [9], Gain ratio, Information Gain and Symmetrical uncertainty [8]. Each univariate measure ranks the available features according to a criterion, which evaluates the effectiveness in discriminating samples belonging to different classes.

The Chi-Square (CS) measure estimates feature merit by using a discretization algorithm on the CS statistic. For each feature, the related values are initially sorted by placing each observed value into its own interval. The next step uses the Chi-square statistic CS to determine whether the relative frequencies of the classes in adjacent intervals are similar enough to justify the merge.

The second considered measure is the Relief (RF), which uses instance-based learning to assign a relevance weight to each feature. The assigned weights reflect the feature ability to distinguish among the different classes at hand. The algorithm works by randomly sampling instances from the training data. For each sampled instance, the nearest instance of the same class (nearest hit) and different class (nearest miss) are found. A feature weight is updated according to how well its values distinguish the sampled instance from its nearest hit and nearest miss. Feature will receive a high weight if it differentiates between instances from different classes and has the same value for instances of the same class.

The last three considered univariate measures, are based on the well known information-theory concept of entropy $H(X)$, which can be used to estimate the uncertainty of the random variable X. This concept can be extended defining the conditional entropy $H(X|Y)$, which represents the randomness of X when the value of Y is known. These quantities can be used to define the information gain (IG) concept:

$$IG = H(C) - H(C|X)$$

IG represents the amount by which the entropy of C decreases when X is given and reflects additional information about C provided by the feature X.

The last two considered univariate measures uses the information gain defined in 3. The first one, called Gain Ratio (GR), is defined as the ratio between the information gain and the entropy of the feature X to be evaluated:

$$GR = IG/H(X)$$

Finally, the last univariate measure taken into account, called Symmetrical Uncertainty (IS), compensates for information gain bias toward attributes with more values and normalizes its value to the range $[0, 1]$:

$$IS = 2.0 \cdot IG/(H(C) + H(X))$$

To compare our results with those attainable by other searching algorithms defined in the literature, we have considered the well-known Best First (BF) search strategy, combined with two different criteria for feature evaluation, namely the Consistency Criterion [10], and the Correlation-based Feature Selection criterion [8].

The Consistency Criterion (CC) provides an effective measure of how well samples belonging to different classes are separated in a feature sub-space, while the Correlation-based Feature Selection criterion (CFS) uses a correlation based heuristic to evaluate feature subset worth. This function takes into account the usefulness of individual features for predicting class labels along with the level of inter-correlation among them. The idea behind this approach is that good subsets contain features highly correlated with the class and uncorrelated with each other. Denoting with X and Y two features, their correlation r_{XY} is:

$$r_{XY} = 2.0 \cdot (H(X) + H(Y) - H(X, Y))/(H(X) + H(Y))$$

Given a feature selection problem in which the patterns are represented by means of a set Y of N features, the CFS function computes the merit of the generic subset $X \subseteq Y$, made of k features, as follows:

$$f_{CFS} = k\overline{r_{cf}}/\sqrt{k + k(k-1)\overline{r_{ff}}}$$

where $\overline{r_{cf}}$ is the average feature-class correlation, and $\overline{r_{ff}}$ is the feature-feature correlation. Note that the numerator estimates the discriminative power of the features in X, whereas the denominator assesses the redundancy among them.

4 Experimental Results

In order to assess the effectiveness of the proposed approach in handwritten character recognition problems, we considered two real-world databases, namely the well-known NIST-SD19 and the RIMES databases.

NIST [7] contains binary images representing alphanumeric characters. We have considered handwritten uppercase and lowercase letters (52 classes). The handwriting sample form hsf4, containing 23941 characters (11941 uppercase and 12000 lowercase), was merged with the form hsf7, containing 23670 characters (12092 uppercase and 11578 lowercase) and used as a unique database of 47611 samples. In each form, characters are isolated, labeled and stored in 128×128 pixel images.

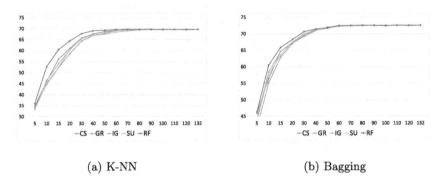

(a) K-NN   (b) Bagging

Fig. 1. Recognition rates on NIST as function of the number of selected features.

RIMES is a publicly available database containing real-world handwritten words and it has been largely adopted for performance evaluation of handwriting recognition systems [6]. The 4047 word images of RIMES were processed in order to extract sub-image containing connected component of ink, which were labeled by six human experts. At the end of this process, from the 9869 labeled samples, a subset of 4768 samples, corresponding to isolated characters has been extracted and used for our experiments.

We performed two sets of experiments and evaluated the effectiveness of the selected feature subsets by using two well-known and widely used different classification schemes, namely K-Nearest Neighbor (K-NN) and Bagging.

In this first set of experiments, we applied the methods for feature evaluation illustrated in Sect. 3. To illustrate our experimental setup, let us first consider the database NIST. We applied the univariate measures illustrated in Sect. 3 to these data, obtaining 5 different feature rankings. Let us consider the ranking provided by the first univariate measure, namely CS: by using this feature ranking, we generated different representations of the database NIST, each containing an increasing number of features. More specifically, we generated 15 datasets in the following way: in the first one, NIST samples were represented by using the first 5 features in the ranking, in the second one by using the first 10 features, in the third one the first 15 features and so on, adding each time the successive 10 features in the ranking. In the last dataset, NIST samples were represented by using all the 132 available features. The same procedure was repeated for the other univariate measures applied to the database NIST. Similarly, this procedure was repeated for RIMES. Summarizing, for each database, we obtained 5 different feature rankings, each used to generate 15 different sets of data with an increasing number of features. Each of them was used in the experiments for evaluating the obtainable classification results.

As regards the classification process, we considered the two classification schemes mentioned above, using a 10-fold validation strategy and performed 20 runs for each experiment. The results reported in the following were obtained by averaging the values over the 20 runs.

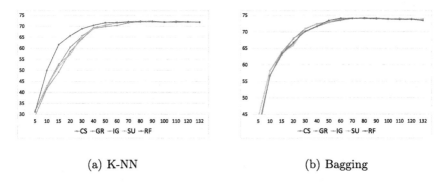

(a) K-NN   (b) Bagging

Fig. 2. Recognition rates on RIMES as function of the number of selected features.

Figure 1 shows the average results on NIST. In each plot, the x-axis reports the number of features used to represent the input samples, while the y-axis reports the corresponding classification results, in terms of recognition rate. Similarly, Fig. 2 shows the results on RIMES.

It is interesting to note that, accepting a reduction of the recognition rate of about 5% with respect to its maximum value, it is possible to select a very small subset of features, namely the first 30 ones in the rankings, strongly reducing the computational complexity of the classification problem. The plots in the figures also show that, using the first 60 features in the rankings (i.e. less than 50% of all the available ones), the reduction of the recognition rate is less than 2%.

For sake of clearness, we have also summarized the obtained classification results in Table 1. The first row in the table shows the recognition rate (RR) obtained with all the available features, while the other ones show the best RR for each feature ranking, together with the corresponding number of selected features (NF). The last two rows of the table show the RR obtained with CFS

Table 1. Best Recognition Rates (RR) and the related number of features (NF).

(a) NIST

	KNN		BAG	
	RR	NF	RR	NF
All	69.56	132	72.51	132
IS	69.60	110	72.52	80
RF	69.70	70	72.57	110
CS	69.64	80	73.61	80
GR	69.64	120	72.58	110
IG	69.63	120	72.57	100
CFS	67.79	54	72.06	54
CC	54.66	16	65.46	16

(b) RIMES

	KNN		BAG	
	RR	NF	RR	NF
All	71.85	132	73.40	132
IS	72.05	80	74.15	80
RF	72.27	90	74.07	80
CS	72.23	110	74.21	80
GR	72.11	110	74.02	70
IG	72.03	80	74.16	90
CFS	69.57	50	73.31	50
CC	52.34	16	66.65	16

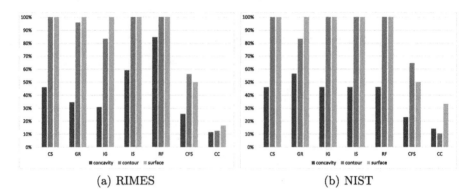

(a) RIMES   (b) NIST

Fig. 3. Percentage of groups (concavity, contour and surface) included in the best feature subsets.

and CC feature selection methods and the corresponding NF. The data in the table show that, in the large majority of the cases, the recognition rates obtained with our feature selection method outperform those obtained by using the other considered feature subset selection methods, as well as those obtained by using all the available features. Moreover, the best results are always achieved using a number of features significantly smaller than 132. In the average, the number of features allowing us to obtain the best results is about 90, i.e. about 70% of the total number of features. Finally, as regards the performance of the subset feature selection methods, CFS provides recognitions slightly worse, but using in the average a smaller number of feature. CC feature selection method, instead, performs significantly worse than all the other methods, selecting in the average a too small number of features.

In the second set of experiments, we analyzed the discriminant power of the groups of features described in Sect. 2 (concavity, contour and character surface). To this aim, we computed the percentages of features of each group that: (i) have been included in the best feature subsets obtained by using the five univariate measures taken into account; (ii) were selected by the two feature subset evaluation methods. The results, shown in Fig. 3, indicate that the features representing contour information and those representing character surface information have very high discriminant power and are almost always selected. On the contrary, the features associated to concavity information, whose number is higher than that of the other categories, seem to be less distinctive and, in most of the cases, more than 50% of such features have been discarded.

5 Conclusions

We have proposed a feature selection method which uses a feature ranking based technique for choosing feature subsets able to provide high classification results. We have used a widely used set of features in handwriting recognition for representing samples of two real-world databases. The experimental results confirmed that it is possible to choose a reduced set of features without affecting the overall classification rates. The results have also shown that it is possible to strongly reduce the number of features, accepting a very limited reduction of the best recognition rate (less than 2%). This opportunity may be very helpful in case of applications where keeping low the computational cost of the classification system is crucial. We have also characterized the type of features that exhibit higher discriminant power among the whole set of available ones.

References

1. Choudhary, A., Rishi, R., Ahlawat, S.: Off-line handwritten character recognition using features extracted from binarization technique. AASRI Procedia **4**, 306–312 (2013)
2. Cilia, N.D., De Stefano, C., Fontanella, F., Scotto di Freca, A.: A ranking-based feature selection approach for handwritten character recognition. Pattern Recogn. Lett. (2018)
3. Cordella, L.P., De Stefano, C., Fontanella, F., Marrocco, C., Scotto di Freca, A.: Combining single class features for improving performance of a two stage classifier. In: 20th International Conference on Pattern Recognition, pp. 4352–4355. IEEE Computer Society (2010)
4. De Stefano, C., Fontanella, F., Marrocco, C.: A GA-based feature selection algorithm for remote sensing images. In: Giacobini, M., et al. (eds.) EvoWorkshops 2008. LNCS, vol. 4974, pp. 285–294. Springer, Heidelberg (2008). https://doi.org/10.1007/978-3-540-78761-7_29
5. De Stefano, C., Fontanella, F., Marrocco, C., Scotto di Freca, A.: A GA-based feature selection approach with an application to handwritten character recognition. Pattern Recogn. Lett. **35**, 130–141 (2014)
6. Grosicki, E., Carre, M., Brodin, J.M., Geoffrois, E.: RIMES evaluation campaign for handwritten mail processing. In: ICFHR 2008: 11th International Conference on Frontiers in Handwriting Recognition, Concordia University, Montreal, Canada, pp. 1–6 (2008). https://hal.archives-ouvertes.fr/hal-01395332
7. Grother, J.: Nist special database 19: Hand printed forms and characters database. Technical report, National Institute of Standards and Technology, Gaithersburg (1995)
8. Hall, M.: Correlation-based feature selection for machine learning. Ph.D. thesis, University of Waikato (1999)
9. Kononenko, I.: Estimating attributes: analysis and extensions of RELIEF. In: Bergadano, F., De Raedt, L. (eds.) ECML 1994. LNCS, vol. 784, pp. 171–182. Springer, Heidelberg (1994). https://doi.org/10.1007/3-540-57868-4_57
10. Liu, H., Setiono, R.: Chi2: feature selection and discretization of numeric attributes. In: Seventh International Conference on Tools with Artificial Intelligence (ICTAI), pp. 388–391. IEEE Computer Society, Washington, DC (1995)
11. Oliveira, L.S., Sabourin, R., Bortolozzi, F., Suen, C.Y.: Automatic recognition of handwritten numerical strings: a recognition and verification strategy. IEEE Trans. Pattern Anal. Mach. Intell. **24**(11), 1438–1454 (2002)
12. Plamondon, R., Srihari, S.N.: Online and off-line handwriting recognition: a comprehensive survey. IEEE Trans. Pattern Anal. Mach. Intell. **22**(1), 63–84 (2000)

13. Surinta, O., Karaaba, M.F., Schomaker, L.R., Wiering, M.A.: Recognition of hand-written characters using local gradient feature descriptors. Eng. Appl. Artif. Intell. **45**, 405–414 (2015)
14. Xue, B., Zhang, M., Browne, W.N., Yao, X.: A survey on evolutionary computation approaches to feature selection. IEEE Trans. Evol. Comput. **20**(4), 606–626 (2016)

Human Interaction

Using Image Processing Techniques and HD-EMG for Upper Limb Prosthesis Gesture Recognition

Roberto Díaz-Amador$^{(\boxtimes)}$ ⓘ, Carlos A. Ferrer-Riesgo ⓘ,
and Juan V. Lorenzo-Ginori ⓘ

Centro de Investigaciones de la Informática, Universidad Central de Las Villas,
Carretera a Camajuaní km 5½, Santa Clara, Cuba
{rdamador, cferrer, juanl}@uclv.edu.cu

Abstract. In this paper we present the results of using image processing techniques for gesture recognition based on High-Density Electromyography (HD-EMG). Here the instantaneous sample of each EMG channel is represented as a pixel of an image that changes with different movements. In this image, various patterns are recognizable as associated to specific gestures. Experiments were performed to compare the use of image feature extraction by dividing the image into patches (blocks). In this case, the effectiveness for gesture recognition of three different patch sizes and locations were tested and compared. The results show the feasibility of using image processing concepts in order to obtain appropriate features for gesture recognition from HD-EMG, in some cases with advantage when compared to conventional methods.

1 Introduction

The control of upper limb prosthesis devices using electromyography signal (EMG) and pattern recognition (PR) has been regarded as a promising approach. The conventional approach in EMG usually uses a limited and very well localized number of electrodes. In contrast, the pattern recognition approach allows the use of a high density electrode array forming a matrix of high density electromyography signals (HD-EMG). In the current paper, we present the results of using image processing techniques for HD-EMG based gesture recognition. We represent the instantaneous sample of each EMG channel as a pixel of an image that changes with different movements. Then the set of pixels obtained in this way forms a pattern associated to the corresponding movement. Notice that the spatial resolution (number of pixels per unit area) is defined by the array electrodes, i.e., the number of electrodes and their inter-electrode distances. This method seeks for an instantaneous spatial-temporal representation of the motor unit action potential (MUAP).

The use of HD-EMG to analyze how muscle activation patterns are composed and distributed and the single MUAP behavior is not new in pattern recognition research [1]. Recently, the use of electrode arrays was extended to classify gestures and decode the intention of motion [2]. In previous works [3], the representation of HD-EMG is done as 2-D arrays called topography EMG or EMG map. Usually, the map is defined

© Springer Nature Switzerland AG 2019
R. Vera-Rodriguez et al. (Eds.): CIARP 2018, LNCS 11401, pp. 913–921, 2019.
https://doi.org/10.1007/978-3-030-13469-3_105

as a time-average 2-D intensity image in which each pixel is either the root mean square (rms) value of a certain channel in a time window or as instantaneous samples of HD-EMG.

In [4] a result of 89.8% and 90.4% of accuracy in the classification of 27 gestures was reported using an 8×24 electrode array. In [5] a deep convolutional network approach obtained 99%, 96.8% and 52.1% of accuracy for three datasets using instantaneous images and instantaneous samples as features.

The current work compares the use of image feature extraction dividing the instantaneous image in patches (blocks), analyzing three different block sizes and locations.

2   Materials and Methods

2.1   HD-EMG Signal Dataset

HD-EMG data were obtained from the sub-database DB-a in CapgMyo database [6]. These data were collected [7] using a non-invasive wearable device consisting of 8 acquisition modules, each of them containing a matrix-type (8×2) differential electrode array. Each electrode has a diameter of 3 mm and was arranged with an inter-electrode distance of 7.5 mm horizontally and 10.05 mm vertically. The silver wet electrodes were disposable and covered with conductive gel, with a contact impedance of less than 3 kΩ. The 8 acquisition modules were fixed around the right forearm with adhesive bands. The first acquisition module was placed on the extensor digitorum communis muscle at the height of the radio-humeral joint; others were equally spaced clockwise (viewing from the subject's perspective), forming an 8×16 electrode array. When collecting HD-EMG, no individual muscle is directly measured, but the combined superposition of all. In this way, each adjacent electrode contains redundant information.

The EMG signals were sampled at 1 kHz, digitized with a 16-bit analog to digital converter and band-pass filtered at 20–380 Hz. The EMG data from the 8 acquisition modules were packed in an ARM controller and transferred to a PC via WIFI [7]. The database contains 8 isometric and isotonic hand gestures obtained from 18 subjects. Subjects were asked to hold each gesture for 3 to 10 s. The considered gestures are shown in Fig. 1 and correspond to classes 13–20 in the NinaPro database [8]. Each gesture was recorded 10 times.

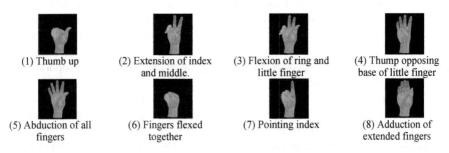

| (1) Thumb up | (2) Extension of index and middle. | (3) Flexion of ring and little finger | (4) Thump opposing base of little finger |
| (5) Abduction of all fingers | (6) Fingers flexed together | (7) Pointing index | (8) Adduction of extended fingers |

Fig. 1. Gestures considered in this study. Numbers in parenthesis represents the corresponding labels in the dataset.

Power-line interference was removed from the EMG signals by using a second-order Butterworth band-stop filter (45–55 Hz). To the purpose of the current research, only the static part of the movement (the middle one-second window for each trial) was used to train and to evaluate the recognition algorithms.

2.2 Experiments

In the current research we apply the standard classification scheme. It consists of a feature extraction, classifier training and classification steps. For feature extraction we evaluated two different alternatives: Experiment (a) used a traditional pattern recognition EMG approach, extracting features channel by channel, while experiment (b) used the image processing approach creating an image from instantaneous samples of HD-EMG and extracting features from the image. Within the approach (b), we compute features from three different scenarios as is showed in Fig. 2: (1) considering the total image to compute global features, i.e., an 8 × 16 array, (2) dividing the image into two blocks, i.e., two 8 × 8 arrays, and (3) dividing the image into four blocks, i.e., four 4 × 8 arrays. It is important to clarify that although the EMG matrix is considered as high definition, the corresponding image is not.

On experiment (a), a time-domain feature set (TD) described in [9] consisting of mean absolute value (MAV), zero-crossings (ZC), waveform length (WL) and slope sign changes (SSC). The TD features used are described from Eqs. (1) to (4).

Mean Absolute Value (MAV)

$$MAV = \frac{1}{N}\sum_{i=1}^{N}|x_i| \tag{1}$$

Zero-crossing (ZC)

$$ZC = \sum Ct;$$
$$Ct = \begin{cases} 1; & x_i > 0 \text{ and } x_{i+1} < 0 \text{ and } |x_i - x_{i+1}| > th \\ 1; & x_i < 0 \text{ and } x_{i+1} > 0 \text{ and } |x_i - x_{i+1}| > th \\ 0; & otherwise \end{cases} \tag{2}$$

Waveform Length (WL)

$$WL = \sum_{i=1}^{N}|\Delta x_i|; \Delta x_i = x_i - x_{i-1} \tag{3}$$

Slope Sign Changes (SSC)

$$SSC = \sum_{i=1}^{N} sgn[-(x_{i+1} - x_i) * (x_{i+2} - x_{i+1})]; sgn = \begin{cases} 1, x > th \\ 0, x < th \end{cases} \tag{4}$$

In Eqs. (1) to (4), x_i represents the amplitude of the sample i of EMG, s N is the length in samples of the analysis window, and th is a threshold taken as the 5% of the MAV on the analysis window.

On experiment (b), in each of the three scenarios of instantaneous images the feature set consists of:

- Pixel-based features: energy by block, maximum intensity value by block, position of maximum intensity by block,

Equations (5) to (7) show the corresponding expressions:
Energy (En)

$$En = \frac{1}{N_1 N_2} \sum_{n_1}^{N_1} \sum_{n_2}^{N_2} (x[n_1, n_2])^2 \tag{5}$$

Maximum Intensity Value (MIV)

$$MIV = \max[x(n_1, n_2)] \tag{6}$$

Position of Maximum Intensity (PMI)

$$PMI = [n_1, n_2]; MIV = \max[x(n_1, n_2)] \tag{7}$$

- Texture-based features: contrast, correlation and homogeneity calculated from the co-occurrence matrix by block.

Equations (8) to (10), show expressions to calculate them:
Contrast

$$Ct = \sum_{n_1, n_2 = 0}^{N-1} P_{n_1 n_2}(n_1 - n_2)^2 \tag{8}$$

Correlation

$$Cr = \sum_{n_1, n_2 = 0}^{N-1} P_{n_1 n_2} \left[\frac{(n_1 - \mu_{n_1})(n_2 - \mu_{n_2})}{\sqrt{(\sigma_{n_1}^2)(\sigma_{n_2}^2)}} \right] \tag{9}$$

Homogeneity

$$Ho = \sum_{n_1, n_2 = 0}^{N-1} \frac{P_{n_1 n_2}}{1 + (n_1 - n_2)^2} \tag{10}$$

In (8) to (10), P is the probability matrix from the co-occurrence matrix.

– Shape-based features: number of pixels actives by block, area and centroid of the major region active by block, after the image is binarized using the Otsu [10] method.

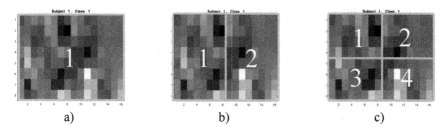

a)   b)   c)

Fig. 2. Three sub-division of instantaneous image to calculate the feature set.

According to the schemes showed in Fig. 2, it is clear that the size of the feature vector increases with the number of blocks. The blocks' sizes and locations were selected following the hypothesis that different gestures should provoke different patterns, which should be associated to certain regions in the arm.

We chose a k-nearest neighbor (kNN) classifier in the classification steps. We evaluated odd values for k from 1 to 11 together with Euclidean distance. In the training phase, we provided a training data set corresponding to the first five repeats of each movement. In the classification phase, we used the remaining five repeats. It is important to clarify that for the purposes of the current research, the data set was balanced which mitigate the effects of unbalanced classes in kNN-based pattern recognition.

3 Results and Discussion

Results of the first experiment, dealing with the classification of HD-EMG using channel by channel time-domain features, are shown in Fig. 3 using a gray bar, showing $87.97 \pm 2.56\%$ of accuracy. Bars in red, green and blue colors represent the results of the image processing approach with blocks of sizes [8 × 16], [8 × 8] and [4 × 8] respectively. Results with [8 × 8] blocks showed the best results $(91.18 \pm 2.23\%)$ compared to [8 × 16] blocks $(90.86 \pm 2.26\%)$ and [4 × 8] blocks $(88.16 \pm 2.65\%)$. Wilcoxon non-parametric test showed statistical differences $(p < 0.01)$ between all paired combinations of methods, except the [8 × 16] and [4 × 8] pair. All of the image-based methods showed better results when compared to the traditional channel by channel method.

We consider that is important to analyze the fact of that dividing the image into two [8 × 8] blocks yielded better results than [8 × 16] and [4 × 8]. These results correspond to the idea that different regions of the image represent the activation of different muscles in the arm. In contrast to that, when using 4 blocks the results become worse.

It can be explained by the fact that in the 4 partitions, blocks 1 and 3, and blocks 2 and 4 probably represent the same muscle since they are longitudinally located in the arm.

Other aspect to point out is the relation between the number of features and the resulting accuracy. Table 1 shows results by number of features. In row one, the number of features is the number of features by channel. In this cases 4 time domain features in 128 channels. In the rest of the methods, the number of features increases when the size of the blocks decreases.

Table 1. Accuracy by methods and number of features.

	Number of features	Accuracy (%)
Channel by channel	4 × 128 = 512	87.97 ± 2.56%
Image-based 1 × [8 × 16]	14	90.86 ± 2.26%
Image-based 2 × [8 × 8]	14 × 2 = 28	91.18 ± 2.23%
Image-based 4 × [4 × 4]	14 × 4 = 56	88.16 ± 2.65%

Experiments performed by other authors [3] addressing similar problems but using rms images, obtained comparable results. In [5] 99% of accuracy was reached, but using a deep neural network and a higher number of features.

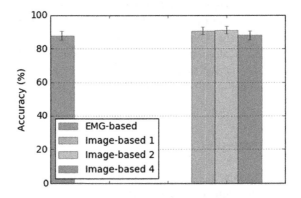

Fig. 3. Results of the experiments.

An important aspect using kNN classifiers is determining the optimal k-value. In the current research we compared different values of k, among which k = 3 showed the best results in all of the approaches under study (Fig. 4).

Finally, comparing the results class by class, it is shown in Table 2 that all classes present a precision around 90%, true positive rate in the range from 83 to 95%, false positive rate less than 2.6% and F1 score higher than 84%. Global correctly classified instances were 91.18%. From class by class results we can say that class 8 presents the worst performance.

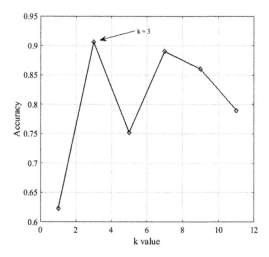

Fig. 4. Results for different values of k for image-based [8 × 8] approach.

Table 2. Detailed performance by class adding all subjects for image-based [8 × 8] approach

Class	TPR	FPR	Pr.	F-Meas.
1	0.955	0.009	0.938	0.946
2	0.924	0.015	0.895	0.909
3	0.898	0.013	0.909	0.930
4	0.865	0.026	0.828	0.846
5	0.901	0.010	0.927	0.914
6	0.967	0.004	0.975	0.971
7	0.949	0.011	0.926	0.937
8	0.834	0.013	0.899	0.865

TPR: True Positive Rate, FPR: False
Positive Rate, PR: Precision, F-Meas:
F1 Score.

In the confusion matrix shown in the Table 3 rows represent the actual class, while columns represent the classification results. The confusion matrix was obtained adding individual results of all cases of all the classes of all of 18 subjects. In this way, the total numbers of cases were 720,000 by class. We can realize that some instances in class 8 were incorrectly classified as classes 4 and 5, which explain the worst performance shown in class 8.

Table 3. Confusion matrix of all 18 subjects together.

		Classification Results							
		1	2	3	4	5	6	7	8
	1	687600	720	5040	8640	5040	5040	5040	2880
	2	2160	665280	10800	12960	7200	3600	8640	9360
	3	13680	18000	646560	14400	5040	2880	7920	11520
Actual Class	4	7200	18720	12240	622800	14400	3	16557	28080
	5	5760	11520	6480	27360	648720	1440	6480	12240
	6	7200	7200	2160	2160	1440	696240	1440	2160
	7	6480	4320	9360	12240	2160	720	683280	1440
	8	2880	17280	18720	51840	15840	4320	8640	600480

4   Conclusions

Results obtained in the current research confirm that image processing techniques can improve accuracy of gesture classification from HD-EMG signals. Comparing different block sizes and locations suggests also that two image blocks can represent adequately the EMG patterns corresponding to a desired gesture. Further testing is being conducted and additional analysis will be performed to confirm these results. Future works should address the relative importance of each EMG channels and search for the optimal number of channels to be used in image analysis from HD-EMG.

Acknowledgement. Supported in part by an Alexander von Humboldt Foundation Fellowship granted to C. Ferrer (Ref 3.2-1164728-CUB-GF-E).

References

1. Merletti, R., Holobar, A., Farina, D.: Analysis of motor units with high-density surface electromyography. J. Electromyogr. Kinesiol. **6**, 879–890 (2008)
2. Rojas-Martínez, M., Mañanas, M., Alonso, J., Merletti, R.: Identification of isometric contractions based on high density EMG maps. J. Electromyogr. Kinesiol. **1**, 33–42 (2013)
3. Rojas-Martínez, M., Mañanas, M., Alonso, J.: High-density surface EMG maps from upper arm and forearm muscles. J. Neuroeng. Rehabil. **1** (2012)
4. Amma, C., Krings, T., Boer, J., Schultz, T.: Advancing muscle-computer interfaces with high-density electromyography. In: Proceedings of the 33rd Annual ACM Conference on Human Factors in Computing Systems, pp. 929–938 (2015)
5. Geng, W., Du, Y., Wenguang, J., Wentao, W., Jiajun, L.: Gesture recognition by instantaneous surface EMG images. Sci. Rep. **6** (2016)
6. Du, Y., Wenguang, J., Wentao, W., Geng, W.: Surface EMG-based inter-session gesture recognition enhanced by deep domain adaptation. Sensors **3** (2017)

7. Du, Y., Wenguang, J., Wentao, W., Geng, W.: CapgMyo: a high density surface electromyography database for gesture recognition. http://zju-capg.org/myo/data/index.html
8. Atzori, M., et al.: Electromyography data for non-invasive naturally-controlled robotic hand prostheses. Sci. Data. **1** (2014)
9. Hudgins, B., Parker, P., Scott, R.N.: A new strategy for multifunction myoelectric control. Biomed. Eng. IEEE Trans. **40**, 82–94 (1993)
10. Otsu, N.: A threshold selection method from gray-level histograms. IEEE Trans. Sys. Man. Cyber. **1**, 62–66 (1979)

An Effective Approach Based on a Subset of Skeleton Joints for Two-Person Interaction Recognition

Sirine Ammar[1]($\boxtimes$), Nizar Zaghden[2], and Mahmoud Neji[1]

[1] MIRACL, University of Sfax, 3018 Sfax, Tunisia
ammarsirine3@gmail.com, mahmoud.neji@gmail.com
[2] ESC, University of Sfax, 3018 Sfax, Tunisia
nizar.zaghden@gmail.com

Abstract. In this article, the problem of human interaction recognition is addressed. A novel methodology is presented to model the interaction between two people using a Kinect sensor. It is proposed to analyse the distances between a subset of skeleton joints to determine their contribution to the recognition of interaction. Subsequently, the most representative joints are taken into account for the formation of a pentagon for each person. Five Euclidean distances are extracted between the vertices of two pentagons corresponding to the people to analyse. Finally, the SVM is used for the recognition of human interaction. Experimental results demonstrate the effectiveness of this work compared to recently published proposals.

Keywords: Human interaction recognition · Kinect · Subset · Skeleton joints · Representative joints · Pentagon · Euclidean distances · SVM

1 Introduction

Human-human interaction recognition has attracted increasing importance in recent years due to its large applications in computer vision fields. However, recognizing human interactions remains a very difficult task especially in realistic environments because of its large intra-variations, lighting changes, clutter, partially or totally occluded target objects. In recent decades, many studies have addressed this issue [1, 2]. Recent work [3–5] has suggested that accuracy of human interaction recognition based on both color images and depth maps can provide better accuracy. In addition, it is known that a human joint sequence is an effective representation for structured movement [6]. Therefore, in this paper we present a new approach for human-human interaction recognition using depth cameras.

This paper proposes a framework for robust human interaction recognition and demonstrates its performance on public benchmark dataset. The two-persons interactions presented are parallel to the Kinect sensor. Each interaction is captured in three different angles (0°, 45° and 135°). Eight two-person interactions are taken into account, namely Approaching, Departing, Kicking, Pushing, Shaking Hands, Hugging, Exchanging and Punching. A pentagon has created for each human for each frame of a

© Springer Nature Switzerland AG 2019
R. Vera-Rodriguez et al. (Eds.): CIARP 2018, LNCS 11401, pp. 922–929, 2019.
https://doi.org/10.1007/978-3-030-13469-3_106

sequence. The pentagon vertices generated by the algorithm have three-dimensional information because the Kinect sensor models the human body using 20 body joint coordinates in three dimensions. For each frame two various pentagons are formed corresponding to two person interaction. We calculated the Euclidean distances between similar vertices of two different persons as features for our algorithm. For the recognition purpose, multi-class support vector machine (SVM) [7, 8] is applied. Experimentally, it is found that recognition rate of our method based on distances between a subset of two persons skeleton Joints outperforms other state of the art method.

Our contributions can be summarized as follows:

- We propose a novel framework for human interaction recognition using depth information including an algorithm to reconstruct depth sequence with as few key frames as possible.
- We extend the low-level features (joint-joint distances) previously used in [9] computed over the entire human skeleton and propose a new person-to-person interaction feature that roughly describe the distances between a subset of joints extracted from skeleton two of two person.

The paper is organized as follows. Related work is reviewed in Sect. 2. Section 3 provides a detailed description of our approach and defines the proposed two-person interaction descriptor. Section 4 presents the experimental results and Sect. 5 concludes the paper.

2 Related Work

Over the last two decades, various approaches have been suggested to focus on different representations of the interaction between two or more persons. In [10], Park et al. propose an algorithm to achieve human activity recognition with distributed camera sensors. In track-level analysis, the gross-level activity patterns are analysed and in body-level analysis, person's activity is analysed in terms of the individual body parts' coordination. In [11], a method is proposed to extract the spatial semantics between the humans, including front, back, face to face, back to back, and left or right. To recognize the interactions between persons, they used context-free grammar. Rehg et al. [12] have proposed the interactions between children and an adult. The extracted Information is combined to acquire the social representations of the interaction. In Kong et al. [13], a method is proposed based on primitive interactive phrases for recognizing complex human interactions. Relationship is described by means of a set of features which are common to different relationships. Raptis and Sigal [14] extract the most discriminative key frames and consider the local temporal context between them. In Blunsden and Fisher [15], the movement is classified using a hidden Markov mode as a feature interaction in a group of people. The body orientation is also taken into account as an important aspect related to the interaction between two persons.

Currently, many studies have applied skeleton-based classification for people interaction recognition. One of the advantages of the depth cameras is the ability to capture human skeleton information in real time and provide the 3D joint coordinates of a human model. Yun et al. [9] present a method based on relational body-pose features which characterize geometric relations between specific joints in a single pose or a short sequence of poses like joint motion, joint distance, velocity and plane. In classification phase, they apply linear SVMs and multiple instance learning (MIL) with a bag of body poses. In [16], a feature descriptor which combines spatial relationship and semantic motion trend similarity is proposed for human-to-human interaction recognition. The motion trend of each skeleton joint is firstly quantified into the specific semantic word and then a Kernel is built for measuring the similarity of either intra or inter body parts by histogram interaction. Chen et al. [17] proposed a two-level hierarchical method based on the skeleton information. In the first layer, the most representative articulations are determined using a part-based clustering feature vector. In the second layer, only relevant joints within specific clusters are used for feature extraction.

This paper presents a new method to describe person-to-person interactions using skeleton-based features. Hence, we present a system, which implements a simple technique to extract pertinent human interaction features adequate for two-interacting persons. Conversely, from other works that extract features based on the whole human skeletons [9], the developed system models an interaction using a few and basic informative postures based on a few selected joints. Our System is tested on SBU Kinect Interaction dataset [9] and shows good performance.

3   Proposed Approach

Our system aims at recognizing human-human interactions based on the distances between two-person skeleton joints extracted from depth images. This skeleton contains the 3-D position of a certain number of joints representing different parts of the human body and provides strong cues to recognize human interaction.

An overview of the proposed methodology is presented in Fig. 1. First, key frames are collected from the video sequence. As skeleton information, we calculate distances between a subset of skeleton joints captured by Microsoft Kinect sensor. For each frame, five Euclidean distances are extracted between two pentagon vertices corresponding to two persons. These features are used for classification using Support Vector Machine classifier to recognize human interactions.

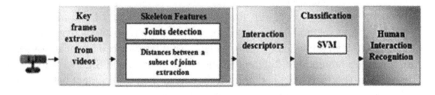

Fig. 1. Architectural diagram of our human interaction recognition system

3.1   Key Frames Extraction

This section explores a method of key-frames extraction algorithm. It is based on two phases: First phase computes threshold using mean and standard deviation of absolute difference of histogram of consecutive image frames. Second phase extracts key frames comparing the threshold against absolute difference of histogram of consecutive image frames. The algorithm starts by extracting frames from video. Next, histogram difference between two consecutive frames is calculated. The threshold (T) is computed using following equation.

$$T = \text{Standard Deviation} + (\text{Mean} * a) \tag{1}$$

Where Standard Deviation and Mean are the standard deviation and mean of absolute difference of histogram respectively and a is constant. Next phase determine the key-frames by comparing the absolute difference of histogram against threshold. If the threshold value is greater than output pair then first image of that pair is considered as key frame otherwise second image of that pair is considered as a key frame. The proposed algorithm is given below:

Implementation Steps
Here input video V is read frame by frame 1st to n^{th} frame.
    Step 1. Read an input video with N frames with n $\times$ n size.
    Step 2. Read consecutive i^{th} and $(i + 1)^{th}$ frames.
    Step 3. Histogram difference between two consecutive frames.
    Step 4. Calculate mean and standard deviation of absolute difference.
    Step 5. Compute threshold.
    Step 6. If difference > T select $(i + 1)^{th}$ frame as key-frame.
    else Discard it.
    Step 7. Repeat this for all frames until the end of the video. Key frames are collected.

3.2   Human Interaction Representation

The human interaction feature extraction step is the core of the system. The input of this module is a temporally ordered key frames of the recorded video extracted previously, representing the most important postures of the original skeleton sequence. One of the advantages of the adoption of skeleton features is that it ensures that the system is not affected by environmental light variations.

Our system is based on the idea that, the limitation of the single person skeleton features is that information about the surrounding humans is not provided. In fact, these could be exploited to model an action with humans by taking into account the relationships between skeletons to represent two-person interaction. This system is an improvement of the work already presented in [9]. The actual implementation differs from the previous one in the use of distances between a subset, instead of using distances between all skeleton joints. Each person is described using a pentagon. The five vertices of the pentagon are formed as follows: The 1st vertex is obtained by averaging head (H) and shoulder centre (SC) joints. The second vertex is calculated using the average values of shoulder right (SR), elbow right (ER), wrist right (WR) and hand right (HR). Similarly, mean values of wrist left (WL), hand left (HL), shoulder left (SL) and elbow left (EL) are scored to generate vertex 3. Vertices 4 and 5 are due to the average values of leg coordinates for right and left legs. Hip right (HR), knee right (KR), ankle right (AR) and foot right (FR) are taken into account for representation of vertex 4. In the same way, hip left (HL), knee left (KL), ankle left (AL) and foot left (FL) are noted and vertex 5 is generated by averaging values of those joints.

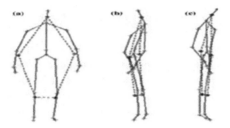

Fig. 2. Human skeleton in three various angles with Microsoft Kinect sensor (a) 0° (b) 45° (c) 135°. (Color figure online)

$$Vertex_1 = \frac{H + SC}{2} \tag{2}$$

$$Vertex_2 = \frac{SR + ER + WR + HR}{4} \tag{3}$$

$$Vertex_3 = \frac{SL + EL + WL + HL}{4} \tag{4}$$

$$Vertex_4 = \frac{HR + KR + AR + FR}{4} \tag{5}$$

$$Vertex_5 = \frac{HL + KL + AL + FL}{4} \tag{6}$$

In Fig. 2, the previous computed pentagon vertices are presented using black stars. The red dashed lines illustrate the edges of the pentagons. For each person, a pentagon is formed at the ith frame. Let the right and left humans are represented using R and L respectively. The Euclidean distance between vertex no i, j is determined by (7).

$$D = ||Li, j - Ri, j|| \tag{7}$$

3.3   Human Interaction Classification Using SVM

In this last step, multiclass SVMs are trained for supervised classification as considered in [18] using human interactions features obtained in the previous step (see Sect. 3.2). We employ the Multi-SVMs classifier that reaches better performances compared with other classifiers types.

4   Experimental Results

4.1   Recognition Results

In this section, we evaluate the proposed method and compare its performance to other methods. We have tested our system on a publicly available dataset: the SBU Kinect Interaction dataset [9]. Eight types of human-human interactions are presented: hugging, kicking, hand shaking, punching, exchanging and pushing. This system acquires a recognition rate of 95 with the use of multi SVM classifier. When the angle of interaction varies with respect to Kinect sensor, i.e. when the angle is 45° or 135°, then the average performance degrades to 81.3. The pentagon formed for each person is described with green dotted lines. The red lines are the illustration of Euclidean distances between the vertices of the two pentagons as presented in Fig. 3.

Fig. 3. Two person interaction modeling for kicking, punching, pushing and hugging using SBU Kinect Interaction dataset [9]. (Color figure online)

Table 1 presents the experimental values obtained for five Euclidean distances compared to other state of the art methods (Table 2 and Fig. 4).

Table 1. Comparison with related work in recent years using the SBU Interaction dataset.

Comparative literature	Features and recognition methods	Recognition rate (%)
Yun et al. [9]	Joint features	80.1
Ji et al. [19]	CFDM	89.4
[20]	Body parts	86.9
Proposed method		95.0

Table 2. Classes and corresponding activities

Class	Activity
1	Approaching
2	Departing
3	Kicking
4	Pushing
5	Shaking hands
6	Hugging
7	Exchanging
8	Punching

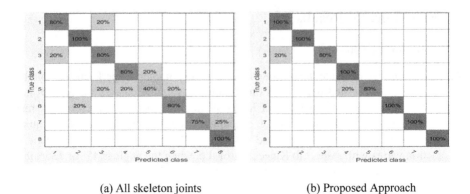

(a) All skeleton joints   (b) Proposed Approach

Fig. 4. Confusion matrix for human interaction recognition on SBU Kinect Interaction dataset.

4.2 Results Discussion

The experimental results are very encouraging and show the potential of the use of the distances between a subset of skeleton joints as features for two-person interaction recognition compared to the use of distances between the whole skeleton joints. In [9], two person interactions are modeled using multiple instance learning and Linear SVMs with achieved maximum recognition of 80%. But in this work, the rotation variance is not taken into account. The proposed method, not only able to produce higher recognition rates than [9] for rotation invariance purpose, but also capable to achieve good results. The limitation of [9] is overcome with high efficiency and also with less timing complexity.

5 Conclusions and Future Work

In this paper, we have presented a new framework for describing two-person interaction based on skeleton characteristics. The distances between a subset of human skeleton joints are calculated to distinguish between these interactions. This subset is obtained using the skeleton joints contributing the most towards an activity. Key frames are extracted from video and a pentagon is constructed for each person. Five Euclidean distances are calculated between two pentagon vertices corresponding to two persons. Feature vectors are composed using the 3D position of these joints as well as the distances between them and are used by SVM for classification. We have been able to reach an accuracy of 95% when using a subset of joints. The recognition accuracy when tracking all skeleton joints is also evaluated for comparison and is found to be lower than our algorithm. Future work may include the case of an activity on which the algorithm has not been previously trained is given as input to the classifier. The SVM, as any other machine learning algorithm, requires training in all possible outcomes. The unknown activity will be labelled as the one it looks like the most from the training set.

References

1. Ryoo, M.S., Aggarwal, J.K.: Semantic representation and recognition of continued and recursive human activities. Int. J. Comptut. Vis. **28**(1), 1–24 (2009)
2. Wang, H., Yuan, C., Hu, W., Ling, H., Yang, W., Sun, C.: Action recognition using nonnegative action component representation and sparse basis selection. IEEE Trans. Image Process. **23**(2), 570–581 (2014)
3. Ni, B., Wang, G., Moulin, P.: RGBD-HuDaAct: a color-depth video database for human daily activity recognition. In: ICCV Workshops (2011)
4. Li, W., Zhang, Z., Liu, Z.: Action recognition based on a bag of 3D points. In: CVPR Workshops (2010)
5. Alcoverro, M., Lopez-Mendez, A., Pardas, M., Casas, J.: Connected operators on 3D data for human body analysis. In: CVPR Workshops (2011)
6. Gu, J., Ding, X., Wang, S., Wu, Y.: Action and gait recognition from recovered 3-D human joints. IEEE Trans. Syst. Man Cybern. **40**, 1021–1033 (2010)
7. Raptis, M., Sigal, L.: Poselet key-framing: a model for human activity recognition. In: Proceedings of the IEEE Conference on Computer Vision and Pattern Recognition, pp. 2650–2657 (2013)
8. Agarwal, A., Triggs, B.: Recovering 3D human pose from monocular images. IEEE Trans. Pattern Anal. Mach. Intell. **28**(1), 44–58 (2006)
9. Yun, K., Honorio, J., Chattopadhyay, D., et al.: Two-person interaction detection using body-pose features and multiple instance learning. In: IEEE Computer Society Conference on Computer Vision and Pattern Recognition Workshops (CVPRW), pp. 28–35 (2012)
10. Park, S., Trivedi, M.: Multi-person interaction and activity analysis: a synergistic track- and body-level analysis framework. Mach. Vis. Appl. **18**, 151–166 (2007)
11. Jin, B., Hu, W., Wang, H.: Human interaction recognition based on transformation of spatial semantics. IEEE Signal Process. Lett. **19**(3), 139–142 (2012)
12. Rehg, J., Abowd, G., Rozga, A., et al.: Decoding children's social behavior. In: Proceedings of the IEEE Conference on Computer Vision and Pattern Recognition, pp. 3414–3421 (2013)
13. Kong, Yu., Jia, Y., Fu, Y.: Learning human interaction by interactive phrases. In: Fitzgibbon, A., Lazebnik, S., Perona, P., Sato, Y., Schmid, C. (eds.) ECCV 2012. LNCS, vol. 7572, pp. 300–313. Springer, Heidelberg (2012). https://doi.org/10.1007/978-3-642-33718-5_22
14. Raptis, M., Sigal, L.: Poselet key-framing: a model for human activity recognition. In: IEEE Conference on Computer Vision and Pattern Recognition, CVPR 2013, pp. 2650–2657 (2013)
15. Blunsden, S., Fisher, R.B.: The behave video dataset: ground truthed video for multi-person behavior classification. Ann. BMVA **4**(1–12), 4 (2010)
16. Liu, B., Cai, H., Ji, X., Liu, H.: Human-human interaction recognition based on spatial and motion trend feature. In: 2017 IEEE International Conference on Image Processing (ICIP), pp. 4547–4551 (2017)
17. Chen, H., Wang, G., Xue, J.H., He, L.: A novel hierarchical framework for human action recognition. Pattern Recogn. **55**, 148–159 (2016)
18. Ammar, S., Zaghden, N., Neji, M.: A framework for people re-identification in multi-camera surveillance system. In: 14th International Conference on Cognition and Exploratory Learning in Digital Age (CELDA 2017), pp. 319–322 (2017)
19. Ji, Y., Cheng, H., Zheng, Y., Li, H.: Learning contrastive feature distribution model for interaction recognition. J. Vis. Commun. Image Represent. **33**, 340–349 (2015)
20. Ji, Y., Ye, G., Cheng, H.: Interactive body part contrast mining for human interaction recognition. In: Multimedia and Expo Workshops (ICMEW). IEEE (2014)

Evaluating Deep Models for Dynamic Brazilian Sign Language Recognition

Lucas Amaral[1], Givanildo L. N. Júnior[1], Tiago Vieira[1], and Thales Vieira[2(✉)]

[1] Institute of Computing, Federal University of Alagoas, Maceió, Brazil
[2] Institute of Mathematics, Federal University of Alagoas, Maceió, Brazil
thales@pos.mat.ufal.br

Abstract. We propose and investigate the use of deep models for dynamic gesture recognition, focusing on the recognition of dynamic signs of the Brazilian Sign Language (Libras) from depth data. We evaluate variants and combinations of convolutional and recurrent neural networks, including LRCNs and 3D CNNs models. Experiments were performed with a novel depth dataset composed of dynamic signs representing letters of the alphabet and common words in Libras. An evaluation of the proposed models reveals that the best performing deep model achieves over 99% accuracy, and greatly outperforms a baseline method.

Keywords: Brazilian Sign Language ·
Dynamic sign language recognition · Deep learning

1 Introduction

Sign languages are visual languages used by deaf communities to communicate. Differently from spoken languages, in which grammar is expressed through sound, sign languages employ hand gestures, movement, orientation of the fingers, arms or body, and facial expressions [2,5]. However, sign languages are still very limited as a social inclusion tool, mainly because most hearing individuals are not knowledgeable in any sign language. Consequently, most deaf people can only communicate with a very limited part of the population, finding difficulties to interact in many daily activities.

In the last decade, with improvements on hardware and computer vision algorithms, real-time recognition of sign languages is becoming feasible. These novel technologies can enable the communication between deaf and hearing people and also potentialize interactions with machines through gestures. While recognizing simple static signs is an easy and well-established problem for many machine learning algorithms [1,4,12], recognizing words represented by complex dynamic interactions between hands, arms, body and facial expressions is rather a difficult task. An intermediate step to achieve a complete solution is developing robust methods to recognize dynamic signs, *i.e.* hand poses in movement.

However, very few studies have aimed to recognize dynamic signs of Libras [3,11,12], and none of them investigated deep models such as recurrent

© Springer Nature Switzerland AG 2019
R. Vera-Rodriguez et al. (Eds.): CIARP 2018, LNCS 11401, pp. 930–937, 2019.
https://doi.org/10.1007/978-3-030-13469-3_107

neural networks. Pizzolato *et al.* [12] presented a two-layer ANN used for automatic finger spelling recognition of Libras signs from RGB images. However, the architecture of the network is a Multi Layer Perceptron (MLP), which is currently an outdated choice for image classification or dynamic gestures recognition. Moreira *et al.* [11] use depth data to recognize all letters of the Libras alphabet, including static and dynamic signs. They also employ neural networks, but as in the previous, only a general MLP is proposed, requiring the optimization of a huge number of weights. Recently, Cardenas and Camara-Chavez [3] proposed a method that fuses deep learning descriptors to recognize dynamic gestures, including experiments on Libras. Depth, RGB and skeleton data are fused in that hybrid approach. Deep features from images are extracted using straightforward 2D CNNs applied to both depth data and image flow. However, according to Tran *et al.* [14], 2D CNNs are not suitable for spatiotemporal feature learning as recent state-of-the-art architectures, which we investigate in this work. It is also worth mentioning that the authors of that work suggested the use of 3D CNNs as future work.

In this paper, we propose to investigate deep models to recognize dynamic signs of the Brazilian Sign Language (Libras) from depth data. To the best of our knowledge, deep models based on learning spatiotemporal features have not been investigated to recognize dynamic signs of Libras. More specifically, we investigate the use of variants of 3D CNNs, which are capable of learning local spatiotemporal features [9]; and LRCNs, which can learn long-term spatial features dependencies [7]. We present experiments to evaluate the ability of variants of both architetures to recognize segmented dynamic Libras signs, and compare them with a baseline method. Another relevant contribution is the acquisition and publication of a large depth dataset composed of dynamic signs of Libras that represent letters of the alphabet and common words in Libras. Although the complete set of dynamic gestures in the Libras language is much higher than the selected signs, they are all composed by combinations of 46 *key handshapes* in movement [13], sharing similarities among them. Thus, the selected set of dynamic signs is still valuable to evaluate the proposed architectures. By finding a very robust deep model to recognize dynamic libras signs, we expect, in a near future, to build more sophisticated methods that would employ such model to recognize more complex interactions.

2 Methodology

We first describe the data acquisiton and pre-processing steps. We consider each dynamic sign as a finite sequence of depth images. In both training and recognition phases, the sequences are preprocessed before being given as input for the deep models. Depth data is acquired from a Intel RealSense sensor [8] at 640×480 spatial resolution, 8 bit depth resolution and 30 frames per second.

Let $f = \{f_1, f_2, \ldots, f_{|s|}\}$ be a dynamic sign, where $f_t[x, y]$ represents the depth (distance to the sensor) of the pixel at column x and row y of the tth image of the sequence. For each image f_t, we initially segment the hand from the background by first identifying the closest distance d_t to the sensor (smallest value of f_t). We consider a depth threshold D ensuring that the hand of most individuals, performing any hand pose, is not incorrectly extracted or cropped from the image, even if some parts of the arm are not extracted from the image. The filtered image $\tilde{f}_t$ is given by

$$\tilde{f}_t[x,y] = \begin{cases} f_t[x,y], & f_t[x,y] \leq d_t + D \\ 0, & f_t[x,y] > d_t + D. \end{cases} \quad (1)$$

We achieve excellent results by empirically setting $D = 20$ cm. Note that, even if the hand is not perfectly segmented, we expect the neural networks to learn how to deal with instances of signs containing regions of the arm, for example.

After segmentation, each image is subsampled to 50×50 of spatial resolution. We empirically found that this resolution is sufficient for a human to identify any sign, and thus we expected the same capability from a neural network.

As the inputs of 3D CNNs are expected to have fixed size, we fix the time dimension T to match the longest example of our collected data set, which is $T = 40$. Instead of oversampling each shorter sequence, we pad them with zero images to fill up the remaining time steps. In what follows, we describe two different classes of deep architectures that are capable of learning features of different nature: 3D-CNNs and LRCNs. We formally describe both, highlighting the advantages of each one.

2.1   3D CNNs

3D Convolutional Neural Networks were initially proposed to recognize human actions in surveillance videos [9]. Later, it was found that such networks are more suitable for spatiotemporal feature learning compared to 2D CNNs, as the latter loses temporal information of the input video right after every convolution operation [14].

The input for 3D CNNs are videos where each frame has a single channel containing depth data with resolution $m \times n \times T$, which can be seen as a cube formed by stacking multiple contiguous frames together. Instead of applying 2D convolutions in each image, as in the classical 2D CNN approach, 3D convolutions are directly applied to the cube. Thus, the extracted features represent spatiotemporal information that combines data from different frames. In contrast, 2D convolutions may only capture spatial information.

In a 3D convolutional layer, a video (or 3D feature map) f^{l-1} from a previous layer $l-1$ is given as input and K^l different 3D feature maps are computed by applying K^l different kernels w_k^l, jointly with a bias b_k^l and an activation σ, as

$$f_k^l[x,y,t] = \sigma((f^{l-1} * w_k^l)[x,y,t] + b_k^l).$$

As shown in Fig. 1, 3D CNNs follow the same structure of 2D CNNs. In this work, given an instance of a dynamic sign of Libras, we give the whole depth video as input to a 3D CNN.

2.2 LRCN

Long-term Recurrent Convolutional Networks were recently proposed and experimented on three applications involving sequences: activity recognition, image captioning, and video description [7]. They combine the power of 2D CNNs to extract relevant spatial features, with LSTMs: a class of recurrent neural networks (RNNs) that can learn long-term temporal dependencies. Consequently, this class of networks is capable of learning dependencies of spatial features over the time. Advantages of recurrent models include the capability of modelling complex temporal dynamics; and directly mapping variable-length inputs, such as videos, to variable-length outputs.

As in classical RNNs, an LSTM unit also has a memory (state) which is updated at each time step of a sequence. However, differently from RNN, LSTM learns when to forget and when to update previous states by incorporating information from the current step. The final output of the network depends on the last updated state. For more details, see the work of Donahue *et al.* [7].

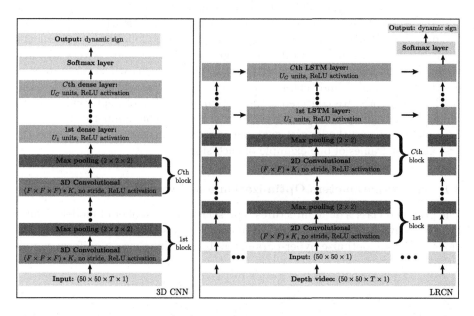

Fig. 1. 3D CNN architecture (left): the whole depth video is given as input to convolutional blocks composed of 3D convolutional layers (each one applying K filters of size $F \times F \times F$), and max pooling layers. Then, flattened features are given to dense layers that precede a softmax layer, which returns the final classification. LRCN architecture (right): Frames from the depth video are processed independently by 2D convolutional blocks. The extracted feature maps are flattened and given as input to the LSTM layers, that update their states. When the last frame is processed, the LSTM states, together with a softmax layer, are used to give the sign classification as output.

Differently from the 3D CNNs, LRCNs receive as input one image per step. Convolutional layers jointly with max pooling layers hierarchically learn features at different scales, similarly to 2D CNNs. Then, the extracted features are flattened and given as input to LSTM layers that update their states and compute partial (until the current time step) outputs. Finally, a dense softmax layer computes the partial probability.

To classify dynamic signs of Libras, we consider that, for each time step, a depth image is given as input and a partial probability is computed by the network. However, only the final probability, *i.e.* the probability distribution given by the softmax layer after the last image of the sign is processed, is considered for classification. The complete architecture is shown in Fig. 1.

3   Experiments

In our experiments we use a novel dataset containing dynamic Libras sign gestures, which is publicly available[1]. Assisted by Libras specialists, we designed a set of 10 classes representing dynamic signs of Libras: the letters H and J; and the words "day", "night", "enter", "all", "again", "start", "course" and "yours". The dynamic signs were chosen to satisfy the following requirements: 5 one-handed signs and 5 two-handed signs; all signs should be very distinct, to increase diversity, except for two pairs of similar signs which are harder to discriminate ("night" and "enter"), to better evaluate the robustness of the models. For each class, we collected a total of 300 examples of depth videos using the hardware and specifications described in Sect. 2. The number of frames per example varies, and the longest example contains 40 frames. Figure 2 shows the first and last frames of one example of each sign.

3.1   Hyper-parameters Optimization and Evaluation

The proposed classes of architectures represent a large number of models defined by several hyper-parameters. Instead of empirically setting values as many previous works, we optimize hyper-parameters by searching over a uniform sample

Fig. 2. Dynamic Libras sign dataset: images showing the first (top) and last (bottom) frames of each trained sign, after background extraction. From the left to right, the one-handed signs are H, "day", "again", "yours", J; and the two handed-signs are "night", "enter", "all", "start", "course".

---

[1] http://im.ufal.br/professor/thales/libras/.

of the search space. We consider the following hyper-parameters for 3D CNNs and LRCNs:

- Number of convolutional layers: $C_{3DCNN} = \{1, 2\}$ and $C_{LRCN} = \{1, 2, 3\}$;
- Filter size of convolutional layers: $F_{3DCNN} = F_{LRCN} = \{3, 5\}$;
- Number of filters of convolutional layers: $K_{3DCNN} = K_{LRCN} = \{16, 32, 64\}$;
- Number of dense/LSTM layers $L_{3DCNN} = L_{LRCN} = \{1, 2, 3\}$;
- Number of units of dense/LSTM layers $U_{3DCNN} = U_{LRCN} = \{100, 200, 300\}$.

Here, we consider both U_{3DCNN} and U_{LRCN} to be three-dimensional vectors containing the number of units up to 3 possible layers. If a layer does not exist, we set the corresponding number to zero. The same applies to F_{3DCNN} and F_{LRCN}. After each convolutional layer of all models, a max pooling layer with pool size $(2, 2)$ and no stride is applied. For all layers of both architectures, we use the ReLU activation function given by $\sigma(x) = \max(0, x)$, with a few exceptions, such as LSTM units and softmax layers.

For each combination of hyper-parameters, we perform a cross-validation experiment by randomly splitting the dataset examples into training and test sets, considering 70% of the examples for training and 30% for testing. The validation accuracy is evaluated after 10 training epochs for LRCNs and 5 training epochs for 3D CNNs. The mean validation accuracy after 10 repetitions is the value to be optimized, representing the robustness of the evaluated model.

We employed the Adam optimization algorithm [10] of the Keras library [6], with an initial learning rate of 0.001. The 5 best performing models of each class of architectures are shown in Table 1. Excellent results were obtained from the best configurations, achieving more than 99% of accuracy in all these cases.

To analyze the sensitivity of both classes of architectures to hyper-parameter calibration, we investigated the accuracies distribution among all performed experiments. Histograms of accuracies for both classes of architectures are exhibited in Fig. 3. Clearly, most accuracies are concentrated near the best results of Table 1. We conclude that the robustness of both classes of architectures is not very sensitive to hyperparameter calibration, with most evaluated configurations achieving more than 90% of accuracy. Consequently, the number of trainable parameters (weights) is a relevant criterion to select the most appropriate model. As shown in Table 1, the best performing LRCN is the best choice, due to the smaller number of weights.

We conclude that both classes of architectures can robustly be applied to the recognition of dynamic Libras signs. The excellent results can be explained by the relatively simplicity of dynamic Libras signs, and give evidence that such models are appropriate to more complex situations, including, larger dictionaries of signs and continuous conversations. However, in contrast to 3D CNNs, LRCNs have the ability to output partial probabilities for each time step, which may be very useful in such situations.

3.2   Comparison

In this section we compare the best performing deep model with a baseline method. The objective is to show that, although most dynamic Libras signs

Table 1. Accuracy of the best evaluated 3DCNNs and LRCNs models.

Class	C_*	F_*	K_*	L_*	U_*	Mean accuracy	Weights
LRCN	2	(3, 3, 0)	64	2	(100, 100)	99.8%	3,256,978
3DCNN	2	(3, 3, 0)	64	3	(300, 200, 100)	99.8%	18,779,658
3DCNN	2	(5, 3, 0)	32	3	(300, 200, 100)	99.6%	5,656,874
LRCN	1	(3, 0, 0)	64	2	(100, 100, 0)	99.7%	14,868,050
LRCN	1	(5, 0, 0)	64	2	(200, 200, 0)	99.7%	27,570,074
LRCN	1	(3, 0, 0)	64	3	(300, 200, 200)	99.7%	45,322,250
LRCN	1	(5, 0, 0)	64	3	(300, 200, 200)	99.6%	41,713,674
3DCNN	2	(3, 3, 0)	32	2	(200, 300, 0)	99.5%	6,287,286
3DCNN	2	(5, 3, 0)	64	2	(300, 100, 0)	99.5%	11,437,938
3DCNN	2	(3, 3, 0)	16	3	(100, 100, 200)	99.5%	6,287,286

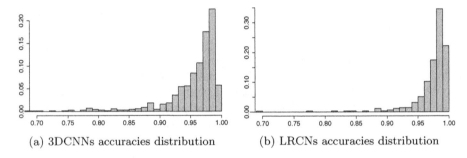

(a) 3DCNNs accuracies distribution   (b) LRCNs accuracies distribution

Fig. 3. Histograms of accuracies of the evaluated deep models. Horizontal axes represent relative accuracies, and vertical axes the relative frequencies.

are relatively easy to be recognized by deep models, a naive classifier will not be appropriate in this situation. In this experiment, we consider that the same inputs given to the 3D CNNs (raw depth video) are given to a multi-class one-versus-all SVM classifier. We adopt the popular rbf kernel, and calibrate both its radius γ and the regularization parameter C. Both parameters are calibrated by exhaustive grid search and cross-validation, using the same fraction of 70% of samples for training and 30% for validation. The best performing model was given by $\gamma = 0.1$ and $C = 1$, achieving only 63% of accuracy, in comparison with 99.8% of the best deep model of Table 1.

4   Conclusion

In this work we proposed and experimented deep models for the recognition of dynamic signs of Libras from depth data. Several variants of LRCNs and 3D CNNs revealed high robustness for the recognition of segmented signs. As future work, we expect the proposed models to be combined with other techniques, such as skeleton trackers, to recognize more complex conversations of Libras, including arms and body movement, so that the machine would be capable of translating a Libras conversation in real-time. The collection of larger datasets would also be required to turn this objective feasible. In addition, research on online recognition methods would also be necessary, in such a way that unsegmented data could be given as input to the machine to identify phrases and words.

Acknowledgements. The authors would like to thank CNPq and FAPEAL for partially financing this research.

References

1. Bastos, I.L., Angelo, M.F., Loula, A.C.: Recognition of static gestures applied to Brazilian sign language (libras). In: SIBGRAPI, pp. 305–312. IEEE (2015)
2. Brito, L.F., Langevin, R.: The sublexical structure of a sign language. Mathematiques Inform. et Sciences Humaines **125**, 17–40 (1994)
3. Escobedo Cardenas, E., Camara-Chavez, G.: Fusion of deep learning descriptors for gesture recognition. In: Mendoza, M., Velastín, S. (eds.) CIARP 2017. LNCS, vol. 10657, pp. 212–219. Springer, Cham (2018). https://doi.org/10.1007/978-3-319-75193-1_26
4. Cardenas, E.J.E., Chávez, G.C.: Finger spelling recognition from depth data using direction cosines and histogram of cumulative magnitudes. In: SIBGRAPI, pp. 173–179. IEEE (2015)
5. Cheok, M.J., Omar, Z., Jaward, M.H.: A review of hand gesture and sign language recognition techniques. Int. J. Mach. Learn. Cybern. **10**(1), 131–153 (2019)
6. Chollet, F., et al.: Keras (2015). https://keras.io
7. Donahue, J., et al.: Long-term recurrent convolutional networks for visual recognition and description. In: Proceedings of the IEEE Conference on Computer Vision and Pattern Recognition, pp. 2625–2634. IEEE (2015)
8. Intel: Intel realsense technology (2018). https://www.intel.com/content/www/us/en/architecture-and-technology/realsense-overview.html
9. Ji, S., Xu, W., Yang, M., Yu, K.: 3D convolutional neural networks for human action recognition. IEEE Trans. Pattern Anal. Mach. Intell. **35**(1), 221–231 (2013)
10. Kingma, D.P., Ba, J.: Adam: a method for stochastic optimization. arXiv preprint arXiv:1412.6980 (2014)
11. de Souza Pereira Moreira, G., Matuck, G.R., Saotome, O., da Cunha, A.M.: Recognizing the Brazilian signs language alphabet with neural networks over visual 3D data sensor. In: Bazzan, A.L.C., Pichara, K. (eds.) IBERAMIA 2014. LNCS (LNAI), vol. 8864, pp. 637–648. Springer, Cham (2014). https://doi.org/10.1007/978-3-319-12027-0_51
12. Pizzolato, E.B., dos Santos Anjo, M., Pedroso, G.C.: Automatic recognition of finger spelling for libras based on a two-layer architecture. In: Proceedings of the 2010 ACM Symposium on Applied Computing, pp. 969–973. ACM (2010)
13. de Quadros, R.M., Karnopp, L.B.: Língua brasileira de sinais: estudos linguísticos. Artmed, Porto Alegre (2004)
14. Tran, D., Bourdev, L., Fergus, R., Torresani, L., Paluri, M.: Learning spatiotemporal features with 3D convolutional networks. In: 2015 IEEE International Conference on Computer Vision (ICCV), pp. 4489–4497. IEEE (2015)

A DTW-Based Representation to Support Static Sign Language Recognition from Binary Images

J. S. Blandon$^{(\boxtimes)}$, A. Alvarez, and A. Orozco

Automatics Research Group, Universidad Tecnológica de Pereira, Pereira, Colombia
jsblandon@utp.edu.co

Abstract. Sign language recognition (SLR) from binary images is a challenging task due to the huge amount of information required to process and the complex variations among classes. Here, we introduced a dynamic time warping (DTW) based representation approach to reveal consistent static SLR patterns from binary images. Indeed, we estimated curvature coefficients sequences (CCSs) from a contour filtering using different step length values. In turn, a DTW feature space is built from CCSs attributes, and a Relief-F-based feature selection stage is carried out to highlight discriminative DTW attributes. Achieved results on a publicly available dataset probe that our strategy attains an 85% classification performance on average. Further, to the best of our knowledge, this is the first attempt to apply dissimilarity-based representations for codifying binary images in SSLR.

1 Introduction

Nowadays, sign language recognition (SLR) is a research field of interest oriented to the development of automatic sign language gestures (SLG) discrimination. Commonly, two kinds of technologies are used in SLR: direct measure devices (data gloves and body trackers like Microsoft Kinect), and 2D Camera Based Systems (CBS) [3]. Indeed, the CBS-based SLR seems to be widely adopted due to its low cost and non-intrusiveness. However, the SLG differs geographically and anatomically according to the subject, not mentioning the natural image and video acquisition issues, i.e., occlusions, noise, lighting conditions, etc., which yield to signs overlapping. Then, efficient pattern recognition methodologies are required to support SLR.

In this sense, different feature representation approaches in SLR tasks have been developed in the literature. For instance, authors in [1] created feature profiles of depth and movement for each sign from depth images obtained by a Microsoft Kinect; next, a Support Vector Machine (SVM) is applied. Besides, authors in [7] proposed an SLR system based on signs tracking and identification, using a serial particle filter, representing the acquired images as covariance matrices. Nonetheless, the system works only if the signer is the single subject for the background. Authors in [8] presents an SLG classification scheme using

R. Vera-Rodriguez et al. (Eds.): CIARP 2018, LNCS 11401, pp. 938–945, 2019.
https://doi.org/10.1007/978-3-030-13469-3_108

geometric features extracted from binary images to separate among Spanish vowels. Other approaches used Convolutional Neural Networks (CNN) to identify hand gestures from videos [12], and static signs from depth images [4]. Notwithstanding, CNN is well known for their propensity to overfitting. Furthermore, sequential-based features are used to code dynamic signs or static ones. Indeed, [6] presents a scheme where features related to hand coordinates respect to face, hand movement, and sign size changes, are computed to classify them from a Statistical Dynamic Time Warping (SDTW) approach. Nonetheless, SDTW gives a poor prior on DTW path shape, inducing a recognition performance decreasing. Also, [11] shows an ensemble of multiples classifiers based on Sequential Pattern Trees, where the features are hands trajectories along gesture description. In [13] authors develop a system of hand gesture recognition based on Hidden Markov Models, using primitive descriptors. Even though these methods consider sequential data, the samples usually are noise free, tend to be homogeneous and reside in a high-dimensional space.

We introduce a DTW-based feature representation strategy to support static SLR - (SSLR). Our algorithm, called DTW-SSLR, includes the estimation of curvature coefficients sequences (CCSs) from binary images. Afterward, a Dynamic Time Warping (DTW) measure is carried out to compare CCSs ruled by Euclidean (EUC) or symmetric Kullback-Leibler (SKL) localized metrics. Since our methodology represents the input binary images as a distance matrix, we include different CCSs by varying the step length parameter. Next, to reveal relevant features of the DTW-based representation, a Relief-F selection is applied. Latter, SSLR is inferred using three different classifiers: Linear Bayes Classifier (LBC), K-Nearest Neighbours (KNN), and Support Vector Machine (SVM), whose performance are measured regarding the classification accuracy. Attained results on a publicly available dataset show that DTW-SSLR obtains an 85% accuracy on average, showing that our novel method, which relies on representing sequential features using dissimilarity spaces, is an alternative strategy to overcome the problem of SLR.

The remainder of this paper is organized as follows: Sect. 2 describes the materials and methods, Sect. 3 the experimental set-up, Sect. 4 the results and discussions, and Sect. 5 the concluding remarks.

2   Materials and Methods

Binary Images Preprocessing and Curvature Estimation. Given a binary image $I \in \mathbb{R}^{W \times H}$ coding a hand gesture shape, a Canny filtering procedure is carried out to highlight the object shape. Afterward, some morphological operations, i.e., opening, closing, and erosion, are applied to prevent non-closed trajectories. Then, to quantify hand shape variations, a curvature vector $x \in \mathbb{R}^N$ holding N coefficients is computed based on first order changes [2]. Indeed, those trajectories are extracted from the farthest horizontal point to the right of the shape centroid, getting each curvature point from this first coordinate in a counterclockwise manner ruled by a step length $\xi \in \mathbb{N}$.

DTW-Based Feature Representation. To compare two different CCSs $x \in \mathbb{R}^N, x' \in \mathbb{R}^M$ extracted from a pair of binary images, we use a Dynamic Time Warping-based distance (DTW). In fact, the DTW allows comparing two sequences of different length based on a localized function: $\zeta : \mathbb{R} \times \mathbb{R} \rightarrow \mathbb{R}^+$. So, if $\zeta(x_n, x'_m)$ is small ($n \in \{1, 2, \ldots, N\}, m \in \{1, 2, \ldots, M\}$), then x_n and y_m code a similar curvature pattern; instead, if $\zeta(x_n, y_n)$ is high, they are dissimilar. Here, the Euclidean and Kullback Leibler-based localized functions are deemed as follows:

$$\zeta_{EUC}(x_n, x'_m) = \sqrt{(x_n - x'_m)^2}, \tag{1}$$

$$\zeta_{SKL}(x_n, x'_m) = (x_n - x'_m)(\log(x_n) - \log(x'_m)). \tag{2}$$

Further, a matrix $\boldsymbol{\Psi} \in \mathbb{R}^{N \times M}$, holding elements $\Psi_{nm} = \zeta(x, x')$, can be built by fixing the localized function ζ. The DTW algorithm searches the alignment between CCSs as the minimum mean cost in $\boldsymbol{\Psi}$. Namely, a warping path set $\{z_k \in \mathbb{N}^{2 \times L_k}\}_{k=1}^K$ is built, where $z_k = [(n_1, m_1), \ldots, (n_{L_k}, m_{L_k})]$ is the k-th path of size $L_k \in \mathbb{N}$ into the matrix $\boldsymbol{\Psi}$, $n_r \in \{1, 2, \ldots, N\}$ and $m_r \in \{1, 2, \ldots, M\}$ depict the sample positions in vectors x and x', respectively, and $r \in \{1, 2, \ldots, L_k\}$. Notably, each path z_k satisfies the boundary, monotonicity, and step size conditions [9]. Besides, a distance function $\gamma : \mathbb{R}^N \times \mathbb{R}^M \rightarrow \mathbb{R}^+$ between CCSs can be defined as follows: $\gamma(x, x') = \min_{k \in K} \psi_k(x, x')$, where $\psi_k(x, x') = \sum_{r=1}^{L_k} \zeta(x_{n_r}, x'_{m_r})$ is the cost for the path k.

Relevance Analysis and Discrimination. Let $\{I_t \in \mathbb{R}^{W \times H}, y_t \in \{1, 2, \ldots, C\}\}_{t=1}^T$ be a set holding T binary images and output labels regarding C static signs. Moreover, let $\{\xi_l \in \mathbb{N}\}_{l=1}^{\eta}$ be a set of step length values used to reveal different curvature relationships within a binary image, a feature space matrix $F \in \mathbb{R}^{T \times Q}$ is built as: $F = [D^{(1)}, D^{(2)}, \ldots, D^{(\nu)}]$, where $D^{(l)} \in \mathbb{R}^{T \times T}$ is a DTW-based matrix with elements: $d_{tt'}^{(l)} = \gamma(x_t(\xi_l), x_{t'}(\xi_l))$, $x_t(\xi_l) \in \mathbb{R}^{N_{tl}}$ is the CCS for the step length value ξ_l, and $Q = T \times \eta$. In practice, F holds a huge number of attributes (features). This fact can yield to overfitting in further classification stages, being necessary to infer a matrix $\hat{F} \in \mathbb{R}^{T \times Q'}$ ($Q' \leq Q$), with the most Q' relevant features favoring the trade-off between system complexity and SSLR performance. To do this, we compute the contribution of each feature in F in terms of the supervised information given by the labels in a relevance vector $\rho \in \mathbb{R}^Q$ based on the Relief-F approach as [14]:

$$\rho_q = \frac{1}{T} \sum_{t=1}^{T} \left(-\frac{1}{\varphi} \sum_{f_{t'} \in \Omega_t^{y_t}} \|f_t - f_{t'}\|_2 + \frac{1}{\varphi} \sum_{c \neq y_t} \frac{p(y = c)}{1 - p(y = y_t)} \sum \|f_t - f_{t'}\|_2 \right), \tag{3}$$

where $\Omega_t^c = \{f_{t'} : t' = 1, 2, \ldots, \varphi\}$ holds the φ-nearest neighbors of f_t, and $p(y = c)$ is the probability that a sample belongs to the c-th class ($c \in \{1, 2, \ldots, C\}$), and $q \in \{1, 2, \ldots, Q\}$. In this manner, the higher the ρ_q value the better the q-th feature for discriminating hand gestures in SSLR. Therefore, a performance curve (in terms of classification accuracy) can be used to find the Q' most relevant features by adding one by one the input attributes concerning the ρ values. Figure 1 summarizes the proposed DTW-based representation approach to support SSLR recognition.

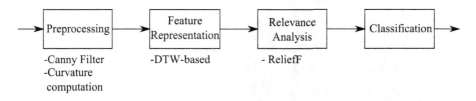

Fig. 1. SSRL recognition using DTW-based representation.

3 Experimental Set-Up

To test the proposed DTW-based representation, called DTW-SSLR, we use the publicly available database *Polish Hand Gesture Recognition*[1] - (PSL-DB), which is composed by 899 binary images representing 25 different hand gestures. Each sample, whose have different resolutions, corresponds to a static PSL. For concrete testing, 6 classes and 25 samples per class are used as suggested by [10], since those samples were well discriminated in their work. Figure 2 shows some examples of the PSL DB. We compute the curvature coefficients sequences varying the curvature step length value ξ_l in an equally spaced grid between 3 to 20. Afterward, for each ξ_l, we compute a pairwise distance between the whole dataset using the DTW approach, which allows changing its metric: EUC or SKL. A feature space holding $T = 150$ inputs and $P = 2700$ attributes are computed. Also, the number of neighbors in Relief-F is fixed at 1. Finally, a nested cross-validation strategy is carried out to train an LBC, KNN, and SVM classifiers using a Hold-Out scheme of $(70 - 30)\%$ and get statistical relevancy for the presented results. The number of neighbors in KNN is searched in a grid from 1 to 15, a Gaussian kernel is utilized for the SVM finding the bandwidth between $0.1\sigma_o$ to σ_o, being $\sigma_o \in \mathbb{R}^+$ the median of the Euclidean distances between input samples, and the regularization value between 0.1 to 1000.

4 Results and Discussion

Figure 2 (Right) shows the curvature estimation of a preprocessed sample of class 4 in the PSL-DB, fixing the curvature step length at $\xi_l = 15$. Each point depicts a curvature coefficient computed as explained in Sect. 2. The plot demonstrates that the CCS represents the main patterns concerning the shape variations, where bluish colors denote low curvature values and reddish the higher ones, whose are related to smooth and sharp changes, respectively. Accordingly, it is clear that the proposed features take essential information described by the morphological structure from the hand gesture. Now, the first row in Fig. 3 shows the

---

[1] http://sun.aei.polsl.pl/~mkawulok/gestures/.

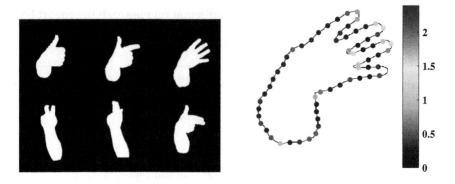

Fig. 2. PLS-DB examples. Left: SL samples of 6 classes: 1, 2, 4, H, K, N. Right: Shows the curvature coefficients for a sample in class 4.

Table 1. Confusion matrix for the LBC using the 851 most relevant DTW-based features (EUC metric). Average ± standard deviation are displayed in percentage.

	1	2	4	H	K	N
1	86 ± 14	7 ± 11	0 ± 0	0 ± 0	0 ± 0	6 ± 9
2	1 ± 4	85 ± 13	0 ± 0	1 ± 4	0 ± 0	13 ± 13
4	0 ± 0	5 ± 6	93 ± 6	0 ± 0	0 ± 0	3 ± 5
H	0 ± 0	0 ± 0	0 ± 0	79 ± 13	17 ± 12	4 ± 6
K	1 ± 4	0 ± 0	0 ± 0	14 ± 14	85 ± 14	0 ± 0
N	1 ± 4	14 ± 9	0 ± 0	1 ± 4	3 ± 5	81 ± 9

classification results obtained by adding one-by-one the sorting features using the Relief-F ranking. Remarkably, the EUC metric shows a better performance than the SKL. This outcome ought to SKL metric does not code the main differences between classes accurately, leading to poor performance results (see the right top in Fig. 2). On the other hand, the EUC captures the relevant differences among CCSs, generating a dissimilarity representation which accurately describes the SSLR patterns. Respecting to classifier performances, the LBC and the SVM show stable results for the two types of dissimilarity spaces. However, KNN does not increase its outcomes using a few attributes, which means that no matter how many features we used in the classifier can not improve its performance. According to the DTW-SSLR results, the highest accuracies for the EUC and SKL are $84.79 \pm 2.95\%$ (851 features using the LBC) and $43.54 \pm 6.55\%$ (1721 features using the SVM).

To get a visual representation of our relevant subsets, we mapped it into a 2D space using the well-known Jensen-Shannon Embedding (JSE) algorithm [5]. As seen, the EUC metric preserves neighborhoods locally, showing that our dissimilarity representation codes the similarity between classes. Notwithstanding, globally our features do not seem to embed well the information per class. However, it is well known that the classification models discriminate the selected features in the high dimensional space, showing that our approach preserves the discriminative ones from the database. Further, the SKL metric retains neither local nor global similarities, which restates that SKL as dissimilarity representation lacks in coding and preserving relevant information.

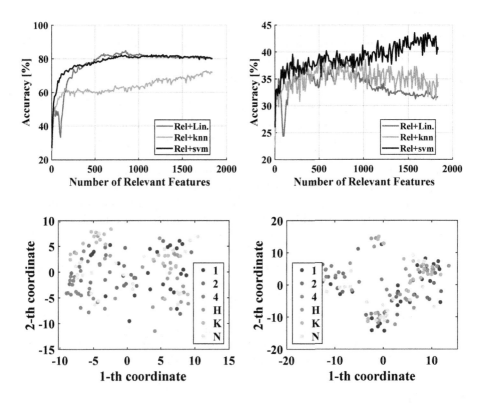

Fig. 3. First row: classification performance vs the number of relevant features. Second row: 2-D embeddings using JSE. First column: EUC metric, Second column: SKL metric.

Table 1 shows the confusion matrix from the best classification results regarding the performance curves in Fig. 3. In particular, the best LBC results are depicted for 851 relevant features according to the EUC metric. First of all, tackling the problem of SSLR from binary images is a difficult task since they present a low degree of homogeneity. Thus, a system which discriminates correctly hands gestures needs to learn mostly each variation from the same sign. Nevertheless, the proposed methodology based in CCS represented by a DTW-based measurement resolves almost well the whole classes. However, between H-K and 2-N gestures tend to compromise the results since these such classes are similar in shape. Furthermore, Table 1 shows that information from small and large scales, e.g., $\xi_l = 3$ and $\xi_l = 20$, allows our system to learn details that between scales differs and determinate how the gesture is performed. Likewise, the EUC metric captures relevant information in the DTW-based representation, obtaining a high-performance per class. Thus, our DTW-SSLR reveals information at different scales which allows classifying hand gestures.

5   Conclusions

We develop a novel DTW-based representation approach to support SSLR. Our method comprises the estimation of CCS coefficients from binary images of hand gestures and a multi-step length feature estimation to reveal both local and global variations towards shape edges. Then, a DTW-based distance is computed to compare CCSs of different length. In turn, a feature selection approach is employed to code consistent patterns regarding the DTW features from different step length CCS. Notably, our proposal allows to code morphologic similarities to varying scales between binary images using data sequences, encouraging the discrimination among static signs. Attained results on a public database probe that we can achieve an 85% classification performance on average. Besides, to the best of our knowledge, this work is the first attempt to apply dissimilarity-based representations to codify sequential data from binary images devoted to SSLR. Moreover, we used a simple set of features and powerful representation techniques to learn data-driven classification models. Future work involves the extension of our approach to separate dynamic hand gestures using enhanced sequential features, and apply our methodology over another statistic sign language databases, e.g. American Sign Language.

Acknowledgments. J.S. Blandon is partially funded by the project E6-18-11 (Vicerrectoría de Investigaciones, Innovación y Extensión) and by Maestría en Ingeniería Eléctrica, both from Universidad Tecnológica de Pereira.

References

1. Agarwal, A., Thakur, M.K.: Sign language recognition using Microsoft Kinect. In: 2013 Sixth Internation Conference on CC, pp. 181–185. IEEE (2013)
2. Bicego, M., Murino, V.: Investigating hidden markov models' capabilities in 2D shape classification. IEEE Trans. Pattern Anal. Mach. Intell. **26**(2), 281–286 (2004)
3. Er-Rady, A., Faizi, R., Thami, R.O.H., Housni, H.: Automatic sign language recognition: a survey. In: 2017 International Conference on ATSIP, pp. 1–7. IEEE (2017)
4. Huang, J., Zhou, W., Li, H., Li, W.: Sign language recognition using 3D convolutional neural networks. In: ICME, pp. 1–6. IEEE (2015)
5. Lee, J.A., Renard, E., Bernard, G., Dupont, P., Verleysen, M.: Type 1 and 2 mixtures of kullback-leibler divergences as cost functions in dimensionality reduction based on similarity preservation. Neurocomputing **112**, 92–108 (2013)
6. Lichtenauer, J., Hendriks, E., Reinders, M.: Sign language recognition by combining statistical dtw and independent classification. IEEE Trans. Pattern Anal. Mach. Intell. **30**, 2040–2046 (2008)

7. Lim, K.M., Tan, A.W., Tan, S.C.: A feature covariance matrix with serial particle filter for isolated sign language recognition. Expert Syst. Appl. **54**, 208–218 (2016)
8. Monsalve, D.J.B., Domínguez, M., González, C.A.M., Ospina, A.E.C.: Automatic classification of vowels in colombian sign language. Revista Tecno Lógicas **21**(41), 103–114 (2018)
9. Müller, M.: Dynamic time warping. In: Müller, M. (ed.) Information Retrieval for Music and Motion, pp. 69–84. Springer, Heidelberg (2007)
10. Nalepa, J., Kawulok, M.: Fast and accurate hand shape classification. In: Kozielski, S., Mrozek, D., Kasprowski, P., Małysiak-Mrozek, B., Kostrzewa, D. (eds.) BDAS 2014. CCIS, vol. 424, pp. 364–373. Springer, Cham (2014). https://doi.org/10.1007/978-3-319-06932-6_35
11. Ong, E.J., Cooper, H., Pugeault, N., Bowden, R.: Sign language recognition using sequential pattern trees. In: 2012 IEEE Conference on CVPR, pp. 2200–2207. IEEE (2012)
12. Pigou, L., Dieleman, S., Kindermans, P.-J., Schrauwen, B.: Sign language recognition using convolutional neural networks. In: Agapito, L., Bronstein, M.M., Rother, C. (eds.) ECCV 2014. LNCS, vol. 8925, pp. 572–578. Springer, Cham (2015). https://doi.org/10.1007/978-3-319-16178-5_40
13. Premaratne, P., Yang, S., Zhou, Z.M., Bandara, N.: Dynamic hand gesture recognition framework. In: Huang, D.-S., Jo, K.-H., Wang, L. (eds.) ICIC 2014. LNCS (LNAI), vol. 8589, pp. 834–845. Springer, Cham (2014). https://doi.org/10.1007/978-3-319-09339-0_84
14. Robnik-Šikonja, M., Kononenko, I.: Theoretical and empirical analysis of ReliefF and RReliefF. Mach. Learn. **53**(1–2), 23–69 (2003)

Human Activity Recognition Using Multi-modal Data Fusion

Andres Felipe Calvo[1]([✉]), German Andres Holguin[1], and Henry Medeiros[2]

[1] Faculty of Engineering, Universidad Tecnológica de Pereira, Pereira, Colombia
{afcalvo,gahol}@utp.edu.co
[2] Department of Electrical and Computer Engineering, Marquette University,
Milwaukee, USA
henry.medeiros@marquette.edu

Abstract. The automated recognition of human activity is an important computer vision task, and it has been the subject of an increasing number of interesting home, sports, security, and industrial applications. Approaches using a single sensor have generally shown unsatisfactory performance. Therefore, an approach that efficiently combines data from a heterogeneous set of sensors is required. In this paper, we propose a new method for human activity recognition fusing data obtained from inertial sensors (IMUs), surface electromyographic recording electrodes (EMGs), and visual depth sensors, such as the Microsoft Kinect®. A network of IMUs and EMGs is scattered on a human body and a depth sensor keeps the human in its field of view. From each sensor, we keep track of a succession of primitive movements over a time window, and combine them to uniquely describe the overall activity performed by the human. We show that the multi-modal fusion of the three sensors offers higher performance in activity recognition than the combination of two or a single sensor. Also, we show that our approach is highly robust against temporary occlusions, data losses due to communication failures, and other events that naturally occur in non-structured environments.

Keywords: Human activity recognition · Multimodal sensors ·
Data fusion · Support vector machine · Hidden Markov Model

1 Introduction

The analysis of human activity is a critical component for applications in fields such as health, security, sports, among others. Performing this task in an automatic manner is challenging and has prompted several researchers to attempt a multitude of approaches [3,5,19]. Among the most common devices used for this task are depth cameras (Kinect®). Some approaches use the spatial coordinates of human body joints and then compute feature vectors that can be used for classification. In [16], the authors use polar coordinates for the characterization of joints in order to achieve higher performance in activity classification. Other

© Springer Nature Switzerland AG 2019
R. Vera-Rodriguez et al. (Eds.): CIARP 2018, LNCS 11401, pp. 946–953, 2019.
https://doi.org/10.1007/978-3-030-13469-3_109

methods use classifiers (K-means, SVM) to generate a codebook with key postures and subsequently employ a Hidden Markov Model (HMM) to recognize the different combinations of postures and thus identify the activity being performed. However, all these methods present limitations caused by partial occlusions of the target [4,15].

Sensors such as Inertial Measurement Units (IMUs) are also used for activity recognition [2,18]. However, these sensors require high processing capabilities [13], and most of the time a single sensor is not sufficient to perform satisfactory detection [1]. Electromyographic signal sensors (EMG) are also useful for activity recognition [6,14]. However, sophisticated signal processing and multiple sensors are also required for adequate detection accuracy. Kang et al. use Mel-Frequency Cepstral Coefficients (MFCC), obtaining an activity recognition accuracy of 85% [11]. Korbinian et al. use an HMM for activity recognition and neural networks for motion segmentation, reporting high accuracy rates between 93% and 100% [12]. There is a consensus that fusing data from different sensors improves human activity recognition systems [5,16]. Also, a single sensor modality is generally not capable of identifying the wide range of human activities. Although several methods for human activity recognition that use multi-modal fusion approaches have been proposed [7,9], few techniques take more than two sensing modalities into account at the same time. Among the few recent works that do use multi-modal approaches, Zhand et al. employ a model that is based on primitive motions to classify movements using Bag of Features (BOF) techniques with histograms of primitive symbols [17]. In particular, to the best of our knowledge, no existing method fuses the information of IMUs, EMGs, and depth sensors simultaneously. Therefore, we propose a fusion method that combines the strengths of each sensor to provide better performance.

2 Proposed Method

This paper proposes an activity recognition method based on primitive motion detection. Our method is comprised of two main steps. First, we analyze the sensor data over a small time window to perform primitive motion classification, creating a motion sequence from each sensor. Second, this sequence of primitives is fed into a Hidden Markov Model that classifies the overall activity. An overview of the prediction and training methods is shown in Fig. 1. To validate our method, we built an annotated database containing 5 different human activities. Each activity was performed 3 times by 16 different individuals. For each subject, we captured raw data from 4 IMUs, 4 EMG sensors, and a Kinect® device. Our dataset is publicly available at https://goo.gl/6F82wd.

2.1 Primitive Motions Recognition

Models based on primitive motions are inspired on techniques from human speech analysis [8]. In speech recognition, phrases are generally divided into isolated phonemes. These phoneme models are used as basic blocks in order to build

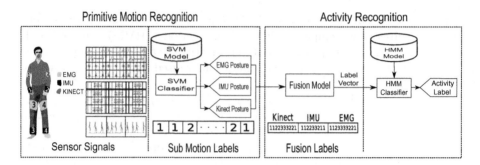

Fig. 1. Overview of the training and classification processes of our proposed approach.

words and phrases in a hierarchical way [10]. Our motion detection model follows a similar idea to that of Zhand et al. [17] in the sense that each activity is represented as a sequence of sub-movements, or primitive motions, generating a unique signature that will be used for classification of the overall activity.

Primitive Motions Encoding. In this work, we propose eight primitive motions to train the HMM system. These motions are: (1) Repose, (2) Partially crouched, (3) Fully crouched, (4) In midair, (5) Quarter rise arm, (6) Three-quarters arm rise, (7) Step forward with right foot and (8) Step forward with left foot.

Feature Extraction. From each sensor modality, a set of features is extracted from the video sequence during a time observation window, which was set experimentally to 3 s. For the Kinect®, the descriptor vector is obtained from the 14 human pivot points. The sensor is able to provide data at 30 samples per second. However, our feature vector is composed of groups of 3 samples, corresponding to an overall rate of 10 samples per second. Given the set of body joints in Cartesian coordinates, all these points are converted to polar coordinates vis-a-vis the center of mass:

$$P_i = [r_1\,\theta_1\,r_2\,\theta_2 \ldots r_{14}\,\theta_{14}], \tag{1}$$

where i is the i-th sample window, with $i = \{1, 2, 3\}$. In addition, the mean m and standard deviation v are computed over all the coordinates. The final feature vector for the Kinect sensor is then defined according to

$$\mathrm{KIT} = [P_1\,P_2\,P_3\,m_x\,m_y\,m_z\,m_r\,m_\theta\,v_x\,v_y\,v_z\,v_r\,v_\theta]. \tag{2}$$

For the IMUs, 4 sensors were attached near the wrists and knees of the subjects. Each IMU provides 30 samples per second. Again, we used the average of 3 samples to compute our features. Therefore, the IMU vector is also available at 10 samples per second. With the IMU data $I_k = [a_x\,a_y\,a_z\,a_\theta\,a_\phi]_{1\times 5}$, where $k = \{1, 2, 3, 4\}$ is the k-th IMU, we compute the following descriptors: (1) Features based on the physical parameters of the human motion [18], and (2) Statistical

Descriptors. The overall IMU descriptor is a combination of the IMU_k descriptor for each of the sensors in the network, i.e.,

$$IMUF = [IMU_1 \, IMU_2 \, IMU_3 \, IMU_4] \, . \tag{3}$$

For the EMGs, we track the activity of 4 body muscles. We obtain the signal E_i from each muscle at a sampling frequency of 2 kHz, where i is the i-th EMG sensor. E_i is segmented by using V_j windows of 200 samples where j is the jth window. Each window V_j is concatenated to form a vector W_i and this vector is characterized by a Daubechies Wavelet transform with 35 orthogonal coefficients and 6 levels, which produces the feature vector $\text{EMG}_{1 \times 1300}$.

Motion Classification. We use three multi-class support vector machines with classification strategy "One-vs-All" with Gaussian kernels to separate the data. The same process is used with the Kinect, IMU, and EMG sensors.

2.2   Activity Recognition

We use our set of primitive motions described in Sect. 2.1 to classify the following activities: (1) Stand still, (2) Squat and stand up, (3) Jump, (4) Raise right hand, and (5) Jog. To classify each activity from this set, the outputs of the three SVMs are used as input to an HMM. An HMM is chosen because it has been successfully used to detect and encode sequences over time (i.e., the ones produced by the SVMs). Deep learning methods can also be explored in a future work.

Hidden Markov Model Classification (HMM). As described in Sect. 2.1, each SVM classifier generates a label that corresponds to the information provided by the different sensors. The vectors EI correspond to the network of IMUs, EK to the Kinect® device, and EE to the EMGs. The data fusion process consists of generating a EF feature vector with the labels from the SVM classifiers. EF is built by concatenating each classifier label during motion capture.

$$EF = [[EK_1 \, EK_2 \ldots EK_{30}] \, [EI_1 \, EI_2 \ldots EI_{30}] \, [EE_1 \, EE_2 \ldots EE_{30}]]_{90 \times 1} \tag{4}$$

2.3   Training and Validation Process

We train our multi-class SVM models using sequential minimal optimization (SMO). For HMM training, we used 24 states and 32 centroids for the construction of the codebook. We evaluate our models using a cross-validation strategy that partitions the database with 70% of the data for training and 30% for evaluation and generate the confusion matrix for each classifier. This process applies a Monte Carlo analysis, where the stop criterion is defined by

$$\|\text{diag}\,(M_k) - \text{diag}\,(M_{k-1})\|_2 < th, \tag{5}$$

where M_k is the confusion matrix at iteration k and th is the error threshold.

3   Results

We show the results to validate the performance of our method as a function of the sensors used to collect the data. Initially, we evaluate the performance of every sensor modality and the different combinations of sensors. The assessment is based on two basic steps: primitive motion analysis and activity recognition analysis. The first step carries out the performance analysis of the SVM classifiers for the proposed primitive motions. The second step validates the human activity classification using an HMM.

Table 1. Traces of the confusion matrices for the primitive motion classification analysis.

Class	Kinect	IMU		EMG	
	All joints	All	For 1, 3 and 4	All	For 1, 3 and 4
C1	86.77 ± 3.79	86.77 ± 0.73	81.33 ± 0.88	72.28 ± 5.83	62.52 ± 5.56
C2	77.57 ± 3.81	78.71 ± 2.10	75.51 ± 2.62	66.51 ± 1.13	67.81 ± 0.26
C3	71.86 ± 8.05	71.46 ± 4.33	69.29 ± 4.60	70.84 ± 4.73	73.57 ± 4.03
C4	89.95 ± 1.46	74.52 ± 0.93	83.87 ± 1.06	71.49 ± 1.33	79.34 ± 1.48
C5	90.47 ± 3.15	76.51 ± 5.25	56.85 ± 5.38	59.43 ± 5.21	45.44 ± 5.05
C6	96.78 ± 1.33	93.07 ± 2.02	0.84 ± 3.53	63.88 ± 2.35	79.03 ± 2.37
C7	75.68 ± 1.95	61.43 ± 2.91	54.68 ± 2.95	50.54 ± 1.84	51.98 ± 1.84
C8	75.63 ± 2.97	57.56 ± 2.73	55.64 ± 2.85	34.08 ± 2.50	55.71 ± 2.51
Average	84.69 ± 3.31	75.00 ± 2.63	59.76 ± 2.98	61.13 ± 3.12	64.43 ± 2.89

3.1   Primitive Motion Analysis

We use the validation approach described in this section to obtain the confusion matrices of the Kinect®, IMU, and EMG sensors. The traces of the recognition confusion matrices of the primitive movements (using all the sensors as well as the minimum number of sensors that guarantees a reliable detection performance) are shown in Table 1. The Kinect® sensor provides the best primitive movement detection results with an average detection value of approximately 85%, which is substantially higher than those of the other sensors. The analysis of the set of IMU sensors demonstrates a comparable performance with the Kinect in the first three primitive movements. While the EMG sensors alone perform relatively poorly, they can still obtain a precision higher than 70% for classes 1, 3 and 4.

We evaluated the performance of the subsets of sensors by systematically removing the features corresponding to each sensor from our classification system. In columns 4 and 6 of Table 1, we report the results obtained from the subsets that showed the best performance. As the table indicates, while removing a single IMU sensor results in a substantial accuracy reduction for class 6 and a more modest reduction for class 5, the other activities remain mostly at the same performance level. The subset of EMG sensors, on the other hand, show comparable performance for most classes.

3.2   Activity Recognition Analysis

Table 2 shows the traces of the confusion matrices for the HMM-based activity recognition for each sensor category. The results correspond to 181 Monte Carlo iterations for each sensor. Our results demonstrate that the Kinect or the IMU sensors alone provide high classification accuracy for all the activities. The EMG sensors show high classification performance for activities 2, 3, 4 and 5. Also shown in the table are the results of 30 Monte Carlo iterations using a single IMU sensor, which demonstrate that it is possible to recognize all the activities with a single sensor.

Table 2. Traces of the confusion matrices for the activity recognition analysis.

Activity	Kinect	IMU		EMG
	All joints	All	For 1	All
1	93.50 ± 10.77	99.80 ± 1.07	100.00 ± 0.00	38.78 ± 16.33
2	90.30 ± 9.06	98.33 ± 3.49	99.49 ± 1.03	90.94 ± 11.23
3	84.96 ± 11.31	96.14 ± 7.09	92.27 ± 9.76	96.16 ± 4.63
4	97.16 ± 7.39	98.43 ± 4.43	99.60 ± 1.02	94.08 ± 3.94
5	94.86 ± 7.90	100.00 ± 0.00	87.34 ± 12.22	89.69 ± 11.07
Average	92.15 ± 9.29	98.18 ± 3.22	95.74 ± 4.81	81.93 ± 8.52

Table 3. Performance comparison for different combinations of sensors.

Sensor group	C1	C2	C3	C4	C5	Average
Kinect®+IMU+EMG	$100.0 \pm$ 0.00%	$99.60 \pm$ 1.53%	$99.62 \pm$ 1.03%	$99.09 \pm$ 1.59%	$95.76 \pm$ 3.36%	$98.81 \pm$ 1.81%
Kinect®+IMU	$100.0 \pm$ 0.00%	$100.0 \pm$ 0.00%	$97.71 \pm$ 2.50%	$97.95 \pm$ 2.36%	$98.39 \pm$ 2.10%	$98.81 \pm$ 1.81%
Kinect®+EMG	$91.00 \pm$ 4.78%	$100.0 \pm$ 0.00%	$98.8 \pm$ 1.82%	$97.68 \pm$ 2.51%	$95.51 \pm$ 3.45%	$96.81 \pm$ 2.93%
IMU+EMG	$100.0 \pm$ 0.00%	$98.14 \pm$ 0.02%	$99.46 \pm$ 1.23%	$99.67 \pm$ 0.96%	$96.65 \pm$ 3.00%	$98.78 \pm$ 1.78%

The results obtained using combined sensors are reported in Table 3, which shows the average value of the main diagonal of the confusion matrices as well as their uncertainty intervals with a confidence rate of 99%. As shown in the table, the Kinect®+IMU+EMG and the Kinect®+IMU combinations show the best overall performance, with a success rate of 100% for class 1 in both cases and comparable results for the other classes. By comparing these results with those shown in Table 2, we can see that combining the Kinect® and EMG sensors improves the activity recognition performance by 4.66% with respect to the Kinect® sensor alone and 14.88% for the EMG sensor. The integration of the IMU and EMG sensors yields a similar performance improvement.

4   Conclusions

We developed an automatic method for human activity recognition based on multi-modal data fusion from a network of IMU and EMG sensors and a Kinect® sensor. Our approach uses multi-class support vector machines for primitive movement detection and subsequently classifies the activity according to the sequences provided by the SVM outputs over a time interval using an HMM. This work studies the contribution of each sensor to the recognition task by evaluating the performance of different sensor configurations. To perform robust activity recognition, it is necessary to use all the sensors due to the potential failures that these devices might show during the process. These failures include partial occlusions or self-occlusions from the Kinect® or connection losses in the wireless communication systems, which are commonly used to acquire data from the IMU or EMG sensors. Multi-modal information from every sensor might mitigate mistakes caused by such failures. The proposed approach was tested in an annotated dataset that was created specifically for this work, because there was no publicly available database with synchronized recording of these three sensor modalities. We made the dataset publicly available to facilitate comparisons and accelerate the research in this area. In the future, the database must be expanded to validate our approach on a wider set of activities.

Acknowledgments. The authors want to thank the support from the Master's program in Electrical Engineering at Universidad Tecnologica de Pereira.

References

1. Bayat, A., Pomplun, M., Tran, D.A.: A study on human activity recognition using accelerometer data from smartphones. In: The 11th International Conference on Mobile Systems and Pervasive Computing (2014)
2. de Castro, D.M.: Aplicación Android para el reconocimiento automático de activi-dades físicas en tiempo real. Master's thesis, Universidad Carlos III de Madrid Departamento de Informática (2012)
3. Leightley, D., Darby, J., Li, B., McPhee, J.S., Yap, M.H.: Human activity recog-nition for physical rehabilitation. In: 2013 IEEE International Conference on Sys-tems, Man, and Cybernetics (SMC), pp. 261–266, October 2013
4. Destelle, F., et al.: Low-cost accurate skeleton tracking based on fusion of kinect and wearable inertial sensors. In: 2014 Proceedings of the 22nd European Signal Processing Conference (EUSIPCO), pp. 371–375, September 2014
5. Feng, S., Murray-Smith, R.: Fusing Kinect sensor and inertial sensors with multi-rate Kalman filter. In: Data Fusion & Target Tracking 2014: Algorithms and Appli-cations (DF&TT 2014), pp. 1–8 (2014)

6. Ferguson, S., Dunlop, R.G.: Grasp recognition from myoelectric signals. In: Australasian Conference on Robotics and Automation, November 2002
7. Gaglio, S., Re, G.L., Morana, M.: Human activity recognition process using 3-D posture data. IEEE Trans. Hum. Mach. Syst. **45**(5), 586–597 (2015)
8. Ghasemzadeh, H., Barnes, J., Guenterberg, E., Jafari, R.: A phonological expression for physical movement monitoring in body sensor networks. In: 5th IEEE International Conference on Mobile Ad Hoc and Sensor Systems, MASS 2008, pp. 58–68, September 2008
9. Helten, T., Muller, M., Seidel, H.P., Theobalt, C.: Real-time body tracking with one depth camera and inertial sensors. In: 2013 IEEE International Conference on Computer Vision (ICCV), pp. 1105–1112, December 2013
10. Huang, X., Acero, A., Hon, H.W.: Spoken Language Processing: A Guide to Theory, Algorithm, and System Development, 1st edn. Prentice Hall PTR, Upper Saddle River (2001)
11. Kang, W.J., Shiu, J.R., Cheng, C.K., Lai, J.S., Tsao, H.W., Kuo, T.S.: The application of cepstral coefficients and maximum likelihood method in emg pattern recognition [movements classification]. IEEE Trans. Biomed. Eng. **42**(8), 777–785 (1995)
12. Frank, K., Nadales, M.J.V., Robertson, P., Angerman, M.: Reliable real-time recognition of motion related human activities using MEMS inertial sensors. In: 23rd International Technical Meeting of the Satellite Division of the Institute of Navigation (2010)
13. Bocksch, M., Seitz, J., Jahn, J.: Pedestrian activity classification to improve human tracking and localization. In: Fourth International Conference on Indoor Positioning and Indoor Navigation (2013)
14. Pancholi, S., Agarwal, R.: Development of low cost EMG data acquisition system for Arm Activities Recognition. In: 2016 International Conference on Advances in Computing, Communications and Informatics (ICACCI), pp. 2465–2469, September 2016
15. Tao, G., Archambault, P., Levin, M.: Evaluation of Kinect skeletal tracking in a virtual reality rehabilitation system for upper limb hemiparesis. In: 2013 International Conference on Virtual Rehabilitation (ICVR), pp. 164–165, August 2013
16. Wu, H., Pan, W., Xiong, X., Xu, S.: Human activity recognition based on the combined svm amp; hmm. In: 2014 IEEE International Conference on Information and Automation (ICIA), pp. 219–224, July 2014
17. Zhang, M., Sawchuk, A.A.: Motion primitive-based human activity recognition using a bag-of-features approach. In: ACM SIGHIT International Health Informatics Symposium, IHI 2012, pp. 631–640. ACM, New York (2012)
18. Zhang, M., Sawchuk, A.A.: A feature selection-based framework for human activity recognition using wearable multimodal sensors. In: International Conference on Body Area Networks (BodyNets), Beijing, China (2011)
19. Zhang, Z., Liu, Y., Li, A., Wang, M.: A novel method for user-defined human posture recognition using Kinect. In: 7th International Congress on Image and Signal Processing (CISP), pp. 736–740, October 2014

Using Scene Context to Improve Action Recognition

Juarez Monteiro[(⊠)], Roger Granada, Felipe Meneguzzi,
and Rodrigo Coelho Barros

School of Technology, Pontifícia Universidade Católica do Rio Grande do Sul,
Av. Ipiranga, 6681, Porto Alegre, RS 90619-900, Brazil
{juarez.monteiro,roger.granada}@acad.pucrs.br,
{felipe.meneguzzi,rodrigo.barros}@pucrs.br

Abstract. Recently action recognition has been used for a variety of applications such as surveillance, smart homes, and in-home elder monitoring. Such applications usually focus on recognizing human actions without taking into account the different scenarios where the action occurs. In this paper, we propose a two-stream architecture that considers not only the movements to identify the action, but also the context scene where the action is performed. Experiments show that the scene context may improve the recognition of certain actions. Our proposed architecture is tested against baselines and the standard two-stream network.

Keywords: Action recognition · Convolutional Neural Networks · Neural networks

1 Introduction

Action recognition is one of the promising tasks in the computer vision area and has been employed in many tasks such as surveillance and assistance of the sick and disabled. Although recognizing actions is a trivial task for the human being, the automation of such task is particularly challenging in the real physical world, since it involves understanding the not only the movements that are being performed but also the context in which the action is happening. In this sense, the contextual information plays an important role, giving cues to disambiguate actions that are performed with the same movements. For example, observing a scene context, a human being can easily identify whether a swing movement is being performed in a tennis or a baseball match. To perform such task autonomously, we need an approach that is able to identify not only the moving parts of the image, but also the background of the image to identify the scene context.

In this paper, we address the problem of recognizing actions from videos by using a two-stream architecture, where two convolutional neural networks run in parallel, merging their features in a late fusion approach. Inspired by Silva *et al.* [12] that improve the object recognition by using the scene context, we

© Springer Nature Switzerland AG 2019
R. Vera-Rodriguez et al. (Eds.): CIARP 2018, LNCS 11401, pp. 954–961, 2019.
https://doi.org/10.1007/978-3-030-13469-3_110

build a two-stream neural network architecture where a stream performs the action recognition and another stream improves this recognition by identifying the context where the action occurs. We perform experiments using our approach in two datasets for action recognition and compare our results with baselines and the state-of-the-art approaches.

This paper is organized as follows. Section 2 describes the related work and introduces the standard two-stream architecture and how it has been employed so far. Section 3 details our deep neural architecture based on two-stream for action recognition, whereas Sect. 4 presents all settings and data we use for assessing the performance of our proposed approach. Results are presented and discussed in Sect. 5 along with a comparison with baselines and the state-of-the-art results for each dataset. We finish this paper with our conclusions and future work directions in Sect. 6.

2   Related Work

Advances in hardware and greater availability of data have allowed deep learning algorithms such as Convolutional Neural Networks (CNNs) [5] to consistently improve on the state-of-the-art results when dealing with image-based tasks such as object recognition [7], detection, and semantic segmentation [3]. Extensions of CNN representations to the action recognition task in videos have been proposed in several recent works [8,13,15]. For example, Wang et al. [15] apply dynamic tracking attention model (DTAM), which is composed by a CNN and a Long-Short Term Memory (LSTM) to perform human action recognition in videos. Their architecture uses the CNN to extract features from images and the LSTM to deal with the sequential information of the actions. DTAM uses local dynamic tracking to identify moving objects, and global dynamic tracking to estimate the motion of the camera and correct the weights of the motion attention model.

Simonyan and Zisserman [13] propose the two-stream convolutional network architecture, which is composed by two streams running in parallel with a late fusion to merge both streams. The idea behind the two-stream is to mimic the visual cortex, which contains the ventral stream (responsible for object recognition) and the dorsal stream (responsible for recognizing motion) as two separate pathways. Thus, videos can be decomposed into spatial and temporal components: the spatial one that carries information about scene context, and the temporal one that conveys the motion across frames, indicating the movement of the observer and objects. Simonyan and Zisserman use the raw images in the spatial stream and pre-computed optical flow features in the temporal stream. Using a two-stream architecture with two different CNNs, Monteiro et al. [8] perform action recognition in a small egocentric dataset. They affirm that a two-stream architecture achieves better results than a single stream because each stream extracts different features from the same image. The extracted features are then merged by a late score fusion using a Support Vector Machine (SVM).

Scene recognition is a fundamental problem in computer vision and recently has been receiving an increasing attention [12,16,17]. As Wang et al. [16] affirm, a scene provides rich semantic information of the global structure providing a meaningful context. As scene context, we can understand as the place in which the objects seat, *i.e.*, the background environment where actions occur. Unlike Monteiro *et al.* [8] and Simonyan and Zisserman [13], in this work, we associate the identification of the action with the scene context since we believe that the scene context may give interesting clues about the action that is being performed.

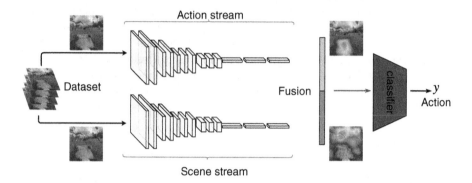

Fig. 1. Two-stream architecture composed by a stream to recognize actions and a stream to recognize the context scene with a late fusion.

3   Recognizing Actions with Scene Context

To address the contextual awareness on action recognition, our approach aims to use the context of the scenes by fusing the information of the background with the information that identifies the action being performed in a two-stream architecture [13]. Our architecture is composed by a stream containing a CNN to identify the action happening in the current frame, and a CNN to identify where (scene context) the action is happening in the current frame, as illustrated in Fig. 1. The idea of this architecture is that the CNN responsible for the action stream focuses on the movements that are being performed to identify an action, while the CNN responsible for the scene stream focuses on the background where the action happens. For example, consider two actions that contain similar movements, such as baseball swing and tennis swing. While the action stream may identify the swing performed in the action, the scene stream identifies the context where the swing is happening, increasing the chance to correctly classify the action. Features from both streams are connected in a late fusion approach and a classifier predicts the action performed on the input image.

Although our architecture allows different networks in each stream, we use two VGG-16 networks [14]. In order to extract features from the background environment (Scene stream), we use the weights of a CNN pre-trained using the Places365 [17] dataset, which contains only images with scenes. For the Action stream, we fine-tune a version of the VGG-16 with the weights pre-trained on the 1.2-million-image ILSVRC 2012 ImageNet dataset [10]. Finally, we train a multi-class Support Vector Machine (SVM) using the concatenation of both streams for the final classification.

Fig. 2. Examples of frames from each class of DogCentric (a) and UCF-11 (b) datasets.

4   Experiments

In this section, we describe the datasets and the main implementation details applied to our experiments.

4.1   Dataset

Our experiments are performed using two freely available datasets that contain a single action in each video. We select the datasets because they contain different characteristics: dataset containing an egocentric viewpoint of actions performed by dogs and a dataset containing a third-person viewpoint performed by humans. We detail each dataset as follows.

DogCentric Activity dataset[1] [4] consists of 209 videos containing 10 different action performed by 4 dogs as illustrated in Fig. 2 (a). The dataset contains first-person videos taken from an egocentric animal viewpoint, *i.e.*, a wearable camera mounted on dogs' back records outdoor and indoor scenes, which are very challenging due to their strong camera motion. Following Monteiro *et al.* [9], we randomly select half of the videos of each action to the test set and the rest of the videos are separated into training and validation sets. Validation set contains 20% of the videos and the rest is separated to the training set.

UCF YouTube Action dataset[2] (hereafter called UCF-11) [6] consists of 1,600 videos extracted from YouTube containing 11 actions as illustrated in Fig. 2 (b). Each video has 320 × 240 pixels and was converted to a frame rate of 29.97 fps and annotations were done accordingly, containing a single action associated with the entire video. As performed by Monteiro *et al.* [9], we divided the UCF-11 dataset into train, validation and test sets.

4.2   Network Settings

In this work, we only train the Action stream, since we use the Scene stream as a feature extractor from a pre-trained version of the CNN. All deep models developed in this work (including baselines) are implemented using *Keras*[3] and

---

[1] http://robotics.ait.kyushu-u.ac.jp/~hyumi/db/first_dog.html.
[2] http://crcv.ucf.edu/data/UCF_YouTube_Action.php.
[3] https://keras.io.

TensorFlow[4] frameworks. We pre-trained the Action stream CNN using the ImageNet dataset with weights being directly loaded from Keras core library. Training phase performs iterations using mini-batches of 128 images, applying mini-batch stochastic gradient with momentum (0.9), and using rectified linear unit (ReLU) as the activation of each convolution. We subtract all pixels from each image by the mean of each pixel from all training images. For all networks, we perform hyperparameter optimization using a grid search for *dropout* on the fully-connected layers and *learning rate* hyperparameters, since they are commonly changed when trying to learn a deep model. Due to space constraints, we show the results only for the setting that achieves the highest results in validation data. The best configuration for the Action stream contains 0.5 of *dropout* and 5e-4 of *learning rate* for the UCF-11 dataset and 0.95 of *dropout* and 5e-3 of *learning rate* for the DogCentric dataset. We limit the number of epochs to 30 with applying early stopping, where most of our experiments took no longer than 15 epochs to finish. The Scene stream contains a VGG-16 using weights of a CNN[5] pre-trained in the Places-365 [17] dataset. For the classification phase, we use the Crammer and Singer [1] implementation of the SVM from *scikit-learn*[6] with the default parameters.

4.3 Baselines

As deep learning approaches have become the state-of-the-art of different computer vision tasks [3,7,8,15], we use as baselines the single stream networks, *i.e.*, only the Action stream and only the Scene stream, and the standard two-stream [13] configuration containing the Action stream and a Temporal stream. For the standard two-stream baseline, the Action stream has the same configuration of the Action stream in our approach. The Temporal stream in the two-stream baseline contains a dense optical flow representation [2] of adjacent frames, *i.e.*, vectors containing both horizontal and vertical displacements, regarding all points within frames. In order to generate the final image for each sequence of frames, we combine the 2-channel optical flow vectors and associate color to their magnitude and direction. Magnitudes are represented by colors and directions through hue values. The training phase of the Temporal stream follows the same settings as the Action stream, but the hyperparameters selected by grid search (*dropout* and *learning rate*). The best configuration for the Temporal stream contains 0.5 of *dropout* and 5e-3 of *learning rate* for both datasets. Due to space constraints, we do not insert in the paper the results achieved with the validation set, but these results, as well as our code, are freely available on our project's website[7].

---

[4] https://www.tensorflow.org.

[5] https://github.com/GKalliatakis/Keras-VGG16-places365.

[6] http://scikit-learn.org/.

[7]   https://github.com/jrzmnt/PlacesInAction.

Table 1. Accuracy ($\mathcal{A}$), Precision ($\mathcal{P}$), Recall ($\mathcal{R}$) and F-measure ($\mathcal{F}$) achieved by the baselines, our approach and the state-of-the-art results.

		$\mathcal{A}$	$\mathcal{P}$	$\mathcal{R}$	$\mathcal{F}$
UCF-11	Action stream	0.71	0.70	0.71	0.70
	Scene stream	0.69	0.68	0.69	0.67
	Two-stream (as in [13])	0.71	0.73	0.71	0.71
	Our approach	**0.75**	**0.78**	**0.75**	**0.75**
	DTAM [15]	0.90	–	–	–
	Visual-DTAM [15]	0.91	–	–	–
DogCentric	Action stream	0.54	0.59	0.54	0.54
	Scene stream	0.48	0.54	0.48	0.48
	Two-stream (as in [13])	0.54	0.62	0.54	0.54
	Our approach	**0.53**	**0.58**	**0.53**	**0.53**
	PoT+ITF [11]	0.75	–	–	–
	2 CNNs-SVM-PP [8]	0.76	0.74	0.76	0.75

5   Results and Discussion

To evaluate our proposal and compare with baselines, we compared the output of each network using the test set. Table 1 shows the accuracy ($\mathcal{A}$), precision ($\mathcal{P}$), recall ($\mathcal{R}$) and F-measure ($\mathcal{F}$) scores for all experiments in each dataset.

In Table 1, we can see that the combination of Scene stream with Action stream performed by our approach increased the results achieved by the Action stream alone in the UCF-11 dataset. The addition of features from the background (Scene stream) increased the accuracy by 4% points and the precision by 8% points indicating that the context of the scene is helpful to identify the action that is being performed. The best results on this dataset are achieved in *Diving* and *Horse riding* actions, with 85% and 81% of accuracy respectively. On the other hand, the approach achieved the lowest accuracy for *Soccer juggling*, indicating that the action may not be dependent on the background. Checking images of this dataset, we can see that the *Soccer juggling* is performed in different places, thus confirming that the scene context is not relevant to identify this action.

Unlike the results achieved on UCF-11, when testing on the DogCentric dataset, our approach seems to be ineffective. The results achieved in the Dog-Centric dataset may be justified since usually the actions performed by a dog are not related to a fixed background as the actions performed by different sports. In fact, the actions that have some relation to the background, such as *Car*, where the dog is outside waiting for a car to pass by, the precision achieved 90%. The second highest precision score was achieved by the action *Drink*, where the background always contains a water bowl in which the dog drinks water. Actions that do not depend on the background, such as *Look left*, *Look right* or *Shake* achieve low precision scores 21%, 14% and 17% respectively.

Above the results achieved by our approach in Table 1, we can see that the baselines achieved lower scores for all measures when compared with our approach in the UCF-11 dataset, indicating that the scene context may improve the action recognition. A comparison with the standard two-stream baseline suggests that the identification of the scene plays an important role when compared with the optical flow representation. Due to the camera movement on the back of the dog in DogCentric dataset, the scene identification is not very effective. The same problem occurs with the optical flow generation in a standard two-stream. Therefore, both approaches achieved approximately the same results when compared with the Action stream alone.

Below our approach in Table 1, we present the results achieved by the state-of-the-art for each dataset. Values containing a dash are not reported by the authors. As illustrated in Table 1, the results achieved by our approach are modest when compared with the results achieved by the state-of-the-art. However, it is important to note that our intention in this paper was not to achieve the state-of-the-art results, but instead, verify whether the scene context improves the action recognition. Wang *et al.* [15] achieved the state-of-the-art results for UCF-11 dataset using a combination of visual attention with dynamic tracking attention model (DTAM). Their approach uses a combination of CNN and LSTM as an attention mechanism, in order to capture the temporal aspect of an action. Monteiro *et al.* [8] uses the DogCentric dataset to apply a two-stream approach containing two different CNNs and a post-processing step which consists of smoothing the predicted classes by assigning to a target frame the majority voting of all frames within a window. This smoothing process intends to eliminate a few correctly predicted classes when they are in the middle of other classes.

6   Conclusions and Future Work

In this work, we developed an architecture for action recognition based on a two-stream CNN architecture. Unlike the standard two-stream architecture, our approach includes a stream focusing on recognizing actions and the other stream focusing on recognizing the context of the scene. Finally, we performed a late fusion using the concatenation of the features extracted from both streams. We performed experiments to validate our architecture and showed that our approach achieves better results when compared with the baselines composed by the streams separately, and a standard two-stream using optical flow in the temporal stream. A preliminary analysis demonstrates the importance of taking into account the context where the action occurs. Our intention in this paper was not to achieve the state-of-the-art results, but check whether the scene identification plays an important role in the action recognition. Thus, in a future work, we intend to expand our architecture by changing the action stream by the state-of-the-art algorithm to recognize actions taking into account the temporal aspect of the video.

Acknowledgement. The authors would like to thank CAPES/FAPERGS and Motorola Mobility for partially funding this research. We gratefully acknowledge the support of NVIDIA Corporation with the donation of the Titan Xp GPU used for this research.

References

1. Crammer, K., Singer, Y.: On the algorithmic implementation of multiclass kernel-based vector machines. JMLR **2**, 265–292 (2001)
2. Farnebäck, G.: Two-frame motion estimation based on polynomial expansion. In: Proceedings of SCIA 2003, pp. 363–370 (2003)
3. Ge, W., Yang, S., Yu, Y.: Multi-evidence filtering and fusion for multi-label classification, object detection and semantic segmentation based on weakly supervised learning. In: Proceedings of CVPR 2018, pp. 1277–1286 (2018)
4. Iwashita, Y., Takamine, A., Kurazume, R., Ryoo, M.: First-person animal activity recognition from egocentric videos. In: Proceedings ICPR 2014, pp. 4310–4315 (2014)
5. LeCun, Y., Bottou, L., Bengio, Y., Haffner, P.: Gradient-based learning applied to document recognition. Proc. IEEE **86**(11), 2278–2324 (1998)
6. Liu, J., Luo, J., Shah, M.: Recognizing realistic actions from videos "in the wild". In: Proceedings of CVPR 2009, pp. 1996–2003 (2009)
7. Lu, C., et al.: Beyond holistic object recognition: enriching image understanding with part states. In: Proceedings of CVPR 2018, pp. 6955–6963 (2018)
8. Monteiro, J., Aires, J.P., Granada, R., Barros, R.C., Meneguzzi, F.: Virtual guide dog: an application to support visually-impaired people through deep convolutional neural networks. In: Proceedings of IJCNN 2017, pp. 2267–2274 (2017)
9. Monteiro, J., Granada, R., Aires, J.P., Barros, R.: Evaluating the feasibility of deep learning for action recognition in small datasets. In: Proceedings of IJCNN 2018, pp. 1596–1603 (2018)
10. Russakovsky, O., et al.: Imagenet large scale visual recognition challenge. Int. J. Comput. Vis. **115**(3), 211–252 (2015)
11. Ryoo, M.S., Rothrock, B., Matthies, L.: Pooled motion features for first-person videos. In: Proceedings of CVPR 2015, pp. 896–904 (2015)
12. Silva, L.P., Granada, R., Monteiro, J., Ruiz, D.: Using scene context to improve object recognition. In: Proceedings of the KDMiLe 2017, pp. 105–112 (2017)
13. Simonyan, K., Zisserman, A.: Two-stream convolutional networks for action recognition in videos. In: Proceedings of NIPS 2014, pp. 568–576 (2014)
14. Simonyan, K., Zisserman, A.: Very deep convolutional networks for large-scale image recognition. arXiv preprint arXiv:1409.1556 (2014)
15. Wang, C.Y., Chiang, C.C., Ding, J.J., Wang, J.C.: Dynamic tracking attention model for action recognition. In: Proceedings of ICASSP 2017, pp. 1617–1621 (2017)
16. Wang, Z., Wang, L., Wang, Y., Zhang, B., Qiao, Y.: Weakly supervised patchnets: describing and aggregating local patches for scene recognition. IEEE Trans. Image Process. **26**(4), 2028–2041 (2017)
17. Zhou, B., Lapedriza, A., Khosla, A., Oliva, A., Torralba, A.: Places: a 10 million image database for scene recognition. IEEE Trans. Pattern Anal. Mach. Intell. **PP**(99), 1–14 (2017)

Empirical Evaluation of the BCOC Method on Multi-Domain Sentiment Analysis Data Sets

Brian Keith Norambuena[(✉)] and Claudio Meneses Villegas

Departamento de Ingeniería de Sistemas y Computación,
Universidad Católica del Norte, Av. Angamos 0610, Antofagasta, Chile
{brian.keith,cmeneses}@ucn.cl

Abstract. Sentiment analysis and opinion mining is an area that has experienced considerable growth over the last decade. This area of research attempts to determine the feelings, opinions, emotions, among other things, of people on something or someone. In particular, this article discusses the task of determining the polarity of reviews using an ordinal classification technique called Barycentric Coordinates for Ordinal Classification (BCOC). The aim of this analysis is to explore the viability of the application of BCOC on the field of sentiment analysis. This method is based on the hypothesis that the ordinal classes can be represented geometrically inside a convex polygon on the real plane by using barycentric coordinates. A set of experiments were conducted to evaluate the capability and performance of the proposed approach relative to a baseline, using accuracy as the general measure of performance. In general, the method is competitive with the baseline. For sentiment analysis with four classes, the results show improvements in the overall accuracy.

Keywords: Opinion mining · Ordinal classification ·
Sentiment analysis · Barycentric coordinates

1 Introduction

Opinions are central to almost all human activities due to their crucial influence on people's behavior. Every time that there is a need to make a decision, human beings seek to know other people's opinions. In the real world, companies and organizations want to know the public's opinion about their products and services. Moreover, shoppers want to know what other customers think about a product before purchasing it. In the past, people turned to their friends and family for opinions, whereas companies relied on surveys or focus groups. However, nowadays the explosive growth of social media and the increase in the available sources of data has made individuals and organizations use the information provided by these to support their decision-making process. The field of sentiment analysis, also known as opinion mining [6] has been developing in this context.

© Springer Nature Switzerland AG 2019
R. Vera-Rodriguez et al. (Eds.): CIARP 2018, LNCS 11401, pp. 962–970, 2019.
https://doi.org/10.1007/978-3-030-13469-3_111

One of the main tasks in sentiment analysis is determining the polarity, though it should be noted that sentiment analysis encompasses several other tasks apart from polarity determination. This can be seen as a classification problem in general, as most of the literature does. The most common approaches to deal with this task are support vector machines and the naive Bayes classifier [8]. A literature review shows that most works focus on binary classification; the multi-class case has not been exhaustively studied [8].

Most works on determining polarity use a binary classification approach [8]. Other studies that use multi-class classification with five levels apply regression methods and then a transformation into the corresponding class [6]. However, recent works such as [10] illustrate that multi-class classification of polarity at the full document level remains elusive, even when using the deep learning approach proposed in that article.

This work seeks to extend the evaluation of the BCOC method [5], since it this method showed promising results in its first evaluation. However, more extensive experimentation is required in order to assess the value of this proposal. Thus, this paper seeks to fill this gap by providing an evaluation of the BCOC method on several sentiment analysis data sets.

In most cases, determining the polarity can be seen as a task of ordinal classification (in the multi-class case, because in the binary case order has no relevance), where the ordering of the different classes corresponds to the natural order provided by their different labels (i.e., the order of the classes is: very negative, negative, neutral, positive and very positive). In spite of the ordinal nature of the problem and that ordinal classification methods have been widely studied, upon reviewing the literature it can be noted that these characteristics of the data have not yet been exploited exhaustively to obtain better classifiers.

The term ordinal classification makes reference to the supervised learning problem of classification where classes have a natural order imposed on them due to the characteristics of the concept studied. When the problem has, in fact, an ordinal nature, it would be expected that this order would also be present in the input space [10]. In contrast to nominal classification, there is an ordinal relationship among the categories and it is different from regression in that the possible number of ranks is finite and the exact differences between each rank are not defined. In this way, ordinal classification lies somewhere between nominal classification and regression [9]. Determining if the problem has an ordinal nature requires knowledge of the domain and problem themselves.

Most of the methods in the field of sentiment analysis correspond to techniques for nominal data, namely, data in which the class labels belong to a set with no natural order. In contrast to this approach, the problem can be tackled with ordinal classification methods (sometimes called ordinal regression), which lies in a middle ground between classic classification and regression [11].

In a problem of authentic ordinal nature, this order is also expected to be present in the input space [4]. Defining a space where the ordinal nature of the data is evident could prove useful for the functioning of a classifier. The hypothesis behind the proposed method is based on the intuition that exploiting the ordinal nature of the classes should bring about a positive effect in a classifier's performance, in particular in problems of multi-class classification.

2   Description of the BCOC Method

In this section the BCOC method is described, taking as reference the original proposal [5]. The central idea of this method arises from the triangular representation used by SentiWordNet 3.0 to model the different terms [1] and could be seen as one possible generalization of it.

The BCOC method uses a barycentric coordinates system [3] as its basis to represent the input and to carry out the classification, this representation gives the method its name. It should be noted that the coordinate transformation is a simple mathematical function. Intuitively, this barycentric coordinates representation is much closer to the structure of opinions. In a certain way, this is implicit in the representation used by SentiWordNet 3.0.

While the triangle could be considered for a problem of 3 classes, the method generalizes to a problem with n classes, taking as a base the case of $n = 3$. While the idea originates from the representation of terms in a sentiment analysis lexicon, the notion is general enough to be used in other classification contexts, given that the labels have an ordinal structure.

The BCOC method is based on the use of the vertices of a convex polygon inscribed in a semi-circumference to represent the different classes. An example can be seen in Fig. 1. Note that the order of the classes is preserved by the relation of distance between the points that represent them. It is clear that the class "−−" is more distant from "++" than from "−" or "+". This is easily confirmed by the geometric intuition of the representation and it is easy to prove by applying the triangle inequality from linear algebra and elementary geometry.

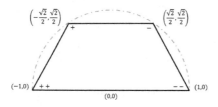

Fig. 1. Representation of four ordinal classes.

The method is based on the construction of n classifiers using a one-vs-all approach. Using these classifiers, an estimate of the probability of belonging to each class must be obtained. The results of these classifiers are transformed into a geometric representation and are then classified using a new classifier that is trained in function of the new representation.

Each class $C_i(i = 1, ..., n)$ is associated with a point x_i which corresponds to a vertex in a convex polygon of n sides (as seen in the example of Fig. 1), then the system of barycentric coordinates is utilized to obtain the position of the example (taking into account the result of all classifiers) within the polygon. Each point x_i can be determined using the formula in Eq. 1. Which generates the vertices of a n-sided polygon inscribed in a semi-circumference. The point $(1, 0)$ is associated with the lowest class and the point $(-1, 0)$ with the highest class with respect to the order of the labels.

$$x_i = \left(\cos \left[\frac{\pi(i-1)}{n-1} \right], \sin \left[\frac{\pi(i-1)}{n-1} \right] \right), \quad i = 1, ..., n \tag{1}$$

Given an example from the data set, a probability p_i is generated for each class i from the lower level classifiers. This probability represents the chance that the current instance belongs to class i (obtained in a one-vs-all fashion). Due to the fact that each probability is obtained using independent classifiers, the sum of the obtained probabilities will not necessarily add up to 1. However, the definition of barycentric coordinates requires that the sum of the weights of each point add up to 1 [3]. Therefore, it is necessary to normalize the resulting probabilities using Eq. 2.

$$\lambda_i = \frac{p_i}{\sum_{j=1}^{n} p_j}, \quad i = 1, ..., n \tag{2}$$

This normalized coefficient is denoted by λ_i and represents the weight of the class i for the current instance. These coefficients in turn correspond with the barycentric coordinates themselves and can be turned directly into a point in the plane inside the convex polygon. According to the generalized version of barycentric coordinates, the formula to obtain the final representation of each point inside a convex polygon is shown in Eq. 3.

$$x = \sum_{i=1}^{n} \lambda_i \cdot x_i = \frac{\sum_{i=1}^{n} p_i \cdot x_i}{\sum_{i=1}^{n} p_i} \tag{3}$$

The point x is finally fed into an additional classifier that is in charge of determining the class. In the exceptional case when $\sum_{i=0}^{n} p_i = 0$, in order to avoid division by zero, x is assigned to the centroid of the polygon. It should be noted that this is equivalent to the case where all $p_i = 1$, but with the assigned classes reversed, in both cases, the result will be assigned to the centroid.

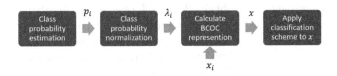

Fig. 2. Process flow of the BCOC method.

The general process flow of the BCOC method is represented in Fig. 2. The training required before applying BCOC can be summarized as follows:

1. For each class train a one-vs-all classifier that can provide probability estimates.
2. For each instance in the data set estimate the class probabilities using the previous classifiers.
3. For each instance in the data set normalize the class probabilities according to Eq. 2.
4. For each instance obtain the new representation in the BCOC two-dimensional space using Eq. 3.
5. Train a multi-class classifier using the new feature space as input.

The application of the BCOC method on a test data set is similar:

1. For each instance in the data set estimate the class probabilities using the previously trained one-vs-all classifiers.
2. For each instance in the data set normalize the class probabilities according to Eq. 2.
3. For each instance obtain the new representation in the BCOC two-dimensional space using Eq. 3.
4. Apply the final multi-class classifier on the new feature space.

3 Materials and Methods

The present section describes the data sets used, the evaluation metrics utilized and the preprocessing of the data sets. The method is evaluated in the task of determining sentiment polarity on various domains, using the Multi-Domain Sentiment Data Set (version 2.0) from the works of Blitzer et al. [2]. This multi-domain data set contains different kinds of reviews. All the data sets have four classes (very negative, negative, positive and very positive) and there is no neutral class. Also, the 2.0 version of the data set has several more domains than the four used in the original work [2].

Standard preprocessing techniques (tokenization, stop-word filtering, and stemming) are applied. Afterwards, a representation is obtained using TF-IDF. The final representation is obtained by applying LSA [6] (using the $n = 100$ most important components, as recommended by scikit-learn documentation [7]).

Regarding the evaluation of the methods, a 10-fold cross-validation approach is utilized, with folds fixed within a domain for the different algorithms. In particular, the overall accuracy obtained by each one of the classifiers generated by the 10-fold cross validation is used as the main metric. Even though accuracy is a simple metric and does not take into account all the aspects of the classification, it allows obtaining a useful estimate to evaluate the performance attained.

The implementation of the methods was carried out in Python using the scikit-learn library [7]. Naive Bayes (NB), Linear Support Vector Classification (SVC) and Ordinal Logistic Regression (LR) methods (adapted for the multi-class case) are used as a comparison baseline. While both NB and SVC are not specialized in ordinal classification, their results on ordinal data sets are competitive with those obtained using more specialized methods, thus they provide a starting point for evaluation. These two methods have been selected because of their wide use in sentiment analysis [8]. On the other hand, LR has been selected due to its innate ability to handle ordinal data sets.

When this method was first introduced, it was only tested against nominal classifiers (NB and SVC) and the selected architectures could have been improved. Thus, this work seeks to improve previous works [5]. Regarding the BCOC method, two architectures are used: NB-LR and LR-LR. The first uses NB classifiers in the lower level and an LR classifier in the superior level (in contrast with the original paper that used a linear support vector machine for the superior level). The second architecture will use both LR in the lower level and the superior level. It is important to note that logistic regression was not evaluated in the previous work, and thus, its effects remain unknown. As in the original proposal [5], the inferior level classifiers are parameterized in the same way as individual classifiers used in the baseline. The superior level classifier is parameterized with the default values of the scikit-learn library.

4   Results and Discussion

Table 1 shows the results obtained on the data sets provided by Blitzer et al. [2]. For an easier presentation of results, the data sets have been grouped into four distinct categories:

- **Data sets with less than 1k instances**: for these data sets, the analysis of results shows no improvements in the case of *automotive* and *tools_&_hardware*. However, there are marginal improvements when the BCOC method is applied in the case of *musical_instruments* and *office_products*. However, due to the small size of these data sets, the variability of these accuracy results makes them less reliable.
- **Data sets with more than 1k instances and less than 5k instances**: for these data sets there are mostly improvements in the results when using the BCOC approach, however this increase of the average accuracy is, in general, not statistically significant. In particular, improvements were found in the *baby, beauty, cellphones & service, gourmet food, grocery* and *outdoor living* data sets. On the other hand, for the data sets of *jewelry & watches, magazines*, and *software* no improvements were found using the proposed BCOC architecture.
- **Data sets with more than 5k instances and less than 10k instances**: for these data sets, the analysis of results found mostly marginal improvements. In particular, the *apparel, camera & photo* and *computer & video games* data sets showed slight improvements in accuracy, while the *health & personal care* and *sports & outdoors* did not present favorable results.
- **Data sets with more than 10k instances**: for these data sets, all the accuracy results (*dvd, electronics, kitchen & housewares, music, toys & games* and *video*) showed at least marginal improvements when using the proposed BCOC architecture.

Table 1. Accuracy (%) results obtained for the baseline and the proposed BCOC architectures on the different data sets.

Data sets	Size	Baseline			BCOC architectures	
		Naive Bayes	Linear SVC	LR	NB-LR	LR-LR
Apparel	9246	64.54 ± 1.99	68.47 ± 2.09	69.53 ± 1.43	64.65 ± 1.54	**70.12 ± 1.49**
Automotive	736	55.03 ± 7.22	62.75 ± 5.53	**63.18 ± 5.28**	57.09 ± 6.32	63.05 ± 3.76
Baby	4256	58.18 ± 2.12	63.98 ± 1.68	64.59 ± 2.09	58.76 ± 1.90	**65.11 ± 3.56**
Beauty	2884	66.92 ± 2.87	71.15 ± 1.78	71.21 ± 2.53	66.82 ± 2.41	**71.84 ± 1.81**
Camera & photo	7408	60.92 ± 1.45	65.24 ± 1.63	65.97 ± 2.41	60.65 ± 0.99	**66.71 ± 1.65**
Cell phones & service	1023	42.32 ± 4.35	58.74 ± 6.41	57.67 ± 3.67	40.86 ± 7.62	**59.34 ± 4.56**
Computer & video games	2771	62.61 ± 2.75	64.42 ± 3.28	64.81 ± 2.84	62.61 ± 2.74	**65.10 ± 3.40**
DVD	124438	60.60 ± 0.48	63.03 ± 0.45	65.31 ± 0.40	60.60 ± 0.29	**65.41 ± 0.36**
Electronics	23009	54.04 ± 1.2	61.00 ± 1.16	62.05 ± 0.92	54.11 ± 1.07	**62.67 ± 0.68**
Gourmet food	1575	72.64 ± 3.93	74.73 ± 3.65	74.16 ± 5.55	72.89 ± 3.51	**74.28 ± 3.33**
Grocery	2632	69.53 ± 3.26	70.82 ± 2.36	71.54 ± 2.74	70.02 ± 2.52	**72.23 ± 1.69**
Health & personal care	7225	57.11 ± 2.00	62.96 ± 2.61	**64.66 ± 1.55**	57.20 ± 1.90	64.55 ± 1.42
Jewelry & watches	1981	59.06 ± 3.22	63.30 ± 1.83	**64.01 ± 4.20**	59.77 ± 3.28	63.81 ± 1.58
Kitchen & housewares	19856	58.71 ± 1.12	65.52 ± 1.19	66.68 ± 0.57	58.69 ± 0.61	**66.72 ± 1.09**
Magazines	4191	59.51 ± 2.23	64.61 ± 2.01	**65.81 ± 2.39**	58.79 ± 2.45	65.55 ± 2.89
Music	174180	70.19 ± 0.38	70.21 ± 0.26	71.39 ± 0.20	70.19 ± 0.18	**71.55 ± 0.38**
Musical instruments	332	57.17 ± 8.91	55.12 ± 10.66	57.21 ± 4.81	54.85 ± 8.53	**61.45 ± 8.29**
Office products	431	65.18 ± 6.73	62.43 ± 7.99	**65.66 ± 9.11**	65.66 ± 5.12	65.65 ± 4.57
Outdoor living	1599	57.53 ± 2.84	64.35 ± 3.89	64.91 ± 4.30	57.35 ± 3.91	**66.04 ± 3.45**
Software	2390	41.21 ± 4.43	58.20 ± 2.72	**60.33 ± 3.14**	40.71 ± 4.47	59.71 ± 1.98
Sports & outdoors	5728	56.32 ± 1.61	62.29 ± 2.42	**63.55 ± 2.04**	56.30 ± 2.67	63.50 ± 1.58
Tools & hardware	112	66.89 ± 15.57	**88.56 ± 15.8**	64.77 ± 13.57	68.71 ± 11.30	64.09 ± 13.81
Toys & games	13147	56.41 ± 1.28	63.35 ± 1.46	63.56 ± 1.49	56.60 ± 1.28	**64.10 ± 0.51**
Video	36180	62.39 ± 0.91	66.73 ± 0.56	67.74 ± 0.88	62.36 ± 1.00	**67.84 ± 0.87**

While differences were mostly marginal and not statistically significant (e.g., LR vs. LR-LR using a t-test for *apparel*), the majority of the best results were given to the BCOC architectures (LR-LR), with basic logistic regression as the runner-up. This result is expected since logistic regression is a decent method for ordinal classification, but on the other hand, BCOC acts as a small ensemble based on logistic regression. As an ensemble of logistic regression units, the BCOC architecture could be interpreted as a pseudo neural network, with some previous knowledge imparted on its weights (i.e., the ordinal structure of the classes through their associated vertices). Under the assumption that this representation helps when representing ordinal data, this should perform relatively well when compared to another scheme that does not consider this information.

5   Conclusions

In this work, we have provided an empirical evaluation of the BCOC method using two architectures in its basic one-vs-all approach, one using Naive Bayes in the lower level classifier and another one using Logistic Regression for its probability estimations. Both of these architectures used Logistic Regression for the high-level classifier. Experiments have been carried out on multi-domain data sets from the field of sentiment analysis. It has been shown that this proposal yields competitive results in multiple domains and in some cases superior results.

The BCOC method is based on a combination of the probabilities from multiple one-vs-all classifiers. Thus, different class distributions may affect the classification probabilities and in turn, might produce different results. This issue has yet to be addressed since in its current state it would seem that the BCOC method that the distribution of the classes is biased toward neutral classes.

It should be noted that several challenges remain, such as exploring the underlying assumptions of the method and defining formal framework to justify the usage of this method. In this context, the relationship between BCOC and other classifiers and machine learning methods must also be studied, considering its similarity to a neural network when using an LR-LR architecture.

Considering the results from previous work [5], it is believed that further experimentation is required in order to determine the applicability of this proposal, but as mentioned before, the insight behind the LR-LR architecture and its similarity to neural networks could provide a starting point for further research.

References

1. Baccianella, S., Esuli, A., Sebastiani, F.: Sentiwordnet 3.0: an enhanced lexical resource for sentiment analysis and opinion mining. In: LREC, vol. 10, pp. 2200–2204 (2010)
2. Blitzer, J., Dredze, M., Pereira, F., et al.: Biographies, bollywood, boom-boxes and blenders: domain adaptation for sentiment classification. In: ACL, vol. 7, pp. 440–447 (2007)
3. Coxeter, H.S.M.: Introduction to Geometry, vol. 136. Wiley, New York (1969)
4. Huhn, J.C., Hullermeier, E.: Is an ordinal class structure useful in classifier learning? Int. J. Data Min. Model. Manag. $1(1)$, 45–67 (2008)
5. Keith, B., Meneses, C.: Barycentric coordinates for ordinal sentiment classification (2017)
6. Liu, B.: Opinion mining and sentiment analysis. In: Liu, B. (ed.) Web Data Mining, pp. 459–526. Springer, Heidelberg (2011). https://doi.org/10.1007/978-3-642-19460-3_11
7. Pedregosa, F., et al.: Scikit-learn: machine learning in Python. J. Mach. Learn. Res. **12**, 2825–2830 (2011)
8. Ravi, K., Ravi, V.: A survey on opinion mining and sentiment analysis: tasks, approaches and applications. Knowl. Based Syst. **89**, 14–46 (2015)
9. Sánchez Monedero, J.: Challenges in ordinal classification: artificial neural networks and projection-based methods (2014)

10. Socher, R., et al.: Recursive deep models for semantic compositionality over a sentiment treebank. In: Proceedings of the Conference on Empirical Methods in Natural Language Processing (EMNLP), vol. 1631, p. 1642. Citeseer (2013)
11. Wang, D., Zhai, J., Zhu, H., Wang, X.: An improved approach to ordinal classification. In: Wang, X., Pedrycz, W., Chan, P., He, Q. (eds.) ICMLC 2014. CCIS, vol. 481, pp. 33–42. Springer, Heidelberg (2014). https://doi.org/10.1007/978-3-662-45652-1_4

Improving Attitude Words Classification for Opinion Mining Using Word Embedding

Reynier Ortega-Bueno[1,2(✉)], José E. Medina-Pagola[3],
Carlos Enrique Muñiz-Cuza[1], and Paolo Rosso[4]

[1] Center for Pattern Recognition and Data Mining, Santiago de Cuba, Cuba
{reynier.ortega,carlos}@cerpamid.co.cu
[2] Computers Science Department, University of Oriente, Santiago de Cuba, Cuba
reynier@uo.edu.cu
[3] University of Informatics Science, Boyeros, Havana, Cuba
jmedinap@uci.cu
[4] PRHLT Research Center, Universitat Politècnica de València, Valencia, Spain
prosso@dsic.upv.es

Abstract. Recognizing and classifying evaluative expressions is an important issue of sentiment analysis. This paper presents a corpus-based method for classifying attitude types (Affect, Judgment and Appreciation) and attitude orientation (positive and negative) of words in Spanish relying on the Attitude system of the Appraisal Theory. The main contribution lies in exploring large and unlabeled corpora using neural network word embedding techniques in order to obtain semantic information among words of the same attitude and orientation class. Experimental results show that the proposed method achieves a good effectiveness and outperforms the state of the art for automatic classification of attitude words in Spanish language.

Keywords: Appraisal Framework · Attitude classification ·
Opinion mining · Neural network word embedding

1 Introduction

The Appraisal Theory presented by Martin [10], provides a useful framework for distinguishing between different types of attitudes (Affect, Judgment or Appreciation) and describes how writers or speakers use the language to reveal their engagement with the reader or hearer, and to amplify or diminish the strength of their attitudes and engagements. This theoretical study has opened an interesting research area to analyze opinions. Even though opinions about a specific target may have a similar polarity, they can differ according to their evaluative purpose. Some of them refer to personal or emotional reactions, others evaluate objects and entities properties by reference to aesthetics aspects, or even, they assess the human behavior by reference to ethical and social norms. Going

© Springer Nature Switzerland AG 2019
R. Vera-Rodriguez et al. (Eds.): CIARP 2018, LNCS 11401, pp. 971–982, 2019.
https://doi.org/10.1007/978-3-030-13469-3_112

beyond opinion's polarity, recognizing attitudes in opinions is a step towards more fine-grained models for sentiment analysis. Considering that, methods and resources for automatically classifying the attitude of the words or phases are a cornerstone for creating knowledge-based systems able to properly identify not only the valence but also determine the evaluative purpose of the opinions. Mining the attitudes behind opinions can enhance other sentiment analysis tasks and it can be useful for decision making.

Actually, some authors have turned their attention to computational treatment of evaluations in language. Taboada and Grieve [16] tried to calculate the strength of its semantic association with pairs of words, *pronoun-copula*, composed by a pronoun and the verb form "was", as follows: *"I was"* for Affect, *"he was"* for Judgment, and *"it was"* for Appreciation using a Point Mutual Information (PMI) and AltaVista Search Engine. Bloom and Argamon (2010) propose an automatic method for complex appraisal extraction patterns [1] in English. They manually created a lexicon of targets commonly used in two given domains (Digital Camera and Movie) and annotated a list of 29 syntactic dependencies to associate these targets to attitudes expression, also to identify targets that were not included in the lexicon [2] based on syntactic dependencies. A notable advance in attitude recognition at sentences level was presented in [12,13]. These works analyze complex contextual attitude on the basis of deep analysis of syntactic and dependence structures, the compositional linguistic rules applied at various grammatical levels, the rules elaborated for semantically distinct verb classes, and a strategy for considering the hierarchy of concepts based on Word-Net. A corpus-based method for classifying attitudinal words in Spanish language was introduced by Hernández *et al.* [7,8]. In these works binary classifiers were trained for recognizing attitude type and orientation at words level. A corpus and lexicon used for training the classifiers were manually created. According to our best knowledge, these works are the first ones that address the problem of attitude words classification in the Spanish language, and constitute the more closely approach to the work introduced in this research.

Previous studies were able to show that mostly approaches are focus on the English language; and rely on prior lexicons with attitude annotation for developing complex models based on machine learning or knowledge-based systems. Hence, the quality and size of these lexicons have implications on the effectiveness of these methods. Considering these limitations, proposing effective algorithms to build new lexicons of attitude words, especially for Spanish, comprises an interesting research direction due to limited advances that have been found in the scientific literature for this task in this language. Two are the main goals of this work: (i) to suggest a new solution for automatic classification of both attitude types and orientations of the words in Spanish better than existing ones; (ii) to explore large unlabeled datasets available on-line using neural network based word embedding techniques in order to obtain a good semantic representation of the words useful for identifying their attitude types and orientations. The remainder of this paper is organized as follows: in Sect. 2, theoretical background about Appraisal Framework is presented. Later, Sect. 3 introduces our proposal for classifying attitude types and orientation at words level. Later, in Sect. 4, experiments and discussion about the results are summarized. Finally, in Sect. 5, conclusions and main directions for future investigation and improvement are presented.

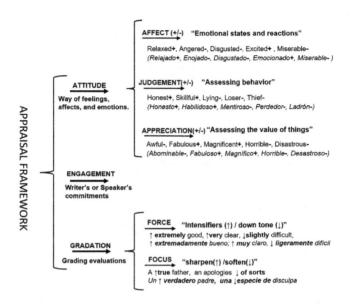

Fig. 1. General structure of the Appraisal Framework

2   Appraisal Framework Background

Appraisals according to Martin's research work [10] can be divided into three distinct systems closely related (cf. Fig. 1): Attitude, Engagement and Gradation. The Attitude system is concerned with words or expression used to reveal feelings, including emotional states or reactions, judgments of behavior and evaluation of things. On the other hand, Engagement is concerned with words or expressions used by the writer or speaker for positioning her statements and point of views. Finally, Gradation considers words that attend to grading (intensify, diminish, soften or sharpen) evaluations insight of language. The central aspect of the Appraisal Framework is the Attitude system and it is divided into three refined subsystems: Affect, Judgment and Appreciation; that define the specific type of appraisal used by the writer for negotiating her feelings and private states. Specifically, Affect deals with language resources (words or expressions) for constructing emotional states and reactions in texts (e.g. the words: *relaxed, disgusted, exited, miserable*). Judgment is concerned with resources for assessing behavior according to various normative principles and ethics rules (e.g. the words: *honest, skillful* and *loser*). Lastly, Appreciation looks at resources for obtaining aesthetic qualities of objects and natural phenomena (e.g. the words: *awful, magnificent, fabulous* and *horrible*). The Attitude system also deals with the orientation of the appraisal and distinguishes whether has a positive or negative semantic orientation. One difficult point that must be considered in the Attitude system is the dependence of type and orientation of appraisal expressions according to the context where these occur. This is a hard challenge also related with subjective language ambiguity and contextual sentiment identification.

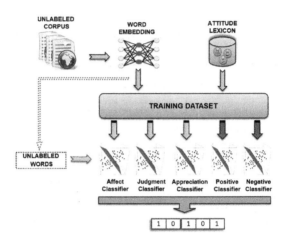

Fig. 2. Overall architecture proposed for the attitude classification method

3   Attitude Word Embedding Classification

This section introduces our method for attitude words classification. It constitutes a step towards more refined methods for understanding evaluative language from the Appraisal Theory perspective, and an advance beyond traditional systems for polarity classification in Spanish language. The Fig. 2 depicts the overall architecture of the proposal. It can be divided into two main parts: the word representation based on neural networks, and the training of one classifier for each attitude type and orientation. As illustrated in Fig. 2 the method takes as input an unlabeled corpus and a lexicon of words annotated with attitude types and orientation. Firstly, the text preprocessing of the corpus is carried out, including sentences recognition, word segmentation, and word stemming by using the FreeLing tool [14]. Once the corpus was preprocessed, it is given as input to the word embedding method in order to obtain a vector representation of the terms. This model aims to create vectors in a much lower dimensional space that the original Vector Space Model (VSM) [15], so it is a more efficient representation. Moreover, it provides more expressiveness because the words are encoded as dense vectors with syntactic and semantic properties. As consequence, semantic related words are close in this new vector space. Having a semantic representation of words, the next step is then using them for solving the problem of attitude classification. To achieve this objective, the words in the lexicon are represented according to the vectors learned in the previous step. Later, considering this representation and the attitude labels associated to each entry in the lexicon, a training set is build for each type of attitude and each type of orientation. By using these training sets, five classifiers are trained in order to automatically recognize the attitude and orientation of unseen terms.

3.1   Unlabeled Corpora and Attitude Lexicon

Our proposal relies on unlabeled background corpora and an attitude lexicon to learn words representation. In contrast to the works presented in [7,8] which use a specific corpus of evaluative sentences (LAM11), in this work SBW16 [4] was considered as an open domain and useful corpus to encode semantic and syntactic information associated to the words based on distributional semantic principle. This has the advantage that a huge volume of textual information can be considered without requiring specific manually tagged corpora which demand great efforts by human experts. In order to establish a comparative analysis, also LAM11 and RMC17 were explored as background corpora. SBW16 consists of raw texts in Spanish language with approximately 1.5 billion words, extracted from different resources from the Web. It replaces all non-alphanumeric characters with whitespaces, all number with the token "DIGITO" and all the multiple whitespaces with only one. The capitalization of the words remain unchanged. LAM11 contains 56970 "attitudinal sentences" in Spanish language having around 1.3 million words. In the corpus creating process, sentences from distinct sources were retrieved. Specifically, movie reviews, Mexican news, letters, stories and poems. Finally, RMC17 is composed by all sentences in LAM11 and SBW16. The aim behind this merge was motivated by the need of taking the advantage of the huge volume of sentences in SBW16 useful for capturing the semantic properties associated to the words, also by considering the appraisal information explicitly encoded in LAM11.

The distribution of sentences, words, and vocabulary size for each corpus is presented in Table 1. As can be observed, SWB16 and RMC17 are much longer than LAM11. This dramatic difference might have a direct impact on word representation, and on the effectiveness of the proposed method.

Table 1. Description of corpora w.r.t. number of sentences, words, and vocabulary size

Corpus	No. Sen	No. Tok	V. Size
LAM11	56970	1358727	19055
SBW16	46925295	1420665810	855514
RMC17	46982265	1422024537	859352

Table 2. Distribution of words in the lexicons w.r.t. to attitude and orientation

Labels	LAM11-LEX
Affect	543
Judgment	2286
Appreciation	1156
Positive	1278
Negative	1796

The Attitude lexicon can be considered as key point because it is used to train and validate the attitude classifiers. Specifically, LAM11-LEX lexicon [8] was considered. It has 3,005 word entries, where each word was manually annotated, considering three integer values: 0, 1, and 2, to establish its polarity (positive (Pos), negative (Neg)) and its correspondence to the Attitude system (i.e., Judgment (Jud), Appreciation (App), Affect (Aff)). Where 0 indicates the lowest and 2 the highest strength. The distribution of words in the lexicon respect to attitude and orientation labels is illustrated in Table 2. Notice that, there is a dramatic disproportion. The affect words (minority class) represent only 23.75% of the judgment words (majority class), also the appreciation words represent 50.56% of the majority class. Regarding positive and negative words, the problem is similar but to a lesser extent than in attitude classes. As consequence, in the process of classification of attitudes the rate of misclassified ones in the minority class might be increased.

3.2 Attitude Word Representation Based on Neural Network Embedding

Unsupervised learned word embedding has been a successful representation in numerous tasks of Natural Language Processing in recent years. This technique has obtained better or similar results to other complex models for representing words such as Latent Semantic Analysis (LSA) [6] and Random Indexing (RI) [9], specifically when large corpora are used to learn word vectors. The major contribution of the words embedding representation underlays in its capability of capturing and encoding semantic similarities between words or phrases based on their distributional properties. In contrast to the representation used in [8], which considers that the vectors of words (VSM) within sentences are good for capturing attitudinal and orientation of the words, this proposal aims at using word embedding as a more semantic-rich representation useful for improving the effectiveness of attitude word classification. To validate this assumption, Word2Vec [11] and FastText [3] were used for words representation.

3.3 Classification Schema Proposed

Considering the theoretical aspects related with the Appraisal Framework, it can be noted that attitude classification is a multi-classes and multi-labels problem due to the great overlapping between words in distinct attitude types (Appreciation, Judgment and Affect). However, in this work the problem was simplified, and we did not treat either attitude type and orientation classification as a multi-classification or multi-labels problem. Instead, the problem is modeled as a single-label binary classification task.

For recognizing attitude type and orientation, five binary classifiers were training in a separate manner, three of them for identifying the type of attitude and the two remainders for classifying the semantic orientation. The training set for each class was built in the following way. Firstly, all words associated to the class that needs to be recognized were taken as positive instances and the remaining words were considered as negative instances of the class[1]. It is important to clarify that words that are in both classes (positive class and negative class) are removed from the negative instances and only considered as instances for the positive class. After that, the words were represented with their vectors obtained through the word embedding method. Once the training set was created, the next problem that was addressed is the imbalance of the minority class (positive) respect to the majority class (negative). For that, an oversampling techniques was applied. Specifically, the method called SMOTE (Synthetic Minority Over Sampling Technique) [5] was applied using the python packages Scikit-Learn-Contrib[2]. It has the purpose of increasing the number of instances in the minority class and hence reduce the problem of imbalance. Finally, different classifiers were trained for identifying each attitude type and orientation of the words. Regarding the classification methods, in this work five distinct models were evaluated. The motivation behind that was to assess the quality of the vectors learned using word embedding over large corpora for attitude word classification. In this work, no great effort to choose the best classification model and its optimal parameters setting was dedicated. Specifically, the implementation of Linear Support Vector Machine (SVM), Random Forest (RF), K-Nearest Neighbor (KNN), Gaussian Naive Bayes (NB) provided by the python package Scikit-Learn[3] were applied. Also an ensemble of classifiers was evaluated combining in a soft voting schema the four previous classifiers.

4   Experiments and Results

The evaluation of the proposed method constitutes a bottleneck, due to the lack of benchmark collections in the scientist literature already used to validate the results and establish a strict comparison with previous approaches. As was explained in Sect. 1, the proposal introduced by Hernández *et al.* (2011) [8] is the most similar to this work. For that reason, the validation strategy followed by them was assumed here. This allows to consider their results as a baseline, and to establish a comparative analysis. The validation process relies on manually annotations provided by the attitude lexicon. In this case, labels associated to each word in the lexicon LAM11-LEX was used as *"gold-standard"*. The words in the lexicon were partitioned in training and test subsets using a stratified five-cross validation. For measuring the effectiveness of our classification method, two global measures were considered, the first one (F1-ATT), that measures the overall quality for recognizing attitude types and the second (F1-SO) for recognizing attitude orientations. Also, F1 measure was reported for each class.

In the validation of the proposed method the main interest was focused on analyzing the impact of using word embedding techniques for representing the

---

[1] Positive and negative in this context refer to samples that belong and do not belong to the class respectively, these concepts are completely different to the concept of positive and negative used for describing the attitude orientation.

[2] https://github.com/scikit-learn-contrib/imbalanced-learn.

[3] http://scikit-learn.org/stable/.

attitudinal words. In this sense, Word2Vec and FastText model were applied on the three background corpora (LAM11, SBW16, and RMC17) with the purpose of learning dense semantic vectors for representing the words. The Word2Vec parameters were modified to consider the skip-gram model and fix at 300 the size of the word embedding vectors; the defaults values of the remainder parameters were maintained as reported in [11]. For FastText the default values as reported in [3] were considered, apart from the vector size, which we set respectively to 300, to match Word2Vec. Notice that, FastText uses the sub-word structure for learning word vectors. For this reason, when this model is used the word stemming task carried out in the preprocess stage was ignored.

Regarding the parameters setting of classifiers methods, in this work not great efforts were made to estimate the optimal parameters. The main goal aims at discovering how the embedding vector representation contributes to the task of attitude word classification. Therefore, a slight modification of parameters was carried out based on empirical knowledge. Specifically, in the case of the Random Forest classifier (RF) the number of trees in the forest was set to 300. For the Nearest Neighbors classifier (KNN) the number of neighbors to consider into neighborhood was set to 3. The linear kernel was chosen for the Support Vector Machine method (SVM), and the Gaussian Naive Bayes classifier (NB) was used with default settings. The classifiers mentioned before were combined in an ensemble (ENS) using a Weighted Voting Schema. The weight assigned to each classifier was empirically set (limiting the coefficient values in the interval [0,1]) taking into account the performance of base methods.

In the first experiment, vector representations for words in the LAM11-LEX were learned using the Word2Vec model over LAM11, SBW16 and RMC17 corpora separately. Based on these representations, the five classifiers were trained and validated using a stratified five-fold cross validation. Table 3 shows the F1-measures by class and the obtained macro-averaged. The first column shows the corpus used for learning the vector representation and the second shows the classification method used. The columns between the third and fifth illustrate the F1 measure achieved for the three types of attitude taken into account in this work, whereas the sixth and seventh show the values of F1-measure for the attitude orientation. The next two columns show the global effectiveness in attitude recognition and orientation classification, respectively. The last column (WV) quantifies the number of words in the lexicon for which were possible to build a vector representation according to the model and corpus used.

Several observations can be made by analyzing the results in Table 3. Firstly, the number of words in LAM11-LEX that can be represented from SBW16 is greater than in LAM11. On the other hand, RMC17 is the corpus that better covers the words in the lexicon, although the vector representations for 193 words could not be built from it. The constraint that a word should appear at least 5 times in the corpus passed as input to Word2Vec model may be the reason why these words were not represented. This problem will be addressed in further research.

Regarding corpora, it is clear that the lowest results were obtained using the LAM11 corpus. This performance could be conditioned by the corpus size. It probably does not provide enough sentences to train adequately the Word2Vec

Table 3. Results achieved for attitude type and orientation classification in LAM11-LEX using Word2Vec model on three distinct background corpora

CORPUS	Classifier	AFF	JUD	APP	POS	NEG	F1-ATT	F1-SO	WV
LAM11	KNN	**0.488**	0.498	**0.507**	**0.501**	**0.505**	**0.498**	**0.503**	2130
	NB	0.440	0.291	0.369	0.404	0.410	0.367	0.407	
	SVM	0.363	**0.522**	0.488	0.473	0.469	0.458	0.471	
	RF	**0.505**	**0.508**	**0.514**	**0.502**	**0.492**	**0.509**	**0.497**	
	ENS	0.481	0.461	0.426	0.439	0.441	0.456	0.440	
SBW16	KNN	0.411	0.417	0.603	0.771	0.770	0.477	0.771	2713
	NB	0.640	0.554	0.681	0.847	0.833	0.625	0.840	
	SVM	**0.682**	**0.640**	**0.754**	0.847	0.856	**0.692**	0.852	
	RF	0.673	0.541	0.728	**0.873**	**0.868**	0.647	**0.871**	
	ENS	**0.702**	**0.607**	**0.741**	0.872	0.864	**0.683**	0.868	
RMC17	KNN	0.350	0.397	0.599	0.714	0.706	0.449	0.71	2812
	NB	0.625	0.548	0.667	0.830	0.808	0.613	0.819	
	SVM	**0.687**	**0.636**	**0.741**	0.844	**0.845**	**0.688**	0.845	
	RF	0.667	0.536	0.725	**0.861**	**0.854**	0.643	**0.858**	
	ENS	**0.690**	**0.593**	**0.730**	0.851	0.842	**0.671**	**0.847**	

model hence noisy vectors associated to the words were obtained. The results achieved using SBW16 showed a considerable increase with respect to those obtained from LAM11. The classes *Appreciation*, *Affect* and *Judgment* are more clearly learned with SVM and ENS methods achieving (0.692) and (0.683) of F1-ATT correspondingly. On the other hand, positive or negative words are better recognized with RF and ENS methods obtaining an effectiveness of 0.871 and 0.868 respectively in terms of F1-SO. The results obtained on RMC17 show a similar performance to those derived from SBW16. Surprisingly, no increase in terms of F1-ATT and F1-SO were obtained when this corpus was considered. The values of F1-ATT (0.688) and F1-SO (0.858) obtained by SVM and RF show a slight drop with respect to previous results. Notice that, through this corpus, 99 words more than in SBW16 were represented and incorporated to the training and the validation sets. Adding these words may be correlated with the decrease of results.

The second experiment follows a similar structure that the previous one. In this case the same classifiers, attitude lexicon and background corpora were used. It differs from the experiment above in the model applied to build the words representation. The main goal aimed to evaluate the impact of using FastText as technique for representing words. Table 4 illustrates the results obtained by using this representation. As can be observed, the number of words represented with this model increase from LAM11 to SBW16 and from SBW16 to RMC17. In case of LAM11, the classifiers that achieved better performance for *Appreciation*, *Affect* and *Judgment* were ENS (0.640) and SVM (0.634) methods, whereas the best values for positive and negative words classification were acquired with

SVM (0.730) and RF (0.722). Remarkable increase in terms of F1-ATT (0.719) and F1-SO (0.886) were achieved when SBW16 was used as background corpus (most words in the LAM11-LEX could be represented). In addition, the most significant improvement in F1-ATT (0.722) and F1-SO (0.889) were achieved using the RMC17 corpus combined with the ENS method. Analyzing Tables 3 and 4 together, several observations can be made. Firstly, the proposed method obtains very good results in terms of macro-weighted F1 for both attitude classification and orientation recognition when the words representation was built on large unlabeled corpora (SBW216 and RMC17). These results support the hypothesis that relying on large unlabeled corpora, good semantic vector representation can be learned by using word embedding techniques to improve the task of attitude words classification in the Spanish language. Secondly, the results achieved with FastText show an important increase in both F1-ATT and F1-SO. Also more words can be represented using it. With respect to the classifiers, in general, SVM, RF and ENS showed the best performance. Contrary to expectations, not significant differences were found among ENS, SVM and RF; this suggests that the weights assigned to each base classifier need to be tuned with the purpose of increasing the quality of the ENS method. Finally, it can be clearly observed that *Appreciation* was the attitude class better recognized whereas the *Judgment* was the most difficult. This could be correlated with the fact that words or phrases used to express judgments are more subjective than words used for evaluating aesthetic aspects of objects even from the Appraisal Theory.

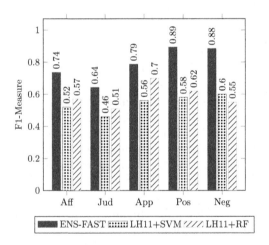

Fig. 3. Comparison w.r.t. F1 measure against the best results achieved by Hernández *et al.* (2011) [8]

Finally, a comparison is made between the best results achieved by the proposed method (henceforth ENS-FAST) and the most significant results (henceforth LH11+SVM and LH11-RF) obtained by Hernández *et al.* (2011) [8]. As it can be seen in Fig. 3 the proposed method obtained a remarkable increase in the recognition of all classes. Particularly, the positive and negative classes were the

Table 4. Results achieved for attitude type and orientation classification in LAM11-LEX using FastText model on three distinct background corpora

CORPUS	Classifier	AFF	JUD	APP	POS	NEG	F1-ATT	F1-SO	WV
LAM11	KNN	0.508	0.524	0.635	0.618	0.615	0.556	0.617	2054
	NB	0.551	0.520	0.669	0.665	0.673	0.58	0.669	
	SVM	0.620	**0.586**	0.696	**0.723**	**0.736**	**0.634**	**0.730**	
	RF	**0.628**	0.553	**0.703**	0.725	0.718	0.628	**0.722**	
	ENS	**0.627**	**0.591**	**0.702**	0.714	**0.719**	**0.640**	0.717	
SBW16	KNN	0.456	0.490	0.686	0.771	0.755	0.544	0.763	2824
	NB	0.669	0.588	0.761	0.876	0.868	0.673	0.872	
	SVM	**0.704**	**0.645**	0.777	0.872	0.871	**0.710**	0.872	
	RF	0.685	0.584	**0.778**	0.886	**0.875**	0.682	**0.881**	
	ENS	**0.729**	**0.642**	**0.787**	0.887	**0.888**	**0.719**	0.886	
RMC17	KNN	0.455	0.485	0.688	0.772	0.737	0.543	0.755	2888
	NB	0.665	0.590	0.760	0.871	0.879	0.672	0.875	
	SVM	**0.707**	**0.654**	0.768	0.872	0.864	**0.710**	0.868	
	RF	0.697	0.595	**0.774**	0.889	0.883	0.689	**0.886**	
	ENS	**0.736**	**0.643**	**0.786**	0.893	0.884	0.722	**0.889**	

most improved by ENS-FAST, whereas the *Affect* was the attitude class with more increase in F1 measure. Based on these considerations, it is possible to conclude that the proposed method overcomes clearly the results achieved by the LH11+SVM and LH11-RF.

5   Conclusions

The task of recognizing and classifying words according to the attitude type and orientation that they convey is an important step in order to apply fine-grained models based on the Appraisal Theory for analyzing evaluative language. In this work we showed an improvement on the automatic classification of attitude type and orientation of Spanish words. These results were achieved using two approaches that rely on neural network word embeddings (Word2Vec and FastText) for learning good vectors on large unlabeled corpora. One of the directions for future work will be to study the impact of different parameter settings of neural network word embedding on the classification method. We also plan to analyze the effectiveness of the proposal for classifying new attitude words out of LAM11-LEX and extending popular Spanish opinion lexicons with attitudes. Also the authors will work on the classification of multi-words, expressions and idioms rather than individual words. Finally, great efforts will be made for tackling the problem with a multi-class and multi-labels approach, considering the overlapping inherent to the Attitude system of the Appraisal Framework.

Acknowledgments. The work of the fourth author was partially supported by the SomEMBED TIN2015-71147-C2-1-P research project (MINECO/FEDER).

References

1. Bloom, K., Argamon, S.: Automated learning of appraisal extraction patterns. In: Gries, S.T., Wulff, S., Davies, M. (eds.) Corpus Linguistic Applications: Current Studies, New Directions, Third edn., pp. 249–260. Rodopi B.V., Amsterdam, New York (2010)
2. Bloom, K., Garg, N., Argamon, S.: Extracting appraisal expressions. In: Proceedings of the Annual Conference of the NAACL-HLT, pp. 308–315. ACL (2007)
3. Bojanowski, P., Grave, E., Joulin, A., Mikolov, T.: Enriching word vectors with subword information. Trans. ACL **5**, 135–146 (2017)
4. Cardellino, C.: Spanish billion words corpus and embeddings (2016)
5. Chawla, N.V., Bowyer, K.W., Hall, L.O., Kegelmeyer, W.P.: SMOTE: synthetic minority over-sampling technique. J. Artif. Intell. Res. **16**, 321–357 (2002)
6. Deerwester, S., Dumais, S., Furnas, G., Landauer, T., Harshman, R.: Indexing by latent semantic analysis. J. Am. Soc. Inf. Sci. **41**(6), 391–407 (1990)
7. Hernández, L., López-Lopez, A., Medina-Pagola, J.E.: Recognizing polarity and attitude of words in text. In: Proceedings of 14th Portuguese Conference on Artificial Intelligence, (EPIA 2009), pp. 525–536. Aveiro, Portugal (2009)
8. Hernández, L., López-Lopez, A., Medina-Pagola, J.E.: Classification of attitude words for opinions mining. Int. J. Comput. Linguist. Appl. **2**(1–2), 267–283 (2011)
9. Kanerva, P., Kristofersson, J., Holst, A.: Random indexing of text samples for latent semantic analysis. In: Proceedings of the 22 Annual Conference of the Cognitive Science Society, vol. 1036, no. 2, pp. 16429–16429 (2000)
10. Martin, J.R., White, P.R.R.: The Language of Evaluation: The Appraisal Framework, 1st edn. Palgrave Macmillan, New York (2005)
11. Mikolov, T., Corrado, G., Chen, K., Dean, J.: Efficient estimation of word representations in vector space. In: International Conference on Learning Representations (ICLR 2013), pp. 1–12 (2013)
12. Neviarouskaya, A., Aono, M., Prendinger, H., Ishizuka, M.: Intelligent interface for textual attitude analysis. J. ACM Trans. Intell. Syst. Technol. **5**(3), 1–20 (2014)
13. Neviarouskaya, A., Prendinger, H., Ishizuka, M.: Attitude sensing in text based on a compositional linguistic approach. Comput. Intell. **31**, 1–45 (2013)
14. Padró, L., Stanilovsky, E.: FreeLing 3.0: towards wider multilinguality. In: Proceedings of the (LREC 2012) (2012)
15. Salton, G., Wong, A., Yang, C.S.: A vector space model for automatic indexing. Commun. ACM **18**(11), 613–620 (1975)
16. Taboada, M., Grieve, J.: Analyzing appraisal automatically. In: Proceedings of AAAI Spring Symposium on Exploring Attitude and Affect in Text, pp. 158–161. American Association for Artificial Intelligence (2004)

Author Index

Printed in the United States
By Bookmasters